THE RANDOM HOUSE THESAURUS OF SLANG

THE RANDOM HOUSE THESAURUS OF SLANG

Esther Lewin and Albert E. Lewin

150,000 uncensored contemporary slang terms, common idioms, and colloquialisms arranged for quick and easy reference

RANDOM HOUSE • NEW YORK

To Talia and Ian
and in memory of
dear Natalie

Library of Congress Cataloging-in-Publication Data

Lewin, Esther.
  The Random House thesaurus of slang.

  Reprint. Originally published: The thesaurus of slang.
New York, N.Y.: Facts on File Publications, © 1988.
  Bibliography: p.
  1. English language — Slang — Dictionaries. 2. English language — Synonyms and antonyms
— Dictionaries.
I. Lewin, Albert E. II. Title.
PE3721.L45   1989   427'.003   89-10254
ISBN 0-679-72700-0

Manufactured in the United States of America

1 2 3 4 5 6 7 8 9

Preface

The Random House Thesaurus of Slang is made up of 12,000 English words listed alphabetically; each is followed by one or more of the 150,000 slang words or phrases contained in this volume. That simple arrangement is what makes this book a useful tool for writers, speakers, students of language and anyone else who might need a quick and easy source of slang.

It has been said that a thesaurus is a book in which you look up the wrong word in order to find the right one. That definition fits this book perfectly. As a thesaurus, it offers a convenient translation from standard English to its slang equivalent. It is by no means a slang dictionary, nor is it meant to be. Using this thesaurus, all or part of a formal English sentence can be rewritten in slang, something almost impossible to do using a slang dictionary. This is not to say that slang dictionaries should be considered superfluous. It is the basic premise that is different; a dictionary is meant to define words, but if the user doesn't know the slang word for which a definition is sought, a slang dictionary is reduced to little more than a volume for browsing. If anything, *The Random House Thesaurus of Slang* should make slang dictionaries more useful. Except in a few instances where the use of an obscure slang term is demonstrated, this thesaurus, since it is not a dictionary, does not define slang words beyond giving them a formal English synonym. For a more precise definition of the words found in this book, a slang dictionary should be used.

In a sense, this volume is similar to a foreign-language dictionary in that it "translates" formal English into the language of slang. To some readers slang can seem like a foreign language and, like a foreign language, there are times when it doesn't translate exactly. The same word or phrase can differ subtly in meaning in different contexts. In an extreme instance a word can be its own antonym; for example, *baddest* can mean "best" or "worst."

While attempting to determine the right formal synonym of a slang term, we often asked which formal English word was the one most likely to occur to a reader searching for a slang synonym. For example, it is not likely a reader would think to find *pot likker* under the entry *residue*. *Soup stock* was more credible. Therefore, for some entries, precision has been sacrificed for ease of use. Where a widely used slang term is not easily translated into standard English, the slang itself is listed at the subject heading. Such a case is *blind date*.

The slang in this collection is based on actual usage culled from a wide variety of sources, such as newspapers, magazines, fiction and nonfiction books, television, radio, trade papers, industry, casual conversation. For the most part, the slang terms in this thesaurus are in current general usage; however, the reader will also find many of the most recent words appearing particularly in the language of young people, technical workers and politicians. In these pages, most readers will discover unfamiliar words and phrases, as well as old words with surprising new definitions.

All of language was once "nonstandard," until the invention of the printing press created the need for standardization and inspired the first dictionary. Slang also originates out of need. New words are continually coming into the language, to stay only as long as they are useful. No attempt was made in this book to rule out "vogue" words. Deciding which of these words are merely passing through the language and which are taking up more-or-less permanent residence was not part of our editorial criteria. Slang is created by all social classes in every kind of circumstance as a more convenient, more private, or more entertaining means of communication. Groups create their own language within a language. The various kinds of slang are a means of identification. Peers recognize each other through its use. Slang is a way of belonging, of "speaking the same language."

The word *slang* itself is said to have once meant "to be abusive." And much slang is abusive, chauvinistic, irreverent, profane, and sexually explicit. This book includes all types of slang, uncensored. For better or worse, this is the slang commonly used in America today.

Experts in linguistics disagree among themselves over matters of definition, and they are certain to disagree with some of the definitions in this work. It is a risk anyone who prepares such a text must take. In those instances where it can be pointed out that we are in error, corrections will be made most gratefully, but for the moment, what the reader finds within these pages is as close to the correct usage of slang, colloquialisms, and the American idiom as we could presently determine.

—Esther and Albert E. Lewin

How to Use This Book

For speakers, writers of fact or fiction, playwrights, screen and television writers, journalists, advertising copy writers, publicists, politicians, members of the clergy—anyone who deals with the expression of ideas through words, *The Random House Thesaurus of Slang* is simple to use. Standard English words are listed in alphabetical order. Under each of these words is a collection of slang synonyms. Suppose you are preparing a speech or an essay and you want to make the following statement less formal, "Freedom of speech is basic to democracy." The operational word is *basic*. Look up the word *basic*.

> **BASIC n.** bottom line, plain vanilla, nitty gritty, where it's at, name, name of the game, nub, meat and potatoes, coal and ice. See also VITAL.

Depending on the level of informality desired, you find a wide range of choices, so the sentence can be written, "Freedom of speech is the meat and potatoes of democracy," or "Freedom of speech is the nub of democracy."

In addition to the listing of slang synonyms under a particular word, the thesaurus also offers a broader selection of words to assist you in finding exactly the sense you seek.

> **ENACT v.** 1. jam, jam through, railroad, railroad through, steamroller through. 2. be on, go on, do a turn, do one's stuff, do a number. See EXECUTE. See also PERFORM.

"Enact" illustrates three of these features. The word *enact* is synonymous with "legislate." Synonyms for that sense of the word are listed under the numeral 1. "Enact" also means to "act." Number 2 provides a selection of "act" words. Following the slang terms there appears "See EXECUTE." and "See also PERFORM." "See" references offer a broader selection of slang synonyms. If you don't find the word you are seeking in the first group, the "See" category can provide many more choices. "See also" references provide a broader selection still, directing you to collateral meanings of the word. As a convenience, there are no listings simply referring the reader to another category without some slang synonyms listed, allowing the reader a choice of synonyms without having to look further.

Still another refinement is offered to aid your search for exactly the right word. A semicolon separates specialized references from the general: such words might refer only to males as opposed to females or might differentiate activities from objects. Wherever possible, the most current, widely used words are listed first.

It is agreed among lexicographers that finding exactly the right synonym for a word is an inexact pursuit. In standard English, no two words carry precisely the same meaning and it is no different with slang, where exact definitions are often as varied as the locales in which the words are used. In many cases, parts of speech are mixed; nouns are listed with adjectives; verbs become nouns and nouns verbs; positives are used as negatives. That's the way you will find it here. Except for the sake of clarity, no attempt has been made to define slang beyond the category heading. The thesaurus should not be considered a dictionary. Where definition is necessary, reference to a good slang dictionary is recommended.

Acknowledgments

Our deep appreciation to:

Eliza Lewin, who kept us current with the youth and music scenes, and who was ever ready to help with the drudgery of checking references, researching, and preparing bibliographies.

Professor Herbert Turman, who was always available to advise, read manuscript, and to provide technical counseling and general encouragement.

Charles Bloch of Bantam Books, for his help in shaping the presentation of the work, for his sage advice and our sadness that he will not see it in its final form.

Joseph Simon, publisher of Ward Ritchie Press, for his technical expertise.

Anthony Borras, who tailored his deftly programmed data base management system, DBMS, to perform so many complex tasks when personal computers were still very primitive.

To our many patient friends, who were unaware of their cooperation as guinea pigs in blind tests of questionable material.

List of Abbreviations

Acad.	academy	N.	Navy
adj.	adjective	n.	noun
Admin.	administration	News.	newspaper
adv.	adverb	N.Y.	New York
A.F.	Air Force	N.Y.C.	New York City
Amer. Ind.	American Indian	Obs.	obsolete
Anon.	anonymous	Obsc.	obscene
Arc.	archaic	Pl.	plural
Ass't.	assistant	Pol.	political
Bl.	black	Porno.	pornographic
Bsbl.	baseball	pron.	pronoun
CB	Citizen's Band Radio	Rel.	religious
C.I.A.	Central Intelligence Agency	Rest.	restaurant
Derog.	derogatory	Rom.	romantic
Elec.	electrical	R.R.	railroad
Esk.	eskimo	Sch.	school
Fem.	female	So.	southern
Fin.	financial	Sp.	Spanish
Ftbl.	football	Stu.	student use
I.R.S.	Internal Revenue Service	The.	theatrical use
Ger.	German	TV	television
Jap.	Japanese	U.	underworld
Joc.	jocular	U.S.S.R.	Union of Soviet Socialist Republics
L.A.	Los Angeles	Usu.	usually
Lt.	lieutenant	v.	verb
M.	male	V.D.	venereal disease
Medic.	medical	WWI	World War I
Mex.	Mexican	WWII	World War II
Mil.	military	Yid.	Yiddish
Ms.	manuscript		

THE
RANDOM
HOUSE
THESAURUS
OF SLANG

A

A n. able, alpha.

ABANDON v. bail out, bow out, chicken out, check out, punk out, drop out, opt out, count out, cop out, sell out, storm out, pull out, butt out, push out, flake out, snake out, but out, nix out, ooze out, peel out, ship out, burn out, walk out on, run out on, leg, leg it out, ease out, fase out, fase, do a fase, fase away, hatup, drift away, dust, fly the coop, ease on, put it to the wind, slide, take French leave (without permission), scratch gravel, duck, heel, haul one's freight, quit the scene, sniff a powder, take a powder, screw, walk, fuck off, bug off, kick off, knock off, slam off, skidoo, go over the side, slough, book, time to book, time to bail, bottle up and go, up stakes, pull up stakes, cheese it, take a walk, dump, cut loose, ditch, shake, leave flat, leave high and dry, leave holding the bag, bag it, leave in the lurch, swear off, pass, pass on, pass up, take the oath, pack in, give in, cave in, give up, throw in the sponge, throw in the towel, pull the pin, pull the plug, pull in one's horns, cry uncle, hang up one's spurs, pack it in, rat, chuck, chuck it, fold, quit cold, quit cold turkey, kick, drop, angle, hang it up, bog down, binch (job), come off, cry off, stand down, drag it, give up the ghost, give up the ship, kiss good-bye, throw over, toss over, throw overboard, wash one's hand of, change one's tune, change one's song, drop like a hot potato, back down, pigeonhole, sideline, sidetrack. See also DESERT, RENOUNCE, RESIGN.

ABANDONED adj. pigeonholed, sidelined, sidetracked, godforsaken, passed up, on the rocks, out in left field, left in the lurch.

ABASH v. discombobulate, ball up, bug, throw into a tizzy, throw into a swivet, fuddle, fuck with. See also BEWILDER.

ABATE v. coast, cool it, cool out, chill out, don't sweat it, eyes to cool it, go with the flow, hang easy, hang loose, lay back, let go, let it all hang out, let it all happen, let it all out, mellow out, take it easy, unlax.

ABBREVIATE v. cut, cut down, cut to the bone, nutshell, put in a nutshell, boil down, trim, get to the meat. See also SHORTEN.

ABBREVIATED adj. for short. See also SHORT.

ABDICATE v. bail out, opt out, sell out, leave high and dry, bag it, leave holding the bag, leave in the lurch, give it up. See RESIGN. See also QUIT.

ABDOMEN n. tummy, gut, pot, belly, potbelly, spare tire, corporation, breadbasket, bay window. See STOMACH.

ABDOMINAL ORGANS n. guts, innards, inners, insides, department of the interior, inner man, inner workings, inner works, spaghetti.

ABDUCT v. grab, shanghai, snatch, put the snatch on one, sneeze, dognap (dog abduction).

ABERRANT adj. flaky, weirdo, psycho, mental, Section 8, off base, off-color, out of line. See also ABNORMAL.

ABHOR v. grossed out on, have no use for, have an allergy to, be allergic to, be down on. See DISLIKE.

ABHORRENT adj. gross, shucky, yucky, icky, total shuck, awful beastly. See DESPICABLE.

ABIDE v. 1. live with, bear with, hear of, put up with, hang in, hang in there, hang tough, sit tight, be big, stand for. See ENDURE. 2. bunk, bunk out, crash, hang out, nest, perch, roost, squat. See INHABIT.

ABILITY n. the stuff, the right stuff, what it takes, cutting the mustard, savvy, the goods, know-how, on the ball. See SKILL.

ABJURE v. swear off, knock off, lay off, turn it off, pass by, pass on, pass up, stay away from, cool it, can it, chuck it, stow it, cut it out, break it off, break it up, drop it, get on the wagon, kick, pigeonhole, shake, sideline.

ABLE adj. all around, paid one's dues, there, right there, up to it, up to speed, up to snuff, up to the mark, have savvy, take care of business, just what the doctor ordered, mad (jazz), wicked, know one's onions, know one's goulash, know one's beans, know backwards and forwards, know the ropes, know all the ins and outs, know the score, know all the answers, know one's oats, know one's bananas, know one's goods, know one's fruit, know one's groceries, know one's oil, know one's [practically anything], fool (e.g., dancing fool, flying fool). See CAPABLE; see also SKILLFUL.

ABNEGATION n. no way, nix, forget it, who me? not by a long shot, fat chance, nothing doing, stonewall. See DENIAL.

ABNORMAL adj. screwy, for weird, weirdo, flaky, off base, off-color, out of line, spaz, grody, grody to the max, gross, fantasmo, funny. See also ECCENTRIC.

ABODE n. pad, crash pad, crib, condo, co-op, coop, joint, den, domi, dommy, flop, digs, diggings, hole. See HOUSE.

ABOLISH v. scrub, nix, call off, call all bets off, kill, kibosh, put the kibosh on, zap. See CANCEL, DESTROY.

ABOMINABLE adj. gross, grody, grody to the max, sleazeball, awful, beastly, grim, hairy, lousy, rotten, stinking. See BAD.

ABORT v. scrub, call it quits, knock it off, break off, break it off, cut off, lay off. See CANCEL; see also STOP.

ABORTION n. pro choice, pro-choicer (pro); right to life, right-to-lifer, pro life, pro-lifer (anti). See also FAILURE.

ABORTION, PERFORM v. pull a rabbit.

ABOUND v. have a full plate, be up to here with, be up to one's ass in, be up to one's ears in, be knee deep in, be alive with, crawl with, be filthy with, be no end of, be no end to, be thick with, be thick as flies, be all over the joint, be all over the place, be more than you can shake a stick at.

ABOUT adv. pretty near, practically, craptically, in the neighborhood of, in the ball park. See also NEAR.

ABOVEBOARD adj. up front, right on, call a spade a spade, make no bones about it, straight from the shoulder. See HONEST.

ABRASIVE adj. rub the wrong way, hard to take, spiky. See IRRITATING.

ABRIDGE v. chop, cut, nutshell, put in a nutshell, snip, blue pencil. See SHORTEN.

ABROGATE v. do in, finish off, knock out, nix, renig, torpedo, scrub, ankle, take a walk, get off the hook. See REPEAL, CANCELED.

ABROGATED adj. scrubbed, killed, shot, shot down, shot down in flames, washed out, wiped out, all bets are off, all off, kaput, zapped. See CANCELED.

ABRUPT adj. snippy, snappy, short.

ABSCOND v. asquatulate, powder, take a powder, take a runout powder, split, take off, hightail, fade, fade out, fade away, git, get, fly the coop, exfiltrate, breeze, clear out, skin out, duck out, duck and run, cut out, cut and run, pull out, dog it, make feet, talk a walk, vamoose, skedaddle, make oneself scarce, get the hell out, make a break for it, take French leave, go AWOL, go south with, skip, skip out, jump, beat it, blow, scram, lam, take it on the lam.

ABSENCE n. no show, hookey, AWOL, a-wol, cut, over the hill, French leave.

ABSENT adj. no-show, hookey, cutting, blitz, bag (Sch.), AWOL, French leave, over the hill, out, out-of-pocket, out of touch, ghost (counted as present), nobody home.

ABSENT v. cut, cut class, ditch, skip class, no show, dope off, fuck off, goof off, play hookey, skip, AWOL, go AWOL, go over the hill, make oneself scarce, not show up, stay away in droves, take French leave, on French leave, turn up missing, flush, buck.

ABSENTMINDED adj. out to lunch, popcorn headed, airheaded, absentminded professor, mooning, moony, pipe dreaming, woolgathering, goofing off, looking out the window, the lights are on but nobody's home, spacey, space cadet. See also FORGETFUL.

ABSOLUTE adj. downright, flat out, straight out, no catch, no fine print, no fine print at the bottom, no holds barred, no ifs ands or buts, no joke, no joker in the deck, no kicker, no strings attached.

ABSOLUTELY adv. absofuckinglutely, right on, positulely, absitively, fucking-A, cert, def, but def, why sure, for sure, fer shure, fer sher, fer shirr, sure thing, surest thing you know, sure as shootin', sure enough, sure as death and taxes, sure as fate, sure as hell, sure as the devil, sure as I live and breathe, sure as can be, sure as God made little green apples, dead sure, dead cert, for dang sure, for a fact, and no mistake, no buts about it, no ifs ands or buts, come hell or high water, flat, flat out, you know, you know it, you better believe it, you said a mouthful, you can say that again, you're not kidding, you're darn tootin', you betcha, you betcher life, you bet, you said it, straight out, no strings attached, no holds barred, no catch, no kicker, with knobs on, with tits on, in a handbasket, the real McCoy, I'll tell the world, I'll tell the cockeyed world, in spades, check, with bells on, on the button, on the money, on the nose, that's the ticket, the very thing, the checker, to a tee, Judy (I understand), on the lemon, on the noggin, it, Is the Pope Catholic?, Does a bear shit in the woods?, Is a bear Catholic?, Does the Pope shit in the woods?, honest to God, indeedy, real, for real, really truly, right-o, right on, right as rain, right you are, rather, stone (stone deaf) almighty.

ABSOLVE v. let off, let one off this time, let one off the hook, let one off easy, let up on, let go, let it go, whitewash, launder, sanitize, bleach, clear, wipe the slate clean, wipe it off, write off, go easy on, blink at, wink at, lifeboat, hand out clemo, spring.

ABSOLVED adj. beat the rap, walked, off the hook, let go, let off, clemo.

ABSORB v. 1. co-opt, take over. 2. get, get into, follow, fershtay, latch onto, soak up, take in. 3. eat (eat the cost). See UNDERSTAND.

ABSORBED adj. eat sleep and breathe [something], really into, gone, up to here in, head over heels in. See ENGROSSED.

ABSORPTION n. hang up.

ABSTAIN v. 1. take the pledge, take the cure, go on the wagon, go on the water wagon. 2. pass, pass up, sit on the fence, sit on one's ass, sit on one's butt, sit on one's duff, sit on one's hands, sit out, fence sit, go by, give the go by, give one or something the go by, quit.

ABSTAINER n. A.A., teetotaler, on the wagon, on the water wagon, on the dry, dry, fence-sitter, wet blanket, Christer.

ABSTINENT adj. on the wagon, on the water wagon, dry, took the pledge.

ABSTRACTED adj. daydreaming, pipe dreaming, mooning, moony, woolgathering, staring into the middle distance. See PREOCCUPIED.

ABSTRUSE adj. clear as mud, clear as dishwater, it beats me, you've got me, Greek to me. See OBSCURE.

ABSURD adj. camp, campy, jokey, joshing, yokky, gagged up, for grins, flaky, freaky, freaked out, goofy, kooky, wacky, screwy, loony, off the wall, batty, cockamamie, cool, crazy, daffy, nutty, sappy, dippy, dizzy, goofus, do the crazy act, do the crazy bit, do the crazy shtick, tomfool, fool around, make a monkey of oneself, make an ass of oneself, fool. See also FOOLISH.

ABSURDITY n. jive, jazz, bull, shit, bullshit, BS, horseshit, total cahcah, crap, applesauce, sour grapes, vanilla, phedinkus, hot air, balloon juice, flapdoodle, flumadiddle. See NONSENSE.

ABUNDANT adj. no end of, up to one's ass in, lousy with, filthy with, stinking with, crawling with, a drug on the market, rolling in, mucho, heavy, plate is full. See PLENTIFUL.

ABUSE n. bad-mouth, shitting on, pissing on, kicking around, pushing around, lousing around, screwing, screwing around, fucking over, buckwheats, honey, hosing, humping, knifing, quinine, skinning alive, signifying, signifyn' shucking and jiving, S'ing n' J'ing.

ABUSE v. 1. mess up, manhandle, roughhouse, rough up, bung, bung up, cut up, shake up, total, wax, hose, hump. 2. trash, bash, bad-mouth, cap, back cap, back bite, rip up the back, bitter mouth, cut down to size, do a number on, pick on, dump on, rag, rag on, tool on, knock, put down, run down, tear down, smear, ride, hurl a brickbat, dozens, play the dozens, play dirty dozens, sound dozens, sound, signify, shuck and jive, give one the finger, give five fingers to one, give a black eye, zing, give one a zinger, give one the cold shoulder, cut to the quick, blow off, cut, chop, get bent, do one wrong, rank out, gross out, cuss out, dish out, dish it out, slam, dig, dig at,

pooh-pooh, slap at, swipe, hassle, break one's balls, push around, louse around, kick one around, mess around with, screw around, screw, yentz, buckwheat, hit with buckwheats, knock up, shag, haircut (by a female), take over the hurdles, shit on, piss on, fuck over.

ABUSED adj. dogged, picked on, shafted, walking wounded, have to scrape one off the sidewalk. See also BATTERED.

ACADEMICIAN n. prof, teach, brain, egghead, nerd, gome, grind, pencil geek, tool, power tool, throat, wonk, auger, bookworm, cereb, cutthroat, grub, ink squirter, spider, squid. See also TEACHER.

ACADEMY n. old Siwash, brainery, halls of ivy, aggie, cow college, fem sem. See SCHOOL.

ACCEDE v. 1. okay, OK, go along with, play ball with, be game for, give the go ahead, give the green light. 2. cave in, give in, cry uncle, fold, throw in the towel, roll over and play dead. See AGREE.

ACCELERATE v. put on the afterburners, put the pedal to the metal, gun, rev, rev up, open 'er up, drop the hammer down, hammer on, nail it, peel rubber, dust, roll, tool, fire up, step on the gas, lay rubber, lay a batch, batch out, railroad, railroad through, make tracks. See SPEED.

ACCELERATOR PEDAL n. hammer.

ACCENTUATE v. spot, spotlight, limelight, highlight, underline, hit, headline.

ACCEPT v. 1. okay, OK, buy, lap up, eat up, set store by, sign, sign off on, thumbs up, check out, check up, put one's John Hancock on, get behind, go for, have eyes for, got to hand it to one, give the nod, give the go ahead, give the green light, give the stamp of approval, rubber-stamp, stroke, pat on the back, hats off to. See also APPROVE. 2. live with, bear with, go along with, put up with, stomach, stand for, sit still for, take, don't make waves, don't rock the boat, fit in, play the game, swim with the tide, toe the mark, when in Rome do as the Romans do. See also ENDURE. 3. take one up on. 4. take as gospel truth, take stock in, swallow, swallow hook line and sinker, take one's lumps, lump it.

ACCEPTABLE adj. cool, coolville, coolsville, A-OK, A-okay, fucking-A, OK, okay, okay dokey, okee doke, reat, all reet, all root, all righty, right on, like a shot, swell, dory, okydory, hunky-dory, ducky, just ducky, George, jake, peachy, peachy keen, sharp, so so, hitting on all six, all to the mustard, on the beam, on the ball, on the right track, up to code, up to snuff, slick, slide by easy, big, large, crasher (boy), drooly, kimble (tries to be), lulu, one of the boys, pop, prom trotter, selling, sizzler, tuff, hip, hep, mod, trendy, in the swim, faddy, masscult, ding ho, ding how, ding hau, ding hao, it's the berries, big deal, chop chop, crazy, copacetic, kopasetic, gas, a gas, gasser, cooking with gas, close, in the groove, groovy, groove, far out, hounds, in orbit, on the beam, on the right track, on the ball, on target, right on, right on the money, frantic, fab, home cooking, hotsie-totsie, in there, ice, ready, sharp, right guy, okay people, kosher, regular.

ACCEPTANCE n.   go-ahead, green light, okay. See APPROVAL.

ACCEPTED adj.   1. okayed, go down. 2. made it, in, in the loop, in like Flynn, that's it, pass, pass current, won one's spurs, arrived. 3. touted, highly touted, okay people, kosher, legit, card-carrying, according to the book, boy scout, good Joe, aces, straight, straight arrow, in line, playing their game, playing it safe, in the groove, in a rut, according to Hoyle.

ACCESS n.   connection, contact, in, open arms, open door.

ACCESSIBLE adj.   the door's always open, come-at-able, getable, getinable.

ACCESSORY n.   stall, insider, plant, shill, ringer.

ACCIDENT n.   total, pileup, crack-up, fender-bender, fender tag, rear ender, stack-up, smash, smashup, rack-up, wrack-up, event (nuclear), fluke, mess 'em up, scratch hit, shunt, slipup, bang 'em up, crack 'em up.

ACCIDENT PRONE adj.   Calamity Jane, butterfingers, klutzy.

ACCLAIM n.   pat on the back, pat on the head, PR, puff, puffing up, pumping up, rave, strokes, stroking, abreaction route, commercial, cow sociology, Doctor Spocking the help, opening up.

ACCLAIM v.   hear it for, kudo, rave, root, beat one's skin, beat one's drum, blow one's horn, stroke, boost, push, puff up, brag about, give a bouquet, give a posy, hand it to, have to hand it to.

ACCLAIMED adj.   hot, highly touted, touted, be a somebody, belled. See also CELEBRITY.

ACCLAMATION n.   hand, big hand, mitt pound, bring down the house, have 'em on their feet.

ACCLIMATED adj.   sea legs, get one's sea legs, settled in. See also ACCUSTOMED.

ACCOMMODATE v.   go with the flow, go by the book, don't make waves, don't rock the boat, play the game, shape up, shape up or ship out, bend over backwards, meet halfway. See CONFORM.

ACCOMMODATING adj.   user friendly, handy, all around, on deck, on tap, be a sport, be a regular fellow. See also INDULGENT.

ACCOMMODATION n.   deal, fifty-fifty, one's own sweet time, whenever. See also COMPROMISE.

ACCOMMODATIONS n.   crash pad, pad, digs, diggings, crib, roof over one's head. See HOUSE.

ACCOMPANIMENT n.   back, back up, backing.

ACCOMPANY v.   1. drag, take out, furp, squire, date. 2. dog, dog one's heels, string along, tag after, tag along, tailgate, draft, spook, shlep along, stick to, shadow.

ACCOMPLICE n.   stall, insider, plant.

ACCOMPLISH v.   make it, pull off, do the trick, put it over, take care of, score, hit, get there, unzip, arrive, bring home the bacon, nail it, do a bang-up job, do one proud, do justice, get out from under, get someplace, get to first base, make hay, make hay while the sun shines, sew up. See ACHIEVE.

ACCOMPLISHED adj.   buttoned up, a wrap, wrapped up, cleaned up, wound up, mopped up, dealt with, have under one's belt, knocked off, pulled it off, polished off, put away, did the trick, turned the trick, put across, put over, came through with, fixed, home, set, shot, wired, all over but the shouting, done for, done to a T, done to a finish, done to a frazzle, washed up, all set, almost home (nearly), home free. See also FINISHED. 2. brainy, savvy, wised up, hep, hip, hip to the jive, cool, sharp, with it, all woke up, knows one's business. See SKILLED, SKILLFUL.

ACCORD n.   1. okay, deal, dicker, pack, Bit 10-4. 2. good vibrations, good vibes, on the same wavelength. See AGREEMENT.

ACCORDION n.   squeeze box, box of teeth, groan box, wind box, lap organ.

ACCOST v.   run into, face off, brace, cross, flag, flag down, whistle for, whistle down. See also CONFRONT.

ACCOUNT n.   1. the picture, the whole picture, run down, lowdown, ABCs, blow by blow, play by play, score, tab, take, make, megillah, whole megillah. See also STORY. 2. tab, cuff, bad news, check, checkeroo, grunt, IOU, score. See also STATEMENT.

ACCOUNT v.   count heads, count noses, cut ice, cut some ice, dope out, figure in, keep tabs, keep score, run down, take account of, tote, tote up. See also COUNT.

ACCOUNTABLE adj.   count on one, on the hook, carry the load, kosher, right guy, Rock of Gibraltar, straight, surefire. See also RESPONSIBLE.

ACCOUNTANT n.   pencil pusher, sharp pencil pusher, pencil shover, pen pusher, pen driver, bean counter, CPA.

ACCOUNTING n.   1. the books, count. 2. score, tab. 3. pitch, story, bomb, spiel, chew one's cabbage, chew one's tobacco, say so, one's two cents' worth. See also STORY, STATEMENT.

ACCRUAL n.   up, upping, buildup, beefing up, boost, hike, ante.

ACCULTURATE v.   go native, hit the beach, fit in.

ACCUMULATE v.   round up, scare up, rack up, clean up, pile up, make a pile, make a bundle, make a killing. See also GET, INCREASE, SAVE.

ACCUMULATION n.   1. buildup, up, upping. 2. chunk, gob, pile, hunk. See also SUM.

ACCURATE adj.   on the nose, on the button, on the numbers, on the money, right on the money, right on, keerect, reet, reat, solid. See CORRECT.

ACCURSED adj.   snakebit, jinxed, damned, all fired, hell fire, hoodooed, voodooed.

ACCUSATION n.   beef, beefing, bitch, gripe, the gripes, a hooha, stink, big stink, dido, kick, blast, holler, roar, rumble, squawk, yell, rap, bum rap (false). See also COMPLAINT.

ACCUSE v.   name, finger, point the finger at, put the finger on, hang something on, pin on one, pin it on one, blow the whistle on one, whistle-blow, frame, frame up, put-up job, lay at one's door, let one have it. See also DENOUNCE.

ACCUSED n.   butt, goat, patsy, fall guy.

ACCUSER n.   whistle-blower, fink. See also IN-FORMER.

ACCUSTOM v.   get one's sea legs, roll with the punches, swim with the tide, come up to scratch, fit in. See CONFORM.

ACCUSTOMED adj.   grooved, in the groove, get one's sea legs, settled in. See CONFORM.

ACHIEVE v.   go to town, go over big, perk, percolate, tear off, tick, make it, make it big, make one's mark, make a name for oneself, make hay, make the grade, make well, make out, make a noise in the world, earn one's wings, have one's wings, pull off, pull it off, beat out, knock off, polish off, romp off with, do the trick, turn the trick, do up brown, do a turn, do to a turn, do to a T, do a number, do one's thing, do oneself proud, do the job, be on, go on, as advertised, get it across, put across, put over, put it over, put away, put the lid on, put it together, one down, one down and two to go, sail through, take care of, T.C.B. (take care of business), deal with, come through with, come out on top of the heap, strut, strut one's stuff, do one's stuff, come on, come on like gangbusters, score, hit, bring down the house, be home free, get away with, get fat, get rich, get well, get over, get ahead, get there, get to first base, clean up, wind up, button up, wrap up, mop up, unzip, pan out, turns out, ring the bell, flop (by trickery), hack it, arrive, bring home the bacon, bring home the groceries, feather one's nest, line one's nest,

knock one for a loop, cream, cream up, hit the bull's-eye, fly, nail it, drive it home, win one's spurs, squeak by (barely), go places, go great guns, luck, step into the shoes of.

ACHIEVED adj.   under one's belt, knocked off, polished off, dealt with, put away, pulled off, put across, put over, cleaned up, wound up, wrapped up, mopped up. See also ACCOMPLISHED, FINISHED.

ACHING adj.   hurting, grabbing, stab in the ———, making like the anvil chorus in one's skull, some hide and hair. See PAINFUL.

ACKNOWLEDGE v.   1. I'll be back to you, I'll get back to you; not give one a flop, not give one a rumble or tumble, cut, pass up (fail to). See also ANSWER. 2. own up, come out of the closet, cop a plea, fess, fess up, out with it, open up, crack, come clean, get it off one's chest. See CONFESS.

ACQUAINT v.   intro, knock down, give a knockdown, do the honors, bring out, come out with, fix up, get together, spring with. See also INTRODUCE.

ACQUIESCE v.   1. okay, pass, pass on, shake on, cut a deal, buy, set, yes one, ditto, play ball with, give one five (slap hands), jibe. 2. come across, come around, give out, put out (sexual); give in, cave in, cry uncle, say uncle, roll over and play dead, fold. See AGREE.

ACQUIESCENT adj.   1. yes-man, ass-kisser, on a string, henpecked, tied to one's apron strings, on a leash, weak sister, Milquetoast, Casper Milquetoast, tail between one's legs, schnook, dance, dance to one's tune, eat crow, eat humble pie, eat shit, putty in one's hands, when in Rome do as the Romans do. See also SUBMIS-SION.

ACQUIRE v.   promote, corral, access, hustle, wangle, grab, get hold of, get one's hands on, latch on to, pick up, lock up, rack up, scare up, snag, catch, cop. See GET.

ACQUISITIVE adj.   grabby, poligot, greedy guts.

ACQUISITIVENESS n.   the grabs, the gimmies.

ACQUIT v.   clear, wipe it off, let go, let off, let off the hook, let off easy, blink at, wink at, whitewash. See ABSOLVE.

ACQUITTED adj.   beat the rap, walked, let off, let off the hook.

ACRIMONIOUS adj.   bitchy, cussed, mean, ornery, salty. See SARCASTIC.

ACT n.   1. routine, shtick, gag, bit, blackout, piece, afterpiece, spot, number, stand-up comedy, dumb act (without words), hoke act. See also PERFORMANCE. 2. shuck and jive, stall, put-on, stunt, bit, false front, fake, phony, crocodile tears, soft soap, sweet talk, chaser, mitzvah (good). 3. papers (legal).

ACT v. 1. go for it, go for broke, go in for, go that route, go to town, move, make one's move, make with (the eyes, feet, etc.), do a number, do one's thing, double, do double duty (two roles), TCB (take care of business), take a flier (impulsively), pull off, fish or cut bait, shit or get off the pot, get in there, get with it, take up, whip up, whip out, tear off, knock off, perk, percolate, cook, it cooks, tick, bag, click, stooge, operate, run with the ball, come one, come on like, do one's stuff, whittle. 2. be on, go on, do a turn, do one's bit, knock off, strut, strut one's stuff, do one's stuff, say one's piece, play one's role, play one's gig, go into one's song and dance, chew the scenery, mug, ham, ham it up, tread the boards, stooge, emote, do black; go over big, put it over, bring down the house, come on like gangbusters (well), beat out, blow; bomb, lay a bomb, lay an egg, go into the toilet (fail). See also PRETEND, IMITATE.

ACTING n. ham acting, hammy acting, hamming, hamming up, improv (improvisation), stooging, thesping. See also ACT.

ACTION n. bag, game, ball game, scene, trip, where the action is, where the rubber hits the road, comin' down, comin' off, goin' down, going, happenin', movin', movin' out, rollin', do, whoop de do, whoop la, hoop a doop, hoop de doop, hoopla, hoopty do, racket, plan, stunt, bit, follow through, big idea, deal, hopper, pipeline, proposition, works, in full swing.

ACTIVATE v. de-mothball, take out of mothballs, trigger, call up. See also ACTUATE, ENERGIZE.

ACTIVE adj. ball of fire, fireball, hyper, whiz, eager beaver, busy as a beaver, busy as a bee, busier than a one-armed paperhanger, perky, chipper, burn, clocked up, in full swing, jumping, on the go, on a merry-go-round, on the hop, on the jump, working one's tail off, running one's ass ragged, running around like a chicken with its head cut off, whirling dervish, tied up, hopped up, hepped up. See also SPIRITED, INDUSTRIOUS.

ACTIVITY n. bag, game, ball game, scene, trip, where the action is, what's comin' down, what's comin' off, what's goin' down, what's going, what's happening, racket, stunt, bit, works, zoo. See ACTION.

ACTOR n. ham, hambone, ham fatter, trouper, legiter, lead, matinee idol, bit player, moppet (child), star, thesp, straight man, feeder, stooge, foil, mugger, baddie, finger wringer, greaseball, barnstormer, dog (bad), hulligan (foreigner), stand-in, extra, lot hopper (film extra), atmosphere, scene chewer, scene sweller, spear carrier, supe, super, walk-on. See also ACTRESS.

ACTOR'S AGENT n. flesh peddler, ten percenter.

ACTRESS n. fem lead, star, love interest, T and A, tits and ass, wampus. See also ACTOR.

ACTUAL adj. for real, honest to God, kosher, sure enough, no buts about it, no ifs ands or buts, honest injun.

ACTUALITY n. what it is, like it is, telling it like it is, the emess, the real world, live, in the flesh, brass tacks, down to earth, no shit, the straight shit, the straight stuff, for real, too good to be true. See also REALITY, TRUTH.

ACTUATE v. turn on, egg on, fire up, key up, work up, work up into a lather, put up to. See also ACTIVATE, ENERGIZE.

ADAGE n. daffodil.

ADAMANT adj. hard-nosed, hang tough, tough nut, set in concrete, carved in stone, pat, stand pat, murder (he's murder). See STUBBORN.

ADAM'S APPLE n. gargle, google (not common).

ADAPT v. play the game, shape up, shape up or ship out, get one's act together, get it all together, come around, come over, if you can't beat 'em join 'em, roll with the punches. See CONFORM.

ADAPTABLE adj. all around, AC/DC, acdac, cosplug, switch hitter, go every which way, can do it all, hang loose, roll with the punches, putty in one's hands.

ADD v. 1. pad, pyramid, tag, tag on, slap on, tack on, hitch on, pour it on, cue in, figure in, piggyback, bump, bump up, beef up, soup up, hop up, heat up, hike, hike up, step up, jazz up, jack up, jump up, put up, run up, charge up, punch up, heat up, hot up, juice up, up, build, build up, spike, flesh out, add bells and whistles, dump on, snow, snowball, snow under, sweeten, sweeten the pot, ante, up the ante, parlay, speed up, boost, press a bet, join together, join up with, hook up with, hook on, plug into, add fuel to the fire. 2. tot, tot up, tote, tote up, reckon up. See also INCREASE.

ADDICT n. AD, A-head, junkie, junker, greasy junkie, user, doper, mainliner, zone, zoner, space cadet, freak, head, hop, hophead, drughead, coke head, acid head, acid freak, dust head, weedhead, pothead, pillhead, methhead, fiend, dope fiend, hooked, hype, hypo, banger, bangster, jabber, jaboff, needle man, needle knight, smack slammer, tripper, dirty, dopenik, straight (after injection), viper, wasted, dynamiter, sick (needs injection), cokey, snifter, tooter, ice creamer, student, Skag Jones, snowbird, snow snorter, station worker, Saturday night habit (occasional), bean popper, joy popper (new or occasional user), campfire boy, tea toker, from Mount Shasta (not common), goof, goof ball, aspirin hound, speedo, speed freak, horse, globetrotter (always moving). See also DRUG USER.

ADDICTED v. hooked, hooked on, on the needle, hyped, spaced out, strung out.

ADDICTION n. habit, hook, monkey, monkey on one's back, Jones, jones, sweet tooth, thing, to be into, hang-up, one's bag, shot, kick.

ADDITION n. options, all the options, bells, bells and whistles, upping, boost, hike.

ADDITIONAL adj. option, all the options, bells and whistles, on the side, perks, padding, spare tire, fifth wheel, plus God knows what, and (implied coffee and), and such, and such and such, and so on, all that sort of thing, and all that, and like that, stuff like that, and what not, and what have you, widow, lagniappe. See also EXTRA.

ADDITIONALLY adv. one mo' time, una mas, come again, chew one's cabbage twice.

ADDLE v. get to, discomboberate, discumbobulate, ball up, rattle, rattle one's cage, throw, throw one, put one on a crosstown bus. See CONFUSE.

ADDLED adj. unglued, slap happy, punchy, shook, shook up, up, balled up, fouled up, fucked up, mixed up, farmisht, fertummeled, woozy, thrown, rattled, out to lunch, gone. See CONFUSED.

ADDRESS n. pitch, spiel, chalk talk, pep talk, soapbox oration. See SPEECH.

ADDRESS v. 1. pitch, spiel, spout, stump, get on a soapbox, hear it for, root for. See SPEAK. 2. dig, hammer away, plug, peg away, go at, go for, have a go at, have at, pitch into. See APPLY ONE'S SELF. See also ATTEMPT. 3. flag, flag down, whistle for, whistle down, flop, give one a flop, give one a toss, give one the glad eye, give one the glad hand, highball, shoulder, tumble. See also GREET.

ADDRESS BOOK n. little black book.

ADEPT adj. sharp, sharp as a tack, smart as a whip, brainy, got it up here (head), no dumbbell, no dummy, nobody's fool, not born yesterday, quick on the trigger, quick on the uptake, crazy like a fox, clean, heads up, on the ball, on the beam, up to speed, phenom, pro, there, whiz, whiz kid, whiz bang, wizard, boss player, has enough ducks in a row, hot, hotshot, know one's onions, know one's stuff, have know-how, slick, smooth, crack, crackerjack, cute, no slouch, savvy. See also SKILLED.

ADHERE v. stick like a barnacle, stick like a leech, stick like glue, stick like a wet shirt, stick like a limpet, freeze to, cling like a burr, cling like ivy, hold on like a bulldog, stay put.

ADHERENT n. flunky, buff, echo, fan, freak, frenzies, nut, hanger-on, ho dad, ho daddy, plaster, shadow, stooge, tail.

ADHESIVE n. stickum, gunk, gummy, spit.

AD HOC adj. ad hockery. See also TEMPORARY.

ADJUST v. 1. fix up, doctor, fine tune, fiddle with. See also CHANGE, MODIFY. 2. get one's act together, get one's shit together, get it together. 3. fit in, play the game, roll with the punches, swim with the tide, grin and bear it, when in Rome do as the Romans do. See CONFORM.

ADJUSTER n. go-between, fixer.

ADMINISTER v. boss, ride herd on, run, run the show, head, head up, hold the reins, sit on top of, be in the driver's seat, be in the saddle, crack the whip, pull the strings, pull the wires. See MANAGE.

ADMINISTRATION n. brass, top brass, front office, people in the front office, upstairs, people upstairs, big brother, one's watch, D.C., the digger, the mighty dome, the Union, Uncle Sam, Washington, the Feds (also Federal Reserve Bank). See also MANAGEMENT.

ADMINISTRATION BUILDING n. ad building, tower of power, HQ, GHQ, CP.

ADMINISTRATOR n. CEO, exec, boss, Prez, prex, prexy (usu. college), POTUS (Pres. of the U.S.), big brother, head, head man, head honcho, brass, man upstairs, front office. See also EXECUTIVE.

ADMIRABLE adj. a 10, A, A-1, A-number one, A-plus, A-OK, okay, ace, aces, ace high, ace of spades, super, super-duper, smashing, gnarly, mega-gnarly, unreal, cool, zero cool, cold, wicked, out of this world, out of sight, gilt-edged, drooly, flash, like wow, best ever, crack, cracking, crackerjack, peacherino, peach, peachy, ginger peachy, peachy keen, keen, salt of the earth, top, tops, top-notch, top-notcher, topflight, top drawer, top of the line, tip top, first class, first chop, first rate, star, boss, stunning, corking, a corker, solid, solid sender, great, greatest, a doozie, a daisy, dilly, bo, boo, tickety boo, deadly, deadly boo, bong, sly, copacetic, kopasetic, the bee's knees, the cat's meow, the cat's whiskers, the cat's pajamas, the butterfly's book, the caterpillar's kimono, George, the real George, down, good show, gear, golden, hard, hummer, humdinger, knock out, mad, mess, mezz, nasty, nifty, the nuts, the nerts, ripping, ripsnorter, sanitary, heavenly, bang-up, like dynamite, fab, in fat city, in orbit, murder, neat, neato, hunky dory, all wool and a yard wide, jam up, slap up, dandy, fine and dandy, just dandy, jim dandy, but good, strictly, a sweetheart, catch, find, plenty, zanzy, beautiful, cuspy, check plus, staller, dream, lollapaloosa, whiz, killer-diller, mean, ducky, hot, spiffy, spiffing, ripping, nobby, delicious, scrumptious, not too shabby, something else, groovy, tough, heavy, bad, marvy, winner, choice, rest, gasser, fab, fabulous, dynamite, far out, funky, state of the art, too much, swell, savage, shirt, shirty, tawny, a whale of a, world beater, pip, pippen, lulu, darb, a honey, a beaut, this is some kinda ———, it's the berries, bully, sharp, the best.

ADMIRE v. be crazy for, be crazy over, be crazy about, be nuts about, be daffy about, be wild about, be whacky about, be mad about, be mad for, go for, fall for, moon for, have the hots, be hot for, have eyes for, carry the torch for, torching, have it for one, be gone on, be far gone on, be sweet on, be stuck on, groove on, be hipped on, get high on, freak out on, have a crush on, have a mash on, have a case on, take to, take a liking to, take a fancy to, take a shine to, cotton to, be serious about, be smitten by, got it bad, rings one's bell, hit it off, nose open, be that way, be wrapped up in, be keen about, have a thing about, be struck by lightning. See also LOVE, APPROVE.

ADMIRED adj. pop, drooly, okay people, big, large, large charge, big man on campus, BMOC, kimble (tries to be).

ADMIRER n. rooter, groupie, buff, fan, autograph hound, booster, bug, freak, junkie, nut, frenzie, crank, culture vulture, fiend, flip, hound, alligator, gator, gate, cat, hep cat, stargazer, blue farouq. See also DEVOTEE, LOVER, SUPPORTER.

ADMISSION TICKET n. admish, board, stub, twofer (half price), pasteboard, chit, deadwood (unsold); pass, freebee, paper, Annie Oakley, Chinee, Chinee ducat, comp (free); dukie, dookie (meal ticket); duck (social event); bid, invite (invitation).

ADMIT v. 1. spill, spill it, spill one's guts, spill the beans, cop a plea, get it off one's chest, get it out of one's system, let it all hang out, open up, fess up, own up, out with it, spit it out, blab, blabber, come clean, give away, give away the show, let the cat out of the bag. See also CONFESS. 2. give the nod, okay, OK, sign, sign off on, thumbs up, be big on, bless, buy. See also ALLOW, CONCEDE.

ADMONISH v. speak to, talk to, tell a thing or two, gig, give what for, give a going over, give a piece of one's mind, give one his comeuppance, call to task, call down, come down on, come down hard on, sit on, jack up, hoist, growl, rap, dance the carpet, call on the carpet, slap one's wrist, rap on the knuckles, glue, ding, draw the line. See also SCOLD.

ADO n. stink, big stink, to-do, commo, scene, big scene, dustup, flap, fofarraw, foofooaw, hell broke loose, kickup, wingding, rhubarb, rowdydow, rumpus, ruckus, ruction, shindy, shivaree, stir, fuss, row, free-for-all, rumble, fuzzbuzzy, haroosh.

ADOLESCENT n. weenie bopper, bobby-soxer, juve, punk, yoot, jailbait (Fem.), teen, teeny, teenybop, teenybopper, petiteen, sub deb, sweet sixteen, twixt teen. See TEENAGER.

ADOPT v. go in for, go native, take up, go down the line, opt, tap.

ADORABLE adj. cute, dishy, hot stuff, hot item, sure fire, sexy, lulu, suave, superfly, dream bait, highly salable, good enough to eat up, good enough to eat with a spoon, a catch (usually husband or wife), after one's heart, wouldn't kick [him/her] out of bed.

ADORATION n. amore, mash, pash, weakness, yen, shine, beaver fever (Obsc.), calf love, puppy love, hankering.

ADORE v. be crazy for, be crazy over, be crazy about, be nuts about, be daffy about, be wild about, be whacky about, be mad about, be mad for, dig, go for, fall for, flip over, be gone on, be far gone on, be sweet on, be stuck on, groove on, be serious about, be smitten with, got it bad, have one's nose open, be that way. See LOVE.

ADORED adj. touted, highly touted. See also ESTEEMED.

ADORN v. doll up, fix up, gussy up, spruce up.

ADORNMENT n. dingbat, doodad, thing, fandangle, jazz, floss, seagoing (large, absurd).

ADROIT adj. quick on the trigger, quick on the uptake, savvy, have know-how, sharp, slick, crack, crackerjack, cute, cutie, foxy, hot tamale, neat, nifty, sharp as a tack, smart as a whip, have good hands, clean, heads up, on the ball, on the beam, up to speed, whiz, wizard. See also SKILLED.

ADULATE v. suck ass (Obsc.), suck up to, kiss up to, kiss ass, brownnose (Obsc.), bootlick, massage, curry below the knee. See FLATTER.

ADULATION n. strokes, bouquet, posy, eyewash, oil, soap, soft soap, blarney, bunkum, butter salve, sweet talk, shot, shot in the arm, shot in the ass. See FLATTERY.

ADULTERATE v. doctor, doctor up, phony up, plant, spike, water, water down, baptize, irrigate, cook, cut, needle, lace, shave.

ADULTERATOR n. needleman (liquor).

ADULTEROUS adj. extracurricular, fast, fast and loose, speedy, messy, two-timing, moonlighting, cheating, double-crossing, two-faced.

ADULTERY n. affair, fling, relationship, musical beds, carrying on, hanky-panky, playing around, nooner, matinee, two-timing, getting some on the side, a little something on the side, dog one around, tip, tip out, working late at the office, yard on, extracurricular activity, extracurricular sex, extracurricular relations, Roman spring (late in life), thing, your place or mine? See also AFFAIR.

ADULTHOOD n. prime, prime of life, dry behind the ears, ripe age, age of consent, drinking age.

ADVANCE n. 1. breakthrough, a break, go ahead. 2. boost, buildup. See also PROMOTION. 3. front money, in front, front-end loading, hike, angel dust, bite, floater, grubstake, jawbone, juice (usurious), score, scratch, take (secure a), touch, stake to. See also LOAN. 4. tip, tip off, feeler, pass, proposition. See also OFFER. 5. up, upping, upgrade. See also IMPROVE.

ADVANCE v. 1. get the green light, get the go-ahead, get over, get well, get ahead, get there, get with it, get one's act together, put it together, go places, go to town, go great guns, go straight, make hay, make well, make the grade, make the scene, make a noise in the world, make a hit, hit the bull's-eye, ring the bell, shape up, run with the ball, romp off with, skyrocket, take off, fly, move out, strike a vein, strike a rich vein, hit, sail through, come through with, cream, cream up, step into the shoes of, catch on, score, be home free, knock one for a loop, arrive, nail it, hack it, do oneself proud, come on, come along, come out on top of the heap, win one's spurs. See also ACHIEVE, SUCCEED, IMPROVE. 2. up, up one's pay, upgrade, boost, boost one's pay, get fat, get rich, strike it rich, strike gold, make a killing, make out, pan out, turn out, break the bank, hit the jackpot, hit pay dirt, kick upstairs. 3. plug, hype, push, splash, spot, throw the spotlight on, puff, boost, ballyhoo, put on the map, make a pitch for, beat the drum for, thump the tub for, get ink for. See SUPPORT.

ADVANCED adj. leading edge, cutting edge, state of the art, avant-garde, break, breakthrough, far out, out of sight.

ADVANCING adj. looking good, looking up, making it, on the upswing, on a roll, rolling, upbeat, on the rise, on the lift, upscaling.

ADVANTAGE n. edge, break, bulge, drag, pull, suction, string, ropes, weight, wire, wire-pulling, clout, winner, over, drop, have the drop on, jump, have a jump on, have a leg up on, bargaining chip, big chip, ace in the hole, card up one's sleeve, play the card, born with a silver spoon in one's mouth, head start, flying start, running start, nose out, in, in on the ground floor, inside track, what's in it for one, in pocket, the percentage, the upper hand, whip hand, a foot in the door, sitting pretty, sitting in the driver's seat, sitting in the catbird seat, steal a march, al joe, alzo, fix, gaff, gimmick, nuts, spot, spark, zinger, all sewed up, loose change (temporary), a lot to do with, a lot to say about.

ADVANTAGE, TAKE v. give one the short end of the stick, get one by the balls, get one by the short hairs, make hay, make hay while the sun shines, kick around, pack it in, trade on, cash in on, pour it on, push, push one's luck, burn up, hump, knock up, put one over on one, pull a fast one, push around, screw, screw around, cop a heel, cop a sneak, double bank, piece off; rim, ream (Obsc.); shave, skin, play for a sucker, take for a ride, take for a sleigh ride, take the bull by the horns, strike while the iron is hot, not be caught flatfooted.

ADVENTURE n. a happening, hap, happenso, a trip, a real trip, scene, a gas.

ADVENTURE v. go out on a limb, go for broke, go off the deep end, step off the deep end, go to sea in a sieve, leave oneself wide open, play with fire, be a fire-eater.

ADVERSARY n. opposish, oppo, opposite number, bad guy, bandit, buddy (sarcasm), buddy-buddy, buddy fucker (Obsc.), crip.

ADVERSE adj. agin, down on, allergic to, have no use for, ornery, stuffy, on the debit side, down side, the bad news.

ADVERSITY n. bummer, downer, can of worms, hobble, crunch, be clobbered, shit, deep shit, shit out of luck, S.O.L., up shit creek, up shit creek without a paddle, tought shit, TC, shit hit the fan, down on one's luck, rotten luck, rough, tough, tough luck, rotten break, tough break, bad break, total shuck, drag, grabber, hurting, the worst, kiss of death, can't even get arrested, cold, hard time, hard knocks, hard row to hoe, up against it, on the skids, gone to pot, gone to the dogs, it shouldn't happen to a dog, unload, rain, rainin', rainy day, run for cover, bugaboo, double whammy, jinx, jonah, evil eye, poison, that's the way the ball bounces, that's the way the cookie crumbles, a bitch, payin' dues, raw deal, tit caught in the wringer, tit in the wringer, tail in a gate, holy mess, unholy mess, messed up, stew, the devil to pay, hell to pay, pain in the ass, pain in the neck, bad news, clutch, jam, pretty pass, pickle, pretty pickle, fine kettle of fish, how do you do, fine how do you do, ticklish spot, tricky spot, sticky wicket, scrape, double trouble, headache, heat's on, hot water, hot grease, jackpot, messed up, screw-up, tsuris, tumul, need it like a hole in the head, rum go, deadman's hand, they're peeing on us and telling us it's raining, next week East Lynne.

ADVERTISE v. plug, pitch, make a pitch for, drum, beat the drum for, hard sell, soft sell, tub-thump, thump the tub for, ballyhoo, bill, billboard, boost, puff, put on the map, hype, push, splash, spot, build up, press agent, throw the spotlight on, get on a soapbox for.

ADVERTISEMENT n. ad, plug, envelope stuffer, flyer, throw away, literature, squib, want ad, advert, commercial.

ADVERTISER n. fairy godmother, sponsor.

ADVERTISING n. Madison Avenue, Mad Avenue, blurb, hype, PR, promo, puff, plug, pluggery, ballyhoo, buildup, pitch, dynamiting, hardsell, blasting, bulldogging, hoopla, pizzazz, squib, screamer, spread. See also PUBLICITY.

ADVERTISING AGENCY n. ad agency, pluggery.

ADVERTISING FRAUD, n. scam, hype, limb, tap, tap game, on, con game, on the bite.

ADVERTISING MAN n.   huckster, adman, ad writer, ballyhooer, ballyhoo man, booster, pitchman, plugger, spieler. See also PUBLICIST.

ADVICE n.   tip, tip-off, steer, bum steer (bad), kibitz, flea in the ear, two cents' worth, word to the wise, telltale.

ADVISE v.   steer, tout, update, level with, clue one in on, lay it on one, lay it on the line, put it on the line, lay it out for, let one in on, let one in on the know, put next to, put one on to, put one on to something hot, put one in the picture, put hip, put hep, put a bug in one's ear, put a bug up one's ass, put a flea in one's ear, put in one's two cents, put one wise, wise one up, put one through the grind, put one through the mill, tip, tip off, give one a tip, give one a pointer, give a pointer to, give one the word, post, keep one posted, pull one's coat, show one the ropes, kibitz, fold an ear, break in, break it to one, lace one's boots. See also INSTRUCT.

ADVISOR n.   spin doctor, tout, tipster, clubhouse lawyer, jailhouse lawyer, guardhouse lawyer, kibitzer, armchair general, Monday morning quarterback, second-guesser, Dutch uncle, rabbi, buttinski, backseat driver, God Committee, God Squad (both Medic.).

ADVISORS, GROUP OF n.   think tank, kitchen cabinet, groupthink, brain trust.

ADVOCATE v.   root for, stump for, thump the tub for, bless, boost, give a boost to, give a leg up, give a lift, go for, go to bat for, hold a brief for, plump for, ride shotgun for, stick up for, run interference for, put a flea in one's ear about, put a bug in one's ear about, push, juice up, build up, plug, tout, spread it around, be in one's corner, back, back up, buck up, brace up, hold with, go with, get on the bandwagon, stick by, say so. See also RECOMMEND, SUPPORT.

AFFABLE adj.   Mr. Nice Guy, one of the boys, one of the guys, clubby, clubbable, breezy.

AFFAIR n.   1. fling, carrying on, goings-on, hanky-panky, holy bedlock, a thing together, a relationship, getting some on the side, playing around, nooner, matinee, two-timing, extracurricular activity, extracurricular sex, extracurricular relations, tip out. 2. hap, happening, happenso. See also PARTY.

AFFECT v.   playact, put up a front, do a bit, fake, lay it on thick, make out like. See IMITATE, PRETEND.

AFFECTATION n.   front, false front, put-on, putting on the dog, putting on the ritz, show, showing out, showing off, Flash Gordon, going Hollywood, neon ribbons. See PRETENSION.

AFFECTED adj.   ham, hammy, schmaltzy, tear-jerking, false, fraud, phony, playactor, gone Hollywood, camp around, campy, artsy, artsy-crafty, artsy-fartsy, chichi, putting on the dog, putting on the ritz, ritzy, stuck

up, airish, crooker, pinky crooker, high falutin', play the ———, put the hat on. See also PRETENTIOUS.

AFFECTING adj.   mind-blowing, out of this world, on the move, feel in one's guts, turned on by, turned on to. See MOVING.

AFFECTION n.   soft spot, crush, case, hooked, amore, mash, pash, mad pash, weakness, yen, mad for, crazy for, wild for, shine, beaver fever (Obsc.), calf love, puppy love, hankering, partial to, spoiling for, itch for.

AFFECTIONATE adj.   lovey-dovey, huggy-huggy, mushy, nutty about, nutty over, all over one, partial to, soft on, big, big for, crazy for, crazy about, crazy over, have one's heart in the right place.

AFFIANCED n.   old lady, old man, main squeeze, dolly, daddy-o, intended, steady, going steady, pinned, bird, donah, donar, future, asked for.

AFFILIATE n.   1. affil (TV), branch, branch house, offshoot. 2. clubber, joiner. See ASSOCIATE.

AFFILIATE v.   team up, team up with, tie up, tie up with, line up with, throw in together, throw in with, go partners with, hook up with, come aboard, plug into. See ASSOCIATE.

AFFILIATION adj.   tie-up, tie-in, have an in with, hookup, gang, mob, ring, syndicate, clan, bunch, crew, crowd, plunderbund, outfit, cahoots. See ASSOCIATION.

AFFINITY n.   thing, bag, groove, in the groove, turned on to, cotton to, flash, weakness for, cup of tea, druthers, hit it off, on the same wavelength, good vibes, good vibrations, simpatico. See INCLINATION.

AFFIRM v.   swear up and down, swear on a stack of bibles, swear till one is blue in the face, cross one's heart and hope to die, cross one's heart and hope to spit, say so, cinch, clinch, ice, put on ice, have a lock on, lock up, nail down, set, okay, put one's John Hancock on, rubber-stamp. See also AGREE.

AFFIRMATION n.   fuckin'-A, go-ahead, green light, okay, right on, stamp of approval. See CONFIRMATION. See also APPROVAL.

AFFIRMED interj.   fuckin'-A, alrighty, all reet, right on, absofuckinglutely, solid, O.K., thumbs up, Rodger Dodger, crazy. See AGREED.

AFFIX v.   tack on, tag, tag on, hitch on, slap on. See also FASTEN.

AFFLUENCE n.   high on the hog, on top of the heap, bed of roses, clover, Easy Street, lap of luxury, the life of Riley, velvet.

AFFLUENT adj.   uptown, upscale, in the chips, livin' high, have money to burn, shittin' in the tall grass, stinking rich, well-heeled, well-fixed, have the wherewithal, flush, fat cat, big boys, upper class, the main line, the haves. See WEALTHY.

AFFRONT n.   put-down, brickbat, left-handed compliment, backhanded compliment, dump, dump on, dirty deed, dozens, dirty dozens. See INSULT.

AFFRONT v.   put down, dump on, give one the finger, give one a zinger, give one the cold shoulder, hit one where he lives. See INSULT.

AFRAID adj.   'fraidy cat, scaredy cat, run scared, scared stiff, scared witless, scared spitless, scared shitless, have cold feet, shit in one's pants, piss in one's pants, spooked, frozen, goose bumpy, asshole suckin' wind, pecker-assed, clutched up, D and D (deaf and dumb, afraid to testify). See FRIGHTENED.

AFTER-EFFECT n.   spin-off, fall out, chain reaction, flak (bad), waves, can of worms.

AFTERMATH n.   chain reaction, waves, flak (bad), upshot, blow-off, payoff. See RESULT.

AFTERNOON n.   this aft.

AGAIN adv.   one mo' time, come again, una mas, chew one's cabbage twice.

AGAINST adj.   agin, down on, anti, con, copper a tip (act against advice). See OPPOSED.

AGAINST, BE v.   knock, pan, put down, thumb down, turn thumbs down on, slam, blackball, be agin, hold no brief for, hit, take a dim view of. See OPPOSE.

AGE n.   mileage, wear and tear.

AGE v.   put mileage on, push, get along, take hair off the dog, pull pages off the calendar.

AGED adj., n.   senior citizen, golden ager, ager, gray power, on the shady side, over the hill, been around, bent, geed up, gone, hairy, passé, oldie, sleazy, raunchy, worse for wear, rusty, creaky, hinges creaking, motheaten, got a few miles on one, shot, back number, antique, oldish, relic, from way back, pop, pops, pappy guy, dad, grandpa, gramps, grandma, gramms, grans, granny, old lady, old girl, old bag, haybag, hag, old dame, old hen, old battle-ax, war-horse, old frump, biddy, O.M., old gent, old chap, old cuss, coot, old bat, old dog, old goat, dodo, fogey, old folks, old-timer, old softy, old smoothie, foozle, fossil, old fossil; old fart, old poop, old crock (Derog.), codger, duffer, old as Methuselah, old as the hills, oldster, alter cocker, A.K., duddy, fuddy-duddy, no chicken, no spring chicken, buzzard, desert rat, mossback, second childhood, the dwindles, on one's last legs, have one foot in the grave, raisin, pruneface, baldie, baldy, gink, gummer, long in the tooth, upper plates, on one's last legs, one foot in the grave.

AGENDA n.   lineup.

AGENT n.   flesh peddler, ten percenter. See also OPERATIVE.

AGGRANDIZE n.   boost, hike, hike up, beef up, jack up, jump up, parlay, ballyhoo, hype, lay it on with a trowel. See EXAGGERATE.

AGGRAVATE v.   bug, needle, hack, wig, drive up the wall, dog, nag, be on the back of, be at, pick on, give a bad time to, get to. See ANNOY.

AGGRAVATION n.   aggro, headache, tsuris, pet peeve, a pain, pain in the ass, hang-up, botheration. See ANNOYANCE.

AGGREGATE n.   the works, whole enchilada, whole ball of wax, whole schmear, whole megillah, whole shooting match. See WHOLE.

AGGRESSION n.   blitz, blitzkrieg, push, dirty deed. See ATTACK.

AGGRESSIVE adj.   ambish, ballsy, bogard, pushy, cheeky, cocky, flip, fresh, crusty, gally, nervy, chutzpadik, biggety, sassy, smart, smart alecky, smart ass, wise ass, brassy, bold as brass, come on, come on like gangbusters, come on strong, enforcer, get up and go, be a go-getter, go after, play for keeps, play hard ball, hard sell, heller, take charge, take over, take the bull by the horns, shoot from the hip. See also AMBITIOUS, ENTERPRISING, BELLIGERENT.

AGGRESSIVENESS n.   guts, push, punch, clout, steam, moxie, spunk, gumption, balls, drive, the stuff, the goods, what it takes, taking it to 'em, in there punching, get up and go, get out and go.

AGGRESSOR n.   bushwhacker, mugger.

AGILE adj.   quick on the draw, quick on the trigger, twinkle toes. See also FAST.

AGITATE v.   adjy, psych, spook, get to, make one flip, flip one out, craze, bug, bug up, burn one up, egg on, push one's buttons, turn one on. See DISTURB. See also EXCITE.

AGITATED adj.   antsy, uptight, shittin' bricks, shook, shook up, wired up, hopped up, hyper, clutched, clutched up, be a wreck, be a basket case. See DISTURBED.

AGITATION n.   creeps, fidgets, jitters, heebie-jeebies, jimjams, jumps, shakes, quivers, trembles, dithers, allovers, flap, fuss, lather, flusteration, pucker, swivet, tizzy, stage fright, buck fever, needles, stew, to-do, zingers, fuzzbuzz (commotion), fuzzbuzzy, haroosh, scene, big scene, foofaraw, wingding, rhubarb, rowdydow, rumpus, ruckus, ruction, shindy, shivaree, stir, row, rumble.

AGITATOR n.   adjy, sparkplug, pusher, fireman, hatchet man, needle man, steam up ghee, stormy petrel, wave maker.

AGO adv.   back, from way back, back when, time was, ages ago, from the year one, since God knows when, since Hector was a pup.

AGONIZE v.   bleed, hurt, carry on, stew over, eat one's heart out, sing the blues, take it big. See LAMENT.

AGREE v.   1. okay, pass on, shake on, shake hands on, sign on, take one up on, clinch, clinch the deal, make a deal, firm a deal, cut a deal, buy, buy into, set, yes one, ditto, take kindly to, get on the bandwagon, track, go along with, go along with the crowd, play ball with, hold with, be in tune with, be on the same wavelength with, be game for, give the go ahead, give the green light, give one a blank check, give one carte blanche, give one's blessing, give one's stamp of approval, give off good vibes, bury the hatchet, check, be game for, give one five (slap hands), jibe, crazy, solid, way to go, there you go, you sold me, you got it, you just ain't whistling Dixie, you said a mouthful, it's a deal, me too, sure thing, I'll drink to that, I hear you, I hear you talkin', like you say, groovey, all the way. See also APPROVE, ENDORSE. 2. come across, come around, give out, put out (sexual); give in, cave in, cry uncle, say uncle, say the word, roll over and play dead, fold, gleek it, throw in the sponge, throw in the towel, toss in the sponge, toss in the towel, toss it in, give away the store, give up, quit, knuckle under, knuckle to, lie down and roll over for, string along. See also SUBMIT.

AGREEABLE adj.   Mr. Nice Guy, be a prince, be a good joe, be a pussycat, breezy, upper, nervous, wild, reet, all reet, all root, all righty, cool, coolsville, crazy, copacetic, kopasetic, okay, A-OK, fucking-A, okey-dokey, okey-doke, ding ho, ding how, swell, dory, okydory, hunky-dory, right, righteous, snazzy, ducky, just ducky, George, jake, sharp, so so, fine, fine as wine, dandy, fine and dandy, just dandy, jim-dandy, peach, peachy, peacherino, peachy keen, keen, swell, fat, neat, nifty, spiffy, spiffing, ripping, nobby, delicious, flyin', creamy, orgasmic, cushy, fetching, home cooking, buzz, buscar (unexpected), but good, up to code, up to snuff, it's the berries, big deal, chop chop, gas, a gas, gasser, far out, in orbit, groove, in the groove, groovy, hip, on the beam, on the right track, on the ball, on target, on the button, on the nose, right on, right on the money, hitting on all six, all to the mustard, just what the doctor ordered, that's the ticket, frantic, fab, in there, in line, ice, ready, hotsie-totsie. See also ACQUIESCENT, CONTENT, WILLING.

AGREED interj.   uh huh, umhuh, yeah, yeah man, yep, yup, yowzah, yessiree, yes indeedy, indeedy, yea bo, si si, fer sher, sure, sure thing, surest thing you know, shore, check, right, right on, all right, alrighty, right-o, reet, all reet, all rightee, okay, okie-doakie, okie bebe doakie, you betcha, you bet, you bet your life, you bet your boots, A, fuckin'-A, absofuckinglutely, for it, give the nod, thumbs up, Rodger Dodger, crazy, fine, like you say, good deal, kee-rect, solid, Charlie, Uncle Charlie, jake with me, you're damn tootin, you're darn tootin, you're the doctor, natch.

AGREEMENT n.   good vibrations, good vibes, on the same wavelength, okay, deal, handshake, pact, ticket, piece of paper, Big 10-4, Four Roger for sure, Ten Roger Four, Ten Roger D, Four Roger, Roger Dodger, me too, go-ahead, green light, get the nod.

AGRICULTURAL COLLEGE n.   aggie, cow college.

AGRICULTURAL STUDENT n.   aggie.

AID n.   leg, leg up, shot in the arm, hand, hand out, boost, juice, on the reservation (political), security blanket, backup, backing,

AID v.   go with, go for, go to bat for, go the route for, stick up for, open doors for, lend a hand, bail out, straighten one out. See HELP. See also SUPPORT.

AIDE n.   girl Friday, man Friday, stooge, shop, crew, troops. See ASSISTANT.

AIL v.   feel awful, feel under the weather, look green around the gills, not feel like anything, come down with, take one's death.

AILING adj.   down, run down, down with, get a bug, under the weather, below par, feel awful, be off one's feed, feel like death warmed over, rocky, seedy, sick as a dog. See ILL.

AILMENT n.   bug, crud, creeping crud, the runs (diarrhea), the screaming shits, that's what's going around, the flu, the pip, dose, double scrudfantods, fascinoma (Medic.), willies (mythical).

AIM n.   where one's heading, ambish. See also OBJECTIVE.

AIM v.   target, zero in, move in, sight, sight on, get one in the cross hairs.

AIMLESSLY adv.   hit or miss, by bits and pieces, by fits and starts, any which way. See ERRATICALLY.

AIR BATTLE n.   dogfight, raid, air raid, scramble.

AIRCRAFT CARRIER n.   flat top, covered wagon, birdfarm, mother, jeep carrier, blackshoe (crew).

AIRFIELD n.   strip, airstrip, landing strip, runway, home plate (A.F.).

AIR FORCE ACADEMY CADET n.   doolie, Mister Doolie, gadget, gomer, gomar.

AIR FORCE PERSONNEL n.   flyboy, goofer, goopher, gimper, kiwi, sky winder, penguin.

AIR FREIGHT n.   birdieback.

AIRPLANE n.   plane, jet, ramjet, scramjet, stretch DC 9, crate, boxcar, fat Albert (jumbo jet), ship, airship, can, big iron (multi-engine), big iron fever (desire to fly big aircraft), cab, kite, cloud buster, crop duster, clay pigeon, coffee grinder, coffin (unsafe), flying coffin, beast, bogie (enemy, target), bus (WWI & II), tail-ass Charlie, bird, bird in the air (unidentified), bird dog (WW II), Gooney Bird (DC-3), bandit (enemy), drone, flivver, flying jenny, grasshopper, heap, hedgehopper, Jenny, Jerry (German), Mig (Russian), pea shooter (WW II), seagull, soup job, wind wagon, Willie Fudd, flying banana, flying boxcar, killer, mosquito, spotter plane, spy plane, zoo (press).

AIRPLANE CONTROLS n.   joy-stick, joy knob.

AIRPLANE CRASH n.   pancake, belly landing, ditch, down, in the drink, splash, thud, washout, wipeout, prang, Chinese three-point landing (one wing low).

AIRPLANE DEPARTURE n.   takeoff, wheels up.

AIRPLANE FLIGHT n.   jump, hop, hedgehop (low), flip.

AIRPLANE GROUND CREW n.   grease monkey, blisterfoot, dust eater, ground gripper, paddlefoot.

AIRPLANE LANDING n.   three point, three pointer, touchdown, touch and go (practice), put her down, grease it in, dead stick, power off; splash, splash down, go in, pancake, ditch (crash). See also AIRPLANE CRASH.

AIRPLANE PARTS n.   eve (rib of wing), flaps (ailerons), greenhouse (cockpit cover), stick, joy stick.

AIRPLANE TAKEOFF n.   scramble (A.F.).

AIRPORT n.   strip, airstrip, landing strip, runway, home plate (A.F.).

AIRPORT HOTEL n.   airtel.

AIR RAID n.   alert, flap (also alert or alarm), mission.

AIRS n.   front, false front, put-on. See also PRETEN-SION.

AIR TRAVEL n.   flight, hop, red eye (overnight). See also TRAVEL.

AIR VICTORY n.   down one, splash one, splash the zeros (WW II).

AKRON, OHIO   Rubber City.

ALABAMA   Cotton State, Lizard State, the Heart of Dixie, Yellow Hammer State.

ALABAMAN n.   Bama.

ALARM n.   Mayday, SOS, flap, flash, high sign, sign, wigwag, wink, nod, tip, tip off, tooter, scramble, a bug in one's ear. See ALERT.

ALARM interj.   fore, watch it, heads up, cheese it, cheese it the cops, chickie, chickie the cops, jigs, jiggers,

jiggers the cops, beat it, look out, amscray, awlay, bleaso, butso, duck, freeze, bird dog.

ALARM v.   spook, scare to death, scare stiff, scare silly, throw a scare into, chill, chill off, give one a turn, make one jump a mile, make one jump out of his skin, toot the tooter (set off mechanical). See FRIGHTEN. See also ALERT, WARN.

ALARM CLOCK n.   alarm, clock radio, chimer, tattler.

ALARMED adj.   pushed the panic button, scared stiff, scared shitless, spooked, up tight, hung up, frozen, goose bumpy, jumped a mile, jumped out of one's skin, given a turn, struck all of a heap. See FRIGHTENED.

ALARMING adj.   hairy, hair-raising, furry, scary, spooky, hot, loaded, dynamite, chancey, dicey, unhealthy, heavy, rugged, on the spot, put on the spot.

ALASKA   Last Frontier, Great Land, North Star State, Sourdough State, Up Over, Seward's Folly.

ALBUQUERQUE, NEW MEXICO   Big A.

ALCATRAZ PRISON n.   the Rock.

ALCOHOL n.   hall, hootch, booze, sauce, alky, moonshine, medicine, oil, rotgut, red-eye, rerun, canned heat, smoke, firewater. See LIQUOR.

ALCOHOLIC n.   drunk, heavy drinker, brown bagger, boozer, dip, dipso, stew, stewbum, rummy, rum bum, wino, lush, barfly, shikker. See DRINKER.

ALCOHOLISM CURE n.   A.A., dry out, kick the habit, go on the wagon, go on the water wagon, take the cure, quit cold turkey.

ALERT adj.   1. sharp, wired, with it, bright-eyed and bushy tailed, jazzed, switched on, on the job, on one's toes, on the qui vive, on the lookout, on the ball, quick on the draw, quick on the trigger, fast on the draw, good hands, have no flies on one, on the beam, Johnny on the spot, keep one's eye on the ball, salty, fly, heads up, hopped up, psyched up, wise, wised up, cagey, leery, hip. See also AWARE, INTELLIGENT, KNOWLEDGEABLE. 2. be all ears, have one's ear to the ground, have eyes in the back of one's head, have a weather eye open, have one's eyes peeled, mind one's p's and q's, scramble.

ALERT n.   Mayday, SOS, flap, high sign, tip off, tooter, scramble. See ALARM.

ALERT v.   flag, wave a red flag, cloud up, give one the high sign, toot the tooter (set off mechanical), pull one's coat, tip, tip off. See also ADVISE, WARN.

ALEUTIAN ISLANDS   Chain.

ALIAS n.   AKA (also known as), handle, moniker, nickname, summer name.

ALIBI n. cop-out, cover, cover up, cover story, stall, fish story, song and dance, airtight alibi. See EXCUSE.

ALIBIER n. Alibi Ike.

ALIEN n. furriner, FOB (fresh off the boat), greenhorn, ginzo, guinzo, gringo, goum, greaseball, jaboney, jiboney, wetback, blow in, bum, face, floater, geepo, weed, strange weed.

ALIENATED adj. turned off, on one's shitlist, in bad with, on the outs, at outs, at sixes and sevens, at loggerheads. See also ALONE.

ALIKE adj. xerox, carbon copy, ditto, double, dead ringer, look-alike, spittin' image, S.O.S. (same old shit), same difference. See SAME.

ALIMONY n. palimony (unmarried).

ALIVE adj. alive and kicking, ticking, warm, here, in the lifestream.

ALL n. jackpot, the works, lock stock and barrel, whole enchilada, whole ball of wax, whole nine yards, whole works, whole schmear, whole show, whole shooting match, wall to wall, across the board. See WHOLE.

ALLAY v. cool, cool out, make nice, play up to, pour oil on troubled waters, schmear, square, take the sting out, take the bite out. See PACIFY.

ALLENTOWN, PENNSYLVANIA Mack City.

ALLEVIATE v. soft-pedal, take the bite out, take the edge off, pour water on troubled waters, take the sting out. See also PACIFY.

ALLIGATOR n. gator.

ALLOCATE v. dish out, divvy, divvy up, cut, slice, slice the melon, split up. See DIVIDE.

ALLOCATION n. piece, a piece of the action, end, divvy, bite, cut, slice, rake off, fifty-fifty, the lion's share. See SHARE.

ALLOT v. cut, cut the pie, cut the melon, slice, shell out, split up, divvy, divvy up. See DIVIDE.

ALLOTMENT n. cut, bite, slice, chunk, split, end, piece, a piece of the action, a cut of the pie, a cut of the melon, rake off. See SHARE.

ALLOW v. okay, pass on, yes one, ditto, take kindly to, be big, free up, go along with, live with, hold with, sit still for, be game for, hear of, give the go-ahead, give the green light, give one a blank check, give one carte blanche, give one's blessing, give one's stamp of approval, give one five (slap hands), check, come around. See also CONCEDE, GRANT.

ALLOWANCE n. cut, cut in, cut up, cut a melon (profits), share, drag, P.C., piece, rake off, taste. See SHARE.

ALL RIGHT adj. no slouch, all reet, okey-dokey, okey-doke, O.K., A-OK, ding how, swell, hunky-dory, ducky, fucking-A, George. See ACCEPTABLE.

ALLURE n. bedroom eyes, come-hither look, come-on, the jazz.

ALLURE v. hook, pull, vamp, suck in, turn one on, come on, give one the come on, sweep off one's feet. See ATTRACT.

ALLURING adj. stacked, built, curvy, be whistle bait, be a looker, be a pussycat, be a sex kitten, be a mink, be a stone, be a stone fox, be a head rush, be a stunner, drop-dead beautiful, knock-out (all women); lady killer, tall dark and handsome (both for a man). See BEAUTIFUL.

ALLY n. friendly, ours, us. See also FRIEND.

ALLY v. play ball with, plug into, line up with, tie in with, throw in with, go partners with, play footsie with, join up with, hook up with, interface with. See ASSOCIATE.

ALMOST adv. by the skin of one's teeth, pretty near, practically, craptically. See NEARLY.

ALMS n. handout, hand, helping hand, do one's part. See DONATION.

ALONE adj. be a loner, be a lone wolf, doe, shag, stag, solo, onliest, Herman the hermit, Crusoe, Robinson Crusoe, traveling light, in solitary, batching it (living alone), be all by one's lonesome, me and my shadow, me myself and I, to chew something over alone, on one's own hook, on one's own say so, ace (Rest.).

ALOOF adj. cool, cool cat, cold, cold fish, loner, lone wolf, dog it, dog up, stuck up, uppity, laid back, offish, standoffish, on ice, put on airs, thick-skinned, hard-boiled, I should worry, hardhearted, Herman the hermit. See also ARROGANT.

ALPHABET n. ABCs.

ALTER v. doctor, phony up, cook, take it in a little, mid-course correction, revamp, tweek, give it a tweek (small), fine tune, dink, dial back, recalibrate. See CHANGE.

ALTERATION n. mid-course correction, about-face, flip-flop, switch, switch-over. See MODIFICATION.

ALTERCATION n. brawl, brush, fracas, flap, hassle, punch out, rhubarb, rumble, run-in, go, set-to, bone of contention, fuss, wrangle, beef, blowup, spat, tiff, words. See ARGUMENT.

ALTERED adj. doctored, cooked, spiked.

ALTERNATE n. back up, sub.

ALTERNATE v. yo-yo, blow hot and cold, shilly-shally, hem and haw.

ALTERNATING CURRENT n. AC.

ALTERNATIVE adj. flipside, other side of the coin, take it or leave it.

ALTERNATIVE n. 1. back-up, redundancy, sub. 2. druthers, go down the line, other fish to fry, other fish in the sea, other pebbles on the beach, take it or leave it. See also CHOICE.

ALTIMETER n. air log.

ALTRUIST n. do-gooder, bleeding heart, good scout, Robin Hood. See also PHILANTHROPIST.

ALTRUISTIC adj. big, big-hearted, all heart, bleeding heart, heart in the right place, do-gooder.

ALUMNUS n. alum, old grad.

ALWAYS adv. for keeps, for ever so long, for a coon's age, for a dog's age, for a month of Sundays, till hell freezes over, till you're blue in the face, till the cows come home, till shrimps learn to whistle, since God was young, since Hector was a pup, when a donkey flies.

AMALGAM n. combo, mishmash, mishmosh, soup (liquid), lorelei, everything but the kitchen sink, duke's mixture (strange).

AMALGAMATE v. pool, team up with, tie up, tie in with, tie up with, join together, come together, hook up with, interface with, network with. See ASSOCIATE.

AMALGAMATION n. megacorp, multinational, pool, bunch, crew, crowd, gang, mob, plunderbund, outfit, ring. See ASSOCIATION.

AMANUENSIS n. sec., girl Friday, man Friday.

AMARILLO, TEXAS Big A, Cactus City.

AMASS v. corral, round up, scare up, clean up, pile up, make a pile, make a killing. See also INCREASE.

AMATEUR n. am, ammie, ham (radio), bush, bush league, jackleg, Sunday——— (Sunday driver, e.g.).

AMATEURISH adj. half-assed, artsy-fartsy, half-baked, half-cocked, Mickey Mouse, Sunday (Sunday driver, etc.). See INCOMPETENT.

AMATEUR PHOTOGRAPHER n. shutterbug.

AMATEUR RADIO OPERATOR n. ham, ham operator.

AMATEUR RADIO n. rig.

AMAZE v. put one away, blow one away, blow one's mind, bowl down, bowl over, flabbergast. See ASTONISH.

AMAZED adj. blown away, mind blown, bug-eyed, floored, could have been knocked over with a feather. See ASTONISHED.

AMAZEMENT n. one for the book, something else, stunner, stopper.

AMAZING adj. mind-blowing, stunning, butt-puckering, something else, something to shout about, something to write home about, one for the book, stunner, grabber, stopper, megadual, helluva note.

AMBASSADOR n. cookie pusher.

AMBIGUOUS adj. clear as mud, clear as dishwater, clear as ditch water.

AMBITION n. fire in the belly, push, right stuff, in there punching, moxie, get up and go, get out and go.

AMBITIOUS adj. ambish, hungry, ballsy, bogard, pushy, pushy hotshot, come on, come on like gangbusters, come on strong, enforcer, get up and go, go-getter, hard sell, hard ball, play hard ball, play for keeps, take charge, take over, on the make, out for a rep, ball of fire, fireball, eager beaver, spark plug, self-starting, self-starter, full of get up and go, looking to glom the stepping dough (U.), raise one's sights, set one's sights high, take the bull by the horns, heller. See also AGGRESSIVE.

AMBLE v. ank, ankle, hoof it, toddle, sashay, gander, percolate, gumshoe, ooze, mope, mooch, boogie. See WALK.

AMBULANCE n. meat wagon, band-aid wagon, butcher wagon, crash wagon, fruit wagon, blood box, bone box.

AMBUSH v. jump, box in, get one in a box, lay for, bushwhack, drygulch, jap, pull a jap. See also ATTACK.

AMELIORATE v. upgrade, step up. See IMPROVE.

AMEND v. square, square up, square a beef, square things, make up for, pay one's dues. See CORRECT. See also IMPROVE, EDIT.

AMERICAN n. Joe, G.I. Joe, Uncle Sam, Yank, Yankee, yanqui, Americano, gringo (Derog.)

AMERICAN FLAG n. Old Glory, Red White and Blue, Star Spangled Banner, Stars and Stripes, Stars and Bars (Confederate).

AMERICAN INDIAN n. redskin; apple, Uncle Tomahawk (friendly to the White Establishment, Derog.).

AMERICAN INDIAN MOVEMENT AIM, red power.

AMERICAN LEAGUE n. junior circuit (Bsbl).

AMERICAN LEGION n. the heroes union (Derog.).

AMERICAN NATIONAL RED CROSS n. Red Cross.

AMIABLE adj. 1. buddy-buddy, clubby, mellow, tight, palsy-walsy, cozy, downright neighborly. See FRIENDLY. 2. Mr. Nice Guy, prince, pussycat, breezy, reet, reat, all reet, all root, all rightee, cool, coolsville, crazy, copacetic, swell, right, righteous, home cooking.

AMICABLE adj. clubby, mellow (close), cozy, right nice, white, regular, square shooter. See FRIENDLY.

AMISS adj. glitched up, haywire, gone haywire. See WRONG, CROOKED.

AMITY n. good vibes, good vibrations, hit it off, in sync, on the same wavelength, simpatico, together, kissing kin. See also HARMONIOUS, SYMPATHETIC.

AMMUNITION n. ammo, iron rations, confetti.

AMMUNITION DEPOT n. ammo dump.

AMNESIA n. out of it, out to lunch, blackout, draw a blank. See also FORGETFULNESS.

AMOROUS adj. horny, pash, sexy, hot, hot for, hot pants, heavy, hot and heavy, hot baby, hot number, hot patootie, sweet for, sweet on, turned on, have a crush on, lovey dovey, boy crazy, girl crazy. See also FOREPLAY, SEXUALLY AROUSED.

AMOROUS ADVANCE n. hit on, come on to, pick up, move, move in on, make one's move, make a play for, make a pass at. See FLIRT.

AMOROUS PLAY n. making out, pass, make a pass, suck face, doing face time, consent, kneesies, footsies, cop a feel, feel one up, dry hump, petting, necking, party, petting party, get physical, parking, monkey business, pitch woo, fling woo, spoon, smooch, perch, lallygag, lollygag, spark, billing and cooing, night baseball. See also SEXUAL RELATIONS.

AMORPHOUS adj. baggy, blobby.

AMOUNT n. 1. price tag, score, tab, list, net, come to, bad news, damage, set one back, to the tune of, tidy sum. See COST. 2. chunk, gob, heap, hunk, mess, pack, hit, load, passle, pile, slat. See also WHOLE.

AMOUNT, LARGE n. ton, mucho, mucho mucho, heap, load, loads, lots, bags, heavy, heavy duty, bo coo, boo coo, boo koos, bocooz, pack, peck, pot, passle, flock, raft, slew, whole slew, scads, score, zillion, jillion, bazillion, skillion, umpteen, umptieth, umpty-umpth, kind (that kind of money), mint, wad, whopper, whopping, bundle, man-sized, king-sized, mess, gang, sockful, shithouse full, fist-full, aplenty, good 'n' plenty, gob, dollop (serving of food), lollop, oodles, oodles and oodles, stinking with, crawling with, alive with, thick with, thick as flies, thick as hail, thick as fleas on a hound dog, drug on the market, galore, money to burn, rolling in, up to one's ass in, coming out of one's ears, knee deep in, all over the place, more than you can shake a stick at, would choke a horse, no end of, no end to, — and then some.

AMOUNT, SMALL n. titch, smidge, smidgen, skoshe, skoshe more, spot, taste, un poco, weenchy, teensy-weensy, teeny-weeny, diddley, diddley shit, shit, chicken shit, chicken feed, peanuts, small change, penny ante, two cents' worth, tad, shoestring, gnat's heel, bite, cut, nip, slice, a hoot, drop in the bucket, drop in the ocean, small beer, hill of beans, row of buttons, row of pins, damn, darn, tinker's damn, smithereen, stump. See also NOTHING.

AMPERE n. amp.

AMPHETAMINE n. A, speed, bam, bombita, cartwheel, chalk, cotton (saturated with Benzadrine), copilot, diet pills, double blue, driver, eye opener, forwards, French blue, hearts, jellybeans, jollybeans, leapers, leepers, lid popper, lightfooted, peaches, pepper, pep pill, ripper, splash, thrusters, truck drivers, up, uppers, wake up, obie.

AMPHETAMINE USE v. amp, overamp.

AMPHETAMINE USER n. A-head, speed freak.

AMPHIBIOUS VEHICLE n. duck (WW II).

AMPLE adj. heavy, galore, no end, up to one's ass in, one's plate is full. See PLENTY. See also AMOUNT, LARGE.

AMPLIFICATION n. boost, buildup, upping, padding. See also EXAGGERATION.

AMPLIFIED adj. beefed up, built up, souped up, hiked up, jacked up, boosted, padded, upped, pyramided. See also EXAGGERATED.

AMPLIFIER n. hamburger helper (linear radio).

AMPLIFIER, LINEAR n. afterburner.

AMPLIFY v. 1. boost, up, beef up, build up, hike, hike up, jack up, jump up, put up, pyramid. See EXPAND. 2. flesh out, spell out. 3. puff, ballyhoo, lay it on thick, blow, blow smoke, make a federal case out of something. See EXAGGERATE.

AMUSE v. crack one up, break one up, fracture one, grab, tumul, panic, put away, wow, slay, kill, knock dead, knock them in the aisles, lay 'em in the aisles, have 'em in the aisles.

AMUSEMENT n. ball, laughs, lots of laughs, action, fun and games, grins, get some grins, just for grins, big time, high time, high old time, picnic, field day, whoopee, hoopla, just for laughs, just for the heck of it, just for the hell of it, just for the devil of it, merry go round. See also ENTERTAINMENT.

AMUSE ONESELF v. have a ball, have a few grins, have lots of laughs, laugh it up, party, get one's kicks, get one's jollies.

AMUSING adj. crack up, ball, for grins, fun, gas, more fun than a barrel of monkeys, cut up, he had 'em in the aisles, knock 'em in the aisles, lay 'em in the aisles, hooper-dooper, hooper-doo, boffo, break one up, tear one apart, a scream, camp, campy, jokey, joshing, yok, yokky, zetser, a hoot, laffer, riot, gagged up, priceless, a million laughs, screaming, screamingly funny, too funny for words, too killing for words, gut-busting, side-splitting.

AMYL NITRITE n. amy, popper, blue, blue angel, blue bird, blue devil, blue heaven, pear, snapper, pearls, poppsies, whiffenpopper.

ANAL INTERCOURSE v. ace fuck, back scuttle, brown, brown hole, corn hole, goin' up the mustard road, Greek, hershey bar way, sit on it, up the old dirt road, up the chocolate highway (all Obsc.). See also SEXUAL IN-TERCOURSE.

ANALINGUS v. browning, bite the brown, reem, rim job (all Obsc.). See also CUNNILINGUS.

ANALYSIS n. on the couch, the couch.

ANALYST n. shrink, shrinker, head shrinker, couch doctor, guy with the net, guy in the white coat, bug doctor (prison), guru, squirrel.

ANALYST, FINANCIAL n. numbers cruncher, bean counter.

ANALYZE v. figure, figure out, sort out, rap, confab, hash, rehash, hash over, chew over, kick around, knock around, get down to cases, get down to brass tacks, spell out, let the daylight in, let the sunlight in, talk game, flog a dead horse, whip a dead horse. See also DE-LIBERATE.

ANCHOR n. hook, mud hook.

ANCHOR v. drop the hook.

ANCHORAGE, ALASKA The Iceberg.

ANCIENT adj. been around, bent, got a few miles on, a lot of mileage, relic, antique, creak, creaker, back number, from way back, oldie, old dodo, fossil, old fossil, old goat, worse for wear, rusty, moth eaten. See also AGED, OLD.

AND conj. 'n', nuh.

AND THEN? So?, Nu? What then?, Vah den?

ANECDOTE n. gag, yarn, long and the short of it, tall story, fish story, cock-and-bull story, cock and bull, tall tale, fairy tale, line of cheese, megillah, wheeze, chestnut, old chestnut, old touches, touches.

ANESTHESIOLOGIST n. goo man.

ANESTHETIC n. dope, gas, shot, spinal.

ANESTHETIZE v. kayo, KO, knock out, dope, drug, put to sleep, freeze.

ANEW adv. one mo' time, una mas, come again.

ANGER n. mad, sore, huff, dander, Irish, pet, tiff, miff, stew, storm, wingding, slow burn, conniption, con-niption fit, cat fit, duck fit, blow up, flare up, boiling point, rise, get a rise out of, more heat than light.

ANGER v. brown off, burn up, rile, miff, make mad, make sore, piss one off, tick off, T-off, frost, needle, give one the needle, blow up, blow one's top, blow one's stack, blow a fuse, blow a gasket, flip, flip out, flip one's lid, fly off the handle, get sore, see red, push one's buttons, get one's back up, get one's balls in an uproar, get hot under the collar, get under one's skin, get in one's hair, get a rise out of one, get one's goat, get into a dither, get into a stew, get one's dander up, get one's Irish up, get one's mad up, get one hot under the collar, make one's blood boil, work up, work oneself into a lather, work oneself into a sweat, have a hemorrhage, have a shit hemorrhage, whip up, fire up, key up, kick up a row, kick up a dust, kick up a shindy, put one's Irish up, put one's dander up, raise one's dander, raise Cain, raise hell, raise the devil, raise the roof, hack, hit the ceiling, egg on, turn on, turn one on, go on make my day, make waves, make a scene, ask for it, stick in one's craw, sound, sound off, burn one off, do a slow burn, reach boiling point, boil over, go into a tailspin.

ANGLE n. dogleg, slant, twist.

ANGLO-SAXON n. WASP, anglo, whitey, ofay, white bread, goy, goyim, shicksa, shagetz.

ANGRY adj. browned off, pissed off, p'd off, p.o.'d, cheesed off, burned one's head, chewed, bent, bent out of shape, pushed outta shape, torqued (A.F.), blow, blow one's cool, blow a fuse, blow a gasket, blow one's stack, blow one's top, blow one's topper, blow one's cork, blow one's noggin, blow one's cap, blow one's wig, blow the roof, blow it out, bouncing, bugged, bummed out, mad, good and mad, mad as a hornet, mad as a wet hen, mad as hops, hacked, sore, steamed, steamed up, let off steam, at the boiling point, boiling over, fried, ticked off, tee'd off, t'd off, t.o.'d, see red, shit blue, shit green, shit hemorrhage, shit on one or something, go ape, go ape shit, go into a tailspin, go up in the air, go ballistic, huffy, miffed, peeved, have a hemorrhage, have a shit hemorrhage, have it in for one, have a conniption, have a conniption fit, have a cat fit, have a kitten, have kittens, cast a kitten, have pups, throw a fit, duck fit, fit to be tied, hit the ceiling, hopped up, hopping mad, sizzling, burned, slow burn, burnt up, burned up, smoke, smok-ing, hot, get hot, get hot under the collar, get hot in the biscuit, get one's back up, get one's dander up, get one's gage up, get up on one's ear, flipped, flip one's wig, flipped one's lid, flip one's razzberry, fly off the handle, shit bricks, so mad one could spit nails, on a short fuse, on the warpath, on the outs, in a stew, in a sweat, in a swivet, in a tizzy, in a lather, in a dither, in a pucker, race one's motor, raise Cain, raise hell, raise the devil, raise the roof, ranting and raving, raving mad, red-assed, riled up, ripped up, roaring mad, run a temperature, salty, jumpin' salty, loaded for bear, look daggers at, geed up, get one's monkey up, plugged, porky, evil, fighting, flare, scream bloody murder, yell bloody murder.

ANGUISHED adj. cut up, tore up, ripped, hurting, worried sick, worried stiff. See DISTRESSED. See also DISTURBED.

ANIMAL n. critter, dog (inferior), mutt, stray (orphaned, deserted), varmint, bad actor (vicious), bum, cob roller.

ANIMAL DOCTOR n. horse doctor, vet.

ANIMAL EXCREMENT n. terd, turd, do, do-do, dog do, dog dew, doggy-do, bird terd, cow plop, cow flop, droppings, golden apples, road apples (horse), hooky, horse hocky.

ANIMATED adj. peppy, zingy, snappy, zippy, zappy, full of piss and vinegar. See SPIRITED.

ANIMATION n. bounce, piss and vinegar, zip, zap.

ANKLETS n. bobby socks, bobby sox.

ANNAPOLIS, MARYLAND Crabtown, crab (resident).

ANNEX v. tack on, tag, tag on, hitch on, slap on, take on, take over, hook on, hook up, hitch up. See also FASTEN, APPROPRIATE.

ANNEXATION n. grab, takeover.

ANNIHILATE v. wipe out, take out, rub out, do in, finish off. See KILL.

ANNIHILATED adj. totalled, wiped out, kaput, hashed up, cooked, sunk, zapped. See KILLED.

ANNOUNCE v. trumpet, call, blast, drum, spread it around, pass the word, sound off, run off at the mouth. See also DECLARE, PROCLAIM.

ANNOUNCEMENT n. poop, poop sheet, flyer.

ANNOUNCER n. deejay, disc jockey, veejay, rip and reader, spieler, talker.

ANNOY v. bug, needle, put the needle in, ride, miff, push, push one's button, push all the buttons, push the right button, hit one where he lives, be at, be on the back of, gross out, eat, shiv, chiv, chivey, chivvy, henpeck, nag, noodge, nudzh, sound, sound off, brown off, tick off, T-off, brass off, cheese off, piss one off, turn one off, talk one's ear off, drug, ask for it, go on make my day, make waves, heat up, hot up, fire up, burn up, burn one off, peeve, cool, give one the finger, flip one the finger, give a bad time to, give one a hard time, give one the business, give one the needle, give one a turn, turn one on, egg on, work on, hit on, what's with, bend one's ear, bore stiff,

burn out, put one to sleep, fuck with one's head, get, get to, get in one's face, get in one's hair, get a rise out of one, get one's goat, put one's dander up, get one's dander up, get one's Irish up, get one's mad up, get one hot under the collar, get under one's skin, make it tough for, make it tough for all, discombobulate, throw into a swivet, throw into a tizzy, flummox, fuzzbuzz, drive one bananas, drive up the wall, drive one up a tree, rile, rattle one's cage, hack, hassle, hound, dog, penny dog, worry, wig, ride, dump on, dog one's case, jump on one's case, get on one's case, get on one's back, put the heat on, start in on, drive up the wall, hock a charnik, hock one's charnik, put the squeeze on one, put the screws on, put one through the ringer, play cat and mouse, pick at, pick on, pressure, rub, rub the wrong way, rub salt in the wound, bone, all right already, graum, yap at, on one's tail, tail, bring one up short, pull one up short, rag, rag on, curdle, gripe, gripe one's ass, gripe one's back, gripe one's balls, gripe one's butt, gripe one's left nut, gripe one's middle kidney, nitpick, picky picky, break one's balls, stick in one's craw, add insult to injury, what's eating one?

ANNOYANCE n. drag, downer, beef, bellyache, bitch, headache, gripe, grouse, holler, howl, kick, rip, tsuris, pet peeve, a pain, pain in the ass, pain in the neck, a nag, nudge, nudzh, noodge, worriment, worriation, hang-up, rough go, handful, drip, flat tire, blister, pill, botheration, bad news.

ANNOYED adj. bugged, hacked, rousted, steamed, defrosted, frosted over, uptight, tightened up, unglued, choked, zonkers, clutched, clutched up, hacked, sketched, discombobulated, pissin', pissed off, peed off, tee'd off, browned off, bummed out, strung out, burned up, hung, hung up, dogged, miffed, peeved, riled, rubbed the wrong way, spooked, all hot and bothered, at the end of one's rope, buffaloed, hard put to it, put to it, picked on, torn down, up the wall, driven up the wall, on edge, bleeding, what's eating one?, fit to be tied.

ANNOYING adj. uncool, heavy, hefty, blivit, bugs one, that gives one a pain, one gives one a pain, pain in the neck, pain in the ass, bitch, son of a bitch, son of a gun, a bit much, too much, flea, pesky, pestiferous. See also WORRISOME.

ANNUL v. scrub, nix, call off, kill, get off the hook. See CANCEL.

ANNULMENT n. breakup, dedomiciling, go phftt, split, split up, couldn't make it, marriage on the rocks. See also DIVORCE.

ANOINT v. lube, slick, slick on, grease the wheels.

ANON adv. by 'n' by, by and by, come Sunday, down the road a piece, down the line, coming down the pike, in a short, short short.

ANONYMITY n. what's its name, whatsis, whatzit, whatchamacallit, what d'ye call it, what's his face, what's his name, I'll never forget what's his name, so and so, such and such, you know who, a whoozit.

ANONYMOUS adj. a certain person, Joe Doakes, Jane Doe, John Doe, Cheap John, Joe Blow, pig in a poke, X, X factor, Mr. X, unk, George Spelvin, so and so, such and such, whatchamacallit, what's his name, I'll never forget what's his name, what's his face, whatsis, whatzit, you know who, incog, bearding.

ANSWER n. 1. owning up. 2. comeback, feedback, snappy comeback, backcap, back talk, crack, crackback, wisecrack, dirty crack, smart crack, nasty crack, topper, cooler, lip, guff, parting shot, you get it, thank-you note. 3. all the right moves, band-aid (temporary, too little), quick fix, on target, pay dirt, the ticket. See also SOLUTION.

ANSWER v. 1. answer back, talk back, back talk, shoot back, snappy comeback, come back at, get back at, come right back at, back at you, get back to one, I'll be back to you, I'll get back to you, be in touch with one, feedback, own up, 'fess up, field the question, sass, squelch, top, settle. 2. crack, deal with, dope, dope out, lick, unzip, work through. See also SOLVE.

ANTAGONIST n. opposish, oppo, opposite number, meat, me and you, bad guy, bandit, buddy (sarcasm), buddy-buddy, buddy fucker, crip, whose side are you on?, angries.

ANTAGONISTIC adj. anti, agin, be agin, con, balky, bitchy, cussed, mean, ornery, scrappy, snorky, limber, flip, catty, waspish, be down on, have no use for, have a chip on one's shoulder, have a bone to pick, have it in for, hard on for (Obsc.), on the muscle, on the outs, at outs, out for a rep, at loggerheads, allergic to, turned off by. See also BELLIGERENT, CONTRARY.

ANTENNA n. rabbit ears (indoor), whip, bullwhip, bird snapper, feelers, sky wire, spike, big mama, ballet dancer, chopped top, hustler, scatterstick, tuning forks, twangers, twin huskies.

ANTI-AIRCRAFT ARTILLERY n. flak, SAM (USSR), silkworm (China).

ANTI-AIRCRAFT-GUN n. AA, ack ack, able able, pom pom, 88 (Ger.), archie, chatterbox, flak hack.

ANTI-BALLISTIC MISSILE n. ABM, MX.

ANTICIPATE v. jump the gun, count one's chickens before they're hatched, cross the bridge before one comes to it, take the words out of one's mouth, lick one's chops, figure, in the cards, it's looking to, see it coming, be afraid, wait for the other shoe to drop. See also PREDICT.

ANTICIPATED adj. as advertised, no big surprise, be just like one, be one all over, not put it past, looking for, in the cards, in the wind, waitin' on, the noose is hanging. See also FORETOLD.

ANTI-COMMUNIST n. red-baiter, hard hat, right winger, real 'merkin, boss class, Archie Bunker, red-neck (all Derog.).

ANTIDOTE n. fix, quick fix.

ANTI-ESTABLISHMENT adj. underground, hippy, yippie.

ANTI-INTELLECTUALISM n. meatballism, know nothing.

ANTINUCLEAR adj. antinuke, antinuker, antibomb.

ANTITANK ROCKET n. bazooka (rocket and launcher).

ANTI-WHITE PREJUDICE n. Crow Jim, Crow Jimism.

ANTI-WOMEN'S LIBERATION Aunt Jane, Aunt Jemima, Aunt Tabby, Aunt Thomasina, Aunt Tom (all Derog.).

ANTIPATHY n. allergy, no use for.

ANTITHESIS n. flip side, other side of the coin. See OPPOSITE. See also CONTRARY.

ANUS n. servant's entrance, asshole, ass, crack, rear, rear end, keester, kazoo, back hole, back way, rip, rosebud, back garden, bucket, snatch, ying-yang, gig, gigi, gee gee, hole, bum, bumhole, bunghole, brown hole, little brown eyeball, round eye, dirt road, exhaust pipe, chocolate highway, Hershey bar route, hoop, food dropper, moon, where the sun doesn't shine. See also BUTTOCKS.

ANXIETY n. worriment, worriation, botheration, downer, drag, jitters, shakes, sweat, cold sweat, shivers, cold shivers, cold creeps, creeps, willies, goose bumps, all-overs, needles, pins and needles, pucker, fidgets, ants, ants in one's pants, nail-biter, heebie-jeebies, jimjams, jumps, quivers, trembles, dithers, butterflies, flap, fuss, lather, stew, to-do, zingers, stage fright, buck fever, cliff-hanging. See also NERVOUSNESS.

ANXIOUS adj. uptight, jittery, jumpy, the jumps, jitters, shaky, bugged, choked, zonkers, pissin', shittin', shittin' bricks, scared shitless, strung out, unglued, hyper, spooked, twitty, fidgety, wreck, nervous wreck, bundle of nerves, nervy, all-overish, wired, wired up, yantsy, antsy, antsy-pantsy, ants in one's pants, about to piss in one's pants, clutched, clutched up, shook up, all shook up, shaking in one's boots, shivery, quivery, hacked, dragged (following drugs), have a short fuse, butterflies, butterflies in one's stomach, coffee head, the jams, the jims, the jimmies, the jimjams, heebie-jeebies, the screaming meemies, the meemies, fall apart, torn down, shot to pieces, basket case, hung up with, tightened up, up the wall, in a lather, in a stew, in a sweat, sweaty, sweat it, sweating bullets, in a swivet, in a tizzy, in a state, in a dither, in one's hair, on edge, on the ragged edge, have one's teeth on edge, on pins and needles, on tenterhooks, on the gog, jumpy as a cat on a hot tin roof, have kittens, cast a kitten, having the leaps, worried sick, worried stiff, biting one's nails, beside oneself, put to it, hard put to it, at the end of one's rope, rarin' to go. See also AFRAID, APPRHENSIVE, NERVOUS.

ANY adj. any which way, whatever, any old ———.

ANYHOW adv. anyhoo.

ANYTHING pron. all, whatever.

APART adj. loner, lone wolf. See ALONE.

APARTMENT n. condo, co-op, coop, crash pad, crib, blue denim crib (nice), dommy, turf, digs, diggings, pad, padhouse, cave, den, flop, joint, box, flat, dump, heave, camp, kip, scatter, walk-up, walk-back (rear), go-down (basement), cold-water flat, cubby, cubbyhole (small), place to hang your hat, place to lay your head and a few friends, roof over one's head. See also HOUSE.

APATHETIC adj. blah, have the blahs, laid back, could care less, couldn't care less, flat, have spring fever, June around, dopey, drippy, draggy, nebbish, wimpy, moony, don't give a shit, don't give a damn, don't give a hoot, what's the diff?, what the hell, so what?, I should worry?, it's all the same to me. See also INDIFFERENT, LANGUID.

APE v. mirror, ditto, do, do like, go like, make like. See IMITATE.

APEX n. ape, the max, far out, the most, tops, the greatest, up there, really up there.

APHORISM n. daffodil.

APHRODISIAC n. love drug, popper, Spanish fly, turn-on, wampole.

APIECE adv. a pop.

APOLOGIZE v. cop a plea, cop out, crawl, square oneself, square a beef, square things, make up for, get down on one's marrowbones. See also EXCUSE.

APPALL v. gross out, throw, get to, faze. See DISCONCERT. See also INSULT.

APPALLING adj. bummer, gross, grody, grody to the max, downer, mean, heavy, the end. See BAD. See also DREADFUL.

APPARATUS n. gismo, widget, outfit, idiot box, black box, conjerod, job, jobby, jobbie, contraption, dealie bob, sucker, bugger, mother; motherfucker, mothafucka (Obsc.), mofo, mother grabber, grabber, gimmick, gaff, stuff, set up, whatchamacallit, whatsis, whatzis, what's its name, whats it, whatchee, whatchy, whoziz, whoose it, whosis, whoosis, whoosamajiggle, jigamaree, gimcrack, thigamajig, thingamajig, thingamajigger, thinguma-jugfer, thingum, thingummy, thingadad, thingumabob, thingumadad, thingumadoo, thingamadoodle, whang-doodle, thingamadodger, thingamadudgeon, thinga-mananny, thingamaree, turnout, doo, doo da dad, doodad, do funny, dofunny, jigger, dojigger, doojigger, dojiggy, domajig, domajigger, hickey, dohickey, doohickey, do hinkey, dowhacky, dowillie, doowillie, dowhistle, doowhistle, doomaflogy, dingbat, dingus, goofus, gasser, gigamaree, gilguy, gilhickey, gilhooley, fandangle, flumadiddle, frobnitz, frobnitzem, kit and kaboodle, hootenanny, hootmallalie, wingding, coil, can opener (vault), Armstrong (requires strength).

APPAREL n. threads, glad rags, rig, getup, drapery, duds, feathers.

APPARENT adj. barefaced, plain as the nose on one's face, clear as the nose on one's face, under one's nose, clear cut, crystal clear, big as life, open and shut, open-and-shut case, out in the open, makes no bones about it, talks turkey, that's a fact Jack, you ain't just whistling Dixie, if it were a snake it would bite you, cheesecloth (person), commando (sex), jazzy, Is the Pope Catholic?, Does a bear shit in the woods? See also CERTAIN.

APPARITION n. spook, haunt, hant, haint, things that go bump in the night.

APPEAL v. hit on, strike. See also BEG, PLEAD.

APPEALING adj. a honey, cher, disky, dreamy, pussycat, head rush, delicious, fetcher, but good, okay. See BEAUTIFUL.

APPEAR v. make the scene, make it, pop up, bob up, turn up, clock in, check in, time in, come to light, drop in, blow in, breeze in, roll in, pop in, punch in, punch the clock, ring in, see the light of day, show, show up, speak of the devil, show a leg, turn out. See also ACT.

APPEARANCE n. front, get one's game together (best), image, screen (deceptive), blind. See also COUNTENANCE.

APPEARANCES n. front, get one's game together (best), image, screen (deceptive), blind. See also COUNTENANCE.

APPEASE v. make matters up, patch things up, meet halfway, pour oil on troubled waters. See PACIFY.

APPELLATION n. handle, John Doe, John Hancock, John Henry, moniker, tag, what's 'is name, what's his face, brand, flag (assumed), front name, label, tab.

APPETITE n. big eyes, itch, sweet tooth, yen, zazzle. See DESIRE.

APPETIZERS n. dip, finger food, spread, munchies.

APPETIZING adj. delish, scrumptious, sweetened, sugar coated, yummy, divine, heavenly, got the juices flowing. See also DELICIOUS.

APPLAUD v. beat one's skin, give a hand, give a big hand, hear it for, kudo, rave, root. See also ACCLAIM.

APPLAUSE n. hand, big hand, mitt pound, bring down the house, have 'em on their feet. See also ACCLAIM.

APPLE PIE n. Eve with the lid on.

APPLICABLE adj. on the button, on the nose, right on, on target, kosher, legit, that's the idea, that's the ticket, just what the doctor ordered. See also SUITABLE.

APPLY v. put in for. See also ASK.

APPLY ONESELF v. take one's best shot, give it one's best shot, give it all one's got, give it the ol' college try, bear down on it, buckle down, knuckle down, hump, bust one's hump, hump it, hump oneself, put one's back into it, hustle, scratch, sweat, hit the ball, pour it on, grind, dig, hammer away, plug, peg away, pull out all the stops. See also ATTEMPT, STRIVE.

APPOINTMENT n. date, heavy date, blind date, blind drag, rendezvous, gig, double date, meet, your place or mine; miss a meet, stand one up, stand one on a corner (fail to keep an); zero hour, triff, treff (secret).

APPOINTMENT, KEEP v. keep a meet, make a meet, take a meet, shape, show.

APPORTION v. divvy, divvy up, slice, split, split up, cut, cut up, piece up. See DIVIDE.

APPRAISE v. check, check out, dig it, eye, look over, peg, read, size, size up, dope out, take account of, figure, figure in, figure out, cut in, cut some ice, guesstimate, have one's number, take one's measure.

APPRECIATE v. 1. flip, flip for, flip over, get high on, freak out on, groove on. See ENJOY. See also GAIN. 2. savvy, with it, catch the drift, see daylight, dig, read. See UNDERSTAND. See also KNOW.

APPREHEND v. 1. collar, take in, bag, grab, nail, run in. See ARREST. 2. get, catch, blow wise, collar the jive, tumble, get the picture, read. See UNDERSTAND.

APPREHENSIVE adj. feel in one's bones, feel in one's guts, get the vibes, have a funny feeling, have a hunch, worried sick, worried stiff, biting one's nails, jitters, jittery, jumpy, shaky, shivery, cold shivers, quivery, trembles, dithers, in a dither, sweat, in a sweat, cold sweat, in a cold sweat, have cold feet, frozen, 'fraidy cat, scaredy cat, run scared, scared buck fever, stage fright, willies, heebie-jeebies, jumps, all-overs, butterflies, uptight, hung up, on the ragged edge, have butterflies in one's stomach, stiff, push the panic button, the willies, spooked, goose bumpy, rabbity, mousy, jellyfish, chicken, chicken out, chicken-hearted, pigeon-hearted, chicken-livered, white-livered, lily-livered, milk-livered, milksop, Milquetoast, Casper Milquetoast, weak-kneed, weak sister, sissy, baby, big baby, nebbish, candy ass, pucker, pucker-assed, pecker-assed, asshole puckerin', asshole suckin' wind, gutless, shake in one's boots, ague, creeps, heebies, leaping heebies, jams, jims, jimjams, jimmies, hung up, clutch up, D and D (deaf and dumb, afraid to testify), punk out. See also ANXIOUS, FEARFUL.

APPRENTICE n. newie, new kid on the block, rookie, rook, greenhorn, tenderfoot, boot, freshie, turkey, flunky, heel, heeler (reporter), peg boy, pratt boy, student. See also NOVICE.

APPRENTICESHIP n. paying one's dues, learning the ropes.

APPRISE v. tip, tip off, wise up, put next to, put one in the picture. See ADVISE. See also INSTRUCT.

APPRISED adj. plugged in, in the picture, in the know, wise to, all woke up, know the score, on the beam, double digs, kept posted. See AWARE. See also KNOWLEDGEABLE.

APPROACH n. wrinkle, new wrinkle, crack, fling, go, lick, stab, shot, whack. See also CONCEPT, PLAN, IDEA, OFFER.

APPROACH v. 1. belly up to, buzz, move in on, come at, contact. 2. make up to, feel, feel one out, give one a flop, give one a play, give one a promote, give one a rumble, give one a tumble, give one a toss, thumb, tumble. See also GREET, PLAN.

APPROACHABLE adj. the door's always open, come-at-able, getable, getinable. See also OBTAINABLE.

APPROBATION n. get the nod, go ahead, okay, OK, crazy, bells. See APPROVAL.

APPROPRIATE adj. just what the doctor ordered, on the button, on the nose, tailor-made, that's the idea, that's the ticket. See also SUITABLE.

APPROPRIATE v. take over, annex, grab, grab hold of, glom on to, snatch, confiscate, liberate, moonlight requisition, borrow, clap hands on, get one's fingers on, get one's hands on, swipe, kipe, highjack, hijack, highgrade. See also CONFISCATE, STEAL, PLAGIARIZE.

APPROPRIATION n. grab, takeover.

APPROVAL n. 1. strokes, stroking, abreaction route, commercial, cow sociology, Doctor Spocking the help, opening up, pat on the back, pat on the head, one's stock has gone up, eyes for, PR, puff, puffing up, pumping up, tasty, dual, megadual, bold rave, rave, radical, way sweet, mondo choice, bells, atta boy, atta girl, that's the boy, that's the girl, that's my boy, that's my girl, George, by George, hubba-hubba, keen, wow. See also AGREE, ENDORSE. 2. okay, OK, get the nod, green light, get the green light, crazy, go ahead, get the go-ahead, bells, that's the boy, that's the girl, that's my boy, that's my girl, atta boy, atta girl, hubba-hubba, keen, wow, George, by George, tasty, bold rave, radical, dual, megadual, eyes for, one's stock has gone up. See also ACCEPT.

APPROVE v.   1. back, bless, dig, groove, buy, buy into, okay, OK, lap up, sign, sign off on, thumbs up, check out, check up, check up on, ditto, get behind, go for, go along with, have eyes for, plump for, push, stump for, hold a brief for, thump the tub for, hear it for, whoop it up for, boost, booster, give a boost to, give the nod, give the go ahead, give the green light, give the stamp of approval, rubber stamp, put one's John Hancock on, carry on over, make a to-do over, take on over, go on about, stroke, hats off to, push, puff up, rave, root for, cracked up to be, brag about, give a bouquet, give a posy, hand it to, have to hand it to. 2. live with, go along with, string along with, put up with, cope, handle, lump it, lump it and like it, stomach something, grin and bear it, face it, take one up on, be big on, roll with the punches.

APPROVED adj.   kosher, okay, okay people, OK'd, get the nod, touted, highly touted.

APPROXIMATELY adv.   around, guesstimate, ball park figure, in the ball park of, upwards of. See NEARLY.

APRICOTS n.   cots, elephant ears (not common).

APROPOS adj.   on the button, on the nose, right on, kosher, legit, that's the idea, that's the ticket, just what the doctor ordered. See also SUITABLE.

APT adj.   quick on the uptake, nobody's fool, no dumbbell, not born yesterday, quick on the trigger, savvy, smart, sharp as a tack, smart as a whip. See also SKILLED, APPLICABLE, SUITABLE.

APTITUDE n.   smarts, savvy, stuff, what it takes, plenty on the ball. See SKILL.

ARAB n.   A-rab, camel jockey, gypo (WW II), rab, sand nigger (Derog.).

ARBITER n.   go-between, fixer, holdout, maven, middleman. See ARBITRATOR.

ARBITRAGEUR n.   arb.

ARBITRARY adj.   bossy, downright, flat out, straight out, no ifs ands or buts, no joke, no joker in the deck.

ARBITRATE v.   come to school, make a deal, hammer out a deal, hack out a deal, work out a deal, meet halfway, play ball with, strike a happy medium, trade off. See also NEGOTIATE.

ARBITRATOR n.   go-between, fixer, holdout, maven, middleman (labor).

ARCH SUPPORTERS n.   happies, arch supports.

ARDENT adj.   lovey-dovey, horny, hot, hot for, hot pants, pash. See AMOROUS.

ARDOR n.   hot pants, weakness, turn on, jazz, oomph, pep talk. See LOVE. See also DESIRE.

ARDUOUS adj.   uphill, heavy, murder, pisser, tough, ballbuster, no picnic. See DIFFICULT.

AREA n.   neck of the woods, the zone, turf, nabe, pit (racing, gambling).

ARENA n.   bowl, gridiron (Ftbl.), diamond (Bsbl.), boards (basketball), ice, rink (hockey), ring, pit.

ARGOT n.   doublespeak, bafflegab, lingo, jive, street talk. See JARGON.

ARGUABLE adj.   iffy.

ARGUE v.   hassle, cross, buck, nix, zap, zapper, take on, lock horns, set to, sock, sock it to one, stick it to one, top, talk back, talk game, in one's face, be agin, go agin, sass, pick a bone, pick an argument, put up an argument, put up a fight, put up a struggle, argufy, row, break with, rhubarb, pettifog, kick around, knock around, hammer, hammer away at, chew over, hash, rehash, hash over, bump heads, cross swords, lock horns, face off, face down, go one on one, one to one, go at, come at, lay at, have at, have at it, have at each other, fly in the face of, pitch into, light into, lay into, wade into, lace into, sail into, lean on, take on, crack down on, gang up on, jump, jump on, jump on one's case, jump down one's throat, come down on, come down hard on one, land on, land all over, lay a finger on, lay out, straighten out, let have it, let have it with both barrels, give one both barrels, blast, rip, rip into, rip up, rip up one side and down the other, mix it up with, tangle with, knock the chip off one's shoulder, push around, make a stink, gripe, griping, gritch, pop off, sound off, squawk, up a squawk, bellyache, blast, crab, cut a beef, grouse, growl, kick, speak one's piece, haul into court, drag into court, beat a dead horse, flog a dead horse (moot). See also CONTEST.

ARGUMENT n.   row, tiff, spat, words, rumpus, ruckus, ruction, brawl, brush, brush-off, shindy, scene, set-to, run-in, scrap, hassle, talking heads, rhubarb, bone, bone of contention, bone to pick, face-off, fuss, flap, go, stew, wrangle, static, beef, spat, words, romp, dustup, hoedown, knockdown, knockdown and drag out, sockdolager, flak session, clincher, crusher, finisher, blow, blowup, brannigan, catamaran, donnybrook, rowdydow, rowdy-dowdy, battle royal, jackpot, gin.

ARGUMENTATIVE adj.   chip on one's shoulder, fire-eater, forecastle lawyer, scrappy, salty, spiky. See BELLIGERENT.

ARID adj. bone dry, dry as a bone, dry as dust.

ARISE v. roll out, rise and shine, hit the deck, pile out, show a leg, turn out, drop your cocks and grab your socks (Obsc.), keep bankers' hours (late).

ARISTOCRAT n. ritzy, upper cruster, blueblood, bluestockings, silk stocking, lace curtain, swell.

ARIZONA Apache State, Aztec State, Baby State, Grand Canyon State, Sand Hill State, Sunset State, Valentine State.

ARKANSAS CITY, ARKANSAS Ark City.

ARKANSAS Bear State, Bowie State, hog country, Hot Water State, Land of Opportunity, Toothpick State, Wonder State.

ARM n. 1. bender, flapper, flipper, fin, wing, hook arm. See also WEAPON. 2. affil (TV), branch, branch house, offshoot.

ARM v. heel, equalize, pack, pack a rod, tote, rod up, heel up, load up, lug iron.

ARMAMENT n. hardware, heat (gun).

ARMED adj. equalized, wired, carrying, carrying the difference, carrying iron, totin', toting a gun, packing a gun, packed, gat up, heeled, heeled up, well-heeled, loaded, armed to the teeth, lugging, lugging iron, lugging a rod, rodded up, packing a rod, packing a heater, packing heat.

ARM INJURY n. glass arm, winged.

ARMORED TRUCK n. money bus, fort.

ARMORY n. dump.

ARMY DISCHARGE n. the paper, ruptured duck, Section 8 (mental), blue ticket (dishonorable), bobtail, bob tail (dishonorable WW I), early out (medical).

ARMY OFFICER n. brass, brass hat, gold braid, barbed wire, chicken colonel, light colonel (lt. colonel), skipper, skip, old man, buck general (brigadier); shavetail, Looey, 90-day wonder (2nd Lt.), butcher (M.D.), padre (chaplain), buggy bitchers (field artillery, cavalry 1930), mustang (risen from the ranks), ossifer, goat, O.D. (officer of the day), dust dust (newly promoted).

ARMY OFFICER, NONCOMMISSIONED n. NCO, one-striper, PFC (private first class), two-striper (corporal), sarge, kick, topkick, first man, first shirt, first soldier (first sergeant).

ARMY PLATOON n. toon, able, baker, charlie, regs, the book.

ARMY TRUCK n. blitzbuggy.

ARMY UNIFORM n. G.I., O.D., olive drab, pinks (officer), full dress, fatigues, khakis, peacoat, A uniform, B uniform.

ARMY, VIETNAM n. ARVN, Arvn, arvin, (Army of the Republic of Vietnam).

AROUSE v. turn on, heat up, wake up, work up, send, fire up. See EXCITE.

AROUSED adj. turned on, hot, hot to trot, hopped up, steamed up, worked up. See EXCITED.

ARRAIGN v. point the finger, point the finger at, lay at one's door, pin on, pin it on one, hang something on one. See also ACCUSE.

ARRANGE v. 1. put in shape, put in good shape, whip into shape, put to rights, put in apple-pie order, clear the decks, fix up, police, police up, spruce, spruce up. 2. hammer out a deal, hack out a deal, work out, work out a deal, iron out, make a connection, promote, quarterback, get one's act together, get one's head together, get one's shit together, pull things together, shape up, straighten up and fly right, pull a wire, put the fix in, frame, tailor. See also PLAN, SCHEME.

ARRANGED adj. packed, stacked, cooked up, in the bag, fixed, framed, set up, cut and dry. See also ORGANIZED, PREARRANGED.

ARRANGEMENT n. 1. game plan, layout, package, package deal, setup, frame-up, pecking order, T. O. (table of organization), down the line. 2. chart, score, lead sheet (music). See also AGREEMENT.

ARRAY n. threads, drapes, duds, feathers, getup, glad rags, rig. See CLOTHING.

ARRAY v. doll up, dog out, dud, dude up, fit out, rag out, rag up, rig out, rig up, suit up, deck, deck out, turn out, tog, drape.

ARREST n. collar, bust, heat, mitt, the mitt, nab, grab, pick up, pinch, pull, pull in, run in, sweep, bag, drop, gaff, glom, glom onto, hook, nail, nick, nip, fall, booby pinch, brodie, crimp, flop, jackpot, jam, knock off, rumble, slough, slough up, snare, snatch, trip, tumble, pickle, accommodation collar (to fill a quota or social or political pressure), humbug (unjustified).

ARREST v. 1. collar, bust, going down, pick up, pinch, pull, pull in, run in, bag, brace, book, hook, get, grab, nab, nail, net, nick, nip, kick, tab, tag, vag, snag, sneeze, slough, slough up, round up, roust, drop, gaff, glom, gloon to, sidetrack, put the arm on, put the claw on, put the cuffs on, put the bite on, put the sleeve on, put the snare on, snatch, put the snatch on, land, come down on, take in, haul in, toss in jail, throw in the clink, slap in the piss can, knock off, knock over, belt out, get one's fingers on, get one's hands on, throw the book at one, accommodation collar (to fill a quota or social or political pressure), humbug (unjustified), pluck chickens, red light, looks like rain (imminent), chill (submit to arrest). 2. scrub, drop, knock off, can it, shut down, freeze. See STOP.

ARRESTED adj. booked, collared, nabbed, nailed, corralled, cornered, hooked, dog meat, dropped, flopped, guzzled, hit the pits, ill, in the pokey with smokey, jammed up, on the peg, sneezed, dead to rights, got one dead to rights, I'm dead, one move and you're dead, come out with your hands up, take a brodie, walk into a collar. See also STOPPED.

ARREST, ESCAPE v. miss a collar, duck a pinch.

ARREST IN THE ACT n. caught red-handed, caught dead to rights, dead bang, dead bang rap, right fall, right rap. See also CAUGHT IN THE ACT.

ARREST ON SUSPICION v. pick up, forty-eight, forty-eighter, highway mopery, mopery, mopery collar, mopery in the first degree, mopery pinch, mopery rap.

ARREST, UNJUST n. bum beef, bum rap, frame, frame-up, hummer, phony collar, phony drop, phony fall, phony grab, phony knock, phony pinch, phony snatch, plant, stiff, wrong drop, wrong fall, wrong pinch.

ARRIVE v. access, clip off, make it, make the scene, hit, hit town, blow in, sky in, breeze in, come breezing in, barge in, bust in, roll in, pull in, check in, sign in, time in, clock in, punch in, punch the clock, drop in, pop in, ring in, spring in, mooch in, drag in, look what the cat dragged in, fall in, fall up, fall by, fall out, fall down, show, show up, bob up, pop up, wind up at, buzz (to announce an arrival). See also APPEAR, ENTER.

ARROGANCE n. brass, cheek, chutzpah, crust, gall, nerve.

ARROGANT adj. cool, cocky, biggety, bossy, dicty, sidity, sidity, sniffy, snippy, snooty, snotty, puffed up, uppish, uppity, upstage, stuck up, stuck on oneself, chesty, too big for one's britches, ego trip, ego-tripping, king shit, high and mighty, high hat, high-hatted, high hatty, high-toned, high-flown, high headed, high-nosed, high-falutin', on one's high horse, put on airs, pull rank, have one's glasses on (Bl.), toplofty, hoity-toity, cold shoulder, crack the whip, throw one's weight around, dog it, cheeky, know-it-all, smarty, smarty pants, smart aleck, smart alecky, smart guy, smart ass, wise ass, wise guy.

ARSENAL n. dump.

ARSON n. torching, touch off.

ARSONIST n. firebug, match, spark, torch, touch-off man, fiero, fire buff, sparkie.

ARTERY n. red pipe, sewer.

ARTFUL adj. foxy, crazy like a fox, slick, smooth, playing politics, politician. See also SLY.

ARTICLE n. 1. piece, think piece, column, scoop, spread, beat, blurb, write-up, story. 2. thingamajig, dojigger, jigger, dohickey, gismo, jobbie, thingamabob. See APPARATUS.

ARTICULATE v. verbalize, mouth, sound off. See also SPEAK.

ARTIFICE n. gimmick, grift, racket, con, know-how, savvy. See also CHEAT, STRATAGEM.

ARTIFICIAL adj. fake, faked, falsie, hyped up, phony, queer. See also COUNTERFEIT.

ARTIFICIAL GRASS n. Astroturf, carpet, rug.

ARTIFICIAL LEG n. peg, peg leg.

ARTILLERY n. AAs, Arty, Divarty (division artillery), big bertha, Big Bertha (WW I), how, grandmother (howitzer, WW I), 88, long Tom, big guns, heavy stuff, tree bursts, rainmakers, bazooka, stovepipe,

ARTILLERYMAN n. guns.

ARTILLERY TERMS ack ack, ashcan, coal box, crump (WW 1); the cosmolines (WW II), fireworks, flak, G.I. can.

ARTISTIC adj. arty, arty crafty, arty farty, artsy-craftsy, artsy fartsy, long-haired.

ARTLESS adj. up front, call a spade a spade, make no bones about it, open, straight shit, call it like it is, talk turkey. See FRANK.

AS, AS IF adv. like (I'll be worse like I might die).

ASCENDANCY n. 1. on top. See AUTHORITY. 2. upper hand, whip hand, drop on one, edge on one, jump on one, leg up on one. See ADVANTAGE.

ASCERTAIN v. check, check out, check up on, double-check, look-see, make sure, eye, eyeball, read, see, dig it, peg, size, size up, pick up, pick up on, get hold of, get into one's head, get it down, get down pat, get down cold, get the hang of, learn the ropes, go through the school of hard knocks.

ASCERTAINED adj. dead sure, for sure, fer sher, fer shirr, for a fact, cold, nailed down, all locked up. See PROVEN.

ASCRIBE v. reference, hang something on, pin on. See ASSIGN.

ASIAN n. Chinaman, Chink, Chinx, gook, Jap, nip, dink, gooney, gooney bird, buddha-head, rag head, skibby, skibo, slant, slant eyes, slope, slope eyes, yellow peril, zip (Derog.). See also CHINESE, JAPANESE, PHILIPPINE.

ASIAN FLU n. Mao flu.

ASIDE n. throw-away.

AS IS adj. as advertised, pat, stand pat, what you see is what you get.

ASK v. 1. grill, roast, sweat, sweat it out of one, sweat out, So?, buzz, give one the third, give one the third degree, put one through the wringer, put the heat on one, put the screws on, go over, pick one's brains, cat haul, hit, strike, pop the question, whistle for (but won't get). See also QUESTION. 2. hit, touch, bite, bum, hustle, promote, mooch, knock. See BEG.

ASKEW adj. topsy-turvey, catawampus, zigzag, cockeyed, yaw ways. See CROOKED.

ASLANT adj. slaunchways, slaunchwise.

ASLEEP adj. crashed, snoozing, out, out cold, out like a light, out of it, flaked out, sacked out, getting some sack time, getting some shut-eye, making zzz's, making a few z's, catching some zees, taking forty winks, on the kip, on the nod, dead, dead to the world, in dreamland, in the land of nod, collaring a nod, in the arms of Morpheus, in the lap of Morpheus, sawing wood, sawing logs, pounding one's ear.

ASPARAGUS n. sparrowgrass.

ASPECT n. slant, twist, gimmick, angle, switch.

ASPERSE v. slam, knock, put down, dig at, slap at, give a black eye. See SLANDER.

ASPERSION n. rap, slam, smear, dump, hit, knock, put-down, black eye, backhanded compliment, dirty dig. See DEFAMATION.

ASPIC n. nervous pudding.

ASPIRANT n. tyro, hopeful, white hope.

ASPIRATION n. fire in the belly, push, right stuff.

ASPIRING adj. ambish, eager beaver, go-getter, on the make, out for a rep. See AMBITIOUS. See also HOPEFUL.

ASS n. Rocky Mountain canary.

ASSAIL v. bash, bust, blister, blast on, lambaste, trash, work over, have at, come at. See ATTACK.

ASSAILANT n. mugger, hit man, trigger man, goon, bushwhacker, oppo, opposite number, meat. See also ENEMY.

ASSASSIN n. hit man, trigger man, piece man, torpedo, enforcer, gorilla, gun, gunman, gunsel, bumpman, button man, hatchet man, bang man, apache, shootist, clipper, plugger, soldier, troop, butcher, knock-off ghee, red hot, dropper (hired).

ASSASSINATE v. liquidate, neutralize, waste, do in, burn, off, take out, erase, kiss off, take care of. See KILL.

ASSASSINATION n. offing, wasting, liquidation, neutralization, taking out, a ride, croaking. See KILLING.

ASSAULT v. 1. bash, blast, haul off on one, slam, trash, zap, jump, go for, slap around, work over, come down on, meat-ax, bushwhack, let one have it, light into. 2. shoot down, jump on one's case, jump down one's throat, take one over the hurdles, blitz. See ATTACK.

ASSAULT AND ROB v. arm, bushwhack, mug, put the arm on, put the muscle on, put the mug on, put the slug on.

ASSAULTER n. mugger, hit man, bushwhacker.

ASSAY v. check, check out, eyeball, read, see, peg, size, size up. See APPRAISE. See also ANALYZE, ATTEMPT.

ASSEMBLE v. corral, round up, scare up, meet up, bunch up, gang up, hang around, hang out, make the scene, poke, punch, capture. See also MEET.

ASSEMBLY n. confab, clambake, coffee klatch, meet, get-together, huddle, sit-in, turnout. See MEETING. See also CROWD.

ASSENT v. 1. okay, pass on, shake on, cut a deal, buy, ditto, give one five (slap hands). 2. give in, cave in, say uncle, give away the store, knuckle under. See AGREE.

ASSERT v. shoot one's wad, shoot one's bolt, shoot off one's mouth, mouth off, pop off, butt in, horn in. See also PROCLAIM.

ASSERTION n. say so, one's stamp of approval, mouthful (you said a mouthful), okay, OK, two cents' worth. See AFFIRMATION.

ASSESS v. check, check out, dig it, figger, figure, nick, peg, size, size up, take one's measure. See also APPRAISE.

ASSESSMENT n. 1. Irish dividend. 2. value judgment.

ASSETS n. bankroll, nut, nest egg, rainy day, sock, stash, stache, mattress-full, kitty, stake, backing, budget, ace in the hole, ace up one's sleeve (hidden), a little something put away, a little something put aside, stuff, goods.

ASSIDUOUS adj. grind, plugger, nose to the grindstone, springbutt, eager beaver, work one's tail off, whiz. See INDUSTRIOUS.

ASSIGN n. 1. name, slot, tab, tag, reference, hang something on, pin on, credit. See also NAME. 2. dish out, fork out, hand out, shell out. See also DIVIDE. 3. task.

ASSIGNATION n. affair, date, heavy date, love nest, matinee, noonie, one-night stand, quickie, rendezvous, triff, treff (secret), your place or mine. See RENDEZVOUS.

ASSIGNMENT n. beat, bum out. See also TASK.

ASSIMILATE v. go native, hit the beach.

ASSIST n. shot in the arm, shot in the ass, boost, leg, leg up, hand, handout, lift, backup. See also SUPPORT.

ASSIST v. boost, give a boost to, give a leg up, give a lift, lend a hand, plug, hype, push, hold a brief for, go with, go for, go to bat for, go to the mat for, go down the line for, go the route for, make a pitch for, beat the drum for, plump for, run interference for, grease the wheels for, thump the tub for, root for, stump for, front for, stand up for, stick up for, ride shotgun for, take care of one for, carry the water for, put a flea in one's ear, put a bug in one's ear, open doors, hand out, spot, throw the spotlight on, puff, ballyhoo, put on the map, press agent, up, backup, bail out, hold one's end up, straighten one out. See also SUPPORT.

ASSISTANT n. girl Friday, gal Friday, man Friday, sec, help, temp, gofer, backup, flunky, furp, apparatchik, squeak, straw boss, home guard, peon, savage, serf, slave, slavey.

ASSISTANTS n. shop, crew, troops.

ASSOCIATE n. 1. affil (TV), branch, branch house, offshoot. 2. buddy, chum, pal, sidekick, playmate, matie, pard, pardner, kissing cousin, one of the boys. See FRIEND. 3. clubber, joiner. 4. dweeb (junior or senior).

ASSOCIATE v. pool, team up, team up with, tie up, tie in, tie-in-tie-up, tie in with, tie up with, throw in together, throw in with, line up with, swing in with, go partners with, go in partners with, be in cahoots with, go in cahoots with, bunch up, gang up, gang up with, pal up with, buddy up with, hang around, hang out with, run with, run around with, truck with, play footsie with, go along with, string along with, take up with, get into, get in on, get in with, get together, come together, join together, join up with, hook up, hook on, hook up with, stand up with, stand in with, get on the in with, interface, interface with, network with, meld with, play ball, play ball with, suit up with (team), sign up, sign on, tag on, tack on, slap on, hitch on, come aboard, deal one in, include me in, plug into, glue oneself to, fraternize.

ASSOCIATED adj. hooked up with, in cahoots with, joined up with, lined up with, partners with, thrown in with, tied in with, plugged into.

ASSOCIATES n. shop, crew, troops.

ASSOCIATION n. syndicate, outfit, tie-up, tie-in, tie-in tie-up, hookup, gang, mob, bunch, crew, ring, circle, clan, tribe, troupe, troops, those one runs with, combination, combo, pool, megacorp, multinational, plunderbund, the company, family, famiglia, rat pack, yoot (teenage), crowd, zoo.

ASSORTMENT n. mixed bag, combo, everything but the kitchen sink, mishmash, mishmosh, garbage, kludge (parts). See also MIXTURE.

ASSUAGE v. cool, cool out, make nice, pour oil on troubled waters, take the edge off, take the sting out of. See PACIFY.

ASSUME v. 1. take over, glom on to, snatch, liberate, confiscate, moonlight requisition, annex, swipe, grab, grab hold of, borrow, clap hands on, get one's fingers on, get one's hands on, highjack, hijack, kipe, highgrade. 2. be afraid, have a hunch, have a sneaking suspicion. See also BELIEVE. 3. take on, take over.

ASSUMPTION n. 1. hunch, shot, shot in the dark, stab, sneaking suspicion. See also BASIS 2. grab, takeover.

ASSURANCE n. lock, lock and win, have a lock on, sure thing, sewed up, cold lay, shoo-in, rain or shine. See CERTAINTY.

ASSURE v. 1. buck up, brace up. See SUPPORT. See also AFFIRM, AVER. 2. ice, put on ice, lock, lock on, lock and win, have a lock on, lock up, cinch, clinch, nail down, set. 3. sell, sell one on, bag, bet on. See also PERSUADE.

ASSURED adj. 1. iceman, ice in one's veins, gutsy, got the faith baby, gung ho, high, high on something, gamble on, keeping the faith, rosy, upbeat, all puffed up, pumped up, glad-hander (overly), looking at the world with rose-colored glasses, looking at something with rose-colored glasses, cocksure. See also IMPERTURBABLE. 2. sure as shit, surefire, nailed down, lock-and-win situation, on ice, bet one's bottom dollar on, in the bag, racked, boat race (horse racing). See CERTAIN.

ASTERISK n. bug.

ASTONISH v. floor, rock, gork, blow away, blow one's mind, boggle the mind, bowl down, bowl over, flabbergast, knock one over, knock one over with a feather, set one on one's ass, strike all of a heap, throw on one's beam ends, spring something on one, throw one a curve, put one away. See also SURPRISE.

ASTONISHED adj. floored, stuck, stumped, thrown, blown away, boggled, bowled down, bowled over, bug-eyed, discombobulated, flabbergasted, could've knocked one over with a feather, set on one's ass, struck all of a heap, thrown off one's beam ends, caught off base, caught with one's pants down, flatfooted, shit blue, shit green, bit one in the ass. See also SURPRISED.

ASTONISHMENT n. one for the book, something else, something to shout about, something to write home about, stunner.

ASTOUND v.   blow away, bowl over, flabbergast, knock one over with a feather, set on one's ass, strike all of a heap, throw on one's beam ends. See ASTONISH.

ASTOUNDED adj.   bug-eyed, set on one's ass, boggled, bowled down, bowled over, flabbergasted, struck all of a heap, blown away, put away. See ASTOUNDED.

ASTOUNDING adj.   mind-blowing, far out, stunning, megadual. See AMAZING.

ASTRONAUT n.   moonman, spaceman.

ASTRONAUT LAUNCH n.   eyeballs in eyeballs out.

ASTUTE adj.   brainy, foxy, sharp as a tack, have smarts, on the ball, quick on the uptake, not born yesterday. See INTELLIGENT, SHREWD.

ASYLUM n.   1. booby hatch, funny farm, nut house, rubber room, soft wall. See INSANE ASYLUM. 2. hideaway, hideout, hole in, hole up, place to hole up, safe house, blowout center, ivory tower, den.

AT prep.   by.

ATHLETE n.   jock, superjock, shoulders, V man, iron man, muscle man; muscle head, meathead, jockey, animal, ape, gorilla, Neanderthal (Derog.); redshirt (eligibility extended), speed merchant, white hope (white contender), sport.

ATHLETIC SUPPORTER n.   jock.

ATLANTA, GEORGIA   Big A, Big South, Hot Lanta, Hotlanta, Hot Town.

ATLANTIC CITY, NEW JERSEY   The Boardwalk.

ATLANTIC OCEAN n.   big drink, the pond, big pond, herring pond, Big Ditch.

ATMOSPHERE n.   scene, space, place, mood, color, local color, color man (TV sports).

ATOM BOMB n.   A-bomb, nuclear bomb, the bomb, doomsday machine, nuke, backpack nuke.

ATOMIC WAR n.   A-war, H-war, nuclear war, the unthinkable, MAD (mutually assured destruction).

ATONE v.   make up for, pay one's dues, square, square a beef, square things, take one's medicine. See also APOLOGIZE, CORRECT, PAY.

ATROCIOUS adj.   gross, grody, grody to the max, awful, beastly, godawful, goshawful, hairy, lousy, rotten. See BAD. See also DREADFUL.

ATTACH v.   hitch up, hitch on, hook on, hook up, slap on, tag on, latch onto. See also FASTEN.

ATTACHED adj.   anchored, nailed.

ATTACHMENT n.   crush, case, amore, mad pash, weakness, yen, shine, hankering, beaver fever (Obsc.), calf love, puppy love. See LOVE.

ATTACK n.   blitz, blitzkrieg, mugging, push, dirty deed, surgical mission (quick), attempting a creep.

ATTACK v.   1. mug, bat, bash, bust, biff, blister, boff, bop, bean, beat, beat the shit out of, beat one to a frazzle, blast, blast on, brain, break one's face, bam wham, whop, soak, slog, storm, wallop, haul off on one, land a haymaker, lambaste, K.O., slam, swat, push, paste, sock, smack, split, trash, whack, wing, zap, zapper, zetz, larrup, yerk, plunk, jump, jump on, slug, heel, punch out, wipe out, work out, work over, lay out, read one out, throw a punch, tangle ass with, gang up, get, shellack, guzzle, go at, go for, go for it, go in for, go out for, go after, go to town on, heat, have at, have a go at, lay at, take a swing at, take a crack at, crack down on, poke, take a poke at, take a swipe at, whack, take a whack at, rush, come at, come down on, come down hard on one, put the bee on one, belt, belt out, blind, blindside, bushwhack, dry gulch, banjax, boot, boot around, bloop, bonk, conk, clout, clip, hit a clip, clump, clunk, clonk, clock, crown, chop down, chill, cold cock, cold pack, cook, con (1850), Chinese, cop, double bank, drop, deck, dump, dust off, flip, flatten, give 'em hell, give one a fat lip, give one both barrels, let one have it with both barrels, let one have it, give one the blanket, give one the works, give a deal to, sock it to one, stick it to one, hand it to one, kick ass, kick the shit out of one, kick the living daylights out of one, kick the bejesus out of, kick one ass over teakettle, kick one on one's ear, kick one into next week, kick one's cruller in, kick one's lemon in, kick one's sconce in, put out one's lamps, put one in the hospital, tip over, knock over, knock off, knock cold, knock dead, knock the bejesus out of one, knock one on one's ass, knock one ass over teakettle, knock one on one's ear, knock on one's kiester, knock one into next week, knock one's block off, knock one for a loop, knock for a row of [anything], knock the beholden out of one, knock the daylights out of one, knock the shit out of one, whale the daylights out of one, floor one, land all over one, measure, meatball, lump, lump up, put the boots to, roast, scorch, skin alive, lace, lace into, lay into, pitch into, light into, sail into, wade into, rip, rip into, rip up, rip up one side and down the other, slap down, fire on, hang one on, lean on, lean against, take on, lay on sap, lay a finger on, lay a glove on, land on, put the slug on, put the slough on, slough, slough around, push around, ring one's bell, pull a joint, pull a Jap (surprise), pepper, plant one. See also SCOLD. 2. shoot down, shoot down an idea, shoot down a thing, jump on one's case, jump down one's throat, you gonna jump on my chest?, do a razor job on, stretch, take one over the hurdles, timber up, blitz, fly in the teeth of.

ATTACKER n.   mugger, bushwhacker, dry gulcher.

ATTAIN v. 1. snag, cop, get one's hands on, glom on to, latch on to, promote. See GET. See also EFFECT. 2. make it, pull off, come through with, score, get fat, get there, unzip, arrive. See ACHIEVE.

ATTAINABLE adj. no sweat, no problem, duck soup, cherry pie, piece of cake, can o' corn. See EASY. See also OBTAINABLE.

ATTEMPT n. all one's got, crack, fling, go, jelly go, header, lick, one's all, one's damnedest, one's darnedest, one's level best, shot, stab, try, whack, dry run, try on, tryout, have a fling at, shakedown, shakedown cruise, workout. See also ENDEAVOR.

ATTEMPT v. make a run at, tackle, take on, look to, make a try, cut and try, try on for size, do it or bust a gut, bust one's ass, break one's ass, break one's neck, break one's back, break one's heart, try one's damnedest, try one's darnedest, give it the old college try, try on for size, give it a try, give it a go, give it a fling, give it one's best shot, take one's best shot, give it a whirl, give a go, give a fling, give it one's all, give it all one's got, bend over backward, lay oneself out, push, knock oneself out, take the bull by the horns, take a shot at, take a fling at, take a crack at, take a whack at, cut, take a cut at, take a stab at, make a stab at, have a go at, have a fling at, have a shot at, on the make, pitch into, in there pitching, do one's level best, go in for, go out for, go all out, go for it, go for broke, go the limit, shoot the works. See also APPLY ONESELF.

ATTEND v. 1. catch, make the scene, bob up, pop up, turn up, show, show up, punch in, punch the clock, clock in, time in, drop in, ring in, check in, come to light, see the light of day, speak of the devil. See also APPEAR. 2. listen up, pick up, catch, get a load of this, get a load of that, give ears, have one's ears on, knock on your lobes. 3. doctor.

ATTENDANCE n. box office, draw, house.

ATTENDANT n. bird dog, alarm clock, baby-sitter.

ATTENTION interj. looky, heads up, Tenhut.

ATTENTION n. big rush, brace, drop a line on one, listen up, pop to, spotlight, tender loving care, TLC.

ATTENTION GETTER n. grabber, hook, billboard, promo.

ATTENTION, PAY v. see to, TCB (take care of business), be on the ball, get one's head out of one's ass, keep a weather eye open, keep one's ear to the ground, keep one's eye on the ball, keep one's eye peeled, listen up, not miss a trick, not overlook a bet, pay mind to, shine me on (to me), watch out. See also HEED.

ATTENTIVE adj. hang on every word, listen up, on the ball, on the job, on one's toes, on the lookout, on the que vive, Johnny on the spot, with a weather eye open, with one's eyes peeled, all ears, glued, hooked, not miss a trick, not overlook a bet, see after, see to. See also WARY.

ATTIC n. sky parlor.

ATTIRE n. threads, glad rags, bib and tucker, drapes, dud, feathers. See CLOTHING

ATTIRE v. dud, rag out, rag up, tog, doll up, dog out, turn out, deck, deck out, fit out, outfit, drape, dude up, suit up.

ATTIRED adj. dolled up, decked out, rigged out, dressed fit to kill. See DRESSED.

ATTITUDE n. head-set, mind-set, mindtrip, routine, where one's head is, where one is at, where it's at, like it is, the size of it, say so, slant, angle, twist, sound, pov, P.O.V. See also OPINION.

ATTITUDINIZE v. do a bit, lay it on thick, playact, put up a front, fake, make out like. See POSTURE. See also PRETEND.

ATTORNEY n. man's mouth, mouthpiece, shyster, ambulance chaser, legal eagle, legal beagle, beagle, beak, fixer, lip, patch, the L.A., tongue, pleader, pettifogger, Philadelphia lawyer, squeal, bomber (divorce), front, mugger, spieler, spouter, tangle jaw, warble, springer, ghost (writes briefs), D.A. cuter, cutter (prosecutor).

ATTORNEY GENERAL n. the A.G.

ATTORNEY, PUBLIC DEFENDER n. state lawyer, state mouthpiece.

ATTORNEY'S FEE n. fall dough, knock off, nut.

ATTRACT n. pull, grab, draw, kill, slay, bait, mousetrap, shill, steer, tout, freak out, knock out, knock dead, send, turn on, turn one on, come on, give one the come on, give one a come-hither look, make a hit with, sweep off one's feet, vamp, hook, bat one's eyes at, bat the eyes at, suck in, rope in, score, wow, humbug, go over big, lead up the garden path. See also LURE.

ATTRACTION, SEXUAL n. chemistry, it.

ATTRACTIVE adj. ten, 10, drop-dead gorgeous, hunk, hooky, looker, good looker, stone, head rush, knock one's eyes out, stunning, beaut, tall dark and handsome. See BEAUTIFUL.

ATTRIBUTE v. reference, hang something on, pin on, credit. See ASSIGN.

AUCTION v. jam.

AUDACIOUS adj. gutty, nervy, brassy, ballsy, smart ass, wise ass, chutzpahdik, cheeky, rind. See DARING.

AUDACIOUSNESS n. balls, brass balls, guts, gutiness, gutsiness, chutzpah, cheek, brass, nerve, moxie, stuff, crust, gall, spunk.

AUDIENCE n. fan, moviegoer, playgoer, showgoer, theatergoer, first-nighter, showcase, standee, turnout, sports fan, buff, clacker, clapper, deadhead, paper (free pass), paper house, one who catches a show, kibitzer, heckler, aficionado, fence-hanger, bleacher bum, knothole gang. See also SPECTATOR.

AUDIT v. sit in.

AUDITION n. demo, tryout, reading, try on.

AUDITORIUM n. hall, barn.

AUGER n. corkscrew.

AUGMENT v. pad, boost, bump (poker), tag on, piggyback, beef up, add bells and whistles, sweeten. See INCREASE.

AUGMENTATION n. beefing up, fleshing out, boost, buildup, hike, up, upping. See also ADDITION.

AUGUR v. read, crystal ball it, call it, call the shots, have a hunch, figure out, psych it out. See PREDICT.

AUGUST adj. highfalutin', high-minded, high-nosed, high-toned, stiff-necked. See also POMPOUS.

AUSPICIOUSLY adv. at the eleventh hour, in the nick of time. See also TIMELY, CONVENIENT.

AUSTERE adj. clean, vanilla, bare-bones, what you see is what you get. See PLAIN.

AUSTRALIA Down Under, Aussie land, Outback.

AUSTRALIA/NEW ZEALAND Anzas.

AUSTRALIAN n. Aussie, Auzzie, Anzac, Ossie; Bill-Jim, Billjim (soldier, WW I), Digger, dinkum (soldier); down under, Sooner.

AUTHENTIC adj. for real, genuine article, legit, the emess, the real McCoy, straight from the horse's mouth, twenty-four carat. See TRUE.

AUTHOR n. scribe, scribbler, scripter, telewriter (TV), ghost, ghostwriter, columnist, ink slinger, word slinger, wordsmith. See WRITER.

AUTHOR v. script, pen, put down, bang out, bat out, make hen tracks. See WRITE.

AUTHORITATIVE adj. 1. legit, on the legit, the emess, the righteous, out of the horse's mouth, straight from the horse's mouth. See FACTUAL. 2. got the horses to do it, Norwegian steam, powerhouse. See POWERFUL.

AUTHORITIES n. Establishment, the feds, the law, brass, top brass, in-group, ins, people in the front office, people upstairs, higher ups, the top, the bosses, power elite, powers that be, them, they, city hall, the man. See also ADMINSTRATOR, MANAGEMENT.

AUTHORITY n. 1. A-number 1, chief, C.O., CEO, exec, executive suite, front office, boss, bosslady, bossman, the old man, czar, governor, the commish, hot stuff, head, head honcho, head man, hammer-man, lead-off man, general, queen bee, the brass, brass hat, top brass, gold braid, rug rank (high), Mr. Big, big player, big chew, big shot, big shit, big weenie, big cheese, the whole cheese, big wig, bigwigged, top, on top, top dog, topper, top hand, top kick, upstairs, high up, higher ups, high priest, king, kingfish, kingpin, king of the hill, bull of the woods, big league, shark, brain, brains, guru, pro, pundit, egghead, ivory dome, ol' professor, old pro, old hand, old war-horse, maven, whiz, wizard, buff, bone man, heart man, big nose man, freak, nut, the fuzz, the man, pigs, the long arm of the law, oink (police), biggest frog in the pond, buddy seat. See also EXECUTIVE, COMMANDER, SUPERVISOR. 2. juice, zap, pow, kicker, pizzazz, the force, moxie, powerhouse, poop, punch, clout, steam, might and main, beef, strong arm, the stuff, the goods, what it takes, upper hand, whip hand, drop on one, edge on one, jump on one, leg up on one, the say, the say so, a lot to say about, a lot to do with, the word, bible, righteous, geets, guts, string, ropes, weight.

AUTHORIZATION n. go ahead, green light, okay, OK. See CONSENT.

AUTHORIZE v. okay, OK, say the word, give the go-ahead, give the green light, give the word, put one's John Hancock on, rubber-stamp, bless. See APPROVE.

AUTHORIZED adj. okayed, OK'd, kosher, legit.

AUTO n. wheels, bug, van, jeep, bus, clunker, jalopy, crate, heap, buggy, hot rod. See AUTOMOBILE.

AUTO RACEWAYS n. Indy, brickyard (Indianapolis), hairpin turn, groove, line, (best route around track), marbles (slippery spot).

AUTO RACING TERMS back off (decelerate), consy (consolation race), dice (close race), endo (end over end crash), fishtail, squirrel (both skid side to side), green flag, grid start, heel and toe (driving technique), hooligan race, nerf (bump during race), pace lap, pick off (pass a car), pole sitter (pole position starter), red flag, reverse start, shunt (collide), sling shot (passing strategy), spinout.

AUTOCRAT n. a Hitler, Simon Legree, slave driver, czar.

AUTOCRATIC adj. bossy, czar, driver, pusher, whip cracker, ass-kicker. See IMPERIOUS.

AUTOGRAPH SEEKER n. autograph hound.

AUTOMATIC adj. knee-jerk reaction.

AUTOMATIC PILOT n. George, Iron Mike.

AUTOMOBILE n. wheels, hoopty, ride, trans, bug, beetle, four-wheeler, fastback, hatchback, go-cart, hard top, ragtop (convertible), no top, benzo (Mercedes-Benz), chrome dome, super skate, compact, pony car, pony (medium sized), short, limo, stretch limo, stretch car (extra length), van, jeep, peep (jeep), Detroit Iron (American), Model T (Ford), tin lizzie, quad (four headlights), long John Silver (one headlight), bus, mean machine, chine, clean 'chine, wheelchair, meat grinder, oil burner, banger, junker, clunker, lemon, crutch, jalopy, tuna wagon, rattletrap, death trap, coffin, cage, hoopy, chugalong, wreck, wreck of the Hesperus, bucket, bucket of bolts, guzzler, gas guzzler, grizzler, crate, egg crate, heap, heap of junk, junk heap, cheap heap, scrap heap, boat, boiler, can, bone shaker, breezer, golfer, gondola, load, rig, rubber, sled, slicker, buggy, gas buggy, gasoline buggy, blitz buggy, zoom buggy, buzz buggy, love buggy, dune buggy, struggle buggy, chopped, chopped car, low rider, raked, stocker, art cart, funny car, scout car, jeepers-creepers, Easter Egg (decorated), midget, midgie, bantam car, soup job, hot rod, bomb, buzz wagon, chariot, job, deuce, flivver, fliv, gig, goat, hog (Cadillac), go it all, grinder, hayburner, one lunger, kemp, Jimmie, jitney, leaping Lena (Obs.), puddle jumper, tub; bent one, rinky (stolen); bear bait, bear food, bear meat (unequipped with citizens band radio), orphan (no longer manufactured), turtle (armored). See also VEHICLE.

AUTOMOBILE ACCIDENT n. total, smashup, smackup, stack-up, pileup, fender-bender, fender tag, crack-up, rack-up, wrack-up. See ACCIDENT.

AUTOMOBILE HOOD n. doghouse.

AUTOMOBILE HORN n. beeper, honker, tooter.

AUTOMOBILE SHOW n. Motorama.

AUTOMOBILE, STOLEN n. a short, hot car, bent one, rinky, trap, slick, gondola (not common); consent job, owner's job (insurance fraud, theft of); move a job, push hot boilers, push hot ones (dispose of), on the schlep (stealing).

AUTOMOBILE TERMS Georgia credit card (hose for siphoning gasoline), California tilt (front end lower); binders, grabbers, clinches (brakes); buggy whip (radio antenna), pits (service area), stack, stick, dash (dashboard), down in the kitchen (low gear), big hole (gear), banger (cylinder), blow (supercharger), bottom end, kill switch (automatic brakes), fishtail, flat (tire), roll bar, make (brand name).

AUTOMOBILE TIRE n. rubber, baldy (worn), retread, skins, shoe; flat, flat hoop, sore foot (punctured), pumpkin (flat), slicks (racing).

AUTOMOBILE WAREHOUSE n. doghouse, drop off, dump, hole, hot boiler farm, hot car farm, plant, stash.

AVAILABLE adj. on tap, come-at-able, getable, getinable, up for grabs, on deck, ready willing and able. See OBTAINABLE.

AVANT-GARDE adj. leading edge, state of the art, far out, beat, way out, hep, hip, new wave. See VANGUARD.

AVARICIOUS adj. grabby, piggy, tight, big-eyed, skinflint, screw, pinchy, poligot. See STINGY. See also GREEDY.

AVENGE v. get even with, come back at, get back at, get hunk, stick it in and break it off, square accounts, give one a dose of one's own medicine. See REVENGE.

AVER v. swear up and down, swear on a stack of bibles, swear till one is blue in the face, cross one's heart and hope to die, say so. See also AFFIRM.

AVERAGE adj. so so, vanilla, white bread, fair, fair to middling, middle of the road, middlebrow, run of the alley, run of the mill, everyday, plastic, boilerplate, garden, garden variety, no great shakes, dime a dozen, nowhere, strictly union, humdrum, rumdum, cotton-pickin', mainstream, starch, boojy, ham and egger, hoddy-doddy, journeyman, in and outer (sports), man on the street, Billy Sixpack, Joe Lunchbucket, Sammy Smith concept, Susie Smith concept, John Smith, Mr. Smith, Mrs. Smith, Mrs. Brown, Mr. Brown, Brown Jones and Robinson, any Tom Dick or Harry, Jane Doe, John Doe, John Q. Public, ordinary Joe, Joe Doakes, plebe, ham and egger.

AVERSE adj. allergic, have no use for.

AVERSION n. allergy, no eyes for, no use for.

AVIATOR n. flyboy, hotshot, jockey, throttle jockey, truck driver, bird legs, birdman, barnstormer, eagle. See PILOT.

AVIATRIX n. birdwoman.

AVID adj. creaming to, dying to, gotta have. See IM-PATIENT.

AVOCATION n. bag, one's bag, into, kick, schtick, shot, thing, be into, do one's thing.

AVOID v. 1. deke, duck, duck out of, hide, lay low, run for cover, bob, weave; janck, jink (enemy planes); juke, stutter step, fake one out, shake, shake off, shake and bake, fish, flicker, ditch, give the slip, get on one's bicycle, shuffle off, jump, skip, skip out on, skip town, get around, sashay around, tiptoe around, dodge, give one the runaround, hang one out to dry, palm off, steer clear of, run for cover, circumlocute, bend the rules, beat around the bush. See also RETREAT. 2. cut, cut dead, cold shoulder, give the cold shoulder to, have no truck with. 3. bag, skip, give a miss to, not touch with a ten-foot pole, give the go by, give a wide berth, pass the buck,

buck pass, buck it over, pass up, stay shy of. See also SNUB.

AVOW v. swear up and down, swear on a stack of bibles, swear till one is blue in the face, cross one's heart and hope to die. See also AFFIRM.

AWAIT v. hang in, hang around, hang out, sweat, sweat it, sweat it out, cool one's heels, it's looking to, wait for the other shoe to drop. See WAIT.

AWAKEN v. roll out, rise and shine, hit the deck, pile out, show a leg, turn out, drop your cocks and grab your socks (Obsc.), get up with the chickens (early), keep bankers' hours (late).

AWARD n. the gold, gold star, the cookies, feather in one's cap, Oscar. See also DONATION.

AWARD v. gift, gift with, hand out, dish out, fork out, shell out, put something in the pot, sweeten the kitty. See GIVE.

AWARDS n. Oscar (film), Tony (theater), Emmy (TV), Grammy (phono record), Obie (Off Broadway), Clio (TV commercial), Effie (advertising), E (for efficiency, WWII).

AWARE adj. plugged in, tuned in, in the picture, be up on, grounded, with it, cool, savvy, sharp, wise to, wised up, on to, hep, hip, hip to the jive, hipped, on the beam, tuned in, into, really into, go-go, all woke up, know-how, groovy, latched on, in the know, know one's stuff, know the ropes, know all the ins and outs, know the score, know all the answers, know what's what, know one's onions, know it all, know one's business, know one's p's and q's, on the beam, double digs, hear tell of, hearsay, kept posted, ear to the ground. See also KNOWLEDGE-ABLE.

AWAY adj. out, out-of-pocket, out of touch. See also ABSENT.

AWE v. blow away, blow one away, knock one's socks off, make one's teeth fall out, showboat, grandstand, hotdog. See IMPRESS.

AWESOME adj. zero cool, far out, megadual, frantic, mean, mind-blowing, gone, real gone, hairy, nervous, something else, clean outta sight. See IMPRESSIVE. See also AMAZING.

AWFUL adj. sucks, sucks a big one, grody, grody to the max, gross, grungy, raunchy, stinking, synthetic, tough, tough nuggies. See BAD.

AWKWARD adj. klutzy, all thumbs, butterfingers, two left hands, two left feet, clodhopper. See CLUMSY.

AWRY adj. catawampus, slaunchways, slaunchwise, zigzag, cockeyed, hell west and crooked. See CROOKED.

AXIOM n. daffodil.

B

B n. Benny, bravo.

BABBLE v. yackety yak, yakking, gas, go on, run on, run off at the mouth, have diarrhea of the mouth, talk through one's hat, spill the beans, bibble babble, bull, bullshit, BS, throw the bull. See also SPEAK.

BABY n. kid, babe, bottle baby, babykins, bambino, cheese factory, crawler, toddler, tot, tad, in diapers, nipper, papoose, drape ape, preemie, button, bundle, bundle from heaven, little darling, little angel, little doll, little cherub, little deduction, little dividend, little write-off, write-off, tax benefit, expense, youngster, angelface, dumpling, buttercup, chick, honeychild, lollypop, rosebud, snooky, snookums, sugar, sugarplum; boomer, baby boomer (post WW II); wet behind the ears, Irish twins (both born within a year).

BABYISH adj. kid stuff.

BACHELOR n. batch, old bach, bachelor girl, old maid, single, single-o, single man, stag, unattached, available, eligible.

BACHELOR v. bach it, batch it.

BACHELOR OF ARTS n. BA.

BACHELOR OF SCIENCE n. BS.

BACK v. 1. angel, bankroll, grubstake, stake. See FINANCE. 2. boost, give a boost, give a leg up, give a lift, go to bat for, stick by, stick up for. See SUPPORT.

BACKACHE n. backachy, back gone out, crick.

BACKER n. the money, angel, sponsor, fairy godmother, grubstaker, staker, meal ticket. See BENEFACTOR.

BACK TALK n. comeback, snappy comeback, feedback, you get it, guff, lip. See ANSWER.

BACKUP adj. spillback.

BACKWARDS adj. ass backwards, bass ackwards, ass over elbows, arsy-varsy, off the cob, topsy-turvy, catawampus. See also REVERSE.

BACKWOODS n. boonies, boondocks, tullies, sticks. See COUNTRY.

BACON n. grunts, sow belly.

BACON AND EGGS ON TOAST n. Adam and Eve on a raft, bride and groom on a raft, cackleberries and grunts.

BACON LETTUCE AND TOMATO n. BLT, BLT on wheels (to take out).

BACTERIA n. bug.

BAD adj. sucks, grody, grody to the max, gross, beastly, dead ass, rat's ass, bad-assed, barfy, grunge, grungy, raunchy, scuzzy, sleazy, sleazeball, foul ball, shitty, crappy, crap, dreck, crud, cruddy, crusty, cheesy, cheap, cheapie, diddly, diddly shit, diddly poo, doodly, doodly poo, chicken shit, ain't worth shit, ain't worth the powder to blow it to hell, ain't worth a hoot, ain't worth a plugged nickel, bad news, bummer, downer, grabber, the pits, the dogs, bottom out, blah, crummy, rough, sad, stinking, synthetic, tough, tough nuggies, eighteen carat, fierce, something fierce, godawful, goshawful, fiddlefucking, worst-case scenario, garbage, icky, yucky, lousy, rotten, murder, murderous, nuts, poison, tripe, bum, dirty, dirty minded, doin'dirt, low-down, mangy, measly, damn, damned, darn, darned, cotton-pickin', stiffo, tin, wood, not so hot, no bargain, no account, no count, no-good, N.G., tripe, turkey, dud, hellish, hell of a note, hipper dipper, dinger, ech, flukum, flookum, on the fritz, white elephant, punk, humpty-dumpty, hump, jeasley, crab, ice, pretzels, bogus, junk, junky, the least, lousy, beans, hill of beans, a lemon, peanuts, bad apple, two bit, short end of the stick, bottom of the barrel, number ten (Korean war), one thou, one thousand (Vietnam war).

BADGE n. shield, button, buzzer, cookie cutter, flash, potsy, tin, white tin, yellow tin. See also IDENTIFICATION.

BADGER v. bug, ride, be at, be on the back of, eat, chiv, noodge, give one the business, work on, fuzzbuzz, hassle. See ANNOY.

BAD PERSON n. bad guy, bastard, prick, mother, motherfucker (Obsc.), mofo, sleazeball, slimeball, slime bucket, fuck face (Obsc.), cock sucker (Obsc.), son of a bitch, SOB, maggot, shithead. See SCOUNDREL.

BAD-TEMPERED adj. bitchy, cussed, mean, ornery, ugly. See IRRITABLE.

BAFFLE v. stick, stump, throw, floor, get, rattle, buffalo. See PUZZLE.

BAFFLED adj. thrown, in a fog, spaced out, beat, bamboozled, buffaloed. See PUZZLED.

BAG n. jiffy bag, keister, valpack, carry-on, tote bag, gear, swag bag, diddie bag (Army), doggie bag (Rest.). See also LUGGAGE.

BAGATELLE n. diddly, diddly shit, shit, chickenshit, chicken feed, peanuts, small change, a hoot, drop in the bucket, drop in the ocean, small beer, hill of beans, row of buttons, row of pins, damn, darn, tinker's dam. See also AMOUNT, SMALL.

BAGGAGE n. bags, carry on, tote, tote bag, things, fortnighter, gear, two-suiter, valpack, keister, meter, peter, slough, jiffy bag, swag bag, turkey.

BAGGAGE HANDLER n. baggage smasher, baggage masher, red cap, skycap. See also PORTER.

BAGGAGE THIEF n. keisterman, keister mark (victim).

BAIL BOND TERMS spring, springer (bondsman); buy new shoes, hop bail, lam, jump bail (run away); charge account (access to bail money), half in stir (free on bail).

BAILIWICK n. turf, territory, stamping grounds, stomping grounds, old stomping grounds, neck of the woods. See NEIGHBORHOOD.

BAIL VIOLATOR n. hot foot, jumper.

BAIT n. come on, drag, shill, B-girl. See LURE.

BAKER n. doughboy, dough head, dough puncher. See also COOK.

BALANCE n. hang, even-steven.

BALANCE v. come out, come out even.

BALCONY, THEATER n. peanut gallery, bloody-nose gallery, nigger heaven, paradise, Ethiopian paradise.

BALD adj. baldy, bald as a coot, bald as an egg, bald as an eagle, cue ball, curly, egghead, skin head.

BALK v. crimp, cramp, cramp one's style, throw one a curve, throw a monkey wrench into the works, spike one's guns, upset one's apple cart. See HINDER.

BALL n. apple, pellet, pill, sphere.

BALL (DANCE) n. prom, hop, jump, mingle, shindig, hoedown, hoedig, hoodang, hog wrestle, brawl. See also PARTY.

BALLET STUDENT n. rat.

BALLOON n. bladder, sky hook.

BALLOON VENDOR n. bag guy.

BALLROOM n. frolic pad, track.

BALTIMORE AND OHIO RR n. beefsteak and onions, old B. and O.

BALTIMORE, MARYLAND Bal City, Balto, B.W.

BALTIMORE RESIDENTS n. Baltimorons.

BAN n. no-no, a don't, off-limits, outta bounds, a thou-shalt-not.

BAN v. blackball, ice out, pass by, pass up, shut out, close down, close up.

BANAL adj. dumb, no place, nowhere, square, stupid, corn, cornball, cornfed, corny, hokum, hokey, tripe, blah, draddy, dull as dishwater, flat, flat as a pancake, ho hum, nothing, pablum, zero. See also TRITE.

BANALITY n. buzzword, boiler plate, dullsville, high camp, hokum, corn, familiar tune, chestnut, old chestnut, saw, old saw, old song, old story, potboiler.

BAND n. 1. combo, group, big band, jazz band, jump band, swing band, blue blowers, jazz blowers, sidemen, backup, ork. 2. those one runs with, bunch, crowd, mob, gang, ring, clan, outfit, tribe, troupe, troops, rat pack, yoot (teenage). See GROUP.

BANDANA n. snot rag, wipe, blower, duster, tear duster, sneezer, sniffer.

BAND LEADER n. monkey, professor.

BANISH v. bounce, kick out, chuck out, chucker out, boot out, throw out on one's ear, give one the heave-ho, give one the old heave-ho, give one the bum's rush, give the mitten, give the hook, fire, kiss off, can. See also EJECT, OSTRACIZE.

BANISHED adj. blackballed, cold shouldered, left out in the cold, left on the outside looking in, not in the picture, shut out, sidelined. See EXCLUDED.

BANJO n. banjer.

BANJOIST n. banjo man, banjo picker, banjo strummer, banjo thrummer, banjo twanger, picker.

BANJO-UKULELE n. banjo uke, banjuke.

BANK n. damper, jay, jug.

BANK ACCOUNT n. nest egg, rainy day, sock, mattress-full.

BANKBOOK n. damper pad.

BANKER n. loan shark, shylock, juice dealer. See also FINANCIER.

BANKROLL n. roll, wad, bundle, shoestring, glory roll, Michigan roll, Philadelphia bankroll. See also MONEY.

BANKRUPT adj. belly up, broke, busted, Chapter 11, on the rocks, to the wall, cleaned out, go to the cleaners, go to the poorhouse. See also DESTITUTE.

BANKRUPT v. belly up, go bust, go Chapter 11, go broke, go under, go up, go to the wall, fold, fold up, close one's doors.

BANKRUPTCY n.   Chapter 11, Chapter 7, Chapter 13, belly up, go belly up, go under, in the toilet, in the tub, take a bath, close the doors.

BANNED adj.   blackballed, no-no, shut out, left out in the cold, not in the picture, out of bounds, left on the outside looking in. See also PROHIBITED, EXCLUDED.

BANNER n.   streamer, screamer.

BANQUET n.   big feed, blow, blowout.

BANTAM n.   banty.

BANTER v.   rap, jive, jolly, josh, kid, kid around, needle, play the dozens, put on, rag, razz, rib, roast. See also JOKE, TEASE.

BANTERER n.   rapper, jiver, jollyer, josher, kidder, kibitzer, needler, ragger, razzer, ribber, roaster.

BAR n.   snake ranch, office, meat rack, meat market (singles bar), beaver palace, candy store, fern bar, fernie, fleshpot, free and easy, gay bar, bird circuit (homosexual), guzzlery, guzzery, guzzle shop, dram shop, grog shop, grog mill, gin mill, fillmill, hideaway, room, rum room, night spot, nitery, dive, joint, after-hours joint, juke joint, juice joint, hop joint, beer joint, tap room, grocery, waterholes, the nineteenth hole, gutbucket, bucket shop, suds shop, slop, slopshop (beer), barrelhouse, gashouse, ale house, beer house, mug house, washer, cheap John, creep dive, deadfall, honky-tonk, speakeasy, blind pig, blind tiger, scatter, gargle factory, water hole, chain locker (dockside), shine box (Bl.).

BAR v.   blackball, ice out, shut out, pass by, pass up. See EXCLUDE.

BARB n.   needle.

BARBAROUS adj.   bad ass, kill-crazy.

BARBED WIRE n.   gooseberry, gooseberry bush (entanglement).

BARBEQUE n.   cookout, smoke out, B.B.Q.

BARBER n.   axeman, butcher, chin polisher, scraper, hair bender.

BARBER v.   get ones ears raised, get one's head scratched, get one's rug beat, mow the lawn.

BARBITURATE n.   barb, blue devils, blue heaven, candy, down, goof ball, peanuts, Phennies, pink lady, purple heart, yellow jacket, abbot, blockbuster, nimby, nebbie, nemmy.

BARE adj.   1. bare-assed, B.A., buck naked, naked as a jaybird, naked as the day one was born, without a stitch, nudie, in one's birthday suit, in the altogether, in the raw, skinny. See NUDE. 2. clean, vanilla, what you see is what you get. See PLAIN.

BARE v.   1. let it all hang out, show, show up, whip out, flash (also used in cards). See EXPOSE. 2. spill, spill one's guts, blab, sing, crack, get it off one's chest, come clean, open up, blow the whistle on. See CONFESS.

BARELY adv.   squeak by, by a hair, by the skin of one's teeth, pretty near, close shave, practically.

BARGAIN n.   buy, steal, a real steal, deal, dicker, a run for one's money, loss leader. See also AGREEMENT, CHEAP.

BARGAIN v.   deal, dicker, hack out a deal, hammer out a deal, make a deal, work out a deal, hondle, Jew down (Derog.), knock down the price. See NEGOTIATE.

BARITONE n.   bary.

BARRACKS n.   hooch (quonset), jeep town.

BARRED adj.   blackballed, cold shouldered, left out in the cold, left on the outside looking in, not in the picture, shut out, sidelined. See also PROHIBITED.

BARREN adj.   godforsaken.

BARTENDER n.   bar keep, apron, B-girl, bar girl, beer jerker, beer slinger, fizzical culturist, mixologist, pour man.

BARTER v.   horse trade, swap, swap horses. See NEGOTIATE.

BASE adj.   sucks, grody, grody to the max, gross, beastly, dead ass, rat's ass, bad-assed, raunchy, scuzzy, sleazy, sleazeball, slimeball.

BASE n.   HQ, GHQ, CP. See also HEADQUARTERS.

BASEBALL, BALL n.   apple, horsehide, cowhide, pill, sphere, spheroid, cantaloupe, casaba, egg, radish, hand grenade, globule (Arc.), emery ball (rough sided, illegal), shine ball (smooth, illegal), voodoo ball, die (fail to roll or bounce).

BASEBALL, BASE ON BALLS   walk, give up a walk, free transportation, free ticket, free trip, handout, four wide ones.

BASEBALL, BASES   bag, sack, cushion, hassock (base), keystone, keystone sack (second base), plate, platter (home), hot corner (third base).

BASEBALL BAT n.   lumber, wood, stick, pole, club, war club, Black Betsy, fungo, fungo stick, swat stick, banana stick.

BASEBALL, BAT v.   up (at bat), switch hit, take one's cut, choke, choke up (grip bat high on handle), hit the dirt (drop to avoid a bad pitch), ahead of the count, looking (not swinging), K. (strikeout), buck ten (low batting average).

BASEBALL ERROR n.   bobble, boot, lose the handle, muff, miscue.

BASEBALL HIT n. 1. poke, pole, belt, clout, touch, fly, pop fly, pop out, pop up, pull (he pulled it to left), fungo, punch, chop, Baltimore chop (high bounce), roller, comebacker, sacrifice, sacrifice fly, bloop single, dying swan, smash, swat (Babe Ruth was the Sultan of Swat), paste, blast, bleeder, scratch hit, fluke, flair, bouncer, Leaping Lena, pinch hit, hopper, hammer, shell (Lefty was shelled for ten hits), safety, slam, lace one (hard hit), sip one, scorcher, smoke one, scald one, atom ball (hit right atom), pull the trigger, lather, banjo hit, can o'corn (high fly), cloudbuster, tater (fly ball), sinker, Texas Leaguer (short fly), cat, clean (a clean hit), clothesline (low hard), hangout the wash, hang out the hump, a rope, drive, blue dart, line drive, drive in (he drove in a run), grounder, daisy cutter, grass cutter, lawn mower, slow roller, skimmer, tag one, crank one out, cream, infield hit, leg hit, fence buster, go for the fences, get good wood on it, slugfest, slugging average, tape measure, pepper, scatter (they scattered six hits against Valenzuela). 2. bunt, drag bunt, squeeze, squeeze bunt, suicide squeeze, dump one, lay down a, sacrifice bunt. 3. single, beat out (get to first base before the throw), bleeder, seeing-eye single. 4. double, two bagger, two-ply poke. 5. triple, go for three, three bagger, three-ply poke. 6. home run, homer, four bagger, grand slam (with bases full), grand slammer, lose one, lose one over the fence, money smash, out of the park, take one downtown, over the fence, round tripper, Babe Ruth, circuit blow, circuit clout, circuit wallop, clean the bases, clean off the bases, dial 8, dial long distance, dinger, tater, tape measure.

BASEBALL HOME RUN n. home run, homer, four bagger, grand slam (with bases full), grand slammer, salami, lose one, lose one over the fence, money smash, out of the park, over the fence, take one downtown, round tripper, Babe Ruth, circuit blow, circuit clout, circuit wallop, clean the bases, clean off the bases, dial 8, dial long distance, dinger, tape measure.

BASEBALL PITCH n. deal, fire, hurl, twirl, stuff, stuff on the ball, stuff on it, Sunday pitch, bringing it to 'em, hummer, hump it in, good cheese, the express, aspirin, beebees, fast ball, fastballing, the express, fireballing, blow, blow one by, burn one over, smoke, smoke ball, steam heat, canned heat, heater, fog, fog it in, split-fingered fast ball, breaking ball, curve, nickel curve, Uncle Charlie (curve), chuck 'n duck (hanging curve), yellow hammer, yakker (curve), crossfire (sidearm), slider, slurve (sliding curve), fader (swerve), jug handle curve, roundhouse (slow curve), hook, fadeaway, junk, throw junk, floater, flutterball, butterfly ball, palm ball, hesitation pitch, slip pitch (off speed), change up, let up, let-up pitch, let-up ball, pull the string, Clyde's ball (slowball), sinker, sinker ball, drop, submarine (under-hand), screwball, turn the ball over (screwball), knuckleball, knuckler, spitball, spitter, Cuban fork ball (spitball), fork ball, emery ball, grease ball, dipsey do,

dipsey doodle, knockdown, brush back, chin music, dust, dust off (high inside), duster, knuckle duster, ear duster, bean ball, head hunter, inshoot, jam (in on the hands), floater, fat (perfect to hit), hanger (failed to curve), gofer ball, gopher ball, groove one (heart of the strike zone), over the plate, automatic take (3 balls, 0 strikes), cripple (thrown with 3 balls, no strikes), away (wide), four wide ones, cheese express, airing it out (pitching well), pinching (umpire conservative call).

BASEBALL PITCHER n. hurler, knuckler, flinger, southpaw, portsider, lefty, chucker, starter, stopper (able to beat any team), fireman (relief), reliever (sub), middle reliever, long man, short man, ace (best), arm (ability, a great arm), side wheeler, fast baller, fireballer, smoke (he throws smoke), junkman (throws slowballs), submariner (underhand), hose (throwing arm), rubber arm (durable), glass arm, barber, cockeye, crooked arm, croakie, fork hander, fork baller, hook arm, hand grenader, cannon (strong throwing arm), cousin (easy to hit); go the route, go the distance, go all the way, in a hole (at a disadvantage); derrick, yank, send him to the showers, chase (replace pitcher); Iron Mike (pitching machine).

BASEBALL PLAY n. on (on base), aboard (on base), jammed, juiced, drunk (bases loaded), die (runner left on base), around the horn (ball thrown third to second to first base), triple play (three outs in one play), double play, double steal, steal, take a lead (move toward next base), go with the pitch, squeeze, safety squeeze, suicide squeeze, safe, beat out, out, cut down (out, he was cut down stealing), pick off, run down (caught off base), gun down, nail (out, nailed at second), hit the dirt (slide), fadeaway slide, fallaway side, fielder's choice, force, force out, shade (adjust field position, Dusty shaded a little to the left), sacrifice, sacrifice fly, shag (chase a ball), caught on the fly, corral, trap, take, gobble, wait for, one hand, under it, a chance, shoestring catch, circus catch, (catch a ball); peg, flip (throw); assist, take (fail to strike at a pitch), bail out (drop away from a wild pitch), bat around (full team bats in an inning), break (unexpected favorable action).

BASEBALL PLAYER n. big leaguer, bush leaguer, bush, busher, sand lotter, baseballer, boys of summer, first sacker, second sacker, third sacker, battery (pitcher/catcher), first string, second string, leadoff, leadoff man (first to bat), slugger, cannon, woodman, fence buster, heavy sticker, clouter, power hitter, long ball hitter, pinch hitter, pinch runner, pull hitter, punch hitter, spray hitter, switch hitter, guess hitter, cleanup (fourth batter); Desi, DH (designated hitter); a good eye; cream puff, banjo hitter (weak); ball hawk, fly catcher, center (center fielder), back-up infielder, glove man (fielder), utility man, platoon player, gardener, butterfingers, bark (coach).

BASEBALL SCORE n. safe, save (relief pitcher game credit), away (one out, one away), die (left on base), behind (balls or strikes to one's disadvantage), blank, pitchers' duel, shutout (held scoreless), laugher (easy win), bring in (a hit brings in a run), give up a run, go ahead run, long count (3 balls, 2 strikes).

BASEBALL STADIUM n. ball park, park, diamond (infield); daisies, garden (outfield); pasture, the yard, Hogan's brickyard, the rockpile (bad infield).

BASEBALL STRIKEOUT n. fan, K, caught looking, punched out, retire, whiff (also strike).

BASEBALL TERMS national pastime, horsehide, nine, play hard ball, rounders, piggy, piggy move up, the majors (major leagues), cactus league, grapefruit league, farm, farm team, farm out (transfer a player to a farm team), sandlot (amateur), cup of coffee (short stay on a team), home stand (play on home grounds), pitching duel, slugfest, hitfest, doubleheader, twin bill (two games), twi-night double header, nightcap (2nd game of double header); raincheck, rainout (postponement); pennant (league championship, they took the pennant), flag (pennant), magic number (formula of victories needed to win pennant), cellar (last place in team standings), lifetime (career record), come off (past record, he comes off a big slump), cousin (easily beaten opponent), chapter (inning), bottom (last half of an inning, the bottom of the sixth); hill, mound, (pitching box); rag, pup (glove); retire the side, pull (remove, he pulled the pitcher), bull pen, slab (pitcher's rubber bar), lineup (batting order), on deck, in the slot (awaiting a turn at bat), bat in a bucket, come through, fungo circle, pepper; the daisies, the garden (outfield); scout (talent scout), Baseball Annie (dates players).

BASEBALL UMPIRE n. ump, the boys in blue, homer, arbiter, blind Tom, the call (decision), the count (balls and strikes), clubhouse lawyer (player).

BASELESS adj. hot air, just talk, bullshit, BS, whataya talking, my eye, you're talking like a man with a paper ass, you're talking through your hat. See GROUNDLESS.

BASHFUL adj. wallflower, mousy, ratty.

BASIC n. bottom line, plain vanilla, nitty gritty, where it's at, name, name of the game, nub, meat and potatoes, coal and ice. See also VITAL.

BASICS n. ABCs, three Rs, nitty-gritty, nuts and bolts, brass tacks, get down, get down to brass tacks, groceries, guts, meat and potatoes, beginners, coal and ice, primo, cut, gutty.

BASIS n. bottom line, nitty-gritty, nuts and bolts, rock bottom, meat and potatoes. See FOUNDATION.

BASKETBALL PLAY n. one on one, low post, high post, assist, give and go, blindside (he blindsided him and stole the ball), fast break, flip pass, hook pass, jump pass, outlet, blind pass (without looking), dish it off (pass), pull the trigger (shoot), turnover (lose possession of the ball), put the ball on the floor (dribble), sag (they sagged to cut off Alajuan), softball pass (underhand), steal (Magic reached in and stole the ball), put him in the popcorn machine (outmaneuver and score).

BASKETBALL PLAYER n. cager, basketballer, basket hanger, hoop man, big man (center), post man, the tall trees (center and forwards), front line (forwards and center), front liner, swing man (plays more than one position), playmaker.

BASKETBALL SHOT n. hoop, lay up, jumper, jump shot, set shot, flip, finger roll, fallaway, hook, three pointer, scoop, stuff, swish, swisher, can one, get one to go down, bomb (long), chippie (easy open shot), garbage (score loose ball), alley oop, dunk, slam dunk, tomahawk (dunk), shoot a pair, charity shot, air ball, a brick (complete miss).

BASKETBALL TERMS cage (the game), five, quint (the team), casaba (ball); the iron, the rack, hoop, hole, (basket), the paint, the key (free throw lane); shoot some hoops (play), sellout (bad play) sweet (smooth player), lineup (players in game), hoop man, the big man, low post, high post, ref, the dirt part (defense), hijack (blocked play), jump ball, bring it in (from out of bounds), outlet pass, pass off, ball handler, hot hand (playing well); flip, bury it, drain (score); box out, screen, tickytack foul, T (technical foul), foul out, bonus situation, charity stripe (free throw line), go to the line, shoot a pair, kill the clock (time out), run out the clock (stall), sit on a lead, sit on the ball, let the air out of the ball (slow down the play).

BASS FIDDLE n. bass, bull fiddle, gut bucket, doghouse, old boomer, vein (double bass).

BASTE v. slather, slop on.

BATH n. tub, shower, jacoozy, splash, light splash.

BATHE v. shower, dunk, tub, splash, swab down.

BATHING SUIT n. bikini, monokini (topless), string, tank suit, kneebusters, clamdiggers, baggies, jammies.

BATHROOM n. can, john, rest room, ladies, ladies' room, women's room, girls' room, little girls' room, powder room, library, sandbox, biffy, throne room, where the dicks hang out (Obsc.). See TOILET.

BATHTUB n. tub, jacoozy, plunger.

BATON ROUGE, LOUISIANA B.R. Town.

BATON n. stick, night stick, bat, billy club (policeman's).

BATTER v. mug, bat, bash, bust, beat the shit out of, blast, lambaste, paste, trash, punch out, work out, work over, kick ass, take one over the hurdles. See HIT.

BATTERED adj. 1. bashed, bashed up, beat up, bunged up, worked over, roughed up. See also ABUSED. 2. geed up, g'd up (coin).

BATTERY n. juice box, can (WW II).

BATTLE n. rumble, rhubarb, knock down and drag out, battle royal, brawl, brannigan, hey rube. See FIGHT.

BATTLE v. brawl, hassle, scrap, roughhouse, bang heads, mix it up, pitch a bitch, raise sand.

BATTLESHIP n. battlewagon, man o' war.

BAUBLE n. gewgaw, junk jewelry.

BAWDY adj. dirty, raunchy, blue, rough, low down and dirty, purple, off-color, salty. See OBSCENE.

BAYONET n. can opener, toothpick, pig sticker, frog sticker, cheese toaster, toasting fork, Rosalie.

BEADS n. junk jewelry, brass (cheap or fake), stones, rocks, sparklers, ice, glass, Christmas, hardware, pennyweight, chocker, choker.

BEAM n. glim, dimmer.

BEAM v. crack a smile, grin from ear to ear, grin like a Cheshire cat, grin like a Chessy cat.

BEANS n. musical fruit, bullets, rib stickers, Arizona strawberries, Arkansas strawberries, Boston strawberries, Mexican strawberries, prairie strawberries.

BEANS AND FRANKFURTERS n. army chicken, beans and tubesteak, beans and franks.

BEAR v. live with, bear with, put up with, roll with the punches, hang on, ride out, stay the course, stand for, be big, grin and bear it. See ENDURE.

BEARD n. beaver, brush, muff, peach fuzz, pez, spinach, face spinach, face lace, bush, shrubbery, alfalfa, chin whiskers, Castro; gallaway (false), galways (stage Irishman). See WHISKERS.

BEARDED adj. brushfaced, muffed, wearin' a muff, alfalfa'd, beavered, brushy, brush peddler, chin whiskered, Castro; galwayed, gallawayed (false); Santa Clausish.

BEARER n. boy, shlepper, Typhoid Mary (disease). See also BAGGAGE HANDLER.

BEARING n. 1. that a way, every which way, forty ways to Sunday, forty ways from Sunday, forty ways for Sunday. 2. brace, brush (Army).

BEARINGS n. fix, how it is, how the land lies, the lay of the land.

BEAST n. 1. critter, dog (inferior), stray (orphaned, deserted), varmint. 2. bad actor (vicious), bum, cob roller.

BEASTIALITY n. animal training.

BEAT (RHYTHMIC) n. pitapat, tick, ticktock.

BEAT v. 1. bash, trash, drub, flax, wax, lather, cane, wipe, hide, tan one's hide, brain, kayo, clobber, cream, paste, waste, beat the shit out of one, put one in the hospital, break one's face, See HIT. 2. bury, blank, skunk, schneider, murder, kill, cook, trim, skin, shellack, squelch, squash, bulldoze, torpedo, put away. See DEFEAT.

BEATEN adj. blanked, burned, busted, beatsville, creamed, clobbered, hosed, licked, ripped, fixed, shut down, you can't buck city hall, you can't beat the system. See DEFEATED.

BEATEN UP adj. 1. bashed, bashed up, beat up, bunged up, roughed up, worked over. 2. geed up, g'd up (coin).

BEATING n. paddling, licking, larruping, walloping, whaling, lathering, leathering, hiding, tanning, shellacking, waxing, lumps, get one's lumps, barrel punishment, dressing down, strap oil, hazel oil, hickory oil, birch oil, dose of strap oil, dose of hazel oil, dose of birch oil, dose of hickory oil. See also DEFEAT.

BEAU n. old man, main squeeze, flame, boyfriend, honey man, lovebird, big moment. See BOYFRIEND.

BEAUTIFUL adj. ten, 10, boss, righteous, such a Mona, traffic stopper, hardbody, stacked, constructed, built, well-built, built for comfort, built like a brick shithouse, curvy, a honey, a lulu, cool, cher, diddly, drooly, dishy, dazzler, dream, dreamy, dreamboat, dream puss, dream bait, drop-dead gorgeous, vicious, whistle bait, angel, angel face, angel puss, phat chick, piece, piece of furniture, nice little piece of furniture, piece of ass, flavor (Bl.), geranium, daisy, glamour girl, looker, good looker, hammer, bunny, pussycat, sex kitten, mink, stone, stone fox, foxy, head rush, crazy, sharp, slick, slick chick, cute, smooth, scrumptious, ducky, nobby, snappy, snappy number, snazzy, solid sender, stunner, stunning, cunning, tip, nifty, number, gimme, peach, peacherino, peachy keen, delicious, pinup, pinup girl, playmate, oomph girl, sweater girl, spiffy, spiffing, ripping, pip, pippin, pipperoo, poundcake, right, reet, reat, neat, fetcher, biscuit, beaut, raving, raving beauty, go-getter, hot shit, keen, look like a million, look fit to kill, killer, killer-diller, lady-killer, killing, knockout, knock dead, knock one dead, knock one's eyes out, eye filling, eyeful, easy on the eyes, sight for sore eyes, treat for sore eyes, not hard to look at, long on looks, a picture, pretty as a picture, centerfold, swell, dandy, fine and dandy, just dandy, jim-dandy, fat, hunky-dory, but good, good enough to eat up, good enough to eat with a spoon, okay, OK, A-OK, oh yeah.

BEAUTIFY v. doll up, fix up, gussy up, pretty up, spruce up.

BEAUTY TREATMENT n.   blow job, blow dry, the works, color, hair done, nails done, perm.

BECOME v.   snowball, mushroom, shoot up.

BED n.   hay, pad, sack, fart sack, flop, joint, kip, snooze bin, work bench (Obsc.), rock, barnacle, camp, dreamer, safety, doss, fleabag.

BEDBUG n.   chinch, crum, crumb, pillow pigeon, wild life.

BEDDING n.   crash pad, roll, California blanket.

BEDEVIL v.   1. hoodoo, voodoo, put the whammy on one or something, put the horns on one or something. 2. bug, ride, be on the back of, noodge, give one the needle, hit on, get, get to, fuzzbuzz, rile, hassle, hound, dog, worry, push, push one's button. See ANNOY.

BEDEVILED adj.   spooked, bugged, bummed out, hacked, hung up, uptight, picked on. See ANNOYED.

BED, GO TO v.   crash, flake out, get some shut-eye, hit the hay, hit the sack, sack out, turn in. See RETIRE.

BEDLAM n.   all hell broke loose, to-do, snarl-up, mishmosh, mishmash, rumpus, ruckus, ruction, shivaree, hoopla, holy mess, unholy mess, bloody mess, mess and a half, rat's nest, every which way, every which way but up, forty ways from Sunday, forty ways for Sunday, galley west, hectic, hassle, pretty kettle of fish, pretty piece of business, nice piece of work, free-for-all. See also TURMOIL.

BEDROLL n.   balloon, biddle, bindle.

BEDROOM SLIPPERS n.   skivvies, mules, scuffs.

BEDSHEET n.   dreamer, lily whites.

BED SHEETS n.   lily whites, dreamer.

BEEF n.   bossy, (roast beef, stew), cow, bull, leather, moo (steak), shoe sole, tiger meat, young horse.

BEER n.   brew, suds, a chill, oil, Alaskan martini, barley pop, belly wash, draw one, blow one, boilermaker (with whiskey chaser), brown bottle, cold coffee, Coney Island head, Coney Island (mostly foam), fluids and electrolytes, (Med. Stu.), head (foam), hops, horse collar, Kool Aid, near beer (non-alcoholic), needle beer, needled beer (alcohol added), pig sweat, pony.

BEER DRINKING v.   having a few, raising a few, pounding a few brews, chugalugging, pub-crawling.

BEFALL v.   come down, go down, action, jell, gel, cook, cook up a storm, cook with gas, shake, smoke. See OCCUR.

BEFITTING adj.   on the button, on the nose, right on, just what the doctor ordered, according to Hoyle, kosher. See SUITABLE.

BEFOULED adj.   cooked (radiation), dirty, exposed, mucked up.

BEFRIEND v.   buddy up, get in with, get on the in with, get chummy with, take up with, case out, come on to, cotton to, hit it off, tuck under one's wing. See also CULTIVATE.

BEFRIENDED adj.   make it with one, on the in with, hit it off.

BEFUDDLED adj.   shook, shook up, dopey, punchy, punch drunk, slaphappy, in a botheration. See CONFUSED.

BEG v.   bum, panhandle, hustle, sponge, schnor, score, cadge, chisel, tap, touch, make, make a touch, mooch, promote, bite, put the bite on, put the bee on one, put the touch on, put the arm on, put the sleeve on, pass the hat, brace, batter, burn, buzz, ding, nick, nickel up, dime up, hit, hit up, hit the bricks, hit the stem, hit the turf, freeload, pivot, pling, grub, knock, needle, hold out for, whistle for (but won't get), drop the lug on one, flag down, slam a gate.

BEGET n.   parenting.

BEGGAR n.   bum, bummer, stumblebum, slum bum, rubber bum, moocher, panhandler, promoter, ragbag, bag lady, bag woman, schnorrer, sponger, freeloader, lumberman, (with crutches), crip (crippled), peggy (one legged), plinger, professor, rustler, muzzler, bindle man, bindlestiff, stiff, mission stiff, bit borrower, blinkie (fakes blindness), chiseler, chroniker, cipher, wingding, dingbat, ding dong, ding donger, dinger, dino, geezo, greaseball, heister, guttersnipe, gutterpup, in the gutter, bo. See also VAGRANT.

BEGGARLY adj.   broke, busted, flat, flat broke, stony, piss poor, hard up, truly needy, strapped, pinched, down and out, down at the heels, on one's uppers, poor as a church mouse, looking for a handout. See DESTITUTE.

BEGIN v.   bow, open, open up, come out, coming out, roll 'em, let it roll, start the ball rolling, get rolling, get things rolling, get going, get into, get in there, get in on the ground floor, start from scratch, get one's feet wet, get the show on the road, get under way, get with it, get on the job, get cracking, let's get cracking, get squared away, buckle down, knuckle down, tackle, from the top, take it from the top, count down, take off, kick off, blast off, sail off, send off, push off, jump off, jump to it, go to it, hop to it, have at it, light into, head into, tear into, sail into, wade into, fall to, cut one's teeth, rev, rev up, fire up, goose, hit for, hit the ground running (in full operation), break in, clock in, ring in, pitch in, dive in, blast away, batch out (accelerate), begin the beguine, break the seal, right out of the gate, break the ice, let fly, play ball, shoot, stanch, stanch out, hang up one's shingle.

BEGINNER n.   starter, boot, student, freshie, newie, new boy, new boy on the block, new kid on the block, break in, gremlin, gremmie, fish, tyro, tenderfoot, foot in the door, green, greenie, greenhorn, rookie, rook, turkey, punk, jice, new jice, heel, heeler (reporter), peg boy, pratt boy, buckwheater, cheechako, chukoko, Johnny come lately, blow-in. See also NOVICE.

BEGINNING n.   preem, bow, curtain-raiser, opener, openers, for openers, opener upper, open up, top, from scratch, square one, day 1, day one, first crack out of the box, countdown, for starters, flying start, running start, right off the bat, from out front, from the top, from the word go, the get go, git go, jump off, kick-off, take-off, send-off, start-off, blast-off, first off, first round, coming out, coming-out party, virgin territory.

BEGRUDGE v.   turn green, eat one's heart out, to die over, I should have such luck.

BEGUILE v.   1. gyp, flam, flimflam, screw, have, take, stick, burn, chisel, con, scam, shave, rook, snow, play for a sucker, diddle, string along, suck in, rope in. See TRICK. 2. vamp, sweep off one's feet, knock dead, knock out, slay, tickle to death, tickle pink, send, wow, turn on. See also ATTRACT.

BEHAVE v.   shape up, shape up or ship out, toe the mark, mind your p's and q's, watch one's step, keep one's nose clean.

BEHAVIOR n.   bag, style.

BEHIND adv.   trailing, backyard, have to play catch up, off the pace, bringing up the rear, eat one's dust.

BEHOLD v.   catch, glim, glom, spot, spy, eye, eyeball, give with the eyes, lay eyes on, flash, lamp, pipe, gun. See SEE.

BEHOLDEN adj.   into, on the tab, in hock, owe one (I owe you one), on the cuff, on the arm, into the shylock, on a string.

BEING n.   life, lifing, rat race, world, journey, the big game, hand (one is dealt).

BELCH v.   burp, repeat.

BELIEF n.   op, say so, slant, POV, P.O.V., gospel truth, stock, store, judgment call, two cents' worth.

BELIEVABLE adj.   straight, straight shit, no shit, no bullshit, up front, above board, honest to God, one's stock has gone up.

BELIEVE v.   feel, sold, stomach (can't stomach something), swallow, swallow it hook line and sinker, take as gospel truth, take stock in, set store by, swear by, okay, OK, buy, bank on, bet on, bet one's bottom dollar on, lay money on, lap up, be afraid, have a hunch, have a sneaking suspicion, got to hand it to one, pat on the back, go along with, string along with.

BELIEVER n.   freak (strong), nut. See DEVOTEE.

BELITTLE v.   run down, put down, downplay, play down, take down, take down a peg, take down a peg or two, take the starch out of, take the shine out of, tear down, shoot down, cut down to size, cut rate, cut to the quick, rip, pan, slam, smear, squash, squelch, hit, blister, roast, scorch, rap, take a rap at, take a swipe at, take the shine out of, fluff off, brush off, dump on, shit on, do a number on, shred, mudsling, needle, give one the needle, knock, knock down, poor mouth, bad mouth, bitter mouth, back cap, back bite, rip up the back, give a black eye, give one one's comeuppance, thumb one's nose at, pooh pooh, rubbish, sour grapes, mark lousy, put the crimpers in, put the hooks in, put the needles in, put the zingers in, put away, put a tuck in one's tail, poke full of holes, shoot full of holes, prick one's balloon, puncture one's balloon, take the wind out of one's sails, blow sky high, knock the bottom out of, knock the chocks out from under, knock the props out from under, knock one off his perch, make one sing small. See also EMBARRASS.

BELITTLED adj.   eat crow, eat dirt, eat humble pie, sing small, crawl, lost face, took down, put down, comedown, dumped on, drummed out, draw in one's horns, egg on one's face, knocked from one's high horse, knocked off one's perch, have a tuck in one's tail, got one's comeuppance. See also DISCREDITED.

BELITTLING n.   sour grapes, crow, humble pie.

BELL n.   ding-dong, dinger, tinkler; hit the dinger, toot the tooter (ring a bell).

BELL BOTTOMS n.   bells.

BELLBOY n.   bellhop, hop, boy, button, baggage smasher, pack rat. See also BAGGAGE HANDLER.

BELLIGERENT adj.   ornery, scrappy, snorky, bitchy, cussed, flip, tetchy, salty, spiky, limber, mean, bad ass, cantankerous, fire-eater, out for a rep, have a bone to pick, have a chip on one's shoulder, have it in for, at loggerheads, at outs, on the outs, on the muscle, hard on for, forecastle lawyer. See also AGGRESSIVE.

BELLOW n.   holler, beller, blast, yawp, yell.

BELLOW v.   holler, holler out, beller, beller out, yell, yell out, blast, yawp.

BELLY n.   tummy, gut, pot, potbelly, melon belly, swagbelly, beerbelly, tank, spare tire, corporation, breadbasket, bay window, front porch. See STOMACH.

BELONG v.   in, in with, run with, swing, swing with, one of the boys.

BELOVED n.   number one, numero uno, B.F., G.F., old lady, old man, one and only, O and O, honey, hon, dearie, baby, doll, doll face, puddin', sweetie, sweetie pie, sweets, sweet pea, sugar, sugar bowl, sugar daddy,

daddy, candyleg, money honey, honey man, biscuit, gold mine, generous keeper, steady, big moment, heartbeat, heart throb, love, love of my life, flame, oyster, jane, toots, tootsie, turtle dove, roller, mule skinner, hat, mat, date, mate, significant other, dumb Dora, patootie, hot patootie, sweet patootie, lambie pie, rave. See also BOYFRIEND.

BELT n. squeeze, stretcher.

BEMOAN v. sing the blues, beat one's breast, cry me a river, cry over spilled milk, go for a crying towel. See LAMENT.

BEMUSED adj. mooning, moony, daydreaming, pipe dreaming, woolgathering, staring into the middle distance.

BENEFACTION n. write off, handout, gifting, lump, poke out.

BENEFACTOR n. the money, angel, sponsor, backer, sugar daddy, fairy godmother, lady bountiful, meal ticket, Santa Claus, staker, grubstaker, pigeon, live one, mark, fan, front. See also PHILANTHROPIST.

BENEFICENT adj. softie, soft touch, a marshmallow, big, big-hearted, be big, loose, Santa Claus, good Joe, have a heart, heart in the right place, prince of a person.

BENEFICIAL adj. good for what ails you, what the doctor ordered.

BENEFIT n. gravy, mitzvah, perk, extras, cakes and ale, gravy train, cream, cream at the top, egg in one's beer. See also PROFIT.

BENEFIT v. pay, pay off, make it, do for one, do the trick, fill the bill, make a killing. See PROFIT. See also HELP.

BENEVOLENT adj. big, big-hearted, bleeding heart, all heart, heart in the right place, do gooder, Santa Claus. See also BENEFICENT.

BENT n. bag, thing, thing for, head-set, mind-set, groove, tilt, druthers, weakness for, have a bump for. See INCLINATION.

BENZEDRINE n. B, benny, benzie, speed, upper, peachies, white.

BENZEDRINE USE v. benny jag.

BERATE v. chew, chew ass, chew out, eat out, cuss out, jump all over, rake over the coals, call down, tell off, give what for, give one hell, scorch, blister. See SCOLD.

BERKELEY, CALIFORNIA Berzerkely.

BESET adj. bugged, dogged, rousted, picked on, driven up the wall. See ANNOYED.

BESET v. hassle, dog, nag, noodge, nudge, nudzh, bug, ride, pick on, start in on, give a bad time to, give a hard time to, give one the needle, give one the business, jump on one's case, on one's case, on one's back, drive up the wall, hock a charnik, put the squeeze on, put the heat on, put one through the ringer, play cat and mouse. See also ANNOY.

BESIEGE v. come at from all sides, bug, buttonhole, work on, work over, put the bee on. See also PERSUADE.

BESPECTACLED adj. four-eyed, four eyes, wearing cheaters.

BEST adj. 1. A, A-1, A-number 1, A-one, number one, numero uno, the fat, the cream, primo, ten, 10, ace, ace hi, aces, world class, greatest, out of sight, out of this world, far out, gonest, hundred proof, mostest, bad, baaadest, bitchin', boss, cool, coolsville, coolville, crack, crackerjack, murder, first chop, super, gilt-edged, gilt-edge, all time, all-time haymaker, stone, terrible, terrific, tops, top gun, top dog, top drawer, topflight, top-notch, tip top, top of the class, top of the list, the most, the almost, endsville, the end, savage, solid gold, winner, champ, king o' the hill, white hope, white knight. See also EXCELLENT. 2. all one's got, all out, balls out, one's all, one's damnedest, one's darnedest, one's level best, best shot, Sunday best.

BEST v. 1. trash, drub, flax, wax, lather, larrup, leather, lambaste, whop, whomp, whip, wipe, hide, tan, tan one's hide, brain, bop, K.O., kayo, drop, deck, dish, total, powder, clobber, cream, zap, paste, waste, hurt, kick ass, whip ass, bust up, clean on, take the wind out of one's sails, take one, take it all, take out, take care of, take down, put down, smack down, shoot down, shoot down in flames, dress one down, shut down, shut out, psych out, rank out, fake out, lay one out, lay one low, wipeout, wipe up the floor with, wipe up the place with, wipe off the map, beat one out, beat up, beat the bejesus out of, beat the tar out of, beat the beholden out of, beat the shit outta, beat the living tar out of, beat the living daylights out of, make mincemeat out of, knock cold, knock off, knock the beholden out of, knock the daylights out of, knock the living daylights out of, knock the shit out of, knock into the next county, knock for a row of [anything], knock one on one's ass, knock one ass over teakettle, knock one on one's ear, knock one into next week, knock one for a loop, deal a knockout blow to, make hamburger out of one, wallop, blast, sock it to one, let have it, floor one, down one, land a haymaker, put one away, put on ice, put it in their eye, put one in the hospital, give a going over. See also DEFEAT. 2. bury, blank, skunk, murder, kill, trim, swamp, skin, bulldoze, roll over, torpedo, meatball. See DEFEAT. See also TRIUMPH.

BEST MAN n. stand up for one.

BESTOW v. gift, gift with, kick in, put out, come through, get it up, get it on. See GIVE.

BET n.   action, down on, odds on, long shot, shot, ante, parlay, play. See WAGER.

BET v.   play, plunge, put up, put up or shut up, shoot, back, cover, make book, book the action, take a flyer, get down on (on a horse). See WAGER.

BETHLEHEM, PENNSYLVANIA   Steel City, Steel Town.

BETRAY v.   knife, stab one in the back, rat, rat on, fink, fink on, sing, sing on, snitch, squeal, stool, spill, finger, double-cross, fuck, blow the whistle, drop a dime on one. See INFORM.

BETRAYAL n.   beat out of, buried, double cross, fucked, fucked over, fucked without a kiss, giveaway, got it up the ass, Judas kiss, letting down, sellout.

BETRAYER n.   rat, rat fink, fink, narc, snitch, snitcher, squealer, stoolie, stool pigeon, blabbermouth, preacher, singer. See INFORMER. See also TRAITOR.

BETROTHED n.   intended, asked for, steady, going steady, pinned, bird, donah, donar, future.

BETTER adj.   souped up, sharpened, over the hump, on the mend, out of the woods, on the comeback trail.

BETTER v.   boost, upgrade, look up, pick up, perk up, dress up, snap up. See IMPROVE.

BETWEEN prep.   in the seam, between a rock and a hard place, between sixes and sevens, between the devil and the deep blue sea, betwixt and between, catch 22, damned if you do and damned if you don't, the rub.

BEVERAGE n.   bug juice, chaser, pop, cooler, drink. See also DRINK, LIQUOR.

BEWAIL v.   take on, sing the blues, eat one's heart out. See LAMENT.

BEWARE v.   keep a weather eye open, keep one's eye peeled, keep one's distance, keep on one's toes, keep one's ear to the ground, watch one's step, watch out, mind one's p's and q's, bend over backwards, handle with kid gloves, walk on eggs.

BEWHISKERED adj.   alfalfa'd, beavered, brushy, brushfaced, brush peddler, chin whiskered, Castro; galwayed, gallawayed (false); Santa Clausish, muffed, wearin' a muff.

BEWILDER v.   rattle, throw, take one's mind, fuck with one's head, mess with one's head, snow, floor. See PUZZLE.

BEWILDERED adj.   unglued, unzipped, unscrewed, punchy, shook up, floored, flipped out, farmisht, thrown, dopey, out to lunch. See PUZZLED.

BEWILDERMENT n.   mix-up, foul-up, fuck-up, snafu, who's minding the store? See CONFUSED.

BEWITCH v.   1. hoodoo, voodoo, put the whammy on one or something, put the horns on one or something. 2. sweep off one's feet, vamp, knock dead, knock out, slay, tickle to death, tickle pink, send, wow, turn on. See ENRAPTURED. See also ENRAPTURE, ATTRACT.

BEWITCHED adj.   hooked, bugged, gone on, fallen for, mad about, gaga about, hung up, head over heels, turned on, have one's nose open, have a bee in one's bonnet, have a bug in one's ear, have a bug up one's ass, have an ax to grind, have a thing about. See also CHARMED.

BEWITCHING adj.   a lulu of a, traffic-stopping, mink, fox, drop dead beautiful. See BEAUTIFUL.

BEYOND adj.   hyper, hypercharged.

BIAS n.   head-set, mind-set, mind trip, spin, spin control, tilt, flash. See INCLINATION.

BIASED adj.   agin, tilted, weighted, loaded, down on, one-sided, cold deck, feel a draft, flash, Jane Crow (against women), homer (umpire favoring home team), red-neck, red-baiter, Jew-baiter, black baiter, a regular Archie Bunker.

BIBLE n.   the Word, the Good Book, the good news.

BIBLIOPHAGE n.   grind, greasy grind, bookworm.

BICARBONATE OF SODA n.   bicarb.

BICEPS n.   guns.

BICKER n.   hassle, scene, tempest in a teapot.

BICKER v.   scrape, pick at, trade zingers, dig, hassle each other. See ARGUE.

BICYCLE n.   bike, cycle, two-wheeler, wheel, wheels.

BICYCLE v.   bike, cycle, pedal.

BICYCLING n.   biking, cycling, pedalling, wheeling.

BICYCLIST n.   cyclist, scorcher, crackerjack.

BID n.   feeler, proposition, pass, hit, offer.

BID v.   1. give the nod, shill, boost (false auctioneering). 2. make a play for, make a pass at, hit on, make a pitch, come up with, pop the question, proposition, speak one's piece.

BIDE v.   hang in, hang around, cool it, hold the phone, sit tight, sweat it. See WAIT.

BIG adj.   gross, humongous, humungous, mungo, king sized, monster, monstro, moby, mother, mother fucker (Obsc.), mofo, big mother, big mama, big daddy, biggy, big ass, big time, big wiz, heavyweight, heavy duty, beefy, hefty, high powered, major league, big league, overgrown, overblown, tall, super, super duper, super colossal, seagoing, jumbo, man-sized, lunker, hoss, buster, bull, blimp, barn door, a whale of a, whaling, whacking, walloping, lolloping, whopping, whopper, hulking, spanking, slapping, strapping, thumper, thumping, thundering, bumping, banging, tidy.

BIGAMIST n.   Brigham Young, captain's paradise.

BIGOT n.   red-neck, no-neck, good old boy, good old boys network, male chauvinist pig, MCP, pig, sexist porker, McCarthyite, Archie Bunker, jingoist, flag-waver, patrioteer, superpatriot.

BIGOTRY n.   feel a draft (recognition of), Jim Crow, Jim Crowism, Jane Crowism.

BILK v.   rook, screw, shaft, frig, rip off, jive, shuck, shuck and jive, fleece, burn, bleed, bleed white, con, pluck, take, take one to the cleaners, milk, sting. See CHEAT.

BILL n.   bad news, check, checkeroo, grunt, IOU, score, tab, knock. See ACCOUNT.

BILL v.   put the squeeze on, put the arm on, put the bite on, chase, bone, see you in the alley.

BILLBOARD n.   three sheet, twenty-four sheet.

BILL OF SALE n.   papers.

BIND n.   box, in a box, crunch, squeeze, tight squeeze, tight spot, hot water, lose-lose situation, no-win situation, pickle, between a rock and a hard place. See PREDICAMENT.

BIND v.   1. hog tie, put a half nelson on, put a lock on, lock up. 2. tack on, hitch on, hook on, hook up.

BIOGRAPHY n.   bio, biog, close up, profile, resume.

BIOLOGY n.   bio, bugs.

BIPHETAMINE n.   black beauties.

BIRD n.   birdie, birdy, feathered friend, boid, banty, biddy, chick, chickabiddy, chickadee.

BIRMINGHAM, ALABAMA   Magic City.

BIRTH n.   blessed event, producing, visit from the stork, drop one.

BIRTH CONTROL n.   Vatican roulette (rhythm method), on the pill.

BIRTH CONTROL DEVICE n.   the pill, BC, IUD, bag, scum bag, cundrum, Trojan, skin, fish skin, rubber, Rameses, safety. See CONTRACEPTIVE.

BISCUIT n.   bullet, cat head, clanker, dingbat, hard tack, sinker, tooth buster, dry cush.

BISEXUAL n.   ac/dc, AC/DC, ambidextrous, ambisextrous, bi, double-gaited, he/she, swings both ways, hits both ways, ki-ki, switch hitter.

BIT n.   bite, gob, blob, chunk, hunk, lump, stump, smithereen, cut, slice, rake off, piece of the pie, slice of the melon, slice of the pie. See also SHARE.

BITE n.   1. chaw, chomp, gob. 2. kick, guts, zap, zip.

BITE v.   sink one's teeth into, take a chunk out of, chaw on, fling a fang into, nab at.

BITS n.   chewed fine, itsy bitsy pieces.

BIZARRE adj.   kooky, grody, grody to the max, off the wall, offbeat, camp, wild, far out, way out. See STRANGE. See also ECCENTRIC.

BLABBER v.   yackety-yak, yakking, blah-blah, blab, gas, go on, run on, run off at the mouth, have diarrhea of the mouth, beat one's gums, talk through one's hat, spill the beans, bibble-babble, bull, bullshit, BS, throw the bull, shoot the breeze. See also SPEAK.

BLACK adj.   black 360 degrees, mantanblack.

BLACK n.   brother, sister, bro, blood, youngblood, blood brother, soul, soul brother, soul sister, member, groid (So. Stu.); spade, ace of spades, moke, smoke, smoky, nigger, coon, darky, buck, buck nigger, boy, beige, ape, blue, blue gum, blue skin, boogie, faded boogie, boogerboo, clink, bones, Mr. Bones, boot, satchel, satchel mouth, dark cloud, dark meat (sexual), shadow, shad, shad mouth, shine, spook, skillet, squasho, scobe, spill, splib, watermelon, zulu, ditty bop, ditty bob, domino, eightball, eight-rock, chocolate, chocolate drop, Hershey bar, alligator bait (Fla., La.), article (slave, Obs.), Gange, Kange, Geechee, boojie, clown, cluck, cuffee, Mose, original, suede, shvartzeh, goonie (Virgin I.), Mau Mau, jungle bunny, chungo bunny, moss, burrhead, hardhead, jarhead, kinkyhead, nap, nappy, nappyhead, woolly head, butterhead, headlight, hod, scuttle, shot, Ethiopian, Guinea, snowball, raisin, ink, inky dink, jazz bo, jig, jigaboo, zig, hoofer, Jim Crow, jit, peola, pink toes, pinky, dinge, conk buster (intellectual), bedbug (pullman porter), bright (light), kelt, keltch (passing as white), tush (mulatto); black and tan, banana, high yella, high yellow, lemon, bird's eye maple (female mulatto); handkerchief head, Uncle Tom, Mister Tom (middle class), Dr. Thomas, Aunt Tom, Aunt Jane, Aunt Jemima, uncle, aunt, auntie, uppity black, pancake (subservient), HN (house nigger), Sam, Sambo, Stepin Fetchit, load of coal (group).

BLACK (FEMALE) n.   sister, soul sister, band, bantam, barbeque, covess dinge, dange broad, black and tan, banana, bird's eye maple, high yella, high yellow, lemon, peola, pink toes; poontang (sexual, Derog.), Aunt, auntie, Aunt Jane, Aunt Jemima, Aunt Tom, Sapphire. (all Derog.)

BLACKBALL n.   ding, thumbs down. See also BANISH, OSTRACIZE.

BLACKBALL v.   ding, zing, thumbs down on one. See also BANISH, OSTRACIZE.

BLACKEN v.   bad-mouth, do a number on, rip, rip up and down, knock, give a black eye, pan-smear. See SLANDER.

BLACK EYE n.   shiner, mouse, goog, shanty.

BLACKGUARD n.   sleazoid, sleazeball, bad ass, bad news, bastard, prick, dick, shit, low-life, bounder, rounder, rotter, scalawag. See SCOUNDREL.

BLACKJACK TABLE POSITIONS   first base, second base, third base, nine o'clock, ten o'clock, eleven o'clock, twelve o'clock, noon, high noon, one o'clock, etc.

BLACKJACK TERMS   George (generous player), hit (card request), hole card, snapper (make blackjack).

BLACKLIST n.   hit list, shitlist. See also OSTRACIZE, BANISH.

BLACKLIST v.   hit list, pipe one off, siwash.

BLACKMAIL v.   shake, shake down, put the shake on one, badger, play the badger game.

BLACKMAILER n.   bloodsucker, leech, shakedown artist, shark.

BLACK MARK n.   gig, ram, rip, skin, demo.

BLACK MARKET adj.   under the counter, under the table.

BLACK OUT v.   1. pass out, zone out, draw a blank, go out like a light. 2. cover up, cut off, hold back, squelch, squash.

BLACKS AND WHITES n.   black and tan, salt and pepper.

BLACKSMITH SHOP n.   pig joint.

BLACKSMITH n.   smithy, smitty, darby cove, iron burner.

BLACK STUDIES n.   Chitlins 101.

BLADDER n.   bag, water tank.

BLADE adj.   shank.

BLAME v.   finger, point the finger, blow the whistle on, cap on, can, carry the can, tie the can on one, blast, blast on, lay on, lay a bad trip on one, lay the body at one's doorstep, put the whammy on one, lower the boom, pass the buck, knock, paste, roast, rap, rap on the knuckles, slap on the wrist, rap one's knuckles, slap one's wrist, let one have it, climb all over, jump all over one, jump down one's throat, put the slug on one, throw the book at one, sock it to one, stick it to one, give one hell, catch it, catch hell, bitch, bitch bitch bitch, sound off, read one out, chew out, go after, take down, call down, come down on, come down hard on, rip, bad-mouth, poor mouth, trash, zing, zap, knock, give one both barrels, rake over the coals, frame, frame up, put up a job, find the smoking gun. See also ACCUSE, DENOUNCE.

BLAMED n.   butt, goat, fall guy, pigeon, who shot John.

BLAND adj.   vanilla, diddly bop, jerky, nerdy, wuss, wimpy, tame, blah, dull as dishwater, flat, flat as a pancake, ho hum, nothing, pablum, white bread, zero. See also MILD.

BLANDISH v.   butter, butter up, stroke, soap, soft soap, play up to, soften up, string along, sweet talk. See CAJOLE.

BLANDISHMENT n.   eyewash, soap, soft soap, a line, sweet talk, baloney, blarney. See FLATTERY.

BLASE adj.   cool, laid back, mellow, fed up, done it all, been around twice, what's the big deal?, BFD (big fucking deal). See INDIFFERENT.

BLASPHEME v.   cuss, damn, darn, drat, flame, put the horns on, put the whammy on one, put the double whammy on one, hoodoo one, voodoo one, talk dirty.

BLAST n.   energetic disassembly.

BLATANT adj.   loud, flashy, screaming, glitzy, pizzazz, snazzy, zappy, showy. See also FLAGRANT, GAUDY, CONSPICUOUS, NOISY.

BLAZE n.   rapid oxidation.

BLEACHER SEATS n.   blues (circus), Ruthville (baseball).

BLEMISH n.   zit, blem, second, beauty spot, bloom, doohickey, dohinky, hickey, sight, dump, blot on the landscape, bug.

BLEMISHED adj.   a few bugs, a glitch, gremlins, a lemon, rank, seconds. See IMPERFECT.

BLEND n.   combo, mishmash, mishmosh, mixed bag, soup (liquid), stew, goulash, lorelei, everything but the kitchen sink.

BLEND v.   interface, feather in, camouflage, marry; dissolve, cross dissolve (film).

BLIGHT n.   sight, dump, eyesore, blot on the landscape.

BLIGHT v.   trash, foul up, fuck up, mess up, glitch up. See also DAMAGE.

BLIND DATE n.   grab bag.

BLINK v.   bat the eyes.

BLISS n.   gone, far out, cool, Nadaville.

BLISSFUL adj.   crazy, groked, mad, cool, zero cool, gone, real gone, sent, stoned, dreamy, floating, flying, high, wicked, wigged, wild, weird, weirded out, out, far out, spaced out, wigged out, blissed out, flipped out, turned on, on cloud seven, on cloud nine, in seventh heaven, in Nadaville, twilight zone. See also HAPPY.

BLITHE adj. up, upbeat, high, perky, chipper, sunny. See CHEERFUL.

BLIZZARD n. whiteout.

BLOCK n. catch, hang-up, jam-up, joker, monkey wrench, gridlock (traffic). See HINDRANCE.

BLOCK v. hang up, hold up, shut out, shut off, close out, close off, stall, stymie, stonewall. See HINDER.

BLOCKAGE n. lock, jam-up, backup, gridlock.

BLOCKHEAD n. twit, goof, ninny, nincompoop, oofus. See also STUPID.

BLONDE adj. dizzy blonde, bottled blonde, bleached blonde, platinum blonde, decided blonde (bleached), peroxide blonde, ash blonde, whitey, towhead, goldilocks (Derog.).

BLOOD n. claret, goo, gravy, red gravy, people juice.

BLOODHOUNDS n. catsup hounds, ketchup dogs, ketchup hounds, beat the pups (evade).

BLOOD VESSEL n. main line.

BLOUSE n. body shirt, tank top, top.

BLOW n. belt, bash, sock, slug, zap, zetz, clip, Sunday punch, blindside (unexpected). See HIT.

BLUDGEON n. club, billy, billy club, stick, nightstick, blackjack, sap, conk crusher. See CLUB.

BLUEPRINT n. blue. See also PLAN.

BLUFF v. bull, bullshit, BS, bunco, bunko, cheek it, con, fake, fake it, fake one out, psych out, four flush, jive, shuck, shucking and jiving, muscle, stiff, throw the bull. See also DECEIVE.

BLUNDER n. flub, flub-up, fluff, muff, gaff, boner, blooper, bloomer, howler, goof, dumb trick, dumb move, dumb thing to do, fool mistake. See MISTAKE.

BLUNDER v. flub, fluff, muff, blow, blow one's lines, foul up, fuck up, mess up, drop the ball, drop one's buckets. See ERR.

BLUNDERER n. goof, goof ball, goofer, goof off, goof up, foul ball, foul-up, fuck-off, fuck-up, muff, muffer, butterfingers, fumble fist, foozler, stumblebum, stumblebunny, klutz, dub, duffer, hick, lummox, lump, rube, slob, Swede.

BLUNT adj. 1. snippy, snappy, short. 2. lay it on the line, put all one's cards on the table, talk turkey, talk like a Dutch uncle, call a spade a spade. See also FRANK.

BLUNTLY adv. cold turkey.

BLUSTER n. bull, bullshit, BS, bunk, bunco, bunkum, talk, big talk, fancy talk, fine talk, tall talk, tall story, fish story, gas, hot air, balls, guts, macho. See also DECEIT.

BLUSTER v. jive, shuck, shuck and jive, hotdog, grandstand, showboat. See BOAST. See also RANT.

BLUSTERER n. bullshitter, bullshooter, bullshit artist, gasbag, blowhard, windbag, big bag of wind. See BRAGGART.

BLUSTERING n. talk, big talk, tall talk, baloney, bull, bullshit, BS, shittin'. See BRAGGING.

BOARD A TRAIN v. hop on board, hop a choo choo, hop a freight, catch a rattler, flip (free, hobo use).

BOARDING HOUSE n. bed and breakfast, bread and board, crumb joint, crumb house, cat house, flophouse, rooming house, doss house, doss, Cheap John, chinch pad, fleabag, flea trap, fort (Stu.).

BOARD OF DIRECTORS n. execs, exec suite, front office, toppers, brass, upstairs.

BOARD OF EXAMINERS n. board, laundry (pass on cadets).

BOARDS n. load of sticks.

BOAST n. bull, bullshit, BS, shittin', bunk, bunco, bunko, bunkum, baloney, talk, big talk, fancy talk, fine talk, tall talk, tall story, fish story, gas, hot air, high falutin', high siding.

BOAST v. jive, shuck, shuck and jive, hot dog, grandstand, showboat, fake, fake it, fake one out, psych out, stiff, four flush, bull, bullshit, BS, throw the bull, sling the bull, sling, sling the crap, shovel the shit, shoot the shit, lay it on thick, sound off, noise off, show off, cheek it, con, muscle, toot one's own horn, blow one's own horn, blow one's own trumpet, blow, blow off, blow smoke, crow, signify, blow hard, pitch, advertise, three sheet, big mouth, talk, talk big, spread oneself, brag oneself up, pat oneself on the back, crack one's jaw, gam, yam, lick one's chops, rub one's nose in, splash, sport, bog wog.

BOASTER n. grandstander, hotdogger, showoff, hotshot, key swinger, blowhard, bullshit artist (Obsc.), hot-air artist. See BRAGGART.

BOASTFUL adj. hot stuff, hotshot; hot shit, bullshit, bullshitting (Obsc.); big talking, biggety, ho dad, ho daddy, key swinging, loudmouth, know-it-all, smart alecky, phony, hubcap, crack one's jaw, crapper, cocky, cock, cock of the walk, chesty, gutbucket, stuffy, stuffed shirt, stuck up, puffed up, gassy, windbag, windy, load of wind, full of hot air, blowhard, blow smoke, gall, ham, hifalutin, highfalutin, high hatty, hinkty, his nibs, snooty, on an ego trip, swell-headed, swell head, big head, big I am, stuck on oneself, a regular I love me, think one is it, think one's shit doesn't stink, too big for one's shoes, too big for one's britches.

BOAT n. tub, bateau, bucket, hooker, cat (catamaran), dink (dinghy). See also SHIP.

BOATSWAIN n. bos'n, pipes.

BODY n. 1. bod, build, built, shape, shaft, chassis, classy chassis, beefcake, built like a brick shithouse, frame, coke frame (Fem.), anatomy, bag of bones, booty. 2. dead meat, cold meat, stiff, loved one, remains, cage, carcass, corpus, croppy (R.R.).

BODYGUARD n. jaboney, jiboney, sidewinder, trigger man. See also GUARD.

BODY ODOR n. B.O.

BOGUS adj. bogue, queer, fake, phony, ersatz, not what it's cracked up to be. See COUNTERFEIT.

BOISE, IDAHO Spud Town.

BOISTEROUS adj. roughhouse, rowdy-dowdy, cowboy, hoopla, loudmouth, rambunctious, rootin' tootin', raise hell, raise cain, raise the roof, ziggy, off base, out of line, out of order.

BOLD adj. gutsy, gritty, nervy, chutzpahdik, spunky, brassy, cheeky, fire-eater, come on strong, smart ass. See FEARLESS. See also DARING.

BOLOGNA n. boloney, horse cock.

BOLSTER v. brace up, buck up, pick up. See SUPPORT.

BOLT v. take off, jump off, drop out, bail out, cut out, opt out, cop out, hightail, hotfoot, skedaddle, make tracks, make a break for it, step on it, run like a scared rabbit, run out on, walk out on, kiss good-bye, cut loose, quit cold, ditch, leave flat, leave high and dry, leave holding the bag, leave in the lurch, dump, give up the ghost, give up the ship. See also GO, FLEE.

BOMB n. the bomb, A-bomb, H-bomb, nucular bomb, slow flyer (cruise missile), doomsday machine, buzz bomb, smart bomb, dumb bomb, nuke, backpack nuke, egg, blockbuster, daisy cutter, firecracker; football, Italian football, guinea football (gangster); Molotov cocktail (homemade), fat Albert, pill, pineapple, ticker, lazy dog, hamburger.

BOMB v. blitz, lay a bomb, lay an egg, prang.

BOMBARDIER n. bubble chaser (WW II).

BOMBARDMENT n. blitz.

BOMBAST n. balderdash, gobbledygook, hifalutin', highfalutin', hot air. See also BLUSTER.

BOMBASTIC adj. bullshitting, big talking, biggety, loudmouth, stuffed shirt, gassy, windbag, windy, full of hot air. See BOASTFUL.

BOMBING MISSION n. milk run (easy), prang (successful).

BOMBING n. blitz.

BOMB MAKER n. can maker.

BONA FIDE adj. for real, kosher, legit, on the legit, all wool and a yard wide, card carrying. See TRUE.

BOND n. 1. gunk, stickum, spit. 2. network, tie-in, hookup. See also ASSOCIATION.

BONDS n. 1. Fannie Mae, Ginnie Mae, Sallie Mae, Freddie Mac, Farmer Mac, muni, municipals, baby bond (less than $1,000 denomination), James Bond (matures in 2007); Bo Derek, ten (Treasury bond maturing in the year 2010); junk bond (low value), double-barreled bond (two sources of repayment), zeroes, Tigr, Cats, Lyon, Strips, gorilla (trader). 2. cuffs, darbies, derbies. See also STOCKS.

BONUS n. fringe benefit, goodies, gravy, perk, golden parachute, button, hat, ice, PM, spiff (salesman). See also EXTRA, GRATUITY.

BOO n. Bronx cheer, raspberry, razz, razzberry, the bird.

BOOK n. best-seller, books with legs, page-turners, potboiler, spyboiler, bible (authoritative).

BOOK v. line up, sew up, pencil in, set up.

BOOKING AGENT n. flesh peddler, ten percenter.

BOOKKEEPER n. CPA, bean counter, sharp pencil pusher, pencil shover, pen pusher, pen driver.

BOOKKEEPING n. books, count.

BOOKMAKER n. book, bookie, customer's man, runner, scalper, banker, C (commission); horse room, poolroom, wire room (place of business).

BOOKWORM n. grind, greasy grind.

BOON n. mitzvah (Yid).

BOORISH adj. bad-assed, bad ass, off base, out of line, out of order, bitchy, cantankerous, cussed, grouchy, grumpy, mean, ornery, tetchy, ugly, loud, loudmouthed, rough. See also COARSE.

BOOST n. lift, shot in the arm, shot in the ass, leg, leg up, hand, handout, backup, buildup, goose. See also SUPPORT.

BOOST v. goose, goose up, pick up, put one on cloud nine, put one on top of the world, give a lift, gazumph (price after sale). See also SUPPORT.

BOOTLEG v.   moonlight, moonshine, under the counter, under the table, rum run.

BOOTLEGGER n.   moonshiner, rumrunner, gangster, legger, dynamiter,

BOOTLEG LIQUOR n.   moonshine, shine, mountain dew, white lightning, white mule, corn, corn likker, panther piss, bathtub gin, Dago red (wine), home brew, hootch, just off the boat. See also LIQUOR.

BOOTS n.   waders, waffle stompers, waters.

BOOTY n.   goods, hot goods, hot items, graft, take, make, pickings, swag, boodle, squeeze.

BORDELLO n.   house, cathouse, call house, poontang palace, snake ranch, chicken ranch, call joint, hook shop, body shop. See BROTHEL.

BORE n.   yawn, major yawn, downer, bummer, wimp, creep, drag, drip, frog, grind, grub, grunge, grunch, Jeff (Bl.), meatball, sklonk, flat tire, headache, a pain, pain in the ass, pain in the neck, wet blanket, blister, deadwood, deadhead, nudge, nag, pill, crashing bore, snooze act, lump, drone, spare tire, stuffed shirt, mince.

BORE v.   turn one off, bend one's ear, bore stiff, burn out, drag, put one to sleep, talk one's ear off.

BORED adj.   ho hum, so what else is new?, bored stiff, fed up, full up, up to here, had it up to here, done it all, been around twice, just going through the motions. See also UNINTERESTED, LANGUID.

BOREDOM n.   ho hums, the blahs, blah-blahs.

BORING adj.   bor-ring, MEGO (mine eyes glaze over), blah, flat, flat tire, flat as a pancake, ho hum, nothing, nothing doing, zero, big zero, drag, draggy, draddy, a yawn, big yawn, yawner, snooze, gasser, icky, the least, downer, bummer, dead, really deadsville, Dullsville, noplaceville, Nadaville, go over like a lead balloon, lay an egg, bomb, diddly bop, nowhere, bore one stiff, tired, wonky, gummy, pablum, beige, drip, grass, grass out, wiped out, grunch, grunge, grungy, neb, nebbish, Irving, Melvin, party pooper, dull as dishwater, stick in the mud, wet blanket.

BORROW v.   touch, tap, hit, hit up, hit one for, bum, burn, appropriate, jawbone, knock, mooch, smooch, sponge, scrounge, cadge, cuff, crab, float one, brace, blitzkrieg, soak, lift, lug, put the lug on one, bite, put the bite on one, put the bee on one, put the arm on one, put the sleeve on one, put the claw on one, dog it, four-flush, go on the hook for, feel a dollar, feel some bread, steal one's stuff, get on the cuff, get on tick.

BORROWER n.   moocher, smoocher, sponge, sponger, scrounger, desperado, four-flusher (does not repay), leech.

BOSOM n.   boobs, boobies, bubs, bubbies, tits, titties, knockers, bazooms, babaloos, cans, jugs, headlights. See BREASTS.

BOSS n.   exec, chief, bosshead, boss lady, bosslady, boss man, honcho, head honcho, head, head man, big shit, big weenie, big cheese, big man, big gun, wheel, top dog, whip hand. See EXECUTIVE.

BOSSY adj.   pulling rank.

BOSTON, MASSACHUSETTS Beantown, highbrowville, hub.

BOSTON RESIDENT n.   Beantowner, Bean Eater, Beaner, Baked Bean, Bowwow.

BOTCH n.   flub, muff, boner, boo boo, blooper, boot, bobble, fumble, dumb trick, fool mistake, fuck-up, put one's foot in it. See MISTAKE.

BOTCH v.   queer, boot, bobble, goof, goof up, hash up, screw up, bollix up, mess up, no way to run a railroad. See ERR.

BOTHER n.   drag, bellyache, bitch, headache, pain in the ass, pain in the neck, a nag, nudge, worriment. See ANNOYANCE.

BOTHER v.   bug, ride, eat, nudge, make waves, give one a hard time, get in one's hair, push one's button, rub the wrong way. See ANNOY.

BOTHERED adj.   bugged, hacked, uptight, pissed off, peed off, tee'd off, browned off, bummed out, burned up, hung up, in a stew, in one's hair, dogged, miffed, peeved, riled, rubbed the wrong way, spooked, screaming meemies, all hot and bothered, at the end of one's rope, buffaloed, hard put to it, put to it, picked on, on pins and needles, on tenterhooks, worried sick, worried stiff, driven up the wall, rousted, sweat it, steamed. See also DISTURBED.

BOTHERSOME adj.   pain, pain in the ass, pain in the neck, bitchy, son of a bitch, son of a gun, messy, pesky, pestiferous, flea. See TROUBLESOME. See also ANNOYING.

BOTTLE n.   bot, soldier, dead soldier (empty).

BOTTLENECK n.   standoff, Mexican standoff. See also HINDRANCE.

BOTTOM n.   the pits, cellar, bottom line, bottom dollar, rock bottom, scraping the bottom of the barrel, low man on the totem pole, ain't no more, that's all there is.

BOUND adj.   hog-tied.

BOUNDLESS adj.   no end of, no end to, wide open, more than you can shake a stick at, no strings, no strings attached, you name it you got it, no holds barred, no catch, no kicker, no joker, no joker in the deck, no ifs ands or buts. See also PLENTIFUL.

BOUNTEOUS adj. 1. big, bighearted, be big, loose, Santa Claus, good Joe, have a heart, heart in the right place. 2. dime a dozen, aplenty, galore, no end in sight, stink with, crawling with, up to one's ass in. See PLENTY.

BOUNTIFUL adj. 1. softie, soft touch, be big, loose, Santa Claus, good Joe, have a heart, heart in the right place. 2. dime a dozen, aplenty, galore, no end, no end in sight, stink with, crawling with, up to one's ass in. See PLENTY.

BOURGEOIS adj. boojy.

BOUT n. set-to, bat, bender, binge, bust, go, tear, toot, wingding. See also BOXING, FIGHT, EVENT, REVEL.

BOVINE n. bossie, Bossy, moo cow, moo moo, Elsie, Nellie.

BOWEL MOVEMENT n. shit, crap, dump, caca, B.M., number two, poop, call, nature's call, turds, dingleberries, big one, boom-boom, business, poo-poo, aah-aah, honey, dreck, being regular, the shits, the runs, trots, shits, GI's, GI shits, turistas, Montezuma's revenge; bird turd, doggy do, buffalo chips, cow chips, cow flops, cow plops, cow pats, golden apples, horse apples, road apples, alley apples, hocky, horse hocky.

BOWEL MOVEMENT v. shit, crap, dump, poop, go to the can, go to the John, shake a few clinkers out, do one's business. See DEFECATE.

BOWLING, SPLITS half Worcester (3,9 or 2,8 pins left standing), horsemen (1,2,4, & 7 or 1,3,6, & 10), lily (5,7 & 10), sour apple (5,7 & 10), spread eagle (2,3,4,6,7 & 10), washout (1,2 & 10), baby split (2 & 7 or 3 & 10 standing), bedpost, goalpost, fencepost (all 7 & 10 left), big four (4,6,7,10), Christmas tree (3,7,10 or 2, 7,10), Cincinnati (8,10), dodo (1 & 7 or 10), double pinochle (4,6,7 & 10), rob the cradle (pick up only one).

BOWLING TERMS big ball (powerful), blow (miss), carry (knockdown pins), cheesecake (a lane grooved for strikes), cherry (miss a spare), the count (pins downed by first ball), creeper (slow ball), flat apple, flat ball, kegler, kegling, maples (pins), pie alley (grand for strikes), spare, strike.

BOXER n. mug, pug, lug, palooka, slugger, punching bag, cauliflower ear, plug. See PRIZEFIGHTER.

BOXING n. the fights, battle, prelim, scrap, slugfest, mill, throw leather. See also FIGHT.

BOXING, KNOCKOUT KO, kayo, TKO, flatten, stopper, stiffener, chill, down for the count, take the count, kiss the canvas, kiss the resin, lower the boom, throw in the towel.

BOXING MATCH n. go, bout.

BOXING PUNCHES KO, stopper (knockout), lower the boom, stiffener, bolo, jab, smear, right cross, rabbit punch, roundhouse punch, sizzler, tee off, uppercut.

BOXING TERMS put on the gloves, go a coupla rounds, swap leather, one-two punch, punchy, duke (win), garden (arena), inning, heat (round), handle (manage); leather, mitt, pillow (glove); thumb (get finger in opponent's eye), cauliflower ear, listener, tin ear, potato trap (mouth), glass jaw, slam bang (hard fight), waltz (easy fight), do-se-do (dull), TKO (technical knockout), back peddle, dance, rock on one's heels, on the ropes, hit the canvas, take the count, saved by the bell; fix (bribed to lose), throw a fight, take a dive, splash, tank act, tank fight, tank job, go in the tank, dump (loss, all fixed).

BOX OFFICE n. B.O., wicket, window.

BOY n. guy, dude, cat, feller, man, boyo, boychik, lad, tad, tadpole, kid, kiddo, sonny, sonnyboy, juvie, JD (juvenile delinquent), punk, punk kid, bub, bubba, bud, buddy, squirt, chap, buck, buster, chip, chip off the old block, cub, sprout, small fry, young fry, bird, duck, stud, joker, character, clown, jasper, runt, half-pint, little shaver, booger, bugger, chicken, wet behind the ears, cokey, gunsel, monkey, pecker, pisser, Peck's bad boy. See also CHILD, YOUNG MAN, YOUTH.

BOYCOTT v. blackball, ice out, pass by, pass up, shut out. See also OSTRACIZE.

BOYFRIEND n. main dude, main man, main squeeze, squeeze, my guy, my man, old man, total babe, baby, stud, John, ace, ace lane, beau, best fella, best fellow, big moment, flame, heart throb, passion ration, sofa lizard, papa, sweet papa, daddy, sugar daddy, sugar bowl, body and soul, Casanova, Lothario, Don Juan, companion, constant companion, jelly roll, kissing cousin, back-door man, honey man, money honey, generous keeper, gold mine, big game, biscuit roller, masher, mule skinner, oyster, lovebird, turtle dove.

BRA PADDING n. falsies, cheaters, deceivers, gay deceivers, props.

BRACE v. buck up, perk up, pick up, chirk up.

BRACER n. pickup, pick-me-up, shot in the arm, tonic, eye-opener, hair of the dog, hair of the dog that bit one.

BRAG v. jive, shuck, shuck and jive, hotdog, grandstand, showboat, blow one's own horn, pat oneself on the back. See BOAST.

BRAGGADOCIO n. talk, big talk, fancy talk, tall talk, bullshit, BS, shittin, hot air. See BLUSTER.

BRAGGART n. grandstander, hotdogger, showoff, hotshot, blowhard, blower, big timer, big mouth, bullshitter, bullshooter, bullshit artist, hot-air artist, crock of shit, pile of shit, earbanger, gasbag, windbag, big bag of wind, windjammer, windy, lover boy, know-it-all, blatherskite, big I am, big I love me, big head, swellhead, swelled head, be on an ego trip, think one is it, think one's shit doesn't stink, hot shot Charlie, get too big for one's britches, biggety, ho dad, ho daddy, key swinging, loudmouth, hub cap, crack one's jaw, crapper, cocky, cock, cock of the walk, chesty, gutbucket, stuffy, stuffed shirt.

BRAGGING n. jive, jazz, snow job, hard sell, blow job, build, buildup, line, spiel, talk, talk big, tall tale, tall story, fish story, fancy talk, fine talk, baloney, phoney baloney, phonus bolonus, crap, bull, bullshit, BS, crock of shit, pile of shit, piece of shit, shit for the birds, shittin, cock-and-bull story, bunk, bunkum, gas, smoke, hot air, high falutin', high siding, riff, garbage, hocky, horse hocky, hogwash, latrine rumor, malarkey, marmalade.

BRAIN n. head, bean, noodle, noggin, pate, sconce, thinker, box, think box, think pot, think tank, knowledge box, dream box, upper story, upstairs, wig, gray matter, little gray cells, wetwear. See also HEAD.

BRAIN-DAMAGED adj. gork, pinhead, spaz, retardo, not all there, soft in the head, weak in the upper story, vegetable. See RETARDED. See also FEEBLE-MINDED.

BRAINY adj. brain, genius, egghead, whiz kid, Einstein, have smarts, smart as a whip, no dumbbell. See INTELLIGENT.

BRAKE v. anchor it, lay down rubber, leave a stripe, give one the wind (suddenly), in short pants, skuffling. See also STOP.

BRAKEMAN n. brakie.

BRAKES n. anchor, binders, cinchers, grab a handful of air.

BRAMBLE n. sticker.

BRAND NAME n. make (usually automobile), label.

BRANDISH v. flash, sport, show off, come on strong, throw one's weight around. See FLAUNT.

BRASH adj. get previous, brassy, cheeky, flip, fly. See also BRAZEN, FEARLESS.

BRASS n. Dutch gold.

BRASSIERE n. bra, harness, lung hammock, uplift, falsies.

BRASS KNUCKLES n. brass knucks, knucks.

BRAT n. JD (juvenile delinquent), punk, punk kid, holy terror, wild one, snot nose, snot nose kid. See also CHILD, BOY, GIRL.

BRAVADO n. balls, guts, macho, talk, big talk, fancy talk, fine talk, tall talk.

BRAVE adj. game, gritty, gutsy, gutty, spunky, nervy, fire-eater, hairy, stand tall, walk tall, bigger'n life. See FEARLESS. See also DARING.

BRAVE v. defi, face off, face down, fly in the face of, put one's life on the line, meet eyeball to eyeball, stand up to, take one on, knock the chip off one's shoulder, step over the line. See CHALLENGE.

BRAVERY n. balls, guts, heart, corazon, nerve, stomach, what it takes, grit, true grit, spunk, backbone, moxie, starch, clock, Dutch courage (intoxicated).

BRAWL n. scrap, rumble, free for all, rhubarb, knock down and drag out, battle royal, duke out, donnybrook, hell broke loose. See FIGHT.

BRAWL v. buck, kick up a row, roughhouse, put up a fight, bang heads, raise Cain, rumble. See FIGHT.

BRAWN n. beef, clout, muscle, punch, sock, kick, moxie, steam, steamroller, strong-arm.

BRAWNY adj. hunk, hulk, husky, hefty, beefy, pumped up, muscle man, he-man, powerhouse. See MUSCULAR. See also STRONG.

BRAZEN adj. cocky, gritty, grit, gutsy, gutty, nervy, spunky, hotshot, come on strong, bold as brass, brassy, smart, smart alecky, smart ass, wise ass, chutzpahdik, crusty, chit, spetters, salty, cheeky, flip, fly, hell of a, hell of a note, helluva nerve. See also FEARLESS.

BRAZIL NUT n. nigger toe.

BREACH v. crash, crash the gates, break in, bust in, kick in, barge in, butt in, chisel in, horn in, muscle in, penetrate, mess over, put in one's oar, shove in one's oar, put one's two cents in. See also PENETRATE.

BREAD n. slab, staff of life, double-o, duffer, dummy, gum wadding, punk, shingle (toasted slice).

BREAD AND BUTTER n. punk and plaster, dough well done with cow to cover (also toast).

BREAD AND WATER n. piss and punk, angel cake and wine, cake and wine, dry.

BREAK n. 1. total bust. 2. coffee break, breakoff, time, time out, time off, downtime, letup, take five, take ten, breather, take a breather, breathing spell, cutoff, happy hour, layoff.

BREAK v. 1. bust, bust up, bust in, wrack up, goof up, bung, bung up, break up, break to smithereens, total, torpedo, trash, fix, fritz, put on the fritz, jim up. See also DAMAGE. 2. break out. See also ESCAPE. 3. break in, break out, kick in, bust in, crack, crack open, jimmy. 4. take out, knock out, KO, squish, squash, scrunch, shoot down, shoot down in flames, finish off, do in, put in the toilet, cook one's goose, cut up, make mincemeat of, romp. See also DEFEAT. 5. gentle. 6. break break, break in, barge in. See also INTERRUPT.

BREAK AND ENTER v. penetrate, crash, toss. See also BURGLARIZE; PENETRATE.

BREAKDOWN n. come apart at the seams, crack-up, conk out, strung out, schizzed out, psyched out, basket case.

BREAKFAST n. brekkie, eat one's wheaties, put on the feedbag, morning chow, brunch (late morning).

BREASTS n. boobs, boobies, kajoobies, bubs, bubbies, tits, titties, knockers, bazooms, torpedoes, babaloos, cans, jugs, eyes, brown eyes, big brown eyes, globes, headlights, knobs, nobs, lungs, maracas, mamas, upper frontal superstructure, racks, tonsils, bags, teacups, plates, bazoongies, bazongas, breastworks, cantaloupes, melons, twins, pair, peach of a pair, apples, lemons, oranges, grapefruits, watermelons, milkers, milk bottles, pumps, hooters, orbs, balloons, sweater full, bra busters, front bumpers, endowed, chichi, droopers, pillows (Obs.), top heavy, growths, raisins, pimples, warts (Derog.).

BREECHES n. jeans, slacks, shorts, Levis, hip huggers, whites, bells, bell bottoms, britches, ducks. See PANTS.

BREED n. likes, likes of, lot, number.

BREEZY adj. hawk stretch.

BRIBE n. fringe benefit, goodies, juice, graft, gravy, perk, perks, payoff, payola, plugola, drugola, gayola, kickback, big one, fix, hush money, envelope, ice, nut, take, on the take, under the table, Mordida, contract, cush, baksheesh, salve, sugar, sweetener, sweetening, shake, soap, hat, smear, schmeer, grease, palm oil, touch, boodle, street money, walking around money, chop, fall dough, freight; laying pipes, Abscam (Pol.); influence peddling, protection, protection money.

BRIBE v. pay off, fix, fix the alzo, put in the fix, take care of, smear, shmeer, grease, grease one's palm, oil, oil one's palm, slip one a buck, reach, get to, get at, get it on the line, put in the bag, come across, take an envelope, take a chicken, fit the mitt, buzz, do business, crack business, make a deal, buy, buy off, piece one off, kick in, put in the zingers, sweeten the pot, sweetener, sweeten one up, see, see the cops, gaff, barry (hiring boss), black market, swing for bread. See also PAY.

BRIBE MONEY n. the payoff, the envelope, payola, drugola, gayola, cough syrup, grease, schmeer, smear, ice, protection, protection money, kickback, the fix, a chicken, mordida, boodle, pound, chop, freight, take, slush, slush fund, sugar. See also PROTECTION MONEY.

BRIBER n. fixer, apple polisher, greasy.

BRIBERY n. juice, payola, drugola, gayola, on contract (police), on the pad, on the take.

BRICKS n. confetti, Irish confetti, load of rocks.

BRIDEGROOM n. man, my man, old man, main man, main on the hitch, ace lane, breadwinner, buffalo. See also BOYFRIEND.

BRIDGE, DENTAL n. mouth jewelry.

BRIEF adj. in a nutshell, boiled down, short and sweet, make a long story short, the long and the short of it, snippy.

BRIEF v. update one, let in on, put next to, put one in the picture, put one wise, tip off, show one the ropes. See ADVISE.

BRIEFING n. backgrounder, rundown, update.

BRIER n. sticker.

BRIG n. can, clink, clinker, cooler, tank, lockup, lock up, slam, slammer, jug, crate, pokey, hoosegow, iron house. See also JAIL, PRISON.

BRIGHT adj. 1. razzle-dazzle, glitzy, flashy, showy. 2. brain, egghead, sharp, whiz kid, Einstein, have smarts, smart as a whip. See INTELLIGENT.

BRIGHTEN v. punch up, shine, buff up.

BRILLIANT adj. 1. razzle-dazzle, glitzy, flashy, showy. 2. brainy, genius, egghead, sharp, whiz kid, Einstein, smart as a whip. See INTELLIGENT.

BRING v. lug, pack, piggyback, ride, shlep, tote, truck, back, birdie back, buck, gun, heel, hump, jag, shoulder.

BRING YOUR OWN BEER v. B.Y.O.B. (also bring your own bottle).

BRING YOUR OWN LIQUOR v. B.Y.O.L.

BRING YOUR OWN WHISKEY v. B.Y.O.W.

BRITAIN n. Blighty, John Bull, Merry Old, Albion, Limeyland, tight little island.

BRITISH n. beefeater, Brit, Britisher, Cockney, limey; Tommy, Tommy Atkins (soldier).

BRITISH FLAG n. Union Jack.

BROADCAST adj. all over the lot, all over the place, from hell to breakfast.

BROADCAST v. colorcast, get out, go on the air, go on the air waves, telecast, televise. See also INFORM, SPEAK.

BROADCAST NETWORK n. net, web, skein, feed (source).

BROADCASTER n.   deejay, disc jockey, veejay, rip and reader, spieler, talker, airer.

BROADCASTING n.   air time.

BROAD-MINDED adj.   open.

BROAD SCALE adj.   shotgun approach.

BROADSIDE n.   literature, flyer, handbill, handout.

BROADWAY n.   Great White Way, Mazda Alley, dream street, the big time.

BROCHURE n.   flyer, handout.

BROKE adj.   flat, flat broke, dead broke, strapped, cleaned out, tap city, tapped out, on one's ass, on one's uppers, down to one's last penny, wiped out. See DESTITUTE.

BROKEN adj.   busted, down, downtime, out, out of commission, on the blink, on the fritz, in the shop, on the shelf, wracked dead, kaput. See DAMAGED.

BROKERAGE, ILLEGAL n.   clearing house, stiff joint, bucket shop.

BRONCHOSCOPE v.   bronck.

BROOD v.   bleed, eat one's heart out, stew over, sweat over, chew the cud. See LAMENT. See also THINK.

BROOK v.   hang in, hang in there, hang tough, sit tight, be big, hear of, live with, bear with, put up with, stand for. See ENDURE.

BROTH n.   bowl, dishwater, splash, water.

BROTHEL n.   house, cathouse, can house, call house, massage parlor, rap club, rap parlor, rap studio, poontang palace, snake ranch, chicken ranch, meat market, camp, zoo, bagnio, beauty parlor, joint, call joint, hook shop, maison joie, house of joy, nautch joint, notchery, notch house, parlor house, sporting house, bawdyhouse, fancy house, gay house, barrelhouse, bed house, peg house (male), house of ill repute, house of ill fame, house of delight, rib joint, sugar hill (Bl.), body shop, stew, dive, den of vice, den of iniquity, sink of iniquity, gooseberry den, doss, doss house, juke, juke house; jag, jag house (homosexual); intimaterie, man trap, pad, place, red light, red lighterie, service station, shooting gallery, sin spot, crib, case (not common), Cheap John, chippie joint, birdcage (not common), fleshpot, honky-tonk.

BROTHEL PROPRIETOR n.   head pimp, sporting girl's manager, stable boss.

BROTHEL PROPRIETRESS n.   madame, housemother, landlady, mama-san, mother, Aunt, Auntie.

BROTHELS, CHAIN OF n.   line, stable.

BROTHER n.   breed, bro, broh, bub, bubba, bud, buddy.

BROWBEAT v.   bulldoze, lean on, put the heat on, put one through the wringer, put the chill on, bad eye. See INTIMIDATE.

BROWNING AUTOMATIC RIFLE   B.A.R.

BROWSE v.   hit the high spots, get the cream, give the once-over, once over lightly.

BRUISE v.   bung, bung up, cut up, do a number on one, hit one where one lives, lay a bad trip on one, zing. See WOUND. See also HIT.

BRUSH v.   brush down (clothes), brush up.

BRUSQUE adj.   snippy, snappy, short.

BRUTAL adj.   bad ass, kill-crazy.

BRUTALITY n.   bear hug, choke hold (police), third degree.

BRUTALLY adv.   something fierce, something terrible.

BUCKET n.   billy can, growler, gutbucket.

BUFFALO, NEW YORK   The Buffer, Polack Town.

BUFFOONERY n.   camp, high camp, low camp, pratfall comedy, slapstick, monkeyshines, shenanigans. See also FOOLISHNESS, ACTING.

BUG n.   seam squirrel, cootie, cutie, cootie garage (hair puffs in which the cootie lives), grayback.

BUGLE n.   misery pipe.

BUGLER n.   hellcat (plays reveille).

BUICK n.   B.I, deuce and a quarter (Electra 225).

BUILD v.   prefab, throw up, throw together, knock together, fudge together, whomp up, cobble up.

BUILDING n.   high rise, skyscraper, tower, towers, pile o' bricks, rockpile, the blindfold lady (court).

BULGARIAN n.   bugger.

BULGE n.   blob.

BULGE v.   pop out, bug out, blob, googly.

BULKY adj.   beefy, hefty.

BULL n.   duke.

BULLDOZER n.   dozer.

BULLET n.   slug, lead, dose, rocket, love letter, pickle, pill, stumer, cap.

BULLETIN n.   what's going down, what's happenin', a flash, break, scoop, skinny, handout, the dope, hot wire. See NEWS. See also REPORT.

BULLET-PROOF VEST n.   corset.

BULLY v.   lean on, push around, bulldoze, buffalo, enforce, showboat, turn on the heat, walk heavy, jackboot. See INTIMIDATE.

BUM n. bummer, bag lady, guttersnipe, gutterpup, in the gutter, bo. See BEGGAR.

BUMBLER n. klutz, dub, all thumbs, butterfingers, two left hands, two left feet, stumblebum, clodhopper, goof ball, not cut out for. See CLUMSY.

BUMP v. bang into, crash, nerf, fender-bender, fender tag, rowdy dowdy, rough and tumble, tumul, push around, bump heads. See also HIT.

BUMS' LODGINGS jungle, skid row, bug house, square, the scratch park, flophouse, fleabag.

BUNCH n. blob, chunk, hunk.

BUNDLE n. a roll, biddle, bindle, load.

BUNGLE n. muff, boo-boo, blooper, boot, bobble, goof-up, fuck-up, louse-up, screw-up, bonehead play, dumb trick. See MISTAKE.

BUNGLE v. flub, muff, boot, bobble, couldn't get a handle on it, lost the handle, drop the ball, go at it ass backwards. See ERR.

BUNGLER n. foul-up, fuck-up, dub, goof, goofball, stumblebum. See BLUNDER.

BUNGLING adj. amateur night, amateur night in Dixie, awful, raunchy. See also CLUMSY.

BUNK n. sack, hay, kip, doss, fleabag (Navy). See also BED.

BUNK MATE n. bunkie, chum, roomie, roomy, old lady, old miss, wife, old man, O.M.

BUNKHOUSE n. dump, bull pen, dice house. See also HOUSE.

BUOYANCY n. bounce, vim and vigor, zip, feelgood.

BUOYANT adj. high wide and handsome, laid back. See CHEERFUL.

BURDEN n. excess baggage, shlepper, ball and chain, albatross, albatross around one's neck. See HINDRANCE. See also RESPONSIBILITY.

BURDEN v. snow, snow under, dump on, give it to one, dish it out, dish out, stick it to one. See also HINDER.

BURDENED adj. stuck, stuck with, stung, snowed.

BURDENSOME adj. bitch, ballbreaker, ballbuster, tough, tough proposition, headache. See TROUBLESOME.

BUREAU n. setup, cave, foundry, salt mines, front office, shop, store.

BUREAUCRACY n. red tape, red tapism, red tapery, foolocracy, gunocracy, mediocracy, moneyocracy. See also ADMINISTRATION, MANAGEMENT, ESTABLISHMENT.

BUREAUCRAT n. paper shuffler, buck passer, apparatchik, empty suit.

BURGLAR n. prowler, crook, second-story man, second-story worker, porch-climber, crasher, flat worker, fly, midnight, midnighter, moonlighter, owl, spider (of house and apartment); cracksman, safecracker. See THIEF.

BURGLAR ALARM n. bug, dinger; slap on a jumper, kill a bug (divert a); bug, put a bug on (install).

BURGLARIZE v. burgle, rip off, lift, liberate, moonlight requisition, promote, appropriate, hustle, snatch, snitch, swipe, pinch, boost. See ROB. See also CRIME, COMMIT A.

BURGLAR'S TOOLS n. jimmy, jumper, nippers, bar, bar spreader, spreader, blade, briars, chopper, double, hardware, james, outsiders, pig, screw, shamus, stem, stick, wire gun.

BURGLARY n. break-in, caper, heist, owl job, prowl, on the prowl, crashing in joints, pushing joints, safeblowing, safecracking, second-story work, shack, sting.

BURGLARY, SAFE OR VAULT n. box work, busting petes, cracking cribs, heavy, heavy time, knocking off peters, peter racket, pete job, pete work, safeblowing, safecracking, taking boxes, the rip.

BURIAL n. deep six, cold meat party, planting.

BURIAL GROUND n. boneyard, bone factory, bone orchard, marble orchard, marble town, cold storage, headstone city.

BURIAL PLACE n. cold storage, deep six, dustbin, planted, pushing up daisies, a daisy, six, six feet under.

BURLESQUE n. topless, T and A, burlesk, burlap, burlicue, burly, burlyque, burlesk, camp, cooch show, coochie show, girlie show, hootchy-kootchy show, leg show, peep show, skin show, skin house, takeoff.

BURLY adj. hunk, hulk, gorilla, husky, hefty, beefy, beefcake, bruiser, muscle man. See MUSCULAR.

BURNISH v. shine, buff up.

BURRO n. mountain canary, Rocky Mountain canary.

BURSAR n. ghee with the boodle, payoff ghee.

BURY v. adios it, cover up, deep six, plant, put six feet under.

BUS n. mini bus, micro bus, avenue tank (double deck), clunker, coffin (unsafe), hack, jitney, jitney bus, kidney buster, rig, rubberneck wagon (sightseeing), two-story lorry; brain train, kiddie car (school). See also AUTOMOBILE.

BUS DRIVER n. bus jockey, hack skinner, skip.

BUS STOP n. flag spot, flag stop.

BUSHFIGHTER n.   bushwacker.

BUSINESS n.   1. bag, game, racket, dodge, line, what one is into, rat race, biz, show biz, gesheft. See OCCUPATION. 2. megacorp, multinational, plunderbund, outfit, setup, set up shop (start), shop, small time, Ma and Pa, Mom and Pop, front door, turnkey operation, shoestring operation, fly-by-night operation, bucket shop, coffee and cake joint, coffee and cake layout, coffee and cake place, coffee and cake spot (petty), white elephant (unsuccessful), gold mine (successful). See also CORPORATION. 3. beeswax, carrying on, goings-on, hanky-panky, hap, happening, ongoing.

BUSINESS ADMINISTRATION n.   bizad.

BUSINESS, GO INTO v.   set up shop, open up, get into, take a fling at, take a flyer, hang up one's shingle.

BUSINESSMAN n.   big-time operator, BTO, big wheel, wheeler-dealer, tycoon; cockroach, nickel and dime operator, small potatoes (small); tradester, baron, robber baron, big butter and egg man, the money.

BUSINESS OPPORTUNITY n.   contact, in.

BUSINESS TRANSACTION v.   buy out, close, deal, wheel and deal, hard sell, make a buck, make a buy, make a killing, put one over, bring home the bacon, raid, takeover, cash in one's chips, chase, fold.

BUST n.   boobs, boobies, tits, knockers, jugs, globes, headlights, knobs, maracas. See BREASTS.

BUSTLE n.   1. fuzzbuzz, do, fuss, rumpus. See ACTION, TURMOIL. 2. bishop (1775-1875), birdcage (1870).

BUSY adj.   in warp one, up to speed, at the speed of heat, run one's ass ragged, clocked up, busy as a beaver, busy as a bee, busier than a one armed paperhanger, on a merry go round, on the hop, on the jump, like Grand Central Station, whirling dervish, tied up, have other fish to fry, head over heels in, up to one's ass in, up to here in, overloaded, snowed, swamped, full plate, enough on one's plate.

BUSYBODY n.   buttinsky, kibitzer, nosey Parker, snoop, snooper, yenta, backseat driver, Paul Pry, little pitcher with big ears, bugger. See also NEWSMONGER.

BUTCHER v.   1. beef up (cow). 2. goof up, hash up, louse up, screw up, bollix up, make a mess of. See ERR.

BUTT n.   turkey, pigeon, clay pigeon, goat, patsy, mark, easy mark, vic, chump, setup, softie, fall guy. See VICTIM.

BUTT v.   buck.

BUTTE, MONTANA   Big Butte.

BUTTER n.   high-priced spread, grease, axle grease, goober grease (peanut), lube, lubricant, marfak, plaster, cow, cow salve, salve.

BUTTERMILK n.   Arizona.

BUTTOCKS n.   buns, fanny, ass, arse, ass end, behind, bottom, bucket, bum, butt, can, cheeks, moon, tail, tailbone, tail end, keester, keister, kazoo, wazoo, derriere, prat, rump, rumpus, seat, rumbleseat, sitter, fern, heinie, heinder, hind end, rear end, tush, tushy, tuchis, tokus, dokus, duff, frances, labonza, gazonga, winkie, culo, back porch, backyard, biscuit, canetta, duster, getaway, pads, spread, rusty dusty, satchel, vestibule, nether cheeks, stern, booty, doo-doo, caboose, gold mine, moneymaker, parking place, poop, Sunday face, handle bars of love.

BUTTRESS v.   beef up, build up, step up, hop up, soup up, jazz up, jack up, heat up, hot up, spike (drink). See SUPPORT.

BUXOM adj.   busty, curvy, zaftig, built, stacked, well-stacked, built like a brick shithouse, built for comfort. See also FAT.

BUY v.   blow oneself to, cop, score, land, make a buy, buy off, buy out, buy into, take up.

BUYER n.   live one, float, walk in, front, head, mark, chump, easy make, pigeon, sucker, end user.

BYGONE adj.   olden days, water under the bridge, water over the dam, down memory lane, when Hector was a pup, when one was knee high to a grasshopper. See PAST.

BYPASS n.   circumbendibus.

BYPASS v.   finesse it, go 'round the barn, go by way of.

BYPASS SURGERY n.   rich man's tonsillectomy, senior citizen tonsillectomy.

BYSTANDER n.   gaper, kibitzer, nark, sidewalk superintendent, watcher.

C

C n. Charlie.

C RATIONS n. Charlie.

CABBAGE n. violets, geraniums.

CABARET n. night spot, nitery, disco, after-hours joint, dive, speakeasy, hideaway. See NIGHTCLUB.

CABIN CRUISER n. stinkpot.

CABOOSE n. little red caboose, bed house, doghouse, bouncer, brain box, clown wagon, glory wagon, crib, crumb, diner, go cart, hack, hearse, hut, kitchen, palace, parlor, perambulator, shack, shanty, van, way car, saloon. See also TRAIN.

CACHE n. kitty, nest egg, stake, stash, stache, plant, drop, drop joint, drop-off, hideout, shade. See also ASSETS.

CACHE v. stash, stache, stash away, plant, park, ditch, duck, bury, squirrel, squirrel away, put in the hole, stick in the hole.

CACOPHONY n. clinker, sour note.

CAD n. shit, shit heel, heel, sleazeball, slimebucket, worm, maggot, bounder, rounder, rotter, dog, rake.

CADAVER n. stiff, cold meat, dead meat, fly bait, body, loved one, remains, cage, carcass, croppy.

CADAVEROUS adj. skin and bones, skeleton, bag of bones, stack of bones, peaked, peaky. See THIN.

CADENCE n. beat, count.

CADET n. kaydet, beast; doolie, gadget, gomer, gomar (A.F. Academy); foundling, find (dismissed), gray legs (West Point), middy (Navy).

CADGER n. bum, moocher, panhandler, promoter, bag lady, schnorrer, sponger, freeloader. See BEGGAR.

CADILLAC n. cad, caddie, caddy, golfer, cat, kitty, cattle train, hog.

CAFE n. eatery, pit stop, burger joint, grease joint, soup house, bistro, noshery. See RESTAURANT.

CAFETERIA n. caf, one-arm joint. See also RESTAURANT.

CAISSON WORKER n. sandhog.

CAJOLE v. stroke, snow, massage, soap, soft soap, simonize, con, jolly, oil, spread it on, lay it on, lay it on thick, lay it on with a trowel, get around, get next to, play up to, shine up to, make up to, act up to, butter, butter up, soften up, schmeikle (Yid.), sweeten up, sweet talk, loud talk, dialogue one, honey, schmeer, rub the right way, work on, work over, brownnose, suck around, suck up to; suck off, suck ass, kiss ass, kiss one's ass, lick ass (all Obsc.), bootlick, boost, pat on the back, build, build up, toss a bouquet, give a posy, give the man a big cigar, gold star, have to hand it to one, puff up, trade last, TL, blarney, buzz, charm, buck, contract, cream, bagplay, hand one a line, shoot a line, shoot the crap, shoot the bull, sling the bull, sling it, sell, shit, bullshit, BS, pull one's leg, over do it, string along, kid along, stooge, yes, be a yes-man, fall all over, fish, play footsie, footsie-wootsie, footie-footie, footsie-footsie, handshake, heel, play Mr. Nice Guy, politic, run after, polish the apple, apple polish, kowtow, caboodle, buddy up, carpet-bag, curry below the knee.

CAJOLERY n. eyewash, grease, oil, snow job, soap, soft soap, sweet talk, blarney, bunkum, butter, banana oil, shit, salve. See FLATTERY.

CAKE PREPARATION n. mix, cake mix.

CALAMITY n. shit, deep shit, total shuck, the worst, blue ruin, curtains, Waterloo, holy mess, unholy mess. See DISASTER.

CALCULATE v. dope out, figure in, figure out, figure up, reckon up, take account of, tote, tote up, tot, tot up, keep tab, keep tabs, size up, take one's measure, work out.

CALCULATOR n. brain, number cruncher.

CALCULUS n. calc.

CALENDAR n. lineup, pipeline.

CALENDAR v. line up, get on line, pencil in, set, set up.

CALIFORNIA Shakeyside, the Golden State, slow track, the Coast.

CALISTHENICS n. aerobics, jazzercise, monkey drill.

CALL n. holler, yawp.

CALL v. 1. blast, give one a blast, give one a blow, beep, bleep, contact, get back to, figure, swing by, fall by, fall down, hit, play, pay a call, crash (uninvited). See also TELEPHONE. 2. holler, holler out, yawp, yoo hoo.

CALLIGRAPHY n. chicken tracks, hen tracks, mark, scrawl, scribble.

CALLING n. racket, line, bag, do, dodge, go, grift, play, hang, nine-to-five shit, rat race, slot, swindle, gig, day gig. See OCCUPATION.

CALLIOPE n. goopus, horse piano.

CALLOUS adj. cold, cool, cool cat, laid back, flat, nowhere, chill, iceman, cold fish, cold-blooded, hard as nails, hard-boiled, thick-skinned, rhinoceros hide, dead ass, mean machine, no heart, butter wouldn't melt in his mouth, got lead balls for eyes, tough.

CALLOUSLY adv. in cold blood.

CALLOW adj. kid, low tech, sophomore, jellybean, green ass, don't know shit from Shinola, not dry behind the ears. See UNSOPHISTICATED.

CALM adj. cool, cool as a cucumber, keep one's cool, keep one's shirt on, unflappable, not turn a hair, ah-ah head, laid back, all quiet on the western front, all quiet on the Potomac. See also ASSURED, IMPERTURBABLE, DISPASSIONATE.

CALM v. cool, cool out, cool it, cool off, stroke, pour oil on troubled waters, take the edge off, take the bite out, take the sting out of, take it easy, lay back, soft-pedal, simmer down. See PACIFY.

CAMBODIAN n. Cambo.

CAMEL n. hump.

CAMERA n. box, pop bottle (inferior).

CAMERAMAN n. lenser, photog, shutterbug, coffee grinder (silent films).

CAMOUFLAGE n. cover up, beard, camel flags (WW I).

CAMOUFLAGE v. cover up, beard, wear cheaters, slap on some glims, flash the gogs, throw on a make up, phony up one's get up.

CAMPAIGN v. run, politick, press the flesh, stump, take the stump, stump the country, hit the campaign trail, whistle-stop, take to the hustings, shake hands and kiss babies, ring doorbells, mend one's fences, mudsling, muckrake.

CAMPAIGN FUNDS n. war chest, slush fund, rainmaker (fund raiser).

CAMPAIGNER n. baby kisser, stumper, stump speaker, stump orator, whistle-stopper. See also POLITICIAN.

CAMPER adj. sourdough tourist, tenderfoot (first time).

CAN n. pop top, gutbucket, gunboat, growler (large for beer).

CAN OPENER n. church key (beer).

CANADIAN n. Canuck, Kanuck, Jack Canuck, Jean Baptiste, pepsi (Fr. Canadian), hoser (north).

CANAL n. choke point, bottleneck.

CANAPES n. dip, finger food, spread, munchies.

CANCEL v. scrub, nix, kill, cut, trim, zap, X-out, do in, do one in, dial back, off, trash, total, torpedo, ax, sink, bog, crab, queer, squash, smash, smash up, finish off, forget it, knock off, knock out, knock the bottom out of, knock the chocks out from under, knock the props out from under, call off, call all bets off, scratch, break, break the lease, blow sky high, tear down, come down on, shoot, shoot down, shoot down in flames, put down, torpedo, spike one's gun, kibosh, put the kibosh on, kayo, KO, blue pencil, rub out, take out, launder, wash out, wipe out, weasel out, worm one's way out of, worm out of, welsh, crawfish, renig, nig, go back on one's word, put something out of action, cook, cook one's goose, upset one's apple cart.

CANCER n. C, big C.

CANDID adj. up front, right up front, frontal, open, call it like it is, straight shit, talk turkey. See FRANK.

CANDIDACY n. running, throwing one's hat in the ring, on the ticket.

CANDIDATE n. hopeful, political hopeful, presidential timber, dark horse, favorite son, handshaker, stalking horse, write-in, lame duck. See also POLITICIAN.

CANDY n. sweets, sweets to the sweet, pogie, pogey bait, commo (prison), hokey-pokey, hokum, jawbreaker.

CANDY FLECKS adj. ants, dots, jimmies, shots, sparkles, sprinkles.

CANDY STORE n. gedunk, sweet shoppe.

CANE n. stick, gimp stick, skinned mush.

CANINE n. mutt, pooch, doggy, pup, puppy, man's best friend, flea hotel, tail wagger. See DOG.

CANNON n. AAs, Arty, Divarty (division artillery), how, 88, long Tom, big guns, heavy stuff, rainmakers, Big Bertha, grandmother (WW I). See ARTILLERY.

CANNY adj. foxy, crazy like a fox, cagey, fancy footwork, full of fancy footwork, slick, slippery, sly boots, smooth, smarts, street smarts, streetwise. See SHREWD.

CANONICALS n. clericals, backward collars.

CANTANKEROUS adj. bitchy, bad-assed, ornery, stuffy, snappish, waspish. See IRRITABLE.

CANTON, OHIO Fame Town.

CAP n. beanie, dink, sky piece; cunt cap, tit cap (Army, Obsc.). See also HAT.

CAP v.   put the lid on, top it off, wrap, wrap up, button up, button down, do to a T, do to a frazzle, clinch, can.

CAPABLE adj.   A, 1-10 (degree, he's a 7), pro, vet, the right stuff, stuff, know one's stuff, dynamite, fireball, one-man band, has what it takes, the formula, the goods, green thumb, fool (i.e., dancing fool), mad (jazz), there, on the ball, something on the ball, know one's way around, know the ropes, know the score, know-how, know one's onions, crisp, up, up to it, up to snuff, up to speed, up to the mark, up one's alley, a pistol, old hand, old-timer, old war-horse, won one's spurs, been around the block a few times. See also QUALIFIED.

CAPACITY n.   1. standing room only, SRO, jam-packed, sardined, up to the rafters, chock full. See FULL. 2. what it takes, the goods, up to it. See SKILL.

CAPER n.   rib, gag, put on, high jinks, hi jinks, hot foot, hot one, monkeyshines, shenanigans. See also REVEL.

CAPER v.   let loose, cut loose, go on a tear, horse around, kick up one's heels, whoop it up, raise hell, blow off the lid. See REVEL.

CAPITAL n.   1. kitty, nest egg, stake. See ASSETS. 2. cap, small cap. 3. the hill, D.C. (Washington).

CAPITALIST n.   the money, moneybags, the boss, the boss class, the one who signs the checks, angel (theater), backer, robber baron, Daddy Warbucks.

CAPITALIZE v.   angel, back, bankroll, juice, grubstake, stake, pick up the check, pick up the tab. See FINANCE.

CAPITALIZED adj.   uppercased.

CAPITULATE v.   fold, cave in, give away the store, knuckle under; come across, put out, give out (sexual). See SURRENDER.

CAPRICE n.   fool notion, flea in one's ear, rib, gag, put on, caper.

CAPRICIOUS adj.   flaky, kinky, fantasmo, gaga, punchy, yo-yo, any way the wind blows, blow hot and cold, up and down, picky, picky picky, helter-skelter, higgledy-piggledy, every which way. See WHIMSICAL.

CAPRICIOUSLY adv.   any which way, fast and loose, hit or miss, all over the shop, by fits and starts. See ERRATICALLY.

CAPSULE n.   cap.

CAPTAIN n.   C.O., boss, exec, skip, skipper, old man, cap, chief, four-striper, owner, head honcho, head man, top, top dog, topkick, topper, higher up, A-1, A-number 1. See also COMMANDER, EXECUTIVE.

CAPTAIN (ARMY) n.   skip, skipper.

CAPTAIN (NAVY) n.   skip, skipper, old man, C.O., cap, chief, four-striper, owner.

CAPTIVATE v.   hook, vamp, rope in, bat one's eyes at, give one the come on, make a hit with, sweep off one's feet, turn one on. See ATTRACT. See also PERSUADE.

CAPTIVATED adj.   turned on, head over heels in, hooked, have one's nose open, fallen for, gaga about, gone on, mad about, crazy about. See also BEWITCHED.

CAPTIVATING adj.   pussycat, stone fox, head rush, dishy, whistle bait, solid sender, stunner, number, oh yeah. See BEAUTIFUL.

CAPTURE n.   collar, bust, nab, grab, pick up, pinch, pull, pull in, run in, sweep, bag, drop, gaff, glom, gloon to, hook, nail, nick, nip, fall, booby pinch, brodie, crimp, flop, jackpot, jam, knock off, pinch, rumble, slough, slough up, snare, snatch, trip, tumble, pickle, accommodation collar (to fill a quota or social or political pressure), humbug (unjustified).

CAPTURE v.   collar, bust, round up, pinch, pick up, pull in, run in, haul in, land, snatch, grab, nab, nail, put the cuffs on. See ARREST.

CAPTURED adj.   collared, nabbed, nailed, cornered, hauled in, picked up, dog meat, I'm dead, come out with your hands up. See ARRESTED.

CAR n.   wheels, ride, bug, beetle, stretch car (extra length), van, peep (jeep), bus, jalopy, bucket, gas guzzler, crate, heap, boat. See AUTOMOBILE. See also VEHICLE.

CAR, RECONNAISSANCE n.   recon car, beep, jeep, peep, half track.

CARBON COPY n.   cc, flimsy, tissue.

CARBONATED WATER n.   soda, club soda, clear soda, white soda; back soda, soda back (chaser); seltzer, sizz water, fizz water, fizzy stuff, for two cents plain, ammonia, maiden's delight (cherry), mixer. See also SODA.

CARBONATED adj.   bubbly, fizzy, fizzly, sparkling.

CARBURETOR n.   duals, pot, twin pots, carbos.

CARCASS n.   body, loved one, remains, stiff, cold meat, dead meat, croppy. See BODY.

CARDIAC MASSAGE v.   CPR, pump a patient (medical).

CARDSHARP n.   mechanic, card shark, capper (Obs).

CARE n.   1. tender loving care, TLC. 2. worriation, worriment.

CARE FOR v.   1. sit, baby-sit, keep an eye on, keep tabs on, ride herd on, watch out for, watch over, watch the store, mind the store. See HEED. 2. crazy about, nuts about, mad for, go for, hot for, gone on, stuck on, groove on, got it bad, nose open. See LOVE.

CAREER n. bag, game, number, racket, thing, dodge. See OCCUPATION.

CAREFREE adj. laid back, cool, feelgood, high wide and handsome.

CAREFUL adj. cover one's ass, play it cool, bend over backwards, handle with kid gloves, hedge one's bets, play safe, walk on eggs, pussyfoot. See CAUTIOUS.

CARELESS adj. slapdash, sloppy, any old way, any which way, by halves, fast and loose, helter-skelter, harum-scarum, devil may care, go out on a limb, fail to cover one's ass, leave oneself wide open, stick one's neck out, play with fire, fire-eating, go for broke, go off the deep end, step off the deep end, jump off the deep end, get in over one's head, goofing off, pay no mind, looking out the window, out to lunch, asleep at the switch, asleep on the job, not on the job, daydreaming, woolgathering, go overboard, go to sea in a sieve, buy a pig in a poke.

CARELESSLY adv. do by halves, knock off, knock out, bat out, shove out, slap out, slap up, slapdash, throw off, toss off, toss out, any old way, any which way, mess around, fast and loose, half-assed, helter-skelter, higgeldy-piggledy. See also ERRATICALLY.

CARESS v. stroke, feel up, feel out, cop a feel, fool around, paw, playing footsie, bear hug, clinch, clutch, grab, grab ass, squeeze.

CARETAKER n. sitter, baby-sitter, house-sitter, super, swamper, crumb boss (hobo and logger).

CARGO HATCH n. bellyhold (airplane).

CARGO PLANE n. goon, pregnant guppy.

CARGO SHIP n. crock, tub, rust bucket, tramp.

CARICATURE n. takeoff, put-on, send-up.

CARNAGE n. offing, wasting, taking out, liquidation, blitz, S and D, search and destroy, a ride, croaking.

CARNIVAL n. carny, carnie (also worker), gilly show, grind show, ragbag.

CAROM v. sideswipe, kiss off.

CAROUSAL n. tear, bender, binge, toot, bat, drunk, jag, paint the town red, on the town, blowout, wingding, bust. See also PARTY, REVEL.

CAROUSE v. go on a toot, go on a bat, go on a spree, whoop it up, hell around, raise Cain, paint the town, paint the town red. See REVEL.

CAROUSER n. playboy, good time Charlie, man about town, rake.

CARP v. lint pick, nitpick, bitch, noodge. See also QUIBBLE.

CARPENTER n. carps (stage), chips (ship), wood butcher.

CARPET n. wall-to-wall.

CARRIAGE n. brace, brush (Army).

CARRIER n. boy, shlepper, Typhoid Mary. See also BAGGAGE HANDLER.

CAROUSEL n. whirligig, merry-go-round.

CARRY v. lug, pack, back, backpack, piggyback, birdie back, heft, hoist, ride, shlep, shlep along, tote, truck, buck, gun, heel, hump (bags of coffee), jag, shoulder.

CARTEL n. megacorp, multinational, plunderbund, bunch, crew, crowd, gang, mob, outfit, ring. See also CORPORATION.

CARVE v. chiv, shiv, whack, hack.

CASH n. cold cash, hard cash, spot cash, buck, bread, long bread, dough, oday, dinero, the ready, the necessary, loot, lucre, filthy lucre, skins, gelt, green, green money, green stamps, greenmail, greenbacks, green stuff, green folding, folding, folding green, long green, folding dough, folding money, folding lettuce, folding cabbage, cabbage, happy cabbage, roll, bankroll, glory roll, Michigan roll, Philadelphia bankroll, wad, paper, soft money, happy money, mad money, moolah, frog hair, frogskin, gee, geech, geetis, geets, geetus, geedus, greedus, gingerbread, glue, gravy, bundle, change, feed, chicken feed, chicken money, hard money, hard stuff, hardtack, coin, iron (silver coin), iron men, jangle, jingle jangle, piece of change, piece of jack, jack, hip gee, ice, kick, lay down, line, grift, handsome ransom, lumps, maine line, mazumah, mezonny, mint, mint leaves, mopus, morphine, offtish, oil of palms, ointment, oof, ooks, ookus, package, pazoza, peanuts, poke, color, cookies, corn, cush, darby, dead president, dib, dibs, dingbat, dust, dirt, fews and twos, rags, rhino, rivets, rock, rocks, salve, scrip, sheets, shekels, black money (illegal), blunt, bob, bomb, bones, boodle, brass, buttons, candy, chump change, clinks, shinplaster, shortbread, shorts, small bread, small potatoes, simoleons, silk, sleeper, soap, soft, the soft, spending snaps, spinach, trading stamps, wampum, adobe dollar, alfalfa, bait, ballast, bark, bat hides (paper), braver bait, beans, beater, bees and honey, beewy, berries, bird (gold coin), biscuit, bite, spon, spondoolicks, spondoolix, taw, tin, tough bud, tusherony, tucheroon. See also MONEY.

CASH v. break a bill, make change.

CASH A CHECK v. float one, smash.

CASH DRAWER n. damper.

CASHIER n. broad on the damper, ghee on the damper, on the damper, on the gun, box man, stick man, man behind the gun, man behind the stick.

CASHIER v. bounce, give the ax, give the gate, give the air, give one his walking papers, pink-slip, sack, drum out. See DISCHARGE.

CASHIERED adj. unfrocked (any profession), drummed out, turned off, fired, canned, laid off, sacked. See DISCHARGED.

CASH ON DELIVERY n. C.O.D.

CASH REGISTER n. register, cash box, chip, damper, dinger, stick.

CASINO n. house, joint, shop, store, big store, toilet, trap, bust out joint, creep joint, creep dive, frolic pad, track.

CASKET n. box, cold meat box, crate, pinto, pine overcoat, wood overcoat, wooden overcoat, Chicago overcoat, wooden coat, wooden kimono, pine drape, pine pajamas, bird's-eye maple pajamas, tree suit.

CASPER, WYOMING Ghost Town.

CAST v. chuck, chunk, fire, heave, lob, peg, pitch sling, toss.

CASTIGATE v. chew out, chew out one's ass, eat out one's ass, bawl out, ream ass, lay out, lean on, jump down one's throat, come down on, read the riot act. See PUNISH.

CAST OFF v. cut loose. See DISCARD.

CASTRATE v. cut off one's balls, deball, fix, alter.

CASUAL adj. laid back, cool, mellow, breezy, easygoing, down home, homey, haimish, folksy, pokesy, sporty, let one's hair down, throwaway, loose, loose as a goose.

CASUAL WEAR n. jeans, denims, dress down, sporty, sports clothes, jogging things, come as you are.

CAT n. kitty, kitty cat, puss, pussy, pussycat, meow meow, Chessycat, coon cat.

CATACLYSM n. deep shit, total shuck, curtains, Waterloo, holy mess, unholy mess, double trouble. See DISASTER. time, tumul, crunch.

CATALOGUE n. charts, drop dead list (fired, expelled, excluded), enemies list, hit list, (punished or ostracized), shitlist, S list. See DIRECTORY.

CATALOGUE v. 1. typecast, tab, button down, peg, chart, spell out, pigeonhole, put away, put down as, put down for. See also ITEMIZE. 2. lane, track (Stu.).

CATALOGUED adj. chapter and verse, by the numbers.

CATALYST n. adjy, spark plug, pusher, fireman, hatchet man, needle man, steam-up ghee, stormy petrel, wave maker.

CATAMITE n. chicken, punk, boy, pratt boy, bindle boy, brat, gazooney. See also HOMOSEXUAL.

CATASTROPHE n. total shuck, bad news, the worst, meltdown, blue ruin, curtains, Waterloo, dead man's hand, tit in the wringer. See DISASTER.

CATCALL n. raspberry, razzberry, razz, Bronx cheer, the bird.

CATCH n. catch 22, joker, nigger in the woodpile. See HINDRANCE.

CATCH v. 1. collar, bust, corral, bag, get one's fingers on, grab, nail, snag, sneeze, looks like rain (imminent). See ARREST. 2. savvy, get, take in, tumble to, wise up to, catch on, catch the drift, get the drift, get the hang of, see daylight. See UNDERSTAND. 3. be on to, be hep to, have one's number, have the goods on, catch with one's pants down, catch flat-footed, catch one dead to rights, get one dead to rights.

CATCH COLD v. take one's death.

CATCH UNAWARE v. blindside, sandbag, snooker.

CATEGORICAL adj. all out, flat out, straight out, no strings attached, no holds barred, no kicker. See UNCONDITIONAL. See also CERTAIN.

CATEGORIZE v. tab, peg, typecast, button down, pigeonhole, put down as, put down for, rank out, size up.

CATERING TRUCK n. roach coach, garbage truck.

CATERPILLAR TRACTOR n. Cat.

CATHARTIC n. cc pills.

CATHOLIC adj. RC, Romish, papish, papist, papistic, popish.

CATHOLIC n. Roman, Jesus lover, cat lick, fish eater, mackerel snapper, Mick, pape, right foot, right-handed.

CATHOLICISM n. papism, papistry, popeism, popery.

CATSKILL RESORT n. borscht belt, Jewish Alps.

CATSUP n. red lead, red paint, kid stuff, growley.

CATTLE n. dogie, longhorn, moo cow, shorthorn, whiteface, dinge (sub standard, unbranded), stray. See also COW, BULL.

CATTLE BRAND n. iron, brand, running iron.

CAUCASIAN n. Anglo, honky, ofay, gray (Bl.), Wasp, white bread, whitey, paleface, blue-eyed, blue-eyed devil, round eyes. See also WHITES.

CAUGHT adj. dog meat, nabbed, nailed, booked, collared, corralled, cornered, dead to rights, got one dead to rights, I'm dead, one move and you're dead, hooked, hook line and sinker, dropped, flopped, guzzled, hit the pits, ill, in the pokey with smokey, in a box, in a fix, in a hole, in a jam, in a pickle, in a scrape, in a stew, in a mess, up a tree, up the creek without a paddle, up shit creek without a paddle, jammed up, on the peg, sneezed, take a brodie, walk into a collar, come out with your hands up, stiffed in, swamped. See also ARRESTED.

CAUGHT IN THE ACT v. caught red-handed, caught with one's hand in the cookie jar, caught with the smoking gun, caught flat-footed, caught with jeans at half mast, caught with one's pants down, caught dead to rights, caught dead bang to rights, caught dead bang, banged to rights, snared flat-footed, snared dead bang, dead pigeon, turkey, had, buried, in the barrel, washed up.

CAUSE v. intro, father, egg on, ring in, start the ball rolling, get things rolling, break the ice, break in, kick off, bow, open, open up, rev, rev up, fire up, cook up, dream up, make up, sound, think up, trump up, come out with, come up with, head trip, brainstorm, spark, spitball, take it off the top of one's head.

CAUSTIC adj. bitchy, cussed, mean, sticking the zingers in, wise guy, smart ass. See SARCASTIC.

CAUTION n. tip, tip-off, flea in one's ear, bug in one's ear. See also ALARM.

CAUTION v. put one wise, wise one up, tip, tip off, give the high sign, flag, wave a red flag, cloud up, pull one's coat. See also ADVISE.

CAUTIOUS adj. pussyfoot, leery, been hit before, cagey, play it cool, play safe, watch one's step, watch out, pay mind to, keep on one's toes, walk on eggs, walk wide, think twice, hedge one's bets, play it close to the vest, take it easy, take it slow, bend over backwards, cover one's ass, not miss a trick, not overlook a bet, not go out on a limb, not stick one's neck out, on the lookout, shine me on, listen up, all ears, keep one's ear to the ground, keep one's eye peeled, keep one's eye on the ball, be on the ball, with a weather eye open, with one's eyes peeled, handle with kid gloves, mind one's p's and q's.

CAVALRY n. bowlegs.

CAVE EXPLORER n. potholer.

CAVIL v. nitpick, lint pick, split hairs, make a big thing about, make a mountain out of a molehill, catch at straws. See also QUIBBLE.

CAVORT v. carry on, go places and do things, fool around, horse around, monkey around, cut loose, cut up. See REVEL.

CB OPERATOR n. apple, CB Stud, channel chump, Dixie cup (Southern), fox jaws (Fe.), signal stopper.

CB RADIO n. ears.

CEASE v. wind up, pack in, drop, drop it, cut it out, break off, back off, knock off, leave off, call it a day, quit cold turkey, close out, shut down. See STOP.

CEASED adj. fini, kaput, dropped, finished up, washed up, wound up, wrapped up, written off, all over but the shouting, signed sealed and delivered, when the fat lady sings. See also STOPPED.

CEASELESSLY adv. round the clock, day and night, on a treadmill. See CONTINUOUSLY.

CEDE v. fold, give in, hand over, fork over, come across with, drop, throw in the sponge, throw in the towel, toss in the sponge, toss in the towel. See also GIVE UP, SURRENDER.

CELEBRATE v. open a bottle, break out the bubbly, paint the town, paint the town red, raise hell, tie one on, party, party down, go on a bender, go on a binge, go on a bust, go on a rip, go on a tear, go on a toot, go on a spree, go on the town. See also REVEL.

CELEBRATED adj. w.k. (well known), number 1, number one, numero uno, large, up there, right up there, big, high powered, double-barreled, touted, highly touted, cut a dash, in the limelight, make a splash, flash in the pan (brief), not to be sneezed at. See also CELEBRITY.

CELEBRATION n. bash, blast, brawl, blowout, hullabaloo, hoopla, jamboree, paint the town red, whoopee, whooper-dooper, wingding. See PARTY. See also REVEL.

CELEBRITY n. celeb, star, superstar, monster, name, champ, a somebody, VIP, face, face card, lion, page-oner, prima donna, great, brass hat, hotshot, hot dog, the late great ———, Mr. Show Biz, Mr. ———, Miss ———, Mr. Big, big name, bigwig, big gun, big noise, big shot, big shit, big timer, big time, big-time operator, B.T.O., wheel, big wheel, big number, big man, big man on campus, B.M.O.C., big stuff, biggie, big boy, big league, major league, big deal, big chew, big player, big one, big ghee, big spud, big cheese, big piece of cheese, real cheese, the cheese, whole cheese, hooper-dooper, knocker, large charge, magoo, shout, visiting fireman, heavy, heavy stuff, heavyweight, gun, high muck, high-muck-a-muck, high-muckety-muck, high-mucky-muck, high monkey monk, high pillow, his nibs, her nibs.

CEMENT n. mud, stickum, gunk.

CEMETERY n. boneyard, bone factory, bone orchard, marble orchard, marble town, cold storage, headstone city.

CENSOR v. bleep, black out, blue pencil, scissor out, cork, put the lid on, decontaminate, launder, sanitize, sterilize, squelch. See REPRESS. See also SUPPRESS.

CENSORSHIP n. blackout, hush up, iron curtain. See SUPPRESSION.

CENSURE v. blow the whistle on, blast, blast on, lay on, lay a bad trip on one, put the whammy on one, lower the boom, drop the boom, paste, roast, rap, tell off, tell one where to get off, speak to, talk to, take down, call down, come down on, come down hard on, turn thumbs down, thumb down, blackball, call to task, call on the carpet, dance the carpet, put one on the carpet, have one on the carpet, have one on the mat. See SCOLD. See also CRITICIZE.

CENSUS n. head count, nose count.

CENTER n. mainstream, middle of the road, straddle the fence. See also MIDDLE.

CENTRAL AMERICAN n. banana.

CENTRAL EUROPEAN n. bohunk, hunky.

CENTRAL INTELLIGENCE AGENCY n. C.I.A., the company, The Company, toy factory, spook (agent).

CENT, ONE n. Indian head, red cent, brown, brown Abe, copper, brownie, peanuts, red, silver, meter money, throw money, wampum, washers.

CENTS, FIVE n. nickel, blip, jit, jitney, buffalo, fish scale, flat.

CENTS, TEN n. dime, thin dime, thin, thin one, thin man, deemar, deemer, demon, dimmer, deece, liberty, sow.

CENTS, TWENTY-FIVE n. two bits, quarter, cuter, kyuter, queter, big George, gas meter, light piece (silver), meter, ruff, shin plaster (paper), squirt.

CENTS, FIFTY n. four bits, half a buck, silver wing.

CENTS, SEVENTY-FIVE n. six bits.

CEREAL n. mush, grits, cush, birdseed.

CERTAIN adj. sure, sure thing, cocksure, sure as shit, for certain, on ice, cold, have down cold, pat, have down pat, nailed down, all locked up, have a lock on, lock-and-win situation, got the faith baby, keepin' the faith, count on it, no buts about it, no ifs ands or buts, open and shut, set, right on, odds on, gamble on, bet on, bet one's bottom dollar on, put your money on, bet the house on, bet the rent on, passed the litmus test, checked and double-checked, racked, taped, cinch, lead-pipe cinch, cinched, clinched, racked, come hell or high water, in the bag, that's death, and no mistake, know damm well, know darn well, boat race (horse racing), the fix is in, Is the Pope Catholic?, Does a bear shit in the woods?, Is a bear Catholic?, Is the Pope Polish?, Does the Pope shit in the woods?, Do they grow corn in Iowa?

CERTAINLY adv. absofuckinglutely, absitively, posolutely, cert, sure as God made little green apples, fer sher, for a fact Jack, you better believe it, right on. See ABSOLUTLEY.

CERTAINTY n. lock, lockup, lock and win, have a lock on, sure thing, dead sure thing, sure bet, sure card, for sure, fer sher, fer shirr, surefire, as sure as shooting, cinch, sewed up, all sewed up, open and shut, open-and-shut case, pushover, stock, store, put stock in, put store by, score, setup, soft touch, wrap-up, nuts, pipe, cinch,

lead-pipe cinch, candy, cold lay, bet your ass, bet your boots, bet your bottom dollar, bet your life, bet your sweet life, shoo-in, gospel truth, ironclad contract, rain or shine.

CERTIFICATE n. shingle, paper.

CERTIFICATE OF DEPOSIT n. CD.

CERTIFICATE OF OWNERSHIP pink, pink slip (car).

CERTIFIED PUBLIC ACCOUNTANT n. CPA, bean counter, sharp pencil pusher, pencil shover, pen pusher, pen driver.

CERTIFY v. okay, OK, rubber-stamp, put one's John Hancock on. See CONFIRM.

CESSATION n. freeze, downtime, time-out, breather, break, break-off, cutoff, layoff, letup, screaming halt, shuddering halt, grinding halt.

CHAIN GANG GUARD n. chain gang Charley, long chain Charley, long line skinner, johnny creep, the johnny.

CHAIN GANG LEG CHAIN n. bull chain, rattler, G-string (leash).

CHAIN n. clinker.

CHAIR n. seat, sling, squatter.

CHAIRMAN n. the chair.

CHAIRPERSON n. the chair.

CHALLENGE n. defy, have one's work cut out for one, when push comes to shove, when you separate the men from the boys.

CHALLENGE v. defi, face off, face down, fuck with, fuck around with, face to face, face the music, brace, cross, fly in the face of, fly in the teeth of, put one's life on the line, eyeball to eyeball, meet eyeball to eyeball, hang in, hang in there, hang tough, stick it out, stick to one's guns, stand up to, stand up and be counted, go one on one, take out, take on, take one on, take one up on, call one's bluff, knock the chip off one's shoulder, make something out of, step over the line, make my day, go on make my day, bite the bullet, keep a stiff upper lip, keep one's chin up, drop a lug, zap.

CHALLENGING adj. furry, hairy. See also EXCITING.

CHAMPAGNE n. bubbly, the bubbly, giggle juice, giggle water, grape, the grape, angel foam, Minnehaha, laughing water, sparkle water, whoopee water.

CHAMPION adj. world class, tops, greatest, cool, out of sight, out of this world, first chop, tip top, top-notch, topflight, top drawer, super, gilt-edged, gilt-edge. See BEST.

CHAMPION n.   champ, number one, numero uno, the greatest, top dog, king o' the hill, king shit, white hope, white knight. See also BEST.

CHAMPION v.   back, go to bat for, ride shotgun for, thump for, beat the drum for. See SUPPORT.

CHANCE adj.   dicey, iffy, risky, chancy, flukey. See RISKY.

CHANCE n.   1. break, breaks, shot at, long shot, fair shake, fighting chance. See WAGER. See also OPPORTUNITY. 2. in the cards, that's the way the cookie crumbles, lucky break, streak of luck, luck out. See LUCK.

CHANCE v.   stick one's neck out, put it on the line, plunge, take the plunge, put one's money where one's mouth is. See WAGER. See also RISK.

CHANGE n.   about-face, flip-flop, turnaround, mid-course correction, switch, switch over, whole new ball game, new deal, new shuffle. See also MODIFICATION, CASH.

CHANGE v.   1. doctor, phony up, switch, switch over, shift gears, cook, take it in a little, mid-course correction, monkey around with, bottom out, transmogrify, do up, revamp, kite stiffs (checks), tweak, give it a tweek (small), fine tune, yoyo, butcher, dink, dial back, recalibrate. See also SHIFT. 2. see the light, come to Jesus, hit the sawdust trail. 3. turn over a new leaf, turn the corner, turn the tables, turnaround, turn one around, do up, about face, flip-flop, sing a different tune. 4. shoot a twenty, break a ten, make change.

CHANGEABLE adj.   yo-yo, seesaw, wishy-washy.

CHANGED adj.   born again, newborn Christian, got religion, saw the light.

CHANT n.   belly music, shout.

CHANT v.   shout.

CHAOS n.   mix-up, holy mess, rat's nest, free-for-all, who's minding the store? See CONFUSION.

CHAOTIC adj.   helter-skelter, harum-scarum, skimble-skamble, every which way, arsy-varsy, topsy-turvy. See CONFUSED. See also ERRATICALLY.

CHAPEL n.   dirge factory, god box, amen corner.

CHAPERON n.   bird dog, alarm clock, baby-sitter.

CHAPLAIN n.   Holy Joe, sky pilot, sky scout, preacher man, sin hound, turn-around collar. See CLERGYMAN.

CHAPTER n.   branch, branch house, offshoot, affil. See ASSOCIATE.

CHARACTER n.   card, creepo, oddball-type, weirdo. See ECCENTRIC.

CHARACTERISTIC n.   1. slant, twist, gimmick, shtick, bit, bag, one's bag, thing, one's thing, nature of the beast, the way of it, the name of that tune, that's one all over, just like one. 2. thumbprint. See also NATURE.

CHARACTERIZE v.   typecast, tab, peg, pigeonhole, button down, put down as, put down for, put away, rank out, size up, take one's measure.

CHARGE n.   1. price tag, bad news, damage, bite, tick, nick, to the tune of, squeeze. See COST. See also FEE. 2. blitz, blitzkrieg, mugging, push, dirty deed, surgical mission (quick), attempting a creep. 3. beef, beefing, bitch, gripe, a hoo-ha, stink, big stink, dido, the gripes, kick, blast. See ACCUSATION. See also CRIMINAL CHARGE.

CHARGE v.   1. put it on one's card, cuff, cuffo, put on the cuff, put on the tab, put on tick, nick, paste, go in hock for. 2. finger, point the finger at, hang something on, whistle-blow, blow the whistle on one, turn on the heat, burn one's ass, drag into court, haul into court, have the law on, law, have up, put one away, pull up, take out after. See also ACCUSE. 3. mug, storm, haul off on one, jump on, blindside, bushwhack, land all over one, lace into. See ATTACK.

CHARISMA n.   pizazz, flash, it, got it, star quality, glamour, the jazz, something, chrismo, chismo, razzle-dazzle, animal magnetism.

CHARITABLE adj.   big, be big, big-hearted, all heart, heart in the right place, bleeding heart, do-gooder, good scout, Robin Hood, Santa Claus.

CHARITY n.   handout, a hand, helping hand, do one's part, chickadee checkoff (donation), write-off, gift, gifting, lump, poke out.

CHARLATAN n.   fake, faker, fraud, four-flusher, phony. See QUACK.

CHARLESTON, SOUTH CAROLINA   Charlie.

CHARLOTTE, NORTH CAROLINA   Queen City.

CHARM n.   1. whammy, chemistry, star quality, something, it, pizazz, the jazz. 2. evil eye, go, hoodoo, jinx, whack, whammy, hocus-pocus, mumbo-jumbo, abracadabra.

CHARM v.   grab, kill, slay, turn on, send, wow, do cute, knock dead, knock out, sweep off one's feet, make a hit with, vamp, bat the eyes at, blow one out of the water, tickle to death, tickle pink. See also PERSUADE, ATTRACT.

CHARMED adj.   sold on, hooked, wowed, turned on, tickled pink, tickled to death, head over heels in, pleased as punch. See also BEWITCHED.

CHARMER n.   vamp, man trap, velvet trap, fetcher, killer, lady-killer, lulu, operator, player, swinger, joy boy, sheik.

CHARMING adj. righteous, dreamy, dishy, drop-dead gorgeous, flavor (Bl.), scrumptious, delicious, good enough to eat with a spoon. See also BEAUTIFUL.

CHARY adj. cagey, leery, mind one's p's and q's. See CAUTIOUS.

CHASE v. shag, take out after, go after, run down, track down, bird-dog (scout), play catch up. See FOLLOW.

CHASTENED adj. ate crow, ate dirt, ate humble pie, got religion, got one's comeuppance. See HUMILIATED.

CHASTISE v. chew out, ream out, lay into, lean on, climb all over, rake up one side and down the other, slap down, ding, settle one's hash. See PUNISH.

CHAT n. rap, rap session, rapping rash, yak, yackety-yak, blah-blah, chinfest, chin music, chitchat, gab, gas, guff, hot air, talkee-talkee, visit. See also SPEAK.

CHAT v. rap, gab, gas, jaw, chin, confab, yak, yackety yak, yakking, go on, run on, bull, bullshit, BS, throw the bull, throw the bullshit, shoot the bull, shoot the shit, shoot the breeze, bat the breeze, bat the chat, bat one's gums, beat one's gums, chew, chew the fat, chew the rag, parley voo, twiddle, visit with. See also SPEAK.

CHATTANOOGA, TENNESSEE Choo Choo Town.

CHATTER n. gab, gas, yak, yackety-yak, talkee-talkee, guff, hot air, blah-blah, bibble-babble. See also SPEECH.

CHATTER v. gas, gab, jaw, yak, yackety-yak, go on, go on and on, run on, run off at the mouth, have diarrhea of the mouth, shoot off one's mouth, shoot off one's face, shoot the breeze, bat the breeze, bat the chat, beat one's gums, talk through one's hat, bull, bullshit, BS, throw the bull, bibble-babble, twiddle. See also SPEAK.

CHATTERBOX n. gabber, gasbag, windbag, windjammer, hot-air artist.

CHAUFFEUR n. wheelman. See also DRIVER.

CHAUTAUQUA n. Brown Top.

CHAUVINIST n. male chauvinist pig, MCP, pig, sexist porker, Archie Bunker, hard hat, hundred percenter, red-neck, flag-waver, jingoist, patrioteer, superpatriot.

CHEAP adj. 1. cheapie, el cheapo, dirt cheap, cheap as dirt, dog cheap, steal, real steal, buy, real buy, low cost, cost nothing, cost next to nothing, easy on the pocketbook, bought for a song, pick up for a song, cut rate, low tariff, dime a dozen. 2. cheesy, chicken shit, crap, crappy, crud, cruddy, crusty, mangy (fur), borax, shit, dime a dozen, dreck, drecky, piece of shit, pile of shit, rinky-dinky, dog, scroungy, small, small time, two bit, raunchy, quick and dirty, kinky, ratty, ratty-tatty, rat's ass, sleazy, gummy, gook, low rent, diddly, diddly poo, diddly shit, doodly, doodly shit, doodly poo, ain't worth diddly shit, ain't worth doodly shit, ain't worth shit, ain't worth the powder to blow it to hell, ain't worth a hoot, ain't worth a plugged nickel, cheapie, el cheapo, Mickey Mouse, cotton-pickin', garbage, schlock, schlocky, plastic, slimpsey, junk, junky, no-good, N.G., no bargain, no account, no 'count, not so hot, the least, lousy, jelly bean, beans, hill of beans, ain't worth a hill of beans, piss-poor, lemon, peanuts, dud, blah, ham, from hunger, flukey, flookum, white elephant, G.I., jeasley, jitney, bogus, minus, punk, stiffo, wood, tripe, turkey, abortion, bum, clinker, cracker box (house), tin, tinhorn. 3. tight, penny-pinching, close, close-fisted, chintzy, stingy, cheap John. See STINGY. 4. glitzy, snazzy, flashy, ticky-tacky, flukum, frog, fishball, gook. See GAUDY.

CHEAPLY adj. nickel and dime it, run on the rims.

CHEAT n. hustle, hassle, con, con game, short con, big con, big store, sting, bunk, bunco, bunko, flam, flimflam, flimflammery, jip, gyp, scam, racket, dodge, stunt, shady deal, sharp deal, wrong number, not kosher, crooked deal, crooked stick, cheatin' heart, honest John, play dirty, low-down and dirty, dirty work, grandstand, razzmatazz, razzle-dazzle, fast shuffle, royal fucking, royal screwing, sellout, bait and switch, the pilgrim drop, handkerchief switch, bum steer, curveball, jazz, jive, shuck, total shuck, balls, hooey, hocky, hokey-pokey, hokum, hogwash, malarkey, marmalade, spinach, banana oil, baloney, bulldog, garbage, cover, cover up, snow job, whitewash, whitewash job, doesn't wash, down and dirty, dirty dealing, dirty work, dirty pool, dirty trick, taradiddle, diddling, fix, Barney, frame, frame-up, plant, hookup, put-on, spoof, stab in the back, two-timing, Judas kiss, cross, double-cross, double-X, XX, double banker, double talk, doublespeak, double shuffle, fast shuffle, shell game, skin game, Murphy game, the old army game, bill of goods, trick, fool, fast one, run around, cutie, claptrap, line of cheese, borax, song, song and dance, string, smoke, tripe, vanilla, bitch, skunk, cake cutter (circus), hanky-panky, hocus-pocus, hugger-muggery, graft, grift, autograph, kiting checks, bucket shop, boiler room, Carrie Watsons, the engineer's daughter, double trays, dipsy doodle, shenanigans, monkeyshines, monkey business, funny business; limb, shit kicker, tap, tap game (advertising).

CHEAT v. rook, fuck, screw, shaft, frig, fork, hype, fudge, deke, hose, hump, pratt, rim, ream, rip off, jerk one off, jerk one around, dick one around, fuck one over, jive, shuck, shuck and jive, frontin', run a game on, snake one in, rope in, do a number on one, disinform, sell wolf cookies, throw the bull, bullshit, bunco, bunko, cheek it, fake, fake one out, four-flush, cross, cross up, cross one up, two-time, trim, caboodle, fast talk, fleece, gas, gum, flam, flimflam, stick, burn, beat, bleed, bleed white, bilk, clip, con, chisel, gouge, gyp, scam, stiff, sting, sandbag, bait and switch, throw one a curve, wrong steer, bum steer, give one a bum steer, hurdy, give one the run around, see one coming, Murphy, pigeondrop, ike, pluck, rope in, take, take one to the cleaners, take one for a ride, take for a sucker, take a dive, splash, throw a fight, throw a game, play games with, play the nine of hearts, play for a sucker, sucker, suck in, sucker into, cream, milk, pull something on one, pull one's leg, pull a quickie, pull a fast one, pull a fast shuffle, double shuffle, double-cross, XX, double clock, double deal, second deal, give one a raw deal, bottom-deal, deal from the bottom of the deck, pack the deal, stack the cards, stack the deck, shave the deck, shave, sting, strip bare, skin, slice, skunk, crib, crimp, set up, doctor, cook up, deacon, duff, hoke up, frame, load, salt, salt a mine, fudge, plant, phony up, queer, promote, string, string along, snow, snow job, cold haul, cold deck, cold cock, buffalo, bamboozle, gazoozle, hocus-pocus, slip one over on, put something over, put something across, put on, put on the check, make a patsy of, make a monkey of, hold up, soak, sell one a bill of goods, sell gold bricks, gold brick, do in, do out of, chouse, chouse out of, fake out, bust out, kiss out, psych out, outfox, fox, kid, pull the wool over one's eyes, have, humbug, hornswoggle, ice, grift, on the grift, rinkydink, score, shag, single-o, ride a pony, diddle, vamp, hook, throw the hooks into, gaff, lead one up the garden path, they're peeing on us and telling us it's raining, go South.

CHEATED adj. stung, been had, taken, been taken, taken for a bundle, taken for a ride, taken for a sleigh ride, took, been took, took a hosing, aced out, fucked, fucked over, jerked around, screwed, screwed blewed and tattooed, gyped, stiffed, stuck, stuck with, skinned, shafted, get the shaft, foxed, conned, disinformed, mousetrapped, strung along, set up, got it up the ass, weenie, weiner, got the short end of the stick, got a raw deal, got a haircut, got trimmed, jived, shucked and jived, sandbagged, suckered, sucked in, sold, sold a bill of goods, saw one coming, easy mark, bearded, fell for, took the bait, flammed, flimflammed, roped in, double-crossed, diddled, clipped, burned, fleeced, shaved, gouged, chiseled, juiced, gassed, bilked, buffaloed, hippoed, snookered, snowed, snowed under, hornswoggled, laid relaid and parlayed.

CHEATER n. 1. hustler, shark, sharp, sharpie, mechanic, faker, phony, fraud, con man, con artist, chiseler, flimflammer, flimflam man, jive ass, gyp, jip, gyp artist, gypper, gypster, crook, crooked stick, bunco, bunco steerer, bunco artist, clip artist, short-change artist, play actor, double-dealer, double-crosser, gouge, whip, stiff, smoothie, smooth apple, smooth article, smooth operator, operator, suede-shoe operator, slick operator, grifter, grafter, blackleg, bilker, diddler, two-timer, two-faced, moonlighter, fast talker, four-flusher, feather merchant, bent, shady, jackleg, horse trader, burglar, Jesse James, honest John, sneakin' deacon, broadsman, boogerboo, shiver, S.L.O.B. (silver-lipped

operator of bullshit), worm, hoser, wrong, wrong number, crust, city slicker, wolf in sheep's clothing, cheese eater, skunker, dingo, not kosher. 2. he had a pony, he used an airplane, equestrian (test cheating).

CHECK n. damper, grunt, holdup, map, rubber check (bad).

CHECK v. 1. knock off, break off, lay off, leave off, shut off, close off, choke, choke off, cut off, cut the shit, cut the crap, cut it out, kick over, call it quits, freeze, box in, get one in a box, bring to a screaming halt, come to a screaming halt, come to a grinding halt, come to a shuddering halt, hold the horses, cool it, can it, turn it off, come off it, let up, break it up, cramp one's style, cut off one's water, turn off one's water, shut out, shut down, close out, peter out, tune out, stonewall, stall, fix one's wagon, take the air out of the ball, saddle with, weigh down, hand like a millstone round one's neck. See also STOP. 2. double O, O.O., case, check out, check it out, frisk, look see, read, candle, scout it out, squack. See also ASCERTAIN. 3. play for time, conk out, die. See also DELAY.

CHECK, BAD n. rubber check (also forged), bad paper; bouncer, check bouncer, kiter (writer), pusher.

CHECKBOOK n. damper pad.

CHECKERED adj. checkeroo.

CHEEKS n. choppers.

CHEER v. 1. buck up, pick up, brace up, chirk up, perk up, give a lift, put one on top of the world, put one on cloud nine, snap out of it, let the sunshine in. See also ENLIVEN. 2. hear it for, sound off for, root for, plug. See ENCOURAGE.

CHEERFUL adj. chipper, chirpy, corky, perky, high, sunny, sunny side up, up, upbeat, upper, Little Merry Sunshine, little Mary Sunshine, grooving, peppy, zippy, zingy, zappy, snappy, rosy, looking at the world with rose-colored glasses, looking at [something] through rose-colored glasses, go-go, bouncy, jumping, rocking, swinging, swingle, juiced up, full of go, full of pep, full of beans, full of hops, full of prunes, full of vinegar, full of piss and vinegar, glad-hander (overly), high, high on something. See also HAPPY.

CHEERLESS adj. draggy, mopey, blue, ass in a sling, down in the mouth, in the dumps. See UNHAPPY.

CHEERS n. bring down the house, have 'em on their feet.

CHEF n. cookie, hasher, hash slinger, belly robber, belly burglar, biscuit roller, builder, stew builder, grub chocker, grease pot, pot slinger, sizzler, jeppo, ninety-nine, boiler (logger). See also BAKER.

CHEMICAL MIXTURE n. soup.

CHEMICAL RESIDUE n. soup.

CHEMICAL SPRAY n. yellow rain (war).

CHEMISE n. shimmy.

CHERRY PIE n. George Washington pie.

CHERRY SODA n. maiden's delight.

CHESHIRE CAT n. Chesycat.

CHEVROLET n. Chev, Chevvy.

CHEW v. chaw, chomp, munch, gum, fling a fang into.

CHEYENNE, WYOMING Rodeo Town.

CHIC adj. sharp, dap, clean, last word, latest thing, spinach, natty. See STYLISH.

CHICAGO, ILLINOIS Chi, Second City, Windy City, Wind City, Big Wind, Big Windy, Chi Town, Big C, Cattle Town, Toddlin' Town, the loop.

CHICAGO RESIDENT n. Chicagoan, Chicagorilla, hog, South Sider, North Sider, West Sider, gangster.

CHICANERY n. hanky-panky, monkey business, song and dance, run-around, dirty pool, whitewash job. See TRICK.

CHICKEN n. biddy, banty, buzzard, chick, chickadee, chickabiddy, gull, gump, sea gull, albatross (WW II), bird.

CHICKEN PARTS n. part that goes over the fence last, pope's nose, parson's nose, white meat, dark meat.

CHICKEN'S TAIL n. part that goes over the fence last, pope's nose, parson's nose.

CHIDE v. call on the carpet, take down, take down a peg, rap one's knuckles, slap on the wrist, speak to, talk to. See REBUKE.

CHIEF n. key player, head honcho, head man, top brass, big shit, big weenie, big gun, big wheel. See EX-ECUTIVE.

CHILD n. kid, little kid, crumbcrusher, shaver, little shaver, squirt, little squirt, little guy, little bugger, little dickens, little darling, little angel, little doll, juvenile delinquent, JD, punk, punk kid, snotnose kid, kiddo, pup, puppy, cub, sonny, sonny boy, bud, buddy, bub, bubba, drape ape (Stu.), house ape, rug ape, rug rat, young chit, sprout, bambino, nipper, small fry, young fry, tad, tadpole, chip off the ole block, anklebiter, godfer (Obs., Brit.), kinch, kinchen, latchkey child. See also BOY, GIRL.

CHILDBIRTH n. blessed event, producing, visit from the stork, drop one.

CHILDISH adj. kid stuff.

CHILD MOLESTER n. short, short eyes.

CHILD PRODIGY n. boy wonder, natural, whiz kid, quiz kid, brain.

CHILDREN n. crumbcrushers, mice, small fry, young fry, offspring, get (animal).

CHILD TENDER n. sitter, baby-sitter, nanny.

CHILLS n. the shakes, the shivers.

CHILLY adj. 1. creeps, cold creeps, coolth, snappy, two-dog night, icebox (place). 2. cool, frost one, frosty, cold tit, tight-assed, butter wouldn't melt in his mouth. See COLD.

CHIMERA n. fool's paradise, pipe dream.

CHIMPANZEE n. chimp.

CHIN n. button, on the button, point, China chin, glass chin, glass jaw (easily knocked out).

CHINA n. bamboo curtain, Red China.

CHINESE n. Chinaman, Chink, Chinky, Chinx, Chinee, chino, chow, ding, almond eyes, flange head (WW II), John, monk, pong, rice belly, riceman, slant, slant eyes, yellow peril, yellow fish (all Derog.).

CHINESE DINNER n. Chinks, Chinx, eat a chinx.

CHINESE IDEOLOGICAL DIVISION n. bamboo curtain.

CHINESE RESTAURANT n. Chinks, Chinx, chop suey joint.

CHIP v. whack, hack.

CHIPPED BEEF ON TOAST n. shit on a shingle.

CHIPS n. barber pole (stacked by color), buy in, checks, blacks ($100), greens, quarters ($25); reds, nickel, ($5); stack (20).

CHIROPRACTOR n. bonecracker.

CHITTERLINGS n. chit'lins, soul food.

CHLORAL HYDRATE n. knockout drops, Mickey, Mickey Finn, little Michael.

CHOCOLATE n. choc.

CHOCOLATE LOVER n. chocoholic.

CHOCOLATE PUDDING n. ant paste.

CHOICE adj. A-one, ten, aces, bitchin', stone, terrible, top drawer, solid gold, winner. See EX-CELLENT.

CHOICE n. bag, cup of tea, druthers, go down the line, flash groove, turned on to, weakness for, say so, take it or leave it, other side of the coin, other fish to fry, other fish in the sea, other pebbles on the beach.

CHOLERIC adj.   bent out of shape, nose out of joint, hot under the collar, blow one's cool, ranting and raving, red-assed, hacked, steamed, ticked off. See ANGRY.

CHOOSE v.   name, slot, tab, tag, tap, finger, go down the line, opt. See SELECT.

CHOOSY adj.   picky, picky-picky, choicy, pernickety, persnickety, fussy. See also PARTICULAR.

CHOP v.   whack, hack.

CHOPPED MEAT n.   burger, beefburger, cheeseburger, Big Mac, big boy, hamburg, superburger, Wimpy, Salisbury steak, ground round, chewed fine, clean up the kitchen (order for hamburger, hash or stew).

CHORAL adj.   sing, sing in, folk sing, hootenanny.

CHORE n.   grind, workout, bone breaker, ball-breaker, ball-wracker, ball-buster, conk buster, bitch, bitch kitty, son of a bitch, fun and games, funsey, funsies, scud, scut, scutwork, shitwork, KP (Army), chickwork (household). See also WORK.

CHOREOGRAPHER n.   terper.

CHORUS GIRL n.   gypsy, in the line, pony, chorine. See DANCER.

CHOSEN adj.   get the nod, tabbed, pegged, called.

CHRYSANTHEMUM n.   mum.

CHUBBY adj.   fatty, hefty, chunky, husky, big, full-figured, ample, pleasingly plump, zaftig, roly-poly, tubby, butterball. See FAT.

CHUCKHOLE n.   chughole, pothole, bump.

CHURCH n.   dirge factory, god box, amen corner.

CHURLISH adj.   snippy, bitchy, bad-assed, bad ass, cantankerous, cussed, grouchy, grumpy, mean, ornery, tetchy, ugly. See IRRITABLE.

CIGAR n.   seegar, stogie, Havana, rope, el ropo, boxfire, broom, gage, gagger, heater, hemp, the hemp, jitney, punk, stinker, torch, weed, Guinea, twofer (cheap).

CIGAR BUTT n.   curbstone cigar, old soldier, snipe.

CIGARETTE n.   butt, cig, ciggie, smoke, kings, ready made, tailor made, slim, straight, nail, coffin nail, fag, faggot, bonfire, boxfire, brain tablet, stick, cancer stick, chalk, commo (prison), deck, deck of butts (package), duck, fire, lung duster, quirley (cowboy), square, roll yer own, weed, snipe, burn, gage, gasper, hump (Camel), pill, slow burners, fast burners (stale), root, cigaroot, drag, spark, ready roll; dope stick, pimp stick, punk, reefer, joint, rope joint.

CIGARETTE BUTT n.   roach, snipe, clipper, clincher, dincher, grounder, hopper, lip burner, bonfire, maggot, old soldier.

CIGARETTE LIGHTER n.   light (also act of lighting cigarette), zippo, cricket.

CIGARETTE PAPER n.   blanket, joint staff, the makings (includes tobacco), tube.

CINCH adj.   snap, no sweat, no problem, pushover, picnic, cinchy, soft, easy as pie. See EASY.

CINCINNATI, OHIO   Cincy, Queen City.

CINEMA n.   1. the movies, silver screen, big screen, pictures, show, picture show, flicks, bijou, nabes. 2. movie theatre, drive-in, ozoner (drive-in), skin house, adult movies, porn house, porn palace, local fleabag, bughouse (cheap), grindhouse, quadriplex, sixplex. See MOTION PICTURE THEATER.

CINNAMON ROLL n.   snail, Danish.

CIPHER n.   1. squat, diddly squat, zip, zippo, goose egg, zot, zilch. 2. wimp, zero, nebbish, pip-squeak, squirt, shrimp, punk, nobody. See NOTHING.

CIRCLE n.   bunch, click, crew, crowd, crush, gang, insiders, mob, outfit, ring. See also ASSOCIATION.

CIRCLE THE EARTH v.   orbit.

CIRCUITOUS adj.   go round the barn, went by way of, long way, long way home.

CIRCULAR n.   handout, handbill, broadside, flyer, insert, literature, throwaway.

CIRCUMSCRIBE v.   nail it down, call a spade a spade.

CIRCUMSPECT adj.   cagey, play safe, watch one's step, handle with kid gloves. See CAUTIOUS.

CIRCUMSTANCE n.   action, hap, happenin', happenso, situash, scene, like it is, where it's at. See CONDITION. See also EVENT.

CIRCUMVENT v.   get around, queer, crimp, cramp, stymie, stump. See PREVENT.

CIRCUMVENTION n.   gamesmanship, one-upsmanship, run-around.

CIRCUS n.   the big top, gilly (small), three ring.

CIRCUS TERMS   big top, big rag, Clown Alley, come in (waiting crowd), cut cake (short change); Clem, hey Rube (call for help, fight, riot, small-town resident), dead cat (lion, tiger, etc. that does not perform), front door (Admin.), backyard (performers), geek (freak act), with it (circus help), cooch (dancer), gaffer (manager), grifter (sideshow concessionaire), barker, grind show, strike it (pull up stakes).

CITATION n.   quote, saying.

CITE v.   get down to cases, get down to brass tacks, spell out, reference.

CITIZEN n. cit, John Q., John Q. Public, Yank, Yankee.

CITY n. urb, burg, apple, Big Town, Big Time, boomer, boom town, dump, slab, two stemmer, tough town, wide open joint, right tank, wrong tank.

CITY DISTRICTS n. barrio, Bowery, Chinatown, hell's half acre, hell's kitchen, tartown, shantytown, Japantown, Koreatown, Little Italy, black belt, niggertown, wrong side of the tracks, other side of the tracks, red-light district, skid road, skid row, inner city, old town, dinkytown, tenderloin, high-rent district, gold coast, mainline, main street, downtown.

CITY DWELLER n. city slicker, cliff dweller, cave dweller, subway rider, straphanger, street people, Broadway baby, townee, towner.

CIVIL AERONAUTICS ADMINISTRATION n. CAA.

CIVIL AIR PATROL n. CAP.

CIVIL SERVANT n. paper shuffler, buck passer, apparatchik.

CIVILIAN n. feather merchant (WW II), civ, civvie.

CIVILIAN CONSERVATION CORPS n. C.C.C., peavie.

CIVILIAN DRESS n. cits, civvies, mufti, plain clothes, street clothes.

CLAIM v. hit, hit up, hold out for, knock, pop the question, whistle for (but won't get), dibs on something.

CLAIRVOYANCE n. ESP, sixth sense.

CLAIRVOYANT n. mitt reader.

CLAMOR n. hubba-hubba, buzz-buzz, hoo-ha, clinker, rowdydow, ruckus, hullabaloo.

CLAMOR v. howl, put up a howl, put up a squawk, holler, raise Cain, raise sand. See COMPLAIN.

CLAMOROUS adj. jumping, yakky, ear popping. See also NOISY.

CLAN n. folks, home folks, kinfolks, insiders, bunch, click, crew, crowd, crush, gang, mob, outfit, ring. See also ASSOCIATION.

CLANDESTINE adj. under wraps, undercover, hush-hush, tref, triff, creep (mission). See SECRET.

CLANDESTINELY adv. on the Q.T., on the quiet, on the sly, undercover, under wraps, hush-hush, strictly hush-hush, in a hole-and-corner way, in holes and corners.

CLAP v. give a hand, give a big hand, hear it for, beat one's skins.

CLAPTRAP n. bafflegab, gobbledygook, poppycock, bosh, bunk, tommyrot, baloney, narrishkeit. See NONSENSE.

CLAQUE n. groupie, buff, fan, frenzie, rooter. See DEVOTEE. See also SUPPORTER.

CLARIFY v. spell out, draw one a picture, make perfectly clear, give a for instance. See EXPLAIN.

CLARINET n. licorice stick, black stick, stick, gob stick, wop stick, agony pipe.

CLASH n. have a go at each other, brawl, donnybrook, jump, mix up, jam, run-in. See FIGHT.

CLASH v. buck, brawl, row, bang heads, mix it up, raise sand. See FIGHT.

CLASP v. grab, grab ass, squeeze, clinch, clutch, bear hug, glom onto. See also GRAB.

CLASS adj. classy, touch of class, chic.

CLASS n. pecking order, place, slot, likes, likes of, lot, number, down the line, the right stuff, the right people.

CLASS DISTINCTION n. pecking order, place, slot.

CLASSICAL adj. long-hair, long-haired.

CLASSICAL MUSIC n. long-hair, long-haired, long underwear.

CLASSIFIED adj. hush-hush, under one's hat, under wraps, family jewels (gov't., CIA), wildcat (plan). See SECRET.

CLASSIFY v. button down, peg, pigeonhole, put away, put down as, put down for, rank out, size up, take one's measure, typecast, tab.

CLAUSE n. catch, joker, kicker, string, a string to it, a string attached to it, fine print, small print, fine print at the bottom, small fine print at the bottom.

CLAUSTROPHOBIA n. stir crazy, stir daffy, stir simple, stir bugs, cabin fever.

CLEAN adj. apple pie, apple-pie order, neat as a button, neat as a pin, slick, squeaky-clean, vanilla.

CLEAN v. straighten up, police, police the area, spruce up, crumb up, pick up, get one's shit together, once over, dobie, doby (by hand), button chop, soogie, sujee, soogie-moogie, sujee-mujee, swab, swab down (Navy and maritime), do the dishes, G.I., G.I. party, clamp down (Navy), garbage collecting, G.C., bus (Rest.), launder (money, title). See also TIDY.

CLEAR adj. open and shut, clear cut, crystal clear, spelled out, plain as the nose on one's face, barefaced. See APPARENT.

CLEAR v. let off, let one off the hook, let go, defog. See ABSOLVE.

CLEARED adj. beat the rap, walked, let off, let go, clemo, off the hook.

CLEARHEADED adj. all there, together, got one's act together, got one's head together, got one's shit together, sharp, with it. See REASONABLE.

CLEAVE v. 1. whack, hack. 2. freeze to, stay put, stick like a barnacle. See ADHERE.

CLEMENCY n. spring, clemo, lifesaver.

CLERGYMAN n. padre, the rev, reverend, Holy Joe, sky pilot, sky scout, sky merchant, bible beater, bible thumper, abbey, black coat, buck, deac, devil dodger, preacher man, fire proofer, gospel ghee, harp polisher, long-haired boy, right buck, sin hound, turn-around collar, glory roader.

CLERICAL WORKER n. white collar, pink collar, pencil pusher, pencil shover, pen driver, pen pusher, paper pusher, paper shuffler, company monkey (Army). See also SECRETARY.

CLEVELAND, OHIO Dirty City, Iron Town, Yap Town.

CLEVER adj. savvy, slick, crack, crackerjack, brain, brainy, egghead, got the smarts, have a head on one's shoulder, have one's head screwed on right, have savvy, have the smarts, nobody's fool, no dummy, no dumbbell, not born yesterday, not so dumb, on the ball, sharp, sharp as a tack, smart as a whip, got it up here, quick on the trigger, quick on the uptake, cute, hot tamale, neat, nifty, quick, foxy, crazy like a fox, phenom, pro, there, whiz bang, whiz kid, wizard, with it, boss player, enough ducks in a row, hot, hotshot, know-how, know one's onions, know one's stuff. See also SKILLED, INTELLIGENT, SHREWD.

CLICHÉ n. buzzword, boiler plate, corn, familiar tune, high camp, chestnut, old chestnut, saw, old saw, old song, old story, potboiler.

CLIENT n. pigeon, sucker, live one, mark, chump, easy make, float, front, head, walk-in.

CLIMAX n. blow off, blow one's wad, shoot one's wad, pay off, capper, topper, critical mass, ape, bitter end, far out.

CLIMAX (SEXUAL) v. come, cum, blow, go off, get off, get off one's rocks, shoot, shoot one's wad, shoot one's load, haul one's ashes, cream one's jeans, get over the mountain, have one's ticket punched, ring one's bell, ring one's chimes (Fem.). See SEXUAL CLIMAX.

CLIMB v. ape up.

CLING v. hang onto, hang in, freeze to, cling like a burr, cling like ivy, hold on like a bulldog, stay put, stick like glue, stick like a barnacle, stick like a leech, stick like a limpet, stick like a wet shirt.

CLINIC n. bone factory, butcher shop, pogey (prison), alley (corridor).

CLIQUE n. insiders, bunch, click, circle, crew, crowd, crush, gang, mob, outfit, ring. See also DEVOTEE.

CLIQUISH adj. high hat, uppity. See also SNOBBISH.

CLITORIS n. clit, clitty, button, little man in the boat, spare tongue (Obsc.).

CLOCK n. tick-tock, chroniker, tattler, ticker, turnip, timepiece, Big Ben.

CLOSE adj. 1. tight, skinflint, pinchfist, chintzy, skimpy, stingy, Scotch. See STINGY. 2. cozy with, tight with, just like this (fingers intertwined), making it with, thick, thick as thieves, chummy, buddy-buddy, pally, palsy, palsy-walsy, in bed with, roommates, sleepin' together, kissin' cousins, trade spit, swap spit. 3. warm, in spitting distance, in the ball park, give or take a little, slicing it thin. See NEAR. 4. clam, clam up, hush-hush, on the q.t., zip one's lips, mum's the word, button up, button up one's lip, between one and the lamppost, tight chops. 5. close shave, slicing it thin, near miss, right apartment house wrong apartment, close but no cigar (miss). See also NEARLY.

CLOSE n. wrap, wind up, sign off, swan song, el foldo, that's all folks. See END.

CLOSE v. 1. wrap up, wrap a joint up, fold, fold a joint, fold up, close down, shut down, wind down, ring down, drop the curtain, shutter, slough a joint, put a lid on, cap, call off, call all bets off, cut loose. 2. clinch, clinch the deal, button down, button up, sew up. See CONSUMMATE. 3. go the route, put to bed, call it a day, clear, down to the short strokes, pack it in. See FINISH.

CLOSED adj. dark (The., sports), gone fishing.

CLOSELY adv. by the skin of one's teeth, stuck to one like glue, fit like wallpaper, any closer he'd be on the other side, the jeans look like they were painted on.

CLOSEMOUTHED adj. clam up, clammed up, dried up, dummied up, hush-hush, on the q.t., zip one's lips, button up, button up one's lip, between one and the lamppost, tight chops, tight-lipped, garbo.

CLOT v. clabber, lopper, glop up.

CLOTHE v. drape, dud, tog, fit out, deck, deck out, dog out, rag out, rag up, rig out, rig up, turn out, doll up, dude up, suit up.

CLOTHED adj. togged, decked out, rigged out, gussied up, all dolled up, in fine feather, in one's best bib and tucker, in one's Sunday best, dressed fit to kill, dressed to the nines. See DRESSED.

CLOTHES n. threads, togs, duds, glad rags, vines, schmotte, drapes, drag, hand-me-downs, Sunday go-to-meetin' clothes. See CLOTHING.

CLOTHES HORSE n. Beau Brummel, fashion plate.

CLOTHESLINE n. berry, gooseberry (hobo use).

CLOTHING n. threads, set of threads, togs, toggery, duds, outfit, rags, glad rags, getup, get out, turnout, feathers, fine feather, full feather, vine, weeds, flute, dry goods, schmotte, sack, tent, granny dress, duster, frame, front, flash, frock, sock frock, rig, gray flannel, pantsuit, jumpsuit, micro, mini, miniskirt, midi, maxi, maxicoat, maxidress, wraparound, pallazzios, honking brown (flashy), basic black, fofarraw, foofooraw, Christmas (ostentatious), ready-made, tailor-made, civvies, cits, mufti, fatigues, Port Arthur tuxedo, khakis, dress blues, whites, ice cream suit, drape, drapery, drapes, set of drapes, drape shape, drape shape with a reet pleet, zoot suit, zoot suit with a reet pleat, cool suit with a loop droop, Nehru jacket, Nehru suit, clobber, harness (leather, especially motorcycle), bomber jacket, drag, boondock (outdoor), racket jacket, Sunday clothes, Sunday suit, Sunday best, Sunday go-to-meeting, bib and tucker, best bib and tucker, secondhand, handout, hand-me-downs, reach-me-downs, bull's wool (stolen), felon sneakers, harem pants, hot pants, pedal pushers, hip huggers, see-through blouse, tie dyes, knee-hi's, legwarmers, bobbysox, Mary Janes, Buster Browns, white ducks, Dr. Dentons.

CLOTHING INDUSTRY n. rag trade, rag business, schmotte business.

CLOTHING STORE n. toggery.

CLOTTED adj. clabbered, loppered, glopped up.

CLOUD n. ol' buttermilk sky, ground clouds.

CLOWN n. 1. Joey, pale face, white face. 2. cutup, gagman, gagster, jokesmith, madcap, wisecracker, life of the party. See also JOKER.

CLOYING adj. sticky, gooey, sappy, sloppy, schmaltzy, mushy, gushy, gushing, teary, beery, namby-pamby. See SENTIMENTAL.

CLUB n. 1. billy, bill club, blackjack, sap, sap stick, stick, nightstick, rosewood, business, cosh, conk buster, conk crusher, convincer, duffy silencer, mace, persuader, rosh, works, shill. 2. hangout, stamping ground, bottle club, henhouse (WW II officer's). See also NIGHTCLUB. 3. gang, ring, mob, crew, bunch, outfit. See ASSOCIATION 4. wood, iron (golf).

CLUBHOUSE n. hangout, stamping ground, the nineteenth hole.

CLUE n. lead, hot lead, tip-off, tell-tale, dead giveaway, print, bum steer (false).

CLUMP n. blob, chunk, hunk.

CLUMSY adj. klutz, klutzy, clunker, clunky, dub, jerk, jerky, flub dub, amateur, amateur night in Dixie, all thumbs, butterfingers, half-assed, ham-fisted, ham-handed, two left hands, two left feet, lead-footed, stumblebum, clodhopper, galoot, goaty (Army), goofball, garbage, garbage time, not cut out for, walrus, bo.

CLUSTER n. blob, chunk, hunk.

CLUSTER v. bunch up, crowd around, gang around.

CLUTCH v. grab, collar, hook, glom, glaum, glom onto, put the snare on, snatch, snag. See GRAB. See also HOLD.

COACH n. old man, skipper.

COACH v. ready, toot, lick into shape, hone, break, break in, put through the grind, put through the mill, pull one's coat, lay it out for. See also ADVISE.

COAGULATE v. clabber, lopper, glop up.

COAL n. black diamonds, diamonds, estate, real estate.

COALESCE v. join up with, hook up with, tie in with, join together, come together.

COALITION n. hookup, tie up, afil. See ASSOCIATION.

COARSE adj. cheap, raw, raunchy, blue, dirty, low-down and dirty, filthy, off-color, rough, foulmouthed, loudmouthed. See OBSCENE.

COAST v. skate, smooth along.

COAST GUARD n. hooligan navy, SPARS (Women's Auxilliary).

COAST GUARDSMAN n. bungalow sailor.

COAT n. threads, flogger, peacoat, greatcoat, broad (Jive, 1935); Eisenhower, Mao.

COAX v. jawbone, arm-twist, work on, come on, con, hook, rope in. See PERSUADE.

COAXIAL CABLE n. co-ax, main line.

COCA-COLA n. coke, dope, fuzz fuzz, drag one through Georgia (chocolate), frown (lemon), maiden's delight (cherry), freak (not common).

COCAINE n. C, Cee, coke, cola, candy, nose candy, crack, rocks (hard), eight track (2.5 grams), sugar, snow, cloud walk, snowball, speedball (plus morphine or heroin), snowbird, white, white cross, white mosquitoes, white Christmas, old lady white, sleighride, toot, toots, Charlie, Cecil, Connie, Corinne, Bernice, Pearl, girl, her, lady, uptown, gin, jam, flake, joy flakes, joy powder, gold dust, happy dust, heaven dust, Peruvian, reindeer dust, cookie, leaf, trey, wings, bloke, big bloke, live (sniffed), whiff, balloon (bag), Cadillac (ounce), row, line (dose).

COCAINE ADDICT n. cokehead, Charlie, on the pipe (free basing), snifter, snow snifter, snowbird, snow snorter, jammer, tooter.

COCAINE AND HEROIN n. C and H, cold and hot, speedball (also cocaine and morphine), dynamite, whizbang.

COCAINE CARRIER n. body packing, mule.

COCAINE USE v. boola, tin, sniff, snort, toot, ski trip, jam; jam house, rock house, stash house, cokeland (source), hit, row, line (single dose).

COCAINE USER n. cokie, cokehead, jammer, snowbird, snow snorter, snow snifter, snifter, sniffer, tooter, horner (tender nose), on the pipe (free basing), high beams on (high).

COCKPIT n. cab, greenhouse, hut, pulpit, office.

COCKSURE adj. hotdogger, hotshot, smart ass, wise ass, wise guy, smart guy, smart aleck, smarty, smarty pants, know-it-all. See SURE. See also CERTAIN, ARROGANT.

COCKTAIL INGREDIENTS n. garbage (olive, cherry, etc.), mixer, setups.

COCKTAIL LOUNGE n. spot, juice joint, gin mill, office, gargle factory, meat market (singles bar), tap room, fillmill. See BAR.

COCKY adj. hotdogger, hotshot, smart ass, wise ass, wise guy, smart guy, smart aleck, smarty, smarty pants, know-it-all. See SURE. See also CERTAIN, ARROGANT.

CODDLED adj. spoiled, spoiled rotten, played up to, made over, stroked.

CODEINE n. schoolboy.

CODFISH n. Cape Cod turkey, sleeve buttons, Hollywood stew (creamed).

COERCE v. lean on, twist one's arm, strong-arm, put the squeeze on, high pressure, make one an offer one can't refuse. See FORCE.

COERCION n. arm, strong-arm, strong-arm tactics, bulldozing, steamroller, beef, clout, punch, kick, sock, pressure, high pressure, squeeze, chill, heat, gaff, gueril, mugg, nuts, shake, moxie, poop, steam. See also FORCE.

COFFEE n. java, decaf, cup a, mocha, moke, jamoke, dope, mud, cawfee, perk, perc, Joe, draw one (Rest. order), barefoot (black), with socks on (cream), blonde and sweet (cream and sugar), slop and slugs (coffee and doughnuts), coffee and (cream or doughnut, Danish, cake), forty-four, forty weight, hot stuff, cowboy coffee, alkali, battery acid, fluid, embalming fluid, paint remover, varnish remover, belly wash, mouthwash, blackout, black strap, ink, bootleg, flit, smoke, black soup, black water, Brazil water; dishwater, blanko water (WW II), bilge water, stump water, driddle water (weak); Norwegian, creekbank, sawmill, shanty, sheepherder's 100-mile coffee (strong), laced (with liqueur), travelin' (outgoing order), to go, with a splash (dark).

COFFEE CAKE n. bear claw, Danish, snail, coffee and.

COFFIN n. box, cold meat box, crate, Chicago overcoat, pine overcoat, wood overcoat, wooden overcoat, wooden coat, wooden kimono, pine drape, pine pajamas, bird's-eye maple pajamas, tree suit, pinto.

COGITATE v. flash on, kick around, brainstorm, head trip, noodle it around, stew over, figger, chew the cud. See THINK.

COGNITIVE adj. hip, hip to the jive, hep, hep to, tuned in, plugged in, with it, on the beam, grounded. See AWARE.

COGNIZANT adj. got, hipped, hip to, hep to, on to, wise to, in the know, in the picture, tuned in, plugged in, up on, savvy, on the beam. See AWARE. See also KNOWLEDGEABLE.

COGNOMEN n. handle, handle to one's name, brand, front name, label, monniker, tab, tag, flag (assumed), John Doe, John Hancock, John Henry.

COHABITATING adj. apartmates, convivante, mingles, roomies, live-ins, LTR, POSSLQ (persons of the opposite sex sharing living quarters, IRS).

COHORT n. stall. See ACCOMPLICE.

COIFFEUR n. 1. *Women's*: do, hairdo, blow dry, 2. *Men's*: trim, cut, razor cut, fuzz cut, cueball (just had a haircut). See HAIRSTYLE.

COIN n. change, small change, silver, chicken feed, meter money. See also CASH.

COIN v. dream up, make up, think up, trump up, spark, spitball, brainstorm, head trip, take it off the top of one's head. See CREATE.

COINCIDE v. sync, sync up, lip sync.

COIN PURSE n. jitney bag.

COITUS n. fuck, screw, lay, hump, boff, bang, jazz, shag, action, balling, roll in the hay, dirty deed, fooling around (all Obsc.). See SEXUAL INTERCOURSE.

COLD adj. 1. have duck bumps, have goose bumps, creeps, cold creeps, snappy, coolth, colder'n a witch's tit, colder than a frozen fish's asshole, colder than a well digger's ass, freeze one's ass off, cold enough to freeze the balls off a brass monkey, freeze one's tits off, freeze one's balls off, one-dog night, two-dog night, three-dog night, icebox (place). 2. cold tit, butter wouldn't melt in his mouth, cool, frost one, frosty, tight-assed, fish-eyed.

COLD n. sniffles, snuffles, common cold.

COLD CUTS n. delicatessen, deli, sandwich fixings, horse cock.

COLDHEARTED adj. cold, cold fish, ice man, mean machine, got lead balls for eyes. See CALLOUS.

COLLABORATE v. team up, team up with, tie in, tie in with, tie up with, throw in together, throw in with, go partners with, go in partners with, be in cahoots with, go in cahoots with, truck with, get together, come together, join together, join up with, hook up, hook on, hook up with, get in bed with, interface, interface with, be hand in glove with, do business with, glue oneself to.

COLLABORATOR n. team player, running dog, fellow traveler, quisling (Pol.). See also WRITER.

COLLAPSE n. crackup, breakdown, conk out, basket case.

COLLAPSE v. break down, break up, belly up, crack up, fold, fold up, cave in, conk out, give in, give out, drop, keel over, fall apart, come apart at the seams, go to pieces.

COLLAPSIBLE adj. breakaway (The.).

COLLAR n. choker, dog collar (priest), horse collar (protective).

COLLECT v. round up, get hold of, scare up, corral, dig up, pass the hat, put down (wine), moonlight requisition. See also ASSEMBLE.

COLLECTED adj. cool, cool as a cucumber, keep one's cool, keep one's shirt on, not turn a hair, unflappable. See CALM.

COLLECTIVE n. family, co-op.

COLLECTOR n. buff, nut, freak, bag man (gangster), skip tracer (loan). See also DEVOTEE.

COLLEGE n. alma mater, brainery, old Siwash, halls of ivy, aggie, East Jesus State (small), cow college, fem sem. See UNIVERSITY.

COLLEGIATE adj. rah rah.

COLLIDE v. crash, crunch, nerf, jolt, crack up, pile up, wrack up, smash up, smash into, bang into, plow into, sideswipe, fender-bend, fender tag.

COLLISION n. smash, crash, crunch, shunt, sideswipe, pileup, rack, up, wrack-up, crack-up, stack-up, smash-up, head-on, rear ender, fender-bender, fender tag, a tuckis full of fenders.

COLLOQUIALISM n. jive, jive talk, street talk, lingo, weasel words, flash (thieves).

COLLOQUY n. confab, groupthink, rap, rap session, buzz session, clambake, flap (urgent), gam, huddle, powwow, think-in, chinfest, talkfest, talkee-talkee. See also TALK.

COLLUDE v. finagle, frame, buy off, cook up, put in a fix, be in cahoots with, work hand in glove with. See SCHEME.

COLLUSION n. con, con game, short con, big con, sting, bunco, bunko, flam, flimflam, gyp, jip, scam, racket, dodge, royal fucking, royal screwing, bait and switch, fast shuffle, double shuffle, double banker, double-cross, shell game, skin game, the old army game, bill of goods, bitch, skunk, whitewash, diddling, graft, grift. See also SCHEME.

COLOGNE n. smell well.

COLOR v. cook, cook up, doctor, fudge, hoke up.

COLORADO Centennial State.

COLORFUL adj. flaky, jazzy, glamorous.

COLOSSAL adj. humongous, humungous, mungo, monstro, super, super-duper, super-colossal, jumbo, blimp, barn door, a whale of a. See BIG.

COLUMBUS, OHIO Capital City.

COMATOSE adj. out, out cold, out to lunch, loxed out, veged out, dead, dead to the world, gorked. See UNCONSCIOUS.

COMB v. beat the bushes, leave no stone unturned, look high and low, search high heaven, turn upside down. See SEARCH.

COMBAT n. battle royal, brush, brush-off, flap, mix-up, shoot-out, jackpot, run-in. See FIGHT.

COMBAT v. buck, put up a fight, cross swords with, shoot it out with, go up against. See FIGHT.

COMBATANT n. 1. champ, mug, pug, lug, palooka, heavy, slugger, tiger, punching bag, cauliflower ear, dancer (coward), plug ugly. See PRIZEFIGHTER. 2. G.I., GI Joe, grunt, hump, leg (infantry, Vietnam), dogface, yardbird, sad sack, buck private, buck-ass private, doughfoot, doughboy, paddlefoot, foot soldier, footslogger, snuff, jazz-bo (Bl.), trooper, Yank, government-inspected meat (homosexual use), bullet bait, cannon fodder, bunion breeder, galoot, gravel agitator, gravel crusher (WW I), red legs (artilleryman (WW I), bluebelly (Union soldier, Derog.), Fed (Union), Johnny Reb, reb (Confederacy), Fritz, Jerry (German soldiers), Tommy, Tommy Atkins (English soldiers).

COMBATIVE adj. bitchy, cantankerous, cussed, ornery, scrappy, hawkish, fire-eater, trigger happy. See BELLIGERENT.

COMBINATION n. combo, (also safe or musical group), mishmash, mishmosh, stew, soup (liquid), dog's breakfast (unpalatable), lorelei, duke's mixture, everything but the kitchen sink. See MIXTURE.

COMBINE n. bunch, crew, crowd, gang, mob, syndicate, outfit, ring, hookup, tie-up, tie-in tie-up, plunderbund. See ASSOCIATION.

COMBINE v. 1. team up with, tie up with, throw in together, bunch up, get together, hook on. See ASSOCIATE. 2. stand in with, interface, interface with, network with, tag on, tack on, slap on, hitch on, plug into, glue oneself to. 3. cross dissolve (film), cue in (scripts, ms., songs), dub, hook in, marry (film), mix (recording).

COMBUSTIBLE n. juice, go juice, motion lotion, motion potion, soup, synfuel (synthetic).

COME v. hit, hit town, blow in, sky in, breeze in, roll in, check in, sign in, time in, clock in, punch in, punch the clock, drop in, pop in, ring in, spring in, drag in, look what the cat dragged in, fall in, fall up, fall by, fall out, fall down, clip off, make it, make the scene, show, show up, bob up, pop up, wind up at, buzz (to announce an arrival). See ARRIVE.

COMEDIAN n. stand-up comic, stooge, banana, top banana, clown, cutup, million laughs, wisecracker. See JOKER.

COMEDIC adj. horseplay, howl, hot one, needle, nifty, rib, rib-tickler, a million laughs, a million laffs, screaming, screamingly funny, too funny for words, too killing for words, gut-busting, side-splitting.

COMEDOWN n. flop, dive, cropper, pratfall, comeuppance, get one's comeuppance. See FAILURE.

COMEDY n. camp, campy, high camp, low camp, baggypants comedy, pratfall comedy, in-one-door-and-out-another comedy, slapstick, send-up, blackouts, sitcom, dramedy (dramatic comedy), afterpieces, boffo schtick, stationhouse bits, takeoff, playon, burlesk, burlap, burly, burlecue, burlycue, ball, action, fun and games, grins, for grins, laughs, lots of laughs, just for laughs, just for the heck of it, just for the hell of it, just for the devil of it, big time, high time, high old time, picnic, field day, whoopee, hoopla, merry-go-round. See also JOKE, AMUSEMENT.

COMELY adj. ten, 10, boss, righteous, head rush, dishy, dreamboat, whistle bait, piece, looker, stunner, gimme. See BEAUTIFUL.

COMESTIBLES n. eats, feed, grub, scoff, go juice, pecks, vittles, goodies. See FOOD.

COMFORT v. buck up, pick up, brace up, chirk up, perk up, give a lift, snap out of it, let the sunshine in. See SUPPORT.

COMFORTABLE adj. fat, fat dumb and happy, comfy, cushy, snug as a bug in a rug, can't complain, have no kick coming. See also WEALTHY.

COMIC adj. camp, campy, jokey, joshing, yokky, boffo, gagged up, for grins, flaky, freaky, freaked out, goofy, kooky, wacky, screwy, loony, off the wall, batty, cockamamie, cockamainie, cockeyed, cool, crazy, daffy, nutty, sappy, dippy, dizzy, goofus, gump, horse's ass, horse's collar, horse's neck, horse's tail, Mickey Mouse, nerky, jerky, do the crazy act, do the crazy bit, do the crazy shtick, tomfool, fool around, make a monkey of oneself, fool, foolheaded. See also AMUSING.

COMIC n. stand-up comic, stooge, banana, top banana, clown, life of the party, card, a million laughs. See JOKER.

COMIC SECTION n. comics, the comics, comix, funnies, funny paper, funny papers.

COMIC STRIP n. comics, the comics, comix, funnies (also comic-strip page or section), funny paper, funny papers.

COMINGLE v. network, pool, come together, throw in together, throw in with, swing in with, mix in with. See ASSOCIATE.

COMMAND v. head, head up, mastermind, run, run the show, deal, deal with, call the play, call the signals, call the shots, call the tune, take over, take her, sit on top of, sitting pretty, be in the driver's seat, be in the saddle, hold the reins, wear the pants, pull the strings, pull the wires, have the say, have the say so, throw one's weight around, walk heavy, lay down the law, put one's foot down, push the buttons, got 'em by the short hair, got 'em by the balls, got 'em by the nuts, read the riot act, crack the whip, pussywhip (female), conn, take the conn (Navy vessel). See also MANAGE.

COMMANDEER v. liberate, moonlight requisition, take over, grab, snatch.

COMMANDER n. CO, exec, skipper, boss, A-number one, head, head honcho, head man, old man, point man, lead-off man, the man, boss man, boss lady, mother, main squeeze, don, mastermind, Mister Big, Mister Right, the brass, top brass, top, top dog, topkick, top hand, top banana, kingfish, kingpin, king, czar, queen bee, guru, rishi, high priest, higher up, cook, his nibs, digger, spark plug, avatar.

COMMANDER PACIFIC FLEET n. CINCPAC.

COMMANDING adj. bossy, in charge, high and mighty, throw one's weight around, out of the horse's mouth, straight from the horse's mouth, on one's high horse.

COMMANDING OFFICER n. CO, CINC, CINCAT, CINCPAC, exec, skipper, boss, A-number one, head, head honcho, head man, old man, point man, lead-off man, the man, boss man, boss lady, first skirt (WACS, WAVES), mother, main squeeze, the brass, brass hat, top brass, top, top dog, topkick.

COMMAND POST n. CP.

COMMENCE v. start the ball rolling, get going, get one's feet wet, get the show on the road, get cracking, tear into, jump into, hit the ground running (in full operation). See BEGIN.

COMMENCEMENT n. preem, bow, opener, tee off, first crack out of the box, curtain-raiser, countdown, from the top, git go, kick-off. See BEGINNING.

COMMEND v. stroke, boost, give a boost to, pat on the back, build, build up, toss a bouquet, give a bouquet, give a posy, give the man a big cigar, hand it to, have to hand it to, gold star, puff up, trade last, TL, hear it for, hats off to. See also APPROVE, ENDORSE.

COMMENDATION n. stroke, strokes, stroking, points, Brownie points, bouquet, posy, shot in the arm, plum, abreaction route, commercial, cow sociology, Doctor Spocking the help, opening up, pat on the back, pat on the head, trade last, TL, PR, puff, puffing up, pumping up, rave. See also APPROVAL.

COMMENT n. crack, backtalk, comeback, wisecrack, one's two cents' worth, input, mouthful (you said a mouthful).

COMMERCIAL adj. potboiler, pulp, slick, hack.

COMMERCIAL n. plug, spot, teleblurb, pitch.

COMMISSION n. commish, vigorish, ante, bite, chunk, end, juice, piece, piece of the action, rake-off, share, skig, slice, cut, cut-in, cutup, cut a melon (profits), drag, P.M., taste. See also SHARE.

COMMISSIONED OFFICER n. top brass, the brass, five-star general, four-star general [etc.], chicken colonel, shavetail, looey, lieut, 90-day wonder.

COMMISSIONER n. commish.

COMMIT v. 1. go in for, go out for, go for broke. See ACT. 2. hold, put away, take one away, put on ice, lag.

COMMITTED adj. set, set in concrete, bound, bound and determined, go for broke, go for it, locked in, mean business. See DETERMINED.

COMMITTEE TO REELECT THE PRESIDENT n. CREEP.

COMMON adj. plastic, garden, garden variety, everyday, vanilla, mainstream, low, cheap, no great shakes, loudmouthed, so so, dime a dozen, run of the mill, run of the alley, rumdum, starch, masscult, cotton-pickin', ham and egger, hoddy-doddy, plebe, Billy Sixpack, Joe Lunchbucket, ordinary Joe, Joe Doakes, Jane Doe, John Doe, John Q. Public, John Smith, Mr. Smith, Mrs. Smith, Mrs. Brown, Mr. Brown, any Tom Dick or Harry. See also AVERAGE.

COMMON-LAW HUSBAND n. old man, main man.

COMMON MAN n. ordinary Joe, Joe Doakes, John Q. Public, John Smith, Mr. Brown, Mr. Smith, Tom Dick and Harry, Brown Jones and Robinson, Billy Sixpack, Joe Lunchbox, the great unwashed, plebe, vox pop, boojy. See also AVERAGE.

COMMONPLACE adj. garden, garden variety, everyday, corn, chestnut, dime a dozen, vanilla, rumdum, starch, mainstream, middle of the road, run of the alley, run of the mill, boiler plate, familiar tune. See also TRITE.

COMMON SENSE adj. cool, commonsensical.

COMMOTION n. commo, flap, stir, big stink, rumpus, all hell broke loose, big scene. See TURMOIL. See also CONFUSION, BEDLAM.

COMMUNE n. family.

COMMUNICATE v. 1. contact, interact, interface, network, connect, mesh, outreach, reach out, reach out and touch someone, relate, touch, touch base, raise, keep in touch, be on the same wavelength, have good vibes, have good vibrations, have truck with, get across, get the message, grok (sympathetically), back channel (secretly). 2. drop a line, drop a note, give one a ring, give one a jingle, give one a call, give one the horn, get one on the horn. See also CORRESPOND. 3. jaw, confab, give a meeting, hold a meet, buzz, open one's face, modjitate, modulate, soapbox, sound off. See SPEAK.

COMMUNICATION n. info, scoop, poop, the hot poop, the inside story, the hot story, pipeline, skinny, lowdown, dope, dope sheet, goods. See INFORMATION. See also TALK.

COMMUNICATIONS SATELLITE n. COMSAT.

COMMUNIQUÉ n. handout, break, beat, scoop, the latest, what's happenin' what's going down, chip, poop, hot poop, dope.

COMMUNIST n. commie, comrade, red, fellow traveler, lefto, leftist, left-winger, lefty, linkydink, pink, pinko, radical, bolshie, bolshevik, comsymp, card-carrying. See also RADICAL.

COMMUNIST SYMPATHIZER n. comsymp, fellow traveler, parlor pink, pink, pinko, lefto, left winger, red fellow.

COMMUNITY n. 1. hood, neighborhood, neck of the woods, stomping ground, territory, turf, ghetto, inner city, jungle, shantytown, skid row, slum, zoo. See also DISTRICTS. 2. family.

COMMUNITY SING n.   sing, sing in, folk sing, hootenanny.

COMMUTATION n.   clemo, commute, spring, lifeboat, lifesaver.

COMMUTED SENTENCE n.   beat the chair, beat the rope, got a commute, got a lifeboat, got an anchor, got bugged, got clemo, made the bughouse.

COMMUTER n.   straphanger.

COMPACT adj.   1. in a nutshell, boiled down, short and sweet, make a long story short. 2. deal, dicker, handshake, ticket, paper, piece of paper. See AGREEMENT.

COMPANION n.   amigo, pal, brother, sister, cuz, cousin, buddy, roomie, pard, mellow (close), playmate, goombah, sidekick. See FRIEND.

COMPANIONABLE adj.   clubby, cozy, cozy with, tight, tight with, buddy buddy, mellow, pally, palsy, palsy-walsy, chuchula-muchula. See INTIMATE. See also SOCIABLE.

COMPANY n.   megacorp, multinational, outfit, syndicate, plunderbund, socks and stocks (non-banking company such as Sears, offering financial services), bunch, crew, crowd, gang, jungle, zoo, gang, mob, ring, clan. See CORPORATION.

COMPANY SPY n.   fink, company man.

COMPARE v.   hang (how does that hang?), hold a candle to, stack up against, match up.

COMPARTMENTALIZE v.   pigeonhole, slot, niche, place, split, piece, break up, divvy, divvy up.

COMPASSIONATE adj.   all heart, bleeding heart (Derog.), old softie, soft-hearted, soft shell, be big, live with, go easy with, go easy on.

COMPATIBLE adj.   hit it off, get along with, on the same wavelength, good vibes, good vibrations, cotton to, in the groove, groovy, simpatico, mix, togetherness, in sync with.

COMPATRIOT n.   landsman, compadre, compasino.

COMPEL v.   put the arm on, squeeze, put the chill on, turn on the heat, crack down, throw one's weight around. See FORCE.

COMPELLED adj.   hung up, bugged, have a bug up one's ass, have a thing about, have a tiger by the tail. See OBSESSED.

COMPELLING adj.   come on strong, push, punch, steamroller, husky, hefty, beefy, gutty, gutsy, take over, take charge. See also URGENT.

COMPENSATE v.   comp, shell out, come down with, plank out, pony up, tickle the palm, pay up, take care of. See PAY.

COMPENSATION n.   1. take, take home, pay, payoff, groceries, bread, sugar, salt, scale, shake, soap, touch, bacon, bacon and eggs, bring home the bacon, eagle shit; boost, hike, jump (raise); peanuts, coffee and cakes, chicken feed (small); fogy, fogey (Mil.). 2. walking-around money, cash on the nail, cash on the barrelhead, money on the side, boodle, hat, hush money, ice, laying pipes (Pol.), street money, chop, fall dough, freight, grease, palm oil, knock off, rake off, nut, schmear, big one, a fix, influence peddling, under the table, on the take, mordida, contract, cush, graft, juice, salve, baksheesh, sweetener, sweetening, piece, split, kickback, payoff, plugola, payola, drugola, gayola. See also BRIBE. 3. strokes, Brownie button (facetious), feather in one's cap, gold star, plum, what's in it for one.

COMPETE v.   jockey for position, scramble for, go for, go for broke, go for the gold, go for the throat, go for the jugular, go after, in the hunt. See also CONTEST.

COMPETENCE n.   hacking it, the right stuff, what it takes, cutting it, cutting the mustard, know-how, makings, making the grade, moxie, savvy, the goods. See SKILL.

COMPETENT adj.   dynamite, fireball, on the ball, one-man band, a pistol, crisp, no slouch, know one's onions, know one's stuff, know one's business, know one's goulash, know one's beans, know backwards and forwards, know the ropes, know all the ins and outs, know the score, know all the answers, know one's oats, know one's bananas, know one's goods, know one's fruit, know one's groceries, know one's oil, know one's [practically anything], have savvy, take care of business, just what the doctor ordered, all around, paid one's dues, mad (jazz), there, up to it, up to snuff, up to speed, up to the mark, wicked, fool (e.g., dancing fool, flying fool), more bang for one's buck, chakra gonged. See also ABLE, CAPABLE.

COMPETING v.   in the hunt, in the rat race, on the merry-go-round.

COMPETITION n.   competish, rat race, horse race (close), dog eat dog, a regular jungle out there, do or die, one on one, go, go for it, go for the gold, run.

COMPETITIVE adj.   dog eat dog, killer, killer instinct, streetwise.

COMPETITOR n.   oppo, opposish, opposite number, meat, me and you, angries, dark horse (unknown).

COMPLAIN v.   beef, where's the beef?, cut a beef, bitch, pitch a bitch, bleed, make a stink, gripe, gripes one's cookies, pop off, sound off, growl, gritch, squawk, put up a squawk, take on, kvetch, bellyache, blast, buck, crab, grouse, growl, kick, yammer, sing, sing the blues, cry the blues, get out the crying towel, rain, run one's mouth, speak one's piece, squeal, carry on, blow the whistle, holler, howl, raise a howl, put up a howl, piss up a storm, push out one's lips, eat one's heart out, raise Cain, raise sand.

COMPLAINER n. bitcher, beefer, bellyacher, griper, kicker, kvetch, squawker, whiner, crab, crank, crybaby, grouse, grouch, hogcaller, pill, plainer, rapper, sorehead, squealer, whistle-blower, blues singer, heat merchant, forecastle lawyer, sourpuss, lemon puss.

COMPLAINT n. beef, where's the beef?, gripe, kick, rap, guff, stink, rumble, CC (chief complaint). See GRIEVANCE.

COMPLETE adj. the works, whole nine yards, whole enchilada, whole megillah, lock stock and barrel, hook line and sinker. See WHOLE. 2. fini, that's it, all over but the shouting, finished off, home free, you've seen my whole spring line. See FINISHED.

COMPLETE v. wrap up, sew up, wind it up, call it a day, put to bed, put away, button down, go the route, get it under one's belt. See FINISH.

COMPLETED adj. set, wired, a wrap, wound up, mopped up, under one's belt, home free. See FINISHED.

COMPLETELY adv. all (all dolled up), from A to Z, from A to Izzard, top to bottom, plenty, royal, whole hog, to a fare-you-well, to a far-thee-well, galley west, shoot the works, six ways to Sunday, slam bang, stone (stone deaf), up the ass, cold turkey, dead, dead right, dead to rights, smack, smack out, flat out, from soup to nuts, from hell to breakfast, all the way, all hollow.

COMPLETION n. wrap-up, windup, curtains, that's all folks, that's all there is there ain't no more, say goodnight Gracie, hips, swan song. See END.

COMPLETION TIME n. turnaround, turnaround time.

COMPLEX adj. 1. can of worms, zoo, gasser, hi tech, rat's nest, snake pit, wheels within wheels, Rube Goldberg, mega factor. See also DIFFICULT. 2. hang-up, a thing about something.

COMPLEXION n. looks, mug, phiz, cut of one's jib, front.

COMPLEXIONED adj. complected.

COMPLIANT adj. pussy whipped, putty in one's hands, ac/dc, acdac, cosplug, when in Rome do as the Romans do. See SUBMISSION. See also OBEDIENT.

COMPLICATE v. make waves, open up a can of worms, foul up, screw up, snafu, add fuel to the fire, make the cheese more binding. See CONFUSE.

COMPLICATED adj. can of worms, gasser, hi tech, rat's nest, snake pit, wheels within wheels, mind blower, mega factor, Rube Goldberg.

COMPLIMENT v. pat on the back, toss a bouquet, give a bouquet, give a posy, trade last, TL, warm fuzzy, blow sunshine up one's ass. See PRAISE.

COMPLIMENTARY adj. comp, Annie Oakley, on the house, free lunch (seems free but isn't). See FREE.

COMPLY v. 1. yes one, ditto, go along with, go along with the crowd, play the game, play ball. See AGREE. 2. come across, come around, give out, put out (sexual); give in, cave in, cry uncle, say uncle, roll over and play dead, fold, gleek it, throw in the sponge, throw in the towel, toss in the sponge, toss in the towel, toss it in, don't make waves, don't rock the boat, go with the flow, go social, give away the store, give up, quit, knuckle under, knuckle to, shape up, shape up or ship out, clean up one's act, come up to scratch, straighten up and fly right, do it according to Hoyle, go by the book, by the numbers, go through channels, fit in, follow the beaten path, stay in line, not get out of line, toe the line, toe the mark, lie down and roll over for, when in Rome do as the Romans do, crazy, solid, way to go, there you go, you sold me, you got it, you just ain't whistling Dixie, you said a mouthful, it's a deal, me too, sure thing, I'll drink to that, I hear you, I hear you talkin, groovy, all the way.

COMPONENT n. making, makin's, fixings, fixin's, part and parcel, board, plug-in, peripheral.

COMPOSE v. comp, clef, tune, author, coin a phrase, cook up, dream up, whip up, whomp up, fudge together, bang out, bat out, scratch out, knock out, knock off, knock out a few pages, knock off hen tracks on a rolltop piano (type), make hen tracks, put down, note down, pen, put pen to paper, script, scriven, scribble, drive a pen, drive a pencil, push a pen, push a pencil, stain a paper, spoil a paper, shed ink, spill ink, grubstreet (hack), ghost, ghostwrite.

COMPOSED adj. together, have one's act together, cool, cool as a cucumber, keep one's cool, keep one's shirt on, keep a stiff upper lip, not turn a hair, unflappable, commonsensical, ah ah head, ice maiden (woman), roll with the punches. See also ASSURED, CALM.

COMPOSER n. tunester, tunesmith, songsmith.

COMPOSITE n. combo, duke's mixture (strange), stew, paste-up.

COMPOSITION n. comp, piece, tune, chart, arrangement, number, score, setup, getup, lead sheet (music).

COMPOSURE n. cool, keep one's cool, polish.

COMPOUND n. combo, mishmash, mishmosh, soup (liquid), lorelei, duke's mixture, stew, goulash.

COMPREHEND v. get, gotya, get the picture, catch, click, tumble, savvy, capeesh, fershtay, dig, read. See UNDERSTAND.

COMPREHENSION n.   aha reaction, double take, slow take, take, take it big.

COMPREHENSIVE adj.   the works, lock stock and barrel, whole shebang, wall to wall, across the board, the picture, the big picture. See WHOLE.

COMPREHENSIVE EMPLOYMENT AND TRAINING ACT n.   CETA.

COMPRESSED adj.   crash, telescoped, stuffed.

COMPROMISE n.   trade-off, deal, fifty-fifty, half and half, happy medium, sellout, copout, win-win situation.

COMPROMISE v.   trade off, make a deal, meet halfway, go fifty-fifty, if you can't fight 'em join 'em, strike a happy medium, come to school, play ball with, sell out, whore, cop out, give in. See also RECONCILE.

COMPULSION n.   hang-up, monkey, have on the brain, tiger, tiger by the tail. See OBSESSION.

COMPUTE v.   dope out, figure, figure in, figure out, take account of, tot, tote, tote up, tot up, count heads, count noses, cut ice, keep tabs, run down, run down some numbers, size up, take one's measure.

COMPUTER n.   PC, brain, number cruncher, micro, mini, mainframe, CPU, laptop; clone, a compatible (using same architecture and operating codes as a leading brand).

COMPUTER CONTROL n.   joy stick, mouse.

COMPUTER OPERATOR n.   gweep, hacker, user.

COMPUTER TERMS   go down, down, crashed, gronked (inoperative), cuspy (excellent), bug, debug (error correction), tweek, dink (modify), mung (change), bagbiter (failure), deadlock (jammed), gigo (garbage in, garbage out), footprint (table top area occupied), docs (instructions), expansion slot, board, breadboard (fits into an expansion slot), macro, windows (divided or superimposed monitor screens), icon (pictographic utility label), floppy, flippy (disks), AI (artificial intelligence), pull-down menu, backup (safety copy), multitasking, multiuser (network unit), transparent (unobtrusive program operation), LAN (local area network), residence (file location), wysiwyg (what you see is what you get), on-line, Silicon Valley.

COMPUTER USE n.   hackerdom.

COMPUTER USER n.   hacker, gweep, user, lurker (illegal).

COMRADE n.   amigo, buddy, bosom buddy, buddyroo, asshole buddy, chum, matie, pal, sidekick. See FRIEND.

CON adj.   agin, be agin, no way, over my dead body.

CONCEAL v.   1. bury, cover up, duck, stash, flatten out, hide out, hole up, plant, put in the hole, stick in the hole. 2. finesse it, launder, palm, paper over, fig leaf it, hold out on, skim (income), keep buttoned up, keep it under one's hat, keep under wraps, con, jerk around, fuck over, put something across, put something over on one, pull the wool over one's eyes. 3. wear cheaters, cover up, slap on some glims, flash the gogs, throw on a make up, phony up one's getup, beard. 4. stonewall, whitewash, put on an act, put up a front, put on a front, put on a false front, pull up a bluff, put up a bluff, play possum, four flush, make like, let on, let on like. See also DISGUISE, HIDE.

CONCEALED adj.   under wraps, incog, on the Q.T., hush-hush, hushed up, covered up, holed up, planted, stashed, doggo, put in the hole.

CONCEALMENT n.   cover-up, beard, fig leaf; drop, dubock, front, laundromat (places used to hide illegal transactions).

CONCEDE v.   1. yes one, ditto, go along with, play ball with, bury the hatchet. See AGREE. 2. give in, cave in, say uncle, fold, throw in the sponge, toss in the towel, go with the flow, quit, knuckle under. See SURRENDER.

CONCEITED adj.   hot shit, hot stuff, hot shot, bullshit, bullshitting, big talking, biggety, ho dad, ho daddy, key swinging, loudmouth, know-it-all, smart alecky, phony, hubcap, crack one's jaw, crapper, cocky, cock of the walk, chesty, gutbucket, stuffy, stuffed shirt, stuck up, puffed up, gassy, windbag, windy, load of wind, full of hot air, blowhard, blow smoke, gall, ham, hog, highfalutin,' high muck-a-muck, high hat, hinkty, his nibs, snooty, on an ego trip, ego-tripping, swell-headed, big head, high nosed, big I am, stuck on oneself, a regular I love me, think one is it, think one's shit doesn't stink, too big for one's shoes, too big for one's britches.

CONCEIVE v.   1. cook up, dream up, make up, think up, trump up, brainstorm, head trip, spark, spitball, take it off the top of one's head. See CREATE. 2. get knocked up (pregnant).

CONCENTRATE v.   1. sweat, head trip, hammer, hammer away at, crack one's brains, pour it on. See THINK. 2. cut, cut down, cut to the bone, nutshell, put in a nutshell, boil down, trim, sharpen, get to the meat, hone in, move in, zero in.

CONCENTRATED adj.   crashed, telescoped, stuffed, boiled down.

CONCEPT n.   slant, twist, approach, big idea, brainchild, wrinkle, brain wave, flash on it, wienie, fool notion, the name of that tune. See IDEA.

CONCERN n.   1. tender loving care, TLC. 2. megacorp, multinational, plunderbund, jungle, zoo, bunch, crew, crowd, gang, mob, outfit, ring. See CORPORATION.

CONCERNED adj. worried sick, in a stew, uptight, biting one's nails, on pins and needles, butterflies in one's stomach, coffee head, all-overish. See ANXIOUS.

CONCERT n. rockfest, gig.

CONCESSION n. 1. store, stand, hole in the wall. 2. rollback, buyback, giveback, takeaway (labor union bargaining), give, give in, copout, deal, fifty-fifty, half and half, happy medium, sellout, trade-off, win-win situation.

CONCIERGE n. super, swamper, watchdog.

CONCILIATE v. cool, fix up, bury the hatchet, kiss and make up, make up, make it up, make matters up, patch things up, get together on, come together, meet halfway. See PACIFY.

CONCILIATOR n. rent-a-judge.

CONCISE adj. in a nutshell, short and sweet, make a long story short, boiled down, cut to the bone.

CONCLAVE n. clambake, confab, meet, flap (urgent), huddle, powwow, eyeball-to-eyeball encounter, buzz session, rap, rap session, gam, get-together. See MEETING.

CONCLUDE v. 1. wrap it up, wind up, close out, drop the curtain, put the lid on, call it a day, knock off, put to bed. See FINISH. 2. figure, figger, add up to, boil down to, have a hunch, be afraid, what one is saying is, the way one sees it. See also BELIEVE.

CONCLUDED adj. wrapped up, fini, buttoned up, home, in the bag, all over but the shouting, signed sealed and delivered. See FINISHED.

CONCLUSION n. wrap, payoff, down to the short strokes, end of the line, that's all folks, when the fat lady sings. See END.

CONCLUSIVE adj. all out, flat out, straight out, no ifs ands or buts, what you see is what you get, litmus test.

CONCOCT v. prefab, throw together, slap together, fudge together, hatch, ad lib. See CREATE.

CONCUR v. 1. okay, pass on, shake on, cut a deal, set, hold with, give one five (slap hands), jibe. See AGREE. 2. you sold me, you got it, you just ain't whistling Dixie, you said a mouthful, it's a deal, I'll drink to that, I hear you, I hear you talkin', groovy, all the way. See also SURRENDER.

CONCURRENCE n. nod, big 10-4, four Roger, for sure, stamp of approval, on the same wavelength, go-ahead, green light, get the nod. See AGREEMENT.

CONCURRENTLY adv. dead heat, in sync, on the beat, with the beat.

CONDEMN v. put down, come down on, thumbs down on, call down, rap on the knuckles, slap on the wrist, name, hang something on, blow the whistle on one, whistle-blow, finger, point the finger, point the finger at, put the finger on, lay at one's door, pin it on one, frame, frame up, let one have it, put away, send up, send up the river, throw the book at, break one's license, clean up the calendar. See also ACCUSE.

CONDENSE v. cut, cut down, cut to the bone, nutshell, put in a nutshell, boil down, trim, get to the meat, chop, snip, blue pencil. See SHORTEN.

CONDENSED adj. crashed, telescoped, stuffed, boiled down.

CONDESCEND v. high hat, toss a few crumbs, act like one of the boys.

CONDESCENDING adj. snooty, uppish, uppity, king shit, have one's glasses on (Bl.), smart ass. See ARROGANT.

CONDITION n. 1. action, hap, happenin,' situash, spot, riff, ball game, scene, way it shapes up, how things shape up, way things are, way of the world, like it is, what it is, where it's at, where one is at, size of it, lay of the land, how the land lies, how things stand, how things stack up, how it goes, how it is, how things are, how de do, how do you do, the go along. 2. catch, joker, kicker, string, a string attached to it, fine print, small print, fine print at the bottom, small fine print at the bottom. 3. cherry (perfect), mint, showroom perfect, ——— city (fat city).

CONDITION v. 1. warm up, loosen up, shape up, toughen up, build up, work up, work over, whip into shape, sharpen. 2. program, brainwash, mind-fuck, head-fuck, fuck with one's head, fuck over one's mind, break down. See also TRAIN.

CONDITIONALLY adv. with a grain of salt, with a catch to it, with a joker to it, with a kicker to it, with a string to it, with a string attached.

CONDITIONED adj. programmed, brainwashed, head-fucked.

CONDITIONING n. warm-up, sharpening up, shaping up, an edge, readying, daily dozen. See PREPARATION.

CONDOM n. rubber, rubber boots, pro, nightcap, raincoat, protection, cadet, safety, bag, scumbag, Trojan, Ramses, armor, skin, fish skin, French letter, French tickler, Frenchy, purse, Manhattan eel.

CONDOMINIUM n. condo, condomarinium (beside a marina).

CONDONE v. okay, OK, buy, lap up, give the green light, go along with, put the Good Housekeeping Seal of Approval on, let it come. See also ACCEPT, ENDURE.

CONDUCT n. bag, channels, red tape, by the numbers, by the book.

CONDUCT v. run, run things, shepherd, ride herd on, call the tune, trailblaze. See MANAGE.

CONFECTION n. cush, sweets, g'dong, gedunk, hickey.

CONFEDERATE SOLDIER n. butternut, reb, Johnny Reb, Grey, the Grey.

CONFEDERATE SYMPATHIZER n. butternut.

CONFER v. 1. confab, give a meeting, take a meeting, have a meet, hold a meet, brainstorm, blitz, toss some ideas around, kick some ideas around, groupthink, get heads together, huddle, go into a huddle, run something by one, pick one's brains, rap, jaw, gab, chin, chew, chew over, chew the fat, chew the rag, rag around, bump one's gums, bat the chat, breeze, bat the breeze, shoot the breeze, shoot the shit, shoot the bull, bull, bullshit, BS, throw the bull, talk turkey, gobble, flap, mouth off. See also DISCUSS. 2. lay on, gift with, put something in the pot, sweeten the kitty. See GIVE.

CONFERENCE n. confab, meet, groupthink, think-in, huddle, powwow, eyeball-to-eyeball encounter, chalk talk (prof and students, informal, sports). See MEET-ING.

CONFESS v. fess, fess up, rat, rat on, fink, fink on, un-load, unload on, croon, sing, sing on, weasel on, sing like a canary, chirp, talk, snitch, dry snitch, squeal, squawk, stool, spill, spill the beans, spill one's guts, finger, leak, buzz (in secret), bury, deal, hose, split, belch, blow, blow the whistle, blow the gaff, drop a dime on one, clue one in, noise off, sound off, pop off, do one dirt, drum, come clean, come through, come out, come out of the closet, dump on, post, keep one posted, put the finger on, put one in the picture, put hep, put hip, put next to, put on to, put a bug in one's ear, put a bug up one's ass, put one wise to, put it on the line, put it on the street, let it all hang out, cop out, spit it out, crack, crack on, let next to, let down, let one's hair down, let down one's side, let the cat out of the bag, take a load off one's mind, take a load off one's chest, spring, spring one's duke, spring with a crack, tip, tip off, tip one's hand, tip one's duke, peach, holler, open up, own up, cough up, dig up, get it off one's chest, get it out of one's system, out with it, switch, update, wise one up, give with, give away, give the show away, give one the word, give it to one up the ass, sock it to one, lay it on one, lay it on the line, sell out, sell down the river, pull a fast one, run one's mouth, have a big mouth, have a big bazoo, blab, blabber, cop a plea, break a story.

CONFESSION n. owning up, squawk, squeal, song, story.

CONFESSOR n. canary, crooner, singer.

CONFIDE v. buzz, crack to, lay the gaff, lay it on, un-load on, spring with the score, bend an ear, spill to, let one in on. See also CONFESS.

CONFIDENCE n. stock, store, sure bet, guts.

CONFIDENCE GAME n. con, con game, sting, bunco, flimflam, Abscam, bait and switch, shell game, the old army game. See CHEAT.

CONFIDENCE MAN n. hustler, shark, mechanic, con man, con artist, jive ass, slick operator, feather merchant, horse trader. See CHEAT.

CONFIDENT adj. 1. cocksure, sure as shit, gamble on, racked, got the faith baby, keeping the faith, bet on, bet one's bottom dollar on. See CERTAIN. 2. iceman, ice in one's veins, gutsy, rosy, upbeat, gung ho, high, high on something, all puffed up, pumped up, glad-hander (over-ly), looking at the world with rose-colored glasses, looking at [something] through rose-colored glasses.

CONFIDENTIAL adj. eyes only, for your eyes only, for the cuff, hush-hush, top secret, classified, under one's hat, inside, off the record. See SECRET.

CONFIDENTIALLY adv. between you and me, between you me and the lamppost, between you and me and the bedpost, between us girls, don't even tell your mother, don't breath it to a soul, don't spread this around, don't let this get around, the ground floor, let one in on it, on the cuff, off the cuff, off the record, on the q.t., take a tip. See also SECRET.

CONFINE v. 1. ice, put on ice, put away, send up. See JAIL. 2. cool, cool off, cool down, hold down, keep the lid on, bottle up, cork, cork up, hog-tie, put a half nelson on. See RESTRAIN.

CONFINED adj. hog-tied, iced, on ice, chilled, grounded, bottled up, corked up. See also JAILED.

CONFIRM v. bless, buy, okay, OK, lap up, sign, sign off on, thumbs up, check out, check up on, double-check, size up, make sure, make doubly sure, put one's John Hancock on, give the nod, give the go-ahead, give the green light, give the stamp of approval, give the high sign, rubber-stamp, crack on one [or something], debunk (prove false). See also ASCERTAIN, VERIFY, AFFIRM.

CONFIRMATION n. fuckin'-A, go ahead, green light, mouthful (you said a mouthful), okay, OK, right on, bet yer life, you bet, you betcha, you can say that again, you said it, say so, one's stamp of approval, Good Housekeep-ing Stamp of Approval, rubber stamp.

CONFISCATE v. contifisticate, annex, grab, glom on to, liberate, moonlight requisition, take over, swipe, kipe, hijack, highgrade, police up. See APPROPRIATE.

CONFLAGRATION n. rapid oxidation, up in smoke.

CONFLICT n. brush, dance, flap, hassle, rhubarb, run-in, row, ruckus, fuss. See FIGHT.

CONFLICT v. brawl, scrap, romp, slug, tangle, tangle ass with, bump heads with, cross swords with, lock horns with, square off with. See FIGHT.

CONFORM v. go with the flow, go by the book, go through channels, don't make waves, don't rock the boat, play the game, shape up, shape up or ship out, get one's act together, clean up one's act, by the numbers, come around, come over, come to school, come up to scratch, straighten up and fly right, if you can't beat 'em join 'em, lean over backwards, make room, meet halfway, move over, find the middle ground, follow the beaten path, swim with the tide, do it according to Hoyle, bend over backwards, fit in, roll with the punches, toe the mark, toe the line, stay in line, Marin (County) Monopoly, when in Rome do as the Romans do, grin and bear it, take it, make a deal, go fifty-fifty.

CONFORMIST n. straight, straight arrow, square, sheep, yes man, organization man, company man, plastic, plastic person, Barbie doll, Ken, Babbitt, Mr. Grundy, Mrs. Grundy. See CONVENTIONAL.

CONFOUND v. discombobulate, ball up, fuck up, screw up, bug, throw, take one's mind, fuck with one's head, fuddle, put one on a crosstown bus. See CON-FUSE.

CONFOUNDED adj. unglued, balled up, screwed up, farmisht, thrown, rattled, in a fog, dizzy, kerflumixed, stuck, stumped, drowning, hugger-mugger. See CON-FUSED.

CONFRONT v. face down, go up against, meet eyeball-to-eyeball, go one-on-one, tell off, call one's bluff, make my day, go on make my day. See BRAVE.

CONFRONT WITH A WEAPON v. draw on, draw down on, get the drop on, pin, hit one with, smack with, spring with.

CONFUSE v. get, get to, discomboberate, discom-bobulate, ball up, foul up, fuck up, cross, louse up, mess up, muck up, screw up, snafu, blow up, bollix up, beat, lick, bug, rattle, rattle one's cage, throw, throw into a tizzy, throw into a swivet, throw a monkey wrench into the works, bamboozle, buffalo, lose momentum, psych out, gross out, take one's mind, fuck with one's head, mess with one's head, mess with one's mind, make a mess of, fuddle, play hob with, put one on a crosstown bus, make waves, open up a can of worms, add fuel to the fire, ball up, heat up, hot up, profundicate, synomaniac (one who complicates), muddy the waters, stir the waters, make hash out of, snow, stump, floor, put off, flummox, upset one's applecart.

CONFUSED adj. unglued, unzipped, unscrewed, come unglued, come unzipped, come apart, come apart at the seams, gonzo, discombobulated, discom-booberated, spaced out, glassy-eyed, slaphappy, punch-drunk, punchy, mind is blown, shook, shook up, all balled up, fouled up, fucked up, snafu, comfu, tarfu, tuifu, fubb (fucked up beyond belief), loused up, messy, messed up, mucked up, mussy, mussed up, sloppy, screwy, screwed up, bugged up, bollixed up, hung up, mixed up, blaaed up, gummixed up, caught short, messed up attic, helter-skelter, galley west, floored, flipped out, farmisht, fertummeled, woozy, thrown, dopey, lost one's cool, fussed, fried (Stu.), rattled, rattlebrained, nuts, higgledy-piggledy, skimble-skamble, half-baked, half-assed, ass backwards, bass ackwards, arsy-varsy, topsy-turvy, upside down, foggy, wandering around in a fog, in a fog, in a sweat, in a panic, in a tizzy, in a botheration, in a fix, in a pickle, in a stew, in a flush, in a lather, in a mess, in a dither, on a merry-go-round, harum-scarum, all hot and bothered, all over hell, all over the place, all over the shop, like a chicken with its head cut off, out to lunch, psyched out, shot, shot to pieces, gone, Mickey Mouse, dizzy, haywire, hell of a note, go blooey, go kerflooie, kerflumixed, flummoxed, don't know from nothing, don't know one's ass from a hole in the ground, don't know one's ass from first base, don't know shit from Shinola, don't know crossways from crosswise, don't know which way is up, licked, stuck, stumped, mocus, double Dutch, boggi-ly-woogily, drowning, hugger-mugger, bamboozled, buffaloed, bowled over, bowled down, struck all of a heap, thrown off one's beam ends, goat fuck (Mil.), Chinese fire drill. See also DISTURBED.

CONFUSION n. goulash, mix-up, foul-up, fuck-up, screw-up, snarl-up, mishmosh, mishmash, holy mess, un-holy mess, bloody mess, mess and a half, all hell broke loose, horseshit and gunsmoke, topsy-turvy, arsy-varsy, ruckus, ruction, shindy, who's minding the store?, flap, hoopla, rat's nest, discombobulation, discombooberation, flusteration, flustration, foofaraw, lather, stew, sweat, swivet, tizzy, hassle, free-for-all, etaoin shrdlu, every which way, every which way but up, forty ways to Sunday, forty ways from Sunday, all over hell, all over the shop, galley west, hectic, harum-scarum, pretty kettle of fish, pretty piece of business, nice piece of work.

CONFUTE v. tap, knock the props out from under, shoot full of holes, blow sky high. See REFUTE.

CONGEAL v. clabber, lopper, glop up.

CONGENIAL adj. clubby, mellow, right neighborly, regular fellow, mixer. See FRIENDLY.

CONGESTED adj. jam-packed, packed like sardines, sardined, mobbed, up to the rafters, gridlocked. See CROWDED.

CONGLOMERATION n. mixed bag, combo, every-thing but the kitchen sink, kludge (parts), duke's mixture (strange), mishmash, mishmosh.

CONGRATULATE v. stroke, boost, pat on the back, toss a bouquet, give a bouquet, give a posy, give the man a big cigar, gold star, have to hand it to one, hear it for. See also PRAISE.

CONGREGATE v. corral, round up, meet up, bunch up, gang up, gang around, hang out, make the scene.

CONGREGATION n. get-together, sit-in, confab, meet, gam, turnout. See MEETING.

CONGRESS n. 1. the Hill, the mighty dome, the house. 2. clambake, confab, meet, huddle, powwow, get-together. See MEETING.

CONGRESS OF RACIAL EQUALITY n. CORE.

CONJECTURE n. guesstimate, hunch, shot, shot in the dark, stab, stab in the dark, sneaking suspicion.

CONJECTURE v. figure, guesstimate, take a stab, take a shot, take a shot in the dark. See SPECULATE.

CONJUNCTIVITIS n. pinkeye.

CONNECT v. 1. tie in, tie up with, come aboard, get into, plug into, interface, join up with, meld with, network with. See ASSOCIATE. See also COMMUNICATE. 2. hook up, hook on, tag, tag on, tack on, slap on, hitch on. See also FASTEN. 3. cross dissolve (film), cue in, (scripts, ms., songs), dub, hook in, marry (film), mix (recording).

CONNECTICUT the Constitution State, the Nutmeg State, Wooden Nutmeg State.

CONNECTION n. network, tie-in, hookup. See also COMMUNICATION.

CONNECTIONS n. contacts, in, inside track, wires, ropes, strings, clout. See INFLUENCE.

CONNIVANCE n. scam, racket, flimflam, graft, whitewash job, diddle. See CHEAT.

CONNIVE v. operate, be in cahoots with, work hand in glove with, frame, frame up, cook up, finagle, angle, promote, wangle, wire, diddle. See SCHEME.

CONNIVER n. operator, hustler, finagler, wire-puller, carpetbagger, on the make. See also CONSPIRATOR.

CONNOISSEUR n. buff, fan, freak, into, nut, maven. See also AUTHORITY.

CONQUER v. trash, total, drub, whip, clobber, cream, zap, whip ass, shut down, wipe off the map. See DEFEAT.

CONQUEST n. big win, grand slam, score, splash, takeover, killing, clean sweep. See TRIUMPH.

CONSCIENTIOUS adj. tough, hanging tough, hanging in, heart and soul into, watch out, watch one's step, keep on one's toes, play safe, walk on eggs, mind one's p's and q's, bend over backwards, keep one's ear to the ground.

CONSCIENTIOUS OBJECTOR n. conchie, C.O., peacenik.

CONSCRIPT n. draftee, rookie, tenderfoot, chicken; barber bait, big Joe, big John, bimbo, bozo (WW II); boot (Navy), draft bait (subject to conscription). See also RECRUIT.

CONSCRIPT v. sign on, sign up, call up.

CONSCRIPTION n. greetings, letter from Uncle Sam.

CONSENT n. go-ahead, green light, mouthful (you said a mouthful), okay, OK, right on, bet yer life, you bet, you can say that again, you said it, say so, stamp of approval, blank check, carte blanche, blessing.

CONSENT v. 1. okay, bless, shake on, sign off on, make a deal, yes one, give the nod. 2. give in, cave in, cry uncle, say uncle, roll over and play dead, fold, gleek it, lump it, throw in the sponge, throw in the towel, toss in the sponge, toss in the towel, toss it in, give away the store, give up, quit, knuckle under, knuckle to, lie down and roll over for, crazy, solid, way to go, there you go, like you say, you sold me, you got it, you just ain't whistling Dixie, you said a mouthful, it's a deal, me too, sure thing, I'll drink to that, I hear you, I hear you talkin, groovy, all the way. See AGREE.

CONSEQUENCE n. fallout, reaction, chain reaction, flak (bad), follow-up, follow through, spin-off, waves, can of worms, bottom line.

CONSERVATIONIST n. duck squeezer, eagle freak, ecofreak, econut, greeny.

CONSERVATIVE adj. right, right wing, right winger, right of center, New Right, radical right, extreme right, hard right, rightist, right angle, right of Attila the Hun, neo-con, red-neck, red-baiter, good ol' boy, real Amerikan, Archie Bunker, hard hat, hard shell, diehard, Bircher, Birchite, John Bircher, caveman, citizen (anyone more conservative than you are), Ivy League, straight arrow, white bread, white bread and mayonnaise, standpatter, old guard, old line, duddy, fuddy-dud, fuddy-duddy, plays close to the vest, storm trooper, witch hunter, Black Shirt, Brown Shirt, Klu Kluxer, lunatic fringe, McCarthyite, Posse Comatatus.

CONSERVE v. stash, scrimp, skimp, cut down on, cut back, sock away, squirrel, squirrel away. See SAVE.

CONSIDER v. feel, kick around, noodle, noodle it around, sweat, sweat over, cool something over, rack one's brains. See THINK.

CONSIDERABLE adj. fab, fat, something, something else, super, super-duper, monstro, unreal, to the max, a doozie, dynamite, like all get out, mad, man-sized, a pip, solid gold, tidy, tits, tuff. See also IMPORTANT.

CONSIDERATE adj. cool, mellow, a sport, regular fellow, a gent, a mensch. See also ACCOMMODATING.

CONSIDERATION n. a little slack, a little something to sweeten the pot. See also FEE, GRATUITY, PAY.

CONSOLIDATE v. 1. pool, tie in, tie up with, throw in together, plug into, bunch up, hook up with, team up with. See ASSOCIATE. 2. hook up, hook on, tag, tag on, tack on, slap on, hitch on. 3. cross dissolve (film), cue in, (scripts, ms., songs), dub, hook in, marry (film), mix (recording).

CONSOLIDATED adj. crashed, telescoped, stuffed.

CONSORT v. run with, run around with, pal, pal with, pal up with, pal around with, take up with, tie up with, clique with, gang up with, hang around with, hang out with, chum with, chum together.

CONSORTIUM n. megacorp, multinational, plunderbund, bunch, crew, crowd, gang, mob, outfit, ring. See CORPORATION.

CONSORT WITH BLACKS v. change one's luck, deal in coal, nigger lover (all Derog.).

CONSPICUOUS adj. flashy, splashy, glitzy, make a big splash, jazzy, showy, loud, screaming, splurgy, candy, candy kid, classy, flossy, toney, high-toned, belled, duded up, all spiffed up, put on the dog, hanging out, live in a glass house, spot one like a lead dime, stick out like a sore thumb. See also APPARENT.

CONSPIRACY n. fix, frame, frame-up, hookup, put-up job, game, little game, Barney. See SCHEME.

CONSPIRATOR n. finagler, operator, wire-puller, wangler, mastermind, brain.

CONSPIRE v. get in bed with, cook up, operate, promote, wangle, wire, hatch, work something out, be in cahoots, put out a contract. See SCHEME.

CONSTABLE n. cop, copper, keystone cop, bull, shamus, flic, cossack (Derog.), dick, pig (Derog.), oink (Derog.), big brother, boy scouts, county Joe, county mounty, county mountie, hick dick, sparrow cop, law, John Law, Johnny Law, arm, long arm, long arm of the law, local boy, local yard, local yokel, local bear, bear, smokey, smokey the bear, little bear (local), road ranger, button, collar, finger, elbow, flatfoot (Derog.), fink (Derog.), cookie cutter, gum foot, headbeater (Derog.), Mulligan, nab, penny, roach (Derog.), the man, the men, men in blue, badge, clown (Derog.), fuzz, fuzzy, Kojak, shoofly, sky. See also POLICE OFFICER.

CONSTANT adj. cool, together, unflappable, solid as a rock, Rock of Gib, Rock of Gibraltar.

CONSTANTLY adv. round the clock, day and night.

CONSTITUENT n. fixin's, makings, part and parcel, board, plug-in. See also BASIC.

CONSTITUTE v. cook up, dream up, fudge together, whomp up.

CONSTRAIN v. cool, cool off, cool down, not go off the deep end, keep the lid on, bottle up, cork, cork up, hog-tie, put a half nelson on, hold down. See RESTRAIN.

CONSTRAINT n. hang-up, jones, monkey, a no-no, a must. See HINDRANCE.

CONSTRUCT v. whip up, trump up, cook up, cobble up, dream up, hoke up, whomp up, throw up, throw together, knock together, fudge together, prefab, put out.

CONSTRUE v. be afraid, figure it to be, one's best guess.

CONSULT v. brainstorm, confab, get heads together, groupthink, huddle, go into a huddle, flap, take a meeting, have a meet, toss some ideas around, kick some ideas around, run something by one, pick one's brains. See also CONFER.

CONSULTATION n. confab, groupthink, rap, rap session, buzz session, skull session, clambake, eyeball-to-eyeball encounter, flap, gam, huddle, powwow, think-in, second opinion. See also MEETING.

CONSUME v. scarf, chow down, scoff, mow (mow a burger), nibble, snack, wolf, bolt, stuff one's face. See EAT.

CONSUMED adj. down the tube, petered out, shot.

CONSUMER n. end user. See also BUYER.

CONSUMMATE v. wrap, wrap up, button down, button up, clean up, mop up, sew up, wind up, fold up, can, jell, clinch, close, sign, come through, knock off, polish off, top it off, all the way, put away, put the lid on, put to bed, get it together, go the route, take care of, call it a day, drop the curtain, ring down the curtain, deal coming down, do to a T, do to a frazzle, do to a finish.

CONSUMMATION n. payoff, wind-up, wrap, wrap-up, cleanup, mop-up, to a T, to a finish, to a frazzle. See END.

CONTACT n. in, connection, cutout, head to head, network, channel, rabbi. See INFLUENCE.

CONTACT v. interface, interact, network, connect, grok, reach out, relate, touch base. See COMMUNI-CATE.

CONTAIN v. cork, cork up, cool, cool off, cool down, hold down, bottle up, hog-tie, not go off the deep end, keep the lid on, put a half nelson on. See RESTRAIN.

CONTAINER n. bucket, hooker, tub, growler. See also BAG.

CONTAMINATED adj. cooked (radiation), dirty, exposed, mucked up, cruddy.

CONTEMPLATE v.   1. percolate, size up, take in, cool something over, chew over, kick around, bat it around. See THINK. 2. in the cards, it's looking to, see it coming, be afraid, wait for the other shoe to drop. See ANTICIPATED.

CONTEMPORARY adj.   state of the art, leading edge, now, contempo, fire new, hot off the press, just out. See NEW.

CONTEMPTIBLE adj.   heel, shit heel, dirty, cocksucking (Obsc.), low-down no-good, gweebo, rat, rat fink, fink, son of a bitch, SOB, fishball, chicken shit, the lowest, Melvin. See DESPICABLE.

CONTEMPTUOUS adj.   cool, cold shoulder, biggety, dicty, sidity, sidity, sniffy, snippy, snooty, snotty, uppish, uppity, upstage, king shit, high and mighty, high hat, high-hatted, high hatty, high-headed, high-nosed, on one's high horse, have one's glasses on (Bl.), crack the whip, throw one's weight around, come down on, dog it, cheeky, hard, hard-nosed, sticking the zingers in (remark). See also ARROGANT.

CONTEND v.   1. jockey for position, scramble for, go for, go for it, go for broke, go for the throat, go for the jugular, go after, make a play for, push, push for, knock oneself out, break one's neck, bust one's ass, shoot for, shoot at, shoot the works, give it one's all, give it all one's got. 2. handle, handle it, get a handle on something, hack, hack it, live with, make it, make a go of it. See ARGUE. 3. cross, take on, sock, sock it to one, break with, fly in the face of, in one's face, be agin, buck, nix, have a bone to pick, pettifog, put up an argument, set to, zap, zapper, pitch into, light into, lay into, wade into, lace into, sail into, come at, go at, lay at, have at, lean on, crack down on, gang up on, jump on, jump on one's case, jump down one's throat, come down on, come down hard on one, land on, lay a finger on, lay out, let have it, let have it with both barrels, give one both barrels, blast, rip, rip into, rip up, rip up one side and down the other, put up a fight, mix it up with, tangle with, bump heads with, cross swords with, lock horns with, stick it to one, push around. See also FIGHT.

CONTENDER n.   dark horse (unknown), white hope. See also COMPETING.

CONTENT adj.   fat dumb and happy, can't complain, have no kick coming, pleased as Punch, tickled, tickled pink, tickled to death. See HAPPY.

CONTENTION n.   hassle, static, beef, run-in, scrap, scene, set-to, bone to pick, bone of contention, flak, flak session, rhubarb, shindy, dead horse, wrangle. See ARGUE, FIGHT.

CONTENTIOUS adj.   salty, spiky, scrappy, bitchy, cantankerous, cussed, ornery, crabby, touchy, tetchy, chip on one's shoulder, fire-eater, forecastle lawyer. See BELLIGERENT.

CONTENTS n.   guts, innards, nub.

CONTEST n.   hassle, static, beef, row, rumble, run-in, scrap, brawl, set-to, duke out, go, bone to pick, bone of contention, battle royal, squelcher, wrangle, when push comes to shove. See ARGUMENT. See also FIGHT.

CONTEST v.   1. jockey for position, scramble for, go for, go for it, go for broke, go for the throat, go for the jugular, go after, go a couple of rounds, make a play for, push, push for, knock one's brains out, knock oneself out, break one's neck, bust one's ass, shoot for, shoot at, shoot the works, give it one's all, give it all one's got, jump on, jump on one's case, jump down one's throat, come down on, come down hard on one, land on, let have it with both barrels, give one both barrels, blast, tangle, tangle ass with, mix it up with, bump heads with, cross swords with, lock horns with, shoot it out with, stick it to one, push around, raise sand. See also ARGUE. 2. row, scrap, square off, square up, kick up a row, hassle, cross, take on, take a poke, sock, sock it to one, break with, fly in the face of, be agin, buck, nix, have a bone to pick, pettifog, put up an argument, set to, zap, zapper, pitch a bitch, pitch into, light into, lay into, wade into, lace into, sail into, come at, go at, lay at, have at, lean on, crack down on, gang up on, lay a finger on, lay out, let have it, duke, duke it out, put up one's dukes, romp, rip, rip into, rip up one side and down the other, slug, put the slug on one, put on the gloves, put up a fight, go up against, hook up with, knuckle with. See also FIGHT. 3. have the law on, law, haul into court, drag into court.

CONTESTANT n.   dark horse (unknown), white hope, hopeful. See also PRIZEFIGHTER.

CONTINGENCY n.   if money, if it's cool.

CONTINUE v.   get on with it, let it ride, keep on trucking. See also PERSIST.

CONTINUOUS adj.   no end of, no end to, on a treadmill, looped, day and night.

CONTINUOUSLY adv.   round the clock, day and night, right and left, for ever so long, for a coon's age, for a dog's age, for a month of Sundays, till hell freezes over, till you're blue in the face, till the cows come home, till shrimps learn to whistle.

CONTRABAND n.   stuff, goods, swag.

CONTRACEPTIVE n.   rubber, pro, pro pack, prophylactic, prophy, nightcap, raincoat, safety, bag, scumbag, Trojan, armor, skin, fish skin, French letter, Frenchy, purse, the pill, minipill; IUD, B.C., shield, pussy butterfly (inter-uterine device, Obsc.); rubber cookie, ring, catcher's mitt, plastic clam (diaphragm).

CONTRACT n.   deal, dicker, handshake, pact, papers. See AGREEMENT.

CONTRACT v. 1. pact, ink, sign, sign up, buy, set, re-up, hammer out a deal, hack out a deal, work out a deal, make a deal, firm a deal, clinch the deal, it's a deal, shake on, shake hands on, go along with, come around, you sold me, you got it. See also SHORTEN. 2. catch, come down with, take one's death.

CONTRADICT v. be agin, buck, cross, fly in the face of, have a bone to pick, take on, thumbs down, turn thumbs down on.

CONTRADICTORY adj. ornery, stuffy, agin, anti, con, no go.

CONTRAPTION n. gismo, gadget, jobby, motherfucker (Obsc.), whatchamacallit, thingamajig, dohickey. See APPARATUS.

CONTRARILY adv. arsy-varsy, on the other hand.

CONTRARY adj. anti, con, ornery, stuffy, no go, ass backwards, bass ackwards, topsy-turvy, be agin, be down on, have a bone to pick, have it in for, on the outs, at outs, at loggerheads, fly in the face of, copper a tip (act against advice), other side of the coin, flip side.

CONTRAST v. hang (how does that hang?), hold a candle to, stack up against, match up.

CONTRIBUTE v. 1. ante up, pony up, get it up, chip in, kick in, come through. See GIVE. 2. have a finger in, have a finger in the pie, get in the act, sit in on, put in one's two cents.

CONTRIBUTION n. handout, a hand, helping hand, write-off, gift, gifting, do one's part, chickadee checkoff, lump, poke out, maxed out (political limit).

CONTRIBUTOR n. angel, Santa Claus, sugar daddy, fairy godmother, lady bountiful, giver, heavy hitter, maxed out (Pol.).

CONTRIVANCE n. 1. angle, dodge, gimmick, slant, trick, twist, switch. 2. widget, contraption, dealie bob, sucker, mother, whatsis, gimcrack. See APPARATUS.

CONTRIVE v. 1. angle, finagle, mastermind, jockey, play games. See SCHEME. 2. cook up, dream up, trump up, whip up, frame up, come up with, throw together. See PLAN.

CONTRIVER n. hustler, finagler.

CONTROL n. juice, string, ropes, weight, clout, the high ground, the driver's seat, a lot to do with, a lot to say about, inside track, wire pulling. See also AUTHORITY.

CONTROL v. head, head up, mastermind, run, run things, run the show, push the buttons, handle, henpeck, quarterback, call the signals, call the play, call the shots, call the tune, deal with, truck with, be in the driver's seat, be in the saddle, ride herd on, crack the whip, wear the pants, rule the roost, keep under one's thumb, lead by the nose, kick one around, throw one's weight around, throw a lot of weight, twist around one's little finger, wind around one's little finger, have the upper hand, have the whip hand, have it covered, have the say, have the say so, have a lot to do with, have a lot to say about, do it your way, hold the aces, hold the reins, pull the ropes, pull the strings, pull the wires, wire-pull, reel one back in, bring to heel, box in, get one in a box, sit on top of, in front of, take the high ground, pussywhip (female). See also MANAGE.

CONTROLLED adj. cool, cool and collected, cool cat, laid back, dealing with, got a handle on it, hip, ice man, in charge, in the driver's seat. See CALM.

CONTROVERSY n. beef, row, scrap, scene, fuss, words, bone of contention, brush, flak, flak session, wrangle. See ARGUMENT.

CONTUSE v. bung, bung up, rough up, belt around, bang up. See WOUND. See also HIT.

CONVENE v. corral, round up, meet up, scare up, get together. See also MEET.

CONVENIENCE n. one's own sweet time, whenever.

CONVENIENT adj. user friendly, handy, all around, on deck, on tap.

CONVENTION n. confab, powwow, show, quadrennial circus, meet, clambake, get together. See MEETING.

CONVENTIONAL adj. straight, straight arrow, uptight, square, squaresville, cubeular, Elk (person), four square, white bread, plastic, lame, stuffy, drippy, rube, Clyde, Babbitt, buster, boy scout, jock, in line, in the groove, in a rut, by the numbers, by the book, according to Hoyle, playing their game, playing it safe, chicken.

CONVERSANT adj. hip, hep, cool, into, plugged in, all woke up, go-go, kept posted, on the beam. See KNOWLEDGEABLE.

CONVERSATION n. rap, yack-yack, gab, small talk, pillow talk (confidential), jive, chin music, eyeball-to-eyeball encounter, visit. See TALK.

CONVERSE v. gab, rap, yack, chew the fat, rag around, modjitate, shoot the shit, schmoose, fold one's ear, bat the chat. See SPEAK.

CONVERSION n. 1. about-face, flip-flop, switch, switchover. 2. come to Jesus, born again, see the light, hit the sawdust trail.

CONVERT v. 1. switch, switch over. See CHANGE. 2. see the light, come to Jesus, hit the sawdust trail, be born again.

CONVERTED adj. born again, got religion, new born Christian, saw the light.

CONVERTIBLE n. chopped top, no top, rag top.

CONVEY v. lug, pack, back, piggyback, birdie back, ride, shlep, shlep along, tote, truck, buck, gun, heel, hump, jag, shoulder, duke, weed, pass it on over.

CONVICT n. con, jailbird, vic, ex-con, lifer, two-time loser, yardbird, chain gang, rock crusher, PW, stir bird, rat, brig rat, goodie, hog, lag, lagger, robuck (bully), trusty, politician (privileged), merchant, eel, slippery eel, center man, real man, right guy, gee, geezo, gorilla, tough, punk, hipster, spear chicken, apple knocker, lane, Square John; fish, fresh one, jice, new jice, hoosier (new); hide out (escapist), short, short eyes (child molester).

CONVICT v. put away, send up, throw the book at, break one's license, frame, frame up. See SENTENCE.

CONVICTION n. 1. judgment call, op, say so, slant, two cents' worth, vox pop. 2. rap, fall.

CONVINCE v. brainwash, sell one on, hook, hook in, put across, turn one's head around, schmeikle, twist one's arm, make a believer out of one. See PERSUADE.

CONVINCED adj. sold, satisfied, bought.

CONVIVIAL adj. glad-hander, clubby, elbow-bender.

CONVOCATION n. get-together, turnout, meet, clambake, confab, powwow. See MEETING.

CONVULSIVE adj. spaz, herky-jerky, have a fit, throw a fit.

COOK n. cookie, hasher, hash slinger, belly burglar, gut burglar, belly robber, biscuit roller, chocker, grease pot, grub chocker, jeppo, ninety-nine, boiler (logger), pot slinger, sizzler, builder, stew builder. See also BAKER.

COOK v. burn, cremate, doctor, ruin, spoil.

COOKIES n. dry cush.

COOLING adj. warming down.

COOPER n. bungs, Jimmy Bungs (ship).

COOPERATE v. partner, go partners, get together, throw in together, be in cahoots with, do business with, work hand in glove with, team up with, throw in with, go along with, get in bed with, live with, play ball, play the game. See also COLLABORATE.

COOPERATIVE adj. team player.

COOPERATIVE n. coop, co-op. See ASSOCIATION.

COORDINATE v. get it together, get one's act together, get one's ducks together, pull together, pull things together, team up, shape up, quarterback. See ARRANGE.

COORDINATES n. fix, spot.

CO-OWNER n. pard, pardner, buddy, buddy-buddy.

CO-OWNERSHIP n. go partners, get-together, throw in together, in cahoots with, team up with, throw in with, join up with, line up with, in the same bed with.

COPE v. hack, hack it, handle, handle it, get a handle on something, make it, make a go of it, live with.

COPILOT n. kid, meter reader, stooge.

COPIOUS adj. heavy, aplenty, a mess, galore, no end, up to one's ass in, coming out of one's ears, alive with, crawling with, thick with. See PLENTY.

COPULATE v. fuck, screw, lay, hump, ball, bang, boff, dork, jazz, shag, shtup, jump on one's bones, make it, make out, go all the way, do the dirty deed, go to bed with, spread for (Fem.), get it on, get to first base, put the boots to, hide the salami, parallel park (all Obsc.). See SEXUAL INTERCOURSE.

COPULATION n. fuck, screw, lay, nookie, balling, go the limit, score, matinee, nooner, quickie, parallel parking, night baseball, a little heavy breathing, roll in the hay, he'n and she'n, fun and games (all Obsc.). See SEXUAL INTERCOURSE.

COPY n. 1. ditto, dupe, xerox, clone, carbon, carbon copy, mimeo, stat, repro, knock off, flimsy. 2. look-alike, work alike, ringer, dead ringer, copycat, spitting image, spit and image, chip off the old block, double, peas in a pod, twin, ——— compatible (P.C. compatible). 3. fake, phony, knock-off, pirate.

COPY v. 1. dupe, xerox, carbon, clone, mimeo, ditto, knock off, stat. 2. act like, do, do like, go like, make like, mirror, take off as, do a take-off, play the ——— (affect a role). 3. pirate, fake, phony, knock-off, steal one's stuff, take a leaf out of one's book.

COQUETTE n. vamp, operator, player, swinger, man trap, velvet trap, cruiser, gold digger, wolverine.

CORDIAL adj. buddy-buddy, clubby, mellow (close), cozy, palsy-walsy, red-carpet treatment. See FRIENDLY.

CORE n. bottom line, heart, meat and potatoes, nitty gritty, nub. See BASIC.

CORNED BEEF n. Irish turkey (with cabbage), horse, red horse, salt horse, young horse.

CORNED BEEF HASH n. corn bill, corn willie, corned willie.

CORNER v. tree, have one up a tree, chase up a tree, chase up a stump, mousetrap.

CORNET n. quail.

CORNETIST n. brass officer, lip splitter.

CORPORATION n. The Company, syndicate, megacorp, multinational, plunderbund, clan, jungle, zoo, hookup, tie in, tie up, bunch, crew, crowd, gang, mob, outfit, ring, shell. See also ASSOCIATION, BUSINESS.

CORPORATION OFFICERS n. CEO, execs, exec suite, board, biggies, big shot, brass, front office, toppers, upstairs. See also EXECUTIVE.

CORPSE n. dead meat, cold meat, fly bait, body, loved one, remains, stiff, cage, carcus, croppy.

CORPULENT adj. fat city, fat slob, beef trust, baby elephant, hefty, blimp, Mr. Five by Five. See FAT.

CORPUS CHRISTI, TEXAS Taco Town.

CORRAL v. poke, punch, sweep.

CORRECT adj. keerect, on the nose, on the button, on the numbers, on the money, right on the money, on the ball, on the beam, on target, on track, on the right track, dead on, right on, righteous, right you are, right as rain, right-o, bull's-eye, good eye, hit the nail on the head, an A, fuckin' A, S.O.P., amen, you better believe it, that's for sure, kosher, okay, OK, right stuff, reet, solid, stone, cut it fine, draw it fine, dot the i's and cross the t's, cook with gas, cook on the front burner, chop-chop, you said a mouthful, you're darn tootin', according to Hoyle. See also CONVENTIONAL.

CORRECT v. 1. debug, doctor, fly speck, launder, scrub, clean up, pick up, shape up, fix up, go over, fiddle with. 2. straighten up and fly right, straighten out, go straight, follow the straight and narrow, clean up one's act, get one's act together, get with it, get on the ball, shape up, upgrade, make first rate, recalibrate, dial back, turn around, turn things around, turn over a new leaf, mat down, take a brace. See also IMPROVE. 2. make up for, pay one's dues, square, square up, square the beef. See also RECOMPENSE.

CORRELATE v. tune in on, be on the same wavelength, have good vibes, have good vibrations.

CORRESPOND v. 1. lip sync, sync, sync up. 2. drop a note, drop a line, scribble a line, scribble a note, drop a kite, tab a kite, fly a kite (airmail, also a letter smuggled in or out of prison), knock out a tab, pen, put pen to paper.

CORRESPONDENT n. stringer, telewriter (TV), news hen, pen pal. See WRITER.

CORROBORATE v. check out, check up, check on, check up on, double check, okay, OK, rubber-stamp, give the nod. See CONFIRM.

CORROBORATION n. go ahead, green light, okay, OK, rubber stamp, check, double check.

CORRUPT adj. on the take, on the pad, money talks bullshit walks, open, wide open, meat-eater, racket up, tainted, something rotten in Denmark, gone to bad, gone to the dogs, gone to hell, fast and loose. See also DISHONEST.

CORRUPT v. brainwash, hook, get one hooked, lead one down the primrose path.

CORRUPTION n. juice, payoff, payoff money, payola, drugola, gayola, under the table, oil, on the take, padding, shake, skimming, squeeze, boodle, hat. See also BRIBE, PROTECTION MONEY.

CORVETTE n. Vette.

COSMETICS n. makeup, paint, war paint, drugstore complexion, glob, globby, glop, gloppy, goo, gook, goonk, goopy, goup, gunk.

COST n. price tag, bad news, damage, score, tab, bite, nut, nick, dues, tick, ticket, squeeze, a throw, set one back, come to, what's it come to?, to the tune of, tidy sum, hummer, bigger bang for the buck, arm and a leg, highway robbery, highway mopery, back, top dollar, bottom dollar, bottom line, below the line, line, nickel and dime (minor), outlay, paid the piper.

COST v. come to, move back, set one back, stood, to the tune of.

COSTLY adj. pricey, cher, dear, steep, stiff, executive, heavy sugar, an arm and a leg, highway robbery. See EXPENSIVE.

COST OF LIVING ADJUSTMENT n. COLA.

COSTUME n. getup, outfit.

COTERIE n. groupies, bunch, click, crew, crowd, crush, gang, mob, outfit, ring, insiders, followers, fans, buddies, rat pack.

COTTON GIN n. flying jinny, jenny.

COUGH n. hack, bark, croup.

COUGH SYRUP n. turps, terps.

COUNCIL n. brain trust, kitchen cabinet, groupthink, gang, mob, ring, clan, outfit, confab, huddle, powwow, meet. See also GROUP MEETING.

COUNSEL n. 1. steer, bum steer, kibitz, flea in the ear, one's two cents' worth, tip, tip-off, word to the wise. 2. mouthpiece, beak, beagle, legal eagle, lip, patch, bomber (divorce). See ATTORNEY.

COUNSEL v. steer, tout, tip, tip off, give one a tip, give a pointer to, put one in the picture, put on to, put on to something hot, put hip, put hep, put a bug in one's ear, put a flea in one's ear, fold an ear, put in one's two cents, put one wise, wise one up, keep posted, show one the ropes, lace one's boots, confab, get heads together, huddle. See also ADVISE.

COUNSELOR n. 1. mouthpiece, man's mouth, beak, beagle, legal beagle, legal eagle, squeal, bomber (divorce), ambulance chaser, shyster, front, lip, mugger, spieler, spouter, tangle jaw, tongue, warble, fixer, springer, ghost (writes briefs), cutor, cutter (prosecutor), the D.A., pleader, pettifogger, Philadelphia lawyer. 2. tout, tipster, clubhouse lawyer, jailhouse lawyer, guardhouse lawyer, kibitzer, armchair general, Monday morning quarterback, Dutch uncle, buttinsky, backseat driver; God Committee, God Squad (both Medic.).

COUNT v. tot, tot up, tote, tote up, run down, tick off, count heads, count noses, count the house, cut ice, cut some ice, keep tab, keep tabs, dope out, figure in, figure out, take account of, reckon up.

COUNTENANCE n. looks, mug, phiz, phizog, kisser, puss, map, mush, moosh, pan, deadpan, poker face, dial, biscuit, clock, conk, chevy chase, gills, index, mask, potato, squash, sourpuss, picklepuss, sugarpuss, cut of one's jib, front.

COUNTENANCE v. 1. live with, go along with, put up with, bear with, cope, handle, hear of, swallow, stomach something, grin and bear it, stand for, sit still for. See also ENDURE. 2. okay, sign off on, thumbs up, put one's John Hancock on, get behind, go for, have eyes for, give the nod, give the green light, give the stamp of approval. See ACCEPT.

COUNTER n. chow line, coffee pot (lunch).

COUNTER v. be agin, go agin, buck, cross, fly in the face of, have a bone to pick, take on, thumbs down, turn thumbs down on, sass, backtalk, top, put the blocks to. See OPPOSE. See also HINDER.

COUNTERCULTURE n. underground, flower children, hippy, yippie, street people, weathermen.

COUNTERFEIT adj. phony, queer, fake, faked, bogue, junque, pseud, pseudo, put on, autobogophobia (fear of bogosity), bogosity, bogotified, hokey, ersatz, pirate goods, pirate labels, bum, bent, falsie, wrong, wrong number, two-faced, fishy, frame, framed, plant, planted (evidence), crock, crock of shit, sincere, not kosher, not what it's cracked up to be, no such animal, soft shell, it won't fly, stiffing it, gil, Hollywood. See also FALSE.

COUNTERFEIT n. bogue, bunco, bunko, bum, junque, phony, pseud, pseudo, actor, put-on. See also FORGERY.

COUNTERFEIT v. fake, phony, phony up, dupe, knock off, xerox, carbon, clone, mimeo, stat, ditto, do, do like, act like, go like, make like, make out like.

COUNTERFEITER n. penman, raiser, designer, maker, scratcher, scratch man, one of a scratch mob, butterfly man, scrip, script writer, short-story writer, connection, queer hustler, cobbler, paperhanger; bill poster, shoe (also passports); penciler, tracer (crude).

COUNTERFEIT MONEY n. paper, wallpaper, funny paper, funny money, phony money, queer, bogus, sourdough, boodle, backs, fronts, hot dough, shuffle, stiff, green goods, long green, gypsy bankroll; plug, slug, cluck, stumer (coin).

COUNTERFEIT MONEY, DISSEMINATE v. pass, pass the queer, shove, shove the queer, paper, lay paper, smack with.

COUNTERMAN n. jerk, soda jerk.

COUNTERPART n. carbon copy, ringer, dead ringer, ditto, spit and image, spitting image, look alikes, peas in a pod, two of a kind. See COPY.

COUNTLESS adj. zillion, jillion, mucho, eleventeen, umpteen, umptieth, umpty-umpth, load, loads, loaded, raft, rafts, slew, whole slew, wad, gobs, scads, mess, mint, mucho, pack, peck, heap, pile, bags of, oodles, lots of, lousy with, stack, stacks, passel, tidy sum, more than one can shake a stick at, no end of, no end to, thick as fleas on a hound dog, thick as flies, thick as hail.

COUNT ON v. bank on, bet on, bet one's bottom dollar on, take as gospel truth, score, tab.

COUNTRY n. boondocks, boonies, sticks, stix, woods, outback, up country.

COUNTRYMAN n. landsman, paesano, paisano.

COUPLE n. item, duo, deuce it, gruesome twosome, team, pair off, twosome, spic and span (Black and Puerto Rican).

COURAGE n. balls, brass balls, guts, gutsiness, guttiness, heart, nerve, stomach, what it takes, grit, true grit, spunk, backbone, moxie, starch, clock, corazon, chutzpah, intestinal fortitude, bottled courage, Dutch courage (intoxicated). See also DARING.

COURAGEOUS adj. game, gritty, gutsy, gutty, spunky, nervy, stand tall, tough it out, bigger'n life, fire eater, hairy, cool hand. See FEARLESS.

COURIER n. bagman, runner, mule, gofer, gopher, speedy, smurf (carries illegal money to launder it).

COURSE n. 1. groove, rut, boards, aisle, byway, stroll. 2. that a way, every which way, forty ways to Sunday, forty ways from Sunday. 3. channels, red tape, by the numbers, by the book. See also PROCEDURE.

COURSE (COLLEGE) n. gut course, pipe course, snap course, slider (easy); hardcore, killer, grinder (hard); rip, pud, undergrad, grad, postgrad, doc, post doc.

COURT n. kangaroo court (mock or harsh small town), train station (traffic).

COURT v. date, go together, go steady, go with, keep company, chase, run after, make time with, rush, head rush, sashay, sashay out with, walk out with, spark, squire, play up to, set one's cap for, snow.

COURTHOUSE n. blindfolded lady with the scales.

COUSIN n. cuz.

COVENANT n. deal, dicker, handshake, pact, papers. See AGREEMENT.

COVER n. drop, dubok, front (all places used to hide illegal transactions), fig leaf.

COVERED adj. under wraps, doggo, incog, q.t.

COVERED WITH adj. lousy with, mangy with, dripping with.

COVERT adj. under wraps, undercover, hush-hush, creep (mission), tref, triff, doggo, incog, q.t., go black. See SECRET.

COVERTLY adv. undercover, under wraps, hush-hush, strictly hush-hush, on the q.t., on the quiet, on the sly, in a hole-and-corner way, in holes and corners, wildcat.

COVER UP v. 1. beard, cover up, wear cheaters, slap on some glims, flash the gogs, throw on a make up, phony up one's get up. 2. cover for, stonewall, take the rap for, whitewash, put on an act, front, front for, put up a front, put on a front, put on a false front, go to the front for, play the goat. 3. finesse it, launder, whitewash, palm, paper over, squash, squelch, keep it under one's hat, keep under wraps, keep the lid on, put the lid on, sweep under the rug, pull the wool over one's eyes.

COVET v. yen, yen for, have the hots for, hard-on for, itch for, spoil for, have one's mouth fixed for, lech, lech for. See DESIRE.

COVETOUS adj. green-eyed, jelly.

COW n. bossie, Bossy, moo cow, moo moo, Nellie, Elsie.

COW v. buffalo, bulldoze, chicken out, enforce, lean on, push around, showboat, turn on the heat, walk heavy. See INTIMIDATE.

COWARD n. chicken, chicken heart, chicken liver, lily liver, white liver, yellow, yellow belly, candy ass, pecker ass, fraid cat, fraidy cat, scaredy cat, jellyfish, weak sister, sissy, baby, big baby, dancer, deuce, piker, mouse, milksop, Milquetoast, Casper Milquetoast, gutless, gutless wonder, nebbish, nerd, turkey. See also WEAKLING.

COWARDLY adj. yellow, 'fraidy cat, run scared, scared shitless, the willies, rabbity, chicken, lily livered, milk candy ass, paper tiger. See AFRAID.

COXSWAIN n. cox.

COZY adj. comfy, cushy, snug as a bug in a rug, in clover, in velvet, on a bed of roses.

CRACKERS n. dog biscuits.

CRAFTY adj. foxy, crazy like a fox, smart, smarts, street smarts, streetwise, cagey, fancy footwork, full of fancy footwork, slick, slippery, sly boots, smooth. See also SHREWD.

CRAM v. 1. jam, jam pack, pack 'em in, pack like sardines, sardine, ram in, chock, chockablock, stuff, fill to the brim, top off. 2. hit the books, megabook, heavy booking, shed, speed, pull an all-nighter, burn the midnight oil. See STUDY.

CRAMP n. charley horse.

CRANIUM n. biscuit, headbone, ivory. See HEAD.

CRANKY adj. bitchy, mean, ornery, tetchy, out of sorts, a bear, cantankerous, cussed, grouchy, grumpy, snappish, ugly, got up on the wrong side of the bed. See IRRITABLE.

CRAPS TERMS snake eyes, boxcars, Big Dick (10), natural, 7 come 11, 8 the hard way, fever, Phoebe (5), little Joe, eighter from Decatur; dominoes, African dominoes, African golf (both Derog.); perfects, bones, ivories, flats (dice); no dice, you're faded, covered, come out, come, crap out, buy the back line.

CRASH n. 1. total, crunch, crack-up, pileup, rack-up, stack-up, smashup, smash into, sideswipe, fenderbender, fender tag, rear ender. 2. pancake, ditch, washout, splashdown, prang (aircraft). See also AIRPLANE CRASH.

CRASH v. 1. crunch, crack up, pile up, smash up, wrack up, sideswipe, fender bend, fender tag, rear end, bang into, nerf. 2. bite the dust, pancake, washout, prang, ditch, splash down, go in, auger in (WW II, aircraft). See also AIRPLANE CRASH.

CRAVAT n. choker, chocker, noose, stretcher.

CRAVE v. yen for, itch for, hanker for, spoil for, give one's eyeteeth for, die for, eat one's heart out. See DESIRE.

CRAVEN adj. wuss, wimp, wimpy, nebbish, weak-kneed. See WEAKLING.

CRAVING n. the munchies (food), yen, yen yen, have one's tongue hanging out for, have one's mouth fixed for, carry a torch for, it is to die for, lech, itch, hurting. See DESIRE.

CRAZE n. kick, in, in-thing, the latest thing, the last word, newest wrinkle, wrinkle. See RAGE.

CRAZINESS n. cloud cuckoo land, battiness, daffiness, goofiness, nuttiness, sappiness, screwiness, whackiness.

CRAZY adj. dippy, dingy, ding-a-ling, kooky, flaky, wacky, whacko, loco, blue loco, unglued, unzipped, unscrewed, screwy, screwball, screwed up, screwloose, have a screw loose, loose in the bean, loose in the upper story, schitzy, schizzed out, schitzoid, psycho, psyched out, freaked out, zonked out, flippo, flipped, flipped out, flipped one's lid, flipped one's wig, flipped one's stack, nobody home, out to lunch, out of one's tree, out of one's gourd, out of one's head, out of one's skull, out of one's mind, baked, totally baked, fried, in the ozone, over the edge, crackers, bananas, banana pie, bonkers, bonkers in the conkus, ape, ape shit, gone ape, gone ape shit, nertz, nuts, nutsy fagan, just plain nuts, nut cake, nutty, fruity, fruitcakey, nutty as a fruitcake, cockeyed, cockamamie, cracked, cracked up, crackpot, freaky, off one's nut, off one's rocker, off one's head, off one's trolley, off the track, off one's hinges, off in the upper story, off the wall, up the wall, minus some buttons, missing a few buttons, not have all one's buttons, missing a few marbles, not have all one's marbles, lost one's marbles, half deck, not playing with a full deck, tetched, touched, touched in the head, bats, batty, bats in the belfry, mad as a hatter, mad as a March hare, mad as a weaver, mad as a coot, crazy as a coot, crazy as a loon, loony, looneytune, crazier than a bedbug, cutting out paper dolls, leak in the think tank, snakes in one's head, hairpin, haywire, funny, birdie (teenage), dotty, potty, cuckoo, in cloud cuckoo land, gone, not all there, not right in the head, meshuga, meshugana, round the bend, squirrelly, yo-yo, sappy, goofy, scatterbrain, lamebrain, dick-brained, a case, snap case, headcase, snapped, sickie, section 8, non compos, non compos mentis, barmy, loopy, beany, buggy, bugs, bughouse, slaphappy, gaga, daffy, daffydill, pixilated.

CRAZY, GO v. crack up, flip out, go ape, go ape shit, come unglued, come unzipped, flake out, schitz out, psych out, freak out, snap, nut up. See INSANE, GO.

CREAM n. come, cum, cow juice, moo juice.

CREAM AND SUGAR n. blonde 'n sweet.

CREAM CHEESE n. shmeer (on a bagel).

CREAMY adj. gloppy, gooey, gook, gooky, goonk, gunk, gunky, goup, goopy.

CREASE v. dog ear.

CREATE v. 1. cook up, dream up, whip up, whomp up, trump up, come up with, hatch, craft, bat out, knock out, knock off, knock together, fudge together, throw together, throw up, blow, blow one's soul, dash off, pull off, get off, come through with, noodle, doodle around. See also DEVISE. 2. head trip, think up, make up, dream up, brainstorm, spark, spitball, take it off the top of one's head. 3. author, bat out, coin a phrase, pen, drive a pencil, knock off hen tracks on a rolltop piano (type), script, scriven, mount (theatrical). See WRITE.

CREATIVE adj. cool, far out, hep, hip, way out, leading edge.

CREATURE n. critter, varmint.

CREDENCE n. gospel truth, stock, store.

CREDENTIALS, FORGED n. button, creed, flash, paper, tin.

CREDIBLE adj. up front, straight, straight shit, no shit, no bullshit, aboveboard, honest to God, one's stock has gone up. See BELIEVABLE.

CREDIT n. 1. have plastic, on the tab, on the cuff, on the arm, on the muscle, on pump, on tick, tick, extension (maximum). 2. points, Brownie points, strokes, pat on the back. See COMMENDATION. 3. gospel truth, stock, store.

CREDIT v. buy, set store by, take as gospel truth, got to hand it to one, take stock in, pat on the back. See BELIEVE.

CREDITABLE adj. not too shabby, gnarly, nasty, organic, doin' a hundred, batting a thousand, a prince of a fellow, pillar of the church, Jesus bread, Christian, true Christian, salt of the earth. See PRAISEWORTHY.

CREDIT CRISIS n. crunch, squeeze, mid course correction.

CREDIT, EXTEND v. lug, finance.

CREDIT RATING n. D and B.

CREDULOUS adj. fall for, swallow whole, swallow hook line and sinker, take the bait, be taken in, easy mark. See GULLIBLE.

CREEP v. gumshoe, pussyfoot, creepy, crawly.

CRESTFALLEN adj. down, taken down, blue, singing the blues, ass in a sling, down in the dumps. See DEPRESSED.

CREW n. bunch, crowd, gang, mob, hands, team.

CRIME n. caper, racket, heavy racket, job, wrongdoing, hit, hit and run, case, caser, hustle, make, move, promote, bloomer, fast one, quickie, sneak, lay, gaff, touch, grift, score, beat, piece of work, dirty work, riffle, trick, keister, mooch, nick.

CRIME, COMMIT A v. cross the line, set up (plans for), spill the lay, lay out, lay the gaff, spring the gaff; give one a steer, give one a send in, tout (supply with leads); blind steer, bum steer, steer wrong, wrong steer, phony steer, steer, press, (supply with faulty leads); cut in for a gapper's bit, cut in on a touch, declare in, ring in, case, caser, case out, spot (inspect site for), clock, peg a joint, smoke a joint, feeler, put the pike on, duke in, tip, tip off, wire (tip leading up to), beat, caper, clout, job, racket, riffle, candy, make, a sweet make, nice thing, red one, tumul, tumuling (regularly engaged in), making a clean buck, turning a smart buck (nonviolent), bend the law, bang to rights; run the roads down, break out, charge out, mooch out on the grift, get out on the hustle, go out on a piece of work, go out on a touch, plunge out on a score, cut out on the stem, step out on a caper, stepping out, go on a trick, hit the heavy time, hit the hard way, hit and run, hit the turf (leave for scene of), in action, on the hustle, on the make, on the move, on the promote, on the turf, on the sail, out for a buck, racketeering, hip up on the score, pull off a job, pull a heist, pull a one-two play, pull a fast one, pull a quickie, pull a sneak, cop a sneak, play a matinee, stick, hump to death, smash and grab, cop and blow (swiftly); blow, bollix, boot, boot around, crab, crab a play, crimp, crumb a deal, jim, jim a deal, shape up, louse up, mess up, burn up, knock up, piss up, piss in a snowbank, play a bloomer, pull a bloomer, queer, rank, rank a joint, rank a mark, rank and lam, rank a play, screw up (bungle); rehash, reload, go back for seconds (against same victim); screw up (exhaust an area); a nice score, a good touch (profitable venture); blank, stiff, bloomer, fritzer, lemon, skunk, stiffo, a t.b., turkey (profitless venture).

CRIME INSTRUCTOR n.   fagin.

CRIME, ORGANIZED n.   Mafia, Mafioso, Cosa Nostra, famiglia, family, Organization, our organization, outfit, the People, syndicate, the mob, the arm, the gang, crime cartel, the commission.

CRIME, PETTY n.   fink caper, lousy caper, rat caper, spitting on the sidewalk, stabbing a horse and stealing his blanket.

CRIMINAL adj.   crooked, heavy, off base, out of line, racket, shady, caught in the act, caught red-handed, caught with one's hand in the cookie jar, dirty, hung up, hung up with, smoking gun, wildcat.

CRIMINAL n.   perp, crook, chiseler, hood, con, ex-con, heavy, heel, hustler, hot, mug, mugger, dropper, bad actor, bad egg, bad guy, the boys, the boys uptown, deuce (small time), dropper, eel, slippery eel, fagin, shylock, F.F.V., finger, finger man, finger mob (gang), fish, jailbird, yardbird, goodie, hog, hoosier (new), lag, vic, muzzler, arm man, blotto, cat burglar, gorilla, guerilla, hep broad, hep ghee, hipster, moll, gun moll, racketeer, in man, inside man, pick man, box man, second-story man, wrong, wrongo, wrong number, gangster, mobster, hoodlum, hooligan, wheel man (driver), mooner, plug ugly, strongarm man, muscle man, goon, gunsel, trigger man, piece man, button man, torpedo, hatchet man, marker; mob marker, prowler, spotter, steerer, ten percenter, tipster (spotter of victims), two-time loser, repeater, all caught up, all washed up. See also THIEF.

CRIMINAL CHARGE n.   pinch, beef, right fall, right beef, stiff beef, stiff rap, right rap, tough rap (supported by ample evidence); mopery in the first degree, mopery collar, mopery rap, walkout rap, wrapup rap (supported by little evidence); bum beef, bum finger, bum rap, frame up, hummer, phony rap, plant, wrong beef, wrong rap (unjust); chill, chill a beef, chill a rap, fix, jerk off a rapper, spike, square a rapper, get the rapper to pull off, square, square a beef, square a pinch, squash a holler, squash a rap, yank a sticker, play the deuce of clubs (quash or withdrawal of charges).

CRIMINAL, IDENTIFY v.   finger, put the finger on, make, make one's kisser, make one's mug, make one's prints (at scene of crime), card, peg, flop, rumble, toss, blow, give one a blow, call the turn, shag, tumble. See IDENTIFY.

CRIMINAL RECORD n.   pedigree, record, cherry (no record).

CRIMINAL RECORDS n.   rap sheet, yellow sheet.

CRIMINAL'S TOOLS n.   books, hardware, pig, stuff.

CRIMINAL VICTIM n.   touch, square John, stiff, sucker, turkey, yuld, grift, light time (nonviolent action), score, trick, blank, payoff ghee, sailor, scissorbill, springfield, come on, degenerate, hoosier, jay, keister mark, mooch; good giver up, soft giver up, lush, sweet mark, soft touch, sweetheart (docile victim); lush who won't go, sucker who kicks over, mark who kicks up, sleeper, tough giver up (victim who resists).

CRIPPLED adj.   crip, gimp, gimpy, game, g'd up, geed up, hamstrung, hog-tied, sidelined, out of commission.

CRISIS n.   crunch, clutch, in a clutch, pinch, in a pinch, squeeze, in a squeeze, crash, bummer, downer, drag, rub, boxed in, in a box, in a fix, in a hole, jam, in a jam, spot, on the spot, put on the spot, tight spot, in a spot, in a tight spot, in a mess, in a pickle, in a scrape, in a stew, in deep water, in over one's head, up the creek, up the creek without a paddle, up shit creek, up shit creek without a paddle, up a tree, behind the eight ball, zero hour, flap, flashpoint, push the panic button, hit the panic button, when the shit hits the fan, fire in the belly, heats on, hurry-up call, matter of life and death, when push comes to shove, when the chips are down, when the going gets tough, when things get tough, tough going, hard going, hard time, hot potato, bitch, hooker, grabber, joker, catch 22, double trouble, hit a snag, cropper, come a cropper, have one's ass in a sling, one small difficulty, sticky wicket, large order, squeeze, crash, glitch; meltdown, China syndrome (nuclear).

CRISIS MANAGEMENT n.   troubleshooter, fireman, fixer.

CRITIC n.   aisle-sitter, Monday morning quarterback, nitpicker, zapper.

CRITICAL adj. hanging by a thread, on slippery ground, on thin ice, touch and go, touchy, chips are down, fire in the belly, heats on, hurry-up call, matter of life and death, behind the eight ball, up the creek, up the creek without a paddle, up shit creek without a paddle.

CRITICISM n. 1. call down, put down, rap, rap on the knuckles, slap on the wrist, cut, cutting, flak, hit, knock. 2. write-up, notice, rave, pan, scorcher, sideswipe, slam, slap, sleighride, static, swipe, the bird, zapper, Bronx cheer, lemon.

CRITICIZE v. trash, bash, zing, zap, rap, knock, nitpick, pan, slam, slug, slog, hit, scorch, blister, roast, clobber, blast, blast on, lambaste, trim, fluff, take down, take down a peg, call down, dress down, put down, run down, come down on, come down hard on, land on, do a number on, sit on, lean on, jump on, jump all over, cut, cut down to size, cut in half, cut to bits, rip, skin alive, bad mouth, poor mouth, sock it to one, swipe at, snipe at, lay out, read one out, go after, let one have it, stick it to one, sail into, tear into, light into, throw the book at one, take a potshot at, take a swipe at, tee off on one, rake, rake up one side and down the other, rake over the coals, haul over the coals, jack up, needle, give one the needle, give one the heat, give a black eye, give it to, give a going over, give what for, give one the raspberry, boo, bronx cheer, attend to, bitch, bitch bitch bitch, sound off, pop off, dim view, take a dim view.

CRITIQUE n. pan, takedown, putdown, rap, flak, slam, slap, write-up, notice, zapper. See CRITICISM.

CRONY n. buddy, bosom buddy, good buddy, asshole buddy, pardner, mellow (close), old man, mate, pal, sidekick. See FRIEND.

CROOKED adj. zigzag, screwy, kinky, agee, agee jawed, wamper jawed, catawampus, slaunchways, slaunchwise, cockeyed, hell west and crooked, jack deuce, skewed, skewgee, topsy-turvy, yaw ways.

CROOKED HORSE RACE n. boat race, fixed, the fix is in, jockey ring, doctor (one who drugs); hop up, slow pill, fast pill (drug); battery, buzzer, joint (all used to shock horse).

CROSS v. be agin, go agin, buck, sass, backtalk, queer, crimp, cramp, put a crimp in, stymie, crab, foul up, fuck up, louse up, snafu, bollix, stonewall, flummox, stump, gum, gum up the works, throw a monkey wrench into the works, spike one's guns, take on, take the wind out of one's sails, knock the bottom out of, knock the chocks from under one, knock the props from under one, have a bone to pick, put the blocks to, put one's nose out of joint, upset one's apple cart.

CROSS EXAMINATION n. third, third degree.

CROSS EXAMINE v. sweat, grill, put the screws to, third degree, put through the third degree. See QUESTION.

CROSS-EYED adj. cockeye, cockeyed.

CROSSING POINT n. checkpoint Charlie (Berlin).

CROTCH n. snatch.

CROUPIER n. dealer, bank, book, box man, cutter, house, man behind the gun, man behind the stick, stick, stickman.

CROWBAR n. bar, James, jimmy, shamus, stick.

CROWD n. jam, jam up, jam pack, mob, push, turnout, blowout, sellout, crush, everybody and his brother, everybody and his uncle, loaded to the rafters, wall-to-wall people, riffraff, cattle, ragtag, ragtag and bobtail, the great unwashed. See also GROUP, MEETING.

CROWD v. jam, jam-pack, pack 'em in, pack like sardines, sardine, stuff, ram in, chock, chockablock, top off.

CROWDED adj. mobbed, mob scene, packed, jammed, jam-packed, filled to the rafters, full up, up to the hilt, full as a tick, full house, right to the roof, SRO, standing room only, sold out; clean, gone clean (The.); topped off, lousy with, crumbed up with, crummy with, stiff with, swagged up with, up to here, fit to bust, packed like sardines, sardined, fanny bumper, wall-to-wall people.

CRUCIAL adj. showdown, face off, hanging by a thread, on slippery ground, on thin ice, touch and go, touchy. See CRITICAL. See also COARSE.

CRUDE adj. grody, grody to the max, knuckle dragger, loud, loud-mouthed, raunchy, raw, tacky, cheap, skank.

CRUDENESS n. raunch.

CRUEL adj. bad ass, bad-assed, wild-assed, bitchy, cussed, dirty, mean, mean machine, ornery, rough, tough, nuts, poison, bum, lousy, murder, murderous, kill-crazy, hard, butter wouldn't melt in his mouth, got lead balls for eyes, doin' dirt, eighteen carat, hellish.

CRUELLY adv. deadpan, in cold blood, with a poker face, with a straight face, something fierce, something terrible.

CRUISE v. gunkhole (sailing ad lib).

CRUSH v. 1. squash, squish, scrunch, kablooey, romp, total. 2. put away, dump, dump on, shit on, hit, hurt. See HUMILIATE. 3. squelch, ice, kill, put the lid on, blow away, blow one out, snow under. See REPRESS.

CRUSHED adj. 1. crawling, draw in one's horns, eat crow, eat dirt, eat humble pie, sing small. See HUMILIATED. 2. busted, in smithereens, totalled, kablooey, scrunched, squished, squashed, bunged up, cut up. 3. down, a downer, down in the dumps, let down, taken down, taken down a peg, blue, in a blue funk, singing the blues. See DEPRESSED. 4. blown away, blown out, blown out of the water, zapped. See DEFEATED.

CRUTCH n. gimp stick.

CRUX n. nub, heart, meat and potatoes, bottom line, nitty-gritty.

CRY n. fuss, holler, hoot and holler, yawp, ruckus.

CRY v. 1. blubber, bawl, break down, boo hoo, let go, let it out, let it all out, shed bitter tears, weep bitter tears, turn on the water works, cry one's eyes out, cry me a river, sing the blues, crack up, die, laugh on the other side of one's face, put on the weeps. 2. holler, holler out, yawp.

CRYING n. waterworks, weeps.

CRYSTALLIZE v. gel, jell, set, set up.

CUBAN n. hatchet thrower, spic.

CUCKOLD v. creep, put the horns on, stretch the rubber, two-time.

CUCUMBER n. cuke.

CUDDLE v. feel up, grab ass (Obsc.).

CUDGEL n. sap, billy, nightstick, mace, shill. See CLUB.

CUE n. 1. high sign, lead, hot lead, nod, tip off. 2. feed, feed line.

CUE CARD n. idiot board, idiot cards, teleprompter.

CUL-DE-SAC n. dead end.

CULMINATE v. top it off, go the route, go over the mountain, blow one's wad, shoot one's wad. See also CONSUMMATE.

CULMINATION n. blow off, capper, critical mass, payoff, all the way.

CULPABLE adj. caught in the act, caught red-handed, caught with one's hand in the cookie jar, dirty, hung up, hung up with, smoking gun, off base, out of line.

CULPRIT n. con, jailbird, goodie, hog, hoosier (new), lag, vic, yardbird, ex-con. See also CRIMINAL.

CULTIST n. frenzie, crazy, moonie. See also DEVOTEE.

CULTIVATE v. shine up to, make up to, play up to, suck up to, brownnose, kiss ass, ass kiss, get in with, get on the in with, get next to, get on the good side of, get on the right side of, run after. See also BEFRIEND.

CULTURED adj. highbrow, long-haired, hoity-toity. See also REFINED.

CUMBERSOME adj. clunk, clunker, clunky, galumphing. See CLUMSY.

CUNNILINGUS n. head, face, face man, face job, hat job, French, French job, French way, box lunch, fruit cup, fur burger, muff dive, seafood, sugar bowl pie, tongue wash, cunt lapping, tuna taco, yodeling in the gully, eating at the Y, clit licker (Obsc.).

CUNNILINGUS v. eat it, eat out, eat pussy, eat at the Y, face job, French, French kiss, give face, give head, go down on, go around the world, have hair pie, fur pie, muff dive, cunt lap, perform, sit on one's face, sixty-nine (all Obsc.).

CUNNING adj. smooth, smarts, street smarts, streetwise, foxy, crazy like a fox, cagey, fancy footwork, full of fancy footwork, slick, slippery, sly boots. See also SHREWD.

CUNNING n. gamesmanship, one-upmanship, know-how, savvy, the big stick, hustle, hanky panky, hokey pokey, con, con game, short con, big con, big store, sting, bunk, bunco, bunko, flam, flimflam, flimflammery, jip, gyp, gyp joint, scam, stunt, fast shuffle, switch, bait and switch, taradiddle, diddling, cheat, frame, frame up, double shuffle, fast shuffle, fast one, run around, song and dance, monkey business, funny business, skullduggery.

CUR n. mutt, Heinz, Heinz 57, Heinz 57 varieties, pooch, dorg, flea hotel. See DOG.

CURATE n. padre, the rev, Holy Joe, sky pilot, sin hound. See CLERGYMAN.

CURATIVE n. pick-me-up, shot in the arm, just what the doctor ordered.

CURATOR n. baby-sitter, house-sitter, sitter.

CURB v. 1. ice, put on ice, put away, scrub, send up, box in, get one in a box, bring to a screaming halt. See REPRESS. See also STOP, PREVENT. 2. cool, cool off, cool down, hold down, bog, bog down, keep the lid on, bottle up, cork, cork up, hog-tie, put a half nelson on. See RESTRAIN.

CURDLE v. clabber, lopper, cheese up, glop up.

CURE n. fix, quick fix.

CURE v. kick, kick the habit, shake, sweat it out, take the cure, bogue, dry out, quit cold, quit cold turkey, become Mr. Fish.

CURIOUS adj. nosy, snoopy. See INQUISITIVE.

CURRENCY n. cold cash, bread, dough, almighty dollar, dinero, moolah, mezumah, the wherewithal, skins, eagle shit, gelt, green stuff, long green, folding, folding money, happy cabbage, wad, chicken feed, chicken money, hard money, hard stuff, hardtack, coin, iron (silver coin), jangle, jingle jangle, piece of change, piece of jack, hip gee, ice, kick, lay down, line, grift, handsome ransom, lumps, main line, mezonny, mint, mint leaves, mopus, morphine, offtish, oil of palms, ointment, oof, ooks, ookus, package, pazoza, peanuts, poke, color, cookies, corn, cush, darby, dead president. See MONEY.

CURRENT adj. trendy, faddy, hip, mod, now, state of the art, the leading edge, what's happening, with it, on the front burner, swinging, in the mainstream, in the swim. See NEW.

CURRENT n. AC, DC, juice.

CURRICULUM VITAE n. brag sheet, vita.

CURRY FAVOR v. suck up to, kiss ass, brownnose, yes, apple-polish, buddy up, fall all over, play footsie, stroke, massage. See FLATTER.

CURSE n. whammy, double whammy, jinx, cuss, cuss word, dirty word, dirty name, four-letter word, no no, swear word, kibosh, hoodoo, kiss of death.

CURSE v. cuss, damn, darn, drat, flame, jinx, put the horns on, put the whammy on one, put the double whammy on one, give one a kine ahora (Yid.), give one the evil eye, hoodoo, hoodoo one, voodoo, voodoo one, talk dirty.

CURSED adj. all fired, hell fire, hoodooed, voodooed, snakebit.

CURSING n. French, pardon my French, cussing, dirty language, dirty talk, cuss, cuss word, dirty word, four-letter word, swear word, no-no, dirty name, bleep.

CURSORY adj. half-assed, half-baked, by bits and pieces, by fits and starts, in dribs and drabs, hit or miss, sloppy. See CARELESS.

CURT adj. snippy, snappy, short.

CURTAIL v. 1, cut, cut down, cut to the bone, nutshell, put in a nutshell, boil down, trim, chop, get to the meat. See SHORTEN. 2. cut back, roll back, dig in, tighten one's belt, downsize, leblang (theater ticket price).

CURTAIN n. rag, oleo (both The.).

CURTAIN CALL n. bend, take a bow.

CURVACEOUS adj. curves, curvy, stacked, built, built for comfort, built like a brick shithouse. See also BEAUTIFUL.

CURVE n. hairpin.

CURVED adj. skewed, curvaceous, curvy.

CUSTARD n. g'dong, gedunk, glop, goop, pud.

CUSTARD PIE n. magoo (for throwing).

CUSTODIAN n. super, swamper, baby-sitter, house-sitter, sitter.

CUSTOM n. thing, into, hang-up, one's bag, shot, kick, swim, grind, daily grind, groove, one's p's and q's, Jones.

CUSTOMARY adj. regular, same old shit, SOS, according to the book, according to Hoyle, by the numbers, playing it safe, in the groove, in a rut, chicken, chicken shit.

CUSTOMER n. pigeon, sucker, live one, mark, chump, easy make, float, front, head, walk-in.

CUSTOM-MADE adj. customized, tailor-made, special order, to order.

CUT v. whack, hack, chiv, shiv.

CYBERNETIC MACHINE n. brain, number cruncher, micro.

CYLINDER n. barrel, can.

CYMBALS n. highhat, potlids.

CZECH n. Chesky.

D

D. Delta, dog.

DABBLE v. mess around, fart around, fiddle with, monkey, monkey around, horse around, kid around, muck around, fool around, fool with, fuck around, play around, screw around, jerk off, dilly-dally, lollygag, go at it half-assed, go at it half-baked, go at it artsy-fartsy, potchky, play games with.

DAFT adj. flaky, wacky, whacko, screwy, in the ozone, baked, totally baked, fried, out of one's gourd, crackers, bonkers, nutty, off the wall. See CRAZY.

DAINTIES n. goodies, high on the hog, boodle (candy, etc., sent to students and soldiers, 1940).

DAIS n. soapbox, stump, bally stand (circus).

DALLAS Big D.

DALLIANCE n. fling, carrying on, relationship, making out, nooner, hanky-panky, fooling around, horsing around, kidding around, messing around, playing around, screwing around, mucking around, farting around, jerking off, billing and cooing, petting, necking, spooning, smooching, lollygagging, a little on the side, working late at the office, Roman spring (late in life). See also AFFAIR, ADULTERY.

DALLY v. 1. dilly-dally, monkey, monkey around, horse around, mess around, kid around, muck around, fart around, fool around, fuck around, play around, screw around, lollygag, jerk off, fool with, play games with. 2. have a fling, carry on, play around, get some on the side. See also FLIRT.

DAMAGE v. ding, wing, tweak, glitch up, bend the goods, total, louse up, mess up, muck up, ball up, bollix, bollix up, bugger, bugger up, foul up, fuck up, wrack up, goof up, gum up, hash up, screw up, jimmy up, slip up, rough up, shake up, snarl up, snafu, blansh, play hob with, play hell with, play merry hell with, play the devil with, cook, foozle, queer, sink, do, do a number on one, do in, get, hit one where he lives, lay a bad trip on one, zing, lean on, wax.

DAMAGED adj. busted, kaput, dinged, totaled, gone, gone haywire, glitched, down, on downtime, on the blink, on the bum, on the fritz, out of action, out of kilter, out of whack, no go, run down, had it, bent, queered, bobbled, bitched up, buggered, buggered up, wracked up, screwed up, fouled up, fucked up, loused up, gummed up, balled up, bollixed up, messed up, hashed up, mucked up, snafued, commfued, cooked, sunk, shot, flubbed, in smithereens.

DAMN v. 1. jinx, put the horns on, put the whammy on one, put the double whammy on one, hoodoo, hoodoo one, voodoo, voodoo one. 2. cuss, darn, drat, flame, talk dirty.

DAMNED adj. all fired, hell fire, hoodooed, voodooed, snakebit. See CURSED.

DAMP adj. sweat box, sticky, steamy, steam bath.

DAMSEL n. chick, doll, babe, frill, frail, skirt, mini skirt, queen, classy chassy, jill, li'l mama, tomato. See GIRL.

DANCE n. 1. prom, hop, sock hop (shoeless), disco, jump, mingle, shindig, hoedown, hoedig, hoodang, hog wrestle, brawl. 2. soft shoe, clog, crawl, hip hop, jitter, jitterbug, samba, swing, rug cutter, shout, break, go-go, alley cat, pogo, rock, rock 'n' roll, shag, boogaloo, twist, frug, funky chicken, shuffle, hustle, square, the big apple, black bottom, boogie woogie, topless, hooch, hootchy cooch, shake, shimmy, bumps, grinds, bumps and grinds, toddle, circus (naked), ballin' the jack, breakdown, bunnyhug, cakewalk, camel walk, Charleston, Lindy hop.

DANCE v. get down, hip hop, body dance, break dance, touch dance, hoof it, groovin' and duckin', hustle, conga, twist, frug, shuffle, boogie, boogie down, boogaloo, juke it, jive, rock, rock 'n' roll, rock out, shake, spin, swing, jitter, jitterbug, truck, cut a rug, lay iron (tap), strut, strut one's stuff, shimmy, stomp, wrestle, bunny hop, trip the light fantastic, cheek to cheek, belly to belly, strip, grind, bump and grind.

DANCE HALL n. frolic pad, track.

DANCER n. hoofer, jitterbug, soft-shoe, break, apache, rug cutter, alligator, stripper, strip tease, strip-tease artist, sizzler, bumper, grinder, coffee grinder, peeler, cement mixer, fanner, song and dance man, terper; the line, gypsy, pony, chorine (chorus).

DANDY n. dude, flash, Dapper Dan, Beau Brummel, sport, swell, dap, toff, snappy dresser, clotheshorse, macaroni. See DUDE.

DANGER n. double trouble, thin ice, hot potato, dynamite, risky business.

DANGEROUS adj. hot, hairy, loaded, dynamite, unhealthy, widow maker, jungle, zoo, heavy, rugged, spot, on the spot, put on the spot, dicey, iffy, chancy, fat chance, hasn't got a Chinaman's chance, not a prayer, a snowball in hell, play with fire, too hot to handle, hot potato, can get burned, go for broke, play Russian roulette, on thin ice, on slippery ground, on a wing and a prayer, out on a limb, Baker flying (Navy), bell the cat, tweak the devil's nose, touchy, touch and go, hanging by a thread, go to sea in a sieve.

DANGER WARNING n.   watch it, heads up, freeze, jiggers, cheese it, mope, nix, smarten up, wise up, zex, snap out of your hop. See ALARM.

DANGER, WARN OF v.   1. flag, wave a red flag, give one the high sign, cloud up, toot the tooter (mechanical), highball. 2. tip, tip off, crack, hep up, hip up, smarten up, wise up. See also ADVISE, ALARM.

DANK adj.   close, sticky, steamy, steam bath, sweat box.

DAPPER adj.   classy, dap, snazzy, spiffy, clean, sharp, natty, nifty, nobby, swank, swanky, posh, ritzy, swell, dressed to kill, dressed to the teeth, dressed to the nines, turned out. See STYLISH.

DARE n.   defi, defy.

DARE v.   make my day, go on make my day, take one on, call one's bluff, knock the chip off one's shoulder, step over the line, face off. See CHALLENGE.

DAREDEVIL n.   fire-eater, harum-scarum.

DARING adj.   gutsy, gutty, gritty, grit, spunky, nervy, pizzazz, cocky, crusty, smart, smart alecky, smart ass, wise ass, hot shot, cheeky, chutzpahdik, spetters, salty, brassy, bold as brass, come on strong, hell of a, hell of a note, helluva nerve, off the deep end, go off the deep end, step off the deep end, go for broke, go out on a limb, go to sea in a sieve, leave oneself wide open, play with fire, fire-eater. See also FEARLESS.

DARING n.   nerve, guts, moxie, stuff, pizzazz, brass, chutzpah, grit, spunk, speed. See also COURAGE.

DARK EYEGLASSES n.   shades, sunshades, wraparounds, glims, mask, peepers, specs, bebop glasses.

DASH v.   make a run for it, make it snappy, get on it, rush act, rush period. See also GO.

DASHBOARD n.   dash.

DASHED adj.   down, a downer, down in the dumps, let down, taken down, taken down a peg, blue, in a blue funk, singing the blues. See DEPRESSED.

DASH OFF v.   1. knock off, throw off, toss off, toss out, knock out, bat out, slap out, shove out, slap up. See WRITE. 2. slapdash, do by halves, mess around, any which way, any old way, fast and loose, helter skelter, sloppy.

DATA n.   info, poop, poop sheet, scoop, score, dope, goods, whole story, brass tacks, chapter and verse, the know, picture. See FACTS. See also INFORMATION.

DATE n.   bird, blind date, blind drag, drag, shag, cradle snatcher, dream bait, egg (Dutch treat), import (out of town), Faust, John, lounge lizard, sofa lizard, earth pig (unattractive). See also APPOINTMENT.

DATE v.   see, deuce it, go together, go around together, go around with, keep company, go steady, make time with, play around, step out, fix up, furp, rob the cradle, snatch the cradle.

DATED adj.   tired, out, out of it, not with it, old hat, joanie, passe, bent, back number, hairy, moth-eaten, moldy, moldy fig, has-been, yesterday, square, squaresville, corn, corny, cornball, corn-fed, off the cob, clown, dinosaur, duddy, fuddy-duddy, foozle, fossil, frog, funky, horse and buggy, icky, razzmatazz, jazzy, of the old school, ticky, ricky tick, rinky dink, rinky-tinky, gasser, chintzy, mince. See also OLD.

DAUGHTER n.   sprout, little beaver.

DAVENPORT, IOWA   Quad Cities.

DAWDLE v.   get no place fast, poke, poke around, poke along, mosey, toddle, shlep along, bum, bum around, hang out, hang around, goof around, stick around, mooch around, scrounge around, jack around, bat around, fool around, fuck around, fuck off, goof off, screw off, rat, rat fuck, R.F., fuck the dog, sit on one's ass, sit on one's butt, sit on one's duff, jelly, tool, tail, bail out, cat, warm a chair, press the bricks, lie down on the job.

DAWDLER n.   slowpoke, foot dragger, stick in the mud, sleepyhead, goof-off, fuck-off, goldbrick, shlepper, slower than the seven-year itch, molasses in January. See also LOAFER.

DAWN n.   bright, early bright, crack of dawn, day peep, sunup.

DAY n.   bright, early bright.

DAYBREAK n.   crack of dawn, day peep, bright, early bright, sunup.

DAYDREAM n.   trip, head trip, mind trip, castle in the air, fool's paradise, pipe dream, stare into the middle distance, pie in the sky, in a zone.

DAYDREAM v.   trip out, build castles in the air, moon, pipe dream, woolgather, stare into the middle distance.

DAY ORIENTED adj.   day people.

DAYTON, OHIO   Gem City.

DAZE n.   gauze, glaze, Nadaville, MEGO (my eyes glaze over).

DAZED adj.   gorked, glazed, gone, dopey, out of it, out to lunch, nebular, spaced out, spacey, trippy, tweaked out, woozy, foggy, in a fog, wandering around in a fog, slaphappy, punchy, punch-drunk; nodding, on the nod (narcotic). See also CONFUSED.

DAZZLE v.   glitz, razzle-dazzle.

DAZZLING adj.   razzle-dazzle, glitzy, flashy, showy.

DEACON n.   deac.

DEAD adj.   bought the farm, had it, offed, cold, stiff, dead meat, belly up, passed on, passed away, checked out, conked out, kicked the bucket, cashed in, cashed in one's chips, bit the dust, pushing up daisies, croaked, went, went to the last roundup, went West, went to the happy hunting grounds, gone, goner, gone west, gone to the happy hunting grounds, gone glimmering, gone to kingdom come, gone to that great (whatever) in the sky, dead and gone, done for, dead and done for, dead as a dodo, dead as a doornail, dead as a herring, dead as mutton, dead duck, stone dead, stone cold, on a slab, down the drain, finished, kaput, six feet under, in Davy Jones's locker, out of range, took one's last curtain call, popped off, boxed.

DEADLINE n.   drop-dead date, time frame, time lock, the clock's running, under the gun.

DEADLOCK n.   standoff, Mexican standoff, catch 22, box, corner, dead end, gridlock, hole, damned if you do and damned if you don't, pickle.

DEAD ON ARRIVAL adj.   D.O.A.

DEAD, THE n.   the majority, the great majority.

DEAF AND DUMB adj.   D and D, dee and dee, dummy.

DEAL v.   1. dicker, hack out a deal, hammer out a deal, make a deal, work out a deal, hondle, handle, horse trade, swap, swap horses, Jew down (Derog.), knock down the price. See NEGOTIATE. 2. come across with, dish out, drop, fork over, network with, connect with, have truck with.

DEAL CARDS v.   deal out, deliver, hit, pitch, run 'em.

DEALER, CARDS n.   clerk, mechanic, subway expert.

DEALER, GAMBLING n.   box man, stick man, fence, stop.

DEALS n.   ropes, strings, wires, wire pulling, irons, irons in the fire, balls in the air.

DEAL WITH v.   hack, hack it, handle, handle it, get a handle on something, make a go of it, make it, live with. See MANAGE.

DEAN n.   tack, dick.

DEAR adj.   1. dearie, honey, baby, toots, tootsie, sugar, sweetie, sweet face, doll face, puddin', lovey, love of my life. See BELOVED. 2. pricey, steep, stiff, cher, high,

fancy, out of sight, an arm and a leg, pretty penny, heavy sugar. See EXPENSIVE.

DEARTH n.   slim pickings.

DEATH n.   curtains, curtains for one, dirt nap, grim reaper, kiss off, the end, fini, finish, lead poison (by shooting), lights out, lumps, crossing the bar, big jump, final thrill, last debt, last roundup, last out, ol' man Mose, -30-, taps, tap city, one's number is up, when the lights go out, buy the farm, a daisy, parole, the hard way, back gate parlor; back door, back gate, back parole (prison).

DEATH CHAMBER n.   dance hall.

DEATH WALK n.   last mile, last waltz, trip up back.

DEBACLE n.   blue ruin, shit hit the fan. See DISASTER.

DEBASE v.   take down, take down a peg, put down, shoot one down, put one away, dump on, shit on, fluff off. See BELITTLE.

DEBASED adj.   put down, took down, dumped on, eat humble pie, in the doghouse, gone to the dogs, gone to hell, gone to bad, in bad, in Dutch, lost face. See BELITTLED.

DEBATABLE adj.   touch and go, chancy, iffy, betwixt and between, between sixes and sevens, between a rock and a hard place, the jury's out. See DOUBTFUL.

DEBATE n.   hassle, wrangle, words, rap, rap session, powwow, bull yard, blah-blah, flak session, spat, tiff, bone, bone of contention, bone to pick. See also ARGUMENT.

DEBATE v.   hassle, lock horns, set to, talk back, talk game, pick a bone, put up an argument, rhubarb, pettifog, kick around, knock around, hammer, hammer away at, chew over, confab, hash, rehash, hash over, bump heads, cross swords, have at it. See also ARGUE, DISCUSS.

DEBAUCHED adj.   gone to the bad, gone to the dogs, gone to hell, down in the gutter. See WANTON.

DEBAUCHER n.   high liver, playboy, swinger, rake, chaser, womanizer, cunt chaser (Obsc.). See LECHER.

DEBAUCHERY n.   tear, bender, binge, toot, bat, blowout, wingding, bust, drunk, jag, high living, fast living, live in the fast lane, life in the fast lane, drive in the fast lane, drive in the fast lane wih no brakes, live fast and leave a beautiful corpse, la dolce vita, burn one's candle at both ends, hellbent, go to hell, go to hell in a handbasket, merry-go-round, paint the town red, on the town. See also REVEL.

DEBIT n.   in the red, red ink, the nut, the cuff. See DEBT.

DEBRIS n.   junk, shit, crap.

DEBT n.   tab, cuff, red ink, bad news, damage, score, bite, price tag, chit, IOU, I owe you, in debt, in the red, in the ketchup, in a hole, in hock, in the barrel, living over one's head, nut, on the nut, off the nut, bottom line, below the line, set one back, come to, to the tune of, hummer, albatross, albatross around one's neck, baggage, dead horse, due bill, dues, stiffed one, highway mopery, nigger rich (borrowing to buy luxuries, Derog.).

DEBTOR n.   leech, momzer, moocher, smoocher, scrounger, sponge, sponger, rabbit, desperado, deadbeat, four-flusher (does not repay).

DEBUT n.   bow, opener, coming out, coming out party. See BEGINNING.

DEBUT v.   bow, open, come out. See BEGIN.

DEBUTANTE n.   deb, subdeb.

DECADENT adj.   gone to the bad, gone to the dogs, gone to hell. See WANTON.

DECAY v.   go to pot, go soft, go downhill, use it or lose it. See DETERIORATE.

DECEASE n.   the end, curtains, grim reaper, crossing the bar, taps, tap city, buy the farm. See DEATH.

DECEASE v.   go, buy the farm, croak, cool off, meet Mr. Jordan, pull the plug, flatline (Medic.), call off all bets, check out, head for the last roundup, deep six, dirt nap, head for a hearse, one-way ticket, dance on air (hang). See DIE.

DECEASED adj.   bought the farm, dead meat, passed on, checked out, kicked the bucket, bit the dust, pushing up daisies, dirt napping, gone, gone to a better place, gone to meet one's Maker, gave up the ghost, closed one's eyes for the last time. See DEAD.

DECEIT n.   smoke and mirrors, dirty dealing, dirty work, dirty pool, dirty trick, sellout, two-timing, crocodile tears, soft soap, sweet talk, spoof, whitewash job. See CHEAT.

DECEITFUL adj.   jive-ass, bent, shady, sharp, wrong, wrong number, double crossing, snake in the grass, worm, two-faced, two-timing, dirty, low-down and dirty, dirty work, crooked, crooked stick, cheatin' heart, fishy, gyp, not kosher, honest John, feather legs, slick, slippery, speak with forked tongue.

DECEIVE v.   screw, shaft, hose, jerk one around, fuck one over, jive, shuck, shuck and jive, disinform, sting, throw one a curve, give one a bum steer, pull one's chain, doctor, cook, cook up, deacon, duff, hoke, hoke up, load, salt, salt a mine, phony up. See CHEAT.

DECEIVED adj.   been had, been taken, fucked, foxed, conned, disinformed, mousetrapped, set up, sandbagged, suckered, double crossed, diddled, snowed. See CHEATED.

DECEIVER n.   con man, con artist, sharpie, smoothie, fake, faker, fraud, phoney, play actor, fast talker, boogerboo, shiever, S.L.O.B. (silver-lipped operator of bullshit), worm, cheese-eater, skunker, hoser, whip, shark. See CHEATER.

DECENT adj.   on the up and up, straight, straight arrow, straight shooter, white, regular, a livin' doll. See VIRTUOUS.

DECEPTION n.   1. hustle, con, con game, sting, flam, scam, fast shuffle, jive, shuck, total shuck, cover-up, snow job, whitewash, whitewash job, doesn't wash, down and dirty, fast one. See CHEAT. 2. crock, fib, story, terminological inexactitude, balls, hogwash, malarkey, baloney. See LIE.

DECEPTIVE adj.   bum, off, way off, fishy, jivey, jive ass, shuckin' and jivin', two faced, gil, Hollywood, slick, sincere, snide, phony, huggery-muggery, reach-me-down, fake, out in left field. See also SHIFTY.

DECIBELS n.   dog biscuits.

DECIDE v.   call the shots, cinch, clinch, nail down, take a decision, go down the line, opt, tap. See DETERMINE.

DECIDED adj.   nailed, on ice, all locked up, cinched, clinched, in the bag, set, for sure, posilutely, absitively. See DETERMINED.

DECIDEDLY adv.   absofuckinglutely, def, but def, cert, sure, real, really, jolly, bloody, stone (stone deaf), terribly, terrifically, almighty, powerful, right, woofing, for a fact, for a fact Jack, that's a fact Jack, you said it, no buts about it, no ifs ands or buts, no strings attached, no holds barred, no catch, no kicker, and no mistake, come hell or high water, flat out, straight out, in spades, sure as God made little green apples, is the Pope Catholic? See also ABSOLUTELY.

DECISION n.   the nod, the call, showdown.

DECISIVE adj.   litmus test, no ifs ands or buts, all out, flat out, straight out.

DECK OF SHIP n.   mat (usually aircraft carrier), topside.

DECKHAND n.   roustabout.

DECLAIM v.   get on a soapbox, spiel, spout, chew the scenery, blow hot air, pile it on, talk big. See ORATE.

DECLARATION n.   spiel, pitch, story, hot air, say so, two cents' worth, bomb. See also PROCLAIM, PROMULGATE, REPORT, ASSERT.

DECLARE v.   blast, sound off, run off at the mouth, get on a soapbox, soapbox, spiel, spout. See PROCLAIM. See also SPEAK.

DECLINE n.   flop, dive, cropper, pratfall, skids, on the skids. See also SLUMP, FAILURE.

DECLINE v. 1. go to pot, go downhill, go to the dogs, hit the skids, come apart at the seams, be on one's last legs, have one foot in the grave and the other on a banana peel. See DETERIORATE. 2. turn down, turn thumbs down on, pass on, not buy, not hear of, not think of. See also REJECT.

DECLINING adj. done, done up, in a bad way, on one's last legs, on the skids, played out, running out of gas.

DÉCOLLETÉ adj. plunging neckline, down to there, let it all hang out.

DECOMPRESSION SICKNESS n. bends.

DECORATE v. doll up, fix up, gussy up, spruce up, jazz up, put on the bells and whistles.

DECORATION n. 1. gingerbread, bells and whistles, fuss, gewgaws, gimcracks, garbage (food), dingbat, doodad, thing, fandangle, jazz, seagoing (large, absurd). 2. fruit salad, scrambled eggs, ruptured duck, purple heart, brag rags, chest hardware, chicken guts (Mil.).

DECOY n. deek, nark, plant, come on man, sitting duck, shill, stoolie, stool pigeon, booster, pusher, bunco steerer, blow off. See also LURE.

DECOY v. bait, come on, con, mousetrap, shill, steer, tout, suck in, rope in, humbug, egg one on, lead up the garden path, chum (fishing). See LURE.

DECREE n. rap, the riot act, say, the word.

DECREE v. lay down the law, put one's foot down, read the riot act. See COMMAND.

DECRY v. pan, slam, hit, rap, take a swipe at, knock, poor-mouth, bad-mouth, do a number on. See CRITICIZE. See also CENSURE, BELITTLE.

DEDICATED adj. old faithful, true blue. See LOYAL.

DEDUCE v. figure, figger, add up to, boil down to, what one is saying is, have a hunch, be afraid, the way one sees it. See CONCLUDE. See also BELIEVE.

DEDUCT v. knock off, cut back, roll back.

DEDUCTION n. deduck (income tax item), cut. See also INFERENCE.

DEED n. 1. papers. 2. stunt, mitzvah (good). 3. happenin', plan, stunt, game, ball game, bit, do, follow through, big idea. See also ACTION.

DEEM v. be afraid, feel, set store by. See BELIEVE.

DEEMPHASIZE v. downplay, play down, gloss over, soft pedal, throwaway, cover up, make light of. See UNDERPLAY.

DEEMPHASIZED adj. down played, played down, glossed over, low-keyed, low profile, soft-pedalled, kept under one's hat. See also UNIMPORTANT.

DEEP adj. heavy. See SERIOUS.

DEER AREA n. antler alley.

DEFACE v. trash, mess up, hash up, screw up, foul up, fuck up, louse up, gum up, muck up. See also DAMAGE.

DEFAMATION n. dirt, dirty linen, dirty wash, dirty laundry, dirty dig, cheap shot, dynamite, mud, slime, smear, sizzler, scorcher, dirty shame, low-down dirty shame, crying shame, burning shame, Watergate, put down, rap, slam, brickbat, dump, hit, knock, dozens, dirty dozens, woofing, slap in the face, black eye, backhanded compliment, left-handed compliment, skeleton in the closet, skeleton in the cupboard, low rent.

DEFAME v. pan, slam, smear, blister, roast, scorch, knock, bad-mouth, do a number on, put the zingers in. See SLANDER.

DEFAMER n. knocker, mudslinger, cat, backbiter.

DEFAULT v. stiff, welch, welsh, skate, skip, skip out on, run out on, see in the alley, meet under the arch, give one the arm, bet on the muscle, put on the cuff, put the sleeve on, shirk out of, button up one's pocket, draw the purse string.

DEFAULTER n. deadbeat, stiff, welcher, welsher, behind, desperado, rabbit, skipper, skedaddler, no show.

DEFEAT n. beating, whipping, licking, paddling, trimming, shellacking, drubbing, embarrassment, trashing, hiding, lathering, lambasting, smearing, pasting, clobbering, larruping, leathering, tanning, walloping, whopping, whomping, whitewashing, waxing, whaling, shutout, washout, Waterloo, disaster, flunk, foozle, lumps, get one's lumps, cuttin' (jazz), upset, shuck, total shuck, total loss, bloody murder, blue murder, poke in the eye, pratfall, shoot one's wad, fizzle, body blow, dressing down, come down, come down in the world, down for the count, down on one's luck, down and out, fall, take a fall. See also TRIUMPH.

DEFEAT v. 1. bash, trash, drub, dish, flax, wax, lather, larrup, leather, lambaste, workover, whop, whomp, whack, whip, whipsaw, tan, tan one's hide, take it all, take it out of one's hide, take it out of one's skin, brain, bloop, bonk, conk, KO, kayo, bust, drop, deck, total, powder, pepper, clobber, cream, zap, zetz, paste, waste, wing, bump, hurt, kick ass, whip ass, clean on, take one, take out, take care of, take the wind out of one's sails, take down, put down, smack down, shoot down, shoot down in flames, tear down, dress one down, shut down, shut out, rank out, punch one out, lay one low, lay one out, wipe out, wipe up the floor with, wipe up the place with, wipe off the map, beat up, beat the bejesus out of one, beat the tar out of, beat the beholden out of one, beat the shit outta, beat the living tar out of, beat the living daylights out of, make mincemeat out of, knock, knock cold, knock off, knock around, knock one out, knock the beholden out of one, knock the daylights out of, knock the living daylights out of, knock the shit out of, knock the bottom out of, knock the chocks out from under, knock the props out from under, knock into the next county, knock for a row of (anything), knock on the head, knock one on one's ass, knock one ass over teakettle, knock one on one's ear, knock one into next week, knock one's block off, knock one's socks off, knock one for a loop, deal a knockout blow to, make hamburger out of one, whale, whale the [anything] out of, wallop, let have it, dust one's jacket, banjax, blast, put on ice, put the slug on one, put one away, floor one, down one, floor, put it in their eye, put one in the hospital. 2. bury, blank, plunk, skunk, schneider, mug, murder, murdalize, kill, cook, cook one's goose, eat one's lunch, go upside one's face, trim, trounce, cap, top, fix, fix one's wagon, swamp, scuttle, sconce, skin, shave, massage, oil, smear, shellac, whitewash, squelch, squash, steamroller, bulldoze, rollover, torpedo, tube, meatball, make one say uncle, do in, lick, lick to a frazzle, beat all hollow, beat the game, beat the system, beat by a nose, nose out, edge out, sneak past, upset, sink the opposition, put the skids to, snow, snow under, plow under, put the kibosh on, finish, finish off, shut off, tee off on, wrack up, blow away, blow off, blow one out, blow one out of the water, blow sky high, pin one's ears back, have it all over, bring home the bacon, take the cake, put one's nose out of joint, poke full of holes, shoot full of holes, run rings around, run circles around, clean on, clean one's clock, throw for a loop, throw a monkey wrench into the works, upset one's apple cart, give one the business, put away, settle, settle one's hash, spike one's guns.

DEFEATED adj.   aced out, blanked, burned, busted, beatsville, bit the dust, creamed, clobbered, cooked, hosed, scooped, topped, trimmed, trounced, lathered, lambasted, licked, lick one's wounds, whipped, whitewashed, murdered, ripped, fixed, zapped, skinned, skinned alive, snowed, snowed under, settled, down, down and out, done in, done for, stymied, shut down, shut off, flameout, get one's lumps, cry uncle, say uncle, all up with, mind blown, blown away, blown out, blown out of the water, been through the mill, thrown for a loss, tail between one's legs, have one's ass in a sling, on the chin, take it, take it on the chin, you can't buck something, you can't buck city hall, you can't beat the system.

DEFECATE v.   crap, shit, go, caca, go caca, poop, poo-poo, go poo-poo, go ah ah, go to the the can, go to the bathroom, go to the John, go to the chic sale, go to the two holer, have a BM, make number two, make caca, make ah ah, squat, take a squat, take a shit, take a crap, play in the sandbox, haul ashes, shake the ashes out, shake a few clinkers out, drop a terd, dump, take a dump, dump a load, answer a call, have a hurry-up call, answer nature's call, do one's business, grunt.

DEFECATION n.   BM, stool, shit, crap, caca, dump, number two, turd, terd, business, call, nature's call. See BOWEL MOVEMENT.

DEFECT n.   bug, kink, catch, glitch, gremlin, irregular, second, blem, not up to scratch, not come up to scratch, not make it, not pass muster, not cut the mustard. See also BLEMISH.

DEFECT v.   pull out, sell out, run out, take a walk, go over the fence, go over the hill. See also GO.

DEFECTIVE adj.   glitched, a few bugs, gremlins, schlock, blems, seconds, on the bum. See IMPERFECT.

DEFEND v.   back, ride shotgun for, go to bat for, go to the mat for, thump for, beat the drum for, stand up for, stick up for, cover, cover up, cover one's ass, stonewall. See also SUPPORT.

DEFENSE n.   copout, jive, song, song and dance, story, whitewash, cleanup, fish, fish story, fish tale, have to see a man about a dog, off-time, cover one's ass. See EXCUSE.

DEFENSE DEPARTMENT TERMS   MAD (Mutually Assured Destruction), mega deaths (one million killed), bonus kill, collateral damage, body count, theatre war, mirved, marved, strategic hamlet (target city), surgically clean strike, ERD, Enhanced Radiation Device (neutron bomb), SDI, Star Wars.

DEFENSELESS adj.   naked, ass out, sitting duck, out on a limb, wide open, one's hands are tied, on the line, in the line of fire, on the spot, pigeon, clay pigeon, stick one's neck out, ready to be taken, sucker for a left, up the creek without a paddle, caught with one's pants down, caught with the smoking gun, caught in the open, with one's face hanging in the breeze.

DEFER v.   1. shelve, put on the back burner, put on hold, hold off, hang fire, cool it, give one a rain check. See DELAY. 2. kiss ass, give into, kowtow to.

DEFERRED adj.   scrubbed, pigeonholed, on hold, on the shelf, on the back burner, in a wait state.

DEFIANCE n.   defy, balls, gas, guts, hot air, macho, big talk, tall talk, back talk, sass, lip.

DEFICIENCY n.   bug, glitch, hack it, not make it, black mark.

DEFICIENT adj.   not up to scratch, not hack it, not make it, not cut out for, outta gas, second fiddle, second string, third string. See also IMPERFECT.

DEFICIT n.   red ink, in the red, in the ketchup, in the hole, in hock, due bill, dues, dead horse. See DEBT.

DEFILE v.   trash, crud up, crumb up, scuzz up, skank, muck up, sleaze up, mess up, piss on, give one a black eye, make one lose face. See also SLANDER.

DEFILED adj.   cooked (radiation), trashed, dirty, exposed, mucked up.

DEFINE v.   label, tag, nail it down, call a spade a spade, lay it out, map out.

DEFINITE adj. absofuckinglutely, on ice, cold, lock and win situation, no ifs ands or buts, set, checked and double checked, in the bag. See CERTAIN.

DEFINITELY adv. cert, absatively, posilutely, come hell or high water, no buts about it, with tits on, in spades. See ABSOLUTELY.

DEFINITIVE adj. nailed down, what you see is what you get, flat out, straight out, downright. See ULTIMATE. See also ABSOLUTE.

DEFLATE v. debunk, knock down, take down, shoot down, cut down to size, let down easy, break one's heart, kick one in the heart, kick in the ass, kick in the stomach, puncture one's balloon, let the air out of one's tires, let the wind out of one's sails. See HUMILIATE.

DEFLATION n. comeuppance, knock, knockdown, takedown, put-down, touché, pan, debunk, kick one in the heart, kick in the ass, kick in the stomach.

DEFLECT v. bounce, bounce off, slip, cover up, give one the hip.

DEFLOWER v. pop one's cherry, break one's cherry, break in. See also SEDUCE.

DEFRAUD v. rook, screw, shaft, hose, rip off, shuck and jive, double clock, fleece, burn, clip, take one to the cleaners, sucker into. See CHEAT.

DEFRAY v. pay up, foot the bill, cough up, pony up, ante up, come up with the necessary, plunk down, shell out, fork over. See PAY.

DEFRAYAL n. payoff, cash on the line, cash on the nail, cash on the barrelhead, kickback, the wherewithal, the necessary, the needful. See also PAYMENT.

DEFT adj. good hands, have know-how, crack, crackerjack, cute.

DEFUNCT adj. dead and done for, done for, down the drain, gone, gone glimmering, had it, kaput. See DEAD.

DEFY v. defi, fly in the face of, meet eyeball to eyeball, make my day, go on make my day, hang tough, take one on, stick, stick fast, won't take no for an answer, kick over the traces. See CHALLENGE.

DEGENERATE n. bad guy, motherfucker (Obsc.), mofo, bad ass, sleazeball, slimebucket, maggot, creep, turd, shit, shithead, shit heel, bad news, freak, geek, mutant See VILLAIN.

DEGENERATE v. go to pieces, go downhill, go to the dogs, come apart at the seams, die on the vine. See DETERIORATE.

DEGRADE v. bump, bust, bench, mudsling, pan, slam, take down, take down a peg or two, shoot down, tear down, run down, put down, cut down to size. See HUMILIATE.

DEGRADED adj. gone to bad, gone to the dogs, gone to hell, crawling, in bad, lost face, drummed out, put down. See DISGRACED.

DEGRADING adj. infra dig.

DEGREE n. sheepskin, shingle, PHT (putting hubby through).

DEHYDRATED adj. cotton mouth, mouth full of cotton, spitting dust.

DEITY n. Dad, Head Knock, Lordy, Man Upstairs.

DEJECTED adj. dragged, down in the mouth, bummed out, hurtin', in the pits, shot down, all torn up, mopey. See DEPRESSED.

DEJECTION n. blahs, blues, blue devils, blue funk, funk, bummer, dolefuls, letdown, downer, down trip, dumps, mumps, mopes, mulligrubs, the mokers.

DELAWARE the Blue Hen State, the Diamond State, the First State.

DELAY n. bind, downtime, hang up, holdup, slow up, tie-up, jam, logjam, showstopper, holding, holding pattern.

DELAY v. 1. fool around, fuck around, futz around, fart around, play around, screw around, stooge around, hang around, hang about, lollygag, play for time, conk out, die, stall, pull a stall, hang, hang back, dally, dilly-dally, hold on, sit tight, stonewall, drag one's heels, drag one's ass, have lead in one's pants, string out, vamp, take the air out of the ball. See also DAWDLE. 2. shelve, put on the shelf, put on the back burner, put on hold, put on ice, put off, hold off, hold up, hold on, hang, hang up, hang fire, pigeonhole, cool, cool one's heels, goldbrick, goof off, stall, fuck off, dilly-dally, shilly-shally, sit on one's hands, sit on one's ass, sit on one's butt, sit on one's duff, give one the run around (repeatedly), give one a rain check, drag out, drag one's feet, drag one's heels, stall, pull a stall, stall around, stooge around, hang back, hold fire, hold the phone, sit tight, stonewall, stretch out, let go to pot, let slide.

DELAYED adj. 1. scrubbed, stabbed, sidelined, sidetracked, passed up, pigeonholed, buttonholed, shelved, on the shelf, on hold, on the back burner. 2. hung up, held up, in a bind, jammed, jammed up, strapped for time, burn the midnight oil, snooze you lose.

DELECTABLE adj. scrumptious, yummy, delish, divine, heavenly.

DELEGATE n. front, rep.

DELETE v. cut, sterilize, sanitize, decontaminate, bleep, bleep out, blue pencil, knock out, X-out, trim, gut, clean up, launder, snip, pass up, drop, rub, squash, squelch. See EDIT.

DELIBERATE v.   noodle it around, hammer away at, cool something over, stew over, sweat over, chew over, chew the cud, rack one's brains, put on one's thinking cap, kick around, knock around, bat it around, run it up the flagpole, pour it on. See also ANALYZE, DISCUSS, THINK.

DELICACIES n.   goodies, high on the hog, boodle (candy, etc. sent to students and soldiers, 1940).

DELICATESSEN n.   deli, delly, goulash, cold cuts.

DELICIOUS adj.   delish, yummy, yummy in the tummy, divine, heavenly, scrumptious.

DELIGHT v.   turn on, freak out, knock out, knock dead, send, slay, grooving, score, wow, hit the spot, be just the ticket, just what the doctor ordered, go over big, tickle pink, tickle to death. See also AMUSE.

DELIGHTED adj.   set up, blow one's mind, handsprings, backflips, flipping, lookin' good, pleased as punch, sold on, tickled pink, tickled to death, wowed, a rush. See THRILLED.

DELIGHT IN v.   groove on, grok, dig, get off on, get high on, get naked (not necessarily sexual), get a boot out of, live a little, live it up. See ENJOY.

DELINQUENT n.   1. JD, juvie, punk, cuddle bunny (young female). 2. welcher, welsher, behind, deadbeat, deadhead, stiff, desperado, rabbit, skipper, skedaddler, no show.

DELIRIOUS adj.   off one's head, out of one's head, out of one's skull, flipped, flipped out, dingy. See also HALLUCINATORY.

DELIRIUM TREMENS n.   DT's, the shakes, the horrors, the heebie jeebies, jimjams, beezie-weezies, screaming meemies, blue johnnies, blue devils, pink elephants, pink spiders, snakes, snakes in the boots, the clanks, the creeps.

DELIVER v.   drop, fork over, pass it on over, hand-carry, hand-walk, put on, put out, dish out, come across with, duke, weed, gimme.

DELIVERANCE n.   getaway, out, powder, break, breakout, beat, figary, mooch, mope, spring, tear away, getaway route.

DELIVERY n.   drop.

DELIVERY BOY n.   speedy, gopher, gofer, driver.

DELUDE v.   disinform, jerk one around, dick one around, jive, shuck, shuck and jive, sell wolf cookies, do a number, caboodle, snow, hype, they're peeing on us and telling us it's raining. See TRICK.

DELUDED adj.   jerked around, fucked over, sucked in, suckered, foxed, conned, disinformed, mousetrapped, strung along. See TRICKED.

DELUGE v.   swamp, flood with, snow, snow under.

DELUSION n.   pipe dream, trip, head trip, fool's paradise.

DELUXE adj.   plush, posh, ritzy, swank, swanky, first cabin. See LUXURIOUS.

DELVE v.   really get into, leave no stone unturned, turn inside out. See SEARCH.

DEMAND v.   hit, hit up, hold out for, knock, pop the question, whistle for (but won't get), dibs on something, fish or cut bait, shit or get off the pot, hurting for.

DEMANDING adj.   ballbreaker, backbreaker, tough, separates the men from the boys. See DIFFICULT.

DEMEAN v.   cut down to size, cut rate, knock down, pan, poor-mouth, bad-mouth, dump on, shit on. See HUMILIATE.

DEMEANED adj.   eat crow, eat dirt, eat humble pie, crawl, put down, dumped on, knocked from one's high horse, knocked off one's perch, have a tuck in one's tail, got one's comeuppance. See BELITTLED.

DEMEANING adj.   infra dig.

DEMENTED adj.   schitzy, schizzed out, schizoid, psycho, flipped out, totally baked, in the ozone, fruity, fruitcakey, nutty as a fruitcake, whacko, ding-a-ling, unglued, out of one's tree, out of one's gourd, bananas, banana pie. See CRAZY.

DEMERIT n.   gig, ram, rip, rap, skin, demo, Brownie (R.R.), black mark.

DEMILITARIZE v.   demob.

DEMILITARIZED ZONE n.   DMZ.

DEMISE n.   the end, lights out, big jump, final thrill, last roundup, last out, -30-, taps, tap city, one's number is up, buy the farm. See DEATH.

DEMOBILIZE v.   demob.

DEMOCRATIC PARTY n.   Demos, donkeys, party of the people.

DEMOCRATS n.   Demos, donkeys.

DEMOCRATS, SOUTHERN n.   solid South, boll weevils, Dixiecrats, Dix.

DEMOLISH v.   trash, total, torpedo, sink, put in the toilet, wipe off the map, take out, take apart, tear down, break the lease, blue ruin. See DESTROY.

DEMOLISHED adj.   down the tube, down the toilet, done for, wiped off the map, kaput, hashed up, shot, totalled. See DESTROYED.

DEMON n.   fiend, hellion, little devil. See DEVIL.

DEMONSTRATE v. 1. show and tell, roll out, trot out. See DISPLAY. 2. walk one through, crack on one or something, give a for instance, debunk (prove false). See EXPLAIN. 3. sit in, lie in, buck it over, march on, stage a walkout. See STRIKE.

DEMONSTRATION n. lie-in, sit-in, love-in, teach-in, walkout, march, rally. See also STRIKE.

DEMONSTRATOR n. angries, peacenik, protestnik, Vietnik.

DEMORALIZE v. psych out, unglue, unzip, get to, blow up, blow out, take apart, take the steam out, send up, send up the balloon. See also DISTURB.

DEMORALIZED adj. caved in, unzipped, come apart, come apart at the seams, psyched out, go to pieces, lost momentum. See DISCOURAGED.

DEMOTE v. bump, bust, break, rif, bench, set back, hold back.

DEMOTED adj. in the bag (police), benched, busted, broken, set down, set back, held back.

DEMOTION n. rif, bust.

DEMUR v. hem and haw, pussyfoot, pussyfoot around, wait and see.

DEN n. rec room, rumpus room, playroom, family room.

DENIAL n. nix, ixnay, no way, no way Jose, no can do, no sale, no soap, no go, no dice, negatory, turndown, thumbs down, lumps, slap in the face, kick in the teeth, kick in the ass, fubis, 86, like fun, like hell, shove it, shove it up your ass, stick it up your ass, stick it, stow it, frig it, forget it, forget you, who me?, you should live so long, include me out, ask me another, N.O., nope, no siree, unh unh, uh uh, ugh ugh, nah, naw, go take a running jump for yourself, go jump in the lake, over my dead body, not on your life, not by a long chalk, not by a long shot, not by a long sight, not by a darn sight, not by a damn sight, not by a darn, not by a damn, not a bit of it, not much, not a chance, not a Chinaman's chance, fat chance, nothing doing, like hell I will, I'll see you in hell first, stonewall, cold shoulder, cut, go by, hard time (sexual).

DENIED adj. nixed, punched out, turned down, no go, blackballed; 86, eighty-six (denied service, too drunk).

DENIGRATE v. blister, roast, mudsling, run down, put down, tear down, knock, knock down, bad mouth, rip up the back, give a black eye, put away, knock one off his perch, make one sing small. See SLANDER.

DENOMINATION n. handle, moniker, tag, slot, brand, flag (assumed), label, tab.

DENOTE v. flash, button down, put down for, tab, tag, make, peg, finger, put the finger on, put one's finger on, hang a sign on.

DENOUNCE v. rat, rat on, fink, fink on, sing on, stool on, name, drop a dime on one, finger, put the finger on, pin it on one, blow the whistle, lay at one's door. See INFORM.

DENOUNCED adj. blasted, damned, panned, killed, fucked over, caught with a hand in the cookie jar, caught with one's pants down.

DENTAL OFFICE n. tooth booth.

DENTAL STUDENT n. dent.

DENTIST n. butcher, fanger, molar masher.

DENVER, COLORADO Mile High, Mile High City.

DENY v. take the fifth (plead the Fifth Amendment), plead a five, stonewall, nix, be agin, blackball, break with, buck, fly in the face of, turn down, thumbs down, turn thumbs down.

DEODORANT n. smoke screen.

DEOXYRIBONUCLEIC ACID n. DNA.

DEPART v. split, beat it, scram, cut out, cut and run, cut ass, haul ass, bag ass, make feet, make a break, hit the road, hit the trail, hit the bricks, bop off, blast off, fuck off, kick off, shove off, move on, move out, ease on out, ooze out, flake out, peel out, skin out, get, git, get git, blow, take off, take a powder, take it on the lam. See GO.

DEPART EARLY v. party pooper.

DEPARTED adj. bought the farm, passed away, kicked the bucket, cashed in one's chips, pushing up daisies, stone cold, on a slab, finished, kaput, six feet under, popped off, boxed. See DEAD.

DEPARTMENT n. slot, wing.

DEPARTMENT OF ENERGY DOE.

DEPARTMENT OF TRANSPORTATION n. DOT.

DEPARTURE adj. 1. getaway, takeoff, walkout, powder, vanishing act, bow out. 2. in thing, last word, latest thing, latest wrinkle, new wrinkle, newie, newfangled contraption, what's happening, what's in. See NEW.

DEPENDABLE adj. carry the load, rock, Rock of Gibraltar, one who delivers, one who comes through, always there in a pinch, count on one. See TRUSTWORTHY.

DEPENDENCY n. habit, hook, monkey, monkey on one's back, jones, Jones, security blanket. See also ADDICTION.

DEPENDENT adj. on one's back, on one's coattails, carrying one, in one's power, in one's pocket, in one's clutches, under one's thumb, under one's spell, at one's mercy, at one's beck and call, at one's feet, a slave to, beholden to, hooked on, led by the nose, tied to one's apron strings, dance to one's tune.

DEPEND ON v. bank on, bet on, bet one's bottom dollar on, gamble on, lay money on, ride on one's coattails, carry the load, carry the mail.

DEPLETE v. bleed, bleed white, suck dry. See also SQUANDER.

DEPLORABLE adj. awful, dirty, godawful, goshawful, grim, lousy, rotten, stinking, shitty, tough shit, TS, bummer, downer, grabber. See also BAD.

DEPLORE v. carry on, take on, eat one's heart out, sing the blues, cry over spilled milk, cry me a river, hurting. See LAMENT.

DEPOSE v. bounce, boot out, kick out, drum out, freeze out, throw out on one's ear, run out of town, ride out on a rail, give the old heave-ho, send packing. See EJECT.

DEPOSED v. unfrocked (any profession), drummed out, turned off, booted out, run out of town, sent packing.

DEPOSIT n. drop.

DEPOSIT v. drop, park, plant, plank, plank down, plunk, plunk down, plop, stash, stache, ditch, duck, squirrel, squirrel away, sock away.

DEPRAVED adj. kinky, dirty, feelthy, gone to the bad, gone to the dogs, gone to hell, dirty-minded. See WANTON.

DEPRECATE v. rip, put down, take down, run down, cut down to size, pooh pooh, poor mouth, mudsling, give a black eye, take a dim view of, hold no brief for, not go for, not get all choked over, throw cold water on, throw a wet blanket on. See SLANDER.

DEPRESS v. bug, drag, drug, turn one off, bum out, put down, run down, play down, beat, beat down, bring one down, damper, put a damper on, put the zingers in, put the hooks in, put the needle in, chill, chill off, faze, throw cold water on, throw a wet blanket on, act like a wet blanket.

DEPRESSANT n. downer, sleeper.

DEPRESSED adj. dragged, ripped, low, destroyed, dragging ass, ass in a sling, have one's ass in a sling, dick in the dirt, blue, blue funk, in a blue funk, funky, grim, got the blue devils, in the toilet, in the dumper, in the dumps, down, a downer, on a downer, let down, taken down, taken down a peg or two, down in the dumps, in the doleful dumps, down and out, down in the mouth, downbeat (movie, song, etc.), low down, crummy, cleek,

sob story, sob stuff, tear jerker, weeper, teardrop special, make like a crocodile, have the blues, singing the blues, crying the blues, hang crepe, on a bummer, bummed out, flaked out, put away, carry the torch, hurtin', bleeding, in pain, in the pits, down on all fours, shook, shot down, should have stood in bed, carry a heavy load, off one's feed, rhino, have the mulligrubs, have the dolefuls, have the blahs, clanked, clanked up, cracked up, tore up, all torn up, droopy, mopey, moony, gloomy Gus, wet blanket, raining on one's parade, sad sacky, killjoy, prunefaced, sourpuss, spring fever.

DEPRESSED AREA n. ghetto, rig city, rigville, shanty town, ghost town, tar town, dinky town, skid row, tent city, rust belt.

DEPRESSION n. 1. bust, hard times, bad times, slump, crash, rainy days, rainin', bear market, bottom out, slide, the big trouble (the 1930s). 2. blahs, blah blahs, blues, blue devils, blue funk, funk, bummer, downer, dolefuls, dismals, dumps, mumps, mopes, mokers, mulligrubs, down trip, letdown, go downhill, go to the dogs, go to pot, go to pieces, go soft, cave in, hit the skids, come apart at the seams, die on the vine.

DEPRIVE v. stiff, hold back, skim, cold turkey (suddenly and completely).

DEPRIVED adj. have-nots, needy, the poor, truly needy. See also DESTITUTE.

DEPTH BOMB n. ash can, can, tin can.

DEPTH CHARGE n. ash can, can, tin can.

DEPUTY n. backup, sub, dogcatcher, white cap.

DERANGED adj. whacko, loco, ape, ape shit, gone ape, gone ape shit, nuts, nutsy Fagan, unglued, unzipped, unscrewed, loose in the upper story, flipped, flipped out, baked, totally baked, fried, not have all one's marbles, leak in the think tank. See CRAZY.

DERELICT n. bum, bummer, stumblebum, skidrow bum, skidrow stiff, drifter, grifter, slimeball, stiff, bag lady, scumbag, floater. See also BEGGAR.

DERIDE v. pan, put-down, put on, dump on, do a number on, jolly, kid, rag, roast, slam, thumb one's nose at one, give five fingers to one, pooh pooh, hurl a brickbat. See RIDICULE.

DERISION n. slap, slam, swipe, jab, dig, dirty dig, dump, put down, Bronx cheer, the bird, raspberry, razzberry, backhanded compliment, left-handed compliment, brickbat, crack, rank out, comeback, parting shot.

DERISIVE adj. flip, fresh, sassy, smart, smart alecky, smart ass, wise ass, biggety, cocky, cheeky, crusty, gally, nervy, out of line. See SARCASTIC.

DERISIVE SOUND n. boo, bird, Bronx cheer, raspberry, razzberry.

DERIVATION n. spin-off, waves.

DERMATOLOGIST n. zit doctor, skin man.

DERRICK n. Christmas tree.

DESCENDANT n. chip off the old block.

DESCENDING ORDER down the line, pecking order.

DESCRIBE v. rundown, run through, track, picture.

DESCRIPTION n. ABCs, blow by blow, run down, make, picture, fingerprint. See also ACCOUNT.

DESECRATE v. trash, crud up, crumb up, scuzz up, skank, muck up, sleaze up, mess up, piss on, give one a black eye, make one lose face.

DESERT v. go AWOL, go A.W.O.L., go over the hill, go west, go over the side, hit the hump, split, fuck off, take off, take the air, drop out, cut out, opt out, cop out, bail out, pull out, check out, flake out, snake out, crawl out, bug out, light, light out, give up the ship, give up the ghost, hightail, hotfoot, skedaddle, make tracks, run out on, walk out on, walk, take a walk, take French leave, kiss good-bye, cut loose, quit cold, ditch, shake, kick, wash one's hands of, leave flat, leave high and dry, leave holding the bag, leave in the lurch, dump, chuck, fade, do a fade, fade out, fade away, rat, duck, heel, collar a broom, cop a broom, quit the scene, take a powder, sniff a powder. See also GO, ABSCOND, ABANDON.

DESERTER n. AWOL, no-show, hookey player.

DESERTS n. what is coming to one, what one has coming, what one was asking for, get hers, get his, comeuppance.

DESERVE v. rate, be in line for, what is coming to one, what one has coming, get one's comeuppance.

DESEXUALIZE v. cut off one's balls, deball, fix, alter.

DESIGN n. 1. doodle, layout, comp, paste-up, dummy. 2. picture, big picture, game, game plan, play, gimmick, angle, action, pitch, proposition, setup, scenario, scene, story, recipe, trick, bit, child, brainchild, booby trap, lay of the land, what's cookin', how one figures it. See PLAN. See also SCHEME.

DESIGN v. cook up, dream up, sketch out, lay out, work something out. See PLAN.

DESIGNATE v. name, slot, tab, tag, make, peg, finger, lay one's finger on, put one's finger on, put the finger on, button down, pin down, put down for.

DESIRABLE adj. ten, 10, untouchable, drop-dead beautiful, piece, piece of furniture, piece of ass, mink, stone, stone fox, head rush, gimme, centerfold, good enough to eat with a spoon, oh yeah. See BEAUTIFUL.

DESIRE n. bag, itch, hard on for, hots, hot pants, in heat, lech, nasties, the urge, amore, mash, pash, shine, hankering, eyes for, mad for, carry a torch for, have one's tongue hanging out for, have one's mouth fixed for, hurting for, die for, beaver fever, sweet tooth, cup of tea, druthers, go down the line, flash groove, turn on, weakness, fire in the belly, the munchies (food), yen, yen-yen, big eyes, calf love, puppy love, zazzle. See also INCLINATION, LOVE.

DESIRE v. yen for, go for, have the hots for, have hot pants for, hard-on for, cream for, lech for, itch, itch for, hanker for, fall for, have eyes for, big eyes for, spoil for, give one's kingdom in hell for, give one's eyeteeth for, have one's mouth fixed for, mad on, mad for, wild for, crazy for, die over, sweet tooth, sweet on, have a crush on, have a mash on, have a case on, have it bad, be smitten, take to, take a liking to, take a shine to, cotton to, partial to, zazzle.

DESIRED adj. wanted.

DESIROUS adj. horny, turned on, pash, sexy, heavy, hot, hot and heavy, hot baby, hot number, hot pants, hot patootie. See AMOROUS. See also SEXUALLY AROUSED, IMPATIENT.

DESK n. workstation.

DES MOINES, IOWA Dez Minnies.

DESOLATE adj. 1. godforsaken, destroyed. 2. blue, blue funk, ass in a sling, dick in the dirt, down, crying the blues, hurting, in pain, in the pits. See DEPRESSED.

DESPAIR v. bum out, destroy, flatten, take down, take one down, let the air out, eat one's heart out, hit rock bottom, lay the blues on.

DESPAIRING adj. 1. at the end of one's rope, runnin' out of time, can't win for losin', no-win situation, not a prayer, up shit creek, up shit creek without a paddle, sunk, in the soup, shot down, no more cards to play. See HOPELESS. 2. have one's ass in a sling, down in the dumps, teardrop special, crying the blues, hang crepe, bummed out, in pain, in the pits, have the mulligrubs, clanked, clanked up, raining on one's parade. See DEPRESSED.

DESPERATE adj. in the soup, in the toilet, in deep shit, up shit creek, up shit creek without a paddle, up the creek, up the creek without a paddle, hard up, up against it, no way, no-win situation, no more cards to play, sunk, gone, goner, gone goose, dead duck, tryin' to stay alive, runnin' out of time, at the end of one's rope, scrapin' the bottom of the barrel, got one's back to the wall, fighting to keep one's head up, trying to keep one's head above water, can't win for losin', not a ghost of a chance, not a Chinaman's chance, not a prayer, not a snowball's chance in hell, not till hell freezes over.

DESPERATELY adv.   like crazy, like mad.

DESPICABLE adj.   sleazy, sleazeball, slimebucket, maggot, the lowest, low-life, low-down, low-down no-good, down, dirty, low-down and dirty, dirtbag, dirtball; fuckhead, buddy fucker, motherfucker, MF, mofo (all Obsc.); mother lover, mother rucker, mother grabber, mother dangler, dweeb, scurve, scuzzo, scuzzbag, gross, grody, grody to the max, icky, yicky, yucky, shucky, total shuck, beastly, awful, godawful, goshawful, grim, hairy, rotten, gooky, gucky, grungy, bad ass, bitchy, son of a b, son of a bitch, SOB, son of a gun, so and so, son of a so and so, bastard, momzer, snake, snake in the grass, double clutcher, triple clutcher, scumsucking, crummy, cruddy, lousy, shitty, shit-ass, shit heel, heel, shit stick, chicken, chicken shit, meanie, stinking, stinker, stinkeroo, stinky, schtoonk, fink, fink caper, rat caper, rat, rat fink; fuck pig, pig fucker (Obsc.); snide, slimey, pissant, pisshead, beats all, body robber.

DESPISE v.   chill, allergic to, have no use for, down on, put down, run down, do a number on, trash, rubbish, wipe out, look down one's nose at, turn up one's nose at, wouldn't touch something with a ten-foot pole.

DESPONDENT adj.   low, in the pits, blue, blue funk, down in the mouth, ass in a sling, low, bummed out, shot down, all torn up. See DEPRESSED.

DESPOT n.   a Hitler, Simon Legree, slave driver, Czar.

DESPOTIC adj.   bossy, driver, pusher, whip cracker, ass-kicker. See IMPERIOUS.

DESSERTS n.   cush, sweets, g'dong, gedunk, hickey.

DESTINED adj.   in the cards, que sera sera, the way the ball bounces, the way the cookie crumbles, the way the beads read, the handwriting on the wall.

DESTINY n.   break, breaks, karma, the beads, the way the cookie crumbles, the way the ball bounces, handwriting on the wall, in the lap of the gods, Lady Luck, Lady Fortune, Dame Fortune, by and by, from now on in, from here in, from here out, just around the corner.

DESTITUTE adj.   flat, flat broke, dead broke, stone broke, stony, busted, belly up, to the wall, totaled, total wipe, wipe out, wiped out, truly needy, blasted, hard up, strapped, beat, oofless, wasted, clean, cleaned out, tapped, tapped out, melted out, locked out, played out, on one's ass, on the rocks, on the edge, on the ragged edge, on one's uppers, on the hog, on the turf, hurting, pinched, feeling the pinch, down and out, down to one's last cent, down to one's last penny, down at the heel, run down at the heels, looking for a handout, have nots, not have one dime to rub against another, at the end of one's rope, in dire straits, in Queer Street, seen better days, pinched, feeling the pinch, poor, dirt poor, poor as a church mouse, coffee and cake time, cold in hand (Bl.), rhino, for the yoke, on the rims, run on the rims.

DESTROY v.   trash, total, nuke, cream, torpedo, kill, axe, sink, zap, bog, crab, squash, smash, smash up, bitch up, botch up, foul up, fuck up, goof up, pile up, wrack up, crack up, louse up, mess up, muck up, screw up, snarl up, bugger, ball up, bollix up, hash up, put in the toilet, wipe out, wipe off the map, take out, take apart, tear down, break, break the lease, floor, nix, X out, wash out, KO, knock out, knock the bottom out of, knock the chocks out from under, knock the props out from under, stamp out, rub out, queer, zing, blue ruin, blow sky high, poke full of holes, throw a monkey wrench into the works, put out of action, put out of commission, Dutch, flub up, flub the dub, gum, gum up, screw up the works, queer the works, deep six (evidence), jim, pickle, rim rock, put the skids under one, spike one's gun, really fix it. 2. settle one's hash, do, do one in, do in, finish, finish off, fix, fix one's wagon, cook one's goose, clip one's wings. See RUIN.

DESTROYED adj.   totalled, down the tube, down the toilet, down the drain, down the spout, down the rathole, out the window, finished, dead and done for, done for, done in, taken out, wiped out, stamped out, wiped off the map, gone to wrack and ruin, gone to the dogs, gone to pot, gone, had it, kaput, queered, screwed, fouled up, fucked up, mucked up, wracked up, loused up, buggered, gummed up, snarled up, balled up, bollixed up, hashed up, messed up, cooked, on the fritz, on the blink, sunk, shot, kiss [something] good-bye, to hell and gone, in smithereens. See also RUINED.

DESTROYER n.   baby-sitter, can, tin can, garbage can, flivver, rust bucket (all Navy).

DESULTORILY adv.   any old way, any which way, do by halves, half-assed, slapdash, knock off, knock out, bat out, shove out, slap out, slap up, throw off, toss off, toss out, fast and loose, mess around, helter-skelter, by bits and pieces, by fits and starts, in dribs and drabs, hit or miss. See also ERRATICALLY.

DETACHED adj.   cool, play it cool, laid back, far out, out of it, out to lunch, spaced out, spacey. See also ALOOF, INDIFFERENT.

DETAIL n.   1. ABCs, ABC of it, blow-by-blow, rundown, spelled out, like it is, make, picture, the numbers, the goods, bottom line, meat and potatoes, chapter and verse, gospel, megillah, scud, scut, nitty-gritty, nuts and bolts, short stroke, what's what, where it's at, the size of it, the straight of it, cue, clue, dope, brass tacks. 2. kitchen police, KP, shit detail (Mil.).

DETAIL v.   spell out, lay out, take it line by line, fly speck, cross the t's and dot the i's, sweat the details, quote chapter and verse, get down to brass tacks, get down to cases.

DETAILS n.   short strokes, down to the short strokes, nitty-gritty, touches, finishing touches.

DETAIN v. ice, put on ice, put away, send up. See JAIL.

DETAINED adj. hung up, held up, buttonholed. See DELAYED.

DETECT v. uncover, spot, smoke out, smell out, nose out, dig up, hit upon, stumble on, tumble to, wise up to. See DISCOVER.

DETECTIVE n. dick, shamus, flatfoot, tec, private eye, P.I., eye, narc, man, G-man, T-man, revenuer, federal, fed, FBI; Pinkerton, Pink, Pinkie, the Eye, the eye (Pinkerton det. or Pinkerton National Detective Agency); peeper, snoop, shoe, gumshoe, gumboot, gumheel, rubber heel, brain, deek, elbow, fink, plumber, sleeper (male), bird dog, op, nab, peeper, eagle eye, hick dick, house dick, shadow, shagger, slewfoot, stag, star, tail, tin star, pounder, bear tracker (plain clothes), hawkshaw, sleuth, sleuthhound, beagle, skip tracer, spotter; fly ball, fly bob, fly bull, fly cop, fly dick, fly mug (aircraft); cinderball (railroad). See also POLICE OFFICER, OPERATIVE.

DETECTIVE STORY n. whodunit, who-done-it, shocker, chiller, chiller-diller, thriller, cliff-hanger, mystery, spyboiler, grabber.

DETECTOR n. bird dog.

DETER v. cool, chill, turn off, put off, throw cold water on, throw a wet blanket on, act like a wet blanket, damper, put a damper on. See PREVENT.

DETERIORATE v. slide, skid, hit the skids, break, go to pot, go soft, go downhill, go to pieces, go to the dogs, go to Hell in a handbasket, crack, crack up, fold, conk out, peter out, poop out, peg out, fizzle out, cave in, lose it, use it or lose it, over the hill, come apart at the seams, die on the vine, be on one's last legs, have one foot in the grave, have one foot in the grave and the other on a banana peel.

DETERMINATION n. drive, guts, guttiness, intestinal fortitude, the right stuff, starch, backbone, heart, moxie, spunk.

DETERMINE v. 1. figure, figger, have a hunch, be afraid, add up to, boil down to, what one is saying is, size, size up, the way one sees it. 2. opt, tap, cinch, clinch, nail down, pin down, go down the line, be in the driver's seat, call the shots, give the litmus test, lay one's finger on, put one's finger on, take a decision.

DETERMINED adj. 1. set, on ice, in the bag, nailed, nailed down, open and shut, all locked up, have a lock on, lock-and-win situation, no buts about it, no ifs ands or buts, bet on, bet one's bottom dollar on, checked and double-checked, cinched, clinched, for damn sure, surefire, sure, surest thing you know, for sure, fer shure, fer sher, that's for sure, posilutely, absitively, for a fact. 2.

hang in, hang in there, hang tough, go for it, go for broke, go the whole hog, hustle, gritty, gutty, gutsy, game, set, dead set on, sot, bound, bound and determined, scratch, sweat, dig, hammer away, plug, peg away, chill out, do or die, have blood in one's eye, be out for blood, playing for blood, playing hard ball, playing for real, stick at nothing, mean business, strictly business, mean serious jelly, no shit, no bird terdin', not playing around, no fooling, getting it straight, set one's cap for, bent on, hell bent on, hell bent for breakfast, hell bent for leather, pour it on, grind, bear down on it, buckle down, knuckle down, hump it, put one's back into it, high water, come hell or high water, money talks bullshit walks, make no bones about it, unflappable, hard as nails, hard nut to crack, hard boiled, hold the fort, hold the line, pat, brick wall, stay put, stand pat, stand by one's guns, stand one's ground, hold one's ground, dig in one's heels, put one's foot down, solid as a rock, stick it out, stick to one's guns, stick at nothing, stop at nothing, spunky, make no bones about it, knock down and drag out, hard-nosed, take the bit in one's mouth, take the bull by the horns, take the tiger by the tail. See also STUBBORN. 3. in the cards, que sera sera, the way the ball bounces, the way the cookie crumbles, that's the way the beads read.

DETEST v. grossed out on, have no use for, have an allergy, allergic to, down on. See DISLIKE.

DETESTABLE adj. gross, grody, grody to the max, slimey, sleazy, sleazeball, slime bucket, maggot, beastly, awful, godawful, lousy, rotten, triple clutcher, low down. See DESPICABLE.

DETONATABLE adj. live (ammunition), live ammo, ready to blow, hair trigger, touchy.

DETONATE v. push the button, go off, go blooey, go flooey, kablooey, kaflooey, let go, va voom.

DETONATED adj. set off, blown, energetically disassembled, launched.

DETONATION n. energetic disassembly.

DETOUR n. circumbendibus.

DETOUR v. finesse it, go round the barn, went by way of. See also DIGRESS.

DETOXIFICATION CENTER n. detox.

DETOXIFY v. detox, become Mr. Fink, bogue, quit cold turkey, dry out, kick the habit, sweat it out, take the cure, have the shakes, have the wet dog shakes.

DETRACT v. pan, slam, blister, do a number on, mudsling, run down, put down, tear down, shoot down, cut rate, backbite, rip up the back, give a black eye, mark lousy. See SLANDER.

DETRACTION n. put down, rap, slam, black eye, brickbat, dump, hit, knock, backhanded compliment, left-handed compliment. See DEFAMATION.

DETROIT, MICHIGAN   Motown, Motor City.

DETUMESCENT adj.   go flat, go limp.

DEVALUATE v.   knock the bottom out of, nose dive, take down, knock off, cut rate.

DEVASTATE v.   1.trash, total, smash, hash up, put in the toilet, wipe off the map, take apart, break the lease, stamp out. See DESTROY. 2. make hash of, do one in, fix one's wagon, put something out of action, jim, put the skids under one. See RUIN.

DEVASTATED adj.   totalled, shucked, trashed, down the tube, down the rathole, stamped out, had it, kaput, shot, to hell and gone. See DESTROYED.

DEVELOPER n.   1. builder, promoter, wheeler dealer, operator. 2. hypo, soup.

DEVELOPING SOLUTION n.   soup.

DEVELOPMENT n.   buildup, boost, hike, up, up-ping. See ADVANCE.

DEVIANT n.   pervo, prevert. See also HOMO-SEXUAL.

DEVIATE v.   circumlocute, bend the rules, get around, drift.

DEVICE n.   1. angle, dodge, gimmick, slant, trick, twist, switch. See also STRATEGY. 2. gismo, gadget, widget, idiot box, black box, dealie, dealie bob, mother, grabber, gimmick, whatzis, thingumabob. See also APPARATUS.

DEVIL n.   fiend, hellion, little devil, debbil, dybuk, the Deuce, the Dickens, Old Harry, Old Nick, Old Ned, Old Horny, Old Scratch, Old Gooseberry, Old Bendy, Old Clootie, Old Poker, Old Gentleman.

DEVIOUS adj.   fishy, shady, not kosher, playing games, playing politics, put on, the big put on, faking one out, fancy footwork, go round the barn, went by way of, long way. See also SLY, SHREWD.

DEVISE v.   1. brainstorm, head trip, spark, spitball, take it off the top of one's head, mastermind, hatch, make up, think up, come up with, cook up, dream up, trump up, craft, whip up, whomp up, frame up, line up, ready up, throw together, fudge together, get one's act together, get off, work something out, noodle, noodle around. See also PLAN. 2. ad lib, off the top of one's head, fake it, play it by ear. See IMPROVISE.

DEVOTED adj.   gone, gone on, stuck on, hipped on, wild about, mad about, crazy about, nuts about, have a thing about, true blue, old faithful, behind one. See LOYAL. See also AFFECTIONATE.

DEVOTEE n.   groupie, junkie, buff, bug, fan, freak, crazies, nut, trendoid, punker (punk rock), metal head (heavy metal), frenzie, crank, culture vulture, fiend, flip, hound, rooter, booster, alligator, gate, gator, cat, hepcat prophet, stargazer, blue farouq, flunky, stooge, eager beaver, great one for, demon, sucker for, filbert, fool. See also SUPPORTER.

DEVOTEES n.   fandom, groupies, frenzies.

DEVOUR v.   scarf down, chow down, pig out, wolf, wolf down, garbage down, bolt down, inhale, gulp, eat like it's going out of style. See EAT.

DEVOUT adj.   Holy Joe, Jasper, knee bender, born again, got religion, Jesus lover, Jesus freak, Mary, goody, goody-goody, goody two-shoes, scoutmaster.

DEXAMYL n.   Christmas trees, purple heart.

DEXEDRINE n.   dex, dexy, dexie, football, heart, oranges.

DEXEDRINE USE v.   dexed.

DEXTEROUS adj.   good hands, have know-how, savvy, sharp, slick, crack, crackerjack, cute. See SKILLFUL.

DEXTROAMPHETAMINE n.   dex, dexie, dexy, football, heart, greenie, oranges.

DIAGRAM n.   picture, big picture, game, game plan. See PLAN.

DIALECT n.   lingo. See also LANGUAGE.

DIALOGUE n.   rap, rap session, chinfest, small talk, confab, flap (urgent), powwow, talkee-talkee; lines, sides, book (The.).

DIAMOND n.   ice, cracked ice, rock, rock candy, headlight, spark, sparkler, a girl's best friend, pennyweight, Simple Simon.

DIAPER n.   didy, didie.

DIAPER COVER n.   soaker.

DIAPHRAGM n.   rubber cookie, ring, catcher's mitt, plastic clam.

DIARRHEA n.   runs, trots, turistas, shits, G.I.'s, G.I. shits, Basra belly, Delhi belly, gypsy tummy, Hong Kong dog, Johnny trots, Aztec two-step, Mexicali revenge, Montezuma's revenge. See also BOWEL MOVEMENT.

DIARY n.   comic book, funny book, swindle sheet.

DICE n.   craps, cubes, dominoes, galloping dominoes, African dominoes, African golf, perfects, ivories, bones, devil's bones, devil's teeth, horses, Mississippi marbles.

DICE, CROOKED n.   flats, bottoms, horses, busters, bustouts, bevels, coolers, edgework, fading dice, wrong dice, right dice, missouts, platinum loaders, repeaters, peeties, shapes, tappers, tops, t's, downhills, uphills, dis-patchers.

DICE GAMBLER n.   roller, high roller, pad roller, cutter, gaffer, dice hustler.

DICE GAME TERMS craps, floating crap game, dominoes, African dominoes, African golf (Derog.), perfects, bones, ivories, snake eyes (two aces), little Joe, little Joe from Kokomo (four), fever, fever in the South (five), natural (seven), eighter from Decatur, niner, niner from Carolina, nina from Carolina (nine), box cars (pair of sixes), crap out, fade, come, buy the back line.

DICKER v. hammer out a deal, hack out a deal, work out a deal, cut a deal, Jew down, hondle. See NEGOTIATE.

DICTATE v. call the play, call the signals, call the tune, lay down the law, put one's foot down, read the riot act, walk heavy, bulldoze, take the reins. See COMMAND.

DICTATOR n. a Hitler, Simon Legree, slave driver, czar.

DICTATORIAL adj. bossy, crack the whip, throw one's weight around. See IMPERIOUS.

DICTATORSHIP n. garrison state.

DIDACTIC adj. preachy.

DIE v. go, kick off, kick the bucket, kick in, buy it, buy the farm, pass away, croak, cool, cool off, bump, bump off, meet one's maker, meet Mr. Jordan, give up the ghost, turn up one's toes, breathe one's last, OD, pull the plug, flatline (Medic.), go west, go north, go down the tube, go to kingdom come, sprout wings, go home feet first, go home in a box, go to the wall, go flooey, go blooey, go belly up, bite the dust, kiss the dust, kiss off, knock off, pop off, slam off, drop off, pipe off, shove off, step off, step off the deep end, go off the deep end, cash in, cash in one's chips, pass in one's chips, pass in one's checks, hand in one's chips, call off all bets, check out, check in, quit the scene, eat it, had it, head for the last roundup, take the last count, take the long count, make the last muster, over the creek, gone across the creek, slip one's cable, push up daisies, grounded for good, strike bedrock, deep six, take a dirt nap, go to Davy Jones's locker (drown), hop the twig, cook, fry, shove over, quit it, up and die, peg out, pass out, strike out, chalk out, flake out, flack, flack out, head for a hearse, back gate, back door parole, get a back-gate commute, one-way ticket, one-way ride, kayoed for keeps, trumped; dance, dance on air, dance on nothing, dance off (hang).

DIEHARD n. bitter ender, standpatter.

DIESEL ENGINE n. smudge pot.

DIET n. chow, snack, bite, eats, go juice, peckings (Bl.), grubbery, goodies, grub. See FOOD.

DIET v. skinny, skinny down, count calories, fall off (lose weight), watch one's weight, slim down.

DIET SPA n. fat farm.

DIFFER v. bump heads, lock horns, go at it, go after each other, hit a clinker, hit a sour note, sound a sour note. See also DISAGREE.

DIFFERENCE n. 1. dif, diff, different strokes, different strokes for different folks. 2. spat, tiff, words, bone to pick, beef, blowup, dustup, hassle, rhubarb, row, run-in, scrap, brawl, brannigan, blow-off, brush, brush-off, catamaran. See ARGUMENT.

DIFFERENT adj. dif, diff, far cry, funky, offbeat, poles apart, weird, whale of a difference, like night and day, march to the beat of a different drummer.

DIFFERENTIATE v. know what's what, know one's ass from a hole in the ground, know one's ass from one's elbow, know a rock from a hard place, know shit from Shinola, split hairs, redline (financial), Jim Crow.

DIFFICULT adj. uphill, uphill battle, wicked, mean, heavy, hairy, murder, pisser, rough, bitch, son of a bitch, son of a gun, stiff, tough, tough one, tough nut to crack, toughie, tough proposition, tough lineup to buck, rough go, separates the men from the boys, hard job, hard pull, hard row to hoe, hard row of stumps, hard way, hi tech, handful, ballbreaker, ballbuster, ass buster, conk buster, backbreaker, headache, large order, tall order, honey, no picnic, no piece of cake, sticky, sticky wicket, can of worms, makes the cheese more binding, heavy sledding, roundabout way.

DIFFICULTIES n. bummer, downer, hard knocks, hard row to hoe, rotten luck, tough luck, raw deal, bad break, rotten break, tough break, up against it, on the skids, down on one's luck. See ADVERSITY.

DIFFICULTY n. shit, deep shit, serious jelly, serious shit, bad news, clutch, hang-up, drag, bind, double bind, tall order, large order, rough go, heavy sledding, rain, ticklish spot, tricky spot, tight spot, tight squeeze, lose-lose situation, no win situation, gasser, pisser, rat's nest, snake pit, box, crunch, catch, catch 22, bitch, handful, headache, bummer, downer, worriment, botheration, grabber, hooker, double trouble, behind the eight ball, boxed in, in a box, in a fix, in a hole, snafu, jam, in a jam, in a clutch, in a mess, in a pickle, scrape, in a scrape, in a spot, in a tight spot, in a hot spot, on the hot seat, hot water, in deep water, in heavy water, stew, in a stew, in over one's head, up a tree, up the creek, up the creek without a paddle, up shit creek, up shit creek without a paddle, pain in the ass, pain in the neck, between a rock and a hard place, tail in a gate, tit in a wringer, mix, mess, holy mess, unholy mess, kettle of fish, fine kettle of fish, a fine mess you've got us into, how do you do, fine how do you do, hobble, pickle, pretty pickle, pretty pass, squeeze, sticky wicket, hard row to hoe, hard row of stumps, hard time, hard pull, heat's on, a mountain out of a molehill, heavy load to haul, the devil to pay, hell to pay, bug, glitch, hitch, puzzler, can of peas, can of worms,

Pandora's box, green hornet (Mil.), hot potato, stinker, tsuris, tumul, what's with, sixty-four dollar question, twister, teaser, sticker, floorer, stumper, bugaboo, crimp, crimp one's style, hump, stinger, hot grease, jackpot, mess up, screw up, need it like a hole in the head, next week East Lynne, rub, push comes to shove, when things get tough, toughie, tough proposition, tough to buck, tough nut to crack, tough going, hard going, joker, scuffle, put on the spot, hit a snag, a hold up, cropper, come a-cropper, one small difficulty.

DIFFIDENT adj. mousy, rabbity.

DIG v. really get into, leave no stone unturned, look all over hell, search high heaven, shake, shake down, turn inside out, turn upside down. See SEARCH.

DIGEST v. cut, cut down, cut to the bone, nutshell, put in a nutshell, boil down, trim, get to the meat. See SHORTEN.

DIGESTIVE TRACT n. plumbing, guts, innards, inners, insides, gizzard, stuffings, spaghetti.

DIGGER n. groundhog, sandhog.

DIGIT n. claw, fang (musician), feeler (middle finger), fish hooks, forks, hooks, lunch hooks, meat hooks, pinkie, poppers, stealers.

DIGNIFIED adj. highfalutin', high-minded, high nosed, high-toned, stiff-necked. See also MAJESTIC, POMPOUS.

DIGRESS v. circumlocute, get sidetracked, all over the map, go round the barn, go by way of, long way, long way home.

DILAPIDATED adj. beat up, crummy, raunchy, tacky, ratty, ramshackle, rinky-dink, rinky-tinky, slummy, frowzy, fruit, dog eared, used up, in a bad way.

DILEMMA n. box, in a box, bind, double bind, up shit creek without a paddle, catch 22, one small difficulty, grabber, hooker, pickle. See PREDICAMENT.

DILETTANTE adj. half-assed, half-baked, half-cocked, artsy fartsy.

DILIGENT adj. grind, plugger, whiz, nose to the grindstone, springbutt, eager beaver, work one's tail off. See INDUSTRIOUS.

DILUTE v. doctor, doctor up, phony up, plant, spike, water, water down, baptize, irrigate, cook, cut, needle, lace, shave.

DIMETHYLTRYPTAMINE n. DMT.

DIMINISH v. 1. soft-pedal, take the bite out, take the edge off, take the sting out, throw a wet blanket on, throw cold water on, whitewash, water down. See QUIET. 2. dump on, run down, put down, tear down, cut down to size, poor-mouth, bad-mouth, put away. See BELITTLE.

DIMINISHED adj. eat crow, eat dirt, eat humble pie, sing small, put down, egg on one's face, knocked from one's high horse, got one's comeuppance. See BELITTLED.

DIMINUTIVE adj. mini, teeny, teensy, bitty, bitsy, itsy-bitsy, wee, peewee, button, yea big, mite, pint-sized. See SMALL.

DIN n. hubba-hubba, hullaballoo, buzz-buzz, boom-boom, hoo-ha, rowdydow, hell broke loose, all hell broke loose.

DINE v. eat out, do lunch. See also EAT.

DINING ROOM n. caf, crumb hall. See also RESTAURANT.

DINNER n. eats, chow, chow fight, major munch, din din, feedbag, ribs, potluck, Early Bird Special. See also FOOD.

DINNER PAIL n. nose bag, feedbag.

DIP v. dunk.

DIPHTHERIA n. dip.

DIPLOMA n. shingle, sheepskin, dip.

DIPLOMAT n. cookie pusher.

DIPPER n. bug (industrial or baker).

DIPROPYLPHYPTAMINE n. DPT

DIPSOMANIAC n. dip, dipso, power drinker, drunk, boozer, boozehound, stewbum, rummy, wino, lush, barfly, souse, shikker, soak, tippler, long hitter, juice head. See DRINKER.

DIRECT adj. 1. open, straight, straight out, straight from the shoulder, from the horse's mouth, calling a spade a spade, talk turkey. See FRANK. 2. nonstop, beeline, as the crow flies, down the alley, down the pipe, in the groove, on the beam.

DIRECT v. 1. head up, boss, shepherd, run things, call the shots, quarterback, be in the driver's seat, conn (Navy vessel), take the reins, have the say. See MANAGE. 2. target, zero in, move in, sight, sight on.

DIRECT ADDRESS n. Man, Son, Sonny, Doc, Mac, Bo, Brother, Sister, doll, jellybean, pussycat, pal, bub, bud, buddy, buddy boy, good buddy, pard, pardner, Jack, Jackson, Joe, Joe Blow, Jim, kid, kiddo, kiddie, keed, buster, Lady (sarcastic), mate, matie, Mister (Derog.), Melvin, Charley, Chester, hey, hey you, motherfucker (Derog.), mother grabber, mofo, mother, ma, mama, pop, pops, dad, daddio, Sir, ma'am, baby, stinky, tubby, fatso, people, shortie, stupid, four eyes, so and so (affectionate or Derog.), sweetheart, sweetie, sweetie pie, buttercup, toots, tootsie, dear, dearie, darling, old bean, old man, old friend, old chap, old boy, old fellow, old fruit, old fart, old goat, old sock, old thing, old top, son of a bitch, son of a gun, son of a sea cook.

DIRECT CURRENT n. DC

DIRECTION n. 1. that a way, every which way, forty ways to Sunday, forty ways from Sunday. 2. tip, steer, bum steer. See also COUNSEL.

DIRECTION FINDER n. HFDF, huff duff.

DIRECTIONS n. dope sheet, DWIM (do what I mean), DTRT (do the right thing), poop sheet.

DIRECTLY adv. slap, smack, plump, slam bang, smack dab, right outta the box.

DIRECTOR n. top brass, head honcho, skipper, old man, Big Daddy, big player, big chew, exec, man upstairs, kingpin, top dog, key player. See EXECUTIVE.

DIRECTORATE n. brass, front office, people in the front office, man upstairs, people upstairs, executive suite, top brass, Big Brother. See MANAGEMENT.

DIRECTORY n. laundry list (agenda), enemies list, black list (punished or ostracized), crap list, hit list, shitlist, S list, drop dead list (fired, expelled, excluded), sucker list, short list, book (pimp's list), black book, little black book, scorecard, lineup, bluebook, white book, plum book (Govt. positions), charts, pap (Annapolis), white pages, yellow pages (telephone).

DIRIGIBLE n. blimp, gasbag.

DIRT n. 1. state, real estate, dust. 2. gook, dreck, crud, gunk, mung, prut, scuz, smut, sleaze.

DIRTY adj. 1. crud, cruddy, crumb, crumby, crummy, crusty, grungy, mung, icky, yecchy, yucky, chili bowl (person), pigpen, barn, stable, stall, scuzzy, skank, raunchy, messy, mess, mess up, muss, muss up, sleazy, sleaze up, mucky, muck up, crud up, crum up. 2. below the belt, not cricket, raw deal.

DIRTY ROOM n. pigpen, pigsty, stable, stall, live-in wastebasket.

DISABLE v. total, wing, ding, tweak, bend the goods, hamstring, queer, shoot down, knock out, take out, hog-tie, bugger, kibosh, put the kibosh on, put out of commission, fuck up, screw up, screw up the works, queer the works, gum up the works, throw a monkey wrench into the works, throw a monkey wrench in the machinery, spike one's guns, put a spoke in one's wheels, clip the wings of, take the wind out of one's sails, knock the props out from under, cut the ground out from under, not leave a leg to stand on. See also SABOTAGE.

DISABLED adj. crip, gimp, gimpy, game, g'd up, geed up, hamstrung, hog-tied, taken out, sidelined, out of commission.

DISADVANTAGE adj. be had by the balls, be had by the short hairs, be had by the tail, dead man's hand, hipped, underdog, knock.

DISADVANTAGED adj. down and out, hard up (also sexual), have-nots, needy, truly needy, the poor, locked out. See DESTITUTE.

DISADVANTAGEOUS adj. debit side, on the debit side, down side, down tick, the bad news. See also UN-PROFITABLE.

DISAGREE v. 1. jockey for position, scramble for, go for, go for it, go for broke, go for the throat, go for the jugular, go at it, go after each other, go after. 2. cross, take on, sock, sock it to one, break with, fly in the face of, be agin, buck, nix, have a bone to pick, pettifog, put up an argument, set to, zap, zapper, pitch into, light into, lay into, wade into, lace into, sail into, come at, go at, lay at, have at, have at it, lean on, crack down on, gang up on, jump, jump on, jump on one's case, jump down one's throat, come down on, come down hard on one, land on, land all over, lay out, let have it, let have it with both barrels, give one both barrels, blast, rip, rip into, rip up, rip up one side and down the other, put up a fight, mix it up with, tangle with, bump heads with, cross swords with, lock horns with, stick it to one, hit a sour note, sound a sour note, hit a clinker, sound a clinker.

DISAGREEABLE adj. 1. bitchy, out of sorts, cantankerous, grouchy, uptight, Mr. Coffee Nerves, beefing, bellyaching. See IRRITABLE. 2. awful, drag, draggy, gummy, pain, pain in the ass, pain in the neck, sleazeball, sour, sourpuss, witch. See OBNOXIOUS.

DISAGREEMENT n. split, spat, tiff, beef, scrap, hassle, rhubarb, fuss, wrangle, brawl, brush, brush-off, row, rumpus, ruckus, ruction, words, flak, far cry, poles apart, whale of a difference, blow-off, blowup, bone, pick a bone, bone to pick, bone of contention, no way, shindy, set to, run-in, brannigan, catamaran. See also ARGU-MENT.

DISALLOW v. kill, ding, zing, nix, put down, pass on. See DISAPPROVE.

DISAPPEAR v. go south, do a vanishing act, fade, fade out of sight, fade away, melt into the scenery, pull a Judge Crater.

DISAPPOINT v. let down, break a date, no show, stand one up. See also FRUSTRATE.

DISAPPOINTED adj. down, let down, a downer, taken down, down in the dumps, in a blue funk. See also UNHAPPY.

DISAPPOINTMENT n. bummer, downer, drag, letdown, fizzle, fizzle out, not hack it, not make it, also ran, bringdown, half-assed, half-baked, a lemon, bitter pill, bitter pill to swallow, set back, the old one two, that's it?, that's all there is there isn't any more?, this is what we came for, this is what it's all about?, you want it should sing too?, what you see is what you get.

DISAPPROVAL n. nix, ding, zing, square, nuts, balls, your mama (Bl.), call down, rap on the knuckles, slap on the wrist, is that so, izzat so, shee-it, blow it out, not on your life, no siree, no way, no you don't, no eyes for.

DISAPPROVE v. pan, slam, knock, hit, rap, kill, ding, zing, nix, pass on, turn thumbs down, thumb down, blackball, call down, put down, take a dim view of, hold no brief for, not go for, not get all choked up over. See also REJECT, FROWN.

DISAPPROVED adj. blasted, damned, over, panned, killed, kissed off, blooming, dadblamed, dadblasted, darn, drat, in the doghouse, out in the cold, left out.

DISARM v. skin.

DISARMAMENT n. take 'em down.

DISARRANGED adj. beat up, messed up, mussed up, messy, mussy, sloppy, grubby, scuzzed, scuzzed up.

DISARRAY n. all over hell, all over the shop, harumscarum, bloody mess, holy mess, unholy mess, topsyturvy, arsy-varsy. See also CHAOS, MISFORTUNE.

DISASSOCIATE v. blow one off, cut loose, drop out, have no truck with, steer clear, back off, back away from. See DISENGAGE. See also SEPARATE.

DISASTER n. bummer, downer, grabber, shit, deep shit, shit hit the fan, total shuck, bad news, the worst, blue ruin, bitch, rough, tough, hot water, curtains, Waterloo, screw up, mess up, holy mess, unholy mess, rainin', double trouble, hard time, headache, hot grease, jackpot, tsuris, need it like a hole in the head, can of worms, crunch. See also MISFORTUNE.

DISAVOW v. dial back, backwater, crawfish, crawfish out, drop out, nig, renig, wash one's hands of, welsh, go back on one's word, weasel out, worm one's way out of, worm out of.

DISAVOWAL n. no way, no way Jose, no go, no dice, N.O., nope, ugh ugh, fat chance, nothing doing. See DENIAL.

DISBARRED adj. unfrocked, drummed out.

DISBELIEF n. balls, blow it out, bull finch, bullshit, bullchitna (Esk.), horseshit, horse hockey, hockey pucks, get outta town, so's your old man, vanilla.

DISBELIEVING adj. cagey, leery, been hit before.

DISBURSE v. pay off, foot the bill, cough up, pony up, ante up, come through, come across, come up with, shell out, put out, fork out. See PAY.

DISCARD v. chuck, chuck out, eighty-six, ditch it, junk, adios, toss, dump, scrap, give the old heave-ho,

throw over, throw overboard, deep six, throw on the junk heap, toss onto the scrap heap, retire, file it in the circular file, kiss, kiss off, kiss [something] good-bye, cut loose, chop out.

DISCERN v. 1. spot, dig, read, focus, take in, get a load of, rubberneck, give one the beady eye, give with the eyes, put the squint on. See SEE. 2. get, read, get the picture, see the light, blow wise, get wise to, dig, I know where you're comin' from, figure out, have one's number. See UNDERSTAND.

DISCERNMENT n. aha reaction, savvy, hep to, wise to, see the light, flash on it, get one's drift, on the same wavelength, I got it, it hit me, it just came to me.

DISCHARGE n. ax, boot, door, gate, pink slip, walking papers, walking ticket, bounce, bum's rush, kicking out, old heave ho. See DISMISSAL.

DISCHARGE v. can, fire, bump, bounce, boot, boot out, kick, kick out, kick upstairs, lay off, rif (reduction in force), bust, nix, X-out, ax, give the ax, give the air, give one his walking papers, hand one his walking papers, sack, give the sack to, give one the old heave-ho, give the bum's rush, give the hook, give the pink-slip, pink slip, give the gate, show the gate, show the door, wash out, drum out, freeze out, lock out, let out, let one go, throw out on one's ear, run out of town, ride out on a rail, get rid of, kiss off, kiss one good-bye, flush, shake, scrub, send packing, send to the showers.

DISCHARGE NOTICE n. pink slip, walking papers, walking ticket.

DISCHARGED adj. 1. beat the rap, walked, let off, let go, section eight. 2. launched, set off, blown, energetically disassembled. 3. fired, canned, kicked out, let out, locked out, laid off, sacked, booted, bounced, dumped, axed, pink-slipped, got the ax, got the gate, got the sack, got the mat, got the burlap, got a pink slip, got it in the neck, shown the door, given the boot, packed it in, unfrocked (by profession), drummed out, turned off, written off, heads rolled.

DISCIPLE n. booster, buff, bug, fan, freak, groupie, junkie, nut, punker (punk rock), crank, culture vulture, fiend, hound, rooter, flunky, stooge. See DEVOTEE.

DISCIPLINARIAN n. chicken shit, chicken shit guy, sundowner.

DISCIPLINE n. chicken shit, lumps, catch hell, salt mines, back to the salt mines, pay through the nose, for it, going over, hell to pay, get yours, comeuppance, get what is coming to one, ass-kicking. See also PUNISHMENT.

DISCIPLINE v. chew, chew ass, chew out, eat out, ream out, straighten out, jump on one's shit, climb one's frame, jawbone, come down on. See PUNISH.

DISC JOCKEY n. deejay, D.J.

DISCLOSE v. fess, fess up, croon, snitch, squeal, stool, spill, leak, buzz (in secret), drop a dime on one, come out of the closet, put it on the street, put one in the picture, go the hang-out road. See CONFESS.

DISCLOSURE n. ABCs, blow by blow, run down, make, picture, handout, leak, showdown, tip, tip-off, squeal, snitch. See also REVELATION.

DISCONCERT v. bug, get to, discomboberate, discombobulate, ball up, foul up, fuck up, psych out, upset one's apple cart. See CONFUSE.

DISCONCERTED adj. unglued, come unzipped, come apart, all shook up, spaced out, hung up, messed up attic, in a botheration, psyched out. See CONFUSED.

DISCONNECT v. break it off, break it up, drop, drop it, sideline. See DISCONNECT.

DISCONSOLATE adj. destroyed, put away, low, hurtin', in pain, in the pits, cracked up, cut up, tore up, ripped. See DEPRESSED.

DISCONTENTED adj. bitching, crabby, kvetching, griping, picky, picky-picky, that's it?, that's all there is there isn't any more?, this is what we came for?, this is what it's all about?, you want it should sing too?, what you see is what you get, down in the mouth, in the dumps, blue, the natives are restless See UNHAPPY.

DISCONTINUE v. scrub, kill, pack in, drop, blow off, knock it off, break off, call all bets off, call it quits, bag it. See STOP.

DISCONTINUOUSLY adv. by bits and piece, by fits and starts, hit or miss, in dribs and drabs, willy-nilly, herky-jerky. See ERRATICALLY.

DISCORD n. 1. diff, split, spat, hassle, static, beef, row, ruckus, ruction, rumpus, run-in, scrap, scene, set-to, fuss, dustup, hoedown, knockdown, bone, pick a bone, bone of contention, no way, far cry, bad vibes, poles apart, sockdolager, flak, clincher, crusher, finisher, rhubarb, shindy, squelcher, dead horse, wrangle, whale of a difference, like night and day, march to the beat of a different drummer. See also ARGUMENT. 2. clinker, sour note.

DISCORDANT adj. clinker, sour note, hit a clinker, hit a sour note, sound a clinker, sound a sour note.

DISCOTHEQUE n. disco.

DISCOUNT n. deduck (income tax item), cut, cut back, rollback, knock off.

DISCOUNTENANCE v. hold no brief for, take a dim view of, not go for, not stand for, not one's kinda guy, not one's cup of tea, include me out.

DISCOURAGE v. cool, chill, turn off, put off, kid out of, talk out of, take the air out of one's balloon, throw cold water on, throw a wet blanket on, put a damper on, put the zingers in. See PREVENT.

DISCOURAGED adj. down, beat, downbeat, beat down, down in the mouth, down in the dumps, in a funk, in a blue funk, caved in, unzipped, unglued, come apart, come apart at the seams, fall apart at the seams, psyched out, shot, shot to pieces, gone to pieces, lost momentum.

DISCOURSE n. rap, rap session, buzz session, hash session, rapping rash, talkfest, gabfest, bull fest, bull session, clambake, huddle, spiel. See SPEAK.

DISCOURSE v. chew, chew over, chew the fat, chew the rag, rag around, modulate, modjitate, kick the gong around, punch the gun, blow change, give a meeting, hold a meet, confab, talk turkey. See SPEAK.

DISCOURTEOUS adj. flip, fresh, sassy, smart alecky, cheeky, crusty, roll over one, cut, cold shoulder, chit. See INSOLENT.

DISCOURTESY n. cheap shot, put down, zinger, back-handed compliment, left-handed compliment, brickbat, dump, low rent.

DISCOVER v. pick up on, dig up, hit upon, be hep to, be on to, stumble on, trip over, tumble to, wise up to, right under one's nose, uncover, strike (oil, gold), spot, spark, smoke out, smell out, nose out, suss out, see the light, bring to light, catch flatfooted, catch red-handed, catch with one's pants down, catch with one's hand in the cookie jar, have dead to rights, have one's number.

DISCOVERY n. a find, luck out, luck into, fall into.

DISCREDIT v. mudsling, run down, put down, tear down, cut rate, pooh-pooh, mark lousy, poke full of holes, knock one off one's perch. See BELITTLE.

DISCREDITED adj. lost face, in bad, in Dutch, in the doghouse, drummed out, paper tiger, crawl, sing small, bad ass. See also BELITTLED.

DISCREET adj. clam, clam up, hush-hush, on the Q.T., zip one's lips, button up, button up one's lip, between one and the lamp post, tight chops, handle with kid gloves, mind one's p's and q's, on the lookout.

DISCREPANCY n. far cry, poles apart, whale of a difference, split.

DISCRETIONARY adj. the call, the judge and jury, call it as one sees it.

DISCRIMINATE v. know what's what, know one's ass from one's elbow, know one's ass from first base, know one's ass from a hole in the ground, know shit from Shinola, know a rock from a hard place, make out, split hairs, redline (Fin.), Jim Crow.

DISCRIMINATING adj. picky, picky picky, choicy, choosey, pernickety, persnickety. See PARTICULAR.

DISCUSS v. rap, chew over, hash, rehash, hash over, let the daylight in, let the sunlight in, talk game, figure, figure out, sort out, blitz, brainstorm, confab, get heads together, groupthink, huddle, go into a huddle, flap, take a meeting, have a meet, toss some ideas around, kick some ideas around, kick around, knock around, rag around, run something by one, pick one's brains. flog a dead horse, whip a dead horse, blow, blow hot air, bounce off one. See also DELIBERATE, CONFER.

DISCUSSION n. meet, confab, huddle, powwow, think-in, groupthink, gam, rap, rap session, buzz session, clambake, eyeball-to-eyeball encounter, flap, bull yard, chalk talk (Prof. and Stu., informal, sports). See also MEETING.

DISDAIN v. chill, put down, run down, look down one's nose at, turn up one's nose at, wouldn't touch [anything] with a ten foot pole, allergic to, down on.

DISDAINFUL adj. cool, dicty, on one's high horse, put on airs, have one's glasses on (Bl.), toplofty, snooty, king shit, high hat, uppity. See ARROGANT.

DISEASE n. bug, crud, creeping crud, the runs, the flu, the pip, what's going around, dose, double scrudfantods, fascinoma (Medic.). See ILLNESS.

DISEASE, MYTHICAL n. the bug, crud, creeping crud, scrud, double scrudfantods, willies, the pip, gaposis (gap in clothing), medical student's disease.

DISENGAGE v. pull the plug, back out, back out of, back off, back away from, opt out, drop out, cut out, cut loose, fink out, poop out, crawfish out, veg out, weasel out, worm out of, crawl out of, wangle out of, backpedal, backwater, draw in one's claws, draw in one's horns, kiss off, blow one off, have no truck with, steer clear, turn tail, turn tail and run, stand down, quit cold, eyes to cool it, leave flat, throw over, crash, pull in one's horns. See also SEPARATE.

DISENTANGLE v. bail one out, get out from under, let go, let off, let off the hook. See FREE.

DISFAVOR v. blackball, turn thumbs down on, put one on one's shitlist, scratch one off one's list, hold no brief for, not get all choked up over. See DISAPPROVE.

DISFAVORED adj. off one's list, on one's list, on one's shitlist, on one's enemies list, on the shelf, in Dutch, in wrong, in bad, in limbo, in the doghouse, in the shithouse, got one's ass in sideways, out in the cold, left out.

DISGORGE v. barf, puke, throw up, upchuck, Ralph, talk to Ralph on the big white phone, York, toss one's tacos, flash one's cookies, pray to the porcelain god, drive the porcelain bus, laugh at the carpet. See VOMIT.

DISGRACE n. comedown, put-down, dump, in the doghouse, black eye, skeleton in the closet, skeleton in the cupboard. See also SCANDAL.

DISGRACE v. lose face, give a black eye. See HUMILIATE. See also DESECRATE.

DISGRACED adj. in bad, in Dutch, in the doghouse, bad ass, gone to bad, gone to the dogs, gone to hell, took down, put down, come down, dumped on, drummed out, crawl, draw in one's horns, eat dirt, eat crow, eat humble pie, lost face, egg on one's face, knocked from one's high horse, knocked off one's perch, put a tuck in one's tail, stumped, stymied, sing small.

DISGRUNTLED adj. beefing, bitching, kicking, bellyaching, crabbing, crabby, kvetching, cranky, griping, grouchy, grousing. See UNHAPPY.

DISGUISE n. cover-up, beard, front, fig leaf, camel flags (WWI).

DISGUISE v. beard, whitewash, wear cheaters, cover up, slap on some glims, flash the gogs, throw on a make up, phony up one's getup, front, put up a front, put on a front, put on a false front, put on an act, put up a bluff, pull up a bluff, make like.

DISGUISED adj. incog., bearded.

DISGUSTED adj. have a bellyful, have a skinful, scuzzed out, grossed out, turned off, grody, grody to the max, frosted, browned off, pissed off, cheesed off, T'd off, ech, eeoooh, fed up, full up, up to here, gives one a pain, gives one a pain in the neck, gives one a pain in the ass.

DISGUSTING adj. gross, grossed out, grody, grody to the max, it stinks, it sucks, scuzzy, scuzzed out, stinking, skank, icky, yecchy, yucky, lousy, rotten, mothering, mother-fucking (Obsc.), mother-grabbing, mother-nudging, turn off, faust, beastly, furry, awful, godawful, goshawful, grim, uncool, draggy, creepy, stinky, rotten, sleazy, sleazeball, nerdy, twerdy, wimpy, spastic, funky (Bl.), drippy, simpy, lousy, specimen, bad case of the uglies, dumb cluck, dummy, gummy, cotton picking, in one's hat, for the birds, gives one a pain, gives one a pain in the neck, gives one a pain in the ass, pesky, pestiferous, bitchy.

DISH n. manhole cover.

DISHEVELED adj. beat up, messed up, mussed up, messy, mussy, sleazy, sloppy, grubby, scuzzy, scuzzed, scuzzed up, hagged out.

DISHONEST adj. crooked, crooked stick, bent, shady, fishy, fish, dog, gyp, racket, sneaky, slick, sharp, shifty, shifty eyed, wrong, wrong number, wrong gee, not kosher, cheatin', cheatin' heart, dirty, low-down and dirty, dirty work, on the make, on the take, on the pad, play hard, fink out, no-good, N.G., no account, no 'count, no bargain, honest John, shitheel, shit hook, worm, tinhorn, convict, copper-hearted, crum, crumb, slimy, trust one as far as one can swing a cat, trust one as far as one can throw an elephant.

DISHONOR v.   give one a black eye, make one lose face. See also DESECRATE, PROFANE.

DISHONORABLE DISCHARGE n.   kick, D.D.

DISHONORED adj.   lost face, drummed out, in the doghouse, eat crow, eat dirt, eat humble pie. See DISGRACED.

DISHWASHER n.   pearl diver, pot walloper, suds buster, deep sea chef (hobo).

DISILLUSION v.   debunk, turn off, talk out of, kid out of, put off, let down easy, puncture one's balloon, kick in the ass, kick in the stomach, kick in the heart, break one's heart, throw cold water on, throw a wet blanket on.

DISINFORMATION n.   con, scam, spiel, bull, bullshit, BS, bullshitting, a line, baloney, horseshit, the big lie (Pol.), borax, they're pissing on us and telling us it's raining.

DISINTERESTED adj.   not give a damn, not give a shit, so? so what? what's the diff? what the hell, clockwatcher. See INDIFFERENT.

DISJOINTED adj.   fuzzy, spacey, spaced out, out of it, out to lunch, play it cool, cool, far out.

DISLIKE v.   turned off by, grossed out on, have no use for, allergic to, have an allergy to, down on, turn thumbs down on, take a dim view of, hold no brief for, not go for, not get all choked over, put one on one's list, put one on one's shit list, scratch one off one's list, for the birds, gives one a pain, gives one a pain in the neck, gives one a pain in the ass, have a hate on for.

DISLIKED PERSON n.   asshole, jackass, horse's ass, sleaze, sleazeball, meatball, mother, muthuh, motherfucker (Obsc.), mofo, weasel, rat, fink, rat fink, prick, cock sucker, peckerwood (B.I.), scumbag (Obsc.), zod, nerd, schmo, jerk, jerk off, twerp, banana, creep, drip, dumb cluck, dummy, gross, loser, winner, mince, mole, moron, nothing, simp, spastic, stinker, stinkpot, turkey, weenie, wimp, yo-yo, zombie, corpse, droop, herkle, prune, specimen, cotton-picker, dipstick, bad case of the uglies, won't give one the time of day, louse.

DISLOCATED adj.   in the wrong box, right church wrong pew, in the right church but the wrong pew, in the wrong pew, like a fish out of water, out of one's element, nowhere.

DISLOYAL adj.   two-timing, cheater, double-crossing, two-faced, snakey, snake in the grass, worm. See UNFAITHFUL.

DISMAL adj.   low, ass in a sling, dick in the dirt, crying the blues, bummed out, flaked out, hurting, in the pits, down in the dumps, out, down in the mouth. See DEPRESSED.

DISMANTLE v.   part out.

DISMAY n.   blues, blahs, blue devils, blue funk, deep funk, funk, bummer, dolefuls, letdown, downer, down trip, dumps, mumps, mopes, miseries, mulligrubs, the mokers, mess and a half, bloody mess, holy mess, unholy mess, hassle, who's minding the store?, pretty kettle of fish, pretty piece of business, nice piece of work. See also FEAR.

DISMAY v.   faze, flummox, get to, throw, throw into a tizzy, ball up, bollix up, foul up, fuck up, louse up, mess up, muck up, screw up, snafu, play hob with. See FRIGHTEN. See also CONFUSE.

DISMAYED adj.   push the panic button, scared stiff, pee in one's pants, spooked, goose bumpy, pucker-assed, given a jar, dragged, blue, got the blue devils, hang crepe, bummed out, shook, shot down, all torn up. See FRIGHTENED.

DISMISS v.   1. can, fire, bump, boot, lay off, give the ax, give one his walking papers, sack, pink-slip, wash out, rif (reduction in force). See DISCHARGE. 2. throw out on one's ear, run out of town, ride out on a rail, get rid of, kiss one good-bye, flush, shake, scrub, send packing, send to the showers. See also EJECT, BANISH.

DISMISSAL n.   ax, pink slip, sack, boot, the gate, door, bounce, grand bounce, lay off, rif (reduction in force), walking papers, walking ticket, housecleaning, bum's rush, kicking out, old heave ho, in the barrel, fluff, brushoff, kiss-off, cold shoulder.

DISMISSED adj.   fired, canned, unfrocked (any profession), let out, drummed out, turned off, sacked, booted, bounced, axed. See DISCHARGED, OUSTER.

DISORDER n.   1. mess, holy mess, rat's nest, topsyturvy, arsy-varsy, every which way, discombobulation, discombooberation. See CONFUSION. 2. flap, fuss, to do, stir, kickup, snarl-up, fuzzbuzz, scene. See TURMOIL.

DISORDERLY adj.   on a tear, raising a rumpus, raising a ruckus, kicking up a row, kicking up a shindy, off base, out of line, out of order.

DISORGANIZATION n.   foul up, fuck up, mix up, screw up, bloody mess, holy mess, unholy mess, rat's nest, topsy-turvy. See CONFUSION.

DISORGANIZED adj.   screwed up, spazzed out, mussed up, unglued, unscrewed, unzipped, Chinese fire drill. See CONFUSED.

DISPARAGE v.   pan, slam, smear, roast, scorch, rap, dump on, run down, put down, tear down, sour grapes, put the hooks in. See BELITTLE.

DISPARAGED adj.   crawl, eat crow, eat dirt, eat humble pie, lost face, drummed out, draw in one's horns, sing small. See BELITTLED.

DISPARATE adj. far cry, poles apart, whale of a difference, like night and day.

DISPARITY n. diff, different strokes, different strokes for different folks.

DISPASSIONATE adj. iceberg, cold fish, cool cat, cool, cool as a cucumber, keep one's cool, unflappable, laid back, keep one's shirt on, not turn a hair, roll with the punches, could care less, flat, tough, fair to middling, butter wouldn't melt in his mouth, got lead balls for eyes, poker-faced, don't give a shit, don't give a damm, don't give a hoot, what's the diff?, what the hell, so what?, it's all the same to me, that's your lookout, that's your pigeon, I should worry?

DISPASSIONATELY adv. deadpan, in cold blood, with a poker face, with a straight face.

DISPATCH n. handout, poop sheet, beat, scoop. See NEWS.

DISPATCH v. railroad, railroad through, walk through, hand-carry, run with, run with the ball. See also SPEED.

DISPEL v. break up, break it up, bust up, split up, scramble.

DISPENSE v. dish out, fork out, shell out, handout, come across with, give with, give away the store. See GIVE.

DISPERSE v. break up, break it up, bust up, split up, scramble, take off in all directions.

DISPERSED adj. all over the lot, all over the place, from hell to breakfast, every which way.

DISPIRITED adj. dragged, low, dick in the dirt, blue, blue funk, downbeat, shot down, funky, bummed out, rhino. See DEPRESSED.

DISPLACE v. step into the shoes of, take over. See also REPLACE.

DISPLACED adj. in the right church but the wrong pew, in the wrong pew, in the wrong box, like a fish out of water, out of one's element, nowhere.

DISPLAY n. 1. expo, exbo, exhib, exhibish, flash (gaudy merchandise or prize), front, fireworks, an act, a scene, for show, frame up. 2. shine, dash, splash, splurge, grandstand play, showboat, showoff.

DISPLAY v. showcase, flash, sport, grandstand, streak, let it all hang out, roll out, trot out, break out, whip out, carry on, show off, show and tell, hotdog, fan it, wave it around, run up the colors, strut one's stuff, do one's stuff, go through one's paces, parade one's wares, make a scene, put on an act, do a number, hit one with, come up with, smack with, spring with, play to the gallery, take it big, come on strong, come the heavy, do the heavy, throw one's weight around, chuck one's weight about.

DISPLEASE v. zing, wing, nick, turn off, cool, cut to the quick, sound, dozens, sounding dozens, play dirty dozens, signify, signifyn', shucking and jiving, S'ing n' J'ing, miff, cap, capping, gross out, curdle, get bent, blow off, lay a bad trip on one, hit one where one lives, hurt one where one lives. See also ANNOY, INSULT.

DISPOSE v. 1. put to rights, put in apple-pie order, tailor, promote. See ARRANGE. 2. shepherd, call the tune, ride herd on, lay down the law, put one's foot down, read the riot act. See MANAGE.

DISPOSED adj. at the drop of a hat, game, game for. See also READY.

DISPOSE OF v. 1. knock off, polish off, cut, cut off, chop, take care of, put away, deal with, do the trick, turn the trick. See FINISH. 2. chuck, chuck out, eighty-six, junk, adios [something], throw over, throw overboard, deep six, throw on the junk heap, toss onto the scrap heap, file it in the circular file, kiss, kiss off, chop out. See DISCARD. See also DISCHARGE.

DISPOSESS v. bounce, boot out, toss out on one's ear, throw out on the street, aadios one, send packing. See EVICT. See also DISCHARGE.

DISPOSITION n. bag, groove, flash, mind-set, thing, type, cup of tea, druthers, turned on to, where one is at. See INCLINATION.

DISPROVE v. blow sky high, knock the bottom out of, knock the chocks out from under, knock the props out from under, poke full of holes, shoot full of holes.

DISPUTANT n. oppo, opposish, opposite number, meat, me and you, angries, bad guy, buddy (sarcasm), guardhouse lawyer, Philadelphia lawyer.

DISPUTE n. beef, tiff, words, row, fuss, a bone, bone of contention, rhubarb, wrangle. See ARGUMENT.

DISPUTE v. take on, lock horns, pick a bone, put up an argument, be agin, bump heads, have at, jump on one's case, haul into court, drag into court. See ARGUE.

DISQUALIFY v. eighty-six, not make the cut.

DISREGARD v. 1. ig, tune out, look the other way, let it go, let one off easy, let one off this time, wink at, live with, pay no mind, pay no never mind, play past, pooh pooh. 2. cut, brush off, cool, not give one the time of day, give the go by, leave out in the cold, look right through. See IGNORE. 3. be asleep at the switch, let go to pot, let slide.

DISREPAIR adj. busted, down, downtime, out of commission, on the fritz, wracked, dead, kaput. See DAMAGED.

DISREPUTABLE adj. dog, in bad, in the doghouse, in Dutch, bad ass, no good. See also BAD.

DISRESPECTFUL adj. fresh, sassy, smart alecky, smart ass, cheeky, nervy, out of line, bold as brass. See INSOLENT.

DISREPUTE adj. sleaze factor.

DISROBE v. strip, strip to the buff, do a strip, do a strip tease, take it off, peel, get all naked, slip out of, shuck, husk.

DISRUPT v. discombobulate, ball up, rattle one's cage, psych out, muddy the waters, put off, upset one's apple cart. See CONFUSE.

DISRUPTED adj. unglued, come unglued, come unzipped, come apart, come apart at the seams, fall apart at the seams, discombobulated, discombooberated, shook, shook up, all shook up, all balled up, balled up, fouled up, fucked up, fubb (fucked up beyond belief), loused up, messed up, mucked up, screwed up, bugged up, bollixed, bollixed up, hung up, mixed up, blaaed up, gummixed up, gummoxed up, helter-skelter, galley west, farmisht, fertummeled, thrown, fussed, rattled, higgledy-piggledy, skimble-skamble, harum-scarum, shot, shot to pieces, gone, haywire, go blooey, go kerflooie, kerflumixed, flummoxed, flabbergasted, stuck, hugger-mugger, messy, bowled down, bowled over, struck all of a heap, thrown off one's beam ends. See also CONFUSED.

DISRUPTIVE adj. off base, out of line, out of order, trouble-making. See also ROWDY.

DISSATISFIED adj. beefing, bitching, crabby, kvetching, griping, grousing, picky, picky picky, that's it?, that's all there is there isn't any more?, this is what we came for?, this is what it's all about?, you want it should sing too?, what you see is what you get. See UNHAPPY.

DISSEMBLE v. stonewall, cover up, whitewash, pass, shuck and jive, signify, gammon, talk trash, double talk, doublespeak, fake, fake it, wear cheaters, slap on some glims, flash the gogs, throw on a make up, phony up one's getup, beard, put a different face on, put up a front, put on a front, put on a false front, put up a smoke screen, put on an act, make like, let on, let on like, play possum, pussyfoot, put on the check, put up a bluff, pull up a bluff, four-flush.

DISSEMBLER n. phony, smoothie, two-way ghee, wishy-washy person, wolf in sheep's clothing. See CHEATER.

DISSEMBLING n. crocodile tears, soft soap, sweet talk, an act. See also FAKERY.

DISSENSION n. bad vibes, static, sour note, beef, scene, fuss, flak, clinker. See DISCORD.

DISSENT n. 1. N.O., nope, no siree, no way, not on your life, not a chance, nothing doing, forget it. See

DENIAL. 2. bad vibes, clinker, sour note, split, spat, bone, pick a bone, bone of contention, hassle, flak. 3. far cry, poles apart, whale of a difference.

DISSENT v. break with, fly in the face of, be agin, buck, pettifog, put up an argument, jump on one's case, put up a fight. See DISAGREE.

DISSENTER n. angries, maverick, marcher, swinger, dropout, beatnik, hippie, yippie, freak, flower child, nature boy, street people, night people, offbeat, bohemian, weirdo, fish out of water, oddball, square peg in a round hole.

DISSENTING adj. anti, agin, con, no go. See NONCONFORMING.

DISSIDENCE n. bad vibes, clinker, sour note. See also DISCORD.

DISSIMILAR adj. far cry, funky, weird, offbeat, march to the beat of a different drummer, poles apart, whale of a difference, like night and day.

DISSIPATE v. piss away, go through, kiss good-bye, blow, dump, pump up (gambling). See SQUANDER, FRITTER AWAY.

DISSIPATED adj. 1. gone bad, gone to the dogs, gone to seed, gone to hell, gone to hell in a handbasket, hellbent. 2. blown, blown out, burnt out, played out, pissed away, diddled away, down the drain, down the toilet, down the rathole, down the spout, down the tube, kiss something good-bye, out the window.

DISSIPATER n. high liver, nighthawk, night owl, playboy, swinger, operator, player, speed. See LECHER.

DISSIPATION n. 1. life in the fast lane, live in the fast lane, drive in the fast lane, drive in the fast lane with no brakes, high living, burn one's candle at both ends, hellbent, go to hell, go to hell in a handbasket. 2. bat, bender, binge, bust, circus, tear, toot, wingding. See REVEL. See also PARTY.

DISSOLUTE adj. high liver, nighthawk, night owl, playboy, swinger, operator, player, meat-eater, on the pad, on the take, open, racket up, driving in the fast lane, driving in the fast lane wih no brakes, living in the fast lane, life in the fast lane, high living, burn one's candle at both ends, gone to bad, gone to the dogs, gone to hell, go to hell, go to hell in a handbasket, hellbent, fast and loose, fast, swift, speedy. See also WANTON.

DISSONANT adj. clinker, sour, sour note.

DISSUADE v. faze, turn off, put off, kid out of, talk out of, chicken out, blink, throw cold water on, throw a wet blanket on, lean on, put the arm on. See also PREVENT.

DISTANCE n. bit, spitting distance, a good ways, stone's throw, Sunday run, tidy step, whoop, two whoops and a holler, a hoot and a holler, a hop skip and a jump, a shlep, a sleeper jump, piece, far piece, fur piece, down the road a piece, country mile.

DISTANT adj. 1. cold, cool, cool cat, dog it, dog up, laid back, offish, standoffish, on ice, put on airs, stuck up, uppity. See ALOOF. 2. ways, piece, far piece, sticks, boonies, tullies, clear to hell and gone, middle of nowhere. See REMOTE.

DISTANT EARLY WARNING LINE n. DEW line.

DISTASTEFUL adj. grody, grody to the max, gross, yucky, icky, yicky. See UNSAVORY.

DISTILL v. 1. cut, cut down, cut to the bone, nutshell, put in a nutshell, boil down, trim, get to the meat. 2. moonshine, moonlight, cook, rerun, turn over.

DISTILL ALCOHOL v. cook, rerun, turn over, moonlight, moonshine.

DISTINCTION n. diff, different strokes, different strokes for different folks.

DISTINCTIVE adj. 1. far cry, offbeat, march to the beat of a different drummer, poles apart. See also UNIQUE. 2. weird, whale of a difference, like night and day, like wow, super, gnarly, mega-gnarly, unreal, zero cool, cold, wicked, flash, this is some kinda ———. See EXCELLENT.

DISTINGUISH v. 1. glom, glim, gun, beam, flash, flash on, spot, spy, dig, read, lamp, pipe, catch, focus, eye, eagle eye, eyeball, take in, get a load of, get an eyeful of, get a hinge, put the squint on, pick up on. See SEE. 2. make out, figure out, know what's what, know one's ass from one's elbow, know a rock from a hard place, know crossways from crosswise. See DISCRIMINATE.

DISTINGUISHED adj. name, champ, number 1, number one, numero uno, VIP, w.k. (well-known), in the limelight, large, brass hat, big name, heavy, heavy stuff, heavyweight. See CELEBRITY.

DISTORT v. snow, give one a snow job, whitewash, doctor, cook, con, scam, put one on, bull, bullshit, fudge, throw one a curve, trump up, hoke up, phony up, fake, gammon, make out like. See also LIE.

DISTORTED adj. cockeyed, double-talk, chewing gum, bum, off, way off, off base, off the beam, screwy, sour, all wet, bum steer, ass backwards, back asswards, bass ackwards, lame.

DISTORTION n. jazz, jive, line, crap, crock of shit, bullshit, BS, phony baloney, smoke, the big lie (Pol.), tall story, latrine rumor. See LIE.

DISTRACT v. catch flies (The.), stall.

DISTRACTED adj. popcorn-headed, air-headed, empty-headed, absentminded professor, pipe dreaming, daydreaming, in a world of one's own, out to lunch, woolgathering, mooning, moony, goofing off, looking out the window, here in body only, a million miles away, building castles in the air, have on the brain, have on one's mind, pay no mind, hung up, asleep at the switch, asleep on the job, not on the job. See also PREOCCUPIED.

DISTRAUGHT adj. unglued, unzipped, unscrewed, shook up, fertummeled, thrown, fussed, rattled, in a panic, like a chicken with its head cut off. See CONFUSED.

DISTRESS n. 1. bummer, downer, drag, grabber, double trouble, can of worms, clutch, jam, shit, deep shit, rainin', rainy day, scrape, hot water, hot grease, jackpot, screw up, crunch, tumul, pickle, pretty pickle, pretty pass, fine kettle of fish, fine how do you do, ticklish spot, tricky spot, sticky wicket, tail in a gate, tit caught in the wringer, mess, holy mess, unholy mess, devil to pay, hell to pay, hobble. 2. hard time, hard knocks, hard row to hoe, tough break, tough luck, rotten luck, rum go, can't even get arrested. 3. heartache, headache, blues, worriment, tsuris, stew, all-overs, cliff-hanging, pins and needles, need it like a hole in the head, pain in the ass, pain in the neck, bad news, next week East Lynne. See also ADVERSITY, WORRY.

DISTRESS v. bug, hack, wig, burn up, brown off, tick off, bone, dog, eat, what's eating one, ride, nag, needle, hound, nudzh, noodge, miff, peeve, get, get to, get one's goat, get in one's hair, get under one's skin, hit on, flummox, fuck with one's head, rattle one's cage, push, push one's button, drive up the wall, be on the back of, be at, penny dog, rile, nitpick, pick on, picky-picky, break one's balls, do a number on one, hit one where he lives, on one's case, stick in one's craw, give one a hard time, give one a turn, give a bad time to, make it tough for, discombobulate, discomboberate, throw into a swivet, throw into a tizzy, lay a bad trip on one, zing. See also DISTURB.

DISTRESSED adj. uptight, tightened up, jittery, jumpy, the jumps, jitters, shaky, bugged, choked, zonkers, pissin', shittin', shittin' bricks, scared shitless, strung out, bummed out, unglued, hyper, spooked, twitty, fidgety, wreck, nervous wreck, bundle of nerves, nervy, all-overish, hurting, wired, wired up, yantsy, antsy, antsy-pantsy, ants in one's pants, about to piss in one's pants, choke, choke up, clutched, clutched up, shook up, shook, all shook up, shaking in one's boots, shivery, quivery, hacked, hit where one lives, dragged (following drugs), butterflies, butterflies in one's stomach, the jams, the jims, the jimmies, jimjams, heebie-jeebies, the screaming meemies, fall apart, torn down, all torn up, tore up, ripped, cut up, shot to pieces, shot down, basket case, miffed, peeved, riled, rubbed the wrong way, burned up, hung up, tightened up, up the wall, up against it, lose one's cool, in a lather, in a stew, in a sweat, sweaty, sweat it, sweating bullets, in a swivet, in a tizzy, in a state, in a dither, in one's hair, flap, in a flap, on edge, on the ragged edge, have one's teeth on edge, on pins and needles, on tenterhooks, on the gog, jumpy as a cat on a hot tin roof, have kittens, cast a kitten, having the leaps, have a fit, discombobulated, worried sick, worried stiff, biting one's nails, a real nail-biter, turn gray, beside oneself, put to it, hard put to it, have a heart attack, at the end of one's rope, on the skids, gone to pot, gone to the dogs, down on one's luck. See also DISTURBED.

DISTRIBUTE v. divvy up, cut up, cut the pie, cut the melon, slice up, dish out, fork out, shell out. See DIVIDE.

DISTRIBUTION SYSTEM n. pipeline, network, net.

DISTRIBUTOR n. distrib, middle man, jobber.

DISTRICT n. territory, turf, hood, neck of the woods, stomping ground, ghetto, inner city, jungle, shanty town, skid row, slum, zoo. See NEIGHBORHOOD.

DISTRICT ATTORNEY n. D.A., cutter.

DISTRICTS n. Shubert Alley, Tin Pan Alley, Broadway, The Great White Way (The.), West End, the City, Wall Street, the Street, Back Bay, Mainline, gold coast, high-rent district, slurb, burbs, Rialto, old town, Storyville, Las Vegas strip, Sunset Strip, the Strip, Bowery, Hell's Kitchen, the Loop, tenderloin, Sugar Hill, heavy lump (Sugar Hill), SoHo, NoHo, Hashbury (Haight-Ashbury), Clown Alley (circus), Lunch Bucket City (working class), territory, turf, hood, neck of the woods, rust belt, black belt, black bottom, ghetto, down the line, garment district, red-light district, Track One (brothel), Track Two (homosexual), skid row, inner city, slum, the jungle (crowded city), shanty town, zoo, shoestore alley, used-car alley, gasoline alley, drunk alley. See also NEIGHBORHOOD.

DISTRUSTFUL adj. cagey, leery, uptight, been hit before. See also CAUTIOUS.

DISTURB v. 1. adjy, psych, psych out, spook, get to, flip, flip out, rattle, floor, fuddle, craze, curdle, bug, bug up, burn up, ball up, fire up, steam up, stir up, key up, kick up a row, put up to, work up, work up into a lather, bring one up short, pull one up short, rile, give one a bad time, give one a hard time, give one a turn, turn off, turn on, pick on, egg on, sound off, make waves, make a scene, make a fuss, fuss, fuzzbuzz, make it a tough go, make it tough for all, put the zingers in, needle, give one the needle, put the needles in, ride, throw, throw into a snit, throw into a stew, throw one a curve, throw into a tizzy, throw into a swivet, throw wood on the fire, add fuel to the flames, raise cain, raise hell, raise the devil, raise the roof, raise a rumpus, raise a ruckus, raise a ruction, rabble-rouse, rattle, floor, throw, get to, discomboberate, discombobulate, discombooberate, drive one bananas,

drive one up a tree, drive one up a wall, piss one off, ask for it, go on make my day, stick in one's craw, get a rise out of one, get one's goat, get under one's skin, get in one's hair, brown off. See also EXCITE. 2. queer, foul up, fuck up, louse up, gum up the works, flummox, throw a monkey wrench into the works, upset one's apple cart, knock the chocks from under one, knock the props from under one, put a crimp in.

DISTURBANCE n. flap, fuss, commo, dustup, to-do, big scene, stink, big stink, haroosh, fuzzbuzz (commotion), foofaraw, rumpus, ruckus, stir, row, rumble. See AGITATION. See also RIOT.

DISTURBED adj. antsy, yantsy, uptight, tightened up, choked, zonkers, discombobulated, pissing, shitting, shitting bricks, shook, shook up, all shook up, wired, wired up, hopped up, hyper, clutched, clutched up, all hot and bothered, all-overish, in a scrape, in a stew, in a sweat, in a swivet, in a tizzy, flustrated, in a flusteration, in a foofaraw, in a lather, in a pucker, in a botheration, fussed, fidgety, jittery, jumpy, jumpy as a cat on a hot tin roof, on pins and needles, on tenterhooks, on the gog, on edge, on the ragged edge, have one's teeth on edge, have kittens, cast a kitten, biting one's nails, having the leaps, the heebie-jeebies, the screaming meemies, the meemies, the jams, the jims, jimjams, the jumps, jitters, nervy, wreck, nervous wreck, bundle of nerves, beside one's self, worried stiff, shot to pieces, fall apart, basket case, spooked, twitty, sweaty, bum trip, thrown. See also BOTHERED, CONFUSED, EXCITED, TROUBLED, UNEASY.

DISUSED adj. godforsaken, shelved, on the shelf, in mothballs, mothballed, down.

DITCHDIGGER n. sewer hog.

DITHER n. flap, flusteration, flustration, foofaraw, lather, pucker, stew, swivet, tizzy. See EXCITEMENT, NERVOUSNESS, ANXIETY.

DIVE n. header, belly bump, belly buster, belly flop, belly whacker, belly whopper, chewalloper.

DIVE v. brodie, gutter, header, take a header, belly bump, belly bust, belly flop, belly whack, belly whop, chewallop, dump altitude (aircraft).

DIVERGENT adj. far cry, poles apart, whale of a difference.

DIVERSE adj. mixed bag, funky, like night and day, dif, diff.

DIVERSION n. 1. ball, laughs, lots of laughs, grins, fun and games, big time, high time, high old time, hoopla, whoopee, picnic, merry-go-round, field day. See AMUSEMENT. See also ENTERTAINMENT. 2. red herring, action, stutter step, fake out.

DIVERSITY n.   mixed bag, diff, different strokes, different strokes for different folks.

DIVERT v.   1. sidetrack, circumlocute, bend the rules, get around, send on a wild-goose chase, catch flies (The.), stall. 2. break one up, fracture one, wow, get one's kicks, get one's jollies, panic, kill 'em, knock 'em dead, put 'em away, slay, lay 'em in the aisles, have 'em in the aisles. See AMUSE.

DIVEST v.   dump, adios, 86, eighty-six, ditch, unload, bleed, bleed white, milk, sell off.

DIVESTED adj.   minus, cut, dumped, eighty-sixed, unloaded, bled, bled white, milked.

DIVIDE v.   dish out, fork out, shell out, hand out, hand over, divvy, divvy up, go halfies, go halvers, go fifty-fifty, go even-steven, slice, slice up, cut the pie, cut the melon, slice the melon, slice the pie, split, split up, cut, cut up, cut in, cut one in, duke one in, cut up the touches, cut up the pipes, cut up the jackpot, piece up, whack up, bump into, size into (chips); buck it over.

DIVIDEND n.   divvy, lagniappe, melon, pie, plum, taste. See also INTEREST, SHARE.

DIVINE n.   the rev, sky pilot, preacher man, harp polisher, glory roader. See CLERGYMAN.

DIVINE adj.   divoon.

DIVINE v.   take a stab, take a stab in the dark, take a shot, take a shot in the dark, talk off the top of one's head, go out on a limb. See also PREDICT.

DIVINITY n.   Dad, Head Knock, Lordy, Man Upstairs.

DIVISION n.   1. affil (TV), branch, branch house, offshoot. See ASSOCIATE. 2. piece, bite, divvy, cut, slice, chunk, end, piece of the action, piece of the pie, slice of the melon, cut of the melon, rake-off, fifty-fifty, halver, bigger half, big end. See INTEREST, SHARE.

DIVORCE n.   breakup, dedomiciling, pffft, phfft, go phftt, Mexicancellation, Reno-vation, split, split-up, splitsville, on the rocks, marriage on the rocks, come to a parting of the ways, couldn't make it, on the out and out, washed up.

DIVORCE v.   split, split up, dedomicile, break up, call it quits, phfttt, go phfttt, untie the knot, Reno-vate, go to Reno, Mexicancel. See also SEPARATE.

DIVORCEE n.   ex (wife or husband), dumpee, grass widow,

DIVULGE v.   fess up, spill the beans, blow the whistle, put it on the street, let it all hang out, let one's hair down, spring, blab, tip off, open up, own up, cough up, give the show away. See CONFESS.

DIZZY adj.   gaga, rocky, woozy, dopey, punchy, punch-drunk, slap-happy, the room going around, head-spinning, light-headed.

DO v.   go for it, move, do one's thing, TCB (take care of business), pull off, get with it, shit or get off the pot, perk, cook, operate, come on like. See ACT.

DOCILE adj.   cool, mellow, laid back. See also SUBMISSIVE.

DOCKHAND n.   dock walloper, roustabout.

DOCTOR n.   M.D., doc, bones, sawbones, bone bender, bone breaker, bone setter, pill pusher, pill roller, pill bag, pill peddler, pill slinger, big eye man, big nose man, big heart man, medic, medico, med, croaker, stick croaker, butcher, quack, bolus (U.), barefoot doctor (rural); Doctor Feelgood, Feelgood, ice tong doctor, right rocker, script writer, (prescribe drugs illegally); cutemup, pills, pill punk, iodine, salts (prison).

DOCTOR OF DIVINITY n.   DD.

DOCTOR OF PHILOSOPHY n.   PhD, PHT (putting hubby through college).

DOCUMENT n.   MS. Ms, ms., script, pages, language.

DOCUMENT v.   crack on one or something, debunk (prove false), pan out, leave a paper trail. See VERIFY.

DOCUMENTARY FILM n.   doc, docudrama, rockumentary (music).

DODGE v.   duck, juke, shake, shake off, put the move on one, ditch, give the slip, skip out on, circumlocute, buck it over, get around; jank, jink (enemy planes). See AVOID.

DODGE CAR n.   ducker.

DOER n.   eager beaver, operator, big-time operator, BTO, workaholic, hustler, ball of fire, live wire, self-starter. See MAN OF ACTION.

DOG n.   mutt, pooch, poochy, pup, doggie, doggy, puppy dog, purp, dorg, fido, bowwow, goop, gyp (female), man's best friend, four-legged friend, Heinz, Heinz 57, Heinz 57 varieties, flea hotel, tail-wagger, bone polisher, bone eater, biscuit eater, pot licker, pot hound, soup hound, hound dog.

DOG EXCREMENT n.   do, dog do, doggy do, dog dew, dog turd, dog hockey, sidewalk obstacle course.

DOGGED adj.   bullhead, bullheaded, bulletheaded, hardheaded, pigheaded, muleheaded, mule, mulish, stubborn as a mule, hard-nosed, stiff-necked, horse, sticky, Turk, tough nut, hang tough, murder (he's murder), has one's Dutch up, the game ain't over till the last man is out. See also TENACIOUS, STUBBORN.

DOGGEDLY adv.   hang in, hang tough, stick it, go for broke, go for it, go all out. See OBSTINATELY.

DOGMATIC adj.   bossy, flaky, iceman, got the faith baby, cocksure, sure as shit, come hell or high water, red neck, a regular Archie Bunker. See also STUBBORN, PREJUDICED.

DOGMATIST n. Archie Bunker, male chauvinist pig, MCP, pig, sexist porker, red-neck, good old boy, good old boys' network, McCarthyite, jingoist, flag-waver, patrioteer, superpatriot.

DOLDRUMS n. blahs, blah-blahs, blues, blue devils, blue funk, funk, bummer, downer, down trip, letdown, dolefuls, dismals, dumps, mumps, mopes, mokers, mulligrubs, miseries (Bl.).

DOLE n. handout.

DOLLAR n. bill, buck, clam, fish, fishskin, one, single, skin, smacker, ace, berry, bob, boffo, bone, case, case buck, case dough, case note, check, cholly, clacker coconut, cucumber, frog, frogskin, hog, hogs, Jewish flag (Derog.), last dollar, lizard, man, peso, plaster, plunk, potato, rag, rock, rutabaga, scrip, simoleon, Simon, slab, slug, smack, scoot, year; cartwheel, iron man, ball, bullet, copeck, D, hardtack, plug, shekel, shiner, sinker, wheel (silver).

DOLLAR, SILVER n. cartwheel, iron man, ball, bullet, copeck, D, hardtack, plug, shekel, shiner, sinker, wheel, Suzzi.

DOLLARS, TWO n. two spot, deuce, deucer, deuce spot, two case note, two cents.

DOLLARS, FIVE n. fin, five, fiver, five spot, finif.

DOLLARS, TEN n. saw, sawbuck, ten, tenner, ten spot, dews, dime note, dix, eagle (gold coin), Abe's Cabe, five-case note; bean, half eagle (gold coin).

DOLLARS, TWENTY n. double sawbuck, twenty, twenty cents, double eagle (gold coin).

DOLLARS, TWENTY-FIVE n. squirt.

DOLLARS, FIFTY n. fifty, half a C, half a century, half a yard.

DOLLARS, ONE HUNDRED n. C, century, century note, C note, hollow note, one bill, yard, hun.

DOLLARS, FIVE HUNDRED n. half grand, five yards, D, five centuries, five C's, half G, small nickel.

DOLLARS, ONE THOUSAND n. big one, one dollar, dime, G, G note, grand, horse, thou, yard.

DOLLARS, FIVE THOUSAND n. big nickel.

DOLLARS, ONE MILLION n. mil, megabucks, kilobucks.

DOLOPHINE n. dolly.

DOLT n. dork, lamebrain, yo-yo, out to lunch, lunchie, dodo, dumdum, airhead, meathead, doesn't know from A to B, stupe, boob, sap, simp, cluck. See STUPID.

DOMAIN n. 1. territory, turf, stomping grounds, old stomping grounds, stamping grounds, home grounds, back home, neck of the woods, bailwick. See also DISTRICTS. 2. slot, wing. See OCCUPATION.

DOMESTIC n. girl, help, woman, cleaning woman, cleaning lady, biddy, furp, tweeny, pillow punk, cabin girl (chambermaid), live-in, slavey, peon, serf, man, boy, houseboy, number one boy, pratt boy.

DOMESTICATE v. bust, gentle.

DOMESTIC CRISIS n. soap, soap opera.

DOMICILE n. domi, dommy, pad, crash pad, crib, condo, co-op, coop, joint, roof over one's head, dump, castle, homeplate, rack, roost. See HOUSE. See also APARTMENT.

DOMINATE v. run, run the show, call the shots, call the tune, rule the roost, wear the pants, lay down the law, lead by the nose, have the whip hand, reel one back in, bring to heel, box in, get one in a box, sit on top of, in front of, take the high ground. See MANAGE.

DOMINATED adj. henpecked, on a string, tied to one's apron strings, pussy whipped, under one's thumb. See SUBJUGATED.

DOMINEER v. run things, run the show, push the buttons, bulldoze, henpeck, pussy whip (female), shoot on, call the shots, call the tune, be in the driver's seat, be in the saddle, ride herd on, crack the whip, wear the pants, wear the trousers, rule the roost, keep under one's thumb, lead by the nose, kick one around, throw one's weight around, throw a lot of weight, have the whip hand, do it one's way, hold the aces, reel one back in, twist around one's little finger, wind around one's little finger, bring to heel, box in, get one in a box, sit on top of.

DOMINEERING adj. bossy, crack the whip, high and mighty, on one's high horse, throw one's weight around, wear the pants, in the driver's seat. See also ARROGANT.

DOMINION n. territory, turf, stomping grounds, old stomping grounds, stamping grounds, one's neck of the woods. See also DISTRICTS.

DON v. suit up, dud, dude, dude up, doll up, dog out, fit out, rag out, rag up, rig out, rig up, turn out, tog, drape.

DONATE v. 1. ante up, pony up, lay on, get it up, put something in the pot, sweeten the pot, sweeten the kitty, feed the kitty, pass the hat, do one's part. See GIVE. 2. have a finger in, have a finger in the pie, get in the act, sit in on, put in one's two cents.

DONATION n. handout, a hand, helping hand, write off, chicadee check off (charity), gift, gifting, do one's part, lump, poke out, maxed out (political limit).

DONE adj. set, wired, fixed, a wrap, buttoned up, all over but the shouting, done to a T, done with. See FINISHED.

DONKEY n. Rocky Mountain canary.

DONOR n. angel, Santa Claus, sugar daddy, fairy godmother, lady bountiful, giver, heavy hitter, maxed out (political limit), backer.

DO NOTHING v. sit on one's hands, let it come, let it go, stand by.

DOOM n. karma, the beads, the way the cookie crumbles, the way the ball bounces, handwriting on the wall, in the lap of the gods.

DOOMED adj. done, done for, dead duck, dead meat, sunk, in the cards, que sera sera, the way the ball bounces, the way the cookie crumbles, the way the beads read, the handwriting on the wall, kiss of death.

DOOMSAYER n. Calamity Jane, Alice under the ax.

DOOR n. slammer.

DOPEMINE n. L. Dopo, El Dopo.

DORMANT adj. on the shelf, on the bench, on the beach, on ice, out of the rat race, out of action, out of the swim, sidelined, closed down, down.

DORMITORY n. dorm, fratority, sorenity, birdcage, bull pen, bullypen, frau shack, henranch, hencoop, quail roost, zoo.

DOSE n. hit, shot, fix, nip, slug, bang, dram.

DOSE v. dose up, doctor, fix, hit, dope, dope up.

DOSSIER n. sheet, rap sheet, dope, file. See DIRECTORY. See also RECORD.

DOUBLE n. 1. stand-in, ringer, dead ringer, look-alike, twin, spitting image, angel (radar). See also COPY. 2. doubleheader (successful two ways), double in brass, wear two hats (two kinds of work), rule of twice, twofers.

DOUBLE BASS n. bull fiddle, doghouse, vein.

DOUBTFUL adj. chancy, iffy, dicey, up for grabs, doubting Thomas, touchy, touch and go, on slippery ground, on ice, on thin ice, long shot, fat chance, hanging by a thread, cagey, leery, been hit before, don't hold your breath, you should live so long, blow hot and cold, sit on the fence, waffling, shilly-shally, stuck, betwixt and between, between sixes and sevens, between a rock and a hard place, dippydro, the jury's out, tics and twitches.

DOUBTLESS adj. posilutely, sure as hell, sure as I live and breathe, fer shirr, that's for sure, no ifs ands or buts, is the Pope Catholic? See CERTAIN.

DOUCHE BAG n. bag.

DOUGHNUT n. sinker, cruller, slug, submarine, knothole, mud ball.

DOUSE v. dunk.

DOVETAIL v. lip sync, sync, sync up.

DOVETAILED adj. 1. in sync. 2. co-ed.

DOWDY adj. frumpy, frowzy, rundown, down at the heels, off the cob, mince, moldy.

DOWNCAST adj. singing the blues, dragged, ass in a sling, down in the dumps, low, bummed out, in pain, in the pits, shot down. See DEPRESSED.

DOWNFALL n. the skids, on the skids, hit the skids, rack and ruin, on the rocks. See FAILURE.

DOWNGRADE v. bump, bust, rif, bench, set back, hold back.

DOWNGRADED adj. in the bag (police), benched, busted, broken, set down, set back, held back.

DOWNRIGHT adj. up front, open, straight, straight shit, talk like a Dutch uncle, call a spade a spade, put all one's cards on the table, make no bones about it, talk turkey. See SINCERE.

DOWNTRODDEN adj. 1. have-nots, the underdog, the needy, truly needy. See DESTITUTE. 2. in one's power, in one's pocket, in one's clutches, under one's thumb, at one's mercy, at one's beck and call, at one's feet, a slave to, led by the nose, dance to one's tune.

DOZE v. snooze, grab a few z's, cop some z's, flake out, cat nap, doss, dozz, doz, calk off, drop off, dope off, cork off, knock off, dig oneself a nod, collar a nod, catch a wink. See SLEEP.

DRAB adj. blah, grungy, rundown, dull as dishwater, dog, gummy, zero, big zero, flat. See BORING.

DRAFT n. greetings, letter from Uncle Sam.

DRAFT v. sign on, sign up, call up.

DRAFT BOARD n. trap.

DRAFTEE n. boot, rookie, tenderfoot, cannon fodder, sad sack. See also RECRUIT.

DRAG v. lug, shlep, truck.

DRAG RACE TRACK n. drag strip, shutdown strip (past finish line), dragway.

DRAG RACING CAR n. dragster, hot rod, funny car, fueler, gasser, altered.

DRAG RACING, MAINTENANCE burnout pit, bleach box, slicks (treadless tires), stuffer (supercharger), shoe (tire), wheelie bar.

DRAG RACING, START hole, hole job, hole shot (get a winning start); burnout (soften tires); wheelie, wheel stand.

DRAG RACING TERMS drag, dragging, banzai (all out), bench racing (race analysis), Christmas tree (starting lights), heads up (no handicap), altered (vehicle class), dump (win).

DRAIN v. bleed, bleed white, suck dry, get every last drop.

DRAINED adj. dead, dead tired, beat, used up, draggin' ass, hung, pooped, wiped out, burned out, hacked. See WEARY.

DRAMATIST n. play doctor, play fixer, telewriter (TV), teleplaywrite, scripter, scribbler, scribe, scrivener, scratcher, word slinger, wordsmith, ghost, ghostwriter, knight of the pen, knight of the plume, knight of the quill. See also WRITER.

DRAMATIZE v. ham it up, play up, lay it on thick, make a production of, splash, play on the heartstrings, throw in the hook, the grabber, the rooting interest, play it don't say it.

DRAW n. standoff, Mexican standoff, push, even steven, dead heat, dead end.

DRAWING n. 1. the numbers, the numbers game. 2. graphics, comp, layout, storyboard, doodle.

DRAWN adj. peaked, peaky, bag of bones, skin and bones, stack of bones. See also THIN.

DREAD n. cold feet, buck fever, goose bumps, creeps, cold creeps, cold shivers, jitters, worriment, stage fright. See FEAR.

DREADFUL adj. beastly, icky, yicky, yucky, mean, hairy, furry, wicked, heavy, gross, grody, grody to the max, godawful, goshawful, grim, lousy, rotten, hair-raising, spooky, spooked, frozen, goose bumpy, asshole puckerin', asshole suckin' wind, pecker-assed, creepy.

DREAM n. pie in the sky, castles in Spain, castles in the air.

DREAM v. head trip, dream up, make up, think up, trump up, spark, spitball, brainstorm, take it off the top of one's head.

DREAMER n. stargazer, scoutmaster.

DREDGER n. groundhog, sandhog.

DREGS adj. bottom of the barrel, scrape the bottom of the barrel, gook, gunk.

DRESS n. 1. threads, set of threads, togs, toggery, duds, outfit, rags, glad rags, weeds, schmotte, schmatteh, frame, front, flash, frock, sock frock, bag, micro, mini, miniskirt, midi, maxi, maxicoat, maxidress, granny dress, Mother Hubbard, drape, drapery, drapes, set of drapes. 2. getup, get out, feathers, fine feather, full feather, vine, flute, dry goods, rig, pantsuit, jumpsuit, pallazzios, honking brown (flashy), fofarraw, foofooraw, Christmas (ostentatious), ready made, gray flannel, tailor made, civvies, cits, mufti, fatigues, Port Arthur tuxedo, khakis, dress blues, whites, fishtail, drape shape, drape shape with a reet pleet, zoot suit, zoot soot, zoot suit with a reet pleat, cool suit with a loop droop, Nehru jacket, Nehru suit, clobber, harness (leather, especially motorcycle), drag, boondock (outdoor), racket jacket, Sunday clothes, Sunday suit, Sunday best, Sunday go-to-meetings, bib and tucker, best bib and tucker, secondhand, handout, hand-me-downs, reach-me-downs, bull's wool (stolen). See also CLOTHING.

DRESS v. turn out, fit out, rig out, rig up, rag out, rag up, tog, suit up, doll up, deck, deck out, dog out, dud, dude, dude up, drape, primp, prink, prank.

DRESSED adj. togged, togged up, slicked up, rigged up, rigged out, ragged up, ragged out, duded up, duded out, decked out, deck up, trick out, trick up, tog out, tog up, rag out, rag up, fig out, fig up, turned out, tricked out, dolled up, fancied up, gussied up, slicked up, spiffed up, spruced up, in fine feather, in high feather, in one's best bib and tucker, looking sharp, mellow back, wearing one's best, dressed fit to kill, dressed to the nines, in one's Sunday best, Sunday go-to-church, Sunday go-to-meeting, put on the dog. See also WELL DRESSED, STYLISH.

DRIFT v. kick around, float, go that a way, go every which way, go forty ways to Sunday, go forty ways from Sunday, anywhere the wind blows. See also WANDER.

DRIFTER n. bum, on the bum, king of the road, bo, stiff, bindle stiff, floater, ragbag. See VAGRANT. See also BEGGAR.

DRILL n. 1. constitutional, daily dozen, workout, gym, warm-up, jazzercise. 2. call, dry run, run through, shakedown, shakedown cruise, tryout, workout, dress. See also TEST.

DRILL v. work out, tune up, lick into shape, get in shape, walk through, hone, break, break in. See PRACTICE.

DRILL INSTRUCTOR n. D.I.

DRINK n. swig, slug, shot, snort, snorter, snifter, spot, nip, drop, wee drop, jigger, pint, pull, toast, fresh one, short one, short dog (cheap wine in a brown paper bag), double, finger, finger or two, cooler, juice, serum, shot in the arm, slam, taste, wash, quickie, quick one, one for the road, one too many, eye-opener, nightcap. See also LIQUOR.

DRINK v. guzzle, guz, down, swig, belt, put away, sponge, lick, liquor, liquor up, booze up, lap, lap up, sop, sop it up, tank up, soak up, bottoms up, beer up, gin up, mug up (coffee), chugalug, on the sauce, hit the sauce, hit the bottle, hit the booze, hit the red-eye, bend one's elbow, tip one's elbow, take a pull, crook one's elbow, crook one's little finger, go on a drunk, go on a bat, go on a binge, go on a toot, go on a bender, paint the town red, have one too many, drown one's troubles, crawl, pub-crawl, joint-hop, pound, knock back, juice back, juice down, crack a six-pack (beer), wash down, swill, belly wash, tipple, belt the grape, wet one's whistle, dip the beak, splice the main brace, get a bun on, get a buzz on, blast, scoff, slurp, pull, fight a bottle, growler rushing, hang a few on, hang on a few, inhale, irrigate, kill, knock off, fall off the wagon.

DRINKER n. lush, lusher, lush hound, souse, dip, dipso, barfly, stew, stewbum, stewie, wino, big drunk, town drunk, brown bagger, boozer, boozehound, hoochhound, ginhound, tippler, alky, jick head, juice head, juicer, groghound, grog blossom, bum, rum, rummy, rum hound, pretzel bender, shikker, guzzler, swiller, soaker, tank, pot, rumpot, lovepot, tosspot, crock, swigger, soak, sponge, long hitter, elbow bender, elbow crooker, barrel house bum, bottle baby, bottle man, stiff, bust, busthead, copper nose, swillbelly, swillpot, swillbowl.

DRINK, SOFT n. pop, coke, dope, bug juice, setup (for alcoholic mix), chaser, mixer, seltzer, penny plain, two-cents plain, cooler.

DRIVE n. 1. get up and go, push, guts, moxie, punch, clout, steam, the stuff, the right stuff, the goods, what it takes, spunk, gumption, fire in the belly. See also ATTACK. 2. spin, whirl, run, joyride, Sunday drive, airing, lift, pickup, burnout (high speed), commute, hitch.

DRIVE v. 1. cruise, roll, tool, tootle around, tip toe, bomb around, heel and toe (racing), burn rubber, burn up the road, burn the breeze, drag, floor it, step on it, lean on it, bear down on it, fire up, lay rubber down, fly, pour it on, pour on the coal, step on the gas, push, scat, tailgate, whoosh, hustle, make the sparks fly, go all out, go full steam ahead, break one's neck, bear down, poke, hump, get cutting. 2. pressure, high pressure, bulldoze, steamroll, lean on, goose, goose up, nerf, nag, jawbone, egg on, sell, sell one, railroad through. See FORCE.

DRIVE-IN THEATER n. drive-in, ozoner, passion pit.

DRIVEL n. hogwash, gobbledygook, poppycock, tripe, rot, tommyrot. See NONSENSE.

DRIVER n. wheelman, cowboy, leadfoot, Harvey Wallbanger (reckless), charger, double clutcher, dump chump (truck), bottle cap (tank truck), dynamiter, fireman, fluffy foot, gypsy, coachy, skinner, mule skinner, hogger, hoghead, shithead, shoe, skate jockey, road jockey, road runner, road hog, Willy Weaver (drunk). See also TRUCK DRIVER.

DRIVING, AUTOMOBILE v. at the wheel, buggy riding, chining, cruising, tooling.

DROLL adj. camp, campy, jokey, joshing, yok, yokky, gagged up, for grins, zetser, laffer, riot, crack up, crack 'em up, break one up. See AMUSING.

DRONE n. mother (plane).

DROP v. 1. nose-dive, dive, flop, do a brody. 2. adios that, bag that, 86 that, eighty-six that, kibosh, off, knock off, put the kibosh on, scrub, wash out, wipe out, waste one, scratch. See also DISCARD.

DROPPED adj. scrubbed, adiosed, washed out, washed up, all washed up, scratched, eight-sixed, offed, wasted.

DROWSE v. zizz, grab a few z's, cop some z's, catnap, dozz, doz, calk off, drop off, dope off, cork off, cop a nod, dig oneself a nod, collar a nod, catch a wink. See SLEEP.

DROWSY adj. dopey, out of it, sleepy head, snoozy, stretchy, on the nod, eye trouble, in sleepsville.

DRUDGE n. nose to the grindstone, workaholic, workhorse, grind, greasy grind.

DRUDGE v. plug, dig, grind, peg away, slave, sweat, back to the salt mines, heel (Stu.), shlep. See PLOD.

DRUDGERY n. grind, daily grind, rat race, elbow grease, shitwork, donkeywork, gruntwork (Army), scud, scut, workout, ballbreaker, ballwracker, ballbuster, bone breaker, backbreaker, ass breaker, conk buster, bitch, bitch kitty, son of a bitch, fun and games.

DRUG n. A-bomb, Anywhere (possession), ammunition, blank (non-narcotic), doll, downer, downs, Finn, hardstuff, knockout drops, fruit salad (mixture), little Michael, little Mike, Mickey Finn, shot, starch, upper, ups, turkey (diluted), magic bullet (Medic.). See AMPHETAMINE, COCAINE, HEROIN, ETC.

DRUG v. blow one's mind, give one knockout drops, slip one a mickey, fix, hit, dope, dope up, dose, dose up.

DRUG ADDICT n. A.D., A-head, head, Scag Jones. See ADDICT.

DRUG ADDICTION n. habit, hook, Jones, jones, sweet tooth, monkey on one's back. See ADDICTION.

DRUG BUY n. bag, dime bag, nickel bag, dime's worth, cap; matchbox, stick (cigarette); quarter bag, can, lid, O.Z., weight (oz.); key, kee, ki (kilo); brick (compressed kilo).

DRUG CURE take the cure, kick the habit, kick, cold turkey, get the monkey off, get the monkey off one's back, off the habit, kill the Chinaman.

DRUG MARKETPLACE n. rock house, Cokeland, Alphabet Town (N.Y.), Sherm Alley (L.A.).

DRUG OVERDOSE v. OD, oh dee, overjolt, overvamp, overamp, overcharge, burn out, freak out, jazz out, rock out, zone out, zonk out.

DRUG PACKET n. bag, deck, lid, bindle, bird's-eye.

DRUG PARAPHERNALIA n. spike, works, head kit, kit, fit, outfit, the business, joint (total equipment), flake spoon, cooker, gun, hook, ken ten (lamp for opium), artillery, banger, hype stick, light artillery, needle, pin, quill (matchbook cover), bong (pipe), marygin (seed remover), roach clip, Woodstock Emergency pipe (aluminum foil); stash bag, stash box, stash jar (marijuana).

DRUG SELLER n.   dealer, pusher, drug pusher, connection, peddler, dope peddler, source, one who's holding, hyp, hype, mother, mule, junker, shover, viper, the Man, heavy man, tea man, reefer man, candy man, swing man, bagman, big man, scagman, bingles, bingler, broker, house connections, juggler, missionary, operator, trafficker, beat artist, fixer.

DRUG TERMS   cut, doctor, phony up (adulterate); cut deck (adulterated); charge, load, skinful; shot, hit, piece, can, deck, phony bingle, carrying (possession); scag trade, factory, underground factory, basement lab.

DRUG TRAFFIC n.   scag trade.

DRUG USE adj.   high, use, up, habit, belly habit (oral), mouth habit (smoke), nose habit, needle habit, needle park, on the needle, on the nod, reentry, floating, twisted, wired, strung out, way out, wigged out, mellowed out, wiped out, zonked out, freaker out, stoned out of one's gourd, charged up, gaged up, geezed up, junked up, teaed up, torn up, hopped up, heeled, high as a kite, loaded, smashed, fires, weedhead, the business, blown away, blown out, happy, thrill, kick, charge, coasting, having a buzz, flying, joy riding, sleigh riding, tripping out, ripped, out of it, ping wing, pin shot, pothead, on the weed, on the hype, on the hype stick, on the light artillery, on a cloud, shooting the pin, pinned (constricted pupils), shooting gallery, snowed, caught in a snowstorm, snowstorm (party), tracks, cokie, coked, coked up, doper, contact high, coast, drive, geed up, g'd up, geezer, goofed, gow, gowed up, hold, hot shot, hype, in orbit, chemical dependency.

DRUG USE v.   drop, pop, use, shoot, shoot up, space out, zone out, tweek out, nod, fix, take a fix, take a drag, hit, take a hit, toke, get high, get off, get up, go up, tall, floating, flying, gone, sniff, snort, blow, blast, bust a cat, boot, cook, mainline, freebase, the big drive, bang, bomb, bomb out, O.D., jab off, joy pop, skin pop, jolt, jolt of junk, kick the mooch around, kick the gong around, shoot the pin, reenter, chase the dragon, do a blow, do a toot, do drugs, dabbling, dossing, dozzing, speedball, lit up, blind, beaming, torn up, hit the pipe, hit the needle, short, sick (need), straighten one (administer), string out, sweet tooth, trip, blow coke, blow snow, cork the air.

DRUG USER n.   A.D., A-head, junkie, junker, greasy junkie, user, doper, mainliner, freak, head, hop, hophead, drughead, coke head, acid head, acid freak, dust head, weedhead, pothead, pillhead, methhead, fiend, dope fiend, hooked, hype, hypo, banger, bangster,

jabber, jaboff, needle man, needle knight, use the needle, smack slammer, tripper, dirty, dopenik, straight (after injection), viper, wasted, dynamiter, sick (needs injection), cokey, snifter, tooter (cocaine), ice creamer, student, Skag Jones, snowbird, snow snorter, station worker; Saturday night habit, chippy (occasional); joy popper (new or occasional user), campfire boy, tea toker, from Mount Shasta (not common), goof, goof ball, aspirin hound, bean popper, AD, speed freak, globetrotter (always moving).

DRUG USE SITE n.   head shop, gallery, shooting gallery, ballroom, balloon room, parachute, spot.

DRUG WITHDRAWAL n.   kicking the habit, drying out, sweating it out, taking the cure, shakes, wet dog shakes, bogue, cold turkey, becoming Mr. Fink.

DRUGGED adj.   stoned, on the nod, nodding, spaced, spaced out, trip, tripping, flyin', stoned out of one's mind, stoned out of one's head, stoned out of one's gourd, snowed, snowed in, snowed up, caught in a snowstorm, sleigh riding, coked, coked up, coasting, floating, twisted, blown away, blown out, wigged out, mellowed out, strung out, wiped out, zonked out, charged up, gaged up, geezed up, junked up, teaed up, torn up, hopped up, heeled, high as a kite, loaded, smashed, happy, flying, joy riding, ripped, out of it, on the needle, on the weed, on the hype, on the hype stick, on the light artillery, on a cloud, pinned (constricted pupils), high, contact high, geed up, g'd up, goofed, gow, gowed up, in orbit, crispy.

DRUGS n.   D&N (drugs and narcotics), junk, shit, goof ball, reds, uppers, downers, stuff, hard stuff, cement, goods, Jones, merchandise, the needle, shot, shot in the arm, fix, bag, lid, charge, shot, card (portion), biddle, bindle, bingle, bing, birdsize, jolt, bundle, nickel bag, Z (ounce), deck, dime bag (ten dollars' worth), cap, West Coast cap, Tijuana cap, Mexican cap, Frisco cap, cold stuff (deadly), dust, dynamite (pure), fix up, bongs, check, fours, mojo, needle candy, score, sugar, candy, cubes, dust, flea powder, ammunition, lucky seven (mixture), psychadelic jelly bean, nixon (poor quality), stallion stick, stums, sweet surrender, corporation cocktail (coal gas bubbled through milk), Allah Supreme, God's medicine, hokus, hook, hop, half load, happenings, ice cream (crystals), brown bomber, casa boom, death boy, death wish.

DRUGS: AMPHETAMINE n.   A, bam, bombita, cartwheel, chalk, cotton (saturated with benzadrine), copilot, diet pills, double blue, driver, eye-opener, forwards, French blue, hearts, jellybeans, jolly beans, leapers, leepers, lid popper, lightfooted, peaches, pepper, pep pill, ripper, splash, speed, thrusters, truck drivers, up, uppers, wake up, obie.

DRUGS: AMYL NITRITE n. amy, popper, blue, blue angel, blue bird, blue devil, blue heaven, pear, snapper, pearls, poppsies. whiffenpopper.

DRUGS: BARBITURATE n. barb, blue devils, blue heaven, candy, down, goof ball, peanuts, Phennies, pink lady, purple heart, yellow jacket, abbot, blockbuster, nimby, nebbie, nemmy.

DRUGS: BENZEDRINE n. B, benny, benzie, speed, upper, peachies, white.

DRUGS: BIPHETAMINE n. black beauties.

DRUGS: CHLORAL HYDRATE n. knockout drops, Mickey, Mickey Finn, little Michael.

DRUGS: COCAINE n. C, Cee, coke, cola, cokey, candy, nose candy, rocks (hard), sugar, snow, snowball, cloud walk, speedball (plus morphine or heroin), snowbird, white, white cross, white mosquitoes, old lady white, sleighride, toot, toots, Charlie, Cecil, Connie, Corinne, Bernice, Pearl, girl, her, lady, uptown, gin, jam, flake, joy flakes, joy powder, gold dust, happy dust, heaven dust, Peruvian, reindeer dust, cookie, leaf, trey, wings, bloke, big bloke, crack, live (sniffed), whiff, balloon (bag), Cadillac (ounce), row, line (dose).

DRUGS: COCAINE AND HEROIN n. C and H, cold and hot, speedball (also cocaine and morphine), dynamite, whizbang.

DRUGS: DEXAMYL n. Christmas trees, purple heart.

DRUGS: DEXEDRINE n. dex, dexy, dexie, football, heart, oranges.

DRUGS: DEXTROAMPHETAMINE n. dex, dexie, dexy, football, heart, greenies, oranges.

DRUGS: DIMETHYLTRYPTAMINE n. DMT.

DRUGS: DIPROPYLPHYPTAMINE n. DPT

DRUGS: FENTANYL n. China white.

DRUGS: HASHISH n. hash, heesh, sheesh, keef, candy, hash head (user).

DRUGS: HEROIN n. C., H., aitch, the big H, horse, snow, sugar, smeck, smack, bag, cadillac, piece, weight (ounce), fix, shit, the tragic magic, liquid sky (with sex), Lady H, yen shee, stuff, hard stuff, white stuff, junk, hook, hot shot (overdose), pack, blanks, bones, boy, brother, brown, brown sugar, Mexican brown, Mexican mud, black tar, Chinese, Chinese red, red chicken, chiva, cobics, crap, doojee, Dojee, doorjee, estuffa, first degree, heroina, powder, joy powder, flea powder, polvo, scag, scar, scramble, tecaba, thing, bombita, dynamite, cold 45, Colt .45, schmee, antifreeze, caballo, deck, salt, him, hero of the underworld, Harry, Big Harry, witch hazel, angel, noise, lemonade, poison, eye-opener (first of day), goldfinger (synthetic).

DRUGS: HEROIN AND COCAINE n. speedball, dynamite.

DRUGS: HEROIN AND MARIJUANA n. atom bomb.

DRUGS: ISOBUTYL NITRITE n. popper.

DRUGS: JIMSON WEED n. Devil's trumpet.

DRUGS: LUMINAL PILL n. purple heart.

DRUGS: LYSERGIC ACID DIETHYLAMIDE n. LSD, acid, candy, cube, trip, LSD-25, 25, cap, flight, big D, coffee, instant Zen, orange, peace, sugar, sugar lump, sunshine, California sunshine, Hawaiian sunshine, sunshine pill, yellow sunshine, yellow, mellow yellow, white lightning, Owsley's, Owsley Acid, paper acid, blue acid, blue cheer, blue flag, blue heaven, domes, dots, flats, Lucy in the sky with diamonds, barrels, blotters, frogs, lids, wedges, windowpanes, tab.

DRUGS: MANDRAKE n. devil's testicle, Satan's apple.

DRUGS: MARIJUANA n. pot, grass, joint, reefer, reefer weed, weed, lone weed, Viper's weed, hash, shit, hemp, T, tea, jay, roach, Mary, Mary Jane, Mary Anne, Mary Wanna, Mary Warner, greefo, griefo, grefa, grafa, sinsemella, hay, Indian hay, mezz, the mighty mezz, Thai stick, Mexican red, Mexican brown, Panamanian red, Panama red, gold, Acapulco gold, Colombian gold, Santa Marta gold, African black, Jersey green, golden leaf, Maui-wowee, beetle, birdwood, bomber, belt, drag, hit, bush, charge, beat, dynamite, fu, gage, stick, stick of gage, herb, dew, goof ball, spliff, jadja, Indian hemp, smoke, joy smoke, giggle smoke, giggle weed, juane, kef, keef, moocah, muggles, mohasky, pod, Texas Tea, splay, red dirt marijuana, salt and pepper, sinsemilla, sensemilla, stuff, snap, snop, boo, gungeon, gunion, black gunion, jabooby, Lipton's (fake), weed tea, yesca, Alice B. Toklas brownies, bush, mootah, mu, panatella, dope, rope, seed, baby, blue sage, dagga, 13-M, bo bo, dew, bar, gold leaf, manicure, sweet Lucy, baby, Banji, bhang, catnip, Coli, sativa, ace, cheeba.

DRUGS: MESCALINE n. big chief, mesc.

DRUGS: METHADONE n. meth, dolls, dollies.

DRUGS: METHAMPHETAMINE n. crystals, Cris, Cristine, crank, elephant, tranquilizer, dynamite, speed.

DRUGS: METHAQUALONE n. pillow, soap, soaper.

DRUGS: METHEDRINE n. crystals.

DRUGS: METHYLENEDIOXYAMPHETAMINE n. MDMA, MDA, ecstasy.

DRUGS: METHYL FENTENYL n. China white.

DRUGS: MORNING GLORY SEED n. flying saucer, heavenly blue.

DRUGS: MORPHINE n. M, morph, cube juice, dime's worth, dreamer, medicine, God's own medicine, God's drug, soldier's drug, happy dust, Ixey, joy powder, Miss Emma, red cross, sugar, snow, white dust, white nurse, mojo, whiz bang (mixed with cocaine).

DRUGS: NEMBUTAL n. purple heart, yellow jacket, blockbuster, pill, nebbie, nemish, nemmie, nimby, abbot.

DRUGS: NEMBUTAL AND MORPHINE n. purple heart.

DRUGS: OPIUM n. O, big O, pop, poppy, pox, grease, pill, Chinese tobacco, gow, ghow, gom, goma, hop, hops, mud, tar, gee, stem, yen, yen shee, pen yan, pen yen, black stuff, dream beads, dream wax, dream gum, dreams, God's own medicine, midnight oil, yam yam, smoke.

DRUGS: PAREGORIC n. blue velvet, black jack.

DRUGS: PEYOTE n. mescal, button.

DRUGS: PHENCYCLIDINE n. PCP, angel dust, Sherms (cigarette), P-stuff, busy bee, crystal, elephant, elephant tranquilizer, monkey dust, scuffle, killer weed, peace pill, rocket fuel, cannabinal, lovely, tic, mist, dust, rock dust, T dust, animal, cadillac, C.J., K.J., goon, sheets, hog, mint, monkey, snorts, Aurora Borealis, dummy, ozone, soma, cyclone, horse, new magic; super joint, super grass (marijuana sprinkled with PCP).

DRUGS: QUAALUDE n. lude, quad, sopor, pillows, wallbanger, vitamin Q, lemon.

DRUGS: SECONAL n. red, red devil, Seccy, Seggy, Secos, pink lady.

DRUGS: TUINAL n. Christmas trees, double trouble, rainbows, tootsies, reds, blues, red and blue.

DRUGS: VALIUM n. volume, downer, mello yello, true blue.

DRUGS, BUY v. make a buy, score, score some, keep the meet, cop, hit, re-up, sail, ten cents, trey, turn.

DRUGS, SELL v. peddle, push, scag trade.

DRUM v. beat out some licks.

DRUMMER n. hide beater, skin beater.

DRUMMING v. press roll.

DRUMS n. skins, hides, snares, bamboula, bongos, booms, sock, suitcase, traps, tubs.

DRUMSTICKS n. boom sticks, brushes (wire), sticks.

DRUNK adj. tight, tipsy, bombed, bombed out, bombed out of one's skull, crocked, cockeyed, soused, stewed, stiff, stinko, stinking, plastered, hammered, pie-eyed, wasted, fractured, looped, loopy, high, high as a kite, higher than a kite, blind, blotto, under the influence, boozed up, juiced, juiced up, stoned, tanked, tanked up, roaring, roaring drunk, dead drunk, rolling drunk, stinking drunk, sloppy drunk, blind drunk, skunk drunk, drunk as a skunk, drunk as a skunk in a trunk, drunk as a lord, potted, fried, smashed, crashed, swacked, polluted, plotzed, turned on, tied one on, zonked, zonked out, zapped, zig zag, loaded, carrying a load, carrying a heavy load, three bricks short of a load, feeling no pain, embalmed, on a tear, on a toot, on a bat, on a bender, on a binge, on a jag, on instruments, on the sauce, on the juice, on the shikker, schikker, shikkered, schnoggered, schnokkered, snokkered, snokkered up, snootful, lubricated, mellow, ossified, paralyzed, petrified, pickled, pissed, pissed as a newt, pissed up to the eyebrows, pissed to the ears, pissy eyed, pissy drunk, potsed, prestoned, padded, pasted, pied, pipped up, vulcanized, wall-eyed, well oiled, wet, whooshed, woofled, woozy, ripped, put to bed with a shovel, shit-faced, illuminated, lit, lit up, lit up like a Christmas tree, lit a bit, lit to the gunnels, merry, hipped, out, out cold, out like a light, out on the roof, boiled, parboiled, balmy, behind the cork, bent, bleary eyed, boozed, boozy, bottled, bunned, buzzed, buzzy, stewed to the gills, boiled to the gills, fried to the gills, soused to the gills, lit to the gills, burned to the ground, canned, canned up, comfortable, piffed, piffled, piflicated, petrificated, pigeon-eyed, pixilated, plonked, potty, preserved, primed, pruned, rocky, rosy, rumdum, rummy, saturated, screaming, screeching, scronched, set up, sent, shellacked, shot, sloppy, sloshed, slugged, smoked, snozzled, soaked, spiffed, spifflicated, spaced out, passed out, wicked faced, giddy, fuddled, muddled, muzzy, dizzy, addled, seeing double, overtaken, corked, corned, cut, crocko, afflicted, jug-bitten, organized, elevated, heading into the wind, three sheets to the wind, three sheets in the wind and the other one flapping, six sheets to the wind, tiddly, full of Dutch courage, with a bun on, cooked, crashed and burned, daquifried, decayed, ding swizzled, teed, twisted, bagged, bongoed, boxed, featured, frozen, glazed, have a brass eye, have a kick in the guts, have a skinfull, have a rubber drink, have a skate on, have a slant on, have a flag out, have a bun on, have a can on, have a glow on, have an edge on; half cocked, half crocked, half shot, half slewed, half sprung, half stewed, half seas over, half under, half shave, half snapped (half drunk); hang one on, happy, heeled, dipsy, off the wagon, fallen off the wagon, horseback, in the bag, leaping, nimtopsical, over the bay, owled, plowed, sozzled, zozzled, bullet proofed, buzzed, hammered, laid out, stretched, tired, walking on rocky socks, blasted, blewed, blued, blindo, boggled, guyed out, flannel mouth, activated, adrip, afloat, aglow, alcoholized, alight, alkied, alkied up, antifreezed, ate the dog, back teeth afloat, baptized, bashed, basted, beerified, beery, bent out of shape, bent and broken, crashed, torn, tore up, tore down, wiped out, aced, discomboobulated, discomfuddled, flying one wing low, foozlified, fossilized, gaffed, galvanized, giggled, greased, grogged, groggy, guttered, had one or two, holding up the wall, honked, hosed, impaired, inpixocated, in orbit, inked, inky poo, intoxed, irrigated, jazzed up, jiggered, jugged up, juicy, Kentucky fried, southern fried, Mexican fried, knee walking drunk, knockered, laced, likkerous, liquified, listing to starboard, little 'round the corner, loud and proud, lushed, lushed up, lushington, spliced, main brace well spliced, mashed, mizzled, noddy headed, oiled up, pretty far gone, ripe, ripped and wrecked, ripped to the tits, schizzed out, seeing pink elephants, sewed, shot down, sizzled, slathered, slewed, smashed out of one's mind, snooted, squiffed, squiffy, starched, steamed, stiffed, stiffo, suffering no pain, swacko, tanked out, tight as a goat, tight as a drum, top heavy, totaled, toxicated, varnished, whiffled, whoozy, gassed, glassy, glass-eyed, had a bun on, had a skinful and a half, had one too many, marinated, maxed out, in the gutter, in one's cups, jagged, jazzed, jolly, jugged, killed, limp, lathered, liquored, liquored up, decks awash, ding swizzled, feel good, fired up, floating, frazzled, fuzzled, fuzzy, gay, geared up, ginned, ginned up, stitched, stone blind, stunned, tangle-footed, teed up, under the table, under the weather.

DRUNKARD adj.   drinker, heavy drinker, drunk, big drunk, dip, dipso, boozer, booze fighter, boozehound, stew, stewbum, stewie, souse, soak, sponge, sop, shikker, bum, rummy, rumbum, rum hound, lush hound, lush, lusher, lushie, barfly, wino, brown bagger, juicehead, power drinker, swillbelly, swillpot, swillbowl, bottle nose, grog blossom, longhitter, hooch hound, ginhound, elbow bender, town drunk, pot, rumpot, tippler, stiff, big stiff, crock, alky, barrel house bum, bottle baby, bottle man, bust, busthead, tank, copper nose, jick head, juicer, bingo-boy (gang). See also DRINKER.

DRUNKEN COURAGE n.   Dutch courage.

DRY adj.   blah, draggy, dull as dishwater, ho hum, bor-ring! See also TRITE.

DRYDOCK n.   jaheemy, geehemy, jaheembie, geeheebee.

DRY-MOUTHED adj.   cotton mouth, mouth full of cotton.

DUAL adj.   twin, doubleheader (successful two ways), double in brass (two kinds of work), rule of twice, wear two hats, twofers, double-dip (two incomes), switch-hit (bisexual).

DUBIOUS adj.   chancy, iffy, touch and go, hanging by a thread, don't hold your breath, you should live so long. See DOUBTFUL.

DUDE n.   hotshot, flash, city slicker, candy kid, hepcat, sport, macaroni, swell, toff, snappy dresser, Dapper Dan, Beau Brummel, clotheshorse.

DUDGEON n.   rise, get a rise out of, sore, huff, dander, Irish, pet, tiff, miff, stew, storm, ruckus, wing-ding, slow burn, conniption, conniption fit, cat fit, duck fit, blowup, flare-up. See PIQUE.

DUE n.   rate, be in line for, comeuppance, what is coming to one, what one has coming, what one was asking for, get hers, get his.

DUE BILL n.   bad news, I.O.U.

DULL adj.   blah, draggy, ho hum, bor-ring, big yawn, yawner, go over like a lead balloon, lay an egg, bombed, phoned in, dead, dealy, deadsville, dullsville, dragsville. See BORING.

DULLARD adj.   dork, nerd, loser, winner, grunge, grunch, birdbrain, rattleweed, nobody home, dumbo, turkey, spaz, schlemiel, schmuck, dipstick, dill, popcorn head, deadneck, flat tire, gumby, doesn't know enough to come in out of the rain. See STUPID.

DULUTH, MINNESOTA   The Little Twin, Twin Forts.

DUMB adj.   dodo, dummy, dumbo, dumdum, dumbbell, dumb bunny, dumb cluck, dumb Dora, dumb head, dumb ox, four-letter man (D.U.M.B.). See STUPID.

DUMBFOUND v.   blow away, blow one's mind, bowl down, bowl over, flabbergast, knock one over with a feather, set one on one's ass, strike all of a heap, throw, throw into a tizzy, throw on one's beam ends. See ASTONISH.

DUMBFOUNDED adj.   blown away, stuck, stumped, bamboozled, buffaloed, beat, floored, licked, bowled down, bowled over, flabbergasted, struck all of a heap, thrown, thrown off one's beam ends. See also ASTONISHED.

DUN AND BRADSTREET n.   D & B.

DUN v.   chase, bone, hock one's charnik, noodge, lean on, put the squeeze on, put the arm on, put the bite on, see in the alley.

DUNCE n.   dork, nerd, lamebrain, jerk, twit, spaz, dodo, ninny, airedale, pointyhead, stoop, yold, deadneck, goof ball, half-baked, nuthin' upstairs. See STUPID.

DUNG n.   buffalo chips, cow chips, cow flops, cow pats, road apples, golden apples, moose beans, moose nuggets, moose pecans, turd, shit, horseshit, horse hockey.

DUNGAREES n.   jeans, blue jeans, Levis, leaves, coveralls, chinos.

DUPE n.   mark, easy mark, pigeon, patsy, sucker, vic, chump, sitting duck, pigeon, clay pigeon, fish, greeny. See VICTIM.

DUPE v.   rook, screw, shaft, rip off, jerk one around, dick one around, fuck one over, shuck and jive, rope in, do a number on one. See TRICK.

DUPED adj.   stung, been had, taken, taken for a bundle, took, been took, aced out, fucked over, stiffed, suckered, diddled, burned. See TRICKED.

DUPLICATE n.   1. ditto, dupe, xerox, clone, carbon, carbon copy, mimeo, stat, repro, knock off, flimsy. 2. look-alike, work-alike, ringer, dead ringer, copycat, spitting image, spit and image, chip off the old block, double, peas in a pod, twin, ——— compatible (P.C. compatible). 3. fake, phony, knock off, pirate. See COPY.

DUPLICATE v.   1. dupe, xerox, carbon, clone, mimeo, ditto, repro, knock off, stat, reinvent the wheel. 2. act like, do, do like, go like, make like, mirror, take off as, do a take off, play the ——— (affect a role). 3. pirate, fake, phony, knock off, steal one's stuff, take a leaf out of one's book. See COPY.

DUPLICITY n.   dirty dealing, dirty work, dirty pool, dirty trick, Judas kiss, stab in the back, skullduggery, gamesmanship, one upsmanship. See CHEAT.

DURABILITY n.   backbone, grit, guts, gutsiness, heart, intestinal fortitude, moxie, starch, stick-to-itiveness, staying power, eat nails, hard as nails.

DUSK n.   dimday.

DUST n.   dustball, house moss, kittens, pussies, slut's wool, dust kitty, dust bunny, beggar's velvet, ghost turds.

DUTCHMAN n.   butter box, Frank (obs.).

DUTY n.   hooked, on a string, owe one one, dues, minding the store, taking care of business, TCB. See also RESPONSIBLE, RESPONSIBILITY.

DWARF n.   little people, little person, shrimp, runt, shorty, shortish, short pint, half-pint, half-portion, dusty butt, peanut, peewee, bantam, sawed off, squirt, knee high, knee high to a grasshopper.

DWELL v.   bunk, bunk out, hang out, crash, nest, perch, roost, squat, hang up one's hat, hang up one's shingle, hole up, locate, park. See INHABIT.

DWELLING n.   pad, crib, cubbyhole, den, domi, flop, digs, diggings, hole in the wall, dump, castle. See HOUSE. See also APARTMENT.

DYING adj.   done for, on one's last legs, checking out, at the end of one's rope, MFC (measure for coffin), heading for the last roundup, one foot in the grave, the other on a banana peel the other in the grave.

DYNAMIC adj.   ballsy, bogard, come on strong, play for keeps, go-getter, play hard ball. See ENTERPRISING.

DYNAMITE n.   dinah, dine, grease, noise, stick.

E

E. n. easy, echo.

EACH pron. a pop, per.

EAGER adj. hot to trot, rarin' to go, gung ho, self-starting, itchy, dying to, needles, ants, antsy, antsy-pantsy, ants in one's pants, not about to let any grass grow under one's feet, ready for Freddie. See IMPATIENT.

EAGERLY adv. at the drop of a hat.

EARDRUM n. drum, pop a drum (rupture).

EARLY adv. previous, a bit previous, bright and early, early bird, early on.

EARMARK v. name, slot, tab, tag. See DEDICATE.

EARN v. make, make a buck, pull, pull down, drag down, cop, clear, hustle, rate, sock, turn, bring home the bacon, bring home the groceries, get along, keep the wolf from the door, pay one's dues, be in line for, pick up, clean up, scare up, wangle, snag, score, cash in on, make a good thing of, make a killing, make it big, make hay, make money hand over fist, feather one's nest, line one's nest, grab, kipe, kype, latch on to something.

EARNEST adj. no fooling, for real, meaningful, serious jelly, no shit, mean business, playing hard ball, money talks bullshit walks. See SERIOUS.

EARNINGS n. net, payoff, bottom line, in the black, gate, melon, take home, groceries, salt, piece of the pie. See INCOME. See also COMPENSATION.

EARPHONES n. cans.

EARRING n. dangler.

EARS n. flappers, flaps, flippers, lugs, mikes, sails, tin ear (deaf), cauliflower, pretty ear (deformed or cauliflower).

EARSPLITTING adj. leather-lunged.

EARTH n. apple, big blue marble, real estate, spaceship Earth, dust, old sod, terra firma.

EARTHY adj. 1. down, down to earth, down home, funky, folksy, home folks, homey, haymish, meat-and-potatoes man. See NATURAL. 2. cheap, raw, raunchy, blue, dirty, low-down and dirty, filthy, off-color, rough, rough stuff, foul mouth, foulmouthed, loudmouthed, in the gutter, salty. See OBSCENE.

EASE v. grease the wheels, run interference for, open doors, walk through, hand-carry.

EASE UP v. lighten up, don't sweat it, cool it, go with the flow, hang loose, let it all hang out, let it all happen, mellow out. See RELAX.

EASILY adv. no sweat, hands down, like nothing, nothing to it, slick as a whistle, swimmingly, piece of cake, at the drop of a hat.

EAST COAST n. dirty side, East.

EAST n. back east, dirty side.

EASTERN EUROPEAN n. bohunk, hunk, hunkie, Litvak.

EASY adj. snap, setup, wired, no sweat, no problem, nothing to it, like nothin', pushover, picnic, cinchy, soft, soft touch, sweet, velvet, pie, cherry pie, easy as pie, easy as falling off a log, easy make, easy digging, duck soup, sitting duck, like shooting ducks in a barrel, turkey shoot, a piece of cake, cream puff, cushy, knack, downhill, fluff, breeze, breeze in, stroll, walkover, walk in the park, win in a walk, win hands down, waltz, picnic, gut course, snap course (college), pud (test or course), child's play, lead-pipe cinch, racket, white meat, whipsaw, whipsaw through, mick, Mickey Mouse, simple as ABC, clear sailing, can o' corn, laid back, toss it off, throwaway, geranium, jelly, free ride, peach. See also OBTAINABLE.

EAT v. scarf, scarf back, scarf down, chow down, scoff, slurp, squff, mow (mow a burger), munch, munch out, nibble, snack, snack on, peck, peck at, pick at, blimp out, pig out, pork out, make a pig of oneself, make a hog of oneself, dig into, chuck, board, gorm, gorp, graze, grease, grease one's chops, wolf, wolf down, garbage down, inhale, kill, gobble, gulp, bolt, dispatch, dispose, nosh, fress, fling a fang, chew, gum, grit, swabble, yam, brown bag it, stuff one's face, feed one's face, fall to, get away with, pitch in, tuck in, tuck away, put away, pack it away, tie on, tie on the nosebag, tie on the feedbag, put on the feedbag, do lunch, break bread with, eat high on the hog, eat high on the joint, eat like a horse, eat one's head off, eat out of house and home, eat like it's going out of style, eat like there's no tomorrow, eat like a bird, eat Chinx (Chinese dinner), go after it, come and get it, grits time, buzz around the barrel, lick the plate, polish off, knock off, collar a hot, surround oneself outside of, put oneself outside of, take it on, make with a knife and fork, foot under the table, mug up.

EATABLES n. chow, snack, eats, feedbag, grub pile, scoffings, chewings, moveable feast, home cooking. See FOOD.

EATER n. chow hound, nosher, star boarder, fresser.

EATING PLACE n. eatery, pit stop, grease joint, greasy spoon, beanery, bistro, noshery, cook shack, chow hall, chow line, mess, one-armed joint, pigpen, caf. See RESTAURANT.

EAVESDROP v. bug, tap, wiretap, be all ears, ears into, Erie, on the Erie, slurp, listen in, tune in on.

EAVESDROPPER n. bugger, kibitzer, nosy Parker, snoop, snooper, yenta, Paul Pry, little pitcher with big ears.

EBULLIENT adj. bouncy, chirpy, chipper, feeling one's oats, full of beans, full of piss and vinegar, zippy. See SPIRITED.

ECCENTRIC adj. freak, freaky, freaked out, geeky, kook, kooky, coo coo, beat, beatnik, beat generation, offbeat, off the beaten track, bent, weird, weirdo, wombat, funky, strange one, oddball, foul ball, goof ball, special, avant-garde, cool, fringy, kinky, speed, hippy, flaky, far out, way out, wild, crazy, funny, funny-looking, off the wall, out in left field, trippy, not wrapped real tight, fly ball, case, goony, gooney bird, birdy, chirp, queer fish, queer duck, strange duck, rare bird, jayhawk, gasser, loner, meshugah, meshuganah, potty, cockeyed, three-dollar bill, crackpot, gonzo, queer potato, queer in the head, herky, screwy, screwball, aired out, jell-brain, jelled, twerp, character, shaky, creepy, whacko, whacky, whacked out, yo-yo, nut, nutcake, nutroll, nutty, nutty as a fruitcake, fruity, fruitcake, full mooner, spacey, spaced out, Asiatic (WW II N.).

ECCENTRICALLY adv. all over the shop, by fits and starts, every which way, here there and everywhere, hit or miss, right and left. See ERRATICALLY.

ECCLESIASTIC n. the rev, Holy Joe, sky pilot, bible thumper, harp polisher, long-haired boy, right buck. See CLERGYMAN.

ECHO v. ditto, rubber-stamp, mirror, make like, do like, go like. See also COPY.

ECONOMICAL adj. 1. cheapie, el cheapo, dirt cheap, cheap as dirt, dog cheap, steal, real steal, buy, real buy, low cost, cost nothing, cost next to nothing, bought for a song, cut rate, low tariff, dime a dozen. 2. tight, close, scrimpy, skimpy, stingy, on the rims, run on the rims, Scotch, nickel nurser. See THRIFTY.

ECONOMICS n. ec, eco, econ.

ECONOMIZE v. scrimp, skimp, penny-pinch, cut corners, cut to the bone, tighten one's belt, stretch a dollar, rub the print off a dollar bill. See SAVE.

ECSTASY n. gone, far out, cool, Nadaville, twilight zone. See also ELATION.

ECSTATIC adj. cool, zero cool, gone, real gone, out, far out, spaced out, wig, wigged out, flipped out, blissed out, sent, crazy, mad, wild, wicked, weird, weirded out, dreamy, turned on, stoned, high, high as a kite, sunny, sunny side up, shook up, hopped up, tea'd up, up, upbeat, flyin', flyin' high, floating, floating on air, on a joy ride, on a cloud, on cloud seven, on cloud nine, in seventh heaven, tickled to death, tickled pink, pleased as punch, sold on, hummy, out of it, blowing one's top, blowing one's roof, popping one's nuts, in Nadaville, in the twilight zone.

EDIBLES n. chow, bite, snack, eats, feed, feedbag, grub, take out, fast food, pogey, scoff, slop, garbage. See FOOD.

EDIFICE n. pile o' bricks, rockpile, skyscraper, towers.

EDIT v. massage, blue pencil, clean up, cut, tighten, fine tune, go over, dial back, recalibrate, fly speck, debug, bleep, bleep out, launder, sanitize, sterilize, decontaminate, scrub.

EDITOR n. ed, blue penciler, cutter (film), play doctor, play fixer.

EDITORIAL adj. thinkpiece, op ed piece, shirttail (column).

EDUCATE v. brainwash, let in on the know, put hip, put hep, put through the grind, show one the ropes, drum into. See INSTRUCT.

EDUCATED adj. double dig, highbrow, brain, brains, brainy, savvy, know all the answers, know what's what, know one's onions. See KNOWLEDGEABLE.

EDUCATION n. ed.

EDUCATOR n. prof, teach.

EERIE adj. spooky, spookish, scary.

EFFACE v. wipe out, wipe off the map, off, X out, zap, kayo, KO, launder, scrub, nix. See CANCEL.

EFFECT n. fallout, reaction, chain reaction, flak (bad), follow up, follow through, can of worms, spin-off, waves. See RESULT.

EFFECT v. make waves, unzip, turn the trick, do the trick, do the job, do up brown, do to a turn, do to a T, do one's stuff, do one's thing, do a number, come through with, get to, buy, sell, get it across, put across, put it over, put away, make it, make it big, pull off, pull it off, knock off, polish off, tear off, tick, take care of, take care of business, T.C.B., deal with, hammer out, hack out, work out, hit, score, clean up, wind up, button up, wrap up, mop up, put the lid on, go to town, perk, percolate.

EFFECTIVE adj. lead in one's pencil, powerhouse, live, wicked, on the ball, play hardball. See also CAPABLE, POWERFUL.

EFFEMINATE adj. gay, faggy, swish, swishy, flyer, flamer, fruity, pansy, pansified, pantywaist, fairy, fagela, lost his cholla, ma, mother, old woman, womanish, nancy, nance, capon, cream puff, camp, sissy, sissified, cookie pusher, Ethel, bait, frame, goody-goody, lacy, lily, limp wrist, Nellie, pimp, pretty boy, puss, weak sister, milksop, music major, twinkie, lah de dah, Mama's boy, mammy boy, Percy boy, Percy pants, fraidy cat, scaredy cat, chicken, chick (all Derog.).

EFFICIENT adj. dynamite, smoking, fireball, on the ball, play hardball, one man band, up, a pistol, crisp, more bang for one's buck, chakra gonged. See COMPETENT.

EFFORT n. push, try, go, fling, shot, crack, whack, stab, all out, balls out, full court press, Sunday punch (best), go the extra mile, go the full yard, go to the wall, in there pitching. See ENDEAVOR.

EFFORTLESS adj. snap, no sweat, no problem, picnic, cinchy, easy as pie, duck soup, piece of cake, child's play. See EASY.

EFFRONTERY n. backchat, backtalk, brass, cheek, cheeky, chutzpah, crust, face, bareface, gall, guff, lip, sauce, sass, out of line, off base, smart, smart ass, the smarts, nerve.

EFFUSIVE adj. all jaw, big mouthed, gabby, gasser, gassy, windy, windbag, load of wind. See TALKATIVE.

EGG n. hen fruit, hen apple, cackle, cackleberry; blindfold a pair, yellow eye, red eyes, over, over easy, sunny side up (fried); dropped (poached); wreck 'em, wreck a pair (scrambled).

EGGS AND HAM n. cluck and grunt.

EGO n. macho trip, power trip.

EGOTIST n. big I am, big I love me, big timer, swellhead, be on an ego trip, go on an ego trip, think one's shit doesn't stink, jit, grandstander, hotdogger, blowhard, know-it-all. See BRAGGART.

EGOTISTIC adj. stuck on oneself, on a ego trip, hubcap, look out for number one, look out for numero uno, take care of number one, take care of numero uno, out for yours truly, shirt up, single-o. See CONCEITED.

EGYPTIAN n. Gypo (WW II).

EIGHT n. eighter, eighter from Decatur.

EIGHTEEN NINETIES n. Gay Nineties, Naughty Nineties, Mauve Decade, Golden Age, Gilded Age.

EJACULATE v. come, cum, come off, blow, shoot, shoot off, shoot one's wad, cream, cream one's jeans, go off, get off, get one's rocks off, get one's nuts off, get over the mountain, haul one's ashes, bust one's nuts, spend, drop one's load, pop one's cookies (all Obsc.).

EJACULATION n. shot, load, cum, blow, wad (all Obsc.). See SEXUAL CLIMAX.

EJECT v. bounce, boot out, kick out, muscle out, chuck out, put out, can, dump, ditch, adios it, fire, flush, give one the old heave-ho, give 'em the old heave ho, give one the bum's rush, give the mitten, give the gate, give the air, give 'em the hook, give' em the 1-2-3, French walk, Spanish walk, get an early shower, send to the showers, send packing, show the door, throw out on one's ear, run out of town, ride out on a rail, kiss good-bye, kiss off, pack off. See also BANISH.

EJECTION n. rush, bum's rush, bounce, boot, heave ho, kiss-off, the gate.

EJECTION SEAT n. panic rack.

EJECTOR n. bouncer, dude heaver, chucker, chucker out, boot giver.

ELABORATE adj. plush, posh, hi tech, wheels within wheels, mega factor, with bells and whistles, with all the extras, with all the options, Rube Goldberg. See also ORNATE.

ELATE v. send, turn on, fire up. See also CHEER.

ELATED adj. flying, high, flying high, turned on, lookin' good, set up, hopped up, fired up. See also HAPPY.

ELATION n. up, upper, cloud nine land, high, buzz, charge, kick, kicks, flash, jollies. See EXCITEMENT.

ELBOW n. hinge, bow, crazy bone, funny bone.

ELBOW v. rough and tumble, push around.

ELDER n. golden ager, senior citizen, senior, pop, pops, dad, gramps, grampa, grandpa, grandma, gramma, gramms, granny, oldster, old fogey, old fart, old-timer, A.K., alte kocker. See OLD MAN, OLD WOMAN.

ELDERLY adj. gray power, been around, bent, lot of mileage, has seen better days, no spring chicken, tired, one foot in the grave, long in the tooth, over the hill, on one's last legs. g'd up. See AGED.

ELECT v. go down the line, opt, tap. See SELECT.

ELECTED adj. in the bag, a shoo-in, nailed down, on ice, open and shut, set, named, home free.

ELECTIONEER v. run, politick, press the flesh, hit the campaign trail, stump, shake hands and kiss babies, mudsling. See CAMPAIGN.

ELECTIONEERING n. running, pressing the flesh, politicking, stumping, whistle-stopping.

ELECTRIC CURRENT n. juice, AC, DC.

ELECTRIC CORD CONNECTOR n juice box, plug, wall plug.

ELECTRIC CHAIR n. the chair, hot seat, hot spot, hot shot, hot squat, old smokey, hummingbird, electric cure, hair curler, permanent wave, manufactured lightning, baker (not common).

ELECTRIC GUITAR ATTACHMENT fuzzbox.

ELECTRICIAN n. gaffer (movie), grunt, hike, juice (stage), juicer.

ELECTRICITY n. juice, AC, DC.

ELECTROCUTE v. burn, fry, go to the chair, get the hot seat, ride old smokey, ride the lightning, sizzle, squat, squat hot, topped, electric cure.

ELECTRONIC MONITOR n. CRT, tube, screen, readout.

ELECTRONIC SURVEILLANCE n. bug, bugging, tap, body mike, wire.

ELECTROSHOCK THERAPY v. zap a patient.

ELEGANT adj. spiffy, classy, snazzy, posh, plush, plushy, ritzy, swanky, snarky, swellelegant, splendiferous, splendacious, fancy shmancy, dressed to kill, dressed to the teeth, dressed to the nines, done to the nines, nobby. See also STYLISH.

ELEMENT n. part and parcel, board, plug in, making, makin's, fixin's.

ELEMENTARY adj. 1. ABC's, three r's, basics, meat and potatoes, primo. See also BASIC. 2. setup, like nothin', easy make, easy digging, duck soup, child's play, simple as ABC, can o' corn. See EASY.

ELEPHANT n. bull, punk (young).

ELEVATE v. boost, bring up, build up, fetch up, jump up, put up, run up, goose, goose up, hike, hike up, jack up, shoot up, pryamid.

ELEVATED adj. high-rise, big-time, heavy.

ELEVATED TRAIN n. el, elevated, L.

ELEVEN n. dinge.

ELICIT v. worm out of one, worm something out of one, wring out, arm-twist, shake, shake a joint, shake down, squeeze, badger, play the badger game, bite, make a citizen's, pull one's leg, lean on, put the arm on, put on the muscle, put the bee on, put the gorilla on, put the handle on, rattle. See also PERSUADE.

ELIMINATE v. 1. junk, chuck, chuck out, adios, eighty-six, deep six, heave-ho, throw away, throw overboard, throw on the junk heap. See ERADICATE. 2. blackball, ice out, elbow out, pass by, pass up, shut out, shake out. 3. do away with, executive fallout (business), ax, liquidate, wipe out, sanitize, sterilize, scrub, scratch, waste. See KILL.

ELIMINATED adj. axed, washed out, washed up, all washed up, scratched, scrubbed, adiosed, eight-sixed, offed, wasted, liquidated, blackballed, iced out, shut out. See also KILLED.

ELITE adj. 1. world class, greatest, cool, out of sight, out of this world, first chop, tops, tip-top, topflight, top drawer, top-notch, super, gilt-edged, Cliveden set, smart money, Boston Brahmins, reform crowd, DAR, coupon clippers See BEST. 2. beautiful people, jet set, smart set, country club set, horsey set, glitterati, cognoscenti, crowd, our crowd, in crowd, the establishment, blue blood, creme de la creme, FFV's, the 400, Four Hundred, main line, old money, upper ten thousand, those in the know, carriage trade, swell, swanky, upper cut, upper crust, high life, high-rise boys, high society, lace curtain, lace-curtain swell, silk stocking.

ELITIST n. Brahmin, egghead, highbrow, high hat, stiff neck, bluenose.

ELONGATE v. fill, pad, spin out, stretch out, put some rubber in it, drag out, drag one's feet. See also EXPAND.

ELONGATED adj. king size, stretch (auto, airplane). See also PROLONGED.

EL PASO, TEXAS Border Town.

ELUCIDATE v. decode, spell out, draw one a picture, make one see daylight, make clear, make perfectly clear, pull one's coat to, get across. See EXPLAIN.

ELUDE v. 1. duck, ditch, give the slip, get around, dodge, give one the runaround, steer clear of. See AVOID. 2. give a miss to, not touch with a ten-foot pole, give the go by, give a wide berth, pass the buck, buck pass, pass up, stay shy of. 3. cop out, cop a plea, jive, shuck, stonewall, hem and haw, run around, give one the run around, stall off, get around, beat around, beat around the bush.

ELUSIVE adj. cagey, greasy, slippery, jivey, jukey, stonewalling.

EMACIATED adj. peaked, peaky, skinny, skin and bones, bag of bones, stack of bones, rattleboned. See THIN.

EMANATION n. vibe, vibes.

EMASCULATE v. cut off one's balls, deball, fix, alter.

EMBARRASS v. bug, discombobulate, discomboberate, hang up, throw, throw into a swivet, throw into a tizzy, put on a spot, put in a spot, put in a hole, catch one short, catch with one's pants down, catch with egg on one's face, fuzzbuzz, give one a bad time, give one a hard time, low grade, cramp one's style, drag one's foot, make one sing small. See also BELITTLE.

EMBARRASSED adj. burned, egg on one's face, red-faced, caught short, crawling, eat crow, eat dirt, eat humble pie, sing small. See HUMILIATED.

EMBARRASSMENT n. boo boo, goof, drop a brick, hot potato, could have sunk into the floor, wished the floor would open up, egg on one's face, shoot oneself in the foot, takedown, put-down.

EMBELLISH v. doll up, fix up, gussy up, spruce up, add bells and whistles.

EMBELLISHMENT n. gingerbread, jazz, garbage (food), frill, frills, fuss, gewgaw, gimcracks, froufrou, bells and whistles, dingbat, doodad, thing, fandangle, seagoing (large, absurd), egg in one's beer, icing on the cake.

EMBEZZLE v. skim, put a hand in the till, put a hand in the cookie jar, work in a bank and take home samples. See also STEAL.

EMBEZZLER n. white-collar thief.

EMBLEM n. logo, brand.

EMBRACE n. bear-hug, squeeze, clinch, lock.

EMBRACE v. 1. grab, grab ass, clinch, clutch, bear hug, squeeze, glom onto. 2. go in for, take up, get into. See also APPROVE, ENDORSE.

EMBROIDER v. 1. doll up, fix up, gussie up, spruce up. 2. puff, blow, yeast, lay it on, spread it on thick, make a mountain out of a molehill, make a federal case out of something. See EXAGGERATE.

EMERALDS n. green ice.

EMERGENCY n. clutch, crunch, in a pinch, in a squeeze, when the shit hits the fan; meltdown, China syndrome (nuclear). See CRISIS.

EMERGENCY SWITCH n. panic button, chicken button, chicken switch, egads button, egads switch.

EMERITUS adj. on the shelf, out of circulation, over the hill, passed it, a once was, has-been, hung up one's spurs, old-timer.

EMIGRATION n. brain drain, brawn drain.

EMINENT adj. celeb, star, superstar, name, champ, VIP, w.k. (well known), lion, page-oner, prima donna, gun, big gun, not to be sneezed at. See CELEBRITY. See also IMPORTANT.

EMISSARY n. rep, hired gun, front.

EMOTION n. gut reaction, vibes, where one is at, where one lives, drive.

EMOTIONAL adj. emote, emoting (simulate), soap, soapy, syrupy, drippy, dust 'em off, hoke, hokum, hokey, icky, mushy, razzmatazz, schmaltzy, slush, softy, soppy, sloppy, soupy, sappy, sticky, gooey, gummy, gushing, teary, tear-jerker, cry crocodile tears, corny, cornball, off the cob, hearts and flowers, beery, namby-pamby, all torn up, all tore up, all shook up, shook, shook up, choked, choked up, feel stuff, fall apart, frantic, funky, touchy,

touchy feely, get one's gage up, give out, gut reaction, gutty, hyper, wreck, nervous wreck, bundle of nerves, hopped up, full up, shot down.

EMOTIONAL RELEASE n. safety valve, abreaction, blow off steam.

EMOTIONLESS adj. cool, cool cat, laid back, flat, nowhere, chill, cold, cold turkey, cold fish, in cold blood, cold-blooded, ice man, deadpan, with a straight face, poker face, stony-eyed, lead balls for eyes, thick-skinned, rhinoceros hide.

EMPATHETIC adj. good vibes, on the same beam, on the same wavelength. See COMPATIBLE.

EMPATHIZE v. tune in, feel for, I hear ya, can get behind it, be on the same wavelength, pick up on, be there for one.

EMPATHY n. soul, hit it off, on the same wavelength, good vibes, good vibrations, cotton to, in the groove, grooving, simpatico.

EMPHASIS n. hard-hitting, underlined, highlighted, headlined.

EMPHASIZE v. spot, spotlight, limelight, highlight, underline, hit, headline.

EMPHATIC adj. sure, sure enough, for a fact Jack, no ifs ands or buts, and no mistake, do they grow corn in Iowa? See CERTAIN.

EMPHATICALLY adv. absofuckinglutely, posilutely, absitively, mighty, terrifically, indeedy, really truly, woofing, sure, why sure, you know it. See ABSOLUTELY.

EMPLOY v. sign on, sign up, take on, ink, bring on board, come on board, truck with.

EMPLOYED adj. on board, come on board, inked, signed, in place. See also BUSY.

EMPLOYEE n. help, breadwinner, working stiff, company man, desk jockey, white collar, pink collar, blue collar, hired gun, peon, ham and egger. See WORKER.

EMPLOYEE REENFORCEMENT n. stroke sessions, opening up, abreaction route, cow sociology, Doctor Spocking the help.

EMPLOYEE STOCK OWNERSHIP PLAN n. ESOP.

EMPLOYER n. chief, CO, meal ticket, head honcho, boss lady, boss man, hammer man, big shit, bull of the woods, old man, juice, slave driver. See EXECUTIVE.

EMPLOYMENT n. bag, beeswax, biz, game, gesheft, job, line, racket, setup, thing, what one is into, number, rat race, coffee-and-cake job. See OCCUPATION.

EMPLOYMENT AGENCY n. flesh peddler (employee or owner), head hunter, slave market.

EMPLOYMENT, SEEK v. pound the pavements, chase, knock on doors, out lookin', lookin' around, circle the want ads.

EMPORIUM n. schlock joint, stand, chain store, outlet, outlet store, co-op, discount house, flea market, thrift shop, cut-rate store, super, superette, supermarket, five and ten, five and dime, Kresges, Woolworth's, 7-11, the grab, boutique, bodega.

EMPOWER v. give the go-ahead, give the green light, give the nod, give the word, okay, OK, say the word. See also APPROVE.

EMPOWERED adj. okayed, OK'd, kosher, legit.

EMPTY adj. dead, dead soldier, dead marine (empty whiskey bottle), deadhead (empty return trip, i.e., bus, taxi, plane, etc.).

EMPTY BOTTLE n. dead soldier, dead marine, an empty.

EMULATE v. mirror, play the ——— (affect a role), ditto, do, do like, go like, make like, steal one's stuff, take a leaf out of one's book, follow in one's footsteps.

EMULSIFY v. clabber, lopper.

EMULSION n. goo, gooey, goop, goopy, glob, globby, gop, glop, gloppy, gook, gunk.

ENACT v. 1. jam, jam through, railroad, railroad through, steamroller through. 2. be on, go on, do a turn, do one's stuff, do a number. See EXECUTE. See also PERFORM.

ENAMOR v. grab, kill, slay, turn on, bat the eyes at, sweep off one's feet, vamp, make a hit with. See ATTRACT.

ENAMORED adj. gone, gone on, hipped on, stuck on, smitten, has a thing about, has one's nose open, hooked, that way. See LOVE, IN.

ENCHANT v. send, wow, slay, kill, grab, turn on, sweep off one's feet, make a hit with, vamp. See ENRAPTURE. See also BEWITCH.

ENCHANTED adj. turned on, head over heels in, hooked, gone goose. See also BEWITCHED.

ENCHANTER n. vamp, operator, player, swinger, joy boy, sheik, mantrap, velvet trap. See also LURE.

ENCHANTMENT n. abracadabra, hocus-pocus, mumbo-jumbo, open sesame, hoodoo, voodoo, evil eye, jinx, whammy, double whammy.

ENCOMPASSING adj. wall to wall, across the board, all the options, whole ball of wax.

ENCOUNTER n. scrap, hassle, rumpus, run in, set to, flap, gin. See ARGUMENT.

ENCOUNTER v. bump into, run into, meet face to face, meet up with, rub eyeballs, run smack into. See MEET. See also FIGHT. strike.

ENCOURAGE v. 1. push, juice, psych up, back up, prop up, boost, give a leg up, egg on. 2. sound off for, root for, plump for, all the way, get behind, stick by. See SUPPORT.

ENCOURAGED adj. up, set up, psyched up, juiced up, fired up.

ENCROACH v. worm in, worm one's way in, squeeze in, elbow in, horn in, chisel in, muscle in, work in, barge in, butt in, put in one's oar, shove in one's oar, put one's two cents in, crash, crash the gates.

ENCUMBER v. saddle with, weigh down, hang up, hold up, hog-tie, drag one's foot, stall. See HINDER.

ENCUMBRANCE n. hang up, baggage, excess baggage, psychological baggage, foot dragging, catch, glitch, joker, one small difficulty. See HINDRANCE.

END n. wrap, wrap-up, wind-up, mop-up, cleanup, sign-off, blow-off, kiss-off, payoff, capper, tag, tag end, butt, butt end, tail end, fag end, bitter end, el foldo, thirty, -30-, hips, swan song, curtain, curtains, down to the short strokes, short stop, end of the line, and that was all she wrote, all there is, there ain't no more, that's all folks, when the balloon goes up, when the fat lady sings, say goodnight Gracie. 2. mark, where one's heading.

END v. wrap, wrap up, sew up, hang it up, pack it in, close out, shut down, nuke, pull the plug, ring off, cut off, cut the crap, scrub, break off, make a break, call it a day, put to bed, send one south, close the books on. See FINISH.

ENDANGER v. lay on the line, put on the spot, stick one's neck in the noose, stick one's neck out, play into one's hands, chance it.

ENDANGERED adj. on the line, on the spot, out on a limb, got one's neck out, caught with one's pants down, have one's ass out.

ENDEARMENT TERMS n. sweetie, sweets, sweetkins, sweetie pie, sweetheart, sweet nothings, hon, honey, honey bunch, honey child, honey pie, sugar, sugar pie, love, luv, doll, baby doll, baby, babe, babyface, chick, chickabiddy, duck, duckling, dove, turtle dove, lamb, lambkins, lambie, lambie pie, snookums, bubie, buttercup, cutey, cupcake, one and only, stinker, little stinker, toots, tootsie-wootsie.

ENDEAVOR n. 1. crack, stab, try, whack, shot, best shot, fling, go, header, lick, all out, all one's got, one's all, one's damndest, one's darndest, one's level best, ol' college try, crash program, crash project, full steam, full blast, push, try, whirl, balls out, full court press; dry run, try on, have a fling at. See also ATTEMPT. 2. baby, bag,

bag one's into, thing, thing one's into, biggie (major), deal, pet project, proposition. See also ACTION.

ENDEAVOR v. make a run at, take on, cut and try, buck, push, hassle, sweat, sweat it, scratch, grind, dig, plug, peg away, hammer away, hustle, hump, hump it, hump oneself, go for broke, pour it on, work one's head off. See ATTEMPT.

ENDED adj. a wrap, wrapped up, pfft, wound up, buttoned up, done with, in the bag, nailed down, all over but the shouting, when the fat lady sings. See FINISHED.

ENDLESS adj. more than you can shake a stick at, no end of, no end to, on a treadmill.

ENDLESSLY adv. round the clock, day and night, for a month of Sundays, till hell freezes over, till you're blue in the face. See INTERMINABLY. See also ALWAYS.

ENDORSE v. back, bless, boost, give a boost to, give the nod, give the go-ahead, give the green light, stand behind, get behind, get on the bandwagon, push, okay, OK, go with, go along with, go along with the crowd, root for, stump for, thump the tub for, go for, plump for, hold a brief for, hold with, put a flea in one's ear, put a bug in one's ear, be big on, buy, sign, sign off on, put one's John Hancock on, thumbs up, take, take kindly to, ditto, rubber-stamp. See also APPROVE.

ENDORSEMENT n. 1. strokes, pat on the back, abreaction route, commercial, cow sociology, hubba-hubba. 2. okay, OK, get the nod, green light, get the green light, crazy, go-ahead, get the go ahead. See APPROVAL.

ENDOW v. lay on, gift with, come through with, put a buck one's way. See GIVE.

ENDOWMENT n. gifting, stake. See also DONATION.

ENDURANCE n. backbone, grit, guts, gutsiness, heart, corazon, moxie, starch, cool, hanging in there, hang tough, legs, intestinal fortitude, staying power, stick-to-itiveness, sitzfleisch. See also TENACITY.

ENDURE v. handle, lump, lump it, lump it and like it, live with, bear with, put up with, roll with the punches, bite the bullet, hang in, hang in there, hang tough, hang on, stick, stick it out, stick with it, win out, ride out, go the limit, sit tight, sit and take it, sit out, sit still for, cool one's heels, sweat, sweat it, sweat it out, sweat out, wait out, staying power, stay the course, hold one's own, hear of, hack it, take it, take it on the chin, face it, face the music, take one's medicine, go along with, string along with, stand for, stand the gaff, stand up, stand up to it, shape up, show one's mettle, show one's stuff, show some starch, be big, be big about, eat shit, pay dues, grin and bear it, not let it get one down, cut it, bleed, hurt, hurt-

ing, carry the torch for one (love), eat one's heart out (envy).

ENDURING adj. set, set in concrete, in for the long haul, hang in, keep one's cool, keep one's shirt on, not hold one's breath.

ENDURINGLY adv. for ages, for a month of Sundays, forever and a day, till hell freezes over. See PERMANENT.

ENEMY n. oppo, opposish, opposite number, meat, bandit, bad guys, buddy (sarcasm), buddy-buddy, buddy fucker, crip, whose side are you on?, me and you, angries.

ENEMY LIST n. hit list, shitlist.

ENERGETIC adj. zippy, zappy, snappy, peppy, got the horses to do it, ball of fire, fair hell, go-go, movers and shakers, wave makers, come on strong. See SPIRITED.

ENERGETICALLY adv. all out, full tilt, full bore, in full swing, full steam ahead, like gangbusters, slam bang, by storm.

ENERGIZE v. zap, jazz up, pep up, zip up, pump up, work up, juice up, turn on the juice, de-mothball, take out of mothballs, trigger, goose, prime. See STIMULATE. See also EXCITE.

ENERGIZED adj. get a lift, juiced up, pepped up, powered up, zipped up, zapped up. See EXCITED.

ENERGY n. juice, go juice, zing, pow, sock, pizzazz, vim, pep, pepper, pepper-upper, piss and vinegar, full head of steam. See POWER.

ENERGY RESEARCH AND DEVELOPMENT ADMINISTRATION n. ERDA.

ENFEEBLE v. clip one's wings, shake up, soften up, wing.

ENFEEBLED adj. out of condition, out of shape, out of steam, out of gas, on the ropes, run down, run to seed, gone to seed, not what one used to be, rusty, soft, good and flabby. See also INCAPACITATED.

ENFOLD v. grab, grab ass, clinch, clutch, bear hug, squeeze.

ENFORCE v. lean on, lean against, arm-twist, strong-arm, put the arm on, sweat one, take care of, high pressure, make one an offer one can't refuse. See FORCE.

ENGAGE v. 1. hook, grab, catch, turn on. 2. sign on, sign up, take on, ink, bring on board, come on board, truck with. 3. tackle, pitch into, go in for, go out for, go for broke, have a go at, have a shot at, have a fling at, take a fling at, take the bull by the horns, give a whirl, give a try, try on for size.

ENGAGED adj. 1. intended, asked for, steady, going steady, pinned, bird, donah, donar, future. 2. tied up, have other fish to fry, head over heels in, into. 3. on board, inked, signed, in place. See BUSY.

ENGAGEMENT n. date, heavy date, double date, blind date, blind drag, get-together, going out, seeing one, rendezvous, gig, meet; miss a meet, stand one up, stand one on a corner (fail to keep an), zero hour, trif, treff (secret). See also BETROTHED.

ENGAGEMENT, ENTERTAINMENT gig, turn, split week, one-night stand, date, playdate.

ENGINE n. horses, power plant, power train, under the hood, barrel (cylinder), maud, pot, putt putt, rubber band, fan (AE), one-lunger (one cylinder).

ENGINE DRIVER n. hogger, hoghead.

ENGINEER n. techie, technie, technonerd, FIDO (aerospace), slideruley type, black gang (ship worker).

ENGINEER v. rig, angle, wangle, work, come up with, upstage, doctor, cook, plant, con, scam, put one on, put one over, jockey, operate, play games, pull strings, pull wires, wire-pull, finagle, fenagle, faniggle. See also MANAGE, PLAN, SCHEME.

ENGINE FAILURE adj. flameout (jet), die.

ENGLAND n. Blighty, John Bull, Merry Old, Albion, Limeyland, Tight Little Island.

ENGLISH n. 1. beefeater, Brit, Britisher, Cockney, limey, lime juicer; Tommy, Tommy Atkins (soldier). 2. the King's English.

ENGRAVING n. scratch.

ENGROSSED adj. gone, hung up, bugged, hooked, into, really into, heavily into, up to here in, head over heels in, all wound up in, wrapped up in, eat sleep and breathe something, turned on, tied up, fiend, have a bee in one's bonnet, have a bug in one's ear, have a bug up one's ass, have an ax to grind, have a thing about, have a tiger by the tail.

ENHANCE v. pad, pyramid, soup up, build up, upgrade, flesh out, add bells and whistles. See EXPAND.

ENIGMA n. cliff-hanger, a grabber, sixty-four dollar question, twister, teaser, sticker, mind-boggler, stumper, hard nut to crack, tough nut to crack.

ENJOY v. groove on, have a ball, ball, funk, grok, dig, dig one or something, dig the most, rat fuck, R.F., get some grins, get it on, adore, be big on, get off on, get high on, get naked (not necessarily sexual), flip, flip for, flip over, freak out on, get a charge out of, get a kick out of, get a lift out of, get a boot out of, get a bang out of, get one's rocks, get one's cookies, drop the bomb, just for kicks, just for laughs, knock oneself out, have oneself a time, hit

the high spots, eat up, eat it up, savvy, with it, kvell, live a little, live it up, take it easy, make a day of it, make a night of it, out on the town, paint the town, paint the town red, down the primrose path, see the sights, step out, on the town.

ENJOYABLE adj. fun (fun party), groovy, just for kicks, just for grins, lots of laughs, just for laughs, just for the heck of it, just for the hell of it, just for the devil of it, fine and mellow, clear sailing.

ENLARGE v. pad, slap on, beef up, jazz up, jack up, blow up, build up, add bells and whistles, snowball. See EXPAND.

ENLARGED adj. boosted, hiked, hiked up, jacked up, jumped up, built up, blown up, pyramided, beefed up, padded, spun out, strung out, dragged out, run out. See also EXAGGERATED.

ENLIGHTEN v. let in on the know, put hip, put one in the picture, put on to, update, give one the word, pull one's coat. See ADVISE.

ENLIGHTENED adj. plugged in, tuned in, in the picture, savvy, sharp, wised up, hip to the jive, all woke up, know what's what. See AWARE.

ENLIST v. join up, sign on, sign up, sign up for, call up, hitch, poggie, take on.

ENLISTED adj. enrollee, enlistee.

ENLISTED MAN n. G.I., G.I. Joe, Joe, Joe Blow, Blow Joe, doughfoot (WW II), E.M., draftee, doughboy (WW I, Mexican war), dogface. See SOLDIER.

ENLIVEN v. jazz up, perk up, pep up, put pep into, zip up, put zip into, snap up, fire up, work up, buck up, pick up, brace up, chirk up, spice, spice up, juice up, juice, turn on the juice, zap, spark, jimjam, give a lift, snap out of it, let the sunshine in. See also EXCITE.

ENMESH v. box in, get one in a box, lay for, lay a trap for.

ENMESHED adj. hooked into, conned into, sucked into, all wound up in.

ENNUI n. ho hums, the blahs, blah-blahs.

ENORMOUS adj. gross, humongous, humungous, mungo, monstro, king-size, mother, motherfucker (Obsc.), big mother, big mama, big daddy, super-colossal, blimp, barn door, whopping. See BIG.

ENOUGH adj. bellyful, had it, up to here, had it up to here, that's it, that'll do, all right already, enough already, enough of that shit, fed up, have a skinful, have a snootful, sick and tired of, punched out, last straw.

ENRAGE v. brown off, rile, piss one off, T-off, needle, get under one's skin, get in one's hair, get one's mad up, whip up, hack, ask for it. See ANGER.

ENRAGED adj. p'd off, p.o.'d, bent, bent out of shape, blow a gasket, mad as a wet hen, steamed, t.o.'d, see red, go ape shit, have a shit hemorrhage. See ANGRY.

ENRAPTURE v. turn on, freak out, knock out, knock dead, send, slay, grooving, score, wow, vamp, sweep off one's feet, make a hit with, hit the spot, be just the ticket, be just what the doctor ordered, go over big, tickle pink, tickle to death. See also ATTRACT.

ENRAPTURED adj. zero cool, gone, real gone, fallen for, gaga about, mad about, turned on, gone on, head over heels, hooked, have one's nose open, freaked out, far out, spaced out, wig, wigged out, flipped out, blissed out, sent, crazy, grocked, mad, wild, wicked, weird, weirded out, dreamy, high, high as a kite, sunny, sunny side up, shook up, hopped up, tea'd up, up, upbeat, flyin', flyin' high, floating, floating on air, on a joy ride, on a cloud, on cloud seven, on cloud nine, all over oneself, come all over oneself, in seventh heaven, tickled to death, tickled pink, pleased as punch, sold on, hummy, out of it, blowing one's top, blowing one's roof, popping one's nuts, in Nadaville, in the twilight zone.

ENRICH v. pad, pyramid, hitch on, pour it on, figure in, beef up, soup up, hop up, hike, hike up, step up, jazz up, jack up, jump up, run up, up, build, build up, builder-upper, upgrade, spike, flesh out, add bells and whistles, sweeten, sweeten the pot, parlay, press a bet.

ENROLL v. sign on, sign up, sign up for, join up, call up, take on.

ENROLLED adj. enrollee, enlistee.

ENSIGN n. insect, ninety-day wonder, one-striper.

ENSLAVE v. get one's hook into, keep under one's thumb. See SUBJUGATE.

ENSNARE v. bag, hook, rope in, suck in, give a come-hither look, come on, bat the eyes at.

ENSUING adv. next off, coming up.

ENSURE v. cinch, clinch, ice, put on ice, lock on, lock up, nail down, set, okay, OK, put one's John Hancock on.

ENTANGLE v. bag, duke in, hook, rope in, embrangle, swindle in, set up, swindle up, foozle, give a come hither look, lead on, come on, bat the eyes at. See INVOLVE.

ENTANGLED adj. all wound up in, dragged into, hooked into, sucked into, suckered into, wrapped up in.

ENTER v. access, penetrate, barge in, blow in, bust in, pop in, mooch in, ace in, horn in, drop in, breeze in, come breezing in, come barging in, come, come busting in, break in, crack, crack a safe. See also ARRIVE.

ENTERPRISE n. happenin', plan, stunt, game, ball game, bit, do, follow through, baby, bag, bag one's into, thing, thing one's into, big idea, biggie (major), deal, pet project, proposition, flier, plunge. See also ACTION, CORPORATION.

ENTERPRISING adj. ambish, ballsy, bogard, come on, come on like gangbusters, come on strong, enforcer, gumption, spunk, balls, drive, guts, go-go, spanking, snappy, zappy, zippy, full of piss and vinegar, full of hot air, full of beans, full of hops, full of prunes, peppy, full of pep, full of get up and go, get out and go, go-getter, get up a head of steam, have lead in one's pencil, pushy, fair hell, heller, moxie, in there punching, taking it to 'em, take charge, take over, take the bull by the horns, hard sell, play hard ball, play for keeps, ball of fire, hotshot, moving out, spark plug, self-starting.

ENTERTAIN v. crack one up, grab, tumul, slay, knock dead, knock them in the aisles. See AMUSE.

ENTERTAINER n. 1. stand-up comic, baggy-pants comic, straight man, stooge, top banana, second banana, clown, a million laughs, gagman. See COMIC. 2. ham, trouper, legiter, matinee idol, bit player, moppet (child), foil, baddie, stand-in, extra, scene-chewer, walk-on. See ACTOR. 3. hoofer, jitterbug, stripper, song and dance man, terper; the line, gypsy, chorine (chorus). See DANCER. 4. long-hair, long underwear, cat, blowing cat, gate, lip-splitter, solid sender, side man, ear man, faker (illiterate); rocker, monster (popular). See MUSICIAN.

ENTERTAIN, SOCIAL v. throw a party, give a party, put on a party, toss a party, have a get-together, have a do, blow one to, on one, I'm buyin', I'll get it (pay the check), pick up the check, pick up the tab, pop, pop for, spring for, stand for.

ENTERTAINING adj. crack up, ball, fun, gas, a scream, yok, a riot, priceless, screamingly funny, too funny for words, side-splitting, gut-busting. See AMUSING.

ENTERTAINMENT n. 1. ball, laughs, lots of laughs, grins, big time, fun and games, high time, high old time, big time, bash, bat, blow out, wingding, brawl, clambake, shindig. See PARTY. 2. hot stuff, long hair, long haired, tear-jerker, show biz.

ENTERTAINMENT FAILURE n. turkey, bomb, bomb out, flop, stinker, stinkeroo, stiff, go down like the Titanic.

ENTERTAINMENT INDUSTRY n. show biz, Broadway, Hollywood, the movies, the Industry.

ENTHRALL v. grab 'em, hook 'em. See ATTRACT.

ENTHUSE v. pump up, carry on over, make a to-do over, take on over, go on about, whoop it up for, turn on.

ENTHUSIASM n. jazz, oomph, pep talk, turn-on.

ENTHUSIAST n. fan, freak, crazies, nut, frenzie, fiend, rooter, gate, great one for. See DEVOTEE.

ENTHUSIASTIC adj. hot, hot for, hot shit, hot to trot, large for, nuts for, nuts over, nutty about, nutty over, bugged, booster, enthuse, dig, flip, flipped, flip one's lid, freaked out, turned on, cracked on, big on, bugs on, gone on, hipped on, up, jacked up, shook up, fired up, steamed up, hepped up, hopped up, upbeat, stoked, all hopped up about, worked up about, steamed up about, stoned, eager beaver, springbutt, in a big way, wig out, overboard, go overboard about, crazy about, wild about, mad about, ape over, ape about, looking good, looking great, glad hander (overly), gung ho, high, high on something, keeping the faith, rosy, looking at the world through rose-colored glasses, looking at something with rose-colored glasses, cooking, cooking with gas, full of piss and vinegar, full of ginger, rarin' to go, eat this shit, fall apart, hung up on, keen, knock oneself out, carry on over, starry-eyed over, gaga over.

ENTICE v. grab, draw, bait, mousetrap, shill, tout, turn on, give one the come on, bat the eyes at, make with the bedroom eyes. See ATTRACT. See also PERSUADE.

ENTICEMENT n. come on, come hither, sweetening, sweetener, bait, mousetrap. See LURE.

ENTICER n. come-on man, deek, nark, plant, sitting duck, shill. See also SEDUCER.

ENTIRETY n. the works, whole enchilada, whole ball of wax, whole nine yards, whole bit, whole schmear, whole megillah, everything including the kitchen sink. See WHOLE.

ENTITLED TO v. rate, be in line for, what one has coming, finders keepers losers weepers.

ENTOMB v. put six feet under, plant, adios it, cover up, deep six.

ENTOMBMENT n. cold meat party, planting.

ENTOMOLOGIST n. bugologist, bug hunter, bug chaser, man with the net, butterfly chaser.

ENTOMOLOGY n. bugology.

ENTRAILS n. chitlins, guts, insides, innards.

ENTRANCE n. slammer.

ENTRANCE HALL n. squat pad.

ENTRAP v. bag, hook, duke in, rope in, swindle in, suck in, box in, get one in a box, lay for, set up, swindle up. See LURE.

ENTRAPPED adj. cornered, hooked, hooked into, dragged into, sucked into, suckered into, left holding the bag.

ENTRÉE n. connection, contact, in, open arms, open door. See INFLUENCE.

ENTRENCH v. dig in, hole up.

ENTRUST v. buzz, crack to, spill to, lay the gaff, lay it on, let one in on, spring with the score, bend an ear.

ENUMERATE v. tick off, count heads, count noses, count the house, dope out, figure in, keep tabs, run down, take account of, tot, tot up, tote, tote up.

ENUMERATED adj. chapter and verse, by the numbers.

ENVIOUS adj. green-eyed, jelly, have big eyes for.

ENVIRONMENT n. hood, neck of the woods, stomping ground, territory, turf, ghetto, inner city, jungle, shanty town, skid row, slum, zoo. See NEIGHBORHOOD.

ENVIRONMENTALIST n. ecofreak, econut, eagle freak, duck squeezer, web-foot, greeny.

ENVIRONS n. hood, neck of the woods, stomping ground, territory, turf, ghetto, inner city, jungle, shanty town, skid row, slum, zoo. See NEIGHBORHOOD.

ENVOY n. cookie pusher.

ENVY v. turn green, eat one's heart out, to die over, I should have such luck.

EPAULETS n. swab downs (Navy).

EPIDEMIC n. what's going around.

EPILEPSY n. wingding, falling sickness.

EPISODE n. goings-on, hap, happening, happenso, scene, seg, doings, what's going down. See EVENT.

EPISODIC adj. soap, soap opera, in segs.

EPISTLE n. line, drop a line, Dear John, dear sir you cur, kite, cannonball, scratch, stiffo, sugar report (love), tab, tag, poison pen letter (malicious, obscene, etc.), memo, thank-you note, get-well card, dead (not deliverable), FYI, invite.

EQUAL adj. stack up with, horse to horse, double, look-alike, like two peas in a pod, spit and image, spittin' image, opposite number, six of one and half a dozen of the other, break even, even-steven, same difference. See also SAME.

EQUAL v. push (bet), hog-tie, come up to. See also EMULATE.

EQUALITY n. fair shake, fair practice.

EQUALIZER n. evener.

EQUATE v. put two and two together, jive.

EQUIDISTANT adj. betwixt and between, halfway in the middle, plump in the middle, smack in the middle, slap in the middle, smack dab in the middle.

EQUILIBRIUM n. cool, keep one's cool, polish. See also CALM.

EQUIP v. fit out, rag out, rag up, rig out, rig up, turn out, fix up, set up, warm up, gear up, psych oneself up, feather one's nest, line one's nest (at the expense of others), stake, heel (money), prep, ready up.

EQUIPMENT n. stuff, kit and kaboodle, outfit, contraption, setup, thing, turnout. See APPARATUS.

EQUITABLE adj. fair shake, square, square deal, even-steven, fair to middling, cricket. See FAIR.

EQUITY n. blindfolded lady with scales, square deal, piece.

EQUIVALENT n. same difference, ditto, dead ringer, spitting image, carbon copy, six of one and half a dozen of the other, no matter how you slice it cut it or dice it. See SAME.

EQUIVOCATE v. beg the question, CYA, cover your ass, pass the buck, blow hot and cold, flip-flop, shilly-shally, sit on the fence, waffle, hem and haw, cop out, cop a plea, shuck, jive, shuck and jive, fudge, jazz, bull, bullshit, BS, shovel the shit, con, con along, schmear, stonewall, cover up, run around, give one the run around, double-talk, pettifog, cloud the issue, throw up a smoke screen, stall off, get around, beat around, beat around the bush, tell a little white lie, talk through one's hat, speak with forked tongue, nitpick, split hairs, make a big thing about, make a federal case out of, make a mountain out of a molehill, catch at straws. See also LIE.

EQUIVOCATION n. routine, cop out, run-around, stonewall, stall, con, cover, cover-up, terminological inexactitude, line of cheese, song, song and dance. See LIE.

ERADICATE v. adios, trash, total, eighty-six, deep six (evidence), do away with, ax, wipe off the map, wipe out, take out, stamp out, rub out, put out of the picture, knock out, KO, sanitize, sterilize, scrub, scratch, squash, wash out, waste, waste one, put in the toilet, torpedo, mow down, shoot down, shoot down in flames, off, kibosh, put the kibosh on. See also KILL.

ERADICATED adj. trashed, totalled, finished, done for, dead and done for, down the drain, gone, had it, kaput, wiped out, stamped out, washed out, washed up, all washed up, scratched, scrubbed, adiosed, eight-sixed, offed, wasted. See also KILLED.

ERASE v. blue pencil, cut, trim, knock off, gut, launder, X-out, scratch out, black out, blot out, stamp out, wipe out. See also CANCEL.

ERASER n. rubber.

ERECT v. whomp up, put up, throw up, throw together, fudge together, knock together, cobble up, prefab.

ERECTION n. hard, hard-on, rod on, stiff on, stiff stander, turned on, bone on, boner, bone, charge, horn, have lead in one's pencil, heart, piss-hard, piss-proud, golden rivet, fuckstick, joystick, cunt stretcher (all Obsc.).

ERIE, PENNSYLVANIA Dead City, Big E.

EROTIC adj. blue, hot, hot stuff, kinky, purple, steamy, dirty, filthy, jerk off, jerk-off material, jack-off material, psycho kick, off base, off-color, out of line, raunchy, raw. See also OBSCENE.

EROTICA n. peep show, porn, porno, hard porn, soft porn, skin flick, skin pix, smut, T and A, Tijuana bible, X-rated, triple X-rated, hard core, soft core, hot stuff, jack-off material, jerk-off material.

ERR v. flub, fluff, muff, muff one's cue, fluff one's lines, blow, blow one's lines, queer, clinker, boot, bobble, boggle, blob, goof, goof up, gum up, gum up the works, hash up, louse up, screw up, foul up, fuck up, muck up, bitch, bitch up, ball up, bollix, bollix up, snarl up, slip up, bugger, bugger up, piss up, mess, mess up, make a mess of, mess and a half, make a boner, boo-boo, make a boo-boo, hash, make a hash of, cook, make a blooper, miss by a mile, screamer, floater, snafu, commfu (monumental), fubar, fubb, fumtu, janfu (joint Army-Navy fuck-up), tarfu, foozle, sink, dub, drop the ball, stumble, pull a blooper, pull a bloomer, pull a boner, pull a boo-boo, put one's foot in it, put one's foot in one's mouth, play the deuce with, play the devil with, play hell with, play merry hell with, play hob with, fall flat on one's face, fall flat on one's ass, donkey act, bark up the wrong tree, count one's chickens before they're hatched, shoot oneself in the foot, shoot down in flames, stub one's toe, go wrong, go at it ass backwards, jump out of the frying pan into the fire, drop a brick, bonehead into it, jim a deal.

ERRAND BOY n. gofer, gopher, leg man.

ERRATIC adj. flaky, kooky, oddball, queer potato, strange duck, blow hot and cold, up and down. See ECCENTRIC.

ERRATICALLY adv. willy-nilly, helter-skelter, higgledy-piggledy, herky-jerky, every which way, any which way, any old way, right and left, all over the shop, all over the lot, all over hell, here there and everywhere, hit or miss, fast and loose, by bits and pieces, by fits and starts, in dribs and drabs, do by halves, half-assed, slapdash, slapped out, slap up, at one's own sweet will, blow hot or cold.

ERRONEOUS adj. all wet, way off, talking like a man with a paper ass, don't know one's ass from a hole in the ground, wrong number, out in left field, have another think coming. See WRONG.

ERROR n. boner, boo-boo, boot, bobble, goof-up, foul-up, fuck-up, screw-up, slipup, typo, fool mistake. See MISTAKE.

ERUCTIVE adj. farty, fart blossom, gassy, windy, nose-closer.

ERUDITE adj. double dig, highbrow, brainy, savvy, wised up, into, really into, in the know, wise to. See KNOWLEDGEABLE.

ERUPTION n. blowup, cat fit, conniption, conniption fit, duck fit, flare-up, wingding, shit hemorrhage. See also ANGER.

ESCAPADE n. rib, gag, caper, high jinks, hi jinks, hot one, monkeyshines, shenanigans, put on. See also ADVENTURE.

ESCAPE n. 1. getaway, out, powder, runout powder, break, breakout, crash out, beat, fadeout, figary, mooch, mope, push, spring, tear away, getaway route, getaway car, absquatulation, exfiltration. See also PRISON ESCAPE. 2. close call, close shave, close squeak, tight squeeze, squeaker, cliff-hanger, get out with one's eyeteeth. 3. kicker (one that negates work, contract, etc.), fine print, small fine print, escape hatch.

ESCAPE v. exfiltrate, hook it, leg it, lam, take it on the lam, amscray, breeze, breeze dust, fade out, heel, hop, vanish, vamoose, scram, smoke, rabbitfoot, spring, head for the hills, hightail, turn tail, jump, skip, skip out, cut out, split, blow, beat it, disappear, duck, dodge, shake, shake off, ditch, run for cover, lay low, fly the coop, go over the wall, mope, cop a mope, cop a plea, hide, hide out, crash out, break out, make a break for it, break away, take a powder, take a run-out powder, hoof it, steal away, get away, slip away, make a getaway, get while the going is good, get on one's bicycle, bob, weave, steer clear of, worm out of, wriggle out of, breathe easy, jink, jank (enemy planes). See also PRISON ESCAPE.

ESCAPEE n. hot, lamster, lammister, on the lam, wanted, have small pox.

ESCHEW v. duck, have no truck with, not touch with a ten-foot pole, give the go by, give a miss to, steer clear of, cut dead. See AVOID.

ESCORT n. bird dog, alarm clock, date, gigolo, shag, tote, john, Johnny. See also BOYFRIEND.

ESCORT v. drag, take out, furp, squire, date.

ESPOUSE v. go in for, take up, get into, back, stand behind. See also ENDORSE, APPROVE.

ESSAY n. 1. paper. 2. crack, fling, go, header, lick, shot, stab, try, whack, one's all, one's damndest, one's darnedest, one's level best, dry run, try on, tryout. See ATTEMPT.

ESSAY v. make a run at, take a stab at, take a whack at, have a shot at, have a go at, take on, make try on for size, give it a go, do it or bust a gut. See ATTEMPT.

ESSENCE n. point, stuff, nub, bottom line, name of the game, nitty-gritty, nuts and bolts, heart, meat, punch line. See BASIC.

ESSENTIAL adj. nub, where it's at, coal and ice, cold, cold turkey, meat and potatoes, nitty-gritty, name of the game. See BASIC.

ESSENTIALS n. ABC's, brass tacks, nitty-gritty, nuts and bolts, groceries, guts, meat and potatoes, beginners, coal and ice, bottom line, rock bottom, at heart. See BASICS.

ESSEX n. Hudson pup.

ESTABLISH v. ring in, set up, start the ball rolling, father. See also BEGIN.

ESTABLISHED adj. set, going concern, up and running, in place. See also PROVEN.

ESTABLISHMENT n. them, they, city hall, good old boys, old boy network, the Man. See also ADMINISTRATION, MANAGEMENT.

ESTEEMED adj. pop, drooly, okay people, touted, highly touted, score, big, large, large charge, BMOC, big man on campus, kimble (tries to be).

ESTIMABLE adj. big, big name, big time, big league, major league, big wig, big-wigged, double-barreled, high-powered, in the limelight, name, not to be sneezed at. See IMPORTANT. See also CELEBRITY.

ESTIMATE n. guesstimate, ballpark figure, in the ballpark of.

ESTIMATE v. size, size up, dope, dope out, take account of, figger, figure, figure in, guesstimate, take an educated guess, take one's measure.

ESTRANGED adj. turned off, on the outs, in bad with, on one's shitlist, pfft, splits, at outs, at loggerheads, at sixes and sevens.

ETCETERA n. whatever, and like that, blah blah-blah.

ETERNALLY adv. for keeps, for ever so long, for a month of Sundays, till hell freezes over, till the cows come home, till shrimps learn to whistle. See ALWAYS.

ETERNITY n. kingdom come, upstairs, up there, wild blue yonder, the old bye and bye, great ad agency [any business] in the sky. See HEAVEN.

ETHICAL adj. square, square shooter, straight, straight shooter, true blue, Christian, kosher, salt of the earth, fly right, nice guy, white, regular, scoutmaster, boy scout, clean as a hound's tooth.

ETIQUETTE n. P's and Q's, mind one's p's and q's.

ETYMOLOGIST n. jargonaut.

EULOGIZE v. give a bouquet, give a posy. See FLATTER.

EUNUCH n.　capon.

EUNUCH v.　alter, deball, fix.

EUPHORIC adj.　gone, blissed out, sent, dreamy, flying, floating, in the twilight zone. See ECSTATIC.

EUROPE n.　abroad, across the drink, across the pond, over there, the old country, Yurp.

EUROPEAN COMMON MARKET n.　Euromart.

EUROPEAN adj.　Euro.

EUTHANASIA n.　mercy killing, pull the plug.

EVACUATE v.　1. cut out, bag ass, shag ass, ooze out, skin out, bail out, pull out, pack up, get git, skidoo, hightail, run for the hills, time to bail. See LEAVE. 2. shit, crap, dump, poop, poo-poo, take a shit, take a crap, take a dump, shake a few clinkers out, do one's business. See DEFECATE.

EVACUATION n.　1. walkout, powder, vanishing act, bow out. See also DEPART.　2. shit, crap, dump, caca, B.M., number two, nature's call, the shits, the runs, being regular, big one, business, aah-aah. See BOWEL MOVEMENT.

EVACUEE n.　boat people, defector, D.P., displaced person.

EVADE v.　1. deek, lay low, stutter step, shake and bake, give the slip, get on one's bicycle, get around, dodge. See AVOID. 2. give a miss to, not touch with a ten-foot pole, give the go by, give a wide berth, give the slip, give the cold shoulder, pass the buck, buck-pass, pass up, stay shy of. 3. jive, shuck, shuck and jive, stonewall, waffle, fudge, hedge one's bet, pussyfoot, cover your ass, CYA, beat around the bush. See HEDGE.

EVALUATE v.　peg, size, size up, check, check out, price out, look over, read, take one's measure, dope out, take account of, figure, figure in, figure out, guesstimate.

EVALUATION n.　guesstimation, take, the Fribbish Scale (business).

EVASION n.　jive, stall, ditch, slip, dodge, routine, copout, run-around, stonewall, fancy footwork, stutter-step. See also LIE.

EVASIVE adj.　cagey, jivey, greasy, slippery, jukey, stonewalling.

EVEN adj.　even-steven, dead even, break even, six of one half a dozen of the other, horse to horse, halfway in the middle, plump in the middle, smack in the middle, smack dab in the middle, slap in the middle.

EVENING n.　dim, early black, dark, black.

EVENT n.　hap, happenso, happening, trip, real trip, thing, do, deal, big deal, scene, bit, piece, routine, come off, go down, goings-on. like it is, where it's at, the size of it, bummer, trial (bad). See also ACTION.

EVEN-TEMPERED adj.　unflappable, cool, cool as a cucumber, keep one's cool, keep one's shirt on, not turn a hair, keep a stiff upper lip, roll with the punches. See IMPERTURBABLE.

EVENTIDE n.　early black, black, dim, dark.

EVENTUAL adj.　down the road, down the pike, in the cards. See FUTURE.

EVENTUALITY n.　case, any case, hap, happenso, happening, go down, goings-on, come off.

EVER adv.　for keeps, till hell freezes over, till the cows come home, till you're blue in the face. See ALWAYS.

EVERYDAY adj.　garden, garden variety, dime a dozen, vanilla, rumdum, starch, mainstream, middle of the road, run of the alley, run of the mill, familiar tune. See ORDINARY.

EVERYTHING adj.　the works, business, fixins', lock stock and barrel, whole enchilada, whole kit and caboodle, everything including the kitchen sink. See WHOLE. See also COMPLETELY.

EVERYWHERE adv.　all over the map, all over creation, all over hell, to hell and gone, to hell and back, from hell to breakfast, from pole to pole, from here till Sunday.

EVICT v.　bounce, kick out, boot out, drum out, freeze out, toss out on one's ear, throw one out on one's ear, throw out on the street, heave-ho, give one the heave-ho, adios one, French walk, send packing, show the door, give the gate, give the air, give one his walking papers, give one the bum's rush, give 'em the 1-2-3.

EVICTION n.　boot, bounce, kicking out, old heave-ho, the gate, walking papers, walking ticket, rush, bum's rush.

EVICTOR n.　bouncer, chucker, chucker out, dude-heaver, boot-giver.

EVIDENCE n.　dope, goods, info, smoking gun (crucial), clincher, cincher, grabber, clue, cue, hold water, the emess, gospel. See FACTS.

EVIDENT adj.　barefaced, plain as the nose on one's face, clear-cut, crystal clear, open and shut, open-and-shut case, that's a fact Jack. See APPARENT.

EVIL adj.　beastly, bad-assed, rat's ass, sleazeball, stinking, murderous, poison, no good, N.G. See BAD.

EVILDOER n.　creepo, turd, shithead, heel, shit heel, sleazoid, rat, mother, mofo, hood, wrong'un. See SCOUNDREL.

EVIL EYE n.　whammy, double whammy.

EVIL-MINDED adj.　dirty, dirty old man, dirty-minded, mind in the gutter.

EVIL SPIRIT n.　fiend, hellion, little devil. See DEVIL.

EVOKE v. worm out of one, worm something out of one, wring out, arm-twist, put the arm on. See ELICIT.

EXACERBATE v. heat up, hot up, egg on, work on, hit on, rattle one's cage, push one's button, rub salt in the wound, add insult to injury, jump out of the frying pan into the fire, go from bad to worse. See ANNOY.

EX-CONVICT n. ex-con, jailbird, lag, lagger.

EXACT adj. on the button, on the numbers, on the money, on target, on the nose, on the noggin, right on, dead on, bull's-eye, a good eye, stone, dot the i's and cross the t's, draw it fine, cut it fine, hit the nail on the head, flat out, straight out, nailed down, downright. See also CORRECT.

EXACT v. bleed, lean on, put the arm on, put the bite on, put the gorilla on, shake, put the shake on, squeeze, bite to death, line up, make a citizen's. See ELICIT.

EXACTING adj. chicken shit, by the book, comma counter, nitpicker, picky, persnickety, stickler. See PRECISELY.

EXACTLY adv. on the button, on the money, on the nose, on the noggin, on the lemon, the ticket, the very thing, the checker, to a tee, Judy (I understand), cert, sure, why sure, sure thing, for sure, fer sher, fer shirr, surest thing you know, that's for sure, for a fact, you said it, no buts about it, no ifs ands or buts, and no mistake.

EXAGGERATE v. boost, build up, hike, hike up, jack up, jump up, put up, pyramid, up, overdo it, talk trash, loud talk, blarney, jolly, lay it on, lay it on thick, lay it on with a trowel, spread it on, spread it on thick, snow, give one a snow job, whitewash, doctor, cook, con, scam, put one on, bull, shit, bullshit, bs, bulldog, throw the bull, shoot the bull, shoot the crap, shoot the shit, shovel the shit, sling the bull, shoot a line, hand one a line, blow, blow smoke, fudge, throw one a curve, trump up, hoke up, phony up, fake, gammon, take it big, puff, ballyhoo, make out like, make a mountain out of a molehill, make a federal case out of something, make a big production.

EXAGGERATED adj. hammy, schmaltzy, tear-jerking, seagoing, overkill, too-too. See also EXCESSIVE.

EXAGGERATION n. con, scam, jazz, jive, line, crap, crapola, shit, piece of shit, shitting, crock, crock of shit, bull, bullshit, BS, horseshit, bullshitting, shit for the birds, hocky, horse hocky, baloney, phony boloney, phonus bolonus, malarkey, marmalade, borax, spiel, spinach, smoke, gas, garbage, guff, hogwash, riff, thick, thin, tripe, vanilla, whopper, hard sell, salve, snow job, blow job, cheese, line of cheese, yeast, fudge, build, buildup, the big lie (Pol.), cock-and-bull story, fish story, story, yarn, tall tale, tall story, big talk, tall talk, bunk flying, latrine rumor, full of hot air, full of beans, full of hops, full of prunes, song and dance, Mother Machree, Mother Macrea (story).

EXAGGERATOR adj. shoveler, blowhard, bullshitter, bullshit artist. See also LIAR, BRAGGART.

EXAMINATION n. 1. physical, checkup, exam. 2. case, double-o, gunning over, gander, pike, eye, ex, hustle, eyeball examination. 3. third, third degree, grill, fishing expedition, legwork. 4. comp (comprehensive), final, oral, orals, prelim, cream (successful), blue book, exam; drop quiz, flash quiz, shotgun quiz, pop quiz (all unannounced).

EXAMINE v. 1. look see, eye, gun, check, check out, case, scope, sweep, read. See SEE. 2. give one the third, sweat it outta one, put one through the wringer, buzz, cat haul, cool out. See QUESTION. 3. frisk, pat down. 4. rap, chew over, confab, hash, rehash, hash over, kick around, knock around, let the daylight in, let the sunlight in. See ANALYZE. See also THINK.

EXAMPLE n. for instance, f'rinstance, excuse.

EXASPERATE v. brown off, piss one off, T-off, get under one's skin, give one a hemorrhage, give one a shit hemorrhage, hack, make waves, stick it in one's craw, sound, sound off, burn one off, send one into a tailspin, drive one up the wall. See ANNOY.

EXASPERATED adj. bugged, hacked, pissed off, peed off, teed off, burned up, miffed, peeved, riled, rubbed the wrong way, driven up the wall, steamed. See ANNOYED.

EXASPERATING adj. bugs one, gives one a pain, pain in the ass, bitch, a bit much, too much, flea, pesky, pestiferous. See ANNOYING.

EXCAVATOR n. groundhog, sandhog.

EXCEEDINGLY adv. awfully, really, too much, stone (stone deaf), terribly, powerful. See VERY.

EXCEL v. shine, top, cap, wax, make it, got a hot hand, in the groove, on a roll, all systems go, go to town, everything going for one, come through, come through with flying colors.

EXCELLENT adj. A, A-1, A-number one, A-plus A-OK, okay, OK, 10, ten, ace, aces, ace high, ace of spades, in spades, bitchin', brutal, super, smashing, gnarly, mega-gnarly, awesome, dynamite, unreal, cool, coolsville, zero cool, cold, chill, stone, terrific, terrible, down, wicked, evil, vicious, winner, choice, rad, radical, reet, gasser, fab, fabulous, far out, funky, state of the art, too much, out of this world, out of sight, gilt-edged, drooly, flash, like wow, not too shabby, something else, groovy, grooby, frantic, tough, tuff, tidy, tits, heavy, bad, baaadest, rat fuck, nose cone, marvy, best ever, top, tops, tip top, top-notch, topflight, top drawer, top of the line, head of the line, head of the class, world class, hundred proof, first class, first chop, first rate, star, boss, stunning, corking, corker, solid, solid sender, great, greatest, the most, the utmost, mostest, gonest, doozie, daisy, dilly, bo, boo, tickety boo, deadly, deadly boo, bong, sly, copacetic, kopesetic, the bee's knees, the cat's meow, the cat's whiskers, the cat's pajamas, the butterfly's book, the caterpillar's kimono, George, real George, good show, gear, golden, hard, hummer, humdinger, knock out, mad, mess, mezz, nasty, nifty, the nuts, the nerts, the end, endsville, hellacious, savage, solid gold, righteous, ripping, ripsnorter, sanitary, heavenly, bang up, in fat city, in orbit, murder, neat, hunky-dory, all wool and a yard wide, jam up, slap up, dandy, fine and dandy, jim dandy, crack, crackerjack, peacherino, peach, peachy, ginger peachy, peachy keen, keen, salt of the earth, but good, strictly, super-duper, hooper-dooper, super-colossal, sweetheart, catch, find, plenty, crack, zanzy, beautiful, cuspy, gimchy, check plus, stellar, dream, lollapaloosa, whiz, killer-diller, mean, ducky, hot, spiffy, nobby, delicious, scrumptious, swell, shirty, tawny, whale of a, world-beater, pip, pippen, lulu, darb, honey, beaut, mean, tubular, toast, this is some kinda———, it's the berries, cracking, bully, sharp, the best, skull, brain.

EXCEPTIONAL adj. world class, job, primo, wizard, high cotton, splash, mother, motherfucker (Obsc.), muthah, muthahfuckah, mofo, skull, brain, grind.

EXCERPT n. quote, saying.

EXCESS n. overruns, overkill, the limit, he's the limit, too much.

EXCESSIVE adj. way out, worst-case scenario, overkill, glorkish, ultra-ultra, out of all bounds, out of sight, too much, too-too, everything but the kitchen sink. See EXTREME.

EXCESSIVELY adv. too much, too-too. See also EXTREMELY.

EXCHANGE n. network, net, LAN, Wall Street, the Street, the Exchange, the Big Board, over the counter.

EXCHANGE v. 1. horse trade, swap, swap horses. See also NEGOTIATE. 2. flip-flop, put the cart before the horse, turn the tables. 3. contact with, have truck with, network, link up, hook up.

EXCISE v. blue pencil, cut, cut up, trim, knock off, lop off, gut, launder, X out, scratch out, black out, blot out, stamp out, wipe out, scissor out.

EXCITABLE adj. high-strung, hot, hot-headed, hot around the collar, hot under the collar, have a short fuse. See also EMOTIONAL.

EXCITE v. jazz, jazz up, juice, juice up, send, zap, grab, hook, fuss, bug up, burn up, heat up, pep up, perk up, pick up, snap up, wake up, zip up, key up, fire up, steam up, stir up, work up, work up into a lather, work oneself into a stew, work oneself into a tizzy, work oneself into a pucker, wig out, adjy, flip, flip one's lid, egg on, turn on, whatever turns you on, whatever makes your boat float, turn one on, switch on, turn on the juice, turn

on the heat, run a temperature, get hot under the collar, race one's motor, open one's nose, blow up, blow one's stack, blow one's top, blow a gasket, blow one away, fly off the handle, hit the ceiling, make waves, rabble rouse, put the zingers in, get one's pratt, needle, put the needles in, throw wood on the fire, add fuel to the flames. See also DISTURB, STIR, ROUSE.

EXCITED adj. hyper, charged, wired, wired up, juiced up, zipped up, zapped up, fired up, keyed up, all keyed up, steamed up, hopped up, hyped-up, pumped up, worked up, get all worked up, worked up into a lather, freaked out, flipped out, spazzed out, had a spaz attack, had a cow, switched on, turned on, headin' up the mountain, horny (sexual), zonkers, stoned, high, high as a kite, fussed, shook, shook up, all shook up, blow one's mind, mind-blowing, mind-bending, hot, hotheaded, hot as a firecracker, hot to trot, hots, hot stuff, hotter than a two-peckered mule, having the hots, hot and bothered, hot under the collar, warm around the collar, steamin' under one's silks, like crazy, like mad, have a fit, have kittens, cast a kitten, go up in the air, hit the ceiling, hog wild, shit in one's pants, have a shit hemorrhage, in a dither, in a lather, in a swivet, in a foofaraw, in a pucker, in a stew, in a tizzy, rooty, ready to cook, ready for Freddy, feel in one's guts, get to one. See also DISTURBED.

EXCITEMENT n. up, upper, cloud nine land, heaven, high, buzz, charge, large charge, rush (get a rush), head rush, bang, kick, kicks, for kicks, big deal, big shit, turn-on, corker, circus, fireworks, flash, flap, jollies, mess, razzle-dazzle, rowdydow, rowdy-dowdy.

EXCITING adj. cool, real cool, zero cool, frantic, wild, far out, mega, megadual, marvy, nifty, spiffy, groove, in the groove, groovy, in the bubble, fab, boss, jazzy, sensay, sensaysh, big splash, jumping, mad, mean, the most, mostest, like wow, reet, reat, mind-blowing, mind-bending, out of this world, out of sight, clean outta sight, turn on, turned on by, turned on to, kicky, wiggy, diddly bop, a gas, gas up something, evil, knockout, all the way live (Stu.), live one, live wire, dolce vita, gone, real gone, barn burner, hot stuff, hairy, large, large charge, nervous, rootin' tootin', snazzy, razzle-dazzle, glitzy, flashy, showy, smashing, bang up, ace high, swell, stunner, stunning, feel in one's guts, grabbed by, solid, solid sender, something, something else, something to shout about, something to write home about, swinging, fine, lush, sizzler, scorcher, one for the book, blood and thunder, chiller, cliff-hanger, cloak and dagger, page-turner, thriller. See also STIRRING.

EXCLAIM v. blast, figure, holler, holler out, beller, yawp.

EXCLAMATION n. holler, beller, yawp.

EXCLUDE v. ding, zing, cut, snip, drop, blackball, eighty-six, 86, kill, sideline, ice out, pass by, pass up, pass on, shut out, cut out, hand one his walking papers, send one to the showers, dump, fluff off, give one the fluff, give one the cold shoulder, shoot down, throw out, throw away, chuck, chuck out, turn thumbs down on, thumb down, adios it, heave-ho, nix, shit on, piss on, put down, shove it, stick it, stow it.

EXCLUDED adj. blackballed, cold-shouldered, out of the loop, left out in the cold, not in the picture, shut out, sidelined, left on the outside looking in.

EXCLUSION n. ding, blackball.

EXCLUSIVE adj. high hat, uppity. See SNOBBISH. See also ALOOF.

EXCLUSIVELY adj. onliest, one and only. See SINGULAR.

EXCRETE v. shit, crap, dump, take a squat, drop a turd, shake a few clinkers out, make number two. See DEFECATE. 2. make number one, pee, pea, piss, leak, take a leak, drain the dew, tap a kidney, go, go wee-wee, go pee-pee, tinkle, piddle. See URINATE. 3. break a sweat, sweat like a horse, sweat like a trooper, get all in a lather.

EXCRETION n. 1. shit, crap, dump, caca, BM, number two, poop, poot (gas), call, nature's call, turd, being regular, big one, boom boom, business, poo-poo, aah-aah, the shits, the runs, trots, shits, GI's, GI shits, turistas, Montezuma's revenge. See also BOWEL MOVEMENT. 2. piss, pee, pee-pee, number one, piddle, pish, tinkle, wee, wee-wee. 3. buffalo chips, cow chips, cow flops, cow plops, cow pats, road apples, golden apples, hocky, horse hocky, shit, horseshit, lawn dressing, moose beans, moose pecans, moose nuggets.

EXCURSION n. Cook's tour, cruise, do Europe [or wherever], go on apex.

EXCUSE n. jive, shuck and jive, stall, song, song and dance, story, whitewash, have to see a man about a dog, off time, cleanup, copout, cover, cover one's ass, cover-up, cover story, fish, fish story, fish tale, Mother Machree, Mother McCrea, routine, airtight alibi, the why and wherefore, the whyfor.

EXCUSE v. 1. cop a plea, cop out, crawl, square oneself, square a beef, square things, make up for, whitewash, alibi out of, crawl out of, worm out of, squirm out of. 2. let one off the hook, let one off this time, let one off easy, let it go, go easy on, wink at, write off. See ABSOLVE.

EXCUSED adj. let off, let go, walked, beat the rap, off the hook.

EXECUTE v. do the job, do the trick, turn the trick, do up brown, do a turn, do to a turn, do to a T, do oneself proud, pull off, pull it off, knock off, polish off, tear off, make it, make out, be on, go on, as advertised, get to first base, earn one's wings, put across, put it over, put away,

put it together, put over, one down, one down and two to go, sail through, take care of, deal with, come through, score, hit, perk, percolate, tick, do one's thing, get over, get there, ring the bell, sail through, go to town, hack it, hit the bull's-eye, fly, nail it, win one's spurs, squeak by (barely), T.C.B. (take care of business), come on like gangbusters (well), strut one's stuff, do one's stuff.

EXECUTED adj. 1. catch rope, dance, go through the trap, hoist, scrag, stretch, strung up, swing, fried, burned. 2. buttoned up, wrapped up, mopped up, dealt with, put over, wired, done to a T. See FINISHED.

EXECUTION n. 1. chops (talent), nuts and bolts, style. 2. necktie party, lynching bee, rub out, hit.

EXECUTIONER n. torpedo, enforcer, gorilla, gunsel, gun, gunman, piece man, hit man, trigger man. See KILLER.

EXECUTIVE n. C.E.O., C.O., exec, key player, A-number 1, chief, bosshead, boss lady, mother, boss man, perkman, point man, old man, papa, super, skipper, czar, godfather, don, governor, hot stuff, honcho, head honcho, head, head man, the man, lead-off man, general, hammer man, perc man, meal ticket, main squeeze, queen bee, the brass, brass hat, top brass, gold braid, rug rank (high), VIP, tycoon, baron, Mr. Big, Charlie, Mister Charlie (Bl.), Mr. Right, his nibs, big brother, big daddy, big gun, gun, big shot, big shit, big player, big boy, big number, big stuff, big noise, big ghee, big chew, big spud, apple, big apple, big weenie, big cheese, the whole cheese, big man, big name, wheel, big wheel, big timer, big-time operator, BTO, wig, big-wigged, top, on top, topper, top hand, topkick, top drawer, top dog, the big bowwow, upstairs, man upstairs, exec suite, front office, higher ups, high priest, king, kingfish, kingpin, king of the hill, cock, cook, chief cook and bottlewasher, bull of the woods, big league, shark, bread, brains, brain box, mastermind, guru, rishi, old man, old pro, old war-horse, old hand, biggest hand, biggest frog in the pond, buddy seat, spark plug, juice, zap, pow, kicker, pizzazz, the force, moxie, powerhouse, poop, punch, clout, steam, might and main, block and tackle, beef, strong arm, the stuff, the goods, upper hand, whip hand, straw boss, pusher, slave driver, Simon Legree, the say, the say so, a lot to say about, a lot to do with, the word, righteous, geets, guts, string, ropes, avatar, wire, wire man, digger, fruit, oink (police), heavy stuff, heavy, weight, where the buck stops, catbird, apparatchik (junior). See also COMMANDER.

EXECUTIVE BENEFITS n. golden parachute, perks.

EXECUTIVE RECRUITER n. headhunter.

EXECUTIVE SUITE n. fast track, front office, upstairs.

EXEMPLARY adj. goodie, tuff, horror show, atsa nice, not bad, bootin' height, neato, bueno, not too shabby, nasty, doin' a hundred, batting a thousand. See PRAISEWORTHY.

EXEMPT v.   let one off the hook, clear, wipe the slate, go easy on, wink at, write off. See ABSOLVE.

EXEMPTED adj.   beat the rap, walked, let off, let go, off the hook.

EXERCISE n.   constitutional, daily dozen, workout, aerobics, gym, warm-up, jazzercise.

EXERCISE v.   lick into shape, put through the grind, put through the mill, tune up, warm up, work out, work up a sweat, walk through, run through, hone, break, break in, dry run.

EXERCISES n.   gym, warm-up, jazzercise, workout, monkey drill.

EXCERCISE CLASS n.   gym, workout.

EXERCISE SUIT n.   body stocking, sweat suit.

EXERT v.   push, sweat it, dig, plug, peg away, bust one's ass, break one's heart, give it all one's got, give it one's best shot, put one's back into it, pour it on. See ATTEMPT.

EXHAUST v.   1. bleed white, suck dry. 2. fag, tucker, poop, poop out, conk out, burn out, fag out, tucker out, knock out, peter out.

EXHAUSTED adj.   bushed, had it, crispy, too pooped to pop, outta gas, outta juice, frazzled, worn to a frazzle, all in, shot, fucked out, at the end of one's rope, bone-weary, dog-tired. See TIRED.

EXHAUSTING adj.   heavy, hefty.

EXHAUSTION n.   brain fag, burnout.

EXHAUSTIVE adv.   do up brown, from A to Z, to a fare-thee-well, the works, not overlook a bet, leave no stone unturned. See THOROUGH.

EXHIBIT v.   let it all hang out, showcase, show and tell, roll out, parade one's wares, wave it around. See DISPLAY.

EXHIBITION n.   expo, exbo, exhib, exhibish, flash (gaudy merchandise or prize), frame up, front, fireworks, an act, a scene, for show.

EXHIBITIONIST   n.   showboat, showoff, grandstander, grandstand player, hot dog, hotdogger, hotshot, flasho, Flash Gordon.

EXHIBITOR n.   exhib.

EXHILARATE v.   send, turn on, jazz up, juice, juice up, pep up, perk up, pick up, snap up, zip up, jim jam, put pep into, put zip into. See EXCITE.

EXHILARATION adj.   a rush (get a rush), head rush. See EXCITEMENT.

EXHILARATED adj.   blow one's mind, charged, flipped out, high, hopped up, hyper, turned on. See EXCITED.

EXHORTIVE adj.   preachy, bible thumpin', fire breathin', high pressure.

EXIST v.   kick, get along, just makin' it, get by.

EXISTENCE n.   lifing, the big game, rat race, world, the real world, journey, hand (one is dealt).

EXISTING adj.   alive and kicking, ticking, warm, here, in the lifestream, making it, hanging in there, still around.

EXIT v.   split, haul ass, fuck off, flake off, move out, ooze out, get, git, blow this pop stand, hotfoot, absquatulate, do a vanishing act, I'm history, I'm outta here. See GO.

EXONERATE v.   let off, let one off the hook, whitewash, sanitize, clear, wipe the slate clean. See ABSOLVE.

EXORBITANT adj.   high, out of sight, pricey, cher, dear, steep, stiff, heavy sugar, big price tag, an arm and a leg, up to here (elbow), over one's head, holdup, highway robbery. See EXPENSIVE.

EXOTIC adj.   kinky, way out, far out, avant garde, weird. See STRANGE. See also ALLURING.

EXPAND v.   pad, slap on, tack on, tag on, hitch on, pour it on, piggyback, beef up, soup up, hop up, heat up, hike, hike up, step up, jazz up, jack up, jump up, run up, up, build, build up, builder upper, pyramid, spike, flesh out, spell out, spin out, string out, drag out, balloon, add bells and whistles, dump on, snow, snowball, sweeten, sweeten the pot, parlay, boost, press a bet, tish, join together, join up with, hook up with, hook on, plug into, add fuel to the fire.

EXPECT v.   figure, in the cards, it's looking to, see it coming, be afraid, wait for the other shoe to drop. See ANTICIPATE. See also BELIEVE.

EXPECTANT adj.   the noose is hanging, looking for, waitin' on, waiting for the other shoe to drop. See also HOPEFUL.

EXPECTED adj.   as advertised, no big surprise, be just like one, be one all over, not put it past, figured in, figgered in. See ANTICIPATED.

EXPECTORATE v.   let fly, hawk, spritz, squirt.

EXPEDIENCE n.   band-aid, dodge, gimmick, trick, easy way out.

EXPEDITE v.   cut red tape, hand-carry, hand-walk, walk it over, walk it through, go to the whip on, fast track, railroad, grease the wheels, run interference for, run with the ball, handle personally. See SPEED.

EXPEDITION n. swing, jaunt, cruise, trek, safari, snofari, Cook's tour.

EXPEL v. 1. can, fire, bump, bust, bounce, boot, kick, kick out, give one his walking papers, give one the old heave ho, give the bum's rush, give the hook, show the door, drum out, send packing, send to the showers. See DISCHARGE. 2. adios one, French walk, chuck out, bounce, boot out, give one the bum's rush, give one the heave ho, throw one out on one's ear. See EJECT.

EXPEL GAS v. fart, break wind, cut one, cut the cheese, leave one, let one fly, backfire, poot, the butler's revenge (silent), nose-closer.

EXPELLED adj. washed out, washed up, all washed up, scratched, scrubbed, adiosed, eighty-sixed, offed, wasted. See also DISCHARGED.

EXPEND v. pay out, foot the bill, blow, dish it out, shell out, put out, fork out, spring for, throw money at. See PAY.

EXPENDED adj. down the tube, down the drain, down the tube, down the spout, down the rathole, fell between the cracks, out the window, pissed away, diddled away, blown, petered out, shot, kiss it good-bye.

EXPENDITURE n. nut, bottom line, a throw, below the line, set one back, come to, to the tune of, hummer, highway mopery, payoff, cash on the nail, cash on the barrelhead, kickback, nickel and dime (minor), outlay.

EXPENSE n. nut, price tag, bite, bottom line, below the line, nickel and dime (minor), outlay, out of pocket, on one's own nickel, on one's own time and own dime. See COST.

EXPENSE ACCOUNT n. fall money, mad money, lulu, out of pocket, scandal sheet, swindle sheet.

EXPENSES, CLEAR v. get off the gun, get off the nut, make the nut, out of the red. See also PROFIT.

EXPENSIVE adj. pricey, cher, dear, uptown, upscale, big ticket, steep, stiff, posh, executive, fancy, high, high rent, plushy, swanky, ritzy, splendiferous, splendacious, heavy sugar, out of sight, out of bounds, high price tag, an arm and a leg, pretty penny, up to here (elbow), holdup, highway robbery, highway mopery, paid through the nose, collectibles, worth its weight in gold, worth a king's ransom.

EXPERIENCE n. happening, happenso, hap, a trip, a real trip, been there, through the mill, been hit before, bummer trails (bad). See EVENT.

EXPERIENCE v. be turned on to, feel in one's bones, feel in one's guts, get in touch, have a funny feeling, have heart, have a hunch, have vibes.

EXPERIENCED adj. 1. pro, vet, the right stuff, stuff, dynamite, fireball, one-man band, know one's stuff, something on the ball, a pistol. See SKILLED. 2. old hand, old-timer, old war-horse, kicked around, been around, been around the block a few times, been there before, been through the mill, sport, city slicker. See SOPHISTICATED.

EXPERIMENT n. R and D, trial run, try-on, tryout, fling at. See also TEST.

EXPERIMENT v. cut and try, fool around with, futz around, play around with, mess around, give a tryout, give a work out, give it a go, shake down, try on, try it on for size. See also TEST.

EXPERIMENTER n. numbers cruncher, mad doctor.

EXPERT adj. savvy, sharp, slick, there, crack, crackerjack, up one's alley, have know-how, know one's onions, know one's stuff, big league, enough ducks in a row. See SKILLFUL.

EXPERT n. shark, phenom, guru, pro, old pro, ol' professor, old hand, maven, whiz, buff, gnome, mean bean, bone man, heart man, big nose man (Medic. specialists), hotshot. See AUTHORITY.

EXPERTISE n. know-how, savvy, sharpness, goods, makings, stuff, chops, oil, one's thing, bag, dodge, line. See SKILL. See also KNOWLEDGE.

EXPIATE v. make up for, pay one's dues, square things. See COMPENSATE.

EXPIRE v. go, kick the bucket, buy it, croak, meet one's maker, give up the ghost, bite the dust, cash in one's chips, deep six, go to Davy Jones's locker (drown). See DIE. fry, shove over, quit it, up and die, peg out, pass out, strike out, chalk out, flake out, head for a hearse, back gate, back-door parole, get a back-gate commute, one-way ticket, one-way ride, kayoed for keeps, trumped; dance, dance on air, dance on nothing, dance off (hang).

EXPIRING adj. at the end of one's rope, done for, MFC (measure for coffin), on one's last legs, checking out, heading for the last roundup, one foot in the grave, one foot in the grave, the other on a banana peel.

EXPLAIN v. spell out, lay out, lay it out for, lay down, break it down, decode, draw one a picture, show and tell, roll out, trot out, make one see daylight, let daylight in, let sunlight in, make clear, make perfectly clear, get across, put across, put one in the picture, put one straight, get over, open one's head, pull one's coat to, spotlight, limelight, highlight, give a for instance, give a frinstance.

EXPLANATION n. rundown, story, cover story, whatfor, whyfor, why and wherefore, the picture, the whole picture, the idea, the big idea, whole megillah.

EXPLETIVE: AGREEMENT absofuckinglutely!, crazy!, solid!, groovy!, reet!, all reet!, right on!, hell yes!, what you say!, you said it!, you said a mouthful!, you just ain't whistling Dixie!, you bet!, you bet your life!, you bet your boots!, you know it!, for sure!, fer sher!, fer shirrr!, for dammed sure!, for darned sure!, for danged sure!, for a fact!, for a fact Jack!, thunderbird!

EXPLETIVE: ANGER shit!, oh shit!, merde!, son of a bitch!, SOB!, bitch!, bastard!, nuts!, hell!, oh hell!, God damn!, damn!, damn it!, darn!, darn it!, dad blasted!, dad blast it!, dad blamed!, dad burned!, doggoned!, dagnabbed!, gosh darn!, goldarned!, goldinged!, ding blasted!, ding dang!, dash it!, dash it all!, crap!, cripes!, crimus!, cripus!, crimeny!, rats!, that bleeping thing!

EXPLETIVE: DISDAIN phooey!, eeyoo!, eeyuck!, yeeuck!, yeeuch!, phew!, pugh!, ugh!, feh!, pish!, hang it in your ear!

EXPLETIVE: HAPPY wow!, way!, way rad!, like wow!, wowie!, zowie!, man!, man-oh-man!, far out!, out of sight!, outta sight!, groovy!, sakes alive!, goody!, goody goody!, goody gumdrops!, boy oh boy!, hot dog!, hot diggety!, hotdiggety dog!, hot ziggety!, keen-o!, keen-o peachy!, cowabonga!, cowabunga!, let the good times roll!, oowhee!, eeehaw!, yeehaw!, yahoo!

EXPLETIVE: HOSTILE asshole!, up yours!, up your ass!, up the wazoo!, shove it!, shove it up your ass!, stick it!, stick it up your ass!, drop dead!, nuts!, nerts!, bull!, bullshit!, horseshit!, baloney!, bury yourself!, big deal!, T.T.!, tough titty!, T.S.!, toughshit!, fuck!, fuck it!, fuck you!, fuck off!, go fuck yourself!, piss!, piss off!, piss on you!, mother!, motherfucker!, mofo!, muthuh fuckuh!, mother grabber!, mother clutcher!, your mother!, your mama!, your mother's mustache!, your father's mustache!, says who!, sez you!, go soak yourself!, go soak your head!, for Pete's sake!, flip one the bird!, blow it out your barracks bag!

EXPLETIVE: IGNORANCE it beats me!, beats me!, beats the shit outta me!, search me!, you got me!, dammed if I know!, God only knows!, Lord knows!, heaven knows!, it's Greek to me!, I pass!, don't look at me!

EXPLETIVE: REJECTION forget you!, shove it!, shove it up your ass!, stick it!, stick it up your ass!, stick it in your ear!, stow it!, put it where the sun don't shine!, shine it!, you know what you can do with it!, nuts to you!, go to!, go to hell!, fuck you!, fuck off!

EXPLETIVE: SURPRISE no kidding!, oh yeah!, go on!, get out!, no shit!, shee-it!, holy Christ!, holy Christmas!, holy mackerel!, holy moley!, holy Moses!, holy smoke!, holy shit!, holy Toledo!, Jeez!, Jees!, Jeezy peezy!, Jiggers!, Jigs!, I'll be jig swiggered!, I'll be jiggered!, what the fuck!, what the hey!, what in Sam Hill!, fuck a duck!, shoo fly!, twenty-three skidoo!, crazy!, search me!, wow!, like wow!, goodness gracious!, mercy!, whammo!, whamo!, for crying out loud!, for crying in a bucket!

EXPLETIVE: UNPLEASANT eeyuk!, yeeuck!, yech!, yich!, yuk!, yucky!, eeoooh!, ick!, ugh!, ach!, bletch!, blechhh!, feh!, phew!, pugh!, phooey!

EXPLICATION n. whatfor, whyfor, why and wherefore, the picture, the whole picture, rundown, story, the idea, the big idea, megillah, whole megillah. See also DESCRIPTION.

EXPLICIT adj. on the nose, all hanging out, don't need no diagrams, no buts about it, no ifs ands or buts. See also OBVIOUS.

EXPLODE v. go off, go blooey, go flooey, kablooey, let go, va voom, hit the fan.

EXPLODED adj. set off, blown, energetically disassembled.

EXPLOIT n. stunt. See ACTION.

EXPLOIT v. work (she worked the Johns for tips), pick one's brains, mine, mining, get mileage out of. See also ADVANTAGE, TAKE.

EXPLOITER n. operator, carpetbagger, wire-puller, one on the make. See also CHEATER.

EXPLORE v. really get into, leave no stone unturned, turn inside out. See also SEARCH, INVESTIGATE.

EXPLOSION n. energetic disassembly, blow up.

EXPLOSIVE n. fireworks, pineapple, satchel charge, soup, power, dinah, grease, mulligan, noise, peter, picric, shot, stew, string, booby trap, Bouncing Betsy.

EXPLOSIVES WORKER n. powder monkey, UXB.

EXPOSE v. crack, dig, dig up, leak, let the cat out of the bag, giveaway, give the show away, show up, spill, spill it, spill the beans, spill one's guts, blab, blabber, make noise, dump on, break, break it to one, tip, tip off, tip one's duke, tip one's hand, show one's hand, lay it on the stick, lay it on one, own up, come clean, come out, come out of the closet, let it all hang out, get it out of one's system, get it off one's chest, out with it, spit it out, open up, blow one's cover, spring, spring one's duke, spring with a crack, peach, burn (spy), debunk, do one dirt, blow up, blow the lid off, blow sky high, blow the whistle, show, whip out, flash (also used in playing cards), moon (buttocks), streak (run naked).

EXPOSED adj. caught with a hand in the cookie jar, caught with one's pants down, caught dead to rights, out on a limb, on the spot, got one's neck out. See CAUGHT. See also DEFENSELESS, NUDE.

EXPOSITION n. expo.

EXPOSURE n. handout, flashing, mooning, streaking. See also DISCLOSURE, REVELATION, PUBLICITY.

EXPRESS v. pop off, shoot off one's mouth, shoot one's wad, shoot one's bolt. See SPEAK.

EXPRESSIONLESS adj. deadpan, poker face, fish eye, straight face, lead eyeballs, nobody home. See EMOTIONLESS.

EXPULSION n. brush, brush-off, rush, bum's rush, bounce, heave-ho, old heave-ho, the gate.

EXPUNGE v. blue pencil, cut, knock off, gut, launder, trim, scrub, X out, take out, zap, kayo, KO, nix, call off, call all bets off, kill, wipe out, blow the deal. See CANCEL. See also EDIT, DESTROY.

EXPUNGED adj. scrubbed, scratched, killed, offed, wasted, shot, shot down, shot down in flames, taken out, washed out, wiped out, all off, all bets off, kaput, zapped, blue penciled, rubbed out.

EXPURGATE v. bleep, bleep out, blue pencil, clean up, cut, decontaminate, launder, sanitize, sterilize, scrub, squash. See REPRESS. See also SUPPRESS.

EX-SOLDIER n. vet, G.I., ex-GI, war-horse, pro, old pro, old hand, old-timer, old salt, old sea dog, shellback, got his ruptured duck.

EXTEMPORANEOUS adj. improv, ad lib, winging it, fake, off the cuff, off the top of one's head, toss off, toss out; jamming, taking it for a ride, thinking out loud. See IMPROMPTU.

EXTEND v. string out, stretch out, drag out, run on, stall, drag one's feet, pad, put some rubber into it, googly. See EXPAND.

EXTENSION n. boost, buildup, hike, up, upping, stretch, pad.

EXTENSIVE adj. across the board, wall to wall.

EXTENT n. elbowroom, leeway, room to swing a cat, here to hell and gone.

EXTENUATE v. sanitize, go easy on, blink at, wink at, write off, cool it, take the edge off, take the bite out, take the sting out. See SOFTEN.

EXTERMINATE v. erase, rub out, stamp out, blow away, knock off, kiss off, send to kingdom come. See KILL.

EXTERMINATED adj. offed, gone, down the drain, finished, kaput, popped off. See KILLED.

EXTINCT adj. had it, passed on, checked out, went, goner, dead and gone, done for, dead as a dodo, dead duck. See DEAD.

EXTINGUISH v. kill (lights, fire or cigarette), choke, douse, knock down, stamp out.

EXTOL v. hats off to, puff up, rave, root, hear it for, brag about, give a bouquet, give a posy, hand it to, have to hand it to, stroke, push, boost, give a boost to. See PRAISE.

EXTORT v. 1. skin, sting, clip, hold up, soak, stick, bleed, fleece, ice, make one pay through the nose, put the shake on, put the arm on, shake down, pull one's leg. 2. squeeze, worm out of one, worm something out of one, wring out. See ELICIT.

EXTORTION n. payoff, payola, drugola, gayola, pressure, protection, shakedown, shake, squeeze, squeeze rates, arm, badger, bite, cooptation, leg pulling.

EXTORTIONIST n. shakedown artist, shake man, shakester, grafter, leech, vulture, shark, bloodsucker, badger, horseman, leg-puller, in line (paying sums to).

EXTRA adj. option, all the options, perks, golden parachute, button, goodies, gravy, hat, ice, PM, spiff (salesman), sweetener, tip, fuss, gingerbread, gewgaws, bells and whistles, padding, spare tire, fifth wheel, widow, gash, lagniappe. See also BENEFIT, GRATUITY.

EXTRA, FILM n. penguin (formal wear), atmosphere.

EXTRACT v. pull out, drag out, yank.

EXTRA DURABLE adj. double duty, heavy metal.

EXTRAMARITAL n. affair, fling, playing around, getting some on the side, carrying on, tip out, extracurricular activity, extracurricular relations. See ADULTERY.

EXTRAORDINARY adj. gnarly, mega-gnarly, zero cool, wicked, a beaut, drop dead——, nose cone, flash, like wow, primo, boss, like dynamite, fab, in orbit, tough, heavy. See EXCELLENT.

EXTRASENSORY PERCEPTION n ESP, sixth sense, gut feeling.

EXTRATERRESTRIAL n. alien, ET, saucerman, spaceman, man from Mars, Martian, little green man.

EXTRAVAGANCE n. frill, frills, egg in one's beer, living high on the hog, icing on the cake.

EXTRAVAGANT adj. steep, stiff, plush, posh, ritzy, swanky, like money was goin' outta style, spreading it around, fancy, high, high on the hog, out of bounds, out of sight, first cabin.

EXTREME adj. far out, way out, gone, worst-case scenario, bitchen, boss, nose cone, ape, crazy, fancy, glorkish, all out, go all out, all get out, all get up, hell of a, hell fired, all fired, in spades, ultra-ultra, flaming, out of bounds, out of sight, out of this world, throw out the baby with the bathwater, KO, kayo punch, the chips are down, last straw, the straw that broke the camel's back, too-too, too much, everything but the kitchen sink, like carrying coals to Newcastle, like teaching one's grandmother to suck eggs, till hell freezes over, chichi, frou-frou, cushy, spiffy, flossy, high, steep, stiff, the end, bitter end, bad news, the pits, the dogs, the least, bottom out, jump off the deep end, short end of the stick, number ten (Korean war), one thou, one thousand (Vietnam war).

EXTREMELY adv.   totally, fucking, too much, plenty, stone (stone deaf), terribly, terrifically, almighty, powerful. See VERY.

EXTRICATE v.   bail one out, get out from under, save one's bacon, save one's neck, let go, let off. See FREE.

EXTROVERT n.   character, Flash Gordon, showboat.

EXUBERANCE n.   bounce, piss and vinegar, zip, zap, pep, juice, go juice, bounce, sock, pepper, get up and go.

EXUBERANT adj.   chipper, bouncy, zingy, zippy, zappy, feeling one's oats, full of piss and vinegar. See SPIRITED.

EXULTANT adj.   set up, hopped up, blow one's mind, flipping, flying, high, turned on, wowed. See ECSTATIC.

EXULTATION n.   do a Rocky, up, upper, high, charge, large charge, bang, fireworks. See EXCITEMENT.

EYE v.   clap eyes on, lay eyes on, set eyes on, give the eye, give the once over, give the OO, give the double O, take in, glom, check out, size up. See SEE.

EYE, GLASS n.   gravel eye.

EYEGLASSES n.   cheaters, glims, lamps, make up, four eyes, shades, specs, goggles, windows, mini specs, sus-specs, nippers, gogs, granny glasses, professor (wearer). See GLASSES.

EYELIDS n.   shutters.

EYES n.   peepers, peekers, baby blues, blinkers, blinders, lamps, cheaters, headlights, deadlights, gagers, gleeps, glims, glimmers, eyeballs, bugeyes, googly eyes, banjo eyes, popeyes, swivel eyes, saucer eyes, cockeyes, walleyes, pies, mince pies, pincers, shutters, slanters, spotters.

EYESORE n.   sight, dump, blot on the landscape. See also UGLY.

F

F n. foxtrot, fox.

FABLE n. 1. yarn, megillah, old chestnut, old saw, old touches, old wives' tale. See STORY. 2. fib, whopper, bunk, for the birds, crock, claptrap, fish story, cock and bull story, fairy tale, hogwash. See LIE.

FABRICATE v. 1. prefab, throw up, throw together, knock together, whomp up, cobble up, whip up, fudge together. 2. brainstorm, head trip, spark, spitball, take it off the top of one's head, cook up, dream up, think up, make up. 3. jive, shuck and jive, maple stick jive, bull, shit, fudge, make like, let on like, talk trash, signify. See LIE.

FABRICATION n. jive, line of jive, jazz, fib, bull, shit, crap, crock of shit, yarn, cock and bull, smoke, line, hogwash, song and dance. See LIE.

FABULOUS adj. fab, rad, way rad, glor, froody, 10, ten, A, A1, A-number one, A-plus, A-OK, okay, OK, ace, aces, ace high, ace of spades, in spades, super, super-colossal, super-duper, hooper-dooper, smashing, gnarly, mega-gnarly, unreal, rat fuck, cool, zero cool, cold, turn-on, wicked, mind-blowing, mind-bending, gone, real gone, out of this world, out of sight, standout, stick-out, sticks out like a sore thumb, nose cone, gilt-edged, drooly, flash, splash, like wow, best ever, primo, crack, crackerjack, peacherino, peachy, ginger peachy, peachy keen, keen, salt of the earth, top, tops, top-notch, topflight, top drawer, top of the line, tip top, first class, first chop, first rate, star, boss, stunning, corking, corker, solid, solid sender, great, greatest, dozer, doozie, daisy, dilly, bo, boo, tickety boo, deadly, bong, sly, copacetic, kopesetic, the bee's knees, the cat's meow, the cat's whiskers, the cat's pajamas, the butterfly's book, the caterpillar's kimono, George, real George, down, good show, gear, golden, solid gold, hard, hummer, humdinger, high cotton, knock out, mad, mess, mezz, nasty, nifty, the nuts, the nerts, ripping, ripsnorter, sanitary, heavenly, bang-up, like dynamite, fat, in fat city, in orbit, murder, neat, kicky, hunky-dory, all wool and a yard wide, jam up, slap up, but good, strictly, sweetheart, catch, find, plenty, zanzy, beautiful, cuspy, check plus, stellar, dream, lollapaloosa, whiz, killer-diller, mean, ducky, hot, spiffy, ripping, nobby, delicious, scrumptious, not too shabby, one for the book, something, something else, something to brag about, something to shout about, something to write home about, groove, in the groove, groovy, tidy, tits, tough, tuff, heavy, bad, terrible, terrific, marvy, winner, choice, reet, a gas, gas up something, gasser, dynamite, far out, funky, state of the art, too much, the most, the utmost, swell, savage, wild, jumping, shirty, tawny, whale of a, world beater, pip, pippen, lulu (often Derog.), darb, honey, beaut, heller, hell of a note, helluva, some (some show!), this is some kinda———, it's the berries, cracking, bully, sharp, wizard, the best, man-sized, like all get out, like mad, like gangbusters, the end.

FACADE n. front, false front, show, window dressing, put-on, fake, phony. See PRETENSION.

FACE n. kisser, puss, map, mug, pan, mush, phiz, phizog, biscuit, clock, dial, conk, chevy chase, gills, index, mask, potato, squash, deadpan, poker face, sourpuss, picklepuss, sugarpuss.

FACE v. run into, face off, square off, face down, face to face, face the music, not take it lying down, take it, take it on the chin, bite the bullet, brace, cross, fly in the face of, fly in the teeth of, straighten out, put one's life on the line, eyeball, eyeball to eyeball, meet eyeball to eyeball, stick it out, stick to one's guns, stand up and be counted, one to one, go one on one, take on, take out, take one on, take one up on, call one's bluff, knock the chip off one's shoulder, make something out of, step over the line, have a bone to pick, make my day, go on make my day, tell off. See also BRAVE, OPPOSE.

FACE POWDER n. flour, paint, makeup.

FACET n. angle, twist, switch.

FACE TREATMENT n. facial, face-lift, nose job, hamburger (mixture).

FACILE adj. 1. flip, fast talk, fast talker, thick slung, slick, slicker, smooth, smoothie, old smoothie, smooth apple, smooth operator, smooth article, gift of gab. 2. nothing to it, pushover, picnic, easy as pie, easy make, turkey shoot, breeze, walkover, child's play. See EASY.

FACILITATE v. grease the wheels, run interference for, open doors, walk through, hand-carry.

FACSIMILE n. 1. dupe, xerox, clone, carbon, carbon copy, mimeo, stat, repro, knock-off, flimsy. 2. look-alike, work alike, ringer, dead ringer, copycat, spitting image, spit and image, chip off the old block, double, peas in a pod, twin, ——— compatible (P.C. compatible).

FACT n. brass tacks, no shit, straight shit, how it is, like it is, bottom line, emess. See TRUTH.

FACTION n.   combination, combo, click, crowd, circle, insiders, the boys, old boys network. See ASSOCIATION.

FACTOR n.   fixin's, makin's, part and parcel, board, plug in.

FACTORY n.   shop, sweatshop, salt mines.

FACTS n.   dope, inside dope, goods, info, scoop, poop, poop sheet, score, story, whole story, brass tacks, Chapter and verse, the know, pﬦ , lowdown, no shit, like it is, the emess, the numbers, the goods, bottom line, meat and potatoes, gospel, nitty-gritty, what's what, the straight stuff, skinny, facts of life, from the horse's mouth, cue, clue, cold turkey. See also INFORMATION.

FACTUAL adj.   for real, honest to God, kosher, legit, on the legit, on the level, card-carrying, the lowdown, the emess, all wool and a yard wide, righteous, straight from the horse's mouth.

FACULTY n.   the right stuff, dynamite, has what it takes, know one's way around, up to snuff, up to the mark, a pistol. See SKILL. See also PROFESSOR, TEACHER.

FAD n.   in, in-thing, kick, newest wrinkle, the latest thing, the last word, wrinkle. See RAGE.

FADDIST n.   freak, groupie, buff, hound, crazies, frenzie, trendoid, great one for, sucker for. See DEVOTEE.

FADE v.   fold, fag out, poop out, tucker out, peter out, peg out, come apart at the seams, die on the vine. See TIRE.

FAIL v.   1. goof, goof up, gum up, gum up the works, hash up, bobble, boot, blow, flub, flub the dub, bugger, boo-boo, bugger up, ball up, screw up, foul up, slip up, louse up, bitch, bitch up, muck up, trip up, crack up, piss up, fuck up, break, dump, pump up (gambling), mess up, mess and a half, make a mess of, make a hash of, make a boner, make a boo-boo, muff, muff one's cue, miss one's cue, fluff one's lines, miss by a mile, miss the boat, foozle, pratfall, brodie, brown off, take the heat, cool, hold the bag, hold the sack, clutch the gunny, blow it, blow the gig, eat one's lunch, drop the ball, draw a blank, put one's foot in one's mouth, put one's foot in it, die, die on the vine, die standing up, die on one's feet, be on one's last legs, have one foot in the grave, have one foot in the grave and the other on a banana peel, go west, roll over, roll over and play dead, croak; flunk, flunk out, flush, flush it (test or course); bust out (expelled), tap out, conk out, peter out, poop out, flake out, veg out, wash out, peg out, fizzle out, fizz out, fink out, turkey out, bilge out, ace out, drawing dead, drop a brick, drop the ball, stub one's toe, trip up, come apart at the seams, come out on the short end of the stick, go soft, get hung up, get out of whack, get out of kilter, get out of commission, go on the blink, go on the fritz, go kaput, go kerplunk, go wrong, go blooey, go

flooey, go sour, go phut, go haywire, go to pieces, tanking (on purpose), go into the tank, take the count, take it, take it on the chin, land on one's ass, fall flat on one's ass, fall flat on one's face, fall down on the job, fall down and go boom, bite the dust, lick the dust, jim a deal, pull a boner, pull a boo-boo, pull a bloomer, pull a blooper, go over like a lead balloon, not hack it, not make it, not work, not come off, not make the grade, not fill the bill, not get to first base, never pass go, have a bad go at, left at the post (lose from the start), lose out, meet one's Waterloo; have a coral sandwich, get sucked up the face (surfing); be on the skids, stiff, stumble, flummox, flag, flag it, gleek it, tube it, come a-cropper, cave in, cut no ice, curdle, blob. 2. belly up, go bust, go Chapter 11, fold, fold up, go broke, tap out, boff out, crap out, be cleaned out, be taken to the cleaners, go to the cleaners, take the knock, lose big, drop, drop a bundle (money), hooked, go under, go up, go to the wall, close one's doors. See also WEAKEN.

FAILED adj.   flop, dead pigeon, turkey, in the dumper, blown out of the water, down the drain, never passed go. See UNSUCCESSFUL.

FAILURE n.   1. deadbeat, beat, bum, turkey, good-for-nothing, moocher, loafer, bringdown, foul ball, has-been, nonstarter, also ran, loser, out of luck, out of it, lumpy, neverwuz, a nobody, fall guy, stiff, stifferoo, booby, defeatee, duck, dues payer, down-and-outer, can't even get arrested, can't even write home for money, can't punch his way out of a paper bag, flash in the pan, flunkee. 2. flop, flopperoo, bomb, blank, bloomer, shellacking, stinkeroo, fluke, flummox, flookum, clambake, false alarm, dud, disaster, abortion, not work, not come off, flunk, flunk out, crap out, strike out, down the drain, down the chute, down-and-out, down the toilet, in the toilet, washout, washed out, washed up, nowhere, A for effort, near miss, no dice, no go, back to the drawing board, phftt, skids, on the skids, hit the skids, on the rocks, on the ropes, totalled, total wipe, wipe out, gutted, wasteland, should have stood in bed, go under, cropper, pratfall, muss up, piss up, fuck-up, foul-up, snafu, put-down, comedown, down for the count, wet smack, misfire, draw a blank, header, in over one's head, in deep water, flat failure, dull thud, brodie, total loss, rack and ruin, blue ruin, foozle, lamo, stinker, lead balloon (idea went over like a lead balloon), lemon, fizzle, frost, bagel, botch, clunker, dog, enema, hash, jumble, pancake, turd, turkey. 3. belly up, Chapter 7, Chapter 11, Chapter 13, foldo, bust, broke.

FAINT adj.   rocky, woozy.

FAINT v.   blackout, go out like a light, keel over, pass out, freak out, flicker (also pretend).

FAIR adj.   1. regular, open, up front, right up front, on the up and up, on the level, even-steven, cricket, dinkum, sport, fair to middling, fair shake, square, square deal, square John, square shooter, real people, saint, straight, straight stuff, straight arrow, straight dope, straight out, straight shooter, straight from the shoulder, white, damn white, Christian, what you see is what you get, call 'em as one sees 'em, honest Injun, boy scout, down home, fly right, Mr. Clean, third rail, strictly union, Sammy Smith concept, Susie Smith concept. 2. beaut, looker, honey, dishy, number, peach, knockout, easy on the eyes, tall dark and handsome. See BEAUTIFUL.

FAIRBANKS, ALASKA n.   Bearflanks.

FAIT ACCOMPLI adj.   wired, all set, fixed.

FAITH n.   stock, store.

FAITHFUL adj.   true blue, true believer, oncer, string along with, dyed in the wool, behind one, on one's side, ace in, ace through, come through, stand up for one, faithful but not blind.

FAITHLESS adj.   cheater, double-crossing, two-faced, two-timing, chippy on one, step out on one, tip, witch. See UNFAITHFUL.

FAKE n.   phony, actor, four-flusher, pseud, pseudo, put on, bogue, bunco, bunko, bum, junque. See also COUNTERFEIT, ACT.

FAKE v.   dive, take a dive, tank, go in the tank, put on, put on an act. See also PRETEND.

FAKERY adv.   put on, scam, flam, flimflam, shell game, skin game, spoof, whitewash job, front, window dressing, jiggery pokery.

FALL n.   header, dive, nose dive, pratfall, belly buster, belly flop, belly whopper.

FALL v.   land on one's ass, tip over, keel over, take a header, take a dive, take a belly whopper, hit the dirt, nose-dive, lose it, do a pratfall, fall down and go boom, belly up, come a-cropper, go ass over teakettle.

FALLACIOUS adj.   bum, off, way off, fishy, jivey, sincere (sarcasm), phony, fakey. See DECEPTIVE.

FALSE adj.   1. bogue, bogus, bogosity, autobogophobia, bogotified, bum, bent, phony, queer, falsie, fake, faked, hokey, ersatz, wrong, wrong number, fishy, frame, framed, plant, planted (evidence), crock, crock of shit, slick, sincere, not kosher, not what it's cracked up to be, pirate goods, pirate labels, dirty work, no such animal, out in left field, soft shell, it won't fly, lame, stiffing it, gil, Hollywood, reach-me-down. 2. shady, sharp, two-faced, gyp, snide, crooked, crooked stick, cheatin' heart. See DECEITFUL.

FALSE BANKROLL n.   Michigan roll.

FALSEHOOD n.   line of jive, fib, whopper, balls, yarn, story, cock-and-bull story, cover-up, line of cheese, hogwash. See LIE.

FALSE MODESTY n.   shit kick.

FALSIFICATION n.   whopper, bogosity, crock of shit, hooey, story, cock-and-bull story, baloney, cover-up, song and dance. See also LIE.

FALSIFIER n.   jive ass, jive turkey, phony, conner, con artist, con man, con merchant, crap merchant, oil merchant, promoter, quack, spieler, bullshitter, bullshit artist.

FALSIFY v.   con, promote, put on an act, put on a false front, fake it, frame up, phony up, cook the books, four-flush, salt, salt a mine. See LIE.

FALTER v.   hem and haw, drop the ball, bobble, fluff one's lines, stub one's toe, trip up, come a-cropper. See FLOUNDER.

FAMILIAR adj.   1. tight, buddy-buddy, palsy-walsy, chummy, thick, thick as thieves. See INTIMATE. 2. plugged in, tuned in, grounded, with it, savvy, go go, latched on, in the know, know one's stuff, kept posted. See KNOWLEDGEABLE. 3. cheeky, fresh, brassy, smart aleck. See INSOLENT.

FAMILIARITY adj.   flip, fresh, sassy, smart, smart alecky, smart ass, wise ass, biggety, cocky, cheeky, crusty, gally, nervy, out of line, brassy, bold as brass, hands trouble, Roman hands, feeler, cop a feel.

FAMILIARIZE v.   1. mix, get together, get with it, get buddy-buddy, break the ice, let down one's hair. 2. post, put one in the picture, let next to, put on to, tip off. 3. get the lowdown on, case, check out, get the lay of the land. See ADVISE.

FAMILY n.   folks, home folks, kinfolks, in-laws, the whole famdamnly, shirt-tail relatives, kissin' cousins, insiders, bunch, click, crew, crowd, crush, gang, mob, outfit, ring, rack, off the same rack. See also GROUP.

FAMISHED adj.   starving, starved, starved to death, empty, fly light, grits time, have a tapeworm, munchies (follows marijuana use), dog-hungry, could eat a horse, could eat the asshole out of a bear.

FAMOUS adj.   w.k. (well known), celeb, star, name, numero uno, face, right up there, big number, biggie, monster. See CELEBRITY.

FANATIC n.   fan, freak, crank, crazies, nut, frenzie, fiend, demon, fool. See DEVOTEE.

FANATICAL adj.   high on, turned on, eat this shit, nuts for, freaked out, bugged, flipped, wig out. See ENTHUSIASTIC.

FANCIER n.   buff, fan, freak, bug, crank, hound, nut, filbert, junkie, culture vulture, fiend, demon, great one for, sucker for. See DEVOTEE.

FANCIFUL adj.   fantasmo, flaky, kinky, offbeat, floating, floating on clouds, on cloud seven, on cloud nine, pipe dream, play with oneself, jack off, pie in the sky, castles in the air, blue sky.

FANCY adj.   chichi, frou frou, cushy, spiffy, frilly, flossy. See also ORNATE.

FANCY n.   1. bag, groove, thing, turned on to, flash, weakness for, cup of tea, druthers, type, fool's paradise, pipe dream, pie in the sky. 2. big eyes, eyes for, hard-on for, itch, hot pants, lech, sweet tooth, yen, zazzle. See DESIRE. See also LOVE.

FANCY v.   1. yen for, have the hots for, lech for, itch for, fall for, spoil for, gone on, groove on, mad for, wild for, crazy about, have it bad. See LOVE. 2. spark, spitball, head trip, dream up, make up, take it off the top of one's head, think up, trump up. See CREATE.

FANTASIZE v.   trip out, head trip, build castles in the air, moon, pipe dream, woolgather.

FANTASTIC adj.   fantasmo, seven-ply gasser, megagnarly, unreal, rat fuck, out of this world, out of sight, like wow, best ever, primo, first class, the cat's meow, hummer, zanzy, delicious, far out. See FABULOUS.

FANTASY n.   trip, head trip, mind trip, castle in the air, stare into the middle distance, fool's paradise, pipe dream, pie in the sky.

FAR adj.   bit, ways, good ways, a good long walk, piece, far piece, fer piece, spitting distance, stone's throw, just down the road, a hop skip and jump, Sunday run, tidy step, whoop, two whoops and a holler, a hoot and a holler, a shlep, sleeper jump, long chalk, sticks, boondocks, boonies, tullies, on the dance floor but can't hear the band, clear to hell and gone, to hell and gone, jumping-off place, godforsaken place, God knows where, middle of nowhere, back of beyond, end of the rainbow, almost over the county line, you can't get there from here.

FARCE n.   camp, high camp, low camp, pratfall comedy, in-one-door-and-out-another comedy.

FARCICAL adj.   camp, campy, joky, joshing, yokky, gagged up, for grins, in the door out the door.

FARE v.   make out, handle.

FAREWELL interj.   bye-bye, see ya, I'll be seeing ya, ciao, so long, later, I'm outta here, good-byee, have a nice day, have a good one, toodle-oo, ta ta, abyssinia, keep the faith baby, peace. See GOOD-BYE.

FAREWELL n.   eighty-eights, swan song. See PARTING.

FARGO, NORTH DAKOTA   Little Twins.

FARM n.   egg orchard.

FARMER n.   hayseed, country boy, clodhopper, apple knocker, plow jockey, hillbilly, Arkie, Oakie, Clem, cob, clay eater (Southern), shit kicker, clover kicker, gully-jumper, rube, hay rube, briar hopper, Bill Shears, dirty neck, dust raiser, hay shaker, swamp angel, backwoods jockey, seed, woohat (Georgia), John Farmer, Alvin, Clyde.

FART v.   break wind, cut one, cut the cheese, leave one, let one fly, backfire, poot, nose-closer, the butler's revenge (silent).

FASCINATE v.   hook, send, wow, slay, bait, turn on, come on, vamp, knock dead. See ATTRACT.

FASCINATED adj.   sold on, hooked, wowed, turned on, sent, gone on, tickled pink, tickled to death, head over heels in, pleased as punch.

FASCINATION n.   bug, hang-up, thing for, grabber. See OBSESSION.

FASHION v.   whomp up, cook up, dream up, throw up, throw together, knock together, fudge together, ad lib.

FASHIONABLE adj.   faddy, trendy, a go-go, in, in-thing, latest thing, last word, mod, now, the rage, spinach, chic. See STYLE. See also NEW.

FASHION TRENDS n.   trendy, faddy, a go-go, spinach, in thing, the last word, latest thing, new wrinkle, newest wrinkle, the New Look (1947).

FAST adj.   hot, scream, screamin', quickie, sizzler, speedball, fly, pronto, snap, snappy, spanking, barrelling, chop chop, on the double, on the double quick, double time, double clutchin', get the lead out, get moving, get a move on, get going, get cracking, get with it, get a wiggle on, hop to it, move your tail, move your fanny, pretty damned quick, PDQ, right off the bat, toot sweet, whip through, hubba-hubba, in a jiffy, wham bam, in nothing flat, in two shakes of a lamb's tail, in two shakes, in half a shake, before you can say Jack Robinson, horseback, don't spare the horses, step on it, snap to it, make it snappy, shake a leg, stir your stumps, haul ass, high ball, peel rubber, burn rubber, really rolling, lickety split, lickety cut, pour it on, speed boy, speed merchant, storm out, hell-bent, hell-bent for election, hell-for-leather, hell to split, break neck, neck-breaking, like a shot, like a shot out of hell, like a house on fire, like sixty, like fury, like sin, like mad, like crazy, like all get out, like a blue streak, like a streak of lightning, like greased lightning, like a big-assed bird, like a BAB, like a scared rabbit, like a bat out of hell, like shit through a goose, going like a raped ape, gone in a cloud of sour owl shit (WW II), to beat the band, to beat the devil, to beat the Dutch, to beat the deuce, good hands, quick on the draw, quick on the trigger, hair trigger, pack the mail, A.S.A.P. (as soon as possible).

FASTEN v.   button, anchor, nail, freeze to, stay put, tack on, slap on, tag, tag on, hook on, hook up, hitch on, hitch up, stick like a barnacle.

FASTENED adj. anchored, nailed, hitched up, hooked up, locked, locked in, buttoned up, buttoned down.

FASTIDIOUS adj. nitpicker, picky, picky picky, stickler, ace, comma counter, fussbudget, fusspot, fancy pants, fuddy-duddy, granny, old woman, old maid, pernickety, persnickety. See also PARTICULAR.

FAT adj. fats, fatso, fatty, fat-assed, fat city, fat stuff, slob, fat slob, roly-poly, jelly-belly, tub, tubby, tubster, tub of guts, tub of lard, lardo, lard-ass, lard-assed, gutbucket, pus gut, blubber guts, spare tire, rubber tire, beerbelly, corporation, bay window, porker, cow, beef, beef trust, walrus, whale, hippo, baby elephant, heavy, horse-heavy, heavy cream, hefty, hippy, hipsters, love handles (hips and thighs), chunky, chunky trunks, pleasingly plump, blimp, bulge, battle of the bulge, butterball, bagels, Mr. Five by Five, Crisco (fat person), broad in the beam, man mountain, two-ton Tessie, tun, tun of flesh, meat, meat show, solid suet, corn-fed, built for comfort, zaftig, avoirdupois, look like ten pounds of shit in a five-pound bag.

FATE n. break, karma, handwriting on the wall, in the lap of the gods, Lady Luck. See DESTINY. See also LUCK.

FATED adj. in the cards, que sera sera, the way the ball bounces, the way the cookie crumbles, the way the beads read, the handwriting on the wall, kiss of death.

FATHER n. old man, O.M., dad, daddy, big daddy, daddio, daddums, pa, papa, pappy, pap, pop, pops, poppa, padre, pater, governor, guv, gaffer, warden, zoo daddy (divorced).

FATIGUE n. brain fag, burnout.

FATIGUE v. fizzle, fizzle out, fag, fag out, poop, poop out, tucker, tucker out, burn out, knock out, peter out, conk out.

FATIGUED adj. bushed, hung, pooped, out of gas, burned out, crispy, played out, flaked out, wore out, fagged, zonked, ass in a sling, beatsville. See TIRED.

FATUOUS adj. jerky, lamebrained, birdbrained, weak in the upper story, bubbleheaded, sappy, shmendrick. See FOOLISH. See also STUPID.

FAULT n. muff, boner, bug, glitch, gremlin, boo-boo, boggle, goof, louse up, muck up, miscue, typo, fox pass, blow card, zit, catch. See MISTAKE. See also BLEMISH.

FAULTFINDER n. bitcher, griper, whiner, crab, crank, pill, plainer, sorehead. See COMPLAINER.

FAULTLESS adj. right on, 10, ten, on target, four-o, in the groove, textbook, to a fare-you-well. See PERFECT.

FAULTY adj. a few bugs, glitch, gremlins, seconds, lemon, rank. See IMPERFECT.

FAUX PAS n. fox paw, fox pass, boo-boo, fuck-up, mess up, goof, flub, flop. See MISTAKE.

FAVOR v. flash, pro, for, for it, go for it, go for, buck for, root for, groove, back, on one's side, be serious, tilt towards, turned on to, take to, take a liking to, take a fancy to, take a shine to, cotton to, hipped on, keen about, have a thing about, have it for one, have eyes for, eat this shit. See also PREFER, LIKE.

FAVORABLE adj. go, okay, okey-dokey, OK, rave, puffy (exaggerated), sitting pretty, sitting in the driver's seat, sitting in the catbird seat.

FAVORED adj. pet, fair-haired boy, golden-haired boy, white-haired boy, blue-eyed boy, sweetheart deal, asshole buddy.

FAVORITE n. 1. pet, teacher's pet, main, main man, fave, fair-haired boy, blue-eyed boy, candy boy, evergreen, golden oldie, number one boy, pratt boy, chalk, asshole buddy. 2. front-runner, shoo-in.

FAWN v. stroke, snow, massage, jolly, oil, lay it on, play up to, butter up, schmeer, suck ass, fall all over, kowtow, buddy up, carpet-bag, curry below the knee.

FEAR n. goose bumps, creeps, cold creeps, cold shivers, cold feet, buck fever, jitters, fidgets, flap, fuss, lather, needles, pins and needles, stew, to-do, zingers, worriment, all-overs, chicken out, pucker, pucker-assed, asshole puckerin', asshole suckin' wind, stage fright.

FEARFUL adj. yellow, have cold feet, run scared, scared spitless, scared shitless, piss in one's pants, goose bumpy, rabbity, mousy, weak-kneed. See AFRAID. nebbish, candy ass, pucker, pucker-assed, asshole puckerin', asshole suckin' wind, pecker-assed, gutless, shake in one's boots, ague, creeps, heebie-jeebies, heebies, leaping heebies, the jams, the jims, the jimjams, the jimmies, jittery, jumpy, shaky, shivery, quivery, in a dither, have butterflies in one's stomach, in a cold sweat, in a sweat, uptight, hung up, clutch up, D and D (deaf and dumb, afraid to testify), punk out, on the ragged edge.

FEARLESS adj. ballsy, gutsy, gutty, gutiness, gutsiness, gritty, game, hairy, nervy, chutzpahdik, spunky, bodacious, brassy, bold as brass, chit, cheeky, crust, gally, fire-eater, cool hand, iceman, ice in one's veins, tough it out, ain't scared of shit, pizzazz, spetters, salty, come on strong, crusty, cocky, cock stuck up, puffed up, chesty, sure, sure as shit, smart, smart ass, smart alecky, wise ass, wise guy, hot shot, whippersnapper, too big for one's britches, biggety, crack, wisecrack, flip, fresh, lippy, sassy, hell of a note, got the faith baby, racked, gamble on. See also DARING.

FEASIBLE adj. no sweat, cinch, snap, pushover, doable, piece of cake, setup, breeze, duck soup, pie, easy as pie, easy as falling off a log, simple as ABC. See EASY.

FEAST n. big feed, blow, blowout, moveable feast.

FEAT n. stunt, mitzvah (good). See also ACTION.

FEATURE n. slant, twist, gimmick, angle, gag. See also ARTICLE, CHARACTERISTIC.

FECES n. shit, crap, dump, caca, B.M., number two, turd; doggy do, cow chips, road apples, horse hocky. See BOWEL MOVEMENT.

FECES, ANIMAL n. horse apples, alley apples, golden apples, horse hocky, bird turd, cow plops, dingleberries, doggy do, dreck, hocky, moose beans, moose nuggets, moose pecans.

FEDERAL AGENCY BOND n. Fannie Mae, Ginnie Mae, Freddie Mac.

FEDERAL AGENT n. fed, Federal, F.B.I., feeb, feeble, G-man, T-man, tax man, sam, narc, revenuer, hard John.

FEDERAL BUREAU OF INVESTIGATION n. F.B.I., Feeb, feeble, FIB, G-men, the Feds, Foley Square, hard John, big department, gazers, spooks, monkey, prohy, whiskers.

FEDERAL COMMUNICATIONS COMMISSION n. FCC, Charlie, Big Charlie, Uncle Charlie, Big Double C, Candy Man, Friendly Candy Company, Funny Candy Company.

FEDERAL HOME LOAN MORTGAGE CORPORA- TION n. Freddie Mac.

FEDERAL NATIONAL MORTGAGE ASSOCIATION n. Fannie Mae.

FEDERAL RESERVE BOARD n. the Fed.

FEDERATION n. bunch, crew, crowd, gang, mob, outfit, ring, family, hookup, tie-up, tie-in, syndication, pool, tribe. See ASSOCIATION.

FEE n. commish, ante, bite, chunk, cut, end, juice, piece, piece of the action, rake-off, share, skig, slice, a little slack, a little something to sweeten the pot. See also CHARGE.

FEEBLE adj. 1. rocky, woozy, dopey, wishy-washy, out of gas, don't have the horses. 2. paper tiger, weak sister, wimp, basket case, chicken, nobody, clown, eight ball, draddy, zero. See WEAK.

FEEBLEMINDED adj. feeb, dork, nerd, nurdy, loser, winner, lamebrain, birdbrain, rattlebrain, rattleweed, nebbish, out to lunch, lunch, lunchie, out of it, a coupla quarts low, nobody home, jerk, lowbrow, dodo, dummy, dumbo, dumdum, dumb bill, dumb bunny, dumb cluck, dumb Dora, dumb head, dumb ox, four-letter man (dumb), bonetop, boob, birk, box, oofus, ninny, nincompoop, airhead, bubblehead, balloonhead, meathead, blockhead, pointyhead, buckethead, bull- head, bumhead, banana head, squarehead, mushhead,

cementhead, pumpkinhead, saphead, lunkhead, mutton- head, fathead, bonehead, knucklehead, shithead, doughhead, hammerhead, jughead, blubberhead, cheesehead, chickenhead, chucklehead, mallethead, lardhead, peahead, pinhead, puddinghead, wooden- head, dunderhead, blunderhead, chowderhead, cabbagehead, potato head, deadhead, flathead, numb- skull, numb-nut, numb-headed, numb-brained, knows from nothing, doesn't know from nothing, doesn't know the time of day, doesn't know from A to B, doesn't know A from izzard, doesn't know which way is up, doesn't know enough to come in out of the rain, turkey, stupe, thick, loogan, schlemiel, schlamozzle, shlump, shlub, shmendrick, shmoe, shnook, shmuck, clod-pated, deadneck, dildo, dill, droop, dud, Elmer, gasser, gonus, good fellow, goofus, goof ball, goon, goopus, got a hole in the head, jackass, knuckle, bloke, captain of the head, soft in the head, half-baked, nuthin' upstairs, boob, sap, mess, mutt, muttontop, meat, mope, weak in the upper story, simp, lead-footed, marble dome, newt, dimwit, nitwit, nougat, one eye, chump, clam, clock, cluck, cluckhead, clunk, dopey, dunce, dodunk, dub, fish, flub.

FEED v. scarf, scoff, munch out, nibble, snack, peck, pig out, fling a fang, feed one's face, tie on the feedbag, put on the feedbag. See EAT.

FEEL v. 1. be turned on to, feel in one's bones, feel in one's guts, have a funny feeling, have heart, have a hunch, have good vibes, have vibes, get vibes, get in touch, know where one is coming from. 2. frisk, feel up, put the feelers on one or something, grab ass.

FEELING adj. feel stuff, vibes, gut reaction, funky, emote, emoting (simulate), feel in one's bones, have a funny feeling, have a hunch, full up, get one's gage up, give out, where one is at, where one lives, shook, shook up, all torn up, all tore up, all shook up, fall apart, frantic, simpatico.

FEES n. take, take-in, gravy, handle, house.

FEET n. dogs, barking dogs (sore), bow wows, tootsies, tugboats, gunboats, canal boats, gondolas, canoes, clodhoppers, earth pads, flats, hocks, hoofs, hounds, pads, pups, barkers, boots, submarines, plates, platters, stompers, trotters.

FEIGN v. stonewall, put on, put on an act, put up a front, fake it, do a bit, phony up, put up a bluff, four-flush, play possum, salt a mine. See PRETEND.

FEIGNED adj. fake, faked, phony. See also COUNTERFEIT.

FEINT n. stutter-step, deek, juke.

FEINT v. deek, juke, fish, flicker, hang one out to dry, shake and bake, stutter step, sucker one, fake out, fake one out. See also PRETEND.

FELINE n. puss, pussy, pussycat, kitty, kitty cat, Chessycat, coon cat, meow meow.

FELLATIO v. suck, cock suck, sucky suck, suck off, scumsuck, blow, blow job, go down on, pearl dive, head, give head, give cone, deep throat, around the world, perform, a shot upstairs, sixty-nine, cannibal (one who performs), bananas and cream, French, French job, gobble, dickie lick, penilingism, peter puff, play the skin flute, cop a joint (all Obsc.).

FELLOW n. guy, dude, hunk, tuna, beefcake, man, feller, pops, daddy, mac, stud, stallion, john, bugger, meat, boyo, boychik, punk, brother. See MAN.

FELON n. vic, yardbird, ex-con, stir bird, brig rat, chain gang, fish, fresh one (new), jailbird, jice, new jice, lane, lifer, rock crusher, short, two-time loser, four-time loser. See also CRIMINAL.

FEMALE n. mama, old woman, old lady (girl friend), broad, dame, filly, skirt, frail, tomato, dutchess, she-stuff, he she, chichi, femme, fox, stone fox, 10, ten, beaut, beauty, my beauty, pinup, cheesecake, cupcake, cutie, babe, wren, jill, sis, kid, hell-cat, battle-ax, heifer, old bat, twat, piece. See WOMAN.

FEMININE adj. she-stuff, twisty.

FEMINISM n. women's lib.

FEMINIST n. bra burner, libber, women's libber.

FENTANYL n. China white.

FENCE n. swagman, swagsman.

FERMENT n. stir, fuss, row, to-do, commo, dustup, flap, fuzzbuzzy, scene, hell broke loose, rhubarb, stink, rumble, fofarraw, foofooraw. See TURMOIL.

FERRET n. monk.

FERRET OUT v. smell out, nose out, smoke out, pick up on, be on to, have dead to rights.

FERRIS WHEEL n. chump heister.

FERTILIZER n. shit, bullshit, horseshit, batshit, cowshit, lawn dressing, buffalo chips, cow chips, cow flops, cow pats, golden apples, alley apples, road apples, turd.

FERVENT adj. hot, hot for, hot to go, hot to trot, gung ho, hopped up, go great guns, creaming to, about to piss one's pants, fall all over oneself, not let any grass grow under one's feet, ready for Freddie, dying to, gotta have. See also ENTHUSIASTIC.

FERVOR n. jazz, oomph, pep talk, hot pants, weakness, turn on. See also LOVE.

FESTIVE adj. jumping, juiced up full, go go, grooving, swinging, rocking, upbeat, chipper, chirpy, perky, peppy, zippy, zingy, zappy, snappy, bouncy. See also HAPPY.

FESTIVITY n. bash, clambake, shindig, blowout, shindy, hoopla, jamboree, whoopee, whooper-dooper, wingding, whinding, finger pop, do. See PARTY. See also REVEL.

FETCH v. lug, pack, ride, piggyback, shlep, shlep along, tote, truck, back, birdie back, buck, gun, heel, hump, jag, shoulder.

FETID adj. lousy, rotten, stinking, gooky, stinko, stinky, strong, high, whiffy, nosy, gross, grody, icky, yechy, yucky. See also FOUL.

FETTER n. clinker, cuffs.

FETTER v. cuff, hang up, hog-tie, hold up, throw a monkey wrench into the works, drag one's foot. See HINDER.

FETTERS n. darbies, derbies, cuffs.

FEVER n. the shakes, burning up, on fire, running a temperature.

FEVERISH adj. 1. the shakes, burning up, on fire, running a temperature. 2. driven, hyper, unglued, unzipped, unscrewed, hot, wired, keyed up, fired up, in a sweat, like crazy, like mad, mind-blowing. See EXCITED.

FEW n. slim pickings. See also AMOUNT, SMALL.

FIANCÉ(E) n. old lady, old man, intended, steady, going steady, pinned, bird, donah, donar, future.

FIASCO n. flop, flopperoo, bomb, bobble, bonehead play, bonehead trick, boob stunt, dud, disaster, mess, Edsel, abortion, should have stood in bed, dumb thing to do, dumb trick. See FAILURE.

FIB n. line of jive, jazz, bunk, bull, bullshit, BS, bullchitna (Esk.), horse hocky, shit for the birds, crock, yarn, story, fairy tale, spinach. See LIE.

FIB v. jive, shuck and jive, shovel the shit, promote, plant, talk trash, tell a little white lie, speak with forked tongue. See LIE.

FIBBER n. jive ass, jive turkey, phony, con artist, con man, con merchant, conner, crap merchant, oil merchant, promoter, quack, spieler, bullshitter, bullshit artist.

FICKLE adj. yo-yo, two-timer, double-crossing, cheat, cheat on, sneakin' deacon, witch. See UNFAITHFUL.

FICTION n. 1. book, yarn, clothesline, cliff-hanger, bodice-ripper (romance), potboiler, spyboiler, toughtec (mystery), old wives' tale. See STORY. 2. jazz, fib, whopper, shit, bullshit, BS, bullchitna (Esk.), crap, crock of shit, hooey, tall story, fish story, banana oil, smoke, terminological inexactitude. See LIE.

FICTITIOUS adj. fake, faked, falsie, hyped up, phony, queer, no such animal, made out of whole cloth.

FIDGETS n. ants, ants in one's pants, antsy, antsy-pantsy, fantobs.

FIDGETY adj. jittery, jumpy, pissin', shittin', hyper, spooked, nervous wreck, wired up, yantsy, antsy, antsy-pantsy, ants in one's pants, basket case, up the wall, on pins and needles, jumpy as a cat on a hot tin roof. See ANXIOUS.

FIELD n. bag, cup of tea, long suit, thing, weakness, racket. See OCCUPATION.

FIEND n. hellion, hellcat, little devil. See DEVIL.

FIERCE adj. blowtop, flipped, kill-crazy, ape, gone ape, hitting out in all directions. See VIOLENT.

FIFTY CENTS n. four bits, half a buck, half a rock, silver wing.

FIFTY DOLLARS n. half a C, half a yard, half a bill, half bill.

FIFTY-FIVE MILES PER HOUR doing the fifty-five, double buffalo, double nickel, five-five, honest numbers, pair of fives, pair of nickels, holding in the reins, on the peg.

FIGHT n. squab, brawl, brannigan, brush, brush-off, rumble, roughhouse, dance, donnybrook, flap, gin, hassle, hey rube, rhubarb, hoedown, jump, mix-up, one-two, the old one-two, punch out, duke out, jackpot, jam, run-in, swindle, battle royal, go, a go at each other, knuckle buster, knuckle duster, rowdydow, rowdy-dowdy, row, rumpus, ruction, ruckus, stew, shindy, set-to, scrap, dustup, knock down and drag out fight, bone of contention, bone to pick, fuss, wrangle, beef, blowup, spat, tiff, words, romp, foofaraw, free-for-all, hell broke loose, raise cain, raise sand, shivaree, socdolager, when push comes to shove. See also ARGUMENT, RIOT, BOXING.

FIGHT v. buck, brawl, hassle, scrap, row, kick up a row, come out swinging, roughhouse, romp, slug, put the slug on one, blindside, smack, shuffle, give one a fat lip, put up a fight, put on the gloves, go a couple of rounds, mano a mano, take on, take one on, take a poke, tangle, tangle with, tangle ass with, bump heads with, cross swords with, lock horns with, hook up with, knuckle with, shoot it out with, fly in the face of, fly in the teeth of, stand up to, set to, have at it, go toe to toe, go after each other, go up against, be agin, nix, bang heads, break the news (police), break it up, beat up, mix it up, knock one's brains out, duke, duke it out, put up one's dukes, open up, square up, square off, pitch a bitch, pitch into, sail into, light into, lay into, lay for one, sweat it, tummel, raise

sand, pettifog, put up an argument, break with, you got four feet? (invitation to fight).

FIGHTER n. mug, pug, lug, palooka, heavy, slugger, fancy Dan, punching bag, cauliflower ear, tanker, plug. See PRIZEFIGHTER.

FIGHT FOR v. go to the wall, go to the mat, go after it. See also ATTEMPT.

FIGURE n. shape, build, built, built like brick shithouse, bod, chassis, classy chassis, classy chassy, frame, V-man.

FIGURE v. tote, tote up, tot, tot up, keep tabs, dope out, figure in, figure out, take account of, count heads, count noses, cut ice, cut some ice, run down, work out, get out the sharp pencil.

FIGUREHEAD n. front, front man, stooge, straw boss, straw man, Charlie McCarthy, dummy.

FILAMENT n. string.

FILCH v. boost, hustle, scrounge, swipe, snitch, promote, appropriate, liberate, palm, bag, nick, snipe. See STEAL.

FILE n. charts, shitlist, S list, crap list, sucker list, enemies list, hit list, (punished or ostracized), briar. See DIRECTORY, DOSSIER.

FILIBUSTER n. talkathon.

FILIPINO n. flip (WW II), goo-goo, gugu, gook, moke.

FILL v. jam, jam-pack, pack 'em in, pack like sardines, sardine, stuff, top, top off, paper (The.).

FILLED adj. 1. packed, jammed, jam packed, packed like sardines, sardined, full up. 2. full house, filled to the rafters, standing room only, SRO, sold out; clean, gone clean (The.). 3. stuffed, stuffed to the gills, topped off, lousy with, crumbed up with, crummy with, stiff with, swagged up with, up to here, fit to bust, full as a tick.

FILM n. flick, flickie, movie, talkie, remake, footage, rushes, dailies, porno flick, skin flick, nudie, fuck film (Obsc.), snuff film, slice and dice film, slasher flick (horror). See MOTION PICTURE.

FILM v. lens, roll, shoot, turn, can, put in the can (complete).

FILM CREW n. behind the camera, backlot, stagehands, gaffer, juicer, grip, best boy, props, dresser, lenser.

FILM DIRECTOR n. megger, helmer, A.D. (ass't.)

FILM EXTRA n. Number One (owns own dress suit), penguin, atmosphere.

FILM FESTIVAL n. filmfest, expo.

FILM OPENING n. preem, premier, bow, opener, break in, first run, first round, first outing, first inning, getaway, unloading, unspooling.

FILM PRODUCTION n. package, venture, project, deal.

FILM SHOWING n. screening, unspooling, sneak (unscheduled test preview).

FILM TERMS roll, roll'em (start camera), cut (stop), track, truck, dolly (move), pan (move across), loosen (move camera back), tighten (move closer), zoom back (increase lens angle), zoom in (decrease lens angle), take, wrap, close up, full shot, long shot, establishing shot, two shot, over the shoulder, reverse angle, fade in, fade out, on location, cover (alternate plans), footage, dailies, rushes, key light. See also MOTION PICTURE.

FILTH n. scuz, smut, sleaze, drek, crud.

FILTHY adj. cruddy, crumb, crummy, crusty, grungy, yecchy, scuzzy, sleazy. See DIRTY.

FINAL adj. bottom line, and that was all she wrote, curtains, curtains for, what you see is what you get, last hurrah, swan song, ass end, the end, bitter end. See ULTIMATE.

FINALE n. closer, closing, when the fat lady sings, chaser, end piece, afterpiece, blow-off, button (last note of a musical), payoff, swan song. See also END.

FINALIZE v. ice, put on ice, clinch, clinch the deal. See CONSUMMATE.

FINALLY adv. already, it's about time, long time coming.

FINANCE v. angel, bankroll, grubstake, stake, back, juice, pick up the check, pick up the tab, knock (Bl.), lay on one, loan shark, piece one off, prime the pump, go for, plow back into. See also GIVE.

FINANCEABLE adj. bankable (film, business, etc.).

FINANCIAL ANALYST n. numbers cruncher, bean counter.

FINANCIAL ASSISTANCE n. bailout.

FINANCIAL DISTRICTS n. Wall Street, the street, the curb, Threadneedle Street, LaSalle Street, the Bourse, Lombard Street.

FINANCIER n. the money, the bankroll, angel, backer, sponsor, fat cat, tycoon, butter and egg man, baron, robber baron, the one who signs the checks, meal ticket, sugar daddy, lady bountiful, fairy godmother, Santa Claus, stakeman, staker, grubstaker. See also BUSINESSMAN.

FIND v. hit upon, see the light, stumble on, collar, corral, smoke out, trip over, right under one's nose, dig up, uncover, strike (oil, gold). See DISCOVER.

FIND FAULT v. lint-pick, nit pick, pick apart, henpeck, blow the whistle on, cap on, lay a bad trip on one, rap, bitch bitch bitch, rip, bad-mouth, poor-mouth, trash, find the smoking gun. See CRITCIZE.

FINE adj. aces, gnarly, unreal, cool, wicked, gilt-edged, crack, solid, great, hummer, neato, mean, spiffy, not too shabby. See EXCELLENT.

FINE n. rip.

FINE v. slap with a fine, hit with a fine, walk off fifteen yards, pay through the nose, throw the book at one, dock. See also SENTENCE.

FINESSE n. know-how, savvy, gamesmanship, one-upsmanship, gimmick, grift, racket, con, run around, the big stick.

FINESSE v. angle, finagle, faniggle, jockey, play games, pull strings, pull wires, operate, rig, wangle, wire-pull.

FINEST adj. number one, world class, greatest, hundred proof, baaadest, coolsville, all-time, tops. See BEST. See also EXCELLENT.

FINGER n. claw, fang (musician), feeler, forks, hooks, fish hooks, lunch hooks, meat hooks, pinkie, poppers, stealers.

FINGERPRINT n. dab, print, calling card.

FINGERPRINT v. print.

FINICKY adj. choosey, comma counter, nitpicker, picky, picky picky, ticky, stickler, fussbudget, fusspot, fuddy-duddy, granny, old woman, old maid, pernickety, persnickety. See also PARTICULAR.

FINISH n. wrap, wrap-up, curtain, curtains, end of the line, when the balloon goes up, and that was all she wrote. See END.

FINISH v. wrap, wrap up, wrap it up, bag it, nuke, scrub, scrag, scratch, fold, fold up, wind up, break it up, mop up, round up, sew up, clinch, let up, cool it, tie it up, hang it up, shutter, close, close up, wipe up, wipe out, wash out, punch out, close out, close down, shut down, shoot down, shoot down in flames, wind down, ring down, drop, drop the curtain, pull the plug, pull the big one, drop it, hold it, put the lid on, kick, shake, cap, can, can it, cut, cut the shit, cut the crap, cut loose, cut it out, cut off, cut off one's water, turn off one's water, lay off, blow off, blow over, blow the whistle on, kiss off, sign off, zap, break off, break it off, break it up, call off, call all bets off, call it a day, call it quits, flag one, cold turkey, leave off, finish off, polish off, knock off, knock it off, turn it off, come off, come off it, come to a screeching halt, come to a screaming halt, come to a grinding halt, come to a shuddering halt, button up, clean up, slough a joint, wrap a joint up, get it under one's belt, get on the wagon, head for the barn, in the home stretch, chuck it, pack it in, roll in, put to bed, put the finisher on, put the kibosh on, put a cork in it, put on the brakes, drop anchor, kayo, KO, kill, be in at the kill, tune out, peter out, go the distance, go the route, that's all there is there ain't no more, deal coming down, jell, send one south, get down to the short strokes.

FINISHED adj. a wrap, wrapped up, set, all set, fini, finished up, wound up, washed up, buttoned up, mopped up, cleaned up, tied up, to a T, to a finish, to a frazzle, done to a T, done to a finish, done to a frazzle, done with, home, home free, almost home (nearly), in the bag, nailed down, on ice, open and shut, shot, wiped out, under one's belt, all over but the shouting, pfft, kaput, signed sealed and delivered, when the fat lady sings, when the balloon goes up, yesterday's news. See also ACCOMPLISH.

FIRE n. rapid oxidation, up in smoke, hot spot, crown fire (treetop), fire running (spreading rapidly).

FIRE v. can, kick out, lay off, hand one his walking papers, sack, give the bum's rush, pink slip, give the gate, let one go. See DISCHARGE.

FIREARM n. blaster, piece, iron, rod, snub nose, Saturday night special, equalizer, difference, speaker, persuader, convincer, hardware, tool, widow maker, zip gun, gat, six-shooter. See GUN.

FIRE AT v. blast, gun, zap, hemstitch (machine gun), trigger, pull the trigger, squeeze one off, open up, shoot 'em up, let go with, let fly, throw lead, trade lead, turn on the heat, pop at, take a pop at, turkey shoot (helicopter Vietnam), drop the hammer, fog away, bang away, give 'em both barrels, beat to the draw, get the drop on.

FIRECRACKER n. cherry bomb, dago bomb, golf ball, squib, China cracker (Obs.), torpedo.

FIRED adj. canned, laid off, written off, bounced, axed, pink slipped, got the ax, got the gate. See DIS-CHARGED.

FIREFIGHTER n. fire-eater, smoke-eater, smoke jumper (airborne firefighter), winkie (volunteer), bake head (marine).

FIREFIGHTING TERMS blow up (sudden increase in fire intensity), cover (any vegetative material), crown fire (treetop), fire running (rapidly spreading), hot spot (particularly active area), mop up, slash (debris left after logging or brush cutting).

FIRE HOSE n. spaghetti.

FIREMAN n. smoke-eater, fire-eater, winkie (volunteer), bake head (R. R.).

FIRE STATION n. snake den.

FIRM adj. hang tough, set, dead set on, stand pat, set in concrete, Rock of Gibraltar, Rock of Gib, hard-nosed. See STUBBORN.

FIRM n. megacorp, multinational, plunderbund, bunch, crew, crowd, gang, mob, outfit, ring. See also CORPORATION.

FIRMAMENT n. lid, the blue, the wild blue yonder.

FIRST adj. numero uno, number one, primo, A-number one, lead off, first off, first class, top of the class, top of the list, at the head of the line, right up front, right off the bat.

FIRSTHAND adj. right from the horse's mouth, straight from the horse's mouth.

FISHING SPEAR n. gig.

FIST n. duke, grabbers, hams, paws, bunch of fives, bunch of knuckles, knuckle sandwich, lilly whites, mitts, five-ouncers, club, five of clubs, deuce of clubs.

FIT adj. wrapped tight, click, fit as a fiddle, up to snuff, up to the mark. See WELL. See also ABLE.

FIT n. blow, blow a fuse, blow a gasket, blow one's top, blow one's topper, blow one's stack, shit hemorrhage, wingding, cat fit, conniption, conniption fit, duck fit. See FRENZY.

FITFULLY adv. by bits and pieces, by fits and starts, in dribs and drabs, hit or miss, herky-jerky, right and left. See ERRATICALLY.

FITTING adj. just what the doctor ordered, on the button, on the nose, right on, that's the idea, that's the ticket. See also SUITABLE.

FIVE CENTS n. blip, buffalo, fish scale, flat.

FIVE DOLLARS n. fin, five, fiver, five-case note, five spot, finif.

FIVE HUNDRED DOLLARS n. D, five centuries, five C's, half a G, half a grand, small nickel.

FIVE THOUSAND DOLLARS n. big nickel, five grand, five dollars.

FIX v. 1. fix up, doctor, fiddle with, face lift, retread, debug, redline (Mil.). See also RESTORE. 2. freeze to, stay put, stick like a barnacle, anchor, nail down, put it in concrete.

FIXATION n. hang-up, have a thing about, have on the brain, tiger by the tail, bug up one's ass; case, crush (Rom.); chuck habit, chuck horrors (prison food). See OBSESSION.

FIXED adj. anchored, nailed, locked, locked in, hitched up, hooked up.

FIXER n. doctor, little Miss Fixit, Mr. Fixit, trouble man, troubleshooter, efficiency expert.

FLABBERGASTED adj. blown away, put away, bowled down, bowled over, struck all of a heap, thrown off one's beam ends. See ASTONISHED.

FLABBY adj. out of condition, out of shape, not what one used to be, run to seed, gone to seed, rusty, soft, good and flabby.

FLAG n. Maggie's drawers, Old Glory, red white and blue, Stars and Stripes, Star-Spangled Banner, old Betsy, Jolly Roger. Stars and Bars (Confederate), screamer, monkey flag (Mil.), rag (semaphore), white (surrender), red (danger).

FLAG, FOREIGN n. Maple Leaf (Canada), Tricolor (France), Meatball (Japan), Union Jack (Great Britain).

FLAGELLATION n. fladge.

FLAGRANT adj. flashy, flaming, gross, grody, grody to the max, hanging out, hot shot, spot one like a lead dime, stick out like a sore thumb. See also CONSPICUOUS, GAUDY.

FLAIR adj. dash, zip, glamour, presence, pizzazz, splash, splurge, have a bump for, have plenty on the ball, have something on the ball, shine at, shine in. See TALENTED.

FLAMBOYANT adj. flashy, flaky, jazzy, glamorous, gassy, high falutin, purple, windy, sporting, sporty. See GAUDY.

FLAME n. rapid oxidation.

FLASHLIGHT n. flash, bull's eye, dimmer, glim, shiner.

FLAT adj. blah, draggy, dull as dishwater, ho hum, vanilla, flat as a pancake, leaves one cold, go over like a lead balloon, lay an egg, bombed. See INSIPID.

FLAT n. condo, co-op, crash pad, dommy, pad, joint, walk up, go down (basement), place to lay your head and a few friends. See APARTMENT.

FLAT TIRE n. flat, blowout, puncture.

FLATTER v. stroke, snow, massage, massage one's ego, soft soap, simonize, con, jolly, oil, spread it on, lay it on, lay it on thick, lay it on with a trowel, get around, get next to, play up to, shine up to, make up to, act up to, butter up, soften up, schmeikle (Yid.), sweeten up, sweet talk, loud talk, dialogue one, honey, schmear, rub the right way, work on, work over; brownnose, suck around, suck up to, suck off, suck ass, kiss ass, lick ass (Obsc.), bootlick, boost, pat on the back, build up, toss a bouquet, give a posy, give the man a big cigar, gold star, have to hand it to one, puff up, trade last, TL, blarney, buzz, charm, buck, contract, cream, bagplay, hand one a line, shoot a line, shoot the crap, shoot the bull, sling the bull, sling it, sell, shit, bullshit, pull one's leg, overdo it, string along, kid along, stooge, yes, be a yes-man, fall over, fall all over, fish, play footsie, footsie-wootsie, footsie-footsie, handshake, heel, play Mr. Nice Guy, politic, run after, polish the apple, apple-polish, kowtow, caboodle, buddy up, carpet-bag, curry below the knee.

FLATTERER n. A.K., ass kisser, ass-licker, brownnoser, fart sniffer, yes-man, simonizer, egg sucker, suck off, ear banger. See SYCOPHANT.

FLATTERY n. stroke, strokes, jive, snow, snow job, smoke, baked wind, a line, drip, abreaction route, hogwash, goo, hoke, hokum, hokey-pokey, attaboy, bouquet, posy, shot in the arm, shot in the ass, trade last, TL, sweet talk, sweet nothings, eyewash, soap, soft soap, butter salve, grease, bullshit, con, short con, sell, buildup, crap, schmear, promote, baloney, blarney, bunk, bunko, bunkum, shit, applesauce, balloon juice, oil, snake oil, banana oil, honey, chicken, horse feathers, hot air, malarkey.

FLATULENT adj. farty, fart blossom, gassy, windy, nose closer.

FLAUNT v. flash, sport, grandstand, showcase, streak, let it all hang out, roll out, trot out, break out, whip out, show off, show and tell, hotdog, fan it, wave it around, strut one's stuff, do one's stuff, go through one's paces, parade one's wares, make a scene, put on an act, hit one with, smack with, spring with, play to the gallery, take it big, come the heavy, do the heavy, throw one's weight around, chuck one's weight about.

FLAVOR v. hot it up, pep it up, zip it up, zap it up.

FLAVORFUL adj. delish, yummy, zesty.

FLAVORLESS adj. blah, dull as dishwater, flat, flat as a pancake, ho hum, nothing, pablum, zero, draddy. See BORING.

FLAW n. bug, glitch, wart, catch, catch 22, gremlin, typo, slipup, not come up to scratch.

FLAWED adj. a lemon, rank, glitched, bugged, mucked up, messed up, loused up. See IMPERFECT.

FLEDGLING n. boot, greenhorn, greenie, rookie, tenderfoot. See NOVICE.

FLEE v. split, blow, make tracks, take off, fuck off, scram, amscray, kick off, knock off, jump off, jump, hightail, hotfoot, rabbit-foot, run like a scared rabbit, step on it, step on the gas, cut and run, cut out, skin out, pull out, clear out, crush out, skip, skip out, fade, fade out, fade away, git, get, get git, get the hell out, get while the going is good, get away, make a getaway, make a break for it, make oneself scarce, beat it, dog it, powder, take a powder, take a runout powder, shove, shove off, vamoose, wail, fly the coop, lam, take it on the lam, exfiltrate, hook it, breeze, dust, smoke, spring, head for the hills, go over the wall, cop a mope, duck and run. See also ABSCOND, GO.

FLEECE v. rook, shaft, hose, jerk one around, dick one around, fuck one over, run a game on, flimflam, burn, clip, gyp, take one to the cleaners. See CHEAT.

FLEECED adj. jived, suckered, skinned, set up, been had, been taken, taken for a bundle, clipped, aced out, snookered, shafted. See CHEATED.

FLEET adj. screamin', speedball, barrelling, on the double, in nothing flat, really rolling, like a house on fire, like greased lightning, like a big-assed bird, going like a raped ape. See FAST.

FLEETING adj. flash in the pan.

FLEXIBLE adj. all around, go every which way, one who can do it all, AC/DC, acdac, cosplug, switch hitter, hang loose, roll with the punches, putty in one's hands, fungible.

FLICKERING adj. flicky.

FLIER n. flyboy, jet jockey, airplane driver, birdman, birdwoman, airedale (Navy), barnstormer. See PILOT.

FLIGHT n. 1. hop, jump, helihop. 2. getaway, out, powder, runout powder, break, breakout, fadeout, get, beat, figary, mooch, mope, push, spring, tear away, getaway route, getaway car, absquatulation, exfiltration.

FLIGHT ATTENDANT n. stew, cow pilot, stew zoo (quarters).

FLIGHTY adj. airhead, airedale, bubbleheaded, balloonhead, popcorn, spaz, dingbat, dingdong, ding-a-ling, rattlebrained, harebrained, birdbrained, twit, chowderhead, chickenhead, gaga.

FLIMSY adj. Mickey Mouse, humpty-dumpty, tacky, ticky-tacky, sleazy, gimcracky, cheap jack, harum-scarum, slapdash, rocky, rickety, rinkydink, held together by spit, held together by chewing gum, house of cards, cracker box (house), crappy, from hunger, el cheapo.

FLINCH v. blink.

FLING v. chuck, chunk, fire, heave, lob, peg, pitch, sling, toss.

FLIPPANT adj. flip, fresh, breezy, nervy, sassy, lippy, smart, smart alecky, smart ass, wise ass, brassy, bold as brass. See INSOLENT.

FLIRT n. player, swinger, vamp, operator, man trap, velvet trap, cruiser, gold digger, wolverine.

FLIRT v. hit on, come on, come on to, lead on, make a pass, proposition, make one's move, move in on, pitch, pick up, tease, vamp, flam, gam (Bl.), eyeball, reckless eyeball, give one the eye, make eyes at, make goo-goo eyes at, make bedroom eyes at, bat one's eyes at, come hither, gold dig, look sweet upon, wolf-whistle, lollygag, dilly-dally, drop hairpins (homosexual conversation). See also DALLY.

FLIRTATION n. cruising, pickup, tease, dropping hairpins (homosexual conversation).

FLOAT v. smooth along.

FLOG v. flax, wax, larrup, leather, paddle, whop, whomp, hide, tan one's hide, take it out of one's hide, belt, whip ass, beat the shit out of one. See HIT.

FLOGGING n. licking, larruping, walloping, whaling, lathering, leathering, hiding, tanning, shellacking, waxing, paddling, lumps, get one's lumps, barrel punishment, dressing down, strap oil, hazel oil, hickory oil, birch oil, dose of strap oil, dose of hazel oil, dose of birch oil, dose of hickory oil.

FLOOR n. boards, mat, canvas, deck.

FLOOR SHOW n. meat show, T and A, tits-and-ass show.

FLORIDA Bikini State, Everglade State, Peninsula State, Sunshine State.

FLORIDIAN n. alligator bait.

FLOUNCE v. nancy, swish, camp.

FLOUNDER v. phumpher, go at it ass backwards, bobble, boot, blow, flub, flub the dub, bugger, boo-boo, bugger up, ball up, screw up, foul up, slip up, louse up, bitch, bitch up, muck up, trip up, crack, crack up, piss up, fuck up, snafu, mess up, make a mess of, make a hash of, muff, muff one's cue, miss one's cue, fluff one's lines, foozle, pratfall, brodie, crash, flop, lay an egg, lay a bomb, blow it, blow the gig, drop the ball, put one's foot in one's mouth, put one's foot in it, drop a brick, drop the ball, stub one's toe, trip up, come apart at the seams, get hung up, go to pieces, land on one's ass, fall flat on one's ass, fall flat on one's face, fall down and go boom, bite the dust, lick the dust, be on the skids, stiff, stumble, flummox, flag, flag it, gleek it, come a-cropper, cave in, curdle, blob.

FLOURISH v. hit it big, get ahead, come along, live high on the hog, have one's place in the sun, be on top of the heap, be fat dumb and happy. See SUCCEED.

FLOW v. smooth along.

FLOWERY adj. gassy, purple, windy, high falutin'.

FLUCTUATE v. yo-yo, blow hot and cold, shilly-shally, hem and haw. See VACILLATE.

FLUFF n. dust ball, kittens, pussies, slut's wool.

FLUID n. juice, bug juice, chaser, cooler, dope (heavy such as sauce), goo, goop.

FLUSTER v. adjy, psych, spook, get to, flip, craze, bug, work up, make waves, stir up, discombobulate. See DISTURB. See also CONFUSE.

FLUSTERED adj. flustrated, in a flusteration, in a flustration. unglued, discombobulated, shook up, bugged up, farmisht, fertummeled, thrown, in a tizzy, in a flush, kerflumixed. See DISTURBED. See also CONFUSED.

FLUTE n. whiffer, stick whistle.

FLY v. jet out, jet over, helihop, take a hop, hop, wing, wing out, wing in, sky out, sky in, seagull (N. air travel), hedgehop (low), buzz, drive, drive an airplane, bend the throttle, whoosh, barnstorm, fly by the seat of one's pants, flathat.

FLYER n. flyboy, jet jockey, throttle jockey, skyman, birdman, birdwoman, airedale (Navy), ace, dodo (Stu.). See PILOT.

FOCUS v. home in, home in on, hone in, hone in on, zero in, zero in on, sharpen, sharpen up on, key on, move in, get one's head together, knuckle down, pour it on, skull drag, sweat. See also THINK.

FOE n. oppo, opposish, opposite number, meat, bandit, bad guys, buddy (sarcasm), buddy-buddy, buddy fucker, crip, whose side are you on?, me and you, angries.

FOG n. ground clouds, London fog, soup, pea soup, pea souper, pea-soup fog, smaze, smog, visibility zero zero.

FOGGY adj. fogged in, socked in, closed in, smazy, smoggy, soupy, pea-soupy, ceiling zero, zero zero.

FOIL v. 1. juke, shake, shake off, shuffle off, ditch, give the slip, jump, skip, skip out on, duck, dodge, get around, give the run-around, run circles around, run rings around. 2. queer, crimp, cramp, stymie, crab, hang up, foul up, fuck up, bollix, throw a monkey wrench into the works, upset one's apple cart, spike one's guns. See PREVENT. See also HINDER.

FOILED adj. hung up on, stymied, through the mill, up the wall, faked out, put away, skinned, queered, crabbed, fouled up, fucked up, bollixed up, crimped, cramped, stonewalled, flummoxed, gridlocked. See also DEFLATED.

FOLD v. dog ear.

FOLK SINGER n. folkie.

FOLLOW v. shadow, tail, trail, track, freeze, shag, onto, put a spot on, put a tail on, tail down, tailgate, hot on one's tail, on one's biscuit, on one's can, on one's pratt, on one's keister, on one's quiff (closely), on the prowl for, play catch up, run down, chase, go after, take out after, dog, dog one's heels, stick to, string along, tag after, tag along, shlep along, draft, spook.

FOLLOWER n. buff, fan, hanger-on, ho dad, ho daddy, go in for, go out for, have a go at, plaster, shadow, echo, stooge, flunky, tail. See SUPPORTER. See also DEVOTEE.

FOLLOWING adj. next off. See also LATER.

FOLLY n. dumbo, dumb de dumb dumb dumb, dumb thing to do, dumb trick, fool trick, fool's trick. See also FOOLISHNESS.

FOND adj. soft on, big, big for, crazy for, crazy about, crazy over, lovey-dovey, mushy, nutty about, nutty over, all over one, partial to, heart in the right place.

FONDLE v. stroke, feel out, feel up, cop a feel, grope, grab ass, fool around, paw, play footsie, bear hug, clutch, squeeze.

FOOD n. chow, bite, snack, eats, feed, feedbag, grub, grub pile, groceries, take out, fast food, soul food, ribs, pogey, scoff, scoffings, cakes, go juice, chuck, slop, scuzz food (junk food), chewings, chop, chop chop, chocker, moveable feast, garbage, glop, blue plate, black plate (soul food), pecks, peckings (Bl.), natural, lump, dry lump, handout, set down, sticks to one's ribs, yum, yum-yum, vittles, grubbery, goodies, goonk, goulie, gubbins, grit, home cooking; punk, piss and punk, punk and white wine, gooby, chick (prison); peelings, swag, short order.

FOOD, CANNED n. flipper, springer, sweller (spoiled).

FOOL n. dork, asshole, ditz, loser, winner, yo-yo, dingbat, out to lunch, lunchie, nobody home, jerk off, dodo, ninny, airedale, airhead, balloonhead, doesn't know from A to B, turkey, semolia (Bl.), schlemiel, half-baked. See STUPID.

FOOL v. kid, fox, outfox, put on, jive, spoof, juke, deek, suck in, scam, con, snow, diddle, fake out, pull a fast one, spoof, hornswoggle, put something over, put something across, slip one over on. See TRICK.

FOOLED adj. foxed, outfoxed, deeked, snowed, conned, jerked, jerked around, fucked over, sucked in, bamboozled, hornswoggled, flimflammed. See TRICKED.

FOOLHARDY adj. leave oneself wide open, go off the deep end, buy a pig in a poke, go out on a limb, devil-may-care. See CARELESS.

FOOLISH adj. screwloose, jerky, nerdy, squirrelly, harebrained, scatterbrained, rattlebrained, lamebrained, birdbrained, cockeyed, dingy, dingy-dingy, weak in the upper story, goopy, flaky, kooky, dippy, punchy, punch-drunk, slappy, slaphappy, whip silly, bubbleheaded, foolheaded, goofus, gump, horse's ass, horse's collar, horse's neck, horse's tail, Mickey Mouse, sappy, screwy, schlemiel, schloomp, schlub, shmendrick, shmoe, schnooky.

FOOLISHNESS n. dumb trick, fool trick, fool's trick, meatballism, poppycock, tommyrot, narrishkeit, fiddlesticks, twaddle, stuff and nonsense, bushwa, bushwah, booshwah, cheese, a line of cheese, claptrap, caca, cahcah, total cahcah, fiddle-faddle, flamdoodle, flapdoodle, balloon juice, horsefeathers, fudge. See also NONSENSE.

FOOT INSPECTION n. dog show (WW II).

FOOTBALL n. leather, pigskin, oval, pumpkin.

FOOTBALL KICK n. boot, hang time, coffin corner (out of bounds inside the five-yard line).

FOOTBALL PASS v. go up on top, take to the air, go to the air, go upstairs, go long, bomb (long), Hail Mary (a desperation, long pass attempt to score), hook, jump pass, loop, looper, pitch out, pop (short pass), safety valve (short pass option), pump (feint), slant in, thread the needle (between defensive players), aerial, blind pass (without looking), button hook, comeback, comebacker, circle, circle pass, flare, down and in, down and out, right on the numbers, right on the money, rainbow (high arc), dump it off, dump off to, unload (get rid of the ball), complete, completion, incomplete, incompletion; pick, pick off (interception), intercept, interception.

FOOTBALL PLAYER n. gridder, beefer, all pro, all star (honors), front line, suicide squad, scatback (ground gainer), scrambler, tailback (backfield), flankerback, nose guard, cornerman, rusher, ground gainer, runner up, booter (kicker), monster, monster back, blitzer (linebacker), jitterbug (defensive back), safety man, reserve (substitute).

FOOTBALL PLAYS ground game, running game, smashball, smashgut, up the gut (through the center), flying wedge, fire out (fast move off the ball), hand off, hit the hole; hold, held (they held them from scoring); long gainer, muff, fumble, naked reverse, fake, fake out, razzle-dazzle, fleaflicker (complex play), boomerooski (trick play), juke (feint), cut back, cut block, run to daylight (any opening), run double posts, run double corners, wide open, drive (consecutive successful plays), shotgun, wishbone, wishbone T, fade away (quarterback move), rollout (quarterback move sideways to pass), slant, belly back (ball carrier feint), belly series, Statue of Liberty play, sweep (a sweep around left) bootleg, break it (long gain), bump and run, carry, scramble (quarterback ball carry), eat the ball (quarterback has no option but to be tackled), cough up (lose ball during play), turnover (lose possession of the ball); dog, red dog, blitz, blow in, check, chicken fight (repeated blocks), jam, nickel defense, read (he read the hand off), safety blitz (by safetyman), shut down (they shut down the offense), shut off, (they shut off the short gain).

FOOTBALL RULES gridiron lawyer, chain (ten-yard measure), chain gang (officials positioning chain), clip (illegal block), crackback (blindside block, illegal), necessary line (gain needed for first down).

FOOTBALL SCORE take it over, take it in, all the way, go all the way, go coast to coast (goal to goal), burn, convert, a conversion, safety, sit on a lead, sit on the ball, yardage.

FOOTBALL SIGNALS call, the call, check off (change the call), audible, automatic (both substitute play call), hike (start).

FOOTBALL TACKLE dump, sack (tackle the quarterback); bring down, nail, shoot the gap (get through to tackle), clip, clothesline, horse collar, schmear, crawling (trying for more yardage after tackle, illegal).

FOOTBALL TERMS grid, gridiron, eleven, huddle, squad, taxi squad, bomb squad, suicide squad, kamikaze corps (special teams), flat (both sides behind the line), front four, red shirts (ineligible players), the pits (line of scrimmage), in the trenches (the line), wide open, bust it wide open, break it, break it open, the pocket (quarterback zone), snap, squib (outside kick), spike (he danced under the goal posts then spiked the ball), straightarm, uprights, grind out (ground play); put it on the ground, put it on the carpet (fumble); whistle down, whistle dead (end the play by a whistle); hear footsteps (distraction, expecting a tackle), kill the clock (timeout), playing a catch-up ball, run out the clock (stall), eat the clock, nutcracker (rough practice), skull practice, chalk talk (lecture session), grandstand quarterback, Monday morning quarterback.

FOOTLIGHTS n. foots.

FOOTWEAR n. clodhoppers, canal boats, gunboats, barkers, earth pads, ground grabbers, clunkers, bottoms. See SHOES.

FOP n. dude, flash, sport, swell, toff, snappy dresser, clotheshorse, Beau Brummel, Dapper Dan, macaroni.

FOR prep. pro.

FORBEARING adj. be big, live with, soft shell, go easy on, go easy with.

FORBID v. cool, cool out, block, hog-tie, stymie, hang up, hold up, lock up, put the chill on, spike, ding, zing, nix, cut off one's water, shut down, freeze. See PROHIBIT.

FORBIDDEN adj. no no, outta bounds, off limits, closed, closed down, closed up.

FORBIDDING adj. hard-boiled, tough. See also UGLY.

FORCE n. 1. pow, sock, the force, beef, clout, punch, steam, the stuff, what it takes, full head of steam, an 800 pound gorilla. See POWER. See also COERCION. 2. shop, crew, troops, soldiers, horses.

FORCE v. pressure, high pressure, strongarm, twist one's arm, arm-twist, lean against, lean on, lean on it, hassle, push around, squeeze, put the squeeze on, put the screws to, put the screws on, put the chill on, put the arm on, put the heat on, put the scare on, gueril, put the gueril on, make it hot, walk heavy, crock down, clamp down, ram down one's throat, cram down one's throat, railroad, railroad through, steamroll, steamroller, roll over, bull in, bulldoze, muscle in, muscle out, take care of, throw one's weight around, throw a scare into, turn on the heat, make one an offer one can't refuse, sweat one, sweat it, rough up, roughhouse, move in on, chisel in, dump on, horn in, pour it on, go to town on, boost, work on, egg on, nag, jawbone, showboat, jackboat, bear down, bear down on it, put one's back into it, come at it from all sides.

FORCEFUL adj. got the horses to do it, hoss, strong as an ox, bull, powerhouse, punch, go-getter, go-go, ball of fire, steamroller, punchy, gutsy, come on strong, take over, take charge. See POWERFUL.

FORCEFULLY adv. by storm, slam-bang, turn on the heat, all out, full tilt, full bore, in full swing, like gangbusters.

FORD CAR n. lizzie, tin lizzie, tin can, Model T, flying bedstead (1920), Henry, spider, sardine box, T-bone, Model A, deuce (1932).

FOREBODING n. vibes (good or bad), feel in one's bone, funny feeling, sinking feeling, wind change, handwriting on the wall, next week East Lynne. See PREMONITION.

FORECAST v. figure, figger, figger out, figure out, dope, dope out, call the turn, in the cards, it's looking to, telegraph, see it coming, see it in the stars. See PREDICT.

FOREFRONT n. 1. state of the art, leading edge, cutting edge. See also NEW. 2. on the line, in the thick of it, in the trenches.

FOREIGN adj. offshore.

FOREIGN CURRENCY n. P, pee, pea (pesos, piasters, etc.).

FOREIGNER n. greenhorn, furriner, FOB, (fresh off the boat); wetback, ginzo, guinzo, gringo, goum, greaseball, jaboney, jibone (all Derog.). See also ALIEN.

FOREKNOWLEDGE n. ESP, sixth sense.

FOREMAN n. head, headman, honcho, head honcho, Big Brother, boss, bosshead, pit boss, straw boss, gaffer, bull, bull of the woods, pusher, slave driver. See also EXECUTIVE.

FOREMOST adj. A-1, A-number 1, A per se, A1, number one, numero uno, primo, chief, hot stuff, hotshot, hotdog, hot shit, hot flash, hooper-dooper, the force, at the cutting edge, at the leading edge, heavy, heavyweight, heavy stuff, we're not talking about nutmeg here. See BEST.

FOREPLAY n. cat, tomcat, charge, chase, cruise, dark setting (Bl.), hit on, footsie, footsie-wootsie, fun and games, neck, pet, pitch woo, fling woo, spoon, smooch, eat face, tease, cock tease, cop, cop a feel, feel, feel-up, bush patrol, muff dive, butterfly kiss, boodle, finger fuck, canoe, dry hump, group grope, get one's buns warmed. See AMOROUS PLAY.

FORESEE v. crystal ball it, call the turn, dope out, psych it out, have a hunch, see it coming. See PREDICT.

FORESEEN adj. as advertised, no big surprise, it's what always happens, true to form, saw it coming, the handwriting was on the wall, it was in the cards, be just like one, be one all over, not put it past.

FORESHADOW v. telegraph, in the wind, the handwriting on the wall.

FORESKIN n. lace curtains (homosexual).

FOREST n. big sticks.

FORESTALL v. cut 'em off at the pass, throw cold water on, spike one's guns, upset one's apple cart, knock the props from under one. See PREVENT.

FORETELL v. call it, call the turn, read, dope, dope out, figure, figure out, psych it out, crystal ball it, make book, it's looking to, see it coming. See PREDICT.

FORETOLD adj. saw it coming, the handwriting was on the wall, as advertised, no big surprise, it's what always happens, true to form. See FORESEEN.

FOREVER adv. for keeps, till hell freezes over, till the cows come home, till you're blue in the face, when the donkey flies, since God was young, since the year one, since Hector was a pup. See ALWAYS.

FOREWARN v. tip, tip off, flag, wave a red flag, telegraph, cloud up, smell a rat, give the high sign, pull one's coat, put one wise, put a bug in one's ear, put a flea in one's ear.

FOREWARNING n. hunch, vibes (good or bad), vibrations, feel in one's bones, funny feeling, sinking feeling, tip off, handwriting on the wall.

FORGE v. make like, fake, scratch, gammon, pirate, hoke, hoke up, phony up. See also COUNTERFEIT.

FORGE AHEAD v. plow ahead.

FORGED adj. phony, queer, pirate goods, pirate labels, fake, hokey, ersatz, scratch, bouncer, funny, funny paper, sour paper, hot paper, not what it's cracked up to be.

FORGED CHECKS, PASS v. bounce, bounce bum paper, bounce sour paper, hang paper, lay paper, lay sour paper, fly kites, hit one with, stiff, smash a stiff, push a stiff, push kites, push paper, smack with.

FORGED CHECKS, PASSER OF n. paper-hanger, paper layer, paper pusher, sheet passer, shover, bill poster, butterfly man, kiteman.

FORGER n. penman, scratcher, scratch man, one of a scratch mob, bill poster, cobbler, shoe (also passports). See COUNTERFEITER.

FORGERY n. carbon, carbon copy, look alike, work alike, not what it's cracked up to be, twin. See also COUNTERFEIT.

FORGERY, CRIMINAL CHARGE OF n. paper-hanging fall, scratch rap.

FORGET v. draw a blank, blow up, go up, go dry, balloon, clean forget, disremember, disrecollect, punt [someone or something] off, blow one's lines (The.).

FORGETFUL adj. out to lunch, popcorn headed, airheaded, absentminded professor, mooning, moony, pipe dreaming, woolgathering, goofing off, not on the job, asleep on the job, asleep at the switch, looking out the window, sloppy, would lose one's head if it wasn't tied on.

FORGETFULNESS n. blackout, block out, blow, blow a line (The.), don't know if one's comin' or goin', go blank, lose one's marbles, brain fade.

FORGIVE v. let off, let it go, let up on, let one off this time, let one off easy, wink at, blink at, write off, whitewash, launder, sanitize, bleach, clear, wipe it off, wipe the slate clean, go easy on, bury the hatchet, lifeboat, hand out clemo, commute, spring. See also CONCILIATE.

FORGIVEN adj. let off, let go, in from the cold.

FORGIVING adj. big, be big, live with. See COMPASSIONATE.

FORGO v. pass, pass on, pass up, sit out, swear off, take the oath, take the cure, go on the wagon, pack in, give in, give up. See ABSTAIN.

FORGOTTEN v. 1. disremembered, disrecollected, draw a blank, clean forgot, clean forgotten, slipped one's mind, slipped between the cracks, fell between the cracks. 2. blown over, gone glimmering. See also PAST.

FORK n. spear.

FORLORN adj. godforsaken, destroyed, draggin' ass, down and out, in the dumps, blue, got the blue devils. See UNHAPPY.

FORM n. 1. sked, by the book, by the numbers, layout, setup, boilerplate, channels, ropes. 2. build, built, built like brick shit house, V-man, tuna. See BODY.

FORM v. whomp up, cook up, dream up, throw up, throw together, bring together, fudge together, knock together, knock out, knock off, dash off, pull off, polish off, come through, mount (The.).

FORMAL adj. stiff, straight arrow, squaresville, by the numbers, playing their game, stuffy. See CONVENTIONAL.

FORMAL ATTIRE n. formal, tux, tails, hammertails, white tie, white tie and tails, bib and tucker, boiled shirt, soup n' fish, monkey suit.

FORMALITIES n. p's and q's, honors.

FORMER adj. ex, X, one time.

FORMERLY adv. away back, back, back when, one shot, time was, olden days, water under the bridge, water over the dam, down memory lane, when Hector was a pup, when one was knee high to a grasshopper.

FORMIDABLE adj. hairy, murder, pisser, rough go, bitch, tough proposition, tall order, ballbuster. See DIFFICULT.

FORMLESS adj. baggy, blobby.

FORNICATE v. fuck, screw, lay, hump, ball, bang, boff, dork, go the limit, get in, get it on, get some, get one's ashes hauled, get one's end wet, get laid, get it off together, jump on one's bones, have one's ticket punched, trim, make out, put out (Female), go all the way (all Obsc.). See SEXUAL INTERCOURSE.

FORNICATION n. fuck, jazz, screw, lay, hump, boff, poke, bang, action, balling, parallel parking, fooling around, dork, jiggle, the dirty deed (all Obsc.). See SEXUAL INTERCOURSE.

FORSAKE v. take the oath, give up, drift away, kiss good-bye, wash one's hands of, change one's tune, change one's song, walk out on, run out on, leave flat, leave high and dry, leave holding the bag. See ABANDON.

FORSAKEN adj. godforsaken, thrown over, left in the lurch, left at the church.

FORT LAUDERDALE, FLORIDA Beach City, Fort Liquordale, Spring Break.

FORTHRIGHT adj. up front, open, real people, like it is, no lie, straight shit, call a spade a spade. See SINCERE.

FORTHRIGHTLY adv. level, deal level, on the level, right up front, put it on the line, lay it on the line, straight, straight from the shoulder, talk turkey.

FORTIFY v. beef up, soup up, charge up, punch up, heat up, hot up, hop up, jazz up, juice up, build up, step up, pour it on, add fuel to the fire, needle, spike (drink).

FORTITUDE n. balls, guts, gutsiness, heart, nerve, stomach, grit, true grit, spunk, backbone, moxie, starch, clock, corazon, intestinal fortitude, hanging in there, staying power, what it takes; bottled courage, Dutch courage (intoxicated).

FORTUITOUS adj. fluke, lucky dog, luck in, luck out, fall into the shithouse and come up with a five-dollar gold piece. See LUCKY.

FORTUNATE adj. hot, hot hand, on a roll, luck in, luck out, get the breaks, hold aces, strike it lucky, all systems go. See LUCKY.

FORTUNE n. 1. break, shot, whack, stab, fighting chance, fifty-fifty, toss up, flier. 2. karma, kismet, in the cards, the roll of the dice, that's the way the ball bounces, that's the way the cookie crumbles, everything's coming up roses, Dame Fortune. 3. scratch, lucky hit, lucky break, good break, run of luck, streak of luck, lucked out, luck into, hot, fluke, mazel (Yid.), mazeltov (good). See LUCK.

FORTUNE TELLER n. mitt reader.

FORWARD adj. ballsy, pushy, fresh, nervy, smart ass, wise ass, brassy, come on strong. See AGGRESSIVE.

FORT WORTH, TEXAS Cow Town.

FOUL adj. 1. icky, yecchy, yucky, barfy, vomity, stinking, skank, raunchy, chili bowl (person), pigpen, barn, stable. See DIRTY. 2. below the belt, not cricket, raw deal.

FOULED UP adj. fucked, fucked up, all fucked up, snafu (situation normal all fouled up), commfu (complete monumental military foul-up), fubar (fouled up beyond all recognition), fumtu (fouled up more than usual), fubb (fouled up beyond belief), janfu (joint army navy foul-up), jaafu (joint Anglo American foul-up), jacfu (joint American Chinese foul up), nabu (nonadjusting ball-up), tarfu (things are really fouled up), tuifu (the ultimate in foul-ups), sapfu (surpassing all previous foul-ups), susfu (situation unchanged still fouled up).

FOUND v. father, ring in, start up, start the ball rolling, get going. See also BEGIN.

FOUNDATION n. bottom line, rock bottom, ABC's, brass tacks, get down, get down to brass tacks, nittygritty, nuts and bolts, groceries, guts, meat and potatoes, beginners, coal and ice, at heart, nub, bred in the bone, dyed in the wool.

FOUNDLING n. drop, fetch, guttersnipe, mudlark, rustle.

FOUNTAIN PEN n. stick, ball point.

FOUNTAINHEAD n. horse's mouth, connection, tipster, tout.

FOUR OF CLUBS n. bedpost, devils's bedpost.

FOUR-WHEEL DRIVE TRUCK n. four by four, four-wheel drive.

FOWL n. banty, biddy, birdie, boid, chick, chickabiddy, chickadee, chicky.

FOYER n. squat pad.

FRACAS n. brawl, row, rumpus, flap, hassle, mix up, run in, rhubarb, ruckus, stew. See ARGUMENT.

FRACTION n. piece, bite, cut, slice, chunk, lion's share, bigger half, big end, halver, fifty-fifty, even-steven. See also SHARE.

FRACTIOUS adj. bitchy, cussed, mean, ornery, tetchy, thin-skinned, scrappy. See IRRITABLE.

FRAGMENT n. 1. hunk, gob, lump, smithereen, bite, cut, slice, chunk. 2. rake-off, lion's share, bigger half, big end, halver, fifty-fifty, even-steven, piece of the pie, slice of the melon, slice of the pie. See SHARE.

FRAGRANCE n. smell well, smell good.

FRAIL adj. 1. weak sister, wishy-washy, wimpy, sad sack, fish, poor fish, rocky, don't have the horses, what the cat dragged in. See WEAK. 2. humpty-dumpty, sleazy, tacky, ticky-tacky, rickety, rinkydink, held together by spit, held together by chewing gum, house of cards. See FLIMSY.

FRAME n. cage, Mr. Bones.

FRANK adj. up front, right up front, open, mellow, real, real people, the real goods, like it is, call it like it is, lay it on the line, on the level, on the up and up, come-at-able, straight, shoot straight, straight dope, the emess, no lie, straight from the shoulder, straight out, straight arrow, straight shit, true blue, talk like a Dutch uncle, call a spade a spade, put all one's cards on the table, make no bones about it, fly right, talk turkey. See also SINCERE.

FRANKFURTER n. frank, hot dog, hot dawg, weenie, tube steak, balloon, beenie, bowwow, bun pup, Coney Island pup, pimp stick, puppy, footlong special.

FRANKLY adv. level, dead level, on the level, dead on the level, put it on the line, lay it on the line, straight, straight from the shoulder, talk turkey.

FRANTIC adj. hyper, unglued, unzipped, unscrewed, gone, real gone, high, mad, wild, wicked, weird, weirded out, far out, out, wigged out, hot, hot and bothered, hot under the collar, spazzed out, having a spazz attack, flipped out, freaked out, zonkers, wired, wired up, keyed up, all keyed up, shook up, all shook up, steamed up, fired up, get all worked up, turned on, in a stew, in a sweat, in a tizzy, in a panic, in a dither, in a lather, in a swivet, in a foofaraw, in a pucker, crazy, like crazy, like mad, hit the ceiling, shit in one's pants, have a fit, have kittens, cast a kitten, go up in the air, mind-blowing, mind-bending.

FRATERNITY n. frat, Greeks, house.

FRATERNITY HOUSE n. house, frat house, animal house, hut, tong.

FRATERNITY MEMBER n. brother, frater, Greek, legacy, pheeze, feeze (join), pledge (pending acceptance).

FRATERNIZE v. mix, take down one's hair, break the ice, loosen up, warm up, open up, gang up, pal up, pal around, hang around with, tie up with, get with, run with, chum with, chum together, make the rounds, floss around.

FRAUD n. 1. gyp, crook, con man, mechanic, four-flusher, phoney, double-dealer, shark, horse trader, cheese eater, skunker, hoser; one had a pony, one used an airplane, equestrian (test cheating). See CHEATER. See also COUNTERFEIT. 2. hustle, con, sting, flimflam, scam, pseud, fast shuffle, fast one, claptrap, line of cheese, borax, song, song and dance, string, smoke, tripe, vanilla, bitch, skunk, cake cutter (circus), hanky-panky, hocus-pocus, hugger-muggery, graft, grift, autograph, kiting checks, bucket shop, boiler room, Carrie Watsons, the engineer's daughter, double trays, dipsy doodle, shenanigans, monkeyshines, monkey business, funny business; limb, shit kicker, tap, tap game (advertising). See SWINDLER.

FREAK n. geek (circus).

FRECKLE n. daisy.

FREE adj. 1. comp, freebie, free ride, for free, for nothing, for love, do it for one's health, twofer, Annie Oakley, paper, paper the house, on the house, on the cuff, cuffo, on the arm, on the ice, hummer, free lunch (seems free but isn't), handout. 2. free-wheeling, on one's own, couldn't care less, don't give a damm, shoot the moon, fly kites, flake, free-spirited, break loose, cut loose, loose wig, down, get down, let down one's hair, go to town, up front, all hanging out, far out, stretched out. 3. freeloader, schnorrer, deadhead, skip out.

FREE v. let go, let off, let off the hook, kiss off, blow one off, spring, turn out, get a floater, get hours, get a twenty-four, put on the pavement, put on the sidewalk, put on the street, put on the bricks, bail one out, get out from under, save one's bacon, save one's neck. See also ABSOLVE.

FREED adj. out, back on the street, beat the rap, walked, let off, let go.

FREEDOM n. run, run of, free run of.

FREE PERIOD n. float (no class, Stu.).

FREE TICKET n. freebie, free ride, pass, free pass, comp, Annie Oakley, chit, paper, twofer, pigeon.

FREE TIME n. off hours, goof-off time, one's own sweet time, time to burn, time to kill.

FREE WILL n. own hook, say so, own say so, own sweet way.

FREEZING adj. freeze one's balls off, freeze one's ass off, freeze one's tits off, snappy, one-dog night, two-dog night, etc. See COLD.

FREIGHTER n. crock, tub, rust bucket, tramp.

FRENCH n. frog, Froggy, frog eater, tadpole (child), Frenchy.

FRENCH CANADIAN n. Canuck, Pepsi.

FRENCH FRIED POTATOES n. fries, shoestrings, matchsticks, steak fries, chips, f.f., fr. f.

FRENCH HORN n. peck horn, pretzel.

FRENETIC adj. hyper, unglued, unscrewed, weirded out, wigged out, spazzed out, having a spazz attack, wired, wired up, in a lather. See FRANTIC.

FRENZY n. blow, blow a fuse, blow a gasket, blow one's top, blow one's topper, blow one's cap, blow one's stack, blow one's cork, blow on's wig, blow one's noggin, blow one's roof, blow one's lump, flip one's lid, cat fit, conniption, conniption fit, duck fit, shit hemorrhage, hell broke loose, all hell broke loose, every which way but up, free for all, rumpus, ruckus, ruction, dithers, all-overs, flap, fuss, lather, needles, stew, to do, zingers, fuzzbuzz (commotion), fuzzbuzzy, haroosh, foofaraw, fofarraw, wingding, rowdydow, stir, row, rumble.

FREQUENT v. hang, hang out at, hang around, hang about, haunt, drop in, hit, play, give a play.

FRESH adj. mint, cherry, comer, now, the latest, state of the art, brand new, newie, just out, what's happening, what's in. See NEW.

FRESHMAN n. frosh, fresh, freshie, fish, crab, dog, frog, fox, green pea, redhead, hound, plebe (1920s); Mister Ducrot, Mister Dumbjohn, Mister Dumbguard (West Point), doolie, Mister Doolie (A.F. Acad.).

FRET v. bleed, take on, eat one's heart out, stew, get into a stew, carry a heavy load, hassle, something is eating at one, something is beating down on one, get into a dither, work oneself into a lather, work oneself into a sweat, sweat it out.

FRETFUL adj. mean, ornery, crabby, cranky, grouchy, Mr. Coffee Nerves, wreck, got up on the wrong side of the bed. See PETULANT.

FRICTION n. bone to pick, flak, hassle, rhubarb, row, ruckus, rumpus, ruction, set-to, bad vibes, clinker, sour note. See DISCORD.

FRIDAY n. four and one, T.G.I.F., getaway day, fish day.

FRIED EGGS n. over, over easy, sunny side up.

FRIEND n. amigo, brother, little brother, sister, buddy, bosom buddy, buddy boy, buddyroo, good buddy, asshole buddy, chum buddy, chum, roomey, roommate, pard, pardner, partner, ace, spare, main man, main squeeze (girl), hamma (girl), family, fella, B.F. guy, mellow (close), old man, old boy, cousin, kissing cousin, playmate, mate, matie, pal, sidekick, sidekicker, better half, Billy, captain, compadre, goombah, cut dub (reformatory), Jack, Jack at a pinch, lightning, go way back, cobber, bodo (1920).

FRIENDLY adj. buddy-buddy, get buddy-buddy, clubby, chummy, mellow, tight, pally, palsy-walsy, cozy, cuchala-muchala, right nice, right neighborly, downright neighborly, white, regular, square shooter, sucking around, kissy-kissy, kissing counsins, kissing up to, mix, get together, get with it, break the ice, let down one's hair, trade spit, swap spit, roommates, living in each other's pockets, sleepin' together, making it with.

FRIGHTEN v. spook, chill, chill off, put the chill on, scare shitless, scare stiff, scare the pants off, scare hell out of, scare the shit out of, scare silly, scare the bejesus out of, scare to death, throw a scare into, give one a turn, make one shit in one's pants, make one jump a mile, make one jump out of his skin, strike all of a heap, bowl down, bowl over, buffalo, bulldoze, chicken out, enforce, lean on, lean against, push around, whip one around (intellectually), showboat, walk heavy, put on the arm, put on the muscle, put the heat on, turn on the heat, put one through the wringer, bad eye, cuff, hang tough, goose, link back. See also STARTLE.

FRIGHTENED adj. uptight, hung up, clutched up, yellow, yellow-bellied, with a yellow streak, a yellow streak down one a yard wide, yellow streak down one's back, yellow stripe down one's back, have cold feet, have a fit, have kittens, 'fraidy cat, scaredy cat, run scared, scared stiff, scared witless, scared spitless, scared shitless, shit, crap out, shit in one's pants, fudge one's pants, fudge one's undies, pee in one's pants, piss in one's pants, push the panic button, jittery, jumpy, shaky, shivery, quivery, in a dither, in a sweat, in a cold sweat, have butterflies in one's stomach, have the willies, spooked, frozen, goose bumpy, wimpy, rabbity, mousy, jellyfish, chicken, chicken out, chicken-hearted, pigeonhearted, chicken-livered, white-livered, lily-livered, milk-livered, milksop, Milquetoast, Casper Milquetoast, weak-kneed, weak sister, sissy, baby, big baby, nebbish, candy ass, pucker, pucker-assed, asshole puckerin', asshole suckin' wind, pecker-assed, gutless, shake in one's boots, ague, creeps, heebie-jeebies, leaping heebies, the jams, the jims, the jimjams, jumped a mile, jumped out of one's skin, give a jolt, bowled down, bowled over, struck all of a heap, D and D (deaf and dumb, afraid to testify), punk out, on the ragged edge.

FRIGHTENING adj. hairy, furry, hair-raising, scary, spooky, grabber, chiller. See also STARTLING.

FRIGID adj. 1. colder'n a witch's tit, colder than a well digger's ass, freeze one's ass off, snappy, three-dog night, icebox (place). 2. cold, cold tit, cold shoulder, tight-assed, butter wouldn't melt in his mouth, frosty, cool. See COLD.

FRIGIDAIRE n. fridge, ice box.

FRILLS n. gingerbread, bells and whistles, fuss, gewgaws, gimcracks, garbage (food), dingbat, doodad, thing, fandangle, jazz, seagoing (large, absurd).

FRINGE BENEFITS n. fringes, perks, golden parachute.

FRISKY adj. feeling one's oats, full of beans, full of piss and vinegar, full of ginger, goosy, trigger happy, jumpy, peppy, zippy. See SPIRITED.

FRITTER AWAY v. piss away, diddle away, run through, go through, blow, throw money around, pump up (gambling). See DISSIPATE.

FROG n. Dutch nightingale.

FROLIC v. let loose, cut loose, let go, go on a tear, go places and do things, fool around, kick up one's heels, whoop it up, raise hell. See REVEL.

FRONT n. put-on, false front, fake, phony.

FRONT PORCH n. stoop.

FRONT ROW n. bald-headed row.

FROWN n. dirty look, bad eye.

FROWN v. burn, burn up, do a slow burn, look daggers, give one a whammy, give one a dirty look, give one the evil eye, dog eye, bad eye, act the lion tamer, make a kisser, cloud up and rain on one.

FRUGAL adj. tight, tightwad, Scotch, nickel-nurser, penny-pincher, bog pocket, last of the big spenders. See STINGY.

FRUITLESS adj. wild goose chase, spinning one's wheels. See USELESS.

FRUIT PICKER n. apple knocker, wetback, bracero.

FRUSTRATE v. crimp, cramp, cramp one's style, stymie, hang up, hold up, foul up, stump, give the run around. See HINDER.

FRUSTRATED adj. hung up on, stymied, through the mill, up the wall, faked out, put away, skinned, queered, crabbed, fouled up, fucked up, bollixed up, crimped, cramped, stonewalled, flummoxed. See also DEFEATED.

FRUSTRATION n. letdown, setback, the old one-two, bitter pill, bitter pill to swallow, bummer, downer, drag, fizzle. See also HINDRANCE, DISAPPOINTED.

FRYING PAN n. spider.

FUEL n. alky, go juice, juice, motion lotion, motion potion, soup, synfuel (synthetic), diesel juice.

FUEL v. fill 'er up, gas 'er up, shoot 'em up.

FUEL ADDITIVE n. juice, pop.

FUGITIVE adj. hot, lammister, on the lam, wanted, have small pox.

FUGITIVE-WANTED POSTER n. dodger, general, mugg on the board, reader, reader with a tail.

FULFILL v. fill the bill, hit the bull's-eye, score, be just the ticket, get one's jollies, get one's kicks, make the grade, make it. See SATISFY.

FULFILLMENT n. you got it, just name it, get off, get off on, kick, kicks, sure shock, just the ticket, just what the doctor ordered.

FULL adj. packed, jammed, jam-packed, filled to the rafters, full up, full as a tick, full house, standing room only, SRO, sold out; clean, gone clean (The.); stuffed, stuffed to the gills, topped off, lousy with, crumbed up with, crummy with, stiff with, swagged up with, up to here, fit to bust, packed like sardines, sardined. See also SATIATED.

FULLY adv. all the way, all out, royal, from A to Z, from soup to nuts. See COMPLETELY.

FUMBLE v. phumpher, fluff, flub, couldn't get a handle on it, lost the handle. See ERR.

FUN n. ball, laughs, lots of laughs, fun and games, grins, get some grins, just for grins, high old time, picnic, field day. See AMUSEMENT. See also ENTERTAIN-MENT.

FUNCTION v. move, make one's move, do one's thing, go to town, TCB (take care of business), get with it, shit or get off the pot, percolate, cook, operate. See ACT.

FUNCTIONARY n. paper shuffler, buck passer, apparatchik, empty suit, lifer (Army), oink (police).

FUNCTIONING adj. hot, on track, on stream, on line, in place, going, a going concern, hit the ground running, percolating, ticking, clicking, in full swing, doing one's thing.

FUND v. angel, bankroll, grubstake, stake, back, juice, pick up the check, pick up the tab, knock (Bl.), lay on one, loan shark, piece one off, prime the pump. See FINANCE. See also GIVE.

FUNDAMENTAL adj. bottom line, coal and ice, cold turkey, meat and potatoes, nitty-gritty, nub, primo, name of the game, where it's at. See BASIC.

FUNDAMENTALS n. ABC's, brass tacks, get down, get down to brass tacks, nitty-gritty, nuts and bolts, groceries, guts, meat and potatoes, beginners, coal and ice, bottom line, rock bottom, at heart, bred in the bone, dyed in the wool. See also BASICS.

FUNDS n. bankroll, nut, backing, budget, kitty, nest egg, stakes, pork barrel, public crib, public till, public trough, rainmaker (fund-raiser). See also ASSETS.

FUNERAL n. cold meat party, planting, deep six (sea).

FUNERAL WAGON n. Black Maria, bone box, dead wagon, glass wagon, meat wagon, last ride.

FUNNEL n. Charley Noble, Charlie Noble (ship).

FUNNY adj. gas, jokey, yokky, for grins, had 'em in the aisles, hooper-dooper, hysterical, a scream, a zetser, laffer, knee-slapper, riot, laugh riot, humdinger, priceless, too funny for words. See AMUSING.

FUR n. dried barkers, skins, skin joint (shop).

FURBELOW n. bells and whistles, fuss, gewgaws, frou-frou, gingerbread, dingbat, doodad, thing, fandangle, jazz.

FURBISH v. doll up, gussy up, fix up, spruce up, deck out, put on the bells and whistles, put on the dog.

FURIOUS adj. browned off, bent out of shape, blow, blow one's cool, bummed out, mad as a wet hen, hacked, steamed, have a conniption fit, fit to be tied, hopping mad, smoking. See ANGRY.

FURIOUSLY adv. like crazy, like mad, something fierce, something terrible, flaky, helter-skelter, holus-bolus, hurry-scurry, ramble-scramble. See also VIOLENTLY.

FURLOUGH n. orchid hunt (WAC), layoff, hiatus. See also LEAVE.

FURNISH v. feather one's nest, line one's nest (at the expense of others), heel (money), fix up. See also EQUIP.

FURNISHINGS n. turnout.

FUROR n. row, big stink, rhubarb, ruckus, commo, free-for-all, hell broke loose, raise cain, raise sand, big scene.

FURTHER v. push, puff, ballyhoo, back up, give a boost to, go with, thump the tub for, take care of one for, open doors, lend a hand, bail out. See SUPPORT.

FURTIVE adj. creep (mission), tref, triff, under wraps, undercover, hush-hush. See SECRET.

FURTIVELY adv. on the q.t., on the quiet, on the sly, undercover, under wraps, hush-hush, strictly hush-hush, in a hole-and-corner way, in holes and corners.

FURY n. mad, sore, huff, dander, Irish, stew, storm, ruckus, wingding, slow burn, conniption, conniption fit, cat fit, duck fit, blowup, flare-up, boiling point, rise, more heat than light. See ANGER.

FUSS n. stink, to-do, commo, scene, flap, kick-up, wingding, fuzzbuzzy. See TURMOIL.

FUSSY adj. choosy, comma counter, nitpicker, picky, picky picky, ticky, stickler, fussbudget, fusspot, fuddy-duddy, granny, old woman, old maid, pernickety, persnickety. See also PARTICULAR.

FUTILE adj. total shuck, goin' round in circles, on a treadmill, out the window, go fight City Hall, locking the barn after the horse is stolen, looking for a needle in a haystack, save one's breath. See USELESS.

FUTURE adj.   down the road, down the pike, down the line, down the road a piece, in the cards, by and by, from now on in, from here in, from here on out, just around the corner. See EVENTUAL.

FUZZ n.   dust ball, kittens, pussies, slut's wool.

G

G n. golf, George.

GAD v. traipse, bum, mooch, knock around, knock about, bat around, bat about, hit the road, hit the trail, walk the tracks, count ties. See WANDER.

GADFLY adj. adjy, spark plug, pusher, operator, player, fireman, hatchet man, needle man, steam-up ghee, stormy petrel, wave maker.

GADGET n. gismo, contraption, sucker, bugger, mother, whatchamacallit, thigamajig, dojigger, dohickey, goofus. See APPARATUS.

GAFFE n. boo-boo, bloomer, clinker, howler, fox paw, fox pass, wrong riff, put one's foot in it, blow card. See MISTAKE.

GAG v. squash, squelch, put the lid on, keep the lid on, shut down on, bottle up, cork, cork up. See SILENCE.

GAIETY n. whoopee, whooper-dooper, wingding, shindig, brawl, grins. See also REVEL.

GAIN n. 1. gravy, payoff, cut, take, velvet, peanuts (small), cush, in the black, rake-off. See INCOME. 2. boost, buildup, hike, up, upping.

GAIN v. 1. clear, score, promote, parlay, snowball, boost, pick up, rack up, build up, make a killing, feather one's nest. See GET. See also PROFIT. 2. beef up, hike up, jack up, jump up, put up, press up, press a bet, pyramid, builder-upper, sweeten the pot.

GAINFUL adj. going, going concern, paid off, red, sweet, in the black.

GAINS n. bundle, harvest, package, skim, velvet, cream. See INCOME.

GAIT n. clip, getalong, lick.

GALA n. ball, bash, blast, brawl, bust, get-together, clambake, shindig, shindy, rub, belly rub (dance), hop, jump, prom, moveable feast, blowout, stag, jag, jig, zig, jamboree, wingding, roast, donkey roast, drag party, do.

GALE n. big blow, chinook, mistral, Mister Hawkins, the hawk.

GALL n. guts, crust, nerve, cheek, chutzpah, brass.

GALLANT adj. fire eater, hairy, stand tall, gritty, bigger'n life.

GALLANT n. old man, Casanova, Don Juan, flame, Lothario, sugar daddy.

GALLERY n. peanut gallery, bloody-nose gallery, nigger heaven (Derog.), paradise, Ethiopian paradise, groot.

GALLEY n. crumb stash, bean gun (mobile, WW II).

GALLIVANT v. traipse, knock around, knock about, bat around, bat about, hit the road, hit the trail. See TRAVEL.

GALOSHES n. goulashes, rubbers, gunboats, pup tents.

GALVANIZE v. turn on, jazz up, pep up, perk up, snap up, zip up, put pep into it, put zip into it, zap. See STIMULATE.

GALVANIZER n. spark plug.

GAMBLE n. spec, long shot, shot in the dark, stab, have a fling at, irons in the fire, outside chance, toss up, action. See WAGER.

GAMBLE v. get down, play, plunge, take the action, take a flyer, shoot the works, put one's money where one's mouth is, ball the jack. See WAGER.

GAMBLER n. hign roller, plunger, dunker, player, big shot, big timer, dealer, wheeler-dealer, carder, cardsharp, card shark, punter, desperado, prof, tin horn, sharp, sharpie, sharper, sport, crap shooter, boneshaker, spec, gunslinger, Broadway boy (small time), lame duck (stocks), scalper (ticket seller), K.G. (known gambler, police use), angel (The.), backer, the money, the bankroll, staker.

GAMBLING CASINO n. house, joint, shop, store, big store, toilet, trap, crib, flat, hell, bust-out joint, creep dive, creep joint.

GAMBLING TERMS action, skim, play it close to the vest, come, come again (repeat winner), copper on copper off; bust out, crap out (lose); black money (income), dead man's hand (aces and eights), trips (three of a kind), boat (full house), fold (go out), bump (raise), shill, ante up, feed the kitty, sandbag, under the gun (first player dealt to).

GAMBOL v. horse around, fool around, kibitz around, carry on, make whoopee, cut loose, let loose, let go, whoop it up, kick up one's heels, cut, cut capers, cut a dido. See also REVEL.

GAMESMANSHIP n. psych out, give one the needle, one-upmanship.

GAME WARDEN n. possum sheriff.

GAMING HOUSE n. house, joint, shop, store, big store, toilet, trap, crib, flat, hell, bust-out joint, creep joint, creep dive.

GANG n. syndicate, outfit, tie up, tie-in, mob, ring, clan, tribe, troupe, bunch, crowd, combination, combo, rat pack, zoo, hui (Hawaiian). See GROUP. See also CRIME, ORGANIZED.

GANG LEADER n. godfather, capo, war councillor.

GANGSTER n. godfather, mafioso, member of the family, goon, goonlet (young), gunsel, hit man, piece man, hood, hoodlum, hooligan, mo ghee, mob ghee, mobster, racketeer, soldier, cowboy, underboss (second in command), big juice, button man (Mafia), pusher, dealer, digits dealer (numbers). See also CRIME, ORGANIZED.

GANGSTER'S GIRL n. squeeze, moll, gun moll, hairpin.

GAPE n. fish eye, gun.

GAPE v. eye, eyeball, get an eyeful, give the eye, eyeballs buggin' out like percolator tops, gawk, get a load of, size up, hold the glims on, take in, beam, pipe, pin, focus, lamp, rubber, gun. See also SEE.

GARAGE n. barn, doghouse.

GARB n. threads, duds, rags, glad rags, feathers, vine, weeds, rig, drapes, bib and tucker. See CLOTHING.

GARB v. turn out, fit out, rig out, rig up, rag out, rag up, tog, suit up, doll up, deck, deck out, dog out, dud, dude, dude up, drape.

GARBAGE n. gash, garbahge, dreck.

GARBAGE COLLECTOR n. san man, G-man, dirt bag (WW II).

GARBAGE TRUCK n. honey wagon.

GARBLED adj. double talk, ass backwards, bass ackwards, back asswards, chewing gum.

GARGANTUAN adj. humongous, humungous, monstro, mungo, big mother, biggy, heavyweight, superduper, super-colossal, jumbo, lolloping, whopping, thumper, thumping. See BIG.

GARISH adj. showy, glitzy, loud, screaming, gussied up, kitschy, lit up like a Christmas tree. See GAUDY.

GARMENTS n. threads, duds, get up, feathers, vine, weeds, schmotte, sock frock, honking brown (flashy), tailor-made, drapes, harness (leather, especially motorcycle). See CLOTHING.

GARNISH n. garbage (food), gingerbread, bells and whistles.

GARNISH v. doll up, fix up, gussy up, spruce up, put on the bells and whistles.

GARRET n. sky parlor.

GARRULOUS adj. yacky, gabby, gassy, long-winded, motormouth, blabbermouth, Chatty Cathy, spieler, flap jaw, gossipy. See TALKATIVE.

GARY, INDIANA Yellow Air, Yellow Breath.

GAS CHAMBER n. dance hall.

GAS MASK n. chick (WW II, Army).

GASOLINE n. gas, juice, bug juice, go juice, ethyl.

GAS PEDAL n. gun, hammer.

GASTROINTESTINAL ORGANS n. guts, innards, inners, insides, inner man, inner works, inner workings, spaghetti, department of the interior.

GATE n. slammer.

GATHER v. bunch up, gang around, gang up, hang out, make the scene, round up, scare up, capture, corral, poke, punch.

GATHERING n. confab, clambake, meet, get-together, huddle, powwow, rap session, turnout. See MEETING.

GATHERING PLACE n. hangout, in-spot, spot, place, in place, stamping ground, the grab.

GAUDY adj. showy, glitzy, ritzy, flossy, flashy, splashy, splurgy, loud, screaming, flaky, jazzy, snazzy, zappy, pizzazz, splendiferous, splendacious, chichi, frou-frou, gussied up, kitschy, putting on the dog, putting on the ritz, lit up like a Christmas tree, sporty. See also PRETENTIOUS.

GAUGE v. check, check out, dig it, eye, have one's number, look over, peg, size, size up, take one's measure, figure, figure in, dope out, take account of, guesstimate. See APPRAISE.

GAUNT adj. rattleboned, bag of bones, stack of bones, skin and bones, skeleton, peaked, peaky. See THIN.

GAY adj. bouncy, chirpy, chipper, zippy, feeling one's oats, full of beans, full of piss and vinegar. See also HAPPY.

GAZE n. fish eye, gun.

GAZE v. eye, eyeball, get an eyeful, give the eye, eyeballs buggin' out like percolator tops, gawk, get a load of, size up, hold the glims on, take in, beam, pipe, pin, lamp, rubber. See also SEE.

GEAR n. 1. grandma (low gear, truck), Rachel (high gear). 2. stuff, kit and kaboodle, outfit, contraption, setup, thing. See also APPARATUS. 3. drapery, feathers, toggery, togs, duds, threads, rags, glad rags. See also CLOTHING.

GEAR SHIFT n.   stick.

GELATIN n.   nervous pudding.

GELD v.   cut off one's balls, deball, fix, alter.

GELDED adj.   altered, deballed, fixed.

GEM n.   sparkler, spark, a girl's best friend, ice, cracked ice, rock, rock candy, headlight, pennyweight, Simple Simon, glass (imitation).

GEMS n.   junk jewelry, stones, rocks, sparklers, ice, Christmas, glass, hardware, pennyweight.

GENDERLESS adj.   unisex.

GENERAL MANAGER n.   G.M.

GENEROSITY n.   heart, all heart.

GENEROUS adj.   1. softie, soft touch, big, be big, bighearted, have a heart, heart in the right place, loose, Santa Claus, good Joe, prince of a person, give one the shirt off one's back. 2. dime a dozen, aplenty, galore, no end, no end in sight, stink with. See PLENTY.

GENIAL adj.   chipper, chirpy, corky, high, sunny, sunny side up, up, upbeat, upper, perky, Little Merry Sunshine, Little Mary Sunshine. See CHEERFUL.

GENITALIA n.   family jewels, parts, private parts, privates, works, apparatus, business, the business, one's business, equipment, gadgets, tool box, machinery, moving parts, ass, pussy, cunt, purse, snatch, twat, beaver, crack, hole, quiff, quim, snapper, snapping pussy, trim, box, fur, gash, nookie, poontang, tail, clam, bearded clam, cabbage, cookie, love muscle, slash, fireplace, oven, Cape Horn, ace, ace of spades, coffee shop, mink, cuzzy, chacha, chocha, twelge, futy, gigi, jazz, jelly roll, jing jang, nautch, notch, piece, cunny, honey pot, fruit cup, shaf, muffin, muff, receiving set, goldmine, moneymaker, puka, meat, dark meat, white meat, pink, the Y; cock, prick, dick, dork, pecker, peter, joint, middle leg, pencil, dummy, meat, weenie, stick, joy-stick, bone, knob, joy knob, bishop, bicho, wang, thing, putz, schmeckel, schmuck, schwantz, pup, rod, pole, pego, pinga (Sp.), pud, dong, dang, dange, banana, shlong, dingus, staff, doodle, gun, head, tool, arm, jack, jock, Mr. Happy, thing, jigger, do jigger, ding, hickey, fag, booboos, jang, jing-jang, ying-yang, tootsie roll, divining rod, snake, one-eyed monster, one-eyed wonder, shaft, jellyroll, meat whistle, skin flute, piccolo, rod of love, root, worm, instrument, machine, nuts and bolts, basket, heart, hotchee, hung (big), hung like a bull, hung like a chicken, hung like a rabbit (all Obsc.).

GENITALIA, FEMALE n.   pussy, cunt, snatch, twat, beaver, crack, hole, quiff, quim, purse, trim, box, muff, meat, the Y. See VAGINA.

GENITALIA, MALE n.   cock, prick, dick, dork, pecker, peter, joint, wang, shlong, tool, jellyroll, love muscle, hung (big). See PENIS, TESTICLES.

GENITAL INSPECTION n.   short arm, short-arm drill, short-arm inspection (general or relaxed penis, orig. Army use), long-arm inspection (erect penis).

GENIUS n.   brain, brains, the brains, whiz kid, quiz kid, the goods, the stuff, the right stuff, what it takes. See also INTELLIGENCE.

GENTILE n.   WASP, goy, goyim (pl.), shegets (M.), shiksa (Fem., all Derog.).

GENTLE adj.   cool, mellow, laid back, tame.

GENTLEMAN n.   1. nice guy, good guy, good Joe, good egg, doll, pussycat, brick, trump, stout fellow. See also MAN. 2. Brahmin, blue blood, lace curtain, silk stocking, swell, upper cruster. See ARISTOCRAT.

GENTLY adv.   handle with care, don't bend the merchandise.

GENUINE adj.   for real, the real McCoy, genuine article, real people, kosher, legit, open, up front, righteous, twenty-four carat. See SINCERE.

GEOGRAPHIC DESIGNATIONS   Coast, East, East Coast, West, West Coast, Wild West, Down East, Down Under, Down South, Down Home, Overseas, Seaside, the shore, the beach, the Carolinas, the lower forty-eight, the Old South, solid south, deep South, the Mountains, the Valley, the Walley (San Fernando), the Old Country, the Panhandle, Sun Belt, Snow Belt, Bible Belt, Borscht Belt, Dust Bowl, the islands.

GEOLOGIST n.   rocksy, roxy, sand smeller.

GEORGIA   the Empire State of the South, the Peach State.

GEORGIAN n.   goober grabber, clay eater.

GERM n.   bug, cootie, crud, creeping crud, the plague, what's going around.

GERMAN n.   Heinie, kraut, krauthead, sauerkraut, cabbagehead, Jerry, Boche, turner, pretzel; schatzi, schanzi (girl); bucket head, sausage (soldier) (all Derog.).

GERMANE adj.   on the button, on the nose, right on, on target, kosher, legit, that's the idea, that's the ticket. See APPLICABLE.

GESTATION n.   knocked up, expecting, infanticipating, in the family way, have a cake in the oven, have a bun in the oven, blessed eventing, expecting a blessed event. See PREGNANT.

GESTURE n.   high sign, body language.

GET v.   clear, score, snag, grab, hustle, wangle, promote, parlay, snowball, cash in on, clean up, pick up, scare up, lock up, rack up, snap up, build, build up, take up, buy up, buy off, buy out, buy into, make a buy, blow one's self to, make a good thing of, make a killing, make it big, make hay, make a haul, feather one's nest, line one's nest, catch, glom onto, get one's hands on, get hold of, latch on to, access, capture (computer data), cop, kipe, corral, boost (all steal).

GHOST n. hant, haunt, haint, spook, things that go bump in the night.

GHOSTLY adj. spooky, spookish, scary.

GHOSTWRITER n. spook, ghost.

GIBBERISH n. gubble, ubble gubble, scat, double talk, blah blah.

GIBE n. dump, put down, rank out, dig, dirty dig, crack, slam, swipe, jab, comeback, parting shot, brickbat.

GIDDY adj. gaga, rocky, woozy, light-headed, bubbleheaded, harebrained, punchy, slaphappy. See also DIZZY.

GIFT n. goodie, stake, giveaway (often prize), write-off, hand, helping hand, handout, mitzvah, gifting, gash (unexpected), lump, poke out. See also DONATION.

GIFTED adj. a lot of nifty, class act, hot, hotshot, mad, phenom, got it, shine at, shine in, have the smarts, have a bump for, have it on the ball, have plenty on the ball, have the goods. See INTELLIGENT.

GIGANTIC adj. gross, humongous, humungous, mungo, monstro, moby, big mother, super-duper, super-colossal, jumbo, blimp, whale of a, whaling. See BIG.

GIGOLO n. gash hound (Obsc.), lady-killer, heavy cake, blade, bun duster, candy kid, fancy Dan, fancy man. See LADIES' MAN.

GIN n. panther, panther piss, white, bathtub gin, geneva, Gordon water (not common), gunpowder, jump steady, juniper juice.

GIN RUMMY TERMS gin, blitz, schneider, a laydown.

GIRL n. sis, kid, kiddo, chick, chicklet, hip chick, spring chicken, biddie, bird, broad, doll, babe, baby doll, destroyer (beautiful), boytoy, whistle bait, jail bait, San Quentin quail, pigeon, squab, canary, bunny, cub, gadget, gidget, gaunch, ginch, wench, gumdrop, floozy, floogy, faloosie, frill, frail, frail eel, frame dame, cover, cupcake, cheese, cutie, skirt, mini skirt, cunt, pussy, gash, muff, bush, cou, couzie, quasar, cock teaser, CT (all Obsc.); queen, classis chassis, classy chassy, import, bag, baggage, package, jill, filly, heifer, teenybopper, bobby-soxer, bubble gum rocker, kitten, kitty, hellcat, piece, sugar-wooga; witch, battle, cow (fat), pigmeat, sweat, hag, dog, beast, lobo (ugly); crock, jane, jellybean, jerry, mort, mott, mouse, wren, rib, li'l mama, she-she, tomboy, twist, missy, little missy, slip, tomato, babe, baby, eatin' stuff (Obsc.), butterfly, square broad, yuppie (young urban professional).

GIRLFRIEND n. G.F., old lady, squeeze, main squeeze, main queen, big moment, body and soul, hamma, mama, sweet mama, sweetie, companion, constant companion, flame, sugar, sugar pie, sugar bowl, jelly roll, kissing cousin, ace, ace lane, baby, total babe, love bird, turtle dove, oyster, armpiece, baby cake, cake, cakie, chick, gussie mollie (not common), patootie, hot patootie, sweet patootie, josan (Korean war), snoff, corn bread, home cooking, stone marten (beautiful).

GIRLIE SHOW n. T and A, tits and ass, jiggle, jiggly-wiggly, leg show, topless, burleque, strip joint, a circus.

GIRL WATCH v. scope the local units, pussy patrol (Obsc.).

GIST n. point, stuff, nub, bottom line, name of the game, nitty gritty, nuts and bolts, the way of it, nature of the beast, drift, heart, meat, nub, score, punch line.

GIVE v. gift, gift with, slip, give up, hand out, hand over, dish out, fork out, fork over, shell out, pony up, put up, put up or shut up, put out, put something in the pot, sweeten the pot, sweeten the kitty, feed the kitty, pass the hat, ante up, get it up, get it on, get it on the line, chip in, kick in, come through, come across, come across with, come down with, come down with the needful, plank down, plunk down, post, see, go, duke, weed, pass it on over, gimme, stake, put a buck one's way, throw, give away the store, run with the ball, do one's part.

GIVER n. angel, backer, Santa Claus, sugar daddy, fairy godmother, lady bountiful, heavy hitter, maxed out (political limit).

GIVE UP v. give in, cave in, throw in the towel, cry uncle, fold, buckle under, drop, take the oath, pull out, bail out, bow out, chicken out, walk out on, wash one's hands of, drop like a hot potato, back down. See ABANDON. See also SURRENDER.

GLAD adj. up, hopped up, floating on air, pleased as Punch, tickled, tickled pink, tickled to death, can't complain. See HAPPY.

GLADIOLA n. glad.

GLAMOUR n. razzle-dazzle, animal magnetism, star quality.

GLAMOROUS adj. ten, 10, boss, righteous, drooly, dishy, drop-dead gorgeous, glamour girl, hammer, stone, stone fox, foxy, nifty, biscuit, look like a million. See BEAUTIFUL.

GLANCE n. flash, gander, bad eye, the glad eye, eyeball, gun, hinge, glom, pike, slant, lamp, look-see, swivel.

GLANCE v.   flash, pipe, eye, eyeball, get an eyeful, bat an eye at, give one the eye, give with the eyes, give it a thumb check, take in, take a gander, take a hinge, get a hinge, get a load of, check it out. See SEE.

GLARE n.   dirty look, bad eye, dog eye.

GLARE v.   do a slow burn, look daggers, give one a dirty look, dog eye, bad eye, act the lion tamer, cloud up and rain on one. See FROWN. See also SEE.

GLASS n.   jigger, pony, snifter.

GLASSES n.   specs, mini specs, nippers, shades, sun specs, sus-specs, cheaters, frames, windows, rims, four eyes, bop glasses, peepers, glims, googs, goggles, mask (sun), grannies, professor (wearer). See also SUN GLASSES.

GLEAM n.   flash, glitz, show, zap, glim, dimmer.

GLIB adj.   flip, gift of gab, gabbo, fast talker, slick, smooth, smooth operator, spieler, all jaw, flap jaw, big hot-air artist. See TALKATIVE.

GLIDE v.   skate, smooth along.

GLIMPSE n.   flash, gander, bad eye, the glad eye, eyeball, eyeball inspection, gun, hinge, glom, pike, slant, lamp, look-see, swivel.

GLIMPSE v.   flash, pipe, eye, eyeball, get an eyeful, bat an eye at, give one the eye, give with the eyes, take in, take a gander, take a hinge, get a hinge, get a load of, check it out. See SEE.

GLISSANDO n.   slurp, smear.

GLITTER n.   flash, glitz, show, zap, tinsel.

GLITTERY adj.   flashy, glitzy, showy, zappy.

GLOAT v.   lick one's chops, rub one's nose in, horse laugh, give one the horse laugh, hee haw.

GLOBE n.   apple, pellet, pill, sphere, big blue marble, real estate, spaceship Earth.

GLOOMY adj.   dragged, low, blue funk, got the blue devils, in the dumper, down in the dumps, hang crepe, sad sacky. See MELANCHOLY.

GLORIFY v.   boost, build up, hike, hike up, jack up, jump up, put up, put on a pedestal. See also EXAGGERATE.

GLOSS v.   soft-pedal, whitewash, cover up.

GLOVE COMPARTMENT n.   hip pocket.

GLUE n.   stickum, gunk, gummy, spit.

GLUM adj.   down in the mouth, in the dumps, in the doleful dumps, blue, in a blue funk. See MELANCHOLY.

GLUTINOUS adj.   gooey, gloppy, globby, gook, gooky, goonk, gummy, gunk.

GLUTTED adj.   full up, packed, lousy with, up to here in, up to one's ass in, coming out of one's ears. See FULL.

GLUTTON n.   hog, pig, bellygod, mean scorfer, greedygut, greedyguts, hefty eater, husky eater, pelican, foodie, fresser.

GLUTTONIZE v.   gobble, gulp, bolt, gross out, munch out, blimp out, pork out, pig out, scarf, scarf out, scarf back, scarf down, scorf down, pig down, bolt down, gobble down, gulp down, chow down, wolf, wolf down, put away, make a pig of oneself, make a hog of oneself, eat like a horse, eat one's head off, eat out of house and home, dispatch, dispose of, do oneself proud, get away with. See also EAT.

GNAT n.   no see um, punkie, punky.

GNAW v.   chaw, munch, chomp, gum, fling a fang into.

GO v.   Split, beat it, fog, cruise, dedomicile, I'm history, I'm outta here, scram, amscray, cut out, cut loose, cut and run, duck and run, cut ass, haul ass, bag ass, hit the road, hit the trail, hit the bricks, jump off, hop off, bop off, push off, blast off, fuck off, flake off, knock off, nip, nip off, tear off, light off, kick off, slam off, move out, bow out, boo out, ooze out, ease on, ease out, ease on out, phase out, flake out, walk out, run out, clear out, storm out, tear out, nix out, butt out, peel out, check out, opt out, catch out, dig out, skin out, bail out, kick out, push out, pull out, duck out, snake out, ship out, burn out, burn rubber, peel rubber, skip, skip out, bug out, bug off, light, light out, barge out, boogie, tool, tool along, vamoose, ankle, get away, get lost, get going, get, git, get git, get the hell out, get the lead out, make oneself scarce, highball, dog it, blow, blow away, blow this pop stand, blow the joint, breeze, drift, drag, drag it, drag one's freight, pull one's freight, haul one's freight, take off, take off in a cloud, take off in a cloud of sour owl shit, take off like a big ass bird, take off like a B.A.B., take the air, skidoo, skidoodle, skidaddle, skedaddale, hotfoot, play on down, scat, shove, shove off, shove in one's clutch, be getting along, trot along, toddle along, stagger along, ball the jack, perk, percolate, absquatulate, exfiltrate, roll, tick, hightail, make tracks, make a break for it, run like a scared rabbit, do a vanishing act, hop it, sashay off, buzz off, buzz along, wing it, powder, take a powder, take a run out powder, sniff a powder, walk, take a walk, walk out on, run out on, kiss good-bye, have to see a man about a dog, screw, slough, truck, truck on out, book, time to book, time to bail, leg, leg it out of here, make it, fade, fade out, do a fade, fade away, drift away, duck, heel, bottle up and go, pull up stakes, up stakes, dust, plow ahead, fly the coop, scramble, scooch, scream, cheese it, step it, get to steppin', get off the dime, eat a worm, hat up, let the doorknob hit you, put it to the wind, slide, swoop, scratch gravel, collar a broom, cop a broom, quit the scene, quit cold, ditch, stay out of one's face, get out of one's sight, head for the barn (home), drift, drift away, fly the coop, leave flat, leave high and dry, take gypsy leave, take

French leave, go A.W.O.L., go over the hill, go over the fence, go over the side, lam, take it on the lam, wail, mosey, mosey off, mosey along. See also DIE, ABSCOND.

GO, COMMAND v. fuck off, FO, stay out of my face, shove off, vamoose, scram, amscray, get, git, get the hell out, get outta here, get lost, blow, beat it, bug out, bug off, push off, buzz off, flake off, on your way, go chase yourself, bag ass, you're excused, split, hit the road Jack, hit the bricks, make yourself scarce, make like a tree and leave, make tracks, clear out, butt out, screw, shove, take a walk, take a powder, take a hike, skedaddle, cheese it, go chase yourself, scoot, up anchor, scat, get on your horse, go peddle your papers.

GOAD v. goose, goose up, egg on, turn on, fire up, spark, key up, put up to, work up, work up into a lather, sound, trigger. See STIMULATE.

GOAL n. 1. gool. 2. zero, ground zero, surgical mission (precise target).

GOALTENDER n. goalie, anchor man.

GOAT n. billy, billy goat, nanny, nanny goat.

GOATEE n. pez. See also BEARD.

GOD n. Dad, Head Knock, Man Upstairs, Lordy.

GODLY adj. born again, got religion, Jesus freak, Holy Joe, Jesus lover, Jasper, knee bender, Mary, Christian, candy ass, goody, goody-goody, goody two-shoes, scoutmaster. See also VIRTUOUS.

GO FREE v. beat the rap, walk, out, get away with murder, get off, let off, let go. See also PARDONED.

GO IN v. access, penetrate, break in, barge in, blow in, bust in, pop in, mooch in, ace in, breeze in, come breezing in, come barging in, come, come busting in.

GOLD n. dust, yellow stuff.

GOLF CLUB n. stick, shovel sticks, baffy, brassie, iron, wood, niblick.

GOLF CLUB BAR ROOM n. nineteenth hole.

GOLF COURSE n. prairie, back nine, blind hole, bunker, cheat sheet (course plan and yardage chart), dogleg, fat (wide part of green), front nine, home hole (final hole).

GOLF SCORE halve (tie), hole (hole one), holeable, hole out, mulligan (extra shot, uncounted), up (he was 3 up on Watson), ace (hole in one), birdie (one stroke under par, got a birdie), bogey (one stroke over par), eagle (2 under par), double bogey (2 over par), dormie (strokes ahead equal to the holes yet to play), gimme (short putt).

GOLF STROKE n. foozle (clumsy), lay up (intentionally short), sandie (out of the trap in one), sclaff (divot digger), short game (approach and putt), slice (ball hit to right), banana ball (slice), hook (ball hit to left, right-handed player), duck hook (low), waggle (she waggled the club to relax), sink, back door (putt), borrow (putt, allow for slope), sidehiller (putt along the slope), yip (bad putt), approach shot, blast (from sand), carry (distance), chippie (approach shot that drops into hole), dub (hit poorly), explosion shot, fat.

GOLF TERMS creep (slow round), punk, pushover (player), scratch player (plays at par), dub, duffer, hooker (inferior player); Nassau (type of wager), rabbit (pro golf qualifier), away (ball farthest from hole), hole out (finish a hole), bunkered (in a hazard), lie (ball location), read the green, rim (the ball rimmed the hole and didn't drop), rub of the green (grain).

GONADS n. nuts, rocks, balls, family jewels, diamonds, bag, ballocks, basket, cajones, boo boos, ears.

GONE adj. fall between the cracks, petered out, dried up, kiss [something] good-bye, out the window, down the tube, down the drain, down the spout, down the rathole. See also DEAD.

GONG n. gut hammer, hammer (usually iron triangle).

GONORRHEA n. V.D., clap, claps, dose, dose of clap, hammer head clap, old clap, old dose (neglected case), the drip, the whites, pissing razor blades, head cold, caught a cold, picked up something, picked up a nail, lulu (painful case), burn, blue balls, social disease, old Joe.

GOOD adj. goodie, neato, teriff, bueno, bad, down, real down, not too shabby, way, rad, way rad, lookin' chilly (Bl.), gnarly, nasty, doin' a hundred, batting a thousand, organic, up to snuff, up to speed, up to the mark, some (that's some doll), some kind of. See PRAISEWORTHY.

GOOD-BYE interj. bye bye, see ya, so long, chow, ciao, later, I'm history, I'm outta here, good-byee, bye now, ta ta, see you, have a nice day, take it easy, dig ya later, see you later alligator, be good, happy landing, take care, toodleoo, cheerio, cherro, cherry, thirty for now, that's thirty, don't take any wooden nickels, eighty-eights, good hunting, see you in church, abyssinia, keep the faith baby, peace, it's been real, olive oil.

GOOD-BYE n. eighty-eights, swan song. See PARTING.

GOOD DEED n. mitzvah (Yid.), making brownie points.

GOOD-LOOKING adj. ten, 10, righteous, drooly, dishy, dreamboat, phat chick, flavor (Bl.), looker, good looker, tall dark and handsome, handsome thing, Adonis, lover boy, pretty boy. See BEAUTIFUL.

GOOD-NATURED adj. Mr. Nice Guy, breezy, good scout, softie, marshmallow. See also NICE.

GOOD NIGHT interj. night, nighty-night, sweet dreams, turn off the light and don't let the bedbugs bite, see you in dreamland.

GOODS n. the goods, material, stuff, jive (gaudy), seconds (flawed).

GOOD TIME n. ball, blast, picnic, rat fuck, high old time, panic.

GOODWILL n. the good side of, the right side of.

GOOSEFLESH n. goose pimples, goose bumps, duck bumps.

GORGE v. gobble, gross out, blimp out, pork out, pig out, scarf back, pig down, make a pig of oneself, eat like a horse. See EAT.

GORGED adj. full up, fed up, fed to the teeth, fed to the gills, stuffed to the gills, packed, jammed, jam packed, with a bellyful, with a skinful, with a snootful.

GORGEOUS adj. drop-dead gorgeous, lulu, dream puss, ten, 10, stone, stone fox, foxy, head rush, knock one's eyes out, beaut, easy on the eyes, centerfold. See BEAUTIFUL.

GOSSIP n. scuttlebutt, talk, grapevine, clothesline, leak, back-fence talk, back-fence gossip, ear loft, earful, ear dust, slime, bibful, hash, gam, latrine rumor, blowup, wire, hot wire, page-oner, vanilla, whispering campaign, dirty linen, dirty wash.

GOSSIP v. bad-mouth, dish, dish the dirt, chew, chew the fat, cut up, cut one up and down, cut one into little pieces, cut one into ribbons, rap, gate-mouth, rattle on, schmoose, schmoozle, wiggle-waggle, bend one's ear, ear duster, bat the chat, bat the breeze, bat one's gums, beat one's gums.

GOSSIPER n. sleaze monger, yenta (Yid.), polly, satch, gasser, gatemouth, load of wind, windbag, busybody, tabby, tattletale.

GOSSIPY adj. catty, all jaw, big-mouthed, evil, gabby, gassy, windy. See also TALKATIVE.

GO TO THE MOVIES v. flick it, take in a movie.

GOUGE v. screw, bleed, bleed white, hold up, soak, stick, sting, clip, make pay through the nose, skin, fleece, fuck, fuck over. See OVERCHARGE.

GOURMAND n. hog, pig, foodie, bellygod, greedygut, greedyguts, hefty eater, husky eater, pelican, mean scorfer, fresser.

GOURMANDIZE v. gobble, gulp, bolt, gross out, munch out, blimp out, pork out, pig out, scarf, scarf out, scarf back, scarf down, scorf down, pig down, bolt down, gobble down, gulp down, chow down, wolf, wolf down, put away, make a pig of oneself, make a hog of oneself, eat like a horse, eat one's head off, eat out of house and home,

dispatch, dispose of, do oneself proud, get away with. See also EAT.

GOVERN v. head, head up, run, run things, run the show, call the shots, call the signals, be in the driver's seat, pull the strings. See MANAGE.

GOVERNMENT n. Big Brother, the Feds, the Union, Uncle Sam, US, USA, D.C., Washington, the mighty dome, the digger.

GOVERNMENT AGENCIES n. alphabet soup.

GOVERNMENT AGENCY Fed, feds, the Feds.

GOVERNMENT EMPLOYEE n. Fed, feds.

GOVERNMENT FUNDS n. pork barrel, public crib, public till, public trough.

GOVERNMENT NATIONAL MORTGAGE ASSOCIATION n. Ginnie Mae.

GOVERNOR n. guv, head, headman, Big Brother, boss. See also EXECUTIVE.

GRAB v. snatch, snag, collar, corral, hook, land, nail, bag, nab, glom, glaum, glahm, glom onto, put the glom on, put the snatch on, put the snare on, clap hands on, get one's fingers on, get one's hands on. See also ARREST.

GRACELESS adj. klutzy, clunky, flubdub, two left hands, two left feet, clodhopper, galoot. See CLUMSY.

GRADE n. Brownie point, ten, 10, five-pointer (high), A: ace, four-pointer. B: three-pointer. C: hook. D: dog. E: eagle. F: fade (low or failing), flag, flunk.

GRADUATE n. grad, old grad, alum.

GRADUATE SCHOOL n. grad school.

GRADUATE STUDENT n. grad, doc, post doc.

GRAFT n. juice, payoff, payoff money, payola, drugola, gayola, under the table, oil, on the take, padding, shake, skimming, squeeze, boodle, hat. See also BRIBE, PROTECTION MONEY.

GRAFTER n. the juice man, flimflammer.

GRAND RAPIDS, MICHIGAN Chair City.

GRAND adj. fab, marvy, unreal, nifty, magnif, something else, smashing, super, super-duper, doozie, dynamite, man-sized, pip, solid gold, spiffy, bang-up, swell, stunning, out of this world. See IMPRESSIVE. See also DIGNIFIED, BIG.

GRANDEE n. upper cruster, blue blood, lace curtain, silk stocking, swell.

GRANDFATHER n. gramps, grandpa, grandpapa, grandpap, grandpappy, granddad, granddaddy, granddada, grampa, gramper, gramp, gramfer, granther, old man.

GRANDILOQUENCE n. big talk, tall talk, purple, high flown.

GRANDIOSE adj. Flash Gordon, high falutin', splendacious, splendiferous, purple, showy, mister big, mister big shot. See also MAGNIFICENT.

GRANDMOTHER n. grandma, grandmama, grandmammy, grandmaw, gramma, grammy, granmam, grannam, granny, nana, nanny, big mama, gammer, gammy, old woman.

GRANT n. handout, gifting, lump, poke out.

GRANT v. 1. put out, drop, gift, gift with, stake, give with, come through, get it on. See GIVE. 2. bless, pass on, shake on, sign on, sign off on, yes one, go along with, give the nod, thumbs up, jibe. See also ALLOW. 3. come across, come around, give out, give in, give away the store, lie down and roll over for. See SURRENDER. 4. like you say, you got it, sure thing, I'll drink to that, I hear you.

GRAPEFRUIT n. cannonball.

GRASP v. 1. snatch, snag, collar, corral, hook, land, nail, bag, nab, glom, glaum, glahm, glom onto, put the glom on, put the snatch on, put the snare on. 2. get, get the picture, get the hang of it, make, catch on, latch on, pick up, blow wise. See UNDERSTAND.

GRASS n. the green deck, carpet, rug.

GRASSHOPPER n. hopper, hoppergrass.

GRATIFICATION n. flash, kick, kicks, mess, hit, velvet, get off, get off on, sure shock, you got it, just name it.

GRATIFIED adj. 1. on cloud nine, in seventh heaven, have no kick coming, tickled pink, tickled to death, hit the spot, just what the doctor ordered, pleased as Punch. See HAPPY. 2. skinful, snootful, bellyful, no more room, fed to the teeth, fed to the gills, stuffed to the gills.

GRATIFIES v. scores, hits the spot, hits the bull's-eye, makes it, thanks I needed that.

GRATIFY v. fill the bill, make a hit, hit the spot, do the trick, get one's jollies, get one's kicks, get off, get off on. See SATISFY.

GRATIFYING adj. kicks, for kicks, mellow, fine and mellow, lush, downhill, nervous, cool, wild.

GRATING n. waffle iron.

GRATIS adj. freebie, free ride, for love, Annie Oakley, on the house, cuffo. See FREE.

GRATUITY n. tip, toke (gambling), chip, cue, somethin', a little somethin', a little something to sweeten the pot, a little slack; subway, bus ride, one way (5 or 10 cent); sweetener, grease, salve, palm oil, gravy, lagniappe, zukes, fringe benefit, goodies, perk, perks, button, hat, ice.

GRAVE adj. strictly business, heavy, heavy number, meaningful, serious talk, serious jelly, serious shit, no shit, no bird terdin', jelly, deadpan, not crack a smile, cold sober, sober as a judge. See SERIOUS.

GRAVE n. cold storage, dust bin, planted, daisy, pushing up daisies, deep six, six, six feet under.

GRAVE-ROBBING n. body-snatching.

GRAVEYARD n. boneyard, bone factory, bone orchard, marble orchard, marble town, headstone city, cold storage.

GRAVY n. dunk sauce, goo, gooey, goop, goopy, glob, globby, glop, gloppy, gop, gunk, gyppo, gippo.

GREASE v. grease the wheels, lube, slick, slick on.

GREASING n. grease job, lube, schmear.

GREAT adj. 1. A number one, aces, super duper, mega-gnarly, rat fuck, zero cool, cold, out of this world, out of sight, gonest, mostest, like dynamite, brutal, fab, tits, tough, heavy, hellacious, bad. See EXCELLENT. 2. humongous, humungous, mungo, monstro, moby, major league, big league, jumbo. See BIG. 3. star, superstar, monster, champ, lion, a somebody. See CELEBRITY.

GREAT BRITAIN Blighty, John Bull, Merry Old, Albion, Limeyland, Tight Little Island.

GREATCOAT n. benny, binny, Benjamin, car coat, horse blanket.

GREATEST adj. gilt-edged, baaadest, balls out, bitchin', boss, cool, terrible, gonest, hundred proof, murder, stone. See also BEST. See also EXCELLENT.

GREAT FALLS, MONTANA High Water.

GREED n. grabby, the gimmies.

GREEDY adj. grabby, big-eye, poligot, greedyguts.

GREEK n. greaseball.

GREEN BAY, WISCONSIN Title Town.

GREENWICH MEAN TIME n. zulu, G.M.T.

GREET v. highball, tumble, flag, shoulder, whistle for, whistle down, flop, give one a flop, give one a toss, give one five, give one the glad eye, give one the glad hand, give one the key to the city, roll out the red carpet.

GREETING interj. hi, hey, ciao, gimme some skin, gimme five, gimme ten, what's happenin'?, what's going down?, what's coming down? what's the skinny? See HELLO.

GREETING n. tumble, rumble, a blow, high five, howdy, highball.

GREGARIOUS adj. clubby, clubbable. See also SOCIABLE.

GRENADE n. pineapple, apple, cookie, Chicago overcoat, potato masher.

GRENADE KILLING n. fragging.

GREYHOUND BUS n. big dog, dog, the hound.

GRIDDLE CAKE n. flapjack, hotcake, blanket, saddle blankets, brown bucks, flats, manhole cover, tire patch, wheat, collision mat (WW II).

GRIDIRON n. field, grid.

GRIEF n. heartache, tsuris (Yid.), blues. See MISERY. See also DISTRESS, MISFORTUNE.

GRIEVANCE n. beef, where's the beef?, bitch, bellyache, grouse, gripe, the gripes, a hoo-ha, stink, big stink, flack, a knock, mix, dido, hurting, pain, pain in the neck, pain in the ass, kick, blast, howl, holler, squawk, yell, roar, rumble, rap, rip, tsuris (Yid.), CC (chief complaint), ax to grind.

GRIEVE v. carry on, eat one's heart out, sing the blues, take it big, take it hard, take on, cry me a river, hang crepe. See MOURN.

GRILL v. roast, go over, put through the third degree, third degree, put on the grill, put the pressure on, put the screws on. See QUESTION.

GRIMACE v. mug, make a face.

GRIME n. gook, dreck, gunk, prut, crud.

GRIMY adj. scuzzy, sleazy, cruddy.

GRIN v. crack a smile, grin from ear to ear, grin like a Cheshire cat, grin like a Chessy cat.

GRIP n. valpack, tote bag, jiffy bag, keister.

GRIP v. glom onto, clap a hand on, get one's fingers on, get one's hands on, nail.

GRIPE n. clutch, crunch, grab.

GRIPPE n. flu, bug.

GRISLY adj. sick, weird, grody, gross, yucky. See BAD.

GROGGY adj. dopey, punchy, punch-drunk, slaphappy, woozy, out of it. See DAZED. See also SLEEPY.

GROOM v. prep, ready, shape up, lick into shape, put through the grind, put through the mill. See TRAIN. See also PREPARE.

GROOMED adj. clean, flowered, ready, set, prepped, slotted.

GROOVE n. grind, daily grind, same old shit, SOS, S.O.S., sked, shtick, one's slot.

GROPE v. phumpher, bonehead into it, go at it ass backwards. See FLOUNDER.

GROSS adj. 1. whole enchilada, whole shebang, whole ball of wax, whole nine yards, whole schmear. See WHOLE. 2. cheap, loud-mouthed, sleazy, raunchy. See VULGAR, UGLY.

GROTESQUE adj. grody, grody to the max, gross, weird, weirdo.

GROUCH n. sourpuss, lemon puss, bug, bug up one's ass, bug up one's nose. See COMPLAINER.

GROUND n. 1. dust, real estate, old sod, terra firma. 2. bottom line, nuts and bolts, rock bottom, nitty-gritty, meat and potatoes, beginners, coal and ice, ABC's, brass tacks, get down, get down to brass tacks.

GROUNDLESS adj. hot air, bullshit, off base, cockeyed, cockamamie, cahcah, coming from nowhere, made up, made up out of whole cloth, who sez?, my eye, just talk, whataya talkin'?, talking through one's hat, you're talkin' like a man with a paper ass, where'd ya get that shit?

GROUND MEAT n. burger, beef burger, cheeseburger, hamburg, superburger, chewed fine, clean up the kitchen (order for hamburger, hash or stew), Wimpy.

GROUNDS n. goods, info, dope, smoking gun (crucial), chapter and verse, the know, straight stuff, the emess, the numbers, gospel. See FACTS.

GROUP n. bunch, crowd, gang, click, crew, crush, mob, outfit, ring, circle, syndicate, hook up, tie up, tie in, tie in tie up, clan, insiders, family, ashram, groupie, pool, those one runs with, the boys, the boys uptown, tribe, troupe, troops, combination, combo; rat pack, yoot (teenage); beef squad (union toughs), clout (auto thieves), debs (girl gang members), zoo. See also ASSOCIATION.

GROUP v. bunch up, gang around, gang up, hang out, make the scene, round up, scare up, corral, poke, punch.

GROUP AGAINST SMOKE AND POLLUTION n. GASP.

GROUP SEX n. gang bang, gang shag, group grope, circle jerk, line up on, moresome (three or more), swinging, daisy chain, pull a train, party (two prostitutes one customer); sugar and spice, vanilla chocolate and pecan (interracial); vanilla and chocolate (one black, one white prostitute, one customer), white meat turkey on pumpernickel (two black prostitutes, one white customer, all Obsc.).

GROUPING n. mixed bag, combo, everything but the kitchen sink, kludge (parts), mishmash.

GROVEL v. eat dirt, eat crow, suck up to, suck ass, kiss ass, lick ass, bootlick, stooge, yes, be a yes-man, fall over, fall all over, kowtow, curry below the knee. See also FLATTER.

GROW v. shoot up, snowball, mushroom, pyramid. See also EXPAND.

GROW OLD v. put mileage on, push, take hair off the dog, pull pages off the calendar.

GROW PLANTS v. green thumb.

GROWTH n. buildup, beefing up, fleshing out, boost, hike, up, upping, sprawl (urban).

GRUDGE n. bone to pick, peeve, pet peeve.

GRUEL n. cush, grits, mush.

GRUELING adj. heavy, hairy, ass-busting. See DIFFICULT.

GRUESOME adj. sick, sicky, weird, gruesome twosome, grody, grody to the max, gross. See also UGLY.

GRUFF adj. snippy, snappy, short.

GRUMBLER n. bitcher, beefer, bellyacher, griper, grouse, crab, crank, cry baby. See COMPLAINER.

GUARANTEE n. lock, a lock on, sure thing, fer shirr, sure as shooting, pipe, lead-pipe cinch, bet your ass, bet your bottom dollar. See CERTAINTY.

GUARANTEE v. angel, back, bankroll, juice, grubstake, pick up the check, pick up the tab, stake, stand up for one, get behind one, sign for, cosign. See also ASSURE.

GUARANTEED adj. sure, sure enough, sure as God made little green apples, sure as the devil, sure as death and taxes, surefire, for sure, for damn sure, for a fact, for a fact Jack, on ice, have a lock on. See CERTAIN.

GUARD n. screw, bouncer, chaser, eyes, hack, herder, hooligan, roach, roller, shields, sky, yard bull, stick, jaboney, jiboney, sidewinder, trigger man, lookout, bugster.

GUARD v. lookout, shotgun, ride shotgun for, lay chickie; cover, cover up, cover one's ass, go to bat for, stonewall.

GUARD DUTY n. tour, watch, graveyard watch.

GUARDED adj. cagey, leery, on the lookout, with a weather eye open, with one's eyes peeled, handle with kid gloves, mind one's p's and q's.

GUARDHOUSE n. brig, clink, lockup, stockade. See also JAIL.

GUARDIAN n. sitter, babysitter, housesitter, cop, bird dog, alarm clock.

GUESS n. guesstimate, ball-park figure, in the ball park, hunch, shot, shot in the dark, stab, stab in the dark, sneaking suspicion.

GUESS v. figure, size up, guesstimate, go out on a limb, take a stab, take a shot. See SPECULATE.

GUEST n. company, out-of-towner, visiting fireman.

GUIDE n. 1. hot lead, lead, tip off, tell tale, print, bum steer (false), by the book, chapter and verse, no-no's, bible (authoritative book), by the numbers. 2. tour guide, bird dog, alarm clock.

GUIDE v. quarterback, mastermind, spearhead, trailblaze, shepherd, have a handle on. See MANAGE.

GUIDEBOOK n. Baedeker.

GUIDELINES n. bibles (TV), formats.

GUILE n. gamesmanship, one-upsmanship, run-around, dirty dealing, dirty work, dirty pool, dirty trick, double-cross, sellout, Judas kiss, stab in the back. See also TRICKERY.

GUILTY adj. caught in the act, caught red-handed, caught with one's hand in the cookie jar, dirty, hung up, hung up with, smoking gun, off base, out of line, damned.

GUITAR n. belly fiddle, box, git, git fiddle, git box, gitter, guinea's harp (not common).

GUITARIST n. plunker, whanger, plink plunker, string whanger.

GULLET n. goozle, guzzle, gargle.

GULLIBLE adj. easy, mark, easy mark, go for, fall for, tumble for, swallow, swallow whole, swallow hook line and sinker, eat up, lap up, bite, take the bait, be taken in, be a sucker, be a patsy, kid oneself, blue eyed, wide-eyed, yold, yoyo, sucker, patsy, green.

GULP v. belt, chugalug, drop (drug), rock one back, swig, toss one back, scarf down, gorm, gorp, wolf, wolf down, inhale, gobble, bolt, dispatch, dispose, swabble. See SWALLOW.

GUN n. artillery, cannon, blaster, gauge (shotgun), gat, piece, iron, rod, snubby, snub nose, snub noser, snub-nosed automatic, lug, Saturday night special, six-gun, six-shooter, bean shooter, peashooter, popper, pop, equalizer, difference, speaker, mister speaker, persuader, convincer, hardware, heater, heat, Betsy, patsy, Bolivar, Oscar, roscoe, mahoska, jerry, canister, canojerod, hog's leg, forty-five, deuce-deuce, trey-eight, smokepole, smoke wagon, zip gun, slim, belly gun, snug, spud, potato, stick, boom stick, tool, noise tool, toy, works, business, blow, bark, barker, bow wow, boom boom (WW II), biscuit, pickle, prod, copper-dropper, crowd-pleaser (police), scatter gun, bear insurance; chopper, chatterbox, Chicago piano, grease gun, burp gun (submachine); dumb gat, gagged gat, hush hush, sissy rod (silencer); stun gun, taser (electric shock); hang (balance).

GUN, CARRY v.   equalized, wired, carrying, carry the difference, totin', toting a gun, packing a gun, packed, gat up, heeled, heeled up, well heeled, loaded, lugging iron, carry iron, lug, lug a rod, rodded up, pack a rod, pack a heater, pack heat.

GUN COVER n.   bloomers.

GUNFIGHT n.   shoot-out, shootemup, fireworks, Fourth of July, war.

GUNFIRE n.   heat, give one the heat, fireworks, gunplay, shoot-out.

GUNMAN n.   gunsel, blaster, hit man, shootist, trigger, trigger man, piece man. See KILLER.

GUNNER n.   guns.

GUNPLAY n.   heat, give one the heat, fireworks, gunplay, shoot-out, shootemup.

GUSH v.   rave, fall all over one, carry on over, make a to-do over, take on over, go on about, whoop it up for.

GUSHY adj.   all over one, bubbling over.

GYMNASIUM n.   gym, sweatshop, health club, spa.

GYMNASTICS n.   gym, tumbling.

GYNECOLOGIST n.   fingersmith.

GYPSY n.   gyp, jip (1890, Obs.), raghead.

H

H n.   hotel, how.

HABIT n.   thing, into, hang-up, one's bag, shot, kick, hook, Jones, monkey, monkey on one's back, grind, daily grind, groove. See also ROUTINE.

HABITAT n.   1. hood, neck of the woods, stomping ground, territory, turf. See NEIGHBORHOOD. 2. pad, box, cave, condo, den, domi, crib, digs, hole, home plate. See HOUSE.

HABITUAL adj.   regular, SOS, same old shit. See also CUSTOMARY.

HABITUÉS OF THE STREET n.   street people, bums, skell.

HACK n.   grind, greasy grind, grubstreet, pro, old pro, work-horse.

HACKNEYED adj.   corny, hokey, tripe, old chestnut, old saw, familiar tune, run of the mill, old hat. See TRITE.

HACKSAW n.   briar.

HADES n.   hell, the other place, down there, hot spot.

HAGGLE v.   dicker, deal, hack out a deal, hammer out a deal, make a deal, work out a deal, hondle, Jew down (Derog.), knock down the price. See NEGOTIATE.

HAIL v.   1. flag, flag down, flop, give one a flop, give one a toss, give one the glad eye, give one the glad hand, highball, shoulder, tumble, holler, holler out, yawp, yoo hoo, whistle for, whistle down. See also HELLO. 2. hear it for, root for. See ACCLAIM.

HAIR n.   grass, pez, righteous moss, wig, wool, nappy (kinky), frizzies (split ends).

HAIR BAND n.   headache band.

HAIRCUT n.   punk, crew, crewcut, butch, mohawk, natural, afro, 'fro, cut, trim, brushcut, chilibowl, Navajo, Caesar, California, Detroit, continental, Elvis, English, duck's ass, D.A., ducktail, cueball (just had a haircut), roach, feather cut, poodle cut, bandhouse clip, double-o, flattop, razor cut, fuzz cut, pachuco, dreadlocks; baldy (Army). See also HAIRSTYLES.

HAIRCUT v.   get ones ears raised, get one's head scratched, get one's rug beat, mow the lawn.

HAIRDRESSER n.   hair bender.

HAIRDRESSING n.   axle grease, conk (Bl.), goo, gooey, goop, goup, goopy, glop, gloppy, glob, globby, gook, gooky, goonk, gunk, slickum.

HAIRLESS adj.   baldy, cue ball, curly, egghead, skinhead, bald as a coot, bald as an egg, bald as an eagle.

HAIRSTYLE n.   1. Women's: do, hairdo, blow dry, punk, spikey, poodle cut, feather cut, pixie cut, pixie, gamin, pageboy, natural, beehive, rat's nest (1950s), pomp (WWII), high hair, streaked, roach, ponytail, horse tail, load of hay (long); fried, made (straightened, Bl.); naps. 2. Men's: trim, cut, razor cut, fuzz cut, brushcut, crewcut, crew, butch, punk, continental, Caesar, California, Detroit, Elvis, English, duck's ass, D.A., ducktail, scone tail, bandhouse clip, double-o, flattop, mohawk, Navajo, pachuco, chilibowl, cueball (just had a haircut); baldy (Army), skinhead, eggbeater. 3. Unisex: punk, punk wave, Italian cut, afro, 'fro, Jewfro, Isfro, righteous moss, dreadlocks.

HAIRSTYLIST n.   hair bender.

HALE adj.   alive and kicking, wrapped tight, chipper, fit as a fiddle, in the pink, sound as a dollar. See HEALTHY.

HALF adj.   halvers, halvies, half and half, even-steven, fifty-fifty.

HALFWAY adj.   betwixt and between, halfway in the middle, plump in the middle, smack in the middle, slap in the middle, smack dab in the middle, middle of the road, over the hill, over the hump.

HALF-WIT n.   dork, numbnut, loser, lamebrain, birdbrain, rattlebrain, out to lunch, lunchie, jerk, dumdum, four-letter man (dumb), oofus, pointyhead. See STUPID.

HALL n.   squat pad.

HALLUCINATE v.   blow one's mind, freak out, trip, go on a trip, head trip.

HALLUCINATING v.   tripping, head-tripping, devil's grandmother, seeing little men who aren't there, pink elephants.

HALLUCINATION n.   trip, head trip, pipe dream, pink elephants.

HALLUCINOGENIC adj.   mind bender, mind-bending, mind-blower, mind-blowing.

HALLWAY n.   squat pad.

HALT adj.   crip, g'd up, geed up, gimp, gimpy, game.

HALT n.   freeze, break, break-off, cutoff, layoff, letup, screaming halt, shuddering halt, grinding halt, stoppage.

HALT v.   cool it, can it, come to a screaming halt, come to a grinding halt, come to a shuddering halt, blow the whistle on, put a cork in it, drop anchor. See STOP.

HAM n.   grunt, squeal, Noah's boy.

HAM AND EGGS n.   cluck and grunt, ham and.

HAMBURGER n.   burger, cheeseburger, beefburger, superburger, Big Mac, big boy, chewed fine, clean up the kitchen (order for hamburger, hash or stew), hamburg, Wimpy, ground round, salisbury steak.

HAMMOCK n.   fleabag (Navy).

HAMPER v.   hang up, tie up, hold up, get in the way, stymie, cramp one's style, drag one's foot. See HINDER. See also PREVENT.

HAMPERED adj.   stuck, stuck with, stung, snowed, hog-tied.

HAND n.   mitt, paw, bunch of fives (fist), duke, fin, flipper, grabber, ham, hook, meat hook, biscuit hook, lily white, potato grabber.

HAND v.   drop, fork over, pass it on over, hand-carry, hand-walk, put on, put out, dish out, come across with, duke, weed, gimme.

HANDBAG n.   bag, clutch, frame, hide, leather, jiffy bag, jitney bag, keister.

HANDBILL n.   handout, literature, throwaway, flyer, dodger.

HANDCUFF v.   cuff, put on the cuffs, put on the bracelets.

HANDCUFFS n.   bracelets, cuffs, cufflinks, thumbs, darbies, derbies, irons, nippers, slave bracelets.

HANDGUN n.   artillery, piece, iron, snubby, Saturday night special, gat, peashooter, equalizer, difference, hardware, roscoe; dumb gat, gagged gat, hush hush, (silencer). See GUN.

HANDICAP n.   hang-up, baggage, psychological baggage, cap (racing).

HANDICAPPED adj.   crip, game, g'd up, geed up, gimp, gimpy, hamstrung, hog-tied, taken out, sidelined, out of commission.

HANDKERCHIEF n.   blower, duster, tear duster, sneezer, sniffer, snot rag, wipe.

HANDLE v.   get a handle on something, hack it, cut the mustard, make out, make the grade, deal with, call the signals, run things. See MANAGE.

HANDLES n.   ears.

HAND ORGAN n.   hurdy-gurdy.

HANDSHAKE n.   gimme five, gimme ten, gimme some skin, give the man some; high five, high fiving celebration (congratulations); the glad hand.

HANDSHAKER n.   glad-hander, duker, fin flipper, mitt glommer.

HANDSOME adj.   hunk, tuna, Adonis, lover boy, pretty boy, tall dark and handsome, handsome thing.

HANDSPRING n.   flip, flip-flop.

HANDWRITING n.   scrawl, scribble, chicken tracks, hen tracks, mark.

HANG v.   stretch, stretch rope, string up, swing, catch rope, dance, go through the trap, hoist, scrag, top, be crooked.

HANGING n.   necktie party, necktie social, necktie sociable, Texas cakewalk, hemp fever.

HANGMAN'S ROPE n.   necktie.

HANGOVER n.   big head, morning after, the shakes, DTs, shot, under the weather, the feebles, the willies, crown fire, a hair of the dog (cure).

HANKER v.   yen for, cream for, have eyes for, have one's mouth fixed for, have a case on, partial to. See DESIRE.

HANKERING n.   the urge, druthers, weakness, fire in the belly, the munchies (food), yen, zazzle. See DESIRE.

HAPHAZARDLY adv.   any old way, willy-nilly, all over the map, higgledy-piggledy. See ERRATICALLY.

HAPLESS adj.   jinxed, hoodooded, behind the eight ball, jonah, snakebit, loser, a winner, sad sack, schlemiel (Yid.), dick in the dirt, poor fish. See UNFORTUNATE.

HAPPEN v.   shake, smoke, what goes, come down, what's coming down, down, what's going down, action, what's happening, what cooks?, what's cooking?, cooking with gas. See OCCUR.

HAPPY adj.   chipper, chirpy, corky, perky, upper, up, hopped up, upbeat, lookin' good, stocked, flyin', flyin' high, floating, floating on air, on a cloud, on cloud seven, on cloud nine, sunny, sunny side up, in seventh heaven, on a joy ride, tea'd up, wowed, pleased as Punch, happy as a clam, tickled, tickled pink, tickled to death, hummy, fat dumb and happy, high, high as a kite, can't complain, gassed, out of it, get one's grits, have no kick coming, blow one's mind, blowing one's roof, popping one's nuts, handsprings, backflips, flipping, hit the spot, just what the doctor ordered, Little Mary Sunshine, Little Merry Sunshine.

HARANGUE n.   spiel, spouting, hassle, reading out, eating out. See SPEECH.

HARANGUE v. get on a soapbox, spiel, spout, chew the scenery, stump, go on about, blow off, dress down, yell one's head off. See ORATE.

HARASS v. bug, ride, eat, noodge, burn, give a bad time to, give one a hard time, give one the needle, work on, get to, rattle one's cage, hassle, jack one around. See ANNOY. See also INTIMIDATE.

HARASSED adj. hacked, tee'd off, browned off, riled, spooked, hard put to it, picked on, torn down, steamed. See ANNOYED.

HARASSING, STOP v. fuck off, cut the shit, cut the comedy, unass one.

HARD adj. 1. cold fish, cold-blooded, hard as nails, hard-boiled, tough, rhinoceros hide, thick-skinned, dead ass, butter wouldn't melt in his mouth, got lead balls for eyes. See CALLOUS. 2. uphill, uphill battle, mean, heavy, hairy, murder, pisser, rough, bitch, tough proposition, hard row of stumps, ballbreaker. See DIFFICULT.

HARDHEADED adj. bullheaded, pigheaded, hard-nosed, hang tough, tough nut, locked in, head in concrete, stand pat. See STUBBORN.

HARD HITTING adj. socko, sockeroo, punchy.

HARDLY adv. by a hair, by the skin of one's teeth, pretty near, practically.

HARD PRESSED adj. back to the wall, in the soup, at the end of one's rope, hard up, up against it, up shit creek, up shit creek without a paddle, scraping the bottom of the barrel, fighting to keep one's head up, tryin' to stay alive, runnin' out of time, no more cards to play. See also DESPERATE.

HARDSHIP n. case, hard knocks, hard row to hoe, tough break, rum go, rainy day, tough luck, rotten luck, down on one's luck, up against it, on the skids, on one's uppers, gone to pot, gone to the dogs, bummer, downer, drag, grabber, can't even get arrested. See also ADVERSITY.

HARDTACK n. dog biscuit.

HARD TIMES n. bust, bad times, pull in one's belt, run for cover, shorten sail, batten down the hatches, rainy days, slack season, slump, crash, the big trouble.

HARDWARE STORE n. pig joint.

HARDWORKING adj. work one's tail off, whiz, eager beaver, grind, greasy grind. See INDUSTRIOUS.

HARKEN v. listen up, pick up, tune in on, catch, get a load of, be all ears, knock on one's lobes. See LISTEN.

HARLEM Soul City, Soulville, Sugar Hill (elite section).

HARLOT n. hooker, call girl, hustler, ho, working girl, model, pro, chippie, prosty, tart, bimbo, hostess, shady lady. See PROSTITUTE.

HARLOTRY n. in the life, the life, world's oldest profession, broad racket, the bottle, hustle, turning a trick, hitting the turf, stepping out, going out for a buck, on the turf, white slavery.

HARM v. 1. ding, wing, nick, tweak, total, louse up, mess up, muck up, ball up, wrack up, hash up, get, zing, bend the goods. See DAMAGE. 2. dump on, put down, pooh pooh, hit one where one lives, do a number on, lay a bad trip on one, get. See WOUND.

HARMLESS adj. paper tiger, pussycat, softie.

HARMONICA n. harp, mouth organ.

HARMONIOUS adj. hit it off, simpatico, mix, togetherness, good vibes, good vibrations, in sync, in tune with, on the same wavelength, kissing kin. See also FRIENDLY.

HARSH adj. hairy, hard-nosed, tough, wicked, bitchy, cussed, mean, hard-boiled, hard shell. See STERN.

HARTFORD, CONNECTICUT Stag City.

HASH n. gook, clean up the kitchen for one, the gentleman will take a chance (order), gooey (WW I), Irish turkey, mystery, slumgudgeon, yesterday today and forever.

HASHISH n. hash, heesh, sheish, keef, candy, hash head (user). See also MARIJUANA.

HASTEN V. hustle, fog, shake a leg, make tracks, hotfoot it, barrel ass, snap shit, put the pedal to the metal, get the lead out of one's ass, get cracking, get a wiggle on. See SPEED.

HASTY adj. quickie, pronto, snappy, chop chop, on the double, double clutchin', pretty damned quick, PDQ, wham bam, get cracking, in nothing flat. See FAST.

HAT n. lid, topper, cap, boater, bowler, chimney, dip, skimmer, bugle warmer, opera (folding), straw, sailor, Panama, deer stalker, plug, plug hat, stove pipe, dicer, rim, sky, sky piece, Stetson, ten-gallon, sombrero, beaver, tit cap, tar bucket, brain bucket, hard hat, iron hat, tin hat, gimme cap, fore and aft (admiral), go-to-hell cap (WW II, Army and Marines), cady (1850 U.), crusher (1929).

HATCH v. cook up, dream up, trump up, whip up, frame up, come up with, throw together, spitball, brainstorm. See PLAN. See also SCHEME.

HATE v. grossed out on, have no use for, have an allergy to, allergic to, down on, have a hate on for, can't stand the guts of, hate one's guts, on one's shit list. See also DISLIKE.

HATEFUL adj.　uncool, unhep, unhipped, awful, beastly, bitchy, cussed, mean, ornery, gross, grody, grody to the max, pesky, pestiferous, funky (Bl.), act like one's shit doesn't stink. See also DESPICABLE.

HATRED n.　allergy to, no use for.

HAUGHTY adj.　biggety, sniffy, snooty, snotty, uppity, stuck up, high hat, on one's high horse, have one's glasses on (Bl.). See ARROGANT.

HAUL v.　lug, pack, piggy back, ride, shlep, shlep along, tote, truck, back, birdie back, buck, gun, heel, hump, jag, shoulder, move.

HAUNT n.　hangout, the place, stamping ground, old stamping ground, stomping ground, ole stomping ground.

HAUNT v.　hant, spook, voodoo, hoodoo. See also FREQUENT.

HAUNTED adj.　hanted, spooked, spooky.

HAVE v.　lock up, get hold of, glom on to, latch on to, bogart, corner, corner the market, get a corner on, hog, get one's hands on, sit on.

HAWAII　Aloha State, the Islands, Wahoo.

HAWKER n.　candy man, pusher, (drugs); cheap jack, cheap john. See VENDOR.

HAZARD n.　1. long shot, hundred to one shot, go at, stab, have a fling at, outside chance, snowball chance, toss up. See WAGER. 2. that's the way the ball bounces, that's the way the cookie crumbles, that's the way [any number of things], lucky hit, lucky break, run of luck, luck into. See LUCK. 3. double trouble, thin ice, hot potato, dynamite, risky business.

HAZARD v.　take a plunge, go for broke, skate on thin ice, go out on a limb. See RISK.

HAZARDOUS adj.　hot, hairy, unhealthy, widow-maker, dicey, chancy, can get burned, touchy. See DANGEROUS.

HAZE n.　ground clouds, smaze, smog, soup.

HAZE v.　needle, put on, rag, razz, rib, roast, jive, jolly, josh, kid, horse. See TEASE. See also JOKE.

HAZY adj.　smoggy, smazy, muzzy, soupy.

HEAD n.　1. bean, old bean, noggin, noodle, noddle, dome, pate, attic, conk, conk piece, top story, upper story, upstairs, block, biscuit, cabbage head, calabash (Arc.), can, chimney (Bl.), cupola, coco, coconut, pimple, potato, poll, pumpkin, punkin, bonnet, cruller, knob, lemon, sconce, squash, thinker, think pot, box, think box, think tank, knowledge box, dream box, gray matter, little gray cells, wet ware (brain), solid ivory, wig. 2. C.O., bosshead, czar, godfather, head honcho, the man, Mister

Charlie (Bl.), top dog, kingfish, lead-off man. See EXECUTIVE.

HEADACHE n.　head, have a head, hangover, a migraine.

HEADLIGHTS n.　glim, glimmers, one eye, eyeballs, quads (four), bright, dims (parking lights).

HEADQUARTERS n.　ad building, tower of power, HQ, GHQ, CP, home office, puzzle palace (higher), Pentagon, toy factory (C.I.A.).

HEADQUARTERS ASSIGNMENT n　palace guard (police).

HEADSTRONG adj.　bullheaded, mule, hard-nosed, hard core, hard shell, Turk, locked in, has one's Dutch up, murder (he's murder). See STUBBORN.

HEALTH, BAD adj.　poorly, one foot in the grave, one foot in the grave and the other on a banana peel, on one's last legs, a walking disease, walking wounded. See ILL.

HEALTHY adj.　alive and kicking, wrapped tight, bright-eyed and bushy-tailed, chipper, together, fit as a fiddle, full of beans, full of piss and vinegar, in fine feather, in fine whack, in high feather, in the pink, sound as a dollar, right, right as rain, solid as a rock, beefy, husky, strong as a horse, strong as a lion, strong as an ox.

HEALTH SPA n.　fat farm, milk farm.

HEAR v.　listen up, pick up, catch, read, get, get a load of, be all ears, have one's ear to the ground, get an earful, hear tell, give ears, knock on one's lobes. See LISTEN.

HEARSAY n.　scuttlebutt, talk, grapevine, clothesline, leak, ear loft, latrine rumor, wire, heard over the backyard fence. See GOSSIP.

HEARSE n.　meat wagon, dead wagon, glass wagon, bone box, last ride, black Maria.

HEARTBEAT n.　back beat, tick, tick tock.

HEART n.　1. pump, ticker, clock, chimer, puffer, pumper, bad pump, bum clock, bum ticker. 2. bottom line, meat and potatoes, nitty-gritty, nub, nuts and bolts, groceries, coal and ice. See BASIC.

HEARTBROKEN adj.　destroyed, sing the blues, cry the blues, hang crepe, bummed out, hurtin', hurting, in pain, in the pits, off one's feed, cracked up, cut up, tore up, all torn up, ripped. See UNHAPPY.

HEARTLESS adj.　cold fish, cold-blooded, hard as nails, thick-skinned, dead ass, butter wouldn't melt in his mouth, got lead balls for eyes. See CALLOUS.

HEAVE v.　peg, chuck, chunk, fire, lob, pitch, sling.

HEAVEN n.　pearly gates, happy hunting ground, promised land, glory, kingdom come, upstairs, up there, blue, Blue Broadway, wild blue yonder, big skip, the old bye and bye, the great ball park in the sky, the great ad [or any business] agency in the sky.

HEAVY adj. hefty, lead-footed, tough, beefy, fatso, two ton Tessie, like lead. See also FAT.

HEAVYSET adj. built, well-stacked, built like a brick shithouse, built for comfort, busty, curvy, zaftig, fatty. See also FAT.

HECTIC adj. jungle, zoo, madhouse, nutsy, all hell broke loose, to do, hassle. See FRANTIC.

HEDGE v. cop out, cop a plea, jive, shuck, shuck and jive, stonewall, hem and haw, blow hot and cold, flip flop, shilly shally, sit on the fence, waffle, fudge, hedge one's bet, pussyfoot, beg the question, cover your ass, CYA, pass the buck, run around, give one the run around, stall off, get around, beat around, beat around the bush.

HEED n. listen up, pop to, spotlight, tender loving care, TLC.

HEED v. 1. sit, baby-sit, keep tab, keep tabs on, ride herd on, mind the store, watch the store, watch over, not get off base, not get out of line, stay in line, toe the line, toe the mark, keep one's distance, keep a weather eye open, keep one's eye peeled, watch one's step, watch out, watch out for. 2. catch, get a load of, give ears, have one's ears on, knock on one's lobes, listen up, pick up, dig, spot, give a ghee a toss, give a thing a toss, give a thing a play, rap, rumble, tumble.

HEEDFUL adj. listen up, not miss a trick, pay mind to, shine me on, glued, hooked, keep on one's toes, walk wide. See CAUTIOUS.

HEEDLESS adj. out to lunch, asleep at the switch, goofing off, daydreaming, fast and loose, slapdash, sloppy. See CARELESS.

HEIGHTEN v. hop up, beef up, jazz up, punch up, soup up, heat up, hot up, add fuel to the fire, pour it on. See INTENSIFY.

HEINOUS adj. gross, grody to the max, beastly, raunchy, sucks, stinking, godawful. See BAD.

HELICOPTER n. chopper, copter, whirley bird, eggbeater, eye in the sky, telecopter (TV news, traffic), trafficopter, gunship, windmill; air bear, bear in the air, dustoff, smokey copter (police); Charlie copter (Govt.), Huey (Mil.), angel (Navy).

HELIUM n. balloon juice.

HELLO interj. hi, hey, hey there, ciao, look out, gimme some skin, gimme five, gimme ten, cherrio, chorro, cherry, what's happenin'?, what's going down?, what's coming down?, what gives?, what's shaking?, what's the skinny?, what's the low down?, what's the scoop?, what's the poop?, what's the rave?, what cooks, what's cookin'?, what's cookin' good-lookin'?, what it is, hi ya, howdy, howdy do, how de do, how do ye do, how do?, hey now, say now, whatayasay?, well a hey, how you doin'?, how's things?, how's tricks?, how goes it?, how's every little thing?, how's the world treating you?, hello Joe what do you know?, long time no see.

HELMET n. brain bucket, hard hat, hat, iron hat, tin hat.

HELP v. 1. mayday. 2. boost, buck up, brace up, give a boost to, give a leg up, give a lift, lend a hand, plug, hype, push, hold a brief for, go with, go for, go to bat for, go to the mat for, go down the line for, go the route for, make a pitch for, beat the drum for, plump for, run interference for, grease the wheels for, thump the tub for, root for, stump for, front for, stand up for, stick up for, ride shotgun for, take care of one for, save one's bacon, put a flea in one's ear, put a bug in one's ear, open doors, hand out, splash, spot, throw the spotlight on, puff, ballyhoo, put on the map, press agent, up, backup, bail out, hold one's end up, straighten one out. 3. pick up the tab, angel, back, bankroll, grubstake, stake, go for. See FINANCE.

HELPER n. help, temp, sec, girl Friday, gal Friday, man Friday, gofer, hired hand, mother's helper, yard man, flunky, home guard, peon, savage, serf, slave, slavey. See ASSISTANT.

HELPLESS adj. handcuffed, with one's hands tied, pinned, basket case, over a barrel, tapped, tapped out, up the creek, up the creek without a paddle, up shit creek, up shit creek without a paddle. See also DEFENSELESS.

HEMORRHOIDS n. grapes.

HEN n. banty, biddy, birdie, chick, chickabiddy, chickadee, chicky, gull, gump, sea gull, albatross (WW II).

HENCHMAN n. flunky, stooge, yes-man, goon, asshole buddy, ass kisser, brownnose, running dog, toad, ward heeler, heller.

HEN HOUSE n. egg orchard.

HERD v. poke, punch, round up, scare up, corral.

HERMAPHRODITE n. morph, morphodite.

HEROIC adj. stand tall, bigger'n life, fire eater, gritty, gutsy, gutty, ballsy, hairy. See DARING.

HEROIN n. C., H., aitch, the big H, horse, snow, sugar, smeck, smack, bag, cadillac, piece, weight (ounce), fix, shit, the tragic magic, liquid sky (with sex), Lady H, yen shee, stuff, hard stuff, white stuff, junk, hook, hot shot (overdose), pack, blanks, bones, boy, brother, brown, brown sugar, Mexican brown, Mexican mud, black tar, Chinese, Chinese red, red chicken, chiva, cobics, crap, doojee, Dojee, doorjee, estuffa, first degree, heroina, powder, joy powder, flea powder, polvo, scag, scar, scramble, tecaba, thing, bombita, dynamite, cold 45, Colt .45, schmee, antifreeze, caballo, deck, salt, him, hero of the underworld, Harry, Big Harry, witch hazel, angel, noise, lemonade, poison, eye opener (first of day), goldfinger (synthetic).

HEROIN ADDICT n.   Scag Jones, smack slammer.

HEROIN AND COCAINE n.   speedball, dynamite.

HEROIN AND MARIJUANA n.   atom bomb.

HEROIN USE v.   chase the dragon, coast, cook, cook it, do up, pop it, jab a vein, sniff nose candy, snort dust.

HEROIN USER n.   smackhead, smack slammer, Scag Jones.

HESITATE v.   pussyfoot, pussyfoot around, hem and haw, straddle, fence straddle, on the fence, sit on the fence, hang on the fence, run hot and cold, blow hot and cold, hedge, hedge off, shilly shally, waffle, tic and twitch.

HETEROSEXUAL n.   straight, right-handed, vanilla, fish (lesbian use), jam (homosexual use).

HEX n.   evil eye, whammy, double whammy, horns, kibosh, hoodoo, voodoo, kiss of death. See CURSE.

HEX v.   cuss, damn, darn, jinx, spook, put the horns on, put the whammy on one, put the double whammy on one, give one a kine ahora (Yid.), hoodoo, hoodoo one, voodoo, voodoo one.

HEXED adj.   spooked, hoodooed, voodooed.

HIDDEN adj.   covered up, holed up, put in the hole, planted, stashed, under wraps, under the fig leaf, doggo, incog, Q.T., hush-hush, hushed up.

HIDE n.   dried barkers, skins, skin joint (shop).

HIDE v.   1. stash, stache, stash away, ditch, duck, plant, squirrel, squirrel away, hike, put in the hole, stick in the hole. 2. whitewash, sweep under the rug, bury, cover, cover up, duck, stonewall, finesse it, palm, paper over, hold out on, keep buttoned up, keep it under one's hat, keep under wraps, skim (income), unload, launder. 3. hide out, hole up, play dead, lie doggo, lie low, sit tight, tunnel, cool off, duck outta sight, melt into the scenery, take it on the lam, do a crouch, flatten out, out, hit the shade, hit the mattresses.

HIDEOUS adj.   animal, beast, gross, plug (M.), plug-ugly, ugly as sin, grimbo (Fem.), hagged out, face would crack a mirror, pruneface, sick, weird. See UGLY.

HIDING PLACE n.   cover, fig leaf, safe house, hideout, hideaway, getaway place, the scatter, hole, plant, shade, sneezer, stash, stache, drop, drop joint, drop off.

HIERARCHY n.   pecking order, place, slot.

HIGH adj.   high rise.

HIGHBALL n.   tall one, fresh one (another).

HIGH FLOWN adj.   high falutin', high-hatted, high nosed, high-toned, toplofty, stuffed shirt, put on airs, dog it, purple, gassy, windy, given to twenty-dollar words, bor-ring, over one's head. See also POMPOUS.

HIGHJACK v.   jack, hijack, skyjack, heist.

HIGHLY adv.   awful, awfully, real, really, but good, jolly, bloody, daisy, so much, mighty, plenty, too much, mucho, so, stone (stone deaf), terribly, terrifically, almighty, powerful, right.

HIGH-MINDED adj.   cocky, puffed up, stuck up, high-flown, high nosed, have one's glasses on (Bl.), dog it, smarty pants, smart ass. See ARROGANT.

HIGH-PRICED adj.   pricey, steep, upscale, uptown, executive, high, pretty penny, up to here (elbow), highway robbery. See EXPENSIVE.

HIGH SCHOOL n.   hi, high.

HIGH SCHOOL STUDENT n.   prep, preppy, preppie; freshie, frosh (first year).

HIGH SOCIETY n.   upper crust, hoity-toity, the big bucks, 400, high hat, rich bitch, jet set, mainliner, FFV's, Mister and Mrs. Gotrocks. See ELITE.

HIGH-SPIRITED adj.   1. chipper, chirpy, corky, high, sunny, sunny side up, up, upbeat, upper, perky, Little Merry Sunshine, Little Mary Sunshine. See HAPPY. 2. full of piss and vinegar, full of beans, full of prunes, full of hops. See SPIRITED.

HIGH-STRUNG adj.   uptight, wired, wired up, hyper, jittery, jumpy, all shook up, clutched up, on pins and needles, on the ragged edge, choked, zonkers. See NERVOUS.

HIGHWAY n.   bricks, pavement, dragway, pike, rip strip, super slab, bowling alley, four lane parking lot, world's longest parking lot. See ROAD.

HIGHWAY POLICE n.   bear, Smokey, Smokey Bear, CHIPS (California).

HIKE n.   constitutional, legwork, shlep, traipse.

HIKE v.   leg it, hoof it, ride shank's mare, stump it, hit the road, hit the dirt, hit the grit. See WALK.

HILARIOUS adj.   crack up, gas, boffo, a scream, yokky, gagged up, laffer, riot, priceless, screamingly funny, gut-busting, for grins. See AMUSING.

HINDER v.   queer, crimp, cramp, put a crimp in, cramp one's style, stymie, get in the way, put a cork in it, skin, crab, hog-tie, tie up, pin, hang up, hold up, bring to a screaming halt, freeze, blow the whistle on, foul up, fuck up, louse up, snafu, bollix, gum, gum up the works, fake out, shut out, shut off, close out, close off, choke,

choke off, stonewall, stall, flag one down, fix one's wagon, saddle with, drag one's feet, put on the brakes, weigh down, hang like a millstone round one's neck, flummox, stump, give one the business, sandbag, torpedo (a plan), throw a monkey wrench into the works, upset one's apple cart, spike one's guns, cut off one's water, turn off one's water, steal one's thunder, trash, take one down, take care of, take the wind out of one's sails, knock the bottom out of, knock the chocks from under one, knock the props from under one, down one, ditch, give the slip, skip out on, duck, dodge, get around, give the run around, run circles around, run rings around, monkey with the buzz saw, monkey with, mix in. See also RESTRAIN, BURDEN.

HINDRANCE n. hang-up, baggage, excess baggage, psychological baggage, foot dragging, stumbling block, catch, catch 22, glitch, joker, one small difficulty, a lock, jam up, gridlock, bugaboo, crimp, crimp one's style, hump, stinger, monkey wrench, albatross, albatross around one's neck, ball and chain, millstone, shlepper, shlep along, get off my side, get off my case, get out of my life, whose side are you on?, with you as a friend I don't need enemies.

HINDSIGHT adj. Monday morning quarterback, second guess.

HINDU n. raghead (Derog.).

HINT n. lead, hot lead, tip off, telltale, print, bum steer (false), flea in one's ear, sneaking suspicion.

HINT v. leak, spring, spring one's duke, tip one's duke, tip one's hand, let the cat out of the bag, put a flea in one's ear, drop hairpins (homosexual). See EXPOSE.

HINTERLAND n. boondock, boondocks, boonies, outback, sticks, stix, woods, up country. See COUNTRY.

HIPPOPOTAMUS n. hippo.

HIRE v. sign on, sign up, take on, ink, pact, bring on board, come on board, truck with.

HIRED adj. on board, inked, signed, pacted.

HIRELING n. help, stiff, apparatchik, flunky, temp, pencil pusher, girl Friday, man Friday, white collar, pink collar, hard hat, blue collar. See WORKER.

HISS n. Bronx cheer, raspberry, razz, the bird.

HISTRIONIC adj. hammy, schmaltzy, hokey, tear-jerking, scenery chewing.

HIT n. belt, clout, cut, chop, whop, wham, whammy, biff, bash, bat, shot, swat, swipe, sock, slug, slog, zap, zetz, zinger, clip, lick, wallop, lollop, haymaker, bonk, dint, dozer, plunk, clump, one-two, one-two punch, one-two blow, roundhouse, roundhouse sidewinder, Sunday punch, the leather, blindside (unexpected).

HIT v. bash, trash, drub, flax, wax, lace, lather, larrup, leather, lambaste, blitz, cane, spank, paddle, work over, wham, bam, whop, whomp, whack, bushwhack, shellack, whip, whipsaw, wipe, hide, tan, tan one's hide, take it out of one's hide, take it out of one's skin, brain, bloop, bonk, conk, pop, bop, boff, biff, bean, belt, bat, bung, blind, K.O., kayo, chill, stretch, bust, dust, dust off, drop, deck, dump, dish, total, sock, slug, slog, smack, poke, powder, pepper, clout, clobber, cream, lump, lump up, clump, clunk, plunk, clonk, clock, crown, clip, flip, flatten, get, soak, zap, zetz, paste, waste, wing, measure, bump, jump, heel, mug, hurt, yerk, bust up, come at, have at, lay at, go for, pitch into, light into, sail into, wade into, lay into, crack down on, lean on, clean on, take one, take out, shot, take a shot, take a whack at, take one over the hurdles, take care of, take down, take one down, put down, slap down, smack down, shoot down, shoot down in flames, chop down, shut down, lay one out, lay one low, lay on sap, lay a glove on, wipe out, hand it to one, punch out, work out, knock, knock cold, knock dead, knock in, knock off, knock around, knock one out, knock the beholden out of one, knock the daylights out of one, knock the shit out of one, knock into the next county, knock one into next week, knock for a row of [anything], knock on the head, knock one on one's ass, knock one ass over teakettle, knock one on one's ear, knock one's block off, knock one for a loop, knock on one's biscuit, knock on one's can, knock on one's keister, knock on one's pratt, knock on one's quiff, knock one on one's wallet, deal a knockout blow to, whale the daylights out of one, whale, wallop, welt, blast, blast on, fire on, throw a punch, slough, slough around, put the slug on one, sock it to one, give one a fat lip, tangle ass with, go up against, let have it, dust one's jacket, give a deal to, give a dose of birch oil, give a dose of strap oil, give a dose of hickory oil, give a dose of hazel oil, floor one, banjax, plant one, down one, wheel and deal, ring one's bell, haul off on one, let one have it, land a haymaker, put the bee on one, boot, boot around, put the boots to, coldcock, cold pack, Chinese, drygulch, double bank, give one the blanket, give one the works, put one in the hospital, give one a going over, break one's face, hit a clip, go to town, kick one's cruller in, kick one's lemon in, kick one's sconce in.

HITCH n. catch, glitch, bug, hang-up, snafu, holdup, joker, one small difficulty. See DIFFICULTY.

HITCHHIKE v. hitch, hitch a ride, thumb, thumb a ride, thumb one's way, bum a ride, cadge a ride, hook a ride, long arm.

HITTER n. slugger, mugger, pile driver, knuckle-duster, lip-splitter. See also FIGHTER.

HOARD v. sock away, squirrel, stash, scrimp, skimp, put aside for a rainy day. See SAVE.

HOARDER n. hog.

HOAX n. 1. hustle, con, con game, sting, flimflam, scam, racket, dodge, fast shuffle, total shuck. See CHEAT. 2. crap, crock, fib, cock-and-bull story, whopper, bunco, hooey, banana oil, snow job, diddling. See LIE.

HOAX v. rook, run a game on, fleece, sting, Murphy, pigeon-drop, play games with, suck in, pull one's leg, set up, frame up, fake out, humbug. See TRICK.

HOBBLE v. gimp; hang up, crimp, put a crimp in, cramp, cramp one's style. See also HINDER.

HOBBY n. bag, thing, kick, schtick, shot, go in for, be into, have a weakness for, do one's thing.

HOBO n. bum, stumblebum, king of the road, bo, stiff, stiffo, bindlestiff, bindleman, deadbeat, floater. See VAGRANT. See also BEGGAR.

HOBO CAMP n. jungle; crum, crumb, crumb roll (bedroll, blanket or pack).

HODGEPODGE n. everything but the kitchen sink, mishmash, mishmosh, duke's mixture, mixed bag, goulash. See MIXTURE.

HOG n. porker, porky, cob roller (young or small).

HOLD v. 1. stay put, cling like a burr, cling like ivy, freeze to, hold on like a bulldog, stick like a barnacle, stick like a leech, stick like a limpet, stick like a wet shirt. 2. bogart, hog, lock up, get hold of, glom on to, latch on to, corner, corner the market, get a corner on, get one's hands on, sit on. 3. swear up and down, swear on a stack of bibles, swear till one is blue in the face, cross one's heart and hope to die, say so. See AFFIRM. 4. take as gospel truth, take stock in, set store by, swear by, okay, OK, buy, bet one's bottom dollar on, lay money on, lap up, have a hunch, have a sneaking suspicion. See BELIEVE. 5. cool, cool off, cool down, hold down, hold off, keep the lid on, get one in a box, bottle up, cork up, lock up, put a lock on. See RESTRAIN. 6. sock away, squirrel, stash, scrimp, skimp, put aside for a rainy day. See SAVE.

HOLD BACK v. fudge, back off, dial back, go back on one's word, weasel out, worm one's way out, worm out of, welsh, renig, nig, back water.

HOLIDAY n. two weeks with pay, liberty, layoff, a few days off, eyes to cool it, gone fishing.

HOLISTIC MEDICINE n. holismo (as a cure all).

HOLLER v. holler out, give a shout, hoot, squawk.

HOLLYWOOD n. Hollyweird, filmdom, Glamour Town, Movieland, Movieville, moviedom, Tinsel City, Tinseltown.

HOLY adj. Holy Joe, Jasper, knee bender, goody, goody-goody, goody two shoes, scoutmaster.

HOME n. pad, crash pad, condo, joint, domi, flop, digs, diggings, hole in the wall, castle, cave, home plate, turf, ole stomping grounds, roost. See HOUSE. See also APARTMENT, NEIGHBORHOOD.

HOME ECONOMICS n. home ec.

HOMELIKE adj. comfy, cushy, homey, folksy, down home, haymish, snug as a bug in a rug.

HOMELY adj. pig, dogface, airedale, animal, beast, gross, plug-ugly, gruesome twosome, face would stop a clock, homely as a mud fence. See UGLY.

HOMESICK adj. rhino.

HOMESPUN adj. vanilla, folksy, homey, haymish (Yid.), open and shut, meat and potatoes man, plain as an old shoe.

HOMICIDE n. offing, ride, wasting, bang job, big chill, bump off, erase, hit, rubout, scragging, the big M, the works, fragging (officer, Mil.). See KILLING.

HOMILY n. bromide, old saw, broken record, daffodil, cracker barrel, chew one's cabbage, chew one's tobacco.

HOMING PIGEON n. homer.

HOMOSEXUAL n. gay, homo, mo, faggot, fag, agfay, fruit, fruitcake, queer, fairy, pansy, lily, flower, auntie, aunt (elderly), nance, butterfly, fly ball, bait, bronco (novice), mandrake, father fucker, out, out of the closet, gunsel, gazoonil, gazooney, gonif, swing the other way, lover, John, lacy, left-handed, lightfooted, Mary, mintie, mother, Nancy, bent, three dollar bill, chicken, chicken delight (young), faunet, faunlet (pre-adolescent boy), chicken hawk, punk, government inspected meat (Mil.), boy, capon, cocksucker, flamer, drag queen, main queen, closet queen, flute, fluter, freak, frit, fooper, gobbler, girl, limp wrist, jocker, maricon, piccolo player, pix, peter puffer, swish, faygeleh, mola, pato (Sp.), out, paleface (white), pogey, bird taker, man's man, third sexer, eye doctor, cannibal, punk, jock, jocky, trapeze artist, tusk, wolf, ring tail, sod, angel, baby, salesman, mason, male oriented, identified, cake eater, sister, three-letter man (fag), four-letter man (homo), lamb, ma, nellie, skippy, rough trade (sadistic), truck driver (rough), twink, willie, geep, fruit ma toot, cruiser, flinch bird, guzzler, muzzler, nibbler, snake charmer, joker, keister bandit, daddy, papa, uncle, prussian, short arm bandit, short arm heister, turk, wheelman, apple pie, bender, bindle boy, brat, Mr. Brown, charity stuff, coozey, flap, floosie, flit (30s), les, lez, dyke, bull dyke, diesel dyke, butch, bitch, boondagger, daisy, fairy lady, Amy, bird, gal officer, lesbine, lesbo, marge, lady lover, double-barreled broad, shemale, top sergeant (all Derog. and Obsc.).

HOMOSEXUAL ACTIVIST n. Gay Lib, Gay Libber.

HOMOSEXUAL CLUB BAR n. gay bar, fag joint, meat market, fruit market, market, camp, gay hangout.

HOMOSEXUAL, FEMALE n. les, lez, lesbine, lesbie, lesbo, dyke, bull dyke, bull dagger, diesel dyke, butch, crested hen (butch), bitch, boondagger, daisy, fairy lady, Amy, bird, gal officer, marge, lady lover, female identified, female oriented, femme, finger artist, double barreled broad, shemale, harpie, Jasper, sergeant, top sergeant (all Derog.).

HOMOSEXUAL GATHERING n. bird circuit, grab party, lavender convention, meat rack.

HOMOSEXUAL GRATIFICATION meat.

HOMOSEXUAL, MALE n. fag, agfay, fairy, pansy, nance, boy, lily, capon, cocksucker, flamer, aunt (elderly), drag queen, main queen, closet queen, flute, fluter, freak, frit, gobbler, girl, limp wrist, jocker, maricon, piccolo player, pix, peter puffer, swish, faygeleh (Yid.), chicken, chicken delight (young), chicken hawk, bronco (novice), left-handed mintie, mola, out, mandrake, paleface (white), pogey, bird taker, man's man, third sexer, eye doctor, cannibal, punk, jock, jocky, trapeze artist, tusk, wolf, ring tail, sod, angel, baby, salesman, mason, male oriented, identified, cake eater, sister, three-letter man (fag), four-letter man (homo), gunsel, gazoonil, lamb, ma, mother, nellie, skippy, rough trade (sadistic), truck driver (rough), twink, willie, geep, fruit ma toot, cruiser, flinch bird, guzzler, muzzler, nibbler, snake charmer, joker, keister bandit, daddy, papa, uncle, prussian, short arm bandit, short arm heister, turk, wheelman, apple pie, bender, bindle boy, brat, Mr. Brown, charity stuff, coozey, flap, floosie, flit (30s) (all Derog. and Obsc.).

HOMOSEXUAL MOVEMENT n. Gay Lib, Gay Liberation.

HOMOSEXUAL REVELATION v. come out, come out of the closet, drop beads, drop a hairpin.

HOMOSEXUAL UNION to be married, to go shot for shot, to play sixty-nine (Obsc.), to swap stew for beans, swap spits, fag bag (woman married to).

HONEST adj. up front, right up front, open, going the hangout route, like it is, call it like it is, lay it on the line, on the up and up, on the level, the emess, no lie, what you see is what you get, WYSIWYG, honest to God, honest injun, sure enough, twenty-four carat, square, square John, square shooter, true blue, righteous, Christian, kosher, boy scout, down home, fly right, Mr. Clean, regular, legit, on the legit, for real, real people, okay people, saint, straight, straight arrow, shoot straight, straight shooter, straight from the shoulder, straight out, straight dope, straight stuff, straight shit, third rail, talk like a Dutch uncle, call a spade a spade, white, damn white, put all one's cards on the table, make no bones

about it, talk turkey, all wool and a yard wide, card carrying, salt of the earth, clean as a hound's tooth. See also SINCERE.

HONESTLY adv. for real, honest to God, indeedy, no buts about it, no ifs ands or buts, real, really truly.

HONOR v. roll out the red carpet, give one the key to the city, give one the glad hand, give one the blue ribbon.

HOOD n. doghouse.

HOODLUM n. hood, con, wrong number, hooligan, crook, tough, toughie, punk, yoot (teenager), soldier, deuce (small time), gorilla, goon, gun, gunsel, torpedo, wise guy. See CRIMINAL.

HOODWINK v. dick one around, run a game on, snake one in, fleece, gas, clip, con, scam, stiff, sting, double shuffle, skunk. See TRICK.

HOODWINKED adj. stung, been taken, taken for a sleigh ride, fucked over, set up, sandbagged, burned, fleeced, snowed, snowed in, snowed under. See TRICKED.

HOOLIGAN n. ape, gorilla, pug, strongarm, mug, goon, muscle, muscle man, hatchet man, hatchet boy, big boy, sleazeball, slimebucket, maggot, heavy, hood, clipper, bad actor, tough, tough cookie, hellion, terror, holy terror, sidewinder, roughneck, bruiser, mugger, ugly customer, plug-ugly. See also CRIMINAL.

HOOT n. Bronx cheer, razz, razzberry, raspberry, the bird, boo.

HOOT v. howl, put up a howl, set up a howl, holler, give a shout, give one the Bronz cheer, give one the raspberry, give one a razzberry, give one the bird, boo.

HOPE n. bright side, fool's paradise, light at the end of the tunnel, pipe dream. See also PROSPECT.

HOPE v. sweat, sweat it, sweat it out, hang in, keep one's fingers crossed, look on the bright side.

HOPEFUL adj. on the make, glad-hander (overly), gung ho, high, high on something, scoutmaster, keeping the faith, rosy, upbeat. See OPTIMISTIC.

HOPELESS adj. no way, no-win situation, can't win for losin', no more cards to play, sunk, shot down, gone, goner, gone goose, dead duck, put the kibosh on it, at the end of one's rope, not a ghost of a chance, not a Chinaman's chance, not a prayer, not a snowball's chance in hell, not til hell freezes over, in the soup, in the toilet, in deep shit, up shit creek, up shit creek without a paddle, up the creek, up the creek without a paddle, hard up, up against it, tryin' to stay alive, runnin' out of time, scrapin' the bottom of the barrel, got one's back to the wall, clutching at straws, spinning one's wheels, fighting to keep one's head up.

HORDE n.   mob, push, turnout, blowout, crush, jam, jam up, everybody and his brother, everybody and his uncle, loaded to the rafters, wall-to-wall people. See CROWD.

HORN n.   pretzel (French).

HORN BLOWING n.   beep, honk, toot.

HORNED TOAD n.   horny toad.

HOROSCOPE n.   signs, scope, Big Zee.

HORRIBLE adj.   awful, beastly, sickie, barfy, furry, hairy, skin crawling, grim, scary. See BAD. See also DREADFUL.

HORRIFY v.   chill off, scare shitless, scare the pants off one, scare the bejesus out of one, scare to death. See FRIGHTEN.

HORROR STORY n.   chiller, chiller-diller, thriller, monster movie, blood and guts, spine tingler.

HORS D'OEUVRES n.   dip, finger food, spread, munchies.

HORSE n.   hoss, hack, nag, bronc, bronco, bangtail, broom tail (mare), old gray mare, old Nellie, pony, bushtail, bum, crab, crip (crippled), crowbait (ugly or mean), refugee from the glue factory (sick, thin), cayuse, daisy cutter, plug, paint horse, old paint, pinto, G.G., geegee, trotter, dobbin, hayburner, plater, jade, crock, crowbait, goat, stiff. See also RACEHORSE.

HORSE MANURE n.   road apples, golden apples, alley apples.

HORSEPLAY n.   monkeyshines, shenanigans, hijinks, fun and games. See also AMUSEMENT.

HORSEPLAY v.   horse around, fuck around, screw around, roughhouse.

HORSEPOWER, ADD v.   soup, soup up, souped up, hop up, hopped up, juice up, juiced up.

HORSE RACE BETTING   across the board (first, second, third), win, on the nose, place (second), show (third), exacta, trifecta (win, place, show pools), daily double, pick six, quinella, out of the money, also ran, parlay, claim agent (bettor), the chalk (smart money), chalk eater (bookie) chalk favorite, odds-on favorite, long shot, layoff bet, if bet, hunch player, line, morning line (early odds), scratch sheet, tipster, tote board, odds board, tout, to tout (the tout touted me off number two), tout sheet, vigorish (track percentage share of betting pool), handle (total betting), OTB (Off Track Betting).

HORSE RACE CARE n.   cooler (light horse blanket), cool out, exercise boy, hot walker, nerved (nerve block to hooves), put down (humane killing), bute (phenylbutazone, painkiller), swipe (a groom).

HORSE RACE RIDING   up, in the irons, acey deucy (right stirrup shorter) win going away, hand-ride, near side (horse's left side).

HORSE, RACING n.   the ponies, pony, the g.g's, nag, gee gee, bangtail, mudder, pig, plater, dark horse (unknown entry), stick out (superior), maiden, chaser (steeplechase racer), claimer, bug (never won; apprentice jockey), beetle, cooler, lizard, getty up, glue pot, goat, hide, weanling, baby, juvenile (2-year-olds), lug in, lug out (rail), lugger, side wheeler, skin, stiff (loser), tacky, stretch runner, break down (injury while racing).

HORSE RACING TERMS   also ran, bear in, bear out, lug in, lug out, wear blinkers (restrict horse's side view), blow out (workout run), break (start from gate), the call, drive (he won under a drive), early foot (fast starter), speedball (fast horse), one-run horse, handily, breeze, post time (starting time), photo (photo finish), scratch (withdraw entry), bat, gad (whip); caller (race announcer); fast, lightning fast, good, heavy, muddy, sloppy, slow, gumbo (track conditions); the flats, flat racing, give away weight (carry extra weight handicap), footing, maiden race, go, run, in the money; pilot, rider (jockey); railbird (spectator), tack (equipment), the track, the charts, boat race, drug store race (drugged or fixed); sweep (sweepstake); golf ball, soup, T, tea (drugs); produce race (unfoaled entries based on bloodlines), Run for the Roses (Kentucky Derby); claimer, seller, selling race (claiming race); starter (an entry), steal (lead all the way), wire to wire (start to finish), hardboot (jockey or fore), green (inexperienced horse), shipper (horse from another track), improving the breed (horse racing), dropping in class, dogs up (early morning workouts).

HORSESHOES n.   barnyard golf.

HOSE n.   Georgia Credit Card (used for siphoning gasoline).

HOSPITABLE adj.   red-carpet treatment, roll out the red carpet, put out the welcome mat, give one the key to the city, break out the champagne.

HOSPITAL n.   bone factory, butcher shop, pogey (prison), alley (corridor).

HOSPITAL ZONE n.   pill hill.

HOST v.   do the honors, spread oneself, throw a party, pick up the check. See also ENTERTAIN, SOCIAL.

HOSTELRY n.   motel, airtel, aquatel, boatel, floatel, fleabag, chinch pad, flophouse, scratch crib.

HOSTILE adj.   ornery, scrappy, snorky, bitchy, waspish, anti, be agin, allergic to, have a chip on one's shoulder, at outs, on the muscle. See ANTAGONISTIC.

HOTCAKE n.   flapjack, blanket, brown bucks, flats, manhole cover, saddle blankets, tire patch, wheat, collision mat (WW II).

HOT CHOCOLATE n.   hot cha, fifty-one, fifty-two (two cups).

HOT ROD n.   bomb, bug (car and driver), can, rod, chopped (low chassis), low rider, hauler, hot iron, raked car. See also AUTOMOBILE.

HOT ROD TERMS   nerf (push a car with a car), sandbag, shaved, speed shop, squirrel (weave from side to side, a novice driver), twin pots, wrinkle rod, fishtail, forked-eight, bent eight.

HOT SPRINGS, ARKANSAS   Hot Water City.

HOTEL n.   motel, shortel (hourly rates), airtel, aquatel, boatel, floatel, chinch pad, flophouse, scratch crib.

HOTEL ROOM n.   flop box.

HOT WEATHER n.   broiler, roaster, scorcher, sizzler, swelterer, sticky, close, steamy, steam box, sweaty, one can fry eggs on the sidewalk, hotter than blue mud.

HOUND n.   hound dog. See also DOG.

HOUND v.   1. hassle, dog, penny dog, dog one's case, jump on one's case, on one's case, on one's back, bug, ride, be at, be on the back of, all right already, graum, yap at, on one's tail, tail, rag, rag on, curdle. See ANNOY. 2. bird dog (scout), scout, beat the bushes, scratch, scratch around, look all over hell, search high heaven, turn upside down, turn inside out, leave no stone unturned, take out after, track down. See also FOLLOW.

HOUNDED adj.   dogged, picked on.

HOUR n.   a chime, a coupla bells, straight up.

HOUSE n.   pad, crash pad, crib, condo, co-op, coop, pied-a-terre, joint, cubbyhole, den, domi, dommy, setup, layout, flop, flophouse, kennel, digs, diggings, roof over one's head, hole, hole in the wall, pigpen, pigsty, shanty, shack, lean-to, sty, dump, castle, box, cave, hi lo (split level), railroad flat, homeplate, palace, rack, roost, turf, old stomping grounds, bullpen, dice house, yurt.

HOUSEBREAK n.   caper, heist.

HOUSECOAT n.   duster.

HOUSE OF CORRECTION n.   jug, slam, slammer, pen, can, pokey, clink, lockup, cooler, brig, maxi (maximum security), pink clink, crossbar hotel, college, up the river, lockup. See JAIL.

HOUSE OF PROSTITUTION n.   house, cathouse, massage parlor, rap club, poontang palace, snake ranch, chicken ranch, hook shop, nautch joint, service station. See BROTHEL.

HOUSE OF REPRESENTATIVES   House.

HOUSEWORK n.   shitwork, chickwork.

HOUSTON, TEXAS   Astrodome City, Dome City.

HOVEL n.   dump, hole, pigpen, pigsty, rattrap, rathole, stall.

HOVERCRAFT n.   flying bathtub, flying crow's nest.

HOW ABOUT?   how's about?

HOWARD JOHNSON RESTAURANTS n.   Hojos.

HUBBUB n.   hubba-hubba, buzz-buzz, boom-boom, hoo ha, rowdydow, all hell broke loose, ruckus, hullabaloo, fuss.

HUCKSTER n.   Arab, pitchman.

HUFF n.   miff, pet, stew, tiff, snit. See PIQUE.

HUG n.   bear hug, squeeze, clinch, lock.

HUG v.   grab, grab ass, clinch, clutch, bear hug, squeeze,

HUGE adj.   gross, humongous, humungous, mungo, monstro, king-size, big mother, super-colossal, jumbo, whopping. See BIG.

HUMAN BEING n.   naked ape, human bean. See also PERSON.

HUMANITARIAN n.   Robin Hood, bleeding heart, do-gooder, good scout, good Sam. See also BENEFACTOR, PHILANTHROPIST.

HUMBLE v.   prick one's balloon, make one sing small, put one away, take down, take down a peg, take the starch out of, cut to the quick, put away. See HUMILIATE.

HUMBLED adj.   crawling, eat crow, eat dirt, eat humble pie, sing small, in bad, in Dutch, in the doghouse, lost face, drummed out, took down, knocked from one's high horse. See HUMILIATED.

HUMDRUM adj.   garden, garden variety, everyday, vanilla, dullsville, bromidic, dime a dozen, square John, Clyde, meat and potatoes man. See BORING.

HUMID adj.   close, boiler, steam bath, steamy, sweat box, sticky.

HUMILIATE v.   tear down, shoot down, cut down to size, cut rate, run down, put down, downplay, play down, take down, take down a peg, take down a peg or two, take the starch out of, take the shine out of, cut to the quick, rip, pan, slam, smear, squash, squelch, hit, blister, roast, scorch, rap, take a rap at, take a swipe at, take the shine out of, fluff off, brush off, dump on, shit on, do a number on, shred, mudsling, needle, give one the needle, knock, knock down, poor-mouth, bad-mouth, bitter mouth, back cap, backbite, rip up the back, give a black eye, give one one's comeuppance, thumb one's nose at, pooh-pooh, rubbish, sour grapes, mark lousy, put the crimpers in, put the hooks in, put the needles in, put the zingers in, put away, put a tuck in one's tail, poke full of holes, shoot full of holes, prick one's balloon, puncture one's balloon, take the wind out of one's sails, blow sky high, knock the bottom out of, knock the chocks out from under, knock the props out from under, knock one off his perch, make one sing small. See also EMBARRASS.

HUMILIATED adj. gone to bad, gone to the dogs, gone to hell, crawling, die, draw in one's horns, eat crow, eat dirt, eat humble pie, sing small, get one's comeuppance, burned, in bad, in Dutch, in the doghouse, lost face, red-faced, drummed out, took down, comedown, put down, stumped, stymied, dumped on, egg on one's face, knocked from one's high horse, knocked off one's perch, tuck in one's tail.

HUMILIATION n. comeuppance, comedown, take down, put down, touche.

HUMORIST n. jokesmith, gagman, gagster, punster, quipster, wisecracker, stand up comic, clown, cutup. See JOKER.

HUMOROUS adj. camp, campy, jokey, joshing, yokky, boffo, gagged up, for grins, priceless, screaming, too funny for words. See AMUSING.

HUNCH n. feel in one's bones, have a funny feeling. See PREMONITION.

HUNDRED n. C, one C, century.

HUNGARIAN n. Hunky, Bohunk.

HUNGER n. big eyes, eyes for, hard-on for, itch, hot pants, lech, sweet tooth, yen, zazzle.

HUNGRY adj. dog hungry, empty, fly light, grits time, have a tapeworm, munchies (follows marijuana use), starving, starved, starved to death, could eat a horse, could eat the asshole out of a bear.

HUNT v. bird dog (scout), beat the bushes, scratch, scratch around, look all over hell, search high heaven, run down. See SEARCH.

HUNTING EXPEDITION n. snofari (snow).

HUNTSVILLE, ALABAMA Rocket City.

HURDLE RACE n. timber topper.

HURL v. chuck, chunk, fire, lob, heave, pitch, sling, fling, gun, peg.

HURRAH interj.

HURRY v. hustle, fog, shake a leg, make tracks, dust, roll, tool, hotfoot it, barrel, tear ass, put on the after burners, split the breeze, move, rip, get on one's horse. See SPEED.

HURRY UP interj. hubba-hubba, haba-haba,(WW II), get the lead out, get the lead out of your ass, shake a leg, move, get moving, get going, get cracking, get with it,

hop to it, move your tail, move your ass, move your fanny, get on the ball, don't spare the horses, get your ass in gear, get your motor running, shake it up, get a move on, get a wiggle on, step on it, snap shit, snap to it, make it snappy, chop chop, stir your stumps.

HURT adj. 1. hurtin', bleedin', damaged, winged, nicked, zinged, cut, bunged up, busted up, burned, burned one's ass, put away, screwed up, walking wounded, have to scrape one off the sidewalk. 2. all torn up, cut up, hit where one lives, shook, shook up, miffed, miffy, shot down, have one's nose out of joint, sore, uptight.

HURT n. ouch, chop, scratch, nick, graze, boo-boo (minor flesh wound), brand, jig cut, mark, rat mark, stool mark (knife), black and blue, down.

HURT v. 1. zing, lean on, put down, hit one where one lives, lay a bad trip on one, give one a left handed compliment, thumb one's nose at, give one the finger, gross out. See WOUND. 2. mess up, rough up, shake up, total, wax, wing, nick, zing, cut up. See DAMAGE.

HUSBAND n. man, my man, old man, main man, mister, on the hitch, ace lane, breadwinner, buffalo.

HYDROGEN BOMB n. H-bomb, the bomb, megabomb, doomsday machine, nuke.

HYDROPLANE n. thunderboat, flying boat.

HYMEN n. maidenhead, cherry, bug (not common), bean, an issue over tissue, big issue over a little tissue.

HYMN n. shout.

HYPERBOLE n. hype, ballyhoo, big talk, tall talk, lay it on, lay it on thick, lay it on with a trowel, make a mountain out of a molehill, puff, P.R. See EXAGGERATE.

HYPERSENSITIVE adj. can't even look at one cross-eyed, thin-skinned, tetchy, touchy, wired, wired up, uptight. See SENSITIVE.

HYPOCHONDRIA n. hypo, medical student's disease.

HYPOCRISY n. soft soap, sweet talk, chicken, chicken shit, goop, hooey, shit, spinach, chewing gum, crocodile tears. See INSINCERITY.

HYPOCRITE n. hook, fake, four-flusher, fraud, playactor, phony, smoothie, two-way ghee, two-faced, wishy-washy person, wolf in sheep's clothing, fluker, mission stiff, psalm-singing muzzler.

HYPOCRITICAL adj. fishy, two-faced, gil, Hollywood, reach me down, slick, sincere, snide, phony, fake, cry crocodile tears, touchy funky, jivey, jive-assed.

HYPODERMIC INJECTION n. booster, booster shot, hypo, shot; bang, main-line bang, shot in the arm, pop, skin pop, hit, fix, nip, dram (narcotics).

HYPODERMIC NEEDLE n. hypo, hype, hype stick, artillery, gun, hook, nail, point, spike, square needle, jabber, bayonet.

HYPOTHESIS n. guesstimate, hunch, shot, shot in the dark, sneaking suspicion, stab, stab in the dark. See also BASIS.

HYPOTHESIZE v. toss out, spitball, brainstorm, go out on a limb, take a shot, take a shot in the dark, take a stab, talk off the top of one's head. See also SPECULATE.

HYSTERICAL adj. flip, flip one's lid, blow a gasket, pop one's cork, come unglued, come apart, weirded out, have a short fuse, work oneself into a stew, work oneself into a lather, work oneself into a tizzy, work oneself into a pucker, get hot under the collar, run a temperature, race one's motor, blow up, blow one's stack, blow one's top, fly off the handle, hit the ceiling. See also DISTURBED.

I

I n.   India, item.

I pro.   yours truly, number one, numero uno, Dudley, Ol' Uncle Dudley, big three (me, myself, and I).

IBM n.   Big Blue.

ICE n.   hail, diamonds, Prudhoe pineapple (bucket).

ICE CREAM n.   ball (single scoop), pop (on a stick), Eskimo, mud pie, white (vanilla), vanilla cow (vanilla soda, shake, malt), black (chocolate), black and white (soda, vanilla ice cream, chocolate sauce), black cow (root beer with vanilla ice cream), all around chocolate, double chocolate (chocolate ice cream with chocolate sauce).

ICE CREAM VENDOR n.   ice cream man, Good Humor man, hokey-pokey.

ICE HOCKEY, PLAY   assist, check, body check, stick check, knee, kneeing, rag (keep possession of puck), shadow (guard closely), slap pass, slap shot, slapper, slash, steal, icing (illegal play).

ICE HOCKEY PLAYER   head hunter, ice man, sextet, anchor man, goalie.

ICE HOCKEY TERMS   sin bin (penalty box), cage (goal), burn (score) deke (deceive), hat trick (3 goals by a single player).

ICING n.   glop, sugary glop, topping.

IDAHO   Gem State.

IDEA n.   child, brainchild, brainstorm, brain wave, spark, spark plug, flash, flash on it, bell-ringer, deep think, flop, rumble, wig, I got it, it hit me, it just come to me, approach, big idea, slant, twist, wrinkle, new wrinkle, wienie, gimmick, angle, action, big play, scenario, scene, story, picture, big picture, pitch, proposition, setup, game plan, layout, bit, what's cookin', how one figures it, what's the action, bug in one's ear, bug up one's ass, bee, bee in one's bonnet, flea in one's nose, judgment call, op, say so, two cents' worth, bad talk (radical), riff (musical), sneaking suspicion, booby trap, tune, the name of that tune.

IDEAL adj.   outrageous righteous and relaxed, pie in the sky, never-never land, Shangri-la, have it all, fuck-you money. See also PERFECT.

IDEALIST n.   stargazer, dreamer, scoutmaster.

IDEALIZE v.   talk through one's hat, build castles in the air, look at the world through rose-colored glasses, gimme a drag on that before you throw it away.

IDENTICAL adj.   double, look-alike, like two peas in a pod, spitting image, six of one and half a dozen of the other, xerox, carbon copy, dead ringer, ditto, same difference. See SAME.

IDENTIFICATION n.   button, buzzer, cookie cutter, flash, potsy, shield, tin, white tin, yellow tin, dog tag, I.D., ID, logo, make, rap, papers, high sign.

IDENTIFICATION TAG n.   tag, dog tag, dog tags (armed forces), bracelet, ident bracelet, I.D.

IDENTIFY v.   make, card, peg, put down for, tab, tag, button down, finger, put the finger on, put one's finger on something. See also CRIMINAL, IDENTIFY.

IDEOLOGICAL DIVISIONS n.   bamboo curtain (China), iron curtain (Russia), silk curtain (Middle East).

IDIOM n.   jive, jive talk, lingo, street talk, weasel words, flash (thieves).

IDIOSYNCRASY n.   bit, shtick, mishegoss. See CHARACTERISTIC.

IDIOSYNCRATIC adj.   weirdo, strange one, kooky, freaky, off the wall, case, whacky, chirp, character, queer fish, rare bird, meshugenah. See ECCENTRIC.

IDIOT n.   dork, yo-yo, twit, kook, out to lunch, dumb ox, meathead, fathead, pinhead, pointy head, numbskull, drop case, doesn't know which way is up, not have all one's marbles, minus some buttons. See STUPID.

IDIOTIC adj.   batty, daffy, gorked, dumdum, dinga-ling, jerk off, jackass, asshole, squirrelly, hare-brained. See FOOLISH.

IDLE adj.   on the shelf, on the bench, out of the rat race, out of action, out of the swim, down, closed down. See UNEMPLOYED.

IDLE v.   bum, bum around, hang out, hang around, goof around, fiddle around, fiddle fart around, stick around, mooch around, scrounge around, jack around, bat around, mess around, hack around, knock around, monkey around, fool around, fuck around, futz around, poot around, fuck off, fake off, goof off, screw off, flub off, flub the dub, rat, R.F., rat fuck, fuck the dog, lurk, sit on one's ass, sit on one's butt, sit on one's duff, jelly, tool, tail, bail out, cat, warm a chair, press the bricks, lie down on the job, get no place fast, poke, poke around, poke along, mosey, toddle, shlep along, potchky, featherbed, float. See also LINGER.

IDLENESS n. goof-off time, fuck-off time, time to burn, time to kill, one's own sweet time.

IDLER n. foot-dragger, goof off, fuck off, goldbrick, shlepper, sleepyhead, beach bum, drugstore cowboy, cake-eater, lounge lizard, john, johnny, good for nothin', lazy good for nothin'. See LOAFER.

IDOL n. dad, Head Knock.

IDOLIZE v. crazy over, nuts about, daffy about, wild about, wacky about, mad for, gone on, have a thing about. See ADMIRE.

IDOLIZED adj. 1. okay people, touted, highly touted, score. 2. gone, gone on, stuck on, hipped on, wild about, fell for, mad about, crazy about, nuts about, keen about, have a thing about, struck by lightning.

IGNORAMUS n. numbnut, asshole, butt hole, loser, winner, twit, lunchie, lowbrow, dodo, dummy, dumbo, dumdum, airhead, bubblehead, balloonhead, pointyhead, doesn't know the score, not know one's ass from one's elbow. See STUPID.

IGNORANCE n. meatballism.

IGNORANT adj. uncool, unhep, unhip, square, airhead, lowbrow, nerd, dope, a mushroom, goaty, in the dark, out to lunch, out of it, blind as a bat, drowning, hard head, bletcherous, half-assed, half-baked, half-cocked, doesn't know from nothing, doesn't know one's ass from first base, doesn't know one's ass from a hole in the ground, a big know-it-all, damned if I know, search me, haven't the foggiest, not have a clue, not know the score, not know the time of day, not know one's ass from one's elbow, not know a rock from a hard place, not know shit from Shinola, not there, not getting it, not be with it.

IGNORANT interj. God knows, God only knows, Lord knows, heaven knows, nobody knows, damned if I know, beats the shit outta me, it beats me, it has me guessing, it's got me guessing, it's Greek to me, search me, you've got me, I give up, I pass, I don't know what, how should I know?, who knows?, don't look at me.

IGNORE v. 1. ig, tune out, dial out, look the other way, let it go, let one off easy, let one off this time, wink at, live with, pay no mind, pay no never mind, play past, pooh-pooh. 2. cut, cut dead, brush off, give one the brush, high hat, not give one the time of day, give the go by, chili, chill, cool, play it cool, cold-shoulder, leave out in the cold, freeze on, ice, ice out, shine one on, look right through. 3. be asleep at the switch, let go to pot, let slide, let ride, fall between the chairs, fall between the cracks.

IGNORED adj. in the cold, out in the cold, passed up, sidelined.

ILK n. likes, likes of, lot, number, birds of a feather.

ILL adj. peaky, peaked, down, run down, down with, got the bug, rocky, punk, a wreck, rotten, feeling rotten, ratty, poorly, seedy, feeling awful, feeling something terrible, under the weather, below par, running a temperature, off-color, off one's feed, off one's feet, sick as a dog, on the sick list, bum, bummy, on the bum, on the blink, laid low, outta action, woozy, bunk fatigue (WW I), the trots, runs, burpy, barfy, pukish, pukey, upchucking, green, green around the gills, blue around the gills, one foot in the grave, one foot in the grave and the other on a banana peel.

ILL-CONSIDERED adj. off the top of one's head, half-assed, half-baked, half-cocked.

ILLEGAL adj. crooked, heavy, off base, out of line, racket, shady, dirty, hung up, hung up with, wildcat, under the counter, under the table.

ILLEGAL CACHE n. drop, cover.

ILLEGAL ENTRY n. black-bag job.

ILLEGAL SEARCH n. bag job.

ILLEGITIMATE adj. 1. bastard, by blow, born on the wrong side of the blanket, come in though a side door, love child, whore's bird. 2. shady, racket, the rackets, under the table, under the counter, hanky-panky, heavy, off base, out of line, wildcat.

ILL FORTUNE n. bummer, downer, can of worms, crunch, deep shit, up shit creek without a paddle, tough shit, TS, drag, can't even get arrested, rainy day, double whammy, need it like a hole in the head. See ADVERSITY.

ILL-HUMORED adj. chip on one's shoulder, fire-eater, scrappy, salty, spiky, bitchy, cantankerous, cussed, mean, ornery, ugly customer. See IRRITABLE.

ILLICIT adj. crooked, heavy, off base, out of line, racket, shady, dirty, hanky-panky, left-handed, wildcat, under the counter, under the table. See also ADULTEROUS.

ILLIMITABLE adj. jillion, zillion, umpteen, more than you can shake a stick at, no end of, no end to, thick as flies, thick as hail. See COUNTLESS.

ILLINOIS Prairie State, Sucker State, Land O' Lincoln.

ILL-MANNERED adj. grody, grody to the max, loud, loud-mouthed, raunchy, raw, tacky, cheap, skank, dipshit, roughneck, galoot, gool, sleazeball. See also VULGAR.

ILL-NATURED adj. bitchy, cussed, dirty, mean, ornery. See IRRITABLE.

ILLNESS adj. bug, crud, creeping crud, the runs, trots, what's going around, the flu, the pip, dose, double scrudfantods, fascinoma (Medic.), burned (VD), willies (mythical).

ILLOGICAL adj. cockeyed, off the wall, off the beam, nuts, nutty, have another think coming, catch 22, pair of ducks. See WRONG.

ILL-TEMPERED adj. crabby, grouchy, grumpy, bitchy, touchy, cantankerous, ugly customer, short fuse, ticking bomb. See IRRITABLE.

ILLUMINATE v. spot, spotlight, limelight, highlight, hit with a light, hit with a spot, hit with a beam.

ILLUSION n. fool's paradise, pipe dream, trip, head trip.

ILLUSORY adj. float, pipe dream, play with oneself, castles in the air, blue sky. See FANCIFUL.

ILLUSTRATE v. get over, lay out, show and tell, draw one a picture, open one's head, get across, spotlight, highlight, limelight, give a frinstance, roll out, trot out. See EXPLAIN.

ILLUSTRATION n. for instance, frinstance.

ILLUSTRIOUS adj. w.k. (well-known), celeb, star, superstar, name, monster, in the limelight, page-oner, big league, knocker, heavy stuff. See CELEBRITY.

IMAGE n. angel (radar), dead ringer, spitting image, carbon, carbon copy. See COPY.

IMAGINARY adj. trumped up, dreamed up, pipe dream, fool's paradise.

IMAGINATION n. brainstorm, brainchild, brain wave, flash on it, wrinkle, new wrinkle, big idea, wienie, bell-ringer. See also IDEA.

IMAGINATIVE adj. head tripping, brain wave, breaking new snow, way out, weird out, far out, fantasmo, flaky, kinky, offbeat, avant-garde, floating on clouds, pipe dream, play with oneself, jack off, pie in the sky, castles in the air, blue sky.

IMAGINE v. brainstorm, spark, spitball, make up, cook up, dream up, trump up, come up with, take it off the top of one's head. See CREATE.

IMAGINED adj. trumped up, dreamed up, cooked up.

IMBECILE n. lamebrain, birdie (teenage), birdbrain, dork, nerd, dodo, dummy, bonetop, pointyhead, banana head, peahead, pinhead, clodpated, dipshit, nuthin' upstairs. See STUPID.

IMBIBE v. down, belt, put away, booze up, tank up, chugalug, exercise the elbow, raise a few, pound, knock back, juice back, toss down, soak up, hang on a few, irrigate. See DRINK.

IMBIBER n. lush, stew, wino, boozer, rummy, brown bagger, shikker, soak, sponge, tosspot, elbow bender. See DRINKER.

IMBROGLIO n. 1. brawl, rhubarb, run in, flack session, punch out, go, knock down and drag out. See ARGUMENT. 2. the plot thickens, soap opera, can of worms, kettle of fish, in the soup.

IMBUE v. brainwash, fuck with one's head, break down, program.

IMITATE v. 1. dupe, xerox, carbon, clone, mimeo, ditto, knock off, stat. 2. act like, do, do like, go like, make like, mirror, takeoff as, do a take-off, put-on, send up, play the ——— (affect a role). 3. pirate, fake, phony, knock off, steal, steal one's stuff, lift, borrow, crib, take a leaf out of one's book.

IMITATION adj. autobogophobia (fear of bogosity), bogosity, bogotified, bogue, not what it's cracked up to be, queer, fake, phony, ersatz, hokey, soft shell. See FALSE.

IMITATION n. 1. ditto, dupe, xerox, clone, carbon, carbon copy, mimeo, stat, repro, knock-off, flimsy. 2. look alike, work alike, ringer, dead ringer, copycat, spitting image, spit and image, chip off the old block, double, peas in a pod, twin, ——— compatible (P.C. compatible). 3. phony, knock off, queer, bogue, bogotified, junque, pseud, pseudo, ersatz, pirate goods, pirate labels. See COUNTERFEIT. 4. take off, put on.

IMITATOR n. copycat, double, stand-in, crock, crowk (radio use, animal).

IMMATERIAL adj. big deal, BFD, big fucking deal, no big deal, don't mean shit, no biggie, no skin off one's nose, mox nix, makes no never mind, immaterial. See UNIMPORTANT.

IMMATURE adj. kid, kid stuff, baby, sophomore, half-assed, half-baked, green, not dry behind the ears, a bit previous. See UNSOPHISTICATED.

IMMEASURABLE adj. no end of, no end to, more than you can shake a stick at, jillion, a jillion at least, zillion, umpteen, umpteeenth, alive with, crawling with, thick as flies. See COUNTLESS.

IMMEDIATELY adv. pronto, on the double, double time, move your ass, like now, toot sweet, at the kick-off, off the pop, on the dot, in a New York minute, in half a mo, in a jiffy, in half a jiffy, in a flash, in nothing flat, in a shake, in half a shake, in two shakes of a lamb's tail, like a shot, like a shot out of hell, like a big-ass bird, like a BAB, right off the bat, first crack out of the box, all of a sudden, PDQ, pretty dammmed quick, before you can say Jack Robinson, abracadabra.

IMMENSE adj. gross, humongous, humungous, mungo, monstro, king-size, moby, mother, motherfucker (Obsc.), big mother, major league, super, jumbo, barn door. See BIG.

IMMERSE v. dunk.

IMMERSED adj. into, really into, up to here in, wrapped up in, eat sleep and breathe something, turned on, tied up. See ENGROSSED.

IMMIGRANT n. F.O.B. (fresh off the boat), greenhorn, greeny, Hunk, Hunkie, bohunk, wetback, bracero, documented, undocumented.

IMMINENT adj. in the cards, in the wind, at hand, see it coming, it's looking to, waiting on, the noose is hanging, handwriting is on the wall. See also ANTICIPATED.

IMMOBILE adj. pat, anchored, nailed, nailed down. See also STUBBORN.

IMMOBILIZE v. freeze, jack up, take one out, put a stopper in, throw a monkey wrench into, tie up, jam up, hang one up, gridlock.

IMMODERATE adj. too-too, too much, out of sight, like crazy, like mad, throw out the baby with the bathwater. See EXTREME.

IMMODEST adj. biggety, cocky, showboat, blowhard, loudmouth, ego-tripping, swell-headed, stuck on oneself. See CONCEITED.

IMMORAL adj. 1. blue, X-rated. See DISSOLUTE. 2. open, wide open, meat-eater, gone to bad, gone to hell, speedy, fast, fast and loose. See OBSCENE. See also DISHONEST.

IMMOVABLE adj. hard-nosed, tough nut to crack, locked in, set in concrete, stand pat, dig in one's heels, stick to one's guns, mule-headed, dead set on, murder (he's murder). See STUBBORN.

IMMUNIZATION n. shot, shot in the arm, shot in the ass, booster, booster shot.

IMMUNIZE v. give a shot, shoot, give one the square needle.

IMMUNIZED adj. binged, got the hook, got the square needle, stabbed in the ass (WW II), jabbed in the ass.

IMP n. hellion, hellcat, fiend.

IMPACT n. crack up, crash, crunch, smash, smashup, kick, hit one, hit one like a ton of bricks.

IMPACT v. register, crack up, jolt, crash, smash, smash up, wrack up, bang into, nerf, kick.

IMPACT SPORT n. contact sport.

IMPAIR v. ding, tweak, bend the goods, total, wrack up, goof up, gum up, hash up, rough up, snarl up, snafu, queer. See DAMAGE.

IMPAIRED adj. down, on downtime, on the blink, no go, had it, busted, kaput, dinged, totalled, gone, a few bugs, glitched, gremlins, on the fritz. See DAMAGED.

IMPARTIAL adj. call 'em as one sees 'em, on the fence, fence sitter, middle of the road, anythingarian, dawk (neither a dove or a hawk), even-steven, mugwumpian, mugwumpish.

IMPASSE n. standoff, Mexican standoff, catch 22, box, corner, dead end, gridlock, hole, damned if you do and damned if you don't, pickle.

IMPASSIONED adj. hot for, hot about, turned on, gone on, steamed up, all hopped up about, worked up about, steamed up, stoned, wild about, ape over, starry eyed over, gaga over. See ENTHUSIASTIC.

IMPATIENCE n. ants, ants in one's pants, fantobs.

IMPATIENT adj. ants, antsy, antsy-pantsy, ants in one's pants, about to piss in one's pants, itchy, ripe, keen, creaming to, dying to, in a lather, in a sweat, on pins and needles, have a short fuse, work oneself into a stew, work oneself into a lather, work oneself into a tizzy, work oneself into a pucker, get hot under the collar, run a temperature, race one's motor, blow up, blow one's stack, blow one's top, flip, flip one's lid, blow a gasket, fly off the handle, hit the ceiling, hot, hot for, hot to go, rarin' to go, full of get up and go, go great guns, gung ho, hopped up, spark plug, self-starting, catawamptious, fall all over oneself, not let any grass grow under one's feet, ready for Freddie. See also ANXIOUS.

IMPECCABLE adj. A-okay, aces, 10, ten, on target, apple pie, four-o, tip-top shape, outrageous righteous and relaxed. See PERFECT.

IMPEDE v. stymie, hang up, hold up, flag one, freeze, shut off, shut down, stonewall, close off, saddle with, cut off one's water, blow the whistle on, cramp one's style. See HINDER.

IMPEDIMENT n. hang-up, baggage, excess baggage, psychological baggage, ball and chain, catch, glitch, gridlock. See HINDRANCE.

IMPELLER n. blower, butter paddle, club, egg-beater, fan, pants stopper, prop, windmill.

IMPENETRABLE adj. bulletproof.

IMPENDING adj. in the cards, in the wind, at hand, see it coming, it's looking to, waiting to, the noose is hanging, the handwriting is on the wall.

IMPERATIVE adj. chips are down, hurry-up call, when you gotta go you gotta go, orders are orders, there's no turning back, matter of life and death. See URGENT.

IMPERFECT adj. 1. a few bugs, a glitch, gremlins. 2. seconds, crap, crappy, junk, shit, crud, cruddy, creep, creepy, clinker, cheap John, borax, dog, dreck, from hunger, funky, lousy, G.I., garbage, dud, gummy, gook, ham, jelly bean, jitney, lemon, Mickey Mouse, piece of shit, punk, rat's ass, piss-poor, schlocky, rinky-dinky, abortion, turkey, bottom of the barrel, scrape the bottom of the barrel, sleazy, tripe, two bit, ticky-tacky, slimpsy, minus, cheesy, grungy, below the mark, it sucks, not up to scratch, not up to snuff, quick and dirty, plastic, cotton-pickin', low, rank, mucked up, messed up, loused up. See also INADEQUATE, CHEAP.

IMPERFECTION n. bug, catch, glitch, gremlin, not come up to scratch, not make it.

IMPERIL v. lay on the line, put on the spot, stick one's neck in the noose, stick one's neck out, play into one's hands, chance it.

IMPERILED adj. on the line, on the spot, out on a limb, got one's neck out, have one's ass out, caught with one's pants down.

IMPERIOUS adj. bossy, driver, pushy, whip cracking, ass kicking, crack the whip, high and mighty, on one's high horse, throw one's weight around, pull rank. See AUTOCRATIC. See also POWERFUL, MASTERFUL.

IMPERMANENT adj. temp, band-aid, throwaway, here today gone tomorrow, fly-by-night.

IMPERSONAL adj. cool, cold, cold turkey, straight, strictly business.

IMPERSONATE v. mirror, play the ——— (affect a role), ditto, do, do like, make like, act like, go like, steal one's stuff, take off, take a leaf out of one's book, fake, hoke, hoke up.

IMPERTINENCE n. back talk, backchat, come back, lip, sass, brass, crust, gall, guff, smart ass, wisecrack, wise guy, chutzpah.

IMPERTINENT adj. fresh, cheeky, sassy, smart alecky, lippy, saucebox, chutzpahdik, out of line, off base. See INSOLENT.

IMPERTURBABLE adj. cool, cool as a cucumber, keep one's cool, keep one's shirt on, not turn a hair, not get one's balls in an uproar, not get one's self in an uproar, roll with the punches, unflappable, cold fish, hard as nails, rhinoceros hide, thick-skinned, dead ass, without a nerve in one's body, keep a stiff upper lip. See also ASSURED.

IMPETUOUS adj. go off the deep end, go off half-cocked, hopped up, itchy, creaming to, jump the gun. See IMPULSIVE.

IMPLAUSIBLE adj. thick, thin, reachy, won't wash, won't hold water, fishy, for the birds, full of holes, too much, far out. See UNBELIEVABLE.

IMPLEMENT n. contraption, can-opener (safe), Armstrong (requires strength). See APPARATUS.

IMPLICATE v. name, finger, point the finger at, hang something on, pin on, blow the whistle on one, frame, frame up, lay at one's door. See INCRIMINATE.

IMPORT n. point, stuff, nub, bottom line, name of the game, nitty-gritty, nuts and bolts, the way of it, nature of the beast, drift, heart, meat, nub, score, punch line.

IMPORTANT adj. 1. heavy, heavy number, meaningful, mean business, strictly business, get down to business, business end of, chill out, serious shit, serious jelly, matter of life and death, something, something else, fab, fat, big league, major league, top drawer, heavyweight, heavy stuff, the big picture, meat and potatoes, high cotton, high profile, buckle down, chips are down, hurry-up call, like all get out, no fooling, no shit, no bird turdin', bound and determined, dead set on, bent on, hell bent on, heat's on, hot flash, hot shit, fire in the belly, not playing around, not to be sneezed at, we're not talking about nutmeg here, money talks, walk heavy, walk tall, big deal, in, stand in with, cut ice, carry a lot of weight, throw a lot of weight, the juice, the force, underlined. 2. name, face card, big, biggie, big player, big chew, big boy, Mr. Big, big name, big one, gun, big gun, big man, big man on campus, B.M.O.C., big noise, big number, big shot, big shit, big timer, wheel, big wheel, wheeler-dealer, big wig, big ghee, big spud, big league, major league, big butter and egg man, big cheese, real cheese, whole cheese, apple, big apple, biggest frog in the pond, his nibs, honcho, magoo, main squeeze, movers and shakers, one who knows where the body's buried, kuhnocker, higher ups, high-muck-a-much, high-muckety-muck, high monkey monk, high pillow, hot shot, hot dog, top dog, topsider, tycoon, baron, brass, top brass, brass hat, VIP, V.I.P., visiting fireman, lion, connection, connection ghee, polly, wire, wire-puller, godfather, a somebody, hoohaw, double-barreled, in the limelight. See also CELEBRITY, EXECUTIVE.

IMPORTUNE v. work on, con, blarney, lay it on, lay it on thick, sell, shit, string along, egg one on, goose, caboodle, bone, hock one's charnik, noodge. See PERSUADE.

IMPOSE v. move in on, chisel in, horn in, muscle in, lay down the law, put one's foot down, read the riot act, dish it out, dish out, dump on, give it to one, stick it to one. See also FORCE.

IMPOSING adj. mind-blowing, mega, megadual, clean outta sight, one for the book, something else, something to write home about. See IMPRESSIVE.

IMPOSITION n. drag, pain in the ass, pain in the neck. See ANNOYANCE.

IMPOSSIBLE adj. it won't fly, no go, no way, can't win for losin', no-win situation, not a prayer, not a ghost of a chance, not a Chinaman's chance, not a chance in hell, not a snowball's chance in hell, not till hell freezes over.

IMPOSTER n. faker, four-flusher, phony, pseud, actor, bogue. See QUACK.

IMPOTENT adj. 1. fire blanks, shoot blanks, blank cartridge, dud, no lead in the pencil, no toothpaste in the tube, can't get it up, don't have the horses, out of gas. 2. paper tiger, wimpy, gutless, nerdy, can't hack it, not have it, can't cut it, can't cut the mustard, can't make the grade. See WEAK.

IMPOVERISH v. bleed, bleed white, suck dry, wipe out, break, take for all one's got, clean one out, take one's last penny.

IMPOVERISHED adj. flat, flat broke, stony, truly needy, strapped, oofless, clean, tapped out, on the rocks, hurting, have-nots, piss-poor, on the rims. See DESTITUTE.

IMPRACTICABLE adj. it won't fly, no go, not a prayer, not a Chinaman's chance, not a chance in hell, not a snowball's chance in hell. See IMPOSSIBLE.

IMPRECATION n. whammy, double whammy, hoodoo, voodoo, jinx, cuss, cuss word, dirty word, dirty name, four-letter word, no-no, swear word. See also EXPLETIVE.

IMPRECISE adj. guesstimate, ball park, ball-park figure, out in left field. See also WRONG.

IMPREGNABLE adj. bulletproof.

IMPREGNATE v. knock up, get in trouble, put in the family way.

IMPRESS v. register, blow away, blow one away, faze, move, score, kill, slay, grab, knock one's socks off, knock one out, knock one for a loop, hit like a ton of bricks, make one's teeth fall out, buffalo, bulldoze, enforce, lean on, push around, turn on the heat, walk heavy, showboat, show off, grandstand, hotdog, make a grandstand play, make a big splash.

IMPRESSED adj. programmed, brainwashed, head-fucked, mind-fucked, boggled.

IMPRESSIVE adj. cool, real cool, zero cool, fab, far out, mega, megadual, marvy, nifty, spiffy, frantic, unreal, dynamite, scandalous, in the groove, groovy, jazzy, jumping, mad, mean, the most, mostest, like wow, reet, mind-blowing, mind-bending, out of this world, turn on, kicky, diddly bop, a gas, live one, live wire, wild, dolce vita, gone, real gone, hot stuff, hairy, large, large charge, nervous, rootin'-tootin', snazzy, solid, solid sender, one for the book, something, something else, something to shout about, something to write home about, swinging, fine, lush, sizzler, scorcher, big splash, out of sight, clean outta sight, razzle-dazzle, glitzy, flashy, showy, smashing, bang-up, ace high, swell, stunner, stunning.

IMPRISON v. put away, hold, lock up, send up, ice, book, cool, cage. See JAIL.

IMPRISONED adj. away, fell, go over, go up, up the river, in the slam, in the slammer, in the pokey, in the clink, in college, out of town, sent up, iced, put on ice, cooped, cooped up, jugged.

IMPROBABILITY n. very iffy, it don't figure, hundred-to-one shot, got two chances: slim and none, not in the cards, not a chance in hell, not a Chinaman's chance, not a snowball's chance in hell, not a snow ball's chance, outside chance, it won't fly.

IMPROMPTU adj. improv, ad lib, wing it, vamp, fake, fake it, off the wall, off the cuff, off the top of the head, off the hip, shoot from the hip, play by ear, dash off, strike off, knock off, throw off, toss off, toss out, whip up, spitball.

IMPROPER adj. bad form, off, way off, off base, off color, off the beam, not cricket, out of line, out in left field, wrong number, put one's foot in it, put one's foot in one's mouth, bend the law.

IMPROVE v. 1. upgrade, polish, sharpen, boost, skyrocket, take off, make first rate, up, doll up, fix up, gussy up, pretty up, spruce up, dress up, look up, pick up, perk up, soup up. 2. step up, step up in class, shape up, get back in shape, get well (monetarily), be on the mend, pick up the pieces, brace up, take a brace, bounce back, come back, make a comeback, on the comeback trail, come from behind, come out of it, pull out of it, snap out of it, turn the corner, bottom out, be out of the woods, come around, come along, come alive. 3. clean up one's act, get one's act together, get with it, get on the ball, go straight, straighten out, straighten up and fly right, turn around, turn things around, turn over a new leaf.

IMPROVED adj. souped up, sharpened, over the hump, out of the woods, on the comeback trail.

IMPROVEMENT n. uptick, upbeat, upgrade, retrofit.

IMPROVING adj. looking good, looking up, on the lift, on the rise, on the upbeat, on the upgrade, on the upswing, bottoming out.

IMPROVISATION n. improv, ad lib, blow room, blow session, hot lick, lick, riff, winging it, vamp, fake, off the wall, off the cuff, off the hip, off the top of one's head, shoot from the hip, spitball, play by ear, dash off, strike off, knock off, throw off, toss off, toss out, whip up, jamming, taking it for a ride.

IMPROVISE v. ad lib, impro, improv, noodle around, play piano, brainstorm, head trip, spark, spitball, off the cuff, off the hip, shoot from the hip, off the top of one's head, wing it, fake, fake it, play it by ear, play it as it lays, jam, shuck, vamp, strike off, get off, throw off, throw out, toss off, toss out, knock off, knock out, dash off, bat out, slap out, slapdash, slap up, shove out, dream up, make up, whip up, cook up, think up, whomp up, trump up, mess around, noodle, noodle around, work something out, put together with spit and chicken wire.

IMPROVISED adj.   ad lib, improv, off the cuff, off the top of the head, band-aid, fly-by-night, hit or miss, Mickey Mouse, rinkydink, slapdash. See IMPROMPTU.

IMPRUDENT adj.   off the deep end, go off the deep end, step off the deep end, put one's foot in it, put one's foot in one's mouth, go to sea in a sieve, go out on a limb, go for broke, buy a pig in a poke, play with fire, leave oneself wide open. See also CARELESS.

IMPUDENCE n.   back chat, back talk, brass, cheek, chutzpah, crust, face, gall, guff, lip, sauce, sass, smarts, smart ass, the smarts, nerve, out of line, off base.

IMPUDENT adj.   get previous, brassy, flip, smart ass, wise ass, off base, chutzpahdik. See INSOLENT.

IMPUGN v.   trash, slam, zing, zap, knock, rap, put down, run down, thumb down, break, come down on, pin on, have something on, swipe at, throw the book at, skin alive, lay out, stick it to, cut to bits, cut to ribbons, blast, tar, smear.

IMPULSE n.   flash, yen.

IMPULSIVE adj.   flaky, mad, ad lib, blow hot and cold, up and down, winging it, off the wall, off the cuff, off the hip, off the top of one's head, shoot from the hip, spitball, play by ear, dash off, strike off, knock off, throw off, toss off, toss out, whip up, go off the deep end, step off the deep end, jump off the deep end, jump the gun, go off half cocked, at one's own sweet will. See also SPONTANEOUS.

IMPUTE v.   reference, hang something on, pin on. See ASSIGN.

INACCESSIBLE adj.   out of pocket, no got.

INACCURATE adj.   off, way off, off the beam, off base, all wet, that doesn't track, have another think coming. See WRONG.

INACTION n.   sit on one's ass, sit on one's butt, sit on one's duff, sit on one's hands, cool one's heels, stand pat, stand by.

INACTIVE adj.   blah, dopey, draggy, drag ass, lox, sack artist, Stepin Fetchit, on the shelf, on the bench, on hold, in a holding pattern, in cold storage, out of the rat race, out of action, out of the swim, down, closed down. See also UNEMPLOYED.

INADEQUATE adj.   a few bugs, a glitch, gremlins, seconds, crappy, junk, shit, cruddy, creepy, clinker, cheap John, borax, dog, dreck, from hunger, funky, lousy, for the birds, G.I., gummy, gook, ham, jelly bean, jitney, lemon, Mickey Mouse, bush league, piece of shit, punk, pile of shit, rat's ass, piss poor, schlocky, bottom of the barrel, scrape the bottom of the barrel, sleazy, tripe, two bit, ticky-tacky, slimpsy, minus, cheesy, grungy, bupkis, chicken shit, too little too late, zilch, below the mark, it sucks, clown, bringdown, fuck-up, loser, nerd, half-assed, half-baked, clunker, also ran, no good, loser, a real loser, a real winner, out to lunch, turkey, dipstick, runt, outta gas, burned out, cooked, low man on the totem pole, have nothing on, nothing on the ball, not up to scratch, not come up to scratch, not up to snuff, not hack it, not have it, not make it, not cut out for, not hold a candle to, quick and dirty, can't cut it, can't cut the mustard, can't make the grade, second fiddle, second string, dime a dozen, all thumbs, a menace, plastic, cotton-pickin', low, rank. See also INEFFECTIVE.

INANE adj.   jerky, nerky, harebrained, lamebrained, birdbrained, ditzy, weak in the upper story, goopy, horse's ass, Mickey Mouse, sappy. See FOOLISH. See also INISPID.

INAPPLICABLE adj.   garbage.

INAPPROPRIATE adj.   bad form, off, way off, off base, off color, off the beam, out of line, out in left field, wrong number, put one's foot in it, put one's foot in one's mouth, bend the law, garbage.

INATTENTIVE adj.   mooning, daydreaming, out to lunch, popcorn headed, asleep at the switch, goofing off, looking out the window. See DISTRACTED.

INAUGURATE v.   ring in, get things rolling, break the ice, break in, kick off, bow, fire up, cook up, dream up, make up, come up with. See BEGIN.

INCALCULABLE adj.   jillion, zillion, umpteen, umpteenth, more than you can shake a stick at, no end of, no end to, thick as flies, thick as hail. See COUNTLESS.

INCANTATION n.   abracadabra, hocus-pocus, mumbo-jumbo, open sesame, ala kazam, hoodoo, voodoo.

INCAPABLE adj.   fumble-fist, butterfingers, muff, muffer, duffer, slob, lummox, lump, dub, uncool, yo-yo, can't hack it, loser, winner, turkey. See INADEQUATE.

INCAPACITATE v.   hamstring, queer, take out, hogtie, put out of commission, throw a monkey wrench into the works, spike one's guns, clip the wings of. See DISABLE.

INCAPACITATED adj.   crip, gimp, gimpy, game, g'd up, geed up, hamstrung, hog tied, taken out, sidelined, out of commission.

INCARCERATE v.   put away, hold, lock up, send up, send up the river, ice, put on ice, book, throw the book at, cool, can, cage, lay the arm on, take one away, settle, slough, slough up, railroad.

INCARCERATED adj.   away, up the river, in the slammer, in college, iced, jugged. See IMPRISONED.

INCAUTIOUS adj.   any old way, fast and loose, pay no mind, put one's foot in it, put one's foot in one's mouth, play with fire, stick one's neck out, leave oneself wide open, devil may care. See CARELESS.

INCENSE v. brown off, piss one off, T-off, get under one's skin, get a rise out of one, fire up, egg on, ask for it, stick in one's craw. See ANGER.

INCENSED adj. bugged, hacked, uptight, pissed off, peed off, tee'd off, browned off, bummed out, burned up, hung up, huffy, in one's hair, dogged, miffed, peeved, riled, rubbed the wrong way, spooked, all hot and bothered, at the end of one's rope, buffaloed, hard put to it, picked on, driven up the wall, rousted, steamed. See also ANGRY.

INCESSANTLY adv. round the clock, day and night, for ever so long. See also ALWAYS.

INCIDENT n. happening, hap, happenso, trip, real trip, like it is, where it's at, the size of it, scene, go down, come off, goings-on. See EVENT.

INCISE v. chiv, shiv.

INCITE v. adjy, psych, spook, get to, flip out, craze, jazz up, juice, send, blow up, trigger, bug, burn up, fire up, key up, kick up a row, put up to, work up, work up into a lather, egg on, turn on, make waves, make a scene, make a fuss, sound off, make it tough for all, put the zingers in, needle, give one the needle, put the needles in, ride, steam up, throw wood on the fire, add fuel to the flames, rabble-rouse, stir up, discombobulate, go on make my day, stick in one's craw, ask for it, get a rise out of one, turn one on, rile, get one's goat, get under one's skin, get in one's hair, brown off.

INCITER n. adjy, spark plug, pusher, fireman, hatchet man, needle man, steam-up ghee, stormy petrel, wave maker.

INCLINATION n. bag, groove, thing, natural at, handy at, shine in, take to something like a duck takes to water, have a bump for, turned on to, flash, weakness for, cup of tea, druthers, type, where one is at, head-set, mind-set, mind trip, tilt, big eyes, eyes for, hard-on for, itch, hot pants, lech, sweet tooth, yen, zazzle. See also DESIRE.

INCLUDE v. cut one in on, duke one in on.

INCLUSION n. hands on, sit in, get in the act.

INCLUSIVE adj. across the board, the whole ball of wax, wall to wall, all the options. See also WHOLE.

INCOGNITO adj. incog, bearding. See also ANONYMOUS.

INCOME n. net, velvet, pay, payoff, rake off, gravy, bottom line, in the black, in the till, cush, cash flow, revenue stream, bottom line, the big time, split, get, gate, handle, melon, peanuts (small), strength, sweetener, sweetening, what's in it for one, take, take in, take home, harvest, cream. See also COMPENSATION.

INCOMMUNICADO adj. on ice, out of touch, out of pocket.

INCOMPATIBLE adj. diff, far cry, funky, offbeat, march to the beat of a different drummer, poles apart, weird, whale of a difference, like night and day.

INCOMPETENT adj. out to lunch, bringdown, amateur night, amateur night in Dixie, can't hack it, can't cut it, can't cut the mustard, can't make the grade, not have it, not cut out for, uncool, Mickey Mouse, bush, bush league, haywire, dead one, lamebrained, dub, flubdub, flub the dub, dud, fuddy-duddy, ham, half-assed, half-baked, hell of a way to run a railroad, fumble-fist, butterfingers, muff, nowhere, out of one's depth, in over one's head, zilch.

INCOMPETENT n. fuck up, nerd, jerk, yo-yo, turkey, clown, dipstick, runt, eightball, winner, real winner, loser, real loser, ham, bull-staller, shmendrick, schmo, muffer, duffer, slob, lummox, lump.

INCOMPREHENSIBLE adj. clear as mud, clear as dishwater, it beats me, beats the shit outta me, it's Greek to me, you've got me, I give up, I pass. See OBSCURE.

INCONCEIVABLE adj. 1. thick, thin, reachy, won't wash, fishy, phoney, rings phoney, in one's hat, pure bullshit, not born yesterday. See UNBELIEVABLE. 2. it won't fly, no-go, no way, not a prayer, not a ghost of a chance, not a Chinaman's chance, not a chance in hell. See IMPOSSIBLE. 3. fantasmo, seven-ply gasser, gnarly, mega-gnarly, unreal, rat fuck, cool, zero cool, cold, out of this world, out of sight, nose cone, like wow, stunning, mad, mess, mezz, fab, in orbit, murder, something, something else, dynamite, far out, funky, too much, the most, the utmost, hell of a note, this is some kinda ———, the end.

INCONSEQUENTIAL adj. 1. big zero, big fucking deal, BFD, no biggie, no great shakes, dinky, two bit, entry level (job), bupkis. 2. wimp, nebbish, shrimp, runt, a nobody, small potatoes, twerp, jerkwater (small town). See UNIMPORTANT.

INCONSISTENCY n. catch, catch 22, pair of ducks.

INCONSPICUOUS adj. low keyed, low profile, soft-pedalled.

INCONSTANT adj. 1. yo-yo, wishy-washy, see-saw, picky, picky picky. 2. two-timer, two-faced, dog one around, yard on, cheat on, chippy on one, step out on one. See UNFAITHFUL.

IN CONTENTION adj. in the hunt.

INCONTROVERTIBLE adj. sure as God made little green apples, sure as death and taxes, sure thing, surefire, sure as shootin', no two ways about it, absofuckinglutely, posilutely, absitively, nailed down, open-and-shut case, and no mistake. See CERTAIN.

INCONVENIENCE v. hang up, give one a bad time, give one a hard time, make it tough for, discombobulate, put in a hole, put in a spot, put on a spot, fuzzbuzz. See also TROUBLE.

INCORPORATE v. pool, tie in, gang up, put together, cross dissolve (film), cue in, (scripts, ms., songs); dub, hook in, marry (film), mix (recording). See ASSOCIATE.

INCORRECT adj. all wet, ass backwards, way off, off the beam, full of beans, that doesn't track, wrong number. See WRONG.

INCORRIGIBLE adj. gross, stinking, too much, beastly, a bit much, too far gone, wrong ghee, three-time loser, loser. See BAD.

INCREASE v. pad, pyramid, slap on, tack on, tag on, hitch on, pour it on, hook on, hook up with, piggyback, mushroom, up, beef up, soup up, hop up, ramp up, heat up, hike, hike up, step up, jazz up, jack up, pick up, jump up, shoot up, put up, run up, tish, build, build up, builder-upper, bring up, fetch up, goose up, spike, flesh out, spin out, string out, drag out, add bells and whistles, dump on, snow, snowball, sweeten, sweeten the pot, parlay, speed up, boost, press a bet, join up with, join together, plug into, add fuel to the fire.

INCREASED adj. beefed up, hiked, hiked up, jacked up, upped, built up, boosted, padded, spun out, strung out, dragged out, run out, pyramided.

INCREDIBLE adj. 1. fab, glor, superfly, outrageous, fantasmo, twitchin', piss-cutter, unreal, skrouk, seven-ply gasser. See FABULOUS. 2. thick, thin, reachy, won't wash, fishy, phoney, rings phoney.

INCRIMINATE v. name, finger, point the finger at, put the finger on, hang something on, pin on, pin it on one, blow the whistle on one, whistle-blow, frame, frame up, put up a job, lay at one's door, let one have it, stick it to one, find the smoking gun.

INCULCATE v. brainwash, head-fuck, mind-fuck, fuck with one's head, break down, program, shape up, work over. See also INSTRUCT.

INCURABLE adj. had it, no more cards to play, nowhere to go, runnin' out of time, in the soup, at the end of one's rope. See HOPELESS.

INDEBTED adj. into, on the tab, on the cuff, on the arm, in hock, into the shylock, hooked, on a string, owe one one, meet in the alley.

INDEBTEDNESS n. IOU, in the red, in hock, on the nut, on the cuff, on the arm, dues. See DEBT.

INDECENT adj. blue, X-rated, raunchy, raw, spark, a circus, foulmouthed, off-color, dirty, filthy, flasher, rough. See OBSCENE.

INDECISIVE adj. pussyfoot, pussyfoot around, weenie, straddle, on the fence, hot and cold, hedge off, shilly-shally, waffle, hem and haw. See UNDECIDED.

INDEED adv. indeedy, yes indeedy, amen, sure thing, you better believe it, you can say that again, for real, right rather. See ABSOLUTELY

INDEFATIGABLE adj. nose to the grindstone, work one's tail off, bound, bound and determined, stick at nothing, dead set on, bent on, hell bent on, ironclad. See INDUSTRIOUS.

INDEFINITELY adj. indef.

INDEPENDENT adj. on one's own, on one's own hook, one's own sweet way, paddle one's own canoe, have fuck-you money, couldn't care less, free wheeling, look out for number one, don't give a damm, mugwumpian, mugwumpish, on the fence, indie (film). See also NONPARTISAN.

INDIAN n. injun, redskin, buck, brave, red man, redskin; apple, Uncle Tomahawk (white establishment oriented).

INDIANA Hoosier State.

INDIANAPOLIS, INDIANA Indy, Naplus, Circle City, Speed Town.

INDIANAPOLIS SPEEDWAY n. Indy, brickyard.

INDIAN RESERVATION n. res.

INDICATE v. name, slot, tab, tag, make, peg, card, finger, lay one's finger on, put one's finger on, put the finger on, button down, pin down, pinpoint, put down for, make a noise, sign, high sign, signal, send a signal, flash.

INDICATION n. high sign, nod, wink. See also HINT.

INDICT v. finger, frame, frame up, put up a job, stick to one, stick it to one, stick one with. See also ACCUSE.

INDIFFERENT adj. iceberg, cold, cold fish, cool cat, cool, cool as a cucumber, keep one's cool, unflappable, laid back, loose, no sweat, don't sweat it, keep one's shirt on, not turn a hair, roll with the punches, go with the flow, could care less, blah, flat, tough, hard-boiled, hard-hearted, hard as nails, rhinoceros hide, thick-skinned, dead ass, fair to middling, butter wouldn't melt in his mouth, got lead balls for eyes, poker-faced, don't give a shit, don't give spit, don't give a damn, don't give a darn, don't give diddly, don't give diddly-shit, don't give a fuck, don't give a flying fuck, don't give a hoot, phone it in, just going through the motions, walk through it, what's the diff?, what the hell, so what?, it's all the same to me, big deal, big fucking deal, BFD, that's your lookout, that's your pigeon, I should worry? See also ALOOF.

INDIFFERENT, BECOME v.   chill, chill off, chill up on, cool off, turn a cold shoulder.

INDIGENCE n.   on the rims, run on the rims, needy, truly needy, through the safety net.

INDIGENOUS adj.   home towner, local, local yokel, landsman, paesano.

INDIGENT adj.   flat, flat broke, busted, hard up, strapped, oofless, wasted, tapped out, on the rocks, down and out, piss-poor, cold in hand (Bl.). See DESTITUTE.

INDIGNANT adj.   browned off, pissed off, p.o.'d, bent out of shape, bugged, steamed, ticked off, tee'd off, t.o.'d, miffed, burned up, run a temperature, make one's blood boil. See ANGRY.

INDIGNATION n.   burning, slow burn, mad, miff, huff, sore, rise, get a rise out of, put out, stew, dander, Irish, pet, more heat than light, boiling point. See also ANGER.

INDIGNITY n.   put-down, brickbat, backhanded compliment, left-handed compliment, dump, dump on, take down. See INSULT.

INDIRECT adj.   go round the barn, went by way of, long way, long way home.

INDISCREET adj.   put one's foot in it, fox paw, bad form.

INDISCRETION n.   goof, misspeak, miscue, hash up, louse up, screw up, foul-up, fuck-up, muck up, bitch, bitch up, slipup, fox paw, fox pass, gaff, blow card, bugger, bugger up, mess, mess up, make a mess of, make a boner, fool mistake, dumb trick, boob stunt, boo-boo, make a boo-boo, bloomer, make a blooper, boot, bobble, drop the ball, stumble, pull a blooper, pull a bloomer, pull a boner, pull a boo boo, diarrhea of the mouth, put one's foot in it, put one's foot in one's mouth, foot in the mouth disease, shoot oneself in the foot, stub one's toe, go at it ass backwards, jump out of the frying pan into the fire, drop a brick. See also LAPSE.

INDISPOSED adj.   down, down with, got a bug, rocky, feeling rotten, poorly, under the weather, below par, on the sick list, outta action, laid up, on the shelf. See ILL.

INDISPOSITION n.   bug, crud, creeping crud, the runs, trots, what's going around, the flu, the pip, dose, fascinoma (Medic.), burned (VD). See ILLNESS.

INDISPUTABLE adj.   sure as shooting, sure as death and taxes, bet your ass, that's a fact Jack, no buts about it, open and shut, checked and double checked, and no mistake. See CERTAIN.

INDIVIDUAL n.   unit, guy, dude, cat, bird, stud, joker, clown, head, ace (good), motherfucker, mofo, hairpin, number (hot number), boot (bl.), poor fish. See PERSON.

INDIVIDUALIST n.   maverick, oddball, freak, crazy, weirdo, an original, nature boy, offbeat, beatnik, hippie, yippie, square peg in a round hole. See ECCENTRIC.

INDIVIDUALISTIC adj.   diff, far cry, cool, funky, offbeat, poles apart, far out, way out, out of sight, hip, hep, weird, whale of a difference, like night and day, march to the beat of a different drummer.

INDIVIDUAL RETIREMENT ACCOUNT n.   IRA, Keogh.

INDOCTRINATE v.   brainwash, mind-fuck, head-fuck, fuck with one's head, break down, program, work over. See also INSTRUCT.

INDOCTRINATED adj.   programmed, brainwashed, head-fucked, mind-fucked. See also KNOWLEDGE-ABLE.

INDOLENT adj.   blah, dopey, draggy, drag ass, lox, sack artist, Stepin Fetchit, on the shelf, on the bench, out of the rat race, out of action, out of the swim, down, closed down. See also LAZY.

INDORSE v.   back, bless, boost, get behind, get on the bandwagon, go with, go for, hold with, buy, ditto, rubber-stamp. See ENDORSE.

INDUBITABLE adj.   sure as shooting, sure as I live and breathe, bet your ass, bet your life, fer sher, dead sure, absitively, for a fact, cold, lock-and-win situation, no ifs ands or buts, open and shut case, know damm well, rain or shine. See CERTAIN.

INDUCE v.   soft-soap, sweet-talk, eat one's mind, duke in, promote, sell one on, iggle, goose, suck in, twist one's arm, squeeze, steamroller. See PERSUADE.

INDUCEMENT n.   come-on, leader, loss leader, con, bait, the Murphy, hook, sell, hard sell, soft soap, snow job, sweet talk, twist one's arm, shovelin' shit, goose, brainwash, See also BRIBE.

INDUCT v.   sign on, sign up, swear in.

INDUCTEE n.   boot, rookie, tenderfoot, draft bait (subject to conscription).

INDUCTION n.   greetings, letter from Uncle Sam.

INDULGE v.   1. live it up, live high on the hog, live on the fat of the land, put on the dog, put on the ritz. See INTEMPERATE. 2. look out for number one, take care of number one, be on an ego trip, ego trip, go on an ego trip. 3. spoil, spoil rotten, go along with, go easy with, go easy on.

INDULGED adj.   spoiled, spoiled rotten, played up to, made over, stroked.

INDULGENT adj.   be big, soft shell, live with, go along with, go easy with, go easy on. See COMPASSIONATE.

INDUSTRIAL GROUPINGS smokestack industries, Sun Belt, Rust Belt, Silicon Valley, Pacific Rim, Motown, oil patch, Establishment, Northern Establishment.

INDUSTRIALIST n. fat cat, baron, robber baron, tycoon. See also BUSINESSMAN.

INDUSTRIOUS adj. grind, plugger, nose to the grindstone, springbutt, eager beaver, work one's tail off, whiz, ball of fire, chipper, burn, fireball, hyper, in full swing, jumping, on the go, perky. See also SPIRITED.

INDUSTRY n. megacorp, multinational, plunderbund, bunch, crew, crowd, gang, mob, outfit, ring. See also BUSINESS, CORPORATION.

INEBRIATED adj. tight, tipsy, bombed, stewed, stiff, stinking, plastered, pie-eyed, wasted, tanked up, blind drunk, fried, smashed, polluted, loaded, feeling no pain, embalmed, shikker, pickled, pissed, three sheets to the wind, have a skin full, in orbit, seeing pink elephants. See DRUNK.

INEFFECTIVE adj. wuss, nobody, nebbish, sad sack, shnook, wimp, limp dick, limp dishrag, clambake, false alarm, flash in the pan, deadbeat, bum, loser, out of luck, lumpy, neverwuz, total shuck, no great shakes, nothing to write home about, kaput, clown, dud, fuddy-duddy, flub the dub, good for nothing, bringdown, down-and-out, foul ball, eightball, half-assed, half-baked, amateur night, amateur night in Dixie, ham, haywire, dead one, lamebrained, lame duck, piss-pour, Mickey Mouse, bull-staller, out of one's depth, in too deep, in over one's head, in a vicious circle, shooting blanks, zilch, go under, go hit your head against the wall, go fight City Hall, go on a wild goose chase, looking for a needle in a haystack, locking the barn after the horse is stolen, no way, no dice, no go, nowhere, get nowhere, fall on one's face, fall on one's ass, fall down, fall down on the job, foldo, flop, down the drain, down the chute, down the toilet, in the toilet, washout, not come off, flunk, flunk out, crap out, strike out, on the skids, on the rocks, A for effort, near miss, back to the drawing board, out of it, out to lunch, missed the boat, can't even get arrested, can't even write home for money, can't punch his way out of a paper bag, should have stood in bed. See also INADEQUATE.

INEFFICIENT adj. can't hack it, can't cut the mustard, not cut out for, Mickey Mouse, haywire, flubdub, dud, fuddy-duddy, half-baked, shooting blanks. See INCOMPETENT.

INEPT adj. all thumbs, butterfingers, fumble-fist, ham-fisted, ham-handed, bo, fuck up, yo-yo, loser, real loser, can't hack it, can't cut it. See INCOMPETENT.

INERT adj. down, closed down, on the shelf, on the bench, on ice, out of action.

INEVITABILITY n. karma, kismet, in the cards, the beads, that's the way the beads read, that's the way the ball bounces, that's the way the cookie crumbles. See also CERTAINTY.

INEVITABLE adj. sure as fate, sure as death, sure as death and taxes, for certain, on ice, cold, pat, all locked up, no buts about it, bet one's bottom dollar on, in the bag, the fix is in, name of the game. See CERTAIN.

INEXACT adj. bum, off, way off. See WRONG.

INEXCITABLE adj. cool, cool as a cucumber, keep one's cool, keep one's shirt on, not turn a hair, roll with the punches, without a nerve in one's body, unflappable. See IMPERTURBABLE.

INEXHAUSTIBLE adj. more than you can shake a stick at, no end of, no end to, jillion, a jillion at least, zillion, umpteen. See PLENTY.

INEXORABLE adj. locked, locked in, no going back, like death and taxes, bound, bound and determined, stick to one's guns, stick at nothing, dead set on, bent on, hell bent on, mean business, ironclad, set, sot, set in concrete, buried in concrete, chiseled in stone, Rocka Gibraltar, Rock of Gibraltar. See also STUBBORN.

INEXPENSIVE adj. cheapie, el cheapo, dirt cheap, cheap as dirt, dog cheap, steal, a real steal, buy, a real buy, low cost, cost nothing, cost next to nothing, bought for a song, cut rate, low tariff, dime a dozen.

INEXPENSIVELY adj. nickel and dime it, on the rims, cheap it out.

INEXPERIENCED adj. virgin, rookie, kid, green, green-ass, amateur night, amateur night in Dixie, gay cat, scut, spring chicken, don't know shit from Shinola, out of one's league, out of one's depth. See SOPHISTICATED.

INEXPRESSIVE adj. deadpan, straight face, poker-faced, fish eye, lead eyeballs, wooden.

INFANT n. kid, babykins, bambino, cheese factory, toddler, nipper, papoose, preemie, bundle, little deduction. See BABY.

INFANTILE adj. kid stuff.

INFANTRYMAN n. G.I., GI Joe, dogface, doughboy, footslogger, grunt, paddlefoot, sad sack, leg (Vietnam). See SOLDIER.

INFATUATED adj. gone, far gone on, hipped on, stuck on, mad about, smitten, has a thing about, hooked. See LOVE, IN.

INFATUATION n. amore, mash, pash, weakness, case, crash, crush, yen, mad for, crazy for, wild for, spoiling for, itch for, hankering, partial to, shine, beaver fever, hot pants, turn-on, calf love, puppy love. See LOVE.

INFECTION n. bug, burned (VD), crud, creeping crud, runs, trots, what's going around.

INFER v. have a hunch, be afraid, figure, figger, add up to, boil down to, what one is saying is, read between the lines, read into, the way one sees it. See also BELIEF, SPECULATE.

INFERENCE n. guesstimate, subtext, hunch, shot, shot in the dark, sneaking suspicion, stab, stab in the dark.

INFERIOR adj. 1. man Friday, pratt boy, peon, serf, droid, slave, slavey, girl Friday, bush league, entry level (employment), low man on the totem pole, bottom man on the totem pole, bottom rung, bottom man, bottom sawyer, back seat, second fiddle, second string, third string, yes man, poor man's something or somebody, hanger-on, flunky, furp, stiff, apparatchik, squeak, last hired first fired, minus, in one's power, in one's pocket, in one's clutches, under one's thumb, at one's mercy, at one's beck and call, at one's feet, a slave to, led by the nose, spear carrier, second banana, infra dig. See also INADEQUATE. 2. seconds, crap, crappy, gummy, junk, shit, borax, dreck, lemon, gook, Mickey Mouse, punk, schlocky, sleazy, two bit, cheesy, low rent, low ride, sad, not up to scratch. See IMPERFECT.

INFERNO n. hell, the other place, down there.

INFERTILE adj. shoot blanks, fire blanks, blank cartridge, dud, no lead in the pencil, no toothpaste in the tube.

INFIDELITY n. affair, carrying on, hanky-panky, playing around, two-timing, getting some on the side, working late at the office, extracurricular activity, thing, your place or mine? See ADULTERY.

INFILTRATE v. penetrate, access, crack. See PENETRATE.

INFILTRATOR n. mole.

INFINITE adj. jillion, a jillion at least, zillion, umpteen, more than you can shake a stick at, no end of, no end to, thick as flies, thick as hail. See COUNTLESS.

INFINITELY adv. for ever so long, for a coon's age, for a dog's age, for a month of Sundays, till hell freezes over, till you're blue in the face, till the cows come home, till shrimps learn to whistle.

INFIRM n. rocky, laid low. See ILL.

INFIRMITY n. bug, crud, creeping crud, the runs, trots, what's going around, the flu, the pip, dose, double scrudfantods, fascinoma (Med.), burned (V.D.), willies (mythical). See ILLNESS.

INFLAME v. turn one on, heat up, steam up, jazz up, work up, switch on, turn on the heat, work up into a lather, fire up. See EXCITE.

INFLAMED adj. juiced up, zipped up, zapped up, all fired up, worked up, turned on. See EXCITED.

INFLATE v. boost, balloon, hike, hike up, jack up, jump up, put up, build up, pyramid, up, beef up, flesh out, pad. See EXPAND.

INFLATION n. boost, buildup, hike, overheated economy, up, upping.

INFLEXIBLE adj. set, dead set on, stand one's ground, brick wall, solid as a rock, set in concrete, stuck in concrete, buried in concrete, chiseled in stone, bound and determined, do or die, hard core, hard line, stiff necked, locked in. See STUBBORN.

INFLICT v. move in on, chisel in, horn in, muscle in, lay down the law, put one's foot down, read the riot act, dish it out, dish out, dump on, give it to one, stick it to one. See also FORCE.

INFLUENCE n. juice, string, ropes, weight, drag, pull, clout, access, fix, grease, alzo, contacts, channels, network, connection, hooks, license, nuts, wire, snow, snow job, suction, suck, a lot to do with, a lot to say about, in, inside track, wire-pulling, con, hook, sell, soft soap, snow job, sweet talk, twisting one's arm, body English, driver's seat. See also POWER.

INFLUENCE v. put a spin on, impact on, con, sell, snow, jawbone, lead by the nose, pull ropes, pull strings, pull wires, throw one's weight around, whitewash, wire-pull, get one's hooks into, twist one's arm. See also PERSUADE.

INFLUENCE PEDDLER n. five percenter, fixer, logroller, wire-puller, connection.

INFLUENTIAL adj. name, big player, big chew, big gun, big noise, big wheel, major league, main squeeze, movers and shakers, one who knows where the body's buried, hot dog, connection, wire. See IMPORTANT.

INFLUENZA n. flu, flue, bug, flu bug, Mao flu, virus, what's going around.

INFORM v. 1. tout, tip, tip off, tip one's duke, spring one's duke, steer, put hip, update, level, clue one in, crank one in, let in on, let in on the know, let next to, put next to, put it on the street, put in one's two cents, put one in the picture, put on to, put one wise, wise one up, put a bug in one's ear, put a flea in one's ear, fold an ear, show one the ropes, give one a tip, give one the word, give a pointer to, post, keep posted, touch base with, pull one's coat, break it to one, lace one's boots, lay it on one, lay it on the line, put it on the line, lay it out for, drum. See also INSTRUCT. 2. leak, blab, blabber, rat, squeal, squawk, stool, talk, verbalize, cop a plea, crack, peach, spit it out, spill, spill one's guts, spill the beans, give away, give with, give the show away, have a big bazoo, have a big mouth, let down one's hair, let it all hang out, let the cat out of the bag, sing, sing like a canary, chirp. 3. deal, double-cross, drop a dime on one, dime one out, fuck, fuck one's buddy, hose, screw, split, knife, stab one in the back, finger, put the finger on, turn on, turn in, rat, rat on, eat cheese, fink, fink on, croon, sing, squeal, squeal on, stool, stool on, weasel on, holler, open up, buzz (in secret), blow, blow the whistle, blow the gaff, belch, sell out, let down, let down one's side, sell down the river, do one dirt, dump on, switch, snitch, dry snitch.

INFORMAL adj. folksy, down home, haymish, homey, laid back, sporty, easygoing, let one's hair down, mellow, pokesy, throwaway, off the cuff, improv, cool, loose, loose as a goose. See CASUAL.

INFORMANT n. fink, nark, snitch, stoolie, canary, source, blabbermouth, tattletale, whistle blower, fat mouth, motor mouth, deep throat, tout. See IN-FORMER.

INFORMATION n. info, leak, network, tie-in, hookup, cue, clue, scoop, poop, hot poop, poop sheet, ammo, pipeline, boot snitch, score, skinny, lowdown, dirt, dope, dope sheet, inside dope, medicine, inside wire, insider, tip, hot tip, hot poo, the know, picture, story, inside story, whole story, chapter and verse, goods, brass tacks, garbage, goulash (false), ear loft, break, beat, the latest, what's what, what's happenin' what's going down, chip, brush-up, earful, ear duster, hash, haymaker, hotshot, hot wire; kick in the ass, shot in the ass (bad); are you ready for this? page-oner. See also FACTS.

INFORMED adj. posted, hip, savvy, with it, tuned in, into, wise to, know the score, know what's what, on top of, kept posted. See KNOWLEDGEABLE.

INFORMER n. rat, rat fink, fink, narc, finger, snitch, snitcher, squealer, stoolie, stool pigeon, canary, chirper, songbird, nightingale, singer, yodeler, source, weasel, blab, blabber, blabberer, blabbermouth, tattler, tattletale, telltale, whistle-blower, whistler, double-crosser, fat mouth, preacher, snake, snake in the grass, buddy fucker, beefer, copper, copper-hearted, cheese bun, cheese-eater, bat-carrier (1925), faded boogie (Bl.), geepo, cat, chalk hat, fork tongue, mouse, punk, ringtail, shamus, flip, deep throat, nose, tout.

INFRARED IMAGE CONVERTER n. snooperscope.

INFRINGE v. 1. lift, steal, borrow, crib, pick one's brains, pirate, rape. 2. chisel in, muscle in, butt in, crash, crash the gates, pirate. See ENCROACH. See also COPY.

INFURIATE v. brown off, burn up, rile, piss one off, T-off, juice, blow one away, get under one's skin, whip up, fire up, steam up, put one's Irish up. See ANGER.

INFURIATED adj. pissed off, p'd off, cheesed off, bent, pushed outta shape, bouncing, mad as a wet hen, hacked, steamed up, see red, go ape shit, have a shit hemorrhage, hit the ceiling, burned up, smoking, hot, on the war path, yell bloody murder. See ANGRY.

INFURIATING adj. a bit much, pesky, pestiferous, too much.

INGENUOUS adj. 1. up front, call a spade a spade, make no bones about it, open, straight dope, straight shit, like it is, call it like it is, talk turkey. See FRANK. 2. babe in the woods, square, green, mark, low tech, uncool, wet behind the ears, shit kicker. See UNSOPHISTICATED.

INGEST v. scarf, scoff, slurp, mow (mow a burger), gorp, graze, wolf down, inhale, stuff one's face, tuck in, pack it away, put oneself outside of. See EAT.

INGRATIATE v. kiss ass, suck ass, suck up to, brownnose, fall all over, apple-polish, bootlick, kowtow, hand one a line. See FLATTER.

INGRATIATING adj. smarmy, kissy ass.

INGREDIENT n. fixin's, makin's, part and parcel.

INHABIT v. bunk, bunk out, hang out, crash, nest, perch, roost, squat, locate, park, hole up, hang up one's hat, hang up one's shingle.

INHALATION n. drag, puff, hit, pull.

INHALE v. snort, sniff, pull.

INHARMONIOUS adj. clinker, hit a clinker, sour, sour note, hit a sour note, sound a clinker, sound a sour note.

INHIBIT v. hang up, hog-tie, stymie, faze, sandbag, cramp one's style, monkey with the buzz saw, put on the brakes, drag one's foot. See HINDER.

INHIBITED adj. uptight, tight-assed, hung up, square, iced, chilled, bottled up, corked up, hog-tied.

INITIALLY adv. right off the bat, for openers, for starters, first crack out of the box.

INITIATE n. boot, newie, boy, new boy on the block, new kid on the block, fish, tenderfoot, greenie, rookie, blow in. See BEGINNER.

INITIATE v. intro, ring in, start the ball rolling, break the ice, kick off, trigger, rev up, fire up, cook up, dream up, make up, come out with, come up with, get one's feet wet. See BEGIN.

INITIATIVE n. gumption, spunk, drive, moxie, punch, push, steam, get up and go.

INJECT v. 1. give a shot, shoot, shoot up, give one the square needle, joy pop, skin pop, mainline, send it home. 2. fudge in, lug in, lug in by the heels, drag in, drag in by the heels, squeeze in, worm in, shoehorn it in.

INJECTED adj. got the hook, got the square needle, binged, stabbed in the ass.

INJECTION n.   the needle, jab, shot, shot in the arm, shot in the ass, booster, booster shot, hit, fix, nip, slug, bang, dram.

INJUDICIOUS adj.   go off the deep end, put one's foot in it, put one's foot in one's mouth, go out on a limb, buy a pig in a poke, play with fire, leave oneself wide open. See RECKLESS.

INJURE v.   1. gotcha, rough up, shake up, hack up, total, wax, wing, ding, nick, zing, tweak, cut up, bend the goods. See DAMAGE. 2. do in, dump on, muck up, queer, hit one where one lives, lay a bad trip on one, give one a left-handed compliment, gross out. See WOUND.

INJURED adj.   1. hurtin', bleedin', damaged, winged, nicked, zinged, cut, bunged up, busted up, burned, burned one's ass, put away, screwed up, walking wounded, have to scrape one off the sidewalk. 2. all torn up, cut up, hit where one lives, shook, shook up, miffed, miffy, shot down, have one's nose out of joint, sore, uptight.

INJURY n.   ouch, chop, scratch, nick, graze, gotcha, boo-boo (minor flesh), brand, jig cut, mark, rat mark, stool mark (knife), black and blue, down.

INJUSTICE n.   raw deal, screwing, fucking, royal screwing, royal fucking, gurdy, hurdy, kick around, railroad, sellout, cheap shot, not cricket, hitting below the belt, dirty pool.

INK n.   pen juice.

INKLING n.   lead, hot lead, tipoff, tell-tale, flea in one's ear, sneaking suspicion, hunch, tip, straw in the wind.

INN n.   motel, airtel, aquatel, boatel, floatel, chinch pad, flophouse, scratch crib.

INNARDS n.   guts, tripes, stuffings.

INNER adj.   innerspace.

INNER CIRCLE n.   insiders, click, circle, the loop, ring, gang, crew, crowd, bunch, the power curve, in-group; inside the beltway (WASHINGTON, D.C.).

INNING n.   go, go at, one's move, one's say, whack, one's turn, break, big break, shot, fling. See OPPORTUNITY.

INNOCENT adj.   low tech, uncool, green, wide-eyed, clean, lily white, softie, square, off the cob, search me. See UNSOPHISTICATED.

INNOCENT n.   pussycat, greenhorn, kid, babe in the woods, hick, wimp, simp, shnook, Golden Bantam, eight ball. See UNSOPHISTICATED.

INNOVATE v.   break out. See ORIGINATE.

INNOVATION n.   leading edge, cutting edge, breaking new snow, avant-garde, in-thing, last word, latest thing, latest wrinkle, new wrinkle, newie, newfangled contraption, what's happening, what's in.

INNOVATIVE adj.   state of the art, leading edge, cutting edge, breaking new ground, contempo, fire new, just out, avant-garde, newfangled. See NEW.

INNUMERABLE adj.   jillion, zillion, umpteen, umpteenth, more than you can shake a stick at, no end of, no end to, thick as flies, thick as hail, alive with, crawling with. See COUNTLESS.

INOCULATE v.   give a shot, shoot, give one the square needle.

INOCULATED adj.   got the hook, got the square needle, binged (WW I), stabbed in the ass (WW II).

INOCULATION n.   shot, booster, booster shot, shot in the arm, shot in the ass.

INOFFENSIVE adj.   clean, white bread, vanilla.

INOPERABLE adj.   crashed, down, go down, out of whack, out of kilter, out of order, out of commission, kaput, on the blink, on the fritz, haywire, conked out, fouled up, fucked up, no go. See DAMAGED.

INORDINATELY adv.   too much, too-too. See also EXCESSIVE.

IN PERSON adj.   in the flesh, live.

INQUIRE v.   hit, hit up, knock, put out a feeler, feel out, test the waters, see which way the wind blows, send up a trial balloon, grill, roast, put the screws on, go over. See QUESTION. See also INVESTIGATE.

INQUIRY n.   third, third degree, what's happening?, what's cooking?, what cooks?, what's with one or something, fishing expedition, witch hunt, Q. and A., wringer, legwork, feeler, trial balloon, poll. See also INVESTIGATION.

INQUISITION n.   third, third degree, witch hunt, wringer.

INQUISITIVE adj.   snoopy, nosey, nosey Parker, rubbernecking, playing the bird with the long neck, on the earie, on the gun, on the i.c. (eye see), on the lake, on the mooch, on the pike, on the prowl, on the squint.

INSANE adj.   whacko, unglued, unzipped, unscrewed, screwy, schitzy, schizzed out, psycho, psyched out, freaked out, flipped one's lid, half deck, totally baked, out of one's gourd, out of one's tree, out of one's bird, off one's chump, in the ozone, crackers, bonkers, bananas, gone ape, nuts, nutty as a fruitcake, whacked out, off one's rocker, lost one's marbles, cutting out paper dolls, section 8, gonzo, gonzxoitis. See CRAZY.

INSANE ASYLUM n.   booby hatch, funny farm, loony bin, bughouse, nut house, crazy house, bat house, funny house, warehouse, rubber room, soft walls, acorn academy, college, nut college, nut factory, nut farm, nut hatch, zoo, ding tank (holding cell).

INSANE, COMMIT TO ASYLUM v.   bug, drop the net on, lag; make the bughouse, get the straw hat and the red tie (be committed).

INSANE, GO v.   crack up, blow, blow a fuse, blow one's top, blow one's cap, blow one's cork, blow one's noggin, blow a gasket, blow one's roof, blow one's stack, blow one's mind, flip, flip out, flip one's lid, flip one's stack, pop one's cork, go ape, go ape shit, go bananas, go bonkers, go nuts, nut up (Stu.), go crackers, go bugs, go coo coo, go daffy, lose one's taffy, go off one's head, go off one's nut, go off one's rocker, go off one's base, go off the track, go off the trolley, slip one's trolley, go out of one's skull, go round the bend, go for soft-wall treatment, head for the funny farm, come unglued, come unzipped, come off the wall, flake out, schizz out, psych out, freak out, snap, lose all one's buttons, lose all one's marbles, cut out paper dolls.

INSCRUTABLE adj.   clear as mud, it beats me, you've got me, it's Greek to me, deep. See OBSCURE.

INSECTICIDE n.   bug bomb.

INSECTS n.   crabs, crum, crumb, grayback, seam squirrel, shimmy lizard; crumby, crummy, cooties, lousy (afflicted with).

INSECURE adj.   shaky, choked, jumpy, touchy, uptight, touch and go, on slippery ground, on thin ice, hanging by a thread.

INSENSITIVE adj.   cold fish, hard as nails, hard hearted, rhinoceros hide, thick-skinned, dead ass, has lead balls for eyes, tough. See CALLOUS.

INSERT v.   stick in, shove it in, shoehorn it in, cut it in, drag in, drag in by the heels, lug in, lug in by the heels, squeeze in, fudge in, worm in.

INSIDE adj.   innerspace.

INSIDIOUS adj.   snake, snake in the grass, worm. See DECEITFUL.

INSIGHT n.   aha reaction, savvy, hep to, wise to, see the light, flash on it, click, get one's drift, on the same wavelength, I got it, it hit me, it just come to me.

INSIGNIA n.   fruit salad, scrambled eggs, ruptured duck, brag rags, chest hardware, chicken guts (trimmings).

INSIGNIAS n.   hardware, hash mark, hash stripe, Hershey bar, jack (Cavalry), monkey flag, tracks, railroad tracks, spam cluster, one-striper, two-striper, three-striper, two-and-a-half striper, travel bars, diag (gold braid, Annapolis), didie pins, (second Lt. gold bars), homing pigeon, hooks (chevrons), the bird (Eagle, Army Colonel, Navy Captain), gold bars (2nd Lt.), r.r. tracks (Army Captain), buzzard (Army, Navy), chicken guts (trimmings), scrambled eggs, fried egg, costume jewelry (WAC), chevrons, strips, crow.

INSIGNIFICANT adj.   1. no big deal, no biggie, Podunk, entry level (job), bottom rung, lower rung, not worth a hill of beans, not worth the powder to blow it to hell. 2. small time, gadget, spear carrier, Mr. Ducrot (West Point), small fry, small beer, small change, small pot, a lightweight, fly speck, flea, a hump, two blink, underwhelming, nickel and dime, penny ante, peanuts, pokerino, shot, scratch, skag, jerkwater (small town). See UNIMPORTANT.

INSINCERE adj.   fishy, jivey, jive-assed, shuckin' and jivin', two-faced, gil, Hollywood, reach-me-down, put on, slick, sincere, snide, phony, fake, cry crocodile tears. See also DISHONEST.

INSINCERITY n.   jazz, jive, chicken, chicken shit, shit, bull, bullshit, throw the bull, shoot the bull, shoot the shit, bullshit artist, bull shooter, bull shot, bull skate, horseshit, piece of shit, crock of shit, chewing gum, goop, hooey, spinach, put on, crocodile tears, soft soap, sweet talk, fast talk, con, hokum, hokey, hokey-pokey, double-dealing, lay it on thick, do a number on one.

INSIPID adj.   blah, beige, draggy, draddy, dull as dishwater, ho hum, bor-ring, bore one stiff, nebbish, rundown, a yawn, big yawn, dead, diddly bop, gasser, gummy, grunch, grungy, icky, the least, nowhere, noplaceville, Nadaville, dullsville, nothing, nothing doing, tired, wiped out, a snooze, flat, flat tire, flat as a pancake, pablum, zero, big zero, big deal, no big deal, big shit, no big shit, winner, real winner, loser, real loser, downer, dog, go over like a lead balloon, lay an egg, bombed.

INSOLENCE n.   back talk, brass, cheek, chutzpah, gall, guff, lip, sass.

INSOLENT adj.   get previous, flip, fly, jazzy, fresh, breezy, nervy, cheeky, sassy, smart, smarty, smarty pants, smart alecky, smart ass, wise ass, wise guy, wiseacre, weisenheimer, brassy, bold as brass, whippersnapper, puppy, barefaced, lippy, minx, hussy, sauce box, gally, biggety, put down, run down, chutzpahdik, cocky, crusty, out of line, off base, give one the business.

INSOLVENCY n.   belly up, go belly up, go under, chapter 7, chapter 11, chapter 13, close the doors, in the toilet, in the tub, take a bath. See BANKRUPTCY.

INSOLVENT adj.   flat broke, stone broke, strapped, clean, tapped out, on one's ass, on the rocks, down to one's last penny, seen better days, piss-poor. See DESTITUTE.

INSPECT v.   scope, clock, flash, flash on, lamp, pipe, eye, eyeball, look-see, scout, give the once over, double O, case, check, check out, kick the tires. See SEE.

INSPECTION n.   Cook's tour, double O, once over, check, frisk, read, flash, eyeball inspection, eyeball examination, look-see, squawk (WW II).

INSPECTION STATION n.   checkpoint, Checkpoint Charlie.

INSPIRATION n.   brainchild, brainstorm, brain wave, spark plug, spark, flash, bell-ringer, deep think, rumble, rah rah, I got it, it hit me, it just come to me, approach, big idea. See IDEA.

INSPIRE v.   jazz up, juice, juice up, fire up, work up, spark, turn on, trigger, zap, give a lift, put one on top of the world, put one on cloud nine. See SUPPORT.

INSPIRED EFFORT v.   play over one's head, knock one's self out, heads up play.

INSPIRED adj.   pumped up, fired up, sparked, fire in the belly, turned on, juiced, juiced up, zapped, get a lift.

INSTALLMENT PLAN n.   buy jawbone, buy on time.

INSTANT n.   sec, split second, mo, half a mo, tick, half a tick, bat of an eye, jiffy, half a jiffy, shake, half a shake, two shakes of a lamb's tail, nothing flat.

INSTANTLY adv.   like now, pronto, double time, move your ass, in half a mo, like a shot, pretty dammmed quick, PDQ, before you can say Jack Robinson. See IMMEDIATELY.

INSTIGATE v.   adjy, fire up, put up to, work up, egg on, turn on, make waves, needle, steam up, throw wood on the fire, add fuel to the flames, rabble-rouse, stir up, turn one on. See STIMULATE.

INSTIGATOR n.   adjy, spark plug, pusher, fireman, hatchet man, needle man, steam-up ghee, stormy petrel, wave maker.

INSTILL v.   brainwash, fuck with one's head, program.

INSTILLED adj.   programmed, brainwashed, head-fucked, mind-fucked.

INSTINCT n.   hang, hang of it, know how, savvy, nose for, nose, good nose, by the seat of one's pants, flying by the seat of one's pants, feel in one's bones, have a funny feeling, have a hunch. See also INCLINATION.

INSTINCTIVE adj.   knee-jerk reaction, by the seat of one's pants.

INSTITUTE v.   intro, ring in, start the ball rolling, get things rolling, break the ice, break in, kick off, bow, open, open up, rev, rev up, fire up, cook up, dream up, make up, come out with, come up with. See BEGIN.

INSTRUCT v.   brainwash, break in, let in on the know, let next to, put next to, put hip, put hep, put through the grind, put through the mill, put in one's two cents, put one in the picture, put on to, put one wise, wise one up,

show one the ropes, update, level, clue one in, fold an ear, put a bug in one's ear, put a flea in one's ear, tip, tip off, tout, steer, give one a tip, give one the word, give a pointer to, post, keep posted, pull one's coat, break it to one, lace one's boots, lay it on one, lay it out for, lay it on the line, drum into.

INSTRUCTED adj.   plugged in, tuned in, grounded, savvy, sharp, wise to, into, really into, go-go, all woke up, in the know, know one's business. See KNOWLEDGEABLE.

INSTRUCTION n.   chalk talk, skull session. See also ADVISE.

INSTRUCTIONS n.   dope sheet, poop sheet, DWIM (do what I mean), DTRT (do the right thing).

INSTRUCTOR n.   prof, teach, baby-sitter, grind, gun, slave driver. See also PROFESSOR.

INSTRUMENT n.   ax, tool, gismo, doodad, thingamajig, thingamabob. See also APPARATUS.

INSUBSTANTIAL adj.   1. cheap jack. 2. pipe dream, pie in the sky, castles in the air, blue sky, fly-by-night, without a leg to stand on.

INSUFFICIENT adj.   bupkis, chicken shit, too little too late, minus, short, half-assed, half-baked. See also INADEQUATE.

INSUFFICIENT FUNDS n.   light, short, shortfall.

INSULT n.   single-digit salute, the finger, put-down, take-down, zinger, brickbat, cheap shot, rap, slam, black eye, hit, dirty dig, dump, dump on, dozens, dirty dozens, woofing, back-handed compliment, left-handed compliment, slap in the face, low rent.

INSULT v.   put down, dump on, single-digit salute, bag (Bl.), give one the finger, give one five fingers, flip one the finger, chop, blister, roast, scorch, burn, wing, nick, cut up, zing, give one a zinger, give one the cold shoulder, give one a backhanded compliment, give one a left handed compliment, thumb one's nose at, slap in the face, hurl brickbats at, play dirty dozens, sound dozens, sound, signify, signifying shucking and jiving, S'ing n' J'ing, woofing, eighty-six, hit one where he lives, blow off, cut, cut to the quick, get bent, skin alive, cap, curdle, gross out, miff, blitz, blitzkrieg, push, go fly a kite, kick one around, mess around with, pooh-pooh.

INSULTED adj.   put down, cut up, blown off, shucked and jived, miffed, miffy, bleeding, on one's ear, get up on one's ear. See also OFFENDED.

INSULTING adj.   flip, fresh, sassy, smart, smart alecky, smart ass, wise ass, biggety, cocky, cheeky, crusty, gally, nervy, out of line, helluva note. See INSOLENT.

INSURANCE POLICY n.   floater, coverage.

INSURANCE RACKETEER n. flopper, repeater, twister.

INSURE v. cover one's ass, hedge, hedge one's bet, lay off. See also ASSURE.

INSURMOUNTABLE adj. no way, no-go, no-win situation, can't win for losing, it won't fly, not a prayer, not a ghost of a chance, not a Chinaman's chance, not a chance in hell, not a snowball's chance in hell, not till hell freezes over, f'get it, forget it.

INTEGRAL n. fixings, makings, part and parcel, nuts and bolts, meat and potatoes, kit and kaboodle, the whole ball of wax. See also WHOLE.

INTEGRATE v. get together, throw in together, come together, meld with, interface. See ASSOCIATE. See also BLEND.

INTELLECT n. savvy, smarts, brains, the goods, good head, the stuff, the right stuff, what it takes. See also BRAIN.

INTELLECTUAL n. nerd, the brain, genius, egghead, gasser, gray matter, whiz, wizard, avant-garde, beard, big think, double dome, ivory dome, highbrow, long-hair, pointyhead, conehead, good head, pundit, skull, thumbsucker, wig, Einstein. See also INTELLIGENT.

INTELLIGENCE n. 1. I.Q. smarts, savvy, stuff, the right stuff, what it takes, with it, have something on the ball, plenty on the ball, have a bump for, green thumb. meal ticket, the goods. 2. info, leak, inside dope, insider, hot tip, picture, lowdown, dirt, clue, brush up, let one in on, poop sheet, inside story, what's going down. See INFORMATION. See also FACTS.

INTELLIGENCE AGENT adj. spook, mole, agent, operative, Mexican infantry (Mil.), sheep dip (military disguised as civilian); company brownnose, keek (industrial). See SPY.

INTELLIGENCE QUOTIENT n. I.Q.

INTELLIGENCE TEST n. I.Q., bug test.

INTELLIGENT adj. brain, brainy, egghead, got the smarts, have savvy, have the smarts, have gray matter, sharp as a tack, smart as a whip, whiz, whiz kid, bright, have a good head on one's shoulders, have a head on one's shoulder, have one's head screwed on right, have all one's marbles, nobody's fool, no dumbbell, not born yesterday, not so dumb, on the ball, have plenty on the ball, have the goods, have the stuff, have the right stuff, have what it takes, rocket scientist, beard, big think, deep, double dome, ivory dome, heavy, highbrow, long-hair, long-haired, pointy-headed, pundit, skull, thumbsucker, wig, IQ, quick on the trigger, nifty, a lot of nifty, together, all together, got it, got it all together, got it up here, quick on the draw, quick on the uptake, commonsensical, got one's

boots on, have horse sense, Philadelphia lawyer, genius, gasser, wizard, Einstein.

INTEMPERANCE n. drive in the fast lane wih no brakes, live in the fast lane, life in the fast lane, high living, burn one's candle at both ends, go to hell, hellbent, go to hell in a handbasket.

INTEMPERATE adj. 1. on a tear, raising a rumpus, raising a ruckus, kicking up a row, kicking up a shindy, kicking up one's heels. 2. burn one's candle at both ends, live in the fast lane, drive in the fast lane, drive in the fast lane with no brakes, go to hell in a handbasket, off base, out of line, out of order.

INTENDED n. steady, going steady, pinned, bird, asked for, donah, donar; future, set, setup, accidentally on purpose.

INTENSIFY v. soup up, beef up, step up, jazz up, hop up, heat up, hot up, punch up, build up, add bells and whistles, add fuel to the fire, jump out of the frying pan into the fire, pour it on, spike (usually drink).

INTENT n. point, stuff, nub, bottom line, name of the game, nitty-gritty, nuts and bolts, the way of it, nature of the beast, drift, heart, meat, nub, score, punch line.

INTENTION n. game plan, gimmick, angle, action, setup, scenario, how one figures it, where one's heading. See PLAN.

INTER v. adios it, cover up, plant, deep six, put six feet under.

INTERACT v. contact, interface, network, relate, connect, mesh, give tit for tat, touch, touch base, keep in touch, reach out, reach out and touch someone, have truck with, get across, get the message, grok, back channel (secretly).

INTERACTION n. teamwork, team play, networking, mesh, tit for tat.

INTERCEDE v. butt in, barge in, stick one's nose in, throw a monkeywrench in, monkey with, mix in. See INTERFERE. See also INTRUDE, MEDIATE.

INTERCEPT v. bug, shortstop, cut off, cut off at the pass, cut in.

INTERCHANGE n. networking, mesh, tit for tat.

INTERCHANGE v. contact, interact, interface, network, relate, connect, mesh, give tit for tat, keep in touch, grok, back channel (secretly). See COMMUNICATE.

INTERCHANGEABLE adj. six of one and half a dozen of the other, compatible, workalike.

INTERCOMMUNICATOR n. intercom, chatterbox, squawk box, growler.

INTERCOURSE n. 1. teamwork, team play, networking, mesh. 2. fuck, jazz, screw, lay, hump, bump, boff, nookie, action, balling, meat injection, the dirty deed, oil change, parallel parking, fooling around. See SEXUAL INTERCOURSE.

INTEREST n. 1. vig, vigorish, juice, flipping (interest on interest), front-end loading, points, commish, drag. See also PERCENTAGE, SHARE. 2. bag, game, into, lookout, racket, thing, fish to fry.

INTEREST v. grab, turn on, turn one on, hook. See INTRIGUE.

INTERESTED adj. buy it, caught, hooked, on the case, sold, into, really into, gone, turned on, up to here in, eat sleep and breathe something. See ENGROSSED.

INTERESTING adj. grabber, turn-on, jazzy, jazzed up. See also EXCITING.

INTERFERE v. mix in, barge in, butt in, chisel in, horn in, muscle in, stick one's nose in, poke one's nose in, jam, hang up, hold up, kibitz, put in one's oar, put one's two cents in, fool with, fool around with, mess with, mess around with, mess over, monkey with, monkey around with, monkey with the buzz saw, throw a monkey wrench into the works, cramp one's style, drag one's foot.

INTERFERE, DON'T v. butt out, keep your nose out of, mind your own business, don't mix in, buzz off, fuck off.

INTERFERENCE n. background, flitter (radar), buckshot, covered up (radio).

INTERIM n. breather, breathing spell, break, break-off, coffee break, downtime, letup, five, ten, time, time-out, freeze, cutoff, layoff.

INTERIOR adj. in house, inner space.

INTERJECT v. stick one's nose in, poke one's nose in, put in one's oar, put one's two cents in, shove in one's oar, fudge in, lug in, lug in by the heels, squeeze in, worm in. See INTERFERE.

INTERLOPER n. buttinsky, crasher, gate crasher.

INTERMEDIARY n. connection, go-between, cutout (secret), fixer. See also INFLUENCE.

INTERMENT n. cold meat party, planting, deep six.

INTERMINABLE adj. more than you can shake a stick at, no end of, no end to, on a treadmill, looped, and then and then, spun out, strung out, dragged out, day and night.

INTERMINABLY adv. round the clock, for ever so long, forever and a day, for a coon's age, for a dog's age, for a month of Sundays, till hell freezes over, till you're blue in the face, till the cows come home, till shrimps learn to whistle.

INTERMINGLE v. network, mesh, pool, swing in with, throw in with, throw together, come together. See ASSOCIATE.

INTERMISSION n. break, break-off, five, ten, time-out, breather, breathing spell, letup, layoff, downtime.

INTERMITTENT adj. herky-jerky, by bits and pieces, by fits and starts, hit or miss, in dribs and drabs, willy-nilly. See ERRATICALLY.

INTERNAL adj. in house.

INTERNAL ORGANS n. guts, innards, insides, inners, works, inner works, inner workings, inner man, spaghetti, kishkes, stuffings, plumbing, department of the interior.

INTERNATIONAL BUSINESS MACHINE n. IBM, Big Blue.

INTERNATIONAL CRIMINAL POLICE ORGANIZATION n. Interpol.

INTERNE n. tern.

INTERNIST n. flea (Medic.).

INTERPLAY n. networking, mesh, tit for tat, teamwork, team play.

INTERPLAY v. interface, network, relate, connect, mesh, give tit for tat, touch, reach out. See INTERACT.

INTERPOSE v. mix in, butt in, horn in, muscle in, poke one's nose in, drag in, fudge in, squeeze in, worm in. See INTERFERE.

INTERROGATE v. grill, roast, work over, go over, sweat out, give one the third, put one through the wringer, put the screws on, hit up, knock. See QUESTION.

INTERROGATION n. third, third degree.

INTERRUPT v. shortstop, cut off, break, break break, breaker breaker, break in, butt in, bust in, barge in, chime in, chip in, cut in, horn in, lean in, close down. See also INTRUDE.

INTERRUPTION n. break, break-off, cutoff, layoff, letup, shortstop, blackout.

INTERSECTION n. mixmaster (highway cloverleaf), cross street.

INTERSTATE COMMERCE COMMISSION ICC, I Can Catch (truck driver use).

INTERTWINE v. network, mesh, connect, relate. See ASSOCIATE.

INTERVAL n. break, breathing spell, downtime, layoff, letup, five, ten, time-out.

INTERVENE v.   mix in, barge in, butt in, chisel in, horn in, muscle in, stick one's nose in, kibitz, put one's two cents in. See INTRUDE.

INTERVIEW n.   call, call back, cattle call (The.).

INTESTINAL ORGANS   guts, innards, inners, insides, inner man, inner works, inner workings, spaghetti, department of the interior.

INTESTINE n.   guts, tripes, stuffings, insides, spaghetti, kishkes.

INTIMATE adj.   buddy-buddy, get buddy-buddy, clubby, mellow, tight, pally, palsy, palsy-walsy, cozy, chuchala-muchala, right nice, right neighborly, downright neighborly, white, regular, square shooter, sucking around, kissing up to, mix, get together, get with it, break the ice, let down one's hair, trade spit, swap spit, roommates, sleepin' together, making it with.

INTIMATE n.   amigo, brother, little brother, sister, buddy, bosom buddy, buddy boy, buddyroo, good buddy, asshole buddy, chum, roomey, main man, main squeeze (girl), family, kissing cousin, pal. See FRIEND.

INTIMATE v.   leak, spring, spring one's duke, spring with a crack, tip one's duke, tip one's hand, let the cat out of the bag, spill the beans, peach, make noise, put a flea in one's ear. See EXPOSE.

INTIMATION n.   1. lead, hot lead, tip-off, telltale, flea in one's ear, bug in one's ear. 2. sinking feeling, sneaking suspicion, feel in one's bones, hunch, have a funny feeling, have a hunch, vibes, vibrations.

INTIMIDATE v.   spook, chill, chill off, put the chill on, scare shitless, scare stiff, scare the pants off, scare hell out of, scare the shit out of, scare silly, scare the bejesus out of, scare to death, throw a scare into, give one a turn, make one shit in one's pants, make one jump a mile, make one jump out of his skin, strike all of a heap, bowl down, bowl over, buffalo, bulldoze, chicken out, enforce, lean on, lean against, push around, whip one around (intellectually), showboat, walk heavy, put on the arm, put on the muscle, put the heat on, turn on the heat, put one through the wringer, bad eye, cuff, hang tough, goose, jackboot, full court press.

INTIMIDATED adj.   scared stiff, scared shitless, have cold feet, clutched up, D and D (deaf and dumb, afraid to testify), bowled down, bowled over, feel the heat. See FRIGHTENED.

INTOLERABLE adj.   a bit much, too much, enough already, last straw, straw that broke the camel's back, that's it, that blows it, that tears it.

INTOLERANT adj.   have a short fuse, agin, one-sided, down on, tilted, weighted, red-neck, red-baiter, Jew-baiter, black-baiter, Archie Bunker, a regular Archie Bunker, jingoist, male chauvinist pig, MCP, pig, good old boys, good old boys network, McCarthyite. See also PREJUDICED, STUBBORN.

INTOXICANT n.   hooch, booze, red-eye, sauce, medicine, poison, firewater, fog cutter, likker, panther piss, rotgut, alky, embalming fluid, kickapoo joy juice. See LIQUOR.

INTOXICATE v.   turn on, whip up, get high; get schnokkered, get a snootful, get pissed, get pissy eyed, get cockeyed, liquor up, booze up, beer up, gin up, hit the sauce, hit the booze, hit the red-eye, go on a drunk, crack a six-pack (beer), belt the grape, get a bun on, get a buzz on, fight a bottle, hang a few on, hang on a few.

INTOXICATED adj.   tight, tipsy, bombed, stewed, stinking, plastered, looped, high as a kite, blind, blotto, juiced up, stoned, tanked up, dead drunk, fried, smashed, swacked, tied one on, feeling no pain, on a bat, shikker, schnokkered, stewed to the gills, sloshed, seeing double, Kentucky fried. See DRUNK.

INTRACTABLE adj.   hard core, hang tough, tough nut, tough nut to crack, locked, locked in, rock-ribbed, pat, stand pat, hardheaded. See STUBBORN.

INTRAMURAL adj.   in-house.

INTRANSIGENT adj.   hang tough, tough nut, tough nut to crack, locked, locked in, head in concrete, chiseled in stone, Rock of Gibraltar, pat, stand pat. See STUBBORN.

INTRAUTERINE DEVICE n.   IUD, pussy butterfly.

INTRAVENOUS RACK n.   ivy pole.

INTREPID adj.   ballsy, gutsy, gutty, gritty, spunky, bodacious, iceman, ice in one's veins. See FEARLESS.

INTRICATE adj.   mega-factor, Rube Goldberg, hi tech, can of worms, gasser, rat's nest, snake pit, wheels within wheels.

INTRIGUE n.   game, little game, fix, frame, frame up, hookup, Barney (fixed), put-up job. See SCHEME.

INTRIGUE v.   1. cook up, finagle, frame up, operate, promote, angle, set up, be in cahoots with, work hand in glove with. See SCHEME. 2. grab, turn on, turn one on, hook, pull, send, wow, draw, bait, mousetrap, vamp, shill, steer, tout, lead one on, give one the come on, give one a come-hither look, make a hit with, sweep off one's feet, knock dead, knock out, bat one's eyes at, suck in, rope in, humbug, con, lead up the garden path.

INTRIGUED adj.   caught, on the hook, hooked, on the case, sold, sold on, buy it, into, really into, gone, turned on. See also BEWITCHED.

INTRIGUER n.   finagler, operator, wangler, wire-puller, mastermind, brain.

INTRODUCE v. intro, knock down, give a knockdown, do the honors, break the ice, open up, get things rolling, start the ball rolling, kick off, boot, bring out, come out with, fix up, get together, spring with. See also ORIGINATE.

INTRODUCTION n. intro, blind date, knockdown, preem.

INTROVERT n. creep, creepy, drip, loner, oddball, weirdo, wet blanket, gool, wimp, mince, nerd.

INTRUDE v. mix in, barge in, butt in, chisel in, horn in, muscle in, stick one's nose in, poke one's nose in, hang up, hold up, kibitz, put in one's oar, put one's two cents in.

INTRUDER n. buttinsky, crasher, gate-crasher.

INTRUSIVE adj. nosey, pushy, snoopy.

INTUIT v. have a hunch, get vibes, have vibes, feel in one's bones, feel in one's guts, have a funny feeling, get in touch, figure, be turned on to.

INTUITION n. ESP, sixth sense, hunch, have a hunch, aha reaction, gut reaction, feel in one's bones, have a funny feeling, a nose, a nose for, a good nose, by the seat of one's pants, flying by the seat of one's pants.

INUNDATE v. snow, snow under, dunk, flood with, swamp.

INVADE v. access, barge in, bust in, horn in, muscle in, go in, penetrate (secret agent), crash, crash the gates. See also RAID.

INVALID adj. below par, down, peaky, peaked, poorly, run down, laid low, outta action, on the sick list. See also ILL.

INVALIDATE v. blow sky high, knock the bottom out of, knock the chocks out from under, knock the props out from under, poke full of holes, shoot full of holes, nix, X-out. See CANCEL.

INVEIGH v. blister, roast, scorch, blast, lambaste, trash, jump on, jump on one's case, jump down one's throat, work over, lay out, read one out, go after, go for, go to town on, have at, lay at, crack down on, come down on, come down hard on one, give 'em hell, give one both barrels, let one have it with both barrels, let one have it, give one the blanket, give one the works, sock it to one, land all over one, get on a soapbox, soapbox, spiel, spout, stump, blow, lay it on, skin alive, lace into, lay into, pitch into, light into, sail into, wade into, rip into, rip up, rip up one side and down the other, slap down, take on, pepper, take one over the hurdles, blitz, fly in the teeth of.

INVEIGLE v. stroke, snow, massage, soap, soft soap, jolly, oil, spread it on, lay it on, lay it on thick, lay it on with a trowel, get around, play up to, butter, butter up, soften up, sweeten up, sweet talk, honey, schmear, work on, work over, get around, buzz, charm, hook, give a come-hither look, come on to, bat the eyes at, rope in, suck in, buck, contract, cream, bagplay, hand one a line, shoot a line, shoot the crap, shoot the bull, sling the bull, sling it, pull one's leg, overdo it, string along, egg one on, goose, kid along, blarney, caboodle. See also ATTRACT, FLATTER.

INVENT v. 1. hatch, think up, come up with, cook up, cobble up, dream up, 2. improv, ad lib, off the cuff, off the hip, off the top of one's head, fake, fake it, jam, shuck, knock off, toss off. See CREATE.

INVENTION n. gismo, black box, dealie bob, mother-grabber, grabber, gimmick, doodad, doowillie, frobnitzem, coil. See APPARATUS.

INVENTIVE adj. breaking new snow, avant-garde. See IMAGINATIVE.

INVENTORIED adj. chapter and verse, by the numbers.

INVERT v. back track, double back, put the cart before the horse, turn the tables, renig, flip-flop, put ass backwards, put bass ackwards, put ack basswards.

INVEST v. angel, back, bankroll, juice, grubstake, buy in, sink money in, get into, plow back into, go in for, plunge, pick up the check, pick up the tab, stake. See FINANCE.

INVESTED adj. in, bought in, tax sheltered.

INVESTIGATE v. bug, tap, wiretap, body mike, slurp, tune in on, buzz, check, check out, check it out, check over, check up, cool out, feel out, eyeball it, give it the once over, give it the double O, give it the OO, double O, OO, run it down, nose around, scrounge around, candle, case, frisk, look-see, read, scout it out, spy out, stake out, squack, listen in, be all ears, ears into, Erie, on the Erie. See also SEARCH, QUESTION, RECONNOITER.

INVESTIGATING adj. loaded for bear, out for bear, nosey, witch hunting, fishing expedition.

INVESTIGATION n. ex, hustle, case, double-o, gunning over, gander, pike, eyeball examination, fishing expedition, legwork. See also INQUIRY.

INVESTIGATOR n. bugger, plumber, sleeper (M.) little pitcher with big ears. See DETECTIVE.

INVESTMENT n. flier, flyer, backing, in on the ground floor, inside, piece, plunge, right money, smart money, spec, stab, flutter, hunch, shot, shot in the dark, bear market, bearish market (low); bull market, bullish market (high). See also STOCKS, BONDS.

INVESTMENT FUND n. go-go, go-go fund, money market.

INVESTMENT TERMS takeover (merger), white knight (friendly bidder in a takeover), gray knight (opportunistic second bidder), greenmail (takeover defense payment), target (a vulnerable company), shark (unfriendly financier forcing takeovers), smoking gun (error by a shark permitting the target escape through an antitrust ruling), shark repellent (takeover defense strategy), repo, uptick, gorilla (bond trader), parking (holding stocks to hide investment).

INVESTOR n.   angel (The.), backer, the money, the bankroll, the one who signs the checks, staker, gunslinger, lame duck (stocks), plunger, scalper (ticket seller), spec. See also FINANCIER.

INVIGORATE v.   jazz up, perk up, pick up, chirk up, snap up, zip up, put zip into, pep up, put pep into, juice up, turn on the juice, zap, trigger, turn on. See STIMU-LATE.

INVIGORATED adj.   charged, flipped out, high, hyper, turned on, get a lift, juiced up, hopped up, pepped up, zipped up, zapped up.

INVINCIBLE adj.   bulletproof.

INVITATION n.   bid, invite, stiff card, do you want an engraved invitation?, pass, paper, rain check (for another time), come-on, give one the eye, wolf whistle, come hither, feeler, proposition, pass, hit. See also LURE.

INVITE v.   come on to, give one the come on, suck in, bat one's eyes at, give one a come hither look, hit on, rope in, sweep off one's feet, vamp. See ATTRACT.

INVOCATION n.   abracadabra, hocus-pocus, mumbo-jumbo, hoodoo, voodoo, open sesame.

INVOLUNTARY adj.   knee-jerk reaction.

INVOLVE v.   get around, charm, hook, give a come-hither look, come on to, bat the eyes at, contract, bag, turn on, duke in, rope in, suck in, swindle in, swindle up, foosle, embrangle, set up, frame, frame up, finger, hang something on, put up a job. See also INCRIMINATE.

INVOLVED adj.   1. into, really into, hooked into, sucked into, heavily into, up to here in, knee deep in, up to one's ass, wrapped up in, eat sleep and breathe [something]. See ENGROSSED. 2. can of worms, gasser, hi tech, rat's nest, snake pit, wheels within wheels, Rube Goldberg.

INVOLVEMENT n.   hands on, sit-in, get in the act, be-hind, get behind (a person or idea).

INVULERNABLE adj.   bulletproof, teflon.

IOTA n.   chewed fine, itsy-bitsy pieces.

IOWA   Hawkeye State, where the tall corn grows.

IRASCIBLE adj.   cantankerous, feisty, grouchy, snappish, bear, ogre, bad-assed, uptight, thin-skinned, ready to fly off the handle, edgy. See IRRITABLE.

IRATE adj.   pissed off, p'd off, p.o.'d, bent out of shape, blow a gasket, blow one's stack, bummed out, steamed, ticked off, tee'd off, t'd off, ape shit, hopping mad. See ANGRY.

IRE n.   slow burn, conniption, conniption fit, cat fit, blowup, boiling point, more heat than light. See ANGER.

IRISH n.   Mick, Paddy, Harp, Irisher, Mulligan, lace-curtain Irish (prosperous), shanty Irish (poor), Greek, shamrock, bog hopper, bog trotter, turf cutter.

IRISH REVOLUTION n.   troubles, the troubles, the Troubles, the throubles.

IRK v.   be at, eat, noodge, piss one off, make waves, give one a hard time, fuck with one's head, get to, all right already. See ANNOY.

IRKSOME adj.   tough, pushy, noodgy, nitpicking, humdrum.

IRONS n.   darbies, derbies, cuffs.

IRRATIONAL adj.   flaky, freaky, kooky, cockamamie, wacky, loony, out to lunch, off the wall, nut job, throw out the baby with the bathwater. See CRAZY.

IRREFUTABLE adj.   checked and double-checked, for a fact Jack, cold lay, no ifs ands or buts, bet your ass, absi-tively, dead to rights, set, right on, odds-on, bet on, bet one's gospel truth, ironclad contract. See CERTAIN.

IRREGULAR adj.   herky-jerky, by bits and pieces, hit or miss, in dribs and drabs, willy-nilly, cockeyed.

IRREGULARLY adv.   herky-jerky, helter-skelter, by fits and starts, hit or miss, willy nilly, slapdash, any old way, any which way, fast and loose. See ERRATICALLY.

IRRELEVANT adj.   garbage. See also UNIM-PORTANT.

IRREPRESSIBLE adj.   scoutmaster, Pollyanna, ray of sunshine, eager beaver, beaver. See also UN-RESTRAINED.

IRRESISTIBLE adj.   traffic stopper, drooly, glamour girl, looker, sex kitten, mink, stone, stone fox, foxy, head rush, scrumptious, stunner, stunning, oh yeah. See BEAUTIFUL. See also COMPELLING.

IRRESOLUTE adj.   fence hanger, on the fence, run hot and cold, shilly-shally, wimpy, wishy-washy, waffly, pussyfooting, pussyfooting around. See UNDECIDED.

IRRESPECTIVE adj.   irregardless.

IRRESPONSIBLE adj.   devil may care, let George do it, pass the buck, no account, don't give a shit. See also RECKLESS.

IRREVERENT adj.   flip, fresh, sassy, smart ass, wise ass, cocky, cheeky, crusty, out of line, off base, off color. See INSOLENT.

IRRITABLE adj.   bitchy, bad ass, mean, ornery, tetchy, cantankerous, cussed, grouchy, grumpy, beefing, bellyaching, bitching, crabby, cranky, grousing, snappish, waspish, scrappy, salty, spiky, bear, ogre, ugly, ugly customer, uptight, sucking eggs, thin-skinned, hotheaded, fire-eater, blowtop, firecracker, short fuse, ticking bomb, ready to fly off the handle, edgy, on the ragged edge, wreck, a bundle of nerves, Mr. Coffee Nerves, pushing out one's lips, outta sorts, got up on the wrong side of the bed.

IRRITATE v.   bug, pain, give one a pain, give a bad time to, give one the business, fuck with one's head, get, get under one's skin, drive one up a tree, rile, rattle one's cage. See ANNOY.

IRRITATED adj.   browned off, pissed off, pushed outta shape, uptight, defrosted, blow one's cool, blow it out, bouncing, bugged, bummed out, driven up the wall, all hot and bothered. See ANGRY.

IRRITATING adj.   rub the wrong way, spiky, pesky, pestiferous, a bit much, too much. See ANNOYING.

IRRITATION n.   drag, a pain, pain in the ass, pain in the neck, wet blanket, headache, dead wood, blister, botheration, worriment. See ANNOYANCE.

IS v.   like (e.g., it's like 90 degrees).

ISOBUTYL NITRITE n.   popper.

ISOLATED adj.   far out, out of it, cool, play it cool, spaced out, out in left field. See also ALONE.

ISOLATION n.   the cold, salt mines, back to the salt mines; the hole, solitary, blue room (prison).

ISSUE n.   offspring, get (animal). See also CHILD.

ISTHMUS n.   choke point, bottleneck.

ITALIAN n.   wop, dago, pizza man, macaroni, spic, spig, spiggoty, spaghetti, spaghetti bender, Eyetalian, Eytie, ringtail, dingbat, dino (laborer), ginzo, guinea, ginney, greaser, greaseball (all Derog.).

ITEM n.   piece, think piece, column, scoop, blurb, write-up, story, bit, scrap.

ITEMIZE v.   spell out, lay out, take it line by line, cross the t's and dot the i's, sweat the details, quote chapter and verse, get down to brass tacks, get down to cases. See also CATALOGUE.

ITEMIZED adj.   chapter and verse, by the numbers.

ITERATE v.   again, come again, ditto, echo, one more time, una mas, run that by me once more, say again, chew one's cabbage twice, do, do like, go like, make like. See REPEAT.

ITINERANT WORKER n.   Okie, wetback, floater.

ITINERARY n.   beat, the bricks (hobo, police, union), run.

IVY LEAGUE n.   Kee, Key.

IVY LEAGUE STUDENT n.   key, shoe, white shoe, white buck, white bucks.

IWW   Wobbly, clear (member, Obs.), dehorn (leave IWW), Wob.

J

J n.   Juliette, jig.

JABBER n.   gab, gas, yak, yackety-yak, talkee-talkee, guff, hot air, blah-blah, bibble-babble. See also SPEECH.

JABBER v.   gas, gab, jaw, yak, yackety-yak, go on, go on and on, run on, run off at the mouth, have diarrhea of the mouth, shoot off one's mouth, shoot off one's face, shoot the breeze, bat the breeze, bat the chat, beat one's gums, talk through one's hat, bull, bullshit, BS, throw the bull, bibble-babble, twiddle. See also SPEAK.

JACKASS n.   Rocky Mountain canary.

JACKET n.   threads, flogger, peacoat, Eisenhower, Mao.

JACKSON, MISSISSIPPI   Capital J.

JACKSONVILLE, FLORIDA   Jax.

JADED adj.   fed up, full up, done it all, been around twice, cool, laid back, mellow, blah, up to here, had it up to here, ho hum, so what else is new. See also INDIFFERENT.

JAGUAR n.   cat, Jag (auto).

JAIL n.   jug, slam, slammer, stir, pen, can, pokey, clink, hoosegow, joint, G. joint (federal), lockup, coop, cooler, bull pen, cage, big cage, booby hatch, chokey, choky, caboose, cally, calaboose, brig, guardhouse (Mil.), dump, eighty-four (N.), icebox, maxi (maximum security), the rack, inside, Camp Adirondack, playhouse (small), pink clink, right joint, mill, crossbar hotel, graybar hotel, crowbar hotel, county hotel, bastille, college, graystone college, hook, hospital, jam, lag, limbo, prod, soak, tough can, jook joint, quad, quod, quads, campus, refrigerator, big joint, big house, sugar house, bug house, iron house, up the river, locked down, statesville, doing time, school, big school, Q (San Quentin), sent up; solitary, the hole (solitary confinement), crate, bandbox, bandhouse, tank, bucket, fish bowl, pokery, calaboose, wire city, the bricks (outside).

JAIL v.   put away, hold, lock up, send up, send up the river, ice, put on ice, book, throw the book at, cool, can, cage, lay the arm on, take one away, settle, slough, slough up, railroad.

JAIL CELL n.   tank, fish tank, drunk tank, bull pen, coop, cage, lockup.

JAILED adj.   away, up the river, in the slammer, in the clink, in college, out of town, iced, put on ice, cooped, cooped up, jugged. See IMPRISONED.

JAILER n.   screw, chaser, eyes, hack, herder, hooligan, roach, roller, slave driver, sky, yard bull. See also WARDEN.

JAIL TRANSFER v.   go round the horn.

JAM n.   red lead.

JAMAICA GINGER n.   jake.

JAMMED adj.   jam-packed, sardined, standing room only, SRO, up to the rafters, mobbed, gridlocked, full as a tick. See CROWDED.

JAMMING n.   background, buckshot, covered up (radio).

JANGLE v.   hit a clinker, hit a sour note, sound a sour note.

JANITOR n.   super, sitter, house sitter, swamper, crumb boss (hobo and logger).

JANUARY n.   first thirty.

JAPANESE n.   Jap, Nip, gook, slant eye, yellow peril (all Derog.), Tojo (soldier), skippy (woman or prostitute).

JAR v.   hit a clinker, hit a sour note, sound a sour note.

JARGON n.   jive, jive talk, street talk, doublespeak, hillspeak, bafflegab, bunkum, buzzwords, federalese, officialese, gobbledygook, lingo, mumbo-jumbo, weasel words, flash (thieves). See also VERNACULAR.

JAUNT n.   Cook's tour, cruise (pleasure trips). See TRAVEL.

JAUNT v.   hit the road, hit the dirt, hit the grit, joyride. See TRAVEL.

JAUNTY adj.   1. in, in thing, now, really now, trendy, sharp, spiffy, nifty, natty, reet, sharpie, swanky, ritzy, dressed to kill, go-go, hip, mod, mellow back (Bl.), snazzy, cat's meow, chichi, chic, fashion plate, knock one's eye out, doggy, jazzbo, dap, high powered, toney. 2. feelgood, high wide and handsome, bouncy, chirpy, chipper, feeling one's oats, full of beans, full of piss and vinegar, zippy. See CHEERFUL.

JAW n.   button, chops, clam shells, glass jaw, point.

JAZZ n.   jive, blues, swing, soul music, progressive, pop, Dixieland, bop, bebop, rebop, boogie woogie, rag, ragtime, race music, barrelhouse, cat house, back alley, jam, jam session, riff, gutbucket, carrying weight (blues), down home (New Orleans), electric, funk, funky, gully low, low down dirty, low-down and dirty, slurred gutbucket, smooth and mellow, tailgate, blaring tailgate, cool jazz, far out, way out, light (sympathetic to), swinging like a gate, long underwear, meet (jam), mellow, mop mop.

JAZZ MUSICAN n.   sideman, cat, cool cat, hep cat, gay cat, blowing cat, blue blower, alligator (white), gate, gator, in orbit (avant-garde), lip-splitter, satchel, sender, solid sender, swinging gate, wig, iron man, band man, paper man, rag man; ear man, faker (illiterate); rocker, monster (popular).

JAZZ TERMS   jam, jam session, riff, jive, blow, blow the blues, blow up a storm, send, sending, combo, grooving, coon shouting, lick, break, coast, flare-up, lumpy (played badly), the Man (leader), get off (solo), push, strictly union.

JEALOUS adj.   green-eyed, jelly, turn green.

JEALOUSY n.   green-eyed monster, sour grapes, eat one's heart out.

JEER n.   dump, put down, put on, rank out, dig, dirty dig, crack, slam, swipe, jab, comeback, parting shot, brickbat.

JEFFERSON CITY, MISSOURI   Jeff City.

JELLO n.   nervous pudding.

JELLY n.   red lead, nervous pudding.

JEOPARDIZE v.   lay it on the line, put on the spot, stick one's neck in the noose, stick one's neck out, play into one's hands, chance it, go out on a limb, fail to cover one's ass.

JEOPARDIZED adj.   on the line, on the spot, out on a limb, got one's neck out, have one's ass out, caught with one's pants down.

JEOPARDY n.   double trouble, out on a limb, on the line, on the spot.

JERK n.   yank, yerk.

JERKY adj.   herky-jerky, by fits and starts, by bits and pieces, in dribs and drabs, higgledy-piggledy.

JEST n.   gag, laugh, one-liner, a funny, nifty, rib, rib-tickler, spoof, jive, crack, wisecrack. See JOKE.

JEST v.   jive, kid, put on, spoof, needle, rib, rag, razz, roast, josh, jolly, pull one's leg, funnin', who you jivin'?, make a funny. See JOKE.

JESTER n.   clown, Joey, pale face, cutup, life of the party, madcap, trickster, card, kibitzer, funster, quipster. See JOKER. See also BANTERER.

JESUIT n.   Jebby.

JESUS CHRIST   J.C., Head Knock, Jeeze, Hay-Soose!, Jerusalem Slim, Jesus H. Christ, Jesus Mariah Christ, One Of Our Boys (Yid.).

JET n.   spritz.

JET ENGINE STALL n.   burnout, flameout.

JET FUEL n.   zip fuel.

JET PLANE n.   jet, ramjet, scramjet, air breather, flamethrower, fizz job, blowtorch, flying blowtorch, heat can, squirt, stove pipe, whale, lightning rod (fighter). See also AIRPLANE.

JETTISON v.   deep six. See also DISCARD.

JEW n.   Jew boy, Hebe, kike, Yid, rabbi, sheeny, mocky, cloak and suiter, eagle beak, hook nose, Abe, Abie, Ikie, Izzie, porker, sammy, Yehuda, Goldberg, Hymie, Jewish American Princess, JAP, member of the tribe, M.O.T., geese, clip, clip cock, clipped dick (all Derog.).

JEWELRY n.   junk jewelry, brass (cheap or fake), stones, rocks, sparklers, ice, glass, Christmas, hardware, pennyweight, gullion.

JEWELRY STORE n.   ice house, ice palace, slum joint, stone joint, gullion joint.

JIGGLE v.   jigger, jigget.

JILT v.   drop, dump, ditch, give one the air, give one the gate, give one the wind, give back one's ring, leave, leave at the church, leave at the altar, leave flat, hand one one's walking papers, throw over, break it off. See also ABANDON, REJECT.

JILTED adj.   left at the church, thrown over, ditched, dumped, out, on the rebound. See also REJECTED.

JIMSON WEED n.   devil's trumpet.

JINX n.   whammy, double whammy, kibosh, hoodoo, voodoo, kiss of death.

JINX v.   cuss, damn, darn, spook, put the horns on, put the whammy on one, put the double whammy on one, give one a kineahora (Yid.), hoodoo, hoodoo one, voodoo, voodoo one.

JOB n.   gig, nine-to-five shit, rat race, grind, racket, swindle, shitwork. See WORK.

JOBBER n.   middleman.

JOBLESS adj.   on layoff, on the dole, out of action, down, closed down, in short pants. See UNEMPLOYED.

JOCKSTRAP n.   jock, cup.

JOCULAR adj.   camp, campy, jokey, joshing, yokky, boffo, gagged up, for grins, flaky, wacky, crazy, daffy, tomfool, fool around. See also AMUSING, WITTY, CHEERFUL.

JOIN v. 1. team up, tie up with, throw in together, get in with, join together, join up with, sign on, come aboard, marry, plug into. See ASSOCIATE. 2. tag on, tack on, slap on, hitch on. See also FASTEN.

JOKE n. gag, laugh, one-liner, throwaway, topper, payoff, boff, boffo, yak, yock, yuck, funny, a ha-ha, horse, horseplay, howl, hot one, needle, nifty, rib, rib-tickler, sizzler, spoof, story, whiz bang, jive, crack, smart crack, wisecrack, chestnut, old chestnut, wheeze, old wheeze, old saw, old turkey, oldie, joke with whiskers, warmed over cabbage, bark, bromide, corn, knee-slapper; an egg, an omelet, a bomb, bombed out, laid there, laid an egg (unfunny).

JOKE v. jive, kid, put on, spoof, needle, rib, rag, razz, roast, josh, jolly, ride, kibitz, kibitz around, kid around, horse around, horseplay, pull one's leg, funnin', who you jivin'?, wisecrack, crack wise, make a funny, get off a joke.

JOKE LINE n. punch line, straight line, feed, feed line, set up, set up line, beat, snapper, zinger, wisecrack, comeback.

JOKER n. stand-up comic, baggy-pants comic, hokum comic, straight man, roaster, stooge, banana, top banana, second banana, clown, Joey, paleface, cutup, life of the party, madcap, trickster, card, a million laughs, kibitzer, booger, bugger, jokesmith, gagman, gagster, funster, punster, quipster, wisecracker. See also BANTERER.

JOLLITY adv. laughs, lots of laughs, grins, get some grins, action, ball, fun and games, big time, high time, high old time, hoopla, picnic, whoopee, whooper-dooper, wingding, shindig, brawl. See AMUSEMENT, PARTY.

JOLLY adj. jokey, joshing, for grins, daffy, lots of laughs, bouncy, chirpy, chipper, zippy. See JOVIAL.

JOLT n. kick in the ass, shot, shot in the ass, whammy, double whammy, from out in left field. See SURPRISE.

JOLT v. rock, gork, floor, shake one up, give one a shot, bowl over, lay out, spring something on one, throw one a curve, knock one over, knock for a row of pins. See SURPRISE.

JOLTED adj. shook, shook up, rocked, gorked, slaphappy, hit like a ton of bricks. See SURPRISED.

JOSH v. jive, kid, put on, spoof, needle, rib, ride, kibitz, kibitz around, wisecrack, crack wise, make a funny, get off a joke. See TEASE, JOKE.

JOSTLE v. push around, bang into, nerf, crash, rowdy-dowdy, rough and tumble, tumul, bump heads.

JOURNAL n. 1. daily, rag, scandal sheet, sheet, bladder, blat, bulldog (earliest edition), chroniker, extra, fish wrapper, snitch sheet, toilet paper. See also MAGAZINE. 2. comic book, funny book. 3. swindle sheet.

JOURNALIST n. scribe, scrivener, columnist, stringer, leg man, news hen, news hound, cub, pen driver, pen pusher, pencil driver, pencil pusher, scratcher, ink slinger. See also WRITER.

JOURNEY n. hop, swing, jaunt, cruise, junket, trek, overnight, weekend, Cook's tour. See TRAVEL.

JOURNEY v. jet, jet around, knock about, bat around, go places, country hop, globe trot, cruise, on the move, junket. See TRAVEL.

JOVIAL adj. jokey, joshing, yokky, boffo, gagged up, for grins, loony, off the wall, crazy, daffy, nutty, dippy, dizzy, lots of laughs, do the crazy act, do the crazy bit, do the crazy shtick, tomfool, fool around, make a monkey of oneself, foolheaded, bouncy, chirpy, chipper, zippy. See also CHEERFUL.

JOYFUL adj. flyin', flyin' high, on a joy ride, high, high as a kite, blow one's mind, flipping, Little Merry Sunshine. See HAPPY.

JOYLESS adj. dragged, low, down in the mouth, in the pits, have the blahs, clanked, droopy, mopey. See UNHAPPY.

JOYOUS adj. upbeat, flyin', sunny, sunny side up, tea'd up, popping one's nuts, doing handsprings, doing backflips. See HAPPY.

JUBILANT adj. set up, hopped up, doing backflips, flipping, pleased as punch, flying, sold on, tickled, tickled to death. See ECSTATIC.

JUBILATION n. upper, cloud nine land, high, buzz, large charge, big deal, big shit, circus, fireworks, flash. See EXCITEMENT.

JUDGE n. 1. hizzoner, beagle, beak, bench nibs, Blackstone, Father Time, tough ghee with too much time, ghee with plenty of numbers, gavel jockey, hanging judge, hard rapper, monk, wig. 2. aisle sitter, Monday Morning quarterback, nitpicker, zapper.

JUDGE v. 1. throw the book at one, let one have it, let one have plenty of numbers, jump all over one, lay on a hard rap, jump down one's throat, knock, lower the boom, lay on, come down on, come down hard on, land on. See also CRITICIZE. 2. size, size up, take one's measure, make the call, take a decision, the way one sees it, run it up the flagpole, run it by one again. See APPRAISE.

JUDGMENT n. 1. call down, put-down, rap, rap on the knuckles, slap on the wrist, fall, cut, cutting, flak, hit, knock. See also CRITICISM. 2. notice, write-up, paper. 3. value judgment, judgment call. See also OPINION, SENTENCE. 4. the riot act, say, the word.

JUG n. bucket, hooker, tub, growler (large for beer), rush the growler.

JUKEBOX n. juke, goola box (Bl.).

JUMBLE adj. goulash, garbage, mishmash, mishmosh.

JUMP v. barge, sky.

JUNCTION n. hookup, tie-in, tie-up, plug-in, interface.

JUNGLE n. zoo.

JUNIOR COLLEGE n. J.C., jaycee.

JUNIOR HIGH SCHOOL n. junior hi, junior high.

JUNK n. gash, hogwash, garbage.

JUNKET n. g'dong, gedunk, glop, goop, pud. See also TRAVEL.

JURISDICTION n. territory, turf, stomping grounds, one's neck of the woods, slot, wing. See also CONTROL.

JURIST n. 1. beagle, beak, bench nibs, Blackstone, Father Time, gavel jockey, hanging judge, hard rapper, monk, wig. 2. mouthpiece, shyster, ambulance chaser, legal eagle, lip, the L.A., Philadelphia lawyer, bomber (divorce). See ATTORNEY.

JUSTICE OF THE PEACE n. JP.

JUSTICE n. 1. beagle, beak, bench nibs, Blackstone, Father Time, gavel jockey, hanging judge, hard rapper, monk, wig, old man. 2. blindfolded lady with scales, square deal, straight.

JUSTIFICATION n. song and dance, story, the idea, the big idea, the whole idea, the whatfor, the why and wherefore, the whyfor. See EXCUSE.

JUSTIFY v. alibi, alibi out of, crawl out of, squirm out of, worm out of, cry sour grapes, crawl, square oneself, square things, cop out, cop a plea, make up for, whitewash, put the best face on, get down on one's marrowbones.

JUT v. stick out, pop out, bug out, googly.

JUVENILE adj. kid stuff.

JUVENILE n. juve, punk, yoot, bobby-soxer, chicken, San Quentin quail, jailbait (Fem.). See also BOY, GIRL, YOUNG MAN, YOUNG WOMAN, YOUTH, TEEN-AGER.

JUVENILE COURT n. short-pants division.

JUVENILE DELINQUENT n. J.D., juvie, juvey, minor, yoot, diaper-rashed punk.

K

K n. kilo, king.

KALAMAZOO, MICHIGAN Zoo Town, Guitar City.

KANSAN n. Jayhawker.

KANSAS The Sunflower State.

KANSAS CITY, KANSAS Casey, Kasey, K.C., K.C.K.

KANSAS CITY, MISSOURI Beef City.

KEEN adj. 1. sharp, whiz, whiz kid, Einstein, quick on the trigger, quick on the uptake, smart as a whip, sharp as a tack, nobody's fool, no dumbbell. See INTELLIGENT. 2. creaming to, dying to, gotta have. See IMPATIENT.

KENTUCKIAN n. colonel.

KENTUCKY the Blue Grass State.

KERNEL n. bottom line, heart, meat and potatoes, nitty gritty, nub.

KETCHUP n. red lead, red paint, kid stuff.

KEY n. hog eye (skeleton), screw, twister.

KEYBOARD n. eighty-eight, ivories.

KICK v. boot, kick ass, give him an ass full of leather, give one a tokus full of toes, kick the bejesus out of, kick the beholden out of, kick the shit outta, kick the daylights out of, give one the foot.

KIDNAP v. grab, shanghai, snatch, put the snatch on one, sneeze, hijack, skyjack, dognap (dog abduction).

KIDNAPPER n. snatch man, sneezer, snatcher, hijacker, highjacker, skyjacker.

KIDNAPPING n. snatch, the snatch, body snatch, grab, put the snatch on, sneeze, hijacking, highjacking, skyjacking.

KILL v. liquidate, neutralize, waste, take out of the box, do, do in, do away with, hit, get, snuff, croak, dust, whack, wax, zap, burn, cook, chill, ice, off, total, cool, go cool, cool out, cool off, wipe off the map, wipe out, X out, take out, knock out, KO, blot out, stamp out, lay out, rub out, erase, iron out, lay one out, wash out, whack out, drop, bop, pop, pop one, pop one off, pay off, bump off, blip off, kiss off, knock off, finish off, polish off, push, push off, push across, put away, put out a contract, put on ice, pull the plug, plug, punch one's ticket, blast, blow one's brains out, blow away, do away with, executive fallout (business), frag (usually hand grenade), scrag, smear, grease, score, fix, dump, drill, gun down, mow down, shoot down, drygulch, fog, guzzle, buy one concrete golashes, clip, cream, take care of, take for an airing, take the wind out of, take for a ride, take one out, give the business, give the works, give one a wood overcoat, lynch (Bl.), pickle, top, let one have it, set over, settle, make one disappear, send to kingdom come.

KILLED adj. iced, wasted, offed, bumped off, knocked off, cooled off, chilled, totalled, wiped out, stamped out, liquidated, neutralized, finished, disappeared, cooked, rubbed out, snuffed, snuffed out, dead and done for, done for, done in, down the drain, down the tube, tubed, sunk, gone, had it, hashed up, kaput, fragged, liquidated, offed.

KILLER n. hit man, trigger, trigger man, piece man, torpedo, enforcer, exterminator, terminator, gorilla, gun, gunman, gunsel, bumpman, button man, hatchet man, bang man, iceman, shootist, clipper, plugger, soldier, troop, butcher, blaster, knock-off ghee, red hot, hired gun, dropper (hired).

KILLING n. off, offing, knock-off, wasting, hit, erase, rubout, taking out, the big M, cool, chill, big chill, bump-off, a ride, croaking, bang job, cut down, fragging (officer, Mil.), scragging, the works, dying of the measles, liquidation, neutralization, kiss-off.

KILL, INTENT TO v. gun for, lug a chiv, lug iron for, pack a chiv for, pack a rod for, have a contract on, set up for a hit.

KILLJOY n. party pooper, drag, drip, wet blanket, crepe hanger, sourpuss, sourbelly, sourball, gloomy Gus, downer, worrywart, Calamity Jane, stick in the mud, moldy fig.

KILOMETER n. click, klick, klik.

KIND adj. big, all heart (Derog.), bleeding heart, heart in the right place, softhearted, old softie.

KIND n. likes, likes of, lot, number.

KINDLE v. fire up, burn up, key up, egg on, turn on, work up, get smoking. See INCITE.

KINDLY adj. cool, mellow.

KINDNESS n. heart, mitzvah.

KINSMAN n. folks, homefolks, kinfolk, kissin' cousin, shirttail kin, blood.

KISMET n. karma, in the cards, the beads, that's the way the beads read, that's the way the ball bounces, that's the way the cookie crumbles. See DESTINY.

KISS n.   peck, smack, smooch, X, buss, mush, muzzle, sugar, soul kiss, butterfly kiss, French kiss, kissy face, kissy-poo, lay one on the lips, mouth music.

KISS v.   peck, pucker up, smack, smash, smooch, eat face, suck face, swap slops, swap spit, buss, French kiss, soul kiss, butterfly kiss, spark, buzz, X, mush, muzzle, sugar, lay one on the lips, mouth music, mouth-to-mouth resuscitation.

KITCHEN n.   crumb stash, bean gun (mobile, WW II).

KITTEN n.   kitty, kitty cat, puss, pussy, pussycat.

KLAXON n.   beeper, honker, tooter.

KLEPTOMANIA n.   light fingers, sticky fingers, taking ways.

KLEPTOMANIAC n.   klepto. See also THIEF.

KNACK n.   hang, hang of it, know-how, savvy, good hands. See SKILL.

KNEES n.   knobs, dukes, deuce of benders, prayer bones, prayer handles.

KNIFE n.   blade, shiv, chib, switch, switchblade, bill (Bl.), Arkansas toothpick, Harlem toothpick, Tennessee toothpick, bylow (Barlow), stick, frog sticker, flick, ripper, steel, shank.

KNIFE v.   slice, stick, cut, cut a new kisser for, shiv, brand, open up, chop down, clip, carve, carve initials in one, jag, shank. See also WOUND.

KNIFE FIGHT n.   chivving match, shivving match, cutting match.

KNOCK DOWN v.   drop, deck, flatten, flip, floor one, down one, take down, take one down, put down, smack down, shoot down, shoot down in flames, lay one out, lay one low, wipe up the floor with, wipe up the place with, knock one on one's ass, knock one ass over teakettle, knock one on one's ear, knock on one's biscuit, knock on one's can, knock on one's keister, knock on one's pratt, knock on one's quiff, knock one on one's wallet, knock one into next week. See also HIT.

KNOCK OUT v.   K.O., kayo, deck, hit the deck, hit the mat, kiss the canvas, total, waste, erase, flatten, floor, smear, lay one out, punch one out, knock cold, knock one out, knock on the head, knock one for a loop, lower the boom, deal a knockout blow to, put away, put the slug on one, ring one's bell, land a haymaker, cold cock, cold pack, curtains for, hearts and flowers, Chinese, drygulch. See also HIT.

KNOW v.   into, got it, getya, gotya, get the idea, get the point, on top of, catch on, booted on, blow wise, have down cold, know one's onions, know the score, collar the jive. See UNDERSTAND.

KNOWING adj.   have smarts, street smarts, wised up, cool, sharp, tuned in, into, really into, all woke up, crack, crackerjack, have savvy, not born yesterday, foxy, crazy like a fox, phenom, pro, whiz kid, enough ducks in a row. See SHREWD. See also INTELLIGENT.

KNOWLEDGE n.   the know, poop, picture, dirt, dope, inside dope, inside story, goulash (false), what's happenin', what's what, what's going down. See INFORMATION.

KNOWLEDGEABLE adj.   cool, posted, hep, hipped, hipster, hepster, hepcat, hip to the jive, brains, brainy, sharp, have savvy, groovy, go-go, with it, all woke up, tuned in, in the picture, booted on, on to, into, really into, plugged in, wise to, wised up, inside, on the inside, have the inside track, have the smarts, have a good head on one's shoulders, have a head on one's shoulder, have one's head screwed on right, have one's ships in a row, smart as a whip, sharp as a tack, not born yesterday, tool, power tool, cereb, IQ, together, got it all together, got it up here, commonsensical, got one's boots on, have horse sense, gray matter, wizard, highbrow, in the know, know-how, know damn well, be up on, have down pat, have down cold, know one's onions, know the score, know the ropes, know all the ins and outs, know it all, know all the answers, know what's what, know one's stuff, know one's business, know one's p's and q's, on, on top of, the smart money, ear to the ground, grounded, on the beam, double digs, hear tell of, hear say, kept posted, nobody's fool, not so dumb, no dumbbell, Philadelphia lawyer. See also ALERT, SKILLED.

KNOXVILLE, TENNESSEE   K Town.

KOREAN (SOUTH) n.   gook, katusa (Korean attached to U.S. Army), ROK.

KOREAN SOLDIER n.   katusa.

KOWTOW v.   lie down and roll over for, roll over and play dead, go social, toe the mark, play ball, fold, give in, give up, go along with, cave in, cry uncle, say uncle, knuckle under, knuckle to. See also FLATTER.

KUDOS n.   strokes, raves, plum, Doctor Spocking the help, pat on the back, pat on the head, PR, puff, puffing up, pumping up. See also FLATTERY.

L

L n. Lima, love.

LABEL n. logo. See also NAME.

LABOR n. grind, daily grind, the salt mines, donkeywork, gruntwork (Army), hemo jo (hard labor), shitwork, day gig, moonlight, rank and file, blue collar. See WORK.

LABOR v. scratch, sweat and slave, plug away, plug along, pour it on, beat one's brains out, bust one's buns, work one's head off, bear down on it, invent the wheel (unnecessary), dog it (inferior). See WORK.

LABORATORY n. lab, chem lab, photo lab, JPL (Jet Propulsion Lab, Pasadena), think tank.

LABORER n. help, hard hat, blue collar, blue-collar worker, dirty neck, breadwinner, workhorse, working stiff, dinner-pailer, prentice, come along (temporary, in-experienced), floater. See WORKER.

LABORIOUS adj. uphill battle, wicked, hairy, bitch, tough one, tough proposition, tough job, rough go, hard pull, hard row to hoe, hard row of stumps, ballbreaker, ballbuster, backbreaker. See DIFFICUILT.

LACK v. no got, minus, 86, eighty-six, out, hurting for, come up short, too little too late, half-assed, half-baked.

LACKADAISICAL adj. laid back, spring fever, moony, daydreaming. See LANGUID.

LACKEY n. stooge, yes-man, flunky, brownnose, ass-kisser, asshole buddy, goon, ward heeler, running dog, toad. See INFERIOR.

LACKING adj. minus, not come up to scratch, not hack it, not make it, can't cut it, can't cut the mustard, short, come up short. See INADEQUATE.

LACKLUSTER adj. blah, draggy, dull as dishwater, vanilla, flat, flat as a pancake, ho hum, nothing, pablum, zero, phoned in, laid back. See INSIPID.

LAD n. tad, kid, kiddo, punk kid, bub, buddy, runt, half-pint, little shaver, bugger, chicken, wet behind the ears, boyo, boychik. See BOY. See also YOUNG MAN, YOUTH.

LADDER n. big stick (firefighter).

LADIES' MAN n. wolf, chaser, gash hound, make-out artist, killer, lady-killer, heavy cake, heavy hitter, blade, parlor snake, poodle faker, prom trotter, sailor, lounge lizard, good-time Charlie, cake-eater, bun duster, candy kid, campus butcher, fancy Dan, fancy man, furper (1930), gay cat, tea hound, stick daddy (police).

LADLE n. bug (industrial or baker).

LADY n. broad, dame, doll, mama, queen, queen bee, frail, frail eel, butterfly, fine fryer, stewer (old), biddie, bag, old bag, doe (alone), mare, harpie, bitch. See WOMAN.

LAG v. shlep along, get no place fast, toddle, jelly, tool, tail. See LINGER.

LAGGARD n. slowpoke, foot-dragger, stick in the mud, goof-off, fuck-off, goldbrick, shlepper. See DAWDLER.

LAME adj. crip, game, g'd up, geed up, gimp, gimpy, hamstrung, hog-tied, sidelined, out of commission.

LAMENT v. bleed, hurt, blubber, boo hoo, eat one's heart out, take it big, take it hard, sing, sing the blues, cry the blues, cry me a river, cry over spilled milk, go for a crying towel, get out the crying towel, kick one's self, beat one's breast, rain, carry on, take on, howl, raise a howl.

LAMENTABLE adj. awful, dirty, godawful, goshawful, grim, lousy, hurting, rotten, stinking, shitty, tough shit, TS. See also BAD, SAD.

LAMP n. dimmer, glim, bitch, bitch lamp (hobo), gump light (miner), kenten (for opium), birdcage, bug, bug torch, hay burner.

LAMPOON n. takeoff, roast, put-on, takedown. See RIDICULE.

LAND n. real estate, terra firma, old sod.

LAND v. touchdown, come in, set her down, put her down, make a three-pointer, splashdown, grease it in, grease job (smooth), go in, ditch, splash, pancake, thump in. See also ARRIVE.

LANDING n. three point, three-pointer, touchdown, touch and go (practice), dead stick, splash, splashdown, power off; pancake, ditch (crash).

LANDING FIELD n. runway, strip, airstrip, landing strip, home plate (A.F.). See AIRPORT.

LANDLORD n. landprop, saw, slumlord.

LANDSMAN n. landlubber, ground gripper.

LANGUAGE n. lingo, bafflegab, doublespeak, double-talk, gobbledygookese; hillspeak, Washingtonese

(Washington, D.C.), officialese, federalese; psychobabble, Urbabbble (city govt.), Yerkish (artificial), Yinglish (English using many Yiddish words), Franglish (French using English words), jive talk, street talk, flash (among thieves).

LANGUID adj. laid back, blah, blahs, dopey, drippy, draggy, nebbish, wimpy, moony, sleepyhead, on the nod, snoozy, stretchy, out of it, have spring fever, June around.

LANGUISH v. fizzle out, fag, fag out, poop, poop out, tucker, tucker out, burn out, knock out, peter out, conk out, peg out, go soft, go to pieces, come apart at the seams, die on the vine. See DETERIORATE.

LANGUOROUS adj. laid back, loose, hang loose, dopey, moony, stretchy. See LANGUID.

LANKY adj. twiggy, bean pole, beanstalk, stilt, hat rack, broomstick, clothes pole, gangly, spindleshanks. See THIN.

LANTERN n. dimmer, glim, birdcage, bug, bug torch, hay burner, bitch, bitch lamp (hobo), gump light (miner), kenten (for opium).

LAPSE n. flub, fluff, muff, boner, boo-boo, blooper, goof, goof up, screw-up, gum up, miscue, slipup, clinker, flap (social), fox paw, fox pass, gaff, klong, bonehead play, fool mistake. See MISTAKE.

LARGE adj. gross, humongous, humungous, mungo, monstro, king-size, big mother, biggy, seagoing, jumbo, man-sized, lunker, blimp, barn door, whopping, thumping, would choke a horse. See BIG.

LARGESS n. gravy, grease, palm oil, salve, sweetener, zukes, tip, toke (gambling), chip, cue, somethin', a little somethin'.

LARK n. 1. binge, ball, bash, bust, caper, tear, blowout, wingding, shindig, carousing, hell around, hell-bender, high old time, high jinks, field day. See REVEL. See also PARTY. 2. gag, rib, put-on, hotfoot, hot one, monkeyshines, shenanigans.

LARYNX n. pipes.

LAS VEGAS, NEVADA Vegas, Lost Wages, Sin City, Dice City, Divorce City, Glitter Gulch (downtown).

LASCIVIOUS adj. filthy, dirty, nasty, blue, X-rated, raunchy, raw, hard core, soft core, steamy, hot, heavy, hot and heavy, hot for, hot stuff, rough, rough stuff, evil-minded, foulmouthed, salty, off-color, low-down, low-down and dirty, in the gutter, turned on, horny, cream jeans, hot pants, lechy, a lech on, letchin'.

LASS n. sis, kid, chick, chicklet, bird, doll, jill, filly, heifer, teenybopper, bobby-soxer, bubble-gum rocker, jellybean, li'l mama, little missy, jailbait, San Quentin quail, pigeon, gidget. See GIRL.

LAST adj. ass end, the end, bitter end, tail ass (A.F.), case (cards), the chips are down, curtains, curtains for, last hurrah, swan song. See ULTIMATE.

LASTING adj. in for the long haul, forever and a day, for a coon's age, for a month of Sundays, time out of mind, till hell freezes over, till shrimps learn to whistle, till the cows come home. See PERMANENT.

LAST MINUTE n. eleventh hour, the nick of time.

LAST RESORT adj. bottom of the barrel, scrape the bottom of the barrel.

LATE adj. hung up, held up, in a bind, jammed, jammed up, strapped for time, burn the midnight oil, snooze you lose.

LATE, TOO adj. gone, blew it, blew one's chance, out of luck, missed the boat, the boat has sailed, let slip through one's fingers, left at the starting gate, left at the post, lock the barn door after the horse is stolen.

LATER adj. by and by, come Sunday, down the line, downstream, down the pike, down the road a piece.

LATEST adj. faddy, trendy, in, in-thing, the thing, latest thing, latest wrinkle, last word, mod, now, really now, up to the minute. See STYLISH.

LATIN AMERICAN n. Latino, Chicano, Chicana; greaser, wetback, spic, dago (working class), spaghetti, spig, spiggoty (all Derog.).

LATITUDE n. run, run of, space, elbowroom, leeway, room to swing a cat.

LATRINE n. can, john, head, facilities, amenities, terlit, piss house, shithouse, shitter, crapper, chamber of commerce, altar room, throne room, showers, where the dicks hang out, old soldiers' home. See also TOILET.

LAUD v. stroke, boost, pat on the back, build up, toss a bouquet, give a posy, give the man a big cigar, have to hand it to, hats off to. See FLATTER.

LAUDABLE adj. pink, stellar, neato, keen, teriff, not bad, not too shabby, gnarly, slick, lookin' chilly (Bl.), nasty, horror show, real mean, beaut, atsa nice, bootin' height, organic, check plus. See PRAISEWORTHY.

LAUGH n. crack-up, yock, yack, yuck, howl, scream, boff, boffo, boffola, belly laugh, guffaw, har-de-har.

LAUGH v. crack up, break up, fracture, die, die laughing, boff, howl, scream, roll in the aisles, tear one apart, snap, split, split one's sides, blow a gut, laugh it up, laugh fit to die, laugh fit to bust, laugh fit to burst, bust a gut laughing, pee in one's pants laughing, fall out laughing, be in stitches, show some teeth.

LAUGHABLE adj. jokey, yok, yokky, gagged up, for grins, camp, campy, joshing, boffo, break one up, tear one apart, lay 'em in the aisles, scream, zetser, laffer, har-har, riot. See AMUSING.

LAUNCH v.   bow, kick off, start the ball rolling, get things rolling, get the show on the road, begin the beguine, break the ice, break the seal. See BEGIN.

LAUNDER v.   dobee, doby (by hand), button chop. See also CLEAN.

LAUNDRY n.   button chopper, Chinks.

LAUNDRYMAN n.   button chopper, button hopper (WW II), Chinaman (ship).

LAUREL n.   the cookies, feather in one's cap, gold star, the gold, Oscar, blue ribbon.

LAVATORY n.   can, john, powder room, reading room, library, head, facilities, terlit, piss house, shithouse, sandbox, biffie, chamber of commerce, holy of holies, his, hers, little girls' room, little boys' room, pissoire. See TOILET.

LAVISH adj.   plush, posh, plushy, ritzy, swanky, splendiferous, splendacious, like money was goin' outta style, spreading it around, fancy, high, high on the hog, too much, ultra-ultra, far out, way out, out of this world, out of bounds, out of sight, no end, no end in sight, stink with, crawling with, up to one's ass in, first cabin.

LAVISH v.   go for a meg, throw money at, throw money around, piss it away, run through, go through, live high on the hog, spend money like water, spend money like it was going out of style. See SQUANDER. See also GIVE.

LAW n.   reg.

LAW-ABIDING adj.   legit, on the legit, on the level, up to code, straight, straight arrow. See also VIRTUOUS.

LAWBREAKER n.   crook, hood, con, heavy, hustler, racketeer, inside man, wrong number, mobster, hoodlum, goon, gunsel, trigger man, repeater. See CRIMINAL.

LAWFUL adj.   legit, kosher, card-carrying, on the legit, on the level, on the up and up, hold water, hold together, hold up in the wash, wash. See LEGAL.

LAWYER n.   mouthpiece, shyster, ambulance chaser, legal eagle, beagle, the L.A., pleader, fixer, bomber (divorce), ghost (writes briefs), cutter (prosecutor). See ATTORNEY.

LAX adj.   sloppy, any old way, any which way, devil may care, leave oneself wide open, goofing off, pay no mind, looking out the window, out to lunch, asleep on the job. See CARELESS.

LAXATIVE n.   cc pills.

LAZY adj.   dopey, out of it, sleepyhead, snoozy, on the nod, stretchy, drag ass, Stepin Fetchit, lox, sack artist, bum, no good bum, blanket presser, lounge lizard. See also INDOLENT.

LEAD n.   edge, bulge, ahead, over, top, on top, spark. See ADVANTAGE.

LEAD v.   head, helm, shepherd, run things, call the shots, call the signals, quarterback, mastermind, get the jump on, go out in front, spearhead, trail-blaze. See MANAGE.

LEADER n.   front runner, chief, C.O., exec, boss lady, boss man, godfather, head honcho, queen bee, top, on top, topper, topkick, kingpin, king of the hill, lead-off man, guru, juice. See EXECUTIVE.

LEADING adj.   number one, numero uno, primo, A-number one, tops, top of the class, top of the list, top drawer, at the head of the line, first off, right up front. See BEST.

LEAFLET n.   broadside, flyer, handout, literature.

LEAGUE n.   bunch, crew, crowd, gang, mob, outfit, ring, hookup, tie-up, circle. See ASSOCIATION.

LEAN adj.   skinny, stick, twiggy, shadow, bag of bones, bean pole, stilt, hat rack, clothes pole, gangling, gangly. See THIN.

LEANING n.   bag, groove, thing, cup of tea, mindset, where one is at, weakness for. See INCLINATION.

LEAN ON v.   bank on, bank upon, bet on, bet one's bottom dollar on, gamble on, lay money on, use as a crutch, ride on one's coattails.

LEAP v.   hippety hop, cut, pass up.

LEARN v.   1. get down, get down pat, get down cold, get hold of, get into one's head, get the hang of, get the knack of, pick up, pick up on, learn the ropes, learn backwards and forwards, go through the school of hard knocks, dig up, uncover, smoke out, stumble upon, suss out, trip over, thread the needle. 2. crack the books, megastudy, grind, cram, skull practice, skull drag, dig, bag some food for the brain, cruise a subject, hardwire (by rote). See STUDY.

LEARNED adj.   brain, brainy, sharp, posted, hip, hep, with it, all woke up, in the picture, booted on, in the know, know all the answers, double digs. See KNOWLEDGEABLE.

LEAST adv.   short end of the stick, sticky end of the stick, entry level, low man on the totem pole, low in the pecking order, at the bottom of the heap, second fiddle, third stringer, in the gutter. See also LOWEST.

LEAVE n.   1. eyes to cool it, layoff, liberty. See also FURLOUGH. 2. go-ahead, green light, okay, OK. See CONSENT.

LEAVE v.   I'm history, I'm outta here, split, let's blaze, do a train, do a ghost, beat it, scram, haul ass, bag ass, hit the road, bop off, fuck off, move out, check out, bail out, light out, get lost, get going, git, get git, blow, blow this pop stand, skedaddale, hotfoot, shove off, percolate, make tracks, let the doorknob hit you. See GO.

LEAVE, COMMAND v.   fuck off, stay out of my face, shove off, forget you, vamoose, scram, get lost, blow, beat it, bug off, make yourself scarce, make like a tree and leave, make tracks, clear out, butt out, screw, shove, take a walk, go chase yourself, scat, go peddle your papers. See GO, COMMAND.

LEAVE TAKING n.   swan song.

LEAVINGS n.   leftovers, broken arm (table scraps).

LECHER n.   letch, lech, old letch, heavy hitter, heavy cake, playboy, player, high liver, nighthawk, night owl, dude, operator, speed, mother, cruiser, smoothie, lookin' to get lucky, lookin' to score, campus butcher, old goat, dirty old man, wolf, tomcat, cat, sharp cat, gay cat, sport, swinger, rake, lover boy, killer, lady-killer, ladies' man, man on the make, make-out artist, chaser, broad chaser, woman chaser, skirt chaser, cunt chaser, tail chaser, cocksman, stick daddy (police), poodle faker, masher, rip, rounder, gay deceiver, gay dog, blade, gay blade, good-time Charlie, whorehound, gash hound, prom trotter, tea hound, bun duster, sailor, Lothario, Don Juan, Casanova, lounge lizard, parlor snake, cake-eater, candy kid, fancy dan, furper, drugstore cowboy.

LECHEROUS adj.   raunchy, low-down and dirty; horny, hot and heavy, cream jeans, a lech on, letchin'. See LASCIVIOUS.

LECTURE n.   pitch, spiel, chalk talk, pep talk, soapbox oration, skull session. See SPEECH.

LECTURE v.   get on a soapbox, spiel, spout. See SPEAK.

LECTURE TOUR n.   rubber-chicken circuit, mashed-potato circuit.

LEECH n.   beat, deadbeat, freeloader, hanger-on, hose, schnorrer, sponge, sponger. See PARASITE.

LEEWAY n.   elbowroom, room to swing a cat.

LEFT-HANDED adj.   lefty, leftie, southpaw, portsider, side wheeler.

LEFT LANE n.   sidedoor, lane one.

LEG IRONS n.   anklets, boot, bull chain, clinkers, lam bean, Oregon boot, rat shackle, rattler, tracer chain.

LEGAL adj.   legit, kosher, card-carrying, sure enough, honest to God, twenty-four carat, all wool and a yard wide, on the legit, on the level, on the up and up, stand up, hold up, hold water, hold together, hang together, hold up in the wash, wash, go, fly, for real, okayed.

LEGAL ACTION n.   heat.

LEGAL ALIEN n.   Green Card, documented.

LEGAL DOCUMENT n.   papers.

LEGALIZE v.   launder (money, title), clean up.

LEGGINGS n.   chaps, chaquata (plus jacket).

LEGISLATE v.   put through; jam through, railroad, railroad through, steamroller through (forced).

LEGISLATURE n.   House.

LEGITIMATE adj.   legit, kosher, on the legit, on the level, on the up and up, front door, twenty-four carat, for real, hold up in the wash, honest to God. See LEGAL.

LEGITIMIZE v.   launder (money, title), clean up.

LEGLESS adj.   halfy.

LEGS n.   gams, gambs, hams, pins, pegs, stems, benders, choppers, drumsticks, hinders, pillars, props, shafts, stilts, sticks, trotters, underpinnings, uprights, hind legs, stumps, wheels, bad wheels (injured or ugly).

LEISURE n.   goof-off time, fuck-off time, time to burn, time to kill, one's own sweet time. See also REST.

LEMONADE n.   lemo, forty-one.

LEND v.   knock (Bl.), lay on one, shark, loan shark, piece one off, stake. See LOAN.

LENDER n.   shark, loan shark, shylock, soft touch, uncle (pawnbroker).

LENDING INSTITUTION n.   damper, jay, jug.

LENGTHEN v.   drag one's feet, drag out, spin out, stretch out, put some rubber in it. See also EXPAND.

LENIENT adj.   go easy with, go easy on, be big, live with, soft shell. See COMPASSIONATE.

LEOPARD n.   cat, spots.

LESBIAN n.   les, lez, lesbine, lesbie, lesbo, dyke, bull dyke, bull dagger, diesel dyke, butch, crested hen (butch), bitch, boondagger, daisy, fairy lady, Amy, bird, gal officer, marge, lady lover, female identified, female oriented, femme, finger artist, double-barreled broad, shemale, harpie, Jasper, sergeant, top sergeant (all Derog.).

LESSEN v.   cutback, roll back, downsize, leblang (theater ticket price), soft-pedal, take the bite out, take the edge off, take the sting out. See REDUCE.

LESSER adj.   bush league, low in the pecking order, low man on the totem pole, bottom man on the totem pole, bottom man, bottom sawyer, second fiddle, second string, third string, a notch under. See INFERIOR.

LESSON n.   chalk talk, skull session.

LET v. sit still for, give the go ahead, give the green light, okay, OK, be big, hear of, live with, free up. See PERMIT.

LETHARGIC adj. laid back, blah, blahs, dopey, drippy, draggy, nebbish, wimpy, moony, sleepyhead, on the nod, snoozy, stretchy, out of it, have spring fever, June around. See LANGUID

LETTER n. line, memo, junk mail, drop a line, thank-you note, Dear John, dead (not deliverable), kite, cannonball, scratch, stiffo, sugar report (love), mash note, tab, tag, poison-pen letter (malicious, obscene, etc.).

LETTER WRITER n. pen pal.

LETTUCE n. grass, rabbit food, leaves.

LEVELHEADED adj. together, got it together, cool, cool as a cucumber, have horse sense, commonsensical, all there, in one's right mind, got all one's marbles.

LEVERAGE n. edge, break, juice, clout, drag, pull, suction, ropes, weight, have a jump on, have a leg up on, bargaining chip, ace in the hole, fix, grease, wire, loose change (temporary). See ADVANTAGE. See also INFLUENCE.

LEVITY n. grins, laughs, lots of laughs, high old time, picnic, hoopla, whoopee. See also AMUSEMENT.

LEWD adj. filthy, dirty, blue, X-rated, raw, hard core, soft core, hot, hot stuff, rough, evil-minded, foulmouthed, off-color, low-down and dirty, purple; hot pants. See OBSCENE.

LIABILITY n. tab, bad news, damage, bite, chit, IOU, in the red, nut, below the line, baggage. See DEBT.

LIAISON n. go-between, cutout (secret intermediary), fixer, connection, in, interface.

LIAR n. jive ass, jive turkey, phony, promoter, con artist, con man, con merchant, conner, crap merchant, oil merchant. bullshitter, bullshit artist, burn notice (warning that a person is a liar).

LIBEL v. blister, roast, scorch, crack, knock, give one a black eye, mark lousy, mark wrong, bad-mouth, do one dirt, put the hooks in, put the needles in, put the zingers in, drag one's name through the mud, sizzle. See SLANDER.

LIBELER n. knocker, mudslinger, backbiter.

LIBERAL adj. 1. softie, soft touch, big, be big, bighearted, have a heart, heart in the right place, loose, Santa Claus, good Joe, prince of a person, free and easy, casual. 2. a dime a dozen, aplenty, galore, no end, no end in sight, stink with. See PLENTY. 3. left, lefty, lefto, left winger, New Left, Old Left, left of center, pink, pinko, parlor pink, radish, fellow traveller, linky dink, bleeding heart, do-gooder, innocent (Bl.), knee-jerk reaction, commie, comsymp, hippie, yippie, radiclib, red, rim, underground, Wobbly.

LIBERATE v. free up, bail one out, get out from under, save one's bacon, save one's neck, save one's ass. See FREE.

LIBERTINE n. 1. playboy, player, nighthawk, cruiser, letch, wolf, tomcat, cunt chaser, cocksman, rounder, sailor. 2. pushover, round heels, easy woman, chippy, floozy, tramp, slut, charity girl, run around, floss around, piece of trade, pigmeat (old). See LECHER.

LIBERTY n. run, run of, free run of.

LIBIDINOUS adj. heavy, horny, hot, hot and heavy, lechy, a lech on. See LASCIVIOUS.

LIBRARY n. lib, libe, Phi Beta House.

LIBRETTO n. book.

LICE n. cooties, bugs, crabs, crotch pheasants, walking dandruff.

LICENSE n. 1. go-ahead, green light, okay, OK. 2. ticket (maritime). See CONSENT.

LICENSE PLATE n. plates, pad, pads, marker, tags.

LICENTIOUS adj. fast, fast and loose, drive in the fast lane wih no brakes, high living, speedy, high liver, swinger. See DISSOLUTE.

LIE n. jive, line of jive, jazz, fib, whopper, bunk, bull, shit, pile of shit, piece of shit, bullshit, BS, bullchitna (Esk.), bulldog, horseshit, horse manure, horse hocky, hocky, shit for the birds, crap, crapola, crock, crock of shit, claptrap, hooey, hokum, balls, yarn, story, tall story, fish story, cock-and-bull story, tall tale, fairy tale, baloney, malarkey, banana oil, ball, thick, thin, con, cover, cover-up, smoke, string, line, line of cheese, marmalade, spinach, tripe, vanilla, garbage, hogwash, doesn't wash, taradiddle, dirty lie, terminological inexactitude, borax, dog it, song, song and dance, no such animal, the big lie (Pol.).

LIE v. jive, shuck and jive, maple stick jive, bull, shit, bullshit, BS, shovel the shit, string along, soft-soap, snow, fudge, jazz, con, promote, schmear, queer, lead up the garden path, put on, put on an act, put up a front, put on a false front, fake, fake it, hoke up, frame, frame up, plant, phony up, put up a bluff, four-flush, lie through one's teeth, make believe, make like, let on, let on like, play possum, talk trash, build up, pass, signify, gammon, tell a little white lie, talk through one's hat, speak with forked tongue, cram, doctor, cook, deacon, duff, flaking, load, salt, salt a mine.

LIEUTENANT (ARMY) n. looey, loot, lieut, shavetail, gold brick, jeeter, john, first john, second john, 1st looey, 2nd looey, ninety-day wonder, tent Johnny.

LIEUTENANT (NAVY) n. first luff, one-and-a-half striper, two-striper.

LIEUTENANT COLONEL n. light colonel.

LIFE n. rat race, the big game, world, the real world, journey, hand (one is dealt).

LIFE JACKET n. Mae West.

LIFELESS adj. blah, draggy, dull as dishwater, flat, flat as a pancake, ho hum, nothing, pablum, zero. See INSIPID. See also DEAD.

LIFE PRESERVER n. Mae West, water wings.

LIFETIME n. all one's born days, womb to tomb, cradle to the grave.

LIFT n. boost, leg, leg up. See ASSIST.

LIFT v. boost, bring up, build up, fetch up, goose, goose up, hike, hike up, jack up, jump up, put up. See SUPPORT.

LIFT WEIGHTS v. bench press, press, press weights, pump iron.

LIGHT adj. up, upbeat, upper, perky, chipper, chirpy, corky, high, sunny, sunny side up, Little Merry Sunshine. See CHEERFUL.

LIGHT n. 1. dimmer, glim. 2. flash, bitch, bitch lamp (hobo), gump light (miner), birdcage, bug, bug torch, hay burner (RR).

LIGHT v. spot, spotlight, limelight, highlight, hit with a spot, hit with a light, hit with a beam.

LIGHTEN v. take a load off, take a load off one's mind, take a load off one's chest.

LIGHTHEADED adj. gaga, rocky, woozy, punchy, the room going around.

LIGHTHEARTED adj. feelgood, high wide and handsome, laid back. See BUOYANT.

LIGHTS n. foots, jewelry, spot, juniors, babies, kliegs.

LIKABLE PERSON n. ace, Mr. Nice, nice guy, right guy, good dude, good head, good egg, good Joe, one-way ghee, sweetheart, sweetie, sweetie pie, pussycat, prince, prince of a fellow, regular fellow, after one's own heart, salt of the earth.

LIKE adj. double, look-alike, like two peas in a pod, six of one and half a dozen of the other, spit and image, spittin' image. See SAME.

LIKE v. 1. go for, fall for, have eyes for, big eyes for, have a thing about, stuck on, have a case on, have eyes for, take to, take a liking to, take a shine to, cotton to, partial to, hit it off. See LOVE. See also DESIRE, FAVOR. 2. groove on, balling, grok, dig the most, rat fuck, R. F., get some grins, get off on, get high on, flip for, drop the bomb. See ENJOY.

LIKED adj. okay people, touted, highly touted, score, make it with one, rate with one, regular, regular guy, one's kind of guy, one of the boys. See also POPULAR.

LIKELIHOOD n. even break, fair shake, fighting chance, fifty-fifty, have a shot at, long shot, hundred-to-one shot, outside chance, not a chance in hell, a coin flip, toss-up, near as one can tell, dollars to doughnuts. See POSSIBILITY.

LIKELY adj. dollars to doughnuts, like as not, like enough, a lead-pipe cinch, bet the ranch on it, bet the house on it, bet the rent on it.

LIKEMINDEDNESS n. groupthink.

LIKENESS n. look-alike, work alike, likes of, ditto, knock-off, xerox, clone, carbon, carbon copy, dead ringer, double, spitting image, peas in a pod, two of a kind, angel (radar), birds of a feather. See COPY.

LIMBO n. nowhere, Siberia, there's no there there (originally Oakland, CA.), no-man's-land, out there, left field, cold storage, Erewhon, Yemensville, Lower Slobbovia, hell and back.

LIMBS n. gams, pins, stems, drumsticks, hind legs, wheels, bad wheels (injured or ugly). See LEGS.

LIMELIGHT n. center stage. See also CELEBRITY.

LIMIT n. the max, ape, far out, the most, tops, bottom line, bottom out (lower limit), cap, fence.

LIMIT v. ice, cap, keep the lid on, bottle up, cork, cork up, draw the line, hog-tie. See RESTRAIN.

LIMITED OBJECTIVE n. surgical mission.

LIMITLESS adj. no end of, no end to, wide open, no strings, no holds barred, no joker, no ifs ands or buts, more than you can shake a stick at. See UNLIMITED. See also COUNTLESS.

LIMP n. floppy, gimp, loose, bad wheels, hitch in one's get along.

LIMP v. gimp.

LINCOLN CAR n. pap, boat.

LINEAR adj. beeline, as the crow flies, down the alley, down the pipe, in the groove, on the beam, slam-bang.

LINGER v. hang around, hang out, hang in, hang on, hang about, stick around, monkey around, fool around, fuck around, fuck off, goof around, goof off, screw off, flub off, flub the dub, rat fuck, R.F., fuck the dog, cool it, cool one's heels, sit on one's ass, sit on one's butt, sit on one's duff, jelly, tool, stall, warm a chair, get no place fast, poke around, poke along, mosey, toddle, shlep along, potchky, put on hold. See also DAWDLE.

LINGERER n. hanger-on, foot-dragger, slowpoke, stick in the mud, shlep.

LINGERIE n. briefs, undies, underthings, unmentionables, bra, panties, teddy, nightie, jammies, PJ's. See UNDERWEAR.

LINK n. network, tie-in, in, interface, hookup, contact, connection, channel.

LINK v. 1. network with, interface, plug into, hook up, throw in with, team up with, go in partners, meld with, swing in with, tie in with, mob up. See ASSOCIATE. 2. tack on, tag on, tag along, slap on, hitch on.

LINT n. dust ball, kittens, pussies, slut's wool.

LION n. Leo, big cat.

LIPS n. chops, kisser, rubies.

LIQUID n. juice, bug juice, goo, goop, dope (heavy, such as sauce).

LIQUIDATE v. cash in, cash out. See also KILL.

LIQUID OXYGEN n. lox.

LIQUOR n. hard liquor, likker, brown bag (concealed), alky, hootch, booze, corn, corn likker, cave corn, moonshine, moon, mountain dew, prairie dew, squirrel dew, red-eye, sauce, rotgut, white, white line, white lightning, chain lightning, Jersey lightning, gray mule, white mule, white horse, potato water, tiger milk, panther, panther piss, panther sweat, tiger sweat, pig sweat, pig iron, scrap iron, gas, drop, wee drop, neat, straight up, on the rocks, medicine, snake medicine, poison, snake poison, rat poison, nightcap, swill, ball, bat and ball, jug, firewater, fogmatic, fog cutter, gargle, short dog (cheap wine in a brown paper bag), dog's nose, hair of the dog, hair of the dog that bit one, pickup, pick-me-up, eye-opener, corpse reviver, donk, heel tap, kong, king kong, rerun, smoke, canned heat, third rail, hall, John Hall, high wine (with Coca-Cola), gage, hardware, scat, magic, hospital alcohol, formaldehyde, fluid, embalming fluid, paint remover, varnish remover, shellac, coffin varnish, brush whiskey, bathtub gin, home brew, homespun, nigger pot, cooler, juice, A-bomb juice, bug juice, cactus juice, happy juice, joy juice, kickapoo joy juice, kickapoo juice, torpedo juice, caper juice, Kool Aid, spot, scrap iron, sheepdip, dehorn, swamp root, blue blazer, boilermaker's delight, damp, bourbon poultice, oil of joy, bottle, boxcar, budge, busthead, conk buster (Bl.), forty rod, bold face, pale face, rumpot, sap, seafood, shine, sneaky pete, stuff, screech, steam, belly wash, catgut, blind tiger, blue run, angel teat, gee, glue, whoopee, giggle bottle, giggle water, goat hair, google eye, hard stuff, hardware, hop toad, load, popskull (home made), stiffener, dirty bird (Old Crow), powder (20s), serum, zombie, finger (amount).

LIQUOR GLASS n. jigger, shot glass, snifter.

LIQUOR STORE n. corn cellar, happy shop.

LIST n. lineup, drop-dead list (fired, expelled, excluded), laundry list (agenda), enemies list, shitlist, S list, pap (Annapolis), loop (distribution list). See DIRECTORY.

LIST v. tab, peg, chart, spell out, type-cast, button down, put down as, put down for.

LISTEN v. catch, listen up, pick up, pick up on, tune in on, get, get a load of this, get a load of that, have an ear cocked, be all ears, give ears, have one's ears on, knock one one's lobes, hear tell. See also OVERHEARD, EAVESDROP.

LISTENING adj. on the earie, on the lake, sails are flapping.

LISTLESS adj. laid back, blah, blahs, dopey, drippy, draggy, nebbish, wimpy, moony, sleepyhead, on the nod, snoozy, stretchy, out of it, have spring fever, have tired blood, June around.

LITERATURE n. lit, lit course, shrink lits (condensed classics).

LITHUANIAN n. Litvak.

LITIGATE v. have the law on, law, take the law on, haul into court, drag into court, drag one's ass into court, see one in court, have up.

LITTERER n. litterbug.

LITTLE adj. teeny, teensy-weensy, itsy-bitsy, junior, shrimp, peanut, runt, dinky, two by four, half-pint, tad, titch. See SMALL.

LITTLE ROCK, ARKANSAS Rock City.

LIVE v. 1. get along, just makin' it, get by. 2. bunk, bunk out, hang out, crash, nest, perch, roost, squat, hang up one's hat, hang up one's shingle, hole up, locate, park. See INHABIT. 3. shack up, shack up with.

LIVELIHOOD n. what one is into, thing, nine-to-five shit, rat race, day gig, beeswax, game, dodge, slot, grind, racket, swindle, grift. See OCCUPATION.

LIVELY adj. perky, bouncy, chipper, zingy, jumping, hyper, snappy, juiced up, ball of fire, go-go, full of beans, full of piss and vinegar. See SPIRITED.

LIVEN v. spice, spice up, zip up, zap up, perk up, pep up, juice up, snap up. See ENLIVEN.

LIVER n. sugar factory.

LIVESTOCK n. dogie, longhorn, moo cow, shorthorn, whiteface, stray, dinge (substandard, unbranded). See also COW, BULL.

LIVE TOGETHER v. shack up, shack up with, LT, LTR, POSSLQ (persons of the opposite sex sharing living quarters, IRS).

LIVE WELL v. piss on ice, eat high on the hog, on velvet, on a bed of roses, live off the fat of the land, have it made.

LIVING adj. alive and kicking, ticking, warm, in the lifestream.

LIVING QUARTERS n. pad, condo, co-op, domi, dommy, roof over one's head, hole in the wall, dump, homeplate, turf. See HOUSE.

LIVING TOGETHER adj. apartmates, convivante, mingles, LTR, POSSLQ (persons of the opposite sex sharing living quarters, IRS).

LOAD n. albatross, albatross around one's neck, excess baggage, shlepper, ball and chain. See HINDRANCE.

LOAD v. top, top off, pile it on, heap on, weigh down, chock, jam pack, ram in.

LOAF v. bum, bum around, hang out, goof around, knock around, fool around, fuck around, futz around, fuck off, goof off, rat fuck, R.F., fuck the dog, sit on one's butt, lie down on the job, drag one's ass, drag one's tail, featherbed. See IDLE.

LOAFER n. goof off, fuck off, goldbrick, beach bum, drugstore cowboy, good for nothin', lazy good for nothin'. See IDLER.

LOAN n. on the cuff, on the muscle, on pump, on the arm, on tick, tick, extension (maximum), angel dust, bite, floater, juice (usurious interest), jawbone, balloon payment (final).

LOAN v. loan shark, score, touch, scratch, take (secure a), stake, grubstake, knock (Bl.), lay on one, piece one off, front-end loading, jawbone, loan out (often refers to film and TV talent under contract).

LOAN COLLECTOR n. juice man, skip tracer.

LOATHE v. allergic to, have an allergy to, have no use for, down on, grossed out on. See DISLIKE.

LOATHSOME adj. stinker, sleazy, sleazeball, wimpy, spastic, funky (Bl.), lousy, bad case of the uglies, gummy, gross, grody, grody to the max, beastly, slime bucket, maggoty, creepy-crawly, uncool, in one's hat, for the birds, gives one a pain, gives one a pain in the neck, gives one a pain in the ass, pesky, pestiferous, bitchy. See also DESPICABLE.

LOBBY n. squat pad.

LOBBY v. hype, plug, push, sell, hard sell, high pressure, soft sell, sell one on, sweet-talk, soft-soap, pitch, make a pitch for, drum, beat the drum for, thump the tub for, goose, juice, juice up, build up, puff, splash, spot, throw the spotlight on, press agent, ballyhoo, bill, billboard, boost, root for, buttonhole, politick, get behind, egg one on, knock on doors, work on, work over, lean on, twist one's arm, put the screws on, put the bee on, put the squeeze on, put on the spot, put on the map, bug, jawbone.

LOBBYIST n. five percenter, knife thrower, rainmaker.

LOCAL n. affil (TV), branch, branch house, offshoot; milk run, meat run (trains).

LOCALE n. turf, scene, spot, X marks the spot, neck of the woods, hole, zone.

LOCATE v. 1. hook, read (radar), pinpoint, scare up, zero in, pick up on, hit upon, stumble on, trip over, right under one's nose, uncover, strike (oil, gold), spot, smoke out, smell out, nose out. 2. park, hang up one's hat, hang up one's shingle, dig in.

LOCATION n. spot, X marks the spot, scene, zone, turf, fix, hole, how the land lies, the lay of the land, neck of the woods, pit (racing, gambling).

LOCK v. button, button up, slough, slough up. See also CLOSE.

LOCOMOTIVE n. choo choo, hog, bull engine, goat (switch), battleship (heavy duty), battlewagon (tender), kettle (small), yard goat. See RAILROAD LOCOMOTIVE.

LODGE v. bunk, bunk out, hang out, crash, nest, perch, roost, squat, hang up one's hat, hang up one's shingle, hole up, locate, park. See INHABIT.

LODGING n. crib, crash pad, digs, diggings, pad, roof over one's head, castle, palace, bed and breakfast, dorm, fratority, sorenity, birdcage, bull pen, bullypen, frau shack, henranch, hencoop, quail roost, zoo; motel, shortel (hourly rates), airtel, aquatel, boatel, floatel, chinch pad, flophouse, scratch crib. See also HOUSE.

LOFT n. sky parlor.

LOFTY adj. high-rise. See also ARROGANT.

LOG n. comic book, funny book, swindle sheet.

LOGICAL adj. commonsensical, hold up, hold water, hold together, hang together, hold up in the wash, wash, fly, legit, kosher, signify, stand up, go, all there.

LOGOTYPE n. logo.

LOGS n. load of sticks.

LOITER v. hang out, hang around, goof around, jack around, monkey around, rat fuck, R.F., get no place fast, poke around. See IDLE.

LOITERER n. goof off, fuck off, goldbrick, shlepper, sleepyhead, beach bum, drugstore cowboy, cake-eater, lounge lizard, john, johnny, good for nothin', lazy good for nothin', stick in the mud. See also DAWDLER.

LOLLIPOP n.   sucker, all day sucker (large).

LONE adj.   onliest, stag, solo. See ALONE.

LONELY adj.   godforsaken, down, bummed out.

LONG adj.   king-size, stretch (car or airplane). See also PROLONGED.

LONG v.   yen for, cream for, itch for, hanker for, spoil for, give one's eyeteeth for, wild to, have a case on. See DESIRE.

LONG DISTANCE n.   way, ways, far piece, long chalk, a sleeper jump, overland route, clear to hell and gone. See FAR.

LONGEVITY n.   in for the long haul, shelf life, golden age, gray power, the dwindles. See also AGED.

LONGING n.   itch, hots, lech, nasties, the urge, sweet tooth, fire in the belly, yen, zazzle. See DESIRE.

LONGSHOREMAN n.   dock walloper, roustabout.

LOOK n.   flash, gander, gun, gunning over, case, pike, hinge, glom, once-over, the OO, the double O, the eye, squint, slant, lamp, look-see, eyeball inspection, pike, swivel, come-hither look, bedroom eyes, the glad eye, bad eye, whammy, a murder-one look.

LOOK v.   flash on, read, lamp, focus, eye, eyeball, lay one's glims on, get a hinge, look-see, scout, tumble, rubberneck, give a thing a toss, give it a thumb check, look one up and down, look at one cross-eyed, go slumming, slum, take in the sights. See SEE.

LOOKING GLASS n.   gaper.

LOOKOUT n.   1. weather eye, peeled eye, eagle eye, gapper, hawk, spotter, tip, anchor, case, gap, jigger, jigger guy, jigger man, outside man, zex man, lay zex, lay butzo, lay jiggers, lay chickie, gander (criminal, not common). 2. O.P. (observation post), catbird seat. See also GUARD.

LOOKOUT v.   1. gun, peg, scope, spot, spy, eagle eye, take a hinge, look-see, check out, check something out, case, size up, keep tab, keep tabs on. 2. keep one's eyes peeled, keep a weather eye peeled, peel one's eyeballs, pick up on, ride shotgun for, shotgun, burn up. See SEE.

LOOKS n.   cut of one's jib, phiz. See COUNTENANCE.

LOOMING adj.   in the cards, in the wind, at hand, see it coming, looking to, the noose is hanging, the handwriting is on the wall.

LOOPHOLE n.   out, kicker (one that negates work, contract, etc.), fine print, small fine print, small fine print at the bottom.

LOOSE adj.   high liver, nighthawk, night owl, playboy, player, swinger, operator, speed; out of control. See DISSOLUTE.

LOOT n.   take, graft, goods, hot goods, hot items, swag, squeeze, boodle, make, pickings.

LOOT v.   grab, smash and grab, rip, rip off, boost, lift, loft, kipe, snatch, snitch, swipe, salvage, appropriate, liberate, requisition, moonlight requisition, buzz, crab, make, take, tip over.

LOQUACIOUS adj.   great talker, yacker, gift of gab, shoots the gab, long-winded, windjammer, ear-bender, all jaw, flapjaw, motormouth, have verbal diarrhea, diarrhea of the mouth. See TALKATIVE.

LORD n.   Dad, Head Knock, Lordy, Man Upstairs.

LORDLY adj.   bossy, crack the whip, high and mighty, on one's high horse, throw one's weight around. See ARROGANT.

LOS ANGELES, CALIFORNIA   L.A., Ellay, Los, LaLa Land, Lotusland, City of the Angels, Angel City, Shaky City, the coast.

LOS ANGELES RESIDENT n.   Angeleno, Angelena, Angelino, Angelina, Angel.

LOSE v.   crap out, boff out, lose out, be taken to the cleaners, drop, drop a bundle (money), bite the dust, take the count, take a bath, take a splash, blow, kiss good-bye, pump up (gambling), drawing dead, come out on the short end of the stick, come out with the short end of the stick, take the heat, be bumped (reservation). See FAIL.

LOSE CONSCIOUSNESS v.   pass out, conk out, zonk out, keel over, black out, go out like a light.

LOSE CONTROL v.   come unglued, come unzipped, schiz out, psych out, flip, flip out, go ape, go bananas, go to pieces, come apart, blow one's cool, have a fit, have a hemorrhage, have a shit hemorrhage, hit the panic button, push the panic button. See also CRAZY, GO.

LOSE ONE'S NERVE v.   psyched out, choke, choke up.

LOSER n.   also ran, neverwuz, fall guy, deadbeat, turkey, down and outer, can't even get arrested, can't even write home for money, can't punch his way out of a paper bag, flunkee. See FAILURE.

LOSING adj.   hurting, cold, dumping, in, into, in for, pump up, wicked, down.

LOSS n.   red ink, fall, beating, trimming, shellacking, trashing, clobbering, walloping, shutout, disaster, flunk, get one's lumps, shuck, total shuck, total loss, come down. See DEFEAT.

LOSSES n.   skunk costs, bundle, package, in the red, red ink.

LOST adj.   1. going in circles, don't know which way is up, bushed (in forest), running by the seat of one's pants. 2. kiss something good-bye, out the window, down the tube, down the toilet, down the drain, down the spout, down the rathole, fall between the cracks.

LOT n. break, breaks, karma, in the cards, the beads, that's the way the beads read, that's the way the cookie crumbles, run of luck, hand (one is dealt). See DESTINY.

LOTTERY n. the numbers, the numbers game.

LOUD adj. leather-lunged, booming, turned up, ear-splitting, ear-poppin', wake up the dead, can't hear one's self think, jumpin', yakky.

LOUDSPEAKER n. P.A. speaker, tweeter, woofer, squawk box, hog caller.

LOUISIANA Lousy Anne, the Creole State, the Pelican State, the Sugar State.

LOUISIANAN n. Pelican.

LOUISVILLE, KENTUCKY Derbyville, Derby Town.

LOUNGE n. 1. squat pad. 2. dive, spot, joint, juke joint, juice joint, after-hours joint, snake ranch, fleshpot, gargle factory, meat market (singles bar), tap room; meat rack, gay bar, (homosexual); water hole, beaver palace, candy store, fern bar, fernie, fillmill, grog mill, guzzery, guzzlery, hideaway, room, rum room. See also BAR.

LOUSE n. cootie, cutie, grayback, seam squirrel, cootie garage (hair puffs in which louse lives).

LOVE n. amore, mash, pash, weakness, case, crash, crush, yen, mad pash, mad for, crazy for, wild for, spoiling for, itch for, hankering, partial to, shine, beaver fever, hot pants, the hots, turn on, calf love, puppy love.

LOVE v. gone on, far gone on, groove on, get high on, freak out on, hipped on, mad on, mad for, mad about, daffy about, wild to, wild for, wild about, crazy about, crazy over, crazy for, queer for, letch, letch for, nuts about, keen, keen on, keen about, have a thing about, wacky about, for, moon for, die over, sweet tooth, sweet on, stuck on, have a case on, have a crush on, have a mash on, have eyes for, have it bad, got it bad, have it for one, be serious, be smitten, that way, carry the torch for, torching, take to, take a liking to, take a shine to, cotton to, partial to, hit it off, wrapped up in, nose open, rings my bell, go for, hot for, have the hots for, have hot pants for, hard-on for, cream for, yen, yen for, itch, itch for, hanker for, fall for, big eyes for, spoil for, give a shit for, give one's kingdom in hell for, give one's eyeteeth for, have one's mouth fixed for, struck by lightning.

LOVE AFFAIR n. 1. affair, a relationship, Roman spring (late in life), thing. 2. hanky-panky, nooner, matinee, tip, tip-out, extracurricular activity, extracurricular sex, extracurricular relations, your place or mine? See AFFAIR.

LOVE, IN adj. gone, gone on, far gone on, hipped on, stuck on, sweet on, wild about, mad about, crazy about, nuts about, gaga about, keen about, struck by lightning, moonstruck, took a fancy to, took a shine to, cottoned to, goofy, goofy about, wrapped up in, smitten, fell for, has a thing about, has a thing for, has one's nose open, head over heels, hooked.

LOVELY adj. drooly, dishy, drop-dead gorgeous, whistle bait, daisy, mink, stone, stone fox, foxy, head rush, scrumptious, stunner, delicious, beaut, knockout, picture. See BEAUTIFUL.

LOVE LETTER n. mash note, Billy do.

LOVE POTION n. love drug, popper, Spanish fly, turn on, wampole.

LOVER n. old lady, squeeze, main squeeze, main dude, main man, ace lane, hamma, mama, sweet mama, sweet papa, daddy, significant other, jelly roll, total babe, back-door man, fancy man, armpiece. See SWEETHEART.

LOVING CARE n. tender loving care, TLC.

LOVING CUP n. pot.

LOW adj. 1. dragged, ass in a sling, dick in the dirt, blue, down, down in the dumps, down and out, down in the mouth, low-down, singing the blues, in the pits, mopey, sad sacky. See DEPRESSED. 2. gross, grody, grody to the max, crumb, creep, turd, heel, shit heel. See OFFENSIVE. 3. blue, off-color, off time. See OBSCENE.

LOWBROW adj. from hunger, galoot, ignoramus, peasant.

LOWER adj. bush league, not hold a candle to, low in the pecking order, low man on the totem pole, second fiddle, second string, poor man's something or one, lower rung. See INFERIOR.

LOWER v. cut back, roll back, downsize, low-ball, leblang (theater ticket price). See REDUCE. See also DEMOTE, BELITTLE.

LOWER CLASS n. peasants, lower cut, the great unwashed, riffraff.

LOWEST adj. the pits, cellar, bottom dollar, bottom rung, bottom man, rock bottom, entry level (job), low man on the totem pole, scraping the bottom of the barrel. See also LEAST.

LOW FIDELITY adj. low fi (Joc.).

LOW LIFE n. sleazeball, crud, gone to bad, gone to the dogs, gone to hell. See VILLAIN.

LOW-MINDED adj. dirty, dirty-minded, dirty old man, mind in the gutter. See also VULGAR.

LOW-PRICED adj. low cost, buy, steal, real steal, cost nothing, cost next to nothing, dirt cheap, cheap as dirt, dog cheap, cheapie, el cheapo, cut rate, low tariff, dime a dozen, bought for a song.

LOYAL adj. true blue, true believer, oncer, string along with, dyed in the wool, behind one, on one's side, ace in, ace through, come through, stand up for one, faithful but not blind.

LSD n. acid, candy, cube, trip, ticket, LSD, LSD-25, 25, cap, flight, big D, coffee, instant Zen, Zen, peace, sugar, sugar lump, sunshine, California sunshine, Hawaiian sunshine, sunshine pill, orange, orange mushrooms, orange wedges, wedges, orange sunshine, yellow sunshine, yellow, mellow yellow, pink, pink swirl, purple flats, purple haze, purple microdots, blue cheer, blue flag, blue heaven, blue mist, strawberry fields, white lightning, clear light, haze, contact lens, Owsley's, Owsley acid, paper acid, blue acid, domes, dots, microdots, brown dots, cherry top, chocolate chips, flats, Lucy in the sky with diamonds, pearly gate, barrels, blotters, frogs, lids, windowpanes, tab.

LSD USE v. baby-sit, copilot, guide (guide one on a trip), experience, trip, head trip, echoes (lingering effect).

LUBRICATE v. grease the wheels, lube, slick, slick on.

LUBRICATION n. grease job, lube, lube job.

LUCID adj. all there, cool, together, got one's head together, in one's right mind. See REASONABLE.

LUCIFER n. the debbil, the Deuce, the Dickens, Old Harry, Old Nick, Old Ned, Old Horny, Old Scratch, Old Gooseberry, Old Bendy, Old Clootie, Old Poker, the Old Gentleman.

LUCK n. Dame Fortune, Lady Luck, run of luck, streak of luck, luck out, lucked out, luck into, lucky strike, lucky scratch, lucky hit, lucky break, break, breaks, big break, good break, mojo (Bl.), fluke, mazel, mazeltov (good), snowball chance, fifty-fifty, toss-up, karma, the beads, in the cards, in the lap of the Gods, that's the way the ball bounces, that's the way the cookie crumbles, that's the way [any number of things].

LUCK, BAD n. snakebit, tough luck, rotten luck, shit out of luck, S.O.L., tough shit, TS, can't even get arrested, up against it, payin' dues, up shit creek, double whammy, bad break, bugaboo. See ADVERSITY.

LUCKY adj. hot, hot hand, on a roll, on a streak, jammy, luck in, luck out, mojo (Bl.), fall into the shithouse and come up with a five-dollar gold piece, get a break, get the breaks, hold aces, turn up trumps, strike oil, strike it rich, strike it lucky, make a lucky strike, golden, hit it, hit it big, lucky dog, all systems go, in the groove, everything's coming up roses, everything going for one; greasing it out, sleazeball, sleazing (tennis shots); door sign, into something.

LUCRATIVE adj. paid off, off the nut, sweet, in the black, cost effective.

LUGGAGE n. bags, carry-on, fortnighter, gear, two-suiter, jiffy bag, keister, valpack, tote, tote bag, meter, peter, slough, swag bag, turkey, things.

LULL n. break, coffee break, break-off, breather, breathing spell, downtime, letup, time-out, layoff.

LULL v. cool, cool out, cool it, cool off, stroke, pour oil on troubled waters, take the edge off, take the bite out, take the sting out of, take it easy, lay back, soft-pedal, put the lid on. See PACIFY.

LUMBER n. load of sticks.

LUMBERING adj. clodhopper, clunker, clunky, two left hands, two left feet, stumblebum, galoot, goaty (Army), goof ball, lead-footed, walrus, klutz, klutzy. See CLUMSY.

LUMINAL PILL n. purple heart.

LUMP n. chunk, gob, goose egg, hickey, hump, hunk, knot, konk.

LUNAR MODULE n. LEM, LM.

LUNAR ROVER n. rover, lunar limo, moon car, moon crawler.

LUNATIC n. zip, dingaling, kook, flake, whacko, screwball, screwloose, schitzo, psycho, freak, nut, nutsy Fagan, nutcake, fruitcake, crackpot, crazy old coot, loon, cuckoo, meshugah, meshugana, squirrel, yo-yo, goof, scatterbrain, lamebrain, a case, snap case, sickie, section 8.

LUNATIC adj. dippy, dingy, kooky, flaky, whacko, loco, screwy, schitzy, schizzed out, schitzoid, psycho, psyched out, freaked out, flipped out, out of one's tree, baked, totally baked, bananas, bonkers, gone ape, off one's rocker, missing a few buttons, lost one's marbles, batty, crazier than a bedbug. See CRAZY.

LUNATIC ASYLUM n. booby hatch, funny farm, nut house, rubber room, soft walk. See INSANE ASYLUM.

LUNCH v. do lunch, do the lunch thing, have a power lunch, brown bag it, grab a bite, take a break, put on the feedbag, brunch (late morning); power lunch, working lunch (business).

LUNCH BOX n. nose bag, brown bag.

LUNCH COUNTER n. fast food, quick and dirty, short order, Coney Island. See also RESTAURANT.

LUNGS n. air bags, wind bags.

LURE n. draw, bait, mousetrap, shill, tout, B-girl, come-on, come-on man, deek, nark, plant, sitting duck, vamp, hook, sweetening, sweetener, humbug. See also INVITATION, BRIBE.

LURE v. pull, grab, draw, bait, mousetrap, shill, steer, tout, drag, turn on, turn one on, hit on, sound on, come on, deek, plant, come on to one, give one the come on, give one a come-hither look, make a hit with, sweep off one's feet, vamp, hook, bat one's eyes at, bat the eyes at, make with bedroom eyes, suck in, rope in, humbug, chum (fishing).

LURID adj. blue, dirty, purple, low-down and dirty, off-color, rough, salty, raunchy. See OBSCENE.

LUSCIOUS adj. delish, yummy, yummy in the tummy, divine, heavenly, scrumptious.

LUST n. bag, itch, hots, hot pants, hot rocks, in heat, lech, nasties, the urge, yen, yen-yen, big eyes, zazzle, weakness, fire in the belly, the munchies (food). See DESIRE.

LUSTFUL adj. horny, heavy, hot, hot and heavy, hot pants, turned on, cream jeans, a lech on, letchin'; hot stuff, filthy, dirty, raunchy, raw, evil-minded, low-down. See LASCIVIOUS.

LUXURIATE v. live high on the hog, live off the fat of the land, live it up, live on easy street, put on the dog, put on the ritz.

LUXURIOUS adj. luxo, plush, plushy, posh, uptown, upscale, ritzy, swanky, fancy, first cabin, ultra-ultra, far out, way out, too much, too-too, high, high on the hog, with all the extras, splendiferous, splendacious, done to the nines. See also WEALTHY, LAVISH, MAGNIFICENT.

LUXURY n. high on the hog, living high on the hog, on top of the heap, lap of luxury, velvet, bed of roses, clover, the life of Riley, Easy Street, egg in one's beer, frill, frills, icing on the cake.

LYING adj. double-crossing, snake in the grass, two-faced, two-timing, jive-assed, sincere, cry crocodile tears.

LYNCH v. stretch, string up, swing, catch rope, dance, go through the trap, hoist, scrag, top, be crooked.

LYNCHING n. necktie party, necktie social, necktie sociable, Texas cakewalk, hemp fever.

LYSERGIC ACID USE v. trip, head trip, flight, experience, on a ride, blow one's mind, guide (guide one on a trip), copilot, baby sit, tripsit, echoes (lingering effect), flashback.

LYSERGIC ACID USER n. acid head, acid dropper, acid user, cube head, Explorer's Club.

M

M n. Mike.

MACABRE adj. spooky, spookish, scary.

MACARONI n. makko, worms, dago.

MACHIAVELLIAN adj. smooth, smarts, street smarts, streetwise, foxy, crazy like a fox, cagey, fancy footwork, full of fancy footwork, slick, slippery, a little gamesmanship, one-upsmanship, sly boots. See also SHREWD.

MACHINATE v. trump up, frame up, come up with, hatch, mastermind, finagle, promote, wangle, play games, pull strings, pull wires. See SCHEME.

MACHINATION n. hanky-panky, monkey business, gamesmanship, one-upsmanship, song and dance, skullduggery, on the make, dirty work, sellout, double shuffle. See also SCHEME.

MACHINATOR n. operator, mastermind, brain, pusher, driver, finagler, wangler, wire-puller, carpetbagger.

MACHINE n. gadget, widget, job, jobby, contraption, dealie bob, sucker, mother, motherfucker, thingumabob, gasser, hootenanny, wingding, coil. See APPARATUS.

MACHINE GUN n. Uzi, tommy, tommy gun, chopper, ack ack, chatterbox, grease gun (submachine gun), lead typer, Chicago piano (Thompson), typewriter, remington.

MACHINE-GUN BULLET n. B.B., bee-bee, hemstitch.

MACHINE GUNNER n. tommy, tommy man, MG.

MACKINTOSH n. mack, fog, slicker.

MAD adj. dingaling, kooky, flaky, whacko, screwball, screwloose, schitzy, schizzed out, schitzoid, psycho, psyched out, flipped one's wig, crackers, nuts, nutsy Fagan, tetched, cutting out paper dolls. See CRAZY.

MADAM n. aunt, Aunt (brothel).

MADDENING adj. 1. uncool, bugs one, pain in the neck, pain in the ass, too much, pesky. See ANNOYING. 2. frantic, wild, cool, real cool, zero cool, mean, mind-blowing, mind-bending, gone, real gone. See EXCITING.

MADHOUSE n. booby hatch, funny farm, loony bin, bughouse, nut house, crazy house, warehouse, nut college, nut farm, zoo. See LUNATIC ASYLUM.

MADLY adv. like crazy, like mad, something fierce, something terrible, flaky, helter-skelter, holus-bolus, hurry-scurry, ramble scramble.

MAFIA n. mafioso, mob, family, famiglia, Cosa Nostra, goombah, outfit, syndicate, gang. See also GANGSTER.

MAGAZINE n. mag, fan mag, fanzine (fan magazine), teenzine, slick, glossy, pulp, joint, limb joint, sheet, rag, throwaway, fuck book (Porno.).

MAGIC n. hocus-pocus, mumbo-jumbo, hoodoo, voodoo, evil eye, go, jinx, whack, whammy, abracadabra.

MAGISTRATE n. beagle, beak, bench nibs, Blackstone, Father Time, gavel jockey, hard rapper, monk, wig, hanging judge.

MAGNANIMITY n. heart, all heart.

MAGNANIMOUS adj. softie, soft touch, big, be big, all heart, bighearted, have a heart, heart in the right place, loose, live with, Santa Claus, good Joe, prince of a person.

MAGNATE n. tycoon, fat cat, the money, big butter and egg man, baron, robber baron. See also BUSINESSMAN.

MAGNIFICENT adj. magnif, magnifico, splendiferous, splendacious, plush, posh, swanky, sooper-dooper, splashy, splurgy, super, super-duper, super-colossal, fab, fat, cool, marvy, unreal, nifty, something, something else, smashing, doozie, dynamite, mad, man-sized, pip, solid gold, tidy, tits, tuff, spiffy, bang-up, ace high, swell, stunning, out of sight, out of this world, like all get out.

MAGNIFY v. pad, pyramid, boost, beef up, hike, hike up, step up, jack up, jump up, run up, up, build up, puff up, blow up, make a federal case out of, snowball, sweeten, sweeten the pot, add fuel to the fire.

MAID n. cleaning lady, cleaning woman, woman, girl, help, live-in, tweeny, pillow puncher, biddy, slavey, cabin girl (chambermaid).

MAIDEN n. 1. cherry, canned goods, bug. 2. chick, chicklet, spring chicken, bird, broad, doll, jailbait, San Quentin quail, frill, frail, cupcake, filly, slip, babe, baby. See GIRL.

MAIL CAR n. blind, blind baggage.

MAIL CLERK n. intermodalist (business).

MAIMED adj. gimp, gimpy, crip, game, g'd up, geed up, hamstrung, hog-tied.

MAINE the Pine Tree State.

MAINE RESIDENT n. Mainiac, down easter.

MAIN OFFICE n. HQ, GHQ, CP. See also HEADQUARTERS.

MAINSTAY n. good right arm, right-hand man, main man, old standby, standby, linchpin.

MAIN STREET n. main artery, main stem, funky Broadway.

MAINTENANCE n. the wherewithal, keep, bread, bread and butter, the bacon, the necessary.

MAJESTIC adj. stunning, cool, fab, marvy, mind-blowing, out of sight, clean outta sight, out of this world, smashing, bang-up, ace high, big splash. See also DIGNIFIED.

MAJOR adj. heavyweight, meaningful, serious shit, serious jelly, matter of life and death, major league, we're not talking about nutmeg here. 2. biggie, big player, big chew, big wheel, major league, movers and shakers, top dog, a somebody. See IMPORTANT.

MAJOR n. leaf (Army or A.F.), star.

MAJORITY n. 1. prime, prime of life, dry behind the ears, ripe age, age of consent, drinking age. See MATURITY. 2. big end, big half, lion's share, big end of the stick, max, maxi, the most, the mostest.

MAJOR ROLE n. fat part, lead, star, mover and shaker, key player.

MAKE v. 1. whip up, whip out, whomp up, cook up, dream up, throw up, throw together, fudge together, knock together, knock out, knock off, dash off, tear off. 2. drag down, make a buck, pull, pull down, clear, hustle, rate, sock, turn, bring home the bacon, bring home the groceries, cop, get along, keep the wolf from the door, pay one's dues, be in line for.

MAKE LOVE v. lallygag, lollygag, rock, roll, rock and roll, date, make it, make out, go all the way, fool around, a little heavy breathing, he'n and she'n, fun and games, do it, do the dirty deed, go to bed with, go the limit, get it on, get it off together. See also SEXUAL INTERCOURSE.

MAKESHIFT adj. band-aid, temp, fly-by-night, hit or miss, Mickey Mouse, rinkydink, dink, slapdash, hugger-mugger, throwaway.

MAKEUP n. drugstore complexion, paint, war paint.

MAKE UP v. 1. ad lib, play it by ear, impro, improv, wing it, fake it, off the cuff, dash off, strike off, knock off, toss off, whip up, cook up, whomp up, fudge together.

See IMPROVISE. 2. put on one's face, put on one's war paint, powder one's nose, fix up, freshen up.

MAKEUP MAN n. grease pusher.

MALADROIT adj. klutzy, clunky, all thumbs, ham-fisted, ham-handed, two left hands, two left feet, stumblebum, garbage time. See CLUMSY.

MALADY n. bug, crud, creeping crud, the flu, virus, the runs, what's going around, the pip, willies (mythical), dose, double scrudfantods, fascinoma (rare, Medic.), blue flu (faking it), Asian flu, summer flu, 24-hour flu, 24-hour virus.

MALCONTENT n. bitcher, bellyacher, kvetch, whiner, crab, crank, pill, plainer, sorehead, nitpicker. See COMPLAINER.

MALE n. dude, hunk, tuna, beefcake, man, big man, papa, macho, jock, caveman, ape, butch, stud, wolf, john, goon, he-man, hombre, bruiser, bozo, tiger. See MAN.

MALEDICTION n. whammy, double whammy, jinx, cuss, cuss word, dirty word, dirty name, four-letter word, no-no, swearword, kibosh, hoodoo.

MALEFACTOR n. crook, hood, heel, mug, bad actor, bad egg, fagin, gorilla, wrong number, hooligan, strongarm man, goon, hatchet man. See CRIMINAL.

MALE PARENT n. old man, O.M., dad, daddy, big daddy, daddio, daddums, pa, papa, pappy, pap, pop, pops, poppa, padre, pater, governor, guv, warden.

MALEVOLENT adj. bad-assed, dirty, rough, tough, nuts, poison, bum, lousy, murder, murderous, kill-crazy, catty, evil, waspish, snake in the grass, doin' dirt, eighteen carat, hellish. See MALICIOUS.

MALFUNCTION n. bug, glitch, gremlins.

MALIBU n. Bu..

MALICIOUS adj. uncool, unhep, unhipped, awful, beastly, bitchy, cussed, mean, ornery, low blow, gross, grody, grody to the max, pesky, pestiferous, funky (Bl.), accidentally on purpose, do one dirt, give one a raw deal. See also MEAN.

MALIGN v. smear, roast, rap, take a swipe at, do a number on, mudsling, run down, run into the ground, poor-mouth, bad-mouth, rip up the back, give a black eye. See SLANDER.

MALINGER v. fuck off, goof off, fluff off, flub off, flub, flub the dub, goldbrick, dog, dog it, fuck the dog, featherbed, lie down on the job, look busy, find Rover (work).

MALINGERER n. fuck-off, goof off, goldbrick, dog, deadwood, buck passer, clock-watcher, coffee cooler, featherbedder, skimper.

MALLEABLE adj. putty in one's hands, go with the flow, roll with the punches. See also SUBMISSIVE.

MALODOROUS adj. stinko, stinky, strong, high, whiffy, phooey, nosey, lousy, rotten, gooky, yechy.

MAN n. guy, dude, hunk, tuna, beefcake, man, big man, feller, pops, papa, cool papa, daddy, daddio, big daddy, sugar daddy, gent, macho, jock, caveman, cat, cap, mac, ape, monkey, fox, bub, buster, butch, chap, chappie, stud, stallion, cock, cocksucker (Obsc.), cocksman, rooster, ass man, jelly roll, wolf, rake, ladies' man, Don Juan, Casanova, Joe, Jack, Joe Blow, Joe Doakes, Joe Zilch, john, poor John (less fortunate), John Doe, Richard Roe, Herman, lounge lizard, cake-eater, cowboy, bucker, buckeroo, clown, cookie, hipster, digger, gate, old softie, old smoothie, customer, goon, mug, colt, duck, gee, hardleg, hairy, he-man, hombre, two-fisted, crud, cuss, dog, dirty dog, bastard, sidewinder, stiff, storch, wise guy, bum, bummer, bugger, bommer (1930), boilermaker, bruiser, bozo, tiger, apple, applehead, Arab, geezer, geezle, gazabo, ginzo, hairpin, meat, pants, lad, boy, boyo, big boy, Broadway boy (gambler), bo, blade, gay blade, bloke, blood (Bl.), bird, brother, prune, cracker, hick (southern), huckleberry, joker, jasper, party, character.

MANACLE v. cuff, put on the cuffs, put on the bracelets.

MANACLES n. bracelets, cuffs, cufflinks, thumbs, darbies, derbies, irons, nippers, slave bracelets.

MANAGE v. 1. fix, finagle, spin control (manage opinion), wangle, push around, mind-fuck, rig, doctor, cook, plant, con, scam, upstage, jockey, play games, pull strings, pull wires, wire-pull, swing, work, put one on, put one over, put over. 2. head, head up, boss, captain, skipper, helm, herd, shepherd, ride herd on, sit on top of, run, run things, run the show, hold the reins, pull the strings, push the buttons, mastermind, quarterback, call the shots, call the signals, call the tune, call the play, lay down the law, be in the driver's seat, be in the saddle, pull the strings, pull the wires, pull things together, take over, take the conn, walk heavy, crack the whip, throw one's weight around, have the say, have the say so, rule the roost, wear the pants, keep under one's thumb, twist around one's little finger, wind around one's little finger. 3. get a handle on something, hack, hack it, get on, get along, come on, come along, cut the mustard, make it, make out, make the grade, make a go of it, live with, deal with, truck with, cool down, cool off, handle, deal, deal with, shape up, straighten up, handle.

MANAGEMENT n. front office, execs, executive suite, man upstairs, people upstairs, people in the front office, micro management (petty), mainframe management, brass, top brass, head, big brother, bosses, boss class ('30s), shakeup (change). See also EXECUTIVE, ADMINISTRATION.

MANAGER n. boss, head man, old man, top dog, top hand, topkick, digger, the man, boss man, boss lady, straw boss, slave driver, zookeeper. See EXECUTIVE.

MANDATE n. blank check, carte blanche, go-ahead, green light.

MANDRAKE n. devil's testicle, Satan's apple.

MANEUVER n. stunt, angle, play, game, plant, one-upsmanship, curveball, fancy footwork, fast shuffle, shenanigans. See STRATAGEM.

MANEUVER v. rig, angle, wangle, work, come up with, upstage, doctor, cook, plant, con, scam, mind-fuck, put one on, put one over, jockey, push around, leave holding the bag, operate, play games, pull strings, pull wires, wire-pull, finagle, back and fill, fence, go around. See also PLAN, SCHEME.

MANEUVERABLE REENTRY VEHICLE n. MRV, MERV.

MANIA n. hang-up, jones, have a thing about, have on the brain, grabber, tiger, tiger by the tail, bee, bee in one's bonnet, bug, bug in one's ear, bug up one's ass, bag, ax to grind. See OBSESSION.

MANIAC n. zip, kook, flake, whacko, screwball, schitzo, schitzoid, psycho, nut, fruitcake, crackpot, cuckoo, sickie, section 8. See CRAZY.

MANIACAL adj. psycho, psyched out, freaked out, flipped, out of one's mind, in the ozone, nutty as a fruitcake, off one's trolley, snakes in one's head, non compos mentis, bughouse. See CRAZY.

MANIC adj. high, up, hopped up, turned on, freaky, freaked out, flipped, flipped out, worked up into a lather. See EXCITED. See also CRAZY.

MANIFEST adj. clear-cut, crystal clear, big as life, open and shut, if it were a snake it would bite you, cheesecloth (person), commando (sex), jazzy. See APPARENT.

MANIFEST v. flash, sport, let it all hang out, showcase, show and tell, parade one's wares, strut one's stuff, wave it around. See DISPLAY.

MANIPULATE v. spin control (opinion), mind-fuck, finagle, massage, push around, upstage, jockey, play games, pull strings, pull wires, wind around one's little finger. See MANAGE.

MANLY adj. he-man, hunk, macho, beefcake, stud, jock, jockstrap, two-fisted, caveman, bucko, hairy, jelly roll, tiger, colt, chrismo, chismo. See FEARLESS. See also MAN.

MANNERED adj. campy, camp around, artsy, artsy-crafty, artsy-fartsy, chichi, putting on the dog, putting on the ritz, ritzy, stuck up, airish, crooker, pinky crooker, high falutin', ham, gone Hollywood, play the ————, put the hat on. See PRETENTIOUS.

MANNERS n. P's and Q's, minding one's p's and q's.

MAN OF ACTION n. go-getter, hustler, ball of fire, live wire, powerhouse, workaholic, beaver, eager beaver, operator, big-time operator, BTO, wheeler-dealer, new broom, take-charge guy, spark plug, mover and shaker, human dynamo, busy bee.

MANSERVANT n. man, man Friday, boy, number one boy, pratt boy, flunky, houseman, houseboy. See also SERVANT.

MANUAL n. bible, cookbook (chem lab).

MANUAL LABOR n. grind, daily grind, grindstone, the salt mines, gruntwork (Army), scutwork, donkeywork, hemo jo (hard labor), shitwork, chickwork (household), elbow grease; rank and file, blue collar. See WORK.

MANUFACTURE v. prefab, throw together, knock together, fudge together, whomp up, cobble up, cook up, trump up, whomp up, throw up, knock up, whip up, put out.

MANURE n. shit, horseshit, cowshit, lawn dressing, meadow muffins, road apples, alley apples, golden apples, buffalo chips, cow chips, cow flops, cow pats, turd, moose beans, moose nuggets, moose pecans.

MANUSCRIPT n. ms., script, pages.

MANY adj. umpteen, jillion, loads, rafts, whole slew, gobs, scads, mess, heaps, bags of, oodles, lousy with, no end of. See AMOUNT, LARGE.

MAR v. ding, tweak, bend the goods, fuck up, foul up, mess up, rough up, shake up, screw up, louse up, hash up, muck up, queer. See DAMAGE.

MARBLES n. migs, mibs, cat's eye, aggies, canicks, shooters, commy (cheap glass), immies, peewees, pottrie, purey, real.

MARCH v. drill, hoof it, boot, boot it, stomp, pound the pavement, move out, stump it, trapse, trapse around, strut one's stuff. See WALK.

MARGARINE n. marge, oleo, hard oil.

MARGIN n. elbowroom, leeway.

MARIJUANA n. pot, grass, joint, reefer, reefer weed, weed, lone weed, viper's weed, hash, shit, hemp, T, tea, jay, roach, Mary, Mary Jane, Mary Anne, Mary Wanna, Mary Warner, greefo, grefa, grafa, greapha, sensemilla, sinsemilla, hay, Indian hay, mezz, the mighty mezz, Thai stick, Mexican red, Mexican brown, Panamanian red, Panama red, gold, Acapulco gold, Colombian gold, Santa Marta gold, African black, Jersey green, golden leaf, Maui-wowee, beetle, belt, birdwood, bomber, belt, drag, hit, bush, charge, beat, dynamite, fu, gauge, stick, stick of gage, herb, goof ball, spliff, jadja, Indian hemp, smoke, joy smoke, giggle smoke, giggle weed, juane, kef, keef, kief, moocah, muggles, mohasky, pod, Texas Tea, splay, red dirt marijuana, salt and pepper, stuff, snap, snop, boo, gungeon, black gunion, jabooby, Lipton's (fake), weed tea, yesca, Alice B. Toklas brownies, Jim Jones (marijuana laced with cocaine dipped in PCP), bush, mootah, mu, panatella, dope, rope, seed, baby, blue sage, dagga, 13-M, bo bo, dew, bar, gold leaf, manicure, sweet Lucy, baby, Banji, bhang, catnip, Coli, sativa, ace, cheeba.

MARIJUANA ADDICT n. hash head, viper, grasshopper.

MARIJUANA AMOUNT n. bag, dime bag, nickel bag, dime's worth, cap; matchbox, stick (cigarette); quarter bag, can, lid, O.Z., weight (oz.); elbow (lb.), key, kee, ki (kilo); brick (compressed kilo).

MARIJUANA CIGARETTE n. joint, reefer, J., jay, J. smoke, mezz, mighty mezz, stick, stick of T, stick of tea, weed, dream stick, tea stick, joy stick, J-stick, jive stick, kick stick, giggle stick, thumbs, drag, gage, stick of gage, gage butt, giggle smoke, good butt, goof butt, gow, greefa, griffa, goifa, greeta, reefer, bomber, hooter, jolt, gyve, jive, gangster, hemp, juju, killer, Mary Jane, Mary Ann, funny cigarette, left-handed cigarette, bomb, bone, fatty, nail, number, rainy day woman, root, mooter, moota, mootie, muggles, number, reefer weed, birdwood, ace, cocktail, dube, dubby, rocket, twist, mezzrole; spliff, straight slim, square (half tobacco); A-bomb (contains heroin or opium), burnies (shared), roach (butt).

MARIJUANA PARAPHERNALIA n. roach clip, airplane, crutch, snap (holder); bong (pipe), marygin (seed remover), stash bag, stash box, stash jar, Woodstock emergency pipe (aluminum foil).

MARIJUANA SELLER n. reefer man, viper, pad (sales place).

MARIJUANA SMOKING SITE n. balloon room, ballroom, head shop, parachute, spot.

MARIJUANA USE v. drag, hit, toke, blow smoke, blow gage, blast, bogart, buzz (effect), catch a buzz, gage, get high, kick the gong around, bang, mainline, hit the mainline, shoot the pin, take a shot, sent, tead up, tea pad, tea party.

MARIJUANA USER n. head, pothead, user, fiend, tripper, doper, freak, junkie, grasshopper, hay burner, tea man, tea toker, Alice B. Toklas, Toklas, viper, belongs to M.J.

MARIMBA n. woodpile.

MARINE n. gyrene, leatherneck, jar head, seagoing bellhop, skinhead (recruit), devil dog, bullet bait (untrained), cannon fodder.

MARINE BASE n. green machine.

MARINER n. mate, shipmate, sea dog, gob, swab, bluejacket, salt, old salt, yachtie.

MARITIME CREW n. grease monkey, grease rat (Navy).

MARK n. logo, brand, X, autograph, sig, fist, ink, John Hancock, John Henry, on the dotted line.

MARK v. brand, X, autograph, sig, ink, put your John Hancock on the dotted line, pinpoint, pin, spot, spotlight, limelight, button down, finger, put the finger on, put one's finger on something, make, peg, put down for, tab, tag. See also INDICATE.

MARKET n. 1. contact, truck, Wall Street, the Exchange, the Big Board, over the counter. 2. supermarket, superette, super, deli, stand, co-op, bodega (liquor or NYC grocery), down to the corner for a bottle. See STORE.

MARKETABLE adj. bankable, hotcake, hot item, hot property, hot ticket.

MARKET, ILLEGAL n. black market, under the counter, the street.

MARRED adj. dinged, fucked up. See DAMAGED.

MARRIAGE n. bells, wedding bells, shotgun wedding, hook.

MARRIAGE BROKER n. matchmaker, schatchen, shotgun.

MARRIED adj. hitched, hooked, tied, wear a hat, have a hat, have papers (Bl.).

MARRIED MAN n. old man, O.M., better half, brown bagger, breadwinner, goonie, shack man, on the hitch.

MARRIED WOMAN n. old lady, O.L., better half, little woman, wiff, roommate, ball and chain, block and tackle, grass widow, War Department. See WIFE.

MARRY v. hitch, get hitched, hitch up, splice, get spliced, hook, tie the knot, merge, middle-aisle it, walk down the aisle, put the clamps on, rob the cradle, cradle-snatch, tie down, land, wedding bell it, snap on the ol' ball and chain, take the plunge, jump off the deep end, jump the hurdle, step off, step off the carpet, settle down.

MARSHAL n. cop, fuzz, copper, shamus, flic, cossack, arm, dick, pig, oink, clown (rural), the man, badge, big brother, boy scouts, county Joe, county mounty, county mountie, hick dick, law, local yard, local yokel, local boy. See POLICE OFFICER.

MART n. 1. discount house, superette, supermarket, the grab, schlock joint, chain store, outlet store, co-op. See STORE. 2. Wall Street, the Exchange, the Big Board, over the counter.

MARTINI n. martooni, see through.

MARVEL n. one for the book, something else, something to shout about, something to write home about, stunner.

MARVELOUS adj. marvy, fab, fantasmo, super, super-duper, bad, terrible, grimey, frantic, solid, solid sender, solid gold, outrageous, out of this world, the greatest, boss, skrouk. See FABULOUS.

MARYLAND Free State, Old Line State, Terrapin State.

MASCULINE adj. hunk, tuna, beefcake, daddio, macho, jock, caveman, ape, stud, stallion, cock, hairy, he-man, hombre, two-fisted, bruiser, bo, blood (Bl.). See MAN.

MASH v. scrunch, squish.

MASK n. fig leaf, cover, cover-up, front, beard.

MASK v. cover, cover up, front (usually illegal activities); beard. See also COVER UP.

MASOCHISM n. M, SM, into SM, leather, into leather, bondage, endo.

MASOCHIST n. glutton for punishment.

MASQUERADER n. fake, faker, four-flusher, fraud, gouge, phony, all front, a put-on. See also CHEATER.

MASS n. hunk, chunk, gob, goose egg, hickey, hump, knot, konk. See also AMOUNT, LARGE.

MASSACHUSETTS Bay State, Old Colony.

MASSAGE n. beating, rub, Rolfe.

MASSAGE v. Rolfe, rub down.

MASSAGE PARLOR n. rap club, rap parlor. See also BROTHEL.

MASSES n. the mob, the great unwashed, the public, John Q. Public, Billy Sixpack, Joe Lunchbucket, hoi polloi.

MASSIVE adj. gross, humongous, humungous, mungo, monstro, doby, big mother, colossal, blimp, barn door, walloping, whopping, whopper. See BIG.

MAST n. pole, stick, tree.

MASTECTOMY n. boob job.

MASTER n. 1. pro, real pro, old pro, ol' professor, old hand, old war-horse, maven, whiz, whiz-bang, wizard, buff. See AUTHORITY. 2. numero uno, chief, head man, skipper, general, Mister Charlie (Bl.), big player, big gun, wheel, big cheese, top hand, topkick, top dog, avatar, pro, old man, spark plug, whip hand, slave driver. See EXECUTIVE.

MASTER v. 1. break, break in, bust, gentle, run the show, call the shots, ride herd on, henpeck, crack the whip, pussywhip (female), rule the roost, keep under one's thumb, lead by the nose, have the upper hand, have it covered, have the say, have the say so, hold the reins, pull the ropes, pull the strings, pull the wires, reel one back in, bring to heel, box in, get one in a box, get one's hooks into, sit on top of. See MANAGE. 2. beat the game, beat the system, run away with, win out, put on ice, blow 'em away, swamp, sink the opposition, make a payday. See WIN. 3. hit the books, megastudy, grind, plug, pour it on, bone up, bury oneself in, cram, skull drag, hardwire (by rote). See STUDY. 4. get down, get down pat, get down cold, get hold of, get into one's head, get the hang of, get the knack of, pick up, learn backwards and forwards, learn the ropes.

MASTER OF CEREMONIES n. emcee, MC, femcee, the chair.

MASTERFUL adj. bossy, crack the whip, high and mighty, on one's high horse, throw one's weight around, dealing with, got a handle on it, ice man, in charge, in the driver's seat. See also IMPERIOUS, POWERFUL.

MASTICATE v. chaw, munch, chomp, gum, fling a fang into.

MASTURBATE v. bop, she-bop, bop one's baloney, jack off, jerk off, beat off, beat the dummy, beat one's meat, pull one's pud, pound one's pud, play with one's self, beat the bishop, whack the bishop, flog the dummy, flog the sausage, flog one's dong, milk, milk the chicken, milk the lizard, choke the chicken, paddle the pickle, jerk the gherkin, fist fuck, fuck Mary Fist, jerk, frig, diddle (female), wank off, screw off, fuck off, fingerfuck, give a hand job, hand jive, play pocket pool, ream, sew, stroke, circle jerk (group) (all Obsc.).

MASTURBATION n. hand job, hand jive, jerking off, bananas and cream, bishop beating, pocket pool, dong flogging, fist fuck, gherkin jerking, chicken milking, lizard milking, Mary Fist, pickle paddling, circle jerk (group) (all Obsc.).

MASTURBATOR n. diddler, jerk, jerk-off.

MATCH n. 1. light, Lucifer, snapper, fire. 2. go.

MATCH v. 1. put two and two together, jive, click. See also EQUAL. 2. lip-sync, sync, sync up.

MATCHED adj. in sync.

MATCHMAKER n. schatchen, shotgun.

MATE n. 1. old man, O.M., old lady, O.L., breadwinner, better half, roommate, ball and chain,

block and tackle, front office. See SPOUSE. 2. amigo, brother, sister, buddy, asshole buddy, chum, roomie, roommate, pard, playmate, matie, pal, sidekick. See FRIEND. 3. like of, likes of, look alikes, peas in a pod, two of a kind.

MATE v. 1. get hitched, get spliced, tie the knot, merge, middle aisle it, land, snap on the ol' ball and chain. See MARRY. 2. fuck, screw, lay, hump, ball, bang, boff, jazz, dork, ride, do the deed, do the dirty deed, bed down, go to bed with, go the limit, get it off together. See SEXUAL INTERCOURSE.

MATHEMATICS n. math, number crunching.

MATING n. fuck, screw, lay, boff, plowin', bang, action, balling, shot, roll in the hay, score, the business, meat injection, night baseball, fooling around, bush patrol, he'n and she'n, she'n and she'n, he'n and he'n, fun and games. See SEXUAL INTERCOURSE.

MATRIMONY n. bells, wedding bells, shotgun wedding, hook.

MATTER n. bag, goings-on, job, lookout, nub, thing. See also SUBSTANCE, PREDICAMENT.

MATTER v. cut ice, cut some ice, carry weight.

MATTRESS n. fleabag, donkey's breakfast (straw).

MATURE v. 1. arrive, get hip, grow up, cut one's eyeteeth, cut one's wisdom teeth, have sown one's wild oats, settle down. 2. snowball, mushroom, shoot up, blossom.

MATURITY n. prime, prime of life, dry behind the ears, ripe age, age of consent, drinking age.

MAUDLIN adj. syrupy, drippy, soap, soapy, slush, teary, cornball, mushy, schmaltzy. See SENTIMENTAL.

MAUL v. work over, wax, skin, take it out of one's hide, take it out of one's skin, muscle, mug, paw, bash, bung, bung up, paste, hurt, kick ass, whip ass, lean on, clean on, take care of, wipe up the floor with, wipe up the place with, make mince meat out of, make hamburger out of, punch one out, knock around, jump all over, let one have it, put one in the hospital, go over, break one's face. See also HIT, WOUND.

MAWKISH adj. sticky, icky, gooey, sappy, sloppy, gushing, teary, beery, namby-pamby. See SENTIMENTAL.

MAXIM n. daffodil.

MAXIMUM adj. max, maxi, the most, the mostest, the end, the livin' end. See also SUPERLATIVE.

MAYONNAISE n. mayo.

MAYOR n. city father, hizzoner.

MDMA n. ecstasy.

ME pro.   big three (me, myself and I), number one, numero uno, yours truly, Dudley, Uncle Dudley, ol' Uncle Dudley.

MEADOW n.   green deck, carpet, rug.

MEAGER adj.   1. bupkis, chicken shit, too little too late, zilch. See NOTHING. See also SCANT. 2. skinny, gangling, gangly, twiggy, rattleboned, bag of bones, stack of bones, skin and bones, gangleshanks, bean pole, bean stalk, broomstick. See THIN.

MEAL n.   chow, chow time, eats, feed, feedbag, nosebag, grub, grub pile, ribs, cookout, brunch, din din, squares, square meal, mess, blue plate, black plate (soul food), pecks, peckings (Bl.), potluck; power lunch, power breakfast, working breakfast (business); hot (hobo). See also FOOD.

MEAL TICKET n.   grazing ticket.

MEAN adj.   meanie, down, dirty, low-down and dirty, low-down no-good, louse, lousy, rat, bitchy, son of a bitch, SOB, so and so, son of a so and so, son of a gun, chicken shit, hard, hard-nosed, snide, the lowest, stinker, stinkeroo, stinking, shtoonk, sucks eggs. See DESPICABLE.

MEAN v.   talking (I'm talking big bucks), cut ice, cut some ice, go into one's dance (The.). See also INFER.

MEANDER v.   get sidetracked, all over the map. See WANDER.

MEANING n.   point, stuff, bottom line, name of the game, nitty-gritty, nuts and bolts, the way of it, nature of the beast, drift, heart, meat, nub, score, punch line, kicker (point of a story, joke, etc.).

MEANINGFUL adj.   heavy, deep. See IMPORTANT.

MEANINGLESS adj.   double-talk, doublespeak, hot air, that doesn't chop any wood, that doesn't cut any ice, big zero, nothing, makes no never mind, nutmeg. See UNIMPORTANT.

MEANS n.   1. bankroll, nut, nest egg, rainy day, sock, mattress full, kitty, stake, backing, budget, ace in the hole, ace up one's sleeve (hidden), stuff. 2. Band-Aid, dodge, gimmick, trick.

MEASURE n.   hit, shot, fix, nip, slug, bang, dram.

MEASURE v.   peg, size, size up, check, check out, dig it, eye, look over, read, have one's number, take one's measure, dope out, take account of, figure, figure in, guesstimate.

MEATLOAF n.   mystery, rubber heels.

MECHANIC n.   grease monkey, wrench.

MECHANICAL adj.   1. go through the motions, phone it in, walk through it, by the numbers. 2. ticky.

MECHANICAL BREAKDOWN n.   down, downtime, on the fritz, on the blink. See DAMAGED.

MECHANICS n.   nuts and bolts.

MECHANISM n.   idiot box, black box, job, jobby, dealie bob, gimmick, thingamajig, dohinkey, dingus, wingding, coil.

MEDALS n.   fruit salad, brag rags, chest hardware, chicken guts (trimmings), gong, gonger, hardware, no clap medal, the gold.

MEDDLE v.   mix in, butt in, horn in, stick one's nose in, kibitz, get on one's case, put one's two cents in, monkey with, fuck around with, futz around with. See INTERFERE.

MEDDLER n.   buttinsky, kibitzer, snoop, yenta, backseat driver, nosey Parker, Paul Pry, crasher, gate-crasher.

MEDDLESOME adj.   nosey, pushy, snoopy.

MEDIATE v.   make a deal, meet halfway, strike a happy medium, go fifty-fifty, can't fight 'm join 'em, come to school, trade off, settle.

MEDIATOR n.   rent-a-judge, middleman, umpire, ref, go-between, fixer.

MEDICAL ATTENDANT n.   candy stripper, medic, bedpan commando (WW II), titless nurse (medical corpsman).

MEDICAL BILL FRAUD n.   ping pong.

MEDICAL EXAMINATION n.   check up, physical, exam.

MEDICAL STUDENT n.   med, pre-med.

MEDICATE v.   doctor, dope, dope up, dose, dose up.

MEDIOCRE adj.   so so, fair, fair to middling, run of the alley, run of the mill, no great shakes, strictly union, humdrum, mainstream, vanilla, starch. See AVERAGE.

MEDIOCRITY n.   meatballism, hamfat.

MEDITATE v.   moon, woolgather, head trip, noodle, noodle it around, put on one's thinking cap, figger, chew the cud, track, blow change. See THINK.

MEDLEY n.   mixed bag, combo, duke's mixture, mishmash, mishmosh, everything but the kitchen sink.

MEEK adj.   weak sister, Milquetoast, Casper Milquetoast, wishy-washy, tail between one's legs, schnook, pablum, zero. See also SUBMISSION.

MEET v.   bump into, run into, run up against, come up against, go up against, meet face to face, meet eyeball to eyeball, meet up with, make a meet, take a meet, have a meet, dig up, pop upon, rub eyeballs, run smack into, strike, rendezvous with, get together, show. See also ASSEMBLE, FACE, QUALIFY, SUFFICE.

MEETING n. 1. confab, one on one, clambake, affair, meet, rally, pep rally, gang, bunch, crowd, get-together, barbeque, huddle, call, cattle call, powwow, session, buzz session, rap, rap session, bull session, bitch session, jam session, gig, sit-in, turnout, ashram, groupie, mob, mess, flap (urgent), showdown, gam; triff, tref, (clandestine); put heads together. 2. date, heavy date, blind date, love nest, matinee, noonie, one-night stand, quickie, rendezvous, meet.

MEETINGHOUSE n. aud, Amen Corner, dirge factory, god box.

MEETING PLACE n. hangout, place, in-place, spot, stamping ground, the grab, big store, dinghe, hideout, hole, jungle, meet, plant, scatter, shebang, spot, stash (U.).

MEET REQUIREMENTS v. come up to snuff, cut it, cut the mustard, check out, make the cut, get by, score, fill the bill, make it, make the grade, pass, pass muster.

MEGRIM n. head, have a head, hangover, migraine.

MELANCHOLIA n. blahs, blah-blahs, blues, blue devils, blue funk, funk, bummer, downer, down trip, letdown, dolefuls, dismals, dumps, mumps, mopes, mokers, mulligrubs.

MELANCHOLY adj. dragged, ripped, low, destroyed, dragging ass, have one's ass in a sling, dick in the dirt, blue, in a blue funk, funky, grim, got the blue devils, in the toilet, in the dumper, in the dumps, down, on a downer, letdown, taken down, taken down a peg, down in the dumps, in the doleful dumps, down and out, down in the mouth, downbeat (movie, song, etc.), low-down, crummy, cleek, sob story, sob stuff, tear-jerker, weeper, teardrop special, make like an alligator, have the blues, singing the blues, crying the blues, hang crepe, on a bummer, bummed out, flaked out, put away, carry the torch, hurtin', bleeding, in pain, in the pits, shook, shot down, should have stood in bed, carry a heavy load, off one's feed, rhino, have the mulligrubs, have the dolefuls, have the blahs, clanked, clanked up, cracked up, tore up, all torn up, droopy, mopey, moony, gloomy Gus, wet blanket, raining on one's parade, sad sacky, killjoy, prunefaced, sourpuss, spring fever. See also DESPAIRING.

MELANCHOLY n. blahs, blah-blahs, blues, blue devils, blue funk, funk, bummer, downer, down trip, letdown, dolefuls, dismals, dumps, mumps, mopes, mokers, mulligrubs.

MELANGE n. everything but the kitchen sink, mishmash, mishmosh, mixed bag, combo, duke's mixture (strange), stew, soup (liquid), lorelei.

MELD v. interface, feather in, camouflage, marry; dissolve, cross dissolve (film). See also ASSOCIATE.

MELIORATE v. 1. upgrade, polish, make first rate, up, doll up, pick up. 2. step up, shape up, turn the corner, be out of the woods, come along. 3. get one's act together, get with it, get on the ball, straighten up and fly right, turn things around. See IMPROVE.

MELLOW v. arrive, get hip, grow up, cut one's eyeteeth, cut one's wisdom teeth, have sown one's wild oats, settle down. See also SOFTEN.

MELODRAMA n. meller, melo, chiller, thriller, cliffhanger, barn-burner, corn, cornball, hoke, grabber, penny dreadful, potboiler, Tom Show. See also PLAY.

MELODRAMATIC adj. blood and thunder, cliffhanging, cloak and dagger, ham, hammy, hokey.

MEMBER n. 1. affil (TV), branch, branch house, offshoot. 2. clubber, joiner, blood, blood brother, brother, sister.

MEMORABLE adj. heavy, heavyweight, heavy number, heavy stuff, meaningful, splash, standout, super, super-duper, terrible, terrific, doozie, the most, the utmost, too much, hooper-dooper, the end, far out, mind-blowing, like wow, boss, bitchin', cool, murder, neat, nose cone, some (some show!), like dynamite, daisy, dilly, A, A-1, ace of spades, bang-up, cold, corker, corking, cracking, crackerjack, chill out, serious shit, serious jelly, matter of life and death, something, something else, big league, major league, top drawer, hot shit, we're not talking about nutmeg here, big deal, underlined.

MEMORANDUM n. memo, chit, note.

MEMORIZE v. get it through one's head, get down, get down cold, learn by heart, get by heart, get letter perfect.

MEMORY n. flashback, flash on.

MEMORY LOSS n. blackout, block out, blow, blow a line (The.), don't know if one's comin' or goin', go blank, lose one's marbles, brain fade.

MEMPHIS, TENNESSEE Big M.

MENACE v. lean on, make one an offer one can't refuse, push around, whip one around (intellectually), put on the arm, put on the muscle, put the heat on, bad eye, spook, chill, scare hell out of, scare the shit out of. See INTIMIDATE.

MENACED adj. feel the heat, heat's on, hot, spooked, frozen, goose bumpy, panicked, run scared, shake in one's boots, given a turn, given a jar, given a jolt. See also FRIGHTENED.

MEND v. fix up, doctor, fiddle with.

MENDACITY n. bull, hocky, crap, crock of shit, claptrap, thick, thin, con, cover, cover-up, smoke, string, line, line of cheese, doesn't wash, dirty lie, terminological inexactitude. See LIE.

MENDICANT n. bum, stumblebum, moocher, panhandler, promoter, bag lady, bag woman, stiff, guttersnipe. See BEGGAR.

MENIAL n. help, live-in, girl, woman, man, boy, houseman, houseboy, biddy, furp, peon, serf, slave, slavey, pancake (Uncle Tom). See SERVANT.

MENOPAUSE n. change of life, hot flashes.

MENSTRUATE v. get the curse, have one's period, have the rag on, on the rag, O.T.R., unwell, under the weather, have the monthlies, fall off the roof, having a visitor, got the painters in, little sister's here, come around (late), flagging it, flying the flag, flying the red flag, the red flag is up, Baker flying, the Red Sea's in, wear a red camellia, visit Redbank.

MENSTRUATION n. curse, curse of Eve, period, have the rag on, on the rag, O.T.R., unwell, under the weather, monthlies, that time, that time of the month, fall off the roof, having a visitor, friend, got the painters in, little sister's here, come around (late), dog days, flagging it, flying the flag, flying the red flag, the red flag is up, Baker flying, the Red Sea's in, red camellia.

MENTAL adj. brainy, got the smarts, have savvy, have the smarts, big think, deep, double dome, heavy, gasser, gray matter. See INTELLECTUAL. See also IN-TELLIGENT.

MENTAL ATTITUDE n. head-set, mind-set, mind trip, routine, where one is at, where it's at, where one's head is.

MENTAL BLOCK n. hang-up, hung, hung up, uptight.

MENTAL FATIGUE n. burnout.

MENTAL HOSPITAL n. booby hatch, funny farm, loony bin, bughouse, nut house, warehouse, soft walls, acorn academy, laughing academy, college, nut college, nut factory, nut farm, zoo, cracker factory. See INSANE ASYLUM.

MENTAL LAPSE n. brain fade.

MENTALLY DEFECTIVE adj. retardo, one eye. See also RETARDED.

MENTALLY ILL adj. dingy, loco, in the ozone, un-glued, unzipped, unscrewed, screwloose, schitzy, schizzed out, schitzoid, psycho, psyched out, freaked out, nobody home, out to lunch, out of one's tree, baked, total-ly baked, ape, nerts, not have all one's buttons, batty, loony, haywire, potty, cuckoo, mental job. See CRAZY.

MERCEDES-BENZ n. MBZ, Benzo.

MERCENARY adj. go with the money, flow with the dough, gold digger, money talks bullshit walks, grabby, poligot, greedyguts.

MERCENARY n. merc, soldier of fortune.

MERCHANDISE n. the goods, material, stuff, hot number, jive (gaudy), seconds.

MERCHANDISE, DAMAGED n. ninety-nine.

MERCHANT n. big-time operator, BTO, big wheel, wheeler-dealer, dealer, middleman, tycoon, cockroach (small), nickle-and-dime operator, small potatoes, tradester, robber baron, big butter and egg man. See TRADER.

MERCI BEAUCOUP messy bucket, murky bucket, mercy buckup.

MERCIFUL adj. all heart, bleeding heart (Derog.), old softie, softhearted, heart in the right place; live with, soft shell, go easy with, go easy on.

MERCILESS adj. cutthroat, go for the jugular, killer instinct, mean machine, dog eat dog, hatchet job, take no prisoners. See also CALLOUS.

MERCURIAL adj. yo-yo, up and down, bubbleheaded, gaga, flaky, mad, ad lib, blow hot and cold, race one's motor, have a short fuse, in a stew, in a lather, in a tizzy, in a pucker, hot under the collar, run a temperature, blow up, blow one's stack, blow one's top, blow a gasket, flip, flip one's lid, fly off the handle, hit the ceiling.

MERCURY n. Merc (auto).

MERCY n. clemo, lifesaver.

MERGE v. 1. pool, tie in, come aboard, throw in together, deal one in, plug into, go partners, interface, mob up, join up with, hook up with, line up with, swing in with, meld with, team up with, network with. See ASSOCIATE. 2. hook up, hook on, tag, tag on, tack on, slap on, hitch on. 3. cross dissolve (film), cue in, (scripts, ms., songs), dub, hook in, marry (film), mix (recording).

MERGER n. takeover, tie-up, tie-in tie-up, hookup, cahoots, lineup.

MERGER TERMS takeover, hostile takeover, acquisitions, Pac-Man, raider, poison pill, greenmail, golden parachute, junk bond, crown jewel option, shark repellent, arbs (abitrageurs).

MERINGUE n. calf slobber.

MERIT v. rate, be in line for, what is coming to one, what one has coming, get one's comeuppance.

MERITORIOUS adj. 10, ten, mega-gnarly, winner, choice, rad, top drawer, first chop, boss, good show, golden, hummer, mad, mess, mezz, nasty, nifty, bang-up, world-beater. See EXCELLENT.

MERRIMENT n.   grins, laughs, lots of laughs, high old time, picnic, hoopla, whoopee. See AMUSEMENT.

MERRY adj.   jumping, go-go, grooving, rocking, perky, zippy, zingy, zappy, bouncy, full of go, full tilt, in full swing, swingle, feeling one's oats. See CHEERFUL.

MERRY-GO-ROUND n.   whirligig, goofus, flying ginny (not common).

MERRYMAKING n.   grins, laughs, lots of laughs, high old time, picnic, wingding, shindig, brawl, whoopee, whooper-dooper, hoopla, fun and games. See also REVEL.

MESCALINE n.   big chief, mesc.

MESS n.   bloody mess, holy mess, unholy mess, rat's nest, arsy-varsy, every which way, galley west, hectic, all over hell, all over the shop, discombooberation. See CONFUSION.

MESSAGE n.   news, poop, dope, earful, hot wire; kick in the ass, shot in the ass (bad); cannonball. See also INFORMATION.

MESSENGER n.   boy, shlepper, bag man, runner, speedy, gofer, gopher, smurf (carries illegal money to launder it).

MESS HALL n.   ptomaine palace, ptomaine domain.

MESS SERGEANT n.   bean, cookie, B-boy.

METER n.   beat.

METHADONE n.   meth, dolls, dollies.

METHAMPHETAMINE n.   crystals, Cris, Cristine, crank, elephant, tranquilizer, dynamite, speed.

METHANOL n.   alky.

METHAQUALONE n.   pillow, soap, soaper.

METHEDRINE n.   crystals.

METHEDRINE PILL n.   businessman's trip, crystal, meth, speed.

METHOD n.   channels, red tape, by the numbers, by the book, wrinkle, new wrinkle, nuts and bolts, style, mechanism. See also PLAN.

METHODICAL adj.   grooved, in a groove, by the numbers, by the book, cut and dry, set up, fixed, framed, together, all together, have one's act together, have one's shit together, have one's head together, have one's head screwed on right, laid on. See also NEAT, ORDERLY.

METHYLENEDIOXYAMPHETAMINE n.   ecstasy, MDA.

METHYL FENTENYL n.   china white.

METICULOUS adj.   nitpicker, picky, stickler, dot the i's and cross the t's, fussbudget, fusspot, persnickety, chicken shit, by the numbers. See PARTICULAR.

METROPOLIS n.   urb, burg, apple, Big Town, big time, boomer, boomtown, right tank, slab, two-stemmer, tough town, wide open joint, dump, right tank, wrong tank.

METTLE n.   backbone, grit, guts, moxie, nerve, spunk, heart, starch. See COURAGE.

MEXICAN n.   Latino, Chicano, Chicana; bean, beaner, bean eater, Mex, chili, chili eater, padre, wetback; bracero, dino (laborer); greaser, oiler, hombre, pepper, spic, spig, spiggoty (all Derog.); Tio Taco (Mexican American).

MEXICAN CUISINE n.   Tex Mex, gringo food; Montezuma's revenge, Mexican heartburn, Mexican two-step (the day after).

MICHIGAN   The Wolverine State, Auto State, Lady of the Lakes, Lake State.

MICHIGAN RESIDENT n.   Michigander.

MICROBE n.   bug, crud, creeping crud, the plague, what's going around.

MICROCOMPUTER n.   P.C., micro.

MICROGRAM n.   mike (drug).

MICROMETER n.   mick.

MICROPHONE n.   mike, bug, lollipop.

MICROSCOPE n.   mike.

MIDDLE adj.   mainstream, middle of the road, betwixt and between, halfway in the middle, plump in the middle, smack in the middle, slap in the middle, smack dab in the middle, straddle the fence.

MIDDLE CLASS adj.   plastic, white bread.

MIDDLE CLASS n.   Main Street, Middle America, suburbia, boorjoisie, MODS (teenage).

MIDDLE EASTERN PEOPLE n.   sand niggers, ragheads (Derog.).

MIDDLE FINGER n.   the finger, give one the finger, flip one the finger, single-digit salute, stink finger, the bird, fuck finger, fuck you, give one the bird.

MIDDLEMAN n.   connection, go-between, fixer. See also INFLUENCE.

MIDGET n.   little people, shorty, shrimp, runt, peanut, peewee, squirt, bantam, sawed off, half-pint, half portion, short pint, shortish, dusty butt, knee high, knee high to a grasshopper.

MIDRIFF n.   midsection, gut, spare tire. See also STOMACH.

MIDSHIPMAN n.   middy (Naval Acad.).

MIDSUMMER n.   dog days.

MIDWAY adj. betwixt and between, halfway in the middle, plump in the middle, smack in the middle, slap in the middle, smack dab in the middle, middle of the road, over the hill, over the hump.

MIEN n. cut of one's jib, image, style, act, front.

MIGHT n. zap, sock, the force, beef, clout, might and main, moxie, punch, steam, powerhouse, the stuff, get up and go. See POWER.

MIGHTY adj. got the horses to do it, hoss, strong as a horse, strong as a lion, strong as an ox, powerhouse, steamroller. See POWERFUL.

MIGRAINE n. head, have a head.

MIGRATION n. brain drain, brawn drain.

MIGRATORY WORKER n. wetback, bracero, Okie, short staker, shuffler, stiff.

MILD adj. cool, mellow, vanilla, blah, draddy, flat, ho hum, nothing, nothing much, pablum, weak sister, Milquetoast, Casper Milquetoast, schnook. See also INSIPID.

MILIEU n. bag, scene, thing, space, place, environment, nabe, turf. See also ATMOSPHERE.

MILITARIST n. hawk, Dr. Strangelove, Strangelove.

MILITARISTIC adj. hawkish.

MILITARY DISCHARGE n. section 8 (mental), ruptured duck.

MILITARY OFFICERS n. brass, top brass, brass collar, brass hat, C.O., CINC, CINCPAC, Joint Chiefs, exec, feather merchant (Naval Reserve), ripple (noncom. Waves), Sam Brown, NCO (noncom.).

MILITARY POLICE n. MP, M.P., snowdrop.

MILITARY VEHICLE n. blitz buggy, half-track, jeep, leapin' lena, puddle jumper, weapons carrier.

MILITARY WEAPONS n. hardware.

MILK n. cow, cow juice, moo juice, laiche, cat beer, bovine extract, chalk, Jersey highball, sweet Alice, five, forty-one; armored cow, armored heifer, city cow, canned cow, tin cow, sea cow (canned milk); black cow (chocolate), drive the cow down (pass the milk).

MILK A COW v. juice.

MILKSOP n. chicken heart, candy ass, pecker ass, jellyfish, weak sister, big baby, gutless wonder, nerd, turkey. See EFFEMINATE. See also COWARD.

MILK TOAST n. graveyard stew.

MILL n. shop, sweatshop.

MILWAUKEE, WISCONSIN Beer City, Beer Town.

MIMIC n. copycat; crock, crowk (radio use, animal).

MIMIC v. mirror, ditto, do, do like, make like, go like, take a leaf out of one's book, fake, play the ——— (affect a role). See IMITATE.

MINCE v. whack, hack.

MIND n. brain, box, thinkbox, thinkpad, clockwork, wig. See also INTELLECT.

MIND v. 1. sit, baby-sit, ride herd on, mind the store, toe the line, watch one's step, watch out. 2. get a load of this, get a load of that, give ears, knock on one's lobes, listen up, dig. See HEED.

MINDFUL adj. 1. be up on, hep, on to, hip, in the know, know all the answers, know all the ins and outs, plugged in, tuned in. See KNOWLEDGEABLE. 2. cagey, handle with kid gloves, leery, on the ball, on the job, on one's toes, with one's eyes peeled. See CAUTIOUS.

MINDLESS adj. out, out to lunch, out of it, spaced out, veged out, mooning, moony, pipe dreaming, day dreaming, woolgathering. See UNAWARE.

MINE n. egg (N.), booby trap, bouncing betsy.

MINER n. groundhog, sandhog, desert rat, hard rocker, sourdough, hard ankle.

MINERAL WATER n. mixer, seltzer, soda back (on the side), penny plain, two-cents plain.

MINGLE v. pool, tie in, gang up, network; work the fence, work the room (political). See ASSOCIATE.

MINIATURE adj. mini, minny, teensy, teensy-weensy, itsy-bitsy, mite, pint-sized. See SMALL.

MINIMIZE v. downplay, play down, put down, cut down to size, cut rate, pooh pooh, knock, knock down, pan, poor-mouth. See BELITTLE. See also UNDERPLAY.

MINION n. ass-kisser, ass-licker, tukis licker, brownie, those aren't freckles on his nose, yes-man, nod guy, flunky, flunkystooge, stooge, hanger-on, waterboy, waterman, lackey, sideman. See SYCOPHANT.

MINISTER n. padre, the rev, sky pilot, bible-beater, gospel pusher, preacher man, sin hound, shepherd, glory roader. See CLERGYMAN.

MINISTER v. 1. do for, watch over. 2. boss, ride herd on, run, run the show, head up, sit on top of, be in the driver's seat, hold the reins. See MANAGE.

MINNEAPOLIS, MINNESOTA Big Twin, Minnie, Twin City.

MINNEAPOLIS, ST. PAUL twin cities.

MINNESOTA the Gopher State, the North Star State.

MINNOW n. minny.

MINOR adj. 1. juve, punk, yoot, jailbait, San Quentin quail (Fem.). 2. two bit, ticky-tacky, slimpsy, minus, below the mark, not up to scratch, not up to snuff, plastic, cotton pickin', low, bush league, low man on the totem pole, poor man's something or someone. See also INFERIOR.

MINSTREL SHOW TERMS Bones, Mr. Bones, Mr. Interlocutor (end man), jig show, plant show, cork opera.

MINUTE adj. teeny, teeny-weeny, eentsy-weentsy, itsy-bitsy, titch, piddling. See SMALL.

MINUTE n. mo, half a mo, min, tick, shake, half a shake, two shakes, two shakes of a lamb's tail, sec, split second, bat of an eye, jiff, jiffy, half a jiffy, nothing flat.

MIRACULOUS adj. fantasmo, too much, the utmost, unreal, heavy, gas, seven-ply gasser, far out, one for the book, something to write home about. See FABULOUS.

MIRE n. goo, gooey, glop, gloppy, Mississippi mud, gunk.

MIRROR n. gaper.

MIRROR v. act like, do, do like, go like, make like, take off as, do a take off, play the ——— (affect a role).

MIRTH n. grins, laughs, kicks, whoopee. See AMUSEMENT.

MIRTHFUL adj. crack-up, ball, fun, gas, jokey, joshing, yokked up, for grins, laffer, riot, priceless, screaming, screamingly funny, gut-busting, side-splitting, million laughs. See AMUSING.

MISBEHAVE v. cut up, act up, horse around, fool around, carry on, carry on something awful, cut up rough, roughhouse, go wrong, sow one's wild oats, bend the law.

MISBEHAVING adj. off base, out of line, out of order, trouble-make. See also ROWDY.

MISCALCULATE v. blow, screw up, fuck up, slip up, piss up, mess up, cook, make a blooper, miss by a mile, drop the ball, stumble, pull a blooper, pull a bloomer, pull a boner, pull a boo-boo, put one's foot in it, shoot oneself in the foot, stub one's toe, get one's signals mixed, misread. See ERR.

MISCALCULATION n. boner, blooper, goof, megamistake (big), hash, hash-up, fool mistake, miss by a mile, have another think coming. See MISTAKE.

MISCELLANY n. mixed bag, combo, kludge (parts), everything but the kitchen sink, mishmash, mishmosh, garbage.

MISCHIEF n. dirty trick, rib, gag, high jinks, shenanigans.

MISCHIEVOUS adj. holy terror, little dickens.

MISCREANT n. shit, shithead, shit heel, louse, motherfucker, buddy fucker, rat, rat fink, fink, stinker, sleazeball, bad egg, bad 'un, wrong 'un, black sheep, bastard, son of a bitch, SOB. See SCOUNDREL.

MISDEED n. dirt, dirty pool, dirty deed, miscue, slipup. See also CRIME.

MISDIRECTION n. bum steer, double-cross, double-talk, runaround, jive. See also CHEAT.

MISER n. skinflint, piker, cheapskate, hard man with a buck, scrooge, pinchfist, pinchgut, penny-pincher, nickel-nurser, sticky fingered one.

MISERABLE adj. hurting, on a downer, on a bummer, destroyed, put away, ass in a sling, godforsaken, dick in the dirt, got the blue devils. See UNHAPPY.

MISERLY adj. cheapskate, close, stingy, tight, last of the big spenders, last of the big-time spenders, fast man with a buck, skinflint, screw. See STINGY.

MISERY n. heartache, headache, hurting, grabbing, blues, worriment, tsuris, stew, all-overs, cliff-hanging, pins and needles, who needs it, this I need yet, need it like a hole in the head, pain in the ass, pain in the neck, bad news, stab in the ———, making like the anvil chorus in one's skull, next week East Lynne.

MISFIT n. zoid, fish out of water, oddball, square peg in a round hole. See also DISSOLUTE.

MISFORTUNE n. rough, tough, tough luck, rotten luck, bad news, rainin', deep shit, shit hit the fan, total shuck, can't even get arrested, on the skids, bad break, tit in the wringer, tsuris, crunch. See ADVERSITY.

MISGUIDE n. jerk around, stonewall, shuck and jive, disinform, bum steer, give one a bum steer, lead one up the garden path, mousetrap, throw one a curve, talk trash, double-talk, doublespeak, fake it, beard, put up a smoke screen. See MISLEAD.

MISHANDLE v. flub, blow, bobble, goof up, make a mess of, put one's foot in it, shoot oneself in the foot, go at it ass backwards. See ERR.

MISINFORM v. cover up, signify, bait and switch, disinform, mousetrap, put on, string one along, wrong steer, double-talk, doublespeak, put on a false front, put up a smoke screen, put on an act, let on like, four-flush. See MISLEAD.

MISINFORMED adj. nuts, out in left field, all wet, off, way off, off base, off the beam. See also WRONG.

MISJUDGE v. miss by a mile, drop the ball, stumble, pull a boner, put one's foot in it, bark up the wrong tree, count one's chickens before they're hatched, go at it ass backwards, bonehead into it, jim a deal. See ERR.

MISLEAD v. rook, screw, shaft, frig, fudge, hose, hump, pratt, rim, rip off, jerk one off, jerk one around, dick one around, fuck one over, jive, shuck, shuck and jive, frontin', run a game on, snake one in, rope in, do a number on, disinform, stonewall, cover up, whitewash, pass, sell wolf cookies, signify, bull, throw the bull, bullshit, bunco, cheek it, fake it, fake one out, four-flush, cross up, cross one up, double-cross, XX, double clock, two-time, caboodle, gammon, talk trash, double-talk, doublespeak, fast talk, fleece, gas, gum, flam, flimflam, stick, burn, beat, bleed, bleed white, bilk, clip, con, chisel, gouge, gyp, scam, sting, sandbag, mousetrap, bait and switch, throw one a curve, give one a bum steer, give one a gurdy, hurdy, give one the run around, Murphy, pigeon-drop, ike, pluck, take, take one to the cleaners, take one for a ride, take for a sucker, play games with, play the nine of hearts, play for a sucker, sucker, suck in, sucker into, cream, pull something on one, pull one's leg, pull a quickie, pull up a bluff, put up a bluff, pull a fast one, pull a fast shuffle, double shuffle, double deal, second deal, give one a raw deal, bottom-deal, deal from the bottom, set up, doctor, cook, cook up, deacon, duff, hoke up, frame, frame up, load, salt, salt a mine, plant, phony up, queer, promote, string, string along, string one along, sleighride, snow, snow job, snow under, cold haul, cold deck, buffalo, bamboozle, gazoozle, hocus, slip one over on, wear cheaters, slap on some glims, flash the gogs, throw on a make up, phony up one's getup, beard, put something over, put something across, put one over on, put on, put on the check, put a different face on, put up a front, put on a front, put up a smoke screen, put on an act, make like, let on, play possum, pussyfoot, hype, soak, sell one a bill of goods, sell gold bricks, chouse, chouse out of, fake out, bust out, kiss out, psych out, outfox, fox, kid, pull the wool over one's eyes, have, humbug, hornswoggle, ice, grift, rinkydink, score, shag, single-o, ride a pony, diddle, vamp, hook, gaff, lead one up the garden path, they're peeing on us and telling us it's raining, go South.

MISMANAGE v. goof, goof up, gum up the works, make a mess of, make a hash of, count one's chickens before they're hatched, shoot oneself in the foot, go at it ass backwards. See ERR.

MISREPRESENT v. shuck and jive, maple stick jive, con, promote, blarney, jolly, lay it on, lay it on thick, lay it on with a trowel, spread it on, snow, give one a snow job, pirate, phony up one's getup, wear cheaters, slap on some glims, flash the gogs, throw on a make up, beard, cover up, put up a bluff, blow, blow smoke, bunk flying, cheese, a line of cheese, yeast, throw one a curve, build up, take it big, puff, ballyhoo. See LIE.

MISREPRESENTATION n. jive, line, line of jive, fig leaf, cover-up, hokum, phoney boloney, the big lie (political), fairy tale. See LIE.

MISS v. 1. close but no cigar, cut, pass up, pay no mind, fall between the chairs, fall between the cracks, let slide. 2. blow, flub the dub, miss one's cue, miss by a mile, miss the boat, drop a brick, drop the ball, trip up, fall flat on one's ass, fall flat on one's face, come a-cropper.

MISS A CUE v. fluff, flub, go up, go up in the air, blow it.

MISS A MEAL v. fly light.

MISSED adj. close but no cigar, cut, passed up.

MISSILE n. bird, bat bomb, dingbat (stone or wood), egg, beast (Army), SAM, telephone pole (SAM), MX, cruise, slow flyer (cruise), stealth, MIRV, MARV.

MISSING adj. short, a.w.o.l., A.W.O.L. See ABSENT.

MISSION n. 1. fishery (Rel.). 2. box-top mission, milk run, scramble (A.F.).

MISSIONARY n. padre, Holy Joe, bible-beater, bible thumper, preacher man, sin hound, glory roader. See CLERGYMAN.

MISSISSIPPI Bayou State, the Magnolia State.

MISSISSIPPI RIVER Old Man River, old man river, old muddy, Old Al, Old Big Strong.

MISSIVE n. line, memo, junk mail, drop a line, thank-you note, kite, cannonball, scratch, stiffo, sugar report (love), tab, tag, poison-pen letter (malicious, obscene, etc.).

MISSOURI the Show-Me State, Puke State (origin 19th Cent.).

MISSPEND v. blow, diddle away, piss away, splurge on the line, run through, go through, spend money like water, spend like it was going out of style. See SQUANDER.

MISSPENT adj. blown, blown out, diddled away, down the drain, down the toilet, down the rathole, down the spout, down the tube, pissed away.

MIST n. ground clouds, soup, visibility zero zero.

MISTAKE n. flub, fluff, muff, boner, bug, glitch, fudge factor, gremlin, megamistake (big), boo-boo, blooper, bloomer, bust, butch, botch up, boot, bobble, boggle, goof, goof up, foul-up, fuck-up, louse up, muck up, screw up, gum up, hash up, slipup, snafu, commfu (monumental), tarfu, tuifu, tofu, plumb (serious), clinker, dumbo, fungo, typo, etaoin shrdlu, howler, screamer, flap (social), foozle, fox paw, fox pass, gaff, hummer, klong, brodie, blob, fathead, floater, bonehead play, bonehead trick, boob stunt, donkey act, dumb trick, dumb thing to do, fool mistake, fool trick, pratfall, wrong riff, go wrong, bark up the wrong tree, miss by a mile, mess up, mess and a half, have another think coming, count one's chickens before they're hatched, put one's foot in it, blow card.

MISTAKEN adj. goofed, boo-booed, fooled out, all wet, way off, off the beam, talking like a man with a paper ass, wrong number, bark up the wrong tree. See WRONG.

MISTREAT v. 1. mess up, manhandle, roughhouse, rough up, bend the goods, bung, bung up, cut up, shake up, total, wax, hose, hump. 2. trash, bash, back cap, backbite, rip up the back, do a number on, dump on, play dirty dozens, give a black eye, chop, do one wrong, break one's balls, push around, kick one around, screw, take over the hurdles. See ABUSE. See also WOUND.

MISTRESS OF CEREMONIES n. femcee, the chair.

MISTRESS n. old lady, ol' lady, main squeeze, best girl, girl friend, G.F., sugar, sweetie, roommate, moll, ball and chain, kept woman, keptie, shack, shack job, skibby, dream girl. See also GIRL FRIEND.

MISTRUSTFUL adj. cagey, leery, pussyfoot, walk on eggs, handle with kid gloves, think twice, watch one's step, keep on one's toes, play safe, not born yesterday, walk wide, on the look out. See CAUTIOUS.

MISTY n. fogged in, socked in, closed in, pea soupy, soupy.

MISUNDERSTAND v. get one's signals mixed, misread.

MISUNDERSTANDING n. spat, tiff, beef, fuss, words, bad vibes, falling out, crossed wires, sour note, blowup, set-to, run-in. See DISCORD. See also ARGUMENT.

MISUSE v. 1. blow, diddle away, piss away, splurge on the line, run through, go through, spend money like water, throw out the baby with the bath water, kill the goose that lays the golden egg. 2. mess up, manhandle, roughhouse, rough up, bung, bung up, cut up, shake up, total, wax, hose, hump. 3. trash, bash, bad-mouth, rip up the back, do a number on, pick on, dump on, rag on, tool on, knock, put down, run down, tear down, do one wrong, kick one around. See ABUSE.

MITIGATE v. cool, cool it, cool out, make it up, come together, meet halfway, pour oil on troubled waters, take the edge off. See SOFTEN. See also EXCUSE, PACIFY.

MIXTURE n. everything but the kitchen sink, mishmash, mishmosh, mixed bag, grab bag, combo, duke's mixture (strange), stew, goulash, soup (liquid), lorelei.

MOBILE HOME n. condo on wheels, condominium on wheels, tin can on wheels, land yacht.

MOCK adj. bogue, bunco, bunko, bum, junque, phony, pseud, pseudo, put on, ersatz, hokey, soft shell. See COUNTERFEIT.

MOCK v. 1. jive, needle, do a number on, kid, kid around, razz, rib, thumb one's nose at one, give five fingers to one. See RIDICULE. 2. mirror, make like, play the ——— (affect a role), ditto, do, do like, go like, steal one's stuff, take a leaf out of one's book, fake, hoke, hoke up.

MOCK COURT n. kangaroo court, moot court.

MODE n. 1. fad, mainstream, in-thing, the thing, latest thing, latest wrinkle, new wrinkle, newest wrinkle, last word, mod, now, really now, the rage, spinach. See also NEW. 2. mechanism, channels, the numbers, the book, wrinkle, new wrinkle, nuts and bolts.

MODEL n. 1. mock-up, setup, layout, paste-up, visual, dummy, game plan, picture, paper doll. 2. look-alike, work alike, ringer, dead ringer, ditto, knock-off, clone, copycat, spitting image, spit and image.

MODEL A FORD n. tin lizzie, Model A, A-bone.

MODERATE adj. cool, mellow, mainstream, middle of the road, straddle the fence.

MODERATE v. 1. soft-pedal, coast, cool out, get together on, meet halfway, take the sting out. See PACIFY.

MODERATOR n. umpire, ref, the chair, M.C., emmcee, femcee, toastmaster, rent-a-judge. See also ARBITRATOR.

MODERN adj. state of the art, the leading edge, the cutting edge, at the cutting edge, now, today, contempo, avant-garde, last word. See NEW.

MODIFICATION n. special, customized, custom job, about face, flip-flop, mid-course correction, switch, switch-over, transmogrification, demon tweak.

MODIFY v. doctor, customize, switch over, shift gears, take it in a little, mid-course correction, transmogrify, tweak, turn over a new leaf, turn the corner, turn one around, turn the tables. See CHANGE.

MODISH adj. faddy, trendy, in, in-thing, the thing, latest thing, latest wrinkle, last word, now, the rage. See STYLISH.

MODULATE v. give it a tweak (small), fine tune, take it in a little, monkey around with, bottom out, revamp, transmogrify, do up, switch, switch over, yo-yo. See CHANGE.

MOGUL n. key player, big chew, tycoon, czar, top brass, big shit, big gun, kingpin, beef. See EXECUTIVE.

MOLD v. shape up, fudge together, whomp up.

MOLE n. beauty mark, beauty spot.

MOLESTER, CHILD n. short, short eyes, chicken hawk.

MOLINE, ILLINOIS Quad City.

MOLLIFY v. cool, cool out, fix up, make matters up, patch things up, pour oil on troubled waters, take the sting out. See PACIFY.

MOLTEN METAL n. soup.

MOMENT n. mo, half a mo, tick, sec, split second, shake, half a shake, two shakes, two shakes of a lamb's tail, jiff, half a jiff, jiffy, nothing flat.

MOMENTOUS adj. heavy, heavy number, serious shit, serious jelly, chips are down, we're not talking about nutmeg here. See IMPORTANT.

MONAURAL adj. mono.

MONEY n. cold cash, hard cash, spot cash, buck, big bucks, megabucks, hard coin, important money, bread, long bread, dough, heavy dough, oday, do re mi, almighty dollar, petrodollars, petrobillions, dinero, the ready, ready cash, the wherewithal, the necessary, needful, mazuma, mon, moolah, loot, lucre, filthy lucre, skins, eagle shit, scratch, gelt, gold, ochre, green, green money, green stamps, greenbacks, green stuff, mean green (Bl.), green folding, folding, folding green, long green, folding dough, folding money, lettuce, folding lettuce, folding cabbage, cabbage, happy cabbage, kale, kale seed, roll, bankroll, glory roll, Michigan roll, Philadelphia bankroll, wad, paper, soft money, happy money, mad money, smackers, frog hair, frogskin, gee, geech, geetis, geets, geedus, greedus, gingerbread, glue, gravy, bundle, change, feed, chicken feed, chicken money, hard money, hard stuff, hardtack, coin, iron (silver coin), hay, jangle, jingle-jangle, hunk of change, piece of change, piece of jack, juice, hip gee, ice, kick, laydown, line, grift, handsome ransom, lumps, maine line, mezonny, mint, mint leaves, mopus, morphine, offtish, oil of palms, ointment, oof, ooks, oofus, ookus, package, pazoza, peanuts, poke, color, cookies, corn, cush, darby, dead president, dibs, dingbat, dust, dirt, fews and twos, rags, rhino, rivets, rocks, salve, scrip, sheets, shekels, payola, pretty penny, black money (illegal), blunt, bob, bomb, bones, boodle, brass, buttons, sugar, candy, chump change, chips, clinks, China, shinplaster, shortbread, shorts, small bread, small potatoes, simoleons, silk, velvet, sleeper, soap, soft, the soft, spending snaps, spinach, trading stamps, wampum, adobe dollar, alfalfa, bait, ballast, bark, bat hides (paper), beans, beater, bees and honey, beewy, berries, bird (gold coin), biscuit, bite, spon, spondoolicks, spondoolix, taw, tin, tough bud, tusherony, tucheroon, the mother's milk of politics.

MONEY: CENT n. red cent, Indian head, peanuts, copper, brown, brown Abe, brownie, red, silver, throw money, wampum, washers.

MONEY: FIVE CENTS n. nickel, blip, buffalo head, fish scale, flat.

MONEY: TEN CENTS n. dime, thin dime, thin, thin one, thin man, deece, deemar, deemer, demon, dimmer, jit, jitney, liberty, saw, silver Jeff, tenth part of a dollar.

MONEY: TWENTY-FIVE CENTS n. quarter, two bits, cuter, kyuter, quetor, big George, squirt, gas meter, meter, ruff, shinplaster (bill), silver Jeff, light piece (silver).

MONEY: FIFTY CENTS n. four bits, half a buck, silver wing.

MONEY: SEVENTY-FIVE CENTS n. six bits.

MONEY: DOLLAR n. bill, buck, single, clam, one, potato, simoleon, slug, skin, greenback, smack, smacker, smackeroo, ace, peso, berry, bob, boffo, bone, case, case buck, case dough, case note, check, clacker dollar, cholly, coconut, cucumber, fish, frog, frogskin, lizard, man, plaster, plunk, rag, rock, rutabaga, scrip, Simon, year, hog, hogs, iron man, Jewish flag, last dollar.

MONEY: SILVER DOLLAR n. cartwheel, wheel, ball, bullet, copek, D, hardtack, iron man, plug, shekel, shiner, sinker.

MONEY: TWO DOLLARS n. two spot, deuce, deucer, deuce spot, two-case note, two cents.

MONEY: FIVE DOLLARS n. five, fiver, five spot, fin, finif, nickel note, Abe's Cabe; half eagle, bean (gold coin).

MONEY: TEN DOLLARS n. ten, tenner, ten spot, sawbuck, saw, dews, dime note, dix, eagle (gold coin).

MONEY: TWENTY DOLLARS n. twenty, twenty cents, double sawbuck, double eagle (gold coin).

MONEY: TWENTY-FIVE DOLLARS n. squirt.

MONEY: FIFTY DOLLARS n. half a C.

MONEY: ONE HUNDRED DOLLARS n. C, C note, century, century note, one bill, yard, hun, hollow note.

MONEY: FIVE HUNDRED DOLLARS n. D, five centuries, five C's, half G, half a grand, small nickel.

MONEY: ONE THOUSAND DOLLARS n. G, G note, grand, dollar, thou, yard, big one, dime, horse.

MONEY: FIVE THOUSAND DOLLARS n. big nickel, five dollars.

MONEY: ONE MILLION DOLLARS n. kilobucks, megabucks, mill.

MONEY BAG n. grouch bag.

MONEY BELT n. boodle belt, skin plaster.

MONEY, BRIBE n. payoff, payola, drugola, gayola, take, under the table, fix, juice, schmear, sugar, Mordida; laying pipes, Abscam (political). See BRIBE.

MONEY, COUNTERFEIT n. bogus, paper, queer, funny money, phony money, wallpaper, boodle, green goods, gypsy bankroll, long green, plug, sourdough. See COUNTERFEIT MONEY.

MONEYED adj. loaded, in the chips, stinking rich, well-heeled, have a mint, coupon clipper, well-to-do, fat cat, the haves, the leisure class, got a buck or two, oofy, uptown, upscale. See WEALTHY.

MONEY LENDER n. shark, loan shark, shylock, uncle, softie.

MONEYLESS adj. flat, stone broke, busted, blasted, hard up, strapped, clean, tapped out, on one's uppers, down to one's last cent, down to one's last penny, down at the heel, not have one dollar to rub against another, not have one dime to rub against another. See DESTITUTE.

MONEY, POOL n. chips, kitty, pot.

MONEY, STOLEN n. swag, take, knockdown, loot, make, mark, sting.

MONGREL n. mutt, pooch, Heinz, Heinz 57, Heinz 57 varieties, flea bag, flea hotel. See DOG.

MONITOR v. track.

MONKEY n. monk, monkee.

MONOGRAM n. mono, chop.

MONOLOGUE n. mono, one-man show, stand-up bit.

MONOMANIA adj. one-track mind.

MONONUCLEOSIS n. mono, kissing disease.

MONOPOLIZE v. bogart, corner, corner the market, get a corner on, hog, take over, lock up, sit on.

MONOTONOUS adj. blah, draddy, dull as dishwater, flat, flat as a pancake, ho hum, nothing, put one to sleep. See BORING.

MONSTER n. frankenstein, hellion, hellcat, little devil.

MONSTER adj. monstro, humongous, humungous, mungo, king-size, moby, big mother, biggy, big ass, super-colossal, jumbo, lunker, hoss, whacking, whopping, thumping. See BIG.

MONTANA the Treasure State, big sky.

MONTGOMERY, ALABAMA Monkey City, Monkey Town.

MONTGOMERY WARD n. Monkey Ward.

MONTH n. deano (thief use), moon.

MOOD n. bit, in the groove, one's bag, scene, soul, color. See TEMPER.

MOODY adj. mooney, up and down, yo-yo, blow hot and cold, have spring fever, let down, out of sorts. See MELANCHOLY.

MOON n. pumpkin, green cheese.

MOONSHINE n. corn, cane corn, mountain dew, white mule, white lightning, jug whiskey. See also LIQUOR.

MOPE n. nerd, wimp, wet blanket, crepe-hanger, drag, sourpuss, sourbelly, downer.

MOPE v. bleed, eat one's heart out, stew over, sweat over, chew the cud.

MORAL adj. square, square shooter, straight, straight shooter, true blue, Christian, kosher, salt of the earth, fly right, nice guy, white, regular, scoutmaster, boy scout, clean as a hound's tooth.

MORBID adj. sick, sick sick sick, sicky.

MORGUE n. icebox, slab, ward X (Medic.), greenhouse (prison).

MORNING n. crack of dawn, day peep, sunup, bright, early bright, early beam, early yawning, early yawning hours, foreday.

MORNING GLORY SEED n. flying saucer, heavenly blue.

MORON n. feeb, dork, nerd, loser, lamebrain, a coupla quarts low, four-letter man (dumb), dumbo, mo-mo, numbskull, doesn't know enough to come in out of the rain, stoop, simp, dimwit. See FEEBLEMINDED.

MOROSE adj. down in the mouth, down in the dumps, blue, in a blue funk, singing the blues, got the blue devils, have the blahs. See MELANCHOLY.

MORPHINE n. M, morph, cube juice, dime's worth, dreamer, medicine, God's own medicine, God's drug, soldier's drug, happy dust, Ixey, joy powder, Miss Emma, red cross, sugar, snow, white dust, white nurse, mojo, whiz bang (mixed with cocaine).

MORSEL n. chaw, chomp, chunk, gob, hunk, lump, smithereen, bite, cut, slice, chunk, gob.

MORTAL n. human bean, naked ape. See also PERSON.

MORTAR n. mud.

MORTGAGE n. Daddy MAC (shared equity mortgage), first, second (I have a first on my home but not a second).

MORTIFICATION n. boo-boo, goof, drop a brick, hot potato, could have sunk into the floor, wished the floor would open up, egg on one's face, shoot oneself in the foot, takedown, put-down.

MORTIFIED adj. die, egg on one's face, lost face, crawl, draw in one's horns, eat crow, eat dirt, eat humble pie, sing small. See HUMILIATED.

MORTIFY v.   put away, shred, put down, take down, shoot one down, prick one's balloon, get one's comeuppance, take the wind out of one's sails, lay one out, let one have it. See HUMILIATE.

MOSQUITO n.   skeeter, Alaskan state bird.

MOST n.   lion's share, bigger half, big end, big end of the stick, max, maxi, the most.

MOTEL n.   shortel (used for assignation). See also HOTEL.

MOTEL ROOM n.   flop box, nap trap.

MOTHER n.   mama, mammy, mam, mater, ma, maw, mom, moms, mommy, mootie, motherkin, motherkins, mumsy, mimsy, mummy, muzzy, old lady, old woman, warden.

MOTHER-IN-LAW n.   battle-ax.

MOTION n.   1. on the go, on the move, movin', moving out, coming down, in full swing. 2. body English, high sign.

MOTION PICTURE n.   film, movie, the movies, pictures, picture show, big screen, pic, pix, flick, flickie, flickers, talkie; horse opera, oater, Western, spaghetti western, sagebrusher (Western); boom boom, bang bang, slice and dice, clacker, remake, sequel, prequel, A, B; deepie, depthie, 3-D (three dimension); cheapie, quickie, short, doc, Mickey Mouse (Army training or VD information film), trailer; porno flick, skin flic, snuff, nudie, smoker, stag film, fuck film.

MOTION PICTURE INDUSTRY n.   Hollywood, dream factory, filmdom, moviedom, the industry, the movies. See also FILM TERMS.

MOTION PICTURE STUDIO n.   dream factory, lot, back lot, studio, set.

MOTION PICTURE THEATER n.   movie, the movies, pictures, picture show, movie theatre, movie house, house, cave, hall, hard top; drive-in, ozoner (drive in); flick, flickers, nickelodeon, bug house, grind house, fleabag, passion pit, screen, big screen, silver screen; skin house, stroke house, porno palace, adult movie, adult theatre (pornographic), all-male show.

MOTION, SLOW n.   slo mo, slomo.

MOTIVATE v.   goose, goose up, egg on, spark, sound. See PERSUADE. See also STIMULATE.

MOTIVATOR n.   trigger, spark plug, the driver, the igniter, mover and a shaker.

MOTIVATION n.   fire in the belly, push, goose, kick in the ass, right stuff, get up and go, action, gimmick, angle.

MOTOR n.   horses, power plant, under the hood, barrel (cylinder), maud, pot, putt-putt, rubber band, eggbeater.

MOTORBOAT n.   outboard, stinkpot, yach, yachet, putt-putt.

MOTORCYCLE n.   bike, chopper, cycle, hog, pig, trike, shovel, horse, grid, heap, iron, iron pony, motocycle, motorbike, road bike, dirt bike, mini bike, micro bike, garlic burner (Italian), rice burner (Japanese), hornet, scrambler, trumpet, wasp, bumble bee, cyclone cycle; bathtub, buddy seat (sidecar).

MOTORCYCLE POLICEMAN n.   Evel Kneivel, chopper copper.

MOTORCYCLE CLOTHES n.   harness (leather clothes and accessories), skid lid (helmet).

MOUNTAIN n.   hump.

MOUNTAINEER n.   ridge runner.

MOURN v.   bleed, hurt, blubber, boo hoo, rain, carry on, eat one's heart out, go for a crying towel, get out the crying towel, cry me a river, cry the blues, sing the blues, take it big, take it hard, take on, beat one's breast, crepe-hang, hang crepe.

MOUTH n.   trap, chops, kisser, bazoo, mush, yap, beak, box, gob, clam, clam shells, clam trap, fish trap, fly trap, potato trap, kissing trap, talk trap, satchel mouth, funnel, dipper, gab, gap, jap, gash, gills, hatch, head, mug, box of dominoes.

MOUTHFUL n.   chaw, chomp, gob.

MOVE v.   1. dedomicile, up stakes, pull up stakes, truck, move out. 2. split, beat it, scram, haul ass, hit the road, move out, clear out, check out, dig out, ship out, skip out, get the hell out, blow this pop stand, shove off, drift away, hat up, quit the scene. See GO. See also ACT, EXCITE, AROUSE, PERSUADE, REMOVE.

MOVED adj.   turned on by, turned on to, feel in one's guts, feel for, get to one, grabbed. See also EXCITED.

MOVER n.   1. drifter, grifter, bo, bum, floater, bindlestiff, gad, gadabout, jet-setter, globe-trotter, rod rider. 2. mover and shaker, operator, spark plug, catalyst, wire-puller, trigger, driver.

MOVING adj.   on the move, cool, real cool, zero cool, fab, far out, mega, megadual, marvy, like wow, reet, mind-blowing, mind-bending, out of this world, turn on, turned on by, turned on to, gone, real gone, hot stuff, hairy, large, large charge, nervous, rootin' tootin', solid, solid sender, one for the book, something, something else, something to shout about, something to write home about, stunner, stunning, feel in one's guts, grabbed by.

MUCH adj.   mega (Stu.), up to one's ass in, loads, galore, scads, mucho, mucho-mucho, lotsa, heaps, plate is full. See PLENTY.

MUCILAGE n.   gunk, stickum, spit, gummy.

MUCILAGINOUS adj. gooey, gloppy, globby, gook, gooky, goonk, gummy, gunk.

MUCK n. goo, gooey, glop, gloppy, Mississippi mud, gunk.

MUCKRAKER n. knocker, mudslinger, sleaze-monger, yellow journalist, whistle-blower.

MUCUS n. bugger, booger, boogie, snot, cream.

MUD n. goo, gooey, glop, gloppy, Mississippi mud, gunk, gumbo.

MUDDLE n. mess, mess and a half, rat's nest, foul-up, fuck-up, screw-up, snarl up, mishmosh, every which way but up. See CONFUSION.

MUDDLE v. discombobulate, ball up, louse up, rattle, throw, psych out, fuck with one's head, put one on a crosstown bus. See CONFUSE.

MUDDLED adj. unglued, discombobulated, slap-happy, punchy, bollixed up, fussed, fried, rattled, rattlebrained, higgledy-piggledy, ass backwards, bass ackwards. See CONFUSED.

MUDDY adj. greasy, gummy, gunky.

MUFFIN n. dingbat, garbo.

MUFFLE v. gag, hush, ice, muzzle, shut down on, put the lid on, sit down on. See SILENCE.

MUFTI n. cits, civvies, street clothes.

MULATTO n. banana, hi yalla, high yella, high yellow, high yeller, lemon, bird's eye maple, poontang, yellow girl, tush (all Derog.). See also BLACK.

MULE n. hay burner, jar head, jug head, hardtail (Army).

MULE DRIVER n. skinner, mule skinner.

MULL v. figger, moon, pipe dream, stew over, sweat over, rack one's brains, crack one's brains, cudgel one's brains, hammer, hammer away at, put on one's thinking cap, chew the cud, woolgather. See also THINK.

MULTIPLE INDEPENDENTLY TARGETED RE-ENTRY VEHICLE n. MIRV.

MULTIPLE ORBIT BOMBARDMENT SYSTEM n. MOBS.

MULTIPLE SCLEROSIS n. MS.

MULTITUDE n. mob, push, turnout, blowout, crush, jam, jam up, everybody and his brother, everybody and his uncle, loaded to the rafters, wall-to-wall people. See CROWD.

MULTITUDINOUS adj. umpteen, zillion, jillion, mucho, eleventeen, whole slew, wads, gobs, scads, heaps, piles, oodles, more than one can shake a stick at. See AMOUNT, LARGE.

MUNICIPAL ASSISTANCE CORPORATION n. Big Mac.

MUNICIPALITY n. urb, burg, apple, Big Town, big time, boomer, boomtown, dump, slab, two-stemmer, tough town, wide open joint, wrong tank, right tank.

MUNIFICENT adj. softie, soft touch, big, be big, bighearted, have a heart, heart in the right place, loose, good Joe, prince of a fellow, Santa Claus.

MURDER n. off, offing, wasting, hit, taking out, the big M, big chill, liquidation, kiss-off. See KILLING.

MURDER v. off, snuff, ice, chill, waste, hit, liquidate, get, fog, take out, rub out, do in, bump off, blow away, kiss-off. See KILL.

MURDERED adj. wasted, offed, cooled off, knocked off, rubbed out, snuffed, liquidated. See KILLED.

MURDERER n. hit man, trigger man, piece man, torpedo, enforcer, gunsel, bumpman, soldier. See KILLER.

MURMUR v. buzz, sotto.

MUSCULAR adj. hunk, hulk, gorilla, husky, hefty, beefy, beefcake, bruiser, big bruiser, bone crusher, tiger, Turk, wicked, down, tough, tough guy, puffed out, pumped up, strong-arm, muscle, muscle man, he-man, powerhouse, strong as a lion, strong as a horse, strong as an ox, sturdy as an ox, built like a brick shithouse, coon (stupid).

MUSE v. feel, moon, percolate, sweat over, cool something over, skull drag, chew over, chew the cud, woolgather, pipe dream, build castles in the air. See THINK.

MUSEUM UNIVERSITY DATA PROCESSING INFORMATION EXCHANGE n. MUDPIE.

MUSICAL ACCOMPANIMENT n. back, backing, backup singers.

MUSICAL COMEDY n. musical, tuner, song and dance show.

MUSICALE n. folk sing, hootenanny, sing, sing-in.

MUSICAL ENSEMBLE n. combo, group, rock group, big band, jazz band, jump band, swing band.

MUSICAL INSTRUMENT n. ax, money number.

MUSICAL NOTE n. bent note, biff, biffer (unsuccessful brass high note), blue note, blow for canines (high, trumpet), clam, clinker (sour or wrong); scooping pitch, slurred note, spots, sting.

MUSICAL PERFORMANCE gig, action, blow, funky, ride, moan, jive, jam, tickle the ivories (piano), burning (play wonderfully), groove, groovy, in the groove; date it (play badly), lumpy (jazz played badly), put it in the alley.

MUSICAL TERMS   strictly union (corny), rocku-mentary (rock music documentary film), video (rock tape), sounds, spots (notes), cornfed (plays or appreciates classical); corny, cornball (country, hillbilly); chops (ability, technique), go man go, groove, in the groove, ickie (unappreciative), charts, maps (sheet music), rideout, ride (improvise jazz), hit a lick (emphasize), scat, set, book.

MUSICAL WORK n.   comp, getup, piece, setup, tune, chart, arrangement, number.

MUSIC DEVOTEE n.   rocker, sender, solid sender, cat, hepcat, hipster, groupie, alligator, gate, swinging gate, 'gater, jitterbug, moldy fig, ragger, rug cutter, sharpie, sweet, with it, woof hound, music buff.

MUSIC FORMS n.   fusion, rock, rock and roll, rock 'n' roll, R. & R., hard rock, soft rock, acid rock, shock rock, heavy rock, AOR (album oriented rock), white rock, heavy metal, ragarock, rockabilly, pop rock, rock steady, soft rock, folk rock, hip hop, doo wop, punk, punk funk, punk rock, new wave, power pop, bop, bebop, rebop, riba, hard bop, Western, country, country Western, bluegrass, disco, jazz, Chicago jazz, New Orleans jazz, blues, barrelhouse, gutbucket, Dixie, Dixieland, soul music, rag, ragtime, honky tonk, pop, swing, big beat, rhythm & blues, R. & B., boogie, boogie woogie, bounce, businessman's bounce, society music, jump, rap music, bubblegum, bubblegum and popcorn music, Motown, reggae, dub, ska, salsa, chaser, run off, chestnut (old), classical, long underwear, longhair, longhair juke, ricky tick, scat, shout, whorehouse piano, piano bar, Muzak, elevator music.

MUSICIAN n.   longhair, long underwear, studio, cat, cool cat, blowing cat, gay cat, alligator (white), gate, gator, in orbit (avant-garde), lip-splitter, satchel, sender, solid sender, swinging gate, wig, loose wig (inspired), muso (superb), sideman, iron man, metallurgist (heavy metal), band man, paper man, rag man; ear man, faker (illiterate); rocker, monster (popular).

MUSTACHE n.   brush, soup strainer, tickler, toothbrush, handlebars, lip fuzz, pez, stash, stache, fox tail (Navy, WW I).

MUSTANG CAR n.   horse.

MUSTARD n.   Coney Island butter, baby shit.

MUSTER n.   head count, nose count, call up, draft.

MUSTER OUT v.   demob, get the ruptured duck.

MUTE v.   gag, hush, keep it down, pipe down, decrease the volume, muzzle, put the damper on, put the lid on, bottle up, cork up, put a cork in it. See SILENCE.

MUTILATE v.   queer, bugger, bugger up, mess up, hash up. See also DAMAGE.

MUTINY v.   kick over the traces.

MUTTON n.   Aussie steak (WW II), billy goat.

MUTUALLY ASSURED DESTRUCTION n.   MAD.

MUZZLE v.   gag, ice, squelch, squash, dummy up, dry up, shut one's face, bottle up, put the damper on, put the lid on, cork up, shut down on, crack down on, clamp down on. See SILENCE.

MY EYES GLAZE OVER v.   MEGO.

MYRIAD adj.   loads, raft, slew, gobs, scads, mint, heap, oodles, stacks, no end of. See COUNTLESS.

MYSELF pro.   big three (me, myself and I), number one, numero uno, yours truly, Dudley, Uncle Dudley, ol' Uncle Dudley.

MYSTERY n.   1. chiller, thriller, chiller-diller, who-dun-it, who-done-it, cliff-hanger, spyboiler, grabber. 2. sixty-four dollar question, twister, teaser, sticker, mind-boggler, stumper, hard nut to crack, tough nut to crack.

MYSTIFIED adj.   stuck, stumped, floored, thrown, flummoxed, kerflumixed, bamboozled, buffaloed, beat, licked, foggy, in a fog, wandering around in a fog. See PUZZLED.

MYSTIFY v.   get to, rattle, throw, buffalo, put one on a crosstown bus, muddy the waters, stump, floor, put off, flummox. See PUZZLE.

N

N n. November, Nan.

NADIR n. the pits, cellar, bottom rung, rock bottom, bottom out, dick in the dirt.

NAG v. bug, hound, be at, be on the back of, eat, noodge, nudge, nudzh, work on, hit on, penny dog, worry, hock a charnik, pick at. See ANNOY.

NAIVE adj. wide-eyed, blue-eyed, babe in the woods, cube, square, lamb, sucker, patsy, virgin, don't know from nothin', don't know crossways from crosswise, search me. See UNSOPHISTICATED.

NAKED adj. bare-assed, bald, nudie, in the altogether, in the buff, au naturel, skinny, starkers. See NUDE.

NAME n. handle, handle to one's name (title), John Doe, John D., John Hancock, John Henry, monicker, tag, what's-his-name, what's-his-face, brand, flag (assumed), front name, label, tab.

NAME v. name, slot, tab, tag, make, peg, finger, lay one's finger on, put one's finger on, put one's finger on something, put the finger on, button down, pin down, put down for.

NAMELESS adj. a certain person, John Doe, X, George Spelvin, whatchamacallit, what d'ye call em, what's-his-face, incog, bearding, I'll never forget what's-his-name. See ANONYMOUS.

NAP n. catnap, forty winks, microsleep, snooze, a few z's, the nod, spot, bye-bye. See SLEEP.

NAP v. snooze, zizz, grab a few z's, cop some z's, log some z's, saw logs, get some shut-eye, catnap, doss, dozz, doz, rack, grab some shut-eye, knock a nod, cop a nod, dig oneself a nod, collar a nod, catch a wink, take forty winks. See SLEEP.

NAPE n. kitchen (Bl.).

NAPKIN n. bib.

NARCOTIC CAPSULE n. cap, doll.

NARCOTICS n. junk, shit, uppers, downers, stuff, hard stuff, hard drugs, cement, goods, Jones, hocus, merchandise, happenings, fix, needle candy, ice cream (crystal), ammunition, God's medicine, death boy, fruit salad (mixture). See DRUG. See also AMPHETAMINE, AMYL NITRITE, BARBITURATE, BENZEDRINE, BIPHETAMINE, CHLORAL HYDRATE, COCAINE, COCAINE AND HEROIN, DEXAMYL, DEXEDRINE, DEXTROAMPHETA-MINE, DIMETHYLTRYPTAMINE, DIPROPYL-PHYPTAMINE, FENTANYL, HASHISH, HEROIN, HEROIN AND COCAINE, HEROIN AND MARIJUANA, ISOBUTYL NITRITE, JIMSON WEED, LUMINAL PILL, LSD, MANDRAKE, MARIJUANA, MDMA, MESCALINE, METHADONE, METHAMPHETAMINE, METHAQUALONE, METHEDRINE, METHYLENEDIOXYAMPHETAMINE, METHYL FENTENYL, MORNING GLORY SEED, MORPHINE, NEMBUTAL, NEMBUTAL AND MORPHINE, OPIUM, PAREGORIC, PEYOTE, PHENCYCLIDINE, QUAALUDE, SECONAL, TUINAL, VALIUM.

NARCOTICS ADDICT n. A.D., A-head, head. See ADDICT.

NARCOTICS ADDICTION n. habit, hook, Jones, jones, sweet tooth, garbage habit (mixtures), monkey, monkey on one's back, hooked. See DRUG ADDICTION.

NARCOTICS AGENT n. narc, narco, dopebull, Big John, Fed, Federal, gazer, people, Sam, uncle, Uncle Sam, whisker.

NARCOTICS BUY v. make a buy, score, score some, keep the meet, cop, hit, re-up, sail, trey, turn.

NARCOTICS BUY n. bag, dime bag, nickel bag, paper, dime's worth, ten cents, foil, cap; matchbox, stick (cigarette); quarter bag, can, lid, O.Z., weight (oz.); key, kee, ki (kilo); half a load (15 bags), brick (compressed kilo), bird's-eye.

NARCOTICS CURE take the cure, kick the habit, kick, cold turkey, get the monkey off, get the monkey off one's back, off the habit, kill the Chinaman.

NARCOTICS DOCTOR n. ice-tong doctor, right rocker.

NARCOTICS MARKETPLACE n. stach house, rock house (fortified), Alphabet Town (N.Y.), Sherm Alley (L.A.), smoke shop.

NARCOTICS OVERDOSE v. OD, oh dee, overjolt, overvamp, overamp, overcharge, burn out, freak out, jazz out, rock out, zone out, zonk out.

NARCOTICS PARAPHERNALIA n. spike, point, works, head kit, kit, fit, outfit, the business, joint (total equipment), flake spoon, cooker, gun, hook, ken ten (lamp for opium), artillery, banger, hype stick, light artillery, needle, pin, quill (matchbook cover), bong (pipe), marygin (seed remover), roach clip, Woodstock emergency pipe (aluminum foil); stash bag, stash box, stash jar (marijuana).

NARCOTICS, SELL v. peddle, push, scag trade.

NARCOTICS SELLER n. dealer, pusher, connection, kilo connection (wholesaler), the people, peddler, dope peddler, source, one who's holding, hyp, hype, hipe, mother, mule, junker, shover, viper, the Man, heavy man, tea man, reefer man, candy man, swing man, ounce man, bagman, big man, scagman, bingles, bingler, broker, house connections, juggler, missionary, operator, trafficker, beat artist, fixer.

NARCOTICS TERMS cut, doctor, phony up (adulterate); cut deck (adulterated); charge, load, skinful; shot, hit, piece, can, deck, phony bingle, carrying (possession); scag trade, factory, underground factory, basement lab, tracks (needle).

NARCOTICS USE adj. use, up, habit, ice cream habit (occasional), on the needle, strung out, mellowed out, junked up, teaed up, hopped up, gonged, goofed, kick, charge, maxed, flying, tripping out, high, flight, on the nod, in the ozone, in the zone, wired, snowstorm (party), chemical dependency. See DRUG USE.

NARCOTICS USE v. drop, pop, use, shoot, shoot up, space out, nod, fix, take a fix, take a drag, hit, hit the dope, toke, get high, trip, get off, get behind, get down, go up, sniff, snort, blow, mainline, freebase, bang, bomb, jolt, joy pop, skin pop, geeze, jack up, do drugs, string out, tie up, ping-wing, pin-shot (injected). See DRUG USE.

NARCOTICS USE SITE n. head shop, gallery, shooting gallery, ballroom, balloon room, kick pad (detoxification site), parachute, spot.

NARCOTICS USER n. A-head, junkie, user, doper, mainliner, freak, head, hophead, drughead, coke head, acid head, pillhead, garbage head (mixture), fiend, needle man, smack slammer, tripper, cokie, Skag Jones, snowbird, goof ball. See DRUG USER.

NARCOTICS WITHDRAWAL n. kick the habit, dry out, sweating it out, take the cure, shakes, wet-dog shakes, bogue, cold turkey, become Mr. Fink.

NARRATIVE n. yarn, line, clothesline, long and the short of it, potboiler, old chestnut, old wives' tale, book. See STORY.

NARROWLY adv. squeak by, by a hair, by the skin of one's teeth, pretty near, close shave, practically.

NARROWS n. bottleneck, choke point.

NASHVILLE, TENNESSEE Guitar Town, Nastyvilly, Opryland.

NASTY adj. grody, grody to the max, mung, gross, beastly, bad-assed, barfy, bitchy, mean, ornery, cussed, grungy, raunchy, rough, stinking, tough, eighteen carat, fierce, something fierce, awful, godawful, icky, yucky, lousy, murder, murderous, nuts, poison, bum, doin' dirt, hellish, hell of a note, hipper-dipper. See also UNSAVORY.

NATIONAL AERONAUTICS AND SPACE ADMINISTRATION n. NASA.

NATIONAL ASSOCIATION OF SECURITIES DEALERS AUTOMATED QUOTATIONS n. NASDAQ.

NATIONAL BROADCASTING COMPANY n. NBC, peacock network.

NATIONAL LEAGUE n. senior circuit (baseball).

NATIONAL ORGANIZATION FOR WOMEN n. NOW, N.O.W.

NATIONAL RAILROAD PASSENGER CORPORATION n. AMTRAK.

NATIONALIST n. arm-waver, flag-waver (super), hard hat, hundred percenter, hundred percent 'merkin, jingoist, patrioteer, scoutmaster.

NATIVE n. home towner, local, local yokel, landsman, paesano.

NATIVE, PACIFIC ISLANDS n guinea, ginny; geechie, cheeckee, goo-goo, gu-gu, gook (WW II, all Derog.).

NATURAL adj. 1. go organic, on the natch. 2. folksy, haymish, homey, with the bark on, all hanging out, up front, free-spirited, down, get down, let down one's hair, break loose, cut loose, loose wig, stretched out, laid back. See also PLAIN.

NATURALIST n. bug hunter, bugologist.

NATURALLY adv. natch, but of course.

NATURE n. 1. like, likes of, thing, one's thing, one's way, the way of it, the way it is, that's one all over, just like one, where one's at, bag, one's bag, the name of that tune, nature of the beast. See also CHARACTERISTIC. 2. point, stuff, nub, drift, heart, meat, score, bottom line, name of the game, nitty-gritty, nuts and bolts, punch line, nature of the beast.

NAUGHT n. zip, zippo, zot, zilch, squat, diddly, diddly squat, doodly squat, egg, duck eggs, goose eggs, shut out, empty, harlot's hello, horse collar, nit. See NOTHING.

NAUGHTY adj. bad-assed, barfy, bum, doin' dirt, raunchy, rough, tough, tough nuggies, tripe, yucky, eighteen carat, hellish, hell of a note, hipper-dipper. 2.

holy terror, little dickens. 3. adult, purple, blue, dirty, hot, porn, porno, steamy, low-down and dirty, off-color, rough, salty, raunchy, fast, fast and loose, loose, speedy. See OBSCENE.

NAUSEOUS adj.   barfy, pukish, pukey, rocky, sick as a dog.

NAUTICAL adj.   salty, seagoing.

NAVAL COMMANDER n.   two-and-a-half striper, two-and-a-one-half striper.

NAVAL OFFICERS n.   gold braid, crow.

NAVEL n.   belly button.

NAVIGATIONAL DATA n.   fix, on track.

NAVIGATOR n.   clerk, pencil pusher, Magellan (aircraft).

NAVY PERSONNEL n.   gob, mate, shipmate, blue jacket, tar, Jack Tar (Obs.), hack driver (chief petty officer), snipe, mule (flight deck handler).

NAVY UNIFORM n.   blues, dress blues, whites, dress whites, bell bottoms, peacoat.

NEAR adj.   around, along toward, screwdriver turn away, warm, hot, burning, whoop, within a whoop and a holler, within two whoops and a holler, within a stone's throw, in spitting distance, in the vicinity of, in the neighborhood of, in the ball park, upwards of, pretty near, hair's breadth, give or take a little, practically, on one's heels, close by, close shave, slicing it thin, near miss, close but no cigar (miss).

NEARLY adv.   around, pretty near, practically, craptically, something like, give or take a little, ball park figure, in the ball park of, in the neighborhood of, upwards of, by the skin of one's teeth, close but no cigar (miss).

NEAT adj.   apple pie, apple-pie order, neat as a button, neat as a pin, slick, to rights, all policed up, in good shape, shipshape. See also ORDERLY, METHODICAL.

NEBRASKA   Beef State, Cornhusker State, Tree Planter State.

NECESSARY adj.   bottom line, plain vanilla, nitty-gritty, where it's at, name, name of the game, cold, cold turkey, nub, meat and potatoes, coal and ice. See also VITAL.

NECK n.   stretcher.

NECKBAND n.   choker, dog collar (priest), horse collar (protective).

NECKLACE n.   chocker, choker, ice.

NECKTIE n.   choker, chocker, noose, stretcher.

NEED n.   itch, the urge, have one's tongue hanging out for, weakness, fire in the belly, the munchies (food). See DESIRE.

NEED v.   hurting for, ache for, drive for, yen for, die for, letch for.

NEEDY adj.   have-nots, truly needy, the poor, piss-poor, flat, dead broke, oofless, on the rocks, down and out, down to one's last cent, down at the heel, seen better days. See DESTITUTE.

NEGATE v.   kill, ding, zing, put down, pass on, nix, be agin, blackball, break with, buck, dump, turn down, turn thumbs down, stuff it, stick it, shove it, cram it up one's ass, stick it up one's ass, shove it up one's ass, stick it in one's ear, fly in the face of, take the fifth (plead the Fifth Amendment), plead a five, stonewall. See also CANCEL.

NEGATION n.   N.O., nix, no way, no way José, no sale, forget it, fat chance, stonewall, negatory, like fun, like hell. See DENIAL.

NEGATIVE adj.   anti, agin, con, ornery, stuffy, draw a blank, not so hot, no go, debit side, on the debit side, on the down side, the bad news, nix, have no use for.

NEGLECT v.   ig, let it go, tune out, fuck off, goof off, dog, dog it, live with, pay no mind, pay no never mind, let go to pot, let slide.

NEGLIGENT adj.   pay no mind, asleep at the switch, slapdash, sloppy, by halves, leave oneself wide open. See CARELESS.

NEGLIGENTLY adv.   any old way, any which way, do by halves, knock off, knock out, bat out, shove out, slap out, slap up, slapdash, throw off, toss off, toss out, mess around, fast and loose, half-assed, helter-skelter, higgledy-piggledy.

NEGOTIATE v.   1. deal, dicker, cut a deal, hack out a deal, hammer out a deal, make a deal, work out a deal, hondle, horse trade, swap, swap horses, Jew down (Derog.), knock down the price, come across with, dish out, drop, fork over, network with, connect with, have truck with. 2. make it, make the grade, make out, pull off, pull it off, do the trick, turn the trick, do the job, put it over, deal with, get there, hack it, squeak by (barely).

NEGOTIATOR n.   go-between, fixer.

NEGRO n.   bro, blood, brother, sister, soul; nigger, member, spade, smoke, coon, darkie, buck, boogie, shine, spook, splib, eightball, geechee, shvartzeh (Yid.), handerkerchief head (all Derog.). See BLACK.

NEGRO (FEMALE) n.   sister, soul sister, band, bantam, barbeque, covess dinge, dange broad, black and tan, banana, bird's eye maple, high yella, high yeller, high yellow, lemon; poontang (sexual, Derog.), Aunt, auntie, Aunt Jane, Aunt Jemima, Aunt Tom, Sapphire (all Derog.).

NEGROPHILE n.   nigger lover, Crow Jimism.

NEIGHBOR n.   homeboy (Bl. ghetto), homey.

NEIGHBORHOOD n.   nabe, hood, the block, the blot, the street, neck of the woods, stamping ground, stomping ground, old stomping grounds, territory, turf, ghetto, inner city, slurb, shanty town, skid row, slum, jungle, zoo. See also DISTRICTS.

NEIGHBORING adj.   around, whoop and a holler, stone's throw, spitting distance, pretty near, close by, just down the road, just down the pike. See NEAR.

NEMBUTAL n.   purple heart, yellow jacket, blockbuster, pill, nebbie, nemish, nemmie, nimby, abbot.

NEMBUTAL AND MORPHINE n.   purple heart.

NEMESIS n.   bugaboo, dues. See also PUNISH-MENT.

NEOPHYTE n.   newie, greeny, punk, rookie boot, new kid on the block, fish, tenderfoot, jice, new jice. See NOVICE.

NERVE n.   balls, guts, heart, stomach, what it takes, grit, spunk, starch, chutzpah, intestinal fortitude, Dutch courage (intoxicated). See COURAGE.

NERVOUS adj.   uptight, wired, wired up, hung up, basket case, hyper, horny (sexual), jittery, jumpy, pissin', shittin', butterflies, goosy, shaky, shivery, quivery, charged, high, spazzed out, flipped out, freaked out, shook up, all shook up, worked up, all worked up, clutched, clutched up, tightened up, hopped up, all keyed up, keyed up, steamed up, strung out, high-strung, trigger-happy, on pins and needles, on tenterhooks, on the ragged edge, all hot and bothered, choked, yantsy, zonkers, twitty, have one's teeth on edge, wreck, nervous wreck, bundle of nerves, nervy, all-overish, jumpy as a cat on a hot tin roof, shot to pieces, fall apart, sweaty, have kittens, cast a kitten, the screaming meemies, the meemies, heebie-jeebies, the jams, the jims, jimjams, the jumps, jitters, on the gog, spooked, in a sweat, in a cold sweat, sweating bullets, shaking in one's boots, in a lather, in a dither, in a swivet, in a tizzy, in a foofaraw, in a pucker, have a short fuse, have the leaps, have butterflies in one's stomach, work oneself into a stew, work oneself into a lather, work oneself into a tizzy, work oneself into a pucker, get hot under the collar, run a temperature, race one's motor, shit in one's pants, fuzzbuzzy.

NERVOUS BREAKDOWN n.   schizzed out, psyched out, basket case, crackup, breakdown, come apart at the seams, conk out, strung out.

NERVOUSNESS n.   creeps, cold creeps, shivers, cold shivers, sweat, cold sweat, fidgets, jitters, willies, heebie-jeebies, jimjams, jumps, shakes, quivers, trembles, dithers, butterflies, all-overs, flap, fuss, lather, needles, stew, to do, zingers, pucker, swivet, tizzy, goose bumps, stage fright, buck fever. See also ANXIETY.

NETHER WORLD n.   hell, hot spot, other place, down there.

NETTLE n.   1. sticker. 2. miff, pet, stew, tiff, snit.

NETWORK n.   net, hookup, LAN (local area network, computer), coast-to-coast hookup.

NETWORK, BROADCAST n.   net, web.

NEUROTIC adj.   screwed up, hung up, uptight, tightened up, clutched, clutched up, wired, wired up, choked, yantsy, zonkers, spooked, sick, sickie, wreck, nervous wreck, shot, shot to pieces, basket case, bundle of nerves, on the ragged edge, on the gog. See also NERVOUS.

NEUTRAL adj.   vanilla, flat, cop out, straddle, nothingarian, anythingarian, dawk (neither a dove or a hawk), neither fish nor fowl, play it cool, could care less, don't care one way or another, don't care one way or t'other, don't give a shit, don't give a damm, don't give a hoot, what's the diff?, what the hell, so what?, it's all the same to me, call 'em as one sees 'em, the middle ground, middle of the road, on the fence, fence-sitter, even-steven, no-man's-land, mugwumpian, mugwumpish.

NEUTRON BOMB n.   cookie cutter, Enhanced Radiation Device, ERD, Wall Street weapon.

NEVADA   Battle Born State, Divorce State, Sagebrush State, Silver State.

NEVER adv.   no way, forget it, not on your life, not on your tintype, you should live so long, don't hold your breath, in a pig's eye, it'll be a cold day in July, it'll be a cold day in hell, till hell freezes over, tomorrow, mañana, one o' these days, any day now, on the 31st of February.

NEW adj.   state of the art, the leading edge, the cutting edge, at the cutting edge, avant-garde, now, the "now" generation, today, with it, what's happening, breaking new snow, breaking new ground, what's in, the in-thing, contempo, mint, cherry, newey, brand-new, spanking new, brand spanking new, fire new, hot off the fire, hot off the griddle, hot off the spit, hot off the press, just out, up to date, up to the minute, last word, the latest, latest thing, latest wrinkle, new wrinkle, newfangled, newfangled contraption, comer, young turk, new boy on the block, new kid on the block.

NEW ENGLAND   down east.

NEW ENGLAND COLLEGES n.   Ivy League, Halls of Ivy.

NEW GUINEA NATIVE n.   Guinea, guinea, Ginney, ginney, Ginnee, ginee, guinie (all Derog.).

NEW HAMPSHIRE Granite State, White Mountain State.

NEW JERSEY Clam State, Garden State, Jersey Blue State, Mosquito State, New Spain.

NEW MEXICO Cactus State, Land of Enchantment, Spanish State, Sunshine State.

NEW ORLEANS, LOUISIANA Dixie Town, Fun City, Jazz City, Orleans, Mardi Gras City, the Big Easy.

NEWCOMER adj. new kid on the block, young turk, turkey, blow in, rook, rookie, wetback, bracero, cheechako, chukoko, Johnny come lately, fish, tenderfoot, greenhorn, greenie, Hunk, Hunkie, Bohunk. See also NOVICE.

NEWFOUNDLANDER n. Newfig, Newfie.

NEWS n. info, infotainment (TV), leak, network, tie-in, hookup, cue, clue, flash, scoop, poop, hot poop, poop sheet, ammo, pipeline, boot snitch, score, skinny, lowdown, dirt, dope, dope sheet, medicine, inside dope, inside wire, insider, tip, hot tip, the know, picture, chip, handout, squib, whole story, chapter and verse, goods, brass tacks, garbage, goulash (false), ear loft, break, breaking story, beat, the latest, what's happenin', what's going down, chip, brush-up, earful, ear duster, hash, haymaker, hotshot, hot wire; kick in the ass, shot in the ass (bad); are you ready for this?, let one in on, page-oner, gone cold (old). See also REPORT.

NEWSMONGER n. sleazemonger, yenta, catty, polly, satch, gasser, load of wind, windbag, busybody, tabby, tattletale.

NEWSPAPER n. daily, rag, scandal sheet, sheet, bladder, blat, bulldog (earliest edition), chroniker, extra, fish wrapper, snitch sheet, toilet paper.

NEWSPAPER OPINION SECTION n. op-ed page.

NEWSPAPER SELLER n. newsie, newsy, newspaper boy, newspaperman.

NEWSPAPERMAN n. scribe, scrivener, columnist, stringer, leg man, news hen, cub, pen driver, pen pusher, pencil driver, pencil pusher, scratcher, ink slinger. See also WRITER.

NEWS RELEASE n. handout, the dope, the goods, scoop, skinny, poop, poopsheet, leak.

NEWSWORTHY adj. splash, newsy, break, hot item.

NEW YORK The Empire State.

NEW YORK CITY n. Big A, Big Apple, Gotham, Big Lady, Fun City; Hymie Town, Jew York (all Derog.); N.Y., NYC, Noo York.

NEW YORK RESIDENT n. Gothamite, Madhattaner, Noo Yawker.

NEW ZEALAND Down Under.

NEW ZEALANDER n. kiwi, Anzac.

NEXT adv. next off, coming up.

NIBBLE v. nab at, munch, munch on, snack, peck, peck at, graze, nosh, eat like a bird. See EAT.

NICE adj. all reet, rightee, ducky, Mr. Nice Guy, good joe, pussycat, coolville, copacetic, okay, fucking-A, okey-doke, hunky-dory, fine and dandy, peachy, swell, fat, neato, nifty, orgasmic, home cooking, gasser, groovy. See AGREEABLE.

NIGGARDLY adj. cheap, close, tight, last of the big-time spenders, fast man with a buck, skinflint, screw, Scrooge, Scotch, squeezing the eagle, piker. See STINGY.

NIGH adj. round, warm, hot, burning, within a whoop and a holler, within a stone's throw, in spitting distance, pretty near, hair's breadth, close by. See NEAR.

NIGHT n. black, dim, after dark, after hours.

NIGHTCLOTHES n. nightie, shortie, baby dolls, jams, jammies, jam jams, P.J.'s, peejays, pygies, sleepers, sleeping suit.

NIGHTCLUB n. night spot, nitery, disco, saloon, joint, after-hours joint, juke joint, juice joint, hop joint, rub joint, right joint, scatter, scatter joint, clip joint, gyp joint, trap, boob trap, drum, dump, dive, spot, hot spot, shine box, honky-tonk, speakeasy, blind pig, blind tiger, crib, fleshpot, frolic pad, free and easy, hideaway, room, rum room.

NIGHTCLUB ACT n. floor show, peep show, girlie show, topless, T and A, tits and ass.

NIGHTCLUB SECURITY n. bouncer.

NIGHTFALL n. black, dim.

NIGHTGOWN n. nightie, shortie, baby dolls. See also NIGHTCLOTHES.

NIGHT ORIENTED adj. night owl, night people, swing shifter, graveyard shifter.

NIGHTTIME n. black, dim.

NIGHT WATCHMAN n. Charley, stick.

NINCOMPOOP n. dork, nobody home, dumdum, bonetop, ninny, airedale, musclehead, blockhead, pointyhead, pinhead, saphead, puddinghead, potato head, numbskull, knows from nothing, doesn't know enough to come in out of the rain, stoop, nuthin' upstairs, nitwit, dope. See STUPID.

NINE n. niner, niner from Caroliner, Nina from Carolina.

NINETEEN-TWENTIES n. roaring twenties, golden twenties, jazz age, age of the red hot mamas, mad decade.

NIP v. nab at, sink one's teeth into, take a chunk out of, chaw on.

NIPPLES n. razzberries, rosebuds (Fem.), nips; bee bites (M.).

NITROGLYCERINE n. nitro, dinah, dine, grease, juice, noise, soup.

NITROMETHANE n. juice, pop, nitro.

NITROUS OXIDE n. laughing gas.

NITWIT n. nerd, numbnut, lamebrain, birdie (teenage), scatterbrain, rattleweed, dumdum, four-letter man (dumb), boob, airedale, airhead, balloonhead, meathead, pointyhead, numbskull, stupe, thick, goofus, leak in the think tank, dunce, dead ass. See STUPID.

NO adv. N.O., nix, no way, no dice, no-go, nope, naw, no siree, no way José, no can do, no sale, no soap, frig it, not on your life, nothing doing, negatory, go jump in the lake, take a hike, like hell, shove it, shove it up your ass, stick it up one's ass, stow it. See DENIAL.

NOBLE adj. 1. big, live with, a mensch. See also VIRTUOUS. 2. blue blood, bluestocking, ritzy.

NOBLE n. blue blood, bluestocking.

NOBLEMAN n. blue blood, lace curtain, silk stocking, swell, upper cruster.

NOBODY n. wimp, wuss, little guy, semi-dork, nebbish, squirt, small potato, nobody, Mr. and Mrs. Nobody, Tom Dick and Harry, zilch, zero, zip, zippo. See UNIMPORTANT.

NOISE n. ruckus, fuss, buzz-buzz, hoo-ha, clinker, rowdydow, hubba-hubba, hullabaloo, fireworks.

NOISE v. squawk, squack, put up a squawk, holler, beef, howl, raise a howl, put up a howl, raise cain, raise a ruckus.

NOISY adj. ear-poppin', ear-splitting, wall-shaking, booming, turned up, can't hear yourself think, raising the roof, screaming, jumpin', loudmouth, leather-lunged, yakky, raising cain, raising hell, rambunctious, rootin'-tootin', rowdy-dowdy, ziggy.

NOMINAL adj. all there, as advertised, right on.

NOMINATE v. tab, tag, peg, put down for, name, slot, slate.

NONADDICTIVE DRUG n. soft drug.

NONAPPEARANCE adj. break a date, no-show, stand one up.

NONCHALANCE n. cool, keeping one's cool, polish.

NONCHALANT adj. cool cat, cool, unflappable, laid back, breezy, mellow, loose, hang loose, not turn a hair, go with the flow, poker-faced, phone it in. See INDIFFERENT.

NONCOMMISSIONED OFFICER n. NCO, noncom, sarge, topkick, tech sarge; ripper, ripple (WAVE).

NONCOMMISSIONED PERSONNEL n. Hollywood corporal, zebra.

NONCOMMITTAL adj. 1. play it cool, it's all the same to me, the middle ground, middle of the road, on the fence, fence-sitter, even-steven, no-man's-land, mugwumpian, mugwumpish. See NEUTRAL. 2. clam, clam up, hush-hush, zip one's lips, button up, button up one's lip, between one and the lamp post, tight chops, play it cool.

NONCONFORM v. drop out, opt out, cop out, get out of line, rock the boat, make waves, leave the beaten path, kick over the traces. See also DISAGREE.

NONCONFORMING adj. anti, agin, con, beat, beatnik, beat generation, offbeat, off the beaten track, off the beaten path, cool, far out, way out, avant-garde, flake, flaky, fringy, kinky, bent, weird, weirdo, cuckoo, cooky, kook, kooky, off the wall, out in left field, zoid, trippy, off base, out of line, march to a different drummer. See also ECCENTRIC.

NONCONFORMIST adj. maverick, oddball, swinger, bohemian, an original, offbeat, beatnik, hippie, yippie, dropout, freak, flower child, nature boy, street people, night people, crazy, weirdo, weirdie, fish out of water, square peg in a round hole.

NONDRINKER n. A.A., teetotaler, on the wagon, on the water wagon, Christer.

NONE n. zip, zippo, zilch, goose eggs, shit-all. See also NOTHING.

NONENTITY n. wimp, little guy, nebbish, pip-squeak, small potato, jackstraw, nobody, zilch, zero, zip, zippo. See UNIMPORTANT.

NONESSENTIAL adj. deadwood, excess baggage, Mickey Mouse, need it like a hole in the head, this I need?, who needs it. See also UNIMPORTANT.

NONFUNCTIONAL adj. crashed, down, go down, on downtime, no go, busted, out of commission, on the blink, on the fritz, kaput, freeze up, frozen, haywire. See DAMAGED.

NONINTERVENTION n. butt out, not butt in, cool one's heels, sit on one's ass, sit on one's butt, sit on one's duff, sit on one's hands, mind your own beeswax, peanut policy (Pol.).

NON-JEW n. goy, goyim, shegets, shiksa (Derog.).

NONPAREIL adj. world class, 10, ten, A number one, ace high, mega-gnarly, zero cool, rad, fab, dynamite, state of the art, flash, tops, first class, first chop, stellar, boss. See BEST.

NO PARKING red zone.

NONPARTICIPANT n. nonstarter, along for the ride.

NONPARTICIPATION n. butt out, not butt in, cool one's heels, sit on one's ass, sit on one's butt, sit on one's duff, sit on one's hands, mind your own beeswax, peanut policy (Pol.).

NONPARTISAN adj. free wheeling, on one's own, nothingarian, anythingarian, dawk (neither a dove or a hawk), play it cool, middle of the road, on the fence, mugwumpian, mugwumpish. See NEUTRAL.

NONPAYER n. deadbeat, deadhead, welcher, welsher, freeloader, load of hay (group), rabbit, stiff, desperado, skipper, skedaddler, no-show, behind.

NONPAYING adj. freeloader, schnorrer, deadhead, skip out, shoot the moon, fly kites, welsher.

NONPLUS v. bug, rattle, rattle one's cage, throw, throw into a tizzy, buffalo, fuck with one's head, mess with one's head, play hob with, floor, flummox. See PUZZLE.

NONPLUSSED adj. unglued, discombobulated, shook up, balled up, hung up, floored, stunned, struck dumb, thrown, rattled, in a fog, bamboozled, buffaloed. See PUZZLED.

NONPROFESSIONAL n. nonpro, am, ammie, ham, bush, bush league, jackleg, Sunday —— (Sunday driver). See AMATEUR.

NONRESISTANT adj. pushover, go along for the ride, go with the flow, wimpy, blah. See also SUBMISSIVE.

NON-SAILOR n. landlubber, ground gripper.

NONSENSE n. jazz, jive, bafflegab, double-talk, gobbledygook, hokum, hoky, hoky-poky, hop, noise, applesauce, poppycock, tommyrot, rot, narrishkeit, fiddlesticks, twaddle, bunch of baloney, baloney, phoney boloney, globaloney, phonus bolonus, spinach, gas, wind, song and dance, bunk, bunko, bunkum, bull, shit, bullshit, BS, horseshit, crap, crapola, shit for the birds, stuff and nonsense, blah, blah-blah, bushwah, boushwah, bosh, banana oil, blarney, chicken, cheese, a line of cheese, claptrap, tripe, pshaw, caca, total cahcah, guff, scat, bop, drool, bilge, piffle, moonshine, fiddle-faddle, flamdoodle, flapdoodle, flumadiddle, balloon juice, hot air, horsefeathers, hooey, fudge, slush, hogwash, garbage, malarkey, full of beans, full of hops, full of hot air, full of prunes, talk through one's hat, talk like a man with a paper ass, tell it to the marines, crackpot, crackers, cockamamie, cockeyed, bughouse, off the wall, wacky, whacko, loco, blue loco, loony, loopy, loose, screwloose, screwy, screwball, squirrelly, birdie (teenage), skag, jerky, batty, sappy, goofy, daffy, kooky, potty, dotty, ding-a-ling, dingy, dippy, dumbo, dumb de dumb dumb dumb, dumb thing to do, dumb trick, fool trick, fool's trick, foolheaded, meatballism, goofy, goo-goo, gaga,

cuckoo, meshuga, meshugana, fruity, fruitcakey, nutty as a fruitcake, nutty, nutsy Fagan, nuts, just plain nuts, nerts, dippy, dizzy, bananas, goofus, bonkers, barmy, beany, buggy, bugs, round the bend, snap case, do the crazy act, do the crazy bit, do the crazy shtick.

NONSUPPORTIVE adj. off the reservation.

NONTIPPER n. stiff, clutch, deadbeat, flathead, George, Eddy, load of hay (party).

NONUNION WORKER n. scab (strikebreaker), red apple, papoose, scissorbill, free rider.

NOOSE n. rope, hemp, the hemp, hemp four-in-hand, hemp bridle, hemp collar, hemp necktie.

NORFOLK, VIRGINIA Sailor City.

NORMAL adj. together, all there, as advertised, right, right in the head, in one's right mind, have all one's buttons, have all one's marbles, have both oars in the water. See also AVERAGE.

NORTH AMERICAN DEFENSE COMMAND n. NORAD.

NORTH ATLANTIC TREATY ORGANIZATION n. NATO.

NORTH CAROLINA Old North State, Tar Heel State.

NORTH DAKOTA Flickertail State, Sioux State.

NOSE n. smeller, schnoz, schnozzola, schnozzle, bazoo, beak, bugle, horn, honker, honk-honk, snoot, nozzle, banana, bill, beezer, boke, conk, handle, sniffer, snuffer, whiffer.

NOSTALGIA n. schmaltz, goo, mush, slop, glop, slush, sob story, tear-jerker, hearts and flowers.

NOSTALGIC adj. 1. syrupy, drippy, soppy, tear-jerker, beery, sticky, sappy, sloppy, gushing, hearts and flowers, cornball, mushy, shmaltz, schmaltzy. See SENTIMENTAL. 2. down memory lane, strike a note, like it was yesterday, old hat, rhino.

NOSTRUM n. fix, quick fix.

NOT adv. N.O., nix, ixnay, no way, no dice, nope, unh unh, uh uh, ugh ugh, nah, naw, no siree, no way José, no can do, no sale, no soap, ask me another, frig it, forget it, forget you, who me?, not on your life, not by a long shot, not by a long chalk, not by a long sight, not by a damm sight, not a bit of it, not much, not a chance, not a Chinaman's chance, fat chance, nothing doing, stonewall, negatory, go take a running jump for yourself, go jump in the lake, fubis, 86, like fun, like hell, shove it, shove it up your ass, stick it, stick it up one's ass, stow it.

NOTABLE adj. heavy, heavy stuff, serious shit, something else, big league, major league, top drawer, high profile, hot flash, underlined. See IMPORTANT.

NOTABLE n. name, biggie, big name, big gun, big man on campus, B.M.O.C., big cheese, magoo, high up, high pillow, hotdog, V.I.P., visiting fireman, lion, a somebody, in the limelight. See IMPORTANT. See also CELEBRITY, EXECUTIVE.

NOT COMPLY v. drop out, opt out, cop out, get out of line, rock the boat, make waves, leave the beaten path, kick over the traces, look the other way, let it go, let one off easy, let one off this time, wink at, pay no mind, pay no never mind, play past, pooh pooh. See also REFUSE.

NOTE n. 1. memo, line, thank-you note, scratch, reminder. 2. football (whole musical note), lick (music). See also LETTER.

NOTE v. flash on, dig, spot, clock, take in, tumble, take a tumble, catch, get an eyeful of, get a load of, pick up on. See SEE.

NOTEBOOK n. little black book.

NOTED adj. celeb, star, name, number 1, number one, numero uno, a somebody, w.k. (well known), face, lion, page-oner, hot dog. See CELEBRITY.

NOTEPAPER n. scratch pad.

NOTEWORTHY adj. heavy, meaningful, splash, stand out, super-duper, terrific, the utmost, the end, mind-blowing, boss, bitchin', cool, murder, serious jelly, something else, big league, major league, high profile, hot shit, we're not talking about nutmeg here, underlined. See IMPORTANT.

NOTHING adj. 1. zero, big zero, zip, zippo, zot, zilch, nix, cipher, goose egg, duck egg, egg, shutout, empty, horse collar, nit, a collar, nada, 86, scratch, squat, diddly, diddly squat, diddly poo, shit, diddly shit, doodly squat, beans, jack, jack shit, borscht, fly speck, flea, chit, chirp, a chromosome, crumb, drip, dinky, measly, minimal to the max, from nothing. 2. Mickey Mouse, gadget, rinkydink, nutmeg, two by four, two bit, nickel and dime, penny ante, peanuts, pissytailed, big deal, no big deal, big shit, no big shit, no biggie, no big thing, no skin off one's nose, never mind, no matter, chicken feed, chicken shit, bupkis, a hump, shot, tinhorn, entry level (job), bottom rung, lower rung, small potatoes, small beer, small change, small time, small pot, pokerino, pinchy, one horse, jerkwater (small town), nowhere, drop in the bucket, drop in the ocean, sucking wind, little go, macht nichts, mox nix, makes no never mind, no great shakes, mere bagatelle, frig it, chuck it, drop it, forget it, let it pass, skip it, not worth a hill of beans, not worth a row of beans, row of buttons, row of pins, damn, darn, tinker's dam, a hoot, got other fish to fry, other fish in the sea, other pebbles on the beach, raggedy act, harlot's hello. 3. wuss, wimp, jerk, semi-dork, sad sack, nebbish, squirt, twerp, shrimp, scrub, runt, little guy, small potatoes, small fry, cipher, zero, nobody, Mr. and Mrs. Nobody,

Brown Jones and Robinson, John Doe and Mary Roe, John Doe and Richard Roe, Tom, Dick and Harry, pushover, winner, real winner, dog, loser, real loser, punk, tinhorn, flat tire, dud, skag, pip-squeak, whippersnapper, whiffet, flash in the pan, jackstraw, man of straw.

NOTICE n. info, tip, score, picture, lowdown, know, goods, cue, clue, dope, dope sheet, poop, poop sheet, squib, write-up, story, whole story. See NEWS. See also ADVERTISEMENT.

NOTICE v. flash on, dig, spot, clock, take in, tumble, catch, get an eyeful of, get a load of, pick up on, rap, rumble. See SEE.

NOTICEABLE adj. big as life, one can't miss it, open and shut, open and shut case, under one's nose, if it was a snake it would bite you. See APPARENT.

NOTIFICATION n. info, tip, hot tip, score, lowdown, goods, cue, clue, dope sheet, poop sheet, let one in on. See INFORMATION.

NOTION n. spark, flash, flash on it, approach, slant, twist, wrinkle, wienie, angle, how one figures it. See IDEA.

NOTORIETY n. 1. flak, ballyhoo, splash, big noise, ink, noise about, pitch, scratch, spread, bell, make a big splash, get ink. 2. flash in the pan, on center stage, in the spotlight.

NOTORIOUS adj. live in a glass house, hanging out, spot one like a lead dime, stick out like a sore thumb, make a splash, page-oner, wanted, candy, candy kid, duded up, belled. See CELEBRITY.

NOUGHT n. zero, big zero, zip, zippo, zot, zilch, cipher, goose egg, horse collar, nada, 86, scratch, squat, beans, borscht. See NOTHING.

NOURISHING adj. sticks to one's ribs.

NOURISHMENT n. eats, feed, grub, go juice, lump, sticks to one's ribs, vittles, grubbery, home cooking. See FOOD.

NOVEL adj. diff, far cry, funky, offbeat, at the cutting edge, breaking new snow, avant-garde, now, contempo, fire new, just out, newfangled. See NEW.

NOVEL n. book, yarn, clothesline, cliff-hanger, bodice-ripper (romance), potboiler, spyboiler. See STORY.

NOVELTY n. an original, crazy, oddball, weird, last word, fire new, newfangled contraption. See NEW.

NOVICE n. newie, greeny, gremlin, gremmie, freshie, turkey, punk, rook, rookie, boot, starter, new boy, new boy on the block, new kid on the block, break in, gazooney (Maritime), fish, greenhorn, student, tenderfoot, heel, heeler (reporter), peg boy, pratt boy, buckwheater, cheechako, chukoko, dub, jice, new jice, john, mark, know from nothing, not know the score, not be with it, not know one's ass from one's elbow, not have the foggiest, first of May. See also APPRENTICE, RECRUIT, BEGINNER.

NOW adv. pronto, on the double, double time, like now, toot sweet, off the pop, in nothing flat, pretty damned quick, PDQ: See IMMEDIATELY.

NUB n. bottom line, heart, meat and potatoes, nitty-gritty. See BASIC.

NUCLEAR ACCIDENT n. event, meltdown, China syndrome.

NUCLEAR PARTICLES n. fallout, zoo.

NUCLEAR WEAPON n. nuke, mininuke, backpack nuke, doomsday machine.

NUCLEAR WEAPONS SYSTEMS MX, Cruise, Stealth, Honest Johns, Marv, Mirv, Goloshes, Scuds, Frogs, Scapegoats, Aphids, Sparrows, Kangaroos, Kitchens, Walleyes, Fishpots, Tweets, Aardvarks.

NUDE adj. bare-assed, B.A., peeled, bald, buck naked, naked as a jaybird, nudie, in one's birthday suit, in the altogether, buff, in the buff, stripped to the buff, raw, in the raw, without a stitch, au naturel, skin, wear a smile.

NUISANCE n. drag, headache, pain, pain in the ass, pain in the neck, blister, nudzh, noodge, nudge, nag, bummer, creep, pill, drip, kibitzer, flat tire. See ANNOYANCE. See also BORE.

NULLIFY v. scrub, kill, zap, trash, cream, torpedo, ax, crab, squash, dial back, forget it, knock out, call all bets off, scratch, blue pencil, wash out, wipe out, stamp out, take out, renig, nig. See CANCEL.

NUMBER v. count noses, count heads, count off, tick off, cut ice, cut some ice, dope out, figure in, keep tabs, run down, take account of, tote, tote up.

NUMBERLESS adj. umpteen, zillion, jillion, eleventeen, rafts, gobs, heaps, bags of, no end of, no end to. See COUNTLESS.

NUMBERS, LARGE adj. zillion, skillion, gillion, jillion, stillion, bazillion, eleventeen, forty' leven, skaty-eight, umpteen, umpteenth, umpty, umpty-umpth, steen, flock of, google, slew, whole slew of, a boodle, whole kit and boodle, caboodle, whole kit and caboodle, everybody and his brother, everyone and his uncle. See also AMOUNT, LARGE.

NUMBERS RACKETEER n. digits dealer.

NUMBERS, SMALL adj. nothing, buttons, peanuts, bupkis, practically nothing, no one, practically no one. See also AMOUNT, SMALL.

NUMEROUS adj. umpteen, zillion, jillion, mucho, gobs, scads, heaps, lousy with, stacks. See AMOUNT, LARGE.

NUN n. hood.

NURSE n. sitter, baby-sitter, nanny, mammy.

NURSE v. sit, baby-sit, watch over, watch out for, keep an eye on, keep tabs on, ride herd on.

NURSEMAID n. sitter, baby-sitter, nanny sitter, mammy, nanny.

NURTURE v. bring up, fetch up, drag up.

NUTRITIOUS adj. sticks to one's ribs.

NYMPHET adj. nymph, nympho, sex job, Lolita, jailbait, San Quentin quail.

NYMPHOMANIAC n. broad, pushover, round heels, easy lay, mink, easy woman, loose woman, woman of easy virtue, chippie, chippy, floozy, tramp, bum, slut, dog, frail, frail sister, blimp, bombshell, charity girl, chaser, run around, floss around, cuddle bunny, fruit, piece of trade, pigmeat (old), flasher.

NYMPHOMANIC adj. nymph, nympho, hot in the ass, hot to trot, sex job, hose monster.

O

O n. Oscar, oboe.

OAF n. numbnut, asshole, loser, winner, lamebrain, birdie (teenage), birdbrain, lunchie, dodo, dummy, dumbo, dumdum, dumb Dora, dumb head, dumb ox, four-letter man (dumb). See STUPID.

OAKLAND, CALIFORNIA Big Oak.

OATH n. cuss, cuss word, dirty word, dirty name, four-letter word, no-no, swear word. See also EXPLETIVE.

OATMEAL n. cush, grits, mush.

OBDURATE adj. 1. cold fish, cold-blooded, mean, rhinoceros hide, thick-skinned, dead ass. See CALLOUS. 2. hard-nosed, hang tough, tough nut to crack, head in concrete, set in concrete, rock-ribbed, hardheaded, bullhead, stubborn as a mule. See STUBBORN.

OBEDIENT adj. in one's power, in one's pocket, in one's clutches, under one's thumb, at one's mercy, at one's beck and call, at one's feet, a slave to, on a string, on a leash, yes-man, ass-kisser, pussy whipped, led by the nose, tied to one's apron's strings, dance to one's tune, putty in one's hands. See also SUBMISSIVE.

OBESE adj. fatso, fat city, whale, hippo, baby elephant, heavy, blimp, butterball, two-ton tessie, avoirdupois. See FAT.

OBEY v. knuckle under, go by the book, go by the numbers, stay in line, not get out of line, toe the line, toe the mark, lie down and roll over for, go along with, give in, don't make waves, don't rock the boat, go with the flow, go social. See COMPLY.

OBFUSCATE v. con, diddle, double-talk, sell wolf cookies, muddy the waters, stir the waters, pettifog, cloud the issue, throw up a smoke screen, stonewall, cover up. See CONFUSE.

OBITUARY n. obit.

OBJECT n. 1. jobby, dealie bob, motherfucker, mofo, mother grabber, gimmick, gismo, widget, do hinkey, dingus, whatchamacallit, whatzis, frobnitzem. See APPARATUS. 2. ground zero, surgical mission (precise target), zero.

OBJECT v. 1. bitch, beef, make a stink, gripe, sound off, gritch, squawk, crab, grouse, kick. See COMPLAIN. 2. be agin, buck, take on, mix it up with, tangle with, cross, go one on one. See OPPOSE.

OBJECTION n. beef, where's the beef?, bitch, kick, squawk, stink, gripe, bellyache, blackball. See GRIEVANCE. See also DISAPPROVAL, CRITICISM.

OBJECTIONABLE adj. 1. it sucks, bummer, take down, bad news, bad scene, godawful, murder, poison, lousy. See UNDESIRABLE. See also OBNOXIOUS. 2. turkey, toad, phrog (person), creep, jerk, drip, chirp, chit, nerd, wet blanket, stinky, twerp, gives one a pain, gives one a pain in the neck, gives one a pain in the ass, gripes one. See UNDESIRABLE PERSON.

OBJECTIVE adj. like it is, call 'em as one sees 'em, cool, cold, cold turkey, strictly business, straight, straight from the shoulder, the emess, no shit, no bull, no bullshit, no bullshitting, on the square, warts and all. See also FAIR, UNEMOTIONAL.

OBJECTIVE n. ground zero, surgical mission (precise target), zero.

OBLIGATED adj. into, on the tab, in hock, hooked, on a string, owe one one.

OBLIGATION n. IOU, in debt, in the red, in hock, on the nut, hooked, chit, due bill, dues. See DEBT. See also RESPONSIBILITY.

OBLIGE V. fit in, fill the bill, be just what the doctor ordered, be just the ticket, make room, meet halfway, go fifty-fifty, find the middle ground, don't rock the boat, don't make waves, roll with the punches, swim with the tide, if you can't beat 'em join 'em, when in Rome do as the Romans do, toe the mark, grin and bear it, take it, come around, come over, move over, bend over backwards, lean over backwards, make a deal.

OBLITERATE v. scrub, nix, kill, cut, blue pencil, X out, axe, zap, trash, total, cream, torpedo, do in, dial back, waste, off, finish, finish off, knock off, knock out, kayo, KO, sink, bog, squash, smash, smash up, bitch up, scratch, shoot down, shoot down in flames, put the kibosh on, wash out, wipe out, wipe off the map, take out, take apart, tear down, stamp out, rub out, blue ruin, blow sky high, fix, fix one's wagon, come down on, cook, cook one's goose, deep six (evidence). See also CANCEL, KILL.

OBLITERATED adj. scrubbed, killed, offed, wasted, shot, shot down, shot down in flames, washed out, wiped out, all bets off, kaput, zapped, totaled, nixed, scratched, blue penciled, rubbed out. See also KILLED.

OBLIVION n. no-man's-land, out there, gone, nowhere.

OBLIVIOUS adj. gorked, gone, zonked, spacey, out to lunch, strung out, not all there, not with it. See UNCONSCIOUS.

OBNOXIOUS adj. rotten, gross, awful, beastly, stinking, grody, grody to the max, pesky, pestiferous, bitchy, cussed, mean, ornery, funky (Bl.), chromo, crumb, creep, turd, nerd, nudnik, pill, heel, shit heel, shit hook, big mouth, gives one a pain, pain in the ass, pain in the neck, hunk of cheese, blue, off-color, off time, zod.

OBOE n. thermometer, snake charmer, ill wind.

OBSCENE adj. filthy, feelthy, dirty, blue, X-rated, adult, porn, porno, porny, raunchy, raw, adult, mature, hard core, soft core, hot, heavy, hot and heavy, hot stuff, jack-off material, jerk-off material, steamy, rough, rough stuff, evil-minded, foul mouth, foulmouthed, salty, off-color, off base, out of line, low-down, low-down and dirty, smutty, jiggly, purple, in the gutter, horny, cream jeans, hot pants, a lech on, lechin's.

OBSCENITY n. scuz, smut, sleaze, cuss, cuss word, dirty word, dirty name, four-letter word, no-no, swear word, porn, porno, soft porn, hard porn, soft core, hard core, skin flick, skin pix, snuff, T and A, Tijuana bible, X-rated, triple X-rated, hot stuff, jack-off material, jerk-off material, peep show.

OBSCURE adj. clear as mud, clear as dishwater, clear as ditch water, heavy, fuzzy, mumbo-jumbo, Greek, it's Greek to me, Choctaw, double Dutch, tough, tough nut to crack, mind-bending, it beats me, beats the shit outta me, you've got me, you got me, I pass, I give up, too much, too deep for one, over one's head.

OBSCURE v. con, diddle, double-talk, muddy the waters, stir the waters, pettifog, cloud the issue, throw up a smoke screen, stonewall, cover up. See also EQUIVOCATE, CONFUSE.

OBSERVANT adj. on the ball, on the job, on one's toes, on the lookout, on the qui vive, not miss a trick, not overlook a bet, see to. See ATTENTIVE.

OBSERVATION n. saying, catch phrase, crack, wisecrack, say so, comeback, mouthful (you said a mouthful).

OBSERVATION POST n. O.P., catbird seat.

OBSERVE v. 1. beam, flash, flash on, spot, spy, dig, read, lamp, catch, eagle eye, eyeball, take in, get an eyeful of, get a load of, pick up on. See SEE. 2. go slumming, slum, take in the sights, gap, jap (crime). 3. mouth off, crack, wisecrack, spring with a crack.

OBSERVER n. kibitzer, nark, sidewalk superintendent, watcher, gaper. See also AUDIENCE.

OBSESSED adj. fiendish, gone, hung up, bugged, hooked, taken over by, into, really into, heavily into, up to here in, head over heels in, all wound up in, wrapped up in, eat sleep and breathe something, turned on, tied up, have a bee in one's bonnet, have a bug in one's ear, have a bug up one's ass, have an ax to grind, have a thing about, have a tiger by the tail.

OBSESSION n. hang-up, jones, monkey, a must, have a thing about, have on the brain, bug, bug up one's ass, bug in one's ear, bag, ax to grind, bee, bee in one's bonnet, head in concrete, set in concrete, one-track mind, tiger, tiger by the tail, case, crush (romantic).

OBSOLETE adj. out, gone, had it, out of it, has-been, old hat, dinosaur, fossil, horse and buggy, icky, back number, of the old school, dead as a dodo, dead and done for, done for, moldy fig, kaput. See also DEAD.

OBSTACLE n. catch, joker, catch 22, hang-up, psychological baggage, stumbling block, monkey wrench, booby trap. See HINDRANCE.

OBSTINATE adj. hard shell, hang in there, hang tough, locked in, head in concrete, set in concrete, chiseled in stone, solid as a rock, brick wall, stand one's ground, dig in one's heels, stick to one's guns, pigheaded, dead set on, has one's Dutch up. See STUBBORN.

OBSTINATELY adv. hang in, hang in there, hang tough, hang on, hang on for dear life, hang on like a bulldog, hang on like a leech, stick it, stick it out, stick to it, stick with it, stick to one's guns, go the whole hog, go all out, go through hell and high water, go for broke, go for it, not give up the ship.

OBSTREPEROUS adj. rambunctious, raising a riot, raising a ruction, raising a rumpus, kicking up a row, out of order, out of line. See also NOISY.

OBSTRUCT v. queer, stymie, crab, hang up, hold up, foul up, fuck up, gum up the works, stonewall, stall, weigh down, drag one's foot, hang like a millstone round one's neck, sandbag, monkey with the buzz saw, monkey with, mix in. See HINDER. See also PREVENT.

OBSTRUCTION n. stumbling block, one small difficulty, a lock, jam up, monkey wrench, booby trap, gridlock. See HINDRANCE.

OBTAIN v. snag, grab, cop, kipe, kype, corral, wangle, promote, latch on to, scare up, snap up, buy up, blow one's self to, access, capture (computer data). See GET.

OBTAINABLE adj. pushover, on tap, on deck, in stock, come-at-able, getable, get-in-able, no sweat, no problem, duck soup, cherry pie, piece of cake, can o' corn, ready willing and able, there for the taking, ready to be plucked, ready to be taken. See also EASY.

OBTUSE adj. nerky, lamebrained, birdbrained, four-letter man (dumb), thick, clodpated, blockheaded, pointyheaded, woodenheaded, deadheaded, flat tire, numbskulled, doesn't know which way is up, doesn't know enough to come in out of the rain, dope, dead ass, dub, drip, farmer, slow on the uptake, slow on the draw. See STUPID.

OBVIOUS adj.   barefaced, plain as the nose on one's face, crystal clear, big as life, open and shut, open and shut case, you know it, cheesecloth (person). See APPARENT.

OCARINA n.   sweet potato.

OCCASION n.   hap, happening, happenso, scene, goings-on, go down, come off, time. See EVENT.

OCCASIONALLY adv.   once in a blue moon, once in a coon's age, every now and then, every once in a while, every so often.

OCCIDENTAL n.   round eye.

OCCUPATION n.   bag, gig, day gig, rig gig (truck driving), beeswax, biz, schmear, game, gesheft, line, line of business, number, go, do, dodge, wheeling & dealin', what one is into, thing, hang, nine-to-five shit, rat race, slot, setup, grind, daily grind, grindstone, lick, moonlight, the salt mines, play, racket, swindle, grift, gyppo, jippo, hemo jo, shitwork, chickwork (household), scutwork, donkeywork, coffee-and-cake job. See also WORK.

OCCUPATIONAL SAFETY AND HEALTH ADMINISTRATION n.   OSHA.

OCCUPIED adj.   at warp one, clocked up, busy as a bee, busier than a one-armed paperhanger, tied up, head over heels in, enough on one's plate. See BUSY.

OCCUR v.   gel, jell, shake, smoke, what goes, what's coming down, what's going down, action, where's the action?, what's happening, cook, cook up a storm, what cooks?, what's cooking?, cooking with gas.

OCCURRENCE n.   happening, hap, happenso, go down, come off, trip, real trip, like it is, where it's at, the size of it, scene, bit, piece, routine, shtick, spot, goings-on. See EVENT.

OCEAN n.   drink, big drink, the pond, big pond, bounding main, deep, the briny, briny deep, Davy Jones's locker, sink, splash.

ODD adj.   kooky, offbeat, funny, weirdo, weirdie, oddball, foul ball, avant-garde, fringy, kinky, flaky, far out, way out, crazy, off the wall, not wrapped real tight, character, spacey. See ECCENTRIC.

ODIOUS adj.   mean, ornery, chromo, crumb, creep, turd, heel, shit heel, pain in the ass, pain in the neck. See OBNOXIOUS.

ODOROUS adj.   stinko, stinky, stinking, whiffy, nosey, strong, loud (strong).

OF prep.   a (piece a cake).

OFFEND v.   zing, turn off, cool, chop, cut up, sound dozens, lay a bad trip on one, flip one the finger, give five fingers to one, hit one where one lives, do a number on one, kick one around. See INSULT.

OFFENDED adj.   burnt up, browned off, bleeding, sore, all torn up, cut up, miffed, miffy, hit where one lives, shook, shook up, shot down, peeved, uptight, have one's nose out of joint. See also INSULTED.

OFFENSE n.   1. put-down, zinger, rap, slam, black eye, hit, dirty dig, left-handed compliment, slap in the face, low rent. See INSULT. 2. blitz, blitzkrieg, push, mugging. 3. sight, dump, blot on the landscape.

OFFENSIVE adj.   1. rotten, gross, stinking, grody, chromo, crumb, turd, blue, off-color, off time. See OBNOXIOUS.

OFFER n.   hit, feeler, proposish, proposition, pass, pitch, action.

OFFER v.   hit on, proposition, make a pitch, put a feeler out, pop the question.

OFFHAND adj.   1. laid back, cool, mellow, breezy, easygoing, down home, homey, haymish, folksy, pokesy, sporty, let one's hair down. See CASUAL. 2. throwaway, ad lib, off the cuff, off the hip, off the top of one's head, shoot from the hip. See IMPROVISE.

OFFICE n.   work station, cave, foundry, salt mines, front office, shop, store, setup.

OFFICEHOLDER n.   pol, politico, glad-hander, handshaker, hack, party hack, satch, war-horse, wheeler-dealer, logroller, boss, man higher up, baby kisser, bell-ringer. See POLITICIAN.

OFFICER n.   cop; slime, slime bucket (Derog.); arm, narc (narcotics), the man, black and white, badge, city kitty, Snow White, county mounty, flatfoot, fly cop, fly dick, shamus. See POLICE OFFICER.

OFFICER'S CLUB n.   henhouse.

OFFICE WORK n.   nine-to-five, nine-to-five shit, white collar, pink collar, catching (police duty), day gig, shitwork, salt mines.

OFFICIAL n.   CEO, exec, exec suite, big shot, upstairs, man upstairs, front office, boss, kingpin, brains, head, headman, old man, papa, Big Daddy, Big Brother, brass, top brass, brass hat, gold braid, the topper, the top, on top, top dog, top drawer, higher ups, perkman, apparatchik (junior), rug rank (high), killjoy, buck passer. See also EXECUTIVE, POLITICIAN, POLICE OFFICER.

OFFICIAL LANGUAGE n.   officialese, legalese, federalese, bafflegab.

OFFICIAL PAPERS n.   ticket.

OFFICIALDOM n. pecking order. See also ADMINISTRATION, BUREAUCRACY, ESTABLISHMENT, MANAGEMENT.

OFFICIALISM n. red tape, red tapism, red tapery, foolocracy, gunocracy, mediocracy, moneyocracy.

OFFICIATE v. do the honors, boss, chair, ride herd on, run, handle. See also MANAGE.

OFF-KEY adj. clinker, hit a clinker, hit a sour note, sour, sour note.

OFF-SEASON adj. fifth season, slack season, pinochle season (clothing industry).

OFFSPRING n. kid, sprout, bambino, nipper, pup, cub, chip off the ole block, little shaver, little bugger. See CHILD.

OGLE v. gun, gawk, glom, hold the glims on, lamp, pipe, get a load of, get an eyeful of, give the double O, smoke, rubber, rubberneck, 87 1/2 (look at a girl, restaurant), give the eye, give a thing a play. See SEE.

OGLER n. girl-watcher, drugstore cowboy, rubberneck, rubbernecker. See also FLIRT.

OHIO Buckeye State.

OIL n. devil's tar, liquid gold, mud, oil patch (oil producing area).

OIL v. lube, grease the wheels, slick, slick on.

OIL-FIELD WORKER n. roughneck, sloper (Alaska).

OILING n. grease job, lube.

OILSKIN n. mack, fog, slicker.

OIL-WELL INVESTOR n. oilie.

OKAY interj. O.K., A-O.K., A-okay, okey-dokey, okey-doke, four, ten four, four ten (emphatic), ding ho, ding how, ding hau, no slouch, all reet, reat, right, all right, solid, aces, aljoe, alzo, swell, dory, okydory, hunky-dory, ducky, just ducky, peachy, peachy-keen, copasetic, twenty-two carat, goods, jake, keen, keeno, kosher, McCoy, nuts, pat, patsy. See also ACCEPTABLE.

OKINAWAN n. Okie (Army use).

OKLAHOMA Sooner State.

OKLAHOMA CITY, OKLAHOMA Okie.

OKLAHOMAN n. Okie.

OLD adj. 1. rusty, moth-eaten, a lot of mileage, been around, bent, gone, hairy, passé, oldie, old as the hills, tired, worse for wear, back number, fossil, antique, relic, from way back, raunchy, shot, sleazy. See also DATED. 2. senior, senior citizen, pop, old fart, old-timer, no spring chicken, got a few miles on one, on one's last legs, over the hill, older than God. See AGED.

OLD AGE adj. golden age, gray power, the dwindles. See also AGED.

OLD-FASHIONED adj. funky, lame (Bl.), tired, out, old hat, passé, back number, moth-eaten, museum piece, square, corny, horse and buggy, of the old school. See DATED.

OLD MAN n. old man, O.M., old boy, oldster, golden ager, senior citizen, senior, pop, pops, dad, gramps, grampa, grandpa, granddad, creak, creaker, back number, antique, relic, fossil, old fossil, geezer, old geezer, dodo, old dodo, duffer, old duffer, gaffer, codger, old codger, coot, old coot, fogy, old fogy, regular old fogey, old fart, old poop, old crock, old-timer, old goat, old bat, old gent, old chap, old cuss, old dog, A.K., alte kocker, alter cocker, baldie, baldy, buzzard, desert rat, duddy, fuddy-duddy, ager, raisin, upper plates, gink, gummer, pappy guy, foozle, mossback. See also AGED.

OLD PERSON n. golden ager, senior citizen, no spring chicken, moth-eaten, a lot of mileage, been around, old fossil, old coot, duffer. See AGED.

OLD WOMAN n. old lady, old girl, oldster, golden ager, senior citizen, senior, grandma, gramma, gramms, granny, old granny, old bag, haybag, old haybag, hag, old hag, old dame, old hen, old battle-ax, war-horse, old frump, biddy, biddie, back number, creak, creaker, antique, relic, fossil, old fossil, dodo, old dodo, old folks, old crock, old-timer, old bat, buzzard, ager, raisin, upper plates, gummer, foozle. See also AGED.

OLEOMARGARINE n. margarine, oleo, hard oil.

OLIVE DRAB adj. O.D.

OMAHA, NEBRASKA Beef City, Big O.

OMAHA RESIDENT n. Omahog.

OMBUDSMAN n. troubleshooter, fireman, fixer.

OMIT v. cut, snip, pass up, drop, X-out, trim, knock off. See also EDIT, EXCLUDE, FORGET.

ONCE adj. time was, back, back when, away back, in the olden days.

ONE n. uno, numero uno, ace (restaurant), uh.

ONE pron. me myself and I, big three (me, myself and I), number one, numero uno, yours truly, a dude, cat, a ghee.

ONE TIME adj. one shot, one-shot deal, once in a lifetime.

ONEROUS adj. heavy, hefty, tough, tough proposition, large order, tall order, backbreaker, ballbreaker, ballbuster, rough go, heavy sledding, bitch, headache, can of worms. See DIFFICULT. See also TROUBLESOME.

ONESELF n. big three (me, myself and I), number one, numero uno, yours truly.

ONION n. breath, skunk egg, stinker, tear gas.

ONION ROLL n. bialystok, bialy, tsibilah.

ONLOOKER n. kibitzer, nark, sidewalk superintendent, watcher, rubbernecker, gaper.

ONLY adj. onliest, one shot, once in a lifetime.

ON STAGE adj. on.

OOZE n. goo, gook, gooey, glop, Mississippi mud, gunk.

OPEN adj. 1. up front, mellow, call it like it is, lay it on the line, on the level, straight from the shoulder, straight arrow, talk like a Dutch uncle, call a spade a spade, talk turkey. See FRANK. See also SINCERE, FREE, TALKATIVE. 2. vanilla, folksy, homey, haymish, meat-and-potatoes man. 3. come-at-able, get-in-able, getable, reachable, on tap, on deck. 4. open and shut, clear as the nose on one's face.

OPEN v. 1. crack, crack open, break out, break in, bust in, kick in, jimmy. See also BREACH, PENETRATE. 2. bow, preem, kick off, ring in, start the ball rolling, get things rolling, raise the curtain on. See BEGIN.

OPENER n. church key (beer).

OPENING n. 1. bow, preem, opener, curtain-raiser, coming out, coming-out party. See also BEGINNING. 2. break, big break, shot, get a shot at, go, go at, a fling at, whack, whack at, cut, cut at, a run at, in the hunt, in the running, iron in the fire, connection. See OPPORTUNITY.

OPENLY adv. in broad daylight, under one s nose, warts and all. See also FRANKLY.

OPERA n. uproar, grand uproar.

OPERATE v. 1. percolate, perk, tick, click, hum, cook, it cooks, whittle, cut (surgical). 2. move, make one's move, do a number, go to town, TCB (take care of business), pull off, get in there, run with the ball. See ACT. 3. head up, sit on top of, run, run things, run the show, call the signals, call the play, be in the driver's seat, be in the saddle, hold the reins, pull the strings, pull the wires, handle. See MANAGE.

OPERATING adj. hot, on track, on stream, on line, all systems go, hit the ground running, going, in full swing, with a full head of steam, doing one's thing, percolating, cooking, cooking on all burners, ticking, clicking.

OPERATING EXPENSE n. nut, outlay.

OPERATING ROOM n. OR, the pit.

OPERATION n. 1. ball game, scene, trip, where the action is, goin' down, happening, movin' out, plan, stunt, bit, deal. See ACTION. 2. going concern. See BUSINESS.

OPERATIVE n. op, agent, spook, mole, beekie, buddy fucker, humint, plant, rug merchant, sheep dip (military disguised as civilian), sleeper; company brownnose, keek (industrial), dick, shamus, flatfoot, tec, private eye, P.I., eye, narc, man, G-man, T-man, revenuer, Federal, fed, FBI; Pinkerton, Pink, Pinkie, the Eye, the eye (Pinkerton detective or Pinkerton National Detective Agency); shoe, gumshoe, gumboot, gumheel, rubber heel, brain, deek, elbow, fink, plumber, sleeper (male), bird dog, nab, peeper, eagle eye, house dick, shadow, shagger, slewfoot, stag, star, tail, pounder, bear tracker (plainclothes), Hawkshaw, sleuth, sleuthhound, beagle, skip tracer, spotter; cutout (secret intermediary).

OPINION n. take, judgment call, value judgment, op, say so, slant, two-cents' worth, one's two-cents' worth, vox pop, another county heard from. See also ATTITUDE.

OPINIONATED adj. tilted, weighted, one-sided, cold deck, hard line, locked in, head in concrete, stick to one's guns, hardheaded, stuffy, set on, bitter ender, puffed up, chesty, cocky, bossy. See STUBBORN. See also CONCEITED.

OPIUM n. O, big O, pop, poppy, pox, grease, pill, Chinese tobacco, gow, ghow, gom, goma, hop, hops, mud, tar, gee, stem, yen, yen shee, pen yan, pen yen, black stuff, dream beads, dream wax, dream gum, dreams, God's own medicine, midnight oil, yam yam, smoke.

OPIUM PIPE n. dream stick, joy stick, hop stick, saxophone, yen hook, stem.

OPIUM USE v. burn the midnight oil, hitting the pipe, kick the engine around, kick the gong around, beat the gong, hit the gong, lamp habit, ken ten (lamp), lay down, lay up, laying on the hip, lie down, on the gonger, on the three taps; pill pad, hopjoint (den).

OPIUM USER n. campfire boy, gongbeater, gong kicker, lobby gow, chef, cook (prepares), sick (needs injection).

OPPONENT n. opposish, oppo, opposite number, bad guy, bandit, buddy-buddy (sarcasm), buddy fucker, crip, meat, me and you, angries, dark horse (unknown). See also PRIZEFIGHTER.

OPPORTUNIST n. hustler, finagler, carpetbagger, on the make, operator, wire-puller, bird dog, one on the make.

OPPORTUNITY n. 1. break, breaks, big break, even break, one's move, one's say, one's turn, shot, shot at, get a shot at, whack, whack at, go, go at, stab, stab at, cut, cut at, have a fling at, run at, in the running, in the hunt, prayer, irons in the fire, connection, fair shake, fighting chance, outside chance, fifty-fifty, toss up, flier, flyer, plunge, play, action, a find. 2. lucky strike, lucky scratch, lucky hit, lucky break, good break, run of luck, luck out, luck into, a fluke. See LUCK.

OPPORTUNITY, LOSE THE v. goof, blow it, boot, boot it, muff, muff it, bobble it, drop the ball, miss the boat, miss the bus, lock the stable door after the horse is stolen.

OPPOSE v. be agin, go agin, buck, sass, backtalk, top, take on, take out, mix it up with, tangle with, break with, bump heads with, cross, cross swords with, lock horns with, tell off, square off, face off, face down, put down, push out your lips at one, go one on one, one to one, have a bone to pick, hold no brief for, hit, take a dim view of, zap, nix, blackball, turn thumbs down on, fly in the face of, put the blocks to, put up a fight, put up a struggle, pan, knock, knock the chip off one's shoulder, straighten out. See also DISAGREE, RESIST, FIGHT, BRAVE.

OPPOSED adj. agin, anti, con, allergic to, down on, have a bone to pick, have no use for, turned off by, copper a tip (act against advice). See also CONTRARY.

OPPOSITE adj. other side of the coin, flip side, anti, agin, con, ass' backwards, bass ackwards, topsy-turvy, copper a tip (act against advice), ornery, stuffy. See also CONTRARY.

OPPOSITION n. oppo, opposish, opposite number, bad guy, the bad guys, angries.

OPPRESS v. bug, ride, pick on, put the squeeze on, put the screws on, put the heat on, put one through the wringer, on one's back, on one's case, dog, dog one's case, drive one up the wall. See also FORCE, DOMINEER, DEPRESS.

OPPRESSIVE adj. 1. heavy, hefty, mean, heavy-handed, tough, tough proposition, backbreaker, ballbreaker, ballbuster, rough go, heavy sledding, bitch, headache. 2. close, sticky, steam bath, steamy, sweatbox.

OPPRESSOR n. a Hitler, Simon Legree, slave driver, czar, cossack.

OPTIMIST n. scoutmaster, Pollyanna, ray of sunshine, cheerleader.

OPTIMISTIC adj. rosy, upbeat, high, high on something, Pollyannaish, sunny, ray of sunshine, keeping the faith, looking at the world through rose-colored glasses, looking at something with rose-colored glasses, looking at the bright side, the game ain't over till the last man is out, one can dream can't one?

OPTIMUM adj. ace hi, world class, greatest, gonest, hundred proof, baaaadest, coolville, gilt-edge, topflight, solid gold. See BEST. See also EXCELLENT.

OPTION n. pickup, take it or leave it, flipside, other side of the coin, other fish to fry, other fish in the sea, other pebbles on the beach. See also CHOICE.

OPULENCE n. high on the hog, living high on the hog, on top of the heap, lap of luxury, velvet, bed of roses, clover, the life of Riley, Easy Street, frill, frills, icing on the cake. See also PLENTY.

ORAL SEX n. head, face, face man, face job, hat job, French, French job, French way, box lunch, fruit cup, fur burger, muff dive, seafood, sugar bowl pie, tongue wash, tuna taco, yodelling in the gully, eating at the Y, blow job, French job, suck, deep throat, shot upstairs, sixty-nine, bananas and cream, penilingism, peter puff (all Obsc.).

ORAL SEX v. eat it, eat out, eat pussy, eat at the Y, French, French kiss, give a face job, give face, give head, go down on, go around the world, have hair pie, muff dive, perform, sit on one's face, sixty-nine, suck, cock suck, sucky suck, suck off, blow, blow job, head, deep throat, cannibal (one who performs), gobble, peter puff, play the skin flute, cop a joint (all Obsc.). See also FELLATIO.

ORANGEADE n. forty-one (Rest.).

ORANGE JUICE n. OJ, squeeze one.

ORATE v. pitch, spiel, spout, stump, soapbox, get on a soapbox, chew the scenery, blow, blow hot air, lay it on, lay it on with a trowel, lay it on thick, pile it on, talk big, talk tall, talk highfalutin'. See also SPEAK.

ORATION n. pitch, spiel, chalk talk, pep talk, soapbox oration. See SPEECH.

ORATOR n. chalk talker, jawsmith, soapboxer, soapbox orator, spieler, spouter, stumper, tub thumper.

ORCHESTRA n. ork, orc, orch, combo, group, sidemen, backup, big band, jump band, swing band, jazz band, jazz blowers, blue blowers.

ORCHESTRA LEADER n. monkey, professor.

ORCHESTRATION n. charts.

ORDAIN v. call the play, call the signals, call the tune, lay down the law, deal, deal with, put one's foot down, read the riot act, walk heavy, bulldoze. See COMMAND.

ORDER n. pecking order, down the line, place, slot. See also SEQUENCE.

ORDER v. lay down the law, pull the strings, call the shots, call the signals, call the tune, crack the whip, rule the roost. See MANAGE.

ORDERLY adj. together, all together, have one's act together, have one's shit together, have one's head together, have one's head screwed on right, apple pie, apple pie order, neat as a button, neat as a pin, slick, to rights, in shape, in good shape, shipshape, all policed up, set up, fixed, framed, it is laid on. See also METHODICAL.

ORDERLY n. dog robber (WW I).

ORDINANCE n. reg, up to code.

ORDINARINESS n. hamfat, meatballism.

ORDINARY adj. garden variety, everyday, generic, plastic, no great shakes, so-so, strictly union, vanilla, rumdum, run of the mill. See AVERAGE.

OREGON the Beaver State, Sunset State, Webfoot State.

ORGAN n. 1. god box, wind box, mighty Wurlitzer. 2. org, insides, guts, parts, nuts and bolts, family jewels.

ORGANIST n. monkey grinder.

ORGANIZATION n. the Company, the Establishment, the Man, syndicate, outfit, T.O., dotted line responsibilty, pecking order, jungle, zoo, org, tie-up, tie-in, tie-in tie-up, hookup, gang, mob, ring, clan, tribe, troupe, combination, combo. See also ASSOCIATION.

ORGANIZATION OF PETROLEUM EXPORTING COUNTRIES n. OPEC.

ORGANIZATION TABLE n. dotted-line responsibility, T.O.

ORGANIZE v. 1. put in shape, clear the decks, button down, tailor, work out a deal, get one's act together, get one's ducks together, pull things together, team up. See ARRANGE. 2. frame, mastermind, line up, set up, lay out, get set for, fix to. See PLAN.

ORGANIZED adj. 1. together, all together, have one's act together, have one's shit together, have one's head together, have one's head screwed on right, cut and dry. 2. set up, all lined up, by the numbers, apple pie, apple-pie order, slick, to rights, in shape, in good shape, shipshape, set up, jumped up (hastily), fixed, framed, it is laid on. See also PLANNED.

ORGANIZED CRIME n. Mafia, Cosa Nostra, the famiglia, the family, syndicate, the organization, our outfit, the rackets, the people, the arm, the commission, crime cartel, dope ring, black market, Black Hand.

ORGASM n. come, blow, get it off, get off, get one's rocks off, shoot, shoot one's wad (all Obsc.). See SEXUAL CLIMAX.

ORGY n. bat, bender, binge, tear, toot, wingding, bust; circle jerk, circus, circus love, gang bang (all Obsc.). See also PARTY, REVEL.

ORIENTAL n. dink, slope, slant eye, gook, gooney, gooney bird, moose (women), rice burger, rice grinder, skibby (all Derog.).

ORIENTATION n. 1. backgrounder, breaking in. 2. fix, how it is, how the land lies, the lay of the land.

ORIGIN n. 1. opener, square one, day 1, day one, first crack out of the box, from the word go, git go, blast off.

See BEGINNING. 2. horse's mouth, connection, tipster, tout.

ORIGINAL adj. breaking new snow, avant garde, cherry. See also NEW.

ORIGINAL TV PROGRAM n. pilot.

ORIGINATE v. intro, father, break the ice, open up, think up, come up with, spark, spitball. See CAUSE, INNOVATE.

ORNAMENT n. gingerbread, bells and whistles, fuss, gewgaws, gimcracks, frou frou, dingbat, do dad, doodad, thing, fandangle, jazz, garbage (food).

ORNAMENT v. doll up, fix up, gussy up, spruce up, pretty up, ungepotch (Yid.).

ORNATE adj. showy, glitzy, flashy, splashy, cushy, spiffy, splendiferous, splendacious, chi chi, frou frou, lit up like a Cristmas tree. See GAUDY. See also ELEGANT, EMBELLISHMENT.

ORPHAN n. drop, fetch, guttersnipe, mudlark, rustle.

ORTHODOX adj. straight, straight arrow, square, by the numbers, in line, in the groove, according to the book. See CONVENTIONAL.

OSCILLATE v. fish tail.

OSCILLATION n. judder, pitch, chatter.

OSCULATE v. peck, pucker up, smack, smash, smooch, eat face, suck face, swap slops, swap spit, buss, French kiss, soul kiss, butterfly kiss, spark, buzz, X, mush, muzzle, sugar, lay one on the lips, mouth music.

OSCULATION n. peck, smack, smooch, X, buss, mush, muzzle, soul kiss, sugar, butterfly kiss, French kiss, lay one on the lips, mouth music.

OSSINING, NEW YORK Stirville, Sing Sing.

OSTENTATION n. shine, splash, splurge, grandstand play, showboat, showoff, show, showing out, for show, false front, put on, put on the dog, flash, Christmas (clothes and jewelry), neon ribbons. See PRETENSION.

OSTENTATIOUS adj. flashy, splashy, showy, uptown, highfalutin', tony, classy, splurgy, duded up. See PRETENTIOUS.

OSTRACIZE v. ding, cut, drop, blackball, ice out, shut out, turn thumbs down on, leave out in the cold. See EXCLUDE. See also BANISH.

OTHERWISE adv. or else.

OUST v. 1. bounce, boot out, kick out, Adios one, give one the old heave-ho, give the bum's rush, give 'em the 1-2-3, throw out on one's ear, send packing. See EVICT. 2. give the gate, pink slip, can, fire, lay off, ax, give the ax, give the air, hand one his walking papers, sack, let one go. See DISCHARGE.

OUSTED adj. unfrocked (any profession), canned, drummed out, turned off, sent packing.

OUSTER n. ax, sack, boot, the gate, door, bounce, grand bounce, layoff, rif (reduction in force), walking papers, bum's rush, old heave-ho. See DISMISSAL.

OUTBOARD MOTOR n. eggbeater, kicker, putt putt.

OUTBURST n. blow, blowup, cat fit, duck fit, conniption, conniption fit, flare-up, wingding, shit hemorrhage. See also ANGER.

OUTCAST adj. blackballed, cold shouldered, left out in the cold, not in the picture, shut out.

OUTCOME n. reaction, chain reaction, flak (bad), upshot, score, blowoff, payoff, fallout, verdict isn't in on that. See RESULT.

OUTCRY n. hoo ha, hullabaloo, flak, hubba-hubba.

OUTDATED adj. tired, out, not with it, old hat, passé, back number, moth-eaten, has-been, square, ricky-tick. See DATED.

OUTDISTANCE v. lap, run away, blow out, break out.

OUTDO v. 1. outgun, beat one's time, top, outfox, end run, fake out, juke, deek, cop a heel on, cop a sneak on, pull a quickie on, pull a fast one. 2. bury, blank, cook, trim, fix one's wagon, shave, bulldoze, torpedo, tube, trash, cream, do in, lick, snow under, blow out, blow off, blow one out of the water, pin one's ears back, have it all over, bring home the bacon, take the cake, put one's nose out of joint, run rings around, run circles around, clean on. See DEFEAT.

OUTDONE adj. aced out, blanked, creamed, clobbered, hosed, topped, murdered, skinned, done in, done for, shut down, shut off, flameout, get one's lumps, cry uncle, say uncle. See DEFEATED.

OUTFIT v. fit out, rig out, rig up, rag out, rag up, turn out, doll up, dog out, dud, dude up, suit up, tog, drape, deck, deck out.

OUTHOUSE n. closet, shithouse, johnny house, necessary, chic sale, one-holer, two-holer. See also TOILET.

OUTLANDER n. blow-in, bum face, floater, geepo, weed, strange weed. See also ALIEN.

OUTLAW n. crook, hood, con, ex-con, mug, bad actor, bad guy, jailbird, racketeer, wrong number, gangster, mobster, drifter, saddle tramp, desperado, hoodlum, hooligan. See CRIMINAL.

OUTLAY n. price tag, bad news, damage, score, tab, bite, nut, bottom line, a throw, below the line, set one back, come to, to the tune of, hummer, highway mopery. See also EXPENSE.

OUTLOOK n. head-set, mind-set, mind trip, routine, where's one's head is, where one is at, where it's at, like it is, the size of it.

OUTMANEUVER v. beat one's time, outfox, con, end run, fake out, juke, cop a heel on, pull a fast one. See OUTWIT.

OUTMODED adj. tired, out, old hat, bent, back number, moth-eaten, has-been, dinosaur, horse and buggy. See DATED.

OUT OF STOCK adj. 86, smack out, clean out, gone clean (The. tickets).

OUTRAGE n. mad, huff, stew, storm, ruckus, conniption, conniption fit, cat fit, duck fit, blowup, flare-up, boiling point. See ANGER.

OUTRAGE v. burn up, whip up, fire up, kick up a row, raise cain, raise hell, raise the devil, hit the ceiling, reach boiling point, boil over. See ANGER.

OUTRAGEOUS adj. ape, crazy, glorkish, out of all bounds, worst-case scenario, last straw, too much, bitter end, the pits. See EXTREME. See also BAD, EXPENSIVE, UNBELIEVABLE.

OUTSIDER n. blow-in, bum face, floater, geepo, weed, strange weed. See also ALIEN.

OUTSKIRTS n. slub, slurb, spread city, bedroom community, sticks, stix.

OUTSMART v. fox, outfox, pull a quickie on, pull a fast one, finagle, work one's points, put one in the cookie jar, put one in the popcorn machine. See OUTWIT.

OUTSPOKEN adj. up front, lay it on the line, talk like a Dutch uncle, call a spade a spade, make no bones about it, talk turkey. See FRANK.

OUTSTANDING adj. A, A-1, A-number 1, A-number one, A-one, number one, numero uno, primo, ten, 10, ace, ace hi, aces, world class, greatest, out of sight, out of this world, far out, gonest, hundred proof, mostest, baaadest, bad, bitchin', boss, cool, zero cool, coolsville, crack, murder, first chop, super; mother, motherfucker, muthah, muthahfuckah, mofo (all Obsc.); gilt-edged, splash, wizard, high cotton, all-time, Sunday best, stone, terrible, terrific, skull, brain, grind, tops, top of the line, top dog, top drawer, topflight, top-notch, tip top, the most, the end, endsville, savage, solid gold, winner, champ, king o' the hill, white hope, white knight.

OUTWIT v. beat one's time, cap, top, fox, outfox, goose, con, short con, gyp, jip, end run, fake out, juke, cop a heel on, cop a sneak on, pull a quickie on, pull a fast one, finagle, work one's points, put one in the cookie jar, put one in the popcorn machine.

OVATION n. bring down the house, have 'em on their feet, hand, big hand, mitt pound.

OVER adj. hyper.

OVERCONFIDENT adj. know it all, wise ass, wise guy, smarty, smarty pants, smart ass, smart guy, smart aleck. See also ARROGANT, CERTAIN.

OVERACT v. mug, ham, ham it up, milk a scene, chew up the scenery. See also OVERDO, DRAMATIZE.

OVERALLS n. Levis, leaves, coveralls.

OVERAWE v. blow one away, knock one's socks off, hit like a ton of bricks, score big, snow, do a snow job, highbrow, cut a swath, fold one's ears back (talk). See IMPRESS.

OVERBEARING adj. cocky, bossy, sniffy, snotty, uppity, king shit, high and mighty, hoity-toity. See ARROGANT.

OVERBLOWN adj. hyped up, puffed up. See also AGED.

OVERCHARGE v. rook, screw, hose, rip off, jerk one off, stick, burn, bleed, bleed white, bilk, clip, con, chisel, gouge, gyp, scam, stiff, sting, pluck, take one to the cleaners, take one for a ride, take for a sucker, cream, milk, give one a raw deal, strip bare, skin, hold up, hype, soak, sell one a bill of goods, do in, do out of, chouse, chouse out of, hornswoggle, hook, throw the hooks into. See also CHEAT.

OVERCHARGED adj. been had, been taken, been took, clipped, fucked, screwed, stung, stuck, stuck with, fleeced, iced, rooked. See also CHEATED.

OVERCOAT n. greatcoat, car coat, horse blanket, benny, binny, Benjamin, threads, flogger; lead sheet, orchestration (Bl.).

OVERCOME adj. blown away, blown out of the water, run over, buried, taken, take down, swamped. See DEFEATED.

OVERCOME v. 1. kick, kick the bug, kick the habit, kick the illness, hit the burner (a crisis). 2. ban jax, flip, get around, blow away, blow one out, blow one's mind, blow one out of the water, snow, snow under, hit, knock one's socks off. See also DEFEAT, TRIUMPH.

OVERDO v. lay it on, lay it on thick, lay it on with a trowel, puff, hype, ballyhoo, talk big, take it big, blow up something, make a big production of something, make a federal case out of, make a mountain out of a molehill, drive it into the ground, go whole hog, go all out, get carried away, flip, flip out, wig out, bust one's nuts, break one's balls, break one's back, break one's ass, bust one's balls, bust one's back, bust one's ass, gweep (one who is overworked), pressure, push; mug, ham it up, chew up the scenery (The.). See also EXAGGERATE, DRAMATIZE.

OVERDOSE v. OD, oh dee, overjolt, overvamp, overamp, overcharge, burn out, freak out, jazz out, rock out, zone out, zonk out.

OVERDRESSED adj. jellybean, sharpie.

OVERDUE adj. held up, hung up, jammed.

OVEREAT v. gross out, blimp out, pork out, pig out, scarf out, pig down, wolf, make a pig of oneself, eat out of house and home. See GLUTTONIZE. See also EAT.

OVERENTHUSIASTIC adj. overboard, steamed up, flipped, freaked out, rarin' to go, throw out the baby with the bathwater. See ENTHUSIASTIC.

OVEREXCITED adj. hyper, wired up, fired up, spazzed out, freaked out, zonkers, like crazy, like mad, hit the ceiling, hog wild, have a shit hemorrhage. See EXCITED.

OVEREXERT v. break one's balls, break one's back, break one's ass, bust one's hump, go all out. See OVERDO.

OVEREXTENDED adj. in too deep, out of one's depth, over one's head, bit off more than one can chew, too many irons in the fire, too many balls in the air.

OVERHAUL n. facelift, retread, fix up, doctor, fiddle with, debug, redline (Mil.).

OVERHEAD n. nut, outlay.

OVERHEAR v. catch, get, read, be all ears, get an earful, hear tell. See also LISTEN, EAVESDROP.

OVERHEAT TIRES v. fry the tires.

OVERINDULGE v. go whole hog, get carried away. See OVERDO. See also EAT.

OVERINDULGED adj. spoiled rotten.

OVERLOOK v. 1. look the other way, ig, tune out, live with, pay no mind, pay no never mind, play past, pooh pooh, go along with, be big, handle, put up with, stomach something, grin and bear it, string along with, roll with the punches, play the game, swim with the tide, bear with, stand for, take. 2. whitewash, wipe the slate clean, let off, let go, let it go, wipe it off, write off, let one off easy, let one off this time, wink at, blink at. See ABSOLVE. See also FORGIVE. 3. be asleep at the switch, let go to pot, let ride, let slide, fall between the chairs, fall between the cracks.

OVERLY adv. too much, too-too.

OVERNICE adj. nicey nice, sticky.

OVERPAY v. pay through the nose.

OVERPLAY v. lay it on thick, blow up something, make a mountain out of a molehill, get carried away; mug, ham it up, chew up the scenery (The.). See OVERDO.

OVERPOWER v. 1. trash, drub, kayo, total, clobber, cream, waste, take out, take care of, lay one out. 2. bury, blank, murder, trounce, swamp, shellack, bulldoze, roll over, torpedo, tube, meatball, make one say uncle, beat all hollow, shut off, blow away, put away. See DEFEAT.

OVERPOWERED adj. blanked, creamed, clobbered, topped, trimmed, trounced, murdered, snowed, snowed under, shut down, blown out, have one's ass in a sling. See DEFEATED.

OVERPRAISE v. snow, spread it on, lay it on, lay it on thick, lay it on with a trowel, work over, suck ass, kiss ass, ballyhoo, phoney up, puff up, bullshit, shoot a line, fall all over. See FLATTER.

OVERPRICE v. rip off, jerk one off, run a game on, rope in, flimflam, stick, burn, bleed, bleed white, bilk, clip, con, chisel, gouge, gyp, stiff, sting, take, take one to the cleaners, give one a raw deal, skin, hold up. See OVERCHARGE.

OVERPRICED adj. out of sight, steep, stiff, heavy sugar, holdup, highway robbery, highway mopery, paid through the nose. See EXPENSIVE.

OVERREACH v. bite off more than one can chew, have too many irons in the fire, have too many balls in the air.

OVERREACT v. take it big, flip, flip out, wig out, get carried away, drive it into the ground, go whole hog, make a mountain out of a molehill; mug, ham it up, chew up the scenery (The.). See also REACT.

OVERRIPE adj. bum, bummy.

OVERSEE v. captain, skipper, herd, shepherd, ride herd on, baby-sit, sit on top of, run the show, call the shots, be in the driver's seat. See MANAGE.

OVERSEER n. boss, big brother, head, head honcho, bosshead, super, skipper, old man, top hand, digger, the man, pit boss, king pin, bull, straw boss, slave driver, pusher. See EXECUTIVE.

OVERSENSITIVE adj. hyper, wired up, uptight, hung up, wreck, nervous wreck, shot to pieces, thin-skinned, can't even look at him cross-eyed. See SENSITIVE.

OVERSHOES n. goulashes, goolashes, rubbers, gunboats, pup tents. See also SHOES.

OVERSIGHT adj. slipup, goof, boot, dumb trick, miscue, fool mistake. See MISTAKE.

OVERSLEEP v. sleep in. See also SLEEP.

OVERSTATE v. talk trash, lay it on, snow, give one a snow job, cook, shovel the shit, puff, ballyhoo, hype, overdo it, hit too hard, make a mountain out of a molehill, make a federal case out of something. See EXAGGERATE.

OVERSTATEMENT n. jazz, jive, hype, line, bullshit, baloney, malarkey, thick, whopper, snow job, blow job, buildup, the big lie (political), tall tale, big talk. See EXAGGERATION.

OVERTALKATIVE adj. all jaw, big-mouthed, gabby, gassy, windy. See TALKATIVE.

OVERTAX v. run into the ground, drive it into the ground, bust one's nuts, gweep (one who is overworked), pressure, push. See OVERDO.

OVERTIME n. burn the midnight oil, pull an all-nighter, golden time, run over, time and a half, double time, triple time.

OVERTIRED adj. bushed, wiped out, wrung out, wore out, draggin' ass, worn to a frazzle, nearly dead, done in, all in, bone tired, bone-weary, dog-tired. See TIRED.

OVERTLY adv. under one's nose, in broad daylight.

OVERTURE n. feeler, pitch, proposition, proposish, openers, big idea (unwelcome).

OVERWEIGHT adj. fatty, tubby, spare tire, heavy, heavy cream, hefty, zaftig. See FAT.

OVERWHELM v. 1. bury, blank, kill, swamp, steamroller, bulldoze, roll over, torpedo, tube, meatball, make one say uncle, do in, beat all hollow, snow, snow under, finish off, blow one out of the water, run rings around, run circles around, clean on. See also ASTONISH. 2. total, take out, shut out, wipe out, wipe off the map, knock the props out from under. See DEFEAT.

OVERWHELMED adj. aced out, blanked, burned, bit the dust, creamed, clobbered, hosed, topped, murdered, snowed, snowed under, done in, blown out, knee deep, in too deep, out of one's depth, over one's head, up to one's ass in, bit off more than one can chew, too many irons in the fire. See DEFEATED. See also ASTONISHED.

OVERWORK v. drive it into the ground, go whole hog, get carried away, bust one's nuts, gweep (one who is overworked), pressure, push. See OVERDO.

OVERWROUGHT adj. spazzed out, wired up, hyper, keyed up, all shook up, hopped up, steamed up, fired up, flipped out, freaked out, high, stoned, zonkers, hot and bothered, hot under the collar, like crazy. See EXCITED.

OVERZEALOUS adj. off the deep end, go off the deep end, step off the deep end, throw out the baby with the bathwater. See ZEALOUS. See also EAGER.

OWE v. be into one for, behind, ducking one, on the cuff, on the tab, on the tick, in hock.

OWED adj.   comeuppance, what is coming to one, what one has coming.

OWNED AND OPERATED adj.   O and O.

OWNER n.   landprop, saw, slumlord, governor.

OWNERSHIP n.   cut, end, piece, piece of a joint, slice, make a grab, muscle in, push in, takeover, unfriendly takeover (by coercion).

OX n.   bull (logger).

OXYGEN n.   oxy, gox (gaseous), lox (liquid).

OXYGEN MASK n.   bag.

P

P n. papa, Peter.

PACE n. 1. clip, lick, getalong. 2. beat, bounce, downbeat, brown-off (break).

PACIFIC OCEAN n. Big Drink.

PACIFIER n. trank, tranx, backwards, dope, goof ball, knockout drop, Mickey Finn, gig, gigi, gee-gee.

PACIFIST n. dove, dove of peace, peacenik.

PACIFY v. cool, cool out, cool it, cool off, stroke, con, schmear, butter up, grease, pour oil on troubled waters, take the edge off, take the bite out, take the sting out of, take it easy, lay back, soft-pedal, put the lid on, square, fix up, bury the hatchet, kiss and make up, make up, make it up, make nice, patch things up, play up to, get together on, come together, meet halfway.

PACK n. bunch, crowd, gang, mob, circle.

PACK v. 1. jam, jam-pack, pack 'em in, pack like sardines, sardine, ram in, chock, chockablock, stuff, top off. 2. lug, tote, truck, piggyback, ride, shlep, shlep along, birdie back, buck, gun, heel, hump, jag, shoulder.

PACKAGE n. roll, biddle, bindle, load.

PACKED adj. jam-packed, mobbed, sardined, packed like sardines, up to the hilt, up to the rafters, right to the roof, chock, chock full, full as a tick, full to bursting, wall-to-wall people.

PACT n. deal, dicker, ticket, paper, piece of paper. See AGREEMENT.

PAD n. scratch, scratch pad.

PADDLE v. sky an oar.

PAGE v. beep.

PAGER n. beeper.

PAID FOR BY v. on (it's on me), popped for, taken care of, handled, put on the line for, laid out.

PAIL n. gutbucket, billy can, growler.

PAIN v. do a number on, dump on, hit one where one lives, lay a bad trip on one, gross out, mess up, nick, zing. See WOUND.

PAINFUL adj. hurting, grabbing, stab in the ———, making like the anvil chorus in one's skull, take some hide and hair.

PAINKILLER n. shot, dope, knockout drop.

PAINSTAKING adj. picky, stickler, dot the i's and cross the t's, fussbudget, fusspot, fuddy-duddy, pernickety, persnickety, chicken shit, by the book, by the numbers. See PARTICULAR.

PAINT v. daub, slap on, slop on, slather on, slather with, cover up, put on a couple of coats, decorate, orange peel (texture).

PAIR n. team, twosome, gruesome twosome, spic and span (Black and Puerto Rican, Derog.).

PAJAMAS n. jams, jammies, jam jams, P.J.'s, peejays, pygies, baby dolls, sleepers, sleeping suit.

PAL n. amigo, brother, bro, blo, buddyroo, good buddy, asshole buddy, chum, old man, old boy, mate, sidekick. See FRIEND.

PALATABLE adj. 1. delish, yummy, divine, heavenly, scrumptious, sweetened, sugar-coated. 2. cool, A-OK, copasetic, hunky-dory, jake, peachy, slide by easy, groovy, home cooking. See ACCEPTABLE.

PALAVER v. rap, yak, jaw, gab, shmooze, chin, chew the fat, bat the chat, shoot the breeze, shoot the shit, bend one's ear, run one's mouth, have diarrhea of the mouth, rattle on. See SPEAK.

PALLIATIVE n. fix, quick fix, band-aid.

PALMIST n. mitt reader.

PALPITATE v. go pitapat.

PALPITATION n. pitapation.

PAMPERED adj. spoiled, spoiled rotten, played up to, made over, stroked.

PAMPHLET n. broadside, flyer, handout.

PANAMA CANAL n. the Big Ditch.

PANCAKE n. flapjack, hotcake, blanket, saddle blankets, flats, brown bucks, manhole cover, tire patch, wheat, collision mat (WW II).

PANDEMONIUM n. all hell broke loose, rumpus, ruckus, bloody mess, hassle. See BEDLAM.

PANDER v. 1. suck, suck around, suck up to, kiss ass, brownnose, play up to, fall all over, play footsie, play Mr. Nice Guy, politic, stroke, massage, snow, soften up, soap, lay it on, spook, fish. See CAJOLE. 2. have a string of hustlers, run a stable, have a sister-in-law, steer, tout. See also PIMP.

PANDERER n. mack, mackman, macko man, hard Mack (violent), dude, hustler, Johnny Ponce, pee eye, P.I., ponce, player, honey man. See PIMP.

PANIC n. crash, bust, slump, rainy days. See also DEPRESSION.

PANIC v. shit, crap out, shit in one's pants, pee in one's pants, piss in one's pants, piss razor blades, pucker-assed, asshole puckerin', asshole suckin' wind (Obsc.), push the panic button, hit the panic button, run scared, have cold feet, have a fit, have kittens, chicken out, pucker, shake in one's boots, clutch up, punk out, come apart, freeze up. See also FRIGHTENED.

PANTS n. slacks, jeans, Levis, denims, cords, ducks, whites, bell bottoms, bells, hip huggers, pedal pushers, Capris, clam diggers, hot pants, shorts, Bermudas, kneebusters, baggies, jammies, chinos, chaps, gaucho pants, dungarees, pegs, striders, strides, britches, high-water pants, pistols (pegged), fatboy pants (down), plus fours (1930), knickers, bloomers, drawers, longies, bags, trousers with the reat pleat.

PAP n. pablum.

PAPER BAG n. jiffy bag, brown bag.

PARACHUTE n. chute, overcoat, umbrella, skyhook.

PARACHUTE v. hit the silk, jump, bail out.

PARACHUTE DROP n. jump, hit the silk, hang out the laundry (WW II).

PARACHUTIST n. chuter, chutist, jumper, smoke jumper, paratrooper (Mil.).

PARADE n. rat race.

PARADE GROUND n. grinder.

PARADISE n. 1. pearly gates, kingdom come, happy hunting ground, promised land, upstairs, up there, the great ball park in the sky. 2. pie in the sky, Nadaville, cloud seven, cloud nine, seventh heaven, fat city, hog heaven. See HEAVEN.

PARADOX n. pair of ducks, catch 22, catch.

PARAGRAPH n. graph, squib.

PARASITE n. beat, deadbeat, freeloader, gremlin, gremmie, hanger-on, leaner, schnorrer, sponge, sponger, hose, ass-kisser, A.K., bun duster, groupie, taker, waterboy, waterman, yes-man, nod guy, sideman; suck, cocksucker, brownie, brownnose, fart sniffer (Obsc.), bootlick, bootlicker, flunky, stooge, flunkystooge, lackey.

PARASITIC adj. on one's back, on one's coattails, carrying one.

PARATROOPER n. airborne, bloomer boy, chutist, chuter, jumper.

PARCEL n. 1. load, bindle, biddle. 2. piece, bite, cut, slice, chunk, piece of the action, piece of the pie, rake-off, halver, lion's share, bigger half, big end, fifty-fifty, even-steven.

PARCEL v. divvy, divvy up, split up, cut up, cut in, cut the melon, slice up, slice the pie. See DIVIDE.

PARCHED adj. dry as dust, cotton mouth.

PARDON n. lifeboat, clemo, commute, spring, lifesaver, anchor.

PARDON v. let off, let one off this time, let one off easy, wink at, blink at, write off, wipe the slate clean, bury the hatchet, lifeboat, hand out clemo, spring. See ABSOLVE.

PARDONED adj. beat the rap, walked, let off, let go, off the hook, in from the cold.

PARE v. knock off, shave.

PAREGORIC n. blue velvet, black jack.

PARENT n. fossil, OM, old man, old lady, folks, old folks, foozle, rent, toad, empty nester (children gone).

PARENTHOOD n. parenting.

PARLANCE n. lingo, bafflegab, doublespeak, double-talk, gobbledygookese, officialese, psychobabble, Urbababble (city govt.). See LANGUAGE.

PARLEY n. confab, meet, get-together, groupthink, powwow, clambake. See MEETING.

PARLEY v. confab, give a meeting, take a meeting, have a meet, hold a meet, brainstorm, toss some ideas around, kick some ideas around, groupthink, get heads together, huddle, go into a huddle, pick one's brains, rap, chew the fat. See CONFER. See also SPEAK.

PARODY n. takeoff, play on.

PARODY v. put on, send up, sheik, take off.

PAROLE n. clemo.

PAROLE v. spring, put out on the street, put out on the bricks, put out on the pavement.

PARSIMONIOUS adj. close, stingy, penny-pinching, tight, tightwad, tight-fisted, last of the big-time spenders, a regular Jack Benny, skinflint, screw, Scotch, squeezing the eagle, chintzy. See STINGY.

PARSON n. padre, reverend, Holy Joe, sky pilot, bible beater, buck, preacher man. See CLERGYMAN.

PART n. 1. chunk, gob, glob, hunk, lump, smithereen. 2. bite, cut, cut in, divvy, lion's share, big end, drag, piece, piece of the action, slice, slice of the pie. See SHARE. 3. stint (role), lead, bit, extra, walk-on, spear carrier. 4. making, makin's, fixings, fixin's.

PART v. 1. blow one off (in anger), split, split up, break, break off, break up, kiss off, wash up, couldn't make it, dedomicile, go pffft. 2. split, beat it, fog, cut out, cut and run, cut ass, haul ass, hit the road, push off, bow out, ooze out, ease on, ease out, clear out, pull out, ship out, haul one's freight, shove, shove off, quit the scene, fly the coop, leave flat, run out on, walk out on. See GO.

PARTAKE v. make the scene, be into, be in on, sit in, sit in on, have a finger in, have a finger in the pie, get in the act, latch on, tune in, give with the eyes. See also EAT.

PARTIALITY n. bag, cup of tea, dish, dish of tea, druthers, flash, thing, type, turned on to, weakness for. See INCLINATION.

PARTICIPANT n. in, player.

PARTICIPATE v. make the scene, be into, be in on, sit in, sit in on, have a finger in, have a finger in the pie, get into the act, latch on, tune in, give with the eyes.

PARTICIPATION n. hands on, sitting in, getting in the act.

PARTICLE n. smithereen.

PARTICLES n. chewed fine, itsy-bitsy pieces.

PARTICULAR adj. choosy, choicy, comma counter, nitpicker, picky, picky-picky, ticky, stickler, stiff, ace, tough, rough, cut it fine, draw it fine, dot the i's and cross the t's, mind one's p's and q's, watch one's step, bend over backwards, handle with kid gloves, fussbudget, fusspot, fuddy-duddy, granny, old woman, old maid, pernickety, persnickety, crab, chicken shit, according to Hoyle, by the book, by the numbers.

PARTICULAR n. the case, what's what, where it's at, chapter and verse, spelled out, nitty-gritty. See DETAIL.

PARTICULARIZE v. spell out, lay out, take it line by line, fly speck, sweat the details, get down to brass tacks, get down to cases. See SPECIFY.

PARTICULARS n. 1. ABC's, ABC of it, blow by blow, rundown, spelled out, like it is, make, picture, the numbers, the goods, bottom line, meat and potatoes, chapter and verse, gospel, megillah, scud, scut, nitty-gritty, nuts and bolts. 2. what's what, know, the straight stuff, facts of life, from the horse's mouth, cue, clue, dope, inside dope, scoop, score, skinny, story, whole story, lowdown, brass tacks, no shit, the emess, cold turkey. See FACTS.

PARTING n. break, breakup, come to a parting of the ways, on the rocks, on the out and out, phfft, pffft, Reno-vating, split-up, splitsville, washed up, eighty-eights, swan song.

PARTITION v. divvy, divvy up, go halfies, go halvers, go fifty-fifty, go even-steven, slice up, cut the pie, cut the melon, slice the melon, slice the pie, slice, split, split up, cut, cut up, cut in, cut into, cut one in, duke one in, cut up the touches, cut up the pipes, cut up the jackpot, piece up, whack up, bump into, size into (chips), buck it over.

PARTNER n. buddy, buddy-buddy, pard, pardner, sidekick, playmate, date. See also WIFE, HUSBAND, FRIEND.

PARTNERSHIP n. hookup, tie-in, tie-up, gang, mob, ring, clan, outfit, syndicate, go partners, in cahoots with, get together, team up with, throw in together, throw in with, join up with, line up with. See also ASSOCIATION.

PARTNERSHIP, ACCEPT count one in, fill, shake on it.

PARTS n. makings, makin's, fixings, fixin's, spares.

PARTURITION n. blessed event, producing, visit from the stork, drop one.

PARTY n. ball, bash, bat, binge, bender, blast, brawl, bust, beer bust, kegger, bow, opener, coming-out, com-ing out party, tailgating, get-together, carousing, clambake, crush, brannigan, shindig, blast party (marijuana), rub, belly rub (dance), hop, jump, mingle, prom, moveable feast, BBQ, barbecue, camp it up, blowout, hen party, stag, jag, jig, zig, hullabaloo, rat race, rent party, skiffle, scramble, shag, set, coffee klatch, smoker, shindy, drunk, drunken brawl, hoopla, jamboree, merry-go-round, on the town, paint the town red, rip, tear, toot, whoopee, whooper-dooper, wing-ding, finger pop, boogaloo, racket, belling, horning, jam, roast, donkey roast, drag party, drag out, do, fight, freeload, flap, gas, gig, hoedown, hoedig, hoodang, hog wrestle, scene, serenade, shivaree, skimmelton. See also REVEL.

PASADENA, CALIFORNIA Pass the doughnuts.

PASS n. freebie, free ride, Annie Oakley, chit, paper, twofer, pigeon, paper, comp.

PASS v. duke, weed, gimme, give the go by, pass up, pass on, pass it on over, buck it over, pass in the dark, masquerade, blow over. See also QUALIFY, APPROVE.

PASS BAD CHECKS v. down paper, paper hang, kite.

PASSBOOK n. damper pad.

PASS COUNTERFEIT MONEY v. push, lay paper, paper, hit one, smack with, pass, pass the queer, shove, shove the queer.

PASSÉ adj. out, out of it, old hat, back number, has-been, yesterday, of the old school. See DATED.

PASSENGER n. drop, line load (taxi), deadhead (free), seat cover.

PASSION n. 1. amore, mash, pash, weakness, case, crash, crush, yen, the hots, emote, emoting (simulate).

See LOVE. 2. jazz, oomph, pep talk, where one is at, drive.

PASSIONATE adj. 1. hot, hot for, horny, turned on, pash, sexy, hot baby, hot number, hot pants, hot patootie, heavy, heavy breathing, hot and heavy. See AMOROUS. 2. all torn up, all tore up, all shook up, feel stuff, fall apart, frantic, full up, funky, get one's gage up, give out, gutty, hopped up, shook, shook up, shot down. See also ENTHUSIASTIC.

PASSIONLESS adj. cold, cold tit, cold shoulder, cold-blooded, tight-assed. See also EMOTIONLESS.

PASSIVE adj. flat, moony, cool, unflappable, laid back, go with the flow, dead ass, poker-faced, phone it in, just going through the motions, walk through it, hands off. See INDIFFERENT.

PASSIVITY n. cool one's heels, sit on one's ass, sit on one's butt, sit on one's duff, sit on one's hands, stand pat.

PASSPORT n. shoe (forged).

PAST adj. ancient history, good old days, olden days, olden daze, olden times, stone age, away back, from way back, way back when, back when, behind one, time was, ages ago, since God knows when, water under the bridge, water over the dam, down memory lane, when Hector was a pup, when one was knee high to a grasshopper.

PASTE n. stickum, gunk, gummy, spit.

PASTIME n. fun and games, rec.

PASTOR n. padre, the rev, Holy Joe, sky pilot, bible beater, preacher man, right buck, shepherd, glory roader. See CLERGYMAN.

PASTURE n. the green deck, carpet, rug.

PATCH n. blob, chunk, hunk, fix, band-aid.

PATCH v. fix up, doctor, fiddle with, retread.

PATE n. bean, noggin, noodle, dome, attic, upper story, chimney (Bl.), coco, knob, think pot, dream box. See HEAD.

PATENT adj. barefaced, plain as the nose on one's face, clear-cut, crystal clear, open and shut, Is the Pope Catholic? See APPARENT.

PATENT MEDICINE n. punk, snake oil.

PATH n. 1. groove, rut; lane, track (Stu.). 2. aisle, byway, stroll, rail.

PATIENCE adj. backbone, grit, guts, gutsiness, heart, moxie, starch, cool, hanging in there, hang tough, legs, intestinal fortitude, staying power, sitzfleisch, stick-to-itiveness.

PATIENTLY adj. keep one's shirt on, not hold one's breath, hang in, keep one's cool, cool it, cool one's heels, sit tight.

PATRICIAN n. blue blood, bluestocking, silk stocking, lace curtain, swell, upper cruster.

PATRIOT n. arm-waver, flag-waver (super), hundred percenter, jingoist, patrioteer, scoutmaster.

PATRIOTIC adj. wrap oneself in the flag, flag-waving.

PATROL v. ride shotgun for, shotgun. See also WATCH.

PATROL CAR n. black and white, fuzzmobile, skunk wagon, bear car, bearmobile, buzz, buzzer, screaming gasser, whistler, catch car; brown bag, plain wrap (unmarked); buggy whip (transmitter).

PATROL WAGON n. battlewagon, paddywagon, Black Maria, Maria, fuzzmobile, black and white, booby hatch, go long, milk wagon, piewagon.

PATRON n. the money, angel, sponsor, backer, sugar daddy, fairy godmother, lady bountiful, meal ticket, Santa Claus, staker, grubstaker, pigeon, live one, mark, front, head, fan, rabbi.

PATRONAGE n. pork barrel.

PATRONIZE v. high hat, toss a few crumbs, act like one of the boys, go along with, look down one's nose at, look down on.

PATRONIZING adj. biggety, dicty, sidity, siditity, sniffy, snippy, snooty, uppish, uppity, upstage, ego-tripping, high-toned. See ARROGANT.

PAUNCHY n. beerbelly, spare tire, rubber tire, bulge, battle of the bulge, corporation, bay window, tub of guts, gutbucket, pus gut, blimp. See FAT.

PAUPER n. bum, bummer, stumblebum, slum bum, rubber bum, ragbag, bag lady, bag woman, in the gutter, bo, weed. See also DESTITUTE.

PAUPERIZE v. bleed, bleed white, suck dry, wipe out, break, take one for all one's got, clean one out, take one's last penny.

PAUPERIZED adj. stone broke, truly needy, oofless, on one's ass, on the rocks, on the edge, down and out, down to one's last cent, down to one's last penny, have-nots, not have one dollar to rub against another, not have one dime to rub against another, in dire straits, piss-poor, dirt poor. See DESTITUTE.

PAUSE n. break, break-off, coffee break, breather, breathing spell, downtime, letup, five, ten, time out, freeze, cutoff, layoff, happy hour. See DELAY.

PAUSE v. put on hold, call time, take a break, take five, take ten, take smoke, break it off, break it up, drop, drop it, pigeonhole, shake, sideline.

PAVEMENT n. the bricks.

PAWN n. cat's paw, mark, patsy, pigeon, stooge.

PAWN v. hook, soak, hock, put in hock, see uncle.

PAWNBROKER n. loan shark, shylock, soft touch, uncle.

PAWNSHOP n. hockshop, three balls, spout.

PAY n. scale, take home, bread, bacon, eagle shit; peanuts, coffee and cakes (small). See COMPENSATION.

PAY v. 1. pay up, pay off, pay out, pay down, put down (begin to pay), pay to the tune of, pay through the nose, foot the bill, pick up the check, pick up the tab, kick in, chip in, cough up, pony up, ante up, come through, come across, come down with, come down with the needful, come up with the necessary, blow, blow out, plank up, plank down, plunk down, clunk, clunk down, cash out, dish it out, shell out, put out, lay out, fork out, fork over, fork up, hand over, spring for, make good, lay on one, lay it on the line, put it on the line, put one's money on the line, throw money at, throw money around, piss it away, iron off, post, go for a meg, go Dutch, Dutch treat. 2. comp, swing for bread, square, square things, square up, square the beef, make up for, sugarcoat, stroke, sweeten, sweeten the pot, tickle the palm, pay the piper, pay one's dues, pay through the nose, slip one a buck, take an envelope, take care of, take a chicken, schmear, grease, grease one's palm, oil, oil one's palm, barry (hiring boss), fix, fix the alzo, put in the fix, piece one off, gaff, fit the mitt, put in the bag, put in the zingers, buzz, crack business, do business, see, see the cops, buy, buy off, iron off, reach, get at, get to. See also SQUANDER.

PAY BACK v. square, square things, square a beef, make up for, pay one's dues, you scratch mine and I'll scratch yours. See also PAY, REVENGE.

PAYDAY n. day, eagle day, day the eagle shits, day the eagle flies, day the eagle screams, when the eagle flies, four and one.

PAY EXTORTION v. pay off, buy off, pay through the nose, pay off on the moosh, kick in on the squash.

PAY FOR v. blow one to, blow, on one, on the house, I'll get it (pay the check), I'm buyin', pick up the check, pick up the tab, pop, pop for, spring for, stand for, set up, stake.

PAYING adj. going, going concern, paying off, cashing in, in the black, red, sweet.

PAYMENT n. drop, payoff, kickback, payola, drugola, gayola, juice, ante, bite, chunk, end, cut, slice, share, piece, piece of the action, rake-off, commish, skig, cash on the line, cash on the nail, cash on the barrelhead, out of pocket, outlay, the wherewithal, the necessary, vig, vigorish, flipping (interest on interest), front-end loading, points. See also BRIBE, COMPENSATION.

PAYROLL n. payoff, payola, scandal sheet.

PAYROLL TIMEKEEPER n. biscuit.

PCP n. P.C.P., Angel Dust, Sherms (cigarette), P-stuff, busy bee, crystal, elephant, elephant tranquilizer, monkey dust, scuffle, killer weed, peace pill, rocket fuel, cannabinal, lovely, tic, mist, dust, rock dust, T dust, animal, cadillac, C.J., K.J., goon, sheets, hog, mint, monkey, snorts, Aurora Borealis, dummy, ozone, soma, cyclone, horse, new magic; super joint, super grass (marijuana sprinkled with PCP).

PEACE ADVOCATE n. peacenik, dove, dove of peace.

PEACE OFFICER n. cop, fuzz, copper, shamus, flic, dick, narc (narcotics), pig, oink, black and white, badge, bluecoat, bluebird (Bl.), flatfoot, harness bull, law, Kojak, smokey, Smokey the Bear. See POLICE OFFICER.

PEACE, MAKE v. bury the hatchet, kiss and make up, make up, offer an olive branch. See PACIFY.

PEACEFUL adj. level vibes, smooth, mellow, all quiet on the Potomac, all quiet on the Western front.

PEAK adj. in full swing, tops, in top form, the greatest, level best, all out, world class. See BEST.

PEAK n. 1. hump. 2. spike (Elec.).

PEANUT n. goober.

PEANUT BUTTER n. goober grease.

PEARLS n. tears, teardrops, oyster berries.

PEAS n. bullets, sheep shit.

PECTORAL adj. pec.

PECULIAR adj. freaky, kooky, beat, bent, weirdie, oddball, fringy, kinky, flaky, far out, way out, off the wall, not wrapped real tight, fly ball, aired out, character, creep, whacky, spacey. See ECCENTRIC.

PECULIARITY n. bit, shtick, slant, twist, gimmick, mishegoss. See CHARACTERISTIC.

PEDANT n. brain, egghead, cereb, gnurd, gome, grind, auger, pencil geek, throat, bookworm, cutthroat, grub, ink squirter, spider, squid, weenie, poler, wig, wonk, moldy fig.

PEDDLER n. Arab, bag guy (balloon), butch, butcher, hawker, pitchman; candy man, pusher, dealer (drugs); cheap jack, cheap john. See VENDOR.

PEDESTRIAN n. boot jockey, gumshoe, jaywalker.

PEEP n. free show, peeping Tom, flash, keek.

PEEP v. flash, flash on, spy, catch, eyeball, take in, get a load of, get an eyeful of, take a squint, have a look-see. See SEE.

PEER n. blue blood, lace curtain, silk stocking, swell, upper cruster.

PEER v. glom, glim, gun, gawk, beam, focus, eye, eagle eye, eyeball, pin, rubber, rubberneck, get a load of, put the squint on, gap. See SEE.

PEERLESS adj. aces, world class, greatest, out of sight, out of this world, gonest, mostest, baaadest, first chop, super, gilt-edge, all-time, tops, solid gold, champ. See EXCELLENT.

PEEVED adj. bugged, hacked, pissed off, peed off, bummed out, burned up, miffed, rubbed the wrong way, all hot and bothered, driven up the wall, steamed. See ANNOYED. See also ANGRY.

PEEVISH adj. bitchy, mean, ornery, tetchy, out of sorts, cantankerous, cussed, grouchy, grumpy, beefing, bellyaching, bitching, crabbing, crabby, cranky, grousing, griping, kicking, snappish, scrappy, kvetchy, bear, ogre, ugly, ugly customer, bad-assed, uptight, thin-skinned, wreck, bundle of nerves, Mr. Coffee Nerves, pushing out one's lips, ready to fly off the handle, edgy, on the ragged edge, got up on the wrong side of the bed.

PELT n. dried barkers, skins, skin joint (shop).

PEN n. stick, ink stick, ball point.

PENALIZE v. dock, slap with a fine, hit with a fine, walk off fifteen yards, pay through the nose, throw the book at one. See also SENTENCE.

PENALTY n. rap, fall, hell to pay, pay dues, rip.

PENCHANT n. a thing for, weakness for, turned on to, druthers, tilt, big eyes, eyes for, itch, sweet tooth, yen, zazzle. See INCLINATION.

PENCIL n. stick.

PENDING adj. in the works, in line, on the board, on the fire, on line.

PENETRATE v. 1. access, barge in, break in, blow in, bust in, pop in, mooch in, breeze in, come breezing in, come barging in, come, come busting in, crack, crack a safe. 2. get over, put over, get across, sink in, soak in, work one's points, ace in.

PENIS n. cock, prick, dick, dork, pecker, peter, pee-pee, pisser, pistol, joint, hose, bazooka, affair, business, agate (small), middle leg, third leg, pencil, dummy, meat, weenie, peenie, stick, joy-stick, dipstick, swizzle stick, bone, enob, knob, joy knob, bishop, bicho, wang, thing, putz, schmeckel, schmuck, schwantz, pup, rod, hot rod, humpmobile, pole, pego, percy, oscar, pinga (Sp.), pud, dong, dang, dagger, banana, cucumber, kosher pickle (circumcised), baloney, sausage, salami, frankfurter, wurst, pork, peppermint stick, shlong, dink, dingus, staff, doodle, gun, head, tool, plunger, fountain pen, arm, short arm, jack, jock, big Ben, Mr. Happy, John Thomas, Johnson, junior, redcap, Rumpleforeskin, jigger, ding, hickey, fag, booboos, yang, ying yang, jang, jing jang, tootsie roll, divining rod, pike, piston, prod, serpent, snake, one-eyed monster, one-eyed wonder, stalk, shaft, prong, spear, sword, jellyroll, meat whistle, skin flute, piccolo, love muscle, rod of love, root, roto rooter, worm, instrument, machine, baby maker, nuts and bolts, banger, poker, hammer, rammer, ramrod, battering ram, charger, stretcher, peace maker, cherry picker, basket, heart, hotchee, log, maypole, pole, pylon, hung (big), hung like a bull, hung like a chicken, hung like a rabbit, stub, dangling participle; meat and two vegetables, Dickie and the boys (penis and testicles) (all Obsc.).

PENITENTIARY n. pen, joint, right joint, big joint, big house, slam, slammer, up the river, statesville, Q (San Quentin), Sing Sing, sent up, maxi (maximum security), inside, school, big school, campus, college, greystone college, graybar hotel, crossbar hotel, crowbar hotel, bastille, lag, G. joint (federal). See also JAIL.

PENMANSHIP n. chicken tracks, hen tracks, mark, scrawl, scribble.

PENNANT n. screamer, streamer, flag (baseball), bean rag (Navy).

PENNILESS adj. flat, broke, flat broke, dead broke, stony, strapped, clean, tapped out, tap city, on one's ass, on one's uppers, down to one's last cent, down to one's last penny, not have one dollar to rub against another, not have one dime to rub against another, over a barrel, piss-poor, dirt poor, on the rims. See DESTITUTE.

PENNSYLVANIA Coal State, Keystone State, Oil State, Pennsy, Quaker State, Steel State.

PENNSYLVANIA RAILROAD n. Pennsy.

PENSIONER n. senior, senior citizen, on the shelf, out of circulation, over the hill, passed it, a once was, has-been, hung up one's spurs, old timer. See also AGED.

PENTAGON n. D.O.D., ground zero, target A, puzzle palace.

PENULTIMATE adj. down to the short strokes.

PENURIOUS adj. cheap, cheapskate, close, stingy, tight, skinflint, skin, screw, Scotch, sticky-fingered, squeezing the eagle, piker, scrimpy, skimpy, pinch-fisted. See STINGY.

PEOPLE n. bodies, cats, dudes, heads, hoi polloi, the public, John Q., John Q. Public, Billy Sixpack, Joe Lunchbucket, Tom Dick and Harry, Brown Jones and Robinson, booboisie, the little guy.

PEPPER n. dirt (Army), hot it up.

PEPPERY adj. shotgun.

PERCEIVE v. 1. flash on, spot, spy, dig, lamp, eyeball, get a load of, take a hinge, have a look-see. See SEE. 2. get it, get the picture, flash on, blow wise, track, feature, dig, pin, copy, read, get the message. See UNDER-STAND.

PERCEIVED adj. hep to, on to, pat, down pat, wise to, pegged, got, got the picture, dug, know where one is coming from, picked up on. See also APPARENT.

PERCENTAGE n. cut, piece, piece of the action, points, end, rake-off, share, commish, vig, vigorish, bite, chunk, juice, skig, slice, cut in, cut up, cut a melon (profits), piece of the pie, drag, P.C., taste. See also INTEREST, SHARE.

PERCEPTION n. brain wave, brainchild, approach, big idea, picture, flash on it, see the light, the light. See IDEA. See also PLAN.

PERCEPTIVE adj. hip, hep, hip to the jive, hep to the jive, a brain, brains, brainy, sharp, savvy, with it, all woke up, tuned in, booted on, wise to, know one's onions, know what's what, know one's stuff, on top of, the smart money, ear to the ground, on the beam, got good antenna. See also AWARE.

PERDITION n. 1. hell, the other place. 2. blue ruin, rack and ruin, totaled, total wipe, wipe out.

PERFECT adj. A-O.K., A-okay, aces, right on, 10, ten, out of this world, bull's-eye, on target, on the button, on the numbers, on the money, dead on, gig, apple pie, four-o, in the groove, outrageous righteous and relaxed, textbook, tip-top shape, to a T, to a turn, to a frazzle, to a fare-thee-well, done up brown, down to the ground, not do by halves. See also CORRECT.

PERFECTIONIST adj. picky, picky picky, stickler, dot the i's and cross the t's, fussbudget, fusspot, pernickety, persnickety, according to Hoyle, by the book, by the numbers. See PARTICULAR.

PERFECT SCORE n. ace, par, scratch (golf).

PERFIDIOUS adj. double-crossing, snake in the grass, two-faced, two-timing, low-down and dirty, dirty work, cheatin' heart, slick, slippery, speak with forked tongue. See DECEITFUL.

PERFORATE v. poke full of holes, shoot full of holes.

PERFORM v. 1. be on, go on, do a turn, do a number, strut one's stuff, play one's gig, go into one's song and dance, chew the scenery, ham, ham it up, tread the boards, emote, bring down the house. 2. go that route, go to town, move, make one's move, do one's thing, TCB (take care of business), take a flier (impulsively), pull off, shit or get off the pot, perk, percolate, tick, operate, run with the ball, come on like, do one's stuff, deliver the goods. See ACT.

PERFORMANCE n. gig, stunt, perf, set (musical), cut (recording), dumb act (without words), high jinks, hi jinks; exhebeesh, exhibicion (sex acts). See also ACT.

PERFORMER n. star, ham, hambone, trouper, legiter, lead, bit player, thesp, straight man, stooge, mugger, baddie. See ACTOR.

PERFUME n. smell well, smell good.

PERFUNCTORY adj. laid back, loose, could care less, don't give shit, don't give a shit, phone it in, just going through the motions, walk through it, asleep at the switch. See INDIFFERENT. See also CARELESS.

PERIL n. double trouble, deep shit, risky business.

PERILOUS adj. hot, hairy, loaded, dynamite, unhealthy, widow maker, jungle, zoo, rugged, dicey, chancy, risky business, play with fire, hot potato, play Russian roulette, on thin ice, touch and go. See DANGEROUS.

PERIODICAL n. mag, pulp, sheet, slick, rag, throwaway, fan mag; joint, limb joint (nonexistent). See also NEWSPAPER.

PERISCOPE n. scope.

PERISH v. go, kick off, kick the bucket, buy the farm, pass away, croak, give up the ghost, OD, pull the plug, bite the dust, kiss off, cash in one's chips, check out, one-way ticket. See DIE.

PERISHED adj. bought the farm, had it, offed, dead meat, stiff, belly up, kicked the bucket, croaked, gone west, gone to that great (whatever) in the sky, stone cold, on a slab, out of range, boxed. See DEAD.

PERMANENT adj. set, set in concrete, in for the long haul, forever and a day, for keeps, for a coon's age, for a month of Sundays, ever so long, time out of mind, till hell freezes over, till one's blue in the face, till shrimps learn to whistle, till the cows come home.

PERMISSIBLE adj. legit, kosher, on the up and up, on the legit. See LEGAL. See also ACCEPTABLE.

PERMISSION n. go-ahead, green light, okay, OK, stamp of approval. See CONSENT.

PERMIT v. bless, buy, okay, OK, sign, sign off on, pass, pass on, shake on, thumbs up, put one's John Hancock on, boost, get behind, go for, give the nod, give the go-ahead, give the green light, it's a deal, like you say, you got it, take kindly to, give the stamp of approval, rubber-stamp, cave in, bear with, live with, hold with, go along with, string along with, put up with, be big, hear of, stand for, sit still for, lump it and like it, stomach something, grin and bear it, face it. See also ALLOW.

PERMITTED adj. legit, kosher, on the legit, on the level, on the up and up, card-carrying. See ACCEPTED.

PERPETRATOR n. perp.

PERPETUALLY adv. for ever so long, for a coon's age, for a dog's age, for a month of Sundays, till hell freezes over, till you're blue in the face, till the cows come home, till shrimps learn to whistle, when a donkey flies.

PERPLEX v. get to, discomboberate, discumbobulate, rattle, rattle one's cage, buffalo, mess with one's head, fuddle, put one on a crosstown bus, muddy the waters, snow, stum, flummox. See PUZZLE.

PERPLEXED adj. unglued, shook up, all balled up, bugged up, bollixed, bollixed up, hung, hung up, mixed up, messed up attic, floored, in a fog, don't know from nothing, don't know which way is up. See PUZZLED.

PERQUISITE n. fringe benefit, goodies, gravy, perk, perks, golden handcuffs, golden parachute, swindle sheet. See also EXTRA.

PERSECUTE v. bug, ride, pick on, put the squeeze on, put the screws on, put the heat on, put one through the wringer, on one's back, on one's case, dog, dog one's case, drive one up the wall. See also ANNOY.

PERSECUTED adj. dogged, picked on.

PERSECUTION n. witch hunting, red-baiting, fishing expedition.

PERSEVERANCE n. backbone, drive, moxie, spunk, gits, grit, guts, cool, keep on keeping on, sitzfleisch, stick-to-itiveness, never say die.

PERSEVERE v. hang tough, hang in, hang in there, stick it, stick it out, stick with it, go for it, go for broke, see it through, leave no stone unturned, stay the course, never say die. See PERSIST.

PERSEVERING adj. stiff-necked, mulish, the game ain't over till the last man is out, tough, game, dead set on, bound, bound and determined, going the whole hog, hanging in, going for broke. See STUBBORN. See also DETERMINED.

PERSIST v. hang tough, hang in, hang in there, hang on for dear life, hold on like a bulldog, hang on like a leech, stick like a leech, stick like a barnacle, stick like a limpet, stick like a wet shirt, stick it, stick it out, stick to it, stick with it, stick to one's guns, tough it out, stay put, go for it, go for broke, go the whole hog, go the limit, go on with the show, go all the way, go to any length, go through fire and water, go through hell and high water, go through with, see through, see it through, carry through, leave no stone unturned, leave no avenue unexplored, follow up, follow through, get on with it, let it ride, plug along, plug away, peg away, stay the course, dig, grind, hammer, move heaven and earth, not give up the ship, never say die, hold the fort. See also ENDURE.

PERSISTENCE n. staying power, hanging in there, hanging tough, stick-to-itiveness, sitzfleisch, cool. See also TENACITY.

PERSISTENT adj. bound, bound and determined, keeps coming back for more, in for the long haul, like a bad penny, always turning up like a bad penny, sticky, hang tough, murder (he's murder), never say die. See DETERMINED. See also STUBBORN.

PERSON n. unit, guy, dude, cat, feller, lad, chap, bird, duck, stud, joker, character, clown, jasper, bugger, bastard, customer, party, certain party, head, ace (good), bad news, type; motherfucker, mofo, mothafucka, mother clutcher, mother grabber (Obsc.), bod, warm body, face, hairpin, job, number (hot number), boogie bear (ugly), boot (Bl.), cake, poor fish, skin, geezer, so and so, ghee, hip ghee, mickey, stiff, fly horse, gapper.

PERSONABLE adj. ace, aces, O.K. guy, good Joe, right guy, all right guy, good guy, nice guy, one's kinda guy, a sweetheart, a prince, white hat, good egg, hipster, sport, big deal, softy, old softy, old smoothy, easygoing, all heart, brick, crackerjack, cutie, got that certain something, snuggle bunny, cher, daisy, doozie, honey, hot stuff, one after one's own heart, true blue, solid citizen, good apple. See also BEAUTIFUL, CHARISMA, PERSUASIVE.

PERSONAGE adj. celeb, star, superstar, monster, name, numero uno, VIP, w.k. (well known), face, page-oner, prima donna, right up there, hot shot, big, big noise, big cheese, knocker, large charge, visiting fireman, gun. See CELEBRITY.

PERSONAL APPEARANCE n. PA, flesh show.

PERSON, DISLIKED n. shit, shit heel, piece of shit, cocksucker, prick, cunt, twat, ass, asshole, jackass, bad ass, shithead, bad medicine, bad news, son of a bitch, S.O.B., mother, motherfucker, mofo, mothuh fuckuh, mother grabber, grabber, mother's cunt (all Obsc.); bad guy, bad actor, bad hat, black hat, bad egg, wrongo, turkey, animal, beast, scumbag, scum, gross, stinker, stink pot, skunk, louse, crud, loser, real winner, a nothing, creep, drip, fink, rat fink, rat bastard, fuckface, heel, hood, hit man, finger man, hatchet man, snitch, snake, rat, bastard, ballbreaker, ballbuster, low-life, double-dealer, double-crosser, wrong ghee, bum, crumb bum, crumb, stumblebum, yo-yo, zombie, banana, dumb cluck, cluck, dumbo, mince, simp, spastic, weenie, wimp, worm, bad case of the uglies, Arkansas lizard, won't give one the time of day.

PERSONNEL n. shop, crew, troops.

PERSPECTIVE n. headset, mindset, mindtrip, where one's head is, where one is at, where it's at, like it is, the size of it, P.O.V., angle.

PERSPIRATION ODOR n. B.O.

PERSPIRE v. break a sweat, sweat like a horse, sweat like a trooper, sweat bullets, get all in a lather.

PERSUADE v. work on, work over, soften up, soft soap, sweet talk, stroke, lay it on, lay it on thick, lay it on with a trowel, schmear, schmeikle, butter, butter up, honey, soap, oil, kid along, play up to, give a come-hither look, come on, bat the eyes at, give with bedroom eyes, get around, turn one's head around, brainwash, eat one's mind, crack one or something, put across, con, duke in, promote, spark, sound, rope in, swindle in, sell, sell one on, hard sell, soft sell, fast talk, snow, snow under, push, goose, goose up, jolly, blarney, caboodle, fire up, key up, suck in, hand one a line, hook, hook in, nag, twist one's arm, egg one on, iggle, lobby, bug, buttonhole, jawbone, put the screws on, put the bee on, lean on, make it hot for, put the squeeze on, put up to, push around, break one's arm, break one's finger, break one's leg, make a believer out of, cream, twist one's arm, sweat one, put on the spot, throw one's weight around, cram down one's throat, ram down one's throat, come at from all sides, high pressure, squeeze, juice, steamroller, bulldoze, knock on doors, politick.

PERSUADED adj. satisfied, bought, sold.

PERSUASION n. sell, hard sell, soft soap, snow job, sweet talk, blow job, shovelin' shit, con, hook, arm-twist, working over, goose, brainwash, promote, squeeze, juice. See also BELIEF.

PERSUASIVE adj. fast talker, gift of gab, slick, smooth, smoothie, old smoothie, smooth article, smooth apple, smooth operator, slicker, spieler.

PERT adj. flip, fresh, breezy, nervy, sassy, smart, smart alecky, smart ass, wise ass, brassy, bold as brass, have a mouth. See also CHEERFUL, INSOLENT.

PERTINENT adj. on the button, on the nose, on target, right on, kosher, legit, that's the idea, that's the ticket, just what the doctor ordered.

PERTURB v. adjy, spook, get to, bug, make waves, make a scene, needle, rabble rouse, stir up. See DISTURB. See also CONFUSE, DISTRESS.

PERTURBED adj. discombobulated, all shook up, bugged, in a stew, in a lather, fussed, have kittens, wreck, shot to pieces, in a botheration. See DISTURBED. See also CONFUSED, DISTRESSED.

PERVASIVE adj. wall to wall, all over the place, all over the lot, stinking with, can't get away from it.

PERVERSE adj. bitchy, ornery, hard-nosed, locked in, stuck in concrete, brick wall, pat, stand pat, mulish, mule, stubborn as a mule, horse, stiff-necked, sticky, bitter ender. See STUBBORN. See also IRRITABLE.

PERVERT n. freak, geek, pervo, prevert, queer, panty thief.

PERVERT v. 1. doctor, doctor up, spike, water, water down, cut, load, salt, salt a mine, fudge, plant, fake, phony up, queer. 2. lead one down the primrose path, brainwash, get one hooked, hook.

PERVERTED adj. foreign, kinky, queer. See also CORRUPT, VICIOUS.

PESO n. adobe dollar, p, pa.

PESSIMISM n. dim view, dark side.

PESSIMIST n. drag, wet blanket, killjoy, crepe hanger, gloomy Gus, downer, sourpuss, sourbelly, sourball, drip, party pooper, dog in the manger, worrywart, Calamity Jane, calamity howler.

PEST n. drag, headache, pain, pain in the ass, pain in the neck, blister, nudge, nudzh, noodge, nag, bummer, creep, pill, drip, kibitzer, flat tire, wet blanket, crashing bore.

PESTER v. bug, ride, be at, noodge, nudge, work on, get in one's hair, hound, dog, nag, worry, hock a charnik, mess with, graum, get on one's nerves. See ANNOY.

PESTICIDE n. bug bomb.

PESTS n. crabs, crum, crumb, grayback, seam squirrel, shimmy lizard; crumby, crummy, lousy (afflicted with).

PET n. fair-haired boy, blue-eyed boy, candy boy, number one boy, pratt boy, evergreen, fave.

PET v. grab ass, ball, make out, smooch, spoon, perch, pitch woo, fling woo, feel up. See also AMOROUS PLAY.

PETITION v. put in for. See REQUEST.

PETRIFIED adj. scared stiff, scared witless, scared shitless, push the panic button, frozen, pucker-assed, asshole suckin' wind, shake in one's boots, struck all of a heap. See FRIGHTENED.

PETRIFY v. spook, chill, chill off, put the chill on, scare shitless, scare stiff, scare silly, strike all of a heap. See FRIGHTEN.

PETROL n. gas, bug juice, juice, go juice, Ethyl.

PETROLEUM n. gas, black gold.

PETTY adj. big zero, no big deal, no biggie, no great shakes, pissytailed, dinky, measly, two bit, tinhorn, chicken shit, frig it, not worth a hill of beans, nickel and dime, penny ante, peanuts, pokerino, shot, scratch, skag. See UNIMPORTANT. See also SELFISH.

PETULANCE n. miff, pet, stew, tiff, snit.

PETULANT adj. bitchy, mean, tetchy, crabby, cranky, kvetchy, whiny, snappish, crybaby, pill, plainer, rapper, sorehead, uptight, thin-skinned, pushing out one's lips, got up on the wrong side of the bed. See PEEVISH.

PEYOTE n. mescal, button.

PHALLUS n. cock, prick, dick, dork, pecker, peter, joint, pencil, meat, weenie, joy stick, bone, knob, joy knob, bishop, wang, thing, putz, schmuck, dong, shlong, dingus, tool, one-eyed monster, hung (big), one-eyed wonder (all Obsc.). See PENIS.

PHANTOM n. haint, hant, spook, things that go bump in the night.

PHENCYCLIDINE n. PCP, P.C.P., water, Angel Dust, Sherms (cigarette), P-stuff, busy bee, crystal, elephant, elephant tranquilizer, monkey dust, scuffle, killer weed, peace pill, rocket fuel, cannabinal, lovely, tic, mist, dust, rock dust, T dust, animal, cadillac, C.J., K.J., goon, sheets, hog, mint, monkey, snorts, Aurora Borealis, dummy, ozone, soma, cyclone, horse, new magic; super joint, super grass (marijuana sprinkled with PCP).

PHENOMENON n. one for the book, something else, something to write home about, stunner.

PHI BETA KAPPA n. Phi Bete, fly bait.

PHILADELPHIA, PENNSYLVANIA Philly, Phillie, Philly Town, City of Brotherly Love, Big Brother, Liberty City, Quaker City, Big Pretzel.

PHILANDER v. dilly-dally, two-time, monkey, monkey around, horse around, mess around, kid around, muck around, fart around, fool around, fuck around, play around, screw around, lollygag, jerk off, fool with, play games with.

PHILANDERER n. playboy, player, nighthawk, dude, operator, cruiser, heavy cake, letch, wolf, tomcat, swinger, lover boy, lady-killer, man on the make, chaser, skirt chaser, tail chaser, rounder, whorehound, Don Juan, good-time Charlie. See LECHER.

PHILANDERING adj. two-timing, moonlighting, cheat, cheater, cheating, playing around, fooling around, extracurricular activities, double-crossing, sneakin' deacon, step out on one, chippy on one, tip, two-faced, witch, yard, hanky-panky.

PHILANTHROPIST n. do-gooder, bleeding heart, good scout, angel, fairy godmother, lady bountiful, Robin Hood, Santa Claus, sugar daddy. See also BENEFACTOR.

PHILIPPINE n. chico, filipino, phillipino, moke (Derog.).

PHILOSOPHICAL adj. cool, cool as a cucumber, keep one's cool, keep one's shirt on, keep a stiff upper lip, not turn a hair, roll with the punches, unflappable, commonsensical, ah ah head.

PHILOSOPHY n. phil.

PHLEGM n. snot, ginder, green ginder, green one.

PHLEGMATIC adj. blah, flat, mopey, dopey, drippy, nebbish, wimpy, what the hell, it's all the same to me, could care less, draggy. See LANGUID. See also INDIFFERENT.

PHOBIA n. have a thing about, have on the brain, hang-up, tiger, tiger by the tail, bee, bee in one's bonnet, bug, bug in one's ear, bug up one's ass, bag, grabber, ax to grind; chuck habit, chuck horrors (prison food).

PHOENIX, ARIZONA Sun City.

PHONOGRAPH n. hi fi, stereo, box, jukebox (commercial), low fi (jocular), noisola, phono, pick, playback.

PHONOGRAPH RECORD n. album, disc, platter, licorice pizza, single, wax, acetate, vinyl, manhole cover.

PHOTOGRAPH n. shot, photo, pic, pix, snap, art (newspaper, criminal), beefcake (male), cheesecake (female), blowup, mug, mug shot, pinup, atta-boy shot (TV sports close-up), French postcard (porno), gow, centerfold (nude), eight by ten glossy, 8x10 glossy, picture gallery (file).

PHOTOGRAPH v. film, lens, shoot, roll, turn, gun, long shot, close-up, mug, snap, get, can.

PHOTOGRAPHER n. fotog, photog, lenser, shutterbug, camera bug, glowworm, mugger, paparazzo.

PHOTOGRAPH GALLERY n. mug joint.

PHYSIC n. cc pills.

PHYSICAL EDUCATION n. phys ed, gym.

PHYSICALLY FIT adj. in the pink, wrapped tight, fit as a fiddle, 1A (Mil. draft).

PHYSICAL THERAPY n. rolfing, workout.

PHYSICALLY UNFIT adj. out of shape, run down, good and flabby, let oneself go, 4F (Mil. draft).

PHYSICIAN n. M.D., medico, doc, quack, bones, sawbones, pill pusher, pill slinger, big eye man, big nose man, big heart man, bone bender, Doctor Feelgood, shrink, head shrinker, ice-tong doctor, script writer (prescribes drugs illegally), back-alley abortionist. See DOCTOR.

PHYSIOGNOMY n. kisser, puss, map, mug, pan, mush, moosh, phiz, phizog, biscuit, clock, dial, conk, chevy chase, gills, index, mask, potato, squash, deadpan, poker face, sourpuss, picklepuss, sugarpuss.

PHYSIQUE n. bod, build, built, shape, shaft, chassis, classy chassis, beefcake, muscle man, muscles, stacked, V man, built like a brick shithouse, cream puff (small, weak), frame, coke frame (Fem.), anatomy, corpus, bag of bones, booty.

PIANIST n. fingers, ivory tickler, ivory thumper, itches a mean ivory, tickles the ivories, thumper, piano kid, professor.

PIANO n. ivories, box, tinkle box, eighty-eight, 88, goola, grand, upright, studio.

PIANO KEYS n. eighty-eights, ivories, goola.

PIANO PLAYER n. fingers, ivory tickler, ivory thumper, itches a mean ivory, tickles the ivories, thumper, piano kid, professor.

PIAZZA n. gallery, front stoop, stoop.

PICAYUNE adj. chicken, chicken shit, nitpicking, picky, picky picky, small, small time, tinhorn, measly, two bit, punk, one horse, two by four, jerkwater. See UNIMPORTANT.

PICK n. bag, cup of tea, druthers, turned on to, weakness for. See CHOICE.

PICK v. opt, tap, finger, name, tab, tag, slot, go down the line, say so, take it or leave it. See SELECT.

PICKAX n. anchor.

PICKET v. hit the bricks, walk out. See STRIKE.

PICKPOCKET n. dip, cannon, tool, wire, mechanic, Catholic, cutpurse, digger, fanner (locates victim), file, forks, five fingers, finger, fingersmith, front gee, gavar, gee, gee whiz (armed), greasy finger, gun, knucker, knucksman, moll buzzer, shot, picks, friskers, hooks, spitter, wise, jostle, jostler, clipper.

PICKPOCKET v. lift, dip, beat, boost, dig, dive, make, make a mark, make a poke, drop the duke, put the duke down, kiss the dog, reef, riffle, whiz, work the get-ons, work the put-offs, work a short, work a spill, work a tip, work the breaks, out on the shorts, jostle, rooting on the cannon.

PICKPOCKET'S ASSISTANT n. bumper, nudger, stall, stick.

PICTURE n. 1. doodle (meaningless pattern), snap (photo), art (News.). 2. angel (radar). 3. dead ringer, spitting image.

PIE n. chocker (large), magoo (custard pie for throwing).

PIECE n. chunk, gob, hunk, lump, smithereen, bite, chaw, chomp, cut, slice, halver. See also INTEREST, SHARE.

PIERCE v. crack, crack open, break in, jimmy.

PIG n. porker, porky, cob roller (young or small).

PILE n. 1. buildup. 2. chunk, gob, hunk.

PILFER v. rip off, appropriate, boost, scrounge, pinch, promote, buzz, cop, kipe, liberate, lift, moonlight requisition, snatch, snitch, swipe, snipe, scoff, glom, glaum, glahm, glue, burn, annex, borrow, palm, bag, nip, snare, pluck. See also STEAL, APPROPRIATE.

PILFERED adj. bent, lifted, kyped, moonlight requisitioned, liberated, hot, hot stuff, hot ice, hot paper, kinky, sizzling, swag (without a gun).

PILL n. doll, jelly bean, amp, bombita, cockleburr (pep), downer, Finn, fruit salad (mixture), lude, Mickey Finn, peter, popper, upper; dizzy wizzy, goof ball (non-narcotic), G.B.

PILOT n. flyboy, jockey, jet jockey, pipe jockey, throttle jockey, airplane driver, bird legs, birdman, birdwoman, goofer, dodo (Stu.), eagle, rotorhead (helicopter). See FLYER.

PILOT HOUSE n. brain box (river towboat).

PIMP n. mack, mackman, macko man, hard Mack (violent), sweet Mack, mac, mackerel, maggot, dude, flesh peddler, hustler, Johnny Ponce, king bung, missionary, outlaw, pee eye, P.I., ponce, brother-in-law, husband, Mr. McGimp, player, rack salesman, skirt man, honey man, sweet man, old man, bull bitch, butch pimp, cadet, driver.

PIMP v. run a stable, have a string of hustlers, have a sister-in-law, steer, tout.

PIMPLE n. hickey, zit, beauty spot, bloom, doohickey, dohinky, blem.

PIMPLY adj. crater face, pizza face.

PINBALL MACHINE n. whiffle board.

PINCE-NEZ n. nippers.

PINCH n. crunch, clutch, box, tight spot, tight squeeze, between a rock and a hard place. See DIFFICULTY.

PINCHED adj. at the end of one's rope, hard up, up against it. See DESTITUTE.

PINE v. carry a torch, hanker for, itch for, yen for, have a yen for, spoil for, give one's kingdom in hell for, give one's eyeteeth for, eat one's heart out. See DESIRE. See also MOURN.

PINEAPPLE SUNDAE n. Chicago (also soda).

PINNACLE n. tops, in top form, in full swing, the greatest, the most, the max, ape. See BEST.

PIONEER v. spearhead, trail-blaze, get the jump on, go out in front. See also BEGIN.

PIOUS adj. born again, got religion, Jesus freak, Holy Joe, Jesus lover, Jasper, knee bender, Mary, goody, goody-goody, goody two-shoes, scoutmaster.

PIPE n. stove, hay burner, bug juice (residue).

PIQUANCY n. guts, kick, zip.

PIQUE n. miff, pet, stew, rise, get a rise out of, tiff, snit, peeve, pet peeve, sore, huff, dander, Irish, miff, storm, ruckus, wingding, slow burn, conniption, conniption fit, cat fit, duck fit, blowup, flare-up, bone to pick.

PIQUE v. 1. bug, piss one off, turn one off, make waves, give a bad time to, give one a hard time, give one the business, give one the needle, hit on, fuck with one's head, get a rise out of one, get one's dander up, get under one's skin. See ANNOY. 2. grab, goose, goose up, egg on, turn on, fire up, key up, put up to, work up, work up into a lather, sound, hook, trigger, pressure, push. See INTRIGUE.

PISTOL n. artillery, cannon, blaster, gat, gee, piece, iron, rod, snubby, snub nose, Saturday night special, bean shooter, peashooter, popper, pop, equalizer, difference, speaker, mister speaker, persuader, convincer, hardware, heater, heat, Betsey, roscoe, forty-five, zip gun, slim, belly gun, snug, spud, potato, tool. See GUN.

PIT AREA n. zoo (racing).

PITCH v. chuck, chunk, fire, lob, heave, pitch, sling, fling, gun, peg, toss.

PITCHER n. growler (large for beer).

PITCHMAN n. barker, booster, plugger, huckster, hucksterer, ad man, ad writer, adsmith, blurbist, ballyhooer, ballyhoo man, grifter, grinder, spieler. See also ADVERTISING MAN, PUBLICIST.

PITFALL n. catch, catch 22, booby trap, bag, hook, swindle, box, setup, come-on.

PITH n. bottom line, heart, meat and potatoes, nitty-gritty, nub.

PITIFUL adj. wimpy, fish, poor fish, what the cat dragged in, nebbish. See also UNHAPPY.

PITILESS adj. cutthroat, go for the jugular, killer instinct, mean machine, dog eat dog, hatchet job, take no prisoners. See also CALLOUS.

PITTSBURGH, PENNSYLVANIA Steel City.

PIZZA n. tza, za, garbage pizza (everything on it).

PLACATE v. cool, stroke, pour oil on troubled waters, take the edge off, soft-pedal, fix up, make matters up, make nice, play up to. See PACIFY.

PLACE n. 1. hangout, joint, lay, layout, plant, dump, digs, scene, fix, hole, spot, X marks the spot, pad, crib, crash pad, roof over one's head, the pits, armpit (undesirable), office, neck of the woods, zone, turf. 2. slot, where one is at, pecking order, down the line.

PLACE v. park, peg, nail, spot, finger, plank, plank down, plunk, plop. See also INDICATE.

PLACED adj. set up, fixed, framed, laid on.

PLACID adj. cool, cool as a cucumber, ah-ah head, unflappable, level vibes. See CALM.

PLAGIARIST n. pirate.

PLAGIARIZE v. pirate, lift, steal, borrow, crib, pick one's brains, rape.

PLAIN adj. 1. vanilla, unvarnished, stripped down, clean, bare bones, with the bark on. 2. folksy, homey, haymish, meat-and-potatoes man. 3. big as life, open and shut, open-and-shut case, under one's nose, if it were a snake it would bite you, makes no bones about it, call a spade a spade, what you see is what you get, plain as the nose on one's face, talk turkey. See APPARENT. 4. plain as a mud fence, plain enough to stop a clock, barefaced, hard on the eyes, short on looks.

PLAINSPOKEN adj. up front, right up front, call it like it is, straight, shoot straight, talk like a Dutch uncle, call a spade a spade, put all one's cards on the table, make no bones about it. See FRANK.

PLAINTIVE adj. bitchy, out of sorts, cantankerous, grumpy, beefing, bellyaching, bitching, crabby, cranky, grousing, ugly customer. See PEEVISH. See also UNHAPPY.

PLAN n. game, game plan, layout, gimmick, angle, action, big picture, picture, pitch, proposition, proposish, dodge, setup, play, scenario, scene, story, bit, child, brainchild, slant, trick, twist, switch, booby trap, lay of the land, what's cookin', how one figures it, what's the action, where one's heading. See also SCHEME.

PLAN v. hatch, mastermind, quarterback, brainstorm, spitball, craft, line up, ready up, set up, cook up, dream up, trump up, frame up, whip up, come up with, up, throw together, get one's act together, lay out, work something out, block out, get set for, fix to. See also SCHEME.

PLANE n. jet, ram jet, crate, boxcar, ship, can, big iron (multi-engine), cloud buster, bird, wind wagon, zoo (press). See AIRPLANE.

PLANET n. apple, big blue marble, real estate, spaceship Earth.

PLANKS n. load of sticks.

PLANNED adj. fixed, wired, rigged, framed, packed, stacked, put up, set up, cooked up, gimmicked up, sewed up, in the bag, on ice, cinched, cut and dry, bagged, gaffed, sacked, spiked, square, had zingers put in. See also PREARRANGED.

PLANNER n. mastermind, brain. See also CONSPIRATOR.

PLANT v. park, plank, plank down, plunk, plop.

PLASTIC CARD n. loid (used to open locks).

PLASTIC COVER n. blister (aircraft).

PLASTIC SURGERY n. facelift, nose job, eye job, tummy tuck, body and fender man (surgeon).

PLATE n. manhole cover.

PLATFORM n. soapbox, stump, bally stand (circus).

PLATITUDE n. buzzword, boiler plate, high camp, hokum, corn, familiar tune, chestnut, old chestnut, saw, old saw, old song, old story, potboiler.

PLATTER n. manhole cover.

PLAUSIBLE adv. like as not, like enough, very likely. See also BELIEVABLE, LOGICAL.

PLAY n. legiter, legit, piece, potboiler, one-acter, book show, dromedy (dramatic comedy), curtain-raiser, meller, minstrel show, cork opera, dumb show, toby show; hit, smash, smash hit, boff, turkey, flop (failure) (also refers to TV, book, radio, movie, etc.).

PLAY v. 1. clown, carry on, horse around, mess around, kibitz, let go, let loose, kick up one's heels, cut up, cut up a few touches, go places and do things, go on a spree. See REVEL. 2. do a turn, do one's bit, strut one's stuff, play one's gig, chew the scenery, ham, ham it up, tread the boards, come on like gangbusters (well); blow, lay a bomb, lay an egg, go into the toilet (badly). See ACT.

PLAYBOY n. player, high liver, night owl, operator, speed, heavy hitter, wolf, tomcat, cat, sport, swinger, lover boy, killer, man on the make, make-out artist, chaser, rounder, gay dog, whorehound, good-time Charlie. See LECHER.

PLAYER n. 1. ham, hambone, trouper, legiter, thesp, lead, star, bit player, stand-in, scene sweller, spear carrier, moppet (child). See ACTOR. 2. jock, animal, ape, gorilla, V man, muscle man, meathead, speed merchant, superjock. See ATHLETE. 3. plunger, piker, tinhorn, tinhorn gambler, two dollar bettor, chalk player, sharp, sharper, sharpie, crap shooter, boneshaker. See GAMBLER. 4. rocker, monster (popular), cool cat, longhair, long underwear, lip-splitter, sender, solid sender, swinging gate, wig. See MUSICIAN.

PLAYFUL adj. zippy, zappy, snappy, peppy, full of pep, full of piss and vinegar, full of beans, full of hops, feeling one's oats, go-go, have lead in one's pencil. See SPIRITED.

PLAYGOER n. fan, house, showcase, standee, theatergoer, turnout. See AUDIENCE.

PLAYHOUSE n. house, four walls, deluxer, legiter, legit, opera house, barn, boards, garlic opera (old, cheap), grind house, mousetrap. See THEATER.

PLAYING-CARD HOLDER n. shoe.

PLAYING CARDS, MARKED n. readers, coolers, paper, hot paper, humps, strippers, low-belly strippers, edgework, lacework, pinwork, greasy aces, B-backs, fish backs, slick backs, broads with ears; shaved deck, cheater, sorts (marked or stacked deck).

PLAYING CARD TERMS bullet (ace), deuce (two), trey (three), John, Johnny (jack), girl bitch, lady (queen), cowboy (king), bug, cuter, cutter (joker); wash (shuffle), deck, California bible, California prayer book (1855), boards; cold deck, shaved deck, stacked deck, cheater (marked or prearranged); player, card sharp, card shark, sit in on a hand, bumblepuppy, goulash (unusual hand); Yarborough, lollapaloser (poor hand); low belly strippers, boards, pasteboard, paint, picture, one-eyed Jacks, wild card (joker), puppy dog feet (clubs), duke mitt (hand), rag, riffle (shuffle), ups and downs, wedges.

PLAY MUSIC v. wail, jam, jazz, jive, blast, blow, lip, rag, tootle, wig, blow one's ass off, blow the roof off (loud), blow up a breeze, blow up a storm, get off (swing), kick it (jazz), hit it up, scratching (records).

PLEA n. cop out, jive, song, song and dance, whitewash, clean up, story, fish, fish story, fish tale, have to see a man about a dog, off time. See EXCUSE.

PLEA BARGAIN v. cop a plea, cop out, do business.

PLEAD v. cop a plea, cop out, crawl, square oneself, square a beef, square things, make up for, get down on one's marrowbones. See also BEG, APPEAL.

PLEAD GUILTY v. ride a beef, cop a plea, cop out, plea bargain.

PLEAD POVERTY v. poor-mouth.

PLEASANT adj. all reet, all righty, coolville, copacetic, fine and mellow, home cooking, all to the mustard, hotsie-totsie, Mr. Nice Guy. See AGREE-ABLE.

PLEASE v. score, wow, grab, kill, slay, turn on, go over big, hit the spot, fill the bill, sell, sell one on, be just the ticket, just what the doctor ordered, make the grade, sweep off one's feet. See also OBLIGE.

PLEASED adj. up, upbeat, flyin', flyin' high, floating on air, in seventh heaven, pleased as Punch, tickled pink, gassed. See HAPPY.

PLEASES v. scores, hits the spot, hits the bull's-eye, makes it, thanks, I needed that.

PLEASURABLE adj. kicks, for kicks, mellow, fine and mellow, lush, nervous, cool, wild, downhill, just for grins, fun (fun party), clear sailing.

PLEASURE n. turn-on, flash, kick, kicks, knocks, mess, velvet, buzz, get off, get off on. See also AMUSEMENT, DESIRE, CHOICE.

PLEAT n. reet pleat.

PLEBE n. ducrot, dumbjohn, Mister Ducrot, Mister Dumbjohn, Mister Dumbguard (all West Point).

PLEBEIAN n. boojy, pleb, Billy Sixpack, Joe Lunchbucket.

PLEDGE v. 1. hook, soak, hock, put in hock. 2. feeze, pheeze (fraternity).

PLEDGED adj. 1. steady, going steady, pinned, bird, donah, donar, future, intended. 2. in the bag, nailed down, on ice, cinched. See also AGREED, DETERMINED.

PLENTY adj. no end, no end of, no end to, up to one's ass in, up to one's ears with, lousy with, filthy with, stink with, crawling with, alive with, stinking with, thick with, thick as flies, thick as hail, thick as fleas on a hound dog, a dime a dozen, a mess, loaded, loads, loads of, plate is full, enough on one's plate, drug on the market, galore, money to burn, scads, rolling in, coming out of one's ears, all over the place, a ton, mucho, mucho mucho, heavy, a raft of, bags of, lots of, lotsa, oodles, oodles and oodles, beaucoup, bocoop, bocoo, boocoo, umpteen, eleventeen, jillion, zillion, knee deep in, sockful, shithouse full, wad, more than one can shake a stick at, coals to Newcastle, egg in one's beer, heaps, passel, flock, aplenty, good 'n plenty.

PLIANT adj. go with the flow, putty in one's hands, hang loose, roll with the punches. See also SUB-MISSIVE.

PLIGHT n. shit, deep shit, serious shit, serious jelly, bad news, double trouble, fix, jam. See PREDICA-MENT.

PLOD v. plug, plug along, plug away, dig, grind, hammer, peg along, peg away, buckle down, knuckle down, put one's nose to the grindstone, slave, sweat, sweat and slave, back to the salt mines, dog it (inferior), mess around, heel (Stu.), scratch, bear down on it, shlep. See also WALK.

PLODDER n. grind, workhorse, greasy grind, nose to the grindstone, workaholic.

PLOT n. 1. line, story, story line, picture, scenario, scene, weenie. 2. fix, frame, frame-up, booby trap, game, little game, setup, scam, lay of the land, put-up job. See SCHEME. See also PLAN.

PLOT v. angle, cook up, finagle, frame, frame up, operate, promote, wangle, wire, put out a contract. See SCHEME. See also PLAN.

PLOTTER n. finagler, operator, brain, mastermind, wire-puller.

PLUCK n. guts, gutsiness, grit, backbone, heart, intestinal fortitude, starch, moxie, nerve, spunk. See COURAGE.

PLUCK v. slap (bass viol strings).

PLUCKY adj. gutsy, gutty, gritty, nervy, spunky, game, tough, cool hand. See FEARLESS. See also DAR-ING.

PLUMP adj. pleasingly plump, roly-poly, heavy cream, hefty, hippy, chunky, battle of the bulge, butterball, built for comfort, zaftig. See FAT.

PLUNDER n. goods, hot goods, hot items, pickings, take, squeeze, make, swag, boodle, graft.

PLUNDER v. grab, smash and grab, lift, loft, kipe, snatch, salvage, appropriate, liberate, requisition, moonlight requisition. See LOOT.

PLUNGE n. header, nose dive, belly buster, belly flop, belly whopper.

PLUNGE v. 1. dunk, nose dive, belly-flop, take a belly whopper, take a header. 2. take a header, go the limit, go whole hog, shoot one's wad, shoot the works, take a flyer. See WAGER.

PNEUMOCONIOSIS n. black lung.

POCATELLO, IDAHO Poca, Pocaloo.

POCKET n. poke, binny (large for shoplifters), coffee bag, frame, hideaway, keister, kick, mouse, prat kick, rat hole.

POCKETBOOK n. bag, clutch, jiffy bag, jitney bag, keister, frame, hide, leather.

PODIUM n. soap box, stump.

POINT n. nub, bottom line, name of the game, nitty-gritty, nuts and bolts, the way of it, drift, heart, meat, stuff, score, punch line, kicker (point of a story, joke, etc.).

POINT v. name, tab, tag, make, peg, finger, lay one's finger on, put one's finger on, put the finger on, button down, pin down, put down for.

POINTED adj. 1. on the button, on the nose, right on, kosher, legit, that's the idea, that's the ticket, just what the doctor ordered. 2. in a nutshell, short and sweet, get right to it, make a long story short, boiled down, drawing one a picture, laying it on the line, make no bones about it, call a spade a spade, talk turkey.

POINTLESS adj. goin' round in circles, in a vicious circle, on a treadmill, going nowhere, locking the barn after the horse is stolen, looking for a needle in a haystack. See USELESS.

POINT OF VIEW n. P.O.V., angle, slant, where one is at, as one sees it, from where one is sitting.

POISE n. cool, keep one's cool, polish.

POKE n. shot, sock, zetz, goose.

POKE v. 1. give one the elbow, goose, give one the goose. 2. mosey, shlep along, get no place fast, toddle. See also IDLE.

POKER CHIPS n. barber pole, checks, stack.

POKER TERMS drop, over, fold, bug (wild card), cut, bingle (chip), case (last of a number), case ace (last ace), ace in the hole, ace high, dead man's hand (two pair, aces and eights), deuce (two), trey (three), Hart Schaffner and Marx (three jacks), Johns, Johnnys, hooks (Jacks), ladies (queens), cowboys (kings), trips (three of a kind), backdoor straight (acquired on last card), made, a run (consecutive cards), wired (hidden pair), split week, straight, busted flush, busted straight, boat (full house), tiger (lowest hand), kicker (unpaired high card), fourth street (fourth card), off suit (two different suits), stand pat, stay, ride 'em, play 'em close to the vest (conservative), pot (bets made), see, blind, sandbag, bump (raise), slow play (bluffing), put one on (guess opponents hand), the gun (dealer), under the gun (first player left of dealer); the flop, on board (face-up cards); lock, nuts (certain to win), sit out, deal one out (waive a hand).

POLE n. Bohunk, Hunkie, Hunky, Polak, Pollack, Pollock, Stash, Stella (all Derog.).

POLICE AIRCRAFT n. air bear, chopper copper, copper chopper, eye in the sky, pie in the sky.

POLICE CAR n. black and white, skunk wagon, fuzzmobile, bear car, bearmobile, buzz, buzzer, catch car, prowl car, cherry top, screaming gasser, whistler; brown bag, plain wrap (unmarked); buggy whip (transmitter), gumball (lights).

POLICE CLUB n. billy, sap stick, stick, nightstick, business, conk buster, conk crusher, convincer, duffy silencer, persuader, rosewood, rosh, works, shill.

POLICE FORCE n. boys in blue, fuzz, goon squad, heat, John Law, long arm of the law, New York's Finest, the force, the law, pigs, boy scouts.

POLICE HELICOPTER n. bear in the air, eye in the sky, chopper copper, copper chopper.

POLICE LEDGER n. blotter, sheet, rap sheet.

POLICE LIEUTENANT n. boss, lieu, lou.

POLICEMAN'S BADGE n. button, buzzer, cookie cutter, flash, tin, white tin, yellow tin.

POLICE OFFICER n. cop, fuzz, fuzzy, copper, slime, slime bucket, bull, shamus, flic, cossack, arm, dick, narc (narcotics), pig, oink, clown (rural), the man, the men, black and white, badge; badge bandit, bike (motocycle); boys in blue, blue man, bluecoat, bluebird (Bl.), big brother, boy scouts, city kitty, county Joe, county mounty, flathead, flatie, flatty, flatfoot, harness bull, harness dick, harness cop, keystone cop, sparrow cop, Evel Knievel, hick dick, law, John Law, Johnny Law, long arm, long arm of the law, Kojak, bear, smokey, Smokey the Bear, lady bear, girlie bear, mama bear, baby bear (rookie), little bear (local), local bear, local yard, local yokel; CHP, CHIPS (California Highway Patrol); bearded buddy, yard bull, cinderbull (railroad), deputy dog, goobie (campus), grasshopper (park), grasseater (corrupt), local boy, mafia, meat-eater (corrupt), nightcrawler, savage, slewfoot, road ranger, button, collar, finger, elbow, fink, cookie cutter, geerus, goms, goon squad, gum foot, headbeater, Mulligan, nab, penny, roach, Charley Goon, Charlie Nebs, Dan O'Leary, claw, fly ball, fly bob, fly bull, fly cop, fly dick, fly mug, shoo fly, sky, grumbler (chief), pounder, sham, shamus, slough, snake, snatcher, stick, stool, geepo, boogle man, foot soldier, hat rack (traffic), infantry, paper hanger, Peter Rabbit, the man with the headache stick, the brass, brass hat, five-0. See also DETECTIVE.

POLICE PATROL WAGON n. battlewagon, paddywagon, black and white, Maria, Black Maria, fuzzmobile, pigmobile, booby hatch, go long, milk wagon, piewagon.

POLICE RECORD n. pedigree, prior, rap sheet.

POLICE SERGEANT n. boss, sarge, desk sarge.

POLICE SPY n. plant, nose, narc (narcotics).

POLICE STATION n. station, station house, glass house, can, cop shop, front office, bear cage, bear cave, lock em up, lockup, cally (hobo).

POLICE TERMS buzzer, cookie cutter, tin (badge); box (telephone operator), the company (metropolitan force), swoop (raid), O.P. (observation post), U.C. (Undercover unit), make, make one (recognize), stake, stakeout, hog (uniform).

POLICEWOMAN n. Dickless Tracy, meter maid, Min, lady bear, girlie bear, mama bear, city kitty, sow.

POLICY n. channels, red tape, by the numbers, by the book. See also PLAN.

POLICY NUMBERS LOTTERY numbers, policy game; bank, banker, number baron, number man, pay off ghee (boss of); play the numbers (make a bet), hit, hit the numbers (win), comptroller, runner (subordinate).

POLIOMYELITIS n. polio.

POLISH n. Polak, Pollack, Pollock, Hunkie, Hunky, Bohunk, blitz (WW II) (all Derog.)

POLISH v. shine, buff up.

POLITIC adj. cool, sharp, tuned in, play it cool, handle with kid gloves, mind one's p's and q's, on the lookout. See also DISCREET.

POLITICAL ACTION COMMITTEE n. PAC.

POLITICAL CAMPAIGN n. politicking, rubberchicken tour, on the stump, stumping the hustings, off kissing babies, pressing the flesh (shaking hands), rainmaker (fund-raiser).

POLITICAL CONVENTION n. powwow, quadrennial circus.

POLITICAL HOLDOVER n. lame duck.

POLITICAL JARGON n. bafflegab, bunkum, federalese, gobbledygook, officialese, Washingtonese, hillspeak.

POLITICAL OPPONENTS n. opposish, enemies list, hit list, shit list.

POLITICAL ORGANIZER n. ward heeler, one of the troops, rainmaker (fund-raiser).

POLITICAL SCIENCE n. poli sci.

POLITICIAN n. pol, politico, two-bit politician, peanut politician, jackleg politician, porkbarrel politician, boys in the backroom, the boys uptown, dark horse (candidate), boodler (corrupt), glad-hander, grandstander, handshaker, hack, party hack, satch, war-horse, wheeler-dealer, logroller, boss, man higher up, ward heeler, flesh presser, party boss, party chieftain, stumper, stump speaker, stump orator, whistle-stopper, baby-kisser, bell-ringer.

POLITICS n. art of the possible, smoke-filled room, backroom politics, jungle, zoo, bossism, peanut politics, kid-glove politics, silk-stocking politics, hotairistocracy.

POLL v. polling the nabes (family and friends), polling the hornrims (staff intellectuals), polling the wiz (computer), trying it out on the dog (public), put out a feeler, test the waters, see which way the wind blows, send up a trial balloon.

POLL-TAKER n. numbers cruncher, pollster, pulse-taker.

POLLUTED adj. dirty, exposed, cooked (radiation), mucked up.

POLYSYLLABIC adj. jawbreaking.

POMADE n. axle grease, conk.

POMPOUS adj. biggety, bossy, dicty, sidity, puffed up, uppity, stuck on oneself, chesty, high and mighty, high hat, high-flown, high falutin', put on airs, have one's glasses on (Bl.), stuffed shirt, windbag, windy, full of hot air, gassy, top lofty. See CONCEITED.

POND n. splash.

PONDER v. figger, moon, noodle it around, put on one's thinking cap, chew the cud, wool gather, pipe dream, build castles in the air. See THINK.

PONDEROUS adj. heavy, hefty, deadly, bor-ring. See also CLUMSY, TROUBLESOME.

PONTIFF n. papa.

POOL OF MONEY n. kitty, pot.

POOL TERMS crip, eight ball, pool parlor, ham joint, scratch (miss), rack 'em up, run 'em (sink all the balls), English, bridge shot, bank shot, the break, ringer, hustler.

POOR adj. needy, truly needy, hard up, tapped, played out, on one's ass, on the rocks, down and out, have-nots, seen better days, piss-poor, dirt poor, the poor, poor as a church mouse. See DESTITUTE.

POPCORN n. old maids (kernels unpopped).

POPE n. papa.

POPSICLE n. pop.

POPULACE n. bodies, cats, dudes, heads, hoi polloi, the public, John Q., John Q. Public, Billy Sixpack, Joe Lunchbucket, the mob, riffraff, cattle, the great un-washed. See PUBLIC.

POPULAR adj. 1. lulu, one of the boys, big man on campus, BMOC, prom trotter, kimble (tries to be), crowd-pleaser, right guy, okay people, regular, big with. See also LIKED. 2. selling, selling like hotcakes, sizzler, tuff, hip, hep, mod, trendy, in the swim, in the mainstream, in, in-thing, the thing, in there, mod, now, really now, the rage, spinach, trendy, faddy, up to the minute, fashion plate, go-go, hip, hep, mellow back, upscale, catch on, caught on, in-spot, happening place, groovy hangout, hot spot, masscult, crazy, gas, a gas, gasser, in the groove, groovy, off the charts, far out, home cooking, hotsie-totsie, ice, sharp. See also NEW, STYLISH.

POPULAR CONCERT n. pop concert, pops.

POPULAR MUSIC RATINGS n. the charts, top ten, hit parade.

PORCH n. stoop, front stoop, gallery.

PORCUPINE n. quill pig.

PORK n. sow belly (bacon, salt pork), squeal, piano (spare ribs), Cincinnati cracklings (scraps), Cincinnati oysters (pigs' feet), Cincinnati quail (fatback).

PORNOGRAPHIC adj. adult, X-rated, purple, blue, dirty, hot, porn, porno, porny, steamy, low-down and dirty, off-color, rough, salty, raunchy. See OBSCENE.

PORNOGRAPHIC BOOKSTORE n. adult bookstore, emporium, sex shoppe.

PORNOGRAPHIC FILM n. X-rated, nudie, porn, porno, pornoflick, soft porn, hard porn, skin flick, flesh flick, adult film, snuff film, stag film, eroductions.

PORNOGRAPHIC PUBLICATIONS n. adult magazines, skin magazines, nudies, Tijuana bible, fuck book.

PORNOGRAPHY n. hard core, soft core, hot stuff, jack-off material, jerk-off material, porn, hard porn, soft porn, X-rated, triple X-rated. See OBSCENITY.

PORRIDGE n. cush, grits, mush.

PORTEND v. call it, call the turn, call one's shots, read, have a hunch, in the cards, it's looking to, see it coming, crystal ball it, psych it out. See PREDICT.

PORTENT n. hunch, vibes (good or bad), feel in one's bones, funny feeling, sinking feeling, in the wind, handwriting on the wall. See PREMONITION.

PORTER n. sky cap, red cap, baggage smasher, baggage masher, flunky, pack rat, punk, razor back, swamper.

PORTION n. 1. hit, shot, fix, slug, bang, dram, chunk, gob, glob, hunk, lump, smithereen. 2. bite, cut, divvy, lagniappe, plum, taste, lion's share, bigger half, drag, P.C., piece, piece of the action. See SHARE.

PORTLAND, OREGON Big Port.

PORTLY adj. beerbelly, bay window, corporation, spare tire, rubber tire, hefty, hippy, broad in the beam, corn-fed, built for comfort, avoirdupois. See FAT.

POSE v. playact, put up a front, do a bit, fake, lay it on thick, make out like, put on, take off as. See POSTURE. See also PRETEND.

POSITION n. 1. spot, the scene, fix (stationary), where it's at, where one is at, X marks the spot, how the land lies, lay of the land. 2. bag, day gig, do, dodge, gig, go, hang, nine-to-five shit, rat race, slot. See OCCUPATION. 3. spot, situash, happenin', like it is, the size of it, the way it shapes up, how things stack up, ball game. See CONDITION. See also BASIS, OPINION, ATTITUDE.

POSITIVE adj. absofuckinglutely, posilutely, absitively, sure as I live and breathe, cocksure, dead sure, surefire, on ice, cold, no buts about it, checked and double checked. See CERTAIN.

POSITIVELY adv. flat, flat out, come hell or high water, cert, amen, sure, why sure, sure thing, fer sure, sure as God made little green apples, absofuckinglutely, absitively, posilutely, you know, you know it, you better believe it, you betcha, you betcher life, you bet, you said it, you said a mouthful, you can say that again, you're not kidding, you're darn tootin', straight out, no strings attached, no holds barred, no catch, no kicker, no buts about it, no ifs ands or buts, with knobs on, with tits on, in a handbasket, the real McCoy, I'll tell the world, I'll tell the cockeyed world, in spades, check, with bells on, on the button, on the money, on the nose, the ticket, the very thing, the checker, to a tee, Judy (I understand), on the lemon, on the noggin, it, is the Pope Catholic?, Does a bear shit in the woods?, Is a bear Catholic?, Does the Pope shit in the woods?, honest to God, indeedy, yes indeedy, for a fact, for a fact Jack, real, for real, really truly, righto, right on, right as rain, right you are, rather, woofing. See ABSOLUTELY.

POSSESS v. lock up, get hold of, glom on to, latch on to, grab, bogart, corner, corner the market, get a corner on, hog, get one's hands on, sit on.

POSSESSED adj. fiendish, gone, hooked, taken over by, into, really into, eat sleep and breathe something. See OBSESSED.

POSSIBLE adj. no sweat, cinch, can do, snap, pushover, piece of cake, setup, breeze, duck soup, easy as pie, easy as falling off a log, simple as ABC. See EASY.

POSSIBILITY n. break, breaks, big break, even break, shot, shot at, get a shot at, have a shot at, long shot, hundred-to-one shot, whack, whack at, go, go at, stab, stab at, have a fling at, prayer, in the running, irons in the fire, fair shake, fighting chance, outside chance, near as one can tell, dollars to doughnuts, a Chinaman's chance, as much chance as a snowball in hell, snowball chance, fifty-fifty, toss-up, play, action, maximax (big return, big loss), maximin (small return, big loss), minimax (safe), fluke.

POST BILLBOARDS v. snipe.

POST EXCHANGE n. PX.

POSTAGE STAMP sticker, hot sticker (counterfeit).

POSTER n. three sheet, twenty-four sheet.

POSTERIOR n. buns, fanny, ass, behind, bottom, butt, can, cheeks, moon, tail, derrière, pratt, rear end, tush, tuchis, tokus, duff. See BUTTOCKS.

POSTGRADUATE n. postgrad.

POST OFFICE n. P.O., APO (Mil.).

POSTPONE v. shelve, put on the back burner, put on hold, hang fire, hold fire, pigeonhole, cool it, give one a rain check. See DELAY.

POSTPONED adj. 1. hung up, held up, scrubbed, slowed up, tied up, pigeonholed, stabbed, buttonholed, shelved, put on the shelf, put on hold, put on the back burner. 2. in a bind, jammed, jammed up, strapped for time.

POSTURE n. brace, brush (Army). See also ATTITUDE, OPINION.

POSTURE v. do a bit, fake, lay it on thick, make out like, playact, put up a front, fake it. See also PRETEND.

POTATO n. spud, murphy, mickey, tater, earth apple, Irish grape.

POTENCY n. juice, snap, zap, zing, zip, sock, kick, moxie, punch, steam, what it takes, piss and vinegar. See POWER.

POTENT adj. zippy, zappy, got the horses to do it, powerhouse, go-getter, on the ball, ball of fire, spanking, punchy, gutsy, have lead in one's pencil. See POWERFUL.

POTPOURRI n. everything but the kitchen sink, mishmash, mishmosh, mixed bag, combo, duke's mixture (strange), stew, goulash, soup (liquid), lorelei.

POVERTY n. on the rims, run on the rims, under the safety net, through the safety net.

POWER n. 1. juice, go juice, bounce, snap, zap, zing, zip, zippo, ginger, pow, sock, kick, kicker, pizzazz, dash, splash, the force, beef, clout, might and main, moxie, punch, steam, powerhouse, poop, hustle, the stuff, the goods, the word, what it takes, grease, alzo, connection, hooks, in, license, wire, a lot to do with, a lot to say about, inside track, wire-pulling, vim, pep, pepper, pepper-upper, picker-upper, pick-me-up, pop, get up and go, piss and vinegar, full head of steam, steamroller. See also INFLUENCE. 2. boss, czar, rug rank (high), big shot, big shit, big cheese, top dog, high up, kingpin, bull of the woods, head, a lot to say about, the say, the say so, a lot to do with. See EXECUTIVE.

POWERFUL adj. 1. wicked, husky, hefty, beefy, gutty, gutsy, got the horses to do it, hoss, powerhouse, hyper, hypercharged, bull, push, punch, go-getter, go-go, play hard ball, ball of fire, hotshot, steamroller, get up a head of steam, Norwegian steam, spanking, punchy, zippy, zappy, snappy, peppy, live, full of beans, double-barreled, mover and shaker, wave maker, have lead in one's pencil, the juice, the force, money talks, pull, in, connected, connections, stand in with, cut ice, throw a lot of weight, carry a lot of weight, sit fat, built like a brick shithouse, sturdy as an ox, strong as a lion, strong as an ox, strong as a horse, come on strong, magnum force, gorilla, bruiser, bone-crusher, beefcake, strong-arm, muscle man, he-man, hulk, hunk, tiger, turk, big bruiser, tough, tough guy, come on like gangbusters, walk heavy, walk tall, take over, take charge, bossy, fair hell, high cotton, hot flash, hot shit, we're not talking about nutmeg here. 2. name, big, biggie, Mr. Big, big name, big time, big-time operator, B.T.O., big-timer, big player, big wheel, wheeler-dealer, big man, big man on campus, B.M.O.C., big boy, big number, big one, big shit, big shot, hotshot, hotdog, top dog, gun, big gun, big noise, big chew, big wig, big-wigged, big butter and egg man, big ghee, big spud, big league, major league, rainmaker, big deal, big stuff, heavy stuff, heavy, 800-pound gorilla, V.I.P., apple, big apple, big cheese, big piece of cheese, real cheese, whole cheese, biggest frog in the pond, his nibs, honcho, hooper-dooper, higher ups, the high-rise boys, high profile, in the limelight, high muck-a-muck, high muckety-muck, high monkey monk, high pillow, lion, knocker, kuhnocker, connection, connection ghee, magoo, main squeeze, one who knows where the body's buried, polly, wire, wire man, wire-puller, a hook (police), godfather, czar, tycoon, baron, brass, top brass, brass hat, topsider, a somebody, something.

POWERLESS adj. 1. paper tiger, weak sister, wishy-washy, wimp, chicken, gutless, nerd, putty in one's hands, can't hack it, not have it, can't cut it, can't cut the mustard, can't make the grade. 2. fire blanks, shoot blanks, blank cartridge, dud, no lead in the pencil, no toothpaste in the tube, can't get it up, don't have the horses, out of gas, over a barrel, tapped, tapped out. See WEAK.

PRACTICAL adj. commonsensical, hardheaded, nuts and bolts, hands on. See also LAZY.

PRACTICE v. dry run, hone, tune up, warm up, work out, call, shakedown, shakedown cruise, tryout, dress, walk through, run through; lick into shape, put through the grind, put through the mill.

PRAGMATIC adj. commonsensical, hardheaded.

PRAISE n. warm fuzzies, pat on the back, pat on the head, PR, puff, puffing up, pumping up, rave, strokes, stroking, abreaction route, commercial, cow sociology, Doctor Spocking the help, opening up. See also FLATTERY.

PRAISE v. hear it for, kudo, rave, root, root for, beat one's skin for, stroke, boost, push, puff up, build, build up, brag about, toss a bouquet, give a bouquet, give a posy, give the man a big cigar, hand it to, have to hand it to, pat on the back, hats off to, gold star, trade last, TL.

PRAISEWORTHY adj. goodie, stellar, neato, keen, teriff, yummy, bad, not bad, not too shabby, gnarly, bueno, slick, lookin' chilly (Bl.), nasty, doin' a hundred, batting a thousand, tuff, tough, horror show, real mean, beaut, atsa nice, bootin' height, cuspy, Jesus bread, mitzvah, organic, fat city, gone, reet, check plus, swell, a prince of a fellow, Christian, true Christian, pillar of the church, salt of the earth. See also ADMIRABLE.

PRANK n. rib, gag, put-on, caper, spoof, high jinks, hi-jinks, hotfoot, hot one, monkeyshines, shenanigans, pull one's leg.

PRANKSTER n. card, cutup.

PRATTLE v. yap, yackety-yak, natter, patter, beat one's chops, beat one's gums, bat the breeze, jibber-jabber, run off at the mouth, run one's mouth, rattle, rattle on. See SPEAK.

PREACH v. get on a soapbox, blow, lay it on, lay it on with a trowel, lay it on thick, pile it on, talk big, talk highfalutin', talk tall.

PREACHER n. padre, Holy Joe, sky pilot, bible thumper, devil dodger, preacher man, glory roader, jackleg preacher (lay). See CLERGYMAN.

PREADOLESCENT n. weeny bopper, teenybopper, bobby-soxer. See also GIRL.

PREAMPLIFIER n. preamp.

PREARRANGE (ILLEGAL) v. fix, rig, frame, frame up, set up, wire, cook, cook up, stack the cards, pack the deal, rig the jury, satchel.

PREARRANGE v. fix, frame, frame up, cook up, sew up, set up, rig, pack, slant, stack the cards, pack the deal, load the dice, put in the bag, put on ice, rig the jury. See PREPARE. See also PLAN, SCHEME.

PREARRANGED adj. wired, bagged, fixed, gaffed, planted, loaded, rigged, sacked, stacked, stacked deck, packed, packed jury, rigged jury, put-up job, cut and dry. See PREPARED.

PRECARIOUS adj. hot, hairy, loaded, dynamite, unhealthy, rugged, dicey, iffy, chancy, too hot to handle, on thin ice, on slippery ground, out on a limb, touch and go, hanging by a thread. See DANGEROUS. See also DOUBTFUL.

PRECEDING adj. ex, X, one time.

PRECIOUS adj. collectibles, worth its weight in gold, worth a king's ransom, worth one's eyeteeth, would give one's eyeteeth for.

PRECIPITATE adj. jump the gun, go off half-cocked, off the hip, off the top of one's head, shoot from the hip. See IMPULSIVE.

PRECIPITATION n. precip, wet stuff, heavy dew, window washer, gully washer, cloud juice, deep water (heavy), drownder. See RAIN.

PRECIPITOUSLY adj. early on, jump the gun. See also IMPULSIVE.

PRECISE adj. on the button, on the nose, choosy, comma counter, nitpicker, picky, picky picky, ticky, stickler, pernickety, persnickety, dot the i's and cross the t's. See EXACT.

PRECISELY adv. on the button, on the money, on the nose, on the noggin, on the lemon, the ticket, the very thing, the checker, to a tee, Judy (I understand), hit the nail on the head, cert, sure, why sure, sure thing, for sure, fer sure, fer sher, fer shirr, surest thing you know, that's for sure, for a fact, you said it, no buts about it, no ifs ands or buts, and no mistake.

PRECISIONIST adj. comma counter, nitpicker, ace, picky, picky picky, pernickety, persnickety, stickler, fussbudget, fusspot, fuddy-duddy, granny, old woman, old maid. See also PARTICULAR.

PRECOCIOUS adj. pushy, cheeky, cocky, flip, fresh, crusty, gally, nervy, chutzpahdik, biggety, sassy, smart, smart alecky, smart ass, wise ass, brassy, bold as brass, the cutes. See also AGGRESSIVE.

PRECOGNIZE v. have a hunch, get vibes, feel in one's bones, have a funny feeling. See SENSE.

PREDICAMENT n. shit, deep shit, serious jelly, serious shit, bad news, clutch, hang-up, drag, bind, double bind, tall order, large order, rough go, heavy sledding, rainin', ticklish spot, tight spot, tight squeeze, lose-lose situation, no-win situation, gasser, pisser, rat's nest, snake pit, box, crunch, catch, catch 22, bitch, handful, headache, bummer, downer, worriment, botheration, grabber, hooker, double trouble, behind the eight ball, boxed in, in a box, in a fix, in a hole, snafu, jam, in a jam, in a clutch, in a mess, in a pickle, scrape, in a scrape, in a spot, in a tight spot, in a hot spot, on the hot seat, hot water, in deep water, in heavy water, in a stew, in over one's head, up a tree, up the creek, up the creek without a paddle, up shit creek, up shit creek without a paddle, pain in the ass, pain in the neck, between a rock and a hard place, tail in a gate, tit in a wringer, mix, mess, holy mess, unholy mess, kettle of fish, fine kettle of fish, a fine mess you've got us into, fine how do you do, hobble, pickle, pretty pickle, pretty pass, squeeze, sticky wicket, hard row to hoe, hard row of stumps, hard time, hard pull, heat's on, a mountain out of a molehill, heavy load to haul, the devil to pay, hell to pay, bug, glitch, puzzler, can of peas, can of worms, Pandora's box, green hornet (Mil.), honey, hot potato, stinker, tsuris, tumul, what's with, sixty-four dollar question, twister, teaser, sticker, floorer, stumper, bugaboo, crimp, crimp one's style, hump, stinger, hot grease, jackpot, mess up, screw up, need it like a hole in the head, next week East Lynne, rub, push comes to shove, when things get tough, toughie, tough proposition, tough to buck, tough nut to crack, tough going, hard going, joker, scuffle, put on the spot, hit a snag, a hold up, come a-cropper, one small difficulty.

PREDICT v. dope, dope out, figure, figger, figger out, figure out, size up, call it, call the turn, call one's shots, call the shots, read, make book, have a hunch, in the cards, it's looking to, telegraph, see it coming, see the handwriting on the wall, crystal ball it, psych it out, be afraid, wait for the other shoe to drop.

PREDICTION n. dope, indicator, tip.

PREDICTOR n. dopester, tipster, tout, touter, oddsmaker.

PREDILECTION n. bag, dish, dish of tea, cup of tea, thing, a thing for, weakness for, turned onto, druthers, flash, groove, type, mind-set, where one is at. See INCLINATION.

PREDISPOSITION n. bag, dish, dish of tea, cup of tea, druthers, flash, groove, thing, turned on to, type, weakness for. See also INCLINATION.

PREEMPT v. bump.

PREFABRICATE v. prefab.

PREFABRICATED adj. prefabbed, ready-made, off the rack.

PREFER v. tag, tap, finger, opt, go down the line, partial to, thing for, turned on to. See also SELECT, DESIRE.

PREFERENCE n. bag, cup of tea, druthers, go down the line, flash, groove, turned on to, weakness for, say so, take it or leave it, other side of the coin, other fish to fry, other fish in the sea, other pebbles on the beach. See also INCLINATION, DESIRE.

PREGNANT adj. knocked up, preggie, expecting, expecting a blessed event, blessed eventing, in a family way, in a delicate condition, on the nest, got one in the oven, got a bun in the oven, have a cake in the oven, bumped, infanticipating, heirapparenting, fragrant, full of heir, have one, join the club, swallow a watermelon seed, watermelon on the vine.

PREGNANT, MAKE v. knock up.

PREJUDICE n. head-set, mind-set, mind trip, tilt, where one is at, cold deck, down on, flash, Jim Crow, Jim Crowism, Jane Crow (against women), feel a draft (recognition of).

PREJUDICED adj. agin, down on, one-sided, tilted, weighted, cold deck, flash, red-neck, red-baiter, Jew-baiter, black baiter, Jim Crow, Jane Crow (against women), a regular Archie Bunker, homer (umpire favoring home team). See also INTOLERANT.

PREMATURE adj. a bit previous, early on, half-assed, half-baked, half-cocked, jump the gun.

PREMATURE BABY n. preemie, preemy.

PREMATURELY adv. previous, a bit previous, bright and early, early bird, early on.

PREMEDICAL adj. pre-med.

PREMEDITATE v. fix, frame up, rig, set up, lay out, put in the bag, sew up, pack the deal, stack the cards, stack the deck. See PLAN.

PREMIER n. preem. See also BEGINNING.

PREMISES n. hangout, joint, lay, layout, plant, dump, digs, scene, fix, hole, spot, X marks the spot, pad, crib, crash pad, roof over one's head, the pits, armpit (undesirable), office, neck of the woods, zone, turf. See also HOUSE, OFFICE.

PREMIUM n. gravy, spiff, P.M., button (salesman's reward). See also EXTRA.

PREMONITION n. hunch, vibes (good or bad), vibrations, feel in one's bone, funny feeling, sinking feeling, worriment, batten down the hatches, winds, in the wind, winds of change, wind change, handwriting on the wall, next week East Lynne.

PREOCCUPATION n. hang-up, have a thing about, have on the brain, have on the mind, bee, bee in one's bonnet, bug, bug in one's ear, bug up one's ass, bag, ax to grind, grabber, tiger, tiger by the tail. See also OBSESSION.

PREOCCUPIED adj. mooning, moony, pipe dreaming, daydreaming, woolgathering, out to lunch, spaced out, popcorn headed, airheaded, absentminded professor, have on the brain, have on one's mind, have a thing about, hung up, have a bee in one's bonnet, have a bug in one's ear, have a bug up one's ass, bugged, asleep at the switch, asleep on the job, not on the job, goofing off, looking out the window, pay no mind. See also OBSESSED.

PREORDAINED adj. in the cards, so it goes, the way the deck is stacked, handwriting on the wall.

PREPARATION n. prep, prepping, readying, readying up, lead time, breaking in, dry run, run through, shakedown, shakedown cruise, tryout, workout; rundown, backgrounder, briefing.

PREPARATORY SCHOOL n. prep school.

PREPARATORY SCHOOL STUDENT n. prep, preppie, preppy, prep scholar.

PREPARE v. 1. prep, warm up, ready, gear up, line up, psych oneself up, set up, get set for, get the juices flowing, loosen up, shape up, sharpen, work over, work up, whip into shape, lick into shape, toughen up, build up, fix to, clear the decks, pave the way, cram, do one's homework, lay out, work something out, pack, stack the cards, pack the deal, put through the grind, put through the mill. See also TRAIN. 2. brief, fill in, fill one in, put on to, put one in the picture, wise up, give a pointer to, let in on the know, keep one posted, frame, frame up, rig, rig up.

PREPARED adj. prepped, wired, bagged, fixed, gaffed, gimmicked up, rigged, sacked, framed, square, had zingers put in, packed, stacked, up, set up, put up, up on, psyched up, cooked up, sewed up, in the bag, on ice, cinched, cut and dry, got it covered, all bases covered, looking to, looking for, waitin' on, the noose is hanging, at the ready, loaded for bear, have one's ducks in a row.

PREPAYMENT n. front money, up front, in front, in the blue, front-end loading (loan interest).

PREPONDERANCE n. lion's share, big half, bigger half, big end, max, maxi, the most, mostest.

PREPOSTEROUS adj. ass backwards, bass ackwards, back asswards, harebrained, lamebrained, thick, reachy, pure bullshit, too much, bubbleheaded, horse's ass, far out, takes the cake. See UNBELIEVABLE.

PREPUCE n. lace curtain (homosexual use).

PRESCRIPTION n. scrip, script, reader.

PRESENT adj. yo, check, dig, made the scene, on board, on deck, on hand, show, show up, there with bells on, there with knobs on, there with tits on.

PRESENT n. goodie, stake, giveaway (often prize), write-off, handout, mitzvah, gifting, gash (unexpected), lump, poke out. See also MODERN.

PRESENT v. 1. do the honors, give a knockdown, knock down, fix up, get together, intro. See INTRO-DUCE. 2. pitch, make a pitch, speak one's piece, put on, roll out, trot out, hit, lay down, lay out, pop the question, proposition. 3. gift, get it up, kick in, give with, gift with, come up with, get it on, lay on, put something in the pot, sweeten the kitty. See GIVE. 4. boot, bring out, come out with, spring with.

PRESENTATION n. pitch, sales pitch, dog and pony show, intro, knockdown.

PRESENTIMENT adj. hunch, vibes (good or bad), feel in one's bone, funny feeling, sinking feeling, worriment, in the wind, handwriting on the wall, no light at the end of the tunnel. See PREMONITION.

PRESENTLY adv. by n' by, come Sunday, down the line, down the road, coming down the pike, in a short, short short, before you know it.

PRESERVATIONIST n. eagle freak, ecofreak, econut, greeny.

PRESIDE v. run, run the show, head, head up, sit on top of, do the honors, call the shots, call the signals, be in the driver's seat, pull the strings. See also MANAGE.

PRESIDENCY n. White House, Oval Office, top job.

PRESIDENT n. Pres, Prez, prex, prexy (usu. college), Great White Father (U.S.), POTUS (Pres. of the U.S.). CINC, C.O., exec, key player, A-number 1, chief, bosshead, head, head honcho, head man, where the buck stops. See also EXECUTIVE.

PRESIDENT'S BLACK BOX n. football.

PRESIDENT OF THE UNITED STATES n. Chief, CINC, POTUS, Great White Father, Prez, Pres.

PRESS n. fourth estate, media.

PRESS v. 1. scrunch, squish. 2. squeeze, put the squeeze on, railroad through, buttonhole, sell, work on, lean on, put the bee on, come at from all sides. See PERSUADE. See also FORCE. 3. bear down on, get cracking after, shag ass, not spare the horses.

PRESS AGENT n. PA, PR, flack, puffer, drum beater, space bandit. See PUBLICIST.

PRESSING adj. chips are down, fire in the belly, heats on, fat's in the fire, hurry up call, matter of life and death. See URGENT.

PRESS PLANE n. zoo.

PRESSURE n. 1. clutch, crunch, heat, if one can't stand the heat get out of the kitchen, pressure cooker, full court press, albatross around one's neck, choke (react to). See also FORCE, COERCION. 2. drag, pull, clout, juice, string, ropes, weight, a lot to do with, a lot to say about, inside track. 3. suction, suck.

PRESSURE v. 1. keep the lid on, bottle up, cork, cork up, hog-tie, hold down, put a half nelson on. 2. sell, high pressure, squeeze, work over, lean on, twist one's arm, put the screws on, push around, come at from all sides, make it hot for, hold one's feet to the fire, throw one's weight around, knock on doors, politick. See PERSUADE. See also FORCE.

PRESSURED adj. choke, in a pressure cooker.

PRESUME v. be afraid, figure, go off half-cocked, jump the gun, it's looking to. See SPECULATE. See also BELIEVE.

PRESUMPTION n. shot, shot in the dark, stab, sneaking suspicion.

PRETEND v. jive, shuck and jive, maple stick jive, shovel the shit, shit, fudge, stonewall, whitewash, jazz, put on, put on an act, put up a front, put on a false front, fake, fake it, fake out, fake one out, deek, juke, fish, flicker, hang one out to dry, shake and bake, stutter step, sucker one, do a number, do a bit, lay it on thick, chuck a dummy, frame, frame up, plant, phony up, put up a bluff, four flush, make believe, make like, let on, let on like, play possum, talk trash, pass, signify, gammon, flaking, load, salt, salt a mine.

PRETENDER n. fake, faker, fraud, four-flusher, phony, playactor, gouge. See QUACK.

PRETENSE n. routine, shtick, gag, shuck and jive, stall, put on, stunt, bit, false front, fake, phony, crocodile tears, soft soap, sweet talk, dumb act (without words), hoke act. See also EXCUSE.

PRETENSION n. front, false front, fake, phony, put on, put on the dog, put on the ritz, big talk, tall talk, show, for show, showboat, showoff, showing out, big shot, splash, flash, Flash Gordon, go Hollywood, live it up, lay it on thick, Christmas (clothes and jewelry), dog, dozer, fofarraw, foofooraw, neon ribbons.

PRETENTIOUS adj. flashy, jazzy, splashy, make a big splash, showy, artsy, artsy-crafty, artsy-fartsy, chichi, kitschy, campy, camp around, uptown, putting on the dog, putting on the ritz, ritzy, stuck up, airish, crooker, pinky crooker, ham, stuffed shirt, highfaluting, splendiferous, splendacious, high-toned, toney, classy, splurgy, candy, flossy, belled, duded up, hanging out, gone Hollywood, play the ———, live in a glass house, hotshot, spot one like a lead dime; stick out like a sore thumb, a somebody.

PRETEXT n. cover, cover-up, cover story, fig leaf, clean up, copout, fish tale, fish story, Mother Machree, Mother McCrea, routine, song and dance, stall. See EXCUSE.

PRETTIFY v. doll up, fix up, gussy up, pretty up, spruce up.

PRETTY adj. ten, 10, boss, lulu, cher, dishy, dreamboat, looker, mink, stone, stone fox, foxy, head rush, cute, number, eyeful, picture. See BEAUTIFUL.

PREVAIL v. 1. get well, get fat, get there, go places, go great guns, make it, make out, ring the bell, take off, move out, strike oil, hit pay dirt, sail through, luck in, luck out, home free, come out on top of the heap. See SUCCEED. See also TRIUMPH. 2. get around, eat one's mind, crack one or something, put across, promote, sell one on, suck in, cram down one's throat, ram down one's throat. See PERSUADE.

PREVAILING adj. regular, by the numbers, SOS, same old shit, according to the book, according to Hoyle, playing it safe, in the groove, in a rut, chicken, chicken shit. See also BEST.

PREVALENT n. trendy, faddy, hip, mod, now, ongoing, state of the art, the latest, last word, latest word, latest wrinkle, the leading edge, up to date, up to the minute, up to the moment, what's happening, with it, on the front burner, swinging, in the swim, in line. See also NEW, STYLISH.

PREVARICATE v. jive, bullshit, shit, con, put on, phony up, tell a white lie, speak with forked tongue. See LIE.

PREVARICATION n. jive, line of jive, fib, BS, bullchitna (Esk.), horse manure, horse hocky, shit for the birds, story, tall story, fish story, baloney, smoke, line, hogwash, terminological inexactitude. See LIE.

PREVARICATOR n. jive ass, jive turkey, phony, promoter, con artist, con man, con merchant, conner, quack, spieler, bullshitter, bullshit artist, crap merchant, oil merchant.

PREVENT v. 1. cool, cool off, cool out, chill, chill off, faze, keep the lid on, block, bottle up, cork, cork up, box in, get one in a box, hog-tie, tie up, jam up, gridlock, lock up, put a lock on, put a stopper in, bring to a screaming halt, put a half nelson on, put the chill on, kill, spike, throw cold water on, throw a wet blanket on, act like a wet blanket, put a damper on, cut off one's water, turn off one's water, put off, turn off, hold (hold the mayo), hold down, strong-arm, put the arm on, twist one's arm, put down, run down, play down, shut down on, sit on, sit down on, take care of, cross up, double-cross, kid out of, talk out of, hedge in. 2. queer, put a crimp in, stymie, snooker, put a cork in it, crab, hang up, hold up, foul up, fuck up, louse up, snafu, box in, get one in a box, freeze,

shut off, stall, flummox, torpedo (a plan), throw a monkey wrench into the works, upset one's apple cart, spike one's guns, take the play away from, knock the bottom out of, blow the whistle on. See also HINDER.

PREVIEW n. sneak.

PREVIOUS adj. ex, X, one time.

PREVIOUSLY adv. away back, back, back when, one shot, time was.

PRICE n. price tag, list, bad news, damage, score, tab, bite, nut, nick, dues, tick, ticket, squeeze, come to, what's it come to?, to the tune of, tidy sum, bottom line, outlay. See COST.

PRICELESS adj. out of sight, out of bounds, out of all bounds, collectible, worth its weight in gold, worth a king's ransom.

PRICE SUPPORTS n. pump priming.

PRIDE n. ego trip, face.

PRIEST n. padre, Holy Joe, sky pilot, abbey, fire proofer, gospel pusher, sin hound, turn-around collar. See CLERGYMAN.

PRIG n. bluenose, goody-goody, goody two-shoes, old maid, Miss Priss, Holy Joe. See also STRAITLACED.

PRIM adj. uptight, straight, tight-assed, short haircut, Jesus freak, bluenose, old maidish, stuffy, choosy, comma counter, nitpicker, picky, ticky, stickler, pernickety, persnickety, dot the i's and cross the t's, draw it fine, cut it fine, goodie, goody-goody, goody two-shoes, Miss Priss, Holy Joe. See also STRAITLACED.

PRIMA DONNA n. prim.

PRIMARY adj. primo, meat and potatoes, ABC's, three R's, basics, right off the bat, first off, numero uno. See also BASIC.

PRIME adj. 10, ten, A-number one, number one, A-plus super duper, mega-gnarly, zero cool, endsville, crackerjack, top of the line, first class, world class, first chop, stellar, gonest, baaadest, fab, hot, tough, heavy, state of the art. See EXCELLENT.

PRIME v. ready, prep, cram, put through the grind, put through the mill. See PREPARE.

PRIMED adj. wired, bagged, rigged, sacked, packed, stacked, set up, psyched up, on ice, cut and dry, got it covered, loaded for bear. See PREPARED.

PRINCIPAL n. CEO, C.O., exec, key player, chief, head, head honcho, head man, queen bee, Mr. Big, high priest, bread, guru, old man. See EXECUTIVE.

PRINCIPLED adj. square, square shooter, straight, straight shooter, true blue, Christian, kosher, salt of the earth, fly right, nice guy, white, regular, clean as a hound's tooth, boy scout, scoutmaster.

PRINTER'S ERROR n. typo, etaoin shrdlu.

PRIORITIES n. laundry list, shopping list.

PRIORITY n. crash program, crash project, on line.

PRISON n. slam, slammer, pen, can, joint, G. joint (federal), big cage, maxi (maximum security), pink clink, mill, crossbar hotel, graybar hotel, crowbar hotel, bastille, college, graystone college, hospital, campus, big house, big joint, up the river, statesville, big school, Q (San Quentin), Sing Sing, sent up. See JAIL.

PRISON CELL n. cage, birdcage, monkey cage, lockup, cooler, bull pen, coop, clink, calaboose, brig, bing, drum, tank, drunk tank, fish tank, hut, daddy tank (lesbian); bank, hole, icebox, iso, izo, klondike, seclusion, solitary, stretch (solitary confinement); the C.C.'s, dancehall (death house or row).

PRISON CHAPLAIN n. bible back, buck, frocker, goody, psalmer, the church.

PRISON DEATH CHAMBER n. up back, in the back, in the backroom, dance hall, schweiner; last mile, last waltz, trip up back (walk to); baker, juice ghee (death chair switch operator).

PRISON DISCHARGE n. spring, check out, cut out, kick out, go, go home, hit the bricks, hit the pavement, hit the sidewalk, hit the street, leave one the bucket.

PRISON DISCIPLINE n. lockup, lock in, double lock, deadlock, keep locked, jam up, standup, sweatbox, barrel, boat, spot, bury, chalk in, walking the line, (harsh), get one right, pencil, take one's number, put in a beef, put in a pinch, hang a rap on, hang a shingle on, hit with a tin, sting.

PRISONER n. con, jailbird, vic, ex-con, lifer, two-time loser, yardbird, chain gang, rock crusher, PW, stir bird, rat, brig rat, goodie, hog, lag, Robuck (bully), SD (troublemaker), politician (privileged), merchant, eel, slippery eel, center man, real man, right guy, gee, geezo, gorilla, tough, punk, hipster, spear chicken, apple knocker, lane, Square John; fish, fresh one, jice, new jice, hoosier (new); hide out (escapist), short, short eyes (child molester).

PRISONER OF WAR n. POW, P.O.W., Kriegie (American in German prison).

PRISON ESCAPE n. break, getaway, over the wall, lam, beat, blow, clemo, crush, crush out, gut, have the measles, on the bush, map a get (plan), mope, mouse; Big Ben, beat whistle, lam whistle (siren); barspreader, blade, briars, chopper, John Sperl (tools).

PRISON ESCAPE v. break, break out, crush out, heel, go over the hill, go over the wall, beat, beat a joint, beat a stir, blow stir, chop a bar, make a break, hang it, lam, lam the joint, take it on the lam, cop a mope, take a mope, hit the hump.

PRISON GUARD n. screw, chaser, eyes, hack, herder, hooligan, roach, roller, slave driver, sky, yard bull.

PRISON SENTENCE n. time, hitch, stretch, do a stretch, term, up, up the river, trick, knock, rap, jolt, ice box, fall, good time, getup, make little ones out of big ones, throw the book at one, sleep, vacation, curtains for; big bit, buried (long); all, do it all, the clock, the book (life); sleeping time (short); newspaper, magazine, calendar, boppo, boffo (one year), spot (year, one spot, two spot); three deuces jammed, three deuces running wild (three two-year terms running concurrently); fistful, handful, five, nickel (five years); nickel to a dime (five to ten years); both hands, dime, tenner, ten spot, (ten years); do a quarter (twenty-five years); break (reduction), butt (remainder), bit, dipsey, B.O.T. (balance of time), lifeboat (commuted).

PRISON TRUSTY n. trusty, big ghee, biggie, big number, big shot, con turnkey, dep, Dep's man, outside man, P.K.'s man, state man, Warden's man, right ghee, number, stockholder.

PRISON UNIFORM n. state-o.

PRISON WARDEN n. king, main ghee, man, the man, skipper, belly robber, gut robber, big noise, big shot, big spud, strib, screw.

PRISSY adj. tight-assed, old maidish, picky, ticky, stickler, pernickety, persnickety, goody-goody, goody two-shoes, Miss Priss, Holy Joe. See PRIM.

PRIVACY n. one's space. See also RETREAT.

PRIVACY, LACK v. in the spotlight, in the limelight, live in a goldfish bowl, live in a glass house.

PRIVATE adj. inside, hush-hush, eyes only, under one's hat, close to one's chest. See SECRET.

PRIVATE INVESTIGATOR n. dick, shamus, flatfoot, private eye, P.I., eye, gumshoe, sleuth. See DETECTIVE.

PRIVATE SCHOOL n. hen pen (girls).

PRIVILEGED adj. 1. okayed, OK'd, kosher, legit. 2. inside, inside info, top secret, for your eyes only, under one's hat, on the QT. See SECRET.

PRIVY n. Andy Gump, one-holer, two-holer, out back, Chick Sale, chic sale, piss house, shithouse, shitter, crapper, can, john, necessary. See TOILET.

PRIZE n. the gold, gold star, the cookies, feather in one's cap, strokes, brownie button (facetious), plum, sweetening, sweetener, what's in it for one.

PRIZEFIGHT n. go, bout, match.

PRIZEFIGHTER n. mug, pug, lug, palooka, heavy, slugger, champ, fancy Dan, knuckle duster, dukester, lip-splitter, tiger, brawler, glass jaw, punching bag, bag puncher, powder puff (cautious), stiff (loser), canvas back, caveman, cavalier, stumblebum, bum (unemployed), cauliflower ear, cutie, cutey, dancer (coward), foul ball, ham and egger, hamburger, catcher (untalented), gladiator, sausage, tanker, loogan, round heels, plug, plug-ugly, water bag (inferior), white hope.

PROBABILITY n.   prayer, shot, have a shot at, outside chance, toss-up, near as one can tell, like as not, snowball chance. See POSSIBILITY.

PROBABLY adv.   dollars to doughnuts, like as not, like enough.

PROBATION n.   pro.

PROBATIONER n.   probe.

PROBE n.   fishing expedition, legwork, third, third degree.

PROBE v.   look-see, double O, double oo, eye, glim, check, check out, check over, check up. See IN-VESTIGATE.

PROBLEM n.   1. shit, deep shit, box, crunch, headache, hitch, worriment, botheration, between a rock and a hard place, scrape, tail in a gate, tit in a wringer, mess, holy mess, hot water, pickle, squeeze, can of peas, hot potato, tsuris, tough nut to crack. See PREDICA-MENT. 2. cliff-hanger, grabber, sixty-four dollar question, twister, teaser, sticker, floorer, stumper, mind-boggler, hard nut to crack, tough nut to crack, tough proposition.

PROBLEMATIC adj.   chancy, iffy, up for grabs, leery, don't hold your breath. See DOUBTFUL.

PROBOSCIS n.   smeller, schnoz, scnozzola, schnozzle, bazoo, beak, bugle, horn, honker, snoot, nozzle, banana, bill, beezer, boke, conk, handle, sniffer, snuffer.

PROCEDURE n.   shtick, sked, grind, daily grind, channels, back channels (secret), red tape, by the numbers, by the book, game plan, same old shit, SOS, layout, setup, gimmick, action, how one figures it, nuts and bolts.

PROCEED v.   get the green light, get the go-ahead, move out. See also ACT, GO.

PROCEEDING n.   go down, come off, goings-on, hap, happening, happenso, come off, through channels, red tape, by the numbers, by the book. See also ACTION.

PROCEEDS n.   handle, in the till, the take, split, gate. See INCOME.

PROCESS n.   channels, red tape, by the numbers, by the book. See also PROCEDURE.

PROCESS, IN adj.   in the hopper, in the pipeline, in the works.

PROCESSING SOLUTION n.   hypo, soup.

PROCLAIM v.   spout, spiel, call, blast, sound off, pop off, trumpet, drum, stump, get on a soapbox, spread it around, pass the word, lay down the law, put one's foot down, read the riot act, chew the scenery, run off at the mouth, shoot off one's mouth. See DECLARE. See also ASSERT, PROMULGATE.

PROCLIVITY n.   turned on to, thing, a thing for, weakness for, bag, cup of tea, dish of tea, druthers, flash, groove, type. See INCLINATION.

PROCRASTINATE v.   hold off, hang fire, cool, goldbrick, shilly-shally, sit on one's ass, give one the run around (repeatedly), drag one's heels, stooge around, let slide. See DELAY.

PROCRASTINATOR n.   goldbrick, goof off, putter-offer.

PROCURE v.   1. score, grab, cop, kipe, kype, corral, wangle, promote, buy up, buy out, make a haul, glom onto, get one's hands on, latch on to. See GET. 2. pimp, fix up, run a stable, have a string of hustlers, have a sister-in-law, steer, tout.

PROCURER n.   mack, mackman, macko man, hard Mack (violent), sweet Mack, mackerel, dude, flesh peddler, hustler, Johnny Ponce, ponce, brother-in-law, rack salesman. See PIMP.

PROD v.   goose, goose up, egg on, spark, sound, turn on, trigger.

PRODIGAL n.   deep pockets, big-time spender, last of the big-time spenders, good-time Charlie, sport, big sport.

PRODIGIOUS adj.   1. gross, humongous, monstro, king-size, moby, biggy, big ass, super-colossal, jumbo, thumping, See BIG. 2. unreal, mega-gnarly, heavy, bad, marvy, fab, state of the art, the utmost, rat fuck, out of this world. See FABULOUS.

PRODIGY n.   child wonder, wonder child, wunderkind, boy wonder, natural.

PRODUCE v.   1. whip up, whomp up, cook up, dream up, throw together, fudge together, knock together, knock out, knock up, dash off, tear off. See CREATE. 2. perk, percolate, tick, put out, do the job, do a number, do the trick, pull off, come through, T.C.B. (take care of business), make it, make it big. See ACT. 3. mount (The.).

PRODUCT GROUP n.   brand, line.

PROFANE v.   trash, tar, mudsling, cuss, damn, darn, drat, flame, put the horns on, put the whammy on one, put the double whammy on one, hoodoo one, voodoo one, talk dirty.

PROFANITY n.   no-no, cuss, cussing, cuss word, four letter word, swearword, dirty word, dirty language, dirty talk, dirty name, French, pardon my French.

PROFESS v. 1. swear up and down, swear on a stack of bibles, swear till one is blue in the face, swear on one's mother, swear on one's mother's grave, cross one's heart and hope to die, say so. 2. come out of the closet, fess, fess up, get it out of one's system, out with it, open up, own up to, get it off one's chest, sing, croon, let it all hang out. 3. get on a soapbox, soapbox, spiel, spout, chew the scenery, stump, blow, blow hot air, lay it on, lay it on with a trowel, lay it on thick, pile it on, talk big, talk highfalutin', talk tall. See also PROCLAIM.

PROFESSION n. bag, biz, game, gesheft, line, line of business, dodge, what one is into, thing, hang, rat race, slot. See OCCUPATION.

PROFESSIONAL adj. sharp, slick, there, crack, crackerjack, on the ball, on the beam, up to speed, have know how, know one's onions, know one's stuff, enough ducks in a row. See SKILLFUL.

PROFESSIONAL n. pro, real pro, old pro, ol' professor, old hand, old war-horse, ringer, whiz, whiz bang, whiz kid, wizard, maven, shark, phenom, pundit, egghead, ivory dome, brain, star, superstar, hotshot, topper, top hand, powerhouse, YAP (young American professional), yuppie (young urban professional), bubbie (black urban professional), yupfie (young urban professional failure), yumpie (young upwardly mobile professional). See also AUTHORITY.

PROFESSOR n. prof, teach, guru, brain, pundit, egghead, ivory dome, maven; quant, rocket scientist (one who has left to work in industry). See also SCHOLAR.

PROFFER n. hit, feeler, proposish, proposition, pass, pitch, action.

PROFFER v. 1. hit on, proposition, make a pitch, put a feeler out, pop the question. 2. gift, gift with. See GIVE.

PROFICIENCY n. the formula, savvy, goods, know-how, makings, stuff, the right stuff, what it takes, on the ball, something on the ball, up one's alley, chops, moxie, oil, meal ticket, green thumb. See SKILL.

PROFICIENT adj. sharp, savvy, hep, go-go, with it, all woke up, a lot of nifty, slick, crack, crackerjack, no slouch, on the ball, on the beam, up to speed, phenom, pro, whiz, know one's stuff, know one's business. See SKILLED.

PROFIT n. net, velvet, payoff, gravy, bottom line, in the black, split, melon, harvest, skim. See INCOME.

PROFIT v. pay, pay off, pay the rent, clean up, clear, score, cash in on, make a good thing of, make a killing, make it, make it big, make hay, make a haul, line one's nest, feather one's nest, do the trick, fill the bill, get mileage out of. See also EARN.

PROFITABLE adj. going, going concern, paid off, off the nut, sweet, in the black, cost effective.

PROFLIGACY n. high living, life in the fast lane, burn one's candle at both ends, hell bent, gone to the dogs. See DISSIPATION.

PROFLIGATE n. speed, sport, big-time spender, last of the big-time spenders, high liver, playboy, swinger, operator, nighthawk, letch, dirty old man, wolf, chaser, make-out artist, old goat, whorehound, tomcat. See LIBERTINE.

PROFOUND adj. deep, heavy, talking serious shit.

PROFUSE adj. no end, galore, aplenty, dime a dozen, drug on the market, alive with, crawling with, thick with, thick as flies, thick as hail. See PLENTY.

PROFUSION n. scads, a ton, mucho, mucho mucho, heavy, stinking with, oodles, oodles and oodles, beaucoup, spreading it around, like money was goin' out of style. See PLENTY.

PROGENY n. offspring, get (animal). See CHILD.

PROGNOSTICATE v. dope out, figure out, call it, read, make book, have a hunch, in the cards, see it coming, crystal ball it. See PREDICT.

PROGNOSTICATOR n. dopester, tipster, tout, touter.

PROGRAM n. lineup. See also PLAN.

PROGRAM v. line up, get on line, pencil in, set, set up.

PROGRAMMER, COMPUTER n. hacker (illegal), bit fiddler, bit tweeker, tweeker.

PROGRESS n. break, breakthrough, boost, buildup, go-ahead, hike, kick upstairs. See ADVANCE.

PROGRESS v. truck, clean up one's act, get with it, turn over a new leaf, get on the ball, straighten up and fly right, shape up, boost, upgrade, make first rate, mat down. See IMPROVE. See also ADVANCE.

PROGRESS, IN adj. in the hopper, in the pipeline, in the works.

PROGRESSING adj. looking good, looking up, look up, making it, rolling, up, upping, uptick, upbeat, on the upbeat, on the upswing, on the upgrade, on the rise, on the lift, come along, perk up, pick up, skyrocket, take off, getting along, getting there.

PROGRESSIVE adj. bleeding heart, do-gooder, left, lefty, left of center, new left, linky dink, pink, pinko, parlor pink, radish, fellow traveler, innocent (Bl.). See LIBERAL.

PROHIBIT v. cool, cool off, cool out, keep the lid on, bottle up, cork, cork up, block, box in, get one in a box, hog-tie, tie up, jam up, gridlock, stymie, hang up, hold up, lock up, put a lock on, put a cork in it, put a stopper in, bring to a screaming halt, put a half nelson on, put the chill on, kill, spike, ding, zing, put the zinger in, nix, put down, pass on, throw cold water on, throw a wet blanket on, cut off one's water, turn off one's water, put off, turn off, put on hold, hold (hold everything), hold down, strong-arm, put the arm on, shut down on, sit on, sit down on, take care of, hedge in, bring to a screaming halt, flag one, freeze, shut out, shut off, close out, throw a monkey wrench into the works, spike one's guns, take one down, take the wind out of one's sails, knock the bottom out of, knock the chocks from under one, knock the props from under one, cramp one's style.

PROHIBITED adj.   no-no, out of bounds, off limits, off base, out of line, crooked, heavy, shady, wildcat, closed down. See also BANNED.

PROHIBITION n.   no-no, a don't, off limits, out of bounds, bleeper, blankety blank (word or expression).

PROHIBITION AGENT n.   prohi, revenuer.

PROHIBITION ERA TERMS   speak, speak easy; bootleg, bootlegger, moonshine, moonshiner, rum runner; bathtub gin, hooch, home brew; wet, dry; Fed, feds (enforcement officer).

PROHIBITIONIST adj.   dry, Volstead actor, Volstead baby, WCTU, bluenose.

PROJECT n.   baby, bag, bag one's into, thing, thing one's into, biggie (major), deal, pet project, proposition, setup.

PROJECT v.   pop out, bug out, googly. See also PREDICT.

PROLETARIAT n.   the mob, riffraff, cattle, ragtag, ragtag and bobtail, the great unwashed.

PROLONG v.   get on with it, let it ride, hold up, stretch, stretch out, pad, stall, vamp, drag one's feet, drag out, drag on, spin out. See DELAY.

PROLONGED adj.   spun out, strung out, dragged out, dragged on, dragged on and on, run out, held off, boosted, padded, in for the long haul.

PROMENADE v.   ankle, ank, toddle, sashay, cruise, traipse, trapse around, ooze, mooch, boogie, air out, beat the rocks, diddly bop, truck, percolate. See WALK.

PROMINENT adj.   1. flashy, candy, candy kid, duded up, hanging out. 2. live in a glass house, spot one like a lead dime, stick out like a sore thumb. 3. world class, big league, major league, high cotton, high profile, throw a lot of weight, the juice, the force, underlined. 4. biggie, big name, big noise, big shot, big timer, big league, major league, knocker, hot dog, VIP, a somebody, in the limelight. See IMPORTANT.

PROMISCUOUS adj.   fast, swinging, swinger, on the make, chippy around, run around, floss around, sleep around, musical beds, two-time, stretch the rubber, put out, put the horns on, pushover, round heels, easy lay, easy make, cheap, loose, loose woman, alley cat, hose monster, for free, bum, tramp, slut, dog, frail, blimp, broad, mink, bombshell, chippie, chaser, fruit, office bike, town bike, town pump, cuddle bunny, charity girl, piece of trade, pigmeat (old), sex job, no better than she should be.

PROMISE v.   1. string, string one along, jerk one along, jerk one around. 2. swear up and down, swear on a stack of bibles, swear till one is blue in the face, cross one's heart and hope to die, say so.

PROMISED adj.   1. steady, going steady, pinned, bird, donah, donar, future, intended. 2. in the bag, nailed down, on ice, cinched.

PROMISSORY NOTE n.   IOU, marker, paper, tab, dog.

PROMOTE v.   1. hype, plug, push, hard sell, make a pitch for, beat the drum for, build up, throw the spotlight on, press agent, ballyhoo, billboard, boost, get behind, put on the map. See ADVERTISE. 2. up, kick upstairs, win one's wings, deadhead (bypass a senior), up one's pay, boost one's pay. See also ADVANCE.

PROMOTER n.   1. player, operator, con, con man, tout, touter. 2. PR man, flack, plugger, puffer, huckster, ballyhoo man, space bandit, space peddler, booster. See PUBLICIST.

PROMOTION n.   1. boost, buildup, bump, jump, jump up, move up, step up, break, breakthrough, go-ahead, hike, kick upstairs. 2. PR, hype, buildup, pitch, promo, hard sell, ballyhoo, hoopla, plug, puff, puffery, pizzazz, squib, screamer, spread, blurb, dynamiting, blasting, bulldogging, Mad Avenue, pluggery. See also PUBLICITY.

PROMPT adj.   on the ball, on the button, on the dot, on the nose.

PROMPTLY adj.   pronto, on the double, move your ass, like now, off the pop, in nothing flat, like a shot, pretty damned quick, PDQ. See IMMEDIATELY.

PROMULGATE v.   spread it around, pass the word, drum, call, trumpet, call the play, call the signals, call the tune. See also PROCLAIM, DECLARE.

PRONE adj.   bag, thing, head-set, mind-set, mind trip, flash, groove, tilt, type, where one is at, cup of tea, druthers, turned on to, weakness for.

PRONOUNCE v.   verbalize, mouth, sound off, blast, spread it around, drum, trumpet, call. See also PROCLAIM, DECLARE, SPEAK.

PROOF n.   dope, goods, info, smoking gun (crucial), clincher, cincher, grabber, paper trail, clue, cue, skinny, scoop, score, chapter and verse, the know, picture, hold water, straight stuff, from the horse's mouth, lowdown, like it is, the emess, the numbers, gospel, nitty-gritty.

PROPAGANDA n. agit prop, informercial, advertorial, hogwash, disinformation.

PROPELLER n. prop, windmill, eggbeater, fan, blower, butter paddle, club, pants stopper.

PROPENSITY n. thing, turned on to, flash, weakness for, where one is at, tilt, eyes for, itch, sweet tooth, yen. See INCLINATION.

PROPER adj. 1. chicken shit, according to Hoyle, according to the book, by the book, by the numbers, in line, kosher. See STRAITLACED. 2. solid, stone, straight, straight arrow, square, squaresville, cubeular, stuffy. 3. on the ball, on target, on the right track, righteous, right you are, right as rain, reet, just what the doctor ordered, on the button, on the nose, that's the idea, that's the ticket. See also CORRECT, SUITABLE.

PROPERTY n. prop, props.

PROPHESY v. crystal ball it, psych it out, call it, call the turn, call the shots, read, make book, have a hunch, see it coming. See PREDICT.

PROPHYLACTIC n. pro, prophy, pro pack, rubber, safety, nightcap, bag, scumbag, Trojan, armor, skin, fish skin, French letter, Frenchy, purse. See CONTRACEPTIVE.

PROPOSAL n. feeler, pitch, proposition, proposish, pass, game plan, setup, layout, angle, big idea (unwelcome), picture, scenario, brain child. See PLAN.

PROPOSE v. proposition, hit on, come up with, I'm talking ———, make a pitch, pop the question, speak one's piece, kibitz, put a flea in one's ear, spitball, try it on for size.

PROPRIETOR n. meal ticket, front office, gyppo, jippo (piecework), landprop, saw, slumlord.

PROSAIC adj. garden variety, everyday, vanilla, nothing, nowhere, clean, square, blah, draddy, draggy, ho hum, dull as dishwater, yawn, big yawn, dead, diddly bop, dullsville, gummy, flat, flat as a pancake, flat tire, pablum, zero, the least, corny, bromidic, old hat, folksy, homey, haymish, dime a dozen, gasser, noplaceville, square John, Clyde, meat-and-potatoes man.

PROSECUTE v. drag into court, haul into court, see one in court, have up, have the law on, law, take the law on, put one away, pull up, take out after, turn on the heat, burn one's ass.

PROSECUTION n. heat.

PROSECUTOR n. cuter, D.A., beak, beagle, legal eagle. See also ATTORNEY.

PROSELYTIZATION n. agit prop, informercial, advertorial, hogwash.

PROSPECT n. irons in the fire, by and by, from now on in, from here in, from here out, just around the corner, in the cards, in the lap of the gods, mark, sucker, white hope. See also CUSTOMER, HOPE, FUTURE.

PROSPECTOR n. desert rat, hard rocker, sourdough.

PROSPER v. get fat, get there, go places, go to town, make it, make a killing, strike it rich, hit it big, hit the jackpot, score, bring home the bacon, arrive, do a land-office business, live off the fat of the land. See SUCCEED.

PROSPERITY n. boom, good times, gravy train, land-office business, high on the hog, on top of the heap, bed of roses, clover, Easy Street, lap of luxury, the life of Riley, velvet.

PROSPEROUS adj. the haves, have it made, on top of the heap, high on the hog, up in the bucks, in the chips, money to burn, lousy rich, well heeled, well fixed, sitting pretty, fat city, fat cat, upper class, main line, uptown, piss on ice. See WEALTHY.

PROSTITUTE n. hooker, call girl, hustler, ho, working broad, working chick, working girl, nok, model, pro, floozie, chippy, prosty, streetwalker, tart, bag, baggage, B-girl, bimbo, broad, chicken, chicken rancher, pavement princess, bat, beast, bitch, blister, blower, bawd, bum, cat, moll, cement mixer, coffee grinder, chile whore, chacha, fallen woman, dog, fish, gull, forty-four, gooh, piccolo player, piece of trade, biscuit, strawberry (receives dope as payment), blouser, flesh peddler, ass peddler, snatch peddler, coozey, merchandise, zook (U.), Hershey bar (WW II), moose (Korean war), dress for sale, flatbacker, quiff, puta, squaw, schatzi, schanzi, wet deck, white slave, creeper, panel worker (thief), chick on the block, orphan (without a pimp), free-lancer, hole, hostess, shady lady, stick, vegetarian (won't perform fellatio); mixer, sitter, taxi drinker (bars), jade, easy woman, easy lay, woman of easy virtue, frail sister, nympho.

PROSTITUTE'S CUSTOMER n. trick, John.

PROSTITUTE, MALE n. cocksman, midnight cowboy, pink pants, pratt boy, snatch peddler, stern wheeler, Mr. Brown, chicken.

PROSTITUTION n. in the life, the life, world's oldest profession, broad racket, the bottle, hustle, turning a trick, hitting the turf, working the street, stepping out, going out for a buck, on the turf, white slavery.

PROTECT v. cover, cover up, cover one's ass, cover all bases, go to bat for, go to the mat for, ride shotgun for, shotgun, stonewall, hedge, hedge one's bet, lay off.

PROTECTION n. fix, hat, umbrella, insurance.

PROTECTION MONEY n. the payoff, the envelope, payola, drugola, gayola, kickback, ice, take, on the take, under the table, protection, the fix, juice, graft, gravy, perk, perks, fringe benefit, goodies, hush money, grease, schmear, smear, salve, palm oil, soap, shake, cough syrup, sugar, sweetener, hat, a chicken, Mordida, boodle, pound, chop, freight, slush, slush fund, nut, contract, cush, baksheesh, touch, street money, walking-around money, chop, fall dough, freight.

PROTÉGÉ n. candy kid, fair-haired boy.

PROTEST n. 1. beef, where's the beef?, bitch, holler, howl, kick, squawk, stink, big stink, flak, knock, nix, gripe, grouse, bellyache, blackball. See GRIEVANCE. 2. demo, march, teach-in, sit-in.

PROTEST v. 1. bitch, beef, make a stink, pop off, sound off, squawk, blast, holler, howl. See COMPLAIN. 2. be agin, go agin, buck, back-talk, blackball, thumbs down, put up a fight. See OPPOSE.

PROTESTANT n. WASP, Wasp, left foot.

PROTESTER n. angries, marcher, beatnik, yippie, freak, offbeat, bohemian, weirdo, oddball. See DISSENTER.

PROTOCOL n. P's and Q's, p's and q's.

PROTRACT v. let it ride, hold up, hold off, put off, put something on hold, cool, cool it, stretch, stretch out, put some rubber in it, pad, stall, vamp, drag out, drag on, spin out, tish. See DELAY. See also DEFER, LENGTHEN.

PROTRACTED adj. in for the long haul, spun out, strung out, dragged out, dragged on, dragged on and on, run out, held off, boosted, padded.

PROTRUDE v. pop out, bug out, googly.

PROUD adj. cool, cocky, biggety, dicty, sidity, sniffy, puffed up, chesty, high and mighty, high-toned, high-nosed, standing tall, walking tall, that's my boy (girl, etc.). See ARROGANT.

PROVE v. add up, check out, check up, check up on, double-check, crack on one or something, debunk (prove false), pan out, stand up, hold one up. See also TEST, CONFIRM.

PROVEN adj. sure, sure as shit, sure enough, sure as fate, sure as shooting, sure as God made little green apples, sure as hell, sure as the devil, sure as I live and breathe, dead sure, dead to rights, sure as death, sure as death and taxes, sure as can be, sure thing, surest thing you know, surefire, for sure, fer sher, that's for sure, for damn sure, for danged sure, for a fact, for certain, cold, have down cold, pat, down pat, have down pat, nailed down, have a lock on, lock-and-win situation, all locked up, no buts about it, no ifs ands or buts, on ice, open and

shut, set, odds on, bet on, bet one's bottom dollar on, checked and double-checked, lead-pipe cinch, cinched, clinched, come hell or high water, in the bag, racked, that's death, and no mistake, know damm well, know darn well, is the Pope Catholic?, does a bear shit in the woods?, do they grow corn in Iowa?

PROVERB n. daffodil.

PROVIDE v. feather one's nest, line one's nest (at the expense of others), heel (money), stake, grubstake, fix up, fix up with. See GIVE.

PROVIDENCE, RHODE ISLAND Ivy Town.

PROVIDENT adj. tight, tightwad, Scotch, nickel-nurser, penny pincher, bog pocket, last of the big spenders. See THRIFTY. See also CAUTIOUS.

PROVIDER n. angel, fairy godmother, lady bountiful, Santa Claus, sugar daddy, giver, heavy hitter. 2. dealer, middleman, tycoon, cockroach (small), nickel-and-dime operator, tradester, robber baron, big butter and egg man.

PROVISION n. catch, catch 22, joker, kicker, string, string to it, a string attached to it, small print, fine print, fine print at the bottom, small fine print, small fine print at the bottom.

PROVISIONALLY adv. with a catch to it, with a grain of salt, with a joker to it, with a kicker to it, with a string attached, with a string to it.

PROVISO n. catch, catch 22, joker, kicker, string, string to it, a string attached to it, small print, fine print, fine print at the bottom, small fine print, small fine print at the bottom.

PROVOCATION n. defi, defy, brickbat, put-down, grabber. See also INSULT.

PROVOKE v. trigger, ride, go on make my day, make waves, fire up, key up, put up to, work up, work up into a lather, flip one the finger, give one the finger, give one five fingers, give one a backhanded compliment, give one a left-handed compliment, dump on, hit one where he lives, get under one's skin, get in one's face, rile, nag, thumb one's nose at, hurl brickbats at. See ANNOY.

PROVOKED adj. hacked, pissed off, riled, rubbed the wrong way, at the end of one's rope, hard put to it, driven up the wall, rousted, steamed. See ANNOYED.

PROWESS n. balls, guts, heart, nerve, stomach, stuff, the right stuff, grit, true grit, spunk, backbone, moxie, starch, clock, corazon, Dutch courage (intoxicated), what it takes. See COURAGE. See also SKILL.

PROWL v. gumshoe, pussyfoot, snake, mooch around, mooch in, mooch out.

PROWL CAR n. black and white, fuzzmobile, skunk wagon, bear car, bearmobile, buzz, buzzer, screaming gasser, whistler, catch car; brown bag, plain wrap (unmarked).

PROXIMATE adj. warm, hot, burning, around, along toward, within a stone's throw, in spitting distance, pretty near. See NEAR.

PROXY n. sub, backup, bench warmer, dog chaser, fill-in, pinch hitter, pinch runner, ringer, stand-in, front, beard.

PRUDE n. bluenose, cube, square, straight, stick, stick in the mud, wet blanket, moldy fig, Christer, nice Nellie, prune, goody-goody, goody two-shoes, old maid, crabapple Annie. See also PRIM.

PRUDENT adj. leery, play it cool, play safe, keep on one's toes, think twice, hedge one's bets, not go out on a limb. See CAUTIOUS.

PRUDISH adj. square, uptight, tight-assed, stuffy, straight, short haircut, Jesus freak, bluenose. See also PRIM.

PRUNE v. knock off, chop, cut, gut.

PRUNES n. strawberries, army strawberries.

PRURIENT adj. dirty, blue, X-rated, raunchy, raw, hard core, soft core, off-color, low-down and dirty, jack-off material, smutty. See OBSCENE.

PRY v. nose around for, nose out, bug, tap, wiretap, be all ears, ears into, really get into, listen in, tune in on, Erie, on the Erie, slurp.

PRYING adj. nosey, snoopy.

PSALM n. shout.

PSEUDO adj. bogue, bogus, phony, queer, falsie, fake, ersatz, sincere, not kosher, not what it's cracked up to be, pirate goods, pirate labels. See FALSE.

PSEUDONYM n. AKA, A.K.A., handle, nickname, summer name.

PSYCHIATRIST n. shrink, headshrinker, shrinker, couch doctor, guy with the net, guy in the white coat, headpeeper, guru, squirrel, nut doctor, bug doctor (prison).

PSYCHOANALYSIS n. the couch.

PSYCHOANALYST n. shrink, headshrinker, shrinker, couch doctor, nut doctor, guy with the net, guy in the white coat, guru, squirrel.

PSYCHOLOGICAL BLOCK n. hang-up, hung, hung up, uptight.

PSYCHOLOGICAL OPERATIONS psy ops.

PSYCHOLOGICAL PROBLEM n. hangup, thing about.

PSYCHOLOGICAL TEST n. bug test, I.Q.

PSYCHOLOGICAL WARFARE n. psyop (action), psywar, The Bell Telephone Hour.

PSYCHOLOGIST n. shrink, head shrinker, shrinker, couch doctor, guy with the net, guy in the white coat, nut doctor, bug doctor (prison), guru, squirrel.

PSYCHOLOGY n. psych, where one is at, where one's head is at.

PSYCHOPATH n. psycho, section 8, wrong number, schitzo, schizoid, hospital H.

PSYCHOPATHIC WARD n. flight deck, psycho ward.

PSYCHOTHERAPIST n. shrink, head shrinker, shrinker, couch doctor, nut doctor, guy with the net, guy in the white coat, bug doctor (prison), guru, squirrel.

PSYCHOTIC adj. psycho, sick, sick sick, sickie, schizzed out, schitzo, schitzy, flippo, over the edge, nutsy fagan, nuts. See also CRAZY.

PUB n. joint, after-hours joint, juice joint, beer joint, tap room, bucket shop, suds shop, gashouse, ale house, beer house, mug house, gin mill. See BAR.

PUBIC HAIR n. muff, mink, beaver, beard, bush, short hairs, beehive, bird's nest, patch, arbor, cotton (Fem.), grass, hat, pubes, merkin (wig).

PUBLIC n. bodies, cats, dudes, heads, hoi polloi, the man in the street, the guy next door, John Doe, Jane Doe, John Q., John Q. Public, Billy Sixpack, Joe Lunchbucket, Joe Doakes, the average Joe, Mr. and Mrs. America, Tom Dick and Harry, Brown Jones and Robinson, booboisie, the little guy, the mob, riffraff, cattle, ragtag, ragtag and bobtail, the great unwashed.

PUBLIC ADDRESS SYSTEM n. P.A., bullhorn, squack box, bitch box, growler, hog caller.

PUBLIC FUNDS n. pork barrel, John Q's pocket, deep pockets, public crib, public trough, public till, public purse.

PUBLIC IMAGE n. front, pose, act, rep.

PUBLICIST n. PR man, flack, plugger, puffer, huckster, ballyhooer, booster, DINFO (Pentagon), space bandit, booster, blurbist, gas man. See also ADVERTISING.

PUBLICITY n. hype, plug, PR, P.R., pub, promo, blurb, puff, puffery, buildup, hoopla, flackery, ballyhoo, big noise, ink, get ink, handout (release), noise about, pitch, scratch, spread. See also ADVERTISING.

PUBLICITY SEEKER n. hotdogger, publicity hound, showoff.

PUBLICIZE v. hype, plug, push, pitch, promote, splash, spot, boost, build up, puff, ballyhoo, press agent, throw the spotlight on, put on the map, make a pitch for, drum, beat the drum for, tub-thump, thump the tub for, hard sell, soft sell, bill, billboard. See ADVERTISING.

PUBLICLY adv. openly, in front of God and everybody, go public, in the limelight, in the spotlight, in Macy's window.

PUBLIC OFFICIAL n. paper shuffler, buck passer, apparatchik (minor).

PUBLIC RELATIONS n. hype, plug, PR, P.R., pub, promo, puffery, flack, flackery, ballyhoo, big noise. See PUBLICITY.

PUBLIC SPEAKER n. soapboxer, soapbox orator, spieler, spouter, stumper, jawsmith, tub thumper, chalk talker.

PUBLIC TREASURY n. pork barrel, John Q's pocket, deep pockets, public crib, public trough, public till, public purse.

PUBLISH v. put to bed, go to bed, roll the presses, go public, get the word around, spread it around, pass the word, drum, call, trumpet.

PUBLISHER n. pub, pubbery.

PUDDING n. g'dong, gedunk, glop, goop, pud.

PUDDLE n. loblolly.

PUDENDUM n. pussy, cunt, snatch, twat, beaver, crack, hole, quim, snapper, box, clam, love muscle, oven, piece, cunny, honey pot, muff, the Y. See VAGINA. See also GENITALIA, MALE.

PUDGY n. roly-poly, tubby, tubster, heavy cream, hefty, love handles (hips and thighs), butterball, zaftig. See FAT.

PUERILE adj. kid stuff.

PUERTO RICAN n. spic, spig, spiggoty, spic and span, spill, hatchet thrower, parakeet.

PUGILIST n. mug, pug, palooka, slugger, fancy Dan, punching bag, glass jaw, bag puncher, cauliflower ear, loogan, plug, plug ugly, white hope. See PRIZEFIGHTER.

PUGNACIOUS adj. dukes up, scrappy, snorky, salty, spiky, cantankerous, out for a rep, have a bone to pick, have a chip on one's shoulder. See BELLIGERENT.

PULITZER PRIZE n. Pullet Surprise, Putziler Prize (for mediocrity).

PULL v. pull out, yank, jerk, lug, schlep, shlep, shlep along, truck.

PULLMAN PORTER n. George, bedbug.

PULSATE v. go pitapat, tick.

PULSE n. pitapation.

PUNCH n. belt, shot, sock, slug, rap, bash, zap, zinger, clip, lollop, plunk, one-two, one-two punch, Sunday punch. See HIT.

PUNCH v. punch out, punch one out, throw a punch, bash, bonk, conk, belt, sock, slug, smack, poke, clip, rap, zap, paste, plant one. See HIT.

PUNCTILIOUS adj. on the button, on the numbers, on the money, on target, on the nose, on the noggin, right on, dead on, bull's-eye, a good eye, chicken shit, by the book, persnickety. See PARTICULAR.

PUNCTUAL adj. on the button, on the dot, on the nose, on the ball.

PUNCTURE v. poke full of holes, shoot full of holes, blow sky high, knock the bottom out of, knock the chocks from under, knock the props from under.

PUNDIT n. prof, teach, guru, brain, egghead, ivory dome, gnurd, gome, grind, auger, tool, power tool, throat, cutthroat, wonk, bookworm, cereb, pencil geek, ink squirter, spider, squid, grub, weenie, maven.

PUNGENT adj. stinko, stinking, stinky, whiffy, nosey, strong, loud (strong), salty, high, pfui, phooey, peeyooey.

PUNISH v. can, carry the can, tie the can on one, knock, drop the boom, lower the boom, rap, rap one's knuckles, slap on the wrist, put the slug one one, sock it to one, stick it to one, go upside one's haid, cloud up and rain on one, let one have it, let fly, fix, fix one's clock, skin, skin alive, scorch, blister, roast, fry, clobber, tear into, draw the line, lambaste, mop up the floor with, wipe up the floor with, jack up, hoist, rag, dig at, jaw, jawbone, chew, chew ass, chew out, eat out, eat out one's ass, kick ass, ball out, bawl out, ream, ream out, ream ass, read one out, cuss out, go after, rip, zap, cap on, lay into, lay out, rank out, straighten out, serve one out, pay out, sound off, lean on, sit on, jump on, jump all over, jump down one's throat, jump on one's shit, climb, climb all over, climb one's frame, light into, land on, rake, rake up one side and down the other, rake over the coals, haul over the coals, trim, have one on the carpet, have one on the mat, call on the carpet, put one on the carpet, dance the carpet, call to task, smack down, slap down, call down, dress down, put down, come down on, come down on hard, take down, take down a peg, downmouth, ding, gig, growl, glue, read the riot act, throw the book at one, speak to, talk to, tell a thing or two, tell off, tell where to get off, tee off on one, attend to, give it to, give what for, give a bawling out, give a going over, give a bit of one's mind, give a piece of one's mind, give one the business, give one both barrels, give one the deuce, give one the devil, give one the dickens, give one hell, give one hail Columbia, give one his lumps, give one his comeuppance, settle, settle one's hash, settle the score, campus, nail to the wall, nail to the cross.

PUNISHMENT n. bawling out, chewing, out, cussing out, speaking to, talking to, going over, catch, catch it, catch hell, hell to pay, pay through the nose, get yours, get hers, get his, get what is coming to one, get it in the neck, what one was asking for, piece of one's mind, bit of one's mind, rap on the knuckles, slap on the wrist, calling down, dressing, dressing down, set down, lumps, take one's lumps, take one's medicine, what for, for it, jacking up, comeuppance.

PUNSTER n. cutup, gagman, gagster, jokesmith, madcap, wisecracker. See also JOKER.

PUNY adj. 1. shrimp, wee, peewee, peanut, runt, short, small fry, small time, dinky, measly, tomtit, shit, chicken shit, chippie, button, wart, mite, piddling, two bit, two by four, pint-sized, half-pint. See SMALL. 2. wimp, wimpy, neb, nebbish, nothing, zero, zilch, wishy-washy, don't have the horses.

PUPIL n. undergrad, grad, doc, prep, preppie, preppy, brain, skull, tool, grind (bookworm), greasy grind, dig, bookbuster, wonk, bone, boner. See STUDENT.

PUPPET adj. 1. stooge, tool, yuld, yold, yo-yo, cat's paw, apple, patsy, pushover, vic, mom, chump, soft touch, fall guy, babe in the woods, boob, schlemiel, jack, duck, goofus, gopher, jay, lobster, prize sap. 2. muppet, Charlie McCarthy.

PURCHASE v. make a buy, blow one's self to, take up, buy out, buy off, buy into, cop.

PURCHASER n. float, head, mark, pigeon, walk-in, live one.

PURE adj. all wool and a yard wide, Christian, kosher, twenty-four carat, wide-eyed, wet behind the ears, cherry, babe in the woods, Bambi, blue-eyed, baby blue eyes, clean, kid, lily white, look as if butter wouldn't melt in one's mouth. See also UNSOPHISTICATED, UN-ADULTERATED, VIRTUOUS.

PURGATIVE n. cc pills.

PURGE v. liquidate, do away with, executive fallout (business), unload the deadwood, wipe off the map, wipe out, clean out, shake out. See KILL.

PURGED adj. liquidated, unfrocked (any profession), drummed out, turned off.

PURITANICAL adj. cube, square, straight, short haircut, goody-goody, goody two-shoes, bluenose, Christer, nice Nellie, crabapple Annie, prune. See STRAITLACED.

PURPORT n. drift, point, heart, meat, nub, score, stuff, bottom line, name of the game, nitty-gritty, nuts and bolts, the way of it, nature of the beast, punch line, kicker (point of a story, joke, etc.).

PURPOSE n. where one's heading, drift, the big idea, idea, the whatfor, the whole idea, the why and wherefore, the whyfor.

PURPOSEFUL adj. mean business, be out for blood, playing hard ball, dead set on, bent on, hell bent on. See DETERMINED.

PURSE n. grouch bag, leather, lizard, pocket, bag, poke, frame, hide, clutch.

PURSE SNATCH v. bushwhack, buzz, glom a leather, make a poke, mollbuzz.

PURSE SNATCHER n. bushwhacker, buzzer, leather glommer, moll buzzer.

PURSUE v. 1. tail, trail, play catch up, run down, run to ground, go after, take out after, tag after. See FOLLOW. 2. bird-dog (scout), scout, beat the bushes, search high heaven, leave no stone unturned, track down. See SEARCH. 3. dog, dog one's case, bug, on one's back, on one's case, put the squeeze on, put one through the wringer, put the screws on, put the heat on, turn on the heat, burn one's ass, drag into court, haul into court, have the law on, have up, law, put one away, pull up, drive one up the wall, take out after, set one's cap for. 4. go in for, go out for, have a go at, get it on with. 5. date, chase, rush, go for, go after, go steady, play up to, hit on, make eyes at. See COURT.

PURSUIT n. biz, beeswax, game, gesheft, line, go, do, dodge, bag, what one is into, thing, hang, racket, swindle, grift. See OCCUPATION.

PUSH n. gumption, spunk, drive, guts, get up and go.

PUSH v. 1. lean on, push around, bear down, pressure, high pressure, strong-arm, squeeze, put the screws on, put the arm on, railroad through, steamroll, muscle in, muscle out, throw one's weight around, move in on, pour it on, go to town on. See FORCE. 2. fire up, key up, put up to, turn on, egg one on, goose, sell one on, jolly, kid along, lay it on. See URGE.

PUSILLANIMOUS adj. wimpy, nerdy, gutless, candy ass, pucker-assed, paper tiger, jellyfish, turkey, weak sister, big baby, yellow-bellied. See COWARDLY.

PUSTULE n. zit, hickey, beauty spot, bloom, doohickey, dohinky.

PUT v. park, peg, nail, plank, plank down, plunk, plunk down, plop.

PUTRID adj. strong, high.

PUTTER v. mess around, potchky, potchky around. See DABBLE.

PUZZLE v. get to, beat, lick, bug, psych out, gross out, take one's mind, fuck with one's head, mess with one's head, mess with one's mind, make a mess of, fuddle, stump, bamboozle, buffalo, ball up, profundicate, synomaniac (one who complicates), muddy the waters, stir the waters, rattle, rattle one's cage, throw, throw a monkey wrench into the works, play hob with, put one on a crosstown bus, make waves, open up a can of worms, make hash out of, snow, floor, put off, flummox.

PUZZLED adj.   all balled up, balled up, spaced out, hung, hung up, mixed up, blaaed up, gummixed up, gummoxed up, unglued, unzipped, unscrewed, come unglued, come unzipped, come apart, come apart at the seams, discombobulated, discombooberated, mind is blown, shook, shook up, fouled up, fucked up, loused up, messed up, mucked up, mussed up, screwed up, bugged up, bollixed, bollixed up, messed up attic, floored, flipped out, farmisht, fertummeled, woozy, thrown, dopey, lost one's cool, fussed, rattled, rattlebrained, foggy, wandering around in a fog, in a fog, in a botheration, like a chicken with its head cut off, out to lunch, psyched out, kerflumixed, licked, stuck, stumped, double Dutch, boggily woogily, drowning, huggermugger, bamboozled, buffaloed, bowled over, bowled down, struck all of a heap, thrown off ones beam ends. See also DISTURBED.

PUZZLER n.   sticker, stumper, teaser, twister, floorer, sixty-four dollar question, hard nut to crack, tough nut to crack, tough proposition.

PYROMANIAC n.   firebug, torch. See ARSONIST.

Q

Q n. Quebec, queen.

QUAALUDE n. lude, quad, sopor, pillows, wall banger, vitamin Q, lemon.

QUACK n. fake, faker, fraud, four-flusher, phony, pseud, pseudo, put-on, actor, playactor, bogue, diddler, S.L.O.B. (silver lipped operator of bullshit), con man, con artist, clip artist, sharpie, flimflammer, flimflam man, bunco, bunco artist, whip, bum, shark, sharp, jackleg, slicker, boogerboo, shiever, hoser.

QUADRANGLE n. quad.

QUADRIPLEGIC n. basket case.

QUAINT adj. offbeat, off the beaten track, weird, weirdo, weirdie, strange one, oddball, goof ball, special, funny, funny looking, rare bird.

QUAKE v. jitter, shake, shiver.

QUAKING n. shakes, shivers, cold shivers, teeth chattering, heebie-jeebies.

QUALIFICATION n. goods, makings, stuff, what it takes. See SKILL.

QUALIFIED adj. pro, vet, war-horse, paid one's dues, won one's spurs, up to speed, up to the mark, up to snuff, up to code, one of the old school, old-timer, been through the mill, have one's ticket punched, have know-how, know one's onions, know one's stuff, know one's business, know one's oats, know one's beans, know one's bananas, know one's fruit, know one's groceries, know one's oil, know one's goods, all around, wasn't born yesterday, didn't come into town on a load of wood, from way back. See also CAPABLE, SKILLFUL.

QUALIFY v. make it, make the cut, make the grade, score, cut it, cut the mustard, come up to snuff, check out, earn one's wings, hack it, pass, pass muster, pass in the dark, fill the bill, get by. See also SUFFICE.

QUALITY n. nature of the beast, the way of it, name of that tune, what you see is what you get. See also NATURE.

QUALITY, HIGH adj. prime, 10, ten, A-number one, ace high, uptown, gnarly, mega-gnarly, zero cool, winner, choice, state of the art, top of the line, first class, greatest, up to snuff, this is some kinda ———, the best. See EXCELLENT.

QUALITY, POOR adj. cheesy, dreck, piece of shit, rinky-dinky, ratty-tatty, ain't worth diddly shit, ain't worth a plugged nickel, el cheapo, cotton pickin', garbage, junk, lousy, not worth a hill of beans, lemon, dud, white elephant, jeasley, bogus, punk, turkey, abortion, bum, cracker box (house), tinhorn, Mickey Mouse, humpty-dumpty, tacky, ticky-tacky, cheap jack, held together by spit, held together by chewing gum, house of cards. See CHEAP.

QUANDARY n. clutch, hang-up, bind, spot, box, catch 22, double trouble, in a box, in a pickle, up a tree, between a rock and a hard place, fine how do you do, tough nut to crack. See PREDICAMENT.

QUANTIFY v. peg, size, size up, check, check out, dig it, eye, look over, have one's number, take one's measure, dope out, take account of, figure, figure in, guesstimate.

QUANTITY n. 1. heap, loads, lots, bags, peck, passel, flock, whole slew, scads, zillion, umpteen, kind (that kind of money), bundle, oodles, crawling with, no end of, no end to. See AMOUNT, LARGE. 2. titch, smidge, skoshe, taste, weenchy, teensy-weensy, bite, cut, nip, slice, smithereen. See AMOUNT, SMALL.

QUARREL n. hassle, blowup, spat, tiff, words, run-in, scene, flak session, rhubarb, wrangle, fireworks. See ARGUMENT.

QUARREL v. hassle, take on, lock horns, set to, row, scrap, bump heads, cross swords, have at it, pick a bone, tangle with, tangle ass with, go up against, pitch a bitch, put up a fight, beat a dead horse, go round and round. See ARGUE.

QUARRELSOME adj. ornery, scrappy, snorky, bitchy, cussed, tetchy, salty, spiky, limber, cantankerous, have a bone to pick, have a chip on one's shoulder, at loggerheads. See BELLIGERENT.

QUARTER n. 1. territory, turf, hood, neck of the woods, stomping ground, old town, ghetto, inner city, slurb, slum, zoo, garment district, skid row. 2. Shubert Alley, Tin Pan Alley, Broadway, The Great White Way (The.), West End, Wall Street, Las Vegas Strip, Sunset Strip, SoHo. See DISTRICTS.

QUARTERS n. dorm, fratority, sorenity, birdcage, bull pen, bullypen, frau shack, hen ranch, hen coop, quail roost, zoo. See HOUSE.

QUASH v. 1. black out, shut down, kill, queer, squelch, hush up, put the lid on, put the damper on, crack down on, clamp down on, cork up, bottle up. 2. squash, squish, scrunch, trash, snow under. See REPRESS.

QUEASY adj. barfy, pukish, pukey, rocky, sick as a dog, under the weather. See ILL.

QUEER adj. flaky, freaky, kooky, offbeat, weird, weirdo, grody, oddball, fringy, kinky, off the wall, trippy, not wrapped real tight, fly ball, queer duck, rare bird, aired out, jell brain, jelled, character, wacky, yo-yo. See ECCENTRIC.

QUELL v. pour oil on troubled waters, black out, shut down, torpedo, kill, queer, squelch, hush up, sit on, put the lid on, crack down on, ding, zing. See REPRESS. See also PACIFY.

QUENCH v. kill (fire or cigarette), choke, douse, knock down, stamp out.

QUERULOUS adj. bitchy, out of sorts, cantankerous, grouchy, grousing, scrappy, bearish, uptight, thin-skinned, whiny, ready to fly off the handle, edgy. See PEEVISH.

QUERY v. hit up, knock, put out a feeler, test the waters, see which way the wind blows, So?, cool out, P. (beer-p? = Want a beer?), what's with one or something?, what's going down?, what gives? See QUESTION.

QUESTION n. sixty-four dollar question, poll, third, third degree, Q. and A., wringer. See also INQUIRY.

QUESTION v. hit, hit up, hold out for, knock, pop the question, toss, whistle for (but won't get), sweat, sweat it out of one, sweat out, third degree, give one the third, give one the third degree, put through the third degree, put one through the wringer, put the heat on one, put on the grill, grill, roast, put the screws on, put the screws to, go over, work over, flutter (give one a lie detector test), pick one's brains, So?, buzz, cat haul, cook, cool, cool out, P. (beer-p? = Want a beer?), yeah?, what's with one or something?, what's going down?, what gives?

QUESTIONABLE adj. chancy, iffy, dicey, touch and go, hanging by a thread, fishy, been hit before, you should live so long, the jury's out. See DOUBTFUL.

QUESTIONS AND ANSWERS n. Q. and A.

QUIBBLE v. lint pick, nitpick, split hairs, make a big thing about, make a mountain out of a molehill, catch at straws, blow hot and cold, flip-flop, shilly-shally, waffle, hem and haw, hassle, set to, talk back, have at it, pick a bone, put up an argument, pettifog. See also EQUIVOCATE.

QUIBBLER n. nitpicker, hair splitter.

QUICK adj. quickie, ASAP, pronto, snappy, on the double, double time, Jim quick, get the lead out, move it, get a move on, get going, get on your motorcycle, get on your bicycle, get on your horse, step on it, step lively, shake a leg, haul ass, like a bat out of hell, like shit through a goose. See FAST.

QUICK-WITTED adj. gasser, sharp, wired, whiz, whiz kid, Einstein, have smarts, have savvy, on the ball, quick on the trigger, quick on the uptake, quick on the draw, smart as a whip, smart as a tack, sharp as a tack. See INTELLIGENT.

QUIESCENT adj. on the shelf, on the bench, out of the rat race, out of action, out of the swim, closed down, down.

QUIET adj. clammed up, buttoned up, iced, keep one's trap shut, not say boo, saved one's breath, dummied up, garbo, could hear a pin drop, ah ah head. See SILENT.

QUIET interj. shut up, knock it off, hold it down, can it, clam up, dummy up, cool it, drop it, stow it, come off it, shush, hush, shut your tater trap, shut your face, shut your mouth, blow your nose, fold up. See SILENCE.

QUIET n. dead air.

QUIET v. 1. gag, ice, muzzle, squelch, squash, shut up, cool it, can it, soft pedal, dummy up, clam up, hold it down, button one's lip. See SILENCE. 2. cool, cool out, cool it, cool off, stroke, fix up, make matters up, patch things up, square, take the bite out. See PACIFY.

QUIET, BE v. shut up, shut one's trap, shut one's head, shut one's face, shut one's mouth, hush one's mouth, put up or shut up, pipe down, bite one's tongue, hold one's tongue, cut it out, clam up, close up, hang up, dummy up, fold up, dry up, choke in, choke up, drag in one's rope, pull in one's ears, rest one's jaw, sign off, ring off, lay off, roll up one's flaps, stow it, save it, chuck it, can it, stifle it, step on it, put a lid on it, button one's lip, zip one's lip, bag one's lip, bag one's head, be cool, cool one's chops, drink one's beer.

QUINTESSENTIAL adj. ten, 10, aces, world class, greatest, gonest, hundred proof, mostest, drop dead [anything], coolsville, gilt-edge, balls out, all time, the most, endsville, solid gold. See BEST.

QUINTUPLET n. quint.

QUIPSTER n. clown, cutup, life of the party, madcap, trickster, card, a million laughs, kibitzer, booger, bugger, jokesmith, gagman, gagster, funster, punster, wisecracker.

QUIT v. 1. wind up, wrap up, sew up, pack in, kick over, kick the habit, take the cure, knock off, break off, cut it out, call all bets off, call it a day, call it quits, quit cold, quit cold turkey, leave flat, run out on, drop out, get on the wagon, put the finisher on, hang it up. See STOP. 2. cut out, cut ass, bag ass, drag ass, drag it, push off, bow out, ooze out, phase out, nix out, check out, drop, drop out, catch out, pull out, get the hell out, take a walk, book, time to book, time to bail, hang it up, run out on, walk out on. See GO.

QUITTER n. deuce, slacker, welsher.

QUIVER v. jitter, shake, shiver.

QUIVERING n. shakes, shivers, cold shivers, heebie-jeebies.

QUIZ n. exam, cream (successful), blue book; drop quiz, shotgun quiz, pop quiz (unannounced).

QUIZ v. pick one's brains.

QUOTA n. cut, bite, slice, chunk, split, end, divvy, piece, a piece of the action, cut of the pie, cut of the melon, slice of the pie, slice of the melon. See also SHARE.

QUOTATION n. quote, saying.

QUOTATION MARK n. quote.

QUOTATION MARKS n. rabbit ears.

QUOTE v. reference.

R

R n. Romeo, Roger.

RABBI n. Reb, sky pilot, sky scout, sky merchant.

RABBLE n. mob, riffraff, cattle, ragtag, ragtag and bobtail, the great unwashed, turnout, blowout, crush, everybody and his brother, everybody and his uncle, loaded to the rafters, wall-to-wall people, jam, jam up, push. See also POPULACE.

RABID adj. 1. bugs on, hot, hot for, nutty about, freaked out, overboard, stoned, bugged, steamed up, flipped, worked up about, jacked up. See ENTHUSI-ASTIC. 2. ranting and raving, raving mad, roaring mad, hopping mad, good and mad, mad as a hornet, mad as a wet hen, hacked, steamed up, at the boiling point, boiling over, see red, shit blue, go ape shit, have a conniption, hit the ceiling, sizzling, smoking. See ANGRY.

RACE n. go, run, competish.

RACE, FIXED n. dead cert, boat race (horse racing).

RACEHORSE n. the ponies, pony, nag, the g.g.'s, gee gee, bangtail, mudder, pig, plater, dark horse (unknown entry), stick out (superior), maiden, chaser (steeplechase racer), claimer, bug (never won), beetle, cooler, lizard, getty-up, glue pot, goat, hide, weanling, baby, juvenile (2-year-olds), lug in, lug out (rail), lugger, side wheeler, skin, stiff (loser), gluepot (old), tacky, stretch runner, break down (injury while racing). See also HORSE.

RACEHORSE RIDER n. jock, jockette (Fem.), up, bug boy (apprentice), postboy.

RACEHORSE TERMS also ran, bear in, bear out, lug in, lug out, wear blinkers (restrict horse's side view), blowout (workout run), break (start from gate), the call, drive (he won under a drive), early foot (fast starter), handily, breeze, post time (starting time), photo (photo finish), scratch (withdraw entry), bat, gad (whip); caller (race announcer), claimer; fast, good, heavy, muddy, sloppy, slow, gumbo (track conditions); flat racing, give away weight (carry extra weight handicap), footing, maiden race, go, run, in the money; pilot, rider (jockey); railbird (spectator), tack (equipment), the ponies, the track, the g.g.'s, charts, dark horse (unknown entry); maiden, bug (horse who has never won); boat race, drug store race (drugged or fixed); sweep (speepstake); golf ball, soup, T, tea (drugs); produce race (unfoaled entries based on bloodlines), Run for the Roses (Kentucky Derby); seller, selling race (claiming race); starter (an entry), steal (lead all the way), wire to wire (start to finish),

cooler (light horse blanket), cool out, exercise boy, hot walker, nerved (nerve block to hooves), put down (humane killing), bute (phenylbutazone, painkiller), swipe (a groom).

RACING CAR n. Indy car, stock, stocker, formula car, formula A, formula B, formula C, formula F (Ford), formula 5000, formula I, formula II, formula III, formula VEE, blown formula Super VEE (supercharged), funny car, hobby car, mule (practice car), pace car, clean (smooth, aerodynamic body).

RACING CAR DRIVER foot, hot shoe (star driver), ride (got a ride).

RACING CAR MAINTENANCE n. blip, gun (race engine briefly); blueprint (rebuild engine to exact stock specifications), prodify (modify a production car), methanol, nitro (nitromethane), wrench (mechanic).

RACING CAR PARTS n. crash box (transmission), footprint, nerf bar (kind of bumper), roll bar, roll cage, pot, scattershield (safety flywheel and clutch housing), slicks (treadless tires).

RACING FORM n. form, sheet, scratch sheet, dope sheet.

RACISM n. feel a draft (recognition of), Jim Crow, Jim Crowism, Jane Crow (against women).

RACKET n. ruckus, ruction, fuss, fuzz buzz, hoo ha, rowdydow, hubba-hubba, hullabaloo, brouhaha. See also COMMOTION, NOISE.

RACKETEER n. hood, hoodlum, hooligan, mo ghee, mob ghee, mobster, big juice, member of the family, goon, underboss (second in command), pusher, dealer, digits dealer (numbers). See GANGSTER. See also CRIMINAL, MAFIA.

RADAR DETECTOR n. brownie (unit), camera (police), electric teeth, fuzzbuster (auto), huff duff (H.F.D.F.), kodak, picture box, polaroid, X-ray machine.

RADAR IMAGE n. blip, angel (echo), bogie, skunk (unidentified or hostile), clutter, flitter (static).

RADICAL adj. far out, way out, gone, left field, flaming, out of all bounds, all get out, too much, ultra ultra, knee-jerk reaction. See EXTREME.

RADICAL n. left, lefty, leftie, lefto, left winger, New Left, Old Left, left of center, pink, pinko, parlor pink, radish, fellow traveller, linky dink, bleeding heart, do-gooder, innocent (Bl.), commie, comsymp, hippie, yippie, radiclib, red, rim, underground, Wobbly, New Right, Bircher, far right.

RADICAL, LEFT n. bleeding heart, commie, fellow traveller, flamer, knee-jerk lefty, left, left wing, lefty, leftie, leftist, lefto, linkydink, pinko, red.

RADICAL, RIGHT n. right, right wing, right winger, extreme right, radical right, stand pat, stand-patter, Bircher, Birchite, John Bircher, Black Shirt, Brown Shirt, diehard, hard hat, Klu Kluxer, lunatic fringe, McCarthyism, old line, Posse Comatatus, red-baiter, red-neck, storm trooper, witch hunter.

RADIO n. stereo, hi fi, box, ghetto blaster, ghetto box, thunderbox, third world attaché case (portable with tape player), walkman, joy box, tube gear, beeper.

RADIOACTIVE adj. dirty, hot.

RADIOACTIVE PARTICLES n. fallout.

RADIO OPERATOR n. ham, ham operator, sparks, dit da artist, dit da jockey, dit da monkey, brass pounder (1925).

RADIO OPERATOR'S ROOM n. shack, radio shack.

RADIO RECEIVER n. stereo, hi fi, box, ghetto blaster, third world attaché case, walkman, joy box, tube gear, beeper.

RADIO SHOW HOST n. D.J. deejay, disc jockey, platter pusher, anchor.

RADIO STATION n. antenna farm, ozoner.

RADIO TELEPHONE n. cellular phone, port-o-phone, remote, cordless, rig, squawkie-talkie, walkie-talkie.

RADIO TRANSMITTER n. squawkie-talkie, walkie-talkie, Gibson Girl (WW II), tower.

RAFFLE n. the numbers, the numbers game.

RAGE n. 1. mad, huff, dander, storm, wingding, conniption fit, shit hemorrhage, blowup, tearing up the pea patch. See ANGER. 2. faddy, trendy, in, in-thing, the thing, latest thing, latest wrinkle, new wrinkle, newest wrinkle, last word, now, really now, the rage, up to the minute, go-go, hip, hep, mellow back, in-spot, happening place, groovy hangout, hot spot, masscult.

RAGE v. burn up, blow up, blow one's top, blow one's topper, blow one's stack, blow a fuse, blow a gasket, blow one's cap, blow one's cork, blow one's wig, blow one's noggin, blow one's roof, blow one's lump, flip, flip out, flip one's lid, fly off the handle, get sore, see red, get hot under the collar, sizzle, get into a dither, get into a stew, get one's dander up, get one's Irish up, get one's mad up, work oneself into a lather, work oneself into a sweat, have a hemorrhage, have a shit hemorrhage, have a bug on,

sport a bug on, bug up, pop off, sound off, raise cain, raise hell, raise the devil, raise the roof, hit the ceiling, sound off, boiling point, boil over, steam up, tear, tear up the pea patch, go into a tailspin.

RAGGED adj. ratty-tatty, beat up, tacky, frowzy, sleazy, dog-eared.

RAGING adj. bent out of shape, blowing one's cool, blowing a fuse, blowing a gasket, blowing one's stack, blowing one's top, blowing the roof, mad as a hornet, mad as a wet hen, at the boiling point, boiling over, see red, shit blue, go ape shit, having a shit hemorrhage, throwing a fit, on the warpath, raising hell, ranting and raving, raving mad, roaring mad. See ANGRY.

RAGOUT n. mulligan, salmagundi, slumgullion, coll, Black Mike (hobo), lorelei.

RAID v. knock off, knock over, tip over, heat, storm, sweep, pull a joint, slough, slough up, slough a joint, lean against, lean on. See also INVADE, LOOT.

RAILROAD BRAKEMAN n. brakie, baby lifter, car catcher, club winder, hind hook, shack stinger, groundhog.

RAILROAD COACH n. ding-dong, rubberneck, (observation), sleeper, the cushions (first-class passenger car).

RAILROAD CONDUCTOR n. dude, drummer, grabber, kayducer, captain, skipper, big O, big ox, brains, chopper, con.

RAILROAD CREW n. hat; hogger, hog head, hog jockey, hog, eagle eye (engineer); bell ringer, clinker, diamond cracker, diamond pusher, diamond thrower, ash can, dust raiser, smoke, tallow pot (fireman); jerry gang, paperweight (clerk), rag (flagman), rail, razorback, snipe, stinger, switch hog; yard bull, yard goat (guard); dishwasher (engine wiper), dog chaser (relief), donkey, gandy dancer (section hand); general, ringmaster, dinger (yardmaster); grunt, snake, bookkeeper (flagman), cinder crusher, cherry picker (switchman), boom stick (itinerant worker), chambermaid (roundhouse machinist), detainer (dispatcher), cinder dick (detective), cinder bull (RR police).

RAILROAD CROSSING SIGN n. clothes tree.

RAILROAD FREIGHT CARS n. riff, reefer freezer (refrigerated); gon, gond, oilcan, boxer, can, rod, dise drag, gory (empty), gunboat, side-door Pullman, rattler.

RAILROAD LOCOMOTIVE n. hog, pig, bull, bull engine, goat (switch), battleship (heavy duty), battlewagon (tender), boiler, iron horse, smoker, calliope, camel, dinge, hay burner, jack, Johnson rod (mythical part), teakettle, pot, kettle, Mother Hubbard, yard goat, moose gooser.

RAILROAD SIGNALS n.   eye, red eye, green eye, wigwag.

RAILROAD TERMS   AMTRAK, brass collar (RR official), bull fighter (empty freight car), bullpen (dormitory), barefoot (without brakes), car toad (service train), cradle (gondola), crumb (work crew bunk car), deck (passenger car roof), breeze (air brakes), first reader (conductor's notebook), garden (yard), gate, gun (warning torpedo), possum belly, jerk (branch line), shuffle them up, highball (high speed), the cushions (first-class passenger car), deadhead (return empty), bumper (coupling).

RAILROAD TRAIN n.   choo choo, choo-choo train, Chattanooga, Chattanooga choo choo, rattler, ball of fire, highballer, jack, rat, meat run, red ball, varnished car, cannonball, cannonball express (fast), AMTRAK, B.&O., Belt Line, Cannonball, Challenger, Commodore Vanderbilt, C.P.R., Daylight, Dixie Cannonball, Green Diamond, Owl, Pennsy, Century, Zephyr.

RAIMENT n.   threads, togs, duds, outfit, rags, glad rags, getup, get out, feathers, vine, weeds, frame, flash, drapery, drapes, Sunday best, hand-me-downs. See CLOTHING.

RAIN n.   precip, pouring, drips, light drips (shower), spit, it's raining cats and dogs, it's raining hammer handles, it's raining pitchforks, really coming down, spit, deep water (heavy), gully washer, window washer, sheets, wet stuff, drownder, goose drownder, heavy dew, California dew, California sunshine, California weather (in Florida), Florida weather (in California), California orange juice, sky juice, cloud juice.

RAINCOAT n.   mack, Fog, slicker.

RAISE n.   boost, leg, leg up, bump, jump, jump up, move up, step up, hold up (salary), win one's wings, hike, hike upstairs.

RAISE v.   1. boost, look up, pick up, perk up, snowball, mushroom, shoot up, build up, fetch up, goose, goose up, hike, hike up, jack up, jump up, put up, run up, pyramid. 2. bring up, drag up.

RAISIN CAKE n.   fly cake.

RAKE n.   playboy, player, lech, wolf, tomcat, cocksman, womanizer, sport, swinger, make-out artist, chaser, woman chaser. See LECHER.

RALLY n.   clambake, pep rally, meet, get-together, powwow. See also MEETING.

RALLY v.   pick up, perk up, shape up, get back in shape, bounce back, make a comeback, come from behind, snap out of it, come along, get one's act together, turn around, turn things around. See IMPROVE. See also ASSEMBLE, INCITE.

RAMBLE v.   1. get sidetracked, get off the track, lose the thread, all over the map. 2. cruise, drift, bum around, traipse, knock around, knock about, bat around, percolate, ooze, ank. See WANDER.

RAMPAGE n.   mad, Irish, storm, ruckus, wingding, conniption fit, blowup, boiling point, tear, tearing up the pea patch, more heat than light. See ANGER.

RANCID adj.   strong, high.

RANDY adj.   heavy, horny, hot, hot and heavy, turned on. See LASCIVIOUS.

RANGE n.   run, run of, space, elbowroom, leeway, room to swing a cat.

RANGE v.   bum around, drift, float, follow one's nose, traipse, knock around, knock about, bat around, bat about, hit the road, hit the trail, globe-trot, trek. See WANDER.

RANK adj.   strong, high.

RANK n.   pecking order, down the line, place, slot.

RANK v.   tab, peg, pigeonhole, button down, put away, put down as, put down for, typecast, rank out, size up, take one's measure.

RANSACK v.   beat the bushes, leave no stone unturned, look all over hell, look high and low, search high heaven, shake, shake down, toss, turn inside out, turn upside down.

RANT v.   carry on, go on, take on, blow one's roof, blow one's top, sizzle, pop off, sound off, get on a soapbox, spiel, spout, chew the scenery, stump, sport a bug on. See also ORATE.

RAPACIOUS adj.   grabby, poligot, greedyguts.

RAPE v.   short-arm heist, gang bang, gang shay, gang shag, line up.

RAPID adj.   screaming, on the double quick, quick as a wink, double time, in nothing flat, really rolling, hell-bent, hell for leather, like a house on fire, like greased lightning, like a big-assed bird, like a BAB, like a bat out of hell, like shit through a goose, like a raped ape. See FAST.

RAPIST n.   arm man, short-arm bandit, keister bandit, pussy bandit, short-arm heister, skin heister, diddler.

RAPPORT n.   simpatico, good vibes, good vibrations, togetherness, soul, on the same wavelength, cotton to, in the groove, groovy, hit it off.

RAPTURE n.   gone, far out, cool, Nadaville.

RAPTUROUS adj.   flying, floating, dreamy, zero cool, gone, in Nadaville, groked, spaced out, zoned out, on cloud nine. See ECSTATIC.

RARE adj.   scarcer than hen's teeth, numerous as

chicken lips.

RASH adj. foolheaded, pay no mind, off the deep end, out on a limb, play with fire, stick one's neck out, leave oneself wide open. See RECKLESS.

RATE v. tab, button down, peg, pigeonhole, put away, put down as, put down for, typecast, size up, score, rank out, take one's measure, stand in with, redline (insurance rate zoning). See also APPRAISE.

RATIFICATION n. fuckin'-A, go-ahead, green light, okay, OK, stamp of approval.

RATIFY v. bless, okay, go for, give the nod, give the go-ahead, give the green light, give the stamp of approval, rubber stamp. See APPROVE.

RATION n. share, bite, divvy, cut, cut of the melon, P.C., p.c., piece, piece of the action, piece of the pie, drag. See SHARE.

RATIONAL adj. together, got it together, cool, have horse sense, commonsensical, evened out, all there, have all one's marbles, have both oars in the water. See REASONABLE.

RATIONALE n. the big idea, the idea, the whole idea, the whatfor, the whyfor, the why and wherefore, story, song and dance, sour grapes. See EXCUSE.

RATTLE v. get to, discomboberate, rattle one's cage, throw, psych out, fuck with one's head, put one on a crosstown bus, put off, flummox. See CONFUSE.

RATTLED adj. unglued, come unzipped, come apart, all shook up, mucked up, mixed up, floored, farmisht, thrown, fussed, rattlebrained, haywire, bamboozled. See CONFUSED.

RAVAGE v. trash, total, cream, sink, smash, wrack up, put in the toilet, wipe out, take apart, take a joint apart, tear down, break the lease, blue ruin, make hash of, fix one's wagon, play hob with. See DESTROY. See also LOOT, SEDUCE.

RAVE v. 1. carry on over, make a to-do over, take on over, fall all over one, go on about, whoop it up for. 2. freak out, flip one's lid, blow one's top, blow one's stack, go ape, go bananas, go bonkers, go off one's head, come unglued, come unzipped. See CRAZY, GO.

RAVENOUS adj. dog-hungry, empty, have a tapeworm, munchies (follows marijuana use), starved to death, could eat a horse, could eat the asshole out of a bear, could eat the asshole out of a bear without ketchup.

RAVISHER n. arm man, short-arm bandit, keister bandit, pussy bandit, short-arm heister, skin heister, diddler.

RAVISHING adj. ten, 10, devastating, drop-dead gorgeous, dishy, dream puss, whistle bait, stone fox, head

rush, knock one's eyes out, scrumptious, stunner, stunning, beaut, raving beauty, hot shit, knockout, knock one's eyes out, centerfold, oh yeah. See BEAUTIFUL.

RAY n. glim, dimmer.

RAZE v. total, wipe out, take the joint apart, break the lease, blue ruin, zap. See DESTROY.

RAZOR n. hook.

REACH v. make it, make the scene, hit, hit town, blow in, sky in, breeze in, roll in, check in, sign in, time in, clock in, check in, ring in, show, show up, bob up, wind up at, buzz (to announce an arrival). See ARRIVE.

REACT v. 1. be turned on to, feel for, feel in one's bones, feel in one's guts, hear one, get in touch, have a funny feeling, have heart, have a hunch, have good vibes, have vibes. 2. answer back, talk back, back talk, shoot back, snappy comeback, come back at, get back at, come right back at, back at you. See ANSWER.

REACTION n. take, take it big, double take, hit, cooler, knee-jerk reaction (expected), vibes, feedback, comeback, snappy comeback, sass, lip, back talk, crackback, wisecrack, kick, kickback, mug (comic). See also RESULT.

REACTIONARY n. right, right winger, radical right, Bircher, diehard, hard hat, lunatic fringe, red-neck. See CONSERVATIVE.

REACTIVATE v. take out of mothballs, demothball.

READILY adv. 1. at the drop of a hat, no sweat, hands down, like nothing, nothing to it, slick as a whistle, swimmingly, piece of cake. 2. toot sweet, in half a mo, in half a tick, in a jiff, in a jiffy, in half a jiffy, quick as a wink, before one can say Jack Robinson, abracadabra. See IMMEDIATELY.

READY adj. wired, bagged, fixed, in place, in the slot, on deck, gaffed, rigged, set up, up on, psyched up, down, ripe, crisp, cut and dry, got it covered, all bases covered, game for, waitin' on, at the ready, hot to trot, loaded for bear. See PREPARED.

READY v. 1. prep, warm up, ready up, gear up, psych oneself up, get set for, clear the decks, pave the way, put through the grind, put through the mill. 2. brief, fill in, fill one in, put on to, put one in the picture, wise up, give a pointer to, let in on the know, keep one posted, post. See PREPARE.

REAL adj. it, for real, real stuff, genuine article, the real goods, real people, live, in the flesh, honest to God, card-carrying, all wool and a yard wide. See SINCERE.

REALITY n. brass tacks, name of the game, bottom line, nuts and bolts, down to earth, the real world, no shit, straight shit, how it is, how things are, the way of it, what's what, where it's at, what it is, like it is, in living color, the word. See ACTUALITY.

REALIZATION n.   aha reaction, slow take, take, double take, take it big, see the light, flash on it, get one's drift, it hit me, it just come to me, it dawned on me.

REALIZE v.   get, get it, gotya, gotchya, get the idea, get the picture, catch, catch on, pick up, get through one's head, tumble, dig, see daylight, came the dawn. See UNDERSTAND.

REALLY adv.   absofuckinglutely, cert, amen, why sure, fer sure, you know, you're not kidding, no shit, no buts about it, indeedy, for real, really truly. See ABSOLUTELY.

REALM n.   territory, turf, stomping grounds, stamping grounds, neck of the woods. See also NEIGHBORHOOD, DISTRICTS.

REAR v.   bring up, fetch up, drag up, raise up.

REASON n.   cover, stall, song and dance, jive, the big idea, the whole idea, sour grapes, the whatfor, the why and wherefore, the whyfor. See EXCUSE.

REASONABLE adj.   together, got it together, cool, cool as a cucumber, have horse sense, commonsensical, all there, in one's right mind, got all one's marbles, have all one's marbles, have all one's buttons, right, right in the head, have both oars in the water, play with a full deck. See also CHEAP.

REASSIGN v.   bump (worker), kick upstairs.

REASSIGNMENT n.   shake-up.

REASSURE v.   buck up, pick up, brace up, chirk up, perk up, give a lift, snap out of it, let the sunshine in. See SUPPORT.

REBATE n.   kickback, payola, drugola, gayola, a payback.

REBATE v.   kick back, give up.

REBEL n.   Johnny Reb, young Turk.

REBEL v.   drop out, opt out, cop out, get out of line, rock the boat, make waves, leave the beaten path, kick over, kick over the traces.

REBELLIOUS adj.   ornery, out of line. See also DISCONTENTED.

REBUFF n.   nix, turndown, no way José, nothing doing, kick in the ass, kick in the teeth, cold shoulder, cut, go by, hard time (sexual). See REJECTION.

REBUFF v.   pass up, cut, drop, cold shoulder, high hat, brush off, fluff off, give one the fluff. See REJECT.

REBUFFED adj.   burned, cut, dead, feel adrift, killed, nixed, dumped, thrown over, passed over, passed on, put down, turned down, got it in the neck, out in the cold, left at the church. See REJECTED.

REBUILD v.   pick up the pieces, face lift, retread, rehab.

REBUKE n.   gig, put-down, comeuppance, rap, slap in the face, bawling out, calling down, going over, ragging, what for, hard time. See ADMONISH. See also SCOLDING.

REBUKE v.   chew, chew ass, chew out, eat out, eat out one's ass, ball out, bawl out, ream, ream out, ream ass, read one out, cuss out, go after, rip, zap, cap on, lay into, lay out, rank out, straighten out, serve one out, pay, pay out, sound off, lean on, sit on, jump on, jump all over, jump down one's throat, jump on one's shit, climb, climb on, climb all over, into, land on, can, tie the can on one, knock, drop the boom, lower the boom, jaw, jawbone, rake, rake up one side and down the other, take up one side and down the other, rake over the coals, haul over the coals, trim, have one on the carpet, have one on the mat, dance the carpet, call to task, smack down, slap down, call down, dress down, put down, come down on, come down on hard, take down, take down a peg, downmouth, ding, gig, growl, glue, rap, rap one's knuckles, slap on the wrist, put the slug on one, sock it to one, stick it to one, go upside one's haid, read the riot act, throw the book at one, speak to, tell a thing or two, tell off, tell where to get off, tee off on one, attend to, give it to, give what for, give a bawling out, give a going over, give a piece of one's mind, give one the business, give one both barrels, give one the deuce, give one the devil, give one the dickens, give one hell, give one hail Columbia, give one his lumps, give one his comeuppance, cloud up and rain on one, let one have it, let fly, fix, fix one's clock, skin, skin alive, scorch, blister, roast, fry, clobber, tear into, draw the line, lambaste, mop up the floor with, wipe up the floor with, jack up, hoist, rag, dig at, settle, settle one's hash, settle the score, campus.

REBUT v.   come back at, get back at, take on, cross, top. See REFUTE.

RECALL v.   flash, flash on, nail it down, rings a bell, it struck a note, all of a sudden it came to me, came to me that, came to me like it was yesterday.

RECANT v.   back off, dial back, go back on one's word, weasel out, worm one's way out, worm out of, welsh, renig, nig, back water, crawfish, crawfish out, eat crow, eat humble pie.

RECAPITULATE v.   recap, rehash, replay, go over the same ground, go the same round. See REPEAT.

RECAPTURE v.   reel one back in. See also REMEMBER.

RECEIPTS n.   take, take in, cash flow, revenue stream, bottom line, net, velvet, cush, get, gate, handle, melon. See INCOME.

RECEIVE v. snag, grab, cop, pull, pull down, get one's hands on, get hold of, latch on to. See GET. See also WELCOME.

RECEIVER OF STOLEN GOODS n. fence, neighborhood connection, shade, shifter (handler).

RECENT adj. today, contempo, newey, hot off the fire, hot off the griddle, hot off the press, just out, up to date, the latest. See NEW.

RECEPTIVE adj. pushover, ready. See also READY.

RECESS n. break, break-off, coffee break, breather, breathing spell, downtime, letup, five, ten, time-out, freeze, cutoff, layoff, happy hour.

RECESS v. put on hold, call time, take a break, take a breather, take five, take ten, take a smoke, break it off, break it up, drop, drop it, pigeonhole, shake, sideline.

RECESSION n. bust, hard times, bad times, bear market, bottom out, slide, rainy days, rainin', the big trouble (the 1930s). See DEPRESSION.

RECIDIVIST n. repeater, habitual, go back for seconds, two-time loser, three-time loser, four-time loser, glutton for punishment.

RECIPROCATE v. scratch one's back, you scratch mine and I'll scratch yours, make up for, pay one's dues, tit for tat, square.

RECITE v. get on a soapbox, spiel, spout, chew the scenery, stump. See ORATE.

RECKLESS adj. squirrely, harebrained, dingy, dingy dingy, flaky, kooky, foolheaded, sappy, screwy, pay no mind, any old way, any which way, fast and loose, helter-skelter, harum-scarum, devil may care, off the deep end, step off the deep end, out on a limb, play with fire, stick one's neck out, leave oneself wide open, go to sea in a sieve, go for broke, cowboy. See also CARELESS.

RECKLESS DRIVER adj. bonzai, squirrel.

RECKLESSLY adv. like crazy, like mad.

RECKON v. tot, tot up, tote, tote up, run down, tick off, count heads, count noses, count the house, cut ice, cut some ice, keep tab, keep tabs, dope out, figure in, figure out, take account of, take one's measure, reckon up, square.

RECKONING n. bad news, check, checkeroo, grunt, IOU, score, tab. See ACCOUNT.

RECOGNITION n. 1. strokes, cow sociology, pat on the back, pat on the head, PR, puff, puffing up, pumping up, rave, one's stock has gone up, plum (job, rank or title given). See COMMENDATION. 2. tumble, double take (sudden, second look), high sign. See also REALIZATION.

RECOGNIZE v. make, peg, tab, tag, make one, flash on, spot, nail, lamp, button down, finger, put the finger on, put one's finger on something, put down for, ring a bell, tumble to. See also UNDERSTAND, REMEMBER.

RECOLLECT v. flash, flash on, nail it down, rings a bell, it struck a note, all of a sudden it came to me, came to me that, came to me like it was yesterday.

RECOLLECTION n. flashback, flash on.

RECOMMEND v. steer, tout, plug, put next to, put on to, put one wise, tip, tip off, get behind, push, spread it around, post. See ADVISE.

RECOMMENDATION n. C.F. proposal, feeler, pass, proposition, tip, steer, bum steer, kibitz, flea in the ear, two cents' worth, plug, say so.

RECOMPENSE n. tip, toke (gambling), chip, cue, somethin', a little somethin'; subway, bus ride (5 or 10 cent tip); sweetener, grease, salve, palm oil, gravy, zukes. See also COMPENSATION.

RECOMPENSE v. 1. comp, cough up, ante up, put out, spring for, kick in, swing for bread, fork up, square, square things, sweeten the pot, tickle the palm, pay up, take care of. 2. chicken, schmear, grease, grease one's palm, oil, oil one's palm, fix, fix the alzo, put in the fix, piece one off, gaff, fit the mitt, put in the bag, put in the zingers, buzz, crack business, do business, see, see the cops, buy, buy off, reach, get at, get to. See PAY.

RECONCILE v. 1. cool, fix up, bury the hatchet, make up, make it up, kiss and make up, make matters up, patch things up, get together on, come together. See PACIFY. 2. come around, trade off, strike a happy medium, meet halfway, can't fight 'em join 'em, come to school, come to the party, don't make waves, fit in, when in Rome do as the Romans do. See CONFORM.

RECONDITION v. face-lift, retread, rehab, retrofit, fix up, doll up, spruce, spruce up, do, do up.

RECONNAISSANCE n. recon, recce, recco, look-see.

RECONNOITER v. recon, case, spy out, stake out, check around, look around, smell around, see what cooks, see what's going down, see what's coming down, see what's happenin'. See also INVESTIGATE.

RECONSIDER v. run that by one one more time, run through, go over, hash over, rehash, polish up, rub up, brush up. See REVIEW.

RECONVERSION n. switch, switch over, born again.

RECONVERT v. switch, switch over, see the light.

RECORD n. 1. comic book, funny book, the book on one, jacket, swindle sheet, track record, paper trail. See also DIRECTORY. 2. disc, platter, licorice pizza, manhole cover, side, wax, cylinder, demo (audition).

RECORD v.   can, tape, wax, cut a wax, cut a track, dub, lay it down, lay down some tracks.

RECORDING DEVICE n.   tap, wiretap, bug, tape, VCR.

RECORDING TERMS   bloop, tape, dub, mix, cut, cut a take, cut a side, make a take, charts, spin, side, thirty-three, forty-five, LP, single, Grammy (award), groove yard (storage).

RECORD SOUND n.   wow, flutter, hiss, rumble.

RECORD SPINNER n.   D.J., deejay, disc jockey, platter pusher.

RECOUNT v.   1. rehash, recap, play back, echo, run that by one once more, say again, chew one's cabbage twice. See REPEAT. 2. run down, run through, track, picture, unload, blab, let one's hair down, verbalize, lay it on one, put it on the street, let it all hang out, spit it out, let one's hair down, spin a yarn, break a story. See RELATE.

RECOUP v.   get out from under, get well, make well, make up for.

RECOVER v.   bounce back, make a comeback, snap out of it, get out from under, get well (monetarily), get over, be out of the woods, turn the corner. See IMPROVE.

RECREATION n.   rec, R. and R., fun and games, playtime, big time, high time, high old time, picnic, merry-go-round, field day, ball, laughs, lots of laughs, grins. See also ENTERTAINMENT.

RECRUIT n.   draftee, boot (Navy), rookie, tenderfoot, yardbird, chicken; barber bait, big Joe, big John, john, Johnny dogface, bimbo, bozo (WW II); plebe, Mr. DumbJohn (Nav. Acad.); Mr Dooley (Air Acad.), croot, dude, jeep, rubber sock, poggie. See also NOVICE.

RECRUIT v.   sign on, sign up, take on, call up, poggie.

RECRUITER n.   headhunter, people plucker, scout, talent scout.

RECTIFY v.   1. debug, doctor, fly speck, launder, scrub, clean up, pick up, shape up, fix up, go over, fiddle with. 2. make up for, pay one's dues, square, square up, square the beef. 3. straighten up and fly right, straighten out, clean up one's act, get on the ball, recalibrate, dial back, turn things around. See CORRECT.

RECTOR adj.   padre, the rev, Holy Joe, sky pilot, gospel ghee, sin hound, glory roader. See CLERGYMAN.

RECTORY n.   aquarium (Catholic).

RECTUM n.   ass, asshole, rear, rear end, brown hole, back way, exhaust pipe, Hershey bar route, little brown eyeball, crack. See ANUS. See also BUTTOCKS.

RECUPERATE v.   bounce back, make a comeback, snap out of it, pull out of it, get well (monetarily), pick up the pieces, be out of the woods, bottom out, be on the mend, turn the corner. See IMPROVE.

RECURRING adj.   string, roll, on a roll, run, streak, come again, row, chain, two-time, three-time, two-time loser.

REDECORATE v.   doll up, fix up, gussy up, spruce up, do, do up, redo, face-lift, retread, rehab.

RED-HAIRED adj.   red, rusty, carrot top, bricktop.

REDISTRICT v.   gerrymander, remap.

REDRESS v.   make up for, pay one's dues, square, square up, square the beef, recalibrate, dial back, turn around, turn things around, turn over a new leaf. See CORRECT.

REDUCE v.   cut, cut down, cut to the bone, nutshell, put in a nutshell, boil down, snip, trim, chop, get to the meat, cut back, roll back, low ball, dig in, tighten one's belt, downsize, leblang (theater ticket price), knock off, bump, bust, rif, bench. See also DIET.

REDUCTION n.   cutback, rollback.

REEKING adj.   stinko, stinking, stinky, whiffy, nosey, strong, loud (strong), high.

RE-ENLIST v.   re-up.

REEXAMINE v.   cool something over, check, check over, double-check, run it by one again, recap, rehash, hash over, go over, go over with a fine-tooth comb, go over the same ground, go the same round. See REVIEW.

REFER v.   ping pong (Medic. patient), reference.

REFEREE n.   ref, zebra, homer. See also ARBITRATOR.

REFERENCE n.   commercial, plug, source, resource.

REFERENCE POINT n.   checkpoint, where one is at, where one's head is at, P.O.V.

REFILL v.   hit, hit again.

REFINE v.   dink, tweak, butcher.

REFINED adj.   highbrow, hoity-toity, spiffy, classy, snazzy, posh, flossy, plush, ritzy, swanky, snarky, swellegant, nobby, blowed in the glass (hobo).

REFINERY n.   cat plant.

REFLECT v.   head trip, noodle, noodle it around, cool something over, stew, stew over, chew over, chew the cud, skull drag. See THINK.

REFLEX adj.   gut reaction, knee-jerk reaction, take, double take.

REFORM n. house cleaning, clean sweep, shake-up.

REFORM v. shape up, clean up, clean up one's act, get one's act together, get with it, get on the ball, turn over a new leaf, turn around, turn things around, switch, switch over, straighten up and fly right, go straight, straighten out, upgrade, make first rate, mat down, come along, come to school, hit the legit, go on the up and up, get religion, sprout wings, see the light, come to Jesus, hit the sawdust trail.

REFORMED adj. born again, got religion, newborn Christian, saw the light, a different person, a changed person.

REFORM SCHOOL n. college, juvey.

REFRAIN v. 1. take the pledge, take the cure, go on the wagon, go on the water wagon. 2. pass, pass up, sit out, sit on one's ass, sit on one's duff, give the go by. See ABSTAIN.

REFRESHER n. go juice, pick-me-up, pickup, shot in the arm.

REFRESHMENT n. bite, feed, nosh, snack, spread, drink, pick-me-up. See also FOOD, DRINK.

REFRIGERATOR n. fridge, frige, cooler, icebox, dugout, reefer.

REFUELING PLANE n. flying gas station, tanker, buddy store (Vietnam).

REFUGE n. hideaway, hideout, hole in, hole up, safe house, blowout center, ivory tower, den.

REFUGEE n. boat people, defector, D.P., displaced person.

REFUND n. kickback, give up, payola, drugola, gayola. See also RESTITUTION.

REFURBISH v. doll up, fix up, gussy up, spruce, spruce up, redo, rehab, retread, face lift.

REFUSAL n. nix, pass, turndown, no way José, like hell I will, cold shoulder, go-by, hard time (sexual). See DENIAL.

REFUSE n. gash, hogwash, junk, dreck, shit.

REFUSE v. nix, turn down, ding, not buy, piss on, brush off, fluff off, take the fifth (plead the Fifth Amendment right to refuse to answer), plead a five, stonewall. See REJECT.

REFUSE CREDIT v. lower the boom, cut off, cut up one's card.

REFUSED adj. nixed, burned, cut, dead, killed, turned down, put down, passed on, passed over, thrown over, left at the church, got it in the neck, kicked in the ass, punched out, out in the cold, feel adrift, thank you but no thank you.

REFUTE v. top, squelch, shoot down, shoot full of holes, poke full of holes, blow sky high, knock the bottom out of, knock the chocks out from under, knock the props out from under; burn, burn down, pass, pass on, pass by, throw out, turn thumbs down on, thumb down, kill.

REGAIN v. get out from under, get well, make well.

REGALE v. party, throw a party, give a party, put on a party, toss a party, have a get-together, have a do, have a ball, have a few grins, have lots of laughs, laugh it up, crack one up, break one up, fracture one, grab, tumul, panic, put away, wow, slay, kill, knock dead, knock them in the aisles, lay 'em in the aisles, have 'em in the aisles, get one's kicks, get one's jollies. See also AMUSE, ENTERTAIN.

REGARD v. eye, eagle eye, eyeball, beam, flash, flash on, spy, dig, read, lamp, pipe, rap, rumble, lay one's glims on, get a hinge, give the eye, get a load of, pipe. See SEE.

REGIMENTATION n. pecking order, down the line.

REGION n. territory, turf, hood, neck of the woods, stomping ground, ghetto, inner city, the jungle (crowded city), skid row, slum, zoo, high-rent district, slurb. See DISTRICTS.

REGISTER v. sign on, sign up, sign up for, weigh in.

REGISTRATION n. sign-up.

REGRESS v. backslide, rollback.

REGRET v. kick oneself, cry over spilled milk.

REGULATE v. pull the strings, pull the wires, pull things together, shape up, straighten up, deal with. See MANAGE.

REGULATION adj. up to code, G.I., according to the book, according to Hoyle, kosher, S.O.P.

REGULATIONS n. regs, by the numbers, by the book, chapter and verse, no-nos, bible (authoritative book).

REGURGITATE v. barf, puke, be sick, throw up, upchuck, urp, whoops, Ralph, Ralph up, talking to ralph on the big white phone, shoot one's cookies, flash one's cookies, blow one's lunch, the technicolor yawn, drive the porcelain bus. See VOMIT.

REHABILITATE v. rehab.

REHABILITATION n. rehab.

REHEARSAL n. call, dry run, run through, shakedown, shakedown cruise, tryout, workout, dress, blocking.

REHEARSE v. dry run, run lines, run through, walk through, take it from the top, tune up, hone, warm up, work out. See also PRACTICE.

REIGN v. head up, boss, helm, ride herd on, sit on top of, run, run things, run the show, be in the driver's seat, rule the roost. See MANAGE.

REIMBURSE v. square, square things, make up for, pay one's dues.

REIMBURSEMENT n. payoff, kickback. See also PAYMENT.

REINFORCE v. 1. boost, stroke, build up, pick up, lend a hand, hype, hold a brief for, go to bat for, stand up for, back up, carry one, prop, prop up. See SUPPORT. 2. beef up, soup up, punch up, heat up, hot up, hop up, jazz up, juice up, build up, add fuel to the fire.

REITERATE v. rehash, recap, recheck, double-check, check and double-check, come again, play back, ditto, echo, one more time, una mas, run that by one once more, say again, go over the same ground, go the same round, chew one's cabbage twice.

REITERATION n. recap, rehash, replay, playback, echo.

REJECT v. 1. eighty-six, adios, heave-ho, junk, throw away, throw out, throw on the junk heap, chuck, chuck out. See DISCARD. 2. pass by, pass on, pass up, nix, put down, turn down, turn thumbs down on, blackball, ice out, kill, burn, burn down, shoot down, not buy, not hear of, break with, blackball, cut, snip, zing, ding, piss on, shit on, drop, cold shoulder, high hat, dump, ditch, air, flush, brush off, fluff off, give one the fluff, send one to the showers, hand one his walking papers, give one the air, give one the gate, give one the wind, stay away from, swear off, kick in the ass, kick in the teeth, slap in the face, buck, hell no, like hell I will, thank you but no thank you, not touch one with a ten-foot pole.

REJECTED adj. nixed, burned, cut, dead, killed, turned down, put down, passed on, passed over, thrown over, left at the church, got it in the neck, kicked in the ass, punched out, out in the cold, feel adrift.

REJECTION n. nix, turndown, putdown, turndown, pass, pass on, ding, thumbsdown, no go, no dice, no way, no way José, nothing doing, you should live so long, the gate, bounce, grand bounce, kick in the ass, kick in the teeth, slap in the face, lumps, include me out, over my dead body, like hell I will, I'll see you in hell first, fubis (fuck you buddy I'm shipping out), brushoff, call-down, cold shoulder, cut, go-by, hard time (sexual), walking papers.

REJOINDER n. lip, sass, topper, talk back, back talk, snappy comeback, wisecrack. See ANSWER

REJUVENATE v. face lift, retread, rehab, doll up, spruce, spruce up, do, do up.

RELATE v. 1. run down, run through, track, picture, sing, spill, spill the beans, unload, bull, bullshit, throw the bull, shoot the bull, shoot the shit, shoot the bullshit, shoot, shoot the breeze, shoot the lemon, let one's hair down, sling the crap, fess, fess up, verbalize, put one in the picture, lay it on the line, lay it out for, let in on, let in on the know, let it all hang out, get it off one's chest, get it out of one's system, give with, give a pointer to, give one the word, break it to one, clue one in, break a story, spin a yarn. 2. connect, contact, have truck with, make up to, in, in with, run with, swing, swing with, be one of the boys. See COMMUNICATE. 3. stack up against, match up, hang (how does that hang?) hold a candle to.

RELATION n. 1. network, tie-in, hookup. 2. kin folk, kissin' cousin, shirttail kin, shirttail relatives, blood.

RELATIONSHIP n. tie-in, network, hookup. See ASSOCIATION.

RELATIVES n. folks, home folks, kin folk, kissin' cousin, shirttail kin, shirtail relatives, blood.

RELAX v. unlax, break, knock off, take a blow, take a break, take a breather, take five, take ten, take it easy, take time out, take the air out of the ball, at ease, neg, veg off, caulk off, catch forty winks, flake out, flop, goof off, recharge one's batteries, coast, cool it, cool out, eyes to cool it, don't sweat it, go with the flow, hang easy, hang loose, lay back, let go, let it all hang out, let it all happen, let it all out, mellow out, lighten up, ease up on, give some slack, go easy on, let up on.

RELAXED adj. cool, loose, loose as a goose, mellow, folksy, homey, haymish, laid back, let one's hair down. See CASUAL.

RELEARN v. brush up, go over, run through, take a refresher.

RELEASE n. 1. handout, the dope, the goods, scoop, leak, poop, poop sheet, skinny. 2. lifeboat, lifesaver, clemo, commute, spring, floater, forty-eight, forty-eighter, turnout, twenty-four, walkout, a D.O.R. (on one's own recognizance).

RELEASE v. 1. go easy on, let up on, wipe the slate clean, lifeboat, hand out clemo, commute, spring, put out on the street, turn out, bail out, get a floater, get hours, get a twenty-four. See FREE. 2. blow one's mind, leak, let go, let off steam, unlax.

RELEASED adj. out, back on the street, beat the rap, sprung, walked, let off, let go.

RELEASE FROM CUSTODY n. spring, turn out, floater, forty-eight, forty-eighter, twenty four, walk-out, a D.O.R. (on one's own recognizance).

RELEASE FROM CUSTODY v. spring, turn out, bail out, get a floater, get hours, get a twenty-four, put on the street, put on the pavement, put on the sidewalk, put on the bricks.

RELENT v.   lighten up, ease up on, give some slack, go easy on, let up on, fold, quit, cool it, cool out, lay back, hang loose, cave in, give up, give in, say uncle, cry uncle, pull in one's horns, go along with, let go, let it all hang out, let it all happen, mellow out. See also SOFTEN, RELAX, SURRENDER.

RELENTLESS adj.   bound, bound and determined, dead set on, hell bent on, stop at nothing, go for broke, hang in, hang tough, mean business. See DETERMINED.

RELEVANT adj.   right on, on the button, on the nose, on target, that's the ticket, just what the doctor ordered.

RELIABLE adj.   there, count on one, one who always delivers, one who always comes through, always there in a pinch, rock, Rock of Gibraltar. See TRUSTWORTHY.

RELIEF n.   light at the end of the tunnel, fix, quick fix.

RELIEVE v.   1. take a load off, take a load off one's mind, take the load off one's chest. 2. yank, pull.

RELIEVED adj.   breathe easy, cool, got it off one's chest, load off one's mind.

RELIGIOUS adj.   born again, got religion, knee bender, Jesus lover, Jesus freak, Mary, Holy Joe, Jasper, goody, goody-goody, goody two-shoes, scoutmaster.

RELINQUISH v.   swear off, give up, quit cold turkey, take the oath, drop, drop out, drop like a hot potato, opt out, back down, stand down, kiss good-bye, dump, cut loose, kick, ditch.

RELY ON v.   1. bank on, bet on, bet one's bottom dollar on, gamble on, lay money on. See BELIEVE. 2. ride on one's coattails, carry the load, carry the mail.

REMAIN v.   sit tight, stay put, stick around, squat, nest, bunk, hang, hang out, perch, put on hold, roost, hold the fort, freeze, deep freeze.

REMAINDER adj.   bottom of the barrel, leftovers, pot likker.

REMAINS n.   1. stiff, cold meat, dead meat, croppy, cage. 2. broken arm (table scraps). 3. leftovers, pot likker.

REMARK n.   crack, one's two cents worth, back talk, comeback, wisecrack.

REMARK v.   1. crack, spring with a crack, wise crack, mouth off. See SPEAK. 2. flash on, get a load of, pick up on, spot, take in, catch. See SEE.

REMARKABLE adj.   10, ten, super, smashing, gnarly, mega-gnarly, motherfucker (Obsc.), zero cool, wicked, nose cone, gilt-edged, splash, primo, world class, solid, greatest, fat. See EXCELLENT.

REMEDY n.   fix, quick fix.

REMEDY v.   1. debug, doctor, fly speck, launder, scrub, clean up, pick up, shape up, fix up, go over, fiddle with. 2. make up for, pay one's dues, square, square up, square the beef. 3. straighten out, clean up one's act, get one's act together, upgrade, recalibrate, dial back, turn things around. See CORRECT.

REMEMBER v.   flash, flash on, nail it down, rings a bell, it struck a note, all of a sudden it came to me, came to me that, came to me like it was yesterday.

REMEMBRANCE n.   flashback, flash on.

REMISS adj.   pay no mind, looking out the window, out to lunch, asleep at the switch, asleep on the job, daydreaming, woolgathering, slapdash, any old way, any which way, by halves. See CARELESS.

REMODEL v.   face lift, retread, redo, rehab, retrofit, doll up, fix up, gussy up, spruce, spruce up, do, do up.

REMONSTRATE v.   pitch a bitch, beef, sound off, rain, push out one's lips. See COMPLAIN.

REMOTE adj.   1. cold, cool, cool cat, on ice, dog it, dog up, laid back, offish, standoffish, put on airs, stuck up, uppity. See ALOOF. 2. gone (from reality), turned off, out to lunch, spaced out. 3. far piece, long chalk, boondocks, boonies, tullies, on the dance floor but can't hear the band, to hell and gone, God knows where, middle of nowhere. See FAR.

REMOVAL n.   ax, boot, bounce, bum's rush, kicking out, old heave-ho, pink slip, the gate, executive fallout (business), walking papers, walking ticket. See DISMISSAL.

REMOVE v.   1. junk, chuck, chuck out, adios, eighty-six, 86, deep six, heave-ho, throw away, throw overboard, throw on the junk heap. See ERADICATE. 2. bounce, kick out, boot out, drum out, give one the old heave-ho, adios one, send packing, show the door, give the gate, give one his walking papers, give 'em the 1-2-3, ice out, lock out (labor dispute), wash out, shut out. See EJECT. 3. liquidate, wipe out, sanitize, sterilize, scratch, waste, off, knock off. See KILL. 4. drag, drag down, take down (bet).

REMOVED adj.   1. unfrocked (any profession), drummed out, turned off, dropped, washed out, washed up, all washed up, scratched, scrubbed, adiosed, eighty-sixed, offed, wasted. 2. gone (from reality), far out, out of it, out to lunch, play it cool, spaced out.

REMUNERATE v.   shell out, come down with, cough up, ante up, plank up, pony up, dish it out, spring for bread, fork up, post, pay off, pay up, pay to the tune of, do business. See PAY.

REMUNERATION n.   1. take, take home, bread, sugar, bacon, bring home the bacon, eagle shit, peanuts, coffee and cakes (small); fogey (Mil.). 2. walking-around money, cash on the nail, hush money, street money, grease, schmear, under the table, on the take, juice. 3. tip, toke (gambling), chip, cue, somethin', a little somethin'; subway, bus ride (small tip), palm oil, gravy, zukes. 4. strokes, brownie button (facetious), feather in one's cap, plum, what's in it for one. See COMPENSATION.

REMUNERATIVE adj. going, going concern, paid off, sweet, in the black.

RENDEZVOUS n. 1. date, heavy date, blind date, gig, double date, meet; miss a meet, stand one up, stand one on a corner (fail to keep a); zero hour, creep, triff, treff (secret). 2. love nest, spot, matinee, noonie, one night stand, quickie, your place or mine.

RENEGADE n. rat, rat fink, double-crosser, Benedict Arnold, fifth columnist, quisling, snake, snake in the grass. See also TRAITOR.

RENEGE v. fudge, back off, dial back, go back on one's word, weasel out, worm one's way out, worm out of, welsh, renig, nig, back water, crawfish, crawfish out, eat crow, eat humble pie.

RENEW v. doll up, fix up, gussy up, spruce, spruce up, do, do up, redo, face lift, retread, rehab.

RENEWAL adj. born again, fresh start, face lift, retread.

RENEWED COMMITMENT n. born again.

RENOUNCE v. 1. swear off, take the pledge, get on the wagon, get on the water wagon. 2. drop out, opt out, dump, throw over, toss over, throw overboard, walk out on, wash one's hands of, change one's tune, change one's song, chuck, cop out, sell out, leave flat, ditch, run out on, shake, ding, piss on, put down. See also ABJURE. 3. heave-ho, hell no, like hell I will, nix, shit on, shove it, stick it, stow it, stick it up one's ass, shove it up one's ass, kiss good-bye, take some hide and hair.

RENOVATE v. doll up, fix up, gussy up, spruce, spruce up, do, do up, face lift, retread.

RENOWNED adj. celeb, star, superstar, name, number one, a somebody, w.k. (well known), face, in the limelight, make a splash, page-oner, monster, big name, biggie, big league, major league, hooper-dooper. See CELEBRATED, CELEBRITY.

RENT PARTY n. shake, percolator.

REORGANIZATION n. house cleaning, sweep, clean sweep, sweep with a broom, shake-up, hatchet man (reorganizer).

REPAIR v. fix up, doctor, fiddle with, face lift, retread, debug, redline (Mil.), easy fix (simple).

REPAIR SHOP n. fix-it shop.

REPARATION n. make up for, make good, square things, pay one's dues.

REPAST n. chow, chow time, feed, bite, snack, snack time, takeout, BBQ, barbecue, cookout, tailgate party, brunch, do lunch, din din, square meal, blue plate, black plate (soul food), Chinx (Chinese), potluck, coffee and, sit-down dinner. See MEAL.

REPAY v. square, square things, square a beef, make up for, pay one's dues, scratch one's back, you scratch mine and I'll scratch yours. See also PAY.

REPEAL v. scrub, nix, call off, call all bets off, renig, kill, shoot down, shoot down in flames, wipe out, blow the deal, forget it, get off the hook, X out, kibosh, put the kibosh on, zap, kayo, KO, wash out, opt out, back out, back out of, backpedal, back water, weasel out, worm out of, crawl out of, wangle out of, crawfish out, pull the plug, pull in one's horns, draw in one's horns, draw in one's claws, cut loose, stand down, quit cold, leave flat, throw over.

REPEALED adj. scrubbed, killed, shot, shot down, shot down in flames, washed out, wiped out, all bets off, all off, kaput, zapped.

REPEAT v. rehash, recap, recheck, double-check, check and double-check, again, come again, play back, ditto, echo, do like, go like, make like, one more time, una mas, run over, run that by one once more, say again, go over the same ground, go the same round, chew one's cabbage twice.

REPEATED adj. string, run, streak, row, straight (seven in a row, seven straight), chain, come again, two-time, two-time loser, three-time.

REPEATER adj. backslider, two-time loser. See also RECIDIVIST.

REPEL v. 1. gross out, turn off, scuzz one out, give one a pain, give one a pain in the neck, give one a pain in the ass. 2. brush off, cut, high hat, cold shoulder, cool, cool off, cool down, put down, turn down, turn thumbs down, not buy, not hear of, kick one in the ass, kick one in the teeth, slap one in the face, no go, nothing doing. See also REJECT.

REPELLED adj. grossed out, turned off, ech, eeeooo, gives one a pain in the ass. See DISGUSTED.

REPELLING adj. gross, grossed out, grody, grody to the max, scank, icky, yecchy, yucky, turn off. See DISGUSTING.

REPERCUSSION n. fallout, reaction, chain reaction, flak (bad), follow up, follow through, can of worms, spin-off, waves, feedback, kick back, shit hit the fan. See RESULT.

REPERTOIRE n. book, rep, routine, schtick.

REPERTORY n. routine, rep, rep show, rep company (The.), shtick, gag, stunt, bit, chaser, afterpiece, stand-up comedy, dumb act (without words), hoke act.

REPLACE v. pinch hit for, sub, sub for, swap places with, sit in, stand in, back up, fill in, take over, front for, ring, ring in, take out, step into the shoes of.

REPLACEMENT n. spare, backup, sub, stand-in, fill-in, pinch hitter, pinch runner, off the bench, bench warmer, ringer, second string, third string, switcheroo, dog chaser (R.R.).

REPLACEMENT DEPOT n. repple depple, rep dep, reppo depot.

REPLICA n. carbon, clone, ditto, dupe, mimeo, stat, xerox, repro, lookalike, workalike, flimsy, chip off the old block.

REPLICATE v. 1. dupe, xerox, carbon, clone, mimeo, ditto, knock off, stat, repro. 2. act like, do, do like, go like, make like, mirror, take off as, do a take-off, play the ———— (affect a role). 3. pirate, knock off, steal one's stuff, take a leaf out of one's book.

REPLY n. vibes, feedback, comeback, snappy comeback, sass, lip, back talk, crackback, wisecrack, cooler, knee-jerk reaction (expected). See also RESPONSE.

REPLY v. answer back, shoot back, come back at, get back to one, be in touch with one, feedback, field the question, sass, squelch, top, crack. See ANSWER.

REPORT n. rundown, handout, the dope, the goods, picture, scoop, poop, ABC's, blow by blow, make, break, beat, earful, ear duster, chip, hash, haymaker, hot shot, hot wire; kick in the ass, shot in the ass (bad); are you ready for this?, page-oner, the latest, what's happenin' what's going down, latrine rumor, scuttlebutt. See also NEWS.

REPORT v. spread it around, pass the word, drum, call, trumpet, track (narrate a sequence of events), debrief, break a story, weigh in. See also ANNOUNCE.

REPORTER n. columnist, anchor, anchorman, anchorwoman, newscaster, leg man, news hen, cub, stringer, ink slinger, scrivener, scribe, pen driver, pen pusher, pencil driver, pencil pusher, scratcher.

REPORTER, NEWSPAPER n. scribe, scrivener, columnist, stringer, leg man, news hen, cub, pen driver, pen pusher, pencil driver, pencil pusher, scratcher, ink slinger.

REPORTER, TV n. anchor, anchorman, anchorwoman, newscaster, leg man, stringer.

REPOSSESS v. repo.

REPRESENT v. 1. rep, front for, stand in for, pinch hit for, sub, carry the water. 2. picture, track, run through, run down.

REPRESENTATIVE adj. 1. rep, hired gun, front. 2. nature of the beast, that's one all over, just like one, what you see is what you get, WYSIWYG.

REPRESENTING v. repping, fronting for, standing in for.

REPRESS v. 1. ice, put on ice, cool, cool off, cool out, cool down, bottle up, cork, cork up, box in, get one in a box, hog-tie, tie up, jam up, bring to a screaming halt, gridlock, lock up, put a lock on, put a stopper in, black out, put the lid on, keep the lid on, keep buttoned up, keep under one's hat, keep under wraps, put a half nelson on, put the chill on, put the damper on, put the kibosh on, queer, kill, spike, squash, squelch, scrub, gag, muzzle, shut up, can it, ding, zing, nix, hush up, throw a monkey wrench into, throw cold water on, throw a wet blanket on, cut off one's water, turn off one's water, put off, turn off, put on hold, hold down, strong-arm, put the arm on, twist one's arm, pressure, put under pressure, put the heat on, put down, crack down on, clamp down on, shut down, sit on, put the scare on, throw a scare into, put the screws on, take care of, kid out of, talk out of, cramp one's style, hedge in, not go off the deep end. 2. bleep, blue pencil, cut, decontaminate, launder, sanitize, sterilize, clean up. 3. keep it down, soft-pedal, dummy up, dry up, clam up, close up like a clam, pipe down, shut one's trap, shut one's mouth, shut one's face, button up, button one's lip, sit on, decrease the volume, mum's the word, drink one's beer. See also SILENCE.

REPRESSED adj. hung up, uptight, tight-assed, square.

REPRIEVE n. anchor, lifeboat, lifesaver, clemo, commute, spring.

REPRIEVE v. let it go, let up on, let one off this time, lifeboat, hand out clemo.

REPRIMAND n. gig, comeuppance, rap, rap on the knuckles, slap on the wrist, piece of one's mind, bawling out, calling down, jacking up, going over, ragging, grooming, what for, hell to pay, hard time, assbite. See ADMONITION. See also SCOLDING.

REPRIMAND v. chew out, eat out, bawl out, ream out, light into, lower the boom, have one on the carpet, have one on the mat, call on the carpet, call down, dress down, come down on, rap one's knuckles, slap on the wrist, tell off, give what for, give a piece of one's mind, give one the dickens, give one hail Columbia. See REBUKE.

REPRINT n.   dupe, xerox, carbon, mimeo, stat, ditto; knock off (illegal).

REPRISE v.   come again, one more time, uno mas.

REPROACH v.   chew out one's ass, bawl out, ream, cuss out, lay out, sit on, light into, jaw, jawbone, rake, trim, call to task, call down, dress down, attend to, give what for, give a going over, give one the devil, give one his comeuppance, rag on. See REBUKE.

REPROBATE n.   sleazeball, bad egg, heel, shit, turd, stinker, louse, rat, creep, black sheep, rotter, rounder. See SCOUNDREL.

REPRODUCE v.   clone, carbon, dupe, mimeo, stat, xerox, ditto; pirate, knock off, steal one's stuff (illegally). See COPY.

REPRODUCTION n.   clone, ditto, dupe, mimeo, stat, xerox, carbon, carbon copy, repro, flimsy, look-alike, fake, not what it's cracked up to be, twin, chip off the old block. See COPY.

REPRODUCTIVE FLUID n.   come, cum, cream, wad, load, gism, jisum, jizum.

REPROOF n.   comeuppance, rap on the knuckles, slap on the wrist, piece of one's mind, calling down, jacking up, going over, ragging, what for, hell to pay, hard time. See ADMONITION.

REPROVE v.   trash, zing, zap, knock, pan, slam, slug, slog, hit, blast on, eat out one's ass, read one out, jump on one's shit, bad-mouth, poor-mouth, ding, give a going over, give a black eye, give one his comeuppance, needle, give one the needle, give one the raspberry, let one have it, cut down to size, sock it to one, stick it to one, swipe at, snipe at, bitch bitch bitch, take a dim view. See SCOLD.

REPUBLICAN PARTY n.   GOP, Grand Old Party.

REPUBLICANS n.   G.O.P., Good Old Party, Grand Old Party, Gypsy Moths, Ripons.

REPUDIATE v.   nix, be agin, dump, break with, fly in the face of, flush, wash one's hands of. See REJECT.

REPUDIATED adj.   burned, cut, dead, feel adrift, killed, thrown over, passed over, passed on, put down.

REPUDIATION n.   nix, slap in the face, stick it up your ass, forget you, over my dead body, you should live so long, not a chance. See DENIAL.

REPUGNANCE n.   allergy to, no use for.

REPUGNANT adj.   creepy, sleazy, sleazeball, slime bucket, maggoty, bad case of the uglies, gross, grody, beastly. See UNDESIRABLE. See also UGLY.

REPULSE n.   nix, turndown, thumbs down, no way José, nothing doing, kick in the ass, kick in the teeth, slap in the face, lumps, brush off, cold shoulder, go by, the gate, hard time (sexual). See REJECTION.

REPULSE v.   heave-ho, nix, put down, brush off, fluff off, kick in the teeth. See REJECT. 2. gross out, turn off, scuzz one out, give one a pain, give one a pain in the neck, give one a pain in the ass.

REPULSIVE adj.   1. creepy, stinky, sleazy, sleazeball, slime bucket, maggot, spastic, funky (Bl.), cruddy, dorky, earth pig, grimbo, gross, grody, off-putting. See UNDESIRABLE. 2. pig, mole, dog, airedale, animal, beast, plug-ugly, bad case of the uglies, hagged out, fart face, pruneface, homely as a mud fence. See UGLY. See also UNDESIRABLE PERSON.

REPUTABLE adj.   Christian, true Christian, mensch, pillar of the church, salt of the earth. See VIRTUOUS.

REPUTATION n.   rep.

REQUEST v.   put in for, hit, hit up, touch, bite, bum, hustle, promote, make, mooch, schnor, score, sponge, nick, burn, pivot, pling, knock, make a touch, put the touch on, put the bite on, put the bee on, put the sleeve on, hold out for, pop the question, whistle for (but won't get). See also BEG.

REQUESTS n.   commercials (band or orchestra).

REQUIRE v.   hurting for. See also DESIRE.

REQUISITION v.   put in for, dibs on something. See also APPROPRIATE.

RESCIND v.   scrub, nix, call off, call all bets off, renig, forget it, X out, wash out, back out of, backpedal, back water, weasel out, worm out of, crawl out of, wangle out of, crawfish out, pull the plug, pull in one's horns. See REPEAL.

RESCUE v.   bail one out, save one's neck, save one's bacon, give one a break, get one out of hock, get one off the hook, spring, pull something out of the fire, pull one's chestnuts out of the fire.

RESEARCH n.   cut and try, legwork, R and D., fishing expedition.

RESEARCH v.   cut and try, give it a go, fool around with, play around with, mess around.

RESEARCH CENTER n.   think tank, lab, chem lab.

RESEARCHER n.   numbers cruncher, mad doctor.

RESEMBLANCE n.   birds of a feather, like of, likes of, look-alike, peas in a pod, two of a kind, ringer, dead ringer, spitting image, carbon, carbon copy, double.

RESEMBLE v. favor, double.

RESENT v. feel sore, have one's nose out of joint, rubbed the wrong way, put off by.

RESENTFUL adj. sore, uptight, have one's nose out of joint, beefing, crabby, cranky, grousing, grouchy, bugged, pissed, pissed off, a bug up one's ass, on one's ear, get up on one's ear. See also DISCONTENTED.

RESENTMENT n. rise, fog, a bug up one's ass.

RESERVATION n. string, string to it, catch, joker, kicker, fine print, fine print at the bottom, with a grain of salt. See RESTRICTION.

RESERVE n. stash, stache, plant, drop, ace in the hole, nest egg. See also ASSETS.

RESERVE v. 1. stash, stache, ditch, duck, plant, squirrel, squirrel away. 2. hold (hold the mayo), hold out on. 3. book, put a hold on, lay away. See SAVE.

RESERVE ASSET n. ace in the hole, ace up one's sleeve, on a string.

RESERVE, IN adj. depth, deep, on a string, string one along.

RESERVE OFFICERS TRAINING CORPS n. ROTC, Rotacy, Rot corps, Rot see, Rotasie.

RESERVED adj. 1. cool, cool customer, cold fish, ice in one's veins, icicle, clam, tight-lipped. See also SHY. 2. booked, held, laid away.

RESERVED SEAT TICKET n. hard ticket.

RESERVES n. bankroll, nut, backing, budget, nest egg, rainy day, sock, mattress full. See ASSETS.

RESIDE v. bunk, bunk out, hang out, crash, nest, perch, roost, squat, locate, park, hole up, hang up one's hat, hang up one's shingle. See INHABIT.

RESIDENCE n. pad, crash pad, box, cave, condo, co-op, coop, domi, dommy, digs, roof over one's head, hole, homeplate, rack, roost. See HOUSE.

RESIDENT n. cliff dweller (apt.), dug in, squatter, local yokel, home guard, townie.

RESIDUE n. leftovers, pot likker.

RESIGN v. ankle, quit cold, quit cold turkey, drop, bow out, chuck, chuck it, fold, give up, hang it up, throw in the towel, throw in the sponge, throw over, toss over, walk out on, wash one's hands of, pull the plug, punk out, pull the pin, pull out, cave in, cry uncle, chicken out, drop out, give up the ship, kiss good-bye, binch, pack in, pack it in, knock off, stand down, cry off, come off, drag it, hang up one's spurs, run out on, walk out on, bail out, opt out, cut loose, kick, swear off, cop out, bag it.

RESILIENCE n. bounce, vim and vigor, zip, staying power.

RESILIENT adj. roll with the punches, snap back, bounce. See also CHEERFUL.

RESIST v. 1. be agin, go agin, buck, stonewall, cross, lock horns with, face off, go one on one, turn thumbs down on. See OPPOSE. 2. cross, fly in the face of, make my day, go on make my day, hang tough, take one on, call one's bluff, stand up and be counted, not take lying down, stick to one's guns. See CONFRONT. 3. buck, tangle with, tangle ass with, bump heads with, cross swords with, lock horns with, put up an argument. See FIGHT. 4. beef, bitch, bleed, make a stink, gripe, griping, pop off, gritch, sound off, squawk, put up a squawk, kvetch, bellyache, blast, crab, cut a beef. See COMPLAIN.

RESISTANT adj. hard-nosed, a wall, stonewall, like talking to the wall, like water off a duck's back, like getting blood from a turnip.

RESOLUTE adj. hang tough, dead set on, stick to one's guns, mean business, mean serious jelly, no bird turdin', be out for blood. See DETERMINED.

RESOLUTION n. all the right moves, pay dirt, the ticket, the nod, the call, quick fix, band-aid (temporary, too little). See RESOLUTION.

RESOLVE v. chill, dope, dope out, pan out, figure out, crack, lick, deal with, make a deal, iron, iron out, nail down, cinch, clinch, unzip, work through, hit it on the nose.

RESORT n. tourist trap, hideaway, hideout, fat farm, banana belt, Borscht Belt.

RESOURCE n. bankroll, nut, nest egg, rainy day, sock, mattress full, kitty, stake, backing, budget, ace in the hole, ace up one's sleeve (hidden), stuff, the goods, basics. See ASSETS. See also MONEY.

RESPECTED adj. okay people, touted, highly touted, score, aces with, in with, daddy (The.).

RESPITE n. five, take five, time, time out, downtime, break, coffee break, breather, breathing spell, freeze, piss call (Mil.), happy hour, letup, layoff.

RESPOND v. 1. be turned on to, feel for, feel in one's bones, feel in one's guts, hear one, get in touch, have a funny feeling, have heart, have a hunch, have good vibes, have vibes. 2. answer back, talk back, shoot back, come back at, get back to one, be in touch with one, feedback, field the question, crack. See ANSWER.

RESPONSE n. vibes, feedback, comeback, snappy comeback, sass, lip, back talk, crackback, wisecrack, kick, kickback, mug (comic), take, take it big, double take, hit, cooler, knee-jerk reaction (expected), gut reaction.

RESPONSIBILITY n. where the buck stops, rap, take the rap, one's ass, one's neck, albatross, albatross around one's neck, can, carry the can, holding the bag, holding the sack. See also DUTY.

RESPONSIBLE adj. 1. minding the store, on the hook, carry the load, on one's back, taking care of business, TCB. 2. there, count on one, right guy, rock, Rock of Gibraltar, straight arrow. See TRUSTWORTHY.

REST n. 1. break, coffee break, lunch break, breakoff, cutoff, layoff, letup, blow, breather, breathing spell, five, ten, time out, downtime, goof-off time, time to burn, time to kill, one's own sweet time, piss call (Mil.), snooze, bunk fatigue (WW II), R and R. 2. leftovers, pot likker, bottom of the barrel.

REST v. unlax, knock off, take a blow, take a break, at ease, flake out, kick it back, lay back, let it all hang out. See RELAX.

RESTATE v. recap, rehash, go over the same ground, go the same round. See REPEAT.

RESTAURANT n. eatery, pit stop, drive-in, hamburger heaven, burger joint, short-order joint, grease joint, ham joint, fast-food joint, McDucks, Mickey-D's, chop suey joint, Chinks, hash house, chop house, soup house, slop house, sloppy Joe, hideaway, ham and eggery, coffee pot, beanery, bean wagon, chuck wagon, dog wagon, greasy spoon, grease ball, grease trough, bistro, water hole, noshery, hashery, hash foundry, doughnut foundry, doughnut factory, doughnut house, doughnut joint, goulash, chew and choke, cook shack, caf, quick and dirty, Coney Island.

RESTAURANT TERMS draw one (coffee), BLT (bacon lettuce and tomato), hold (hold the mayo), burn one (coke), stretch it (large), hang a draw (large root beer), squeeze one (orange juice), fish eggs (tapioca pudding), sweep up the kitchen for one (hash), Adam and Eve on a raft (poached eggs on toast), wreck 'em (scramble eggs), eighty-six (out of item), on wheels, to go (take out).

RESTITUTION n. square things, pay one's dues, make up for, make good. See also REFUND.

RESTLESS adj. jittery, jumpy, strung out, twitty, bundle of nerves, yantsy, antsy, antsy-pantsy, ants in one's pants, itchy, in a dither, on edge, rarin' to go, on pins and needles, on tenterhooks. See ANXIOUS.

RESTLESSNESS n. ants, ants in one's pants, antsy, antsy-pantsy, fantobs.

RESTORATIVE v. go juice, pick-me-up, pickup, shot in the arm.

RESTORE v. doll up, fix up, gussy up, spruce, spruce up, do, do up, face lift, retread, rehab, pick up the pieces. See also FIX.

REST PERIOD n. five, take five, take ten, time, time out, break, coffee break, breather, breathing spell, freeze, piss call (Mil.), happy hour, letup, goof off, fuck-off, layoff.

RESTRAIN v. cool, cool off, cool out, cool down, keep the lid on, bottle up, cork, cork up, box in, get one in a box, cuff, hog-tie, tie up, jam up, gridlock, lock up, put a lock on, put a stopper in, bring to a screaming halt, put a half nelson on, put the chill on, kill, spike, throw a monkey wrench into, throw cold water on, throw a wet blanket on, cut off one's water, turn off one's water, put off, turn off, hold, hold down, strong-arm, put the arm on, twist one's arm, pressure, put under pressure, put the heat on, shut down on, sit on, sit down on, put the scare on, throw a scare into, put the screws on, take care of, kid out of, talk out of, cramp one's style, hedge in, not go off the deep end. See also HINDER.

RESTRAINED adj. 1. cool, cool and collected, laid back, dealing with, got a handle on it, hip, ice man, in charge, in the driver's seat. See CALM. 2. hung up, square, tight-assed, uptight, iced, chilled, bottled up, corked up, hog-tied. See JAILED.

RESTRAINT n. 1. hang up, catch, lock, excess baggage, stumbling block, foot dragging, glitch, joker, one small difficulty. 2. juice, string, rope, weight. See HINDRANCE. See also PROHIBITION.

RESTRICT v. 1. ice, put on ice, put away, send up. See JAIL. 2. cool down, hold down, hold back, hang up, bottle up, cork up, box in, hog-tie, gridlock, lock up, put a half nelson on, hedge in. See RESTRAIN.

RESTRICTED adj. 1. hog-tied, iced, chilled, bottled up, corked up, held down, held back, hung up, in a box, boxed in, shut down, fenced in, hedged in. 2. top secret, eyes only, for your eyes only, hush-hush, inside info, on the QT, under wraps, keep buttoned up. See SECRET.

RESTRICTION n. no-no, off limits, out of bounds, closed down, closed up, hang-up, catch, lock, excess baggage, stumbling block, foot dragging, glitch, joker, one small difficulty, string to it, kicker, fine print, fine print at the bottom, with a grain of salt.

REST ROOM n. can, john, Men's, Ladies, ladies' room, women's room, girls' room, little girls' room, powder room, men's room, boys' room, little boys' room, reading room, library, head, facilities, amenities, throne room, where the dicks hang out. See TOILET.

RESTUDY v. brush up, go over, polish up, rehash, rub up.

RESULT n. chain reaction, waves, flak (bad), upshot, score, blow-off, spin-off, payoff, punch line, fallout, follow-up, follow through, kickback, shit hit the fan, verdict isn't in on that, can of worms, bottom line.

RÉSUMÉ n. brag sheet.

RESURGENT adj. born again.

RETALIATE v. get, get even with, settle the score, settle one's hash, square accounts, fix one's wagon, give one tit for tat, get back at, turn the tables on, give one a dose of one's own medicine.

RETALIATION n. tit for tat, eye for an eye, get even.

RETARD v. bog, bog down, lose steam, back off, let up, hang up, hold up, bring to a screaming halt, flag one, gum up the works, shut off, shut down, shut 'em down, close off, choke, choke off, put on the shelf (business use), put on the back burner, stall, drag one's heels, drag one's foot, saddle with, weigh down, hang like a millstone round one's neck, throw a monkey wrench into the works, upset one's apple cart, down one, take one down, take care of, take the wind out of one's sails, crimp, put a crimp in, cramp one's style.

RETARDED adj. retardo, pinhead, lamebrain, birdbrain, harebrained, rattlebrain, scatterbrain, dopey, dumbo, dumdum, dumbbell, dumb Dora, dumbhead, blockhead, fathead, bonehead, knucklehead, numbskull, rattleweed, yo-yo, sappy, not all there, soft in the head, weak in the upper story, gorked. See also FEEBLE-MINDED.

RETELL v. rehash, recap, come again, play back, ditto, echo, one more time, una mas, run that by one once more, say again, go over the same ground, go the same round, chew one's cabbage twice. See REPEAT.

RETICENT adj. clam, clammed up, dried up, dummied up, garbo, tight-lipped, close-mouthed.

RETIRE v. 1. crash, flake out, flop, turn in, crawl in, get some shut eye, get forty winks, grab a few winks, hit the hay, hit the pad, hit the nod, hit the sack, sack, sack up, sack out, pad out, make some z's, knock a nod, knock the pad, go night-night, go bye-bye, go beddy-bye. 2. get the gold watch, hang up the gloves, hang it up, call it quits. 3. get the hell out, make oneself scarce, vamoose, highball, dog it, skip, skip out, powder, take a powder, take a run-out powder, fade, fade out, do a fade.

RETIRED adj. on the shelf, out of circulation, out to pasture, over the hill, passed it, a once was, has-been, hung up one's spurs, old-timer.

RETOOL v. switch, switch over, upgrade, modernize.

RETORT n. back talk, comeback, crack, crackback, wisecrack, dirty crack, smart crack, nasty crack, snappy comeback, topper, cooler, lip, parting shot. See ANSWER.

RETORT v. talk back, back talk, shoot back, snappy comeback, come back at, come right back at, sass, squelch, top, crack. See ANSWER.

RETRACT v. welsh, renig, nig, back off, call off, call off all bets, dial back, forget it, go back on one's word, weasel out, worm one's way out, worm out of, back water, crawfish, crawfish out, eat crow, eat humble pie, eat one's words, eat one's hat.

RETREAT n. blowout center, ivory tower, hideaway, hideout, den, place to hole up, hole in, hole up, safe house.

RETREAT v. 1. fold, quit, cave in, give in, go along with, opt out, back out, back out of, backpedal, back water, back slide, weasel out, crawl out of, pull the plug, pull in one's horns, draw in one's horns, draw in one's claws, cut loose, stand down. 2. bail out, turn chicken, chicken out, check out, drop, drop out, cut out, cut and run, tail between one's legs, get the hell out, run like a scared rabbit, do a vanishing act, fade, fade out, do a fade, fade away, drift away. See GO.

RETRENCH v. dig in, roll back, cut corners, tighten one's belt, pull together, circle the wagons.

RETRIBUTION n. comeuppance, just desserts, what for, what one has coming, tit for tat, eye for an eye.

RETROGRESS v. backslide.

RETURN n. 1. ball's in your court, call back, call in, comeback (merchandise to store). 2. net, velvet, pay, gravy, bottom line, cush, get, gate, handle, peanuts (small), take, take in. See INCOME.

RETURN v. 1. bounce back, double back, back at you, call in, show up, dust 'em off (after absence). 2. clean up, clear, score, cash in on, make a good thing of, make a killing, make it big, make hay. See EARN.

RETURNED n. returnee.

REUNITE v. fix up, patch up, patch things up, make up, make it up, kiss and make up, make matters up.

REUSE v. rejase, recycle.

REVEAL v. 1. flash (also used in cards), debunk, blow one's cover, blow the lid off, give the show away, go public. See EXPOSE. 2. talk, leak, tip off, tip one's hand, let the cat out of the bag, put hep, put hip, put it on the street, come out of the closet, open up, fess, fess up, croon, sing, sing like a canary, snitch, squeal, spill, spill the beans, have a big mouth, blab, break, break a story. See CONFESS.

REVEL n. bat, bender, binge, ball, bash, bust, beer bust, buzz, drunk, jag, caper, go, tear, toot, blowout, hoopla, whoopee, jamboree, wingding, shindig, brannigan, rip, merry-go-round, paint the town red, on the town, carousing, growler rushing, hell around, hell bender, high jinks, whooper-dooper, big time, high time, high old time, larking, field day. See also PARTY.

REVEL v. 1. let go, let loose, cut loose, make whoopee, whoop it up, go on a rip, go on a tear, go on a toot, go on a bat, go on a bender, go on a low-flying mission, go on a bombing mission, binge, go on a binge, go on a bust, go on a spree, go on R. and R., lark, go on a lark, go places and do things, step out, paint the town, paint the town red, go on the town, go on the merry-go-round, go the dizzy rounds, carry on, hit the high spots, pub-crawl, run around, kick up one's heels, fool around, horse around, monkey around, kid around, hell around, raise hell, raise a rumpus, raise a storm, raise the devil, raise the deuce, raise the dickens, raise the roof, tear up the pea patch, blow off the lid, cut capers, cut up, cut a dido, cut a few touches, cut up a few touches, live a little, live it up, make a day of it, make a night of it, down the primrose path, see the sights, step out. 2. groove on, have a ball, balling, funk, grok, dig, dig one or something, dig the most, rat fuck, R. F., get some grins, adore, be big on, get off on, get high on, get naked (not necessarily sexual), flip, flip for, flip over, freak out on, get a charge out of, get a kick out of, get a lift out of, get a boot out of, get a bang out of, drop the bomb, just for kicks, just for laughs, knock oneself out, have oneself a time, eat up, eat it up, savvy, with it, kvell (Yid.).

REVELATION n.   the latest, what's happenin', what's going down, leak, catch, break, beat, blow by blow, scoop, poop, chip, dope, earful, ear duster, clue, tip, cue, eye-opener, joker, kicker, bolt from the blue, bolt out of the blue, hash, haymaker, hot shot, hot wire; kick in the ass, shot in the ass (bad); are you ready for this?, page-oner, handout, showdown. See also SURPRISE.

REVELER n.   good-time Charlie, playboy, man about town.

REVENGE n.   tit for tat, eye for an eye.

REVENGE v.   get even with, settle, settle with, settle the score, settle one's hash, settle accounts, square accounts, square, square things, fix, fix one's wagon, give one tit for tat, come back at, get back at, dish it back, hit back at, get hunk, kick back, stick it to one, stick it in and break it off, turn the tables on, give one what is coming to one, give one a dose of one's own medicine, give back as good as one got.

REVENUE n.   cash flow, revenue stream, net, velvet, pay, payoff, gravy, bottom line, cush, split, get, gate, handle, melon, strength, take, take in. See INCOME.

REVEREND n.   padre, the rev, Holy Joe, sky pilot, preacher man, fire proofer, shepherd, glory roader. See CLERGYMAN.

REVERIE n.   trip, head trip, mind trip, castle in the air, fool's paradise, pipe dream, stare into the middle distance, pie in the sky.

REVERSAL n.   1. about face, turn around, switcheroo, flip-flop, bottom out. 2. bath, take a bath (financial).

REVERSE v.   flip-flop, back track, backpedal, double back, put the cart before the horse, turn the tables, renig.

REVERSED adj.   ass over elbows, arsy-varsy, ass backwards, bass ackwards, back asswards, topsy-turvy, catawampus.

REVERSED COLLAR n.   dog collar.

REVERSE ORDER n.   ass backwards, bass ackwards, back asswards, arsy-varsy, flip-flop.

REVERSE SIDE adj.   flip side, other side of the coin.

REVERT v.   about face, backslide, flip-flop, fall off the wagon.

REVIEW n.   blurb, mention, notice, pan (bad), write-up. See also CRITICISM.

REVIEW v.   1. cool something over, chew over, chew the cud, check, check out, check over, cop, crack one's brains, hammer, hammer away at, bat it around, kick around, knock around, run it up the flagpole, run it by one again, run through, debrief, recap, rehash, hash over, go over, go over with a fine-tooth comb, go over the same ground, go the same round, revisit, brush up, polish up, rub up. 2. rave, pan, boo, take down, put down, come down on, come down hard on, rip, skin alive, lay out, needle, give one the needle, Bronx cheer, slam, bad-mouth, poor-mouth, trash, zing, zap, knock, rap, sock it to one, swipe at. See also CRITICIZE.

REVIEWER n.   aisle-sitter, Monday morning quarterback, nitpicker, zapper.

REVILE v.   rank out, dump on, rake over the coals, scorch, blister, tear into, lambaste, slam, rag, rag on, give a black eye, swipe, roast, skin alive. See SCOLD. See also RIDICULE.

REVISE v.   dial back, recalibrate, blue pencil, cut, debug, fly speck, launder, scrub, clean up, tighten, go over. See EDIT.

REVIVAL n.   retro.

REVIVAL MEETING n.   shout.

REVIVE v.   come around, come round, come back, come from behind, bounce back, make a comeback, pull out of it, regroup, snap out of it, turn the corner, be out of the woods, get back in shape, get a lift, pick up, perk up, brace up.

REVOKE v.   scrub, nix, call off, call all bets off, back out of, backpedal, back water, Indian gift. See REPEAL.

REVOKED adj.   scrubbed, killed, shot, shot down, shot down in flames, washed out, wiped out, all bets off, all off, kaput, zapped.

REVOLT v.   1. kick over, kick over the traces, drop out, opt out, cop out, get out of line, rock the boat, make waves, leave the beaten path. 2. gross out, turn off, scuzz one out, give one a pain, give one a pain [somewhere].

REVOLTED adj.   grossed out, scuzzed out, turned off. See DISGUSTED.

REVOLTING adj.   gross, grody, grody to the max, godawful, stinky, rotten, sleazy, sleazeball, bad case of the uglies, gummy. See DISGUSTING.

REVOLUTIONARY n. reb, Yankee Doodle, commie, red, ratfuck.

REVOLUTIONARY adj. avant-garde, breaking new ground, breaking new snow, new wrinkle, newfangle, newfangled, newfangled contraption.

REVOLVER n. artillery, cannon, blaster, gat, piece, iron, rod, snubby, snub nose, Saturday night special, bean shooter, peashooter, popper, pop, equalizer, difference, speaker, mister speaker, persuader, convincer, hardware, heater, heat, Betsy, roscoe, mahoska. See GUN.

REWARD n. fringe benefit, goodies, perk, perks, strokes, brownie button (facetious), feather in one's cap, plum, sweetening, sweetener, grease, salve, palm oil, gravy, zukes, what's in it for one, tip, toke (gambling), chip, cue, somethin', a little somethin'; subway, bus ride (5 or 10 cent tip). See also BRIBE.

REWARD v. stroke, sugarcoat, slip one a buck, take care of, oil one's palm, piece one off.

RHAPSODIZE v. carry on over, make a to-do over, take on over, fall all over, go on about, whoop it up for, turn on.

RHETORIC n. hot air, balderdash, gobbledygook, big talk, tall talk.

RHEUMATISM n. rheumatics, rheumatiz.

RHINOCEROS n. rhino.

RHODE ISLAND Little Rhody, Mini State, Ocean State, Plantation State.

RHYTHM n. beat, bounce, downbeat, brown off (break).

RHYTHM AND BLUES n. R and B.

RIBALD adj. blue, dirty, filthy, feelthy, low down and dirty, rough, raunchy, raw, purple, salty, off base, off-color, out of line. See OBSCENE.

RIBALDRY n. scuz, smut, sleaze, cussing, dirty talk, porn, X-rated, hot stuff, jack-off material. See OBSCENITY.

RIBS n. slats.

RICE n. weevil.

RICE WINE n. Saki, bamboo juice (WW II).

RICH adj. the haves, up in the bucks, in the bucks, in the chips, rollin' in it, rolling in dough, money to burn, stinking rich, well-heeled, plush, flush, loaded, made one's pile, uptown, upscale. See WEALTHY.

RICHES n. high on the hog, on top of the heap, on a bed of roses, in clover, on Easy Street, in the lap of luxury, the life of Riley, on velvet. See WEALTH.

RICKETY adj. rocky.

RID v. 1. 86, eighty-six, junk, adios something, adios it, adios one, fire, heave-ho, throw on the junk heap, toss onto the scrap heap, scrap, chuck out. See DISCARD. 2. give one the heave-ho, give one the bum's rush, give one the brush, give one the brush off, give the mitten, give the hook, gate, give the gate, give the air, give 'em the hook, give 'em the 1-2-3, bounce, chase, duke out, boot out, kick out, kick it, muscle out, throw out on one's ear, French walk, send packing, show the door, lug, roust, put the skids to, skid (rid self of undesirable persons). See EJECT. 3. chill, put the chill on, dust off, fluff off, kiss off, California kiss-off, kiss good-bye, chop out, take one for a ride. See KILL. 4. can, dump, ditch, shake, shake one. See DISCHARGE.

RIDDLE n. sixty-four dollar question, twister, teaser, sticker, floorer, stumper, mind-boggler, hard nut to crack, tough nut to crack, tough proposition.

RIDE n. lift, commute, hitch, pickup, joyride, spin, whirl, run, burnout (high speed), airing, Sunday drive.

RIDE v. cruise, roll, tool around, bomb around, hitch a ride, thumb a ride, hitchhike, go for a spin, go for a whirl. See DRIVE.

RIDE A HORSE v. up, on top, in the irons, back in the saddle, beefsteak (badly), fag along (fast).

RIDE FREIGHT TRAINS v. ride the rails, ride the rods, hit the rods, grab a handful of rods, grab an armful of box cars, hop a ride, hop a freighter, hop a rattler, catch a rattler.

RIDER n. drop, line load (taxi), deadhead (free), seatcover.

RIDICULE n. put-on, putdown, rank out, dump, dirty dig, crack, slam, swipe, jab, dig, comeback, parting shot, brickbat.

RIDICULE v. jive, kid, kid around, needle, rag, razz, rib, roast, jolly, josh, ride, pan, pooh-pooh, guy, put on, put down, take down, slap at, swipe at, dig at, do a number on, flip on the bird, give one the bird, give one the Bronx cheer, give one the razzberry, make sport of, pull one's leg. See also TEASE.

RIDICULOUS adj. ridic, jerky, nerky, nutty, wacky, squirrely, harebrained, daffy, goofy, slappy, slaphappy, whip silly, foolheaded, horse's ass, horse's collar, horse's neck, horse's tail, sappy. See also FOOLISH, IMPOSSIBLE.

RIFLE n. artillery, equalizer, difference, persuader, convincer, hardware, Winchester, pop gun, B.A.R., flintlock, flint stick, aught two, breechloader (19th Cent.), blowpipe, long rod, peashooter, smokepole, smoke wagon, slim, stick, boom stick, tool, noise tool, works, business, iron betsy, boom boom (WW II), prod, crowd-pleaser (police), scatter-gun, bear insurance. See also GUN.

RIFLE v. grab, smash and grab, rip, rip off, take, tip over. See LOOT.

RIFLEMAN n. dogface, G.I. doughfoot, B.A.R. man, bolo (unskilled, Army 1930).

RIGGED adj. in the bag, it's in the bag, fix is in, boat race (horse race).

RIGHT adj. 1. on the nose, on the money, right on, righteous, right you are, right as rain, righto, hit the nail on the head, fuckin' A, amen, right stuff, keerect, reet, cooking on the front burner, according to Hoyle. See CORRECT. 2. hold up, stand up, go, hold water, hold together, stick together, hold up in the wash, wash, fly, no buts about it, no ifs ands or buts. 3. right wing, neo-con, extreme right, rightist, hard right, radical right, Birchite, John Bircher, Black Shirt, Brown Shirt, Klu Kluxer, lunatic fringe, McCarthyism, Posse Comatatus, storm trooper. See CONSERVATIVE.

RIGHT v. 1. debug, doctor, fly speck, launder, scrub, clean up, pick up, shape up, fix up, go over, fiddle with. 2. make up for, pay one's dues, square, square up, square the beef. 3. straighten out, go straight, clean up one's act, make first rate, recalibrate, dial back, turn around, turn things around. See CORRECT.

RIGHTEOUS adj. candy ass, Christian, goody-goody, goody two-shoes, nice Nellie, Crabapple Annie, bluenose. See VIRTUOUS.

RIGHTFUL adj. legit, kosher, card-carrying, honest to God, twenty-four carat, on the level, on the up and up, hold water, hold up in the wash. See LEGAL.

RIGHT-HANDED adj. righty.

RIGID adj. 1. locked in, head in concrete, set in concrete, stuck in concrete, buried in concrete, chiseled in stone, solid as a rock, rock-ribbed, brick wall, ironclad, dig in one's heels, hold the line, hang tough, tough nut to crack, bullheaded, dead set on. See STUBBORN. See also STRICT. 2. crab, chicken shit, by the book, stiff, tough, rough. See PARTICULAR.

RING n. 1. band, handcuffs (wedding), hoop, rock, sparkler. 2. mob, clan, tribe, troupe, bunch, crowd, combination, combo, rat pack, syndicate, outfit, those one runs with. See ASSOCIATION.

RIOT n. flap, fuss, free-for-all, brawl, all hell broke loose, to-do, row, stir, big stink, run-in, rhubarb, rowdydow, rumble, rumpus, ruckus, ruction, shindy, shivaree, commo, dustup, hoopla, hassle, fofarraw, mix-up, kick-up, snarl-up, wingding, raise cain, raise sand, fuzzbuzz, haroosh, big scene, gin, branigan, donnybrook, hey rube, dance, hoedown, jump, jackpot, stew. See also FIGHT.

RIOT v. kick over, kick over the traces. See also LOOT.

RIOTOUS adj. on a tear, raising a rumpus, raising a ruckus, raising the roof, kicking up a row, kicking up a shindy, off base, out of line, out of order.

RISE v. 1. take off, perk up, pick up, bottom out, go through the roof, uptick (small). 2. rise and shine, roll out, turn out, pile out, hit the deck, show a leg, drop your cocks and grab your socks, keep bankers hours (late). See AWAKEN.

RISK n. flier, flyer, flutter, header, plunge, spec, stab, on (on a horse), shot in the dark, brinksmanship. See WAGER.

RISK v. take the action, take a flyer, play, get down, lay it on the line, put it on the line, put up, put up or shut up, put one's money where one's mouth is, put on the spot, tackle, take on, take a plunge, plunge, play the market, take a header, have a fling at, give a fling, take a fling at, have a go at, give a go, give a whirl, take a crack at, take a whack at, make a stab at, have a shot at, jump off the deep end, stick one's neck out, stick one's neck in the noose, play into one's hands, go out on a limb, go the limit, go whole hog, go on the hook for, go for the long ball, shoot the works, ball the jack, make book, book the action, shoot one's wad, grift, on the grift, stake, backstrap, cheesebox, parlay, cap (add illegally), lay off (relay bet), spitball, chance it, skate on thin ice. See also WAGER.

RISKY adj. dicey, iffy, rocky, touchy, touch and go, long shot, chancy, fat chance, not a prayer, on a wing and a prayer, on slippery ground, on thin ice, out on a limb, go out on a limb, on the spot, hanging by a thread, off the deep end, go off the deep end, step off the deep end, go for broke, leave oneself wide open, play with fire, hot potato, one could get burned, too hot to handle, a snowball in hell, hasn't got a Chinaman's chance, go to sea in a sieve.

RISQUÉ adj. blue, dirty, filthy, off base, off-color, out of line, X-rated, jiggle, jiggly, spark. See also OBSCENE.

RIVAL n. opposish, oppo, opposite number, bad guy, bandit, buddy-buddy (sarcasm), buddy fucker, crip, meat, me and you, angries, dark horse (unknown).

RIVAL v. jockey for position, scramble for, go for, go after, in the hunt. See also EQUAL.

RIVALRY n. competish, rat race, dog eat dog, a regular jungle out there, do or die, one on one.

RIVER n. drink.

RIVET n. bullet.

ROAD n. pike, rip strip, dragway, main drag, main stem, main line, back alley, back street, straightways, super slab, pavement, the bricks, byway, trail, stroll, groove, aisle, bowling alley, world's longest parking lot, four-lane parking lot, roller coaster, kidney buster, washboard, boardwalk (rough), licorice stick, skid row.

ROAD HAZARD n. pothole, chuckhole, church hole.

ROAM v. bum, bum around, drift, follow one's nose, traipse, knock about, bat around, take to the road, hit the road, globe-trot, trek. See WANDER.

ROAR v. blast, holler, holler out.

ROB v. rip off, mug (rob and beat), appropriate, boost, scrounge, pinch, promote, buzz, cop, kipe, liberate, lift, palm, moonlight requisition, snatch, snitch, swipe, snipe, glom, glaum, glahm, glue, skim, hijack, heist, hoist, high grade, elevate, make, make off with, burn, annex, borrow, bag, nip, snare, stick up, kick over, tip over, knock off, knock over, shoot a jug, put up, root, put the arm on, take off, pluck, put a hand in the till, put a hand in the cookie jar, have one's hand in the cookie jar, loid, make an entry, make an in, push in, penetrate, blow a safe, burgle, clip a joint, crack a crib, slough, cold slough, crack a safe, hot slough, jimmy, shack, work in a bank and take home samples, give one a haircut, take to the cleaners, sting, score, clip, crash, cream, clout, charge, jackroll, hustle, kife, crook, crab, crib, cabbage, steal one blind, hook, hooky, maverick, nick, move, salvage, smooch, go south with something, fall (unsuccessful).

ROBBER n. punk, holdup man, stickup man, mugger, lush diver, lush roller (of drunkards); prowler, crook, gonif, operator, safecracker, booster. See THIEF, BURGLAR.

ROBBERY n. rip-off, snatch, snitch, caper, heist, grab, filch, pinch, lift, job, hustle, boost, stickup, holdup, holdup job, stickup job, liberation, annexation, moonlight requisition, knock-over, break-in, push-in, crashing in joints, pushing joints, crib crime, crib job, cream, weed (from employers), mugging, cowboy job (amateur), coffee-and-cake time (right time and place), hoist, stand, jug heist, jug rap, hijacking, owl job, prowl, on the prowl, safeblowing, safecracking, second-story work, shack, sting, cattle lifting, cattle rustling. See also BURGLARY, SAFE OR VAULT.

ROBBERY COMMAND v. hands up, stick 'em up, hold 'em up, get 'em up, reach, reach for the ceiling, hang your nose on the wall, belly the wall, belly up, dance, elevate.

ROBOT n. mobot, steel-collar worker, cybernaut, droid.

ROBUST adj. 1. in the pink, fit as a fiddle, in good shape, got the horses to do it, powerhouse, bull, built like a brick shithouse, muscle man, he-man, hulk, hunk, tiger, Turk, strong as a lion, strong as an ox, strong as a horse. 2. zippy, zappy, snappy, peppy, live, wicked, husky, hefty, beefy, full of piss and vinegar. See STRONG. See also HEALTHY.

ROCHESTER, MINNESOTA Doctor Town.

ROCK n. alley apple, ground apple, ground biscuit, Irish confetti, love letter (thrown).

ROCKET n. bird, mouse (small); screaming meemie (small, Army use), vehicle, Roman candle.

ROCKET BOMB n. doodlebug, bumblebomb, buzzbomb.

ROCKET EMERGENCY BUTTON n. chicken switch, chicken button, egads switch, egads button.

ROCKET FUEL n. plasma, lox.

ROCKET LAUNCH n. countdown, blast-off, insertion, moon shot, shot.

ROCKET LAUNCHER n. Minnie Mouse launcher, mousetrap.

ROCK 'N' ROLL adj. R and R, R 'n' R, fish music.

RODS n. macaroni.

ROGUE n. hooligan, booger, bugger, black sheep, cutup, scalawag, bounder, rotter, rounder, bad news, bad egg, bad 'un. See SCOUNDREL.

ROLE n. act, bit, game, piece, spiel, stint, whatever one is into.

ROLE, THEATER n. star, fat part, villain, hero, heroine, juvenile, bit, bit player, bit part, walk-on, spear carrier, one-side part, super, extra, atmosphere, scenery chewer, top banana, second banana, third banana, baggy-pants comic, straight man.

ROLL CALL n. head count, nose count.

ROMAN CATHOLIC n. papish, papist, papistic, RC, Romish.

ROMAN COLLAR n. dog collar.

ROMANCE n. fling, affair, carrying on, hanky-panky, holy bedlock, a thing together, a relationship, playing around, goings-on. See also AFFAIR.

ROMANIAN n. Romaniac.

ROMANTIC adj. syrupy, drippy, soapy, soppy, soupy, tear-jerker, gushing, hearts and flowers, corny, off the cob, mushy, schmaltzy. See SENTIMENTAL.

ROMANTICISM n. deep sugar, glop, hearts and flowers, schmaltz, mush, slush, slop, goo, sob story, tear-jerker.

ROMANTICIZE v. talk through one's hat, build castles in the air, build castles in Spain, look at the world through rose-colored glasses.

ROMP v. fool around, kid around, hell around, cut up, kick up one's heels, whoop it up, let loose, go on the town. See REVEL.

ROOF n. tar beach.

ROOK v. screw, shaft, frig, hose, rim, rip off, jerk one around, dick one around, fuck one over, jive, shuck, shuck and jive, fleece, flam, flimflam, burn, bilk, clip, con, chisel, gouge, gyp, stiff, sting, sucker, hold up, hype. See CHEAT.

ROOKED adj. fell for, fucked over, suckered, sandbagged, been had, taken, stuck, aced out, snookered, shafted, got a haircut, screwed. See CHEATED.

ROOM n. 1. elbowroom, room to swing a cat. 2. pad, crash pad, cinch pad, box, flop, joint, cave, den, crib, cubby, cubbyhole, go-down, balloon room (marijuana), rack, birdcage, heave, hot bed, padhouse, scatter, setup, walk-up, turf. See also APARTMENT.

ROOMMATE n. roomie, roomy, bunkie, chum, old lady, old miss, old man, O.M., wife. See also FRIEND.

ROOT BEER n. black cow, fifty-five.

ROOT BEER SODA n. black cow, root beer float.

ROSTER n. head count, nose count. See also LIST.

ROSTRUM adj. soapbox, stump, bally stand (circus).

ROT v. go to pot, go downhill, use it or lose it. See DETERIORATE.

ROTTEN adj. gross, stinking, strong, high, loud. See also CORRUPT.

ROUÉ n. player, high liver, operator, heavy hitter, lech, dirty old man, sport, swinger, rounder. See LECHER.

ROUGH adj. 1. mean, hairy, tough, tough customer, roughneck, hard-boiled egg, ballsy, bad guy, bad actor, hooligan, commando, welcome to the NFL. 2. cheap, loud, loudmouth, loudmouthed, foul mouth, foul-mouthed. See TOUGH. See also DIFFICULT.

ROUNDABOUT adj. go round the barn, went by way of, long way, long way home.

ROUSE v. 1. craze, bug, fire up, key up, steam up, stir up, work up, trigger, rabble-rouse, make waves, needle, go on make my day, ask for it, rile. See INCITE. 2. heat up, pep up, wake up, zip up, buck up, turn on the heat, run a temperature, get hot under the collar, jazz, jazz up, juice, send, grab, open one's nose. See EXCITE.

ROUT n. beating, whipping, licking, trimming, shellacking, trashing, smearing, clobbering, embarrassment, shutout, washout, disaster, upset, shuck, total shuck, comedown. See DEFEAT.

ROUT v. bash, trash, bury, blank, skunk, murder, kill, trounce, swamp, scuttle, shellack, bulldoze, roll over, torpedo, meatball, beat all hollow, finish, blow one out of the water, drub, larrup, whomp, whip, wipe, total, cream, zap, paste, kick ass, shut out, wipe up the floor with, wipe off the map. See DEFEAT.

ROUTE n. 1. groove, rut. 2. beat, the bricks (hobo, police, union), run. 3. pike, rip strip, dragway, super slab, pavement, the bricks, byway, trail, stroll, groove, aisle, bowling alley, four-lane parking lot, roller coaster, kidney buster, washboard, boardwalk (rough), short cut, beeline.

ROUTINE n. same old shit, SOS, shtick, sked, grind, daily grind, groove, channels, cut and dried, G.I., red tape, donkey work. See also ACT, AVERAGE.

ROVE v. bum, bum around, drift, float, follow one's nose, hopscotch, knock around, bat about, trek. See WANDER.

ROVER n. bum, floater, gad, gadabout, globe-trotter. See also VAGRANT.

ROW n. baldheaded man's row, crotch row (row A, theater). See also ARGUMENT, FIGHT.

ROW v. sky an oar.

ROWDINESS n. rowdydow, rowdy-dowdy, a rhubarb.

ROWDY adj. hell-raising, rambunctious, rootin'-tootin', roughhouse, hoopla, rowdy-dowdy, cowboy, loudmouth, ziggy, harum-scarum, off base, out of line, out of order.

ROWDY n. bullyboy, bucko, hellcat, hell-raiser, hellion, terror, holy terror. See also THUG, VILLAIN.

RUBBISH n. gash, hogwash, junk, dreck, shit.

RUDE adj. fresh, cheeky, sassy, snippy, short, smart alecky, smart ass, brassy, lippy, gally, chutzpadik, cocky, out of line, off base, cut, cold shoulder, give one the business, roll over one. See INSOLENT.

RUDIMENTARY adj. ABC's, three r's, basic, primo. See BASIC.

RUDIMENTS n. ABC's, three R's, nuts and bolts. See BASICS.

RUE v. kick oneself, cry over spilled milk.

RUFFIAN n. mug, mugger, gorilla, ape, bodyguard, pug, heavy, goon, bullyboy, bucko, roughneck, tough cookie, bruiser, ugly customer. See THUG.

RUFFLE v. get to, discomboberate, discumbobulate, rattle one's cage, throw into a tizzy, fuddle, put one on a crosstown bus, stump, floor, put off, flummox. See CONFUSE.

RUG n. wall-to-wall.

RUGGED adj. 1. uphill, mean, heavy, hairy, murder, pisser, bitch, son of a bitch, SOB, tough one, tough proposition, ballbuster, large order, no picnic, heavy sledding. See DIFFICULT. 2. hairy, tough, tough customer, roughneck, hard-boiled, ballsy, enforcer, commando, welcome to the NFL. 3. gutsy, gutty, nervy, spunky, tough it out, cool hand, beefy, hairy, hefty, husky, mean, strong as a horse, strong as a lion, strong as an ox, wicked. See TOUGH.

RUIN n.   wasteland. See also FAILURE.

RUIN v.   1. trash, total, cream, torpedo, kill, ax, sink, smash up, pile up, wrack up, take apart, break the lease, blue ruin, blow sky high, put out of commission. See DESTROY, WRECK. 2. ding, wing, tweak, total, louse up, mess up, muck up, make hash of, snafu. See DAMAGE. 3. settle one's hash, put in the toilet, kibosh, put the kibosh on, fix, fix one's wagon, poke full of holes, do, do a number on one, do in, get, finish, finish off, cook one's goose, shoot down, shoot down in flames, clip one's wings.

RUINATION n.   belly up, go belly up, go under, chapter 7, chapter 11, chapter 13, close the doors, in the tub, take a bath, the skids, on the skids, hit the skids.

RUINED adj.   1. gutted, queered, busted, dinged, totaled, gone, cooked, sunk, shot, flubbed, kaput, on the fritz, down, on downtime, on the blink, on the bum, out of action, no-go, run down, had it, glitched, gremlins, queered, bobbled, bitched, bitched up, buggered, buggered up, wracked up, screwed up, fouled up, fucked up, fucked, loused up, gummed up, balled up, bollixed up, messed up, hashed up, mucked up, fouled up, all fucked up, all fouled up, fubar (fouled up beyond all recognition), fubb (fouled up beyond belief), fumtu (fouled up more than usual), tuifu (the ultimate in foul-ups), nabu (nonadjusting ball-up), sapfu (surpassing all previous foul-ups), snafu (situation normal all fouled up), susfu (situation unchanged still fouled up), tarfu (things are really fouled up), down the tube, down the drain, down the toilet, in the toilet, done for, done in, gone to the dogs, gone to pot, gone to wrack and ruin, gone to bad, gone to hell, gone to the devil, gone to perdition, gone to glory, up in smoke. See also DESTROYED. 2. flat, broke, flat broke, busted, totaled, cleaned out, on one's ass, on the rocks, down and out, down to one's last cent, down to one's last penny, in dire straits, on the rims, go to the wall. See DESTITUTE. See also BANKRUPT.

RULE v.   sit on top of, run, run things, run the show, hold the reins, lay down the law, be in the driver's seat, take over, crack the whip, rule the roost, keep under one's thumb. See MANAGE.

RULES n.   by the book, by the numbers, chapter and verse, no-no's, bible (authoritative book).

RUM n.   myrrh.

RUMANIAN n.   Rumaniac.

RUMINATE v.   brainstorm, head trip, use one's head, noodle, noodle it around, stew over, chew over, rack one's brains, figger. See THINK.

RUMMAGE v.   beat the bushes, leave no stone unturned, look all over hell, look high and low, search high heaven, shake, shake down, toss, turn inside out, turn upside down.

RUMMY TERMS   run (consecutive order), knock, schneider, blitz (win all the points), a laydown.

RUMOR n.   scuttlebutt, talk, grapevine, clothesline, back-fence talk, earful, latrine rumor, wire, hot wire, vanilla. See GOSSIP.

RUMP n.   buns, fanny, ass, behind, bottom, bum, butt, can, moon, tail, keister, derriere, prat, rump, seat, rear end, tushy, tuchis, duff. See BUTTOCKS.

RUMPLED adj.   messed up, mussed up, messy, mussy, sloppy, grubby, scuzzed, scuzzed up, beat up.

RUN v.   1. jog, joggin', cut ass, haul ass, bag ass, barrel, barrel-ass, tear-ass, shag-ass, stir one's stumps, nip off, tear off, tear out, dig out, light, light off, light out, get going, highball, trot along, hightail, make tracks, hop it, hoof it, hotfoot, hotfoot it, smoke, rabbitfoot, greyhound, leg, leg it, step, step along, step it, get to steppin', knees pumpin', pick 'em up and lay 'em down, locomoting, move, pedalling with both feet, scramble, hit the grit, scratch gravel, pack the mail, motor. 2. split, take off, fuck off, hightail, hotfoot, run like a scared rabbit, step on it, step on the gas, cut and run, cut out, get git, take off in a cloud, take off in a cloud of sour owl shit, take off like a big-ass bird, take off like a B.A.B., smoke, haul it. See GO. 3. run things, run the show, pull the strings, mastermind, head up, boss, helm, ride herd on, be in the driver's seat, be in the saddle, take the conn. See MANAGE. 4. politick, press the flesh, stump, take the stump, stump the country, hit the campaign trail, whistle-stop, take to the hustings, shake hands and kiss babies, ring doorbells.

RUN AGROUND v.   pile up (boat).

RUNAWAY n.   hot, lammister, wanted.

RUNDOWN adj.   beat up, ratty, tacky, frowzy, fruit, dog eared, used up, in a bad way, ramshackle. See also UNHEALTHY, TIRED.

RUNNING START adj.   hit the ground running.

RURAL COMMUNITY n.   jerktown, jerkwater town, tank town, Hickville, South Succotash, boondocks, boonies, sticks, stix, bushes, bush league, pumpkin, wide place in the road, tall timbers. See SMALL TOWN.

RUSE n.   angle, dodge, twist, switch, stunt, scenario, game plan, game, little game, shenanigans, curveball, booby trap. See STRATEGEM.

RUSH n.   rush act, bum's rush, blitz, blitzkrieg.

RUSH v.   hustle, shake a leg, roll, tool, fire up, hotfoot, barrel-ass, tear-ass, step on the gas, open 'er up, put on the afterburners, get the lead out of one's ass, get cracking, go like greased lightning, go like a big-assed bird, streak, eat up the road. See SPEED. See also GO.

RUSSIA Russky, Iron Curtain, behind the Iron Curtain, the original borscht belt.

RUSSIAN n. comrade, Roosky, Russky, Ruskie, red, tovarich, Moscovite.

RUSSIAN PLANE n. Mig.

RUSSIAN SATELLITE n. sputnik, muttnik.

RUST n. cancer.

RUSTIC n. hillbilly, hick, plow jockey, country boy, country cousin, hayseed, hay shaker, cornfed, rube, peckerwood (Southern), hecker, wahoo, yahoo, brush ape. See YOKEL.

RUT n. daily grind, grind, groove, hang-up, same old shit, SOS, cut and dried, red tape.

RUTHLESS adj. cutthroat, go for the jugular, killer instinct, mean machine, dog eat dog, hatchet job, take no prisoners, it's a regular jungle out there. See also CRUEL.

S

S n. Sierra, sugar.

SABOTAGE v. torpedo, crab, take out, blue ruin, blow sky high, do, do one in, do in, dutch, screw up the works, queer, queer the works, throw a monkey wrench into the works, toss a monkey wrench into, throw a monkey wrench in the machinery, throw a wrench in the machinery, put a spoke in one's wheels, put something out of action, put out of commission, put the skids under one, gum up, gum up the works, foul up, fuck up, wrack up, louse up, mess up, muck up, ball up, bollix, bollix up, bugger, bugger up, jim, pickle, mess with, do a number on, do in, deep six (evidence). See also DISABLE.

SACRAMENTO, CALIFORNIA Sac, Sacto.

SAD adj. blue, in the dumper, down in the mouth, tear-jerker, hurting, in pain, gloomy Gus, sad sacky. See UN-HAPPY.

SADDEN v. drag, turn one off, bum out, down, bring one down, damper, put a damper on, faze, throw cold water on, throw a wet blanket on, act like a wet blanket. See DEPRESS.

SADDLE n. pimple.

SADISTIC adj. S, SM, into SM, into leather.

SADNESS n. blahs, blah-blahs, blues, blue devils, blue funk, funk, bummer, downer, down trip, letdown, dolefuls, dismals, dumps, mumps, mopes, mokers, mulligrubs, tsuris, heartache.

SADOMASOCHISM n. SM, S and M, B/D (bondage and discipline), C/P (corporal punishment), D/T (dominance training), heavy leather, into domination, into leather, into submission, nice and nasty, R/S (rough stuff), Sadie-Maisie, slaves and masters; water sports, showers, golden showers (urinating on partner), brown showers (defecating on partner).

SAD SONG n. tear-jerker, weeper, blues.

SAD STORY n. sob story, tear-jerker, weeper, downer.

SAFARI n. snofari (snow).

SAFE adj. home free, safe and sound, coast is clear, cuchee, cushy, sitting pretty, buttoned down, buttoned up.

SAFE n. box, crib, coffin, gopher, jug, keister, pete, pete box, pocket, sock, trap (hidden).

SAFE BURGLARY n. heavy, heavy time, box work, taking boxes, cracking cribs, knocking off peters, peter racket, busting petes, pete job, pete work, the rip.

SAFE-DEPOSIT BOX n. damper.

SAFEGUARD v. ride shotgun for, shotgun.

SAFE OPENER n. safecracker, boxman, heavy G, heavy man, jug heavy, mechanic, gopher, pete blower, peteman, peterman.

SAFE-OPENING DEVICE n. can opener, hard ass, ripper, stick (blow); pull the box, punch the box.

SAFE SITE n. deep cover, safe house.

SAFETY BELT n. scare strap, submarine belt.

SAGACIOUS adj. cool, tuned in, all woke up, sharp, shark, smoothie, whiz, have smarts, street smart, foxy, have savvy, have one's head screwed on right, wise to, hip, in the picture, on the beam. See SHREWD.

SAGE adj. beard, big think, deep, double dome, pundit, savvy, have the smarts, tool, power tool, cereb, got it all together, got one's boots on, know what's what. See INTELLIGENT.

SAIL n. rag, skyscraper.

SAIL v. gunkhole, gunkholing (inlet sailing), give her beans.

SAILING TERMS hike out, hiking board, hiking seat, hiking stick, hiking strap, tack, reach, cruise, jibe, a bone in her teeth (foamy bow wave), rooster tail.

SAILOR n. mate, shipmate, gob, swab, swabbie, swabber, bluejacket, jack, jacky, jack afloat, jack tar, tar, salt, old salt, sea dog, water dog, bullet bait (untrained), cannon fodder, feather merchant (office job), flange face, flat foot (not common), geep, home guard (married), sand pounder, lobscouser, limey, limejuicer (English), OD, AB, shellback, barnacle back, yachtie.

SALABLE adj. hotcake, hot item, hot ticket.

SALACIOUS adj. dirty, blue, purple, X-rated, raunchy, raw, hot, heavy, hot stuff, steamy, off-color, low-down. See OBSCENE.

SALAD n. grass, rabbit, rabbit food.

SALAMI n. horse cock, donkey dick (Mil.).

SALARY n. scale, take, take home, bread, eagle shit, bring home the bacon. See COMPENSATION.

SALE adj.   hit the shelves (go on sale).

SALES BILL OR CHECK n.   beef, tab, big ticket (expensive).

SALESPERSON n.   peddler, drummer, bell ringer, ——— dog (e.g., shoe dog), medicine man, pitchman, skig, spieler, tinge, Arab, bag guy (balloon), butch, butcher, hawker, farm salesman (pharmaceutical).

SALES TALK n.   pitch, sales pitch, story, sell, hard sell, soft sell, bally, ballyhoo, spiel; belly stand, bally stand, belly platform, grind (circus).

SALMON n.   deep sea turkey, goldfish (canned), squaw candy (smoked), nova.

SALOON n.   gin mill, rum room, dive, joint, juice joint, beer joint, tap room, bucket shop, suds shop, ale house, speakeasy, water hole, chain locker (dockside). See BAR.

SALT n.   sand.

SALT LAKE CITY, UTAH   Big Salty.

SALT PORK n.   sow belly.

SALUTATION interj.   hi, hey, yo, ciao, gimme five, gimme ten, what's happenin'?, what's going down?, what's coming down?, what cooks?, what gives?, hi ya, how you doing? See HELLO.

SALUTE n.   tumble, blow, high five, howdy, highball, pump handle.

SALUTE v.   highball, tumble, flag, give one the key to the city, roll out the red carpet. See GREET.

SALVAGE YARD n.   chop shop (illegal), dump.

SALVATION ARMY   Sal, Sally, Sally Anne.

SAME adj.   xerox, dupe, clone, carbon, carbon copy, copycat, ditto, double, ringer, dead ringer, look-alike, work-alike, compatible (P.C. compatible), like two peas in a pod, six of one and half a dozen of the other, spit and image, spittin' image, one beat, S.O.S. (same old shit), same difference, no matter how you slice it cut it or dice it.

SAN ANTONIO, TEXAS   Chili Switch.

SAN BERNARDINO, CALIFORNIA   Berdoo, San Berdoo.

SANATORIUM n.   funny farm, funny house (alcohol or drugs), fat farm.

SANCTIMONIOUS adj.   goody, goody-goody, goody two-shoes, holy Joe, holier than thou, stuffy, noble, square John.

SANCTION n.   okay, OK, get the nod, green light, get the green light, get the go-ahead, the word. See APPROVAL.

SANCTION v.   bless, okay, get behind, go for, hear it for, give the nod, give the go-ahead, give the green light. See APPROVE.

SANCTIONED adj.   legit, okayed, kosher. See ACCEPTED.

SANCTUARY n.   hideout, hideaway, hole in, hole up, place to hole up, den, safe house, blowout center, ivory tower.

SANDALS n.   flip-flops, mules, thongs, Jesus boots.

SAN DIEGO, CALIFORNIA   Dago, Swabby Town.

SANDWICH n.   san, burger, dog, hot dog, Coney Island, Texas hot weiner, chili dog, submarine, hero, Italian hero, Cuban hero, po-boy, cowboy, double-decker, open-face, grinder, falafel, pocket, highpockets, Philly (steak sandwich), croissandwich, hoagie, B.L.T. (bacon, lettuce and tomato), B.T. (bacon and tomato), slab, ball lump, dukee, skyscraper, torpedo, Dagwood.

SANE adj.   together, got it together, commonsensical, all there, in one's right mind, got all one's marbles, have all one's buttons, have both oars in the water, play with a full deck. See REASONABLE.

SAN FRANCISCO, CALIFORNIA   Frisco, San Fran, Bagdad by the bay, Bay City, Quake City.

SANITARY NAPKIN n.   rag, Kotex.

SANTA BARBARA, CALIFORNIA   Channel City.

SARCASM n.   wisecrack, comeback, grind, put-down, cut, dig.

SARCASTIC adj.   bitchy, cussed, mean, ornery, salty, needle, evil, crack, crimpers (U.), hooks, sticking the zingers in (remark), wise guy, smart ass, smart aleck, smart alecky, smarty, weisenheimer, wiseheimer. See also DERISIVE.

SATAN n.   fiend, hellion, little devil, debbil, the Deuce, the Dickens, Old Harry, Old Ned, Old Gentleman. See DEVIL.

SATED adj.   bellyful, full up, fed up, fed to the gills, fed to the teeth, skinful, snootful, stuffed to the gills, topped off, packed. See also JADED.

SATELLITE TRANSMISSION n.   bird feed, feed, get on the bird.

SATELLITE n.   eye in the sky, spy in the sky, bird, Domsat, Comsat, Intelsat, Syncom, Telstar.

SATIATED adj.   fed up, fed to the gills, fed to the teeth, stuffed to the gills, bellyful, skinful, snootful, up to here, much of a muchness. See also FULL.

SATIRE n.   takeoff, play on, put-on, send-up, spoof.

SATIRIZE v.   put on, send up, sheik, take off, spoof, kid, roast.

SATISFACTION n. get off, get off on, a rush, kick, kicks, sure shock, hit, velvet.

SATISFACTORY adj. cool, A-okay, fucking-A, jake, hunky-dory, ducky, on the ball, up crazy, groovy, on the beam. See ACCEPTABLE.

SATISFIED adj. 1. sold on, can't complain, have no kick coming, hit the spot, just the ticket, just what the doctor ordered. See HAPPY. 2. skinful, snootful, bellyfull, no more room, fed up, fed to the teeth, fed to the gills, stuffed to the gills.

SATISFIES v. scores, hits the spot, hits the bull's eye, makes it, thanks I needed that.

SATISFY v. fill the bill, make a hit, hit the spot, go over big, do the trick, hack it, make the grade, score, pass in the dark, sell, sell one on, get by, get one's jollies, get one's kicks, get off, get off on, be just the ticket, be just what the doctor ordered.

SATYR n. playboy, dude, operator, speed, cruiser, heavy hitter, letch, old goat, wolf, tomcat, sport, swinger, killer, cunt-chaser, tail-chaser, rounder, Don Juan. See LECHER.

SAUCE n. dip, glob, glop, goo, goop, goup, gunk.

SAUCY adj. flip, fresh, sassy, smarty pants, cheeky, nervy, minx, hussy, saucebox, pup, puppy, bold as brass. See INSOLENT.

SAUERKRAUT n. kraut, hog, liberty cabbage, shrubbery.

SAUNTER v. ankle, ank, toddle, sashay, traipse, traipse around, trill, ooze, strut one's stuff, mope, mooch, boogie, diddy bop, pimpin', percolate, tool, stump it. See WALK.

SAUSAGE n. dog, hot dog, hot dawg, weinie, weenie, frank, tube steak, special, balloon, beenie, bowwow, bun pup, Coney Island pup, puppy, pimp stick, beagle gut; donkey dick, horse cock (Mil.).

SAVAGE adj. bad ass, wild ass, kill crazy, hog crazy. See also VIOLENT.

SAVAGELY adv. something fierce, something terrible, in cold blood.

SAVANT n. brain, egghead, gnurd, gnome, grind, pencil geek, power tool, throat, wonk, auger, bookworm, cereb, cutthroat, grub, ink squirter, spider, squid, tool, weenie.

SAVE v. 1. scrimp, skimp, penny-pinch, cut corners, cut to the bone, go easy on the pocketbook, make ends meet, roll back, tighten one's belt, rub the print off a dollar bill, rub the picture off a nickel, save for a rainy day, put away for a rainy day, squirrel, squirrel away, sock away, salt away, salt down, rat hole, stache, stash. 2. bail one out, save one's neck, save one's bacon, give one a break, get one out of hock, get one off the hook, spring, pull something out of the fire, pull one's chestnuts out of the fire.

SAVED adj. let off, bailed out, off the hook, out of hock.

SAVINGS n. kitty, nest egg, stake, rainy-day account, sock, a little something put away, mattress full, ace in the hole. See ASSETS.

SAVOIR FAIRE n. know-how, savvy, the big stick.

SAVORY adj. delish, yummy, divine, heavenly, scrumptious, sweetened, sugarcoated.

SAVORY n. cush, sweets, g'dong, gedunk, hickey.

SAW n. brad (small).

SAWDUST n. chewed fine, macaroni.

SAXAPHONE n. pipe, sax, ax, axe, barry, big pipe (baritone), small pipe (alto), fishhorn, foghorn, gobble pipe, peck horn.

SAY n. own say so, own sweet way, say so.

SAY v. go, goes, gab, rap, yak, yock, verbalize, spiel, jaw, lip, modjitate, splib, splib de wib, slide one's jib, shoot, flap, run one's mouth, blow, trash. See SPEAK.

SAYING n. daffodil.

SCAMP n. turd, fart, stinker, bastard, black sheep, cut-up, scalawag, bounder, a dick, rotter, rounder, sleazeball, low-life, bad news, bad egg, bad 'un. See VILLAIN.

SCAN v. 1. flash, flash on, get a hinge, take a hinge, take a squint, look-see, have a look-see, take a gander, take a tumble, tumble, give a thing a toss, give the once-over, once over lightly, hit the high spots, thumb through. See also SCRUTINZE.

SCANDAL n. dirt, dirty linen, dirty wash, dirty laundry, dirty shame, low-down dirty shame, crying shame, burning shame, mud, slime, dynamite, sizzler, scorcher, skeleton, family skeleton, skeleton in the closet, skeleton in the cupboard, Watergate, Irangate, ——— gate (anything gate). See also GOSSIP.

SCANDALMONGER n. busybody, yenta (Yid.), cat, muckracker, mudslinger, sleazemonger, source, tabby, tattletale, snitcher, snitch, chalk hat, fork tongue, mouse, punk, ringtail, shamus, songbird, polly, weasel, yodeler, blab, blabber, blabbermouth, peacher.

SCANDALOUS adj. hot, too hot to handle, red hot.

SCANDINAVIAN n. Scandahoovian, Scandinoovian; squarehead, herring choker (Derog.).

SCANT adj. scarce as hen's teeth, numerous as chicken lips, slim pickings.

SCAPEGOAT n.   fall guy, goat, patsy, sucker, whipping boy, the one left holding the bag.

SCAR n.   crater, track.

SCARCE adj.   scarcer than hen's teeth, numerous as chicken lips, slim pickings.

SCARCELY adv.   by the skin of one's teeth, pretty near, practically, craptically.

SCARE v.   spook, chill, scare shitless, scare stiff, scare the pants off one, scare hell out of, scare the shit out of, scare silly, scare the bejesus out of one, scare to death, throw a scare into, lean on, push around. See FRIGHTEN.

SCARED adj.   run scared, scared stiff, scared witless, scared spitless, scared shitless, scared still, scared silly, jump out of one's skin, piss in one's pants, have cold feet, D and D (deaf and dumb, afraid to testify). See AFRAID.

SCARS n.   tracks.

SCATTER v.   break up, break it up, bust up, scramble, split up, take off in all directions.

SCATTERED adj.   all over the lot, all over the place, from hell to breakfast, every which way.

SCAVENGE v.   scrounge, moonlight requisition.

SCENARIO n.   book, the words, pages, sides, the shit. See also STORY.

SCENE n.   bit, blackout, piece, routine, shtick, spot. See also ACT.

SCENE-STEAL v.   upstage, ham it up.

SCENERY (THE.) n.   flat, flats.

SCENT n.   smell well, smell good.

SCHEDULE n.   lineup, sked.

SCHEDULE v.   line up, get on line, sew up, set, set up, pencil in. See also ROUTINE.

SCHEME n.   game, little game, game plan, layout, gimmick, angle, action, big picture, picture, pitch, proposition, proposish, dodge, setup, put-up job, lay of the land, what's cookin', how one figures it, what's the action, where one's heading, play, scenario, scene, story, bit, child, brainchild, slant, trick, twist, switch, hustle, hype, booby trap, fix, frame, frame-up, hookup, skullduggery, bug in one's ear.

SCHEME v.   angle, finagle, jockey, play games, pull strings, pull wires, figure, figger, hustle, hatch, operate, promote, wangle, quarterback, mastermind, craft, line up, ready up, cook up, dream up, trump up, whip up, come up with, throw together, get one's act together, lay out, work something out, get set for, fix to, put in a fix, be in cahoots with, get in bed with, work hand in glove with,

rig, dodge, set up, frame, frame up, buy off, pack, pack the deal, stack the deck, stack the cards, put in the bag, put out a contract.

SCHEMER n.   operator, finagler, wangler, wire-puller, mastermind, brain.

SCHIZOID adj.   schizo, schizzy. See also CRAZY.

SCHIZOPHRENIA n.   schiz, schizo.

SCHIZOPHRENIC adj.   schiz, schizo, schizzy.

SCHOLAR n.   brain, brains, brainy, egghead, professor, gnurd, gnome, grind, pencil geek, power tool, throat, wonk, auger, bookworm, cereb, cutthroat, grub, ink squirter, spider, squid, tool, weenie, poler, wig.

SCHOLARSHIP n.   full ride.

SCHOOL n.   alma mater, old Siwash, brainery, aggie, cow college, fem sem, Ivy League, halls of ivy.

SCHOOL BUS n.   kiddie car.

SCHOOL GRADES n.   ace (A), flunk, flag (F), hook (C), gentleman's C, E (no grade, take over).

SCHOOL NOTES AND BOOKS n.   bricks and mortar.

SCHOOL, PRIVATE n.   hen pen (girls).

SCHOOL, PUBLIC n.   blackboard jungle, jail, knowledge box, konk class.

SCHOOLTEACHER n.   baby-sitter, prof, professor, guru, teach, grind, slave driver.

SCIENCE n.   sci.

SCIENCE FICTION n.   sci fi, space fiction, space opera.

SCION n.   chip off the old block, sun and air, junior, June bug, sprout.

SCOFF n.   put-on, put-down, dig, dirty dig, crack, slam, slap, swipe, jab, comeback, parting shot, brickbat, backhanded compliment, left-handed compliment.

SCOFF v.   rag, roast, josh, ride, pan, dig at, rank out, slap at, swipe at, pooh-pooh, give one the bird. See RIDICULE.

SCOLD n.   bitch, hellion, battle-ax, fishwife, biddy, old biddy, screech, she-devil, she-wolf, wet hen.

SCOLD v.   chew ass, chew out, eat out, ream out, lay out, jump down one's throat, climb all over, light into, rake up one side and down the other, slap down, sock it to one, read the riot act, give a going over, cloud up and rain on one. See REBUKE.

SCOLDING n.   chewing, chewing out, cussing out, going over, piece of one's mind, bit of one's mind, what for, rap on the knuckles, slap on the wrist, bawling out, set down, calling down, dressing, dressing down, the business, catch, catch it, catch hell, speaking to, talking to, jacking up.

SCOOP n. pooper-scooper (for dog droppings).

SCOPE n. 1. run, run of, space, elbowroom, leeway, room to swing a cat. 2. bag, cup of tea, long suit, thing, weakness.

SCORE n. 1. points, tab. 2. charts (musical).

SCORE v. 1. get on the board, put something on the board, get something on the board, make it, get Brownie points, ring the bell, ring the gong, get into pay dirt, ace (high), hang up (sports). 2. count heads, count noses, cut ice, cut some ice, dope out, figure in, keep tab, keep tabs, run down, take account of, tote, tote up. 3. click, connect, put across, put over, get fat, get into pay dirt, go over big, make out, make a killing, make the grade, hit it big, hit pay dirt, luck in, luck out, pull off, take the cake, get Brownie points. See SUCCEED. 4. chew out, eat out, bawl out, tell where to get off, give what for, give a going over, climb all over one, come down on, give one Hail Columbia. See REBUKE.

SCORE, MUSICAL n. charts.

SCORN v. put down, run down, do a number on, trash, rubbish, wipe out, BFD (big fucking deal).

SCOTCH v. queer, crab, louse up, foul up, fuck up, snafu, bollix up, gum up, put a crimp in, spike one's guns, upset one's applecart, knock the bottom out of. See HINDER.

SCOUNDREL n. sleazeball, slime bucket, maggot, bad ass, creep, low-life, bad news, bad egg; prick, dick, shit heel, mofo, motherfucker (Obsc.); black sheep, cutup, scalawag, bounder, rotter, rounder.

SCOUR v. beat the bushes, leave no stone unturned, look all over hell, look high and low, turn inside out, scratch around, track down. See SEARCH.

SCOUT v. case, case a joint, spot, spy out, check out, stake out, recon, get a load of, take in, get an eyeful of, set eyes on, clap eyes on, eyeball, have a look-see. See also RECONNOITER, INVESTIGATE.

SCOWL n. dirty look, bad eye.

SCOWL v. look daggers, dog eye, bad eye, cloud up and rain on one, make a face, act the lion tamer, make a kisser, push out one's lips at. See FROWN.

SCRAMBLE EGGS v. shipwreck, wreck a pair.

SCRAP n. butt, end, stump, gob, glob, chunk, hunk, lump, smithereen, bite, cut, slice. See also ARGUMENT.

SCRAP v. junk, throw on the junk heap, retire, chuck out, adios, kiss off, do away with, send out to pasture. See DISCARD. See also ARGUE, FIGHT.

SCRAPS n. junk, leftovers, odds and ends, bits and pieces, cats and dogs, broken arm (table scraps).

SCREAM n. holler.

SCREAM v. beller, holler, holler out.

SCREEN v. scrub.

SCREW n. blower, fan, prop, windmill.

SCRIBE n. scribbler, scripter, scratcher, news hen, telewriter (TV), ink slinger, ink spiller, pen pusher, pencil driver. See WRITER.

SCRIMP v. penny-pinch, tighten one's belt, rub the print off a dollar bill, rub the picture off a nickel. See STINT.

SCRIPT n. book, pages, sides, the words, the shit.

SCROTUM n. bag, basket, the family jewels, future.

SCRUB v. soogie, sujee, soujge, soogie-moogie, sujee-mujee (mostly U.S.N. and maritime).

SCRUPULOUS adj. mind one's p's and q's, think twice. See also PARTICULAR.

SCRUTINIZE v. check, check out, check over, peg, scope, burn up, pike off, smoke, candle, put under a microscope, get a load of, get down to nuts and bolts, take the measure of. See SEE. See also SURVEY.

SCRUTINY n. look-see, double O, double OO, close-up, the eye, eyeball, eyeball inspection, long hard look, size-up, watchpot.

SCUFFLE n. brawl, jump, mix-up, go, rowdydow, rumpus, ruction, ruckus, shindy, scrap, dustup, fuss, wrangle. See FIGHT.

SCULPTURE v. sculp, sculpt.

SCURRY v. dust, hotfoot it, barrel, step along, rip, zip, whiz along, get going, get a hustle on, get a wiggle on, pedalling with both feet, hop along. See SPEED.

SEA n. drink, big drink, big pond, deep, briny deep, the briny, the pond, Davy Jones's locker, sink, splash, bounding main.

SEALED WITH A KISS n. S.W.A.K., SWAK.

SEAMAN n. mate, gob, swab, swabbie, bluejacket, jack, salt, old salt, sea dog, yachtie. See SAILOR.

SEARCH n. 1. shakedown, frisking, skin search, bag job (illegal). 2. on the prowl, chase, legwork, fishing expedition.

SEARCH v. 1. beat the bushes, really get into it, leave no stone unturned, look all over hell, look high and low, search high heaven, shake, shake down, toss, turn inside out, turn upside down, dog, bird dog (scout), scout, scratch, scratch around, scratch for, track down, nose around. 2. frisk, pat one down, pad down, skin search, feel out, jack up (body), furp up, fan. 3. chase, comb the streets, throw out the dragnet, fan, sweep, put the feelers on one, prowl, prowl around, sniff around.

SEARCH, ILLEGAL v.   penetrate, break in.

SEASICK adj.   feeding the fishes, hanging over the side, riding the rail, blue around the gills, green around the gills. See also VOMIT.

SEASON v.   hot it up, pep it up, zip it up, zap it up.

SEASONED adj.   vet, been through the wars, longtime, pro, old pro, been around the block, been around the block a few times. See SOPHISTICATED. See also SKILLED.

SEASONING n.   guts, kick, zip, zap.

SEAT n.   crotch row (row A), McCoys (choice, The.).

SECONAL n.   red, red devil, Seccy, Seggy, Secos, pink lady.

SECOND adj.   deuce it (come in second), place, runner up, second fiddle, second stringer, second off.

SECOND n.   sec, split second, tick, half a mo, half a shake, bat of an eye, shake, two shakes, two shakes of a lamb's tail, jiff, jiffy, half a jiffy, nothing flat.

SECONDARY SCHOOL n.   hi, hi school, high school, prep school, senior hi, senior high.

SECONDARY SCHOOLER n.   preppie, hi schooler, high schooler.

SECONDHAND adj.   cheapie, hand-me-down, reach-me-down, secondhand Rose.

SECRET adj.   top secret, for your eyes only, hush-hush, strictly hush-hush, classified, classified info, family jewels (govt., CIA), inside, inside info, on the QT, under one's hat, hold out on, under wraps, undercover, doggo, incog, covered up, holed up, pull the ladder up behind one, keep buttoned up, planted, closet, stashed, close to one's chest, something up one's sleeve, for the cuff, for the hat, creep (mission); tref, triff, wildcat (plan).

SECRETARY n.   sec, girl, gal Friday, girl Friday, pink collar, pink-collar worker. See also CLERICAL WORKER.

SECRETE v.   1. stash, stash away, stache, ditch, duck, plant, squirrel, squirrel away, hike, put in the hole, stick in the hole. 2. whitewash, sweep under the rug, bury, cover, cover up, duck, stonewall, finesse it, palm, paper over, hold out on, keep buttoned up, keep it under one's hat, keep under wraps, 3. hide out, hole up, play dead, lie doggo, lie low, sit tight, tunnel, cool off, duck out of sight, take it on the lam, do a crouch, flatten out, hit the shade, hit the mattresses.

SECRETED adj.   planted, stashed, doggo, under wraps, holed up.

SECRETIVE adj.   garbo, tight-lipped, close-mouthed, tight chops, clam, clam up, clammed up, dried up, dummied up, buttoned up, button up one's lips, zip one's lip, on the q.t., between one and the lamp post.

SECRETIVELY adv.   on the quiet, on the q.t., on the sly, in a hole-and-corner way, in holes and corners, wildcat, play close to the chest.

SECTION n.   1. Tin Pan Alley, The Great White Way, West End, Wall Street, Las Vegas Strip, Sunset Strip, SoHo, NoHo, high-rent district, garment district, red-light district.. See DISTRICTS. 2. chunk, gob, glob, hunk, lump, smithereen. 3. slot, wing. 4. seg, bite, end, split, drag, piece.

SECTION v.   whack up, bump into, size into (chips); divvy, divvy up, slice, slice up, slice the melon, cut the pie, split up, cut up, piece up. See DIVIDE.

SECURE adj.   1. got a lock on something, nailed down, on ice, sure thing, as sure as shooting, cinch, all sewed up, cold lay, bet your ass, shoo-in, ironclad contract, rain or shine. See CERTAIN. 2. solid as a rock, anchored, nailed, hard nut to crack, locked, locked in. 3. buttoned down, buttoned up, button up one's lip, coast is clear, cushy, home free, safe and sound. 4. sitting pretty. See WEALTHY.

SECURE v.   1. access, promote, wangle, get one's hands on, glom on to, pick up, lock up, rack up, buy up, buy out. See GET. 2. feather one's nest, line one's nest. 3. back, back up, cosign, cover, cover up, cover one's ass, cover all bases, ride shotgun for, stand up for, stick up for. 4. button, button down, anchor, nail, nail down, freeze to, stay put, tack on, tack down, slap on, hook on, hook up, hitch on, hitch up, slough, stick like a barnacle. 5. lock, lock up, lock and win, have a lock on. See ASSURE. See also GUARANTEE. 6. hook, sign on, sign up, take on, catch.

SECURED adj.   in the bag, nailed down, on ice, cinched. See CERTAIN.

SECURITIES n.   convertible, baby bond (less than $1,000 denomination), Ginnie Mae, Fannie Mae, Freddie Mac, Muni, minicipals, James Bond (matures in 2007); Bo Derek ten (Treasury bond maturing in the year 2010); double-barreled bond (two sources of repayment); paper, wall paper (defunct); blue chips, blue-chip performer (solid); cats and dogs, fancies, high flier; air-pocket stock (dropping), over the counter, downturn, making a Dow line; bear market, bearish market (low), bull market, bullish market (high), top side, top out (high); bottom out (low); buy sign, sell sign, wash out, get caught.

SECURITIES, STOLEN n.   stiff.

SECURITY GUARD n. company cop, lookout, lay chickie, bugster, rent-a-pig, rent-a-cop.

SEDATE adj. laid back, cool, cool as a cucumber, not crack a smile, wipe the smile off one's face, cold sober, sober as a judge. See SERIOUS.

SEDATIVE n. dope, downer, goof ball, knockout drop, Mickey Finn, pill, pain-killer, pain pill, sleeper, barb, yellow jacket, yellow, nemmie, red, red devil, M, morph.

SEDIMENT n. gook, gunk.

SEDUCE v. pull, grab, draw, kill, slay, bait, mousetrap, shill, steer, tout, give one the come-on, come on to one, sweep off one's feet, vamp, hook, make it with one, make out, suck in, rope in, score, reach home plate, get lucky, get over. See LURE. See also ATTRACT.

SEDUCER n. speed, mother, cruiser, heavy hitter, heavy cake, operator, smoothie, lookin' to get lucky, lookin' to score, letch, lech, old letch, old goat, dirty old man, wolf, vamp, man trap, velvet trap, party girl, player, pusher, swinger, sheik, dude, tomcat, cat, sharp cat, gay cat, sport, scorer, lover boy, joy boy, party boy, killer, lady-killer, ladies' man, man on the make, make-out artist, chaser, broad chaser, woman chaser, skirt chaser, cunt chaser, tail chaser, masher, rip, rounder, gay deceiver, gay dog, whorehound, gash hound, tea hound, blade, Lothario, Don Juan, Casanova, good-time Charlie, parlor snake, campus butcher, lounge lizard, cake-eater, poodle faker, prom trotter, sailor, stick daddy (police), bun duster, arm man, diddler, keister bandit, short-arm bandit, short-arm heister, skin heister, pussy bandit, candy kid (1925), fancy Dan, furper (1930), drugstore cowboy.

SEDUCTIVE adj. stacked, whistle bait, piece, piece of ass, flavor (Bl.), sex kitten, mink, tip, hot shit, centerfold, good enough to eat up. See BEAUTIFUL.

SEDUCTRESS n. hooker, flirt, man eater, operator, party girl, player, swinger, vamp.

SEDULOUS adj. grind, nose to the grindstone, plugger, springbutt, eager beaver, whiz, work one's tail off. See INDUSTRIOUS.

SEE v. 1. scope, clock, glom, glim, gun, gawk, beam, peg, flash, flash on, spot, spy, dig, read, lamp, candle, pipe, rap, rumble, spot, catch, focus, eye, eagle eye, eyeball, check, check over, check up, clap eyes on, lay eyes on, set eyes on, lay one's glims on, hold the glims on, take in, get a load of, get an eyeful of, get a hinge, take a hinge, take a squint, have a look-see, take a gander, take a tumble, tumble, give the once-over, give the double-O, give the OO, check, check out, check something out, pin, size up, burn up, pike off, smoke, rubber, rubberneck, kibitz, 871/2 (look at a girl, restaurant), give the eye, give one the eye, give one the beady eye, give one the fish eye, give with the eyes, give a ghee a toss, give a thing a play, give a thing a toss, get a load of, pipe, put the squint on, keep tab, keep tabs on, keep one's eyes peeled, pick up on, gap, jap (crime). See also SPY, SURVEY. 2. catch, catch on, get, get it, read, get the picture, blow wise, get hip, collar the jive, capeesh, fershtay, see daylight, dig, I know where you're comin' from, take in. See UNDERSTAND.

SEEDY adj. beat up, ratty, ratty-tatty, tacky, frowzy, fruit, dog-eared, used up, in a bad way.

SEEK v. 1. beat the bushes, leave no stone unturned, look high and low, scout, scratch, scratch around, scratch for. See SEARCH. 2. chase, comb the streets, throw out the dragnet, fan, put the feelers on one, prowl, prowl around, sniff around, track down, nose around, fish, fishing expedition.

SEESAW n. teeter-totter, jinky board, joggling board.

SEETHING adj. steamed up, boiling over, see red, browned off, blow one's stack, mad as a hornet, mad as a wet hen, ape shit, have a shit hemorrhage, hit the ceiling, hot, flipped one's wig, on the warpath, red-assed, loaded for bear. See ANGRY.

SEGMENT n. seg, hunk, chunk, bite, end, finger, piece, slice, split, cut, cut of the melon, cut of the pie. See SHARE.

SEGMENT v. divvy, divvy up, slice, slice up, cut the pie, split up, cut up, piece up. See DIVIDE.

SEGREGATION n. feel a draft (recognition of), Jim Crow, Jim Crowism, outseg, seg.

SEGREGATIONIST n. seg, seggie, Klu Kluxer.

SEIZE v. 1. snag, glom on to, latch on to, pick up, take up. See TAKE. See also APPROPRIATE. 2. bust, collar, pick up, pinch, bag, grab, nab, nail, snag, put the arm on, put the claw on, put the cuffs on. See ARREST. 3. grab, shanghai, snatch, put the snatch on one, sneeze, hijack, highjack, skyjack, dognap (dog abduction).

SEIZURE n. collar, mitt, bust, brodie, drop, glom, grab, hook, pinch, run-in, snatch. See ARREST.

SELECT adj. world class, number one, numero uno, gonest, mostest, baaadest, boss, cool, terrible, tops, savage, winner. See BEST. See also ELITE.

SELECT v. name, slot, opt, tap, tab, tag, make, peg, finger, lay one's finger on, put one's finger on, put one's finger on something, put the finger on, button down, pin down, put down for, go down the line, say so, take it or leave it.

SELECTIVE adj. choicy, choosey, pernickety, persnickety, picky, picky picky, fussy. See PARTICULAR.

SELF n. number one, numero uno, yours truly, me myself and I.

SELF-CENTERED adj. 1. big I am, big I love me, big timer, swelled head, be on an ego trip, go on an ego trip, think one's shit doesn't stink, grandstander, hotdogger, blowhard, know-it-all. See BRAGGART. 2. stuck on oneself, on an ego trip, hubcap, look out for number one, look out for numero uno, take care of number one, out for yours truly, shirt up, single-o. See CONCEITED.

SELF-CONFIDENT adj. hotshot, hotdogger, know-it-all. See also ARROGANT, CERTAIN.

SELF-CONTROLLED adj. together, have one's act together, cool, cool as a cucumber, keep one's cool, keep one's shirt on, keep a stiff upper lip, not turn a hair, unflappable, commonsensical, ah-ah head, roll with the punches. See also ASSURED, CALM.

SELF-DECEPTION n. bury one's head in the sand, kid oneself, talk oneself into it, jive turkey.

SELF-DESTRUCTION n. O.D., take oneself out, take a rope, wrap up, solitaire, Brodie (off a bridge), gorging out, hang-up, hit oneself in the bonnet, hit oneself out, pack in, string up, swing, back-gate commute.

SELF-GRATIFICATION adj. ego trip, dolce vita.

SELF-IMPORTANT adj. cocky, puffed up, ego-tripping, king shit, big head, on one's high horse, full of hot air, hotshot. See CONCEITED.

SELF-INDULGENT adj. look after number one, look after numero uno, take care of number one, shirt up, single-o. See also INTEMPERATE.

SELFISH adj. hog, got the gimmies, look out for number one, look out for numero uno, out for yours truly, take care of number one, shirt up, single-o.

SELF-POSSESSED adj. laid back, cool, cool as a cucumber, keep one's cool, keep one's shirt on, not turn a hair, unflappable. See CALM. See also ASSURED.

SELF-RELIANCE n. stock, store, sure bet, guts, walking tall.

SELF-RELIANT adj. iceman, gutsy, got the faith baby, cocksure, sure as shit, racked. See also SELF-SUFFICIENT.

SELF-RIGHTEOUS adj. goody, goody-goody, goody two-shoes, holier than thou, holy Joe, noble, square John.

SELF-SUFFICIENT adj. on one's own, on one's own hook, one's own sweet way, do one's own thing, paddle one's own canoe, look out for number one. See INDEPENDENT.

SELL v. push, drum, hustle, pitch, move, unload, dump, hit on, go clean, sell out, soft sell, hard sell, soft soap, sweet talk, snow, close, close the deal, clinch the deal, puff, boost, plug, ballyhoo, spiel, jam, beat the drum, thump the tub, put on the map. See also ADVERTISE, PERSUADE.

SELTZER n. mixer, soda back (on the side), penny plain, two-cents plain. See also CARBONATED WATER.

SEMEN n. come, cum, wad, load, cream, home brew, hocky, hookey, jack, gism, jism, jisum, jizz, love liquid, love juice, man juice, pecker tracks, protein, blecch, scum, sugar, charge, crud (dried).

SEMICONSCIOUS adj. out of it, one's bell rung, not all there, punchy.

SEMILIQUID adj. slurpy, gloppy, gooey, gooky, goopy, gunky.

SEMINAL FLUID n. come, cum, cream, hocky, home brew, hookey, jack, jism, jisum, jizz, pecker tracks, protein, scum, sugar, crud (dried).

SEMINARY n. alma mater, old Siwash, brainery, aggie, cow college, fem sem.

SENATE n. the hill.

SENIOR n. golden ager, senior citizen, pops, gramps, granny, creak, back number, relic, old fossil, old geezer, old folks, old-timer, A.K., alte kocker, mossback. See AGED.

SENIOR HIGH SCHOOL n. hi, hi school, high school, prep school, senior hi, senior high.

SENIORITY adj. pappy guy, grandfather in.

SENSATION n. 1. vibes, high, rush, head rush, kick, charge, boot, bang, lift, jollies, gut reaction, where one lives. 2. barnburner, flash, hit.

SENSATIONAL adj. 1. sensay, sensaysh, zero cool, the most, mostest, mind-blowing, out of this world, turn on, gone, real gone, solid sender, sizzler, scorcher, drop dead, cliff-hanger, dynamite, hot off the press, one for the book, page-oner, something to write home about, page-turner, thriller. See FABULOUS. 2. blue, purple, dirty, low-down and dirty, off-color, rough, salty, raunchy, X-rated. See OBSCENE.

SENSE n. 1. drift, point, meat, stuff, heart, get to the point, nitty-gritty, nub, nuts and bolts, bottom line, punch line, name of the game, the way of it, nature of the beast. 2. guts, gut reaction, vibes, where one lives.

SENSE v. 1. have a hunch, have vibes (good or bad), get vibes (good or bad), feel in one's bones, feel in one's guts, have a funny feeling, be turned on to. 2. read, savvy, dig, take in, pick up, be with it, be with one, catch, catch on, catch the drift, get, get the drift, get the hang of, get the idea, get the picture.

SENSELESS adj. 1. dead, dead to the world, gorked, loxed out, veged out, out cold, out of it, out to lunch, out like a light, on the nod. See UNCONSCIOUS. 2. doubletalk, doublespeak, hot air, that doesn't chop any wood, that doesn't cut any ice. 3. cockeyed, batty, daffy, goofy, flaky, kooky, loony, sappy, wacky, whacko, harebrained, balloon brained, airheaded, cockamamie, screwy, nutty. See FOOLISH.

SENSIBILITY n.   gut reaction, vibes, where one lives.

SENSIBLE adj.   together, got it together, cool, cool as a cucumber, have horse sense, commonsensical, all there, in one's right mind, got all one's marbles.

SENSITIVE adj.   choked, yantsy, feel stuff, touchy feely, get the vibes, simpatico, hyper, nervy, twitty, tightened up, wired up, uptight, hung up, wreck, nervous wreck, bundle of nerves, have one's teeth on edge, on the ragged edge, tetchy, goosey, jumpy as a cat on a hot tin roof, shot to pieces, all-overish, rabbit ears, hit one where one lives, thin-skinned, grumpy, ugly, crabby, grouchy, got up on the wrong side of the bed, bitchy, cantankerous, can't even look at one cross-eyed.

SENSITIVITY TRAINING n.   acidless trip, bod biz.

SENSUAL adj.   hot, heavy, hot and heavy, hot stuff, rough, rough stuff, steamy, blue, purple, X-rated. See LASCIVIOUS.

SENSUOUS adj.   slinky, gully low, low down, low down and dirty.

SENTENCE n.   time, hitch, stretch, term, up, up the river, trick, knock, rap, jolt, icebox, fall, good time, getup, sleep, vacation, curtains for; big bit, buried (long); all, do it all, the clock, the book (life); sleeping time (short); newspaper, magazine, calendar, boppo, boffo (one year). See PRISON SENTENCE.

SENTENCE v.   put away, send up, send up the river, ice, put on ice, throw the book at, put one away, take one away, take the fall, break one's license, clean up the calendar, settle, slough, slough up, railroad. See also FINE.

SENTIMENT n.   mush, slush, slop, goo, glop, deep sugar, schmaltz, hearts and flowers.

SENTIMENTAL adj.   syrupy, drippy, soapy, softie, soft on, soppy, soupy, slush, tear-jerker, teary, beery, sticky, gummy, gooey, sappy, sloppy, gushing, namby-pamby, hearts and flowers, corny, cornball, off the cob, hoke, hokey, hokum, icky, mushy, schmaltzy, lovey-dovey, big, big for, crazy for, crazy about, crazy over, nutty about, nutty over, all over one.

SENTINEL n.   lookout, weather eye, eagle eye, spotter, tip, lay butzo, lay chickie, zex man, jigger, outside man, hawk, gap. See LOOKOUT. See also GUARD.

SEPARATE v.   1. split, split up, break, break off, break up, kiss off, wash up, pull out, dedomicile, untie the knot, Reno-vate, go to Reno, go pffft. 2. break it off, break it up, drop, drop it, put daylight between, sideline. See also DISENGAGE.

SEPARATED adj.   on the outs, in bad with, on one's shitlist, at outs, at loggerheads, at sixes and sevens.

SEPARATION n.   breakup, dedomiciling, pffft, go phftt, split, splitsville, split-up, on the rocks, marriage on the rocks, come to a parting of the ways, couldn't make it, on the out and out, washed up. See also DIVORCE.

SEQUEL n.   spin-off, son of ——— (son of Dracula), The ——— Out West (The Draculas Out West).

SEQUENCE n.   run, skein, streak, pecking order, down the line, time-line, track.

SERENDIPITY n.   find, luck out, luck into.

SERENE adj.   laid back, cool, cool as a cucumber, ah-ah head, unflappable. See CALM.

SERENITY n.   cool.

SERGEANT n.   sarge, top, topkick, third lieutenant, third looey, three-striper, first man.

SERIAL n.   soap, soap opera.

SERIES n.   time-line, run, string, skein, streak.

SERIOUS adj.   1. heavy, heavy number, meaningful, jelly, serious jelly, serious talk, serious shit, no shit, no bird turdin', no fooling, am I laughing?, chill out, buckle down, getting it straight, not playing around, playing for real, playing hard ball, playing for blood, have blood in one's eye, be out for blood, dropping the green flag, smoking, get down, strictly business, mean business, taking care of business, TCB, get down to business. 2. deadpan, draggy, downbeat, sourpuss, am I laughing?, I kid you not, not crack a smile, wipe the smile off one's face, wipe it off, frozen-faced, cold sober, sober as a judge. 3. heavyweight, heavy stuff, nuclear, matter of life and death, something, something else, big league, major league, high powered, double-barreled, high cotton, chips are down, money talks bullshit walks, we're not talking about nutmeg here, not to be sneezed at. 4. bound, bound and determined, set, dead set on, bent on, hell bent on, make no bones about it, go for broke.

SERIOUSLY adv.   for serious, cool it, cut the comedy, quit horsing around, straighten out, save it, simmer down.

SERMON n.   angel food.

SERVANT n.   help, live-in, girl, woman, cleaning woman, cleaning lady, man, boy, houseman, houseboy, pratt boy, biddy, cabin girl (chambermaid), pillow puncher, dog robber (Army orderly), flunky, tweeny, furp, peon, serf, slave, slavey, pancake (Uncle Tom).

SERVE v.   do for, hit (drink). See also HELP.

SERVE FOOD v.   sling hash, chase.

SERVICEMAN n.   G.I., GI Joe, grunt, leg (infantry, Vietnam), dogface, sad sack, buck-ass private, doughboy, footslogger, jazz bo (Bl.), Yank, cannon fodder. See SOLDIER.

SERVICE STRIPE n.   hash mark, Hershey bar.

SERVILE adj.   dance, dance to one's tune, eat crow, eat humble pie, eat shit; handkerchief head, Stepin Fetchit, Uncle Tom (Bl.). See SUBSERVIENT. See also SUB-MISSIVE.

SESSION n.   confab, clambake, affair, meet, get-together, huddle, buzz session, rap, rap session, bull session, bitch session, jam session, showdown, put heads together. See MEETING.

SET adj.   locked in, stuck in concrete, chiseled in stone, solid as a rock, brick wall, ironclad, pat, dig in one's heels, stick to one's guns, hang tough, stiff-necked, unflappable, dead set on. See STUBBORN.

SET n.   bunch, crowd, mob, crew, gang, the boys, the boys uptown, those one runs with, rat pack. See ASSOCIATION.

SET v.   park, plank, plank down, plunk, plop.

SETBACK n.   back to square one, back to the drawing board, whole new ball game, about face, switcheroo, flip-flop, bottom out; bath, take a bath (financial).

SETDOWN n.   comeuppance, take down, put-down, touché. See BELITTLED. See also ADMONITION.

SETDOWN v.   top, take down, put down, put one away, get one's comeuppance, shoot one down, prick one's balloon, take the wind out of one's sails. See BELITTLE. See also ADMONISH.

SET THE TABLE v.   set up.

SETTING n.   location, jungle, zoo. See also LOCA-TION.

SETTLE v.   1. pay up, pay off, pick up the tab, pony up, ante up, come through, come across, come down with the needful, come up with the necessary, cash out, spring for, make good. See PAY. 2. call the shots, cinch, clinch, make a deal, nail down, take a decision. See DETERMINE. 3. square, square things, square up, square the beef, make up for, sugarcoat, pay the piper, pay one's dues, take care of. 4. grease, back off, cool it, pour oil on troubled waters, fix up, bury the hatchet, make up, make it up, make matters up, even the score, have a showdown. See PACIFY. 4. locate, park, hang up one's hat, hang up one's shingle.

SETTLED adj.   on ice, in the bag, nailed down, all locked up, no buts about it, clinched, for sure, que sera sera, the way the ball bounces. See DETERMINED.

SETTLEMENT n.   1. deal, payoff, showdown, cash on the barrelhead, cash on the line, cash on the nail. 2. cop out, deal, fifty-fifty, half and half, happy medium, sellout, trade-off. See also AGREEMENT.

SEVEN n.   sevener.

SEVER v.   chiv, shiv.

SEVERANCE PAY n.   golden parachute.

SEVERE adj.   heavy, hefty, hard shell, hairy, hardnosed, mean, tough, wicked, jump off the deep end. See also DIFFICULT.

SEX APPEAL adj.   S.A., it, hot pants, chemistry, creamy, bedroom eyes, come on, bitchy, it girl, oomph, oomph girl, what it takes.

SEX APPEAL, LACK OF n.   turn-off, iceberg, cold tit, cold fish, cold biscuit, dog.

SEX, GROUP n.   gang bang, gang shag, gang shay, sloppy seconds, group grope, daisy chain, pulling a train.

SEXIST n.   male chauvinist pig, MCP.

SEX OFFENDER n.   shut eyes, short eyes (child molester).

SEXUAL ADVANCE v.   hit, hit on, feeler, proposition, pass, vamp, come on to, come hither, come-hither look, bat eyes at. See FLIRT.

SEXUAL ATTRACTIVENESS n.   candy, leckerish, sweet tooth.

SEXUAL CLIMAX n.   cum, come, come off, blow, bust one's nuts, go off, get it off, get off, get one's nuts off, get one's rocks off, score, shoot, shoot off, shoot one's wad, haul one's ashes, go over the mountain, get over the mountain, explode, cookies, pop one's cookies. See also EJACULATE.

SEXUAL DESIRE n.   cream for, hard-on for, bag, itch, hots, hot pants, in heat, lech, nasties, the urge, sweet tooth, cup of tea, druthers, go down the line, flash groove, turn on, weakness, fire in the belly, yen, yen-yen, big eyes, zazzle.

SEXUAL ENTERTAINMENT n.   circus, dig, exhibi-tion, exhibish, gazupi, peep show, trick a track, trip to the red sea, show.

SEXUAL EXPLOITATION n.   SexPo, sexploitation.

SEXUAL INTERCOURSE n.   fuck, jazz, screw, lay, hump, boff, nookie, nookey, plowin', poke, ass, piece of ass, bang, action, balling, cock, leg, stroking, roll in the hay, have one, go the limit, quickie, score, any (get any?), yum-yum, bouncy-bouncy, rocking chair, the business, meat injection, beef injection, dirty deed, oil change, missionary position, one-night stand, noonie, nooner, matinee, parallel parking, night baseball, fooling around, laps around the track, bush patrol, ground rations, ball, score, quickie, dork, diddle, deliver, jive, jig-jig, gig, jing-jang, shtup, yentz, plow, jump, jump on one's bones, bump bones, homework, work, trim, tumble, tip, hit, horsing, bareback, bareback rider, ride, canoe, crawl, cook, cush, pound, pussywhippin', frisk, jiggle, knock, batter, gombo, grind; ground rations, mug (Bl.); lallygag, lollygag, one shot, pluck, pom-pom (W.W.II), rock, roll, rock and roll, dating, easy make, a little heavy breathing, he'n and she'n, she'n and she'n, he'n and he'n, fun and games, wingding, the deed, the dirty deed, frail job, sex job, the limit, belly to belly, in the box, in the saddle, wham, wham bam thank you ma'm, slam bam, slam bam thank you ma'am, ram bam thank you ma'm, bunny fuck, dry fuck, dry hump, dry run (contraceptive used), dog fashion, dog style, shot, shot downstairs, shot at the front door; shot at the back door, asshole fucking, Greek, the Greek way, Greek fashion, Hershey bar route, corn hole, bugger, brown, brown hole, bunghole, back door (anal); French, French way, half and half, head, bush patrol, lunch, box lunch, eat at the Y, go down, blow job, fudge, futy, fingerfuck, petting party, body rub, half hour, pleasure immersion, keeping company, like the birds and the bees; group grope, gang bang, gang shag, gang shay, daisy chain, doing, a scene, pulling a train, sixty-nine, head, blow job.

SEXUAL INTERCOURSE v. fuck, screw, lay, hump, ball, bang, boff, jazz, score, dork, pork, diddle, deliver, jive, jam, lay pipe, bed down, go to bed with, make the sheets sing, go the limit, spread for, come through, turn out, give it to one, do it, do the deed, do the dirty deed, belly to belly, get it, get it on, get it up, get some, get in, get one's ashes hauled, get one's nuts cracked, get one's oil changed, get one's banana peeled, get to first base, get a taste, get it off together, jig-jig, gig, jing-jang, shtup, yentz, plow, jump, jump on one's bones, bump bones, bone, poke, work, trim, tumble, tip, hit, bareback, ride, canoe, crawl, cook, cush, pound, pussywhippin', frisk, jiggle, knock, batter, gombo, grind, mug (Bl.), liberate (with native of occupied country), lallygag, lollygag, one shot, pluck, pom-pom (W.W.II), rock, roll, rock and roll, date, make it, make out, put out, go all the way, fool around, honey fuck, wingding, fire her up, ring one's bell, dip one's wick, empty one's trash, hide the salami, hide the weenie, parallel park, throw a bop into one, change one's luck, wham, wham bam thank you ma'm, slam bam, slam bam thank you ma'am, ram bam thank you ma'm, bunny fuck, dry fuck, dry hump, dry run (contraceptive used), fire blanks, laps around the track, see a man about a dog, see a dog about a man, have a party, go down the line, visit the red-light district, French, give head, pearl dive, lunch, eat at the Y, go down, blow job, fudge, futy, fingerfuck, keep company, make like the birds and the bees; group grope, gang bang, gang shag, gang shay, morsesome (three or more), daisy chain, do a scene, pull a train.

SEXUAL INTERCOURSE, ANAL n. corn hole, bugger, brown, brown hole, bunghole, asshole fucking, the Greek way, Greek fashion, Greek, Hershey bar route, up the chocolate highway, back door, shot at the back door.

SEXUAL INVITATION n. pass, proposition, bat one's eyes at, come hither, come-hither look, come on, feeler, make eyes at, vamp. See FLIRT.

SEXUALLY AROUSED adj. turned on, horny, creaming, creaming one's jeans, wet and willing, hot, hot for, hot pants, red hot, the hots, having the hots, hot as a firecracker, hot to trot, hot in the biscuit, hot in the ass, ready, rooty, have a hard-on, have a lech on, steamed up. See also AMOROUS PLAY.

SEXUALLY ATTRACTIVE adj. chicken delight (young), hot stuff, armful, sex kitten, stone fox, chemistry, cutie, cute trick, it, oomph, pinup, playmate, make one's teeth fall out, a turn-on, traffic stopper.

SEXUALLY DEPRIVED adj. hard up, cock strong.

SEXUALLY OBSESSED adj. cunt struck.

SEXUAL PARAPHERNALIA n. dildo, vibe, whips, chains, French tickler, leather.

SEXUAL PURSUIT n. cruising, pussy patrol, trim hunt, cunt hunt.

SEXUAL RELATIONS n. fuck, screw, lay, hump, boff, ass, bang, balling, dork, diddle, shtup, dating, gettin' it on, a little heavy breathing, fun and games, wingding, the deed, the dirty deed, frail job, sex job, the limit, belly to belly, in the box, in the saddle, parallel park, bouncy-bouncy. See SEXUAL INTERCOURSE. See also AMOROUS PLAY.

SEXY adj. 1. blue, dirty, filthy, off base, off-color, out of line, steamy, hot stuff, adult, mature. See OBSCENE. 2. horny, hot, hot for, hot pants, turned on, nasty. See LASCIVIOUS.

SEXY MALE n. beefcake, hunk, hunky, tuna, fox, good fuck, good lay, hot ticket, cock hound, lady-killer, man about town, Sam, satisfier, stud, tomcat, trade, wolf.

SEXY WOMAN n. hot, hot stuff, hot pants, hot number, hot mama, hot baby, hot patootie, hot tamale, sheba, stone, stone fox, foxy, foxy lady, pinup, pinup girl, sweater girl; poontang, brown sugar (Bl. or mulatto); sex job, sex pot, sex kitten, sizzler, scorcher, slinky, stuff, tease, teaser, cock teaser, CT (Obsc.); tomato, table grade, trade, vamp, bint, cobra, glamour girl, oomph, oomph girl, nymph, nymphet, jailbait, San Quentin quail.

SHABBY adj. beat up, crummy, raunchy, tacky, ratty, ratty-tatty, ramshackle, rinky-dink, rinky-tinky, slummy, frowzy, fruit, dog-eared, used up, in a bad way.

SHACKLE v. hog-tie, tie up, lock up, cool out, put the chill on, bottle up, cork up, hold down, cuff. See RESTRAIN.

SHACKLES n. darbies, derbies, cuffs.

SHACKS n. shanty town, Hooverville, shanties.

SHAKE v. jitter, shiver, have the shakes, have the jitters, have the shivers, have the quivers, have the cold shivers. 2. shimmy. 3. bring one up short, give one a turn, throw, throw one a curve, make waves, knock the chocks from under one, knock the props from under one. See DISTURB.

SHAKE HANDS v. shake, gimme five, gimme ten, high five, low five, gimme some skin, slip me some skin, press the flesh, lay it there, put it there, mitt, pump the stump, touch gloves (boxing). See also GREET.

SHAKEN adj. shook, shook up, bowled down, bowled over, discombobulated, discomboberated, come apart, come apart at the seams, crack up, have the jitters. See DISTURBED.

SHAKILY adv. herky-jerky.

SHALLOW adj. half-assed, half-baked. See also SUPERFICIAL.

SHAM n. bunco, flimflam, jive, shuck, cover-up, snow job, whitewash, whitewash job, a cheat, smoke. See TRICK.

SHAM v. fake, fake it, jive, shuck and jive, put up a front, sucker one, do a number, make like. See PRETEND.

SHAME v. cut down to size, do a number on, give a black eye, dump on, shoot one down, take down, take the shine out of. See HUMILIATE.

SHAMED adj. lost face, drummed out, eat crow, eat dirt, sing small, draw in one's horns. See DISGRACED.

SHANKS n. gams, gambs, hams, pins, pegs, stems, props, shafts, stilts, trotters. See LEGS.

SHAPE n. build, built, built like a brick shithouse, V-man, bag of bones, bod, chassis, classy chassy, frame.

SHAPE v. throw together, bring together, fudge together, knock together. See also PLAN.

SHAPELESS adj. baggy, blobby.

SHAPELY adj. curvy, stacked, well stacked, busty, zaftig, built, built for comfort, built like a brick shithouse. See also BEAUTIFUL.

SHARE n. points, split, end, bite, seg, cut, cut in, cut up, melon, cut of the melon, divvy, lagniappe, plum, taste, halver, lion's share, bigger half, big end, fifty-fifty, even-steven, drag, rake-off, p.c., piece, piece of the action, piece of the pie, slice, slice of the melon, slice of the pie, cut of the pie, fingers, finger in the pie, bit, chunk.

SHARE v. 1. divvy, divvy up, go halfies, go halvers, slice up, cut the pie, slice the melon, slice, split up, piece up, whack up, bump into, size into (chips), buck it over. See DIVIDE. 2. be into, be in on, sit in, sit in on, have a finger in, have a finger in the pie, get into the act.

SHARECROPPER n. halfer.

SHAREHOLDER n. coupon clipper. See also INVESTOR.

SHARING v. togetherness.

SHARP adj. 1. have smarts, have savvy, on the ball, quick, quick on the trigger, quick on the uptake, smart as a whip, smart as a tack, sharp as a tack, foxy, crazy like a fox, not born yesterday. See SHREWD. 2. snippy, ornery, salty. 3. bent, shady, slick, slippery, snake in the grass, two-faced, feather legs, speak with forked tongue. See DECEITFUL.

SHARPEN v. punch up, soup up, heat up, hop up, hot up, spike, jazz up, pour it on, add fuel to the fire. See STIMULATE.

SHARPER n. 1. carder, cardsharp, card shark, mechanic, high roller, plunger, player, desperado, boneshaker, Broadway boy (small time). See GAMBLER. 2. shark, sharpie, bunco, bunco steerer, bunco artist, clip artist, double-dealer, operator, slick operator, horse trader. See CHEATER.

SHATTER v. total, kablooey, scrunch, crunch, wrack up, bust to bits, break to smithereens, make mincemeat of, smash to smithereens. See also DESTROY.

SHATTERED adj. totalled, busted, in smithereens, kablooey, scrunched. See also DESTROYED.

SHAVE v. knock off, knock off the whiskers, chiv, shiv.

SHAVE, FACE OR HEAD n. scalping, scraping.

SHEEP n. wool on the hoof, wool on the run, wooly, lawn mower.

SHEET n. dreamer, white lilies, lily whites.

SHELL n. flak, G.I. can, screaming mimi, Black Maria (WW II).

SHELTER n. 1. pad, crib, condo, co-op, coop, joint, den, domi, dommy, digs, diggings, roof over one's head, hole in the wall, cave, homeplate, pen, dice house, rack, roost, turf. See HOUSE. 2. fix, hat, umbrella, insurance.

SHELTER v. cover, cover up.

SHELVE v. put on the back burner, put on ice, pigeonhole, cool it, sideline, wooden stake (executive). See DELAY.

SHELVED adj. pigeonholed, passed up, sidelined, sidetracked, put up, hung up, held up, put on hold, put on the back burner, scrubbed, slowed up, tied up, stabbed.

SHEPHERD v. baby-sit, keep tab on, keep tabs on, ride herd on. See also ESCORT, MANAGE.

SHERIFF n. cop, fuzz, bull, shamus, arm, pig, oink, clown (rural), the man, star, badge, county Joe, county mounty, hick dick, long arm of the law, bear, smokey, Smokey the Bear, local boy, road ranger. See POLICE OFFICER.

SHIELD v. cover, cover up, cover one's ass, cover all bases, go to bat for, go to the mat for, ride shotgun for, shotgun, stonewall.

SHIFT v. 1. switch, switch over, shift gears, blow hot and cold, flip-flop, shilly-shally, waffle, hem and haw, drift, cook, bottom out, transmogrify, dial back, recalibrate, yo-yo. See also AVOID, VACILLATE. 2. turn over a new leaf, turn the corner, turn the tables, turn one around, do up, about face, flip-flop, sing a different tune. 3. swap places with, fill in, take over, step into the shoes of.

SHIFT BLAME v. pass the buck, buck it on.

SHIFT GEARS v. double clutch, mash in.

SHIFTILY adv. on the quiet, on the q.t., in a hole-and-corner way, in holes and corners.

SHIFTY adj. crooked stick, shady, cagey, foxy, sneaky, slick, sharp, shifty-eyed, Honest John, slimy, trust one as far as one can swing a cat, trust one as far as one can throw an elephant. See DISHONEST. See also SHREWD, DECEITFUL.

SHILL n. booster, pusher, bunco steerer, blow-off, nark, come-on man, plant, deek, stoolie, stool pigeon.

SHINE n. flash, glitz, show, zap.

SHINE v. buff up.

SHIP n. steamer, liner, tramp, tub, bathtub, bucket, rust bucket, hooker, can, ol' lady, wagon, battlewagon, fig (frigate), jeep, oil burner, sieve, bateau, limey (English ship).

SHIP v. drop (merchandise). See also HAUL.

SHIP'S DECK n. mat (usually aircraft carrier).

SHIP'S FUNNEL n. stack, smokestack, noble, Charlie Noble.

SHIPMATE n. matie, matey.

SHIP'S STORE n. slop chest.

SHIPWRECK v. pile up.

SHIRK v. 1. fuck off, goof off, fluff off, flub off, flub, flub the dub, sluff off, goldbrick, dog, dog it, fuck the dog, featherbed, lie down on the job, find Rover (work). 2. get around, dodge.

SHIRKER n. fuck-off, goof, off, goldbrick, buck passer, clock-watcher, coffee cooler, featherbedder, deuce, welsher, skimper.

SHIRT n. boiled rag, boiled shirt, fried shirt.

SHIVER v. have the shakes, have the quivers, have the shivers, have the cold shivers.

SHIVERING n. shivers, cold shivers, shakes, heebie-jeebies, willies.

SHOCK n. jolt, whammy, double whammy, eye-opener, turn, shot in the ass, kick in the ass, bolt out of the blue, from out in left field. See also SURPRISE.

SHOCK v. rock, gork, floor, shake one up, give one a turn, bowl over, throw one a curve, knock one over with a feather. See SURPRISE.

SHOCKED adj. shook, shook up, all shook up, rocked, gorked, thunderstruck, floored, thrown, unglued, flabbergasted, bowled over, hit like a ton of bricks, bit one in the ass. See SURPRISED.

SHODDY adj. cheesy, borax, schlocky, drecky, gummy, ticky-tacky, ratty-tatty, sleazy, junk, jeasley, slimpsy, crappy, below the mark, not up to scratch, not up to snuff, quick and dirty, plastic, comin' apart at the seams. See CHEAP.

SHOE LIFTS n. lifties, Adler elevators (1930-1950).

SHOES n. sneakers, tennies, canal boats, clodhoppers, gunboats, barkers, platforms, slides, stompers, tooting stomps, wedgies, weejuns, pinchers, treaders, dagger points, earth pads, fiddle cases, violin cases, goldies, ground grabbers, kemels, kicks, kickers, bottoms, brogans, wing tips, flats, Chicago flats, St. Louis flats, creepers, crabs, clunks, clunkers, coffins (large), flip-flops, marshmallow shoes, white ducks, jelly shoes, pyramids, camp (dress), easy walkers, ends, goulashes, gruesome twosome (Army).

SHOE SALESMAN n. shoe dog.

SHOE STORE n. bootique.

SHOE WIDTHS adj. A: Al, B: Benny, C: Charley, D: Dave, David, E: Eddy, Edgar.

SHOOT v. blast, gun, zap, hemstitch (machine gun), trigger, pull the trigger, squeeze one off, open up, shoot 'em up, let go with, let fly, throw lead, turn on the heat, pop at, take a pop at, turkey shoot (helicopter, Vietnam), drop the hammer, fog away, bang away, beat to the draw, burn down, gun down, put a slug in, give 'em both barrels, give one lead poisoning, get the drop on.

SHOOTING n. heat, give one the heat, fireworks, gunplay, shoot out, firefight, bustin' (exit shooting), ride on (drive by shooting).

SHOP n. supermarket, superette, super, deli, stand, chain store, outlet store, co-op, discount house, head shop, ma and pa grocery, mom and pop grocery, bodega (liquor or NYC grocery), the grab, schlock joint, five-and-ten, five-and-dime.

SHOPLIFT v. boost, lift, kipe, swipe, snatch, grab, hook.

SHOPLIFTER n. booster, derrick, dragger, hoister, crotch walker, pennyweighter, skinworker.

SHOPLIFTING n. people's crime.

SHOPPER n. chump, easy make, float, front, head, mark, pigeon, sucker, walk-in.

SHOPPING CENTER n. mall.

SHOPTALK n. lingo, officialese, federalese, doublespeak, hillspeak, bafflegab, bunkum, buzzwords, gobbledygook, mumbo-jumbo.

SHORE LEAVE n. liberty, Cinderella liberty (till midnight), forty-eight (weekend).

SHORT adj. 1. in a nutshell, short and sweet, make a long story short, boiled down, cut to the bone. See also SHORT PERSON. 2. snippy, snappy.

SHORTCHANGE v. duke (circus).

SHORTCOMING n. bug, catch, not come up to scratch, not make it.

SHORT DISTANCE n. pretty near, within a whoop and a holler, within a stone's throw, in spitting distance, just up the road a piece, in the ball park, hair's breadth, practically, close by. See NEAR.

SHORTEN v. cut, cut down, cut to the bone, nutshell, put in a nutshell, boil down, trim, get to the meat, chop, snip, blue pencil.

SHORT PERSON n. shorty, shrimp, peewee, peanut, runt, small fry, wart, mite, pint-sized, half-pint, short pint, squirt, duck-butt, dusty-butt, tad, teeny, teeny-weeny, sawed off, knee high, knee high to a grasshopper.

SHORTS n. Bermudas, cut-offs, kneebusters, clamdiggers, baggies, jammies. See also PANTS.

SHORT TERM adj. short stop.

SHORT WAVE RADIO TERMS ham, send, 10-4, over and out, do you read me?, pound brass (key), C.Q. (call), Mayday!

SHOT, adj. caught slugs, caught it, bought it, take a hit.

SHOTGUN n. artillery, blaster, boom boom, scatter, scattergun, iron, hardware, Betsy, slim, boom stick, works, business, copper-dropper, crowd-pleaser (police), bear insurance. See also GUN.

SHOULDERS n. brace of broads.

SHOUT n. holler, holler out, yawp.

SHOVE v. boost, buck.

SHOVEL n. banjo, Irish banjo, Irish fan, jo, hemo jo, joe, muck stick, clam shovel (short), pooper-scooper.

SHOW n. exbo, expo, exhib, exhibish, grandstand play, showboat, flash (gaudy merchandise or prize), shine, splash, front, fireworks. See DISPLAY.

SHOW v. flash, hot dog, sport, streak, let it all hang out, show off, showcase, do one's stuff, wave it around. See DISPLAY.

SHOW BUSINESS n. show biz, the Industry, the theater, Broadway.

SHOWER v. drips, light drips, spit, it's raining cats and dogs, it's raining hammer handles, it's raining pitchforks, pour, really coming down. See also RAIN.

SHOW GIRL n. gypsy, pony, chorine, floor lamp, parade girl, Ziegfeld Girl, in the line. See also DANCER.

SHOWER BATH n. rain locker.

SHOWY adj. 1. glitzy, flossy, flashy, loud, screaming, flaky, jazzy, snazzy, zappy, pizzazz, frou-frou, gussied up, kitschy, lit up like a Christmas tree. 2. splashy, splurgy, splendiferous, splendacious, tony, classy, chichi, putting on the dog, putting on the ritz. See PRETENTIOUS.

SHRAPNEL n. shrap.

SHREVEPORT, LOUISIANA Sugar Town.

SHREW n. bitch, hellion, battle-ax, fishwife, biddy, old biddy, screech, she-devil, she-wolf, wet hen.

SHREWD adj. 1. cagey, foxy, crazy like a fox, sharp, sharpie, sharp stuff, shark, ringer, slicker, slick, slippery, smooth, smoothie, cute, cutie, fly, smarts, got the smarts, street smarts, streetwise, wised up, inside, on the inside, have the inside track, in the know, be up on, on the beam, on top of, the smart money, ear to the ground, playing politics, double digs, sly boots, hot tamale, hot, hotshot, Philadelphia lawyer. 2. brain, double dome, gasser, bright, whiz, wizard, gray matter, nifty. See INTELLIGENT.

SHUDDER v. jitter, judder.

SHUDDERING n. cold shivers, shakes, shivers, heebie-jeebies.

SHUFFLE CARDS v. wash, break the deck.

SHUN v. dodge, duck, cut, cut dead, ditch, duck out of, pass up, get around, palm off, cold shoulder, give the cold shoulder to, give one the runaround, give the go by, give a miss to, give a wide berth, stay shy of, steer clear of, have no truck with, not touch with a ten-foot pole, hide out, shake, shake off, stall off. See also AVOID, SNUB.

SHUNT v. circumlocute, bend the rules, get around.

SHUT v. wrap a joint up, fold, fold a joint, fold up, close down, shut down, ring down, drop the curtain, shutter. See CLOSE.

SHY adj. mousy, rabbity, wallflower, loner, lone wolf, Herman the hermit.

SIBLING n. sib, sis, sissy, bro, breed, bub, bubba, bud, buddy, rack (off the same rack).

SICK adj. peaked, run down, down with, got the bug, feeling rotten, poorly, under the weather, barfy, green around the gills, blue around the gills. See ILL.

SICKEN v. gross out, feel awful, feel under the weather, look green around the gills, not feel like anything, come down with, take one's death.

SICKENING adj. faust, gross, grossed out, grody, grody to the max, it stinks; mother fucking, mother grabbing (Obsc.), rotten, scuzzed out, stinking, turn-off.

SICK LIST n. binnacle list (USN), sick call (Mil.).

SICKLY adj. draggin', draggin' one's ass, rocky, seedy, down, run down, laid low, below par, peaky, peaked, poorly, out of action, out of shape, good and flabby, Four F.

SICKNESS n. bug, crud, creeping crud, the runs, trots, what's going around, the flu, the pip, dose, double scrudfantods, fascinoma (Medic.), burned (VD.), willies (mythical).

SIDE EFFECT n. fallout.

SIDESHOW n. bally show, kid show, kid top (tent).

SIDELINE n. left field, moonlighting, bench. See also AVOCATION.

SIDESHOW FREAK n. geek.

SIDESTEP v. pussyfoot, duck, stutter step.

SIDEWALK n. bricks, byway, cruncher, pavement, turf.

SIGHT-SEEING n. rubbernecking, slumming, seeing how the other half lives. See also TRAVELING.

SIGHTSEER n. rubberneck, rubbernecker, jet-setter, globe-trotter. See also TRAVELER.

SIGN n. high sign, nod, wink.

SIGN v. ink, put one's John Hancock on, put one's John Henry on, rubber-stamp.

SIGNAL n. high sign, sign, nod, wigwag, wink, bleep, yapper, Mayday, SOS. See ALARM.

SIGNAL v. flag, flash, give the high sign, give the nod, wink.

SIGNALING DEVICE n. beeper, bleeper, wigwag, flasher.

SIGNATURE n. autograph, sig, X, fist, ink, John Hancock, John Henry, on the dotted line.

SIGNIFICANCE n. point, heart, meat, nub, score, stuff, bottom line, name of the game, nitty-gritty, nuts and bolts, the way of it, nature of the beast, drift, punch line, kicker (point of a story, joke, etc.).

SIGNIFICANT adj. heavy, meaningful, serious jelly, serious shit, high cotton, cut ice, carry a lot of weight, the juice, the force. See IMPORTANT.

SIGNIFY v. talking (I'm talking big bucks), sign, high sign, flash, give the nod, wink. See also INDICATE.

SIGN OFF v. blow out, close down, wrap, wrap up.

SILENCE interj. shut up, knock it off, hold it down, can it, button your lip, zip your lip, put a zipper on it, zipper up, hang up, lay off, spit, clam up, dummy up, dummy up and deal (gambling), bag your head, cool it, forget it, skip it, drop it, come off it, never mind, mum's the word, blow your nose, chop, d.d., fold up, get hep, get hip, get under the bed. See also TALKING, STOP.

SILENCE n. dead air.

SILENCE v. gag, ice, muzzle, squelch, squash, shut up, cool it, can it, keep it down, hush-hush, soft-pedal, dummy up, dry up, clam, clam up, close up like a clam, pipe down, hold it down, shut one's trap, shut one's mouth, hush one's mouth, shut one's face, button up, button one's lip, sit on, sit down on, forget it, never mind, decrease the volume, lump it, save one's breath, mum, mum's the word, bottle up, breeze off, cut the mouth, drink one's beer, see the chaplain, chuck it, put the damper on, put the kibosh on, put the lid on, put a lid on that garbage, keep the lid on, put a half nelson on, cork, cork up, shut down on, jump on, crack down on, clamp down on, hog-tie. See also REPRESS.

SILENT adj. clammed up, closed up like a clam, buttoned up, iced, keep one's trap shut, keep one's yap shut, not let out a peep, not say boo, saved one's breath, dried up, dummy up, dummied up, garbo, tight-lipped, like a grave, could hear a pin drop, cool, cool as a cucumber, keep one's cool, keep one's shirt on, unflappable, not turn a hair, ah-ah head.

SILK n. worm.

SILLINESS n. poppycock, tommyrot, narrishkeit, twaddle, stuff and nonsense, claptrap, total cahcah, flapdoodle, balloon juice, horsefeathers, fudge. See NONSENSE.

SILLY adj. jerky, nerky, squirrely, dingy, flaky, kooky, dippy, punchy, slappy, slaphappy, bubbleheaded, sappy. See FOOLISH.

SIMILARITY n. like of, likes of, look-alikes, peas in a pod, two of a kind, ringer, dead ringer, spitting image, birds of a feather.

SIMPLE adj. 1. snap, no sweat, no problem, like nothin', picnic, easy as pie, turkey shoot, piece of cake, breeze, walkover, child's play, lead-pipe cinch. See EASY. 2. vanilla, clean, what you see is what you get. 3. folksy, homey, haymish, open and shut, meat-and-potatoes man. See PROSAIC.

SIMPLETON n. dork, nerd, loser, birdbrain, yo-yo, twit, lowbrow, dodo, dumbo, dumb bunny, ninny, airhead, bubblehead, deadhead, knows from nothing, doesn't know from A to B, doesn't know enough to come in out of the rain, stoop, dimwit, farmer, jay. See STUPID.

SIMPLIFY v. break it down, cut the shit, cut the bullshit, cut the frills, cut the bells and whistles, get down to basics, get down to the meat, hit the high spots, clean it up, lay out, spell out, draw one a picture, dumb down, put one straight, let daylight in, let sunlight in, make clear, make perfectly clear, KISS (keep it simple stupid). See also EXPLAIN.

SIMULATE v. 1. act like, do, do like, go like, make like, mirror, take off as, do a take-off, put on, put on an act, send up, play the ——— (affect a role). 2. pirate, fake, phony, knock off, steal, steal one's stuff, lift, borrow, crib, take a leaf out of one's book. See IMITATE. 3. put up a front, put on a false front, fake, fake it, make like, let on, let on like, play possum. See PRETEND.

SIMULATED adj. phony, queer, fake, faked, bogue, bogosity, bogotified, hokey, ersatz, pirate goods, pirate labels, soft shell, not what it's cracked up to be. See COUNTERFEIT.

SIMULATION n. 1. look-alike, work alike, ringer, dead ringer, copycat, carbon, carbon copy, spitting image, spit and image, double, ——— compatible (P.C. compatible). 2. queer, fake, bogue, pseud, ersatz, pirate, pirate goods, pirate labels. See COUNTERFEIT. 3. take-off, put-on.

SIMULTANEOUSLY adv. dead heat, in sync, on the beat, with the beat.

SINCE adv. back, back when, from away back, since God knows when, since Hector was a pup. See PAST.

SINCERE adj. up front, open, like it is, call it like it is, lay it on the line, on the up and up, on the level, dead level, the emess, what you see is what you get, blowed in the glass, honest to God, honest injun, sure enough, twenty-four carat, mellow, square, square John, square shooter, true blue, righteous, Christian, kosher, boy scout, fly right, Mr. Clean, saint, down home, regular, legit, on the legit, real, for real, playing for real, the real goods, real people, okay people, straight, straight arrow, shoot straight, straight shooter, straight from the shoulder, straight out, straight dope, straight stuff, straight shit, third rail, talk like a Dutch uncle, call a spade a spade, put all one's cards on the table, make no bones about it, talk turkey, all wool and a yard wide, card-carrying, salt of the earth, no fooling, no shit, no bird turdin'. See also TRUSTWORTHY.

SING v. groan, moan, scat, shout, wail, throw a tonsil, chirp, croon, do a canary, canary, yodel, give out, belt out, line out.

SINGER n. crooner, groaner, canary, chanteuse, monster (popular), songbird, thrush, warbler, bad pipes (bad), belter, coon shouter, folkie, shouter (gospel).

SINGING GROUP n. group, barbershop quartet.

SINGING STYLES n. blues, rhythm and blues, R & B, bebop, punk, country, western, country western, down home, rock 'n' roll, R and R, shout (gospel), scat, croon.

SINGLE PERSON n. single, solo, single-o, swingle, swinger, loner, Crusoe, Robinson Crusoe, ace (restaurant). See also UNMARRIED.

SINGULAR adj. 1. onliest, strange one, oddball, special, an original, cool, rare bird, loner, three-dollar bill. See UNIQUE. 2. breaking new snow, avant-garde.

SIOUX FALLS, SOUTH DAKOTA The Sioux.

SIRE n. old man, O.M., dad, daddy, big daddy, daddio, daddums, pa, papa, pappy, pap, pop, pops, poppa, padre, pater, governor, guv, warden.

SIREN n. flirt, man eater, man trap, velvet trap, operator, party girl, player, swinger, vamp. See also SEDUCER.

SISSY adj. faggy, swishy, pantywaist, creampuff, sissified, cookie pusher, goody-goody, pretty boy, weak sister, Mama's boy. See EFFEMINATE.

SISTER n. sis, sissie, sissy, moose, hood (Rel.).

SIT v. squat, cop a squat, park, park it, park yer carcus, put it there, grab a chair, grab a seat, take a load off, take a load off one's feet, give one's feet a rest.

SIT DOWN (command) v. set, sit your ass down, put it there, park it, park yer carcus.

SITE n. spot, scene, slot, X marks the spot, armpit (undesirable), hangout, lay, layout, fix.

SITUATION n. situash, hap, like it is, where it's at, size of it, how things stack up, scene, ball game. See CONDITION.

SIX n. sixer, Captain Hicks, sise.

SIXTY-FOUR n. sixty-fourmo, 64 mo.

SIZABLE adj. gross, humongous, mungo, humungous, monstro, moby, big mother, beefy, hefty, seagoing, jumbo, whopping, tidy. See BIG.

SKATEBOARD TERMS backyard ramp, catch air (become airborne), skate rock (skateboard dancing to music); road rash, beef (injury from fall).

SKELETON n. cage, Mr. Bones.

SKETCH n. 1. bit, blackout, piece, afterpiece, routine, shtick, spot, stand-up routine, stand-up comedy, dumb act (without words), hoke act. 2. doodle (meaningless pattern).

SKETCH v. 1. doodle (meaningless pattern). 2. run down, run through, picture.

SKI n. slats, sticks, boards, bad dog (stunt performer), schuss boom (speed), shuss boomer (fast skier), sitzmark, mogul (snow mound).

SKID n. gilhooley (auto racing).

SKID v. drift (four wheel).

SKIER n. ski bum, shuss boomer, ski bunny, snow bunny.

SKILL n. 1. one's thing, bag, dodge, line, what one does, what one's into. 2. the stuff, the right stuff, what it takes, cutting it, cutting the mustard, clout, makings, making the grade, moxie, smarts, savvy, the goods, up to it, up to snuff, up one's alley, chops, meal ticket, oil, thing, bit, something on the ball, throwin' stuff (Bsbl.), A, 1–10 (degree, he's a 4), know one's way around, know the ropes, know the score, know-how, know one's onions, know one's stuff, has what it takes, on the ball, plenty on the ball, something on the ball, a bump for, the formula, green thumb.

SKILLED adj. sharp, sharp as a tack, smart as a whip, brainy, brain, brains, savvy, wised up, hep, hepster, hip, hipster, hip to the jive, hipped, cool, sharp, tuned in, into, really into, go-go, with it, all woke up, groovy, in the picture, got it up here, a lot of nifty, slick, smooth, crack, crackerjack, cute, no slouch, no dumbbell, no dummy, nobody's fool, not born yesterday, quick on the trigger, quick on the uptake, heads up, on the ball, on the beam, up to speed, up to snuff, phenom, pro, there, whiz, whiz kid, whiz bang, wizard, boss player, shine at, shine in, enough ducks in a row, hot, hotshot, know one's stuff, know the ropes, know one's way around, know all the ins and outs, know the score, know all the answers, know what's what, know one's onions, know it all, know one's business, know one's p's and q's, in the know, have know-how, have a bump for, have plenty on the ball.

SKILLET n. spider.

SKILLFUL adj. good hands, savvy, sharp, slick, smooth, mellow, there, crack, crackerjack, cute, clean, heads up, on the ball, on the beam, all around, up to the mark, up to snuff, up to speed, tuned in, no slouch, up one's alley, have know-how, know one's onions, know one's stuff, know one's business, know one's oats, know one's beans, know one's bananas, know one's goods, know one's fruit, know one's groceries, know one's oil, big league, enough ducks in a row, won one's spurs.

SKIM v. 1. skate, smooth along. 2. get the cream, give the once-over, hit the high spots, once over lightly, thumb through.

SKIMP v. scrimp, penny-pinch, cut corners, cut to the bone, make ends meet, roll back, tighten one's belt. See STINT.

SKIN n. bark, enamel, rind.

SKIN DIVER n. frogman, schorkeller.

SKIP v. 1. hippety hop. 2. cut, pass up, knock off.

SKIRT n. midi, midiskirt (mid-length), mini, miniskirt (short), drap, handkerchief hem. See also CLOTHING.

SKITTISH adj. 1. feeling one's oats, full of beans, full of piss and vinegar, full of ginger, peppy, zippy. See SPIRITED. 2. rabbity, jumpy. See also FEARFUL, EXCITED, SENSITIVE.

SKULK v. prowl, pussyfoot, gumshoe, snake, case, get around, mooch around, mooch in, mooch out. See also SLINK.

SKULL n. biscuit, headbone, ivory.

SKULLDUGGERY n. game, little game, double-cross, fast one, double shuffle, shenanigans, dirty tricks. See TRICK.

SKUNK n. polecat, wood pussy.

SKY n. lid, the blue, the wild blue yonder.

SKYSCRAPER n. high rise, cloud buster.

SLACK v. fuck off, goof off, fluff off, flub off, flub, flub the dub, goldbrick, dog, dog it, fuck the dog, featherbed, lie down on the job, find Rover (work). See also RELAX.

SLACKER n. fuck-off, goof off, goldbrick, buck passer, clock-watcher, coffee cooler, featherbedder, deuce, welsher, skimper.

SLAIN adj. wasted, chilled, totalled, wiped out, rubbed out, snuffed, done for, gone, had it. See KILLED.

SLANDER n. dirt, dirty linen, mud, slime, rap, slam, smear, hit, knock, black eye. See DEFAMATION.

SLANDER v. pan, slam, smear, hit, blister, roast, scorch, crack, rap, take a rap at, take a swipe at, dump, dump on, shit on, mudsling, run down, put down, tear down, shoot down, cut down to size, cut up, cut rate, cut to the quick, chop, zing, give one a zinger, needle, give one the needle, dozens, play dirty dozens, sound dozens, sound, signifying, signifyn' shucking and jiving, S'ing n' J'ing, woofing, knock, knock down, knock one off his perch, poor-mouth, bad-mouth, bitter mouth, cap, back cap, backbite, rip, rip up and down, rip up the back, cut, skin alive, give one a black eye, make one lose face, pooh-pooh, rubbish, sour grapes, curdle, kick one around, do a number on, mark wrong, mark lousy, put the crimpers in, put the hooks in, put the needles in, put the zingers in, sizzle, put away, hurt one where one lives, hit one where one lives, hurl brickbats at, make one sing small. See also SLUR.

SLANDERER n. knocker, mudslinger, backbiter.

SLANG n. jive, jive talk, lingo, street talk, weasel words, flash (thieves). See also LANGUAGE.

SLANTED adj. slaunchways, slaunchwise.

SLAP n. crack, slam, smack, splap, potch, zetz.

SLAPDASH adv. slam bang, slap bang. See also CARELESSLY.

SLAPSTICK n. baggypants comedy, pratfall comedy, afterpieces, boffo schtick, stationhouse bits. See also FARCE.

SLASH v. carve, carve initials in one, chop, chop down, clip, chiv, shiv, slice, stick, cut, cut a new kisser for, open up. See also WOUND.

SLATE n. lineup, ticket (Pol.).

SLATE v. line up, get on line, pencil in, set up.

SLAUGHTER n. offing, wasting, taking out, a ride, liquidation, chill, kiss-off. See KILLING.

SLAUGHTER v. 1. beef up (cow).

SLAY v. liquidate, neutralize, waste, do, do in, hit, snuff, burn, cook, chill, ice, off, cool out, take out, rub out, erase, knock off, blow away. See KILL.

SLAYER n. hit man, trigger man, piece man, torpedo, enforcer, gorilla, gun, gunsel, hatchet man. See KILLER.

SLAYING n. chill, big chill, offing, hit, knock off, rub out, the works, waste. See KILLING.

SLED n. belly whopper, pig sticker.

SLEDDING v. belly flop, belly flopper, belly whopper, belly bust, belly busting, belly bumping, belly smacking.

SLEEP n. catnap, forty winks, microsleep, snooze, a few z's, winks, shut-eye, the nod, sleepville, sack time, sack duty, duty time, pad duty, blanket drill, bunk fatigue, bunk habit, in the arms of Morpheus, bye-bye, beddy-bye, beauty sleep.

SLEEP v. snooze, zizz, grab a few z's, cop some z's, log some z's, saw logs, saw wood, get some shut-eye, get some sack time, sack up, sack in, sack out, conk out, zonk out, fall out, flack out, flake out, pad out, rack out, tube out, catnap, cooping (police), doss, doz, crash, calk off, drop off, dope off, cork off, knock off, grab some shut-eye, huddle, knock a nod, cop a nod, dig oneself a nod, collar a nod, catch a wink, catch forty winks, blanket drill (Army), bunk fatigue (WW II), duty time, flop, kip, pound one's ear, pad down, cup, get horizontal, rest in the arms of Morpheus, plow the deep, in dreamland, sleep in (late).

SLEEP, GO TO hit the hay, hit the sack, hit the pad, knock the pad, mixout, sack out, flack out, flake out. See RETIRE.

SLEEPER n. bunk lizard, goldbrick.

SLEEPING adj. making z's, sawing wood, collaring a nod, dead to the world, flaked out, out of it. See ASLEEP.

SLEEPING BAG n. fleabag, fart sack.

SLEEPING PAD n. corking mat (USN, WW II).

SLEEPING PILL n. dope, goof ball, goofy ball (Nembutal), knockout drop, Mickey Finn.

SLEEPY adj. dopey, out of it, sleepyhead, snoozy, stretchy, on the nod, eye trouble, in sleepville, blah, blahs, drippy, wimpy, draggy.

SLENDER adj. skinny, skeleton, stick, twiggy, bean pole, beanstalk, stilt, broomstick, gangleshanks. See THIN.

SLEUTH n. dick, tec, private eye, P.I., eye, narc; Pink, the Eye (Pinkerton detective or Pinkerton National Detective Agency); shoe, gumshoe, op, house dick, Hawkshaw, beagle. See DETECTIVE.

SLICE v. chiv, shiv, whack, hack.

SLICK adj. 1. smooth, smarts, street smarts, streetwise, foxy, crazy like a fox, cagey, fancy footwork, full of fancy footwork, slippery, sly boots. See SHREWD. 2. greasy.

SLIDE v. skate, smooth along, scooch.

SLIDE RULE n. stick, slipstick, cheat stick, guess stick, swindle stick.

SLIDE TROMBONE n. sliphorn.

SLIGHT adj. skinny, skeleton, stick, twiggy, shadow, bag of bones, stack of bones, hat rack, broomstick, rattlebones. See THIN. See also AMOUNT, SMALL.

SLIGHT n. brush-off, call-down, cold shoulder, cut, go by, kick in the ass, put-down. See also REJECTION.

SLIGHT v. cut, cut dead, brush off, give one the brush, high hat, not give one the time of day, chill, cool, cold shoulder, ice out. See SNUB. See also NEGLECT, REJECT.

SLIGHTED adj. in the cold, out in the cold, passed up, sidelined. See SNUBBED. See also REJECTED.

SLIGHTLY adv. somewhat, pretty, kind of.

SLIM adj. skinny, slinky, stick, twiggy, shadow, bean pole, stilt, hat rack, broomstick. See THIN.

SLIME n. goo, gooey, glop, gloppy, Mississippi mud, gunk.

SLIMY adj. scummy.

SLING v. chuck, chunk, fire, heave, lob, peg, pitch sling, toss.

SLINGSHOT n. flipper.

SLINK v. gumshoe, pussyfoot, snake, mooch around, mooch in, mooch out. See also SKULK.

SLIP n. flub, fluff, muff, boner, boo-boo, bobble, goof, foul-up, fuck-up, screw up, slip up, plumb (serious), howler, flap (social), fox paw, fox pass, gaff. See MISTAKE.

SLIP v. 1. skate, smooth along. 2. let ride, let slide, slip up. 3. flub, fluff, muff, goof, goof up, slip up, make a boner, make a boo-boo, make a blooper, drop the ball, stumble, put one's foot in it, put one's foot in one's mouth, stub one's toe. See ERR.

SLIPPERS n. skivvies, mules, scuffs, thongs, flip-flops, zoris. See also SHOES.

SLIPPERY adj. 1. cagey, crazy like a fox, foxy, slick, smooth. See SHREWD. 2. greasy, skating rink.

SLIPSHOD adj. sloppy, slapdash, junky, fly-by-night, messy, half-assed, do by halves, any old way, mess around, honky-tonk, cold haul, a lick and a promise. See CARELESS. See also SLOVENLY.

SLOG v. 1. plug, plug along, plug away, dig, grind, hammer, slave, sweat, sweat and slave, bear down on it. See PLOD. 2. hoof it, go by hand, boot it, stump it, beat the rocks, press the bricks. See WALK.

SLOPING adj. slaunchways, slaunchwise.

SLOT MACHINE n. one-arm bandit, one-armed bandit, slot, slots.

SLOTHFUL adj. drag ass, lox, sack artist, Stepin Fetchit. See also LAZY.

SLOVENLY adj. sloppy, grubby, grungy, groaty, grotty, grody, grunch, grunge, grubby, tacky, chili bowl, icky, scuzzy, scuzzed, scuzzed up, sleazy, sleazeball, sludgeball, mess, messed up, mussed up, messy, mussy, bloody mess, holy mess, unholy mess, rat's nest, topsy-turvy, arsy-varsy, discombobulated, slob, fat slob, ragmop, scraggly, piggy, pigpen, dip, jeeter, poky, seedy, draggle-tailed, drabble-tailed, down at the heel, out at the heels, out at the elbows. See also SLIPSHOD.

SLOW adj. 1. pokey, slowpoke, draggy, drag ass, foot dragger, shlepper, valium picnic (slow day), banana boat, klupper, slower than the seven-year itch, stepin fetchit, stick in the mud, molasses in January, lox, sack artist. 2. draggy, ho hum, bor-ring, a yawn, big yawn, bore one stiff, dullsville, noplaceville, phoned in, big deal, no big deal, flat. See BORING.

SLOW v. bog, bog down, lose steam, back off, let up, anchor it, brake, hit the brakes, put on the brakes, lay down rubber, leave a stripe, let down the flaps, give one the wind (suddenly), back off the pedal, lay back, cool it, choke, choke in, choke up, ease off. See also DELAY, HINDER, RETARD.

SLOWLY adv. flaps down, stick in the mud, get no place fast, mosey, toddle, plug along, poke along, shlep, drag tail (also move with difficulty), drag ass, drag one's tail, slo-mo, have lead in one's pants, overland route, by pony express, slowpoke, move like a slug, foot dragger, slower than the seven-year itch, in short pants, skuffling.

SLOW MATURATION n. late bloomer.

SLOW-WITTED adj. dorky, nerdy, lamebrain, birdbrain, out to lunch, four-letter man (dumb), stoop, stupe, spaz, thick, lob, dill, dud, ninny, nincompoop, airhead, balloonhead, meatball, bonehead, nuthin' upstairs, weak in the upper story. See STUPID.

SLUDGE n. gook, gunk, glop.

SLUGGISH adj. 1. laid back, blah, dopey, drippy, mooney, sleepyhead, stretchy, have spring fever. See LANGUID. 2. pokey, draggy, drag ass, shlepper, slower than the seven-year itch, molasses in January, lox. See SLOW.

SLUM n. back alley, back street, hogsville, skid row, shanty town.

SLUMBER n. forty winks, sleepville, sack time, sack duty, duty, duty time, pad duty, bunk habit, beauty sleep. See SLEEP.

SLUMBER v. make some z's, log some z's, saw logs, saw wood, get some sack time, grab some shut eye, catch forty winks, blanket drill (Army). See SLEEP.

SLUMP n. 1. bust, hard times, bad times, crash, rainy days, rainin', bear market, bottom out, slide, Black Monday (October 19, 1987), Black and Blue Monday (October 26, 1987), the big trouble (the 1930s). 2. blue devils, blue funk, funk, downer, dumps, down trip, letdown, hit the skids, die on the vine. See DEPRESSION.

SLUR n. put-down, zinger, brickbat, rap, slam, knock, black eye, hit, dirty dig, dump, dozens, dirty dozens, woofing. See DEFAMATION.

SLUR v. put down, dump on, flip one the finger, give one the finger, give one five fingers, chop, blister, roast, scorch, cut up, do a number on, zing, give one a zinger, give one the cold shoulder, give one a backhanded compliment, give one a left-handed compliment, give one a black eye, give one a dirty dig, thumb one's nose, slap in the face, hurl brickbats at, dozens, play dirty dozens, sound dozens, sound, signify, signifyn' shucking and jiving, S'ing n' J'ing, woofing, eighty-six, hurt one where he lives, hit one where he lives, blow off, cut, cut to the quick, skin alive, cap, curdle, gross out, miff, push, kick one around, pooh-pooh. See also SLANDER.

SLUSH n. gook, gunk, glop.

SLY adj. smooth, smarts, street smarts, streetwise, foxy, crazy like a fox, cagey, fancy footwork, slick, slippery, greasy, greaseball, fishy, sly boots, shady, sharp, snake in the grass, cheatin' heart, not kosher, honest John, feather legs, speak with forked tongue. See also SHREWD.

SLYLY adv. undercover, under wraps, hush-hush, strictly hush-hush, on the q.t., on the quiet, on the sly, in a hole-and-corner way, in holes and corners.

SMALL adj. mini, minny, teeny, teeny-weeny, teensy, teensy-weensy, eentsy-weentsy, bitty, bitsy, little bitty, little bitsy, itsy-bitsy, itsy-witsy, shrimp, wee, peewee, peanut, runt, short, small fry, small time, dinky, measly, banty, tomtit, shot, shit, chicken shit, horseshit, bullshit, chippie, button, one horse, yea big, yea high, wart, mite, piddling, two bit, two by four, pint-sized, half-pint, knee high, knee high to a grasshopper, penny ante, tad, titch, tich, jerkwater (town).

SMALL PLACE n. hole in the wall, pigeonhole, cubbyhole, tight pinch, tight spot, tight squeeze.

SMALL TOWN n. jerkwater town, hick town, rube town, hoosier town, one-horse town, tank town, tank station, South Succotash, East Jesus, Podunk, jumping-off place, hickville, burg, whistle stop, whistle snort, noplaceville, filling station, wide place in the road, hideaway, the bushes, the boondocks, boonies, sticks, stix, bush leagues, pumpkin, the rhubarbs.

SMART adj. 1. brain, brainy, egghead, got the smarts, have the smarts, smart as a whip, whiz, whiz kid, bright, long-haired, skull, genius, rocket scientist, Einstein. See INTELLIGENT. 2. sharp, dap, last word, latest thing, nobby, natty, dressed to kill. See STYLISH.

SMASH v. 1. scrunch, crunch, bust to bits, break to smithereens, make mincemeat of, smash to smithereens, trash, squash, squish, smash up, take a joint apart, break the lease, put something out of action, put out of commission, bend the goods. See DESTROY.

SMEAR v. pan, slam, hit, blister, scorch, rap, mudsling, poor-mouth, bad-mouth, rip up the back, give a black eye, pooh-pooh, rubbish, sour grapes, do a number on, put the zingers in. See SLANDER.

SMELLING SALTS n. dope.

SMELLY adj. stinko, whiffy, nosey, strong, stinking, stinky, loud (strong), P.U., what died?

SMELT n. hooligan.

SMILE v. crack a smile, grin from ear to ear, grin like a Cheshire cat, grin like a Chessy cat.

SMIRK v. grin like a Cheshire cat, grin like a Chessy cat.

SMOCK n. Mother Hubbard.

SMOKE v. light up, blow, drag, take a drag, inhale, pull, do up, puff, poke, toat, toke, torch up, hit, take a hit, blow a stick, blow smoke rings, chain-smoke, dinch (extinguish cigarette), have a pipeful, fog, fog up, French inhale, fume, fumigate.

SMOKED ALASKAN SALMON n. squaw candy.

SMOKE-FOG n. smog.

SMOKE-HAZE n. smaze.

SMOKER n. chain smoker, fag hag (Fem.), chimney.

SMOKING ROOM n. butt room.

SMOOTH v. 1. cool, cool out, cool it, cool off, stroke, pour oil on troubled waters, take the edge off, take the sting out of, put the lid on. See PACIFY. 2. grease the wheels, run interference for, open doors, walk through, hand-carry.

SMOOTHLY adv. like nothin', soft touch, velvet, pie, cherry pie, easy as pie, duck soup, piece of cake, fluff, breeze, walkover, waltz, slick as a whistle, swimmingly. See also EASY.

SMOTHER v. kill (fire or cigarette), choke, douse, knock down, stamp out. See REPRESS.

SMUG adj. stuffy, top lofty, hoity-toity, hot shit, hot stuff, hotshot, cock of the walk, think one is it, think one's shit doesn't stink. See CONCEITED.

SMUGGLE v. move the laundry, rum run, run rum, snake one in, whip over, push.

SMUGGLER n. bootlegger, legger, rum runner, monkey runner, sneaker (motorboat), coyote (illegal aliens).

SMUGGLE LIQUOR v. rum run, run rum, whip over.

SMUTTY adj. raw, raunchy, X-rated, filthy, in the gutter, off-color, rough, rough stuff, salty. See OBSCENE.

SNACK n. bite, gorp, nash, nosh, nibble, midnight snack, snack time, eats, grub, pecks, peckings (Bl.), pick-me-up, yum, yum-yum, goodies, munchies. See also FOOD, MEAL.

SNACK BAR n. fast food, quick and dirty, short order.

SNAG n. bug, glitch, fix, hole, pickle, scrape, stew, hang-up, spot, tight spot, crunch, catch 22, joker, cropper, up a tree, tail in a gate, tit in a wringer, puzzler. See DIFFICULTY.

SNAG v. hook, nail, net, gaff, pick up, put the claw on, haul in. See GRAB.

SNAKE CHARMER n. geek.

SNAPPISH adj. snippy, snappy, short.

SNAPSHOT n. photo, snap, shot, pic, pix, print, glossy.

SNARE v. bag, net, land, get one's fingers on, corral, pull in, round up. See GRAB. See also ARREST.

SNATCH v. snag, collar, bag, glom, glom onto, put the snatch on, clap hands on, get one's fingers on, get one's hands on. See GRAB.

SNEAK v. gumshoe, pussyfoot, prowl, snake, case, get around, mooch around, mooch in, mooch out.

SNEAK ATTACK n. Pearl Harbor.

SNEAKILY adv. on the quiet, on the q.t., gumshoeing, pussyfooting, in a hole-and-corner way, in holes and corners.

SNEER n. put-on, dump, put-down, rank out, dig, dirty dig, crack, slam, swipe, jab, comeback, parting shot, brickbat.

SNOB n. Brahmin, highbrow, high hat, smarty pants, stiff neck.

SNOBBISH adj. snooty, uppity, uppish, swanky, snotty, toney, dicty, put on airs, stuck up, hoity-toity, persnickety, sniffy, snippy, high hog, high hat, high-hatted, hinkty, top lofty, high-nosed, sidity, sidity. See also ARROGANT.

SNOOP n. nosey Parker, busybody, Paul Pry, Peeping Tom, gumshoe.

SNOOPING adj. nosing around, peeping. See also INQUISITIVE.

SNORE v. saw gourds, saw logs, saw wood, make z's. See also SLEEP.

SNOUT n. smeller, schnoz, schnozzola, schnozzle, beak, bugle, horn, honker, snoot, nozzle, bazoo, banana, bill, beezer, boke, conk, handle, sniffer, snuffer, whiffer.

SNOW n. powder, whiteout, dandruff, fluff stuff, corn (man made), termination dust (first of season, Alaska).

SNOWMOBILE n. snowgo.

SNOWSTORM n. whiteout.

SNUB v. cut, cut dead, brush off, give one the brush, go by, pass up, high hat, chill, put the chill on, ice, ice out, frost, burr, cool, play it cool, act cool, leave out in the cold, put the freeze on, not give one the time of day, not give one a flop, not give one a rumble, not give one a tumble, look right through, cold shoulder, give one the cold shoulder, cold duke, duck, fluff, give one the fluff, fluff off, kiss off, scratch, scratch off the list, upstage, shine one on, look right through, kick in the ass. See also SHUN.

SNUBBED adj. cut, cold shouldered, out in the cold, chilled, brushed off, fluffed off, got it in the neck, kicked in the ass, slapped in the face. See also REJECTED.

SNUFF n. dust, heifer dust (Arc.), snoose.

SNUG adj. comfy, cushy, snug as a bug in a rug, homey, tight.

SOAKING n. dunking.

SOAP n. soogie, sujee, soujge.

SOB v. blubber, bawl, break down, boo hoo, weep bitter tears, turn on the waterworks, cry one's eyes out, cry me a river. See CRY.

SOBER adj. 1. cold sober, sober as a judge, able to walk the chalk line, on the wagon, on the water wagon, dry, took the pledge. 2. strictly business, heavy, heavy number, am I laughing?, not playing around, sourpuss, frozen faced. See SERIOUS.

SOCIABLE adj. mix, get together, right nice, right neighborly, downright neighborly, white, regular, square shooter, sucking around, kissing up to, get with it, break the ice, clubby, clubbable. See also COMPANIONABLE.

SOCIAL adj. elbow-bender, glad-hander.

SOCIAL DISEASE n. AIDS, VD, clap, dose, dose up, dose of clap, old dose (neglected case), package, picked up something, picked up a nail, brothel sprouts, Cupid's itch, Venus's curse, crotch pheasants, lobster tails, full house (combination of), short-arm inspection (examination of males for). See VENEREAL DISEASE.

SOCIAL GATHERING n. ball, bash, blast, bust, get-together, clambake, crush, shindig, rub, jump, mingle, blowout, coffee klatsch, shindy, merry-go-round, wingding, jam, do, freeload, gig, scene. See PARTY.

SOCIAL GRACE n. polish.

SOCIALIST n. left, lefty, lefto, left winger, Old Left, left of center, pink, pinko, parlor pink, radish, fellow traveller, linky dink, bleeding heart, do-gooder, innocent (Bl.), knee-jerk reaction, comsymp, Wobbly.

SOCIALIZE v. mix, tie up with, gang up, pal up, pal around, hang around with, run with, chum with, chum together, make the rounds, floss around, on the go, gadabout. See also FRATERNIZE.

SOCIALLY ACCEPTABLE adj. housebroken, in.

SOCiALLY ADROIT adj. operator, swinger, player, street smart, streetwise.

SOCIAL REGISTER n. blue book.

SOCIAL WORKER n. streetworker.

SOCIETY n. 1. the 400, the four hundred, beautiful people, glitterati, upper crust, high-rise boys, high society, main line, jet set. See ELITE. 2. hookup, tie-in, tie-up, gang, mob, ring, clan, outfit, syndicate. See ASSOCIATION. 3. jungle, zoo, rat race.

SOCIOECONOMIC GROUPS n. baby boomer, blue collar, white collar, dik (double income, have children), dink (double income, have no children), sik (single income with children), sink (single income, no children), zink (zero income, no children), yup, yuppie, buppie (black urban professional), guppie (gay urban professional), yumpie (young, upwardly mobile professional), yuffie (young urban failure), yavis (young, attractive, verbal, intelligent, successful), the establishment, upper ten thousand, the 400, Four Hundred.

SOCIOLOGY n. soc, sosh.

SOCKS n. bobby socks, bobby sox.

SODA n. pop, club soda, clear soda, soda back (chaser); seltzer, sizz water, fizz water, penny plain, black cow, double chocolate. See SOFT DRINK.

SODA FOUNTAIN WORKER n. jerk, soda jerk, soda jerker, squirt, ninety-eight (mgr.).

SODOMIST n. bugger.

SODOMY n. 1. ace fuck, brown, brown hole, corn hole, burgle, goin' up the mustard road, Greek, Hershey bar way, sit on it, ride the deck, up the old dirt road, bite the brown, reem, rim job. See also SEXUAL RELATIONS. 2. suck, cock suck, sucky suck, blow, blow job, go down on, head, give head, a shot upstairs, gobble, peter puff, play the skin flute. See FELLATIO. 3. face, face job, hat job, French job, box lunch, fur burger, muff dive, eating at the Y (all Obsc.). See CUNNILINGUS.

SOFT adj. 1. gone to seed, not what one used to be, out of condition, out of shape, run to seed, rusty, good and flabby. 2. cool, mellow, gravy.

SOFT DRINK n. coke, pop, club soda, clear soda, white soda; chaser, back soda, soda back (chaser); seltzer, sizz water, fizz water, fizzy stuff, penny plain, two-cents plain, ammonia, maiden's delight (cherry), mixer, cream, egg cream, phosphate, black cow, double chocolate, float, cooler, bug juice.

SOFT DRINK POWDER n. flukum, flookem, flookum.

SOFTEN v. soft-pedal, cool, cool it, cool out, fix up, make up, make it up, make matters up, patch things up, get together on, come together, meet halfway, pour oil on troubled waters, take the edge off, take the bite out, take the sting out.

SOFTHEARTED adj. softie, teddy bear, pussycat, nice guy, Mr. Nice, marshmallow. See also KIND.

SOIL v. crud, sleaze up, crumb up, muck up, mess, mess up, muss, muss up.

SOILED adj. cruddy, grungy, raunchy, messy, messed up, mussed up, sleazy, sleazed up. See DIRTY.

SOJOURN v. bunk, hang out, nest, perch, roost, squat, bunk out, crash. See INHABIT.

SOLDIER n. G.I., GI Joe, Joe, Joe Blow, Blow Joe, dogface, doughfoot (WW II), E.M., draftee, doughboy (WW I, Mexican war), footsoldier, footslogger, grunt, hump, paddlefoot, buck-ass private, trooper, leg (infantry, Vietnam), red legs (artilleryman, WW I), retread (recalled to duty), sad sack, snuff, yardbird, bunion breeder, gravel agitator, gravel crusher (WW I), Yank, jazz bo (Bl.), bulletbait, cannon fodder, fuck off, government inspected meat (homosexual use), lifer (career), Fed (Union), bluebelly (Union soldier, Derog.), dolly dancer (easy duty), barracks lawyer, guardhouse lawyer, galoot, crunchie, clerks and jerks (rear echelon).

SOLD OUT adj. sellout, SRO, go clean, clean house.

SOLE onliest, ace (restaurant). See ALONE.

SOLELY adj. onliest. See ALONE.

SOLEMN adj. 1. heavy, heavy number, matter of life and death, no fooling, mean business. 2. downbeat, am I laughing?, cold sober, sober as a judge. See SERIOUS.

SOLICIT v. 1. hit on, pop the question, whistle for (but won't get). 2. steer, tout, run a stable, have a string of hustlers, have a sister-in-law. 3. bum, panhandle, hustle, sponge, schnorr, cadge, touch, mooch, promote, put the bite on, pass the hat, hit up. See BEG.

SOLICITOR n. 1. mouthpiece, shyster, ambulance chaser, legal eagle, beagle, lip, tongue, squeal, spieler, spouter, springer. See ATTORNEY. 2. mack, mackman, macko man, mac, mackerel, maggot, dude, hustler, Johnny Ponce, pee eye, P.I., brother-in-law, honey man. See PIMP, PROSTITUTE.

SOLICITOUS adj. heart in the right place, worried sick, worried stiff, beside oneself, all overish. See also CONSIDERATE.

SOLICITUDE n. tender loving care, TLC.

SOLID adj. 1. solid as a rock, Rocka Gibraltar, Rock of Gibraltar, Rock of Gib, brick wall, set in concrete, stuck in concrete, buried in concrete, chiseled in stone. 2. set, stay put, unflappable, hard core, hard line, rock-ribbed. See STUBBORN. 3. sound as a dollar, in the black. See also WEALTHY. 4. big time, big league, major league, heavyweight, high powered, double-barreled. See IMPORTANT. 5. husky, hefty, heavy, hunk, hulk. See STRONG.

SOLITARY adj. loner, lone wolf, solo, stag, all by one's lonesome, in solitary, chew something alone, traveling light. See ALONE.

SOLITARY CONFINEMENT n. bury, plant, ice, put on ice, put in the hole, salt, throw the key away, do penance, slap in the box, hit the box, hit izo, hit isolation, hit the beach, hit the icebox, hit the plant, a month in Congress, P and Q (peace and quiet), on the shelf, tending the bar (standing handcuffed), time out.

SOLO adj. loner, single, single-o, swingle, go it alone, Crusoe, Robinson Crusoe, ace (Rest.), get off (swing music: improvised). See also ALONE.

SOLUTION n. all the right moves, on target, pay dirt, the ticket, the nod, the call, quick fix, band-aid (temporary, too little).

SOLVE v. chill, dope, dope out, pan out, figure out, crack, lick, deal with, make a deal, iron, iron out, nail down, cinch, clinch, unzip, work through, hit it on the nose.

SOLVENT adj. sound as a dollar, in the black. See also WEALTHY.

SOMBER adj. dragged, ass in a sling, blue, got the blue devils, down, hang crepe, hurting, carry a heavy load, gloomy Gus, not crack a smile, wipe the smile off one's face, prunefaced, sourpuss. See UNHAPPY.

SOMERSAULT v. endo.

SOMETIMES adv. once in a blue moon, once in a coon's age, every now and then, every once in a while, every so often.

SOMNOLENT adj. dopey, out of it, sleepyhead, snoozy, stretchy, on the nod, eye trouble, in sleepville, blah, blahs, drippy, wimpy, draggy. See also LANGUID.

SON n. chip off the old block, junior, sprout, sun and air, June bug.

SONG n. tune, oldie, golden oldie, holler, holler song, torch song, belly music, chartbursting hit.

SONGWRITER n. cleffer, songster, tunesmith, tunester.

SONOROUS adj. leather-lunged. See also LOUD.

SOON adv. by 'n' by, in a short, short short, coming down the pike. See ANON.

SOOTHE v. cool, cool off, stroke, butter up, make nice, play up to, pour oil on troubled waters, square, take the edge off, take the sting out of, make matters up, patch things up. See PACIFY.

SOOTHING cool, mellow, flannel (manner). See also TRANQUILIZER.

SOPHISTICATE n. cat, sharp cat, hep cat, hip cat, tomcat, hipster, dude, sport, swinger, slicker, city slicker, man about town. See also VETERAN.

SOPHISTICATED adj. with it, wised up, wise to, hep to, hep, hip, sharp cat, tomcat, dude, on to, on the beam, down by law, uptown, go-go, in, into, really into, groovy, swinging, mod, street smart, streetwise, uppity, execu-tive, sport, city slicker, laid back, cool, cool and collected, on, switched on, kicked around, been around, been hit before, been there before, been around the block, been around the block a few times, didn't come into town on a load of hay, wasn't born yesterday, cut a few touches, in the know, knows the score, knows the ropes, knows which side is up, knows which side his bread is buttered on, knows which side his head is battered on, dolce vita.

SOPHOMORE n. soph.

SORCERY n. evil eye, go, hoodoo, voodoo, jinx, whack, whammy, hocus-pocus, mumbo-jumbo, abracadabra.

SORE THROAT n. bad pipes.

SORORITY HOUSE n. house, soror house, snake house, zoo, frau shack, animal farm, bull pen.

SORORITY MEMBER n. soror, sister, pheeze (pledge).

SORROW n. heartache, blues, tsuris, rain, rainin', trouble, big trouble, bad news. See MISERY.

SORROW v. carry on, eat one's heart out, hang crepe, sing the blues, take on, cry me a river. See MOURN.

SORROWFUL adj. sob story, sob stuff, tear-jerker, weeper, teardrop special, sing the blues, crying the blues, hang crepe, bummed out, hurting, in pain, in the pits, carry a heavy load, raining on one's parade, sad sacky. See UNHAPPY.

SORT n. likes, likes of, lot, number.

SORT v. peg, pigeonhole, typecast, tab, button down, put down as, put down for, size up, put in shape, put to rights, put in apple-pie order. See also ARRANGE.

SOT n. drinker, heavy drinker, drunk, big drunk, boozer, boozehound, dipso, brown bagger, souse, sponge, lush, wino, juicehead, town drunk, stiff, juicer. See DRINKER.

SOUND adj. 1. up to snuff, up to the mark, wrapped tight, alive and kicking, in fine whack, in the pink, sound as a dollar, right as rain. See HEALTHY. 2. together, got it together, cool, commonsensical, all there, in one's right mind, have all one's marbles, have all one's buttons. See REASONABLE. 3. wash, fly, go, legit, kosher, signify, stand up, hold up, hold water, hold together, hang together, hold up in the wash, all there.

SOUP n. bowl, dishwater, splash, water.

SOUP STOCK n. pot liquor (residue).

SOURCE n. horse's mouth, connection, tipster, tout.

SOUTH n. Dixie, the cotton curtain, 'bama, below the Mason-Dixon line, down home, Old South, Galilee, sunny South, way down South, deep South.

SOUTH AMERICAN n.   Latino, south of the border; greaseball, spic (Derog.)

SOUTH BEND, INDIANA   Irish City.

SOUTH CAROLINA   Free State, Gamecock State, Palmetto State, Rice State, Swamp State, Sand-lapper.

SOUTH CAROLINA RESIDENT n.   clay eater.

SOUTH DAKOTA   Coyote State, Sunshine State.

SOUTHEAST ASIA TREATY ORGANIZATION n.   SEATO.

SOUTHERN adj.   cornpone, down home.

SOUTHERNER n.   cracker, magnolia blossom, redneck, good ole boy, Dixiecrat, ridge runner, chiv, cornpone, grit, hardboot, hardhead; jig chaser, peckerwood, white trash, clay eater, Reb, Rebel (Derog.).

SOVIET BLOC BORDER n.   iron curtain.

SOVIET CITIZEN n.   comrade, Roosky, Russky, Ruskie, Red, tovarich, Moscovite.

SOVIET JEW n.   refusenik.

SOVIET UNION   reds, Russky, iron curtain, behind the iron curtain, the original borscht belt.

SOW n.   porker, porky, cob roller (young or small).

SPA n.   fat farm, watering hole.

SPACE n.   1. slot, spot, zone, turf, territory. 2. elbowroom, room to swing a cat, leeway. 3. outer space, deep space.

SPACE OBJECTS n.   garbage (Obs.).

SPACESHIP n.   bird, Roman candle, flying saucer, LEM, LM, UFO.

SPACESHIP SEA LANDING n.   splashdown.

SPACE SHUTTLE n.   Ace Trucking Company.

SPACE SUIT n.   penguin suit.

SPACE TERMS   lift off, all systems go, A-OK, fly by wire (automatic pilot), decay (lose momentum), chicken switch (abort switch), chicken button (pilot eject switch), critically one.

SPADE n.   banjo, clam shovel (short), Irish banjo, Irish fan, jo, hemo jo, joe, muck stick, pooper-scooper.

SPAGHETTI n.   lead pipe, worms, pisghetti.

SPANIARD n.   spic, spick, greaseball, hatchet thrower, hombre (all Derog.).

SPANK v.   whup, whup ass, whale, whop, wallop, swinge, lick, larrup, clobber, welt, trim, flax, lather, leather, hide, paddle, paddle one's ass, botch, potch, fan,

tan, tan one's hide, take it out of one's hide, take it out of one's skin, dust one's pants, dust one's trousers, give a dose of birch oil, give a dose of strap oil, give a dose of hickory oil, give a dose of hazel oil. See also HIT.

SPANKING n.   licking, paddling, larruping, walloping, whupping, whaling, lathering, leathering, hiding, tanning, dose of strap oil, dose of hazel oil, dose of hickory oil, dose of birch oil. See also BEATING.

SPARE adj.   1. skinny, stick, twiggy, shadow, beanstalk, stilt, hat rack, broomstick. See THIN. 2. widow. 3. option, all the options, spare tire, fifth wheel, backup, gash, lagniappe, bells and whistles. See also EXTRA.

SPARE v.   let go, let off, let off the hook, bail one out, save one's neck, save one's bacon, give one a break, get one out of hock, get one off the hook, spring, pull something out of the fire, pull one's chestnuts out of the fire. See also FORGIVE.

SPARED adj.   let off, bailed out, off the hook, out of hock.

SPARE RIBS n.   piano.

SPARE TIME n.   goof-off time, fuck-off time, time to burn, time to kill, one's own sweet time.

SPARKLE n.   flash, glitz, show, zap.

SPASM n.   yank, yerk.

SPASMODIC adj.   choppy, herky-jerky, fits and starts.

SPASMODICALLY adv.   by bits and pieces, by fits and starts, herky-jerky. See ERRATICALLY.

SPASTIC adj.   spaz, spas, herky-jerky.

SPAT n.   hassle, static, brush, flap, tiff, words, run-in, fuss, bone to pick, bone of contention. See ARGUMENT.

SPAY v.   alter, fix, neuter.

SPEAK v.   1. go, gab, rap, yackety-yak, yada-yada, yada, yatata-yatata, yak-yak, yak, yack, yock, yuk, yuck, yam, yap, yawp, yaup, yatter, patter, natter, wig, spout, spout off, spiel, jaw, lip, chin, gas, chaff, chew, chew over, chew the fat, chew the rag, rag around, modulate, modjitate, splib, splib de wib, slide one's jib, sing, spill, spill the beans, bull, bullshit, throw the bull, shoot the bull, shoot the shit, shoot the bullshit, shoot, shoot the breeze, shoot the lemon, shoot one's wad, shoot off one's mouth, shoot off one's trap, shoot off one's yap, shoot off one's face, shoot one's bazoo off, shoot one's kisser off, let off steam, blow off steam, unload, blab, blab off, pop off, noise off, sound off, flip one's lip (idle), flap, flap one's lip, flap one's jaw, flap one's chops, flap one's jowls, grind, gum, let one's hair down, jibber-jabber, mush mouth, rattle, schmoose, schmoozle, fat mouth, run one's mouth, run off at the mouth, diarrhea of the mouth, have verbal diarrhea, fold one's ear, bend one's ear, interact, interface, network, reach out, relate, talk one's ear off, do a barber, woof, beef, chop it up, chop up jackpots, slice chops, cut up jackies, crack, spring with a crack, cut it up, kick the gong around, punch the gun, sling the crap, sling the lingo, blow, blow hot air, blow change (radical), blow off one's mouth, blow off one's trap, blow off one's yap, bat one's gums, beat one's gums, chew one's gums, bump one's gums, beat around the bush, beat the drum, beat one's chops, bat the chat, bat the breeze, breeze, buzz, chip the ivories, sass, trash, knock, blitz, bad-mouth, bad-talk, sweet-talk, fast-talk, drool, open one's face, some pig, gobble, talk turkey, wag the tongue, parley voo, twiddle, touch, keep in touch, touch base, have truck with, visit, visit with. 2. grok, back channel (secretly), pitch, spiel, spout, stump, get across, get on a soapbox.

SPEAKEASY n. speak, gin mill, saloon, boozery, blind pig. See also BAR.

SPEAKER n. spieler, spouter, tub thumper, jawsmith, soapboxer, soapbox orator, chalk talker, roaster (uncomplimentary tribute).

SPEAK LOUDER v. increase the volume.

SPECIAL adj. 1. A number one, 10, ten, super-duper, smashing, gnarly, unreal, zero cool, wicked, out of this world, out of sight, flash, primo, crack, solid gold, beautiful, mean, not too shabby, heavy, terrible, state of the art, this is some kinda———. See EXCELLENT. 2. world class, job, wizard, high cotton, splash; mother, motherfucker, muthah, muthahfuckah (Obsc.), skull, brain, grind. See also BEST. 3. nature of the beast, that's one all over, just like one.

SPECIAL FORCE n. swat team, commandos, flying squad, goon squad, rangers.

SPECIALIST n. pro, old pro, old hand, old war-horse, maven, bone man, heart man, big nose man, high priest, guru. See AUTHORITY.

SPECIALIZE v. be into, do one's thing, go in for, have a weakness for, get down to brass tacks, get down to cases.

SPECIAL, TV n. spec.

SPECIALTY n. bag, case, cup of tea, game, long suit, number, racket, thing, up one's alley, weakness. See also OCCUPATION.

SPECIAL WEAPONS AND TACTICS n. SWAT, SWAT team.

SPECIES n. likes, likes of, lot, number.

SPECIFIC adj. on the button, on the numbers, on the money, on target, on the nose, on the noggin, right on, dead on, bull's eye, good eye, dot the i's and cross the t's, draw it fine, cut it fine, lay pipe, hit the nail on the head, flat out, straight out, nailed down, downright.

SPECIFICATIONS n. specs, Mil specs (Mil.).

SPECIFY v. 1. name, slot, tab, tag, make, peg, finger, lay one's finger on, put one's finger on, put one's finger on something, put the finger on, button down, pin down, put down for. 2. spell out, lay out, tick off, draw one a picture, take it line by line, cross the T's and dot the I's, sweat the details, get down to brass tacks. See PARTICULARIZE.

SPECKS n. chewed fine, itsy-bitsy pieces.

SPECTACLE n. ball, circus, to-do.

SPECTACLES n. specs, shades, sun specs, cheaters, frames, rims, glims, grannies. See GLASSES.

SPECTACULAR adj. eye-opener, butchy, bitchin', razzle-dazzle. See also PRETENTIOUS, ASTONISHING.

SPECTATOR n. 1. kibitzer, nark, sidewalk superintendent, gaper, watcher. 2. moviegoer, playgoer, showgoer, theatergoer, fan, sports fan, standee, clacker, clapper, deadhead, paper (free pass), one catches a show, fence-hanger.

SPECTER n. haint, hant, spook, things that go bump in the night.

SPECULATE v. 1. spec, play, play the market, plunge, take a flier, take a fling at, make book, stick one's neck out, go on the hook for, ball the jack. See WAGER. 2. figger, cool something over, brainstorm, kick around, run it up the flagpole, head trip, chew over, pipe dream, build castles in the air. See THINK. 3. guesstimate, dope, dope out, figger, figure, figure out, size up, call it, call the turn, call one's shots, call the shots, read, read between the lines, make book, have a hunch, in the cards, it's looking to, see it coming, crystal ball it, psych it out, be afraid.

SPECULATION n. 1. guesstimate, hunch, shot, shot in the dark, sneaking suspicion, stab, stab in the dark. 2. flier, backing, in on the ground floor, inside, piece, plunge, right money, smart money, spec, stab, flutter, hunch, shot, shot in the dark, bear market, bearish market (low); bull market, bullish market (high). See also WAGER.

SPECULATIVE adj. dicey, iffy, touchy, touch and go, long shot, chancy, fat chance, hasn't got a Chinaman's chance, a prayer, on a wing and a prayer, on slippery ground, on thin ice, out on a limb, on the spot, hanging by a thread, off the deep end, go for broke, leave oneself wide open, play with fire, hot potato, one could get burned, too hot to handle, a snowball in hell, up for grabs, go to sea in a sieve. See also DOUBTFUL.

SPECULATOR n. spec, hign roller, plunger, player, dealer, wheeler-dealer, sharper, crap shooter, boneshaker, gunslinger, the bankroll, staker. See GAMBLER.

SPEECH n. 1. lingo, bafflegab, doublespeak, double-talk, gobbledygookese, hillspeak (Washington, D.C.), officialese, psychobabble, Urbabbble (city govt.), Yerkish (artificial), Yinglish (English using many Yiddish words). 2. spiel, chalk talk, pep talk, pitch, soapbox oration, skull session. 3. yack-yack, gab, gas, talkee-talkee, jive, chin music, spiel, rag chewing, gum beating. See TALK.

SPEECHLESS adj. clammed up, closed up like a clam, buttoned up, iced, keep one's trap shut, keep one's yap shut, not let out a peep, not say boo, saved one's breath, dried up, dummy up, garbo, tight-lipped, like a grave, could hear a pin drop, cool, cool as a cucumber, keep one's cool, keep one's shirt on, unflappable, not turn a hair, ah-ah head.

SPEED n. clip, lick, ton.

SPEED v. 1. put the pedal to the metal, gun, rev, rev up, open 'er up, drop the hammer down, hammer on, haze the tires, hook up, stand on it, wheelie, wheelstand, peel rubber, hop up, put on the afterburners, wing it, clip, spank along, cut along, get a move on, get moving, get going, get the lead out, get the lead out of one's ass, get one's ass in gear, get cracking, get a hustle on, get a wiggle on, get a hump on, let's move it, haul ass, haul the mail, hustle, hustle up, chop chop, what's keepin' ya?, fog, whale one's butt, shake a leg, shake it up, bounce, dust, roll, tool, fire up, hotfoot it, bear down on it, hump it, hump oneself, barrel, barrel ass, tear ass, shag ass, stir one's stumps, in a jiffy, snap, snap shit, snap to it, snap into it, snap it up, step, step along, step on the gas, step up, step on it, step on its tail, railroad, railroad through, break one's neck, fall all over oneself, charge, go like greased lightning, go like a big-assed bird, go like a BAB, go hell bent for election, go full blast, full gate, full bore, go like hell, go like a bat outta hell, go to the whip, crackin' the whip, floor, floor it, push, push it, push it to the floor, push it to the floorboard, put it to the floor, flying, burn rubber, burn up the road, burn the breeze, burn leather, lay rubber, lay rubber down, split the breeze, streak, truckin', wheeling it, whistling, diggin' one's spurs, hit the high spots, flat out, let 'er out, let it out, let it all hang out, slack out, hang your leg on it, drag, locomoting, move, pedalling with both feet, rolling, shoveling coal, smoking, give one or something the goose, give it the gun, give 'er the gas, give it the juice, really rolling, highball, make tracks, carry the mail, hop along, run like a scared rabbit, run like mad, breeze, breeze along, tear up the track, tear up the road, eat up the track, eat up the road, scorch, sizzle, rip, zip, whiz, whiz along, nip, zing, ball the jack, scat, beat the band, bend the needle, flash, don't spare the horses, lay a batch, blip, prune, soup up, hurry up, knock the gun, jazz up. 2. hand-carry, hand-walk, walk it over, walk it through, handle personally, cut red tape, fast track, grease the wheels, run interference for, run with the ball, railroad.

SPEEDER n. lead foot, heavy foot, hell driver, hummer, hustler, scorcher, sizzler, speed demon, speed maniac, speed merchant.

SPEEDY adj. sizzler, speedball, fly, make it snappy, shake a leg, stir your stumps, haul ass, highball, speed boy, speed merchant, like sixty, like crazy, like a scared rabbit, beat the devil, beat the deuce. See FAST.

SPELL n. 1. evil eye, hoodoo, voodoo, jinx, whack, whammy, hocus-pocus, mumbo-jumbo, abracadabra. 2. jag (crying jag).

SPEND v. 1. pay down, put down, pay to the tune of, cough up, pony up, ante up, come through, come across, come down with, blow, cash out, shell out, spring for, throw money at, throw money around, piss it away, drop some iron. 2. square, square things, square up, square the beef, sweeten the pot, tickle the palm, pay the piper, pay one's dues, pay through the nose, slip one a buck, schmear, grease, fix the alzo, piece one off, do business, buy off, reach, get to. See PAY. 3. run through, go through, live high on the hog, spend like a drunken sailor, spend money like water, spend money like it was going out of style, spend like there was no tomorrow. See SQUANDER.

SPENDER n. sport, big sport, live one, live wire, fast one with a buck, high roller, big-time spender, last of the big-time spenders, good-time Charlie.

SPENT adj. 1. blown, blown out, diddled away, pissed away, thrown away, down the drain, down the tube, down the rathole, down the spout, down the toilet. 2. had it, pooped, fagged out, dragged, dragging one's ass, dead, beat up, shot, hacked, dog-tired, cooked. See TIRED.

SPERM n. come, cum, scum, cream, jism, jisum, jizz, blecch, crud (dried), hocky, home brew, hookey, jack, pecker tracks, protein, sugar.

SPEW v. 1. blow, spritz, let fly, hawk. 2. barf, puke, throw up, upchuck, urp, whoops, Ralph up, York, buick, feed the fish, blow one's groceries, kiss the porcelain god, drive the bus. See VOMIT.

SPHERE n. 1. apple, big blue marble, real estate, spaceship Earth. 2. apple, pellet, pill. 3. bag, cup of tea, long suit, thing, racket. 4. hood, neck of the woods, stomping ground, old stomping grounds, territory, turf, ghetto, inner city, jungle, shanty town, skid row, slum, zoo.

SPICE n. guts, kick, zip, zap.

SPICE v. hot it up, pep it up, zip it up, zap it up.

SPICY adj. 1. shotgun, zippy, peppy. 2. hot, too hot to handle, red hot, blue, dirty, filthy, off base, off-color, out of line, X-rated, jiggle, jiggly, spark. See also OBSCENE.

SPINACH n. marsh grass, Popeye, seaweed.

SPINSTER n. old maid, single, single-o, cherry, canned goods, bug.

SPIRIT n. 1. jazz, oomph, gumption, balls, guts, heart, nerve, stomach, what it takes, grit, true grit, spunk, backbone, moxie, starch, clock, corazon, Dutch courage (intoxicated). 2. spook, haint, hant, fiend, hellion, little devil. See also DEVIL.

SPIRITED adj.   perky, bouncy, chirpy, chipper, peppy, grooving, zingy, zappy, zippy, snappy, jumping, hyper, swinging, swingle, rocking, salty, juiced up, upbeat, burning, red hot, powerhouse, bull, push, punch, fireball, ball of fire, hot to trot, hotshot, all out, go-getter, go-go, on the go, full tilt, full of go, full of pep, full of beans, full of vinegar, full of piss and vinegar, full of ginger, full of hops, full of prunes, in full swing, feeling one's oats, got the horses to do it, steamroller, get up a head of steam, Norwegian steam, spanking, punchy, gutsy, have lead in one's pencil, come on strong, come on like gangbusters, take over, take charge, fair hell.

SPIRITLESS adj.   1. blah, flat, have spring fever, dopey, drippy, moony, flat tire, zero, big zero, don't give a shit, don't give a damm, could care less, draggy. See INDIFFERENT. 2. dick in the dirt, down, down in the mouth, low, bummed out, flaked out, have the blahs, droopy, mopey. See DEPRESSED. 3. dull as dishwater, ho hum, bor-ring, yawn, big yawn, dead, nowhere, noplaceville, Nadaville, nothing, nothing doing, tired. See BORING. 4. beige, drip, grass, grass out, Irving, Melvin, party-pooper, stick in the mud, wet blanket, wonky.

SPIRITS n.   hard liquor, likker, alky, hootch, booze, moonshine, mountain dew, red-eye, sauce, panther piss, medicine, poison, firewater, embalming fluid, giggle water, hard stuff. See LIQUOR.

SPIRITUAL n.   shout.

SPIT v.   let fly, hawk, hawking loogies (phlegm), spritz.

SPITE n.   bone to pick, peeve, pet peeve.

SPITE v.   cramp one's style, snooker, crab, hang up, foul up, fuck up, louse up, fake out, give one the business, upset one's apple cart, spike one's guns, get even with one, do one dirt. See THWART.

SPITEFUL adj.   bitchy, cussed, catty, evil, waspish, dirty, mean, ornery, accidentally on purpose, do one dirt. See MALICIOUS.

SPITOON n.   gaboon, goboon, garboon.

SPLENDID adj.   splendiferous, splendacious, magnif, magnifico, plush, posh, swanky, splashy, splurgy, fab, fat, elegant, mad, solid gold. See MAGNIFICENT.

SPLINTER v.   break to smithereens, smash to smithereens, bust to bits.

SPLIT v.   1. chiv, shiv, whack, hack. 2. split up, divvy, divvy up, go halfies, go halvers, go fifty-fifty, go even-steven, slice up, cut the pie, cut the melon, slice the melon. See DIVIDE.

SPOIL v.   bitch up, fuck up, hash up, ding, mess up, muck up, make hash of, put in the toilet, play hob with, queer, put the skids under one, blow up in one's face, cut the ground out from under, put out of commission, screw up the works, put a spoke in one's wheels, trash, squash, smash, take apart, zing, break the lease, cook one's goose, bend the goods. See DESTROY, RUIN.

SPOILED adj.   1. screwed up, fouled up, fucked up, loused up, messed up, hashed up, busted, kaput, dinged, bent, totaled, sunk, shot. See DAMAGED. 2. spoiled rotten. 3. strong, high, loud, gross, stinking, bum, rummy.

SPOILS n.   take, graft, goods, hot goods, hot items, swag, squeeze, boodle, make, cut, loot, pickings, booty, melon, pie.

SPOILSPORT n.   party-pooper, drag, drip, wet blanket, crepe hanger, sourpuss, sourbelly, sour ball, dog in the manger, gloomy Gus, killjoy, stick in the mud, moldy fig, worrywart, Calamity Jane, calamity howler.

SPOKANE, WASHINGTON   Spoke.

SPOKESPERSON n.   mouthpiece.

SPONGER n.   beat, bummer, cheapskate, cadger, deadbeat, freeloader, lounge lizard, moocher, schnorrer, sponge, hanger-on, hose. See also PARASITE.

SPONSOR n.   angel, backer, fairy godfather, fairy godmother, grubstaker, lady bountiful, meal ticket, Santa Claus, staker, sugar daddy, rabbi. See FINANCIER.

SPONSOR v.   angel, bankroll, grubstake, stake, back. See FINANCE.

SPONTANEOUS adj.   ad lib, up front, off the cuff, off the top of one's head, shoot from the hip, off the hip, spitball, pop off, cold turkey, down, get down, all hanging out, free spirited, far out, stretched out, break loose, cut loose, loose wig, let down one's hair. See also IMPULSIVE.

SPOON n.   shovel, bug (industrial or baker).

SPORADICALLY adv.   by bits and pieces, by fits and starts, hit or miss, helter-skelter. See ERRATICALLY.

SPORT n.   rec, action, ball, big time, fun and games, get some grins, grins, high old time, high time, hoopla, laughs, lots of laughs, picnic, whoopee. See also GAMBLER.

SPORT v.   fool around, monkey around, hell around, step out, paint the town red, go places and do things, go on a spree, whoop it up, kick up one's heels, raise hell. See REVEL.

SPORTING adj.   square dealing, square shooting, straight shooting. See FAIR.

SPORTS BROADCASTING n.   color, colorcaster, color man, play-by-play man.

SPORTS DEFEAT n. blown out, shut out, down, dump, pasting, sieve, horse collar (zero), sudden death, sudden death finish (tie-breaker), tank, go into the tank (intentional loss).

SPORTS, GAMBLING n. action, favorite, long shot, point spread, underdog, make book, lay off, overlay, odds on favorite, vigorish.

SPORTS INJURY n. charley horse (leg muscle injury), iron man (plays in spite of injury).

SPORTSMAN n. 1. animal, jock, superjock, ape, muscle head, muscle man, meathead, shoulders, Neanderthal. See ATHLETE. 2. high roller, K.G. (known gambler, police use), big timer, sharper, sport. See GAMBLER.

SPORTSMANLIKE adj. square dealing, square shooting, straight shooting. See FAIR.

SPORTS PERFORMANCE n. grandstander, grandstand play, hot dog, hot dogging (showing off), groove (groove your swing), header (fall head first), heads up play, heads up player (wide awake), real pro, journeyman, hustle, iron man (durable competitor), up (ready for anything, winning), on (at one's best), troops (good players); clutch player, money player (best under stress); choke (psychological disadvantage); picture book, picture perfect (classic), sandbag (fake early weakness then overwhelm the opponent), scrappy (spirited), telegraph (reveal next move), dog it, go flat out, pull it out, full bore, hot, hustle, make a run at, break it open, September swoon.

SPORTS, PSYCHOLOGICAL v. choke, choke up, clutch, clutch up (all poor performance under tension); psych, psych out (distract an opponent); charge up, psych up (inspire); sucker play (entrap).

SPORTS RECORDS n. all time (best ever), cellar (last place), the gold (gold medal), lifetime, world class, All American.

SPORTS SCORING n. blowout (overwhelm the opponent), card (score card), chalk up, chalk up one (score), draw first blood, the gold (gold medal), horse collar (zero), ice, on ice (assure victory), a laugher (lopsided victory), make a run at (concentrated effort to outscore opponent), point spread (betting odds), runaway, runaway and hide (outdistance opponent), run off (score consecutive points), sudden death, sudden death finish (tie-breaker).

SPORTS SPECTATOR n. backer, booster, bench (players' seat), blackout (local television broadcast restriction), bleachers, bleacherite, fan, scout (sports spy).

SPORTS SUBSTITUTES n. backup, backup player, bench, bench jockey, extra horses, ringer (illegal), sideliner, sub, bull pen, reliefer, fireman.

SPORTS TERMS meet (contest), barnburner (exciting contest), away (play at opponent's arena), host (the Yanks host Detroit), beat out, break it open, dominate (win), walkaway, walkover, win (victory), the gold (gold medal), cellar (last place), paste (defeat), shut out, sieve (scoreless), stiffener, dead heat, scrub (tie); ref, ump, zebra (referee); call (referee's decision); call time, chalk talk (discussion of plays); starter, vet, rookie (first-year player), jayvee (junior varsity), homebrew (locally bred player), redshirt (elegibility extended), white hope (Caucasian contender), ringer (higher rated player illegally entered), suit up (ready to play), benched, cut (remove player from team), thin (no reserve players), first string, front line (starting players), horses (power), firepower, book (data on opponents), free wheeling (formless style of play), dog (guard opponent closely), that dog can run (fast man); bobble, foozle (error); bum, clutch, turnover, kick (error), choke, choke up; chapter, canto, frame, lap (division); round, stanza (time period); get, gate, take (receipts); card (scorecard), card (program), wild card (playoff qualifier), October Classic (World Series), greenie (stimulant pill), enduro (endurance race) jock, jog, jogger, jogging, spikes (shoes worn for certain sports), black belt (karate expert), action (gun mechanism for loading and firing), wave (crowd cheer).

SPORTS, WINNING n. sudden death, sudden death finish (tie-breaker); sweep (the Lakers swept the series), top dog, up, the upper hand, blow out of the water, blow out (overwhelm an opponent), chalk up one, clinch, edge, the gold (gold medal), ice (they had the game iced) on ice, a laugher (18 to 1, it was a laugher), runaway, runaway and hide (outdistance).

SPOT n. where one is at, X marks the spot, hangout, joint, lay, layout, plant, office, dump, digs, scene, slot, hole, pad, crib, crash pad, roof over one's head, digs, the pits, armpit (undesirable). See also BLEMISH, LOCATION, HOUSE, BAR.

SPOTLIGHT n. center stage.

SPOUSE n. man, my man, old man, main man, man on the hitch, ace lane, breadwinner, buffalo, old lady, O.L., roommate, mama, missus, better half, little woman, the wifey, missus, little missus, wiff, chief of staff, rib, ball and chain, block and tackle, front office, golf widow, grass widow, headache, War Department, mat, hat, sea gull, slave driver, squaw, headquarters, apron, main queen, old saw, first sergeant, fishwife, fag bag (married to homosexual).

SPRAY v. dust (crops), spritz, shoot (paint).

SPREE n. bat, bender, binge, ball, bash, bust, beer bust, buzz, drunk, jag, caper, go, tear, toot, blowout, hoopla, whoopee, jamboree, wingding, shindig, branigan, rip, merry-go-round, paint the town red, on the town, carousing, growler rushing, hell around, hell bender, high jinks, whooper-dooper, big time, high time, high old time, larking, field day. See also PARTY, REVEL.

SPRIGHTLINESS n. bounce, piss and vinegar, zip, zap.

SPRIGHTLY adj. perky, bouncy, chirpy, chipper, peppy, grooving, zingy, zappy, zippy, jumping, hyper, swinging, go-go, full of ginger, feeling one's oats. See SPIRITED.

SPRING v. hippety hop.

SPRINKLE v. dust (crops), spritz.

SPRUCE adj. classy, dap, nifty, snazzy, spiffy. See also STYLISH, CLEAN.

SPRY adj. 1. quick on the draw, quick on the trigger, twinkle toes. 2. zappy, zippy, rocking, go-go, on the go, full of go, full of pep, full of ginger, in full swing, feeling one's oats. See also SPIRITED.

SPUR n. needle, goose, trigger, turn on, fire in the belly.

SPUR v. goose, goose up, fire up, key up, work up, work up into a lather, put up to, spark, egg on, turn on, trigger, sound. See STIMULATE.

SPURIOUS adj. bogue, bogus, bogosity, bum, hyped up, bent, phony, falsie, fake, faked, framed, made out of whole cloth, not what it's cracked up to be, pirate goods, Hollywood. See COUNTERFEIT.

SPURN v. pass by, steer clear of, nix, turn down, turn thumbs down on, not buy, not hear of, have no truck with, cut, piss on, shit on, drop, cold shoulder, dump, air, flush, give one the air, give one the wind, thank you but no thank you. See REJECT. See also SNUB.

SPURNED adj. nixed, burned, cut, turned down, put down, passed over, left at the church, out in the cold. See REJECTED. See also SNUBBED.

SPURS n. pothooks.

SPURT n. spritz.

SPURT v. spritz.

SPY n. agent, spook, mole, beekie, snark, buddy fucker, humint, operative, plant, rug merchant, sheep dip (military disguised as civilian), cutout (secret intermediary), sleeper; company brown nose, keek (industrial). See also OPERATIVE.

SPY v. case, case a joint, spot, spy out, stake out, snark, recon, get a load of, take in, get an eyeful of, set eyes on, clap eyes on, eyeball, have a look-see. See also RECONNOITER.

SPYING DEVICE n. asset, bug, wire, body mike, eye in the sky, spy in the sky.

SPY SATELLITE n. eye in the sky, spy in the sky.

SQUABBLE n. hassle, flap, spat, tiff, words, row, scrap, scene, set-to, fuss, flack session, rhubarb, wrangle. See ARGUMENT.

SQUABBLE v. lock horns, row, scrap, bump heads, cross swords, pick a bone, put up an argument, go round and round. See ARGUMENT.

SQUAD CAR n. black and white, skunk wagon, fuzzmobile, bearmobile, bear car, buzz, buzzer, screaming gasser, whistler, catch car; brown bag, plain wrap (unmarked), buggy whip (transmitter).

SQUALID adj. cruddy, crudded up, crumby, crummy, crummed up, crusty, grungy, icky, yecchy, yucky, barfy, vomity, pig pen, barn, stable, stinking, stall, scuzzy, skank, raunchy, sleazy, sleazed up, mucked up. See also SLOVENLY.

SQUANDER v. blow, fork out, put out, shell out, spring for, go for a meg, throw money at, throw money around, piss it away, blow out, cash out, diddle away, run through, go through, live high on the hog, spend like a drunken sailor, spend money like water, spend money like it was going out of style, spend like there was no tomorrow. See also PAY.

SQUANDERED adj. blown, pissed away, thrown away, diddled away, down the drain, down the toilet, down the rathole, down the spout, tubed, down the tube.

SQUASH v. 1. scrunch, squish, 2. squelch, ice, kill, put the kibosh on, put the lid on, shut down on, put the damper on. See REPRESS. See also SILENCE.

SQUEAMISH adj. barfy, pukish, pukey, rocky, sick as a dog. See also FASTIDIOUS.

SQUEEZE n. clutch, crunch.

SQUEEZE v. scrunch, squish, juice, lean on. See also PERSUADE.

SQUELCH v. black out, kibosh, kill, sit on, put the kibosh on, put the lid on, settle one's hash, squash. See also SILENCE.

SQUINT v. squinch, scrunch up one's eyes.

SQUIRT v. spritz.

ST. LOUIS, MISSOURI Big Arch, The Gateway.

ST. PAUL, MINNESOTA Twin City.

STAB v. knife, cut, carve, open up, slice, stick, jag, brand, carve initials in one, chiv, shiv, chop, chop down, clip, shank, cut a new kisser for. See also WOUND.

STABILIZE v. firm up, pour oil on troubled waters, cool, freeze. See also PACIFY.

STABLE adj. 1. set, sot, stay put, together, brick wall, solid as a rock, set in concrete, chiseled in stone, Rocka

Gibraltar, Rock of Gibraltar, Rock of Gib, anchored, nailed, nailed down. See also PERMANENT, TRUST-WORTHY. 2. unflappable, cool, keep one's cool, cool as a cucumber, keep one's shirt on, not turn a hair, without a nerve in one's body, together. 3. set, going concern.

STADIUM n. bowl, gridiron (Ftbl.), diamond (Bsbl.), ring, pit.

STAFF n. help, shop, crew, troops, flunky, furp, apparatchik, squeak, home guard, peon, savage, serf, slave, slavey, girl Friday, gal friday, man Friday.

STAGE n. legit, show biz, Broadway, off Broadway, boards, straw-hat circuit, the Fabulous Invalid, Toby Show. See THEATER.

STAGE v. mount, put on.

STAGEHAND n. deck hand.

STAID adj. stuffy, not crack a smile, wipe the smile off one's face, cold sober, sober as a judge.

STAKES n. pot (games). See also WAGER.

STALE adj. 1. flat, flat as a pancake. See INSIPID. 2. tired, out, old hat, past it, passé, bent, back number, moth-eaten, moldy fig, yesterday, corny, dinosaur, horse and buggy. See also DATED.

STALEMATE adj. standoff, Mexican standoff, gridlock, deadlock, catch 22, damned if you do and damned if you don't.

STALL v. play for time, conk out, die. See also DELAY.

STALWART adj. 1. hoss, powerhouse, steamroller, double-barreled, mover and shaker, wave maker, have lead in one's pencil, juice, force, come on strong, walk heavy, walk tall. See also STRONG. 2. gutsy, gutty, gritty, nervy, spunky, tough it out, cool hand, ain't scared of shit. See FEARLESS. 3. dead set on, bound, bound and determined, brick wall, stonewall, dig in one's heels, solid as a rock, hang tough. See STUBBORN.

STAMINA n. backbone, grit, guts, gutsiness, heart, moxie, starch, cool, hanging in there, hang tough, legs, intestinal fortitude, staying power, sitzfleisch.

STANCE n. 1. say so, slant. 2. brace, brush (Army).

STAND n. 1. bally stand (circus), soapbox, stump. 2. P.O.V., slant, sound, twist, angle, two-cents worth, say so, where one is at, where's one's head is, another county heard from.

STAND v. stand for, stand the gaff, stand up, stand up to it, handle, live with, bear with, put up with, hang in, hang in there, hang tough, hang on, stay the course, take it on the chin, be big, grin and bear it. See ENDURE.

STANDARD adj. garden variety, everyday, vanilla, strictly union, boiler plate, run of the mill, starch. See AVERAGE.

STANDARDIZE v. homogenize.

STANDARDIZED adj. PX.

STANDING n. how things stack up, how things stand, place, slot, pecking order, like it is, where it's at, size of it, the scene, how the land lies, lay of the land.

STANDSTILL n. gridlock, box, corner, dead end, hole, standoff, Mexican standoff, damned if you do and damned if you don't.

STAR n. superstar, monster, topliner, headliner, luminary, box office, celeb, face, in the limelight, prima donna, right up there; eight hundred pounder, gorilla (TV news). See CELEBRITY.

STAR TREK DEVOTÉE n. Trekkie.

STARE n. fish eye, gun.

STARE v. gawk, glom, glim, gun, eye, eyeball, get an eyeful, give the eye, eagle eye, beam, pipe, focus, clap eyes on, lay eyes on, set eyes on, lay one's glims on, hold the glims on, take in, get a load of, get an eyeful of, pin, rubber, rubberneck, 87 1/2 (look at a girl, restaurant), give one the eye, give one the beady eye, give one the fish eye, give with the eyes, eyeballs buggin' out like percolator tops, keep one's eyes peeled. See also SEE.

START n. preem, bow, opener, openers, square one, day 1, day one, first crack out of the box, countdown, for starters, flying start, running start, jump off, kickoff, takeoff, start off. See BEGINNING.

START v. bow, open, open up, come out, roll 'em, start the ball rolling, get one's feet wet, get the show on the road, get cracking, get off the dime, take it from the top, kick off, hit out, head out, ring in, blast away, hang up one's shingle. See BEGIN.

START, FALSE jump the gun.

STARTLE v. 1. spook, scare to death, scare the shit out of, put the chill on, give one a turn, make one jump a mile, spring something on one. See FRIGHTEN. 2. rock, gork, floor, shake one up, blow away, blow one's mind, from out in left field, hit them where they ain't, knock one over with a feather. See SURPRISE.

STARTLED adj. spooked, frozen, pucker-assed, jumped a mile, jumped out of one's skin, given a turn, given a jar, given a jolt. See FRIGHTENED, SURPRISED.

STARTLING adj. grabber, hairy, hair-raising, scary, spooky, mind-blowing, stunning, hell of a note, helluva note. See also IMPRESSIVE.

STARVED adj. dog-hungry, empty, peaked, peaky, rattleboned, skinny, skin and bones.

STARVING adj. dog-hungry, empty, fly light, grits time, have a tapeworm, munchies (follows marijuana use), starved, starved to death, could eat a horse, could eat the asshole out of a bear.

STATE n. 1. big brother, D.C., the digger, the mighty dome, the Feds, the Union, Uncle Sam, US, USA, US of A, Washington. 2. situash, like it is, where it's at, the size of it, way of the world, how the land lies, fix (stationary). See CONDITON. 3. cherry (perfect), mint, showroom perfect, —— city (fat city).

STATE DEPARTMENT n. Foggy Bottom, State.

STATE DEPARTMENT OFFICIAL n. cookie pusher.

STATEMENT n. ABC's, blow by blow, rundown, make, picture, bomb, spiel, pitch, story, say so, two-cents worth. See also ACCOUNT.

STATE OF AFFAIRS n. stacks up, shapes up, how things stack up, how things stand, like it is, where it's at, way things are, how it goes, size of it, how the land lies, lay of the land.

STATE OF MIND n. where one's at, where one's coming from, where one's head is at, mind-set.

STATE OF NEW YORK MORTGAGE AGENCY n. Sonny Mae.

STATELY adj. highfalutin', high-minded, high-nosed, high-toned, stiff-necked. See also MAJESTIC, POMPOUS.

STATES' RIGHTS DEMOCRATIC PARTY n. Dixiecrats.

STATIC n. background, buckshot, breaking up, covered up (radio).

STATIONARY adj. pat, anchored, nailed, nailed down.

STATION WAGON n. woody.

STATUETTE n. Oscar (any small statue especially an award or Academy Award).

STATUS n. where it's at, where one is at, the way it shapes up, lay of the land, black eye (low). See CONDITION.

STAY v. sit tight, stay put, let it ride, stick around, squat, nest, bunk, hang, hang out, hang in, hang around, hang about, perch, roost, save it, sweat it, sweat, sweat it out, hold the fort. See also WAIT, STOP, DELAY, INHABIT.

STEADFAST adj. unflappable, bound, bound and determined, brick wall, stick it out, stand by one's guns, solid as a rock, hang tough, Rock of Gibraltar. See STUBBORN. See also LOYAL, TRUSTWORTHY, DETERMINED.

STEADY adj. solid as a rock, Rocka Gibraltar, Rock of Gibraltar, Rock of Gib, brick wall, set in concrete, stuck in concrete, buried in concrete, chiseled in stone. See also LOYAL, TRUSTWORTHY.

STEAK n. rubber, shoe leather (tough).

STEAL v. rip off, appropriate, boost, scrounge, pinch, promote, buzz, cop, kipe, liberate, lift, moonlight requisition, snatch, snitch, swipe, snipe, glom, glaum, glahm, glue, skim, high grade, hijack, skyjack, heist, hoist, elevate, make, make off with, burn, annex, borrow, palm, bag, nip, snare, stick up, kick over, tip over, knock off, knock over, shoot a jug, truck lift, boost a car, gleep a cage (auto), put up, root, scuffle, throw, throw up, tumul, put the arm on, take off, pluck, put a hand in the till, put a hand in the cookie jar, have one's hand in the cookie jar, work in a bank and take home samples, give one a haircut, take to the cleaners, sting, score, clip, crash, cream, clout, charge, mug (rob and beat), jackroll, hustle, kife, crook, crab, crib, cabbage, steal one blind, hook, hooky, maverick, nick, move, salvage, smooch, go south with something, fall (unsuccessful). See also APPROPRIATE; ROB; CRIME, COMMIT A.

STEALING, DOG v. dognapping, pooch snatch, yip snatch.

STEALTHILY adv. in a hole-and-corner way, in holes and corners, on the q.t., on the quiet, on the sly, undercover, under wraps, hush-hush, strictly hush-hush.

STEALTHY adj. creep (mission); tref, triff, under wraps, undercover, hush-hush.

STEAM CALLIOPE n. horse piano.

STEAMER n. crock, tub, rust bucket, tramp. See also SHIP.

STEER v. helm, captain, skipper, take her, take over, take the conn, herd, shepherd, ride herd on, sit on top of, run, run things, take the reins, pull the strings, pull the wires. See MANAGE.

STEERING CONTROL n. joy knob, joy-stick, wheel.

STENOGRAPHER n. steno, girl, girl Friday, man Friday.

STEREOTYPE n. boiler plate.

STERILE adj. fire blanks, no lead in the pencil, no toothpaste in the tube.

STERN adj. crab, chicken shit, by the book, stiff, tough, tough nut, tough nut to crack, rough, hard-nosed, hard core, hard shell, hard line, hard-boiled, hardheaded, bulletheaded, bullhead, bullheaded, pigheaded, mule-headed, mulish, mule, stubborn as a mule, stiff-necked, dyed in the wool, hang in, hang in there, hang tough.

STEROIDS n. gorilla juice.

STET v. check that, play the ink (The.).

STETHOSCOPE n. ears.

STEVEDORE n. dock walloper, roustabout.

STEW n. mulligan, coll, lorelei, salmagundi, slumgullion, Black Mike (hobo).

STEWARDESS n. stew, cow pilot.

STICK n. nightstick, billy, billy club, blackjack, club, sap, sap stick. See CLUB.

STICK v. freeze to, stay put, hold on like a bulldog, stick like a barnacle, stick like a leech, stick like a wet shirt, cling like ivy, cling like a burr, stick like a limpet.

STICKLER n. 1. nitpicker, picky, picky picky, ace, comma counter, fussbudget, fusspot, granny, old maid, pernickety, persnickety. See PARTICULAR. 2. hard-nosed, hard core, hard shell, hard-line, locked in, pat, stand pat, stay put, stick to one's guns, stiff-necked, stuffy, sticky, set, sot, dead set on. See STUBBORN.

STICKY adj. gooey, gloppy, globby, gook, gooky, goonk, gummy, gunk.

STIFFNESS n. charley, charley horse, tennis elbow.

STIFLE v. 1. gag, ice, muzzle, squelch, squash, shut up, dry up, clam up, hold it down, shut one's face, button up, sit on, put the lid on, cork up, clamp down on. 2. torpedo, kill, queer, spike, squash, squelch, hush up, black out, put in the toilet, keep under wraps, ding, zing, hog-tie, tie up, jam up, bring to a screaming halt, put a stopper in, throw cold water on, cut off one's water, put the heat on, crack down on. See REPRESS.

STIFLING adj. broiler, roaster, scorcher, sizzler, swelterer, sticky, steamy, steam box, sweaty, sweat box, close, one can fry eggs on the sidewalk, hotter than blue mud.

STIGMA n. black eye, lost face.

STIGMATIZE v. trash, crud up, crumb up, scuzz up, skank, muck up, sleaze up, mess up, piss on, blackball, give one a black mark, give one a black eye, make one lose face.

STILL adj. buttoned up, clammed up, closed up like a clam, iced, sealed lipped, close-mouthed, not let out a peep, not say boo, saved one's breath. See SILENT.

STILL n. barrel house, boiler, plant, sneaker.

STILL v. gag, muzzle, squelch, squash, shut up, soft-pedal, dummy up, clam up, sit on, decrease the volume, bottle up, cut the mouth, drink one's beer, put the damper on, put the lid on, cork up, shut down on. See SILENCE.

STIMULANT n. doll, spark plug, upper, pick-me-up, shot in the arm, coke, snow, pep pill, jolly bean, bennie, benzie, dexie, heart, football, purple heart, meth, speed, crystal, businessman's trip. See also DRUGS, TONIC.

STIMULATE v. jazz, jazz up, juice, juice up, turn on the juice, send, grab, spark, trigger, hook, fuss, bug up, pep up, put pep into, perk up, snap up, wake up, zip up, put zip into, key up, fire up, steam up, stir up, work up, work up into a lather, work into a stew, work into a tizzy, work into a pucker, pick up, chirk up, wig out, adjy, flip, egg on, turn on, turn one on, switch on, turn on the heat, give one a hotfoot, race one's motor, open one's nose, make waves, rabble-rouse, needle, put the needles in, throw wood on the fire, add fuel to the flames. See also EXCITE.

STIMULATED adj. charged, charged up, higher 'n a kite, hyper, steamed up, juiced up, jacked up, headin' up the mountain (sexual), rooty, ready to cook. See EXCITED.

STIMULUS n. upper, charge, large charge, bang, kick, turn-on, needle, fireworks, flash, jollies, razzle-dazzle, kick in the ass, eye-opener. See also DRUGS, SPUR.

STINGY adj. cheap, cheapskate, close, penny-pinching, nickel-nursing, tight, tightwad, tight-fisted, so tight one squeaks, last of the big spenders, last of the big-time spenders, fast man with a buck, a regular Jack Benny, tight as a drum, tight as O'Reilly's balls, tight as Kelsey's nuts, skinflint, Scotch, sticky-fingered, crumb, bog pocket, dead one, squeezing the eagle, piker, chintzy, chinchy, scrimpy, skimpy, pinch-fisted, hardfisted, pinchy.

STINKING adj. stinko, whiffy, nosey, strong, P.U., phew, high.

STINT v. scrimp, penny-pinch, cut corners, cut to the bone, go easy on the pocketbook, make ends meet, roll back, tighten one's belt, rub the print off a dollar bill, rub the picture off a nickel, save for a rainy day, sock away, squirrel, stash.

STIPEND n. take, take home, bread, sugar, shake, soap, touch, bacon, bacon and eggs, eagle shit, peanuts, coffee and cakes (small). See COMPENSATION.

STIPULATE v. name, slot, tab, tag, make, peg, finger, lay one's finger on, put one's finger on, put one's finger on something, put the finger on, spell out, button down, pin down, put down for.

STIPULATION n. joker, kicker, string, string to it, a string attached to it, small print, fine print, fine print at the bottom, small fine print, small fine print at the bottom.

STIR n. scene, to-do, fuss, dustup, flap, row, fuzzbuzz (commotion), fuzzbuzzy, kickup. See TURMOIL. See also EXCITEMENT, ACTION.

STIR v. 1. adjy, psych, spook, get to, flip out, craze, bug, bug up, fire up, work up, rabble-rouse, stir up, make waves, make a scene, make a fuss, steam up, throw wood on the fire, add fuel to the flames, rile. See DISTURB. 2. jazz up, juice up, spark, trigger, pep up, zip up, switch on, turn on the heat, race one's motor, open one's nose. See EXCITE.

STIRRED adj. hyper, charged, wired, wired up, fired up, keyed up, all keyed up, steamed up, hopped up, worked up, turned on, horny (sexual), stoned, shook up, hot and bothered, in a tizzy. See EXCITED.

STIRRING adj. marvy, like wow, mind-blowing, mind-bending, out of this world, turned on by, large, large charge, solid, solid sender, something, something else, something to shout about, something to write home about, sizzler, scorcher, big splash, out of sight, flashy, showy, bang-up, feel in one's guts, grabbed by. See EXCITING.

STOCKBROKERAGE n. brokerage, boiler room, bucket shop, wire house.

STOCKCAR n. stocker.

STOCK EXCHANGE n. Big Board, Exchange, the market, the Street, Wall Street.

STOCKHOLDER n. coupon clipper.

STOCKINGS n. nylons, first national bank (woman's), gam cases, leg sacks.

STOCK MARKET DECLINE n. correction, dip, downturn, falling out of bed, nosedive, plummet, sell-off, crash, Black Monday (October 19, 1987), Black and Blue Monday (October 26, 1987), slide.

STOCK MARKET TERMS bear market, bearish market (low), bull market, bullish market (high), top side, top out (high), bottoming out, making highs, touch bottom, downturn, making a Dow line, buy sign, sell sign, wash out, get caught, pull back, a squeeze on profits, shallow river running deep (rising price, basis unknown), arbs (arbitrageurs), socks and stocks (nonbanking company such as Sears offering financial services).

STOCK OPTION n. alligator spread (profitless), going naked (short sale), guts (buying and selling simultaneously), strangle (guts situation failing).

STOCKS n. blue chips, cats and dogs, paper, wallpaper (defunct); over the counter, convertible, fancies, high flier, fallen angels (out-of-favor stocks at bargain prices). See also BONDS.

STOCK TICKER n. tape, ticker.

STODGY adj. square, squaresville, duddy, fuddy-duddy.

STOICAL adj. cool, cool as a cucumber, keep one's cool, keep one's shirt on, not turn a hair, roll with the punches, unflappable.

STOKER n. bakehead, smoke agent.

STOLEN AUTOMOBILE n. a short, hot car, bent one, rinky, trap, slick, gondola (not common); consent job,

owner's job (insurance fraud, theft of); move a job, push hot boilers, push hot ones (dispose of), on the schlep (stealing).

STOLEN MERCHANDISE n. make, take, stuff, swag, bull's wool, five-finger discount, poke, waif (abandoned in flight).

STOMACH n. tummy, gut, pot, potgut, pusgut, belly, potbelly, melon belly, swagbelly, beerbelly, keg, pail, tank, solar plexus, spare tire, corporation, breadbasket, bay window, kishkes, crammer, kitchen, labonza, pantry, balcony, basement, bay, bag, basket, dinner pail, feedbag, feedbox, front porch, locker, navy chest, garbage can, chicken cemetery, below the belt, German goiter, Milwaukee goiter.

STOMACH v. live with, bear with, put up with, roll with the punches, bite the bullet, hang in, hang on, sweat it, take it, grin and bear it. See ENDURE.

STOMACHACHE n. bellyache, gut ache, tummyache.

STONE n. egg, brickbat, Irish confetti.

STONES, PRECIOUS n. rocks, sparklers, ice, Christmas, glass, hardware, pennyweight, junk jewelry (cheap or fake).

STOOL n. 1. seat, squatter. 2. BM, ca ca, crap, dingleberry, honey, shit, turd. See BOWEL MOVEMENT.

STOP n. freeze, break, break off, cutoff, layoff, letup, screaming halt, shuddering halt, grinding halt.

STOP v. gronk out, wind, wind up, wrap, wrap up, sew up, scrub, kill, chop, pack in, kick, kick over, kick the habit, kayo, KO, drop, drop it, blow off, kiss off, turn it off, knock off, knock it off, chuck it, hold it, cool it, quit cold, cold turkey, quit cold turkey, close up, close out, can it, can, cut (film), cut the crap, cut the shit, cut off (baseball), cut off one's water, turn off one's water, break off, break it off, sign off, choke, choke off, gag, bottle up, hush hush, ice, muzzle, put the damper on, stall, stuff it, shove it, break it up, cut it out, cut out the something, lay off, cry off, come off, come off it, back off, leave off, call off, call all bets off, call it a day, call it quits, cave in, throw in the sponge, throw in the towel, throw over, cry uncle, take the cure, give up, let up, cork, cork up, put a cork in it, pack it in, fold, fold one's hand, drop out, butt out, tune out, punk out, chicken out, peter out, bow out, pull the pin, pull the plug, pull the plug on one, get on the wagon, come to a screeching halt, come to a screaming halt, come to a grinding halt, come to a shuddering halt, stop on a dime, put on the brakes, put the lid on, put the finisher on, kibosh, put the kibosh on, put a stop to, clamp down on, put to bed, drop anchor, shut out, shut off, shut down, shut 'em down, stand down, ring down, drop the curtain, cash in one's chips, flag one, freeze, stow it, drag it, pig it, hang it up, hang up one's spurs, binch (job), hold one's horses.

STOPGAP adj. temp, band-aid, throwaway.

STOP HARASSING v. cool it, lay off, knock it off, butt out, get off one's back, sign off, cut the crap, cut the shit, change your act, don't bug one, all right already, give it a rest, come off it, stop hocking, stop hocking a charnik (Yid.)

STOPPAGE n. down, downtime, shutdown, walkout, lockout, sit-down.

STOPPED adj. dropped, sidelined, gronked out, shut out, shut down, stonewalled, iced, scrubbed, killed, shot, shot down, shot down in flames, washed out, wiped out, all bets off, all off, kaput, zapped, dead in the water.

STORAGE BATTERY n. can (WW II).

STORE n. supermarket, superette, deli, super, chain store, outlet, outlet store, discount house, co-op, bodega (liquor or NYC grocery), stand, down to the corner for a bottle, the grab, schlock joint, five-and-ten, five-and-dime.

STORE v. stash, stache, plant, park, squirrel, squirrel away, sock away, salt away, salt down, rat hole, put away for a rainy day. See SAVE. See also ACCUMULATE.

STOREHOUSE n. Fort Knox, stash house.

STORM n. blow, coming down, gully washer, heavy wet, heavy dew, precip, raining cats and dogs, raining puppies and kittens, whiteout.

STORM v. 1. blow, come down, rain cats and dogs, rain puppies and kittens. 2. blow one's top, sizzle, sound off, burn up, steam up, tear, tear up the pea patch, carry on, go on, take on. See RAGE. 3. gang up on, come at, come down on, rip, rip into, rip up, rip up one side and down the other, blitz, fly in the teeth of, pull a Jap (surprise).

STORMY adj. blowy, gully washer, wet, raining cats and dogs, raining puppies and kittens, coming down.

STORY n. book, beat, scoop, yarn, clothesline, cliffhanger, bodice-ripper (romance), potboiler, spyboiler, gag, long and the short of it, megillah, spiel, wheeze, heavy lard, chestnut, old chestnut, old wive's tale, old saw, old touches, touches.

STOUT adj. fat-assed, lard-assed, beef trust, Mr. Five by Five, built for comfort, zaftig. See FAT.

STOVE n. belly stove, hot plate, coal pot.

STOW v. stash, stache, jam, jam pack, pack 'em in, pack like sardines, sardine, ram in, chock, chockablock, stuff, fill to the brim, top off. See also SECRETE.

STRADIVARIUS n. Strad.

STRAFE v. on a rhubarb.

STRAGGLE v. get no place fast, poke, poke around, tail, go all over the map, goof off, rat fuck, R.F. See DAWDLE.

STRAIGHT adj. on the beam, slam bang, beeline, as the crow flies, down the alley, down the pipe, in the groove.

STRAIGHTEN HAIR v. fry (Bl.).

STRAIGHTFORWARD adj. up front, open, mellow, like it is, lay it on the line, right on, level, what you see is what you get, square shooter, Mr. Clean, straight arrow, talk like a Dutch uncle, call a spade a spade, talk turkey, all wool and a yard wide. See SINCERE.

STRAIN n. pressure cooker, burnout, brain fog. See also NERVOUSNESS.

STRAIN v. push, hassle, sweat, sweat it, scratch, grind, dig, plug, peg away, hammer away, hustle, hump, hump oneself, bust a gut, bust one's ass, break one's neck, break one's back, bear down, put one's back into it, go for broke. See STRUGGLE.

STRAINED adj. uptight, choked, strung out, unglued, wreck, nervous wreck, bundle of nerves, wired, wired up, clutched up, basket case, sweating bullets, in a state, hard put to it, at the end of one's rope. See TENSE.

STRAIT n. bottleneck, choke point. See also PREDICAMENT.

STRAITJACKET n. camisole, jacket, tuxedo.

STRAITLACED adj. square, squaresville, cubeular, uptight, candy ass, tight-assed, stuffy, stick, in line, straight, straight arrow, short haircut, bible thumper, Christer, Jesus freak, nice Nellie, Crabapple Annie, prune, goody-goody, goody two shoes, old maid, bluenose, crab, chicken, chicken shit, by the numbers, by the book, according to the book, according to Hoyle, stiff, rock-ribbed, hard-nosed, hard core, hard shell, hard-line, hardheaded, bulletheaded, bullhead, bullheaded, pigheaded, mule-headed, mulish, mule, stubborn as a mule, horse, Turk, stiff-necked, stuffy, sticky, set, sot, unflappable, dead set on, dyed in the wool.

STRANDED adj. godforsaken, passed up, left in the lurch, sidelined, sidetracked, on the rocks, out in left field, left high and dry, left at the altar, left God knows where.

STRANGE adj. archfreak, freaky, freaked out, flake, flaky, fringy, kinky, kooky, cooky, camp, cuckcoo, semi-dork, creepo, yo-yo, nut, nutcake, nutroll, oddball, foul ball, goof ball, whack, whacko, weird, for weird, weirdo, weirdie, fly ball, case, hippy, beat, beatnik, beat generation, offbeat, off the beaten track, gooney bird, screwball, loner, chirp, queer fish, queer duck, strange duck, rare bird, jayhawk, three-dollar bill, crackpot, gonzo, queer potato, jell brain, twerp, character, fantasmo, bent, grody, grody to the max, gross, special, avant-garde, wrinkle, new wrinkle, cool, speed, far out, way out, out of sight, wild, crazy, funny, funny-looking, off the wall, out in left field, trippy, not wrapped real tight, gooey, gooney, gasser, meshuga, meshugana, potty, cockeyed, queer in the head, herky, screwy, aired out, jelled, shaky, creepy, wacky, whacky, whacked out, nutty, nutty as a fruitcake, fruity, fruitcake, spacey, cockamamie, Asiatic (WW II, Navy). See also ECCENTRIC.

STRAPPING adj. husky, hefty, beefy, gorilla, hunk, hulk, powerhouse, muscle man, he man, bruiser, big bruiser, ox, beefcake, built like a brick shithouse. See STRONG.

STRATEGEM n. angle, dodge, slant, trick, twist, switch, pitch, proposition, setup, layout, lay of the land, action, what's the action, play, scenario, scene, story, bit, child, brainchild, game plan, game, little game, gamesmanship, one-upmanship, booby trap, grift, racket, con, gimmick, what's cookin', how one figures it. See also PLAN.

STRATEGIC ARMS LIMITATIONS TREATY n. SALT.

STATEGIC ARMS REDUCTION TALKS n. START.

STRATEGIC DEFENSE INITIATIVE n. Star Wars, SDI.

STRATEGIST n. mastermind, brain, finagler, operator, wire-puller.

STRATEGY n. game plan, layout, angle, action, play, scenario, scene, story, brainchild, how one figures it, what's the action. See PLAN.

STRAY n. drop, fetch, guttersnipe, mudlark, ragamuffin, rustle.

STRAY v. circumlocute, get sidetracked, all over the map. See WANDER.

STREAM n. spritz.

STREAMLINE v. clean it up, break it down, cut the shit, cut the bullshit, cut the frills, cut the bells and whistles, get down to basics, get down to the meat. See SIMPLIFY.

STREET n. pavement, bricks, main drag, main line, turf, back alley, byway, trail, stroll, groove. See ROAD.

STREET PEOPLE n. player, bum, pusher, hooker, pimp, operator, drifter, runaway, throwaway, squatter, hippie.

STRENGTH n. 1. juice, pow, sock, kick, the force, beef, clout, might and main, powerhouse, strong arm, steamroller. 2. upper hand, whip hand, connection, hooks, in, license, wire, guts, intestinal fortitude, string, ropes, weight. See POWER.

STRENGTHEN v. beef up, soup up, charge up, punch up, heat up, hot up, hop up, jazz up, juice up, build up, step up, pour it on, add fuel to the fire, needle, spike (drink).

STRESS n. clutch, crunch, heat, pressure cooker, albatross around one's neck; choke, if one can't stand the heat get out of the kitchen, (react to).

STRESS v. spot, spotlight, limelight, underline, headline, hit.

STRESSED adj. uptight, choked, clutched, clutched up, strung out, unglued, hyper, spooked, wreck, nervous wreck, bundle of nerves, wired, wired up, yantsy, shot to pieces, basket case, hung up with, up the wall, in a tizzy, in a state, on edge, worried sick, worried stiff, biting one's nails, at the end of one's rope. See TENSE.

STRESSFUL adj. bummer, downer, grabber.

STRETCH v. 1. pad, fill, spin out, string out, drag out, run out, stretch out, build up, beef up, drag one's feet. 2. boost, build up, pyramid, lay it on, spread it on, make a mountain out of a molehill, make a federal case out of something. See EXPAND.

STRETCHED adj. padded, spun out, strung out, dragged out, run out, boosted, hiked, hiked up, built up, beefed up, jacked up.

STRETCHER CASE n. carry, have to scrape one off the pavement.

STRETCHER BEARER n. body snatcher (WW 11).

STRICKEN adj. 1. hurting, bleedin', damaged, winged, nicked, zinged, cut, grabbing, bunged up, busted up, put away, walking wounded, have to scrape one off the sidewalk. See also ILL. 2. all torn up, cut up, hit where one lives, shook, shook up, screwed up, miffed, miffy, burned, burned one's ass, shot down, have one's nose out of joint, sore, uptight. See also UNHAPPY, UN-NERVED.

STRICT adj. 1. square, cubeular, uptight, tight-assed, stuffy, in line, straight, straight arrow, short haircut, bluenose, chicken shit, by the numbers, by the book, according to the book, according to Hoyle, stuffy, sticky, set, sot, unflappable, dead set on. 2. nitpicker, picky, picky picky, stickler, ace, comma counter, fussbudget, fusspot, fancy pants, fuddy-duddy, granny, old woman, old maid, pernickety, persnickety. See STERN.

STRICTURE n. hang-up, catch, stumbling block, glitch, joker, one small difficulty, bottleneck, choke point. See HINDRANCE.

STRIDE n. clip, lick. See also WALK.

STRIDE v. leg it, hoof it, stomp, pound the beat, pound the pavement, boot it, stump it, traipse, trapse, traipse around, ooze, strut one's stuff, beat the rocks, press the bricks, broom, drill. See also WALK.

STRIFE n. 1. hassle, row, blowup, blowoff, spat, words, rhubarb, ruckus, ruction, rumpus, run-in, static, flap, fuss, flak, wrangle. See ARGUMENT. 2. brawl, brush, scrap, scene, set-to, rumble, knockdown, knockdown and drag out, mix-up, battle royal, stew, shindy, catamaran. See FIGHT.

STRIKE n.   1. walkout, sit-down, sit-in, tie-up, hit the bricks, lockout, holdout, sick-in, sick-out, blue flu (police), skippy strike, quickie; outlaw strike, wildcat (unsanctioned). 2. blitz, push. 3. belt, chop, bam, boff, bop, biff, bash, swat, sock, slug, zap, zetz, wallop, lollop, haymaker, bonk, blindside (unexpected). See HIT.

STRIKE v.   1. walk out, sit down, sit in, skippy strike, locked out, wildcat strike, outlaw strike, hit the bricks, tie up, sick in, sick out, blue flu, hold out. 2. bash, whop, whack, bonk, conk, bop, boff, biff, bean, belt, bung, sock, slug, smack, poke, clip, wallop, throw a punch, sock it to one, plant one, haul off on one, let one have it, land a haymaker. See HIT. 3. cut, bleep, bleep out, blue pencil, knock out, X out, trim, gut, clean up, launder, sterilize, sanitize, decontaminate, snip, pass up, drop, rub, squash, squelch.

STRIKEBREAKER n.   scab, fink, rat, rat fink, goon, goon squad, flying squad, flying squadron, scissorbill, boll weevil, missionary worker.

STRIKER n.   holdout, picket.

STRIKING adj.   1. flashy, jazzy, splashy, make a big splash, showy, splurgy, candy, classy, flossy, toney, high-toned, belled, duded up, hotshot, stand out, spot one like a lead dime, stick out, stick out like a sore thumb, somebody. 2. boss, bitchin', stunning, primo, A number one, 10, ten, super colossal, smashing, gnarly, unreal, motherfucker (Obsc.), zero cool, far out, out of this world, out of sight, corking, doozy, dynamite, in orbit, something, something else, mind-blowing, groovy, heavy, too much. See FABULOUS. See also BEAUTIFUL, POWERFUL.

STRING MUSICIAN n.   fiddler, banjo picker, picker, strummer, thrummer, twanger.

STRINGENT adj.   1. chicken shit, by the numbers, by the book, according to the book, according to Hoyle, stiff, tough, rough, brick wall, ironclad, stick to one's guns, put one's foot down, hard-nosed, set, sot, dead set on, dyed in the wool. See STERN. 2. nitpicking, picky, picky-picky, stickler, pernickety, persnickety. See PARTICULAR.

STRIP v.   do a strip tease, do a strip, strip to the buff, slip out of, take it off, peel, shuck, husk, get all naked.

STRIPPED adj.   bare assed, B.A., bald, naked as a jaybird, nudie, in one's birthday suit, in the altogether, in the buff, in the raw, wear a smile. See NUDE.

STRIPTEASE n.   strip, stripper, tits and ass, T and A, bumps, grinds, bumps and grinds; pastie, pasty, g-string (costume).

STRIPTEASER n.   burlesque queen, exotic dancer, peeler, stripper, stripteuse.

STRIVE v.   1. tackle, take on, cut and try, buck, hassle, sweat, sweat it, sweat and slave, dig, plug, peg away, bust a gut, break one's ass, bear down, put one's back into it, bend over backward, knock oneself out, go all out, go for broke, go the limit, pour it on, work one's head off. See APPLY ONE'S SELF, ATTEMPT. 2. jockey for position, scramble for, go for the throat, go for the jugular, go after, make a play for, push, push for, shoot for, shoot at, shoot the works. See also CONTEST. 3. cross, take on, fly in the face of, be agin, buck, nix, have a bone to pick, put up an argument, put up a fight, mix it up with, tangle with, bump heads with, cross swords with, lock horns with, stick it to one, push around. See FIGHT.

STRIVING adj.   in there, in there pitching, hanging in, going for it.

STROLL v.   ankle, ank, toddle, sashay, traipse, trapse, trapse around, ooze, cruise, air out, mope, mooch, trill, percolate. See WALK.

STRONG adj.   1. husky, hefty, heavy, beefy, gorilla, hunk, hulk, bull, powerhouse, muscle man, he-man, bruiser, ox, beefcake, bone crusher, enforcer, hard-boiled, hooligan, tough customer, plug-ugly, roughneck, big stiff, ballbreaker, ballbuster, backbreaker, built like a brick shithouse, got the horses to do it, hoss, strong as a horse, strong as a lion, strong as an ox, sturdy as an ox. 2. wicked, mean, hairy, hardball, hard-nosed, ballsy, Chicago, bitch, handful, push, punch, go-getter, go-go, ball of fire, hotshot, steamroller, get up a head of steam, Norwegian steam, spanking, punchy, gutty, gutsy, mover and shaker, wave maker, full of piss and vinegar, full of beans, full of hops, have lead in one's pencil, come on strong, come on like gangbusters, take over, take charge, fair hell. See also POWERFUL.

STRONGBOX n.   box, crib, coffin, gopher, jug, keister, pete, peat, pete box, pocket, sock, trap (hidden).

STRONG-WILLED adj.   1. hang tough, tough nut, tough nut to crack, head in concrete, stand one's ground, mule-headed, set, sot, unflappable, dead set on, cussed, ornery, murder (he's murder). See STUBBORN. 2. got the horses to do it, powerhouse, go-getter, steamroller, gutsy, movers and shaker, wave maker, take over, take charge, fair hell, moving out. See STRONG. 3. bound, bound and determined, hang tough, unflappable, set, dead set on, hell bent on, stand by one's guns, put one's foot down, strictly business, mean serious jelly, no shit, no bird turdin', not playing around, no fooling, have blood in one's eye, be out for blood. See DETERMINED.

STRUCTURE n.   1. pile o' bricks, rockpile, cage, the blindfold lady (court). 2. pecking order, T.O. See also ORGANIZATION.

STRUCTURED adj.   have one's act together, have one's shit together, have one's head together, have one's head screwed on right, together, all together. See ORGANIZED. See also ORGANIZATION.

STRUGGLE n. 1. grind, daily grind, grindstone, rat race, the salt mines. 2. hassle, wrangle, beef, brush, rumble, roughhouse, free for all, donnybrook, flap, jump, mix-up, jam, run-in, go, rowdy-dowdy, row, rumpus, ruction, ruckus, stew, shindy, set-to, scrap, when push comes to shove. See FIGHT.

STRUGGLE v. 1. hustle, scratch, slave, sweat, sweat and slave, sweat it, grind, dig, plug, plug away, hassle, take on, have one's nose to the grindstone, bust a gut, bust one's conk, back to the salt mines. See WORK. See also APPLY ONESELF. 2. buck, brawl, hassle, scrap, row, kick up a row, roughhouse, romp, slug, smack, shuffle, put up a fight, tangle ass with, bump heads with, cross swords with, lock horns with, go up against, be agin. See FIGHT. 3. fly in the face of, fly in the teeth of, tummel, raise sand, pettifog, put up an argument. See ARGUE. 4. make a run at, tackle, take on, look to, make a try, cut and try, try on for size, do it or bust a gut, bust one's ass, break one's ass, break one's neck, break one's back, break one's heart, try one's damndest, give it the old college try, try on for size, give it a try, give it a go, give it one's best shot, take one's best shot, give it a whirl, give it one's all, give it all one's got, bend over backward, lay oneself out, push, knock oneself out, take the bull by the horns, take a shot at, take a fling at, take a crack at, take a whack at, take a cut at, take a stab at, make a stab at, have a go at, have a fling at, have a shot at, on the make, pitch into, in there pitching, do one's level best, go all out, go for it, go for broke, go the limit, shoot the works. 4. push, hump it, hump oneself, bear down, buckle down, put one's back into it, bend over backward, pour it on, work one's head off. See ATTEMPT. 5. phumpher, crash, crack up, flop, blow the gig, get hung up, make a hash of, go to pieces, come a-cropper. See FLOUNDER.

STRUMPET n. hooker, call girl, hustler, ho, working broad, working girl, nok, model, pro, floozie, chippie, prosty, tart, baggage, B-girl, bimbo, broad, chacha, fallen woman, ass peddler, hussy. See PROSTITUTE.

STRUT v. sashay, boot, ank, boogie, show off, grandstand, hot dog, put up a front, put on airs, put on, put on the dog, ritz it, look big, shoot the agate, swank, play to the gallery, parade one's wares, strut one's stuff. See also WALK.

STUBBORN adj. hard-nosed, hard core, hard shell, hard ass, hard-line, hang in, hang in there, hang tough, tough nut, tough nut to crack, hard nut to crack, turk, locked, locked in, head in concrete, set in concrete, stuck in concrete, buried in concrete, chiseled in stone, solid as a rock, Rock of Gib, Rock of Gibraltar, rock-ribbed, brick wall, pat, stand pat, stay put, stand one's ground, hold one's ground, dig in one's heels, stick it out, stick to one's guns, put one's foot down, hold the fort, hold the line, do

or die, mean business, come hell or high water, money talks bullshit walks, hard as nails, hardheaded, bulletheaded, bullheaded, pigheaded, mule-headed, mulish, stubborn as a mule, stiff-necked, sticky, set, sot, unflappable, dead set on, bitter ender, dyed in the wool, has one's Dutch up, cussed, ornery, murder (he's murder).

STUDEBAKER n. Studie, Studey.

STUDENT n. wonk, tool, power tool, grind, greasy grind, gunner, weenie, grub, throat, super strap, swat, brown bagger, mug, file boner, plug, plugger, dig, poler, brain, skull, four-pointer, five-pointer, bookbuster, curve-killer (superior), flunky (failing), shark, coed, undergrad, grad, doc, post doc, prep, preppie, grandfather (senior), soph (sophmore); frosh, dewdrop, rat (freshman); rhinie (prep. school freshman), bone, boner, Flunkenstein, jock, jockey, horse (athlete), big man on campus, B.M.O.C., big-time operator, B.T.O., big wheel, key, key swinger, frat (square), ginny (glamorous), blood (college), Joe College, Joe Yale, white shoe (Ivy League), aggie (agricultural), Christer (prude, nondrinker), Jasper (theological), donkey (Rel.), cad, crib (cheats), dryball, doughball, mothball, party boy, party girl, calico, cosmo (foreign).

STUDENT DOCTOR n. tern.

STUDENT LOAN MORTGAGE ASSOCIATION n. Sally Mae.

STUDENT NON-VIOLENT CO-ORDINATING COMMITTEE n. SNCC, Snick.

STUDIOUS adj. wonk, tool, power tool, bookworm, throat, cutthroat, gome, grub, pencil geek, poler, professor, squid, weenie, wig.

STUDY v. 1. heavy booking, crack the books, hit the books, pound the books, go book, megabook, megastudy, grind, plug, shed, speed, pour it on, bone, bone up, pull an all-nighter, burn the midnight oil, bury oneself in, blitz, cram, cram session, skull practice, skull drag, dig, dust 'em off, rack, bag some food for the brain, cruise a subject, wade through, plunge into, polish up, kick around, knock around, worm, hardwire (by rote), get down, get down pat, get down cold, get hold of, get into one's head, pick up, pick up on, learn the ropes, learn backwards and forwards. 2. look-see, double-O, OO, eye, gun, glim, check, check out, check it out, check over, check up, case, keep tab, keep tabs on, peg, scope, read, scout it out, squack, spot, burn up, eagle eye, pike off, smoke, candle, case. See also SEE. 3. figure, figure out, sort out, kick around, bat it around, brainstorm, head trip, stew over, chew over, run it by one again. See THINK.

STUFF n. 1. junk. 2. goods, schmatte. 3. bottom line, nitty-gritty, nuts and bolts, heart, meat.

STUFFED adj. 1. packed, jam-packed, full up, topped off, up to here, fit to bust, packed like sardines, sardined. See CROWDED. 2. fed up, fed to the gills, fed to the teeth, stuffed to the gills, skinful, snootful, bellyful, with a bellyful, with a skinful, with a snootful.

STUN v. rock, gork, floor, shake one up, give one a shot, give one a turn, blow away, blow one's mind, bowl over, throw one a curve, knock one over, set on one's ass. See SURPRISE.

STUNNED adj. shook up, all shook up, gorked, punchy, slaphappy, bug-eyed, thunderstruck, floored, thrown, unglued, flabbergasted, boggled, bowled over, hit like a ton of bricks, caught with one's pants down. See SURPRISED.

STUNTED adj. shrimp, wee, peewee, peanut, runt, short, small fry, small time, dinky, measly, banty, tomtit, shot, yea big, yea high, wart, mite, piddling, two bit, two by four, pint-sized, half-pint, knee high, knee high to a grasshopper.

STUNT MAN n. bump man.

STUPEFIED adj. gorked, glazed, MEGO (my eyes glaze over), gone, dopey, out of it, out to lunch, spaced, spaced out, spacey, trippy, tweeked out, woozy, foggy, in a fog, wandering around in a fog, punchy, punch drunk. See DAZED.

STUPEFY v. rock, gork, zone out, floor, blow away, blow one's mind, bowl over, bowl down, set on one's ass, set back on one's heels, put one away. See SURPRISE.

STUPENDOUS adj. rad, way rad, fab, glor, fantasmo, fat, super, superfly, too much, the utmost, unreal, zero cool, dynamite, marvy, terrif, bitchin', seven-ply gasser, pisseroo, shirty, aggressive, the greatest, skrouk, smashing, something else, hot shit, out of this world, out of sight. See FABULOUS. See also BIG, IMPORTANT.

STUPID adj. dork, nerd, nurdy, numbnut, loser, winner, knuckle dragger, asshole, chili bowl, lamebrain, birdbrain, birdie (teenage), scatterbrain, rattlebrain, rattleweed, yo-yo, nebbish, out to lunch, lunchie, out of it, zonked out, nobody home, the lights are on but nobody's home, pod people, troll, jerk, lowbrow, dodo, dummy, dumbo, dumdum, dumbbell, dumb bunny, dumb cluck, dumb Dora, dumb head, dumb ox, four-letter man (dumb), bonetop, boob, birk, box, oofus, ninny, nincompoop, airhead, bubblehead, baloonhead, meathead, musclehead, blockhead, pointyhead, cone-head, buckethead, bullhead, bumhead, butterhead, banana head, squarehead, mushhead, cementhead, dungeonhead, pumpkinhead, saphead, lunkhead, mut-tonhead, fathead, bonehead, knucklehead, shithead, doughhead, hammerhead, jughead, blubberhead, cheesehead, chickenhead, chucklehead, mallethead, lardhead, peahead, pinhead, puddinghead, wooden-head, stupidhead, dunderhead, blunderhead, chowder-head, cabbagehead, beetlehead, potato head, deadhead, flathead, numbskull, numbhead, numb brained, not all there, minus some buttons, missing a few buttons, not have all one's buttons, missing a few marbles, not have all one's marbles, lost one's marbles, non compos, non compos mentis, knows from nothing, doesn't know from nothing, doesn't know the time of day, doesn't know from A to B, doesn't know A from izzard, doesn't know which way is up, doesn't know from straight up, doesn't know enough to come in out of the rain, case, turkey, goop, stoop, stupe, thick, loogan, schlemiel, schlamozzle, schlump, schlub, shmendrick, shmoe, shnook, schmuck, stiff, big stiff, clodpated, dipshit, dipstick, deadneck, dildo, dill, load, lob, pack horse, droop, dud, Elmer, gasser, gonus, good fellow, goofy, goofus, goof ball, goon, goopus, got a hole in the head, leak in the think tank, nuthin' upstairs, jackass, knuckle, bloke, bohunk, baloney, captain of the head, caspar, soft in the head, half-baked, boob, sappy, slaphappy, fat dumb and happy, mess, mutt, muttontop, meat, meatball, mope, weak in the upper story, simp, klutzy, jaggie, head up, jay, jiggens, juggins, lead-footed, marble dome, newt, nitwit, nougat, one eye, chump, clam, clock, cluck, cluckhead, world's prize cluck, clunk, dopey, dunce, dead ass, dimwit, dodunk, dub, fish, flub, farmer, melon farmer, shit stick, popcorn, sausage, duck soup, slow on the uptake, slow on the draw.

STURDY adj. 1. husky, hefty, heavy, beefy, gorilla, hunk, hulk, bull, powerhouse, muscle man, he-man, strong-arm, bruiser, strong as an ox, strong as a horse, beefcake, bone crusher, built like a brick shithouse. See STRONG. 2. hard-boiled egg, tough, roughneck, ballbreaker, ballbuster, backbreaker. See TOUGH.

STUTTER v. dribble.

STYLE n. bag, cup of tea, druthers, flash, groove, number, thing, type, turned on to, bump for, plenty on the ball, something on the ball, shine at, shine in, dash, splash, splurge. See also FLAIR.

STYLISH adj. faddy, trendy, in, in the mainstream, in thing, the thing, latest thing, latest wrinkle, new wrinkle, newest wrinkle, last word, mod, now, really now, the rage, spinach, up to the minute, in the swim, masscult, fashion plate, chichi, chic, natty, dap, sharp, snazzy, beautiful, clean, go-go, hip, hep, mellow back, swinger, swingle, upscale, uptown, ritzy, plush, posh, spiffy, classy, high class, toney, nifty, swanky, swell, nobby, city slicker, kicky, to be bad, dicty, doggy, dog it, go-getter, jazzy, jazzbo, reat, sharpie, cheesy, cat's meow, knock one's eye out, dressed to kill, dressed to the teeth, dressed to the nines, clotheshorse, catch on, in-spot, happening place, groovy hangout, hotspot.

STYLUS n. stick, ball point.

STYMIE v. 1. choke off, cut off, queer, crab, hang up, hold up, crimp, cramp one's style, throw a monkey wrench into the works, stall, stonewall. See PREVENT. See also HINDER. 2. shelve, put on the shelf, put on the back burner, put on hold, put on ice, hold off, hang fire, pigeonhole, corner, dead end, give one the run around (repeatedly). See DELAY.

SUBCONTRACT v. farm out.

SUBCULTURE n. punk, street people, hippy, yippie, underground.

SUBDEBUTANTE n. deb, subdeb.

SUBDUE v. 1. break, break in, bust, gentle. See SOFTEN. 2. squash, squelch, goof up, queer, sideways over a cliff, put down. 3. trash, drub, whip, drop, deck, clobber, cream, zap, waste, take the wind out of one's sails, take down, put down, smack down, shut down, shut out, rank out. 4. bury, blank, skunk, trim, trounce, fix one's wagon, scuttle, shave, massage, shellack, squelch, squash, make one say uncle, do in, lick to a frazzle, beat all hollow, shut off, blow away, blow one out of the water, put away, settle one's hash. See DEFEAT.

SUBJECT n. guinea pig.

SUBJUGATE v. ride herd on, henpeck, crack the whip, pussywhip (Fem.), wear the pants, wear the trousers, rule the roost, keep under one's thumb, lead by the nose, kick one around, throw one's weight around, throw a lot of weight, twist around one's little finger, wind around one's little finger, have the upper hand, have the whip hand, have it covered, have the say so, hold the reins, pull the ropes, pull the strings, pull the wires, wire-pull, reel one back in, bring to heel, box in, get one in a box, get one's hook into, sit on top of, break in, bust, gentle.

SUBJUGATED adj. in one's power, in one's pocket, in one's clutches, under one's thumb, at one's mercy, at one's beck and call, at one's feet, a slave to, led by the nose, putty in one's hands, tied to one's apron's strings, dance to one's tune, peon, serf, slave, slavey, pratt boy, worker bee.

SUBLIME adj. fab, fantasmo, fat, super, super fly, gross, evil, terrible, too much, the most, zero cool, heavy, dynamite, marvy, terrif, solid gold, outrageous, far out, the greatest, stunner, heavenly, out of this world, out of sight. See FABULOUS.

SUBMARINE n. navy shark, pig boat, tin can, tin fish, tin shack, boomer (missile).

SUBMARINE TERMS Christmas tree (control panel), the creeps (itch from low pressure), pull the plug (submerge).

SUBMERGE v. dunk, pull the plug (submarine).

SUBMERSE v. dunk.

SUBMERSION n. dunking.

SUBMISSIVE adj. yes-man, ass-kisser, on a string, henpecked, tied to one's apron strings, on a leash, weak sister, Milquetoast, Casper Milquetoast, tail between one's legs, schnook, dance, dance to one's tune, eat crow, eat humble pie, eat shit, putty in one's hands, when in Rome do as the Romans do.

SUBMIT v. 1. fold, quit, cave in, give in, say uncle, cry uncle, throw in the sponge, pack it in, kiss ass, eat crow, eat dirt, knuckle under, kowtow, lie down and roll over for, give away the store. See SURRENDER. 2. go with the flow, don't make waves, don't rock the boat, play the game, play ball with, shape up, not get out of line, go social. See COMPLY. 3. proposition, make a pitch, put a feeler out, pop the question.

SUBORDINATE n. peon, serf, slave, slavey, girl Friday, man Friday, low man on the totem pole, second fiddle, second string, third string, flunky, stiff, dweeb, apparatchik, running dog. See INFERIOR.

SUBORDINATION n. pecking order, down the line.

SUBPOENA n. plaster, papers.

SUBSCRIBE v. 1. back, bless, boost, give the nod, give the go-ahead, give the green light, give one's stamp of approval, get behind, okay, go along with, hold a brief for, hold with, put one's John Hancock on, thumbs up, take, take kindly to, yes one, ditto, rubber-stamp. See ENDORSE. 2. ante up, pony up, get it up, put up, put something in the pot, sweeten the pot, sweeten the kitty, do one's part. See GIVE. 3. okay, OK, sign on, make a deal, firm a deal, cut a deal, buy, set, play ball with.

SUBSCRIBER n. angel, Santa Claus, sugar daddy, fairy godmother, lady bountiful, giver, heavy hitter, maxed out (political limit).

SUBSERVIENT adj. 1. bush league, low in the pecking order, flunky, furp, handkerchief head, stepin fetchit, Uncle Tom (Bl.). See INFERIOR. 2. dance, dance to one's tune, eat crow, eat humble pie, eat shit, in one's power, in one's pocket, in one's clutches, under one's thumb, at one's mercy, at one's beck and call, at one's feet, a slave to, led by the nose. See SUBJUGATE.

SUBSIDIARY n. branch, subsid.

SUBSIDIZE v. angel, back, bankroll, juice, grubstake, pick up the check, pick up the tab, stake, prime the pump, knock (Bl.). See FINANCE. See also GIVE.

SUBSIST v. 1. get along, just makin' it, get by. 2. hang in, hang in there, hang tough, hang on, stick, stick it out, stick with it, ride out. See also MANAGE.

SUBSISTENCE n. the wherewithal, bread, bread and butter, the bacon, the necessary.

SUBSTANCE n.   1. point, stuff, nub, bottom line, ABC's, nitty-gritty, nuts and bolts, brass tacks, coal and ice, guts, innards, name of the game, the way of it, nature of the beast, drift, heart, meat. 2. hunk, chunk, gob.

SUBSTANDARD adj.   crap, junk, shit, G.I., lemon, Mickey Mouse, piss-poor, schlocky, bottom of the barrel, sleazy, slimpsy, below the mark, not up to scratch, not up to snuff, seconds. See IMPERFECT.

SUBSTANTIAL adj.   1. sound as a dollar, solid as a rock. 2. heavy, heavyweight, big league, major league, we're not talking about nutmeg here, big deal. 3. biggie, Mr. Big, big gun, big noise, big shit, big timer, big wheel, big wig, real cheese, mover and shaker, high-muck-a-muck, tycoon, baron, brass, V.I.P., connection, wire, godfather, a somebody, double-barreled, big daddy, major league, big league. See IMPORTANT. 4. legit, card-carrying, sure enough, honest to God, twenty-four carat, all wool and a yard wide, for real, righteous.

SUBSTANTIATE v.   1. check out, check up, check up on, debunk (prove false). 2. try, try out, try on. See also TEST, CONFIRM.

SUBSTANTIVE adj.   meaningful, meaningful experience, heavy. See also BASIC.

SUBSTITUTE n.   spare, backup, sub, stand-in, fill-in, pinch hitter, pinch runner, off the bench, bench warmer, ringer, redundancy, second string, third string, switcheroo, dog chaser (R.R.); front.

SUBSTITUTE v.   pinch hit for, sub, sub for, swap places with, sit in, stand in, back up, fill in, take over, front for, ring, ring in, take out, step into the shoes of, cover for.

SUBSTITUTION n.   switcheroo, sub.

SUBTERFUGE n.   1. angle, dodge, slant, trick, twist, switch, pitch, proposition, setup, layout, lay of the land, what's the action, play, scenario, scene, story, bit, child, brainchild, game plan, game, little game, gamesmanship, one-upmanship, booby trap, grift, racket, con, jazz, jive, shuck, total shuck, balls, bunco, hooey, hocky, hoke, hokey-pokey, hokum, hogwash, malarkey, marmalade, spinach, banana oil, baloney, bulldog, garbage, snow job, whitewash, whitewash job, doesn't wash, plant, hookup, put-on, spoof, shell game, skin game, trick, fool, fast one, run around, cutie, claptrap, line of cheese, borax, song, song and dance, string, smoke, tripe, vanilla, gimmick, what's cookin', how one figures it. 2. cover, cover-up, cover story, fig leaf, clean up, cop out, fish tale, fish story, cock-and-bull story, tall story, tall tale, fairy tale, whopper, yarn, dirty lie, terminological inexactitude, Mother Machree, Mother McCrea, routine, stall. 3. hustle, hassle, con, con game, big store, sting, bunk, bunco, flam, flimflam, flimflammery, jip, gyp, scam, racket, dodge, stunt, fast shuffle, bait and switch. See TRICK.

SUBTRACT v.   knock off, take away.

SUBTRACTION n.   deduck (income tax item), cut.

SUBURB n.   slub, slurb, spread city, bedroom community, sticks, stix.

SUBWAY n.   hole, hole in the ground, metro, tube.

SUCCEED v.   click, connect, put across, put it together, put over, pull it off, pull it out (despite adversity), get over, get well, get fat, get rich, get ahead, get away with, get on, get something on the board, get there, get into pay dirt, get the breaks, break the bank, go places, go to town, go great guns, go over, go over big, win out, check out, make out, make the cut, make it, make a killing, make hay, make well, make the grade, make good, make a noise in the world, be heard from, make a hit, hit, hit it big, hit the jackpot, hit the bull's-eye, hit pay dirt, strike it rich, strike oil, strike gold, strike a vein, make a lucky strike, strike it lucky, luck, luck in, luck out, fall into the shithouse and come up with a five-dollar gold piece, shit in high cotton, ace, ace the easy, hold aces, turn up trumps, move out, take off, fly, skyrocket, flash in the pan (brief), ring the bell, score, hang up (sports), win hands down, win going away, win in a walk, win in a waltz, waltz off with, breeze home, romp home, romp off with, run with the ball, blow away, blow out of the water, cream, clean sweep, skunk, KO, knock one for a loop, walk over, be a gas, be a gasser, bring home the bacon, bring home the groceries, have it made, turn the trick, got it made, pull off, bring off, carry off, catch on, pass muster, fill the bill, get by, pass in the dark, arrive, nail it, hack it, win one's spurs, do the job, do oneself proud, do all right by oneself, do a land-office business, come on, come along, be fat dumb and happy, live high on the hog, live off the fat of the land, live the life of Riley, live on Easy Street, live in clover, live on velvet, have one's place in the sun, come out on top of the heap, lie on a bed of roses, take the cake, get Brownie points, break the back of, light at the end of the tunnel, over the hump.

SUCCEEDING adj.   next off, next up, next in line for.

SUCCESS n.   1. winner, grand slam, big hit, sockeroo, killing, laugher, hot run, daily double (series of successes), sleeper (unexpected), howling success, pay dirt. See TRIUMPH. 2. boom, good times, gravy train, land-office business, high on the hog, on top of the heap, bed of roses, clover, Easy Street, lap of luxury, the life of Riley, velvet.

SUCCESSFUL adj.   1. smoking, really smoking, really popping, it cooks, got legs, chill, have it made, have a mint, have the wherewithal, have one's place in the sun, on Easy Street, on velvet, on top of the heap, on a bed of roses, everything's coming up roses, high on the hog, right up there, in the bucks, in the money, in the chips, in the lap of luxury, in the clover, rolling in clover, a pig in clover, on a roll, really rolling, rollin' in it, rollin' in dough, rolling in money, lousy with money, tall money, money to burn, really cooking, cooking with gas, lousy rich, stinking rich, stinky pie rich, holding, well-heeled, well fixed, well-to-do, well set up, set up, sitting pretty, sit fat, fat, fat city, fat cat, arrived, plush, lush, flush, loaded, booming, going strong, going great guns, gold mine (successful business), mining the gold, Midas touch, golden, made it, made it big, made one's pile, did all right by oneself, home free, laughing all the way to the bank, ride the gravy train, gravy boat, jammy, good ticket; yuppie (young urban professional), buppie (Bl.), yumpie (young upwardly mobile professional), yavis (young attractive verbal intelligent succcessful), dicty, big, biggie, big shot, long hitter, king of the hill, duke of the catwalk, Daddy Warbucks, scissorbill, swell, lace curtain, coupon clipper, big butter and egg man, rich as Croesus, the establishment, big boys, the 400, upper class, the beautiful people, main line, large, oofy, uptown, upscale, piss on ice; greasing it out, sleazeball, sleazing (tennis shots). 2. blow one away, blow one out of the water, have one by the balls, have one by the short hairs, have one by the tail.

SUCCESSFULLY adv. with a bang, swimmingly.

SUCCESSION n. pecking order, down the line, timeline.

SUCCINCT adj. in a nutshell, short and sweet, make a long story short, boiled down, cut to the bone.

SUCCOR v. boost, buck up, brace up, up, back up, give a leg up, give a lift, lend a hand, go to bat for, go to the mat for, bail out, hold one's end up. See AID.

SUCCULENT adj. yummy, yummy in the tummy, delish, divoon, divine, heavenly.

SUCCUMB v. 1. go, kick off, kick the bucket, buy the farm, pass away, croak, meet one's maker, give up the ghost, breathe one's last, go west, pop off, cash in one's chips, check out, up and die. See DIE. 2. fold, quit, cave in, give in, give into, say uncle, cry uncle, toss in the towel, throw in the sponge, pack it in, eat crow, eat dirt, eat humble pie, knuckle under. See SURRENDER. 3. go with the flow, don't make waves, don't rock the boat, play the game, shape up, clean up one's act, straighten up and fly right, stay in line, not get out of line, when in Rome do as the Romans do. See COMPLY.

SUDDEN adj. flash, from out in left field, from out of the blue, like a bolt from the blue.

SUE v. drag into court, haul into court, see one in court, have the law on, take the law on, take out after, have up, put one away, pull up.

SUFFER v. live with, bear with, put up with, bite the bullet, sweat, sweat it, wait out, take it, sit and take it, take it on the chin, grin and bear it, not let it get one

down, bleed, hurt, carry the torch for one (love), eat one's heart out (envy). See ENDURE.

SUFFERING adj. hurting, grabbing, bleeding, stab in the ———, making like the anvil chorus in one's skull, who needs it, this I need yet, need it like a hole in the head, take some hide and hair, biting the bullet, carrying the torch, torching. See also DISTRESSED.

SUFFICE v. fill the bill, make a hit, hit the spot, go over big, do the trick, hack it, make the grade, get by, be just the ticket, be just what the doctor ordered. See SATISFY. See also QUALIFY.

SUFFICIENCY n. a ton, mucho, mucho-mucho, heavy, stinking with, oodles, oodles and oodles, beaucoup. See also ENOUGH.

SUFFICIENT adj. no end, up to one's ass in, a dime a dozen, a mess, aplenty, drug on the market, galore, money to burn, bellyful, had it, up to here, that's it, all right already, enough already, enough of that shit, fed up, have a skinful, have a snootful, sick and tired of, punched out, last straw.

SUGAR n. dirt, dominoes (cubes), sand, white gold, sawdust.

SUGAR BOWL n. gravel train (not common).

SUGGEST v. 1. steer, tout, plug, let in on, put on to something hot, put a bug in one's ear, put in one's two cents, tip, tip off, give one a tip, fold an ear. See ADVISE. See also PROPOSE. 2. favor, double for.

SUGGESTIBLE adj. sucker, patsy, mark, easy mark, pigeon, sitting duck, pushover, swallow anything, swallow whole, be taken in, wide open. See SUSCEPTIBLE.

SUGGESTION n. 1. tip, steer, hot lead, lead, tip-off, telltale, bum steer (false). 2. touch, titch, tad, smell, two cents' worth. 3. angle, gimmick, big idea (unwelcome), feeler, pitch, proposition, proposish, game plan, setup, how one figures it, bit, brainchild, sneaking suspicion.

SUGGESTIVE adj. blue, dirty, filthy, off base, off-color, out of line, jiggle, jiggly, spark. See also OBSCENE.

SUICIDE n. OD, take oneself out, take a rope, wrap up, solitaire, Brodie (off a bridge), gorging out, hang up, hit in the bonnet, hit out, pack in, string up, swing, back-gate commute.

SUICIDE, COMMIT v. OD, Brodie (off a bridge), gorge out, hang up, hit oneself in the bonnet, hit oneself out, pack in, swing, take a back-gate commute, take a rope, wrap up.

SUIT n. threads, set of threads, vine, flute, gray flannel, front, getup, rig, zoot suit, ice cream suit (white), drapes, set of drapes, drape, drape shape with a reet pleet, flash, frame, frock, sock frock. See also CLOTHING

SUIT v. 1. fit in, go by the book, roll with the punches, swim with the tide, come up to scratch, do it according to Hoyle, play the game, toe the mark. See CONFORM. 2. make it, make the cut, make the grade, cut the mustard, check out, hack it, pass muster, fill the bill, get by, pass in the dark. See SUCCEED.

SUITABLE adj. 1. user friendly, handy, all around. 2. right stuff, keerect, reet, reat, all reet, all root, all rightee, allrightie, all righty, cool, coolville, crazy, copacetic, copasetic, kopasetic, O.K. okay, A-O.K., A-okay, fucking-A, okey-dokey, okey-doke, ding ho, ding how, ding hau, ding hao, swell, dory, okydory, hunky-dory, right, righteous, hit the nail on the head, an A., S.O.P., kosher, according to Hoyle, up to code, up to snuff, it's the berries, in the groove, groovy, dead on, right on, on the nose, on the button, on the numbers, on the money, right on the money, on the ball, on the beam, on target, on track, on the right track, hitting on all six, all to the mustard, just what the doctor ordered, that's it, that's the idea, that's the ticket, that's the thing, that's just the thing, that's the very thing.

SUITCASE n. jiffy bag, keister, valpack, tote bag, carry-on.

SUITOR n. old man, squeeze, main squeeze, main dude, main man, boyfriend, B.F., ace, big moment, papa, sweet papa, date mate, honey, hon, back-door man. See BOY FRIEND.

SULKY adj. mopey, moony, downer, taken down, down in the mouth, out of sorts. See UNHAPPY.

SULLEN adj. bitchy, mean, ornery, out of sorts, grouchy, grumpy, cranky, bear, ogre, ugly, ugly customer, uptight, pushing out one's lips, got up on the wrong side of the bed. 2. mopey, moony, low, ass in a sling, dick in the dirt, in a blue funk, a downer, bummed out, hurting, off one's feed, killjoy, prunefaced. See MELANCHOLY.

SULLIED adj. dirty, exposed, mucked up, cruddy, scuzzy, raunchy, sleazy, sleazed up, crudded up, crummed up. See DIRTY.

SULLY v. 1. crud, sleaze up, crumb up, muck up, mess, mess up, muss, muss up. 2. put down, pan, knock, slam, hit, rap, give one a black eye, make one lose face. See SLANDER.

SULTRY adj. 1. close, sticky, stuffy, broiler, roaster, scorcher, sizzler, swelterer. 2. heavy, hot and heavy, hot stuff, steamy, blue, purple, X-rated, low-down, low-down dirty, low-down and dirty, turned on, nasty. See also OBSCENE.

SUM n. fixins', fixings, shebang, the whole enchillada, the works, the whole megillah, whole shebang, whole schmeer, whole works, lump sum (money). See WHOLE.

SUMMARIZE v. 1. run down, run over, run through, rehash, recap, make a long story short, get down to cases, get down to brass tacks. 2. cut, cut down, cut to the bone, nutshell, put in a nutshell, boil down, trim, get to the meat, chop, snip.

SUMMARY adj. 1. recap, rehash, run down, run through. 2. short and sweet, boiled down, in a nutshell, make a long story short.

SUMMER n. heat time, heavy heat stretch, riot time.

SUMMER DAY n. broiler, roaster, scorcher, sizzler, swelterer, sticky, close, one can fry eggs on the sidewalk.

SUMMER STOCK n. strawhat, strawhat circuit.

SUMMIT n. tops, the max, the most, up there, really up there.

SUMMON v. beep.

SUMMONS n. plaster, papers, greetings.

SUMPTUOUS adj. plush, posh, ritzy, swanky, splendiferous, splendacious, with all the extras, ultra-ultra, out of this world, out of bounds. See LUXURIOUS.

SUN n. rays, Old Sol, ol' sol, bean, Betsy, Betsey, pumpkin.

SUNBATHE v. bag some rays, tan.

SUNGLASSES n. shades, sunshades, glims, mask, peepers, specs, wraparounds. See also GLASSES.

SUNRISE n. bright, early bright, crack of dawn, day peep, sunup.

SUNSHINE n. rays, UV.

SUPERABUNDANT adj. ton, mucho, mucho-mucho, no end, up to one's ass in, lousy with, crawling with, mess, loaded, scads, shithouse full, wad, heaps. See AMOUNT, LARGE.

SUPERANNUATED adj. put out to pasture, out, back number, has-been, old hat, foozle, fossil, on the shelf, out of circulation, over the hill, passed it, a once-was, hung up one's spurs, old-timer.

SUPERB adj. aces, mega-gnarly, zero cool, rad, way rad, fab, state of the art, tops, stunning, solid, greatest, the real George, hummer, in orbit, this is some kinda ———, the best. See EXCELLENT.

SUPERCILIOUS adj. high and mighty, on one's high horse, dog it, put on airs, toplofty, sniffy, snooty, snotty, hoity-toity, uppish, uppity, bossy, high-toned, smart, cocky, gally, nervy. See ARROGANT.

SUPERFICIAL adj. flash, flash in the pan, glib, half-assed, half-baked, half-cocked, ditsy, bubbleheaded, quick fix, slick, tip of the iceberg.

SUPERFICIALLY adv. hit the high spots, once over lightly, skim, lick and a promise.

SUPERFLUITY n. overruns, the limit, he's the limit, too much. See also PLENTY.

SUPERFLUOUS adj. blivit, fifth wheel.

SUPERINTENDENT n. 1. super, sitter, house-sitter. 2. head, headman, hired gun, Big Brother, boss, bosshead, pit boss, pusher, straw boss, slave driver, governor, bull, bull of the woods, swamper, crumb boss (hobo and logger), zookeeper (racing). See also EXECUTIVE.

SUPERIOR adj. 1. in spades, super, mega-gnarly, cool, zero cool, winner, rad, radical, state of the art, gilt-edged, tops, top of the line, first class, golden, heavy, bad, marvy. See EXCELLENT. 2. cool, cocky, biggety, bossy, dicty, sniffy, snooty, snotty, uppity, upstage, stuck up, king shit, high and mighty, high hat, high falutin', put on airs, have one's glasses on (Bl.), throw one's weight around, smarty pants, wise ass. See ARROGANT. 3. have one by the balls, have one by the tail, have one by the short hairs.

SUPERIOR n. CEO, C.O., exec, key player, chief, bossman, czar, head honcho, the brass, VIP, Mr. Big, big cheese, big gun, big wheel, big player, big chew, top dog, bowwow, superfly, rabbi, higher up, higher ups, guru, buddy seat, the say, the word. See EXECUTIVE.

SUPERIORITY n. edge, ahead, over, top, on top, bulge, spark. See ADVANTAGE.

SUPERLATIVE adj. A, A-1, number one, numero uno, ten, 10, world class, greatest, gonest, hundred proof, mostest, baaadest, first chop, super, gilt-edge, all time, tops, top dog, endsville, the end, solid gold, winner. See BEST.

SUPERNUMERARY n. extra, spear carrier, supe, super, walking gentleman, walking lady, walk-on, atmosphere. See also ACTOR.

SUPERSTAR n. big box office, box office, B.O., box-office champ, box-office name, champ, one to pull 'em in, sure sell, bankable one, draw, big draw, big name, monster, celeb, name, household name, number one, prima donna, great, large, right up there, big-timer, biggie. See CELEBRITY.

SUPERVISE v. ride herd on, sit on top of, run, run things, run the show, call the shots, call the play, be in the driver's seat, be in the saddle, deal with, crack the whip. See MANAGE.

SUPERVISOR n. super, boss, brass hat, big brother, head, top dog, big weenie, big cheese, bull of the woods, king of the hill, big shot, big shit, pit boss (gambling), straw boss, slave driver, zookeeper (racing). See also EXECUTIVE.

SUPPER n. chow, chow time, din din, bite, eats, feed, feedbag, ribs (hot), grub, takeout, sit-down, blue plate, black plate (soul food), cook out, BBQ, barbecue, Chinx (Chinese, Derog.), potluck. See also FOOD.

SUPPLANT v. pinch hit for, sub for, swap places with, sit in, stand in, back up, fill in, take over, front for, ring, ring in, take out, step into the shoes of.

SUPPLANTED adj. has-been, out.

SUPPLEMENT n. spin-off, options, bells, bells and whistles. See also ADDITION.

SUPPLEMENT v. pad, bump, bump up, beef up, soup up, charge up, punch up, heat up, hot up, hop up, jazz up, juice up, build up, step up, pour it on, add fuel to the fire. See ADD.

SUPPLEMENTARY adj. padding, spare tire, fifth wheel, widow, gash, lagniappe, goody, perk, all the options, bells and whistles. See also ADDITIONAL.

SUPPLY v. heel (money), fix up, fix up with, drop (usually illegal or contraband goods), give with, pony up, put up, put out, get it up, kick in, come across with, come through, duke, weed, stake, put a buck one's way. See GIVE.

SUPPLY BASE n. buddy store (Vietnam).

SUPPORT n. 1. backup, backing, the wherewithal, bread, bread and butter, the bacon, the necessary. 2. security blanket, old standby, standby, juice, on the reservation (Pol.). 3. lift, shot in the arm, shot in the ass. See also ASSIST.

SUPPORT v. 1. boost, stroke, buck up, brace up, juice, juice up, key up, psych up, egg on, turn on, build, build up, chirk up, perk up, pick up, put up to, give a boost to, give a leg up, give a lift, lend a hand, plug, hype, ballyhoo, push, goose, hold a brief for, go with, go for, go to bat for, go to the mat for, go down the line for, go the route for, make a pitch for, beat the drum for, plump for, run interference for, grease the wheels for, thump the tub for, root for, stump for, get on the bandwagon, front for, stand up for, stick by, stick up for, ride shotgun for, take care of one, open doors, up, back, back up, pat on the back, toss a bouquet, give a bouquet, give a posy, give the man a big cigar, hand it to, give one the spotlight, gold star, puff up, trade last, TL, hear it for, hats off to, bail out, tin cupping (seeking management support), carry one, prop, prop up, hold one's end up. 2. angel, bankroll, grubstake, stake, back, juice, pick up the check, pick up the tab, knock (Bl.), lay on one, piece one off, prime the pump, go for. See FINANCE. 3. turn on, spark, trigger, zap, beef up, soup up, punch up, fire up, add fuel to the fire, heat up, hot up, hop up, jazz up, build up, juice, juice up, work up, give a lift, put one on top of the world, put on one cloud nine, brace up, chirk up, buck up, pick up, perk up, zip up, snap up. 4. handle, lump it, live with, bear with, put up with, bite the bullet, hang in, hang in there, hang tough, hang on, stick it out, ride out, sit and take it, sweat out, wait out, stay the course, stand up to it, be big, grin and bear it. See ENDURE.

SUPPORTER n. 1. backer, angel, staker, grubstaker, meal ticket, fairy godmother, lady bountiful, sugar daddy, Santa Claus. 2. fan, freak, booster, frenzies, nut, buff, hanger-on, sideman, ho dad, ho daddy, go in for, go out for, have a go at, plaster, shadow, echo, stooge, flunky, tail.

SUPPOSE v. 1. be afraid, have a hunch, have a sneaking suspicion, take as gospel truth, take stock in, swear by. See BELIEVE. 2. go out on a limb, take a stab, take a stab in the dark, take a shot, take a shot in the dark, figure, size up, guesstimate. 3. head trip, cook up, dream up, make up, think up, trump up, spark, toss out, spitball, brainstorm, take it off the top of one's head, talk off the top of one's head.

SUPPOSITION n. guesstimate, hunch, shot, shot in the dark, sneaking suspicion, stab, stab in the dark.

SUPPRESS v. black out, kill, squash, squelch, hush up, put the lid on, crack down on, keep under wraps, keep buttoned up. See REPRESS.

SUPPRESSED adj. 1. hung up, square, tight-assed, uptight. 2. bottled up, corked up, squashed, squelched, blacked out, kept under wraps, hushed up, shut down, killed, buttoned up. See also SECRET. 3. in one's power, in one's pocket, in one's clutches, under one's thumb, at one's mercy, at one's feet, putty in one's hands, dance to one's tune, slavey. See SUBJUGATED.

SUPPRESSION n. no-no, a don't, off limits, outta bounds, bleeper, blankety blank [word or expression], blackout, hush up, clampdown, crackdown.

SUPREME COURT n. Nine Old Men, SCOTUS.

SUPREME HEADQUARTERS WW II n. SHEAF.

SURCEASE n. break, breather, breathing spell, coffee break, five, ten, downtime, timeout, break-off, cutoff, layoff, letup, screaming halt, shuddering halt, grinding halt, freeze. See also END, STOP.

SURE adj. 1. sure enough, sure as fate, sure as shooting, sure as God made little green apples, sure as hell, sure as the devil, sure as I live and breathe, sure as death and taxes, sure as can be, sure as shit, sure thing, surest thing you know, surefire, for sure, fer sher, fer shirr, that's for sure, for damn sure, for danged sure, dead sure, for a fact, for a fact Jack, for certain, on ice, cold, down pat, nailed down, got the faith baby. See CERTAIN. 2. iceman, ice in one's veins, gutsy, high, all puffed up, pumped up, looking at the world through rose-colored glasses. See ASSURED, CONFIDENT, COCKSURE.

SURELY adv. absofuckinglutely, posilutely, absitively, cert, amen, sure, why sure, fer sure, fer sher, and no mistake, you know, you know it, you better believe it, you betcha, you betcher life, you bet, you can say that again, you're darn tootin', no catch, no kicker, no buts about it, no ifs ands or buts, is the Pope Catholic?, does a bear shit in the woods?, indeedy, yes indeedy, for real, right-o. See ABSOLUTELY.

SURFBOARD n. gun, double ender, hot dogging board, spoon, stick, popout.

SURFEIT n. bellyful, had it, skinful, snootful, up to here, dose, much of a muchness. See also FULL.

SURFEITED adj. done it all, been around twice, sick and tired of, had it up to here, fed up, fed to the teeth, fed to the gills, stuffed to the gills, skinful, bellyful, snootful.

SURFER n. gremlin, gremmie, hot dogger, surf bum, wahine (Fem.).

SURFING STYLES n. hang five, hang ten, hot dog, goofy foot (right foot forward), reverse kickout, ride the nose.

SURFING TERMS back out, bomb, bomb out, wipe out, gas out, get the ax, grab a rail, kamikaze (voluntary wipe), pull out, left slide, pearling (nose-down dive), catch a rail, take gas, soup, cowabunga, beach bunny, gun, heavy, skim board, pipe, tube, greenback, ho dad; kneebusters, clamdiggers, baggies, jammies (pants).

SURFING WAVES n. surf's up, heavy, the green, blown out, junk surf, looper, soup (foam), wake surf, tasty waves, wall up (the waves walled up to ten feet before curling).

SURGEON n. M.D., doc, bones, sawbones, bone bender, bone breaker, big eye man, big nose man, big heart man, croaker, medic, medico, stick croaker, butcher, blade, knife man, body and fender man (plastic).

SURGERY n. OR, the pit.

SURMISE n. out on a limb, a stab, a stab in the dark, a shot, a shot in the dark, guesstimate, hunch, sneaking suspicion.

SURMISE v. have a sneaking suspicion, take a stab, take a shot, take a shot in the dark, guesstimate, spitball. See SPECULATE.

SURPLUS n. overruns, the limit, too much, drug on the market.

SURPRISE n. whammy, double whammy, glork, jolt, bolt out of the blue, from out in left field, eye-opener, curveball, ace in the hole, bite one in the ass, kick in the ass, shot in the ass, sleeper (unexpected success).

SURPRISE v. 1. rock, glork, floor, shake one up, give one a shot, give one a turn, blow away, blow one's mind, bowl over, bowl down, strike all of a heap, flabbergast, put one away, make one jump out of his skin, spring something on one, from out in left field, throw one a curve, hit them where they ain't, knock one over, knock one over with a feather, set on one's ass, set back on one's heels, put one away, throw off one's beam ends. 2. drop in on.

SURPRISED adj. shook, shook up, all shook up, rocked, glorked, discombobulated, discombooberated, bug-eyed, thunderstruck, floored, thrown, fussed, gassed, shit, shit blue, shit green, unglued, come unglued, come unzipped, come apart, come apart at the seams, fall apart, fall out, flatfooted, caught flatfooted, galley west, higgledy-piggledy, skimble-skamble, in a flush, shot, shot to pieces, kerflumixed, flummoxed, flabbergasted, boggily-woogily, bowled down, bowled over, hit like a ton of bricks, struck all of a heap, thrown off one's beam ends, caught off base, caught with one's pants down, bit one in the ass.

SURPRISE ENDING n. catch, kicker, joker, payoff.

SURPRISING adj. mind-blowing, stunning, grabber, hell of a note, megadual.

SURRENDER v. 1. fold, quit, cave in, give up, give in, say uncle, cry uncle, toss in the towel, toss in the sponge, throw in the towel, throw in the sponge, toss it in, pack in, pack it in, buckle under, lump it, gleek it, eat crow, eat dirt, eat humble pie, pull in one's horns, knuckle to, knuckle under, drop, kowtow, lie down and roll over for, roll over and play dead, go along with. 2. come across, come across with, give out, put out (sexual); fork over, give away the store. See also GIVE UP.

SURREPTITIOUSLY adj. undercover, under wraps, hush-hush, strictly hush-hush, on the q.t., on the quiet, on the sly, in a hole-and-corner way, in holes and corners.

SURROUNDED adj. boxed in.

SURVEILLANCE n. bug, bugging, eye in the sky, spy in the sky, stakeout, tail, tap, track, wiretap, body mike.

SURVEY v. 1. eye, eyeball, scope, read, case, case the joint, check, check out, check over, check up, size up, spy out, stake out, give it the once over, scout it out, squack, candle, put under a microscope, get down to nuts and bolts, take the measure of. See SEE. See also RECONNOITER. 2. put out a feeler, test the waters, see which way the wind blows, send up a trial balloon.

SURVIVE v. 1. cut it, make the cut, handle, lump, lump it, live with, bear with, put up with, roll with the punches, bite the bullet, hang in, hang in there, hang tough, hang on, hang on for dear life, hang on like a bulldog, hold on like a bulldog, hang on like a leech, stick like a leech, stick like a barnacle, stick like a limpet, stick like a wet shirt, stick, stick it out, stick with it, win out, ride out, get by, go the limit, sit tight, sit and take it, sweat, sweat it, sweat it out, sweat out, staying power, stay the course, hack it, take it, stand for, stand the gaff,

stand up, stand up to it, shape up, show one's mettle, show one's stuff, be big, be big about, pay dues, grin and bear it, not let it get one down, tough it out, go the limit, go all the way, see through, see it through, carry through, see it out, not give up the ship, never say die. See also ENDURE, PERSIST. 2. bounce back, make a comeback, come around, come round, come back, come from behind, pull out of it, snap out of it, turn the corner, be out of the woods, get back in shape. See IMPROVE.

SUSCEPTIBLE adj. sucker, patsy, mark, easy mark, pigeon, clay pigeon, sitting duck, pushover, sucker for, fall for, tumble for, swallow anything, swallow whole, swallow hook line and sinker, be taken in, stick one's neck out, out on a limb, ready to be taken, putty in one's hands, wide open, sucker for a left.

SUSPECT adj. pseudo.

SUSPECT v. be afraid, expect, have a hunch, have a sneaking suspicion, smell a rat. See also BELIEVE.

SUSPEND v. 1. can, fire, lay off, ax, give the ax, give the air, give one his walking papers, sack, pink-slip, show the door, drum out, throw out on one's ear. See DISCHARGE. 2. shelve, put on the back burner, put on hold, put on ice, put off, hold off, hold up, hang, hang up, hang fire, pigeonhole. See DELAY.

SUSPENDERS n. braces, galluses, gaters, pulleys, stretches.

SUSPENSEFUL adj. blood and thunder, thriller, chiller, cliff-hanger, cloak and dagger, page-turner, potboiler, spyboiler, grabber, twisting in the wind.

SUSPENSION n. 1. ax, pink slip, sack, boot, the gate, door, layoff, rif (reduction in force), walking papers, old heave-ho. See DISMISSED. 2. break, break-off, coffee break, breather, breathing spell, downtime, letup, five, ten, timeout, freeze, cutoff, layoff, letup, happy hour.

SUSPICION n. funny feeling, hunch, sneaking suspicion. See also INTIMATION.

SUSPICIOUS adj. 1. cagey, leery, been hit before, not born yesterday, on the lookout, with a weather eye open, with one's eyes peeled. See CAUTIOUS. 2. uptight, green-eyed, jelly. 3. fishy, funny, not kosher, reachy, won't wash, phony, rings phony, too much, something's rotten in Denmark, stink to high heaven.

SUSTAIN v. 1. angel, bankroll, grubstake, stake, back, juice, pick up the check, pick up the tab, knock (Bl.), piece one off, prime the pump, go for. 2. buck up, brace up, lend a hand, plug, go with, front for, stand up for, stick up for, carry one, prop up. See SUPPORT. 3. beef up, soup up, punch up, heat up, hot up, hop up, jazz up, juice up, build up, add fuel to the fire. 4. live with, bear with, put up with, bite the bullet, hang in, take it, stand up to it. See ENDURE.

SUSTAINING adj.   stick to one's ribs.

SUSTENANCE n.   the wherewithal, bread, bread and butter, the bacon, the necessary.

SWAGGER v.   sashay, boot, ank, boogie, show off, grandstand, hot dog, put up a front, put on airs, put on, put on the dog, ritz it, look big, shoot the agate, swank, play to the gallery, parade one's wares, strut one's stuff. See also WALK.

SWAIN n.   main dude, main man, main squeeze, squeeze, my guy, my man, old man, stud, John, ace, ace lane, beau, big moment, flame, heartthrob. See BOYFRIEND.

SWALLOW n.   belt, swig, shot, gulp, chugalug.

SWALLOW v.   belt, chugalug, drop (drug), rock one back, swig, toss one back, slurp, scarf down, gorm, gorp, wolf, wolf down, inhale, gobble, gulp, bolt, dispatch, dispose, swabble, tuck in, tuck away, put away, put it away, pack it away, surround oneself outside of, put oneself outside of. See also ENDURE.

SWAMP DWELLER n.   swamp angel.

SWARM n.   jam, jam up, mob, push, turnout, blowout, crush, everybody and his brother, everybody and his uncle, loaded to the rafters, wall-to-wall people.

SWARMING adj.   alive with, crawling with, thick with.

SWAY v.   1. work on, soften up, turn one's head around, brainwash, eat one's mind, crack one, put across, sell, sell one on, suck in, hook. See PERSUADE. 2. impact on, lead by the nose, pull ropes, pull strings, pull wires, throw one's weight around, whitewash, wire-pull, get one's hooks into, twist one's arm. 3. yo-yo, blow hot and cold, shilly-shally, hem and haw.

SWEAR v.   1. cuss, damn, darn, drat, flame, talk dirty. 2. cross one's heart and hope to die, swear till one is blue in the face, swear up and down, swear on a stack of bibles, say so.

SWEARING n.   cuss, cussing, cuss word, dirty word, four-letter word, swearword, no-no, dirty name, French, pardon my French, dirty language, dirty talk.

SWEARWORD n.   four-letter word, cuss word.

SWEAT v.   get all in a lather, sweat like a horse, sweat like a trooper.

SWEATER n.   pullover, pull-on, poorboy, bulky, sloppy Joe.

SWEATY adj.   sticky, stinky, wet, drippy, bathed in sweat, perspiry.

SWEDE n.   squarehead.

SWEEPER n.   mop jockey, broom jockey.

SWEEPING adj.   across the board, wall to wall. See also WHOLE.

SWEET POTATOES n.   sweets.

SWEET ROLL n.   Danish, coffee and ———, mud ball.

SWEETENING n.   dirt, dominoes (cubes), sand, white gold.

SWEETHEART n.   old lady, old man, squeeze, main squeeze, main queen, main dude, main man, my guy, my man, best girl, dream girl, girl friend, G.F., boyfriend, B.F., jane, stud, John, ace, ace lane, beau, best fella, significant other, number one, numero uno, hat, mat, big moment, heartthrob, heartbeat, body and soul, one and only, hamma, mama, sweet mama, chick, papa, sweet papa, daddy, sugar, sugar daddy, casanova, Lothario, Don Juan, date mate, companion, constant companion, couple, gruesome twosome, flame, passion ration, sugar bowl, honey, hon, jelly roll, kissing cousin, baby, total babe, lovebird, turtle dove, lambie pie, back-door man, honey man, money honey, generous keeper, gold mine, big game, biscuit roller, rave, masher, mule skinner, oyster, armpiece, baby cake, cake, candyleg, gussie mollie (not common), patootie, hot patootie, sweet patootie, josan (Korean war), snoff, corn bread, home cooking, stone marten (beautiful).

SWEETS n.   cush, g'dong, gedunk, hickey, goodies, yum yum.

SWELTERING adj.   close, sticky, stuffy, broiler, roaster, scorcher, sizzler, swelterer, one can fry eggs on the sidewalk.

SWIFT adj.   screaming, sizzler, speedball, pronto, snappy, barrelling, on the double, get a move on, get cracking, move your tail, in nothing flat, step on it, make it snappy, shake a leg, pour it on, like mad, like crazy, like shit through a goose. See FAST.

SWIM v.   dog paddle, skinny-dip.

SWIMMER n.   fanny dipper.

SWIMSUIT n.   bikini, monokini (topless), string, tank suit.

SWINDLE n.   hustle, con, sting, flam, gyp, scam, racket, shady deal, crooked deal, fast shuffle, royal fucking, jive, shuck, hoke, dirty pool, frame-up, double-cross, shell game, skin game, fast one. See CHEAT.

SWINDLE v.   sting, rook, screw, shaft, frig, fudge, hose, hump, rim, rip off, jerk one off, dick one around, fuck one over, jive, shuck, shuck and jive, run a game on, fleece, flam, flimflam, clip, con, chisel, gouge, scam, stiff, sandbag, pluck, take, sucker, suck in, stack the deck, sting, skin, skunk, set up, frame, promote, hold up, soak, fox, ice, score. See CHEAT.

SWINDLED adj.   fell for, jerked around, fucked over, sucked in, taken, been taken, taken for a sleigh ride, clipped, stung, got the shaft, got the short end of the stick, got a haircut, screwed, tattooed, laid relaid and parlayed, bearded. See CHEATED.

SWINDLER n.   shark, sharp, sharpie, mechanic, con man, chiseler, flimflammer, gyp, gyp artist, crook, double-dealer, whip, operator, cheese-eater. See CHEATER.

SWINE n.   porker, porky, cob roller (young or small).

SWITCHBOARD n.   board, PBX, phones.

SWITCH OFF LIGHTS v.   save 'em, dim the glims, kill the lights.

SWOON v.   blackout, go out like a light, keel over, pass out, freak out, flicker (also pretend).

SWORD n.   pig sticker.

SYCOPHANCY n.   jive, snow, snow job, baked wind, abreaction route, soap, soft soap, bullshit, con, promote, applesauce, balloon juice, banana oil, hot air, malarkey. See FLATTERER, TOADY, MINION.

SYCOPHANT n.   ass kisser, A.K., bun duster, bootlick, bootlicker, footlicker, ass licker, tuchis licker, yes-man, nod guy, schmeikler, fan, groupie, gofer, backslapper, back scratcher, glad-hander, handshaker, apple polisher, apple shiner, Simonizer, brownie; brownnoser, those aren't freckles on his nose, fart sniffer, cocksucker (all Obsc.); egg sucker, earbanger, heeler, ho dad, ho daddy, honey cooler, politician, flunky, flunkystooge, stooge, hanger-on, waterboy, lackey, sideman.

SYMBOL n.   logo.

SYMPATHETIC adj.   1. old softie, softhearted, heart in the right place; bleeding heart, all heart (Derog.). 2. grokking, on the same beam, on the same wavelength, simpatico, tuned in, cool, down, have a heart, hip.

SYMPATHIZE v.   tune in, grok, I hear ya, can get behind it, be on the same wavelength, pick up on, feel for, be there for one.

SYMPATHY n.   heart, grandstand play.

SYMPOSIUM n.   confab, rap, rap session, buzz session, clambake, gam, powwow, think-in, chinfest, talkfest, talkee-talkee, skull session. See also MEETING.

SYNAGOGUE n.   Amen Corner, dirge factory, god box.

SYNCHRONIZE v.   1. lip sync, sync, sync up. 2. get it together, get one's act together, team up, pull together, jive, click.

SYNCHRONIZED adj.   in sync.

SYNCOPATE v.   play jazz, play jive, play rag, play swing.

SYNCOPATED adj.   hot, jazzed, jazzed up, jazzy, ragtimey, swingy.

SYNDICATE n.   organization, megacorp, multinationals, bunch, crew, crowd, gang, mob, plunderbund, outfit, ring.

SYNOPSIS n.   1. capsule, recap, rundown, runthrough. 2. short and sweet, boiled down.

SYNOPSIZE v.   1. run down, run over, run through, rehash, recap, make a long story short, get down to cases, get down to brass tacks. 2. cut, cut down, cut to the bone, nutshell, put in a nutshell, boil down, trim, get to the meat, chop, snip, blue pencil.

SYNTHETIC adj.   ersatz, hokey, plastic.

SYNTHETIC FUEL n.   synfuel.

SYPHILIS n.   VD, syph, dose, boogie, chankers, shankers, chank, shank, crud, blood disease, the French sickness, old Joe, the ral, ral up, rahl, rahl up, the rail, Cupid's itch, Venus's curse. See also VENEREAL DISEASE.

SYRUP n.   googlum, goozlum, goop, glop, machine oil.

SYRUPY adj.   goo, gooey, goop, goopy, glop, gloppy, goozlum.

SYSTEM n.   the Company, the Establishment, the Man, channels, cut and dried, G.I., red tape, same old shit, SOS, shtick, sked, grind, daily grind, environment.

SYSTEMATIZE v.   pull things together, shape up, straighten up and fly right, get one's act together, get one's head together, get one's shit together, tighten up, unzip.

SYSTEMATIZED adj.   together, all together, have one's act together, have one's shit together, have one's head together, have one's head screwed on right.

T

T n. tango, tare.

TAB n. logo.

TABLE v. shelve, put on the shelf put on the back burner, put on hold, put on ice, put off, hold off, hold up, hang, hang up, hang fire, pigeonhole, cool, cool it. See DELAY.

TABLE OF ORGANIZATION n. dotted line responsibility, T.O.

TABLET n. scratch, scratch pad.

TABOO n. no-no, a don't, off limits, out of bounds, bleeper, blankety blank [word or expression], thou shalt not.

TACHOMETER n. tach.

TACITURN adj. clammed up, dried up, dummied up, garbo, tight-lipped.

TACKLE v. make a run at, take on, cut and try, try on for size, give it a try, give it a go, give it a whirl, take a shot at, take a fling at, take a stab at, pitch into, go for it. See ATTEMPT.

TACTICS n. channels, red tape, by the numbers, by the book.

TAG n. logo.

TAILOR n. Abie, schneider (Derog.), needle worker.

TAINT v. 1. doctor, doctor up, spike, water, water down, cut, cook. 2. trash, crud up, crumb up, scuzz up, skank, muck up, sleaze up, mess up, piss on. 3. give one a black eye, make one lose face.

TAINTED adj. 1. cooked (radiation), dirty, exposed, mucked up, doctored. 2. strong, high, loud, gross, stinking.

TAKE v. 1. get, get one's fingers on, grab, glom, nab, nail, snag, bag, pick up, take in, haul in, pull in, carve out. See SEIZE. See also APPROPRIATE. 2. rip off, boost, cop, liberate, lift, contifisticate, snatch, snitch, make off with, annex, borrow, nip, snare, pluck, salvage. See STEAL. 3. lug, pack, piggyback, ride, shlep, shlep along, tote, truck, back, birdie back, buck, gun, heel, hump, jag, shoulder, move. 4. stand for, lump it, live with, bear with, put up with, hang in, hang in there, hang tough, hang on, stick it out, ride out, take it, take it on the chin, be big, be big about, grin and bear it. See ENDURE.

TAKE BLAME v. take the rap, take the fall.

TAKE COVER v. hide out, hole up, play dead, lie doggo, lie low, tunnel, cool off, duck out of sight, do a crouch, flatten out, hit the shade, hit the mattresses. See HIDE.

TAKEOUT ORDER n. to go, on wheels, let it walk.

TALE n. yarn, clothesline, long and the short of it, megillah, cliff-hanger, potboiler, chestnut, heavy lard, touches, book. See STORY.

TALEBEARER n. rat, fink, rat fink, narc, finger, snitch, squealer, stoolie, stool pigeon, canary, songbird, weasel, blabbermouth, tattletale, whistle-blower, fat mouth, preacher, deep throat. See INFORMER. See also GOSSIPER.

TALEBEARING n. scuttlebutt, talk, grapevine, clothesline, back-fence talk, back-fence gossip, latrine rumor, wire, hot wire, whispering campaign, dirty linen, dirty wash. See GOSSIP.

TALENT n. the goods, the stuff, the right stuff, star power, what it takes, the formula, know-how, up one's alley, savvy, with it, green thumb, smarts, something on the ball, plenty on the ball, a bump for, have a way with, have a knack for, have a head for, bag, thing, bit, chops, dash, splash, splurge, throwin' stuff (baseball), meal ticket. See also SKILL.

TALENTED adj. A, 1–10 (degree, he's a 9), sharp, sharp as a tack, smart as a whip, brainy, brains, savvy, wised up, hep, hepster, hipster, hip to the jive, hipped, cool, sharp, tuned in, into, go-go, with it, all woke up, got it, got it up here (head), a lot of nifty, class act, slick, smooth, crack, crackerjack, cute, no slouch, no dumbbell, no dummy, nobody's fool, not born yesterday, quick on the trigger, quick on the uptake, heads up, something on the ball, on the ball, on the beam, up to speed, phenom, pro, there, whiz, whiz kid, whiz bang, wizard, gasser, boss player, shine at, shine in, enough ducks in a row, hot, hotshot, know one's stuff, know the ropes, know all the ins and outs, know the score, know all the answers, know what's what, know one's onions, know it all, know one's business, know one's p's and q's, have know-how, have the goods, have the stuff, have the right stuff, have what it takes, have a bump for, have it on the ball, have plenty on the ball.

TALENT POOL n. stable.

TALENT SCOUT n. ivory dome.

TALISMAN n. gig, security blanket, gigi, gee-gee.

TALK n. rap, rap session, buzz session, hash session, rapping rash, yak, yakkety yak, yack-yack, yatata-yatata, yawp, blah-blah, chinfest, chitchat, gab, gas, guff, lip, hot air, small talk, straight talk, pillow talk (confidential), talkee-talkee, talkfest, gabfest, bullfest, bull, bull session, bullshit, B.S., bilge, jazz, jive, garbage, gam, gobbledygook, podspeak (meaningless automatic response), apple butter, fluff, malarkey, mush, chin music, chinjaw, flapjaw, flap (urgent), riff, some pig, clambake, eyeball-to-eyeball encounter, confab, huddle, powwow, earful, bibful, spiel, rag-chewing, gum-beating, visit. See also SPEECH.

TALK v. 1. gab, rap, yackety-yak, yap, spout, spout off, spiel, modulate, modjitate, splib, splib de wib, slide one's jib, blab, noise, noise off, drool, flip one's lip (idle), run one's mouth, fat-mouth, talk one's ear off, cut up jackies, sling the lingo, blow, beat one's gums, yammer, bad-talk, sweet-talk, fast-talk, talk turkey. 2. contact, interact, interface, network, reach out, relate, touch, touch base, keep in touch, have truck with, grok, groupthink, go into a huddle, huddle, have a meet, confab. 3. pitch, spiel, stump. See SPEAK. 4. fess, fess up, rat, rat on, fink, fink on, croon, sing, sing like a canary, snitch, squeal, stool, spill, leak, blow the whistle, drop a dime on one, put it on the street. See CONFESS; INFORM.

TALKATIVE adj. talker, great talker, fast talker, yacker, yacky, yackety-yak, gabby, gabber, gift of gab, shoots the gab, gasbag, gasser, CBS, blowhard, windy, long-winded, windbag, bag of wind, windjammer, bullshitter, barber, flip, loudmouth, big-mouthed, bucket mouth, blabbermouth, chatty Cathy, gum-beater, ear-bender, rattle on, spieler, all jaw, flap jaw, ratchet jaw, ratchet mouth, hot-air artist, thick slung, slick tongue, slick, slicker, smooth, smoothie, old smoothie, smooth apple, smooth operator, smooth article, ear duster, drooler, beefer, gossipy, waxer, have verbal diarrhea, diarrhea of the mouth.

TALK BACK v. give one the lip, lip, sass.

TALKER n. gabby, windbag, jawsmith, soapboxer, soapbox orator, spieler, spouter.

TALKING, STOP v. shut up, shut one's trap, shut one's head, shut one's face, shut one's mouth, hush one's mouth, put up or shut up, pipe down, bite one's tongue, hold one's tongue, cut it out, clam up, close up, hang up, dummy up, fold up, dry up, choke, choke in, choke up, drag in one's rope, pull in one's ears, rest one's jaw, sign off, ring off, lay off, roll up one's flaps, stow it, save it, chuck it, can it, stifle, stifle it, step on it, put a lid on it, button one's lip, zip, zip one's lip, bag one's lip, bag one's head, be cool, cool one's chops, drink one's beer.

TALK SHOW HOST n. talk jockey, T.J.

TALL adj. tall drink of water, long drink of water, flanker (West Point), highpockets, bean pole, beanstalk, stick, longlegs, longshanks, Long John.

TALL AND SLIM adj. long drink of water, Long John, skeleton, stringbean, bean pole, beanstalk, broomstick, clothes pole, hat rack, stilt, stick, twiggy. See THIN.

TALLY n. score, tab.

TAME v. break, break in, bust, gentle.

TAMPA, FLORIDA Big T, Cigar City.

TAMPER v. doctor, doctor up, phony up, fiddle around with, fiddle with, plant, spike, water, water down, baptize, irrigate, cook, cut, needle.

TAMPERED adj. doctored, cooked.

TANG n. guts, kick, zip.

TANK n. alligator, duck (amphibious); bus (WW I), doodle bug, hell buggy, iron horse.

TANKER n. crock, tub, rust bucket, tramp, buddy store (Vietnam). See also SHIP.

TANTRUM n. cat fit, duck fit, conniption, conniption fit, shit hemorrhage, dander up, Irish, Irish up, in a huff, in a pet, in high dudgeon, on a tear, have a devil in one, possessed by the devil. See TEMPER.

TAPE, DUCT n. racer's tape, 200 MPH tape, two hundred miles per hour tape, gray tape, silver tape.

TAPE PLAYER n. deck, ghetto blaster, hi fi, stereo, third world attaché case.

TAPIOCA PUDDING n. cat's eye, fish eyes, fish eggs.

TARDY adj. hung up, held up, in a bind, jammed, jammed up, strapped for time, snooze you lose.

TARGET n. ground zero, sitting duck (easy), Maggie's drawers (missed, Mil.).

TARGET v. get one in the cross hairs, zero in on.

TARPAULIN n. tarp.

TARRY v. get no place fast, put on hold, hold the phone, stall, hang around, hang in, hang about, goof around, stick around, mooch around, monkey around, fuck the dog, cool one's heels, sit on one's ass, jelly, tool, tail, warm a chair. See LINGER.

TART adj. snippy, snappy, short.

TASK n. gig, grind, daily grind, grindstone, scutwork, donkeywork, hemo jo (hard labor). See WORK.

TASK, DIFFICULT n. grind, daily grind, rat race, elbow grease, shitwork, donkeywork, gruntwork (army), scud, scut, workout, ballbreaker, ball wracker, ballbuster, bone breaker, backbreaker, ass breaker, conk buster, bitch, bitch kitty, son of a bitch, fun and games.

TASK, EASY n. breeze, lead-pipe cinch, piece of cake, pie, meat, white meat, wrap up, chicken, clay pigeon, angel teat, around the bend (almost completed), alyo (routine).

TASKMASTER n.   boss, big brother, head, head man, head honcho, bosshead, super, skipper, old man, papa, Big Daddy, Big Brother, top dog, top hand, topkick, mother, the man, boss man, boss lady, bull, bull of the woods, ballbreaker, straw boss, slave driver, pusher, Elmer. See also EXECUTIVE.

TASTE n.   1. bag, cup of tea, druthers, flash, groove, thing, turned on to, type, weakness. See INCLINATION. 2. chaw, chomp, gob.

TASTE, BAD adj.   tacky, gross, bad form, off base, off-color, borax, taboo, blue, skank.

TASTEFUL adj.   spiffy, classy, snazzy, posh, plush, plushy, ritzy, uptown, swank, swanky, snarky, swellegant, splendiferous, splendacious, nobby.

TASTELESS adj.   1. cheap, loud, skank, tacky, raunchy, dirty, low-down and dirty, off-color, rough. See VULGAR. 2. blah, draddy, plain vanilla, nowhere, flat, pablum, zero, big zero. See INSIPID.

TASTY adj.   delish, divine, divoon, heavenly, scrumptious, sweetened, sugarcoated, yummy, yummy in the tummy.

TATTERED adj.   ratty-tatty, beat up, tacky, dog-eared, frowzy.

TATTLE v.   leak, blab, blabber, talk, crack on, peach, spill, spill it, spill the beans, give away, give the show away, have a big bazoo, have a big mouth, do one dirt, snitch. See INFORM. See also GOSSIP.

TATTLETALE n.   1. sleaze monger, yenta, polly, satch, gasser, load of wind, windbag, busybody, tabby. See GOSSIP. 2. snitch, snitcher, squealer, blab, blabber, blabberer, blabbermouth, tattler, telltale, whistle-blower, whistler, fat mouth, peacher, squealer. See INFORMER.

TAUNT n.   dump, put down, rank out, dig, dirty dig, dozens, dirty dozens, crack, slap, slam, swipe, jab, comeback, parting shot, brickbat, backhanded compliment, left-handed compliment.

TAVERN n.   beer joint, tap room, grocery, the nineteenth hole, gutbucket, bucket shop, suds shop, slop, slopshop (beer), office, guzzlery, guzzery, guzzle shop, dram shop, grog shop, grog mill, gin mill, fillmill, hideaway, room, rum room, night spot, nitery, dive, joint, after-hours joint, juke joint, juice joint, hop joint, barrel house, gashouse, ale house, beer house, mug house, washer, cheap John, creep dive, deadfall, honky tonk, speakeasy, blind pig, blind tiger, scatter, gargle factory, water hole, chain locker (dockside). See also BAR.

TAWDRY adj.   tinhorn, showy, glitzy, flossy, flashy, splurgy, loud, junky, jeasley, jazzy, gussied up, lit up like a Christmas tree, sporty. See GAUDY.

TAX n.   nick, bite, sin tax (tobacco and liquor), Irish dividend.

TAX BENEFIT n.   shelter, write-off.

TAXICAB n.   cab, checker, gypsy (without license), hack, taxi, yellow, dimbox, short.

TAXICAB DRIVER n.   cabby, hack driver, hackie, hacker, jockey, skip, boulevard westerner, boulevard cowboy.

TEA n.   Boston coffee, belly wash, dishwater, boiled leaves (not common).

TEACH v.   break in, let in on the know, put through the grind, put through the mill, show one the ropes, pull one's coat, drum, drum into. See INSTRUCT.

TEACHER n.   prof, teach, baby-sitter, grind, guru, slave driver, snap. See also SCHOLAR.

TEACHING n.   chalk talk, skull session.

TEAM n.   varsity, junior varsity, frosh, pro, first string, second string, third string. See also COUPLE.

TEAMMATE n.   buddy, buddy-buddy, playmate, sidekick, sidekicker, pard, pardner.

TEAMSTER n.   skinner, trucker, hair pounder.

TEARFUL adj.   blubbery, cry one's eyes out, cry, good cry, weepy.

TEAR GAS n.   bug juice, eyewash.

TEARS n.   waterworks, weeps.

TEASE n.   nag, kibitzer, clown, nudge, nudzh, noodge, nudge, nudzh, nudnik; cock teaser, C.T., prick teaser, P.T., teaser (all Obsc.).

TEASE v.   ride, razz, roast, jive, snap, guy, needle, give one the needle, pick on, bug, hack, worry, wig, dog, rag, rag on, rib, spoof, dump on, put one on, sound, rank out, slap at, slam, play dozens, hurl a brickbat, pooh-pooh, shiv, chiv, chivey, chivvy, noodge, nudge, nudzh, kibitz, kibitz around, horse around, funnin', send up, sheik, be on the back of, be at, give a bad time to, swipe at, dig at, josh, poke fun at, clown, clown around, fool, fool around, jack around, jack someone around, kid, kid around, play games, pull one's leg, jolly, fake one out, give a bad time to, give one a hard time, give one the business, get under one's skin, fuzzbuzz, drive one bananas, drive one up a tree, rattle one's cage, fart around, futz around, push one's button, push all the buttons, push the right button, mess with, bone, all right already (stop). See also JOKE.

TEATS n.   boobs, boobies, kajoobies, bubs, tits, titties, knockers, bazooms, cans, eyes, globes, headlights, knobs, maracas, cantaloupes, melons, pair, balloons. See BREASTS.

TECHNICAL adj. techie, hi tech (style).

TECHNICAL INSTITUTE n. tech.

TECHNICALITY, LEGAL teck.

TECHNOLOGY n. tech, hi tech.

TEDIOUS adj. draggy, dragsville, drippy, dull as dish water, ho hum, bor-ring, noplaceville, deadsville, snooze, pablum. See BORING.

TEENAGER n. teen, teeny, teenybop, teenybopper, creepybopper, weenie teenie, teeniebop, weenie bopper, Valley girl, jive (associated with jive music, movie, etc.), bobby soxer, petiteen, sub deb, sweet sixteen, twixt teen, jailbait, San Quentin quail, juve, juvenile delinquent, JD, punk, punk kid, punker, punk rocker, bubblegum, bubblegummer, bubblegum rocker, man, boyo, yoot, cokey, duck, gunsel, monkey, pecker, pisser, young fry, youngblood, salad days; twink, twinkle, twinky (homosexual).

TEETH n. china, chops, choppers, fangs, snappers, buck, barn doors (prominent), chewers, crockery, dominoes, gummers, ivories, porcelain.

TEETOTALER n. A.A., dry, on the wagon, on the water wagon, on the dry, fence-sitter, wet blanket, Christer.

TEGUCIGALPA, HONDURAS Goose City.

TELEGRAM n. wire.

TELEGRAPH v. telex, cable, wire, send a wire.

TELEGRAPHER n. sparks, op, brass pounder, lightning slinger, dit-da artist, fist (touch), glass arm (cramped).

TELEGRAPH KEY n. bug (semiautomatic).

TELEGRAPH OPERATOR n. sparks, op, brass pounder, dit-da artist, lightning slinger, fist (touch), glass arm (cramped).

TELEPHONE n. phone, horn, Ma Bell, Ameche, pipe, double-L, voice line, hot line (emergency).

TELEPHONE v. phone, buzz, ring, call, get one on the line, get one on the horn, it's your nickel (you talk), ring off the hook, jingle, tinkle, put in a call, make a call, call up, ring up, give a ring, give a buzz, give one a jingle, give one a honk, touch base with, reach out and touch someone, blast, contact, pick up (answer), get back to; ring off (hang up).

TELEPHONE BOOK n. phone book, Yellow Pages, fluff log, little black book.

TELEPHONE CALL n. buzz, call, phone call, ring.

TELEPHONE LINE n. clothesline.

TELEPHONE SERVICE LINE n. WATS line.

TELESCOPE n. sniperscope, snooperscope.

TELETYPING n. mux.

TELEVISION n. TV, tube, boob tube, vid, video, telly, box, idiot box, goggle box, big eye, eye, one-eyed monster, baby-sitter, flickering blue parent, kidvid (children's).

TELEVISION PROGRAM n. spec, spex, special, infotainment (news), spectacular, miniseries, soap, soaper, sudser, talk show, sitcom, pilot, docudrama, dramedy, kidvid, music video, MTV, skein (series), freevee, livingroom gig, late show, late late show, reruns, telethon.

TELEVISION RECEPTION n. blooping, ghost, snow, snowstorm.

TELEVISION TERMS, TECH. garbage can (microwave relay transmitter), ghost, ike (iconoscope), bloom (glare from a white object), gobo (back screen), talking head, blizzard head (blonde actress).

TELEVISION, VIEW v. catch a show, eye the big eye, see what's on, tube it, tube it up, tube up.

TELEVISION WATCHER n. vidiot, infomaniac (news addict).

TELEVISION WRITER n. telewriter, teleplaywright, telescripter, scripter.

TELL v. 1. spout, spout off, jaw, splib de wib, spill, spill the beans, unload, blab, run one's mouth, crack, open one's face, wag the tongue. See TALK. 2. stab one in the back, rat, rat on, fink, fink on, croon, sing, chirp, talk, snitch, squeal, squeal on, squawk, stool, spill, belch, blow, blow the whistle, tip off, drop a dime on one. See INFORM. 3. fess, fess up, come clean, come through, come out, come out of the closet, put it on the street, let it all hang out, let one's hair down, open up, own up, cough up, get it off one's chest, get it out of one's system, give away, give the show away, blab, blabber, blab off. See CONFESS.

TEMPER n. 1. miff, pet, stew, tiff, snit, cat fit, conniption, conniption fit, shit hemorrhage, dander, dander up, Irish, Irish up, short fuse, slow burn, in a huff, in a pet, in a sniff, in a snit, in a tizzy, in a stew, in a pucker, in a wax, in high dudgeon, duck fit, tear, on a tear, have a devil in one, possessed by the devil, foaming at the mouth. 2. where one's at, bit, in the groove, one's bag, scene, soul.

TEMPER v. 1. soft-pedal, cool, cool out, take the edge off, take the bite out, take the sting out. See SOFTEN. 2. tweek, give it a tweek (small), fine tune, take it in a little, midcourse correction, monkey around with, bottom out, switch, switch over, about face, flip-flop, turn over a new leaf, turn the corner, turn the tables, turn one around, revamp, transmogrify.

TEMPERAMENTAL adj. bitchy, cussed, mean, ornery, tetchy, thin-skinned, scrappy. See also EMOTIONAL, IRRITABLE, CAPRICIOUS.

TEMPLE n. Amen Corner, dirge factory, god box.

TEMPO n. beat, bounce, downbeat, brown off (break).

TEMPORARY adj. temp, here today gone tomorrow, band-aid, fly-by-night, hit or miss, Mickey Mouse, rinkydink, slapdash, throwaway, haywire.

TEMPORIZE v. fudge, play for time, vamp, hedge one's bet, pussyfoot, trade off, make a deal, meet halfway, go fifty-fifty, can't fight 'm join 'em, strike a happy medium, play ball with. See also HEDGE.

TEMPT v. 1. bait, mousetrap, give one the come on, give one a come-hither look, vamp, hook, bat one's eyes at, bat the eyes at. See ATTRACT. See also LURE. 2. schmeer, schmeikle, butter, butter up, honey, soap, oil, kid along, play up to, get around, turn one's head around, eat one's mind, crack one or something, con, duke in, promote, swindle in, sell, sell one on, hard sell, soft sell, fast-talk, snow, snow under, jolly, hand one a line. See also PERSUADE.

TEMPTED adj. on the hook, sucked in, hooked, roped in.

TEMPTER n. cruiser, heavy hitter, operator, wolf, vamp, man trap, velvet trap, swinger, sheik, sport, lady-killer. See SEDUCER.

TEMPTING adj. delish, yummy, yummy in the tummy, divine, heavenly, scrumptious.

TEMPTRESS n. hooker, flirt, man-eater, operator, party girl, player, swinger, vamp.

TEN n. both hands, two fives; Dixie, sawbuck (money).

TENACIOUS adj. mulish, stubborn as a mule, the game ain't over til the last man is out, game, spunky, dead set on, bent on, hell bent on, mean business, bound, bound and determined, set, sot, stand by one's guns, stick to one's guns, going the whole hog, going all the way, going for broke, stick like glue, stick it out, dig in one's heels. See DETERMINED. See also STUBBORN.

TENACITY n. 1. stick-to-itiveness. 2. balls, guts, gutsiness, guttiness, heart, nerve, stomach, what it takes, grit, true grit, spunk, backbone, moxie, starch, clock, corazon, chutzpah, intestinal fortitude, Dutch courage (intoxicated).

TEND v. sit, baby-sit, watch over, watch out for, keep an eye on, keep tabs on, keep on a leash, ride herd on, poke, punch, check out, do for. See HEED.

TENDENCY n. bag, groove, thing, thing for, turned on to, flash, weakness for, cup of tea, druthers, type, mind-set. See INCLINATION.

TENDER adj. lovey-dovey, mushy, all over one, tender loving care, TLC, all heart (Derog.), bleeding heart, heart in the right place, old softie, softhearted. See also AFFECTIONATE.

TENDER n. hit, feeler, proposish, proposition, pass, pitch, action.

TENDER v. make a pitch, make a pass, pop the question, proposition, speak one's piece, put a feeler out, hit, hit on. See also GIVE.

TEND TO BUSINESS v. mind the store, watch the store, who's minding the store?, who's watching the store?, take care of business, TCB.

TENNESSEE Monkey State, Volunteer State.

TENNESSEEAN n. mud head.

TENNIS, SCORING n. ad (advantage), ad in, ad out, deuce (tied at 40), break (win a game against opponent's serve), break point (opportunity to break opponent's serve), line ball, line call.

TENNIS TERMS kill, cave, cream, dust, powder, tube, eat their lunch, on their heads (defeat); dink, garbage (soft tricky returns); sweet spot, hack, hacker; passing shot, put away (scoring opportunities); overhead, overhead smash, ace (missed return of serve), daisy cutter, deef (default); tree, zoning (excellent play); tanking (lose on purpose), greasing it out, sleezeball, sleezing (easy or lucky); clip, hook, roast (cheat), furniture (racket frame), exho (exhibition), Wimby (Wimbledon).

TENOR n. Irish nightingale, whiskey tenor.

TENSE adj. wired, wired up, clutched, clutched up, uptight, jittery, jumpy, the jumps, jitters, shaky, bugged, choked, zonkers, pissin', shittin', shittin' bricks, white knuckle, strung out, hyper, twitty, fidgety, wreck, nervous wreck, bundle of nerves, nervy, all-overish, have a short fuse, butterflies, butterflies in one's stomach, butterflyish, coffee head, the jams, the jims, the jimmies, jimjams, heebie-jeebies, the screaming meemies, the meemies, fall apart, torn down, shot to pieces, basket case, hung up with, tightened up, up the wall, in a lather, in a stew, in a sweat, sweaty, sweat it, sweating bullets, in a swivet, in a tizzy, in a state, in a dither, on edge, on the ragged edge, have one's teeth on edge, on pins and needles, on tenterhooks, on the gog, jumpy as a cat on a hot tin roof, have kittens, cast a kitten, having the leaps, worried sick, worried stiff, biting one's nails, beside oneself, put to it, hard put to it, at the end of one's rope. See also AFRAID, APPREHENSIVE, NERVOUS.

TENSION adj. jitters, jumps, shakes, ants, ants in one's pants, a real nail-biter, cliff-hanging, pins and needles, worriment. See ANXIETY.

TENT n. dog tent, pup tent, top, big top, boudoir, pyramid (Army, WW II).

TERM n. 1. string, string attached, string to it, ball game, catch, catch 22, ——— city [fat city], fine print, small print, small fine print, fine print at the bottom, bottom line, joker, kicker. 2. one's watch (of office), hitch, stretch, time. See also PRISON SENTENCE.

TERMINAL adj. 1. that's all she wrote, and that was all she wrote, and that was it, curtains for, last hurrah, ass end, bitter end, period, the chips are down. See ULTIMATE. 2. done for, on one's last legs, on the way out, checking out, at the end of one's rope, MFC (measure for coffin), heading for the last roundup, one's number is up, one foot in the grave, one foot on a banana peel the other in the grave.

TERMINATE v. wrap, wrap up, nuke, scrub, scratch, fold, wind up, sew up, clinch, hang it up, shutter, close, wash out, close out, close down, shut down, pull the plug, put the lid on, cap, can it, cut off one's water, blow the whistle on, call it a day, kayo, get down to the short strokes. See FINISH.

TERMINATED adj. set, wired, fixed, wrapped up, wound up, buttoned up, washed up, all over but the shouting, fini, kaput, wiped out. See FINISHED.

TERMINATION n. wrap-up, windup, mop-up, blow-off, kiss-off, fag end, thirty, –30–, curtain, curtains, down to the short strokes, end of the line, when the balloon goes up, when the fat lady sings. See END.

TERMS n. what it is, the size of it, nitty-gritty, small fine print at the bottom. See CONDITION.

TERRA FIRMA n. dust, real estate, old sod.

TERRIBLE adj. sucks, grody, grody to the max, gross, dead ass, rat's ass, barfy, grunge, grungy, scuzzy, sleazy, sleazeball, shitty, something fierce, wicked, heavy, bummer, downer, hairy, bad news, the pits. See BAD.

TERRIFIED adj. run scared, scared stiff, scared out of one's head, scared out of one's mind, scared witless, scared shitless, shitting peas, petrified, D and D (deaf and dumb, afraid to testify), jumped out of one's skin, bowled over. See FRIGHTENED.

TERRIFY v. spook, chill, chill off, put the chill on, scare stiff, scare the pants off one, scare the shit out of, scare silly, make one jump out of his skin, lean against, put the arm on, put the heat on. See FRIGHTEN.

TERRIFYING adj. hairy, hair-raising, furry, scary, spooky. See FRIGHTENING.

TERRITORY n. turf, hood, neck of the woods, stomping ground, old stomping grounds, stamping grounds, the block, the street, neck of the woods. See NEIGHBOR-HOOD. See also DISTRICTS.

TERSE adj. 1. in a nutshell, short and sweet, make a long story short, boiled down, cut to the bone. 2. tight-lipped.

TEST n. 1. exam, final, oral, orals, blue book, comp (comprehensive), cream (successful); drop quiz, shotgun quiz, pop test, pop quiz (unnanounced); prelim. 2. try, go, fling, shot, crack, whack, stab, lick, tryout, try on, beta test, trial balloon, feeler, workout, dry run, shakedown, shakedown cruise, whiz, showcase, have a fling at, run that by.

TEST v. 1. cut and try, try on, try it on for size, give a tryout, give a workout, give it a go, shake down, prove out, mess around, fool around with, play around with, run it up the flagpole and see if anyone salutes, see how the cookie crumbles, see how it flies, see how the ball bounces, run this (idea) by one. 2. hang (how does that hang?), hold a candle to, stack up against, match up.

TEST ANSWERS n. bicycle, pony, crib, cheat sheet, gouge, hobby, horse, jack, jockey (student who cribs).

TESTEE n. guinea pig.

TESTES n. balls, nuts, rocks, cajones, boo-boos, ears, diamonds, family jewels, bag, ballocks, basket. See also GENITALIA, MALE.

TESTICLES n. 1. balls, nuts, rocks, stones, cajones, eggs, marbles, boo-boos, ears, diamonds, family jewels, bag, ballocks, basket. See also GENITALIA, MALE. 2. Rocky Mountain oysters, mountain oysters (lamb, pork, beef testicles used as food), prairie oysters, bull fries, swinging steak, bull balls, bull nuts (beef).

TESTIFY v. 1. go to bat against, rat on, squeal on, sing. 2. swear up and down, swear on a stack of bibles, swear till one is blue in the face, cross one's heart and hope to die, say so.

TESTIMONIAL n. plug, say so.

TESTY adj. bitchy, mean, ornery, tetchy, out of sorts, cantankerous, grouchy, grumpy, crabby, cranky, uptight, thin-skinned, pushing out one's lips, ready to fly off the handle, edgy, got up on the wrong side of the bed. See IRRITABLE.

TEXAN n. Tex, chub, redneck, shit kicker, country boy, longhorn.

TEXAS Lone Star State.

TEXT n. book, words.

THANKS n. gramercy, mercy buckup, thank you much, thanks a million, messy bucket, merky bucket.

THE art. a, uh.

THEATER n. 1. movie, the movies, movie theatre, drive-in, skin house, stroke house (pornographic). See MOTION PICTURE THEATER. 2. Broadway, off Broadway, main stem, main kick, house, four walls, legit, legiter, boards, deluxer, paper house, barn, strawhat, strawhat circuit, the Fabulous Invalid, opera house, garlic opera (old, cheap); the big time, two-a-day, the circuit (vaudeville); T and A, tits and ass, strip joint, burlesque, leg show, grind house, honky-tonk, mousetrap, jiggle, a circus (girlie shows); minstrel show, cork opera, Toby Show.

THEATERGOER n.   buff, fan, standee. See AUDI-ENCE.

THEATRICAL adj.   hammy, schmaltzy, tear-jerking, scenery chewing.

THEATRICAL AGENT n.   flesh peddler, ten percenter.

THEATRICAL BUSINESS n.   show biz, B.O., box office, take, angel, butter and egg man, paper, Annie Oakley, SRO, fairy godfather, ghost, pack in, pack them in, paper the house, paper house, split week, roadie (manager), four wall (lease).

THEATRICAL PROPERTY n.   prop, props.

THEFT n.   rip-off, snatch, snitch, caper, heist, grab, filch, pinch, lift, job, hustle, boost, stickup, holdup, holdup job, annexation, break-in, weed (from employers). See ROBBERY.

THEOLOGICAL SCHOOL n.   angel factory.

THEORY n.   shot, shot in the dark, stab, judgment call, op, say so, slant, two cents' worth.

THERAPIST n.   shrink, head shrinker, couch doctor, guy with the net, guy in the white coat, sexpert (sex), bug doctor (prison), guru, squirrel, avatar.

THERAPY, GROUP n.   blowout center, who you're screaming with.

THESPIAN n.   thesp, star, straight man, feeder, stooge, foil, legiter, ham, hambone, ham fatter, trouper, lead, bit player, moppet (child), mugger. See ACTOR.

THICK adj.   gooey, gloppy, globby, gooky, gozzle, goupy, gunky, goonky, gummy, clabbered, loppered.

THICKEN v.   goonk up, gum up, clabber, lopper.

THIEF n.   punk, holdup man, stickup man, mugger, jigger, push-up ghee, stickup ghee, throw-up ghee (armed); lush diver, lush roller (of drunkards); prowler, crook, scrounger, off artist, lifter, derrick, sniper, clip, gonif, ganef, gon, heel, high grader, jackroller, operator, pack rat, alley rat; second-story man, second-story worker, porch climber, cold-slough worker, hot-slough worker, crasher, flat worker, fly, midnight, midnighter, moonlighter, owl, shacker, spider (of house and apartment); iceman, crib man, loid man, cracksman, safecracker, screwman, pete man, peterman, pete blower, yegg, reader, gopher, one of a gopher mob, damper mob, heavy, jug heavy, one of a jug mob (of banks); light-fingered, sticky-fingered, sticky fingers, five finger, five fingers, footpad; cannon, booster, gun, grifter, heister, heist man, hist man, hijacker, chain man (watch), pennyweighter (jewel); loft man, one of a loft mob, loft worker, worm worker (specialist in fur and silk lofts).

THIN adj.   skinny, skin and bones, skeleton, peaked, peaky, slinky, stick, twiggy, shadow, bag of bones, stack of bones, bean pole, beanstalk, stilt, hat rack, broomstick, clothes pole, rattlebones, gangling, gangly, gangle-shanks, spindleshanks, spindlelegs, lathlegs, sticklegs, birdlegs, turkey legs.

THIN v.   water, water down, baptize, irrigate, cook, cut, spike, needle, lace, doctor, doctor up, phony up, shave.

THING n.   thingy, thingamajig, thingumajugfer, thing-um, thingummy, thingadad, thingumabob, thinguma-dad, thingumadoo, thingamadodger, thingamadudgeon, thingamananny, thingamaree, gismo, gadget, widget, black box, job, jobby, contraption, dealie bob, sucker, bugger; momma, mother, motherfucker, mofo, mother-jumper (Obsc.); whatchamacallit, whatzis, whoziz. See APPARATUS.

THINGS n.   junk, props.

THINK v.   feel, spark, spitball, sweat, flash on, figger, figure out, sort out, noodle, noodle it around, percolate, perk, head trip, use one's head, use one's noodle, track, hammer, hammer away at, um, craft, take stock in, hone in, knuckle down, skull practice, skull drag, cool something over, hash, rehash, hash over, stew, stew over, sweat over, chew over, chew the cud, cop, crack one's brains, rack one's brains, get one's head together, put on one's thinking cap, brainstorm, kick around, knock around, knock it around, bat it around, run it up the flagpole, run it by one again, pour it on, dream up, make up, think up, trump up, take it off the top of one's head, blow change (radical). See also RECALL.

THINKER n.   the brain, genius, egghead, beard, big think, double dome, ivory dome, highbrow, long-hair, pointy head, good head, skull, thumbsucker, professor, wig, trig wig (fast), Einstein, gasser, gray matter, whiz, wizard, avant-garde. See INTELLECTUAL. See also SCHOLAR.

THINNED adj.   watered, watered down, baptized, irrigated, cooked, cut, spiked, needled, laced, doctored, doctored up, phonied up, shaved.

THIRSTY adj.   cotton-mouthed, mouth full of cotton, dry as dust.

THIRTEEN n.   baker's dozen, devil's dozen, long dozen.

THIRTY-TWO n.   thirty-twomo, 32mo.

THORN n.   sticker.

THOROUGH adj. slam bang, all out, whole hog, go the limit, do up brown, open all stops, from A to Z, plenty, royal, hanging in, tough, heart and soul into, all the way, whole hog, to a-fare-thee-well, galley west, the works, not overlook a bet, move heaven and earth, leave no stone unturned, six ways to Sunday, you name it, from hell to breakfast, from soup to nuts.

THOROUGHBRED adj. graded.

THOROUGHFARE n. rip strip, dragway, pavement, the bricks, byway, aisle, bowling alley. See ROAD.

THOROUGHLY adv. all (all dolled up), from A to Z, top to bottom, whole hog, slam bang, smack, smack out, flat out, from soup to nuts. See COMPLETELY.

THOUGHT n. child, brainchild, brainstorm, brain wave, spark, spark plug, flash, bell-ringer, deep think, it hit me, big idea, how one figures it, op, two cents' worth. See IDEA.

THOUGHTFUL adj. cool, mellow, play it cool. See also SERIOUS.

THOUGHTLESS adj. 1. pay no mind, out to lunch, asleep at the switch, daydreaming, woolgathering, any old way, go off half-cocked, devil may care. See CARELESS. See also VACUOUS 2. flaky, mad, ad lib, winging it, off the wall, off the cuff, off the hip, off the top of one's head, shoot from the hip, spitball, play by ear, dash off, strike off, knock off, toss off, toss out. See IMPULSIVE.

THOUSAND n. G, grand, K, M, thou, yard, horse (dollars).

THRASH v. 1. bash, trash, drub, lather, larrup, leather, lambaste, cane, work over, whip, tan one's hide, take it out of one's hide, take it out of one's skin, clobber, kick ass, wipe out, beat up, beat the bejesus out of one, beat the shit out of one, whale the daylights out of one, whale, wallop, welt. See HIT. 2. bury, blank, plunk, skunk, schneider, murder, kill, cook, trim, trounce, fix one's wagon, shellack, bulldoze, roll over, torpedo, meatball, make one say uncle, beat all hollow, finish off, wrack up, blow out, pin one's ears back. See DEFEAT.

THREADBARE adj. beat up, ratty, tacky, frowzy, dog-eared, used up, in a bad way.

THREAT n. fix, fix one's wagon, else, or else, I'm gonna break your face, he's gonna have me popped, defi, defy.

THREATEN v. enforce, lean on, flex one's muscles, whip one around (intellectually), walk heavy, put the arm on, put the heat on, hang tough, spook, chill off, bulldoze. See INTIMIDATE.

THREATENED adj. feel the heat, heat's on, hot, spooked, frozen, goose bumpy, shit in one's pants, panicked, run scared, shake in one's boots, given a turn, given a jar, given a jolt. See also FRIGHTENED.

THREATENING adj. in the cards, in the wind, at hand, see it coming, it's looking to, the noose is hanging.

THREE n. trey, ace-deuce.

THREE DIMENSIONAL adj. 3D.

THRIFTY adj. 1. cheapie, el cheapo, dirt cheap, cheap as dirt, dog cheap, steal, a real steal, buy, a real buy, low cost, cost nothing, cost next to nothing, bought for a song, cut rate, low tariff. 2. tight, so tight one squeaks, penny-pinching, pinchy, close, close-fisted, chinchy, chintzy, scrimpy, skimpy, stingy, on the rims, run on the rims, bog pocket, Scotch, nickel-nurser, last of the big spenders.

THRILL n. upper, blast, wallop, belt, boot, blow one's mind, blown away, charge, large charge, bang, get a bang out of, kick, kicks, for kicks, turn on, circus, fireworks, flash. See EXCITEMENT.

THRILL v. 1. juice, send, grab, key up, fire up, steam up, stir up, turn one on, switch on, get hot under the collar, race one's motor, open one's nose. See EXCITE. 2. freak out, wig out, blow one away, turn on, knock out, knock dead, knock the socks off one, send, slay, score, wow, just what the doctor ordered, go over big. See DELIGHT.

THRILLED adj. high, hyper, turned on, freaked out, charged, hopped up, sent, gassed, flipped, backflips, flipping, blew one's mind, mind-blowing, in seventh heaven, on cloud nine, got one's grits, got one's jollies, set up, handsprings, lookin' good, pleased as Punch, sold on, tickled pink, tickled to death, wowed, a rush. See also EXCITED.

THRILLING adj. zero cool, frantic, wild, fab, boss, mad, like wow, mind-blowing, mind-bending, turn on, kicky, knockout, live one, large, large charge, nervous, swinging, lush, sizzler, scorcher, thriller, sensay, sensaysh. See EXCITING.

THRIVE v. get well, get fat, get there, go great guns, make hay, make well, make out, put it together, home free, hack it, do all right by oneself, live off the fat of the land. See SUCCEED.

THRIVING adj. have it made, have a mint, have the wherewithal, on top of the heap, living high on the hog, right up there, up in the bucks, in the chips, really rolling, money to burn, really cooking, lousy rich, well-fixed, well set up, sitting pretty, fat dumb and happy, arrived, booming, going strong, going great guns, mining the gold, home free, laughing all the way to the bank, oofy, uptown. See SUCCESSFUL.

THROAT n. pipes, gargle, google, goozle, guzzle.

THROB n. pitapation.

THROB v. go pit-a-pat, tick.

THRONG n. mob, push, turnout, blowout, crush, jam, jam up, everybody and his brother, everybody and his uncle, loaded to the rafters, wall-to-wall people, sellout.

THROTTLE n. gun.

THROUGH adj. wrapped up, fini, wound up, buttoned up, done to a T, in the bag, nailed down, on ice, all over but the shouting, signed sealed and delivered. See FINISHED.

THROW v. chuck, chunk, fire, heave, lob, peg, pitch, sling, toss.

THROW AWAY v. chuck, deep six, eighty-six, junk, nox out, give the old heave-ho, throw on the junk heap. See DISCARD.

THRUST n. boost, speedup, blitz, jump, push.

THRUST v. chuck, chunk, fire, heave, lob, peg, pitch, sling, toss, hump, boost, buck, charge, bear down on it, push it, give it the gun, pour it on, zing, go to town on, railroad through.

THUG n. mug, mugger, hood, hoodlum, gorilla, ape, bodyguard, pug, sleazeball, heavy, clipper, big boy, bad actor, goon, greaser, bullyboy, bucko, hellcat, hellraiser, hellion, holy terror, roughneck, tough cookie, bruiser, ugly customer, plug-ugly, hooligan, strong-arm man, muscle man, hit man, hatchet man, hatchet boy, sidewinder.

THUNDERBIRD n. T-Bird.

THUNDEROUS adj. leather-lunged. See also LOUD.

THWART v. queer, crimp, cramp, put a crimp in, cramp one's style, stymie, skin, snooker, crab, hang up, hold up, foul up, fuck up, louse up, snafu, bollix, gum up the works, fake out, flummox, stump, cross, cross up, double-cross, give one the business, throw a monkey wrench into the works, upset one's apple cart, spike one's guns, steal one's thunder, trash, take one down, take care of, take the wind out of one's sails, knock the bottom out of, knock the chocks from under one, knock the props from under one, down one, ditch, give the slip, skip out on, duck, dodge, get around, give the run around, run circles around, run rings around. See also HINDER.

THWARTED adj. hung up on, stymied, through the mill, up the wall, faked out, put away, skinned, queered, crabbed, fouled up, fucked up, bollixed up, crimped, cramped, stonewalled, flummoxed. See also DEFEATED.

TICKET n. admish, board, stub, twofer (half price), pasteboard, chit, deadwood (unsold); pass, freebee, paper, Annie Oakley, Chinee ducat, comp (free); throwaway (traffic), dookie (meal ticket); duck (social event); bid, invite (invitation).

TICKET BROKER n. scalper.

TICKET SELLER n. pitchman.

TICKET TAKER n. chopper, ducat snatcher.

TIDINGS n. info, poop, skinny, lowdown, dirt, dope, dope sheet, inside dope, the know, whole story, the latest, what's happenin', what's going down, earful, hot wire; are you ready for this? See NEWS.

TIDY adj. apple pie, apple-pie order, neat as a button, neat as a pin, slick, to rights, all policed up, in good shape, shipshape.

TIDY v. put in shape, put in good shape, whip into shape, put to rights, put in apple-pie order, clear the decks, fix up, police, police up, spruce, spruce up, get one's act together, get one's head together, get one's shit together, pull things together, shape up, straighten up and fly right, frame. See also CLEAN.

TIE n. 1. dead heat, push, photo finish, standoff, Mexican standoff. 2. string, four-in-hand. 3. tie-up, tie-in, tie-in tie-up, hookup, network, outfit, gang. See ASSOCIATION.

TIE v. 1. hog-tie, put a half nelson on, put a lock on, lock up. 2. push (bet), hog-tie.

TIE PIN n. prop.

TIGER n. cat, big cat, stripes.

TIGHT adj. quick.

TIGHT-LIPPED adj. clammed up, dried up, dummied up, garbo. See SILENT.

TILTED adj. raked (auto), slaunchways, slaunchwise.

TIMBER n. load of sticks.

TIMBERLAND n. big sticks.

TIME n. ticks, half a mo, half a shake, jiffy, zero hour, bells (nautical), age, ages; on the button, right on the button, on the nose (on time); at this moment in time, ol' man Mose, coon's age, a dog's age, many a moon, a month of Sundays, once in a blue moon, hitch, stretch, since Hector was a pup, up at the crack of one's back, on the dot; fucking off, goofing off, fucking the dog (kill time); bad time, hard time, movin' through (time passage), count one's thumbs, twiddle one's thumbs (waiting); time to bail, time to book (time to go); on the nose, on the button, right on the button (on time).

TIME v. clock.

TIMELY adj. now, with it, up to the minute, hard-hitting, high-powered.

TIMELY adv. at the eleventh hour, in the nick of time.

TIME PERIOD n. time frame, window, float (Fin.).

TIMEPIECE n. ticker, turnip, kettle turnip (pocket), chroniker, Albert (with chain), Big Ben, totter.

TIMID adj. have cold feet, 'fraidy cat, scaredy cat, run scared, goose bumpy, rabbity, mousy, weenie, jellyfish, chicken, chicken-hearted, lily-livered, milksop, Casper Milquetoast, weak-kneed, weak sister, sissy, baby, big baby, pucker-assed, candy ass. See FRIGHTENED. See also COWARDLY, SHY.

TINFOIL n. Christmas, window (WW II, dropped to confuse radar).

TINKER v. mess around, monkey around, fiddle with, potchky. See DABBLE.

TINY adj. mini, teeny, teeny-weeny, teensy, teensy-weensy, bitty, bitsy, itsy-bitsy, wee, peewee, tomtit, yea big, pint-sized, knee high to a grasshopper. See SMALL.

TIP n. 1. toke, chip, cue, somethin', subway, bus ride (five or ten cents), lagniappe, one way (five cents), sweetener. See GRATUITY. 2. tip off, steer, bum steer, kibitz, flea in the ear, one's two cents' worth, word to the wise, wise up; feedbag information, feedbox information (horse racing); on the Bill Daley.

TIPPLE v. swig, hit the bottle, bend one's elbow, tip one's elbow, crook one's elbow, wet one's whistle, dip the beak, hang a few on, irrigate. See DRINK.

TIPPLER n. barfly, juicer, guzzler, tosspot, soak, elbow-bender, elbow crooker, pretzel bender, bottle baby, bottle sucker. See DRINKER.

TIPSTER n. tout.

TIPSY adj. tight, crocked, loopy, high, high as a kite, tied one on, loaded, feeling no pain, on a toot, lubricated, mellow, wet, lit, lit up like a Christmas tree, boozy, buzzy, piffled, addled, tiddly, happy, beery, flying with one wing low, groggy, had one or two, irrigated, seeing pink elephants, whoozy, had one too many. See DRUNK.

TIRE n. shoe, skins, slicks, flat, flat hoop, sore foot (punctured), pumpkin (flat).

TIRE v. fag, fold, tucker, poop, poop out, burn out, fag out, tucker out, knock out, peter out, fizzle out, conk out, peg out, cave in, go soft, go to pieces, come apart at the seams, die on the vine, be on one's last legs.

TIRED adj. 1. dopey, out of it, sleepyhead, snoozy, stretchy, on the nod, eye trouble, in sleepville, blah, blahs, drippy, wimpy, draggy. 2. bushed, had it, hung, pooped, too pooped to pop, out of gas, out of juice, knocked out, wiped out, wrung out, burned out, crispy, played out, crapped out, down and out, flaked out, wore out, worn out, gave out, petered out, pegged out, dragged out, crumped out, conked out, fagged, fagged out, tuckered out, washed out, whacked out, zonked, dragged, dragging one's ass, draggin' ass, have one's ass in a sling, a wreck, worn to a frazzle, foozled, nearly dead, dead, dead tired, dead beat, beat, beat to the ground, beat down to the ankles, beat to the socks, beatsville,

pissed up, used up, done up, done in, all in, in a bad way, on one's last legs, whipped, whupped, licked, guffed, dished, punchy, low, crumped, shot, shot one's load, shot down, at the end of one's rope, at row's end, clanked, clanked out, hacked, bone-tired, bone-weary, dog-tired, dog-weary, ratty, cooked. 3. fed up, up to here, had it up to here, done it all, been around twice. See also JADED.

TIRELESS adj. grind, plugger, springbutt, eager beaver, work one's tail off, ball of fire, fireball, hyper, jumping, on the go, perky. See also SPIRITED.

TIRES n. duals (includes wheels), rags, runners, skates, whitewalls, slicks, radials, shoes, skins.

TIRESOME adj. 1. uncool, heavy, hefty, that bugs me, gives one a pain, pain in the neck, pain in the ass, bitch, son of a bitch, son of a gun, a bit much, too much. 2. borring, ho hum, drag, draggy, yawn, big yawn, yawner, nowhere, bore one stiff, tired, wonky, gummy. See BORING.

TITILLATE v. 1. turn on, switch on, grab, hook. 2. crack one up, break one up, fracture one, get one's kicks, get one's jollies, tickle pink. See EXCITE. See also AMUSE, ENTERTAIN.

TITILLATED adj. caught, hooked, into, sold, turned on, tickled pink.

TITLE n. handle, handle to one's name, tag, brand, flag (assumed), front name, label, tab, moniker, what's his name, what's his face.

TOADY n. A.K., ass-kisser, bootlick, ass-licker, tuchis licker, brownie, brownnoser, fart sniffer (Obsc.), yesman, nod guy, schmeikler, groupie, gofer, waterboy. See SYCOPHANT.

TOADY v. soft soap, jolly, oil, lay it on, lay it on thick, lay it on with a trowel, play up to, butter up, sweeten up; brownnose, suck around, suck ass, kiss ass, bootlick, fall all over, kowtow. See FLATTER.

TOAST n. down, shingle.

TOASTED adj. down.

TOASTMASTER n. the chair, MC, emcee.

TOASTS cheers, cheerio, prosit!, here's looking at you, here's to ya, l'chayim, à votre santé, salud, bottoms up, happy days, mud in your eye, down the hatch, chugalug, absent friends.

TOBACCO n. plug, bull, hay, alfalfa, Bull Durham, dust, freckles, gage, weed, filthy weed, commo (prison); wad, cheekful, chaw (chewing); rock hound candy, pinch (snuff), niggerhead, coal pot (pipe), bug juice (residue).

TOBACCO CHEWER n. bell-ringer.

TODDLER n. kid, babe, bottle baby, babykins, bambino, tot, tad, in diapers, nipper, button, little darling. See BABY.

TOES n. piggy, ten.

TOGETHER adv. in sync, on the beat, with the beat, witha one witha two witha three, witha one anda two anda three. See also COMPATIBLE.

TOIL n. grind, scutwork, donkeywork, hemo jo (hard labor), shitwork, chickwork (household), elbow grease, gig, nine-to-five shit. See WORK.

TOIL v. sweat it, plug away, peg away, put one's nose to the grindstone, beat one's brains out, bust a gut, work one's head off. See WORK.

TOILET n. can, Cannes, john, johnny, johnny house, rest room, Men's, Ladies', ladies' room, women's room, girls' room, little girls' room, powder room, men's room, boys' room, little boys' room, reading room, library, head, facilities, amenities, comfort station, terlit, piss house, shithouse, shitter, crapper, WC, loo, sandbox, play in the sandbox (go to), biffie, biffy, bippy, bank, chamber of commerce, altar, altar room, holy of holies, throne, throne room, donagher, donniker, Andy Gump, bucket, privy, two-holer, fireless cooker, out back, Chick Sale, honeywagon, honeypot, pisspot, pot, potty, potty chair, cat box, thunder box, thunder mug, joe, jane, flusher, kazoo, gazoo, gazool, showers, where the dicks hang out, old soldiers' home.

TOILET PAPER BALLS n. dingleberries.

TOLEDO, OHIO Scale City.

TOLERANT adj. big, soft shell, easy with, easy on.

TOLERATE v. bear with, live with, go along with, string along with, put up with, hear of, stand for, sit still for, stomach something, grin and bear it, sit and take it, stay the course, stand for, stand the gaff, stand up, be big, be big about, not let it get one down. See also ENDURE.

TOLL BOOTH n. cash register, piggy bank.

TOMATO n. love apple, tommy.

TOMATO SOUP n. red noise.

TOMB n. cold storage, dustbin.

TOMFOOLERY n. monkeyshines, shenanigans, hijinks.

TONE n. football (whole musical note), lick (music).

TONE DEAF adj. tin ear.

TONGUE n. stinger.

TONGUE KISS n. tongue sushi, French kiss, soul kiss.

TONIC n. pick-me-up, pick-up, shot in the arm, go juice. See also DRINK.

TOO BAD adj. tough nuggies, tough shit, TS.

TOOL n. gismo, gadget, widget, job, contraption, dealie bob, sucker, bugger; mother, motherfucker, mofo

(Obsc.), whatchamacallit, whatsis, jigamaree, dojigger, Armstrong (requires strength). See APPARATUS.

TOOTHPICK n. lumber.

TOOTHSOME adj. delish, yummy, divine, heavenly, scrumptious, sweetened, sugarcoated, yummy in the tummy.

TOP v. 1. cap (add to bet), piggyback. 2. bury, skunk, schneider, trounce, swamp, shellack, bash, trash, drub, total, clobber, cream, beat all hollow, plow under, blow out, run rings around, run circles around, put away, shut out, rank out, wipe out, put one in the cookie jar, put one in the popcorn machine. See DEFEAT. 3. beat one's time, fox, outfox, goose, con, short con, end run, fake out, juke, cop a heel on, cop a sneak on, pull a quickie on, pull a fast one, finagle, work one's points. See also EXCEL.

TOPCOAT n. car coat, horse blanket, threads, benny, binny, Benjamin, flogger, fog.

TOPEKA, KANSAS Railroad City.

TOPER n. lush, souse, stew, wino, big drunk, brown bagger, boozer, boozehound, alky, juice head, dipso, rummy, shikker, tosspot, soak, sponge, elbow-bender, bottle baby. See DRINKER.

TOP FORM n. up, wrapped tight, ready, fine tuned.

TOP SECRET adj. hush-hush, classified, under one's hat, under wraps, eyes only, for your eyes only, closet, family jewels (govt, CIA), pull the ladder up behind one, something up one's sleeve, wildcat (plan). See SECRET.

TOPPING n. glop, gunk, ice.

TOPPLE n. header, nose dive, pratfall, belly buster, belly flop, belly whopper, pancake landing.

TOPPLE v. take a header, tip over, belly up, nose-dive, lose it, do a pratfall, fall down and go boom, land on one's ass, hit the dirt, come-a-cropper, go ass over teakettle.

TORMENT v. give a bad time to, drive one bananas, hassle, hound, give a hard time to, put the heat on, drive up the wall, put the squeeze on one, put one through the wringer, play cat and mouse, rub salt in the wound, bone, break one's balls. See ANNOY.

TORNADO n. twister.

TORONTO, ONTARIO n. TO.

TORPEDO n. fish, tin fish, torp, firecracker, pickle, pineapple (German), torp.

TOSS v. 1. heave, lob, peg, pitch, sling, chuck, chunk, fire. 2. chuck, deep six, eighty-six, junk, nox out, give the old heave-ho, throw on the junk heap. See DISCARD.

TOT n. kid, little kid, shaver, little shaver, squirt, little squirt, little guy, little bugger, little dickens, little darling, cub, sonny, sprout, bambino, nipper, tad, ankle biter. See CHILD. See also BABY.

TOTAL n.   jackpot, the works, whole enchilada, whole ball of wax, whole nine yards, whole shebang, whole works, flat out, everything including the kitchen sink, lock stock and barrel. See WHOLE.

TOTAL v.   tot, tot up, tote, tote up, reckon up, go (gambling).

TOTALIZATOR n.   tote, tote board, big board.

TOTALLY adv.   top to bottom, whole hog, full blast, stone (stone deaf), smack out, flat out, flat ass, from soup to nuts. See COMPLETELY.

TOUCH v.   1. frisk, feel up, put the feelers on one or something, grab ass, fool around, paw, playing footsie. See also CARESS. 2. reach, get in touch, touch base, keep in touch, interact, connect, grok, reach out, relate, get across. See COMMUNICATE. 3. get to, grab, stroke, feel out, have a funny feeling, have heart, have good vibes, have vibes, get vibes, know where one is coming from.

TOUCHED adj.   got to, grabbed, feel for, feel in one's guts, turned on by, turned on to.

TOUCHING adj.   stunner, stunning, mind-blowing, out of this world, feel in one's guts, grabbed by. See MOVING.

TOUCHY adj.   1. goosy, jumpy as a cat on a hot tin roof, yantsy, wired up, uptight, hung up, wreck, nervous wreck, bundle of nerves, thin-skinned, bitchy, cantankerous, mean, ornery, can't even look at one cross-eyed. See SENSITIVE. 2. unhealthy, widow maker, heavy, dicey, iffy, chancy, too hot to handle, hot potato, on thin ice, on slippery ground, touch and go. See DANGEROUS.

TOUGH adj.   1. mean, hairy, tough customer, roughneck, wicked, hard-nosed, hard shell, hard-boiled, hardball, ballsy, ballbuster, ballbreaker, eat nails, bad guy, bad actor, John Wayne, bogard, down, enforcer, hooligan, plug-ugly, stiff, cob, commando, Chicago, welcome to the NFL, gutsy, gutty, nervy, spunky, cool hand, beefy, hairy, hefty, husky, mean, strong as a horse, strong as a lion, strong as an ox, wicked. 2. uphill battle, heavy, bitch, tough nut to crack, toughie, hard row of stumps, the hard way, handful, ballbreaker, backbreaker, honey, no piece of cake, heavy sledding. See DIFFICULT.

TOUPEE n.   rug, toup, piece, sky piece, sky rug, fur, brush, divot, mucket, doily, dome doily, scalp doily, headpiece, muff, head falsie.

TOUR n.   1. hop, swing, jaunt, cruise, junket, trek, overnight, weekend, getaway, Cook's tour. See TRAVEL. 2. the road, the circuit; stump, whistle-stop, mashed-potato circuit, rubber-chicken circuit (Pol.). 3. hitch, stretch, time.

TOUR v.   1. jet around, go on Apex, hop, city hop, country hop, globe-trot, cruise, do the continent, do Europe (or wherever), junket, Cook's tour, swing, barnstorm. See TRAVEL. 2. go on the road, stump (Pol.).

TOURING adj.   globe-trotting, rubbernecking, cruising, doing the continent, on the road, on the circuit, on the hustings, on the go, barnstorming, stumping. See TRAVELING.

TOURIST n.   jet-setter, globe-trotter, rubberneck, rubbernecker, dude (bus), snowbird, snowflake, sunflower.

TOUSLED adj.   beat up, messed up, mussed up, messy, mussy, sloppy, grubby, scuzzed, scuzzed up.

TOUT v.   steer, boost, give a boost to, push, let in on, let in on the know, put next to, put on to, put on to something hot, put one in the picture, put hep, tip, tip off, give one a tip. See ADVISE.

TOW CAR n.   draggin' wagon, the motor club.

TOWER n.   high rise, cloud buster.

TOWN n.   burg, apple, Big Town, big time, boomer, boomtown, dump, tough town, wide open joint, tank town, tank station, wrong tank, right tank, slab, two stemmer, urb, patch, jerkwater town, hick town, rube town, hoosier town, one-horse town, ghost town, South Succotash, East Jesus, Podunk, jumping off place, hickville, whistle-stop, whistle snort, noplaceville, filling station, wide place in the road, hideaway, the bushes, the boondocks, boonies, sticks, stix, bush leagues, pumpkin, the rhubarbs.

TOWNSPERSON n.   townee, towner, local local. See also CITY DWELLER.

TOY v.   fool with, play games with, dilly-dally, play around, fool around, jerk off, lead one on, string one along. See DALLY. See also DABBLE.

TRACK n.   boards (indoor), groove, rut.

TRACK v.   1. dog, bird-dog (scout), scout, beat the bushes, run down, leave no stone unturned, track down. See SEARCH. 2. shadow, tail, trail, tail down, hot on one's tail, go after, dog one's heels, stick to. See FOLLOW.

TRACK AND FIELD TERMS   anchor, anchor man (heavy man in tug o' war or last runner in relay race), anchor leg (last segment of relay race); breast the tape (win), bunch start (crouch), hand off (relay race conversion).

TRACT n.   broadside, flyer, handout.

TRACTABLE adj.   putty in one's hands, game, go along with, hang loose, roll with the punches. See also FLEXIBLE.

TRACTOR n. cat, cat skinner (operator), horse, kitty cat.

TRADE n. bag, gig, day gig, beeswax, biz, game, gesheft, line, line of business, dodge, what one is into, thing, nine-to-five shit, racket. See OCCUPATION. 2. Wall Street, the Exchange, the Big Board, over the counter.

TRADE v. dicker, hack out a deal, hammer out a deal, make a deal, work out a deal, wheel and deal, hondle, horse trade, swap. See NEGOTIATE.

TRADEMARK n. logo.

TRADER n. dealer, middleman, big-time operator, BTO, big wheel, wheeler-dealer, tycoon, cockroach (small), nickel-and-dime operator, small potatoes, tradester, robber baron, big butter and egg man, peddler, drummer, bell-ringer, ——— dog (e.g., shoe dog), medicine man, pitchman, skig, spieler, tinge, Arab, bag guy (balloon), butch, butcher, hawker.

TRADITIONAL adj. trad. See also CONVENTIONAL.

TRAFFIC CITATION n. ticket, tag, coupon, green stamps, bit on the britches, Christmas card, feed the bears.

TRAFFIC JAM n. gridlock, gawker's block, gaper's block, curiosity creep, slow and go, jam, parking lot, stall ball, level F, cone zone (working area).

TRAFFIC SIGN n. magic marker.

TRAFFIC TERMS make the light (go through on green or yellow), run a light (go through on red); ticket, tag, coupon, (court summons); pulled over, joyride, cruisin', Sunday driver (inept), Hollywood stop (roll through a legal stop), speed bump (a bump placed to slow speeding cars), sleeping policeman (speed bump).

TRAFFIC WITH v. 1. contact, interact, interface, network, reach out, relate, touch, touch base, have truck with, connect with. See COMMUNICATE. 2. dicker, make a deal, cut a deal, work out a deal, horse trade, swap, swap horses. See also NEGOTIATE.

TRAGEDY n. bummer, curtains, downer, grabber, total shuck, Waterloo, the worst, blue ruin, shit hit the fan. See DISASTER. See also MISFORTUNE.

TRAIL n. aisle, byway, stroll, groove rut.

TRAIL v. 1. dog, leave no stone unturned, take out after, track down. See SEARCH. 2. shadow, tail, shag, hot on one's tail, on one's quiff (closely), dog one's heels, tag after, spook. See FOLLOW. 3. get no place fast, poke, poke around, poke along, shlep along, play catch up, string along, tag along.

TRAILER CAMP n. mo-camp.

TRAILER PARK n. galvanized ghetto.

TRAIN n. choo choo, choo-choo train, rattler, ball of fire, highballer, jack, rat, meat run, milk run, red ball, cannonball, AMTRAK. See RAILROAD TRAIN.

TRAIN v. 1. work out, warm up, tune up, lick into shape, get in shape, put through the grind, put through the mill, run through, walk through, take it from the top, dry run, hone, sharpen, break, break in. See also PREPARE. 2. brainwash, break, break in, put one in the picture, put one wise, wise one up, show one the ropes, update, level, clue one in, give a pointer to, drum, drum into.

TRAIN CONDUCTOR n. big O, big ox, brains, captain, chopper, con, dude, drummer, grabber, kayducer.

TRAINED adj. up to snuff, up to speed, up to code, been through the mill, from way back, pro, vet, warhorse, won one's spurs, one of the old school, old-timer, has know-how, knows the ropes, knows one's onions, knows one's ps and qs. See also KNOWLEDGEABLE.

TRAINEE n. boot, rookie, tenderfoot, flunky, heel, heeler (reporter), peg boy, pratt boy. See NOVICE. See also RECRUIT.

TRAINER n. old man, skipper.

TRAINING n. workout, warm-up, sharpening up, shaping up, an edge, readying, breaking in, daily dozen, chalk talk, skull session. See also PREPARATION.

TRAINING CENTER n. boot camp.

TRAIT n. thing, one's thing, nature of the beast, the way of it, the name of that tune, that's one all over, just like one. See also CHARACTERISTIC.

TRAITOR n. Benedict Arnold, fifth columnist, quisling, rat, rat fink, fink, double-crosser, snake, snake in the grass, narc, snitch, squealer, stoolie, stool pigeon, snitcher, tattletale, whistle-blower (U.). See INFORMER.

TRAITOROUS adj. double-crossing, snake in the grass, two-faced, two-timing, low-down and dirty, dirty work, cheatin' heart, slick, slippery, speak with forked tongue.

TRAMP n. bum, on the bum, king of the road, bo, stiff, bindleman, floater, ragbag, road agent. See VAGRANT.

TRAMP v. hoof it, go by hand, burn shoe leather, hit the road, press the bricks, air out, beat the rocks, navigate, count ties (hobo). See WALK.

TRANCE n. gone, far out, cool, Nadaville, gauze, glaze, MEGO (my eyes glaze over).

TRANQUIL adj. cool, cool as a cucumber, keep one's cool, keep one's shirt on, not turn a hair, unflappable, ah-

ah head, all quiet on the Potomac, all quiet on the Western front.

TRANQUILIZER n. trank, tranx, backwards, volume, dope, goof ball, knockout drop, Mickey Finn. See also SEDATIVE.

TRANS-ALASKA PIPELINE n. TAPS.

TRANSACT v. 1. hammer out a deal, hack out a deal, cut a deal, work out a deal, wrap up, close, sew up, button down, button up, jell, take care of, clinch. See NEGOTIATE. See also FINISH. 2. move, make one's move, effectuate, TCB (take care of business), take a flier (impulsively), pull off, fish or cut bait, get with it, shit or get off the pot, perk, tick, operate, run with the ball, do one's stuff. See ACT.

TRANSACTION n. carrying on, goings-on, hanky-panky, hap, happening, ongoing, play, irons, irons in the fire, little deal (often unethical).

TRANSACTIONAL ANALYSIS n. TA.

TRANSCENDENTAL MEDITATION n. TM.

TRANSFIX v. nail down, pin down, stick.

TRANSFORM v. 1. doctor, phony up, switch, switch over, shift gears, cook, transmogrify, revamp. 2. turn over a new leaf, turn the corner, turn the tables, turn one around, do up, about face, flip-flop, sing a different tune. See CHANGE.

TRANSFORMATION n. 1. born again, got religion, new born Christian, saw the light. 2. about face, flip-flop, switch, switch over, transmogrification.

TRANSITORY adj. flash in the pan, here today gone tomorrow, fly-by-night.

TRANSMIT v. 1. duke, weed, pass it over, get across, get the message, back channel (secretly). 2. drop a line, drop a note, give one a ring, give one a jingle, give one a call, get one on the horn. See also DELIVER, DISPATCH.

TRANSMITTER n. rig.

TRANSPIRE v. gel, jell, shake, smoke, what goes, come down, what's coming down, go down, what's going down, where's the action? See OCCUR.

TRANSPORT v. lug, pack, back, piggyback, birdie back, fishyback (by water), ride, shlep, shlep along, tote, truck, buck, gun, heel, hump, jag, shoulder, move.

TRANSPORT DRUGS v. carryin', carry the mail, body pack.

TRANSPOSE v. flip-flop, backtrack, double back, turn the tables, put the cart before the horse, put ass backwards, put bass ackwards, put ack basswards.

TRANSVESTITE n. TV, T.V.

TRANSVESTITE CLOTHING n. drag (also transvestite party).

TRAP v. collar, corral, grab, hook, land, nail, bag, nab, rope in, suck in, box in, get one in a box, lay for. See also AMBUSH.

TRAPEZE ARTIST n. flier.

TRAPPED adj. dog meat, nabbed, nailed, cornered, in a box, in a hole, up a tree, jammed up, on the peg, stiffed in, swamped. See CAUGHT.

TRASH n. gash, hogwash, junk, dreck, shit.

TRASH COLLECTOR n. San man.

TRAVEL n. hop, swing, jaunt, cruise, junket, trek, overnight, weekend, Cook's tour.

TRAVEL v. jet, jet in, jet out, sky in, sky out, jet around, get around, knock around, knock about, belt around, bat around, bat about, swing, go places, go on Apex, on the go, take off, hop, city-hop, country-hop, globe-trot, tripping, cruise, hit the road, on the road, on the move, on the trail, hit the trail, traipse, trek, do the continent, do Europe (or wherever), jaunt, junket, junketing, overnight, weekend, beat one's way, barnstorm, bum, bum around, bum a ride, thumb, thumb a ride, lam, hitch, hitchhike, hitch a ride, hopscotch, breeze, dog it, drive in, hit the dirt, hit the grit, walk the tracks, count ties.

TRAVELER n. jet-setter, globe-trotter, deadhead (free), seatcover, dude (bus), drop, line load (taxi), rubberneck, rubbernecker, snowbird, snowflake, sunflower.

TRAVELING adj. jetting, globe-trotting, cruising, doing the continent, on the road, on the circuit, on the go, on the jump, on the gad, on the bum, rubbernecking, knocking around, knocking about, batting around, batting about, barnstorming, stumping.

TRAVELING CASE n. jiffy bag, tote, tote bag, carry-on, valpack, keister.

TRAVESTY n. take-off, play on, put-on, roast.

TREACHEROUS adj. double-crossing, snake in the grass, two-faced, two-timing, slick, slippery, speak with forked tongue. See DECEITFUL. See also DISHONEST.

TREACHERY n. dirty dealing, dirty work, dirty pool, dirty trick, double-cross, sellout, put-on, scam, fake, flam, flimflam, racket, dodge, royal fucking, royal screwing, bunco, bunko, fast shuffle, double shuffle, gyp, jip, double banker, diddle, diddling, grift, shell game, skin game, Judas kiss, stab in the back, two-timing, crocodile tears, soft soap, sweet talk, spoof, whitewash job, cake cutter (circus). See also CHEAT.

TREASURER n. ghee with the boodle, payoff ghee.

TREASURY n. damper, Fort Knox.

TREASURY AGENT n. narc, T man.

TREASURY SECURITY n. baby bond (less than $1,000 denomination), James Bond (matures in 2007), Bo Derek, ten, (Treasury Bond maturing in the year 2010); double-barreled bond (two sources of repayment). See also BONDS.

TREAT n. cush, sweets, g'dong, gedunk, hickey.

TREAT v. 1. doctor. 2. blow, blow one to, on one, on the house, I'll get it (pay the check), I'm buyin', pick up the check, pick up the tab, pop, pop for, spring for, stand for, set up, stake.

TREATED BY v. on (it's on me), on the house.

TREE n. twig.

TREK v. on the road, on the move, on the trail, hit the trail, beat one's way, hit the dirt, hit the grit. See also TRAVEL.

TREMBLE v. jitter, shake, shiver, have the shakes, have the quivers, have the shivers, have the cold shivers.

TREMENDOUS adj. humongous, mungo, monstro, big mother, super colossal, jumbo, blimp, barn door, whale of a, whopper, whopping. See BIG.

TRENCH n. foxhole, dug in, bughouse (WW I).

TRENCHCOAT n. mack, Fog.

TREND n. 1. in, in-thing, the latest thing, kick, newest wrinkle, the rage, swim. See RAGE. 2. drift, swing.

TREPIDATION n. goose bumps, creeps, cold creeps, cold shivers, jitters, worriment, pucker-assed, asshole puckerin', asshole suckin' wind. See FEAR. See also AGITATION.

TRESPASS v. 1. mix in, butt in, chisel in, horn in, muscle in, stick one's nose in, poke one's nose in, kibitz, put in one's oar, put in one's two cents in, shove in one's oar. 2. crash, crash the gates, penetrate (secret agent).

TRESPASSER n. buttinski, buttinsky, crasher, gate-crasher.

TRIAL n. 1. try, go, fling, fling at, shot, crack, whack, stab, lick, R and D, showcase, tryout, try on, workout, dry 'run, trial run, shakedown, shakedown cruise, run that by. 2. drag, downer, bitch, headache, tsuris, pain, pain in the ass, pain in the neck, nag, nudge, nudzh, noodge, worriment, worriation, hang-up, rough go, handful, blister, pill, botheration. See also PREDICAMENT.

TRIAL BY JURY, UNDERGO v. go up, go to bat.

TRIBULATION n. bummer, downer, shit, deep shit, tough shit, TS, drag, hard time, hard knocks, up against it, rain, rainin', rainy day, double whammy, headache, tsuris, they're peeing on us and telling us it's raining, next week East Lynne.

TRICK n. dodge, stunt, bait and switch, the pilgrim drop, handkerchief switch, bum steer, curveball, dirty pool, dirty trick, taradiddle, diddling, fix, Barney, frame, frame-up, plant, hookup, put-on, spoof, cross, double-cross, double-X, XX, double banker, double shuffle, fast shuffle, shell game, skin game, fast one, run around, cutie, smoke, hanky-panky, hocus-pocus, hugger-muggery, double trays, dipsy doodle, shenanigans, monkeyshines, monkey business, funny business.

TRICK v. rook, screw, shaft, frig, fudge, deke, hose, jerk one off, jerk one around, dick one around, fuck one over, jive, shuck, shuck and jive, run a game on, snake one in, disinform, sell wolf cookies, fake, fake it, fake one out, flam, flimflam, scam, sandbag, throw a game, play games with, play the nine of hearts, play for a sucker, double shuffle, double deal, second deal, deal from the bottom, shave a deck, set up, hocus, hocus-pocus, slip one over on. See CHEAT.

TRICKED adj. been had, jerked around, foxed, disinformed, mousetrapped, strung along, set up, suckered, sucked in, sold, sold a bill of goods, bearded, fell for, took the bait, roped in, double-crossed, diddled, shaved, buffaloed, hippoed.

TRICKERY n. con, sting, flimflam, gyp, scam, dodge, stunt, razzle-dazzle, fast shuffle, royal fucking, royal screwing, bait and switch, fast shuffle, shell game, skin game, Murphy game, the old army game, hocus-pocus, shenanigans, monkeyshines, monkey business, funny business; limb, shit kicker, tap, tap game (advertising). See TRICK.

TRICKSTER n. card, phony, play actor, shark, sharp, hustler, mechanic, faker, flimflammer, flimflam man, gyp, jip, gyp artist, gypster, con artist, clip artist, double-dealer, two-timer, two-faced, smoothie, smooth apple, smooth article, smooth operator, operator, suede-shoe operator, slick operator, diddler, fast talker, slicker.

TRICKY adj. foxy, cagey, crazy like a fox, fancy footwork, full of fancy footwork, slick, slippery, sly boots, smarts, smooth, street smarts, streetwise, shady, greasy. See also DECEITFUL, SHREWD.

TRIFLE n. squat, diddly squat, diddly shit, beans, borscht, fly speck, minimal to the max, from nothing, two bit, big deal, big fucking deal, BFD, no big shit, no biggie, no great shakes. See NOTHING. See also AMOUNT, SMALL.

TRIFLE v. dilly-dally, monkey, play around, lollygag, jerk off, play games with. See DABBLE. See also DALLY.

TRIFLING adj. big zero, big deal, big fucking deal, BFD, no big deal, no biggie, no big thing, no big shit, no count, pissy assed, dinky, measly, chicken shit, bupkis, forget it, makes no never mind, little go. See UNIMPORTANT.

TRIM adj. 1. in good shape, in fine fettle, slick. 2. clean, apple-pie order, neat as a button, neat as a pin, slick, to rights, all policed up, in good shape, shipshape.

TRIM n. gingerbread, bells and whistles, gewgaws, garbage (food). See ORNAMENT.

TRIM v. 1. doll up, fix up, gussy up, spruce up, pretty up. See ORNAMENT. 2. cut, cut down, cut to the bone, put in a nutshell, boil down, get to the meat, chop, snip, blue pencil.

TRIMMING n. fuss, gingerbread, gewgaws, bells and whistles, options, gadget, jazz, widget. See ORNAMENT.

TRINKETS n. gewgaws, junk jewelry, brass (cheap or fake), stones, rocks, sparklers, ice, Christmas, glass, hardware, pennyweight.

TRIP n. hop, swing, jaunt, cruise, junket, trek, overnight, weekend, Cook's tour. See TRAVEL.

TRIP, GO ON A v. jet, jet in, jet out, sky in, sky out, jet around, knock around, go places, take off, tripping, cruise, hit the road, on the move, hit the trail, trek, do the continent, do Europe (or wherever), junket. See TRAVEL.

TRITE adj. corn, corny, cornball, corn-fed, hokum, hokey, tripe, chestnut, old chestnut, old saw, old song, old story, familiar tune, garden variety, everyday, dime a dozen, rumdum, run of the alley, run of the mill, boiler plate, pulp, slick, bromide, Clyde, old hat.

TRIUMPH n. KO, win, big win, win all the marbles, do a Rocky, grab the gold, nose out, beat the competish, rake in the pot, bring home the bacon, bull's-eye, slam, grand slam, homer, hole in one, hit, big hit, smash hit, bomb, bombshell, score, sell, sock, socko, sockeroo, boff, boffo, splash, takeover, walkaway, walkover, kill, killing, clean sweep, picnic, laugher (lopsided score), wow, pushover, sitting duck, winning streak, hot run, daily double (series of successes), one-two sweep (win two things at once), sleeper (unexpected), easy digging, pay dirt, howling success, roaring success, gas, gasser, riot, sensation, gold star, feather in one's cap, cinch, lead-pipe cinch, shoo-in, sure thing, sure bet, splashed the zeros (A.F., WW II).

TRIUMPH v. win out, make a killing, strike it lucky, win hands down, clean sweep, skunk, take it all, schneider, sweep, trounce, beat the game, beat the system, blow out, sink the opposition, win all the marbles, take the cake, get the last dance. See WIN.

TRIUMPHANT adj. lookin' good, set up, luck out (against all odds), on top of the heap. See VICTORIOUS. See also SUCCESSFUL.

TRIVIA n. chicken shit, peanuts, chicken feed, small beer, small change, not count for spit. See also TRIFLE.

TRIVIAL adj. big deal, big fucking deal, BFD, no biggie, no big shit, no great shakes, pissy assed, dinky, measly, two bit, tinhorn, chicken feed, bupkis, makes no never mind, nutmeg, nit-picking, picky picky, little go, fly speck. See UNIMPORTANT.

TRIVIALITY n. minimal to the max, big deal, no big deal, big shit, no big shit, no biggie, no big thing, no matter, small potatoes, small beer, small change, small pot, drop in the bucket, drop in the ocean, no great shakes, mere bagatelle. See also FOOLISHNESS, UNIMPORTANT.

TROLLOP n. hooker, call girl, hustler, ho, working girl, model, pro, floozie, chippy, prostie, tart, bag, baggage, B-girl, broad, chicken rancher, bawd, jade. See PROSTITUTE.

TROMBONE n. slip horn, slipstick, slush pump, T bone, trom, bone, gas pipe, grunt horn, piston, push pipe, syringe.

TROPHY n. the cookies, feather in one's cap, gold star, the gold, Oscar, blue ribbon.

TROPICAL adj. close, sticky, steamy, sweat box, hotter than blue mud.

TROTSKYITES n. Trots.

TROUBLE n. shit, deep shit, serious jelly, serious shit, bad news, clutch, hang up, jam, in a jam, in a clutch, in a mess, in a pickle, scrape, in a scrape, in a spot, in a tight spot, in a hot spot, on the hot seat, hot water, in deep water, in heavy water, stew, in a stew, in over one's head, up a tree, up the creek, up the creek without a paddle, up shit creek, up shit creek without a paddle, drag, bind, double bind, rough go, heavy sledding, rainin', spot, ticklish spot, tricky spot, tight spot, tight squeeze, lose-lose situation, no win situation, gasser, pisser, rat's nest, snake pit, box, crunch, catch, catch 22, bitch, handful, headache, bummer, downer, worriment, botheration, grabber, hooker, double trouble, behind the eight ball, boxed in, in a box, in a fix, in a hole, snafu, pain in the ass, pain in the neck, between a rock and a hard place, tail in a gate, tit in a wringer, mix, mess, holy mess, unholy mess, kettle of fish, fine kettle of fish, a fine mess you've got us into, how do you do, fine how do you do, hobble, pickle, pretty pickle, pretty pass, squeeze, sticky wicket, hard row to hoe, hard row of stumps, hard time, hard pull, heat's on, a mountain out of a molehill, heavy load to haul, the devil to pay, hell to pay, bug, glitch, puzzler, can of peas, can of worms, Pandora's box, green hornet (Mil.), honey, hot potato, stinker, tsuris, tumul, what's with, sixty-four dollar question, twister, sticker, floorer, stumper, bugaboo, crimp, crimp one's style, hump, stinger, hot grease, jackpot, mess up, screw up, need it like a hole in the head, next week East Lynne, rub, push comes to shove, when things get tough, toughie, tough proposition, tough nut to crack, tough going, hard going, joker, scuffle, put on the spot, hit a snag, a holdup, cropper, come a-cropper, one small difficulty.

TROUBLE v. adjy, psych, spook, get to, flip out, craze, bug, bug up, burn up, fire up, make waves, make a scene, make a fuss, fuss, fuzzbuzz, give one a bad time, give one a hard time, make it a tough go, stir up, drive one bananas, drive one up a wall. See DISTURB.

TROUBLED adj. uptight, tightened up, bugged, choked, clutched, clutched up, bummed out, burned up, hung up, miffed, peeved, riled, rubbed the wrong way, discombobulated, in a lather, in a stew, on edge, on pins and needles, on tenterhooks, worried stiff, biting one's nails, beside oneself, put to it, hard put to it, at the end of one's rope. See also ANXIOUS, DISTURBED.

TROUBLE, IN adj. in the soup, in deep, in deep shit, in deep kim chee, in deep water, in heavy water, in sour, in over one's head, in the barrel, in the center, in the middle, in a jackpot, in a swindle, in a heavy place, in Dutch, in a jam, in a scrape, in a mess, in a hole, in a corner, in a box, in a bind, ih a fix, in a pickle, in a pretty pickle, in a spot, in a tight spot, fucked, hurting, coming undone, coming unglued, coming unzipped, behind the eight ball, on a one-way street, on the shitlist, on Queer Street, got one's ass in a sling, got one's ass in a bind, one's ass in new-mown grass, up against it, up the creek, up shit creek, up shit creek without a paddle, messed up, screwed up, hung up, hard up, jackied up, jammed up, all balled up, all bollixed up, fighting to keep one's head up, out on a limb, out of one's depth, out of line, have a case, looks like curtains, sack, satchel, swamped, under the gun, panic is on, panicked out, squeezed, hit a snag, come a-cropper, at the end of one's rope, scrape the bottom of the barrel, over a barrel, back to the wall, tryin' to stay alive, runnin' out of time, no more cards to play, buried, holding the bag, be a dead pigeon, put one's foot in it, paint oneself in a corner.

TROUBLE, LOOKING FOR v. cruisin' for a bruisin', fuck with, mess with, kick up a fuss.

TROUBLEMAKER n. gremlin, gremmie, wise guy, smart aleck, punk, smart ass, dog, eel, false alarm, muzzler, one who cries wolf, one who is pea soup, gummio, iceman, mutt, phony, loose cannon, shit heel, snake, weasel. See also AGITATOR.

TROUBLESOME adj. pesky, pestiferous, uphill, uphill battle, wicked, mean, messy, heavy, hairy, murder, pisser, pain in the ass, pain in the neck, rough, uncool, bitch, son of a bitch, son of a gun, stiff, tough, tough nut to crack, toughie, tough proposition, tough lineup to buck, tough job, rough go, hard job, hard pull, hard row to hoe, hard row of stumps, the hard way, hi-

tech, handful, ballbreaker, ballbuster, conk buster, backbreaker, headache, large order, tall order, honey, no picnic, no piece of cake, sticky, sticky wicket, can of worms, heavy sledding.

TROUNCE v. 1. bash, trash, drub, flax, wax, lather, lambaste, whip, bust, dust, total, clobber, cream, paste, waste, smack down, shoot down, wipe out, wipe off the map, beat the shit out of one, put one in the hospital, jack one up. 2. bury, blank, skunk, schneider, murder, cook one's goose, trim, cap, top, fix one's wagon, swamp, scuttle, skin, shellack, roll over, tube, blow away, blow out, put away. See DEFEAT.

TROUPER n. ham, hambone, ham fatter, lead, bit player, star, thesp, straight man, barnstormer, spear carrier, super, walk on. See ACTOR.

TROUSERS n. slacks, jeans, Levis, ducks, whites, bells, hip huggers, kneebusters, dungarees, pegs, pistols (pegged). See PANTS.

TRUANCY n. AWOL, cut, French leave, hooky.

TRUANT n. no-show, hookey, cutting, blitz, bag (Sch.), A.W.O.L., French, French leave, over the hill, out, out of pocket, out of touch.

TRUCK n. wheels, four by four, four by eight, quarter ton, eighteen wheeler, semi, Big Mack, oil burner (diesel), dump, box (trailer), draggin' wagon, dragon wagon (tow), bug (Army, WW II), pickemup, gypsy, horse, cement mixer (noisy), kidney buster, bucket of bolts, scow, straight job, carry-all, fat load (overweight), beaver trap, bedbug hauler (moving van), freight box, bushel basket (freight), crate of sand (sugar), muck truck (cement), barn yard (cattle), big orange, bottle popper (beverage); branch bank, money bus, loot limo (armored); pig rig (hogs), portable barnyard, rolling ranch, bull dog, bull rack (animals), ice box, cold rig (refrigerator), fun run (empty), portable pipeline, thermos bottle (tank), gas station (tanker), go-devil, honey wagon (beer), mobile forest (logging), portable parking lot, mobile parking lot (auto), roach coach (catering and garbage), garbage truck (catering), salt shaker, sand blaster, (salt); scrub brush (street cleaner). See also AUTOMOBILE.

TRUCK DRIVER n. trucker, teamster, hack hand, jeep jockey, spinner, skinner, boll weevil (inexperienced), bottle cap (tank), dump chump (dump), fat daddy, pop top (beverage), road runner, gypsy, hair pounder (1925).

TRUCK STOP n. book store, chuck wagon, cook shack, water hole.

TRUCK TRACTOR n. bobtail (without semi trailer), widow maker (double trailered), horse.

TRUCULENT adj. ornery, scrappy, snorky, bitchy, cussed, salty, spiky, mean, cantankerous, fire-eater, have it in for, at loggerheads, trigger happy. See BELLI-GERENT.

TRUDGE v.   plug along, shlep. See also WALK.

TRUE adj.   1. hold up, stand up, go, hold water, hold together, stick together, hold up in the wash, wash, fly, no buts about it, no ifs ands or buts. See also CORRECT. 2. true blue, true believer, dyed in the wool, faithful but not blind. 3. it, for real, the real McCoy, real stuff, genuine article, real goods, in the flesh, honest to God, kosher, legit, on the level, on the up and up, twenty-four carat. See SINCERE. 4. up front, right up front, straight, on the up and up, no lie, what you see is what you get, honest Injun, square John, square shooter, boy scout, Mr. Clean. See TRUSTWORTHY.

TRULY adv.   amen, sure, why sure, sure thing, fer sure, you better believe it, no buts about it, on the money, on the nose, indeedy, yes indeedy, for real, really truly, cross my heart, cross my heart and hope to die, I'm not shittin' you, so help me. See ABSOLUTELY.

TRUMPET n.   iron horn, horn, piston, plumber, plumbing, quail, screamer, squeeze horn.

TRUMPET PLAYER n.   Gabriel, lip-splitter.

TRUNK n.   keister.

TRUNKS n.   baggies, jammies, clamdiggers, kneebusters, (swimming); skivvies, boxers, shorts, jockey, jockeys (underwear). See also PANTS.

TRUST n.   1. gospel truth, stock, store. 2. megacorp, multinational, bunch, crew, crowd, gang, mob, plunderbund, outfit, ring.

TRUST v.   bank on, bet on, bet one's bottom dollar on, gamble on, lay money on, string along with. See BELIEVE.

TRUSTFUL adj.   sucker, swallow anything, patsy, mark, easy, easy mark, wide-eyed, blue-eyed, yold. See GULLIBLE.

TRUSTWORTHY adj.   1. minding the store, on the hook, carry the load, on one's back. 2. there, count on one, one who always delivers, one who always comes through, always there in a pinch, surefire, all right, all right guy, right guy, boy scout, down home, up front, right up front, on the up and up, on the level, Christian, fly right, Mr. Clean, open, real people, saint, rock, Rock of Gibraltar, straight, straight arrow, true blue, oncer, kosher, third rail, square John, square shooter, gimper (Air Force). See also SINCERE.

TRUTH n.   dope, scoop, score, picture, whole story, lowdown, brass tacks, meat and potatoes, name of the game, hangout route, nitty-gritty, point, stuff, nub, bottom line, the numbers, nuts and bolts, down to earth, the real world, for real, no shit, straight shit, straight stuff, straight of it, straight goods, the goods, the case, scene, size of it, how it is, how things are, the way of it, what's what, where it's at, tell it like it is, nature of the beast, live, in the flesh, the real emess, the real McCoy, skinny, from the horse's mouth, that's a fact Jack, cross my heart and hope to die, the goods, honest-to-God truth, God's truth, bible, the word, gospel, cold turkey, you ain't just whistling Dixie.

TRUTHFUL adj.   like it is, call it like it is, on the up and up, on the level, honest Injun, square, square shooter, true blue, righteous, Christian, kosher, boy scout, legit, straight, call a spade a spade, white, damn white, put all one's cards on the table, talk turkey. See SINCERE.

TRUTHFULLY adv.   flat out, level, on the level, on the dead level, give it on the up and up, spring with the legit, spill the works, come out with it, straight, no foolin', say a mouthful (you said a mouthful), cross my heart, cross my heart and hope to die, I'm not shittin' you, indeedy, no buts about it, really truly, so help me.

TRUTH, TELL THE v.   level, level with, dead level, on the level, go the hangout route, blow soul, fack (Bl.), guts, play it straight.

TRY n.   all one's got, crack, go, jelly go, one's all, one's damndest, one's darndest, one's best shot, shot, stab, whack. See ATTEMPT.

TRY v.   make a run at, tackle, take on, make a try, cut and try, try on for size, bust one's ass, break one's neck, give it all one's got, try one's damndest, try one's darndest, give it the old college try, try on for size, give it a try, bend over backward, go for it, go for broke, shoot the works. See ATTEMPT.

TRYST n.   1. date, heavy date, rendezvous, meet, zero hour, creep, triff, treff (secret). 2. love nest, spot, matinee, noonie, one-night stand, quickie. See RENDEZVOUS.

TRYSTING PLACE n.   love nest, place, spot, your place or mine.

TUBA n.   oompah, grunt box, grunt horn, grunt iron.

TUBERCULOSIS n.   TB, con, galloping consumption, lunger (person with disease).

TUBING n.   macaroni.

TUGBOAT n.   tug, cider barrel (oceangoing).

TUINAL n.   Christmas trees, double trouble, rainbows, tooies, reds, blues.

TULSA, OKLAHOMA   Oil City.

TUMBLE n.   header, nose dive, pratfall, belly buster, belly flop, belly whopper.

TUMBLE v.   take a header, nose-dive, lose it, do a pratfall, land on one's ass, go ass over teakettle, tip over, belly up, fall down and go boom, come a cropper, take a belly whopper, hit the dirt.

TUMULT n. flap, fuss, to-do, row, stir, stink, big stink, rhubarb, rowdydow, rumble, rumpus, ruckus, ruction, commo, hell broke loose, all hell broke loose, scene, big scene. See TURMOIL.

TUNE UP v. lick one's chops (music).

TUNNEL n. hole in the wall.

TURBULENCE n. dirty air, bumps, bumpy, air pockets.

TURKEY n. buzzard, gobbler, turk.

TURMOIL n. 1. topsy-turvy, mix-up, every which way, galley west, hectic, discombobulation, flusteration, flustration. See CONFUSION. 2. flap, fuss, to-do, row, stir, stink, big stink, rhubarb, rowdydow, rumble, rumpus, ruckus, ruction, shindy, shivaree, commo, dustup, foofooraw, free-for-all, brawl, all hell broke loose, kickup, wingding, raise cain, raise sand, roughhouse, fuzzbuzz, haroosh, big scene, storm, blast, blowup, flare-up, tear. 3. circus, fireworks, mess, razzle-dazzle.

TURN n. go, go around, one's move, one's say, whack, bit, routine, shtick, act. See OPPORTUNITY.

TURN v. cut, hang a right, hang a left, swivel, make a right, make a left.

TURNABOUT n. about-face, switcheroo, flip-flop.

TURNCOAT n. rat, rat fink, double-crosser, Benedict Arnold, fifth columnist, quisling, snake, snake in the grass. See also INFORMER.

TUSSLE n. brush, rumble, roughhouse, donnybrook, flap, gin, hassle, mix-up, go, row, rumpus, ruckus, shindy, set-to, scrap, wrangle. See FIGHT.

TUTOR n. baby-sitter, grind, guru, prof, slave driver, snap, teach.

TUTOR v. let in on the know, let next to, put hip, put hep, put through the grind, put through the mill, update, ready, lick into shape, clue one in, lay it out for, drum, drum into. See INSTRUCT.

TUXEDO n. tux, black tie, clothes, monkey clothes, monkey suit, smoking, bib and tucker, soup and fish.

TV n. video, tube, idiot box, boob tube, big eye, baby-sitter, telly.

TWEAK n. yank, yerk.

TWELVE n. boxcars, twelvemo, 12mo, box cars (dice).

TWENTY-FOUR n. twenty-formo, 24mo.

TWIST n. yank, yerk.

TWISTED adj. cockeyed.

TWIT v. jive, needle, rag, razz, rib, jolly, josh, ride, put on, make sport of, pull one's leg. See RIDICULE.

TWITCH n. yank, yerk.

TWO n. double, deuce, doubleheader, double in brass, a couple, a pair, a team, a brace, twosome, duo.

TWOFOLD adj. wear two hats, twin, doubleheader (successful two ways), double in brass (two kinds of work), rule of twice, twofers.

TWOSOME n. item, duo, deuce it, couple, gruesome twosome, team, pair off, spic and span (Black and Puerto Rican, Derog.).

TYPE n. likes, likes of, lot, number.

TYPE v. tab, peg, button down, pigeonhole, put away, put down as, put down for, typecast.

TYPEWRITE v. touch, hunt 'n' peck, bat out, beat out.

TYPEWRITER n. chatterbox, desk piano, office piano.

TYPICAL adj. nature of the beast, that's one all over, just like one.

TYPIST n. steno, woodpecker.

TYPOGRAPHICAL ERROR n. typo.

TYRANNIZE v. rule the roost, keep under one's thumb, throw one's weight around, bring to heel, bulldoze, henpeck, pussywhip (Fem.), crack the whip, wear the pants. See DOMINEER.

TYRANT n. a Hitler, Simon Legree, slave driver, czar.

TYRO n. newie, greeny, freshie, turkey, punk, rook, rookie, boot, new kid on the block, fish, greenhorn, tenderfoot, jice, first of May. See NOVICE.

U

U n. uniform, uncle.

UBIQUITOUS adj. wall to wall.

U-BOAT n. navy shark, pig boat, tin can, tin fish, tin shack. See SUBMARINE.

UGLY adj. pig, dog, dogface, airedale, animal, beast, grody, gross, plug, plug-ugly, ugly as sin, grimbo, hagged out, hard on the eyes, fartface, bad head, beaujeeful, a face only a mother could love, face that would crack a mirror, face that would stop a clock, pruneface, homely as a mud fence, mud duck (girl), chromo, short on looks, schacks, boogie bear, from hunger, awful, grungy, death warmed over, gruesome twosome.

UKULELE n. uke, tipple.

ULTIMATE adj. max, maxi, the most, the mostest, bottom line, the end, drop dead —— [anything], the livin' end, ass end, bitter end, tail ass (A.F.), curtains, curtains for, final curtain, blow off, capper, critical mass, payoff, last hurrah, swan song, far out, nose cone, go over the mountain, shoot one's wad, the chips are down.

ULTRA adj. ultra-ultra, too-too, too much, all out, gone, glorkish, out of bounds, out of all bounds, out of this world. See EXTREME. See also RADICAL.

ULTRANATIONALIST n. flag-waver, hundred percenter, hard hat, jingoist, patrioteer, superpatriot, wraps oneself in the flag. See also CONSERVATIVE.

UMBRELLA n. bumbershoot, mush, shower stick.

UMBRELLA THIEF n. mush faker.

UNABLE adj. uncool, not cut out for, can't hack it, can't cut it, can't cut the mustard, can't make the grade, sidelined, out of commission, no can do, hog-tied. See INCOMPETENT. See also INADEQUATE.

UNACCEPTABLE adj. not up to scratch, not up to snuff, doesn't hack it, won't do, half-assed, half-baked, lemon, seconds, crappy, dreck, lousy, Mickey Mouse, piss-poor, rat-fuck, schlocky, sleazy, slimpsy, below the mark, damaged goods, a reject, a clinker, God forbid, heaven forbid it, no way, by no means, not on your life, take it away, perish the thought, I'll be hanged if. See INADEQUATE.

UNACCOMPANIED adj. loner, lone wolf, doe, shag, stag, solo, onliest, Herman the hermit, Crusoe, Robinson Crusoe, traveling light. See ALONE.

UNADORNED adj. clean, vanilla, what you see is what you get, folksy, homey, haymish, open and shut, bare bones, no frills, meat and potatoes. See PLAIN.

UNADULTERATED adj. neat, straight, uncut, right out of the bottle, legit, on the legit, honest to God, Christian, kosher, the emess, righteous, straight dope, straight from the horse's mouth, sure enough, too good to be true, twenty-four carat, all wool and a yard wide, blowed in the glass. See also PLAIN.

UNAFFECTED adj. 1. go organic, on the natch. 2. folksy, homey, up front, laid back, no sweat, don't sweat it, cool, cool cat. See NATURAL. See also CASUAL. 3. not to worry, I should worry, thick-skinned, hard-boiled, hardhearted, cold fish. See CALLOUS.

UNAFRAID adj. game, gritty, gutsy, gutty, spunky, nervy, stand tall, tough it out, bigger'n life, fire-eater, hairy, cool hand. See FEARLESS.

UNALTERABLE adj. hard-nosed, tough nut, tough nut to crack, locked in, head in concrete, set in concrete, solid as a rock, rock-ribbed, brick wall, bullheaded, pigheaded, stubborn as a mule, set, dead set on. See STUBBORN.

UNAMBIGUOUS adj. dead sure, dead to rights, for sure, fer shirr, for damn sure, for a fact Jack, positulely, no buts about it, checked and double-checked, and no mistake, know damm well. See CERTAIN.

UNANTICIPATED adj. from out in left field, from out of the blue, bolt from the blue, sleeper, payoff.

UNAPPETIZING adj. grody to the max, gross, yucky, icky, yicky, barfy, stinky, hocky, hooky, gooky. See UNSAVORY.

UNARMED adj. skinned, clean. See also DEFENSELESS.

UNASSAILABLE adj. bulletproof, covered.

UNATTACHED adj. loner, traveling light, solo, on one's own, paddling one's own canoe, batching it, stag, free-wheeling.

UNATTAINABLE adj. it won't fly, no go, don't have the horses, not a prayer, not a Chinaman's chance, not a chance in hell, beating a dead horse, out of pocket, no got.

UNATTENDED adj. stag, solo, by one's lonesome, on one's own.

UNATTRACTIVE adj. gross, grody, grody to the max, grimbo, roachy, earth pig, pig, dog, beast, cold biscuit, sad sack, witch, flat tire, no bargain, weird, yucky, icky, yicky, wonky. See UGLY.

UNAUTHENTIC adj. phony, queer, fake, ersatz, pirate goods, pirate labels, not what it's cracked up to be. See COUNTERFEIT.

UNAUTHORIZED adj. pirated, no-no, crooked, off base, out of line, out of bounds, over the line, racket, shady, dirty, wildcat, under the counter, under the table.

UNAVAILABLE adj. out of pocket, eighty-six, 86, pie in the sky, no got, ungettable.

UNAVAILING adj. 1. goin' round in circles, going nowhere, can't win for losin', go fight City Hall, save one's breath, not a prayer, not a snowball's chance in hell. 2. out of luck, out to lunch, never wuz, total shuck, good for nothing, shooting blanks, not work, not come off, out of it, missed the boat, can't even get arrested, can't even write home for money, can't punch his way out of a paper bag, should have stood in bed. See USELESS.

UNAVOIDABLE adj. sure as fate, sure as God made little green apples, sure as I live and breathe, all locked up, open and shut, set, come hell or high water, and no mistake. See CERTAIN.

UNAWARE adj. 1. loxed out, veged out, gorked, stoned, zonked, zonked out, spacey, spaced out, out of it, out to lunch, strung out, out cold, out like a light, on the nod, doped, mooning, moony, pipe dreaming, daydreaming, woolgathering, not all there, not with it, dead, dead to the world. 2. unhep, unhip, blind as a bat, doesn't know from nothing, haven't the foggiest, not know the score, not know the time of day, not know shit from shinola. See IGNORANT.

UNBALANCED adj. kooky, flaky, wacky, unglued, unzipped, unscrewed, have a screw loose, loose in the bean, loose in the upper story, nobody home, out to lunch, cockeyed, cockamamie, freaky, off one's head, off one's trolley, missing a few marbles, touched in the head, leak in the think tank, not all there. See CRAZY.

UNBEARABLE adj. too much, a bit much, heavy-handed, the last straw, the straw that broke the camel's back, that's it, that blows it, enough already.

UNBELIEVABLE adj. thick, thin, reachy, won't wash, won't hold water, phony, rings phony, fishy, for the birds, full of holes, for real, pure bullshit, too much, cockamamie, cockeyed, topsy-turvy, screwloose, jerky, nerky, batty, squirrely, harebrained, scatterbrained, rattlebrained, lamebrained, birdbrained, dingy, flaky, freaky, whacky, kooky, dippy, bubbleheaded, foolheaded, goofus, gump, horse's ass, horse's collar, horse's neck, horse's tail, sappy, screwy, off the wall, far out, takes the cake, beats the Dutch, not on a stack of Bibles.

UNBENDING adj. stand pat, stand by one's guns, stand one's ground, hold one's ground, hold the fort, hold the line, brick wall, stick to one's guns, dig in one's heels, set in concrete, do or die, come hell or high water, hard as nails, hard nut to crack, locked in. See STUBBORN.

UNBIASED adj. 1. call 'em as one sees 'em, straight, even-steven. 2. color blind, cold, cold turkey, the emess, on the fence, mugwumpian, mugwumpish.

UNBURDEN v. own up, fess, fess up, out with it, get it off one's chest, let it all hang out, let one's hair down. See CONFESS.

UNBUTTON v. unslough, strip.

UNCANNY adj. spooky, spookish, scary.

UNCARING adj. cold fish, cool cat, could care less, hard-boiled, hard as nails, thick-skinned, dead ass, don't give shit, just going through the motions, I should worry? See INDIFFERENT.

UNCEREMONIOUS adj. folksy, down home, laid back, easygoing, off the cuff, improv. See CASUAL. See also OFFHAND.

UNCERTAIN adj. 1. chancy, iffy, up for grabs, doubting Thomas, touchy, touch and go, on slippery ground, on ice, on thin ice, hanging by a thread. See also DANGEROUS. 2. wishy-washy, leery, pussyfoot around, run hot and cold, blow hot and cold, straddle the fence, shilly-shally, the jury's out. See DOUBTFUL.

UNCHALLENGING adj. snap, no sweat, no problem, nothing to it, like nothin', pushover, picnic, cinchy, easy as pie, duck soup, piece of cake, breeze, walkover, win in a walk, win hands down, kid stuff, child's play, lead-pipe cinch, clear sailing, free ride. See EASY.

UNCHECKED adj. runaway, wide open, loose, on the loose, let loose, cut loose, all out, funky, jag (laughing jag, crying jag), go to town. See also FREE, UNCONTROLLED.

UNCIRCUMCISED adj. blind.

UNCIRCUMSCRIBED adj. straight out, straight from the shoulder, no catch, no joker, no ifs ands or buts. See UNCONDITIONAL.

UNCIVIL adj. flip, fresh, nervy, cheeky, sassy, snippy, short, smart, smart alecky, lippy, cocky, crusty, out of line, off base. See INSOLENT.

UNCIVILIZED adj. 1. bad ass, wild ass, kill-crazy, hog-crazy. 2. boondocks, boonies, sticks, stix, wild west (anywhere west of New York).

UNCLE n. unc, unk, uncs, unks, nuncle, nunks, nunky.

UNCLEAN adj. grungy, pigpen, barn, stable, stall, scuzzy, skank, mucky. See DIRTY.

UNCLEAR adj. clouded, fuzzy, spacey. See OBSCURE.

UNCLOTHE v. peel, strip, strip to the buff, do a strip, do a striptease, get all naked, take it off, husk, shuck.

UNCLOTHED adj. bare-assed, B.A., peeled, naked as a jaybird, in one's birthday suit, in the altogether, buff, in the buff, in the raw, au naturel, skinny, wear a smile. See NUDE.

UNCOMMITTED adj. 1. cop out, don't care one way or another, don't give a shit, it's all the same to me, middle ground, middle of the road, on the fence, fence-sitter, mugwumpian, mugwumpish. See NEUTRAL. 2. free-wheeling, free-spirited, on one's own, flake, break loose, cut loose, loose wig, nonstarter. See FREE.

UNCOMMON adj. 1. kinky, kooky, freaky, offbeat, off the wall, far out, way out, out of sight, wild, screwball. See also NEW. 2. scarcer than hen's teeth, numerous as chicken lips. See STRANGE.

UNCOMMUNICATIVE adj. hush-hush, tight-lipped, close-mouthed, tight chops, clammed up, dried up, dummied up, buttoned up, garbo, on the q.t., play it close to the chest, between one and the lamp post.

UNCOMPASSIONATE adj. cutthroat, go for the jugular, killer instinct, mean machine, dog eat dog, hatchet job, take no prisoners. See also UNSYMPATHETIC.

UNCOMPREHENDING adj. nerdy, in the dark, out to lunch, out of it, blind as a bat, doesn't know one's ass from a hole in the ground, search me, haven't the foggiest, not know the score, not getting it, not be with it. See IGNORANT.

UNCOMPROMISING adj. hard line, hard core, locked, locked in, set in concrete, chiseled in stone, rock-ribbed, brick wall, dig in one's heels, stick to one's guns, hold the line, stand by one's guns, pigheaded, stubborn as a mule, stiff-necked. See STUBBORN.

UNCONCERNED adj. could care less, hard-boiled, hardhearted, hard as nails, don't give shit, don't give a hoot, it's all the same to me, that's your lookout, that's your pigeon. See INDIFFERENT.

UNCONDITIONAL adj. open, wide open, all out, flat out, straight out, straight from the shoulder, what you see is what you get, no strings, no strings attached, no holds barred, no catch, no joker, no kicker, no joker in the deck, no ifs ands or buts, no buts about it, no small print, no fine print, no small fine print, no fine print at the bottom, downright.

UNCONNECTED adj. free-wheeling, on one's own, paddle one's own canoe, indie (film).

UNCONSCIOUS adj. out, blacked out, loxed out, veged out, gorked, stoned, zonked, zonked out, spacey, spaced out, out of it, out to lunch, strung out, bombed out, out cold, out like a light, put away, on the canvas, knocked for a loop, hearing birdies, cuckoo, cooked, in a gauze, cold-cocked, flattened, feeling no pain, passed out, passed out cold, on the nod, doped, mooning, moony, pipe dreaming, daydreaming, woolgathering, not all there, not with it, dead, dead to the world, cockeyed, blotto, auger in, crump, crimped out (from drinking).

UNCONTROLLABLE adj. loose cannon, having a spaz attack, freaked, freaked out. See also EXCITED.

UNCONTROLLED adj. ape shit, go ape, hemorrhage, jerked about, off the wall, on a tear, kicking up a row, burn one's candle at both ends, out of order. See UNRESTRAINED.

UNCONVENTIONAL adj. freaky, kooky, beat, beatnik, offbeat, off the beaten track, weirdo, weirdie, oddball, avant-garde, fringy, kinky, hippy, far out, way out, wild, crazy, off the wall, out in left field. See ECCENTRIC.

UNCONVINCING adj. cut no ice, fishy, thin, thick, iffy. See also DOUBTFUL.

UNCOORDINATED adj. klutzy, clunky, flubdub, all thumbs, butterfingers, ham-fisted, two left hands, two left feet, clodhopper, galoot. See CLUMSY.

UNCOUNTABLE adj. lots, zillion, jillion, umpteen, oodles, oodles and oodles. See COUNTLESS.

UNCOUTH adj. cheap, loud, loud-mouthed, raw, skank, tacky, raunchy.

UNCOVER v. 1. hit upon, spark, strike (oil, gold), see the light, stumble on, spotlight, limelight. 2. crack, break, leak, dig up, let the cat out of the bag, giveaway, give the show away, spill the beans, tip one's hand, let it all hang out, open up, blow one's cover, blow the lid off, blow the whistle, mooning (buttocks), streak. See EXPOSE. 3. catch flatfooted, catch red-handed, catch with one's pants down, catch with one's hand in the cookie jar. See DISCOVER. See also CAUGHT IN THE ACT.

UNCOVERED adj. 1. bare-assed, buck naked, naked as a jaybird, in one's birthday suit, in the altogether, in the raw, without a stitch on, au naturel. See NUDE. 2. ass out, neck stuck out, wide open, sitting duck, on the line, on the spot, out on a limb, up the creek without a paddle. See also CAUGHT.

UNCTUOUS adj. 1. greasy, plummy, smarmy. 2. gift of gab, great talker, slick, smooth, smoothie, smooth apple, smooth operator, smooth article, waxer. See also HYPOCRITICAL, SANCTIMONIOUS.

UNDAUNTED adj. spunky, fire-eater, iceman, ice in one's veins, come on strong, got the faith baby. See FEARLESS.

UNDECIDED adj.   iffy, fence straddle, fence hanger, on the fence, sit on the fence, run hot and cold, blow hot and cold, hedge, hedge off, shilly-shally, wimpy, wishy-washy, waffle, waffling, hem and haw, pussyfoot, pussyfoot around, betwixt and between, hanging fire, stuck, the jury's out, up for grabs, up in the air, between sixes and sevens, dipypdro.

UNDEMONSTRATIVE adj.   cool, cool customer, cold fish, ice in one's veins, icicle.

UNDENIABLE adj.   absofuckinglutely, posilutely, absitively, sure as can be, sure thing, surest thing you know, surefire, for sure, fer sher, fer shure, fer shirr, for damn sure, for a fact, on ice, have down cold, no buts about it, no ifs ands or buts, open and shut, checked and double-checked. See CERTAIN.

UNDEPENDABLE adj.   1. wrong number, loose, fly-by-night, no-good, N.G., no account, no bargain, trust one as far as one can swing a cat, trust one as far as one can throw an elephant. See DISHONEST. 2. honest John, rat, fink, rat fink, stool pigeon, stoolie, shit heel, shit hook, worm, tinhorn, bum, clown, convict. See also DANGEROUS.

UNDERACT v.   throw away.

UNDER CONSIDERATION adj.   on the table, on the line, in the works, on the boards, on the fire, jury is out.

UNDERCAPITALIZED adj.   on a shoestring, hand-to-mouth operation.

UNDERCOVER adj.   creep (mission), tref, triff, under wraps, hush-hush, doggo, incog, q.t., on the q.t. on the quiet, in a hole-and-corner way, in holes and corners, wildcat. See also SECRET.

UNDERGARMENTS n.   undies, underthings, unmentionables, bra, briefs, bikinis, panties, bodystocking, teddy, woollies, shorts, jockey shorts, jockeys. See UNDERWEAR.

UNDERGRADUATE n.   undergrad.

UNDERGROUND adj.   in a hole-and-corner way, in holes and corners, on the q.t., on the quiet, on the sly, undercover, under wraps, hush-hush, strictly hush-hush. See also SECRET.

UNDERHANDED adj.   1. shady, double-crossing, snake in the grass, two-faced, two-timing, dirty-dealing, dirty pool, slippery. 2. undercover, under wraps, hush-hush, strictly hush-hush, on the q.t., on the quiet, on the sly, in a hole-and-corner way, in holes and corners, wildcat. See DECEITFUL. See also SECRET.

UNDERLING n.   peon, serf, slave, girl Friday, gofer, dweeb, yes-man, stooge, running dog, low man on the totem pole, second fiddle, second string, third string, flunky, spear carrier, second banana. See INFERIOR.

UNDERLYING adj.   bottom line, nitty-gritty, where it's at, name, name of the game, cold, cold turkey, nub, meat and potatoes, coal and ice. See BASIC.

UNDERMINE v.   blow sky high, knock the bottom out of, knock the chocks out from under, knock the props out from under, poke full of holes, shoot full of holes, clip one's wings, soften up, sandbag, torpedo (a plan), toss in a monkey wrench. See also SABOTAGE.

UNDERPLAY v.   downplay, play down, gloss over, soft-pedal, throw away, cover up, lay back, play it cool, make light of, take it lightly, take it like water off a duck's back, not bat an eye, not blink an eye, just stand there with a mouth full of teeth.

UNDERPRICED adj.   cheapie, el cheapo, dirt cheap, cheap as dirt, dog cheap, steal, a real steal, buy, a real buy, low cost, cost nothing, cost next to nothing, bought for a song, cut rate, low tariff.

UNDERPRIVILEGED n.   truly needy, hard up, oof-less, down and out, have-nots, in dire straits, in Queer Street, seen better days, piss-poor, dirt-poor, poor as a church mouse, cold in hand (Bl.), for the yoke. See also DESTITUTE.

UNDERREACT v.   lay back, play it cool, make light of, take it lightly, not bat an eye, just stand there with a mouth full of teeth. See UNDERPLAY.

UNDERSIZED adj.   mini, minny, teeny, teeny-weeny, bitty, bitsy, shrimpy, wee, peewee, runty, small fry, measly, piddling, pint-sized, half-pint. See SMALL.

UNDERSTAND v.   get, get it, grok, gotcha, get the idea, get the point, get the picture, get a handle on it, get the hang of it, get next to, get next to oneself, get jerry, get through one's head, get through one's thick head, get into, get into one's head, get it into one's thick skull, hive (West Point), get across, get over, get it down, have down cold, have down pat, get down pat, get down cold, get the hang of, get the message, get the drift, catch the drift, catch, catch on, flash, flash on, latch on, latch on to something, get hold of, pick up, pick up on, wise up, wise up to, blow wise, get wise to, hep to, hep up, hip up, soak up, get hep, get hip, be hip to, follow, track, feature, cop, collar, collar the jive, colly (Bl.), compy, wake up and smell the coffee, take, take in, tumble, tumble to, quick on the draw, quick on the uptake, savvy, capeesh, fershtay, dig, I dig you, make, pin, copy, read, I read you, read someone loud and clear, hear, hear it, I hear you, I hear you talkin', I know where you're coming from, see the light, see daylight, are one's boots laced?, have one's boots laced, peg, peg a setup, figure out, be with it, be with one, be on the beam, right on, right-o, give one some slack, rumble, know what's what, know one's ass from one's elbow, know a rock from a hard place, know crossways from crosswise, have dead to rights, have one's number.

UNDERSTANDABLE adj. open and shut, clear as the nose on one's face, plain as the nose on one's face. See APPARENT.

UNDERSTANDING n. 1. tuned in, cool, down, simpatico, on the same beam, on the same wavelength, grokking, have a heart. 2. aha reaction, savvy, hep to, wise to, see the light, flash on it, get one's drift, I got it, it hit me, it just come to me, double take, slow take, take, take it big, get it through one's thick skull. 3. deal, dicker, handshake. See AGREEMENT.

UNDERSTATE v. throw away.

UNDERSTATED adj. low profile, soft-pedalled, glossed over.

UNDERSTOOD adj. roger, roger dodger, grokked, gotcha, got, got it, got the picture, hep to, on to, pat, down pat, wise to, pegged, dug, know where one is coming from, picked up on.

UNDERSTUDY n. backup, backup man, pinch hitter, stand-in, sub. See also SUBSTITUTE.

UNDERSTUDY v. back up, pinch hit for, stand in for, sub, take over for, fill in for. See also SUBSTITUTE.

UNDERTAKE v. tackle, take on, make a run at, give it a try, give it a go, give it a whirl, take a shot at, have a go at, go in for, go for broke. See ATTEMPT.

UNDERTAKEN adv. in the hopper, in the pipeline, in the works, taken on.

UNDERTAKER n. body snatcher, crepe hanger, black coat, Digger O'Dell.

UNDERTAKING n. 1. crack, fling, go, jelly go, shot, stab, try, whack, fling, header. See ATTEMPT. 2. proposition, deal, racket, thing, grift, play, beeswax, job, what one is into, biz, gesheft, outfit, setup, shop, turnkey operation, carrying on, goings-on, hap, happening. See also ENTERPRISE.

UNDERWEAR n. undies, underthings, unmentionables, bra, briefs, bikinis, panties, bodystocking, teddy, step-ins, drawers, BVD's, beeveedees, woollies, skivvies, shorts, jockey shorts, jockeys; big eights (Bl.), longies, John L's, long-handle underwear, long Johns, long ones (long).

UNDERWEIGHT adj. skinny, skeleton, shadow, bag of bones, stack of bones, rattlebones, gangly. See THIN.

UNDERWORLD n. the rackets, the mob, the syndicate, Mafia, Cosa Nostra, Black Hand, blaht, blot. See also HELL.

UNDERWRITE v. angel, bankroll, grubstake, stake, back. See FINANCE.

UNDESIRABLE adj. 1. fat city, motherfucking, mother grabbing, nowhere, sucks, it sucks, grody, grody to the max, gross, grossed out, uncool, rotten, beastly, sleazy, yucky, icky, yicky, hairy, bitchy, goonk, bummer, bum trip, bad news, bad scene, godawful, goshawful, left-handed, eighteen carat, murder, nuts, poison, rough, sad, fierce, something fierce, hard time, lousy, who needs it, need it like a hole in the head, this I need yet?, from hunger, for the birds, Nimby (not in my backyard), excess baggage, drug on the market. 2. blackballed, cold-shouldered, left out in the cold, not in the picture, shut out.

UNDESIRABLE PERSON n. creep, dork, rat, wrongo, drip, stinker, stinkpot, shit, shithead, sleaze, sleazeball, slime bucket, maggot, turkey, jerk, fink, gross, loser, louse, lousy, meatball, nerd, schmo, shmoe, weirdo, goon, bad case of the uglies, banana, out, out of it, dumb cluck, dummy, mince, mole, nothing, simp, spastic, weenie, wimp, cotton-picker, dipstick, arrowhead, for the birds, twerp, yo-yo, zombie, corpse, droop, herkle, prune, specimen, roach, toad, phrog, potato digger, won't give one the time of day, gives one a pain, gives one a pain in the neck, gives one a pain in the ass, gripes one's ass, wallflower, can't see one for dust, ho dad, ho daddy, funky, Joe Sad (Bl.).

UNDESIRED adj. lousy, who needs it, need it like a hole in the head, this I need yet? from hunger, for the birds, Nimby (not in my backyard), excess baggage, drug on the market.

UNDETERMINED adj. iffy, on the fence, run hot and cold, blow hot and cold, hedge off, shilly-shally, betwixt and between, hanging fire, the jury's out, up for grabs. See UNDECIDED.

UNDEVELOPED adj. half-assed, half-baked, half-cocked.

UNDEVIATING adj. as the crow flies, beeline, down the alley, down the pipe, in the groove, on the beam, slam bang.

UNDILUTED adj. neat, straight, uncut, right outta the bottle, all wool and a yard wide, honest to God, twenty-four carat.

UNDISGUISED adj. barefaced, plain as the nose on one's face, under one's nose, big as life, out in the open, open and shut, if it were a snake it would bite you. See OBVIOUS.

UNDISTINGUISHED adj. vanilla, plain vanilla, garden variety, rumdum, run of the alley, run of the mill, starch, no great shakes. See AVERAGE.

UNDIVIDED adj. jackpot, the works, lock stock and barrel, whole enchilada, whole ball of wax, whole nine yards, whole shebang, whole shooting match, everything including the kitchen sink. See WHOLE.

UNDO v. 1. adjy, get to, flip out, craze, bug, make waves, make a scene, make a fuss, give one a turn, give one a bad time, give one a hard time, put the needles in, stir up, rattle, discombobulate, discombobulate. See AGITATE. 2. queer, crimp, cramp, stymie, skin, snooker, crab, hang up, hold up, fuck up, bollix, gum up the works, upset one's apple cart, spike one's guns, take care of. See CANCEL. See also DEFEAT. 3. psych out, unglue, unzip, get to, blow up, blow out, take apart, take the steam out, send up, send up the balloon.

UNDONE adj. 1. rattled, thrown, fussed, shook up, lost one's cool, shot, shot to pieces, psyched out, unglued, unscrewed, unzipped. 2. sunk, gone, goner, dead duck, can't win for losin', no more cards to play, at the end of one's rope, in deep shit, runnin' out of time, got one's back to the wall, fighting to keep one's head up. See also DEFEATED.

UNDRESS v. peel, strip, strip to the buff, do a strip, do a striptease, get all naked, slip out of, take it off, husk, shuck.

UNEARTH v. hit upon, spark, strike (oil, gold), see the light, stumble on, dig up, spotlight, limelight.

UNEARTHLY adj. spooky, spookish, scary.

UNEASY adj. uptight, jittery, jumpy, strung out, unglued, hyper, spooked, wreck, nervous wreck, bundle of nerves, yantsy, antsy, in a state, in a dither, on edge, biting one's nails. See ANXIOUS. See also DISTURBED, TROUBLED.

UNEDUCATED adj. galoot, lowbrow, ignoramus.

UNEMOTIONAL adj. 1. cool, laid back, flat, cold, cold fish, cool cat, ice man, iceberg, mean machine, thick-skinned, dead ass, deadpan. See CALLOUS. 2. wimpy, blah, go along for the ride, go with the flow.

UNEMOTIONALLY adv. deadpan, in cold blood, with a poker face, with a straight face.

UNEMPLOYED adj. at liberty, between engagements, on layoff, on the shelf, on the bench, on the beach, on the dole, on the turf, out of the rat race, out of action, out of the swim, down, closed down, bum, in short pants, shuffler, skuffling.

UNENCUMBERED adj. traveling light, no strings, fancy free. See FREE.

UNENDURABLE adj. bit much, too much, enough already, had it up to here, last straw, straw that broke the camel's back, that's it, that blows it.

UNENLIGHTENED adj. uncool, unhep, unhip, mushroom, in the dark, out to lunch, doesn't know one's ass from first base, haven't the foggiest, not know a rock from a hard place, not know shit from shinola. See IGNORANT.

UNENTERTAINING adj. draggy, draddy, ho hum, bor-ring, bore one stiff, yawn, big yawn, zero, big zero. See BORING.

UNEQUAL adj. diff, poles apart, weird, whale of a difference, like night and day, march to the beat of a different drummer.

UNEQUIVOCAL adj. tell it like it is, flat out, straight out, absofuckinglutely, no strings attached, no holds barred, no catch, no joker, no kicker, no fine print at the bottom, no ifs ands or buts, no buts about it, downright, straight, straight dope, right on, open and shut. See CERTAIN.

UNEQUIVOCALLY adv. flat out, come hell or high water, cert, amen, sure, why sure, you know it, you better believe it, you betcher life, no strings attached, no holds barred, no catch, no kicker, no buts about it, no ifs ands or buts, in spades. See ABSOLUTELY.

UNESSENTIAL adj. minimal to the max, gadget, never mind, no matter, chicken feed, chicken shit, macht nichts, mox nix, makes no never mind, no great shakes, mere bagatelle, row of buttons, row of pins. See UNIMPORTANT.

UNETHICAL adj. 1. bent, shady, sharp, wrong, double-crossing, motherdangle, motherfucking, mother rucking, hanky-panky, snake in the grass, two-faced, two-timing, dirty, low-down and dirty, dirty work, dirty-dealing, dirty pool, dirty trick, crooked, crooked stick, cheatin', cheatin' heart, fishy, gyp, not kosher, wrong number, wrong gee, Honest John, feather-legs, slick, slippery, speak with forked tongue, sellout, put-on, scam, fake, flam, flimflam, shell game, skin game, fly-by-night, Judas kiss, stab in the back, crocodile tears, whitewash job. 2. on the sly, in a hole-and-corner way, in holes and corners.

UNEXCEPTIONAL adj. so-so, fair, fair to middling, run of the mill, garden variety, no great shakes, strictly union, vanilla. See AVERAGE.

UNEXCITABLE adj. cool, cool as a cucumber, keep one's cool, keep one's shirt on, not turn a hair, roll with the punches, unflappable. See also CALM.

UNEXCITING adj. draggy, draddy, dull as dishwater, ho hum, bor-ring, yawn, big yawn, nowhere, noplaceville, Nadaville, dullsville, flat tire, flat as a pancake, pablum, dog. See BORING.

UNEXPECTED adj. from out in left field, from out of the blue, bolt from the blue, sleeper, payoff.

UNEXPLODED adj. dud, UXB.

UNFAILING adj. there, count on one, one who always delivers, one who always comes through, always there in a pinch, rock, Rock of Gibraltar, Rocka Gibraltar, Rocka Gib, The Rock, straight arrow, dyed in the wool. See TRUSTWORTHY.

UNFAIR adj. fix, fixed, low, low blow, below the belt, hitting below the belt, not cricket, raw deal, dirty, dirty trick, dirty pool, low-down, low-down and dirty, cheap shot, cold duck, dog, feather-legs, half a shake.

UNFAITHFUL adj. double-crossing, snaky, snake in the grass, worm, two-faced, two-timing, cheating, cheating heart, moonlighting, chippy on one, sneakin' deacon, stepping out on one, tip, witch, dog one around, working late at the office, yard on. See also INFIDELITY.

UNFALTERING adj. dead set on, bent on, hell bent on, mean business, bound, bound and determined, stick at nothing, set, sot, unflappable, bulletheaded, pigheaded, stiff-necked, mulish, stubborn as a mule, the game ain't over til the last man is out, sticking to one's guns, hanging in, going all the way. See also CERTAIN.

UNFASHIONABLE adj. tired, out, not with it, old hat, passé, back number, moth-eaten, moldy fig, corny, horse and buggy, ricky-tick, gasser. See DATED.

UNFASTEN v. unslough, strip.

UNFATHOMABLE adj. heavy, too deep for one, clear as mud, it beats me, I pass, tough nut to crack. See OBSCURE.

UNFAVORABLE adj. debit side, on the debit side, down side, the bad news.

UNFEELING adj. cold, cold fish, cool cat, cold-blooded, ice man, thick-skinned, dead ass, deadpan, with a straight face, poker face. See CALLOUS.

UNFINISHED adj. half-assed, half-baked, half-cocked, holiday (task).

UNFIT adj. 1. draggin', draggin' one's ass, rocky, seedy, down, run down, laid low, below par, peaked, poorly, outta action, out of shape, good and flabby, 4-F. See also ILL. 2. uncool, not cut out for, can't hack it, can't cut it, can't cut the mustard, can't make the grade, sidelined, out of commission, hog-tied. See also INAPPROPRIATE. 3. out to lunch, bringdown, amateur night, amateur night in Dixie, not have it, Mickey Mouse, bush, bush league, haywire, dead one, lame brained, dub, flubdub, half-assed, half-baked, fumble-fist, butterfingers, muff. See INCOMPETENT.

UNFITTING adj. bad form, off base, off-color, out of line, garbage.

UNFLINCHING adj. spunk, spunky, bodacious, brass, brassy, bold as brass, ballsy, gutsy, gutty, gutiness, gutsiness, grit, gritty, nerve, nervy, chutzpahdik, tough it out, fire-eater, cool hand, iceman, ice in one's veins. See also FEARLESS, STUBBORN.

UNFORMED adj. baggy, blobby.

UNFORSEEN adj. from out in left field, bolt from the blue.

UNFORTUNATE adj. 1. jinxed, hoodooded, voodooed, behind the eight ball, jonah, joner, snakebit,

loser, sure loser, winner, real winner, fuck up, sad sack, dick in the dirt, schlemiel, schlemazel, hard case, down on one's luck, tough luck, rotten luck, shit out of luck, S.O.L., bad break, rotten break, tough break, out of luck, hard-luck guy, flop, bust, loser, goner, dead, dead duck, beat, deadbeat, dead pigeon, bum, turkey, poor fish, in the toilet, in deep water, in the dumper, in above one's head, blown out of the water, down, down the drain, down and out, out of it, clambake, also ran, losing streak, went down like the Titanic, get nowhere, never passed, never passed go, missed the boat, on the skids, back to the drawing board, can't even get arrested, can't even write home for money, can't punch his way out of a paper bag, should have stood in bed, fall on one's face, fall flat on one's face, fall on one's ass, washout, washed out, washed up. 2. abortion, hurting, clinker, cruller, brodie, foldo, down the drain, down the chute, down the toilet, chapter eleven, go chapter eleven, behind the eight ball, lumpy, on the rocks.

UNFOUNDED adj. bullshit, hot air, off base, cockeyed, who sez?, my eye, just talk, whataya talkin', you're talkin' like a man with a paper ass, where'd ya get that shit?, pie in the sky. See GROUNDLESS.

UNFRIENDLY adj. 1. cool, cold, cold fish, loner, lone wolf, laid back, stuck up, uppity, offish, standoffish. See ALOOF. 2. scrappy, bitchy, salty, spiky, cantankerous, fire-eater, have a chip on one's shoulder, at outs, on the outs, allergic to, down on, turned off by. See ANTAGONISTIC.

UNGAINLY adj. klutzy, clunky, all thumbs, butterfingers, two left hands, two left feet, galoot. See CLUMSY.

UNGENEROUS adj. close, stingy, penny-pinching, tight, tightwad, last of the big spenders, tight as a drum, skinflint, skin, screw, Scotch, piker, chintzy, scrimpy, skimpy. See STINGY.

UNGRAMMATICAL adj. murder the King's English, murder the Queen's English, Mrs. Malaprop.

UNHAMPERED adj. 1. no strings, no strings attached, no holds barred, no catch, no joker, no kicker, no joker in the deck. See UNCONDITIONAL. 2. footloose, footloose and fancy free, free-wheeling, break loose, cut loose, loose wig, on one's own, shoot the moon, all hanging out. See FREE.

UNHANDY adj. klutz, clunker, dub, jerk, flubdub, amateur, amateur night in Dixie, all thumbs, butterfingers, two left hands, two left feet, not cut out for. See CLUMSY.

UNHAPPY adj. 1. dragged, ripped, low, destroyed, dragging ass, ass in a sling, have one's ass in a sling, dick in the dirt, blue, blue funk, in a blue funk, funky, grim, got the blue devils, in the toilet, in the dumper, in the dumps, down, a downer, on a downer, let down, taken down, taken down a peg, taken down a peg or two, down in the dumps, in the doleful dumps, down and out, down in the mouth, downbeat (movie, song, etc.), low-down, crummy, cleek, pruneface, sob story, sob stuff, tear jerker, weeper, teardrop special, make like an alligator, have the blues, singing the blues, crying the blues, hang crepe, on a bummer, bummed out, flaked out, put away, carry the torch, hurting, bleeding, in pain, in the pits, shook, shot down, should have stood in bed, carry a heavy load, off one's feed, rhino, have the mulligrubs, have the dolefuls, have the blahs, clanked, clanked up, cracked up, tore up, all torn up, droopy, mopey, moony, gloomy Gus, wet blanket, raining on one's parade, sad sacky, killjoy, pruneface, prunefaced, sourpuss, spring fever. See also DESPAIRING. 2. sour, beefing, bitching, kicking, bellyaching, crabbing, crabby, kvetching, cranky, griping, grouchy, grousing, raining on one's parade.

UNHEALTHY adj.   draggin', draggin' one's ass, rocky, seedy, down, run down, laid low, below par, peaky, peaked, poorly, out of action, out of shape, good and flabby, 4-F. See also ILL.

UNHEEDING adj.   1. slapdash, sloppy, any old way, any which way, helter-skelter, devil may care, leave oneself wide open, play with fire, go overboard. See CARELESS. 2. pay no mind, looking out the window, out to lunch, asleep at the switch, daydreaming, mooning, airheaded. See PREOCCUPIED.

UNHINDERED adj.   1. no strings, no strings attached, no holds barred, no catch, no joker, no kicker, no joker in the deck. 2. footloose, footloose and fancy free, free-spirited, free-wheeling, loose wig, on one's own, let down one's hair, all hanging out. See FREE.

UNHINGED adj.   dingy, dingaling, unglued, unzipped, unscrewed, loose in the upper story, schitzy, schizzed out, schitzoid, psycho, psyched out, freaked out, flipped out, out of one's gourd, in the ozone, cracked up, off one's nut, off one's rocker, off one's trolley, cutting out paper dolls, cuckoo, gone, not all there, round the bend, squirrelly. See CRAZY.

UNHURRIED adj.   pokey, slowpoke, draggy, shlepper, banana boat, slower than the seven-year itch. See SLOW.

UNIDENTIFIED FLYING OBJECT n.   UFO, flying saucer, spaceship.

UNIFICATION CHURCH MEMBER n.   Moonie.

UNIFORM adj.   xerox, carbon copy, ditto, double, dead ringer, lookalike, like two peas in a pod, spit and image, spittin' image, one beat, same difference.

UNIFORM n.   O.D., khakis, the suit, olive drab, bag, in the bag (in uniform), pickle suit (Marines), getup, monkey clothes, monkey jacket, state o, tar bucket, tit cap, harness, sailor suit, soldier suit, stripes (prison).

UNIMAGINATIVE adj.   pablum, zero, bromidic, vanilla, square, ho hum, dull as dishwater, flat, flat as a pancake, dime a dozen, noplaceville, meat-and-potatoes man. See PROSAIC.

UNIMPEDED adj.   1. no holds barred, no catch, no joker, no kicker, no joker in the deck, no strings, no strings attached. See UNCONDITIONAL. 2. footloose, footloose and fancy free, free-spirited, free-wheeling, break loose, cut loose, loose wig, wide open. See FREE.

UNIMPORTANT adj.   1. diddly, squat, diddly squat, diddly poo, doodly squat, shit, beans, Jack, borscht, 86, nada, nix, zero, big zero, zip, zippo, zilch, nothing, cipher, goose egg, collar, horse collar, fly speck, flea, chit, chirp, chromosome, crum, crumb, drip, dinky, measly, minimal to the max, from nothing, Mickey Mouse, gadget, rinkydink, nutmeg, two by four, two bit, nickel and dime, penny ante, peanuts, pissy-tailed, pissy-assed, scratch, big deal, big fucking deal, BFD, no big deal, big shit, no biggie, no big thing, no skin off one's nose, never mind, no matter, chicken feed, chicken shit, bupkis, hump, shot, tinhorn, bottom rung, lower rung, small potatoes, small beer, small change, small time, small pot, pokerino, pinchy, one horse, nowhere, drop in the bucket, drop in the ocean, sucking wind, little go, mox nix, makes no never mind, no great shakes, mere bagatelle, frig it, chuck it, drop it, forget it, let it pass, skip it, doesn't amount to a bucket of warm piss, not worth a hill of beans, not worth a row of beans, row of buttons, row of pins, damn, darn, tinker's dam, hoot, got other fish to fry, other fish in the sea, other pebbles on the beach, raggedy act, harlot's hello. 2. wimpy, wuss, jerky, sad sack, semi-dork, nebbish, squirt, twerp, shrimp, scrub, runt, little guy, small potatoes, small fry, low level Munchkin, cipher, zilch, zip, zippo, zero, big zero, nobody, Mr. and Mrs. Nobody, Brown Jones and Robinson, John Doe and Mary Roe, Jane Doe and Richard Roe, Tom Dick and Harry, spear carrier, pushover, winner, real winner, dog, loser, real loser, punk, tinhorn, flat tire, dud, skag, pip-squeak, whippersnapper, whiffet, flash in the pan, man with a paper ass, jackstraw, man of straw.

UNIMPRESSIVE adj.   big zero, underwhelming, nowhere, dog, loser, real loser, winner, real winner, cut no ice, big deal, no big deal, big shit, no big shit, downer, dullsville, flat, flat tire, does nothing for one. See also SMALL, UNIMPORTANT.

UNINFORMED adj.   uncool, unhep, unhip, airhead, a mushroom, in the dark, doesn't know from nothing, doesn't know one's ass from first base, doesn't know one's ass from a hole in the ground, big know-it-all, not be with it. See IGNORANT.

UNINHIBITED adj.   off the cuff, all hanging out, break loose, cut loose, loose wig, footloose, footloose and fancy free, free-wheeling, no holds barred, fly kites, let down one's hair, off the wall. See SPONTANEOUS.

UNINITIATED adj.   cherry.

UNINSPIRED adj.   phoned in, corny, bromidic, old hat, everyday, square, ho hum, yawn, big yawn, flat, flat as a pancake, flat tire. See PROSAIC.

UNINSURED adj.   go bare.

UNINTELLIGENT adj.   nerdy, numbnut, lamebrain, birdbrain, nobody home, dummy, dumbo, dumdum, dumb bunny, dumb cluck, dumb Dora, dumb head, four-letter man (dumb), bonetop, boob, nincompoop, musclehead, blockhead, fathead, bonehead, numb brained, doesn't know from A to B, doesn't know which way is up, stoop, stupe, got a hole in the head, leak in the think tank, nuthin' upstairs, jackass, dimwit. See STUPID.

UNINTELLIGIBLE adj.   clear as mud, double Dutch, Greek, unreadable, breaking up (radio signal). See OBSCURE.

UNINTERESTED adj.   don't give a shit, don't give a damm, don't give a hoot, phone it in, could care less, bored stiff, hard-boiled, hardhearted, rhinoceros hide, thick-skinned, dead ass, just going through the motions, walk through it, what's the diff?, what the hell, so what?, so what else is new?, it's all the same to me, that's your lookout, that's your pigeon, I should worry, clock-watcher, turned off. See also INDIFFERENT.

UNINTERESTING adj.   1. blah, draggy, dull as dishwater, ho hum, bor-ring, big yawn, nowhere, noplaceville, Nadaville, Dullsville, nothing, tired, flat, big zero. See BORING. 2. beige, drip, grass, grass out, Irving, Melvin, party-pooper, stick in the mud, wet blanket, wonky.

UNINTIMIDATED adj.   ballsy, gutsy, gritty, nervy, spunky, brassy, bold as brass, fire-eater, ice in one's veins, come on strong, cocky, cocksure, cool hand. See FEARLESS.

UNINVITED adj.   buttinsky, crasher, gate-crasher.

UNION n.   1. local, syndicate. 2. tie-up, tie-in, tie-in tie-up, hookup. See ASSOCIATION.

UNION CARD n.   pie card.

UNION LABEL n.   bug, union bug (printing).

UNION MEETING n.   chapel, chapel meeting.

UNION MEMBER n.   brother, sister, pork chopper, Jimmie Higgins.

UNION ORGANIZER n.   labor skate.

UNIQUE adj.   1. onliest, offbeat, off the beaten track, bent, weird, weirdo, grody, grody to the max, strange one, oddball, goof ball, special, wrinkle, new wrinkle, an original, cool, fringy, flaky, far out, way out, out of sight, wild, crazy, off the wall, out in left field, trippy, fly ball, gooney, gooney bird, rare bird, loner, three-dollar bill,

gonzo, character, scarcer than hen's teeth, numerous as chicken lips. 2. unreal, out of sight, standout, best ever, primo, something else, far out, the most, the utmost, the end. See EXCELLENT. 3. state of the art, the leading edge, the cutting edge, breaking new snow, avant-garde, last word, the latest, latest thing, latest wrinkle. See NEW.

UNIT n.   bunch, crew, crowd, gang, mob, outfit, ring.

UNITE v.   1. tag on, tack on, slap on, hitch on, piggyback, plug into, cross dissolve (film), cue in (scripts, ms., songs), dub, hook in, marry (film), mix (recording). 2. pool, hook up, go partners with, take up with, get in with, get together, join up with, meld with, play ball with, throw in with, gang up with. See ASSOCIATE.

UNITED adj.   hooked up with, in cahoots with, joined up with, lined up with, partners with, thrown in with, tied in with, plugged into.

UNITED NATIONS CHILDREN'S FUND n.   UNICEF.

UNITED NATIONS EDUCATIONAL, SCIENTIFIC, AND CULTURAL ORGANIZATION n.   UNESCO.

UNITED STATES   U.S., U.S.A., States, stateside, lower forty-eight, Lower 48, Mainland, CONUS (continental United States), coast to coast, Uncle Sam, Uncle Sap, Uncle Sham, Uncle Sugar, Uncle Whiskers, Whiskers, Mr. Whiskers, the old man with the whiskers, Yankee land, Brother Jonathan, melting pot.

UNITED STATES ARMY RANKS   brass, brass hat, gold braid, barbed wire, skipper, skip, old man, buck general (brigadier); chicken colonel, bird colonel, buzzard colonel; lieut, looey, second looey, shavetail, 90 day wonder (2nd Lt.); butcher (M.D.), buggy bitchers (field artillery, cavalry 1930), mustang (risen from the ranks), ossifer, goat, dust dust (newly promoted); buckass private, NCO, one-striper, PFC (private first class), poor fucking civilian, two-striper (corporal), sarge, kick, topkick.

UNITED STATES CAPITOL n.   the hill.

UNITED STATES DEPARTMENT OF HOUSING AND URBAN DEVELOPMENT n.   HUD.

UNITED STATES DEPARTMENT OF STATE n.   Foggy Bottom, State.

UNITED STATES FLAG n.   Stars and Stripes, red white and blue, Star-Spangled Banner, Old Glory, Old Betsy, Stars and Bars (Confederacy).

UNITED STATES GOVERNMENT n.   feds, Uncle Sam, Uncle Sugar, Washington.

UNITED STATES MARINE BASE n.   green machine.

UNITED STATES NAVY RANKS   scrambled eggs (Commander and up), crow (chief or captain), broken striper (warrant officer), buffer (chief boatswain's mate); hack driver, C.P.O. (chief petty officer).

UNIVERSAL adj. multinational, anational.

UNIVERSITY n. alma mater, old Siwash, brainery, aggie, cow college, fem sem, Ivy League, halls of ivy.

UNJUST adj. fixed, raw deal, dirty pool, low-down and dirty, hitting below the belt, cheap shot. See UNFAIR.

UNKEMPT adj. sloppy, grubby, grungy, chili bowl, scuzzy, scuzzed up, messed up, mussed up, messy, mussy, seedy, down at the heel, out at the heels, out at the elbows. See SLOVENLY.

UNKNOWN adj. 1. unk-unks, pig in a poke, X, x factor, whatsis, what's its name, whatzit. 2. certain person, Joe Doakes, Jane Doe, John Doe, Cheap John, Joe Blow, Mr. X, George Spelvin, so and so, such and such, whatchamacallit, what d'ya call em, what's his name, what's his face, you know who, incog, bearding. 3. off the map, over the edge, off the street, points west.

UNLICENSED adj. wildcat, bandit (taxicab).

UNLIKE adj. diff, far cry, funky, offbeat, poles apart, weird, whale of a difference, like night and day, march to the beat of a different drummer.

UNLIKELIHOOD n. hundred-to-one shot, it don't figure, not in the cards, not a chance in hell, outside chance. See IMPROBABILITY.

UNLIMITED adj. no end of, no end to, wide open, no strings, no strings attached, no holds barred, no catch, no joker, no kicker, no joker in the deck, no ifs ands or buts, more than you can shake a stick at. See also COUNT-LESS.

UNLOAD v. dump, get it off one's chest, take the load off one's chest, take a load off, take the load off one's mind. See also SELL.

UNLOCK v. loid, jimmy.

UNLUCKY adj. hoodooded, behind the eight ball, snakebit, hard-luck guy, down on one's luck, tough luck, rotten luck, bad break, left-handed, poor fish, dead pigeon. See UNFORTUNATE.

UNMAN v. cut off one's balls, deball, fix, alter.

UNMANLY adv. 1. faggy, swishy, pansy, pantywaist, old woman, sissy, goody-goody, pretty boy, weak sister, mama's boy. See EFFEMINATE. 2. wimpy, yellow-bellied, 'fraidy cat, scaredy cat, rabbity, mousy, jellyfish, chicken, lily-livered, Casper Milquetoast, weak sister, nerd, candy ass, pucker-assed. See COWARDLY.

UNMARKETABLE adj. stuck with, white elephant, gotta eat it.

UNMARRIED adj. batch, old batch, old maid, single, single-o, cherry, canned goods, bug.

UNMASK v. give away, give the show away, spill the beans, come out, come out of the closet, let it all hang out, blow one's cover, spring, spring one's duke, debunk, blow the lid off, blow the whistle. See EXPOSE.

UNMETHODICALLY adv. any old way, any which way, hit or miss, slapdash, half-assed, all over the shop. See ERRATICALLY.

UNMINDFUL adj. pay no mind, out to lunch, asleep at the switch, woolgathering, popcorn headed, airheaded. See FORGETFUL.

UNMISTAKABLE adj. no buts about it, no ifs ands or buts, open and shut, for certain, absofuckinglutely, posilutely, absitively, dead sure, dead to rights. See CERTAIN.

UNMOVED adj. unflappable, not turn a hair, could care less, strong-faced, hard-boiled, hardhearted, hard as nails, rhinoceros hide, dead ass, butter wouldn't melt in one's mouth, poker-faced, don't give shit, so what? See INDIFFERENT.

UNNAMED adj. 1. X, X factor, brand X, whatsis, what's its name, whatzit, unk-unks, pig in a poke. 2. Jane Doe, John Doe, Joe Blow, Mr. X, whatchamacallit, what's-his-name, what's-his-face, incog, bearding. See ANONYMOUS.

UNNATURAL adj. 1. oddball, queer in the head, queer potato, strange duck, weird, for weird, weirdo, bent. See also ECCENTRIC. 2. hammy, schmaltzy, phony, gone Hollywood, camp around, artsy, artsy-crafty, artsy-fartsy, chichi, putting on the dog, airish, play the ————. See AFFECTED.

UNNECESSARY adj. deadwood, excess baggage, Mickey Mouse, need it like a hole in the head, this I need?, who needs it.

UNNERVE v. 1. psych, psych out, spook, get to, bug, needle, put the needles in, ride, rattle, floor, throw, discomboberate, discombobulate, give one a turn, give one a bad time. See DISTURB. 2. spook, chill, give one a turn, scare the pants off one, scare hell out of, bowl over, buffalo, whip one around (intellectually), put one through the wringer, bad eye. See FRIGHTEN.

UNNERVED adj. thrown, psyched out, unglued, un-screwed, unzipped, spazzed out, choked, come apart, come apart at the seams, shot, shot to pieces. See also FRIGHTENED.

UNNOTEWORTHY adj. 1. no great shakes, strictly union, so-so, run of the alley, run of the mill, garden variety, humdrum, rumdum, vanilla, two bit, one horse. 2. pip-squeak, Tom Dick and Harry, Mr. and Mrs. Nobody, nobody, spear carrier, small fry, small beer, small change, small potatoes, chromosome, twerp, fly speck. 3. never mind, mox nix, makes no never mind, no matter, not worth a hill of beans, no big deal, no biggie. See UNIMPORTANT.

UNNOTICEABLE adj.   low keyed, low profile, soft-pedalled.

UNOBSTRUCTED adj.   wide open.

UNOBTAINABLE adj.   1. pie in the sky, blue sky, ungettable, no got. 2. out of pocket.

UNOBTRUSIVE adj.   low keyed, low profile, soft-pedalled.

UNOBTRUSIVELY adv.   under wraps, hush hush, strictly hush hush, on the q.t., on the quiet, on the sly, undercover, in a hole-and-corner way, in holes and corners.

UNORGANIZED adj.   any old way, any which way, hit or miss, willy-nilly, helter-skelter, higgledy-piggledy, slapdash, all over the shop. See also UNPREPARED, ERRATICALLY.

UNORTHODOX adj.   beat, beatnik, beat generation, bohemian, off the beaten path, weirdo, avant-garde, fringy, kinky, hippy, flaky, far out, way out, crazy, rare bird, three-dollar bill. See ECCENTRIC. See also NONCONFORMIST.

UNPAID adj.   comeuppance, what is coming to one, what one has coming.

UNPAINTED adj.   holiday (spot missed).

UNPALATABLE adj.   grody, grody to the max, gross, yucky, icky, yicky, barfy, slimy, fishy, synthetic, gooky. See UNSAVORY.

UNPARALLELED adj.   ten, 10, world class, greatest, gonest, hundred proof, mostest, baaadest, all time, all-time haymaker, tops, the most, the end, solid gold, winner, champ. See BEST.

UNPERTURBED adj.   cool, cool as a cucumber, keep one's cool, keep one's shirt on, unflappable, not turn a hair, ah-ah head. See CALM.

UNPLANNED adj.   improv, ad lib, fake it, off the wall, off the top of the head, play it by ear, cold, caught flatfooted, caught off base. See IMPROMPTU.

UNPLEASANT adj.   sucks, it sucks, grody, gross, uncool, yucky, bad news, bad scene, poison, sad, fierce, hard time, lousy. See UNDESIRABLE.

UNPLEASANT PLACE n.   hellhole, hole, joint, dump.

UNPOPULAR PERSON n.   creep, rat, drip, stinker, stinkpot, shit, shithead, sleaze, sleazeball, hairball, turkey, fink, gross, loser, louse, meatball, nerd, zod, schmo, weirdo, goon, bad case of the uglies, banana, out, out of the loop, out of it, dumb cluck, dummy, mince, mole, nothing, simp, spastic, weenie, wimp, cotton-picker, dipstick, arrowhead, for the birds, twerp, yo-yo, zombie, corpse, droop, herkle, prune, specimen, roach, toad, won't give one the time of day, gives one a pain, gives one a pain in the neck, gives one a pain in the ass, wallflower, can't see one for dust, ho dad, ho daddy, Joe Sad (Bl.). See also DISLIKED PERSON.

UNPREDICTABLE adj.   1. from out in left field, bolt from the blue. 2. chancy, iffy, up for grabs, touchy, touch and go, flukey, on slippery ground, on ice, on thin ice, hanging by a thread, the jury's out. See DOUBTFUL. See also RISKY.

UNPREJUDICED adj.   1. call 'em as one sees 'em, straight, even-steven. See FAIR. 2. color blind, cold, cold turkey, the emess, on the fence, mugwumpian, mugwumpish.

UNPREPARED adj.   cold, flatfooted, caught flatfooted, caught off base, caught napping, caught with one's pants down, improv, ad lib, vamp, fake, fake it, wing it, off the wall, off the cuff, off the hip, off the top of the head, play it by ear, go off half-cocked. See also IMPROMPTU.

UNPRETENTIOUS adj.   folksy, down, down home, home folks, homey, haymish, with the bark on, all hanging out, up front, free-spirited, get down, let down one's hair, stretched out, laid back.

UNPRINCIPLED adj.   1. bent, shady, double-crossing, snake in the grass, two-faced, two-timing, low-down and dirty, dirty-dealing, crooked stick, cheatin' heart, speak with forked tongue. 2. on the sly, in a hole-and-corner way, in holes and corners. See UNETHICAL.

UNPROCURABLE adj.   pie in the sky, ungettable, no got.

UNPROFITABLE adj.   red ink, in the red, total shuck, debit side, on the debit side, down side, the bad news, wild goose chase. See also USELESS.

UNPRONOUNCEABLE adj.   jawbreaker, jaw cracker, tongue twister.

UNPROSPEROUS adj.   1. flat, broke, stony, hard up, strapped, tapped, on the rocks, on one's uppers, hurting, feeling the pinch, down and out, seen better days, on the rims. See DESTITUTE. 2. missed the boat, on the skids, behind the eight ball, foldo, washout, washed up, go under, go chapter eleven, flop, fall down on the job. See UNSUCCESSFUL.

UNPROTECTED adj.   naked, ass out, neck stuck out, sitting duck, wide open, on the line, on the spot, out on a limb, up the creek without a paddle.

UNPUNISHED adj.   walk, get away with, get away with murder, get a slap on the wrist.

UNQUALIFIED adj. 1. amateur night, nonstarter, didn't make the cut, can't cut it, not cut out for, bush, bush league. See INCOMPETENT. 2. flat out, no catch, no joker, no kicker, no small print, no fine print at the bottom, no ifs ands or buts. See UNCONDITIONAL.

UNQUESTIONABLE adj. absofuckinglutely, posilutely, absitively, for certain, cold, have down cold, pat, down pat, no buts about it, no ifs ands or buts, open and shut, bet one's bottom dollar on, checked and double-checked, and no mistake. See CERTAIN.

UNRAVEL v. dope, dope out, pan out, figure out, crack, lick, deal with, unzip, iron out, work through, hit it on the nose. See also EXPLAIN, SIMPLIFY.

UNREADY adj. cold, flatfooted, caught flatfooted, caught off base, caught napping, caught with one's pants down, go off half-cocked. See UNPREPARED.

UNREALISTIC adj. gone, reachy, play with oneself, pipe dream, float, floating on clouds, on cloud seven, on cloud nine, pie in the sky, castles in the air, blue sky. See also IMPOSSIBLE.

UNREASONABLE adj. 1. far out, way out, overkill, out of bounds, out of all bounds, throw out the baby with the bath water, too-too, too much. See EXTREME. 2. all wet, off the wall, off base, off the beam, full of beans, full of hot air, miss by a mile, have another think coming. See WRONG. 3. pricey, cher, dear, steep, stiff, posh, heavy sugar, an arm and a leg, up to here (elbow), holdup, highway robbery. See EXPENSIVE.

UNREFINED adj. cheap, loud, loud-mouthed, raw, skank, tacky, raunchy, rough. See also COARSE.

UNREGULATED adj. open, wide open.

UNREHEARSED adj. improv, ad lib, winging it, vamping, off the top of the head, off the hip, played by ear, tossed off, tossed out, spitballed. See IMPROMPTU.

UNRELENTING adj. bound, bound and determined, hard-nosed, hard line, hang tough, rock-ribbed, brick wall, pat, stand pat, stand one's ground, stick to one's guns, staying power, hardheaded, bullheaded, stiff-necked, set, dead set on, murder (he's murder). See STUBBORN.

UNRELIABLE adj. bent, shady, fishy, sneaky, slick, sharp, shifty, shifty-eyed, loose, fly-by-night, Mickey Mouse, no account, slimy, trust one as far as one can swing a cat, trust one as far as one can throw an elephant. See DISHONEST. See also DANGEROUS.

UNREMARKABLE adj. 1. no great shakes, nowhere, strictly union, so-so, fair to middling, run of the alley, run of the mill, garden variety, vanilla. 2. wimpy, pipsqueak, Tom Dick and Harry, nobody, small change, small potatoes, drip, twerp, flea, hoddy-doddy, 3. not worth a hill of beans, row of pins, nutmeg, little go, big zero, no big deal, no biggie, no big thing, no big shit. See UNIMPORTANT.

UNREQUITED LOVE n. torch, carry a torch.

UNRESERVED adj. 1. open, call it like it is, shoot straight, call a spade a spade, put all one's cards on the table, make no bones about it, talk turkey. See FRANK. 2. all out, flat out, no holds barred, no joker in the deck. See UNCONDITIONAL.

UNRESOLVED adj. run hot and cold, blow hot and cold, shilly-shally, waffling, pussyfoot around, betwixt and between, hanging fire, the jury's out, between sixes and sevens. See UNDECIDED.

UNRESTRAINED adj. 1. free-wheeling, free-spirited, break loose, cut loose, loose cannon, loose wig, having a spaz attack, freaked out, don't give a damm, shoot the moon, fly kites, flake. See FREE. 2. on a tear, raising a rumpus, raising a ruckus, kicking up a row, kicking up one's heels, burn one's candle at both ends, drive in the fast lane. See UNCONTROLLABLE.

UNRESTRICTED adj. 1. wide open, all out, flat out, no strings attached, no fine print at the bottom, no holds barred, no catch, no ifs ands or buts. See UNCONDITIONAL. 2. free-wheeling, break loose, cut loose, let down one's hair, go to town, all hanging out. See FREE.

UNREWARDING adj. fungo, should have stood in bed, wild goose chase. See USELESS.

UNRUFFLED adj. cool, cool as a cucumber, keep one's cool, keep one's shirt on, unflappable, not turn a hair, ah-ah head. See CALM. See also DISPASSIONATE.

UNRULY adj. on a tear, raising a rumpus, raising a ruckus, raising the roof, kicking up a row, kicking up a shindy, off base, out of line, out of order. See also UNRESTRAINED, VIOLENT.

UNSAFE adj. widow maker, on thin ice, on slippery ground, on a wing and a prayer, out on a limb, touchy, touch and go, hanging by a thread. See DANGEROUS. See also DOUBTFUL.

UNSALABLE adj. white elephant, stuck with.

UNSANCTIONED adj. pirated, no-no, crooked, heavy, off base, out of line, out of bounds, over the line, under the counter, under the table, racket, shady, dirty, wildcat.

UNSATISFACTORY adj. seconds, damaged goods, crappy, junk, shit, piece of shit, rat's ass, piss-poor, schlocky, sleazy, ticky-tacky, slimpsy, minus, no good, from hunger, for the birds, Mickey Mouse, it sucks, not up to scratch, not come up to scratch, not up to snuff. See INADEQUATE.

UNSAVORY adj. 1. grody, grody to the max, gross, grungy, yucky, icky, yicky, barfy, raunchy, creepy, cruddy, rough, sad, stinky, stinking, lousy, slimy, shady, fishy, sneaky, slick, sharp, shifty, synthetic, tough nuggies, tripe, hocky, hooky, gooky. 2. bad-assed, creep, shifty-eyed, wrong, wrong number, wrong gee, not kosher, doin' dirt, dirty, low-down and dirty, dirty work, no-good, N.G., no account, shit heel, shit hook, bum, worm, convict, copper-hearted, eighteen carat, crum, crumb, hellish, hell of a note, hipper dipper. See also NASTY.

UNSCRAMBLE v. 1. dope, dope out, pan out, figure out, crack, lick, deal with, unzip, work through, hit it on the nose. 2. break it down, get down to basics, get down to the meat, clean it up, lay out, spell out, make perfectly clear. See SIMPLIFY.

UNSCRUPULOUS adj. 1. shady, sharp, double-crossing, two-faced, two-timing, low-down and dirty, dirty-dealing, crooked stick, featherlegs, slippery, fly-by-night. 2. on the sly, in a hole-and-corner way, in holes and corners. See UNETHICAL.

UNSEATED adj. unfrocked (any profession), drummed out, turned off, blackballed.

UNSECURABLE adj. pie in the sky, ungettable, no got, out of pocket.

UNSEEING adj. 1. blind as a bat. 2. in the dark, not know the score, not know the time of day, not know shit from shinola, doesn't know from nothing. See IGNORANT.

UNSENTIMENTAL adj. hard-boiled, hard-headed, commonsensical.

UNSETTLE v. 1. psych out, spook, get to, flip out, bug, fuss, fuzzbuzz, give one a bad time, give one a hard time, make it tough for all, needle, rattle, floor, throw. See DISTURB. 2. bollix, gum, gum up the works, put off, fuddle, throw a monkey wrench into the works, upset one's apple cart, take the wind out of one's sails, knock the props from under one, down one. See UPSET.

UNSETTLED adj. 1. betwixt and between, hanging fire, on ice, the jury's out, up for grabs, waffling. See UNDECIDED. 2. rattled, thrown, fussed, shook up, all shook up, antsy, fidgety, on pins and needles, all hot and bothered, Chinese fire drill. See CONFUSED. 3. dragged, got the blue devils, bummed out, flaked out, payched out, out of sorts, shot to pieces, going to pieces, droopy, mopey. See UNHAPPY.

UNSEXED adj. cut off one's balls, deballed, fixed, altered.

UNSHAKEABLE adj. set, sot, dead set on, set in concrete, pat, stand pat, brick wall, locked in, unflappable, bound and determined, stand one's ground, dig in one's heels, hang tough. See STUBBORN. See also DETERMINED.

UNSIGHTLY adj. grody, gross, plug-ugly, ugly as sin, grimbo, hagged out, hard on the eyes, beaujeeful, chromo, short on looks, crappy, cruddy, death warmed over. See UGLY.

UNSKILLED adj. virgin, green, greenhorn, green ass, wet behind the ears, rookie, boot, hayseed, raw, fish, first of May, ham, amateur, amateur night, amateur night in Dixie, bush, bush leaguer, crufty, sour apples (can't do something for sour apples); cokey (Bl.). See also INCOMPETENT.

UNSMILING adj. sourpuss, frozen-faced, not crack a smile, wipe the smile off one's face. See SERIOUS.

UNSOCIABLE adj. cool, cool cat, cold, cold fish, loner, lone wolf, dog it, dog up, stuck up, uppity, laid back, offish, standoffish. See ALOOF.

UNSOLICITED adj. through the transom, under the door.

UNSOPHISTICATED adj. 1. go organic, on the natch, low tech, folksy, haymish, homey, corny, cornball, corn-fed, off the cob, on the cob, Golden Bantam, cracker barrel, mossback. 2. uncool, low tech, clean, cube, square, L7, 'bama, raw, boob, hayseed, buster, Jasper, Babbitt, rookie, green, greenhorn, green ass, nowhere, out to lunch, eight ball, wide-eyed, wet behind the ears, not dry behind the ears, kid, babe in the woods, Bambi, blue eyes, blue-eyed, kid, lily white, mark, easy mark, pigeon, Clyde, Ed, Elk, fish, first of May, gunsel (boy), sophomore, bush, bush leaguer, country girl, country boy, hick, shit kicker, chintzy, clodhopper, hoosier, jay, jellybean, clown, lame, swallow anything, swallow hook line and sinker, take the bait, go for, fall for, tumble for, don't know shit from shoe polish, don't know shit from Shinola, don't know from nothin', don't know one's ass from a hole in the ground, don't know one's ass from first base, don't know crossways from crosswise, don't know from nothin', don't know what day it is. See also PLAIN, RUSTIC.

UNSPORTSMANLIKE adj. cheap shot, hitting below the belt, not cricket, raw deal, dirty pool, low-down, low-down and dirty, half a shake. See UNFAIR.

UNSTEADY adj. 1. yo-yo. 2. rocky, dicey, iffy, chancy, on thin ice, on slippery ground, on a wing and a prayer, out on a limb, Baker flying (N.), touchy, touch and go, hanging by a thread. See RISKY.

UNSUBSTANTIAL adj. gimcrack, gimcracky, Mickey Mouse, rocky, rickety, rinkydink, held together by spit, held together by chewing gum, house of cards. See FLIMSY.

UNSUCCESSFUL adj. 1. dead, dead duck, beat, turkey, good for nothing, foul ball, loser, never wuz, also ran, stiff, stifferoo, booby, can't even get arrested, flash in the pan. See FAILURE. 2. bust, flop, floppo, flopperoo, bomb, blank, bloomer, shellacking, stinkeroo, fluke, flummox, flookum, clambake, false alarm, dud, disaster, abortion, not work, not come off, flunk, flunk out, crap out, strike out, down, down the drain, down the chute, down and out, down the toilet, in the toilet, in the dumper, washout, washed out, washed up, nowhere, never passed go, A for effort, a miss, near miss, missed the boat, no dice, no-go, back to the drawing board, phftt, on the skids, on the rocks, should have stood in bed, go under, cropper, pratfall, muss up, piss up, fuck up, foul up, snafu, put down, come down, went down like the Titanic, wet smack, misfire, drew a blank, blown out of the water, header, in over one's head, in deep water, fall on one's face, fall flat on one's face, fall on one's ass, flat failure, also ran, dull thud, brodie, total loss, foozle, lamo, stinker, lead balloon (idea went over like a lead balloon), lemon, fizzle, frost, bagel, botch, clunker, dog, enema, hash, jumble, pancake, turd, turkey. 3. belly up, chapter 7, chapter 11, chapter 13, foldo, broke.

UNSUITABLE adj. cockamamie, bad form, off base, off color, out of line. See also UNDESIRABLE.

UNSUPPORTED adj. left twisting in the wind, left holding the bag. See also GROUNDLESS.

UNSURE adj. 1. iffy, up for grabs, touch and go, on slippery ground, on thin ice. 2. wimpy, pussyfoot around, blow hot and cold, on the fence, betwixt and between, between a rock and a hard place. See DOUBTFUL.

UNSURPASSED adj. A, A-1, A-number 1, number one, numero uno, ten, 10, out of sight, out of this world, gonest, crack, tops, winner, champ. See BEST.

UNSUSPECTING adj. bite, fall for, be taken in, swallow hook line and sinker, patsy, easy mark. See GULLIBLE.

UNSYMMETRICAL adj. agee, agee jawed, wamper jawed, jack deuce.

UNSYMPATHETIC adj. 1. tough nuggies, tough shit, TS, too bad, that's the way the ball bounces, that's the way the cookie crumbles. 2. cool, chill, cold, cold fish, cold-blooded, ice man, hard instinct, mean machine, butter wouldn't melt in his mouth. See also UNCOMPASSIONATE, CALLOUS, PITILESS.

UNSYSTEMATICALLY adv. any old way, any which way, hit or miss, willy-nilly, by fits and starts, helter-skelter, higgledy-piggledy. See ERRATICALLY.

UNTALKATIVE adj. clammed up, dried up, dummied up, garbo, tight-lipped. See SILENT.

UNTIDY adj. sloppy, grubby, scuzzed up, mess, messed up, mussed up, messy, mussy, bloody mess, holy mess, unholy mess, rat's nest, pigpen. See SLOVENLY.

UNTIMELY adv. previous, a bit previous, bright and early, early bird, early on.

UNTIRING adj. grind, plugger, springbutt, eager beaver, ball of fire, fireball, hyper, jumping, go-go, perky. See also SPIRITED.

UNTITLED adj. 1. X, X factor, whatsis, what's-its-name, whatzit, unk-unks, pig in a poke. 2. a certain person, Joe Doakes, Jane Doe, John Doe, Cheap John, Joe Blow, Mr. X, George Spelvin, so and so, such and such, whatchamacallit, what d'ya call em, what's-his-name, what's-his-face, you know who.

UNTRUE adj. 1. it won't fly, it stinks, crock, crock of shit, no such animal. 2. two-timing, cheating heart, moonlighting, chippy on one, sneakin' deacon, step out on one, tip, working late at the office. See UNFAITHFUL.

UNTRUSTWORTHY adj. rat, fink, rat fink, stool pigeon, stoolie, crooked, shady, sneaky, sharp, shifty, shifty-eyed, honest John, trust one as far as one can swing a cat, trust one as far as one can throw an elephant. See DISHONEST.

UNTRUTHFUL adj. fishy, jivey, jive-assed, shuckin' and jivin', two-faced, gil, Hollywood, reach-me-down, put-on, slick, sincere, snide, phony, fake, cry crocodile tears.

UNUSABLE adj. crashed, down, gronked, busted, out of order, out of commission, kaput, haywire, no go. See DAMAGED.

UNUSUAL adj. 1. kooky, kinky, far out, way out, out of this world, out of sight, out in left field, offbeat, off the beaten track, bent, weird, wild, crazy, off the wall. See STRANGE. 2. gnarly, mega-gnarley, unreal, rat fuck, cool, zero cool, cold, wicked, nose cone, catch, find, stellar, dream, lollapaloosa, not too shabby, something, something else, state of the art, too much, the utmost, shirt, shirty, tawny. See also EXCELLENT, NEW. 3. scarcer than hen's teeth, numerous as chicken lips.

UNUSUALLY adv. awful, awfully, real, really, daisy, mighty, plenty, so, so much, too much, terribly, terrifically, almighty, powerful, right.

UNVARNISHED adj. 1. vanilla, folksy, homey, haymish, open and shut, meat and potatoes, clean, what you see is what you get. See PLAIN. 2. it, for real, the real McCoy, real stuff, genuine article, the real goods, honest to God, legit. See GENUINE.

UNVEIL v. come out, come out of the closet, let it all hang out, spring, spring one's duke, tip one's hand, tip one's duke, open up, give the show away. See EXPOSE.

UNWANTED adj. lousy, who needs it, need it like a hole in the head, this I need yet?, from hunger, for the birds, Nimby (not in my backyard), excess baggage, drug on the market.

UNWAVERING adj. set, dead set on, buried in concrete, solid as a rock, Rock of Gibraltar, pat, stand pat, stay put, brick wall, unflappable. See STUBBORN.

UNWED adj. batch, old batch, old maid, single, single-o.

UNWELCOME adj. 1. blackballed, cold-shouldered, left out in the cold, not in the picture, shut out. 2. lousy, who needs it, need it like a hole in the head, this I need yet?, from hunger, for the birds, Nimby (not in my backyard), excess baggage, drug on the market.

UNWELL adj. draggin', draggin' one's ass, peaky, run down, down with, got a bug, got the bug, rocky, punk, feeling rotten, poorly, feeling awful, under the weather, below par, off one's feed, sick as a dog, laid low. See ILL.

UNWORKABLE adj. crashed, down, go down, out of whack, out of kilter, out of order, out of commission, kaput, on the fritz, conked out, no go. See DAMAGED.

UNWORLDLY adj. 1. low tech, folksy, haymish, homey, corny, cornball, corn-fed, off the cob, on the cob, Golden Bantam, cracker barrel, mossback. 2. uncool, clean, cube, square, boob, hayseed, green ass, eight ball, wide-eyed, wet behind the ears, babe in the woods, Bambi, bush league, country, hick, shit kicker, don't know shit from Shinola, don't know one's ass from a hole in the ground. See UNSOPHISTICATED.

UNWRAPPED adj. bald.

UNYIELDING adj. hard-nosed, hard core, hard shell, hard-line, tough nut, locked in, dig in one's heels, hold the fort, hold the line, hardheaded, pigheaded, stiff-necked, dead set on. See STUBBORN.

UPBRAID v. chew, chew ass, chew out, eat out, ball out, cuss out, lay into, jump down one's throat, climb all over, rake, rake up one side and down the other, take up one side and down the other, rake over the coals, have one on the carpet, call to task, dress down, read the riot act, tell where to get off, give one hail Columbia, let one have it, settle one's hash. See REBUKE.

UPHEAVAL n. 1. blue ruin, shit hit the fan. See also DISASTER. 2. about-face, flip-flop, turnaround, switch, switch over, shakeout (business), new ball game, new deal, new shuffle.

UPHOLD v. stick by, stick up for, backup, pat on the back, hear it for, prop up, hold one's end up, hold a brief for, boost. See SUPPORT.

UPLIFT n. uptick, upping, boost, pickup.

UPLIFT v. 1. buck up, pick up, brace up, chirk up, perk up, give a lift, put one on top of the world, put one on cloud nine, snap out of it, let the sunshine in. 2. hear it for, sound off for, root for.

UPLIFTED adj. float, float on air, cloud seven, cloud nine, flying.

UPPER CLASS n. the 400, the four hundred, the beautiful people, glitterati, upper crust, blue blood, FFV's, high society, smart set, jet set, our crowd, the establishment. See ELITE.

UPPERMOST adj. 1. high up, higher ups, high muck, high-muck-a-muck, high pillow, top brass, big number, big shot, big shit, big wheel, head honcho, main squeeze. See EXECUTIVE. 2. world class, greatest, out of sight, out of this world, bitchin', boss, tops, the most, endsville, the end, solid gold, winner. See BEST. See also EXCELLENT.

UPRIGHT adj. up front, square shooter, true blue, righteous, Christian, kosher, Mr. Clean, real people, straight, straight arrow, third rail, all wool and a yard wide. See VIRTUOUS.

UPROAR n. flap, fuss, to-do, row, stir, stink, big stink, rhubarb, hoo-ha, hubba-hubba, hullabaloo, rowdydow, rumble, rumpus, ruckus, ruction, shindy, shivaree, commo, dustup, fofarraw, free-for-all, brawl, all hell broke loose, kickup, wingding, raise cain, raise sand, roughhouse, buzz buzz, fuzzbuzz, haroosh, big scene. See also TURMOIL.

UPSET adj. 1. rattled, thrown, fussed, shook up, antsy, jittery, jumpy, charged up, in a botheration, in a stew, fidgety, on pins and needles, lost one's cool. See DISTURBED. 2. dragged, low, ass in a sling, dick in the dirt, blue, got the blue devils, sob story, sob stuff, tear-jerker, weeper, teardrop special, flaked out, psyched out, shot to pieces, all torn up, broken up, cut up, unglued, unscrewed, unzipped, come apart at the seams. See UNHAPPY.

UPSET n. foul-up, fuck-up, screw-up, mishmosh, mishmash, goulash, mess and a half, flusteration, flustration, stew, sweat, tizzy, hassle, free-for-all. See TURMOIL.

UPSET v. 1. adjy, psych, spook, get to, flip, flip out, craze, curdle, bug, bug up, fire up, key up, egg on, turn on, pick on, make waves, make a scene, give one a turn, give one a hard time, stir up, rattle, floor, throw. See DISTURB. 2. queer, crimp, cramp, put a crimp in, cramp one's style, stymie, skin, snooker, crab, hang up, hold up, foul up, fuck up, louse up, snafu, bollix, gum, gum up the works, fake out, put off, flummox, buffalo, bamboozle, fuddle, stump, cross, cross up, double-cross, give one the business, throw a monkey wrench into the works, upset one's apple cart, spike one's guns, steal one's thunder, trash, take one down, take care of, take the wind out of one's sails, knock the bottom out of, knock the chocks from under one, knock the props from under one, down one, ditch, give the slip, skip out on, duck, dodge, get around, give the run around, run circles around, run rings around.

UPSETTING adj. drag, downer, bummer, bringdown, bring one down, slump, blue funk, crash.

UP TO DATE adj. state of the art, the leading edge, the cutting edge, at the cutting edge, now, today, with it, what's happening, what's in, the in-thing, contempo, avant-garde, last word, the latest, newfangled. See NEW.

URBANITE n. city slicker, cliff dweller, cave dweller, subway rider, straphanger, street people, Broadway baby, townee, towner.

URCHIN n. J.D.(juvenile delinquent), punk, snot nose, snot-nose kid, holy terror, guttersnipe, mudlark, raggedy muffin. See also CHILD.

URETHRA n. pipe, plumbing.

URGE n. itch, hard-on, lech, nasties, beaver fever, sweet tooth, druthers, weakness, fire in the belly, the munchies (food), yen. See DESIRE.

URGE v. fire up, put up to, turn on, egg one on, goose, bug, sell one on, work on, put the bee on, twist one's arm, lay it on thick. See PERSUADE, PUSH.

URGENT adj. heavy, heavy number, heavyweight heavy stuff, serious jelly, fire in the belly, heat's on, hurry-up call, matter of life and death, chips are down, like all get out, hot flash, touch and go, touchy.

URINAL n. duck (bed). See also TOILET.

URINATE v. pee, pea, piss, leak, take a leak, go, go wee-wee, go pee-pee, tinkle, wee, wee-wee, make wee-wee, make pee-pee, pish, number one, make number one, spend a penny, powder one's nose, go to the john, go to the can, go to the Chic Sale, lift a leg, drain the dew, drain the dew from one's lily, wet one's pants, call, nature's call, let fly, piddle, make water, make a pit stop, take a whizz, sis-sis, siss, see a man about a dog, go play in the sandbox, answer nature's call, answer the call, one's back teeth are floating (urgent need to).

URINE n. pee, pee-pee, number one, piddle, pish, piss, tinkle, wee, wee-wee.

USE n. thing, Jones, into, hang-up, one's bag, shot, kick.

USE v. 1. truck with, sign on, sign up, take on, ink, bring on board, come on board. 2. pick one's brains, mine. 3. eat up (use entirely), chew up.

USED CAR n. cream puff (good), lemon (bad).

USED UP adj. down the tube, petered out, eighty-six, 86, out, cheapie, hand-me-down, reach-me-down, secondhand, secondhand Rose, shot, experienced, had, recycled.

USELESS adj. 1. junk, rat's ass, no-good, N.G., lousy, hill of beans, crap, lemon, dreck, two bit, diddly, diddly poo, doodly, doodly poo, down, on downtime, on the blink, on the bum, out of action, no-go, run down, dead ass, dinger, busted, had it, on the fritz, kaput, garbage, white elephant, humpty-dumpty, hump, jeasley, no bargain, ice, pretzels, ain't worth shit, ain't worth the powder to blow it to hell, ain't worth a hoot, ain't worth a plugged nickel, blah, stiffo, tin, wood, dead wood, dreck, dud, foul ball, flat tire. 2. total shuck, goin' round in circles, in a vicious circle, on a treadmill, going nowhere, goner, gone goose, dead duck, wild-goose chase, on a wild-goose chase, no way, can't win for losin', no-win situation, shoulda stood in bed, go fight City Hall, might as well talk to the wall, go hit your head against the wall, locking the barn after the horse is stolen, looking for a needle in a haystack, save one's breath, not a ghost of a chance, not a Chinaman's chance, not a prayer, not a snowball's chance in hell, not till hell freezes over, who needs it?, I need it like a hole in the head, This I need yet? See also INEFFECTIVE.

USUAL adj. 1. same old shit, SOS, sked, grind, daily grind, groove, channels, cut and dried, G.I., playing it safe, in the groove, in a rut, chicken, according to Hoyle. 2. garden variety, everyday, plastic, cotton-pickin', so-so, vanilla, mainstream, run of the mill. See AVERAGE.

USURER n. shark, loan shark, shylock, juice dealer.

USURP v. 1. take over, annex, grab, grab hold of, glom on to, clap hands on, get one's fingers on, get one's hands on, swipe, kipe, highjack, hijack, highgrade. See APPROPRIATE. 2. worm in, worm one's way in, squeeze in, elbow in, horn in, chisel in, muscle in, work in, barge in, butt in.

UTAH Beehive State, Mormon State.

UTENSIL n. gismo, gadget, widget, sucker, mother-fucker, mofo, grabber, gimmick, whatchamacallit, what's it, whatchee, thingamajig, thingumabob, dojigger, domajig, dohickey, dingbat, dingus, goofus, gasser. See APPARATUS.

UTENSILS n. fighting tools (knife, fork and spoon, WW II), tools (table).

UTILITARIAN adj. commonsensical, hardheaded, nuts and bolts.

UTMOST adj. 1. worst case scenario, gorkish, ultra-ultra, out of bounds, out of sight, out of this world, last straw, the straw that broke the camel's back, too-too, too much, bitter end, the pits, the dogs, the least. See EXTREME. 2. number one, numero uno, ten, 10, ace high, aces, world class, the most, mostest, greatest, baaadest, bitchin', tops. See BEST.

UTOPIA n. Erehwon, pie in the sky, Shangri-la.

UTOPIAN adj. pie in the sky.

UTTER v. go, spiel, jaw, lip, chin, gas, chaff, modulate, modjitate, splib, splib de wib, slide one's jib, cut it up, verbalize, mouth. See SPANK.

V

V n. Victor.

VACANT LOT n. prairie (midwest).

VACATION n. two weeks with pay, time off, layoff, a few days off, eyes to cool it, liberty, gone fishing.

VACATIONER n. jet-setter, globe-trotter, out of towner; snowbird, snowflake, sunflower (south for the winter).

VACCINATE v. give a shot, shoot, give one the square needle, give one the hook, hook, stick one.

VACCINATED adj. stabbed in the ass, got the hook, got the square needle, binged (WW I).

VACCINATION n. shot, shot in the arm, shot in the ass, stab in the ass, booster, booster shot.

VACILLATE v. straddle, fence-stradde, fence hanger, on the fence, sit on the fence, yo-yo, hot and cold, run hot and cold, hedge, hedge off, blow hot and cold, shilly-shally, wimpy, wishy-washy, waffle, hem and haw, pussyfoot around.

VACILLATING adj. wishy-washy, waffling.

VACUOUS adj. dorky, nerdy, numb nutty, lamebrain, birdbrain, rattleweed, nebbish, out to lunch, lunchie, out of it, nobody home, dumdum, dumbbell, dumb bunny, bonetop, airheaded, bubbleheaded, baloonheaded, minus some buttons, missing a few marbles, nuthin' upstairs, half-baked. See STUPID.

VACUUM n. vac.

VACUUM CLEANER n. bagpipe.

VACUUM TUBE n. bottle.

VAGABOND n. on the bum, king of the road, bo, floater, ragbag, road agent. See VAGRANT.

VAGINA n. pussy, cunt, snatch, twat, beaver, crack, hole, cockpit, quiff, quim, purse, snapper, snapping pussy, trim, ginch, box, fur, fur pie, furburger, furrow, gash, slash, nookie, poontang, tail, clam, bearded clam, tuna, lower lips, lotus, cabbage, cookie, love muscle, love canal, fireplace, oven, Cape Horn, ace, ace of spades, coffee shop, mink, cuzzy, cooz, coozy, cooch, chacha, chocha, twelge, futy, futz, gigi, giggy, geegee, jazz, jelly roll, jing-jang, nautch, notch, piece, cunny, honey pot, fruit cup, shaf, muffin, muff, mount, receiving set, gold mine, moneymaker, altar of love, puka, meat, dark meat, white meat, pink, the Y, middle eye, Venus-flytrap, cavern.

VAGRANCY n. vag.

VAGRANT n. vag, tomato can vag, bum, on the bum, stumblebum, tramp, hard road freak, hobo, ragbag, bag lady, bag woman, dock rat, drifter, king of the road, bo, bust, stiff, stiffo, blanket stiff, bindle stiff, bindleman, deadbeat, dead one (ex), floater, dingbat, ding-donger, gay cat, jungle buzzard, road agent, on the burrola (U., 1930). See also BEGGAR.

VAGUE adj. 1. fuzzy, out to lunch, spacey. 2. double-talk, doublespeak, hot air, that doesn't chop any wood, that doesn't cut any ice.

VAIN adj. puffed up, stuck on oneself, ego-tripping, high and mighty, big head, have one's glasses on (Bl.), puffed up, big I am, stuck on oneself, think one's shit doesn't stink. See CONCEITED.

VAIN, IN adj. 1. total shuck, goin' round in circles, in a vicious circle, on a treadmill, going nowhere, wild goose chase. 2. no way, can't win for losin', no-win situation, go fight City Hall, not a ghost of a chance, not a prayer, not a snowball's chance in hell, looking for a needle in a haystack, save one's breath. See USELESS.

VALIANT adj. game, gritty, gutsy, gutty, spunky, nervy, stand tall, tough it out, bigger'n life, fire-eater, hairy, cool hand. See FEARLESS.

VALID adj. 1. legit, kosher, card-carrying, sure enough, honest to God, twenty-four carat, all wool and a yard wide, on the legit, on the level, on the up and up, stand up, hold up, hold water, hold together, hang together, hold up in the wash, wash, go, fly, okayed. 2. for real, honest to God, the lowdown, the emess, righteous, out of the horse's mouth, straight from the horse's mouth.

VALIDATE v. make something stick, okay, OK, sign off on, put one's John Hancock on, give the nod, give the go-ahead, give the green light, give the stamp of approval, rubber-stamp. See CONFIRM.

VALIDATION n. okay, OK, go-ahead, green light, mouthful (you said a mouthful), say so, one's stamp of approval, Good Housekeeping Stamp of Approval, rubber stamp. See CONFIRMATION.

VALISE n. jiffy bag, keister, valpack, tote bag.

VALIUM n. volume, downer, mello yello, true blue.

VALOR n. balls, guts, heart, nerve, stomach, what it takes, grit, true grit, spunk, backbone, moxie, starch, clock, corazon, Dutch courage (intoxicated).

VALOROUS adj.   game, gritty, gutsy, gutty, spunky. See also COURAGEOUS.

VALUABLE adj.   collectibles, worth its weight in gold, worth a king's ransom, hot property, high price tag, big price tag, worth an arm and a leg. See also EXPENSIVE.

VALUATE v.   check, check out, price out, dig it, eye, look over, peg, size, size up, dope out, take account of, figure, figure in, guesstimate, have one's number, take one's measure.

VALUE v.   dope out, guesstimate, figure, figure in, figure out, cut ice, cut some ice, keep tab, keep tabs, size up, take one's measure. See also APPRAISE.

VALUELESS adj.   diddly, diddly shit, ain't worth shit, ain't worth the powder to blow it to hell, ain't worth a hoot, ain't worth a plugged nickel, ain't worth a hill of beans, garbage, junk, no count, from hunger, white elephant, jeasley, tinhorn. See USELESS.

VAMPIRE n.   vamp.

VANDALIZE v.   trash, smash, smash up, foul up, crud up, scuzz up, mess up, wrack up, take a joint apart, break the lease, blue ruin. See DESTROY.

VANGUARD adj.   leading edge, cutting edge, state of the art, cool, far out, beat, beat generation, beatnik, way out, hep, hip, hipster, hippie, yippie, crazies, beard, cool cat, new wave. See also NEW.

VANILLA adj.   van.

VANISH v.   do a vanishing act, fade, fade out of sight, fade away, pull a Judge Crater.

VANITY n.   ego trip.

VAPID adj.   the least, nowhere, noplaceville, Nadaville, nothing, nothing doing, wiped out, flat tire, zero, big zero. See INSIPID.

VARIABLE adj.   yo-yo, iffy, waffling.

VARIANCE n.   1. about-face, flip-flop, mid-course correction, switch, switch over, transmogrification. See MODIFICATION. 2. diff, different strokes, different strokes for different folks.

VARIETY n.   mishmash, mishmosh, mixed bag, combo, everything but the kitchen sink, duke's mixture (strange), stew, soup (liquid), lorelei.

VARIETY STORE n.   dime store, five-and-dime, five-and-ten, five-and-ten-cent store, Kresses, Woolworth's, drugstore.

VARNISH v.   soft-pedal, whitewash, cover up. See LIE. See also CONCEAL.

VARY v.   yo-yo, blow hot and cold, hem and haw, shilly-shally. See VACILLATE.

VAST adj.   humongous, humungous, mungo, moby; mother, motherfucker, big mother (Obsc.); big mama, big daddy, super, super-duper, super-colossal, seagoing, jumbo, lunker, blimp, barn door, whale of a, whaling, whacking, walloping, lolloping, whopping, whopper. See also BIG.

VAUDEVILLE n.   two-a-day, six-a-day, the big time, small time, the circuit, Orpheum Circuit, Orpheum time, peeler. See also THEATER.

VAULT n.   box, crib, peter, biscuit, can.

VEER v.   1. cut, hang a right, hang a left, make a right, make a left, swivel, sideslip. 2. drift, get around.

VEGETABLES n.   veggies.

VEGETARIAN n.   veggy, sproutsy (Stu.).

VEHEMENT adj.   1. hot, hot for, blowtop, raising a rumpus, raising a ruckus, kicking up a row, kicking up a shindy, hopped up, catawamptious, come out swinging, come on like gangbusters, come on strong, enforcer, on the make, out for a rep, ball of fire, fireball, heller, hyper.

VEHEMENTLY adv.   like crazy, like mad, terrifically, really truly, fer sure, you know it, straight out, no buts about it, no ifs ands or buts, in spades, with bells on, with knobs on, with tits on, in a handbasket, I'll tell the world, I'll tell the cockeyed world, come hell or high water.

VEHICLE n.   1. wheels, van, jeep, bus, chine, wheelchair, jalopy, crate, junk heap, jitney, boat, buggy, hot rod, chariot, flivver. See also AUTOMOBILE. 2. four by four, four by eight, quarter ton, eighteen wheeler, semi, Big Mack, oil burner (diesel), dump, draggin' wagon, pickemup, horse, kidney buster, scow, carry-all, freight box. See also TRUCK.

VEIL v.   1. cover up, wear cheaters, slap on some glims, flash the gogs, beard. 2. stonewall, whitewash, put up a front. 3. finesse it, launder, paper over, sweep under the rug. See COVER UP.

VENAL adj.   go with the money, money talks bullshit walks, on the take, on the pad, open, wide open, meat-eater, racket up, something rotten in Denmark.

VENDOR n.   peddler, drummer, bell-ringer, ——— dog (i.e., shoe dog), medicine man, pitchman, skig, spieler, tinge, Arab, bag guy (balloon), butch, butcher, hawker, cheap jack, Cheap John; candy man, pusher (drugs), dealer.

VENEREAL DISEASE n.   VD, AIDS, clap, dose, dose up, dose of claps, old clap, old dose (neglected case), package, hammer head clap, the drip, blue balls, crud, scrud, double scrud, syph, head cold, caught a cold, picked up something, picked up a nail, lulu (painful case), pissing razor blades, burn, shank, chanck, dog, old dog, ten-year-old dog, the rahl, rahl up, brothel sprouts,

Cupid's itch, Venus's curse, crotch pheasants, lobster tails, full house (combination of), set one up (infect), short-arm inspection (examination of males for). See also SYPHILIS, GONORRHEA.

VENERY n. 1. fuck, jazz, screw, lay, hump, boff, nooky, poke, piece of ass, bang, action, balling, shot, roll in the hay, go the limit, score, yum-yum, dirty deed, oil change, noonie, matinee, parallel parking, night baseball, fooling around, laps around the track, bush patrol. See SEXUAL INTERCOURSE. 2. high living, life in the fast lane, burn one's candle at both ends, go to hell in a handbasket. See DISSOLUTE.

VENGEANCE n. tit for tat, eye for an eye, get even.

VENOMOUS adj. bitchy, cussed, catty, evil, waspish, dirty, mean, ornery, accidentally on purpose, do one dirt. See also ANTAGONISTIC, MALEVOLENT.

VENTURE n. 1. baby, bag, bag one's into, thing, thing one's into, biggie (major), deal, pet project, proposition, setup. See also BUSINESS. 2. flyer, flutter, header, plunge, on spec, spec, stab, shot, maximax (big return, big loss), maximin (small return, big loss), minimax (safe). See WAGER.

VENTURE v. take the action, take a flyer, play, get down, get on, lay it on the line, put up, take a plunge, play the market, have a fling at, give a whirl, take a crack at, make a stab at, stick one's neck out, go out on a limb. See RISK. See also WAGER.

VENTURESOME adj. 1. dicey, chancy, on thin ice, out on a limb, off the deep end, one could get burned. See DANGEROUS. 2. ambish, ballsy, bogard, come-on, come on like gangbusters, come on strong, gumption, spunk, balls, drive, guts, go-go, full of piss and vinegar, full of get up and go, get out and go, go-getter, pushy, fair hell, heller, moxie, taking it to 'em, take charge, take over, take the bull by the horns, play hard ball, play for keeps, ball of fire, hotshot, moving out.

VERACIOUS adj. up front, right up front, open, like it is, call it like it is, lay it on the line, on the up and up, on the level, the emess, no lie, what you see is what you get, honest to God, true blue, righteous, kosher, boy scout, Mr. Clean, straight arrow, straight shooter. See TRUTHFUL.

VERACITY n. honest-to-God truth, the word, gospel, no shit, straight shit, straight stuff, straight goods, how things are, like it is, the real emess, the real McCoy. See TRUTH.

VERANDA n. gallery, front stoop, stoop.

VERBOSE adj. talker, great talker, yacker, gabby, windy, long-winded, windbag, bag of wind, load of wind, windjammer, barber, have verbal diarrhea, diarrhea of the mouth. See TALKATIVE.

VERIFICATION n. dope, goods, info, smoking gun (crucial), clincher, grabber, chapter and verse, straight stuff, from the horse's mouth. See PROOF.

VERIFY v. dig it, eye, eyeball, peg, look-see, make sure, size, size up, add up, check out, check up, check up on, double-check, crack on one or something, debunk (prove false), pan out, stand up, hold one up.

VERITABLE adj. for real, the real McCoy, genuine article, the real goods, honest to God, on the legit, on the level, the emess, straight dope, no buts about it. See TRUE.

VERMIN n. cootie, cutie, cootie garage (hair puffs in which cootie lives), grayback, seam squirrel, crabs, crum, shimmy lizard; crumby, lousy (afflicted with).

VERMONT Green Mountain State.

VERNACULAR n. jive talk, lingo, street talk, flash (thieves), gobbledygookese, hillspeak (Washington, D.C.), psychobabble, Urbabbble (city govt.). See LANGUAGE.

VERSATILE adj. all around, AC/DC, acdac, cosplug, switch hitter, go every which way, one who can do it all, hang loose, roll with the punches, putty in one's hands, fungible.

VERSED adj. hip, hip to the jive, savvy, with it, all woke up, tuned in, in the picture, booted on, on the inside, in the know, enough ducks in a row. See KNOWLEDGEABLE.

VERTIGO n. wooziness, woozy.

VERVE adj. go juice, bounce, snap, zap, zing, zip, pow, sock, pizzazz, splash, moxie, punch, vim, pepper, get up and go, piss and vinegar. See EXUBERANCE.

VERY adv. awful, awfully, gosh awful, mucho, something, real, really, but, jolly, bloody, daisy, mighty, plenty, so, so much, too much, stone (stone deaf), terribly, terrifically, almighty, powerful, right.

VESSEL n. steamer, liner, tramp, tub, bathtub, bucket, rust bucket, hooker, can, ol'lady, wagon, battlewagon, jeep, oil burner, sieve, bateau.

VESTIBULE n. squat pad.

VESTMENTS n. 1. clericals. 2. threads, togs, toggery, duds, outfit, rags, glad rags, get up, get out, vine, weeds, dry goods, flash, rig, ready-made, drape, drapery, drapes, set of drapes, bib and tucker. See CLOTHING.

VEST POCKET n. sky pocket.

VETERAN adj. pro, vet, longtime, hep, hip, has what it takes, knows one's stuff, knows one's way around, knows the ropes, knows the score, knows which side is up, knows which side his bread is buttered on, knows which side his head is battered on, knows how, knows one's onions, up, wised up, up to snuff, up to speed, to the mark, up one's alley, from way back, one of the old school, won one's spurs, kicked around, been around, been around the block, been around the block a few times, been hit before, been there before, been through the mill, been through the wars, cut a few touches, wasn't born yesterday, didn't come into town on a load of wood.

VETERAN n.   1. vet, G.I., ex-GI, got his ruptured duck (WW II.), war-horse, pro, old pro, old hand, old-timer, old salt, old sea dog, shellback. 2. cat, hep cat, hip cat, sport, city slicker. See SOPHISTICATED.

VETERINARIAN n.   horse doctor, vet.

VETO n.   ding, zing, blackball.

VETO v.   kill, burn, burn down, shoot down, pass, pass on, pass by, throw out, throw away, chuck, chuck out, heave-ho, cut, ding, zing, nix, put down, turn thumbs down, thumb down, blackball, not go for, adios it, eighty-six, 86, hell no. See also NEGATE.

VEX v.   bug, ride, be at, be on the back of, eat, shiv, noodge, brown off, tick off, piss one off, turn one off, go on make my day, give one a hard time, get in one's hair, get under one's skin, drive one up a tree, rile, hack, hassle, push the right button, rub the wrong way. See ANNOY.

VEXATION n.   rise, botheration, downer, worriment, bad news, headache, pain in the ass, pain in the neck, tsuris. See ANNOYANCE.

VEXED adj.   bugged, hacked, steamed, uptight, clutched up, hacked, pissed off, peed off, tee'd off, browned off, riled, rubbed the wrong way. See ANNOYED.

VIBRAHARP n.   vibes.

VIBRAPHONE n.   vibes, bells.

VIBRATION n.   judder, shimmy.

VIBRATO adj.   wah-wah.

VICAR n.   padre, the rev, Holy Joe, sky pilot, sky scout, preacher man, sin hound. See CLERGYMAN.

VICE-PRESIDENT n.   V.P. Veep, veepost.

VICE SQUAD n.   pussy posse.

VICINITY n.   1. hood, nabe, neck of the woods, territory, turf. See NEIGHBORHOOD. 2. around, pretty near, practically, in the ball park of, in the neighborhood of. See NEAR.

VICIOUS adj.   bad-assed, bitchy, cussed, dirty, mean, ornery, rough, tough, nuts, poison, bum, lousy, murderous, kill-crazy, doin' dirt, eighteen carat, hellish. See also MEAN.

VICISSITUDE n.   about-face, flip-flop, turnaround, mid-course correction, switch, switchover, new ball game, new deal, new shuffle.

VICTIM n.   mark, easy mark, easy make, pigeon, patsy, pushover, sucker, turkey, vic, lame, mom, chump, square, clown, cousin, setup, soft touch, fall guy, sitting duck, babe in the woods, boob, schlemiel, stooge, cat's paw, jack, duck, goofus, gopher, jay, lobster, roundheeled, sweetheart, quick push, softie, sweet pea, tool, tourist, yuld, yold, yo-yo, apple, clay pigeon, angel (criminal), fish, sausage, fruit, lamb, Clyde, dumbjohn, Winchell, Bates, John Bates, Mr. Bates, babe, cinch, lead-pipe cinch, grunt, score, storch, greeny, greener, sap, saphead, prize sap, addict, eggs, comedown (pickpocket).

VICTIMIZE v.   fuck, frig, jerk one around, jerk one's chain, fuck one over, shuck and jive, run a game on, rope in, fleece, stick, burn, bilk, clip, con, chisel, gouge, stiff, sting, sucker into, double shuffle, stack the cards, set up, snow under. See TRICK.

VICTIMIZED adj.   stung, stuck, been had, taken, fucked over, screwed, stiffed, ripped off, got a haircut, got trimmed, rooked, burned, juiced, snowed under. See TRICKED.

VICTOR n.   champ, king o' the hill, number one, numero uno, the greatest, top dog, medallist, gold medallist, takes the gold, takes the cake, shoo-in, title holder. See also SUCCESSFUL.

VICTORIOUS adj.   on top of the heap, arrived, fat, fat city, king of the hill, duke of the catwalk, blow one away, blow one out of the water, have one by the balls, have one by the short hairs, have one by the tail, have it made, lucked out (against all odds).

VICTORY n.   win, do a Rocky, grab the gold, nose out, beat the competish, bring home the bacon, bull's-eye, slam, grand slam, hole in one, hit, killing, clean sweep, upset, pay dirt. See TRIUMPH.

VICTUALS n.   vittles, chow, bite, snack, grub, fast food, pogey, scoff, go juice, chuck, blue plate, black plate (soul food), pecks, grubbery. See FOOD.

VIDEO CASSETTE RECORDER n   VCR, homevid, home video.

VIDEO MASTER OF CEREMONIES n.   video jockey, V.J., veejay.

VIE v.   scramble for, go for, go for broke, go for the throat, go for the jugular, go for the gold, jockey for position, buck, push, hassle, sweat, sweat it.

VIET CONG n.   V.C., Charlie, Cong, Victor Charlie (also soldier).

VIETNAM   Nam.

VIETNAMESE n. dink, gook, slope, zip.

VIETNAMESE HOUSE OR HUT n. hooch.

VIEW n. 1. judgment call, value judgment, op, say so, slant, two cents' worth, vox pop, another county heard from, another country heard from. See also ATTITUDE. 2. close-up, C.U., slant, twist. 3. flash, gander, gun, hinge, glom, squint, slant, lamp, look-see, eyeball inspection, pike, swivel.

VIEW v. 1. glom, glim, gun, beam, flash, flash on, scope, spot, spy, dig, read, pipe, rap, eye, eagle eye, clap eyes on, lay eyes on, set eyes on, get a load of, get an eyeful of, rubberneck. See SEE. 2. go slumming, slum, take in the sights.

VIEWER n. kibitzer, nark, sidewalk superintendent, watcher.

VIEWPOINT n. P.O.V., slant, sound, twist, angle, two cents' worth, where one is at, where one's head is, another county heard from.

VIGILANT adj. on the ball, on the job, on one's toes, with a weather eye open, with one's eyes peeled, on the lookout, on the que vive, got it covered, all bases covered, looking to, looking for, waiting on, the noose is hanging, at the ready, loaded for bear. See also ATTENTIVE.

VIGILANTES n. death squad.

VIGOR n. juice, bounce, zing, sock, kick, ginger, clout, punch, steam, hustle, the stuff, get up and go, piss and vinegar, full head of steam. See POWER.

VIGOROUS adj. zippy, zappy, snappy, peppy, got the horses to do it, strong as a horse, strong as a lion, strong as an ox, ball of fire, steamroller, spanking, punchy, come on strong, come on like gangbusters, take over, take charge. See STRONG. See also HEALTHY.

VIGOROUSLY adv. turn on the heat, full tilt, full swing, full steam ahead, all out, slam bang, by storm, like gangbusters.

VILE adj. rat's ass, grungy, raunchy, scuzzy, sleazy, sleazeball, shitty, cruddy, cheesy, the pits, stinking, garbage, the least. See BAD.

VILIFY v. 1. pan, slam, blister, scorch, rap, mudsling, knock, rip up the back, give a black eye, mark lousy. See SLANDER. 2. dump on, call down, dress down, put down, scorch, blister, tear into, slam, rag on, dig at, give a black eye, roast, skin alive. See SCOLD. 3. cuss, damn, darn, drat, flame, jinx, put the horns on, put the whammy on one, put the double whammy on one, give one a kine ahora (Yid.), hoodoo, hoodoo one, voodoo, voodoo one.

VILLAIN n. creep, shit, shitheel, sleazeball, sleazoid, slime bucket, wrongo, buddy fucker, bad ass, bad guy, meanie, black hat, dirty dog, scalawag. See SCOUNDREL.

VILLAINOUS adj. bad-assed, rat's ass, sucks, scuzzy, sleazy, sleazeball, bad news, murderous, poison, dirty, doin' dirt, low-down, no-good. See BAD.

VIM n. bounce, snap, zap, zing, zip, zippo, pow, sock, kick, pizzazz, the force, moxie, pepper, get up and go, piss and vinegar. See POWER.

VINDICATION n. the whatfor, the why and wherefore, the whyfor, tit for tat, eye for an eye. See also EXCUSE.

VIOLA n. chin bass.

VIOLENCE n. storm, ruckus, ruction, rumble, rumpus, shivaree, wingding, blast, blow, blowup, flare-up, dustup, flap, foofaraw, free-for-all, fuss, tear, hell broke loose, raise cain, raise sand, roughhouse, rowdydow. See also ANGER.

VIOLENT adj. blowtop, flipped, kill-crazy, ape, gone ape, on a tear, raising a rumpus, raising a ruckus, kicking up a row, kicking up a shindy, hitting out in all directions.

VIOLENTLY adv. like crazy, like mad, bulldoze, take by storm, steamroll, steamroller tactics, strong-arm, strong-arm tactics, rockem and sockem, slam bang, galley west, hell west and crooked (Obs.). See also VEHEMENTLY.

VIOLIN n. fiddle, strad, scratch box.

VIOLINIST n. fiddler, mice, squeaker.

VIOLIN, PLAY v. saw, scrape.

VIRGIN n. cherry, canned goods, bug, old maid.

VIRGINIA Cavalier State, Mother of Presidents, Mother of States, Old Dominion.

VIRGINITY n. unspoiled, clean; cop a cherry, cop her cherry, pop her cherry (take away).

VIRILE adj. he-man, hunk, tuna, macho, beefcake, stud, jock, jockstrap, two-fisted, caveman, bucko, hairy, jelly roll, tiger, two-fisted, colt, chrismo, chismo. See also MAN, POWERFUL.

VIRTUALLY adv. around, give or take a little, guesstimate, ball park figure, in the ball park of, in the neighborhood of, practically, something like, upwards of. See NEARLY.

VIRTUOSO n. brain, pro, pundit, old pro, old hand, ol' professor, egghead, maven, ringer, shark, sharp, natural, ace, star, superstar, hotshot, hot stuff, tuned in, whiz, wizard, crackerjack, champ, no slouch, know one's onions, know one's stuff, big league, enough ducks in a row. See also AUTHORITY, PRODIGY, INTELLIGENT, MUSICIAN, CELEBRITY.

VIRTUOUS adj. up front, right up front, on the up and up, on the level, honest to God, honest Injun, square,

square John, square shooter, true blue, righteous, Christian, kosher, boy scout, Mr. Clean, regular, legit, on the legit, for real, real people, okay people, saint, straight, straight arrow, straight shooter, straight from the shoulder, straight out, straight dope, straight stuff, straight shit, third rail, white, damn white, all wool and a yard wide, card-carrying, salt of the earth, a prince of a fellow, pillar of the church.

VIRUS n. bug, plague, crud, creeping crud, trots, turistas, runs, Montezuma's revenge, what's going around.

VISAGE n. mug, pan, kisser, puss, map, phiz, phizog, biscuit, clock, mask, dial. See FACE.

VISCOUS adj. gooey, gloppy, globby, gooky, gozzle, goupy, gunky, goonky, gummy.

VISIBLE adj. big as life, out in the open, barefaced, plain as the nose on one's face, under one's nose, if it were a snake it would bite you. See APPARENT.

VISION n. 1. spook, haunt, hant, haint, things that go bump in the night. 2. trip, head trip, mind trip, castle in the air, fool's paradise, pipe dream, stare into the middle distance, pie in the sky. See also DREAM. 3. dazzler, dream, dreamy, dreamboat, dream puss, dream bait, angel, angel face, angel puss, head rush, stunner, stunning, look like a million, eye-filling, eyeful, a picture, pretty as a picture, centerfold. See BEAUTIFUL.

VISIONARY n. stargazer, dreamer.

VISIT v. swing by, fall by, fall down, fall up (Bl.), hit, play, pay a call, crash (uninvited). See also APPEAR.

VISITOR n. company, out-of-towner, visiting fireman, ET, little green men, man from Mars.

VISUALIZE v. dream up, get the picture, head trip. See also THINK, CREATE.

VITAL adj. 1. bottom line, meat and potatoes, nitty-gritty, coal and ice, gutty, name, name of the game. See BASIC. 2. heavy, heavy number, meaningful, business end of, serious shit, serious jelly, matter of life and death, chips are down, underlined. See IMPORTANT.

VITALITY adj. go juice, bounce, bang, zing, zip, sock, pizzazz, the force, clout, steam, the stuff, full of piss and vinegar, full of p and v. See POWER. See also SPIRITED.

VIVACIOUS adj. bouncy, grooving, jumping, hyper, swinging, swingle, rocking, salty, upbeat, red hot, fireball, ball of fire, go-go, full of go. See SPIRITED.

VIXEN n. bitch, bitch kitty, battle-ax, fishwife, hellion, hellcat, she-devil, she-wolf, biddy, old biddy, pain in the ass, screech, wet hen.

VOCAL CHORDS n. pipes.

VOCALIST n. chanteuse, chantoosie, crooner, groaner, canary, warbler, songbird, thrush, nightingale, belter, folkie, monster (popular), shouter (gospel), coon shouter, bad pipes (bad).

VOCALIZE v. croon, groan, moan, chirp, canary, do a canary, yodel, give out, belt out a song, belt out a number, scat, shout, throw a tonsil.

VOCATION n. bag, gig, biz, game, gesheft, line, line of business, number, go, do, dodge, what one is into, thing, hang, nine-to-five shit, racket. See OCCUPATION.

VOGUE, IN adj. faddy, trendy, what's happening, in, in-thing, the thing, with it, mod, now, state of the art, the latest, last word, the rage, up to the minute. See STYLISH.

VOID v. 1. ding, zing, nix, wipe out, take out, knock out, KO, black out, torpedo, kill, queer, shoot down, shoot down in flames, wipe off the map. See CANCEL. 2. cut, sterilize, sanitize, decontaminate, bleep, bleep out, blue pencil, knock out, X-out, trim, gut, clean up, launder, snip, pass up, drop, rub, squash, squelch. 3. shit, crap, dump, poop, go, go to the can, go to the john, go caca, make poo-poo, shake a few clinkers out; pee, piss, leak, take a leak, go, go wee-wee, go pee-pee, tinkle, make wee-wee, pish, drain the dew, piddle, go play in the sandbox. See BOWEL MOVEMENT, URINATE.

VOLKSWAGEN n. beetle, bug, Nazi go-cart, VW.

VOLUBLE adj. gabby, gasser, yacker, CBS, windy, windbag, bag of wind, load of wind, windjammer, big-mouthed, bucket mouth, motor mouth, gum beater, all jaw, flap jaw, ear duster. See TALKATIVE.

VOLUNTEER n. walk-on.

VOMIT v. barf, puke, be sick, throw up, throw up one's guts, bring up, chuck up, upchuck, urp, whoops, Ralph, Ralph up, talk to Ralph, talk to Ralph on the big white phone, talk on the big white phone, York, buick, boot, power boot, bof, woof, shoot one's breakfast (etc.), shoot one's cookies, toss one's cookies, toss one's tacos, drop one's cookies, flash, flash one's cookies, flash one's food, feed the fish, lose it, lose one's lunch, blow one's lunch, lose one's doughnuts, blow one's doughnuts, blow one's groceries, blow grits, blow chunks, the technicolor yawn, instant boot camp, kiss the porcelain god, pray to the porcelain god, drive the bus, drive the porcelain bus, drive the big white bus, laugh at the carpet, air one's belly, heave, cast the gorge, heave the gorge, good stick (heroin induced).

VOODOO n. hoodoo, hocus-pocus, mumbo-jumbo, abracadabra, hoochey-coochey (practitioner).

VORACIOUS adj. dog-hungry, empty, fly light, grits time, have a tapeworm, munchies (follows marijuana use), starving, starved, starved to death, could eat a horse, could eat the asshole out of a bear, piggy, greedyguts.

VOUCH v. 1. swear up and down, swear on a stack of Bibles, swear till one is blue in the face, cross one's heart and hope to die, say so. See SWEAR. 2. stand up for one, back, get behind one, okay, OK, sign for, cosign, put one's John Hancock on, rubber-stamp, hold one up, go to bat for. See also SUPPORT.

VOW v. cross one's heart and hope to die, swear till one is blue in the face, swear up and down. See SWEAR.

VOYAGE n. hop, swing, jaunt, cruise, junket, trek, overnight, weekend, Cook's tour. See TRAVEL.

VOYAGE v. jet around, go places, hop, city-hop, country-hop, globe-trot, tripping, cruise, hit the road, on the move, trek, do the continent, do Europe (or wherever), junket. See TRAVEL.

VOYAGER n. jet-setter, globe-trotter, deadhead (free), seatcover, dude (bus), drop, line load (taxi), rubberneck, rubbernecker, snowbird, snowflake, sunflower.

VOYEUR n. peek freak, peeping Tom.

VULGAR adj. 1. cheap, loud, loud-mouthed, foul mouth, foulmouthed, raw, skank, tacky, raunchy, X-rated, hard core, soft core, blue, dirty, filthy, low-down and dirty, in the gutter, off-color, rough, rough stuff, salty. 2. garden variety, run of the mill, everyday, dime a dozen, plastic, cotton-pickin', chit, low.

VULGARITY n. raunch.

VULNERABLE adj. pigeon, clay pigeon, sitting duck, naked, ass out, neck stuck out, ready to be taken, wide open, on the line, on the spot, out on a limb, sucker for a left.

VULVA n. pussy, cunt, snatch, twat, beaver, crack, hole, quiff, quim, box, fur, fur pie, tail, clam, nautch, piece, cunny, cooch, muff, receiving set, the Y. See VAGINA.

W

W n. whiskey, William.

WAFER n. dry cush.

WAFFLE n. collision mat (N.).

WAG n. cutup, life of the party, madcap, trickster, card, a million laughs, kibitzer, funster, punster, quipster, wisecracker. See JOKER.

WAG v. fish tail.

WAGER n. spec, break, breaks, big break, even break, shot, shot at, get a shot at, long shot, shot in the dark, hundred-to-one shot, odds on, whack, whack at, go, go at, stab, stab at, have a fling at, prayer, hunch, in the running, irons in the fire, fair shake, fighting chance, outside chance, Chinaman's chance, as much chance as a snowball in hell, snowball chance, fifty-fifty, toss-up, flier, header, plunge, brodie, play, action, ante, down on, chunk, parlay, brinksmanship, maximax (big return, big loss), maximin (small return, big loss), minimax (safe); standoff, push (tie); hedge, hedge off, layoff, handle (total).

WAGER v. play, plunge, put up, put up or shut up, lay on the line, put it on the line, put on the spot, put one's money where one's mouth is, parlay, take a flier, take a plunge, take a header, chance it, jump off the deep end, take the action, book the action, make book, get down, get down on, on (on a horse), play the ponies, play the market, spec, on spec, go the limit, go whole hog, shoot, shoot one's wad, shoot the works, go for a chunk, go out on a limb, go on the hook for, skate on thin ice, stick one's neck out, hustle, ball the jack, grift, on the grift, stake, backstrap, cheesebox, cap (add illegally); hedge, lay off (relay bet).

WAGES n. take, take home, bread, sugar, bacon, bacon and eggs, bring home the bacon, eagle shit. See COMPENSATION.

WAGE SCALE n. scale, going rate, top of the show (TV), cheat stick (worker, logger).

WAIF n. drop, fetch, guttersnipe, mudlark, raggedy muffin, rustle.

WAIL v. blubber, sing the blues, cry the blues, go for a crying towel, beat one's breast, rain, carry on, howl, raise a howl. See LAMENT.

WAIST n. midsection, spare tire, bulge, battle of the bulge. See also STOMACH.

WAIT n. hold, on hold, holdup, down, downtime.

WAIT v. cool it, cool one's heels, sweat, sweat it, sweat it out, sweat out, wait out, put on ice, put on hold, hold the phone, hold the line, hold on, hold everything, hold fire, save it, stall, hang, hang in, hang on, hang out, hang onto your hat, hang around, hang about, stick around, sit, sit tight, sit and take it, sit out, sit it out, sit on one's ass, sit on one's butt, sit on one's duff, warm a chair, lay dead, play dead, keep one's shirt on, hold your horses, see which way the cookie crumbles, champ, champ at the bit, chomp at the bit, wait for the other shoe to drop, play the waiting game.

WAITER n. garçon, hasher, boy, carhop, coffee bean, punk, soup jockey. See also WAITRESS.

WAITING adj. 1. looking for, waitin' on, waiting for the other shoe to drop, the noose is hanging. 2. in the wings, in the cards, in the wind, at hand, see it coming, it's looking to.

WAITING ROOM n. squat pad, icebox, dugout, bull pen, green room (The.).

WAIT ON TABLE v. hash, sling hash, deal them off the arm, gun.

WAITRESS n. hasher, girl, miss, biscuit shooter, carhop, coffee bean, curbie, heaver, soup jockey, topless. See also WAITER.

WAKE n. cold meat party.

WAKE UP v. 1. rise and shine, roll out, turn out, pile out, hit the deck, show a leg, drop your cocks and grab your socks, keep bankers' hours (late). See AWAKEN. 2. jazz up, juice up, pep up, zip up, key up, fire up, steam up, stir up, switch on, turn on the heat, rabble-rouse. See EXCITE.

WAKE UP, COMMAND piss call, rise and shine, roll out, pile out, turn out, hit the deck, show a leg, drop your cocks and grab your socks.

WALK n. 1. constitutional, legwork, shlep, traipse. 2. pavement, the bricks, byway, trail, stroll, aisle, boardwalk.

WALK v. ankle, ank, leg it, hoof it, toddle, hotfoot, go by hand, sashay, boot, boot it, foot it, burn shoe leather, shanks' mare, ride shanks' mare, stomp, pound the beat, pound the pavement, hit the road, hit the bricks, hit the dirt, hit the grit, move out, stump it, traipse, trapse,

trapse around, ooze, strut one's stuff, cruise, air out, beat the rocks, gumshoe, navigate, mope, mooch, press the bricks, boogie, Spanish walk, walk Spanish, trill, hippety hop, broom, diddy bop, truck, percolate, count ties (hobo), drill, jaywalk.

WALKER n.   boot jockey, gumshoe, jaywalker.

WALLET n.   poke, frame, leather, lizard, pig, okus, skin, cush (found or stolen).

WALLOP v.   bash, wham, bam, whop, whomp, whack, bushwhack, hide, tan, take it out of one's hide, take it out of one's skin, bop, boff, belt, sock, slug, slog, smack, clobber, zap, zetz, paste, take out, take a whack at, plant one, land a haymaker, beat the bejesus out of one. See HIT.

WALLOPING n.   licking, larruping, whaling, lathering, leathering, hiding, tanning, shellacking, waxing, get one's lumps, strap oil, dose of strap oil. See BEATING. See also DEFEAT.

WANDER v.   1. cruise, drift, float, bum, bum around, sashay, traipse, trapse, trapse around, knock around, knock about, bat around, bat about, hop scotch, percolate, air out, beat the rocks, press the bricks, gumshoe, take to the road, hit the road, hit the trail, hit the dirt, hit the grit, walk the tracks, count ties, ooze, mope, navigate, mooch, ank, boogie, follow one's nose, globe-trot, trek, circumlocute. 2. get off the track, get sidetracked, all over the map. See also DRIFT.

WANDERER n.   drifter, bum, floater, gad, gadabout, globe-trotter. See also VAGRANT.

WANT v.   yen for, have the hots for, cream for, lech for, itch for, hanker for, have eyes for, spoil for, give one's eyeteeth for, have one's mouth fixed for, die over. See DESIRE.

WANTING adj.   1. burned out, outta gas, cooked, not come up to scratch, not hack it, not make it, not cut out for, second fiddle, second stringer, third stringer, low man on the totem pole. See also INADEQUATE, IMPERFECT. 2. short, come up short, minus, bupkis, chicken shit, too little too late, half-assed, half-baked. 3. horny, turned on, pash, sexy, heavy, hot, hot and heavy, hot baby, hot number, hot pants, hot patootie.

WANTON adj.   1. loose, fast, fast and loose, speedy, swinging, cheap, for free, chippy around, sleep around, two-timing, extracurricular, on the make, put out, put the horns on, no better than she should be. 2. filthy, dirty, blue, X-rated, raunchy, raw, hard core, soft core, hot, heavy, hot and heavy, hot stuff, rough, rough stuff, evil-minded, foul mouth, foulmouthed, salty, off-color, low-down, low-down dirty, low-down and dirty, purple, in the gutter; horny, cream jeans, hot pants, a lech on, lechin's. 3. on the take, on the pad, open, wide open, meat-eater,

racket up, something rotten in Denmark, gone to bad, gone to the dogs, gone to hell, double-crossing. 4. flaky, kinky, fantasmo, gaga, punchy, yo-yo, any way the wind blows, blow hot and cold, up and down, every which way. 5. cussed, evil, mean, ornery, accidentally on purpose, do one dirt.

WANTON n.   swinger, pushover, roundheels, easy lay, chippie, floozy, cuddle bunny, pigmeat (old). See LECHER.

WAR n.   cold war, hot war, police action, strike, first strike, preemptive strike, surgical mission, the big one (WW I, W II).

WAR ADVOCATE n.   hawk.

WARBLE v.   chirp, canary, do a canary, yodel.

WARDEN n.   man, the Man, king, main ghee, skipper, belly robber, gut robber, big shot, big noise, big spud, strib, screw. See also JAILER.

WARDEN'S DEPUTY n.   dogcatcher, whitecap.

WARDROBE n.   threads, togs, toggery, duds, rags, vine, weeds, dry goods, drapery, drapes. See CLOTHING.

WAREHOUSE n.   stash house.

WARES n.   the goods, material, stuff, hot number, jive (gaudy), seconds.

WARM adj.   close, toasty, sticky, broiler, roaster, scorcher, sizzler, swelterer, one can fry eggs on the sidewalk.

WARMHEARTED adj.   clubby, mellow (close), tight, palsy, palsy-walsy, cozy, pally, right nice, right friendly, regular. See also KIND.

WARMONGER n.   hawk, Dr. Strangelove, Strangelove.

WARN v.   1. lay it on one, lay it out for, let in on, put one wise, wise up, tip, tip off, post. See ADVISE. 2. flag, wave a red flag, highball, cloud up, give one the high sign, toot the tooter.

WARNING n.   1. Mayday, SOS, high sign, sign, wigwag, wink, bleep, ixnay, tip, tip-off, burn notice (warning that a person is a liar), a bug in one's ear. See ALARM. See also PREMONITION. 2. fore, watch it, heads up, cheese it the cops, jiggers, beat it, look out, amscray. See ALARM. 3. set down, speaking to, talking to, calling down, jacking up, chewing, cussing out, going over, rap on the knuckles, slap on the wrist. See also SCOLD.

WARRANT n.   1. shingle, plaster, sticker, ticket, tag, chit, hooker, ducat, general, reader, reader with a tail. 2. go-ahead, green light, OK, okay, the word.

WARRIOR n.   cannon fodder, bullet bait, G.I., GI Joe, dogface, doughboy, footslogger, grunt, paddlefoot, buckass private, trooper. See SOLDIER.

WART n.   beauty spot.

WARY adj.   cagey, leery, walk on eggs, handle with kid gloves, watch one's step, watch out, keep on one's toes, think twice, hedge one's bets, on the lookout. See CAUTIOUS.

WASH v.   dobee, doby (by hand), button chop, soogie, sujee, soujge, soogie-moogie, sujee-mujee, swab, swab down (N. and maritime). See also CLEAN.

WASH CLOTHES v.   button chop, boil up (hobo).

WASH DISHES v.   do the dishes, pearl-dive, K.P., China clipper, bubble dance, bubble dancer (WW II).

WASHINGTON   Chinook State, Evergreen State.

WASHINGTON, D.C.   D.C., the Capital, Capital City, the hill, inside the beltway.

WASHROOM n.   can, john, rest room, Men's, Ladies', ladies' room, women's room, girls' room, little girls' room, powder room, men's room, boys' room, little boys' room, head, facilities, piss house, crapper, WC, loo, sandbox, altar room, throne room, donagher, donniker, Andy Gump, bucket, privy, two-holer, out back, Chic Sale, honeywagon, honeypot, piss pot, pot, potty, potty chair, cat box, thunder box, thunder mug, joe, jane, showers, where the dicks hang out. See TOILET.

WASTE n.   1. gash, hogwash, junk, dreck, shit. 2. BM, crap, shit, caca, turd, dingleberry. See EXCRETION.

WASTE v.   piss away, flush down the toilet, run through, spend money like it was going out of style, throw out the baby with the bathwater, kill the goose that lays the golden egg. See SQUANDER.

WASTEBASKET n.   file, circular file, round file; file thirteen, file seventeen, skid box (WW 11).

WASTED adj.   blown, blown out, diddled away, pissed away, petered out, shot, down the toilet, down the tube, down the drain, down the spout, down the rathole, going in circles, out the window.

WASTE OF TIME n.   total shuck, wild goose chase, goin' round in circles, can't win for losin', no-win situation, go fight City Hall, go hit your head against the wall, locking the barn after the horse is stolen, not a prayer. See USELESS.

WASTE TIME v.   hang out, hang around, goof around, monkey around, fool around, goof off, screw off, fuck the dog, sit on one's ass, jelly, tool, tail, lie down on the job. See IDLE. See also DAWDLE.

WASTREL n.   big-time spender, last of the big-time spenders, sport, good-time Charley.

WATCH n.   1. ticker, timepiece, turnip, kettle turnip (pocket), chroniker, Albert (with chain). 2. weather eye, peeled eye, eagle eye, gapper, hawk, spotter, tip, anchor, case, gap, jigger, jigger guy, jigger man, outside man, zex man, lay zex, lay butzo, lay jiggers, lay chickie, gander.

WATCH v.   1. scope, spy, pipe, focus, eye, eagle-eye, hold the glims on, take in, get a load of, have a look-see, give the once over, check out, check something out, case, rubber, rubberneck, 87 1/2 (look at a girl, restaurant), keep an eye on, keep tab, keep tabs on. See SEE. 2. keep one's eyes peeled, keep a weather eye peeled, peel your eyeballs, pick up on, ride shotgun for, shotgun, burn up, gap, jap (crime); go slumming, slum, kibitz, take in the sights, peeping Tom.

WATCHFUL adj.   on the lookout, on the que vive, on the ball, on the job, on one's toes, with a weather eye open, with one's eyes peeled, all ears, keep one's ear to the ground, glued, hooked, not miss a trick, not overlook a bet, see after, see to, mind one's p's and q's. See also CAUTIOUS.

WATCHMAN n.   lookout, lay chickie, bugster; Charley, stick (night watchman). See also GUARD, LOOKOUT.

WATER n.   drink, the drink, aqua, H2O, Adam's ale, Adam's water; eighty, eighty-two, eighty-six (glass of water); hobo cocktail, sky juice, splash, ammonia, fizz water, fizzy stuff, seltzer, for two cents plain (carbonated).

WATER v.   doctor, doctor up, phony up, plant, spike, water, water down, baptize, irrigate, cook, cut, needle, lace, shave.

WATERMELON n.   piss chunk.

WAVER v.   yo-yo, waffle, hem and haw, pussyfoot around, run hot and cold, blow hot and cold, shilly-shally, the jury's out, hedge, hedge off. See VACILLATE.

WAVES n.   tasty waves (good surf), foam, breakers, rollers.

WAY n.   1. thataway, every which way, forty ways to Sunday, forty ways from Sunday, forty ways for Sunday. 2. bit, spitting distance, stone's throw, Sunday run, tidy step, whoop, two whoops and a holler, a shlep, sleeper jump, piece, far piece, fer piece, fur piece. 3. groove, thing, Jones, into, hang-up, bag, one's bag, shot, kick, style, hook. See STYLE. See also ROUTINE, PLAN.

WAYFARER n.   jet-setter, globe-trotter, gadabout, deadhead (free), seatcover, dude (bus), drop, line load (taxi), rubberneck, rubbernecker, snowbird, snowflake, sunflower.

WAYLAY v.   jump, lay for, bushwhack, drygulch, jap, pull a jap, box, get one in a box. See AMBUSH.

WEAK adj.   1. rocky, wussy, woozy, dopey, wishy-washy, out of gas, don't have the horses. 2. paper tiger, turkey, weak sister, wimp, wimpy, dopey, laid back, moony, basket case, chicken, gutless, jerky, nerd, nerdy, neb, nebbish, nobody, sad sack, shnook, slob, fish, poor fish, clown, dud, fuddy-duddy, dead one, eight ball, lamebrained, half-baked, rocky, blah, draddy, pablum, nothing, zero, zilch, diddly bop, flub the dub, half-assed, pigeon, clay pigeon, sitting duck, lame duck, shooting blanks, out on a limb, out of gas, out of one's depth, in over one's head, don't have the horses, ready to be taken, wide open, sucker for a left, putty in one's hands, what the cat dragged in.

WEAKEN v. 1. cut, irrigate, baptize. See DILUTE. 2. blow sky high, knock the bottom out of, knock the chocks out from under, knock the props out from under, poke full of holes, shoot full of holes. 3. break, crack, crack up, fold, cave in, go soft, go to pieces, poop out, peg out, fizzle out, come apart at the seams, be on one's last legs, have one foot in the grave, have one foot in the grave and the other on a banana peel. See DETERIORATE. 4. clip one's wings, shake up, soften up, take the edge off, take the bit out, take the sting out.

WEAKENED adj. 1. draggin', draggin' one's ass, rocky, seedy, down, run down, laid low, below par, peaky, peaked, poorly, out of action, out of condition, out of shape, good and flabby, 4 F. 2. out of gas, out of juice, wiped out, wrung out, burned out, played out, nearly dead, used up, in a bad way. See TIRED. 3. cut, spiked, watered down, baptized, irrigated, needled, laced, shaved.

WEAKLING n. wimp, wuss, wuss-puss, chicken, chicken heart, chicken liver, lily liver, white liver, yellow, yellow belly, paper tiger, poor tool, weak tool, droop, glass arm, candy ass, pecker ass, fraidy cat, scaredy cat, jellyfish, cream puff, ladyfinger, skinny, softy, weak sister, sissy, pantywaist, pushover, baby, big baby, crybaby, namby-pamby, dancer, deuce, piker, mouse, milksop, Casper Milquetoast, tootie fruitie, gutless, gutless wonder, drip, sad sack, neb, nebbish, nerd, turkey, doormat, cookie cutter, cookie pusher, punk, putty in one's hands, lame duck.

WEAKNESS n. soft spot, bag, cup of tea, a thing for, soft underbelly, glass chin, Achilles' heel. See also LOVE.

WEALTH n. high on the hog, on top of the heap, bed of roses, clover, velvet, Easy Street, lap of luxury, the life of Riley.

WEALTHY adj. uptown, upscale, the haves, have it made, have a mint, have the wherewithal, have one's place in the sun, on Easy Street, on velvet, on top of the heap, on a bed of roses, everything's coming up roses, high on the hog, right up there, in the bucks, in the money, in the chips, in the lap of luxury, in clover, rolling in clover, on a roll, really rolling, rolling in dough, rolling

in money, lousy with money, tall money, moneybags, money to burn, burner, really cooking, cooking with gas, lousy rich, stinking rich, filthy, filthy rich, holding, well-heeled, well-fixed, well-to-do, well set up, set up, sitting pretty, sit fat, fat city, fat cat, arrived, plush, lush, flush, heavy sugar, big bucks, loaded, booming, going strong, going great guns, mining the gold, Midas touch, golden, made it big, made one's pile, did all right by oneself, home free, laughing all the way to the bank, ride the gravy train, gravy boat, jammy, good ticket, dicty, big, biggie, big shot, long hitter, king of the hill, duke of the catwalk, life of Reilly, live off the fat of the land, Fat Daddy Greenbacks, Daddy Warbucks, scissorbill, swell, curtain, lace curtain, coupon clipper, big butter and egg man, rich as Croesus, the establishment, big boys, the 400, upper class, the beautiful people, main line, large, oofy, piss on ice.

WEAPON n. dingbat, hardware, heat (gun).

WEAPONLESS adj. skinned, clean.

WEAR v. turn out, fit out, rig out, rig up, rag out, rag up, tog, suit up, doll up, dog out, dud, dude, dude up, sport.

WEARINESS adj. brain fag, burnout.

WEARING APPAREL n. threads, set of threads, togs, toggery, duds, outfit, rags, glad rags, getup, get out, vine, weeds, dry goods, flash, ready-made, tailor-made, bib and tucker. See CLOTHING.

WEARY adj. 1. bushed, had it, pooped, out of gas, out of juice, knocked out, wiped out, burned out, crispy, flaked out, zonked, draggin' ass, dead tired, beat, done in, all in, punchy, bone-tired, dog-tired. 2. ho hum, so what else is new?, bored stiff, fed up, full up, up to here, had it up to here, done it all, been around twice. See TIRED. See also JADED.

WEARY v. fizzle, fizzle out, fag, tucker, poop, poop out, burn out, fag out, tucker out, knock out, peter out. See TIRE.

WED v. middle-aisle it, get hitched, get spliced, say I do, ball and chain up.

WEDDING n. bells, shotgun wedding, hook.

WEE adj. teeny, peewee, peanut, small fry, banty, mite, pint-sized, knee high. See SMALL.

WEEK n. double trey (workweek), stanza.

WEEP v. blubber, bawl, break down, boo hoo, let go, let it out, turn on the waterworks, cry one's eyes out, cry me a river, crack-up. See CRY.

WEEPER n. crybaby, crying jag.

WEEPING n. waterworks, weeps.

WEIGH v.   1. kick around, bat it around, brainstorm, head trip, noodle, noodle it around, knock around, put on one's thinking cap, cop, track, run it up the flagpole, run it by one again, blow change, sort out, hash, rehash, hash over, stew, stew over, sweat, sweat over, cool something over, chew over, chew the cud. See ANALYZE. 2. hang (how does that hang?), hold a candle to, stack up against, match up. 3. heft.

WEIGH STATION n.   chicken coop, pig pen.

WEIGHT n.   1. beef, beefiness, heft, heftiness, avoirdupois. 2. albatross, albatross around one's neck, excess baggage, shlepper, ball and chain. See HINDRANCE. 3. juice, string, ropes, drag, pull, clout, access, fix, grease, connection, in, a lot to do with, a lot to say about, inside track, wire-pulling. See INFLUENCE. 4. iron.

WEIGHT LIFTER n.   iron pumper.

WEIGHTY adj.   1. heavy, hefty, beefy, lead-footed. See also FAT. 2. heavy, heavyweight, heavy stuff, heavy number, meaningful, mean business, matter of life and death, serious jelly, talk serious shit, we're not talking about nutmeg here, money talks, no fooling, no shit, no bird turdin'. See SERIOUS. 3. big league, major league, walk heavy, big deal, carry a lot of weight, the juice, the force, underlined. See IMPORTANT.

WEIRD adj.   weirdo, archfreak, semi-dork, creepo, freaky, funky, kinky, kooky, birdie, flaky, off the wall. See STRANGE. See also ECCENTRIC.

WELCOME n.   tumble, rumble, blow, high five, low five, hello, howdy, highball, red carpet, red-carpet treatment, welcome mat, key to the city.

WELCOME v.   highball, tumble, flop, give one a flop, give one a toss, flag, shoulder, whistle for, whistle down, give one the glad eye, give one the glad hand, give one the key to the city, roll out the red carpet.

WELDER n.   smoke-eater.

WELL adj.   wrapped tight, alive and kicking, bright-eyed and bushy tailed, chipper, together, up to snuff, up to the mark, fit as a fiddle, full of beans, full of piss and vinegar, in fine feather, in fine whack, in high feather, in the pink, sound as a dollar, right, right as rain, solid as a rock, beefy, husky, strong as a horse, strong as a lion, strong as an ox.

WELLBORN adj.   born with a silver spoon in one's mouth, blue blood, lace curtain, silk stocking, upper crust, upper cut, FFV, 400, four hundred.

WELL-BRED adj.   blue blood, lace curtain, silk stocking, upper crust, upper cut, FFV, 400, four hundred.

WELL-CONNECTED adj.   in, wired, well wired.

WELL-DRESSED adj.   looking sharp, looking spiffy, looking classy, looking nifty, looking snazzy, looking swanky, looking posh, looking ritzy, looking swell, looking nobby, togged, togged up, togged out, togged to the bricks, slicked up, rigged up, rigged out, ragged up, ragged out, duded up, duded out, decked out, tricked out, tricked up, figged out, figged up, turned out, dolled up, fancied up, gussied up, slicked up, spiffed up, spruced up, in fine feather, in high feather, in one's best bib and tucker, mellow back, wearing one's best, dressed fit to kill, dressed to kill, dressed to the teeth, dressed to the nines, in one's Sunday best, Sunday go-to-church, Sunday go-to-meeting, putting on the dog. See also STYLISH.

WELL-GROOMED adj.   1. classy, dap, nifty, snazzy, spiffy, smooth, dressed to kill, dressed to the teeth, dressed to the nines, sharp, swank, posh, ritzy, swell, nobby. See WELL-DRESSED. See also STYLISH. 2. neat as a pin, clean, pressed, in apple-pie order.

WELL-INFORMED adj.   posted, hip, hep, hip to the jive, savvy, all woke up, in the picture, booted on, wise to, inside, in the know, know the score, know-it-all, know all the answers. See INFORMED.

WELL-KNOWN adj.   WK, w.k., celeb, star, superstar, name, somebody, VIP, face, in the limelight, make a splash, page-oner, large, right up there, big, big name, biggie. See CELEBRITY, CELEBRATED.

WELL-MEANING adj.   bleeding heart, old softie, soft-hearted, heart in the right place, all heart (Derog.), have a heart.

WELL-WISHING n.   send-off, royal send-off.

WELSH RAREBIT n.   rabbit, bunny, blushing bunny (with tomato sauce or soup).

WELTER n.   goulash, mishmash, mishmosh, garbage, everything but the kitchen sink.

WEST COAST n.   left coast, the Coast.

WESTERN FILM n.   horse opera, oater, shoot 'em up, spaghetti Western (made in Italy), sukiyaki Western (Japanese version).

WEST INDIAN n.   conch, jig, zig.

WEST POINT CADET n.   gray legs, yearling.

WEST VIRGINIA   Mountain State, Panhandle State.

WHALE'S PENIS n.   Pink Floyd.

WHAT pron.   whu?, whuh?, come again?, howzat?, huh?, nu?, so?, what then?, I'll bite.

WHEEDLE v.   snow, soap, soft soap, jolly, oil, spread it on, lay it on, butter up, soften up, sweeten up, work on, brownnose, suck ass, polish the apple, apple-polish, kowtow, buddy up, curry below the knee. See CAJOLE.

WHEEDLING n.   jive, snow, snow job, smoke, baked wind, line, abreaction route, goo, hoke, eyewash, soap, soft soap, bullshit, con, sell, applesauce, balloon juice, snake oil. See FLATTERY.

WHIM n. fool notion, bee in one's bonnet, flea in one's ear, spur of the moment. See also DESIRE.

WHIMSICAL adj. fantasmo, flaky, kinky, impomanic, blow hot and cold, up and down. See CAPRICIOUS.

WHINER n. bitcher, bellyacher, griper, kvetch, plainer. See COMPLAINER.

WHIP n. bat (jockey).

WHIP v. 1. bash, trash, drub, lather, larrup, whop, whomp, hide, tan, tan one's hide, take it out of one's hide, take it out of one's skin, whip ass, beat the shit out of one, beat the living daylights out of. 2. bury, blank, skunk, schneider, murder, kill, cook, cook one's goose, trim, trounce, top, fix one's wagon, skin, shellack, tube, make one say uncle, do in, lick, beat all hollow, blow one out, run rings around, run circles around, put away, settle one's hash. See DEFEAT.

WHIPPED CREAM n. snowstorm, in a snowstorm, in the snow.

WHISKERS n. beaver, brush, muff, peach fuzz, pez, spinach, face spinach, face lace, bush, shrubbery, alfalfa, chin whiskers, Castro; gallaway, galways (stage Irishman).

WHISKEY n. hard liquor, likker, alky, alchy, hooch, booze, corn, cave corn, red-eye, moonshine, mountain dew, prairie dew, squirrel dew, sauce, wee drop, coffin varnish, brush whiskey, nigger pot, damp bourbon poultice, dirty bird (Old Crow). See also LIQUOR.

WHISPER v. buzz, sotto.

WHITES n. WASP, white bread, face, paleface, citizen, vanilla, fay, ofay, ofaginzy, gringo, anglo, honky, white honky, white meat, whitey, the Man, Mister Charley, Chuck, white trash, poor white trash, haole (Hawaiian), kelt, keltch, blue-eyed, blue-eyed devil, round eye, cracker, Florida cracker, Georgia Cracker, great white father, gray, hack, hay eater, peck, peckerwood, silk girl, silk broad, li'l Eva, marshmallow, Miss Ann, pale, Sylvester, bale of straw (blonde), beasts, buckra, fade, hack, hard head, pink, jeff, Paddy, patty, patty boy, spook, steel, wig, jig chaser (all Derog.).

WHITEWASH v. launder.

WHOLE n. jackpot, the works, lock stock and barrel, hook line and sinker, fixin's, whole enchilada, whole ball of wax, whole nine yards, whole shebang, whole works, whole bit, whole deal, whole schmeer, whole show, whole shtick, megillah, whole megillah, whole shooting match, whole bunch, whole mess, caboodle, whole caboodle, whole kit and caboodle, whole hog, everything including the kitchen sink, lump sum (money), the picture, the big picture, you've seen my whole spring line, across the board, wall to wall.

WHOLESOME adj. right, right as rain, together, all there, in the pink, fit as a fiddle, in fine feather, sound as a dollar. See HEALTHY. See also MORAL.

WHOLLY adv. from A to Z, from A to Izzard, top to bottom, shoot the works, stone (stone deaf), from hell to breakfast, all the way, all hollow. See COMPLETELY.

WHOOP n. holler.

WHOOP v. holler, holler out.

WHORE n. hooker, call girl, hustler, ho, working broad, working girl, nok, model, pro, floozie, chippy, prostie, streetwalker, baggage, broad, chicken rancher, chile whore, chacha, ass peddler, coozey, vegetarian (won't perform fellatio). See PROSTITUTE.

WHOREDOM n. world's oldest profession, broad racket, the bottle, hustle, the life, in the life, turning a trick, on the turf, hitting the turf, stepping out, going out for a buck, white slavery.

WHOREHOUSE n. house, cathouse, can house, call house, massage parlor, rap parlor, poontang palace, snake ranch, chicken ranch, meat market, camp, zoo, joint, call joint, hook shop, rib joint, body shop, service station. See BROTHEL.

WHOREMONGER n. mack, mackman, macko man, hard Mack (violent), sweet Mack, mac, mackerel, dude, flesh peddler, king bung, pee eye, P.I., ponce, Johnny Ponce, husband. See PIMP.

WHY adv. howcome?, howcum?

WICKED adj. bad-assed, rat's ass, sucks, scuzzy, sleazy, sleazeball, bad news, tough, tough nuggies, fierce, lousy, murder, poison, dirty, low-down. See BAD.

WICKED PLACE n. hellhole, hole, joint, den, den of iniquity, sink, sink of corruption.

WIDE-EYED adj. bug-eyed, pop-eyed, eyes like percolator tops.

WIDESPREAD adj. all over the lot, all over the place, from hell to breakfast, across the board, wall to wall.

WIENER n. frank, hot dog, hot dawg, wienie, weenie, tube steak, balloon, beenie, bowwow, bun pup, Coney Island pup, pimp stick, puppy, special.

WIFE n. old lady, O.L., roommate, mama, missus, better half, little woman, the wifey, little missus, wiff, chief of staff, rib, ball and chain, block and tackle, front office, golf widow, grass widow, headache, War Department, mat, hat, seagull, slave driver, squaw, headquarters, apron, main queen, old saw, first sergeant, baby, fishwife, fag bag (married to homosexual).

WIG n. rug, sky piece, toup, brush, doily, dome doily, scalp doily, headpiece, muff, head falsie, merkin (pubic hair piece).

WILD adj. funky, gonzo, harum-scarum, hog-wild, rat fuck, wild ass, like crazy, like mad, flaky, kill-crazy, hog-crazy. See also VIOLENT, UNRESTRAINED.

WILDERNESS n. boondocks, boonies, bush, outback, sticks.

WILDLY adv. like crazy, like mad, something fierce, something terrible, helter-skelter, holus-bolus, hurry-scurry, ramble-scramble.

WILE n. angle, dodge, slant, trick, twist, switch, set-up, game, little game, booby trap, grift, racket, con, gimmick, curveball, monkeyshines, shenanigans, stunt. See also CUNNING, TRICK.

WILINESS n. hustle, gamesmanship, one-upmanship, con, double shuffle, fast shuffle, fast one, run around, song and dance, monkey business, funny business. See CUNNING.

WILLING adj. game, go along with, on. See also READY.

WILLINGLY adv. at the drop of a hat, game for.

WILY adj. 1. smooth, street smarts, streetwise, foxy, crazy like a fox, cagey, fancy footwork, slick, slippery, greasy, greaseball, sly boots, sharp. See SLY. 2. nifty, Philadelphia lawyer, sharpie, sharp stuff, shark, ringer, slicker, smoothie, got the smarts, got one's boots on, tuned in, nobody's fool, not born yesterday. See INTELLIGENT.

WIMBLEDON n. Wimby.

WIN n. slam, grand slam, bombshell, score, walkaway, kill, killing, clean sweep, laugher, hot run, pay dirt, gold medal, gold star. See TRIUMPH.

WIN v. beat the competish, beat the game, beat the system, beat like a drum, beat all hollow, beat by a nose, nose out, edge out, sneak past, upset, put the skids to, snow under, plow under, put the kibosh on, finish off, shut off, wrack up, blow out, blow off, sink the opposition, pin one's ears back, have it knocked, have it locked, all locked up, lock-and-win situation, walk off with, walk away with, walk over, run away with, run rings around, run circles around, breeze in, rake in the pot, break the tape, grab the brass ring, grab the gold, clean on, clean one, clean out, clean up, clean sweep, break the book, put away, rake it in, make a payday, take one, take one to the cleaners, take it all, take all the marbles, take out, take one out, take care of, shoot down, shoot one down, shoot down in flames, shut down, shut out, lay one low, wipe out, wipe off the map, do a Rocky, bury, blast, blank, plunk, skunk, schneider, sweep, cook, cook one's goose, trounce, top, swamp, scuttle, sconce, skin, smear, shellack, whitewash, squelch, squash, steamroller, bulldoze, roll over, torpedo, tube, meatball, make one say uncle, do in, lick, lick to a frazzle, ring the bell, ring

the gong, score, hang up, win hands down, win going away, win in a walk, win in a canter, win in a waltz, waltz off with, win all the marbles, win one's spurs, breeze home, romp home, romp off with, click, connect, put across, put it together, put over, get over, get well, get fat, get rich, get ahead, get away with, get something on the board, get there, get the last dance, get into pay dirt, get a break, get the breaks, break the bank, go places, go to town, go great guns, go over, go over big, win out, check out, make out, make the cut, make it, make a killing, make hay, make well, make the grade, make good, make a noise in the world, make a hit, hit, hit it big, hit the jackpot, hit the bull's-eye, hit pay dirt, strike it rich, strike oil, strike gold, strike a vein, strike a rich vein, make a lucky strike, strike it lucky, luck, luck in, luck out, fall into the shithouse and come up with a five dollar gold piece, shit in high cotton, ace, ace the easy, hold aces, turn up trumps, move out, take off, fly, skyrocket, flash in the pan (brief), run with the ball, blow away, blow out of the water, cream, cream up, clean sweep, skunk, KO, knock one for a loop, walk over, walk away, push over, picnic, winning streak, laugher, be a gas, be a gasser, bring home the bacon, bring home the groceries, home free, have it made, turn the trick, pull off, bring off, carry off, catch on, pass muster, fill the bill, get by, pass in the dark, arrive, nail it, hack it, win one's spurs, put a feather in one's cap, do the job, do oneself proud, do all right by oneself, do a land-office business, come on, come along, be fat dumb and happy, live off the fat of the land, live the life of Riley, live on Easy Street, have one's place in the sun, come out on top of the heap, lie on a bed of roses, take the cake, get Brownie points, break the back of, end in sight, got it made, light at the end of the tunnel, over the hump, K.O., kayo, waste, take the wind out of one's sails.

WIN APPROVAL v. go over, kill, slay, wow, have 'em eating out of one's hand.

WIND n. big blow, chinook, mistral, Mister Hawkins, the hawk.

WINDBREAKER n. peacoat, Eisenhower. See also JACKET.

WIND CONE n. wind sock, condom.

WINDFALL n. gravy, goodies, perks, hat, ice, button, PM spiff (salesman).

WINDOW n. gazer.

WINDPIPE n. Sunday throat.

WINDSHIELD WIPERS n. slappers.

WINDY adj. hawk stretch.

WINE n. vino, grape, jug wine, juice, alley juice (cheap), white, dago red (Italian or any cheap red), ink, red ink, King Kong, plonk, plunk, pluck, plug, sneaky pete, split, vinblink, vinegar blink, pop wine, soda pop wine (fruit flavored).

WINE AND BARBITURATES n. ripples and reds.

WINK v. bat the eyes.

WINNER n. champ, king o' the hill, number one, numero uno, the greatest, top dog, medallist, gold medallist, takes the gold, takes the cake, shoo-in, title holder.

WINNINGS n. velvet, payoff, rake-off, gravy, cush, bundle, package, skim, take. See INCOME.

WINSTON SALEM, NORTH CAROLINA Tobacco City, Twin City.

WINTER VACATIONER n. snowbird, snowflake, sunflower.

WINTRY adj. snappy, colder than a well-digger's ass, freeze one's ass off, three-dog night, icebox (place). See COLD.

WIRE n. string.

WIRELESS ROOM n. shack, radio shack.

WIRETAP v. bug, tap, body mike.

WISCONSIN Badger State, America's Dairyland.

WISE adj. sharp, with it, all woke up, posted, savvy, have one's head screwed on right, not born yesterday, tool, power tool, cereb, gray matter, wised up. See KNOWLEDGEABLE.

WISEACRE n. smart aleck, smart ass, wisenheimer, wise guy.

WISECRACK n. one-liner, throwaway, topper, pay-off, comeback, needle, nifty, rib, crack, smart crack. See JOKE.

WISECRACKER n. cutup, life of the party, madcap, trickster, card, million laughs, kibitzer, funster, punster, quipster. See JOKER.

WISH v. yen, yen for, itch, itch for, hanker for, spoil for, give one's kingdom in hell for, give one's eyeteeth for. See DESIRE.

WIT n. clown, cutup, life of the party, madcap, trickster, card, a million laughs, kibitzer, booger, bugger, jokesmith, gagman, gagster, funster, punster, quipster. See also JOKER.

WITCH n. bitch kitty, hellcat, she-devil, she-wolf, hoochey-coochey.

WITCHCRAFT n. hoodoo, voodoo, evil eye, jinx, whack, whammy, hocus-pocus, mumbo-jumbo, abracadabra.

WITH prep. by (by me).

WITHDRAW v. 1. bow out, ooze out, ease out, phase out, check out, drop out, bail out, pull out, get lost, make oneself scarce, exfiltrate, do a vanishing act, take a walk, book, time to book, fade, fade out, do a fade, fade away. See GO. 2. fold, quit, opt out, back out, back out of, punt (Stu.), backpedal, back water, back slide, weasel out, fink out, crawl out of, worm out of, wangle out of, crawfish out, bail out, turn chicken, chicken out. See RETREAT. 3. call off, call all bets off, renig, forget it. See RETRACT.

WITHDRAWAL (DRUG) n. cold turkey, kicking the habit, sweating it out, taking the cure, becoming Mr. Fish, bogue, belly habit (pain), crash.

WITHDRAWAL SYMPTOMS n. cartwheel, circus, figure eight, twister, wingding, sweats.

WITHHOLD v. kill, spike, hold (hold the mayo), hold out on, keep it under one's hat, keep under wraps, keep buttoned up, dummy up, clam up. See also ABSTAIN.

WITHHOLD PAYMENT v. hold out, nick.

WITH ICE adj. on the rocks.

WITHOUT prep. hold (hold the mayo).

WITHOUT ICE adj. straight up, neat.

WITHSTAND v. 1. put up with, hang tough, hang on, win out, ride out, sit and take it, take it, stand the gaff, stand up to it. 2. brace, cross, fly in the face of, fly in the teeth of, meet eyeball to eyeball, take one on, stand up to, stick, stick fast, stick it out. 3. top, take out, face down, put the blocks to, put up a fight, put up a struggle, not take lying down. See ENDURE.

WITNESS n. wit, rapper, gawker.

WITNESS v. flash on, spot, spy, read, eyeball, take in, get a load of, get an eyeful of, have a look-see, pipe, pick up on. See SEE.

WITNESS CHAIR n. hot seat.

WITTICISM n. laugh, one-liner, throwaway, topper, payoff, funny, a haha, howl, hot one, needle, nifty, rib, rib tickler, knee-slapper, sizzler, spoof, story, whiz bang, jive, crack, smart crack, wisecrack; an egg, an omelet, a bomb, bombed out, died, laid there, laid an egg (unfunny). See also JOKE.

WITTY adj. jokey, joshing, yokky, gagged up, for grins, camp, campy, cool, crazy, priceless, screaming, screamingly funny, too funny for words, too killing for words.

WIZARDRY n. hocus-pocus, mumbo-jumbo, hoodoo, voodoo, evil eye, go, jinx, whack, whammy, abracadabra.

WOE n. 1. heartache, blues, shit, deep shit, bad news, clutch, hang-up, drag, rough go, heavy sledding, rain, rainin', crunch, bitch, handful, headache, bummer, downer. See MISERY. 2. worriment, in deep water, in over one's head, up shit creek, up shit creek without a paddle, up against it, between a rock and a hard place. See TROUBLE, TROUBLE, IN.

WOEBEGONE adj.   low, ass in a sling, dick in the dirt, blue, grim, got the blue devils, in the toilet, down in the mouth, hang crepe, bummed out, hurting, in pain, in the pits, shot down, carry a heavy load, prunefaced. See UN-HAPPY.

WOMAN n.   chick, mama, hama, old woman, old lady (girl friend), dame, doll, skirt, broad, frill, frail, jane, tomato, mouse, twist, kitten, kitty, sugar-wooga, rib, leg, li'l mama, she-stuff, she-she, chi-chi, femme, fox, stone fox, beauty, my beauty, pin up, cheesecake, cupcake, cutie, cutie pie, classis chassis, classy chassy, body, the body, bombshell, blonde, blond bombshell, brick, miniskirt, calico, sweater girl, bloomer girl, slick chick, chicken delight (young), spring chicken, cookie, bunny, ski bunny, snow bunny, babbling brook, peach, eel, frail eel, babe, baby, baby doll, bird, pigeon, chicken, wren, fine fryer, fly chick, cub, gadget, jill, tootsie, sis, kid, kiddo, slip, bantam, band, bezark, bag, bitch, bitch kitty, bad bitch, nothin' ass bitch, bear, bear cat, hellcat, witch, harpie, battle, battle-ax, two bagger, Zelda, bucket (ugly), beetle, beast, pig, pigmeat, sow, scow, heifer, cow, gaunch, ginch, pot, blimp, old maid, old bitch, old bag, bat, old bat, biddie, biddy, old biddy, hen, old hen, stewer, crow, old crow, baggage, excess baggage, cunt, C, pussy, muff, twat, twitch, snatch, ass, piece, piece of ass, piece of tail, meat, dark meat, white meat, tuna, squab, quail, San Quentin quail, jailbait, whistle bait, wench, gumdrop, floozie, floozy, floogy, faloosie, demi-rep, lay, mat, make, roundheels, gimme, wet hen, alley cat, B-girl, bawd, biscuit, blister, baloney, barlow, barnacle, motorcycle, stallion (Bl.), pit popsie, groundcloth (promiscuous), frame dame, cover, bim, bimbo, bimmy, bimmo, fish, jerry, mort, mott, moll, gun moll, jellybean, queen, queen bee, butterfly, doe (alone), mare, raggle, quasar, hip chick, head, head chick (fellationist), fine dinner (Obs.), bachelor girl, lobo, tomboy, les, lez, dyke, bull dyke, bull bitch, shemale.

WOMANISH adv.   faggy, swishy, fruity, ma, mother, old woman, Ethel, pretty boy, weak sister. See EFFEMINATE.

WOMEN'S ARMED SERVICES n.   WAC, Wacs (Army), WAVE, Waves (N.), WAF, Wafs (A.F.), WAM (Marines).

WOMEN'S ARMY CORPS n.   WAC, WACS, the First Skirt (Commanding Officer).

WOMEN'S LIBERATIONIST n.   libber, women's libber, bra burner.

WOMEN'S RIGHTS n.   women's lib.

WONDERFUL adj.   fab, fantasmo, awesome, rare, fat, froody, superfly, hellacious, boffo, evil, too much, unreal, cool, zero cool, heavy, dynamite, marvy, pisseroo, outrageous, tits, tawny, aggressive, prince, wailing, something else, something to brag about, something to shout about, something to write home about, hot shit. See FABULOUS.

WONT n.   thing, Jones, into, hang-up, one's bag, shot, kick, hook.

WOO v.   date, chase, run after, make time with, rush, spark, play up to. See COURT.

WOOD n.   big sticks, load of sticks.

WOODEN LEG n.   peg, peg leg.

WOODS n.   big sticks.

WORDY adj.   talky, yacky, yackety-yak, gabby, shoots the gab, gassy, CBS, blowhard, windy, long-winded, windbag, bag of wind, windjammer, barber, chatty Cathy, gum beater, verbal diarrhea, diarrhea of the mouth. See TALKATIVE.

WORK n.   line, line of business, bag, dodge, do, gig, day gig, go, hang, moonlight, nine-to-five shit, one's thing, what one does, slot, what one's into, rat race, grind, daily grind, grindstone, the salt mines, shitwork, chickwork (household), gruntwork (Army), scud, scut, scutwork, donkeywork, bull work, hemo jo (hard labor), lick, lick of work, stitch of work, racket, swindle, gyppo, jippo, elbow grease. See also OCCUPATION.

WORK v.   hustle, scratch, slave, sweat, sweat and slave, sweat, sweat it, buckle down, knuckle down, grind, dig, plug, plug away, plug along, hammer, peg away, cook, it cooks, percolate, perk, tick, moonlight, daylight, buck, hassle, take on, pour it on, put one's nose to the grindstone, beat one's brains out, bust a gut, bust one's conk, bust one's buns, knock oneself out, work one's head off, do for, do one's stuff, do one's thing, do one's number, do the trick, fill the bill, hit the ball, bear down on it, hold down a job, bull work, back to the salt mines, dog it (inferior), featherbed, jet up, mess around, make a buck, make change, hang out one's shingle, whittle, heel (Stu.). See also ACT.

WORKABLE adj.   no sweat, cinch, snap, pushover, piece of cake, setup, breeze, duck soup, pie, easy as pie, easy as falling off a log, simple as ABC. See also EASY.

WORKER n.   help, breadwinner, beaver, eager beaver, workhorse, stiff, working stiff, grind, greasy grind, nose to the grindstone, workaholic, company man, apparatchik, boll weevil, flunky, temp, pencil pusher, desk jockey, girl Friday, man Friday, nine-to-fiver, white collar, pink collar, hard hat, blue collar, dirty neck, jerry, razorback, phantom (under assumed name), chump, dinner pailer, legit ghee, legit stiff, furp, home guard, peasant, peon, savage, serf, slave, slavey, scissorbill, square, square John, square plug, up-and-up ghee, pork chopper, wearing two hats, dig, prentice, come along (temporary, inexperienced), fish, floater, glass arm, grease monkey, gyppo, jippo, ham and egger, gandy dancer, hunky chunk (Central European), deadwood (unnecessary).

WORKING adj. going, tasking, in full swing, hot, on track.

WORKING HOURS n. strictly 9-to-5, flex time (flexible hours).

WORKING PARENT'S CHILD n. latchkey child.

WORKOUT n. constitutional, daily dozen, aerobics, warm-up, jazzercise.

WORKPLACE n. shop, mines, salt mines, the store, the office, trenches, firing line.

WORK SHIFT n. day, nine-to-five, graveyard, graveyard shift, moonlight, hoot owl, swing shift, lobster shift, lobster trick, tour, flex time (flexible hours).

WORK, SLOWLY v. slowdown, drag one's ass, drag one's foot, have lead in one's pants, dog it, jake it.

WORLD n. apple, big blue marble, real estate, spaceship Earth.

WORLDLY adj. hep, hip, on to, uptown, swinging, mod, executive, cool, been around, been hit before, been around the block a few times, knows the score. See SOPHISTICATED.

WORLDWIDE adj. multinational, anational.

WORN OUT adj. 1. bushed, had it, pooped, too pooped to pop, out of gas, out of juice, knocked out, wiped, wiped out, wrung out, burned out, wore out, pegged out, wrung out, dragging ass, beat. See TIRED. 2. had it, busted, kaput, dinged, totaled, gone, glitched, shot, ratty-tatty, hand-me-down, reach-me-down, secondhand, experienced.

WORRIED adj. uptight, clutched, sweat it, sweat bullets, on edge, on pins and needles, on tenterhooks, worried stiff, biting one's nails, beside oneself. See DISTURBED. See also ANXIOUS, NERVOUS.

WORRIER adj. worrywart, nail-biter, nervous Nellie.

WORRY n. nag, noodge, bitch, headache, tsuris, pain, pain in the ass, pain in the neck, ants, nail-biter, worriment, worriation, cliff-hanger, bad news. See ANXIETY. See also PREDICAMENT.

WORRY v. 1. bleed, take on, eat one's heart out, have a heart attack, stew, carry a heavy load, work oneself into a lather. 2. be at, be on the back of, eat, chivvy, noodge, nudge, nudzh, give a bad time to, give one a hard time, hassle, hound, dog, nag. See ANNOY. See also DISTRESS.

WORSHIPER n. freak, booster, buff, fan, groupie, rooter, crazie. See DEVOTEE.

WORTHLESS adj. diddly squat, ain't worth doodly shit, ain't worth shit, ain't worth the powder to blow it to hell, stiffo, tripe, garbage, junk, beans, borscht, nada, big zero, measly, minimal to the max, two bit, nickel and dime, penny ante, peanuts, chicken shit, bupkis, pokerino, white elephant, no prize package, not worth a hill of beans, from hunger. See USELESS.

WORTHY adj. A, A-1, aces, ace high, winner, choice, gilt-edged, best ever, salt of the earth, top, tops, topnotch, topflight, top drawer, first class, first chop, first rate, solid, not too shabby, something else, heavy, worldbeater, the best. See ADMIRABLE.

WOUND v. 1. chop, scratch, ouch, bung, bung up, cut, cut one, cut up, jig cut, cut a new kisser for, open up, shiv, chiv, slice, stick, boo-boo (minor flesh), mark, rat mark, stool mark (knife), nick, brand, carve, carve initials in one, chop down, clip, zing, ding, total, wax, tweak. See also MISTREAT. 2. get, gotcha, zing, curdle, do, do in, do a number on, lean on, dump on, put down, rough up, hit one where one lives, hurl brickbats at, lay a bad trip on one, thumb one's nose at, gross out, mess up, shake up, cut, cut up, cut to the quick, total, wax, wing, nick, turn off, cool, chop, sound, dozens, sounding dozens, play dirty dozens, signify, signify shucking and jiving, S'ing n' J'ing, miff, cap, pooh-pooh, get bent, blow off, give one a backhanded compliment, give one a left-handed compliment, give one the cold shoulder, hurt one where one lives, kick one around, mess around with.

WOUNDED adj. 1. hurting, bleeding, damaged, winged, nicked, zinged, cut, bunged up, busted up, burned, burned one's ass, put away, screwed up, walking wounded, have to scrape one off the sidewalk. 2. burnt up, browned off, bleeding, all torn up, cut up, hit where one lives, shook, shook up, miffed, miffy, shot down, have one's nose out of joint, sore, uptight.

WRANGLE n. blowup, brawl, flap, branigan, donnybrook, row, rowdydow, ruckus, ruction, rumpus, scene, blow-off, dustup, rumble, knockdown and drag out, battle royal, flack session, rhubarb. See ARGUMENT.

WRANGLE v. brawl, buck, take on, lock horns, set to, row, bump heads, cross swords, have at it, pick a bone, kick up a row, tangle with, tangle ass with, pitch a bitch, put up a fight. See ARGUE.

WRATH n. mad, huff, dander, Irish, miff, stew, storm, wingding, conniption, cat fit, blowup, flare-up, boiling point, rise, more heat than light. See ANGER.

WRECK n. fender bender, rear ender, pileup, stack up, wrack up, crack-up, smash, smashup, total. See ACCIDENT.

WRECK v. trash, total, cream, smash, smash up, pile up, wrack up, crack up, take out, take apart, take a joint apart, break, break the lease, put out of commission, put in the toilet, bend the goods. See DESTROY.

WRECKED adj. gutted, busted, totaled, gone, cooked, sunk, shot, kaput, no-go, bitched up, buggered, wracked up, hashed up, mucked up, down the tube, down the toilet, out the window, done in, gone to wrack and ruin. See DESTROYED.

WRENCH n. knuckle buster (crescent).

WRESTLE n. rassle, grunt, grunt and groan.

WRESTLER n. grunt, grunt and groaner, pretzel bender, bone breaker, bone cracker, bone crusher. See also PRIZEFIGHTER.

WRETCH n. 1. creep, sleazeball, sleazoid, prick, dick, fart, rat, stinker, muthahfuckah, mofo, bad news, bad egg, bad'un, wrong'un, black sheep, bounder, bastard, son of a bitch, a dirty so-and-so, low-life. See SCOUNDREL. 2. jinx, hoodoo, voodoo, eight ball, jerk, jonah, joner, snakebit, loser, sure loser, winner, real winner, fuck-up, sad sack, schlemiel, schlemazel, hard case, hard-luck guy, flop, bust, loser, goner, dead, dead duck, beat, deadbeat, dead pigeon, bum, turkey, poor fish.

WRETCHED adj. low, ass in a sling, dick in the dirt, down and out, down in the mouth, low, long face, singing the blues, crying the blues, bummed out, hurting, in the pits, clanked, all torn up, raining on one's parade. See UNHAPPY.

WRINKLE v. prune up.

WRINKLES n. crow's feet.

WRIT, LEGAL n. paper.

WRIT OF HABEAS CORPUS n. hapas capas.

WRIT OF MANDAMUS n. goddamus.

WRITE v. push a pen, push a pencil, drive a pen, drive a pencil, drop a note, drop a line, script, scriven, pen, put pen to paper, put down, note down, dash off, toss off, bang out, bat out, knock out, knock out a few pages, shove out, knock off, knock off hen tracks on a rolltop piano (type), make hen tracks, ghost, ghostwrite, grubstreet (hack), stain a paper, spoil a paper, shed ink, spill ink, sling ink, coin a phrase; comp, clef, tune. See also COMPOSE.

WRITE A LETTER v. drop a note, drop a line, drop a kite, knock out a tab, pen. See CORRESPOND.

WRITER n. scribbler, scribe, scripter, scrivener, scratcher, word slinger, wordsmith, free lance, pen driver, pen pusher, pencil driver, pencil pusher, ink slinger, inkspiller, ghost, ghostwriter, knight of the pen, knight of the plume, knight of the quill; telewriter, teleplaywright (TV); legman, columnist, stringer, cub, news hen, play doctor, play fixer.

WRITING n. bilge, hen tracks, chicken tracks, scribble, stuff.

WRITING PAPER n. scratch, the blank page.

WRITING TABLET n. scratch, scratch pad.

WRONG adj. goofed, fluffed, duffed, boo-booed, put one's foot in it, put one's foot in one's mouth, muffed one's cue, fluffed one's lines, bletcherous, cretinous (computer), all wet, cockeyed, ass backwards, back asswards, fouled up, fucked up, glitched up, haywire, gone haywire, off, way off, off base, off the beam, full of beans, full of hops, full of hot air, full of prunes, talking through one's hat, talking like a man with a paper ass, don't know one's ass from a hole in the ground, don't know one's ass from first base, don't know one's ass from one's elbow, don't know shit from Shinola, don't know from shit, don't know from nothing, nutty, off one's nut, that doesn't track, screwy, all wasted, bum, bum steer, wrong number, fell flat on one's face, fell flat on one's ass, dropped the ball, out in left field, miss by a mile, on a fool's errand, have another think coming, count one's chickens before they're hatched, bark up the wrong tree, back the wrong horse.

WRONGDOER n. creep, shit, turd, shithead, heel, shitheel, sleazeball, sleazoid, slime bucket, maggot, prick, dick, fart, louse, rat, stinker, motherfucker, mofo, hood, hooligan, bad news, bad egg, low-life. See SCOUNDREL. See also CRIMINAL.

WROUGHT UP adj. hyper, charged, wired, wired up, fired up, keyed up, all keyed up, steamed up, hopped up, worked up, freaked out, flipped out, spazzed out, had a spaz attack, all shook up, mind-blowing, mind-bending, in a lather, in a tizzy.

WYOMING Equality State, Suffrage State.

X

X n. X-ray, X ray.

XYLOPHONE n. woodpile.

Y

Y.   Yankee, yoke.

YACHT n.   goldplater, yatch, stinkpot, a hole in the water, a hole in the water into which one throws money.

YACHTSMAN n.   yachtie, yachty, yottie, yotty, skipper.

YAMS n.   sweets.

YARN n.   tall story, fish story, cock-and-bull story, cock and bull, tall tale, fairy tale, potboiler, string, line, line of cheese, song, song and dance, chestnut, old chestnut.

YAWN v.   catch flies.

YEAR n.   boffo (prison).

YEARN v.   yen for, carry a torch for, hurting for, hanker for, have eyes for, wild for, die over, got to have, sweet on, have a crush on, have a case on, have it bad, eat one's heart out. See DESIRE.

YEARNING n.   itch, yen, yen-yen, mash, pash, hankering, hots, hot pants, in heat, nasties, the urge, sweet tooth, flash groove, fire in the belly, the munchies (food), beaver fever. See DESIRE.

YELL n.   holler.

YELL v.   holler, holler out, squawk.

YES interj.   yeah, yeah man, yowzah, yeh, yep, yup, yessiree, si si, A, fuckin' A, all right, all rightee, alrighty, all reet, reat, right, right on, right-o, rather, A-O.K., A-okay, O.K., okay, okey-dokey, okey-doke, okie ·bebe doakie, dory, okydory, hunky-dory, ding ho, ding how, ding hau, ducky, just ducky, solid, swell, absofuckinglutely, like you say, good deal, kee-rect, right you are, right as rain, for a fact, that's for sure, for sure, fer sher, fer shirr, shore, sure, sure thing, surest thing you know, you betcha, you bet, and no mistake, come hell or high water, no buts about it, no ifs ands or buts about it, check, for it, give the nod, thumbs up, indeedy, yes indeedy, Rodger Dodger, really truly, crazy, copasetic, uh huh, umhuh, fine, amen, you better believe it, you said it, you said a mouthful, you can say that again, you're not kidding, you bet your life, you bet your boots, you're damn tootin, you're dern tootin, you're the doctor, natch, yea bo, Charlie, Uncle Charlie, George, jake, jake with me, like a shot.

YIELD v.   1. fold, quit, cave in, give up, give in, buy, say uncle, cry uncle, toss in the towel, throw in the towel, pack it in, eat shit, eat crow, eat dirt, eat humble pie, knuckle to, lie down and roll over for; come across, come across with, give out, put out (sexual). See SURRENDER. 2. go along with, go along with the crowd, go with the flow, don't make waves, don't rock the boat, play the game, fit in, toe the line, toe the mark. See COMPLY.

YIELDING adj.   putty in one's hands. See also SUBMISSIVE.

YOKEL n.   hillbilly, hick, plow jockey, country, country boy, country cousin, local yokel, hayseed, hay shaker, cornfed, boob, rube, shitkicker, clodhopper, clown, brush ape, busher, bush leaguer, clay eater (Southern), cracker barrel, Bill Shears, Alvin, Reuben, galoot, gil, goober grabber, goofus, hay rube, hecker, hoosier, swamp angel, wahoo, yahoo, bucolic, woodhick, Herkimer Jerkimer.

YOUNG adj.   juve, punk, yoot, Y-person, bobby-soxer, jailbait (Fem.), green, green ass, spring chicken, wet behind the ears, still wet behind the ears, yuppie (young urban professional), YUP, yuffie (young urban professional failure), yumpie (young upwardly mobile professional), yavis (young attractive verbal intelligent successful), salad days.

YOUNG MAN n.   kid, kiddo, sonny, bub, punk, punk kid, yute, bud, buddy, rock, rocker, stud, stallion, cock, colt, squirt, bugger, booger, chicken, wet behind the ears, man, cokey, duck, gunsel, monkey, pecker, pisser, lad, boy, boyo, boychick, buck, buster, Joe College, bummer, butch, chip, crasher, crock (disliked), junior, yuppie (young urban professional), YUP, yumpie (young upwardly mobile professional), rookie, dollface (good looking), drape (hip clothing), fruit, buddy gee (1930), pachuco (1942, Mex.), jerk (1945), frat, gazooney, glad lad, chico, glamor puss, hell pup. See also BOY, YOUTH.

YOUNG URBAN PROFESSIONAL n.   YUP, yuppie, yumpie (young upwardly mobile professional), buppie (Bl.), yavis (young attractive verbal intelligent successful).

YOUNG WOMAN n.   chick, chicken delight, broad, babe, doll, jailbait, frail, skirt, pussy, piece, tomato. See GIRL.

YOUNGER adj.   kid (sister, brother).

YOUNGSTER n.   kid, little kid, little guy, little bugger, shaver, little shaver, squirt, little squirt, snotnose kid, juve, juvenile delinquent, JD, punk, punk kid, pup, puppy, cub, junior, J.R. sonny, sonny boy, bud, buddy, bub, bubba, young fry, small fry, chit.

YOUNGSTOWN, OHIO   Baseball City.

YOU'RE WELCOME   de nada, no problem, no sweat, think nothing of it, forget it, hey, doy tashey mashtay (Jap.).

YOURS pron.   it's you, you got it, got your name on it.

YOUTH n.   kid, Y-person, shaver, squirt, juve, juvenile delinquent, JD, punk, kiddo, pup, sonny, sonny boy, bud, buddy, bub, bubba, bubblegum rocker, teen, teenie, teenybopper, weenie bopper, creepybopper, jive (associated with jive music, movie, etc.), Valley girl, petiteen, sub deb, sweet sixteen, twixt teen, bobby-soxer, boyo, cokey, duck, gunsel, monkey, pecker, pisser, young fry, youngblood, wet behind the ears, what's wasted on the young, salad days, twink, twinkle, twinky (homosexual).

YUGOSLAVIAN n.   Hunkie, Hunky, bohunk, Slav.

Z

Z n. Zulu, zebra.

ZANY n. gagman, gagster, jokesmith, Joey, pale face, cutup, madcap, wisecracker.

ZANY adj. camp, campy, jokey, joshing, yokky, boffo, gagged up, for grins, goofy, kooky, loony, crazy, sappy, goofus, screamingly funny, tomfool, fool, foolheaded. See FOOLISH.

ZEALOT n. 1. fan, freak, groupie, hound, crazies, nut, frenzie, junkie, punker (punk rock), culture vulture, fiend, demon, eager beaver, sucker for, fool. See DEVOTEE. 2. arm-waver, flag-waver, superpatriot, patrioteer, hundred percenter, jingoist, scout master.

ZEALOUS adj. pushy, pushy hotshot, hot, hot for, hot to go, hot to trot, gung ho, hopped up, ants, antsy, antsypantsy, ants in one's pants, catawamptious, itchy, keen, ripe, creaming to, ready for Freddie, fall all over oneself to, go great guns, come on like gangbusters, come on strong, enforcer, get up and go, go-getter, on the make, out for a rep, ball of fire, eager beaver, fireball, spark plug, self-starting, full of get up and go, heller, not let any grass grow under one's feet. See also ENTHUSIASTIC.

ZEBRA n. convict (circus).

ZEN BUDDHISM n. Zen, Zen hipster.

ZENITH n. blow-off, capper, topper, critical mass, payoff, ape, bitter end, blow one's wad, far out, go over the mountain, shoot one's wad.

ZEPPELIN n. Zepp, blimp.

ZERO adj. big zero, zip, zippo, zot, zilch, nix, cipher, goose egg, duck egg, egg, shutout, nada, 86, scratch, minimal to the max, from nothing. See NOTHING. See also UNIMPORTANT.

ZEST n. guts, kick, zip, zap, moxie, pep, bounce, piss and vinegar.

ZESTFUL adj. 1. perky, bouncy, chirpy, chipper, peppy, zingy, zappy, zippy, jumping, hyper, swinging, swingle, rocking, snappy, salty, juiced up, upbeat, burning, red hot, fireball, ball of fire. 2. hot, hot for, hot to go, hot to trot, rarin' to go, full of get up and go, go great guns, gung ho, hopped up, spark plug, self-starter. See SPIRITED.

BIBLIOGRAPHY

Adams, Ramon F. *The Cowboy Says It Salty.* Tucson: University of Arizona Press, 1971.

Alexander, Clifton J., and Alexander, Sally. *How to Kick the Habit.* New York: Frederick Fell, 1972.

Alexander, Don, and Block, John. *The Racer's Dictionary.* Santa Ana, Calif.: Steve Smith Autosports, 1980.

Allen, Jay Presson. *Just Tell Me What You Want.* New York: E.P. Dutton & Co., 1975.

American Association of Fund Raising Counsel, National Society of Fund Raisers, National Association for Hospital Development. *A Glossary of Fund-Raising Terms.*

American Marketing Association. *Marketing Definitions, A Glossary of Marketing Terms.*

Andrews, Malachi, and Owens, Paul T. *Black Language.* Berkeley, Calif.: Seymour Smith Publishing, 1973.

Barnett, Lincoln. *The Treasure of Our Tongue.* New York: Alfred A. Knopf, 1967.

Barnhart, Clarence L., Steinmetz, Sol, and Barnhart, Robert K. *The Barnhart Dictionary of New English Since 1963.* New York: Barnhart/Harper & Row, 1973.

————. *The Second Barnhart Dictionary of New English.* New York: Barnhart/Harper & Row, 1980.

Boatner, Maxine Tull, and Gates, John Edward. *A Dictionary of American Idioms.* Woodbury, N.Y.: Barron's Educational Series, 1975.

Bombeck, Erma. *Los Angeles Times,* January 28, 1986.

Brandeth, Gyles. *The Joy of Lex.* New York: William Morrow, 1980.

"Cagney & Lacey" TV segment. June 18, 1984.

Carillo, Mary. "I Deef, You Deef, He Deefs." *World Tennis,* February 1982.

CB Fact Book and Language Dictionary. Milwaukee: DMR Publications, 1977.

Chapman, Bruce. *Why Do We Say Such Things?* New York: Miles-Emmett, 1947.

Chapman, Robert L. *New Dictionary of American Slang.* New York: Harper & Row, 1986.

Cohen, John. *The Essential Lenny Bruce.* New York: Ballantine Books, 1967.

Cohen, Sidney. *The Drug Dilemma.* New York: McGraw-Hill, 1969.

Cohen, Stanley. "Cop Talk—New York Style." *Writer,* November, 1980.

Collins, Glen. "Doing a Number on Words." *New York Times Magazine,* February 13, 1977.

Cox, Terrance C., Jacobs, Michael R., Le Blanc, A. Eugene, and Marshman, Joan A. *Drugs and Drug Abuse.* Toronto: Addiction Research Foundation, 1983.

Cross, Donna Woolfolk. *Word Abuse.* New York: Coward, McCann, Geoghegan, 1979.

"A Cursory Glossary to the Off-beat Side of Now." *Harper's Bazaar,* April, 1965.

Dahl, Hartvig. *Word Frequencies of Spoken American English.* Essex, Conn.: Verbatim Books, 1979.

Daily Variety, March 10, March 12, November 19, 1986.

"Dear Abby," *Los Angeles Times,* November 30, 1983.

Dennis, Paul, and Barry, Carolyn. *The Marijuana Catalogue.* Chicago: Playboy Press, 1978.

Dickson, Paul. *Words.* New York: Delacorte Press, 1982.

Dills, Lanie, and Silver, Robert M. *CB Slanguage Language Dictionary.* New York: Louis J. Martin & Associates, 1976.

Ditlea, Steve. "Word Processing." *Personal Computing,* October 1986.

Dohan, Mary Helen. *Our Own Words.* New York: Alfred A. Knopf, 1974.

Dreyfus, Patricia A. "Broker Babble." *Anchorage Daily News,* November 19, 1984.

Dusek, Dorothy, and Girdano, Daniel A. *Drugs—A Factual Account,* 3rd Ed. Reading, Mass.: Addison-Wesley Publishing, 1980.

Espy, Willard R. *Thou Improper, Thou Uncommon Noun.* New York: Clarkson N. Potter, 1978.

Fager, Chuck. "Hillspeak—The Secret Language of Policy Makers in Washington." *Christian Century,* May, 13, 1981.

Fast, Howard. *The Outsider.* Boston: Houghton Mifflin, 1984.

Fast Times at Ridgemont High. Film, 1982.

"Flamingo Hilton Gaming Guide." Las Vegas, Nev.

Fleming, Thomas J. "Space Language." *American Weekly*, August 30, 1959.

Flexner, Stuart Berg. *I Hear America Talking*. New York: Van Nostrand Reinhold, 1976.

48 Hours. Film. 1982.

Free. *Revolution for the Hell of It*. New York: Dial Press, 1968.

Freeman, David. *A Hollywood Education*. New York: G.P. Putnam's Sons, 1986.

Funk, Charles Earle. *Heavens to Betsy*. New York: Harper & Brothers, 1955.

———. *A Hog on Ice*. New York: Harper & Brothers, 1948.

Gannon, Frank. "A Portrait of the Artist as a Young Californian." *New Yorker*, March 25, 1985.

Goldin, Hyman G., O'Leary, Frank, Lipsius, Morris. *Dictionary of Underworld Lingo*. New York: Twayne Publishers, 1950.

Goldman, William. *Adventures in the Skin Trade*. New York: Warner Books, 1983.

"Hardcastle and McCormick" TV segment. November 13, 1983.

Holt, Alfred H. *Phrase Origins*. New York: Thomas Y. Crowell, 1936.

Homer, Joel. "Big Business Talk." *Atlantic Monthly*, December, 1979.

———. "Helpful Talk." *Atlantic Monthly*, November 1979.

Infoworld Magazine, December 3, December 17, 1984, March 24, 1986.

"Jack and Mike" TV segment. November 11, 1986.

"Jeopardy" TV segment. June 20, 1985.

KNBC News. December 2, 1983, September 12, 1984, April 7, 1986, September 30, 1986.

KNXT News. May 19, 1984, March 17, May 2, 1985.

Kagos, Fred. *A Dictionary of Yiddish Slang and Idioms*. Secaucus, N.J.: Citadel Press, 1966, 1967.

Lambodian, William. *Doublespeak Dictionary*. Los Angeles: Pinnacle Books, 1979.

Landy, Eugene E. *The Underground Dictionary*. New York: Simon & Schuster, 1971.

Levy, Steven. *Hackers*. Garden City, N.Y.: Anchor Press, Doubleday, 1984.

Limbacher, James L. *Sexuality in World Cinema*. Metuchen, N.J., and London: Scarecrow Press. 1983.

Lit, Hy. *Hy Lit's Unbelievable Dictionary*. Philadelphia: Hyski Press, 1968.

Los Angeles Times, May 27, 1982—Jan 26, 1987.

Louria, Donald B. *The Drug Scene*. New York: McGraw-Hill, 1968.

MacNeil, Lehrer Report. KCET, July 26, 1984.

Mager, N.H. and S.K. *The Morrow Book of New Words*. New York: William Morrow, 1982.

Major, Clarence. *The Dictionary of Afro-American Slang*. New York: International Publishers, 1970.

Marshman, Joan A. *Drugs and Drug Abuse*. Toronto: Addiction Research Foundation, 1983.

Matthews, Mitford M. *American Words*. Cleveland and New York: World Publishing, 1959.

McCarthy, Abigail. "Can We Rescue Language?" *Commonweal*, January 28, 1983.

McFadden, Cyra. *The Serial*. New York: Signet Book/New American Library, 1978.

McWilliams, Peter A. *The Personal Computer Book*. Los Angeles: Prelude Press, 1983.

Mencken, H.L. *The American Language*. New York: Alfred A. Knopf, 1963.

Middleton, Thomas H. "Light Refractions." *Saturday Review*, November, 25, 1978.

Miller, Don Ethan. *The Book of Jargon*. New York: Macmillan, 1981.

Miller, Merl K. and Sippl, Charles, J. *Home Computers: A Beginners Glossary and Guide*. Portland, Ore.: Dilithium Press, 1978.

Morrow, Lance. "If Slang Is Not Sin." Time, November 8, 1982.

Neaman, Judith S. and Silver, Carole S. *Kind Words, A Thesaurus of Euphemisms*. New York: Facts On File, 1983.

Newman, Edwin. *A Civil Tongue*. Indianapolis/New York: Bobbs-Merrill, 1976.

———. *Strictly Speaking*. Indianapolis/New York: Bobbs-Merrill, 1974.

"Nightline" TV segment. October 23, 1985, December 17, 1986.

Novak, William and Waldoks, Moshe. *The Big Book of Jewish Humor*. New York: Harper & Row, 1981

Opdycke, John Baker. *Say What You Mean*. New York: Funk & Wagnalls, 1944.

Overmeyer, Eric. *Native Speech*, play produced by LAAT. June 1983.

Partridge, Eric. *A Dictionary of Slang and Unconventional English*. New York: Macmillan, 1972.

———. *Slang Today and Yesterday*. New York: Barnes & Noble, 4th Ed., 1970.

Pei, Mario. *Double-Speak in America*. New York: Hawthorn Books, 1973.

———. *Words in Sheep's Clothing*. New York: Hawthorn Books, 1969.

Petievich, Gerald. *Money Men*. New York: Harcourt Brace Jovanovich, 1981.

Pimp Talk: A Dictionary of Black Hustling Slang.

Porky's. Film, 1982.

Rawson, Hugh. *A Dictionary of Euphemisms and Other Doubletalk*. New York: Crown, 1981.

Roberts, Hermese E. *The Third Ear: A Black Glossary*. Better Speech Institute of America, 1971.

Rosten, Leo. *The Joys of Yiddish*. New York: McGraw-Hill, 1968.

Rusche, Sue. "The Drug Scene". *Los Angeles Times*, November 11, 1984.

Safire, William. *On Language*. New York: Times Books, 1980.

———. "On Language." *New York Times Magazine*, March 6, 1983–January 11, 1987.

———. *What's the Good Word?* New York: Times Books, 1982.

Sanders, Lawrence. *The Fourth Deadly Sin*. New York: G.P. Putnam's Sons, 1985.

Sanoff, Alvin P. "Everything from Airheads to Zoids." *U.S. News & World Report*, November 3, 1986.

Schell, Jonathan. "History in Sherman Park." *New Yorker*, January 12, 1987.

Severn, Bill. *Place Words*. New York: Ives Washburn, 1969.

Simmons, J. I. and Winograd, Barry. *It's Happening*. Santa Barbara, Calif.: M/L Marc-Laird Publications. 1967.

Simon, John. *Paradigms Lost*. New York: Clarkson N. Potter, 1976–1980.

Sitbon, Guy. "The Cocaine Society." *World Press Review*, February 1983.

Slansky, David. *Hold 'Em Poker*. Las Vegas, Nev.: GBC Press.

Spears, Richard A. *Slang and Euphemism*. Middle Village, N.Y.: Jonathan David Publishers, 1981.

"Spenser: For Hire" TV segment. September 21, 1986.

Taylor, Marjorie A. *The Language of World War II*. Bronx, N.Y.: H. W. Wilson, 1944.

Testament, TV film. November 26, 1984.

Thompson, Hunter S. *Fear and Loathing in Las Vegas*. New York: Random House, 1971.

Thorndike, Edward L., and Lorge, Irving. *The Teacher's Word Book of 30,000 Words*. New York: Columbia University Teachers College, Bureau of Publications, 1963.

Time, November 8, 1982, January 3, 1983, November 3, 1986.

Trudeau, Garry. "Doonesbury" comic strip. January 6, 1985, June 6, 1986, September 23, 1986, December 18, 1986.

Tuotti, Joseph Dolan. *Big Time Buck White*. New York: Grove Press, 1969.

Urdang, Laurence and LaRoche, Nancy. *Picturesque Expressions, A Thematic Dictionary*. Detroit: Gale Research, 1980.

Watts, Peter. *A Dictionary of the Old West*. New York: Alfred A. Knopf, 1977.

Webster's Sports Dictionary. Springfield, Mass.: G. & C. Merriam, 1976.

Wentworth, Harold and Flexner, Stuart Berg. *Dictionary of American Slang*, 2nd Supp. New York: Thomas Y. Crowell, 1975.

Wolkomis, Richard. "Slipping the Mitten to a Catawamptious Wally: The Slang Gap Revisited." *Smithsonian*, March 1983.

Wouk, Herman. *Inside, Outside*. Boston–Toronto: Little, Brown, 1985.